Business Communication

Helen Rothschild Ewald
Iowa State University

Rebecca E. Burnett
Iowa State University

PRENTICE HALL
Upper Saddle River, NJ 07458

Acquisitions Editor: Donald J. Hull
Development Editor: Patricia D. Taylor
Assistant Editor: John Larkin
Editorial Assistant: Jim Campbell
Editor-in-Chief: James Boyd
Director of Development: Steve Deitmer
Senior Project Manager/Liaison: Linda M. DeLorenzo
Production Editor: Richard Lange, GTS Graphics
Production Coordinator: Renee Pelletier
Managing Editor: Valerie Q. Lentz
Manufacturing Supervisor: Arnold Vila
Manufacturing Manager: Vincent Scelta
Design Director: Patricia H. Wosczyk
Senior Designer: Ann France
Interior Design: Lisa Delgado/Lorraine Castellano
Cover Design: Lorraine Castellano
Cover Image: © 90W. Whitehurst Electronics/The Stock Market

Credits and acknowledgments for materials borrowed from other sources and reproduced, with permission, in this textbook appear on page C-1.

Library of Congress Cataloging-in-Publication Data

Ewald, Helen Rothschild.
Business communication / Helen Rothschild Ewald, Rebecca E. Burnett.
p. cm.
Includes bibliographical references and index.
ISBN 0-205-16243-6
1. Business communication. I. Burnett, Rebecca E. II. Title.
HF5718.E93 1996
658.4'5—dc20 96-46561
CIP

Prentice-Hall International (UK) Limited, London
Prentice-Hall of Australia Pty. Limited, Sydney
Prentice-Hall Canada, Inc., Toronto
Prentice-Hall Hispanoamericaña, S.A., Mexico
Prentice-Hall of India Private Limited, New Delhi
Prentice-Hall of Japan, Inc., Tokyo
Simon & Schuster Asia Pte. Ltd., Singapore
Editora Prentice-Hall do Brasil, Ltda., Rio de Janeiro

Printed in the United States of America

10 9 8 7 6 5 4 3 2 1

To past, present, and future students

About the Authors . . .

OUR GOALS IN WRITING *BUSINESS COMMUNICATION*

We started this book with a vision of what a business communication textbook could be—one that recognizes the importance of context in communicating business messages and encourages students to understand that communication is necessarily affected by the occasion, audience, writer, and message. But more than that, we wanted students to recognize that business communication is not a chore, but a challenge.

In helping our own students address these challenges, it's been our experience that students benefit both from learning business conventions and knowing when to depart from these conventions. We also found that students appreciate hearing about traditional businesses as well as marginalized organizations: small companies, entrepreneurial businesses, and educational institutions. We are thankful to our students who, over the past 25 years, have shared their experiences as they analyzed workplace documents and each others' work.

HELEN ROTHSCHILD EWALD

An Associate Professor at Iowa State University, Helen teaches both undergraduate and graduate courses in rhetoric and professional communication. Among her publications, she has written a textbook for use in first-year writing programs entitled *Writing as Process: Invention and Convention,* and she especially welcomes the opportunity to teach business communication in computer intensive environments. Her present research includes looking into what kind of language we use in our classrooms and how that discourse can help teachers and students work together to make and share knowledge. She lives with her husband Bob, who, as an attorney, contributed a few examples to this book; her children James and Jessica, who at this time are still in elementary school; and her golden retriever, Daisy. When she is not writing and teaching, Helen enjoys playing tennis, searching out bargains at garage sales, and refinishing antique furniture.

REBECCA E. BURNETT

An Associate Professor at Iowa State University, Rebecca teaches both undergraduate and graduate courses in rhetoric and professional communication. Among her publications, she has written a textbook for use in third- and fourth-year writing programs entitled *Technical Communication.* She especially welcomes the opportunity to teach business communication students who complete internships in business and industry. Her present research includes examining ways that teams in international corporations manage various kinds of conflict as they produce English-language documents. She regularly corresponds by e-mail with her systems development engineer son, Bob, who contributed a few examples to this book. She lives with her saved-from-certain-death-at-the-animal-shelter kitties, Quintilian and Hildegard. When she is not writing and teaching, Rebecca enjoys working in her garden, riding her new mountain bike, and taking photographs during international travels.

Brief Contents

PART I COMMUNICATING IN A DIVERSE GLOBAL WORKPLACE 1

1 Organizational Culture and Communication 1
2 Communication Processes in Organizations 32
3 Communicating with Technology 61
Communication Spotlights 90

PART II THE WRITING PROCESS 98

4 Planning Business Documents by Considering Audience 98
5 Planning Business Documents by Considering Purpose 129
6 Conventions in Correspondence: Common Strategies for Organization and Development, and Ways to Adapt Them 160
7 Planning Business Messages 186
Communication Spotlights 212

PART III WRITING BUSINESS CORRESPONDENCE 220

8 Letters, Memos, and Other Documents That Assume Audience Cooperation: Routine, Positive, and Goodwill Messages 220
9 Letters and Memos That Anticipate Audience Resistance: Negative Messages 250
10 Documents That Anticipate Audience Resistance: Persuasive Messages, Sales Messages, and Promotional Packages 279
Communication Spotlights 304

PART IV DESIGNING BUSINESS DOCUMENTS 314

11 Collecting and Interpreting Information 314
12 Designing Pages and Documents 342
13 Designing and Incorporating Visuals 366
Communication Spotlights 398

PART V PREPARING REPORTS, PROPOSALS, MANUALS, AND PRESENTATIONS 405

14 Functions and Structures of Reports 405
15 Proposals and Feasibility Reports 436
16 Instructional Documents 466
17 Oral Presentations 491
Communication Spotlights 520

PART VI PREPARING EMPLOYMENT AND ADMINISTRATIVE MESSAGES 533

18 Employment Messages: Resumes and Letters of Application 533
19 Job Interviews and Performance Appraisals 562
Communication Spotlights 589

Appendix A Formats for Business Documents A-1
Appendix B Documentation and Citation A-25
Appendix C Usage Handbook A-35

Notes N-1
Sources S-1
Index I-1
Credits C-1

Contents

PART I COMMUNICATING IN A DIVERSE GLOBAL WORKPLACE 1

1 ORGANIZATIONAL CULTURE AND COMMUNICATION 1

Organizational Culture Expressed in Communication: The UPS Response to NAFTA 3
Organizational Culture 5
SKILLS & STRATEGIES: Establishing Goals and Criteria 7
Establishing Corporate Direction 7
Corporate Goals, Mission Statements, and Strategic Plans 7
Criteria and Codes of Ethics 9
ETHICS: Tattletales, Sneaks, and Other Cultural Vermin 12
Stylesheets 12
MULTICULTURAL: The Unlucky Number 4 13
International Communication 14
Verbal and Nonverbal Communication 15
Three Accounts of Intercultural Communication 16
TECHNOLOGY: The Virtual Corporation: A Company of the Moment 18
Corporate Image 19
Corporate Image and the Community 21
Corporate Image and Corporate Communications 22
RESPONSE SHEET: Intercultural Communication 27
ACTIVITIES, EXERCISES, AND ASSIGNMENTS 28
Case: Censorship, Cultural Values, and Codes of Ethics 30

2 COMMUNICATION PROCESSES IN ORGANIZATIONS 32

Communication Style Within a Corporate Framework: Kate Kramer and Certified Mail 34
The Communication Process: Existing Views 35
Transmission Models 35
Reciprocal Models 37
Models Highlighting Assumptions 38
Communication Problems and the Three Types of Models 39
Communication Networks 41
What Normally Happens: Formal and Informal Channels 41
What Is Possible: Boundaries and Aids 43
ETHICS: Who's Been Reading My Mail? 45
Management Styles 46
Organizational Climate 46
Directives 46
Meetings 46
MULTICULTURAL: Planning for Multicultural Management 48
Listening 48
Agenda and Minutes 48
TECHNOLOGY: Meetings and Computer Decision Making 49
The Composing Process Within Organizations 51

SKILLS & STRATEGIES: Naming Your Subject 52
RESPONSE SHEET: Communication Models and Problems 57
ACTIVITIES, EXERCISES, AND ASSIGNMENTS 58
Case: American Surgical Products, Inc. 59

3 COMMUNICATING WITH TECHNOLOGY 61

Geist Software E-Mail Exchange 62
Electronic Communication Technologies 68
Telephone Systems 69
Facsimile Equipment 71
Computers and Computer Networks 72
SKILLS & STRATEGIES: Overcoming Computer Anxiety 72
ETHICS: Who Owns the Clock on the Internet? 74
TECHNOLOGY: ". . . Now Insert Disc C in Drive A" 76
MULTICULTURAL: International Iconography 79
Issues Relating to Communicating with Electronic Technologies 81
Information Overload 81
Anonymity 82
Lack of Interpersonal Contact 82
Organizational Values 83
Technology's Impact on Business Communication 84
RESPONSE SHEET: Using Technology 86
ACTIVITIES, EXERCISES, AND ASSIGNMENTS 87
Case: Hotel or Shelter? 88

COMMUNICATION SPOTLIGHT: COLLABORATION 90
Roles and Responsibilities for Teams and Groups 90
Traditional Teams 90
Nonhierarchical Teams 91
Webs and Networks 92
Activities and Questions for Discussion 93

COMMUNICATION SPOTLIGHT: REVISION 94
Establishing Guidelines and Standards 94
Sources of Style Manuals 94
Applying Guidelines and Standards 96
Editing and Reviewing 96
Activities and Questions for Discussion 97

PART II THE WRITING PROCESS 98

4 PLANNING BUSINESS DOCUMENTS BY CONSIDERING AUDIENCE 98

Why Audience Analysis Matters: The Bellencamp Story 100
Factors Basic to Audience Analysis 102
Factors Tied to Reader Characteristics 102
MULTICULTURAL: Target Audiences, Demographics, and Language Choice 103
ETHICS: Ethical Issues in Using Mailing Lists 104
TECHNOLOGY: Communicating to *Large* Audiences 105
Factors Tied to the Writer-Reader Relationship 107

Factors Tied to the Message 107
Factors Tied to the Occasion 107
Understanding How Audience Analysis Affects Writing Strategies 108
You-attitude 110
Pronoun Use 110
Positive Wording 112
Reader Benefit 112
Reader Use 113
Organizational Sequencing 114
Detail Selection 116
Document Design and Format Selection 117
Selection of Style 117
Readability 118
Document-Based Features 118
Reader Expectations and Attitudes 121
Context-Based Aspect 122
SKILLS & STRATEGIES: Avoiding Language That Is Offensive to Your Audience 122
RESPONSE SHEET: Analyzing an Audience 123
RESPONSE SHEET: You-attitude, Reader Use, and Readability 124
ACTIVITIES, EXERCISES, AND ASSIGNMENTS 125
Case: Hamilton Construction 127

5 PLANNING BUSINESS DOCUMENTS BY CONSIDERING PURPOSE 129

Why Purpose Is Important: The Cannes Dew Story 131
Characteristics of Purpose 133
Ties to the Main Idea 133
The Inclusion of Audience 134
Presentation of Purposes 134
Types of Purposes 135
Purposes Tied to the Communicator 135
Purposes Tied to the Message 136
Purposes Tied to the Occasion 136
Purposes Tied to the Audience 137
TECHNOLOGY: E-Mail Is Great, but Not for Everything . . . 137
ETHICS: Should I Be Polite or Right? Knowing Your Purpose for Communicating 138
Appeals and Purposes 138
Appeal to the Communicator's Character 139
Appeal to the Audience's Emotions and Values 144
MULTICULTURAL: The Impact of Cultural Concepts on Communication Goals and Purposes 146
Appeal to the Integrity of the Communication 148
Appeals, Purposes, and Planning 151
SKILLS & STRATEGIES: The Use and Abuse of Passive Voice 152
RESPONSE SHEET: Establishing a Purpose 153
RESPONSE SHEET: Appeals and Purposes 154
ACTIVITIES, EXERCISES, AND ASSIGNMENTS 155
Case: Booker Paper Company 158

6 CONVENTIONS IN CORRESPONDENCE: COMMON STRATEGIES FOR ORGANIZATION AND DEVELOPMENT, AND WAYS TO ADAPT THEM 160

Major Factors Influencing the Use of Conventions: Nick Sanger's Choice 162

Why Knowing About Conventions Matters 163

Aiding Communicator Decisions 163

Facilitating Reader Use 164

Establishing a Secure Writer-Reader Relationship 164

MULTICULTURAL: Differences in Convention Use Between Native and Nonnative Speakers of English 164

Defining the Communication Context 165

TECHNOLOGY: Internet Conventions 165

Conventional Organizational Strategies **166**

Deductive Sequences 166

Inductive Organization 167

Common Strategies for Development **167**

Common Logical Patterns 168

Developmental Patterns 168

SKILLS & STRATEGIES: Conventions and Lists 172

Issues Involving the Use of Conventions **174**

Departing from Convention 174

ETHICS: Promises, Promises: Is Deception Worth the Cost? 177

Ineffective Departures from Convention 177

Factors to Remember When Departing from Convention 179

RESPONSE SHEET: Conventions in Correspondence 180

ACTIVITIES, EXERCISES, AND ASSIGNMENTS 181

Case: Cross Pointe Consultants 183

7 PLANNING BUSINESS MESSAGES 186

Expert Planning: Hsing-Luen's Story 188

Defining Tasks, Planning Documents, and Structuring Arguments 189

The Nature of Planning 189

Claims in Argument 191

MULTICULTURAL: Considerations in International Documentation 193

Line of Argument 194

Components of Argument 197

ETHICS: Do Companies Really Live Up to Corporate Mission Statements? 197

Collaborative Planning 202

SKILLS & STRATEGIES: How to Be a Constructive Contributor 203

Visual Tools for Organizing Business Messages 204

Warnier-Orr Diagrams 204

Flow Charts 204

Project Management Tools 204

TECHNOLOGY: Projects by Computer 207

RESPONSE SHEET: Planning Business Messages 208

ACTIVITIES, EXERCISES, AND ASSIGNMENTS 209

Case: The Wymark Admissions Dilemma 210

COMMUNICATION SPOTLIGHT: COLLABORATION 212

Conflict: What to Encourage, What to Discourage 212

Affective Conflicts 212

Procedural Conflicts 212
Substantive Conflicts 214
Activities and Questions for Discussion 215
COMMUNICATION SPOTLIGHT: REVISION 216
Detecting, Diagnosing, and Revising: Bailing Out of Revision 216
Activities and Questions for Discussion 219

PART III WRITING BUSINESS CORRESPONDENCE 220

8 LETTERS, MEMOS, AND OTHER DOCUMENTS THAT ASSUME AUDIENCE COOPERATION: ROUTINE, POSITIVE, AND GOODWILL MESSAGES 220

Aspects of Audience Cooperation: Street Resurfacing in American City 222
Audience Cooperation 223
Strategies to Encourage Audience Cooperation 223
MULTICULTURAL: Cultural Differences in Business Letters 223
SKILLS & STRATEGIES: Maintaining Cross-Cultural Goodwill 227
Messages That Assume Audience Cooperation 227
Routine or Neutral Messages 227
Announcements, Reminders, and Simple Transmittals 227
Inquiries and Direct Requests 229
Positive Messages 232
Positive Responses 232
TECHNOLOGY: How to Stay Home, Save Money, and Conduct Business Long-Distance 233
Credit Approvals 233
Order Acknowledgments 234
Goodwill Messages 234
Public Relations Messages or Greetings 234
Welcome Messages and Invitations 236
Congratulations and Thank-Yous 239
ETHICS: What Hidden Agenda? Practical Concerns Behind Positive Messages 239
Document Webs and Series 240
RESPONSE SHEET: Inquiries/Direct Requests 245
RESPONSE SHEET: Positive Response 246
ACTIVITIES, EXERCISES, AND ASSIGNMENTS 247
Case: Worchester Family Clinic (WFC) 249

9 LETTERS AND MEMOS THAT ANTICIPATE AUDIENCE RESISTANCE: NEGATIVE MESSAGES 250

The Nature of Reader Resistance: Response to Jamison Cable 252
Reasons for Audience Resistance 253
Old and New Information 253
Traditional Practice versus Change 254
TECHNOLOGY: Where's the Superhighway Going? 254
Organizational Hierarchy 256
Group Membership and Shared Goals 256
Expertise 258

Overcoming Audience Resistance 258
Composing Negative Messages 259
Conventional Organizational Components 259
ETHICS: Can Bad News Be Good News? Phrasing Negative Messages 261
SKILLS & STRATEGIES: How to Say No 262
Negative Responses 264
Bad News about Orders 264
Claim Letters and Complaints 265
Negative Claim Adjustments 269
MULTICULTURAL: The Non-Western Negative Face 272
Adjusting Common Structures 272
RESPONSE SHEET: Reader Resistance and Negative Messages 274
ACTIVITIES, EXERCISES, AND ASSIGNMENTS 275
Case: A New Franchise for Major League Baseball 277

10 DOCUMENTS THAT ANTICIPATE AUDIENCE RESISTANCE: PERSUASIVE MESSAGES, SALES MESSAGES, AND PROMOTIONAL PACKAGES 279
SKILLS & STRATEGIES: Designing a Brochure with the Main Selling Point in Mind 281
Selecting the Main Selling Point: Tedlock Advertising 282
Persuasive Messages 283
The Implied Reader 284
Persuasive Requests 286
ETHICS: Cheers or Jeers—The Ethics of Junk Mail Appeals 288
Fund-Raising Letters 288
Collections 289
Sales Messages 292
Sales Letters 292
Humor in Sales Messages 293
Direct Mail 294
TECHNOLOGY: Internet Ads—A Big No-No? 295
MULTICULTURAL: The Importance of Being "Pop" in International Marketing 296
Promotional Packages 297
Promoting Goods and Services 297
Promoting a Particular Action or Behavior 298
Promoting Company Image 299
RESPONSE SHEET: Reader Resistance, Persuasive Messages, Sales Messages, Promotional Packages 300
ACTIVITIES, EXERCISES, AND ASSIGNMENTS 301
Case: Promoting Trust in Financial Trust 303

COMMUNICATION SPOTLIGHT: COLLABORATION 304
Negotiation on Workplace Teams 304
Separate the People from the Problem 306
Focus on Interests, Not Positions 306
Generate Alternatives 307
Establish Criteria 307
Activities and Questions for Discussion 308

COMMUNICATION SPOTLIGHT: REVISION 309
Using Global Revision to Strengthen Business Documents 309
Activities and Questions for Discussion 313

PART IV DESIGNING BUSINESS DOCUMENTS 314

11 COLLECTING AND INTERPRETING INFORMATION 314

How Pamphlet, Inc., Collected and Interpreted Information 316

Locating and Selecting Sources of Information 317

Library Resources 318

SKILLS & STRATEGIES: Selecting the Right Kind of Database 323

Computerized Databases 323

E-Mail 323

Internet 325

Informational Interviews 325

Focus Groups 328

Surveys 328

MULTICULTURAL: How Managers Can Better Understand Foreign-Born Employees 328

Interpreting Information 329

Recognizing Your Stance 330

TECHNOLOGY: Number Crunching 331

Recognizing the Importance of Question Structure 332

Assessing Errors in Logic 332

ETHICS: Data Massage: The Ethics of Graphics Displays 336

RESPONSE SHEET: Informational Interviews 337

ACTIVITIES, EXERCISES, AND ASSIGNMENTS 338

Case: Energy Commission Recommendation 339

12 DESIGNING PAGES AND DOCUMENTS 342

Designing a Conference Program: How Susan Foley Transformed Text 344

Applying Functions and Principles of Design 346

TECHNOLOGY: Desktop Publishing 347

Applying Design Principles to Business Documents 348

Chunking Information 348

Labeling the Chunks 352

Creating Visual Coherence 353

SKILLS & STRATEGIES: Using Serif and Sans Serif Typefaces 355

ETHICS: Considering Fine Print? The Ethics of Sleight-of-Hand Text 357

Establishing Emphasis 357

Redesigning Documents 360

MULTICULTURAL: Cultural Associations of Color 361

RESPONSE SHEET: Designing Pages and Documents 362

ACTIVITIES, EXERCISES, AND ASSIGNMENTS 363

Case: Thompson Appliances—A Design for Safety Instructions 363

13 DESIGNING AND INCORPORATING VISUALS 366

Choosing Visuals to Convey Image and Content: The Story of a Municipal Booklet 368

Adapting Visuals to Audience Needs 369

MULTICULTURAL: Graphics for International Documents 370

Functions of Visuals 370

SKILLS & STRATEGIES: Conventions for Creating Visuals 371

Organizing Data 372

Identifying Chronology 374
Identifying Relationships 377
TECHNOLOGY: Business Graphics 378
Showing Appearance 383
Identifying Location 385
Creating Appeal 386
Use and Misuse of Visuals 386
Manipulation and Distortion 386
ETHICS: Thou Shalt Not Pirate: The Ethics of Softlifting 389
Chartjunk versus Design Appeal 389
RESPONSE SHEET: Designing and Incorporating Visuals 393
ACTIVITIES, EXERCISES, AND ASSIGNMENTS 394
Case: Rock Springs Art Gallery/Historical Museum 396

COMMUNICATION SPOTLIGHT: COLLABORATION 398
Developing Productive Team Skills 398
Tuning In 398
Listening 399
Asking Questions 399
Sharing 400
Reflecting 400
Working Together 401
Activities and Questions for Discussion 401

COMMUNICATION SPOTLIGHT: REVISION 402
Eliminating Problems in Team-Written Documents 402
Failure to Create a Group Plan 402
Failure to Allow Time for Reading and Revising 402
Revision on a Team 404
Activities and Questions for Discussion 404

PART V PREPARING REPORTS, PROPOSALS, MANUALS, AND PRESENTATIONS 405

14 FUNCTIONS AND STRUCTURES OF REPORTS 405
Reports to Reinforce a Healthy Business Relationship 407
ETHICS: The Ethics in Corporate Voice: Annual Reports Speak About More Than Money 407
Purposes of Reports 408
Documentary Reports 409
Investigative Reports 413
Evaluative Reports 413
Functions of Conventional Components 416
Orienting Readers of Reports 417
TECHNOLOGY: Automatic Style 419
MULTICULTURAL: The Effects of Culture on Report Writing 421
Providing an Introduction for Readers 421
SKILLS & STRATEGIES: Does Your Document's Outline Work? 425
Persuading Readers 426
Including Details for Readers 427
A Sample Report 429
RESPONSE SHEET: Planning Reports 432
ACTIVITIES, EXERCISES, AND ASSIGNMENTS 433
Case: A New Social Services Program 434

15 PROPOSALS AND FEASIBILITY REPORTS 436

Connections Between Proposals and Feasibility Studies: The Solar Industries Reports 437
Characteristics of Proposals and Feasibility Reports 438
SKILLS & STRATEGIES: When Who You Are Counts as Much as What You Have in Mind 439
Conventional Segments of Proposals and Feasibility Reports 440
Proposal Components 440
Background 440
MULTICULTURAL: High- and Low-Context Cultures: How Much Information Is Enough? 441
Needs 442
Idea Section 444
Benefits 444
TECHNOLOGY: Creating Manageable Computer-Generated Presentations 445
Additional Benefits 445
Implementation 445
Recommendation 446
Conventional Segments of Feasibility Reports 448
Criteria 448
Overview of Alternatives 448
Assessment 449
Implementation 451
Principles of Argument in Proposals and Feasibility Reports 452
Argumentative Elements 452
Single-Option Feasibility Reports as Recommendation Reports 452
How Proposals and Feasibility Reports Are Evaluated 453
ETHICS: Ethics in Proposal Writing: Funding or Fleecing? 455
Example of a Proposal 456
RESPONSE SHEET: Proposals 461
RESPONSE SHEET: Feasibility Reports 462
ACTIVITIES, EXERCISES, AND ASSIGNMENTS 463
Case: Pizza Place Policy 464

16 INSTRUCTIONAL DOCUMENTS 466

Instructions for a New Market 468
Types of Instructional Documents 469
Informational and Instructional Sheets 469
Instructional Brochures 471
MULTICULTURAL: Using Symbols in International Documentation 472
Manuals 473
Reviews 476
Planning Instructional Documents 477
Analyzing Task and Purpose in Composing Instructions 478
Analyzing the Audience 479
Responding to the Occasion 479
Managing Constraints 480
Testing the Document 480

Using Conventional Elements in Instructional Documents 481
Orienting Readers 481
TECHNOLOGY: On-Line Documentation 481
Selecting Alternative Structures 484
SKILLS & STRATEGIES: Guidelines for Writing Instructional Material About Products 484
Considering Liability 485
ETHICS: What Are the Ethics of Warning? 486
RESPONSE SHEET: Instructional Documents 488
ACTIVITIES, EXERCISES, AND ASSIGNMENTS 489
Case: Lake View T-Shirt Controversy 490

17 ORAL PRESENTATIONS 491

Presentation Preparation: The Perils of Ignoring Time 492
Active Listening: Engaging Your Audience 496
Consider the Way People Listen 496
Reduce Distractions 497
Focus on the Audience 497
Encourage Audience Involvement 498
Make Information Accessible and Memorable 499
Vary Pacing in a Presentation 499
Purposes of Presentations 499
ETHICS: Oral Presentations as Reflections of Corporate and Personal Ethics 501
Preparing a Professional Presentation 501
Discovering What to Say: Invention 501
Deciding How to Arrange Information: Organization 502
Choosing the Right Words: Style 505
Learning the Presentation: Memory 506
TECHNOLOGY: Multimedia Presentations 507
Using Appearance, Voice, and Body Language: Delivery 508
SKILLS & STRATEGIES: Handling Questions from the Audience 510
Preparing Visuals and Other Support Materials 511
Functions of Visuals in Presentations 511
Handouts to Accompany Presentations 512
Types of Visuals for Presentations 513
Evaluating Presentations 514
MULTICULTURAL: Oral Presentation to an International Audience 516
RESPONSE SHEET: Oral Presentations 517
ACTIVITIES, EXERCISES, AND ASSIGNMENTS 518
Case: Intel's Flawed Pentium Chip—A Public Relations Quandary 518

COMMUNICATION SPOTLIGHT: COLLABORATION 520
Influences on Multicultural Teams 520
What Influences Attitudes about Group Interaction? 521
What Influences Leadership Decisions? 522
Where Do Team Members Get Their Information? 523
How Can Nonverbal Factors Be Misread? 524
Activities and Questions for Discussion 526

COMMUNICATION SPOTLIGHT: REVISION 527
Using Local Revision to Strengthen Business Documents 527
Agreement 528
Parallel Structure 528
Active and Passive Voice 528
Dangling Modifiers 530

Wordiness 530
Final Proofreading 530
Activities and Questions for Discussion 532

PART VI PREPARING EMPLOYMENT AND ADMINISTRATIVE MESSAGES 533

18 EMPLOYMENT MESSAGES: RESUMES AND LETTERS OF APPLICATION 533

A Job Search: The Jeff Foster Story 536
The Problem-Solving Nature of the Job Search 536
Planning Documents 537
Personal Inventories 537
TECHNOLOGY: Career Software Is Helpful, But . . . 539
Job and Company Description 540
MULTICULTURAL: What Kind of People Do Corporations Want for International Assignments? 540
SKILLS & STRATEGIES: Writing for Resume Banks 543
Resumes 544
Essential Information 544
Effective Information 547
ETHICS: What About Warts? The Ethics of Omission in Employment Communication 549
Elicited Information 549
Chronological and Functional Resumes 549
Letters of Application 551
Opening 552
Selling Your Credentials 552
Portfolios 553
RESPONSE SHEET: Letter of Application 555
RESPONSE SHEET: Resume 556
ACTIVITIES, EXERCISES, AND ASSIGNMENTS 557
Case: Pursuing Maxwell Financial Group 559

19 JOB INTERVIEWS AND PERFORMANCE APPRAISALS 562

A Company in Search of a Writer: Associated Insurance Selects a Job Candidate 564
Interviewing 564
Questions Asked by Interviewers 565
SKILLS & STRATEGIES: Dress for Success 565
Questions Asked by Applicants 567
MULTICULTURAL: An Example of Chinese Modesty 568
Interview Basics and Conventions 568
Difficult Interview Situations 569
ETHICS: What Can I Ask? The Ethics of Disclosure in an Employment Interview 570
Follow-Up 571
Performance Reviews 572
A Traditional Performance Review Situation 572
Approaches to Performance Review 573
Accountabilities and Measures 573
Performance Appraisal Documents 575

Alternatives to Traditional Performance Appraisals 577
TECHNOLOGY: Evaluating Employees by Computer? 579
Letters Addressing Employment Concerns 579
Letters of Recommendation 579
Letters of Resignation 581
RESPONSE SHEET: Job Interview Preparation 582
RESPONSE SHEET: Performance Review 583
ACTIVITIES, EXERCISES, AND ASSIGNMENTS 584
Case: A Performance Review for Pat Reardon 587

COMMUNICATION SPOTLIGHT: COLLABORATION 589
Designing Successful Teams 589
Reasons for Collaboration 589
Team Structure: How Is It Organized? 590
Activities and Questions for Discussion 592

COMMUNICATION SPOTLIGHT: REVISION 593
Revising, Editing, and Evaluating—Conducting Document Testing 593
Purpose of Document Testing 593
Types of Document Testing 593
Create a Testing Plan 595
Use the Results of Document Testing 596
Activities and Questions for Discussion 596

APPENDIX A FORMATS FOR BUSINESS DOCUMENTS A-1

APPENDIX B DOCUMENTATION AND CITATION A-25

APPENDIX C USAGE HANDBOOK A-35

NOTES N-1

SOURCES S-1

INDEX I-1

CREDITS C-1

Preface

Business Communication provides users with a fundamental yet complex picture of how to create effective messages within organizations. It is fundamental in that it covers various conventions used to address occasions for communicating in business and industry. It is complex in that it considers how the communicator, audience, message, and occasion all interact to define what will work well in a specific writing or speaking situation.

THE CONTEXT

We started writing this book to help a broad range of students with both the conventions and the complexities of business communication. We think that the elements of communicator, audience, message, and occasion are useful in explaining our rationale for this book.

Communicators

In writing this book, we have drawn on our combined experience of more than 50 years as teachers and workplace communicators. Our experiences range from teaching business communication in traditional classrooms and networked computer labs to working with business professionals in national and international companies. Sometimes our classrooms have been in community colleges, sometimes in small four-year colleges, sometimes in large research universities—and sometimes in corporate training programs. Some of our business experiences have been with traditional industries, some with multinational corporations, some with high-tech firms, some with government agencies, some with not-for-profit organizations, some with entrepreneurial businesses. From this melange of experience, we offer our own observations and suggestions, but we also draw ideas from useful research and from excellent workplace practices. So the voice in the book is ours, but we acknowledge a community of resources that contributes to our voice.

Audience

The primary audience for this book is students in business communication. While we know that each student is distinctive, with personal aspirations and ideas, we also assume that students have certain things in common. Specifically, we assume that students bring with them classroom and perhaps workplace experience, ambition to be successful professionals, and curiosity about how business communication can help them be more successful. Students may begin as inexperienced communicators hoping to develop some measure of proficiency, or they may be more experienced communicators who want to strengthen and refine their skill in dealing with complex communication situations. In any case, we hope students will leave this book having developed competence and confidence as business communicators.

Message

We believe, however, that learning the conventions of business communication isn't enough. Without also understanding the interaction among communicator, audience, message, and occasion, a workplace communicator will simply fall short. Thus, our primary goal in this book is to teach fundamentals of business communication without oversimplifying the rich texture of the situations that communicators find themselves in when speaking, writing, and reading in a corporate environment. Our main goal is to keep communicator, audience, message, and occasion at the forefront of our discussion of business communication conventions and strategies.

One of our secondary goals is to help students picture in detail particular occasions for both oral and written business communication. Another secondary goal is to explore workplace communication issues involving ethics, technology, and multicultural communication. Another is to offer students an ongoing discussion of two aspects important to composing business messages: collaboration and revision.

Yet another goal is to expand the range of organizations featured in business communication textbooks beyond the expected Fortune 500 companies and nationally recognized organizations to include small local businesses, entrepreneurial agencies, health-care offices, educational institutions, and municipalities that contribute to the complex world of business communication.

Occasion

Because this is a textbook, we have included certain features—both conventional and distinctive—for the purpose of making the content accessible and usable for the occasion of learning about and practicing business communication.

We are particularly concerned that students understand the complex contexts of business. As a result, we have several features that emphasize situations in which communication occurs.

- ***Narratives*** at the beginning of each chapter describe particular business situations relevant to the main subject of the chapter.
- ***Context boxes*** preceding many examples explain situational factors that are important to understanding the document.
- A chapter-length discussion of ***organizational culture*** situates presenting and writing business messages.
- Research-based ***sidebars*** about ***ethics, technology,*** and ***multicultural communication issues*** are related to the content in every chapter.

We believe that students will understand the conventions and complexity of business communication more quickly if they examine documents from actual companies as well as examples written by students much like themselves.

- Examples and models from feature companies—including ***3M, Northwest Airlines, Philips Media OptImage, Tedlock Advertising, UPS, and Dr. Wass Orthodontic Offices***—show up repeatedly throughout the book. Other organizations that have provided examples include ***Celestial Seasonings, Eastman Kodak, Iowa State University,*** and ***Working Assets.***
- Examples from ***students in business communication classes,*** especially examples in which students sought workplace clients or responded to realistic simulation activities, are found throughout the book.
- The rich selection of examples—both those from companies and those from students—are ***annotated*** to focus on the ways in which writers handle elements of audience, message, and occasion.

We are also concerned that students understand the processes as well as the skills and strategies to be successful business communicators.

- Twelve ***Communication Spotlights***—two at the end of each of the six parts of the book—discuss strategies for collaboration and revision in composing business messages.
- Discussions of key ***skills and strategies*** are presented in sidebars throughout the book.

Business Communication has distinctive features that make it easy to use and interesting to read. Those features also will make the book useful for occasions long after the course where it's first used.

- The overall ***approach*** is ***consistent.*** In every chapter, with every example, the discussion focuses on how the communicator, audience, message, and occasion influence business communication.
- Well-designed ***visuals***—tables, charts, graphs, diagrams—present principles and examples of effective business communication.
- Important ***key terms*** are signaled in boldface italics and then defined to help users expand their understanding of business communication.
- Highly ***readable discussions*** make it possible to quickly and easily understand the points in each chapter.

THE PARTS AND CHAPTERS

With these special features in mind, we'd like to preview how the six different parts of the book and the individual chapters link together to form a picture of business communication.

Parts

The book is separated into six parts. While each part has a specific focus, the elements of communicator, audience, message, and occasion are always part of the discussion.

1. ***Part I: Communicating in a Diverse Global Workplace*** (Chapters 1–3) introduces the contextual nature of communication in the workplace.
2. ***Part II: The Writing Process*** (Chapters 4–7) explores how audience, purpose, conventions, and planning strategies and tools affect your communication and help in planning business messages.

3. ***Part III: Writing Business Correspondence*** (Chapters 8–10) considers how writing or presenting various business messages is influenced by anticipated audience cooperation or audience resistance.
4. ***Part IV: Designing Business Documents.*** (Chapters 11–13) introduces a range of design issues—from what information to select to how to interpret and present it.
5. ***Part V: Preparing Reports, Proposals, Manuals, and Presentations*** (Chapters 14–17) shows how to prepare and present a range of longer business documents and types of talks.
6. ***Part VI: Preparing Employment and Administrative Messages*** (Chapters 18–19) shows how professionals can best present themselves when seeking a job and when facing a performance review.

Chapters

These elements should help you understand the principles of business communication through concrete stories and examples taken from actual business situations and through ample opportunities for writing and speaking practice. Each chapter contains six distinctive elements:

1. An ***introductory outline*** summarizes the main sections of the chapter.
2. The ***opening example*** highlights one or several issues important to the chapter.
3. A ***narrative*** or story about an actual business situation (sometimes pseudonyms are used) introduces topics covered in the chapter.
4. The ***body of the chapter,*** organized deductively with a bulleted forecast, models and examples from both feature companies and from students, and discussion of key points and examples—all illustrating workable principles of business communication.
5. ***Response sheets*** serve as an interactive review or checklist of specific principles of business communication presented in the chapter.
6. Apparatus at the end of each chapter includes ***in-class activities, individual and group exercises, out-of-class assignments,*** and a ***detailed case for analysis.***

While moving through the nineteen chapters in the book provides a complete, cohesive picture of business communication, it is possible to use the chapters in a different sequence that meets specific needs and interests.

THE SUPPLEMENTS

In order to help users increase their opportunities for understanding and using business communication, the textbook comes with a series of supplemental materials.

- ***Instructor's Manual:*** The 263-page *Instructor's Manual* is valuable both for instructors new to teaching business communication and for those with years of experience. The *Instructor's Manual* has a number of special features:
  ~ suggestions for class discussions in each chapter
  ~ summary notes for lectures for each chapter
  ~ suggested approaches for the end-of-chapter cases
  ~ suggested syllabi for both quarter and semester courses
  ~ answer keys for all exercises
  ~ reprints of selected essays about critical aspects of business communication
  ~ annotated bibliography for the topics in each chapter
- ***Test Item File:*** The TIF includes approximately 1000 multiple choice, short answer and true/false questions. Questions will also be classed by degree of difficulty. In the new test item file, short scenarios will be used for some questions. Page references will be provided for all questions.
- ***Prentice Hall Custom Test, Windows Version:*** Based on a state-of-the-art test generation software program developed by Engineering Software Associates (ESA), *Prentice Hall Custom Test* is suitable for your course and can be customized to your class needs. You can originate tests quickly, easily, and error-free. You can create an exam, administer it traditionally or on-line, evaluate and track students' results, and analyze the success of the exam.
- ***Color Transparencies:*** Full-color transparencies highlight key concepts for presentation and class discussion and analysis. Each transparency is accompanied by a full page of teaching notes that includes relevant key terms and discussion points from the chapters as well as additional material from supplementary sources.
- ***Communication Briefings Video Series & Video Guide:*** Accompanying the text is a series of videos from Communications Briefings, a firm known for its monthly newsletter and its video series. The eight-video set is available at no cost to teachers using *Business Communication.*

Included in the series are the following videos:

Building Cooperation: How Everyone Can Win at Work
How to See Opportunity in a Changing Workplace
How to Tap Employee Idea-Power
Resolving Conflicts: Strategies for a Winning Team
Listen & Win: How to Keep Customers Coming Back
Make the Phone Work for You
Make Presentations Work for You
Better Business Grammar

To order the set, call 1-800-388-8433. In addition, a separate video guide is available. Features include synopses of each video and discussion questions.

- ***Study Guide:*** The *Study Guide* features include a chapter overview, key terms and definitions, and true/false and multiple choice review questions. All answers can be found in the *Study Guide.*

THE ACKNOWLEDGMENTS

We'd like to thank the following people for their contributions to the book:

- the researchers and writers who worked with us
  - ~ David Clark, Lee Tesdell, Christianna White, and Rue Yuan, all of Iowa State University, and Michael Hassett, Boise State University, who helped with research issues
  - ~ Andrea Breemer Frantz, Iowa State University, and Judy Hamilton, Iowa Central Community College, who contributed the cases
  - ~ Jack Vivrett who wrote the format appendix
- the people and companies who shared their documents and stories
  - ~ Jon Austin and Jeff Smith, Northwest Airlines
  - ~ Walden Miller, OptImage
  - ~ Dave Tedlock, Tedlock Advertising
  - ~ Stephen Sanchez, 3M
  - ~ Bill Perry, UPS
  - ~ Kim Wass, Wass Orthodontics
- the students in our classes, some of whom are credited on their documents and some of whom preferred to remain anonymous
- the many reviewers who provided valuable suggestions for improving the manuscript
  - ~ Larry R Honl, University of Wisconsin–Eau Claire
  - ~ Lila Prigge, University of North Dakota
  - ~ George H Douglas, University of Illinois at Urbana–Champaign
  - ~ Henry Roubicek, University of Houston–Downtown
  - ~ Edward B. Versluis, Southern Oregon State College
  - ~ Kristin R. Woolever, Northeastern University
  - ~ Charles Marsh, University of Kansas
  - ~ Stuart C. Brown, New Mexico State University
  - ~ Roberta Allen, Western Michigan University
  - ~ John G. Bryan, University of Cincinnati
  - ~ James S. O'Rourke, IV, University of Notre Dame
  - ~ Judy McClain, Indiana University
  - ~ Geraldine E. Hynes, University of Missouri–St. Louis
  - ~ John Beard, Wayne State University
  - ~ Barbara Alpern, Walsh College
  - ~ Charles Marsh, The University of Kansas
  - ~ Binford H. Peeples, Fogelman College of Business and Economics
  - ~ Linda McAdams, Westark Community College

- ~ Sandra Littleton-Uetz, Purdue University–Calumet
- ~ Ronald J. Nelson, James Madison University
- ~ Katherine Staples, Austin Community College
- ~ Mrs. Mary Jane Patchin, Mankato State University
- ~ Larry R. Smeltzer, Arizona State University

- the folks at Prentice-Hall
  - ~ Among the many people at Prentice Hall who helped publish this book are Jim Boyd, Jim Campbell, John Chillingworth, Steve Deitmer, Linda DeLorenzo, Don Hull, John Larkin, and Pat Wosczyk. Special thanks go to Patricia Taylor, development editor, and Richard Lange, production editor at GTS Graphics, who put so much time into this project.

Business Communication

PART I
COMMUNICATING IN A DIVERSE GLOBAL WORKPLACE

CHAPTER

1

Organizational Culture and Communication

OUTLINE

Organizational Culture Expressed in Communication: The UPS Response to NAFTA

Organizational Culture

Statements of Corporate Direction

Intercultural Communication

Corporate Image

CRITERIA FOR EXPLORING CHAPTER 1

What we cover in this chapter	What you will be able to do after reading this chapter
Definitions of corporate culture	Discuss approaches to organizational culture and the roles communication plays
Statements of corporate direction	Discuss the roles various communication documents play in defining an organization's culture
Intercultural communication	Understand how national cultural factors influence intercultural communication
Corporate image	Discuss how communication helps build corporate image

"The shared values among employees, the heroes they create and stories they tell, the structure on which an organization centers—all these elements create a dynamic mix called corporate culture."—William J. Corbett, Vice President, Communications, American Institute of Certified Public Accountants, New York

Effective communicators recognize that communication fosters connections between different components within an organization, among separate organizations, and between organizations and the larger culture in which they operate. But effective communicators also recognize that communication actually creates, defines, and sustains culture in the corporation, the nation, and the world.

CONTEXT

The message shown in Figure 1.1 below appeared in the international edition of Northwest Airlines' *World Traveler*. Figure 1.2 (on the next page), which did *not* appear in the magazine, provides a translation of the vice president of Northwest Airlines Pacific Division Malcolm Bromham's message. Such communication provides insights into the nature of a corporation.

Figure 1.1 Letter Appearing in International Edition of Northwest Airlines' Magazine

NORTHWEST AIRLINES

ノースウエスト航空へようこそ

ノースウエスト航空が実施するリサイクリング・プログラムは、航空業界でも高い評価を得ています。当社は、毎年、機内から整備工場にいたるまで環境・資源保護の新しい方法を採用しています。全世界４万３千名にのぼるノースウエスト航空の社員が一丸となって、環境・資源保護のための努力を重ねているのです。

たとえば、ノースウエスト航空の客室乗務員は、現在、機内において缶、カップ、ナプキン等を分類して回収しています。リサイクリング会社はそれをさらに細分化し、最終的には、缶、ガラス、プラスチック等の素材に分類し、再生資源として再利用されることになります。

さらにノースウエスト航空では「アンダー・アワー・ウイング（翼のもとに)」と呼ばれるプログラムを導入し、機内食工場から余剰食品を全米のコミュニティーセンターに寄付しています。このプログラムにより、1993年だけで13万ポンド（約60トン）にものぼる食料品を寄付し、またガラス食器、紙ナプキン、ジュース・ソーダ類もあわせて寄付されています。

アメリカ国内路線では、機内食メニューとして、「ア・ラ・カルテ・メニュー」がこのたび導入されました。お客様は、メニューからお好きな物をお好きなだけお選びいただけますので、結果的に「食べ残し」が減り、資源保護の推進に役立つことになります。また「ビュッフェ・スタイル」のア・ラ・カルテも機内食にかかるパッケージの簡素化に大きく貢献しています。このようにア・ラ・カルテの導入で、機内食の「無駄」が従来に比べ約20%も削減されました。

地上においては「スマート・プログラム」と呼ばれるリサイクリング・プログラムを実施しています。主に機体整備工場において実施されているプログラムですが、機内のシートカバー、カーペット、その他備品のリサイクリング推進を目的としています。

上記に紹介しましたのは、ノースウエスト航空が、環境・資源保護を目的として実施しているプログラムの一部で、1993年だけでも当社は、毎月３百トンにのぼる資源リサイクリングを達成しています。

より清潔で、より健康な生活環境を実現すべく、当社はさらなる努力をしてまいります。

ノースウエスト航空
太平洋地区統括副社長

マルコム・ブラハム

Figure 1.2 Translation Provided by Main Office of Northwest Airlines

Northwest Airlines is recognized in the airline industry as a leader in recycling programs. Each year, we are finding more ways to protect our environment through recycling both on board the aircraft and at our maintenance facilities. Worldwide, our 43,000 employees are achieving goals that exemplify their commitment to this environmental philosophy.

On board the aircraft, our flight attendants use specially marked bags to gather cans, cups, napkins and other materials for recycling. A recycling company performs the final sorting of these objects and breaks them down into their recyclable components. The recycled materials are then sold to produce items including cans, glass and plastics.

Through a program called "Under Our Wing," extra food from Northwest flight kitchens is donated to food banks for distribution to community centers throughout the United States. In 1993, Northwest donated approximately 130,000 pounds of excess food. Other items donated include glassware and paper products, juices and sodas.

On Northwest flights throughout the United States, we recently introduced an A La Carte menu selection that lets passengers choose what and how much they want to eat, thereby reducing waste of unwanted items. Packaging of the in-flight meal was also reduced because it is served "buffet style." A La Carte has reduced by approximately 20 percent the waste introduced into the waste system from in-flight food service.

On the ground, we have a waste reduction and recycling program called SMARRT (Save Money and Recycle and Reclaim Today). The program is administered by employees at our maintenance facilities. Their goal is to recycle the majority of all materials removed from the aircraft, including paper, seat covers and carpeting.

These are just a few examples of how Northwest is taking action to help preserve the environment. In 1993 alone, Northwest recycled over 300 tons of materials per month. Our goal is a cleaner, healthier environment in which we all can live and work.

1. What story does Figure 1.1 tell about Northwest Airlines?
2. Why do you think this story is being told to a Japanese audience (or at least to readers of Japanese flying Northwest)?
3. In your opinion, what makes environmental responsibility a trait worth mentioning in the international edition of a magazine published by a major airline company? What does the publication of this story say about the corporate culture of Northwest Airlines? About cultures worldwide?

Malcolm Bromham's letter suggests various issues that are ultimately important to all communicators:

- How do the concepts of organizational and international culture help us understand business documents?
- How do communicators within companies implement criteria found in corporate mission statements, strategic plans, and codes of ethics? How do companies through such publications create and use stories about themselves?
- What factors are important to any given culture? What factors make each culture unique? How are these factors expressed or even shaped in communications?

ORGANIZATIONAL CULTURE EXPRESSED IN COMMUNICATION: THE UPS RESPONSE TO NAFTA

The United States Congress passed the North American Free Trade Agreement (NAFTA) in late November 1993. On November 4, 1993, all United Parcel Service (UPS) management people received the set of communications shown in Figures 1.3 through 1.5 (pages 4–6), which indicates that UPS anticipated NAFTA's passage and planned accordingly.

Jim Kelsey's memo (Figure 1.3), although brief, lends a great deal of insight into UPS as an organization:

- UPS has Prework Communications Meetings (PCMs).
- Management receives background and outline information regarding these meetings from corporate headquarters.
- These meetings involve management at every level of the corporation: officials at national headquarters, managers of various UPS regional sites, and managers of local operations.
- All UPS employees attend PCMs.
- Questions about PCMs are handled by the national office.

Figure 1.3 Cover Memo Regarding UPS's New and Enhanced Service

Prework
Communications
Meeting

Date: November 4, 1993

To: Corporate Headquarters Managers and Supervisors

From: Jim Kelsey

Subj: UPS's New and Enhanced Service to Canada and Mexico

Attached are a Prework Communications Meeting (PCM) Management Background and outline regarding UPS Service to Canada and Mexico.

Please duplicate and distribute this PCM to appropriate department, division and center managers. The PCM is scheduled to be given on Friday, November 12.

If you have any questions regarding this PCM, please contact Tom Farswath at ATLAS, 555-7745 in Corporate Communications.

Kelsey's memo signals that daily communication among all levels and parts of the company is an important element of company life. In fact, Prework Communications Meetings—three minutes of paid time—are scheduled for all employees (package car drivers, general operations personnel such as dispatchers, and employees in air operations) at the beginning of each shift. In addition to conveying information about timely topics, such as the new and enhanced service to Canada and Mexico, these meetings provide locally relevant information about the weather, sorting, and special events. UPS internal surveys have shown that UPS people prefer to get their information from their immediate supervisor. Through the daily PCMs, employees receive important information, and they receive it from their preferred source. UPS believes that communication is essential to the success of its operation.

Moreover, the particular occasion for writing (the new and enhanced service to Canada and Mexico) reveals that UPS has done a lot of work in anticipation of NAFTA's passage. In other words, UPS is responsive to developments at the national and international level.

The Management Background sheet for the PCM about the new and enhanced service provides an overview of the topic for management (Figure 1.4). As stated in the sheet's note, the purpose of the overview is to help managers "understand the PCM topic and answer questions." The background, which gives more details than the outline, is not read to all employees. This selective distribution of information ensures managers will be able to answer employee questions and enables PCMs to stay within 3 minutes.

The Management Background document tells us that information in the organization is filtered down on a need-to-know basis and that top management decides who needs to know what. This impression is reinforced by the outline (Figure 1.5 on page 6), which designates the key points to be conveyed to all parties and then singles out certain additional information to be given to specified audiences (and not to others).

This set of communications reveals quite a bit about corporate culture at UPS. The memos suggest that UPS operates hierarchically. They also suggest that communication within this structure is frequently top-down, with the national office very much in charge of detailed aspects of local operations. As suggested by the management background sheet, the further up you go in the corporate hierarchy, the more you know: at least, you receive more background information on a daily basis. In other words, communication not only reflects relationships, but also creates them within organizational culture. In the UPS case, the filter-down approach to communication creates and sustains separate groups or subcultures within the larger organization. At the same time, Prework Communications Meetings themselves represent a corporate practice aimed at creating common ground, since they are attended by all employees.

To fully understand this set of communications, however, you need to know more about

Figure 1.4 Management Background Sheet

The "remember" and "as we've discussed" cover a multitude of management meetings on the subject of new services to Canada and Mexico.

Separate meetings and publications are to cover details such as the actual rates and procedures. This sheet is simply an outline to inform all employees of the new services to be offered.

Prework Communications Meeting

MANAGEMENT BACKGROUND

(Please note: The Management Background provides more detail than the PCM outline. It will help you understand the PCM topic and answer questions. The Management Background should not be read to the group.)

UPS'S NEW AND ENHANCED SERVICE TO CANADA AND MEXICO

Remember, beginning Monday, the new and enhanced services to Canada and Mexico go into effect.

As we've discussed, U.S. customers shipping to North America now have the benefit of:

- Three services
  - Express
  - Expedited
  - Standard
- Efficient scheduling of shipments
- Computerized tracking
- Expert customs clearance service
- Additional billing options
- Shipment pricing.

Also on November 15, customers in Canada and Mexico will be offered a new portfolio of services for their North American shipments.

Rate/Zone Changes

A number of rate and zone changes will take effect as a result of the new and enhanced services to Canada and Mexico.

For service to Canada, new rates have been developed for Express and Standard, depending on shipping location and shipment destination. However, shippers will see substantial savings with the availability of shipment pricing for multiple-piece shipments.

For service to Mexico, zones for Express service have been renumbered. Rates will also change — customers will see a slight rate increase for lower weight shipments and a significant rate reduction for heavier weight shipments.

Procedures for Handling International Packages

The Worldwide Services and Service to Canada and Mexico training programs reviewed procedures for handling international packages, specifically those to or from Canada and Mexico. The attached PCM reviews the highlights of these training programs.

UPS itself, ranging from the type of company it is to how Prework Communications Meetings are conducted and perceived, and about the larger context, including how UPS's competitors are responding to the trade agreement. Further, you need to understand the implications of the trade agreement for U.S. corporations at large and, broader still, for the world economy. In short, even a brief business message, such as Jim Kelsey's quarter-page memo (Figure 1.3), exists within a complex cultural framework. The memo serves as both a response to and the result of a complicated social context. The memo provides a small piece in the picture of how this company works.

ORGANIZATIONAL CULTURE

Culture is the array of arts, concepts, habits, skills, tools, and institutions associated with a given group at a given time. Studies in individual cultures analyze the way a group confronts problems and challenges at a given point in its history.[1] Studies in **organizational culture** focus on individual corporations as one such group. If you were to study the culture of a particular organization, such as UPS, for example, you might examine company documents as one way of understanding that organization's response to the problems and challenges offered by a particular historical event, such as NAFTA.

Figure 1.5 Prework Communications Meeting Outline, Excerpted

The key points articulate the differences between express service, expedited service, and standard service under the new service.

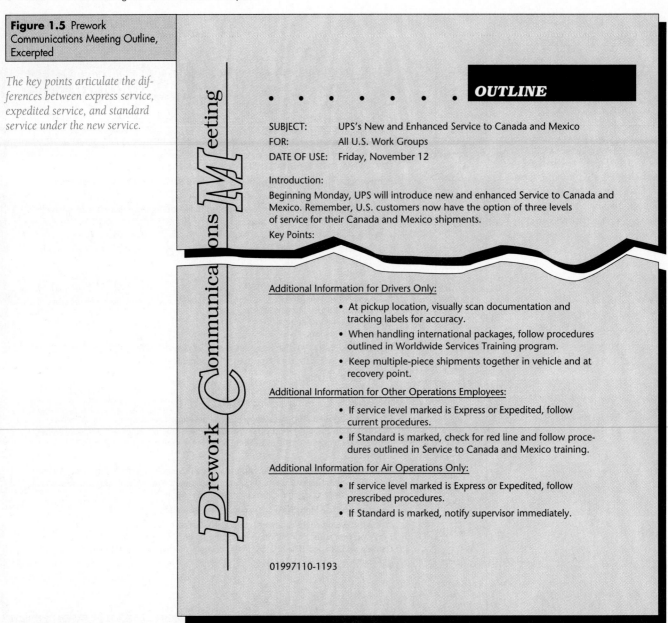

Prework Communications Meeting

OUTLINE

SUBJECT: UPS's New and Enhanced Service to Canada and Mexico
FOR: All U.S. Work Groups
DATE OF USE: Friday, November 12

Introduction:

Beginning Monday, UPS will introduce new and enhanced Service to Canada and Mexico. Remember, U.S. customers now have the option of three levels of service for their Canada and Mexico shipments.

Key Points:

Additional Information for Drivers Only:

- At pickup location, visually scan documentation and tracking labels for accuracy.
- When handling international packages, follow procedures outlined in Worldwide Services Training program.
- Keep multiple-piece shipments together in vehicle and at recovery point.

Additional Information for Other Operations Employees:

- If service level marked is Express or Expedited, follow current procedures.
- If Standard is marked, check for red line and follow procedures outlined in Service to Canada and Mexico training.

Additional Information for Air Operations Only:

- If service level marked is Express or Expedited, follow prescribed procedures.
- If Standard is marked, notify supervisor immediately.

01997110-1193

When doing research on an organization's culture, you might take one of two major approaches:

- focusing on shared factors or points of agreement
- focusing on elements of diversity or points of difference

If you took the approach that emphasizes *shared factors*, you might focus on the communication that promotes consistency, coherence, and shared values within the corporation, such as corporate mission statements that set goals for the company or stylesheets that encourage conformity in the firm's documents. More specifically, you might examine how Prework Communications Meetings help define common company goals, while at the same time instilling company pride at every level in the corporation. Certainly, the fact that these PCMs are a shared experience for every employee every workday at every UPS site contributes to a unified company culture.

If you chose to focus on *diversity* within a culture, you might explore aspects that help explain how a corporation operates within multidimensional situations. In doing so, you might study the complexity of the organizational webs within the organization or the various subcultures within it. You would examine the tensions that naturally exist within and

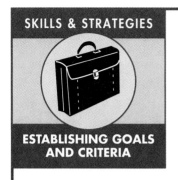

SKILLS & STRATEGIES

ESTABLISHING GOALS AND CRITERIA

Every year, *Fortune* magazine ranks over 400 corporations in its Corporate Reputations Survey, which uses eight key attributes (see pages 19–20) as *criteria* for evaluation. Many companies have adopted the *goal* of improving their performance in some or all of these categories.

The trick to *establishing goals* is to set them at an appropriate level. Linda Flower and John Hayes, who deal with goal setting in their classic 1981 article on composing, report that "middle-range" goals are crucial. Ineffective writers, for example, are able to set "high-level" goals (such as producing an A paper) and "low-level" goals (such as proofreading carefully) but have trouble setting the middle-range goals—defining parts of the task, providing an accurate picture of what each part entails and a realistic time frame for completing each part, and setting priorities of what must be done first, for example.

"Improving our company's rating in *Fortune* for innovativeness" is a high-level goal. It has the advantage of capturing the essence of what you are trying to do, but has the disadvantage of not telling you what is needed to get the job done. Corporations write strategic plans to ensure that they have middle-range goals. Middle-range goals for improving innovativeness might include soliciting employee input, discovering what companies highly rated for innovativeness do, and finding ways to target and support cutting-edge research and development.

Setting criteria presents similar challenges. If, for example, you are evaluating members of your collaborative team, you could have a high-level criterion ("good participation") or a low-level criterion ("on time to every meeting"). But middle-range criteria, such as "contributed on-point ideas that eventually aided in the organization and development of the final document," create a concrete game plan for group action.

You can set such criteria (and goals, for that matter) inductively or deductively. When Celestial Seasonings wanted to build a new corporate headquarters, it used both methods to determine design criteria. Celestial *discovered* criteria by meeting with interested agency and community groups to learn what was important to them. Celestial also approached the project with *up-front* criteria it drew from its corporate mission statement and strategic plan and made these criteria available to the firm designing the new building (see Figure 1.18 on page 22).

among cultures. For example, you might explore the potential effects, positive and negative, of the UPS practice of managing information so that communication progressively streamlines information as it makes its way down the chain to the diverse groups of employees within the company. In fact, the diversity approach might explore corporate managers, division managers, and various employee groups as separate subcultures operating with divergent interests within the organizational culture at UPS. In any case, looking at corporate communication would become a powerful tool for understanding these subcultures.

In terms of business communication, much of what we discuss in this book incorporates both perspectives. That is, this text balances the presentation of what has been successful in past corporate communication practice (what your documents have in common with documents written in response to similar occasions) with the recognition that variation and change from past practice is essential in reflecting the diversity and difference of each communication situation.

Whether focusing on shared factors or diversity, you should recognize that business messages are key objects in organizational culture. Ranging from insider jokes and company war stories to press releases and formal annual reports, these communications express the values held in the culture and represent the shared understanding of its members. You should also recognize that communication defines and supports corporate action. There are certain actions associated with corporate life, including career "rituals," such as entering an organization at an entry level position and then "coming up through the ranks." Each action entails communication. Initial employee job applications and interviews, for example, provide entry into an organization. Periodic employee review keeps track of an employee's progress and entails oral and written communication to evaluate performance (see Chapter 19).

ESTABLISHING CORPORATE DIRECTION

In studying corporate culture, you will discover that establishing objectives and criteria is very important. Objectives are aims or goals. Criteria are standards or tests for evaluating whether objectives have been met. Organizational goals explicitly appear in mission statements and strategic plans. Statements of criteria explicitly and implicitly appear in a range of corporate documents, including codes of ethics.

Corporate Goals, Mission Statements, and Strategic Plans

Corporate mission statements provide goals for employees and make a statement about the organization to shareholders and the general public. 3M, for example, includes a mission statement in its standard press package. The front side of the mission statement document

(Figure 1.6a) provides a broad summary of 3M's goals and objectives. The reverse side (Figure 1.6b) suggests how 3M's goals and objectives are met through

- its principles of management, success based on "new and useful products and services"
- an enhanced quality of life for its customers
- a positive work environment for its employees
- good citizenship for the corporation

Figure 1.6a 3M Statement of Corporate Goals

Corporate Goals and Objectives

3M is an organization of employees and stockholders who have combined their resources to pursue common goals in providing useful products and services, creating rewarding employment, assuring an adequate return to investors and contributing toward a better social and economic environment for the public generally.

3M

Figure 1.6b Specific Principles and Objectives from 3M Mission Statement

3M

In pursuing these goals, certain fundamental principles of management characterize 3M.

The first principle is the promotion of entrepreneurship and insistence upon freedom in the work place to pursue innovative ideas. Policies, practices and organizational structure have been flexible and characterized by mutual trust and cooperation.

Second is the adherence to uncompromising honesty and integrity. This is manifested in the commitment to the highest standards of ethics throughout the organization and in all aspects of 3M's operations.

Third is the preservation of individual identity in an organizational structure which embraces widely diverse businesses and operates in different political and economic systems throughout the world. From this endeavor there have developed an identifiable 3M spirit and a sense of belonging to the 3M family.

It is upon these principles that the following objectives are based:

Profits/Growth: 3M Management will endeavor to maintain optimum profit margins in all product lines in order to finance 3M's future growth and to provide an adequate return to stockholders. Expansion will not be an end in itself, but dictated by needs and requirements of the marketplace for new and useful products and services. In meeting this objective, 3M Management will work for the preservation and improvement of the profit system. It advocates free market principles.

Products/Customers: It is 3M Management's objective to develop and sell unique products and services of high quality and reliability that are genuinely useful to customers and consumers. In this mission, 3M contributes to a better quality of life and a higher standard of living for its employees and the public generally.

Human Resources: 3M Management believes that it is essential to provide an organizational structure and work climate which respect the dignity and worth of individuals, encourage initiative, challenge individual capacities, provide equal opportunity for development and equitably reward effort and contribution. It will endeavor to provide a stable work environment which promotes career employment. It believes 3M employees are the Corporation's most valuable resource.

Citizenship: 3M Management recognizes that 3M's business operations have broad societal impact. It will endeavor to be sensitive to public attitudes and social concerns in the work place, the community, the environment and within the different political and economic systems where 3M conducts business. It will strive to keep the public, employees and investors well informed about 3M business operations.

3M Public Relations Department

L. D. DeSimone, Chairman of the Board and Chief Executive Officer of 3M, summarizes 3M's mission this way:

> At 3M, we are committed to satisfying our customers with superior quality and value; providing investors with an attractive return through sustained, high-quality growth; respecting our social and physical environment; and being a company of which employees are proud.

3M communications promote shared company values. For example, in a six-page brochure entitled *Who We Are*, 3M expressly defines itself as an innovative culture based on initiative and positive relationships (Figure 1.7 presents two panels of the brochure). Such statements, in turn, provide a standard for future corporate action. In this case, the standards or criteria essentially say that 3M can continue to tell its story about being an innovative organization as long as it continues to follow a "cooperative path" in making "customers' lives easier and better."

Overall, such communication defines a particular organization's culture. In this case, the brochure *Who We Are* openly defines 3M as an "innovative culture" that benefits both from unity (shared values, policy of innovation) and from diversity (diverse markets and technologies, "individual and cultural differences").

Figure 1.7 Specific Principles and Objectives from 3M Brochure *Who We Are*

Notice the attempts to link past, present and future to the shared goal of innovativeness.

Top
3M medical laser imaging systems help both large institutions and small practices control health care costs by avoiding surgery and hospital stays.

Middle
The "McKnight Principles," issued in 1941, have become a cornerstone of 3M's values and culture.

Bottom
Masking tape is one of the earliest examples of 3M's practical approach to getting the job done better and more simply.

"Those men and women to whom we delegate authority and responsibility, if they are good people, are going to want to do their jobs in their own way. . . .

"Mistakes will be made, but if a person is essentially right, the mistakes he or she makes are not as serious in the long run as the mistakes management will make if it is dictatorial and undertakes to tell those under its authority exactly how they must do their job.

"Management that is destructively critical when mistakes are made kills initiative, and it is essential that we have people with initiative if we are to continue to grow."

from his "Philosophy of Management," a paper presented in 1941 by William L. McKnight, former President, 3M

Our Innovative Culture

3M's markets and technologies are diverse, but we are strong and united because of our shared values. Innovation, for example, is required at 3M. Thirty percent of each year's sales must come from products less than four years old.

But innovation is more than products, it's the way 3Mers do business.

In the early days of home video, many consumers were bewildered and frustrated by their machines. A creative Memory Technologies customer service supervisor used radio to explain video, appearing on talk shows to explain how to program your VCR and how to choose the right video tape.

The imagination of a practical 3M designer made possible the transfer of technology from automobile dashboards to the hospital darkroom. He recommended using electroluminescence (EL) panels (which typically illuminate automotive displays) in the safelight for the 3M Laser Imager. He knew EL panels were reliable. After all, he had installed one as a night light in the bathroom when his children were small. By the time the safelight project was launched, the children were grown and the EL panel in his bathroom was still glowing.

Of course, these 3Mers weren't working alone. Cooperation was essential. At 3M, we pride ourselves in forming innovative relationships within our own organization, with suppliers and customers, between domestic and international business units—relationships that respect individual and cultural differences and result in products that make life better for all of us.

Criteria and Codes of Ethics

Criteria are the means by which organizations measure whether they have met their objectives. Criteria are also the means by which communicators see whether they have met theirs. If, for example, your goal as a communicator is to be an effective business writer, one criterion you might use to evaluate your success in meeting this goal is whether document

Figure 1.8 Guidelines for Use of Letterhead

Note that Miller discourages writing form letters. This advice correlates with subsequent appeals for quality and courtesy in UPS correspondence.

GUIDELINES FOR USING UPS LETTERHEAD STATIONERY

- Only authorized people may send letters representing the company.
  - Any letter written on UPS letterhead represents the company.
  - The region/district manager designates who is authorized for the region/district.
  - The corporate department manager designates who is authorized for his or her department.
- A letter intended for a specific person should not be copied from a form letter but should be written with personalized information specific to that individual.
- All company letters should meet high standards of quality.
- Company letters should be:
  - Courteous
  - Friendly
  - Neat in appearance
  - Clearly worded
  - Carefully edited
  - Free of grammatical errors
- Letterhead stationery is distributed to the regions and districts through region supply, which submits all requests for reprints and typographical changes to the Communications Department in Corporate Headquarters for quality control.
- All letters, whether they are company letters or not, should be reviewed by someone other than the writer before they are sent.
- Letterhead stationery should never be used for an internal memo.

CONTEXT

With the growth in correspondence with people outside UPS, Communications Manager Mike Miller thought it important to issue guidelines regarding the use of UPS letterhead (Figure 1.8). In a cover memo, Miller stated that the purpose of the guidelines was to "ensure that people in the regions and districts generate UPS correspondence that maximizes their chances of creating a favorable impression and minimizes the chances of creating an unfavorable one."

testing (see the Communication Spotlight for Part VI, pages 593–597) establishes that your readers come away with a clear understanding of your message. Criteria are standards by which you measure your performance. Two basic types of criteria are

- **Common criteria:** standards important to *any* given situation. In communication, criteria such as whether the needs of the reader have been met can be applied to all documents.
- **Situated criteria:** criteria that may be good across situations, but are not present in every situation. In communications, corporate stylesheets present constraints that specify how particular company documents are to look and to sound.

Communication is essential in establishing the criteria (both common and situated) that are important to a corporation.

As a business communication text, this book provides you with criteria for business communication *that hold across situations*. For example, this book shows how considering audience and purpose is crucial to planning any given business presentation or document. Considering audience and purpose is important to you as a communicator, regardless of the organization you may represent now or in the future. Indeed, considering audience and purpose is important to communication outside of business as well.

The book also shows how criteria can be tied to a specific situation. Figure 1.8 suggests how *criteria can be situated in business*. This set of guidelines specifies when to use company letterhead on documents. The guidelines mentioned in this memo are specific to UPS and may or may not apply to other corporations.

Furthermore, Figure 1.9 shows how criteria may be specific to a single occasion. An **occasion** is a specific time, fact, event, or state of affairs that creates an opportunity for communication. In this example, the consultants for BIOBeef, a firm that offers strategic planning for ranchers and farmers, prepare notes about a particular proposal to J.D., the owner of a cattle operation. The notes reveal a number of criteria important to this particular reader and this single occasion for communication. In these notes, the situated criteria concern both the writers' tasks and the reader's assessment of this particular occasion:

- Writers must plan a report that considers both economic and strategic aspects of feasibility.
- Writers must gather data that include both grazing and feedlot operations.
- Both writers and reader apparently share the criterion that any proposal should be environmentally sound. Related to this is J.D.'s concern for conservation.
- The reader will assess the feasibility of the option based on the criteria of cost, scope, and ease of implementation.
- The reader will assess the acceptability of the option based on the criterion of its opportunities for economic modeling. (An idea may be feasible, or doable, but nevertheless unacceptable because of a reader's beliefs and preferences.)
- The writers' analysis suggests that the reader has ranked the criteria: cost and economic modeling are primary concerns, and scope and ease are secondary. Although tied to the issue of economic modeling, the stipulation that both grazing and feedlot operations be involved is a

Figure 1.9 Consultant Notes Showing Situated Criteria

Economic feasibility and strategic feasibility are criteria for the writers evaluating the option.

The fact that data must include both grazing and feedlot operations is another criterion for writing.

Conservation and cost represent criteria of equal rank for the reader. Scope and ease of implementation are additional criteria. Economic modeling is another criterion.

Purpose: To convince J.D. that diversification on a large scale is most appropriate to his situation.

Notes: This option (large-scale diversification) should be both economically and strategically feasible; since his decision will be based on the findings of this report, J.D. will be intent on having accurate data on the impact to both grazing and feedlot operations.

Fortunately, J.D. comes to this report with a positive attitude toward environmental approaches, as represented by large-scale diversification. He is also equally concerned about conservation and cost. The drought the past three years has been hard on cattle, land, and profits.

J.D. sees his alternatives as full commitment to the drug-free program, partial dedication involving only marginal areas of the current beef production operations, or total rejection of the drug-free beef program.

J.D. will evaluate the proposal mostly on feedlot cost figures, with scope and ease of implementation being secondary concerns. Although the grazing operation factors represent low-level concerns, they are important to the larger concern for economic modeling, which is a primary factor in J.D.'s evaluation.

low-level concern, indicating that J.D. apparently will take recommendations that focus on one operation or the other. With these ranked criteria, both writers and reader will evaluate which alternative for beef production (paragraph 3) is best for his ranch.

Figure 1.10 shows how these situated criteria appeared in the finished document.

Another example of situated criteria is **codes of ethics,** which set standards for ethical action within a particular organization. These criteria may cover multiple occasions for action, but are still situated according to profession and to organizational expectations. To be *ethical*, you would have to conform to the standards of conduct of a given profession. These standards sometimes, but not always, deal with *morality* in the sense of considering certain actions either "right" or "wrong." For example, it is not *ethical* for a judge to hear a case involving her own interests. But such conflict of interest is defined differently by every profession and is a concept that changes over time. It *might* be ethical, for example, for a chief executive officer of a major corporation to consult on a project that includes, in part, goods and services provided by his corporation. What is unethical for a judge might be fine for a CEO. And, by extension, what is unethical for a company providing goods to the civilian market might, in fact, be ethical for a company providing goods for the Defense Department. Moreover, what is acceptable in either market can change over time.

Because of the industry-specific or "situated" nature of ethical criteria, many corporations and institutions provide a written code of ethics for all employees that specifies how to act in their particular organization. These codes can cover a range of areas, including communication. For example, a financial institution's code of conduct might state:

> Extreme care must be exercised to avoid any statements that could be interpreted as the giving of legal or tax advice. The customers should always be encouraged to consult with their own attorneys and consultants.

The institution thus makes appropriate communication a part of its code. A company's code of ethics becomes a set of criteria for evaluating performance.

As the 3M example suggests, goals and criteria are closely related. Goals can be interpreted as a set of standards to measure company performance. For 3M, innovativeness is a corporate goal. For those evaluating 3M, innovativeness becomes a criterion for evaluating 3M's performance. Because goals can become criteria, the two are easily confused. Take, for example, an excerpt of a letter to employees of The Stanley Works that names the four goals or "pillars" of the corporation (Figure 1.11 on page 12).[2] These pillars represent objectives

Figure 1.10 Situated Criteria Expressed Explicitly in Report

The writers include specific level criteria in their bullets.

The writers also incorporate what they know about the reader's priorities in how they relate the criteria to each other hierarchically.

CRITERIA

We will evaluate each of these three alternatives according to four criteria:

- cost
- conservation
- opportunities for economic modeling
- scope of adoption necessary
- ease of implementation.

These criteria are rank-ordered, with cost and modeling opportunities being primary. Scope and implementation will involve both feedlot and grazing operations, with the grazing factors important mainly to modeling opportunities.

ETHICS

TATTLETALES, SNEAKS, AND OTHER CULTURAL VERMIN

Are whistleblowers tattletales, sneaks, and troublemakers? Or are they well-educated, well-liked, and committed employees? Although research shows the latter to be true, whistleblowers "continue to be ostracized and humiliated by the companies they hope to improve." (Etorre 8)

Although every corporate action has possible ethical and legal consequences, whistleblowing can bring out the worst in people. "Fear of bad publicity, expensive litigation, and loss of business can make a company hostile and defensive, usually at the expense of the whistleblower's personal or professional reputation." (Etorre 19–20) For example, when A. Ernest Fitzgerald, a financial analyst for the Air Force, testified before Congress about $7 claw hammers costing $436 and 25-cent washers costing $693 each, he was fired from his position, his staff was labeled "attic fanatics" (their cramped offices were on the upper floor of the Pentagon), and it took Fitzgerald 13 years to get his old job back.

Employees need to understand that the ethical stances of a company are not always completely reflected in the official code of ethics, but are also picked up as part of learning the ropes at a particular corporation. To be able to blow the whistle without coming under attack, employees need an organizational climate that "both discourages illegal (or other objectionable) conduct and promotes internal reporting and resolution of wrongdoing." (Smith & Oseth 188–89) They also need to be aware of certain dos and don'ts:

Do	Don't
Make sure your allegation is correct. Something may look fishy but be allowable under a technicality you don't understand. Also, find out whether your state provides protection for whistleblowers. The law may require that you follow special procedures.	Assume a federal or state law will protect you as the "good guy." Legal protection for private-sector workers is often inadequate and varies widely from state to state. Most federal protection covers only government workers.
Keep careful records. Document what you've observed—and your attempts to rectify the problem or alert a supervisor. Keep copies outside the office.	Run to the media. You may be giving up certain rights or risking a defamation suit. Check with an attorney before contacting any reporters.
Be realistic about your future. Talk to your family and make sure you're prepared for a worst-case scenario, which can include loss of job, severe financial burdens, and blacklisting in your field. Even if you're not fired, you may be treated with suspicion by colleagues and management alike.	Expect a windfall if you're fired. Although some states allow punitive damages, you may be eligible for back pay and reinstatement—in a place where you probably don't want to work anyway.

that guide both the internal and external actions of the organization and suggest that the same courtesy afforded customers, suppliers, competitors, and investors should govern relations between employees.

The corporate principles in Figure 1.11 are objectives: to produce valuable products and services, to conduct the company's relations with integrity, to treat associates with respect, and to make quality the watchword of the organization. However, these goals can become criteria for evaluating any given action within the company. All actions of employees and of the corporation itself must meet the criteria of value, integrity, respect, and quality. For example, an annual report that did not include accurate earnings data would not fulfill the criteria of integrity and quality and, therefore, would be unacceptable according to company standards. These criteria would apply to *any* Stanley Works communication, product, or service.

Figure 1.11 Set of Corporate Principles to Guide Actions

- Making available to our customers needed products and services of real *value*.
- Conducting all of our business and community relations with *integrity*.
- Treating our employees, suppliers, customers and all with whom we associate with *respect*.
- In all matters, whether it be the products we make, the services we provide, the people we hire or the way we conduct ourselves—to make certain that *quality* is the glue that holds together everything that happens here at Stanley.

Stylesheets

Stylesheets are in-house publications that set standards or establish criteria for corporate communication. The prospect of conforming to company standards might seem alien to Americans, who have lived in a culture that champions individuality. But, as *Fortune* reporter

Figure 1.12 Stylesheet Concerns

STYLESHEET TOPIC AREA	EXAMPLE
Common criteria (these involve communication principles or rhetorical concerns)	The stylesheet for Digital Equipment Corporation begins with a section about the importance of audience and purpose, and establishes an emphasis on clear thinking and a positive perspective. The second section deals with ways the writer fits into the "interests, schedules, and responsibilities" of other people in the corporation.
Format; page layout	The Stone & Webster Engineering Corporation (SWEC) establishes uniform standards for letters, memos, transmittals, conference notes, resumes, experience records, proposals, general reports, and technical reports. These standards include specifications for margins, type font and size, and other instructions such as "Except for proposal letters, SWEC business letters bear no complimentary close."
Style and usage	Stylesheets in general contain information about such aspects as whether certain words are to be hyphenated or not ("use 'coauthor,' not 'co-author'"), how to punctuate ("do not repeat the dollar sign [$] in lists"), and whether to use company names or their trademarks ("use MTAB• for Structural Analysis, Inc.").
Content	Some stylesheets specify how to handle content. A literal example of this is the stylesheet for the U.S. Coast Guard that specifies that a security classification must be assigned to every message and located just before the text of the message. Similarly, the AT&T stylesheet provides guidelines for indicating proprietary statements (those statements considered the property of the organization). In a different respect, the SWEC stylesheet specifies how attendees are to be alphabetically listed in conference notes: (1) client personnel, (2) outside companies or organizations and personnel, (3) other non-SWEC personnel, and (4) SWEC personnel.

Richard Pascale puts it, "getting recruits to adopt the corporate collection of shared values, beliefs, and practices as their own" plays an acknowledged role in the process of becoming part of an organization's culture.[3] Adopting a shared way of communicating is an important step in "learning the ropes" in any corporation.

Stylesheets prescribe the way a company's communication should look, and the organization expects each communicator in the firm to conform to the guidelines established in its stylesheet. The emphasis on conformity at some corporations is very strong. For example, communication guidelines at Procter & Gamble are very specific. Messages conform to such a highly detailed stylesheet that a corporate executive once remarked, "You can take the writings of five hundred men [sic], and in twenty minutes, you can find the P&G guy."[4]

Stylesheets frequently comment on a range of concerns and reflect individual company preferences (Figure 1.12). In addition, stylesheets can be quite detailed in what they do cover. Philips Media OptImage, a computer software firm headquartered in Des Moines, has an extensive stylesheet running 210 pages. The table of contents shows the following separate detailed chapters:

- Principles and Style
- Manual Organization
- Templates, Formats, and Fonts
- Lists
- Graphics and Tables
- "Nuts and Bolts."

A separate appendix covers commonly misspelled words.

MULTICULTURAL

THE UNLUCKY NUMBER 4

Did you know that the number 4 is similar in Japanese culture to the unlucky 13 in Western culture? Did you know that in many Asian and Native American cultures, it is impolite to look someone in the eye? Did you know that foreign companies doing business in Eastern Europe have to be conscious of dialects when writing product labels?

Each of these questions raises potential problems in verbal and nonverbal communication when you are doing business in a multicultural setting. Northwest Airlines, for example, dropped Flight 4 from its schedule when it discovered the cultural implications of the number 4 to the Japanese. Businesspeople operating with Pacific Rim companies keep their eyes lowered when conducting business face to face. And Americans doing business in Eastern Europe discovered that in Poland foreign companies should write their labels in imperfect Polish to show that they are trying to fit in but aren't quick enough to be fluent. But in the Czech Republic and elsewhere, labels are written in perfect English or High German because labels in local dialects are associated with poor product quality.

Figure 1.13 OptImage Stylesheet: Principles or Common Criteria

The "this" referred to here is having effective documents from the outset (no trial and error at the consumer's expense).

◆◆◆ Principles and Style

We accomplish this by approaching each manual with the following principles firmly in mind:

- Users must consciously and conscientiously work at learning about our products and how to use them. This means that, contrary to popular jargon, our products are not intuitive.
- Users are intelligent people, but they are not mind readers. Thus, implied information cannot be trusted, and what is obvious to a creator is not always obvious to a user.
- Users should be treated as amicable peers, not unruly children—explicate, don't patronize.
- Presenting information in the context of its use is preferable to presenting it as raw information—the former encourages active learning, the latter only passive memorization.
- Repeating key information is desirable, especially if the repetition puts the information in the context of its use.
- Text and graphics are functional and educational, not artistic and entertaining. However, functional and educational work can be designed artistically.
- Organizational consistency within a manual and across manuals is important, but "A foolish consistency is the hobgoblin of little minds" (Ralph Waldo Emerson).
- Documentation conventions—both in-house and industry-wide—should be broken only if doing so works to the user's advantage.

The order in which these principles are given demonstrates the hierarchy of our concerns.

Users are first—what works for them, works for us.

Information is second—descriptions are okay, procedures are essential.

Conformity is third—if a pattern or convention works, use it.

CONTEXT

OptImage strives for its documents to have "an appropriate look and feel" from the beginning. Because OptImage produces "complex multimedia tools that are components of intricate systems for creating interactive titles," writers face the task of making their writing complex enough that it reflects the richness of the software and simple enough that the user can create finished products with the information provided.

Sample pages from this stylesheet show that communicators in this organization are provided with both common and situated criteria for evaluating corporate documents (Figures 1.13 and 1.14, respectively).

Figure 1.14 OptImage Stylesheet: Bulleted Lists or Situated Criteria

Among other things, the stylesheet distinguishes between bulleted and numbered lists, and when to use each.

Bulleted lists

We use bulleted lists extensively for two purposes: itemization and explanation. Although each purpose has distinctive stylistic features, all bulleted lists have the following features in common:

- an introductory sentence or sentence fragment that ends with a colon
- diamond-shaped bullets
- bullets left-aligned with the paragraph that contains the introductory sentence
- text indented .25 inch from the paragraph that contains the introductory sentence
- two or more specific elements, each of which has a separate bullet
- an utter disregard for sequence

This last feature is especially important, for a bulleted list should never be used to set out a list of items in which sequence is significant. Sequential lists should be numbered.

INTERCULTURAL COMMUNICATION

Intercultural communication, or communication between distinct cultures, is commonly equated with international communication—people of one nation communicating with those of another. But intercultural communication can occur even when the communicators are from the same country or even from the same organization.

Although the culture of a particular organization can be defined by the organization's common goals—examples are 3M's "innovativeness" and its shared practices, such as observing a specific stylesheet—the culture of organizations is not necessarily uniform. Various subcultures can exist within a single organization. Diverse distinguishing traits, such as gender, race, age, or ethnicity, can make for distinct subcultures. Power relationships and status or class also work to set up subcultures within an organization. Even geography (branch offices at different sites) can result in subcultures defined by different goals and practices. When members of subcultures communicate, there is intercultural communication. Occasions for intercultural communication thus include

- communication between two organizations from different countries
- communication between two organizations within the same country
- communication between employees who are part of the same multinational corporation but who are working at different sites
- communication between subcultures within an organization (for example, engineering and marketing, or the "Chicago group" and the "Boulder group," or management and labor)
- communication between employees within the same organization who are part of the same subculture but have distinct ethnic backgrounds (for example, a first-generation American project engineer with Palestinian roots, a Jewish software engineer, a Chinese-national software engineer with her "green card," and a test engineer whose mother is a member of the Daughters of the American Revolution)

To understand the impact that culture has on communication, we present three scenarios:

1. SNAP Hardware and Ramirez Rope, where differences in national identity lead to miscues in verbal and nonverbal communication.
2. ABC/DEF, Inc., where members of the merged corporations of ABC and DEF constituted different "ethnic" groups or subcultures within the newly formed company and where the dominant group expressed its power by using verbal and nonverbal communication to define company goals and practices in its own terms.
3. The Apple Valley Transit Authority (AVTA), where ethnic, racial, and gender differences as well as conflicting power structures contributed to offensive communicative practices, personified by "shoptalk."

Before presenting these scenarios, however, we provide a brief definition of verbal and nonverbal communication, both of which play a role in each of the scenarios.

Verbal and Nonverbal Communication

For our purposes, **verbal communication** encompasses both oral and written communication, because each uses words as a way of conveying meaning. This book focuses on how to use words successfully in business.

Nonverbal communication depends on factors other than words to communicate a message. As upcoming narratives suggest (pages 16–19), nonverbal communication can range from appointing minorities to management positions to designing the corporate headquarters to "make a statement" about corporate values. It can include the type of accommodations you provide corporate guests and the kind of mentoring you provide employees. It can be seen in the speed at which you reply to requests and the time that you devote to a joint venture or project. Nonverbal communication can involve the clothes that you wear, as well as a host of other factors, including body language and tone of voice.

Between 65 and 90 percent of what we communicate is nonverbal. Nonverbal behavior is culturally based. Communicators, therefore, need to be aware of how their gestures will be interpreted in another culture. In Buddhist cultures, for example, you must never touch anyone's head, since the head is considered sacred. In Muslim cultures, you must never touch, pass, receive, or eat with the left hand, which is considered unclean. The American circular "A-OK" gesture is considered vulgar in Brazil, Paraguay, Singapore, and Russia. Crossing your ankle over your knee is considered rude in Indonesia, Thailand, and Syria. Pointing your index finger toward yourself insults the other person in Germany, the Netherlands, and Switzerland.

You also need to be aware of how you interpret others' gestures. Chinese stick out their tongues to show surprise, Japanese hiss through their teeth to indicate embarrassment or "no," Hondurans touch a finger below their eyes to indicate disbelief, and Vietnamese look at the ground to show respect. Closely related to gestures is the acceptability of touching. Anglos usually avoid contact, while Latinos tend to prefer substantial touching. Hearty handshakes are the norm in Australia, while light shakes are common in France. In Asia, bows replace handshakes as a greeting. (See the Communication Spotlight for Part V, on cultural differences, pages 520–526.) In short, communicators cannot take the interpretation of certain nonverbal behaviors for granted.

Three Accounts of Intercultural Communication

1. SNAP Hardware and Ramirez Rope.[5] The story of SNAP Hardware and Ramirez Rope suggests particular difficulties that emerge when cultures that are diverse internationally try to communicate.

> Between 1985 and 1988, SNAP, a family-owned hardware firm in Chicago, attempted several joint ventures with Latin American companies. SNAP, which had an international agreement with a company in Taiwan, was now seeking to expand its markets.
>
> At a 1985 trade show, the president of SNAP met the two Ramirez brothers, owners of a large Mexican rope manufacturing firm. (Rope is a logically related product for a firm such as SNAP that sells attachment hardware.) SNAP and Ramirez Rope agreed to explore the possibility of a joint venture under which Ramirez Rope would manufacture braided rope for SNAP and SNAP would market the rope as attachment hardware in the United States and abroad. Afterward, the president of SNAP estimated that his company could enjoy a 20 percent cost saving and expected speedy implementation of the joint venture.
>
> But progress was slow. The Ramirez brothers had little time to devote to the project except during the two one-week trips SNAP executives spent in their factory. Ramirez Rope did not hire new employees to handle SNAP's prospective business, nor did it purchase the equipment necessary to make the polypropylene braided rope SNAP needed. For its part, SNAP did not think to explore the possibility of locating and perhaps purchasing used equipment that Ramirez could use. After a number of exchange trips that involved SNAP's president and vice president, the president of SNAP decided the venture was a "no go" when he discovered that Ramirez Rope had also been talking with another U.S. firm that SNAP considered its competitor.
>
> Although Snap's president several times expressed his concern that he "didn't want to offend the Mexicans," his behavior (as indicated in the table that follows) might not have always been consistent with that goal. The table also suggests that communication barriers involve more than just language differences and that lack of cultural knowledge can communicate itself in a number of verbal and nonverbal ways.
>
> Underpinning these communication difficulties were differences in cultural values concerning time, social class, gender roles, and risk taking.

As a result of unsolved difficulties in intercultural communication, the proposed joint venture between SNAP Hardware and Ramirez Rope collapsed. But as the next two accounts show, the communication difficulties in this international setting are no more serious in nature than the problems experienced when various subcultures try to communicate. The two accounts of United States firms that follow demonstrate how differences among subcultures can undermine attempts to create a workplace that is at once culturally diverse and productive.

COMMUNICATION DIFFICULTIES	
Verbal communication	• Both Ramirez brothers spoke English, although none of their employees did. No one in the SNAP office spoke Spanish well enough to conduct business. The brothers did not phone on a regular basis. SNAP officials phoned but could not talk to the secretaries if neither Ramirez brother happened to be in the office. They could not tell if the brothers were at the bank for 15 minutes or out of town for a week. SNAP made no attempt to bring a bilingual employee on board the project. • On one trip, the brothers took the president and vice president of SNAP to an elegant restaurant on Lake Patzchero, where small fish, a local specialty, were served. The president refused to eat any, joking, "Back home, we use fish that size for bait." The Ramirez brothers, although gracious, were not amused.
Nonverbal communication	• In Mexico, Ramirez Rope housed SNAP officials in an elegant resort overlooking the city and paid for their food and transportation as well. In Chicago, SNAP lodged the brothers in a businessperson's basic suburban motel chain and paid per diem expenses. The standard accommodations were normal for U.S. businesspeople, but were several cuts below those provided by Ramirez.

CONTRASTING CULTURAL EXPECTATIONS	
Time	• The president of SNAP expected action on the joint venture within 90 days and viewed the Ramirez delays as "laziness." The Ramirez brothers were busy meeting domestic production and exploring other joint ventures, and devoted only designated weeks to the project when SNAP officials were there.
Social class and gender roles	• SNAP officials never fully appreciated that while they were upper-middle-class American businesspeople, the Ramirez brothers were members of the local elite and should have been treated as such. The Ramirez brothers were uncomfortable with the concept of women, especially wives, taking part in business. They expressed serious concern that the vice president of SNAP, a woman, should leave her 7-year-old at home when she flew to Mexico on business. The vice president of SNAP expressed concern that she would be expected to "play tour guide" to the Ramirezes' wives if they made a trip to Chicago with their husbands.
Risk taking	• SNAP executives viewed the $20,000 they sunk into this project as a necessary cost of doing business and expanding their markets. The Ramirez brothers were concerned that they were being asked to expand their production and purchase additional machinery and raw materials to make rope that they could not sell in their domestic market—all by prospective partners whom they had known for less than a year.

2. Nonverbal Behavior and "Corporate Ethnicity" at ABC/DEF, Inc.[6] The story of ABC/DEF, Inc., shows that organizational membership can be like membership in an ethnic group. The account suggests how communication can express deeply held differences in "corporate ethnicity." In this case, members from two different corporations have been united as part of a corporate merger and become subcultures within the newly formed corporation.

> ABC/DEF, Inc., which manufactures, markets, sells, and distributes a line of nationally known products, has fewer than 1,000 employees: 60 percent work in the headquarters of a large southwestern city, another 15 percent work in the manufacturing plant, and the remaining 25 percent are sales and quality control personnel scattered across the country. Although, functionally, ABC and DEF *merged* in 1986, in practical terms, ABC took over DEF.
>
> After analyzing the DEF culture, ABC management determined that DEF elements had to be radically changed to fit with the ABC culture. Even so, two years after the merger the employees perceived the companies as having two separate identities and cultures, although only four employees from the original DEF headquarters remained and the DEF company was restructured to run like the dominant ABC company. Divided loyalties, alienation, and hostility prevailed.
>
> The following nonverbal behavior at company headquarters convinced DEF employees that they were being discriminated against:
>
> - the dismissal of the strong 27-employee Sales Planning and Administration Department, a DEF department that had been left intact in the merger and was led by a former DEF employee
> - awarding of all promotions from within to ABC people and none to DEF people
> - unequal access to support staff *("We have a presentation to give next week just as ABC does. Guess whose materials were completed first by the support staff.")*
> - changes in reporting systems so that all forms and documents looked like ABC's, even though some DEF communications were excellent *("It's a major victory to get two words changed in an ABC form.")*
>
> Verbal behavior reflected the fact that ABC employees, who considered themselves "lean and mean," continued to perceive DEF people as wasteful and indulgent:
>
> - DEF was repeatedly referred to as "all wings and no feet." *("DEFers come up with high-flying ideas without any discipline or structure.")*
> - ABCers liked to tell a story about one new DEF executive who was given an annual bonus. The new executive objected because his department had not met its goals. The DEF executive in charge said, "It doesn't matter; just take it and keep quiet." *(DEF had an incentive bonus plan not based on performance.)*

TECHNOLOGY

THE VIRTUAL CORPORATION: A COMPANY OF THE MOMENT

In today's extremely competitive global market, companies have increasingly come to collaborate with other companies. Companies form alliances to create a **virtual corporation:** a company without buildings or offices that represents a combination of divisions from various organizations and often exists just long enough to produce a product.

Take TelePad Corporation, for example. Formed in 1991 to produce handheld computers, TelePad, which employs only a handful of engineers and designers, collaborates extensively: Intel Corp. does the processing, a battery maker provides the power source, and IBM supplies the manufacturing facilities. TelePad concentrates on what it does best and gets others to do everything else. In exchange, the collaborating firms get a foothold in the burgeoning handheld computer market.

The success of virtual corporations might mean that the corporate practice of maintaining a marketing department, a production department, and a shipping department all under the same roof could eventually disappear. Organizations might specialize in joint ventures, choosing to concentrate on what they do best and saving themselves overhead and serving their customers better in the process.

- ABCers made a point of recalling that DEF had boxes and crates full of unopened audiovisual equipment—so much that ABC/DEF, Inc., equipped its new expanded space, including even the break rooms, with this equipment and had some left over.

> ABCers refused to change or even compromise. ABC management personnel tried to force DEFers to make all the changes, for better or for worse. At the same time, employees of each group tried to hold on to the practices and values of their original corporations. The members of each group ate together, worked together, and socialized together, *pointedly excluding* members of the other group, whose offices were mere feet from their own. Intercommunication between the two groups was minimal.

At ABC/DEF, Inc., it is clear that one subculture is intent on dominating the other. This situation is clearly revealed through nonverbal communication: ABCers are strategically placed to advance to upper management at ABC/DEF, Inc., while DEFers are fired or excluded from prominent positions. This situation also shows a culture (ABC) resisting change in an attempt to reproduce (or clone) itself. Verbal and nonverbal expressions of this resistance abound. Verbally, ABCers dismiss the progressive and creative thinking of DEFers as "all wings and no feet." Nonverbally, ABCers eliminate systems and benefits just because they were part of DEF culture. The unequal access to support personnel and the insistence on the ABC stylesheet also dramatize ABCers' attempt to preserve their culture without change.

3. "Shoptalk" and Chaos at the Apple Valley Transportation Authority.[7] The story of Apple Valley Transportation Authority (AVTA) demonstrates how the evolution of cultural expectations can involve communication difficulties. At AVTA, the integration of minorities into the workforce, mandated by developments in the U.S. culture at large, creates havoc within the organizational culture. In addition, the old top-down models of control used by both corporate and union management at AVTA foster conflict rather than communication between the various subcultures.

> Michele Wender Zak, a consultant to the Apple Valley Transportation Authority (AVTA), reported that in the struggle to integrate the AVTA's workforce, the firm's once homogeneous (white male) and orderly vehicle maintenance staff was in chaos: "Within the space of a month, over 60 charges of race and sex discrimination and harassment had been filed by maintenance employees—against management but also against each other, and against each other and management jointly. Worse still, some minor acts of violence among the employees had occurred and threats of violence were proliferating."
>
> Corporate officials tried to deal with the difficulties by using an authoritarian management structure that had evolved after World War II as military veterans filled management slots in the company. Management focused communication downward (through orders and directives issued from the top), and the communication itself ranged from guarded to hostile. Most significantly, management did not offer a core group of white male employees, who felt displaced by women and African-American and Latino subcultures, any opportunities "to participate in reframing the organizational culture in the face of the new demographics."
>
> The core-group rank-and-file employees responded by practicing "exaggerated forms of behaviors, speech, and working patterns long familiar, if less flagrantly practiced in maintenance yards in earlier years." They became "enthusiastic perpetrators of obscene and

abusive language that they tellingly called 'shoptalk,'. . . [which] bespoke raw power of superior strength, sexual prowess, and racial and gender superiority." Shoptalk became a gauntlet thrown at the feet of management and new workers: "Take away shoptalk through your new work rules and sexual harassment regulations, and you betray the community that built AVTA and, in fact, furnished the fertile ground for the new order that seeks to displace us." Like management, union leadership was ineffectual. *Every* male employee, regardless of race and ethnicity, was subject to harassment and hazing, some of it violent, if he was not part of the core group. Yet, union officials refused to see the problem as serious and continued to focus on traditional concerns, such as benefits.

The setting produced a highly charged atmosphere where upper-management efforts to address the situation backfired. Acting unilaterally, upper management made these decisions:

- fired an executive director and appointed a low-key female manager to replace him
- fired one supervisor named in litigation growing out of charges of harassment and placed other named supervisors under probation and surveillance
- called a mass meeting of agency employees—middle managers and rank and file alike—and announced a zero tolerance policy for racially or sexually discriminatory behavior, with termination as the outcome for infractions of the policy

Rank-and-file employees felt that real issues dividing the various groups were "ignored in the undifferentiated reprimand and threat of reprisal." Middle managers felt their efforts to solve the problems were "being repudiated." Upper management's tendency to command rather than to communicate—that is, to consult, collaborate, and negotiate—turned out to be a corporate practice leading to chaos.

At AVTA, the old power structures of both the corporation and the union were inadequate to the task of reinventing the newly diverse corporation, represented by the various subcultures. The top-down communication from both the corporate and the union hierarchy failed to rally the troops. Employees could not successfully communicate their concerns to management, to the union, or to each other. Employees within the hierarchical structure became polarized: core group versus non-core group. The division between employees thus cut across racial and ethnic lines. The organizational structure no longer represented stable communication relationships among the employees, and constructive communication ground to a halt.

All three of the foregoing accounts show how cultural differences are created by and reflected in communication. With SNAP Hardware and Ramirez Rope, different ingrained cultural understandings of nonverbal behavior (for example, Ramirez' "slow" response to SNAP's proposal or SNAP's selection of basic rather than elegant accommodations for Ramirez) in each case created the sense that one company was undervaluing the other. In addition, SNAP's president's comment about small fish and Ramirez' disapproval of the SNAP vice president's leaving her children behind reflected cultural differences between the parties. At ABC/DEF, Inc., ABCers defined corporate practice by taking control of the corporate stylesheet. The informal communication networks reflected the differences between ABC and DEF subcultures. The ABC and DEF networks were mutually exclusive. At AVTA, a particular type of communication—shoptalk—defined the division between the core group and all other subcultures at the company. Shoptalk also created division between the various groups when it escalated into harassment, confrontation, and violence. All three accounts speak to the complexities of intercultural communication.

CORPORATE IMAGE

One aspect of organizational culture that is shared by organizations worldwide is a concern for corporate image. **Corporate image** refers to the reputation that a company develops and nurtures over time. It is the story a corporation tells about itself. To be sure, it matters who is telling the story. At ABC/DEF, Inc., for example, the corporate image would most likely be the picture of a unified company, benefiting from the merger of two diverse companies. And it would be *the story according to ABC*. Even so, both ABCers and DEFers would benefit from a positive corporate image for ABC/DEF, Inc., despite its not telling the whole story.

Corporate image is a very important company asset. Recognizing its importance, *Fortune* runs an annual survey to determine corporate reputation for a sample of the largest U.S. corporations. *Fortune* rates companies according to eight criteria:

1. Financial soundness
2. Value as a long-term investment
3. Wise use of corporate assets
4. Innovativeness

5. Ability to attract, develop, and keep talented people
6. Quality of products or services
7. Quality of management
8. Community and environmental responsibility[8]

Fortune's final rating on corporate reputation or image is the average of the separate scores a company gets on these factors. *Fortune*'s factors have become criteria by which companies evaluate themselves. 3M, for example, emphasizes innovativeness as a key element in its corporate identity and success (see Figure 1.7 on page 9).

A positive corporate image attracts top-notch personnel, customers, and investors: three key elements in creating a successful business. It can also see a corporation through times of crisis and can help a company gain or regain public trust. A strong corporate image helped Johnson & Johnson survive the Tylenol crisis in 1982, caused when someone packed cyanide into capsules in Chicago, killing seven people; and it has likewise helped ARCO maintain positive public relations despite its involvement in "big oil."[9] We see the importance of corporate image as an asset in the growing number of commercials on television and in magazines that in no way offer a product but, instead, sell the image of the entire organization.

Figure 1.15 Initial Letter for Input on Company Name

TEDLOCK
ADVERTISING & PUBLIC RELATIONS

[date]

[inside address]

Dear [first and last name here]:

As a highly valued [friend/dealer/distributor—select one], you're in a position to offer us some important input during an exciting and dynamic time at Simmons Pump.

Over the past 26 years, Simmons Pump Corporation of Arizona has grown and changed. As you may know, we began as a small company associated with Simmons Pump of Lubbock, Texas.

Today, we are the independent manufacturers of a wide array of engineered pumps. Our agricultural customers remain very important to us; our growth is also due to our expansion into manufacturing pumps for industrial uses.

Because of our growth and our developing product line, we've decided to change our name. We've retained an outside marketing consultant, Dave Tedlock, to assist us in our name change. Within a few days, you'll be receiving some material from Dave as well as a call from him.

We'd appreciate your responding to Dave's questions about some new company names we are considering. Changing our name offers us a great opportunity to get your feedback, grow more rapidly, and become even better able to serve our customers.

If you have any questions or concerns, please feel free to call me or our General Manager, Ken Brightwell, at (602) 555-2273. Thanks, in advance, for your input. You'll be hearing more from us about our name change in the near future.

Sincerely yours,

6303 E. Tanque Verde • Suite 210 • Tucson, Arizona 85715 • (602) 555-1598 • Fax (602) 555-0955
Member: American Association of Advertising Agencies (AAAA)

Communication, in fact, is a key factor in developing and maintaining a good corporate image. It involves

- preparing and distributing written and multimedia materials to clients and consumers
- responding to customer inquiries and complaints courteously and quickly
- developing an internal communications system to allow employees to ask questions about policies and practices
- reporting on community participation and corporate philanthropy in annual publications
- developing a body of public relations materials that establish corporate identity
- using various channels to communicate and promote that identity within the company and to the general public

Corporate Image and the Community

Corporate image creates a meeting ground where company culture and community cultures address the same values. Key public sectors to consider in developing a corporate image include customers, employees (and possibly their representatives, such as union leaders), stockholders, the general public, opinion makers (such as educators and the media), financial analysts, governmental agencies, and special-interest groups (such as environmentalists).[10]

For example, friends, dealers, and distributors were the public entities addressed by Simmons Pump in its search for a new company name. Name development is a crucial part of corporate image. There are firms devoted solely to corporate name development, like NameLab in San Francisco; and other firms, like Lippincott & Margulies, which deal with the gamut of corporate identity issues.[11] In this case, Simmons Pump wanted a new company name to account for an expansion in its product line. Simmons Pump retained Tedlock Advertising to get the job done. (See Figures 1.15 and 1.16.) The letter in Figure 1.15 appears on Tedlock letterhead instead of Simmons letterhead, because readers are to respond to Tedlock about the name change. When in final form, the letter in Figure 1.16 will go out under Simmons' new name and logo.

While the Simmons Pump example shows the business community getting involved in a corporate identity issue, corporations also get involved in communities as part of building a corporate image. The UPS Community Internship Program is an example of a community program designed to contribute to a positive corporate image. The program, in existence since 1967, places company managers at various community sites, like inner-city schools and drug rehabilitation centers, for four weeks. The program is reciprocal in that

Figure 1.16 Second Letter Regarding Company Name

Dear [first (and possibly last) name here of dealer or distributor]:

Recently you should've received a copy of the enclosed announcement about our changing our name to Simflo Pumps. We've kept the "Sim" in Simflo to remind people of our 26 years of success in the pump business. We added the "flo" to emphasize that we're on the move.

To give you the best opportunity to serve your current "Simmons" customers and continue to promote our pumps to current prospects, we are completing our name change quickly.

Many important qualities about our company remain the same. As you know, ownership and management here have always been one and the same. That's still true—our ownership, and therefore our management, remains the same.

It's also true that we will continue to:

- Manufacture all the "Simmons" pumps in our product line
- Maintain our extensive parts inventory
- Manufacture all of our own engineered pumps and custom work right here in our own plant—not everybody can say that!

We all benefit from our new name. One benefit is that our pumps and parts will no longer be confused with Simmons of Lubbock. Now, when your buyers specify and/or buy a Simflo pump, we can all be sure it's one of ours.

Our name change also gives you a great opportunity to get your name in front of your current customers and prospects. One way to do that is to send out our attention-getting announcements (sample enclosed), with your business card inserted in the slot provided.

We'll provide all the announcements and envelopes you need at no charge—just call us with your order. Plus, you'll be getting additional marketing help from us soon. We are producing a new brochure, and we've got another surprise for you coming in the mail in a few weeks.

Thanks again for your support. We are looking forward to working with you in making 1993 a record year in sales for both of us.

Sincerely yours,

both managers and communities benefit. It helps managers gain firsthand knowledge of the effects of social ills and helps the community by providing aid to people in need. UPS publications regarding this program link its objectives to the UPS corporate mission. The introduction to the *1993 Community Internship* publication (Figure 1.17) establishes that link in a letter from Kent C. Nelson, then CEO. The 70-page publication then goes on to dramatize interns in action at one of four sites: Henry Street Settlement House, on Manhattan's Lower East Side; St. Margaret of Scotland, on Chicago's South Side; facilities for the physically and mentally challenged at the University of Tennessee in Chattanooga; and social service agencies in McAllen, Texas, in the Rio Grande Valley.

Figure 1.17 Corporate Objectives and Corporate Image

As providers of distribution solutions for a global community, UPS strives to understand and respond to the needs of a diverse population. This commitment to understanding challenges us to address the socioeconomic issues facing individuals—both in the communities we serve and in our own company.

Corporate Image and Corporate Communications

Corporate image, which is built and maintained in part through such community programs, is communicated in a variety of ways, both verbal and nonverbal. For example, in the early 1980s, Celestial Seasonings, Inc., developed a master plan for its organization that included the construction of a new corporate headquarters in Boulder, Colorado. Written documents reveal how the *design* of the new building (a nonverbal element) was to *make a clear statement about the corporation itself*. Figure 1.18 shows the design criteria as they appeared in a "Master Plan" report.

Figure 1.18 Design Criteria Reflecting Corporate Goals and Promoting Company Image

Prior to the commencement of Master Plan activities, Celestial Seasonings developed design criteria to guide Master Planning. These follow:

"Celestial Seasonings' building and grounds must make a clear statement about ourselves. They must take the following elements into consideration in the following priority:

- Commitment to the efficient and effective flow of work both in the office and in manufacturing. In reflecting this, the facility must not be a monument, but reflect an economical and yet highly creative use of resources both in the construction of the building and in the systems which our employees will be utilizing. In addition, as a food plant, it must meet all appropriate GMP regulations.
- Commitment to teamwork. The facility should encourage and support people's ability to work together and should not create undue distinctions between classes of employees. This should be true not only for groups within the office and manufacturing functions, but also to encourage interaction between the office and manufacturing functions. The facility must convey the love and respect that we have for all our employees in providing a safe and stimulating environment in which they may work.
- Concern over the use of natural resources. The facility should be as energy efficient as practically possible while allowing as much natural light as possible into all work areas.
- Dedication to herbs and botanicals. Our facility should convey a natural, serene atmosphere, yet represent the vitality of the organization. Additionally, it should make a clear statement about the importance of botanicals to us as an organization.
- Love of our customer and consumer. Our facility should welcome visitors and tell them things about the company that words can't. In this vein, the facility should provide for the ability to conduct tours of our operation and incorporate a retail store.
- Love of art and uplifting philosophy. Our style is that of realistic fantasy, and the facility should provide a proper atmosphere to convey this.
- Commitment to health. In keeping with our commitment to health, both in our products and in our employees, recreational facilities should be a part of the overall plan."

While every communication coming out of an organization contributes to corporate image, some publications are designed specifically to build and promote that image:

- annual reports
- press releases
- newsletters
- company newspapers

Annual Reports. **Annual reports** summarize a company's financial situation. Although companies initially wrote these reports to satisfy Securities and Exchange Commission requirements, corporations are increasingly using annual reports as a tool for building and promoting company image.

Eastman Kodak, for example, uses its red and yellow corporate colors as a nonverbal rally point in its annual report (Figure 1.19). Complementing the identity established by the familiar red and yellow is the mention of Kodak's goals for health-based products and employee health care: quality, access, and cost-effectiveness. These corporate goals encourage an image of a quality-minded, accessible, cost-conscious, and caring organization.

In addition to financial data, annual reports now include a message from the CEO, detail about corporate achievements, information about employees, a summary of fiscal highlights, and other elements designed to create a positive corporate identity. Annual reports are becoming a standard component in corporate promotional packages (see Chapter 10).

Figure 1.19 Community Action Building Corporate Image at Eastman Kodak

SILVER
Kodak
Health care in the 1990s means three things: Quality, access and cost-effectiveness. Kodak's health businesses work together to achieve positive patient outcomes and, ultimately, improved quality of life.
Health: A commitment to a dynamic, $2 trillion global market.
17

Press Releases. **Press releases** present good news about a corporation to opinion makers, primarily the media. Such releases generally anticipate reader cooperation (Chapter 8) and are arranged deductively, with the good news first, followed by details and a positive close. Press releases follow other conventions. For example, press releases characteristically contain a date and an opening summary that specifies who, what, where, when, why and how (journalism's 5Ws and an H). Attachments giving specific data are common. When reader resistance is anticipated (see Chapters 9 and 10), releases open with an attention getter. Releases are usually triple-spaced for electronic media and double-spaced for print media for clarity and reading ease. Releases always name a contact person with whom the media can consult.

Occasions for press releases at Northwest Airlines (Figure 1.20) are fairly typical of those for businesses nationwide.

Figure 1.21 is an excerpt from a press release reporting company performance at 3M. The entire release runs two pages, with an additional three pages of numerical data showing (1) the sales change analysis for the third quarter, (2) a consolidated statement of

Figure 1.20 Occasions for Press Releases

PRESS RELEASE OCCASIONS	NORTHWEST EXAMPLES
Change in personnel	Ken Levinson, formerly Vice President for Tax, Risk Management and Insurance, is named to new position of Vice President of finance and planning of cargo and charter division.
Improvement in services	NWA/KLM doubles its joint service from Detroit and Minneapolis–St. Paul to Amsterdam. NWA increases service to Osaka, Japan.
Recognition of excellence	NWA receives award for best in-flight audio programming and best in-flight original program of nearly 40 airlines evaluated by a 12-judge panel. Gold Clio Award goes to NWA and KLM for best television music spot of the year.
Change in business partnerships	The advertising agency relationship between NWA and Fallon McElligott is terminated. NWA selects Meredith Publishing to publish in-flight magazine, *World Traveler.*
Change in financial factors	NWA has firm commitments for purchase of approximately 70% of jet fuel for 4th quarter 1994.
Change in policies	NWA announces no-smoking policy for new Seattle/Tacoma–Hong Kong nonstop service. NWA makes improvement in frequent flier program.
Report of performance	October 1994—NWA reports 4.88 billion revenue passenger miles in September, up 2% from September 1993.
Short-term offer	NWA introduces one-day Mall of America fares, companion fares, and mystery trips.
Change in equipment, materials, training, etc.	NWA announces agreement with United Technologies Pratt & Whitney for the purchase of 40 hushkits for 40 McDonnell Douglas DC9-30 aircraft powered with Pratt & Whitney JT8D engines, with option to purchase as many as 90 more. Northwest Aerospace Training Corp., subsidiary of NWA, begins 15-month Boeing 757 simulator training program for more than 100 Continental pilots.
Corporate response to union position	NWA reports its response to IAM District 143 lawsuit.
Impact of government decision	U.S. Department of Transportation ruling affirms NWA's increased service to the People's Republic of China.
Improvement in public image	NWA initiates promotion of charitable partner, SightFirst (Lions Club project to eliminate preventable blindness); other charitable partners in previous years include Make-a-Wish, Pediatric AIDS Foundation, Big Brothers/Big Sisters, Boys and Girls Clubs.

Figure 1.21 Excerpt of 3M Press Release Showing Conventional Components

Who: 3M.

What: Record sales and earnings.

When: Third quarter.

How: The figures show how the record sales and earnings were made.

Why: There was solid growth in unit sales and continued productivity.

3M News

Contact: Jon Greer
(612) 555-1915

IMMEDIATE RELEASE

3M Reports Record Third-Quarter Sales and Earnings

ST. PAUL, Minn., Oct. 24 — 3M today reported record sales,net income and earnings per share for any third quarter.

Sales totaled $3.820 billion, up 9.7 percent from the third quarter last year.

Pre-tax income totaled $553 million, an increase of 10.0 percent from the third quarter last year. Net income was $341 million, compared with $316 million in the year-earlier quarter. Earnings were 81 cents a share,* up 11.0 percent from the comparable quarter last year.

L. D. DeSimone, chairman and chief executive officer, said, "Our operations in the United States and internationally both contributed to the increase in earnings. Earnings benefited from solid growth in unit sales and from continued productivity improvement."

In the United States, 3M's unit volume increased about 9 percent, with growth well-balanced among the company's business sectors.

income, and (3) a consolidated balance sheet. The asterisk (Figure 1.21) refers to a notation on the second page: "All share and per-share data reflect a two-for-one stock split effective March 15, 1994." The press release concludes with the optimistic forecast that good earnings will continue into the fourth quarter.

Newsletters. Although it is beyond the scope of this book to explain in detail how to write newsletters, you should nevertheless be aware that newsletters are important to developing and maintaining corporate image.

Newsletters can cover a variety of topics and concerns, and, like press releases, generally feature good news about the company. Even so, newsletters can serve a variety of functions, from reporting a company's earnings and activities to introducing new products and publicizing a company's community service activities. Newsletters range from slick, multi-page documents to simple bi-fold affairs. (Chapter 12 shows how design plays an important role in producing these publications.)

Even a simple publication can help create and maintain a business's image. Figure 1.22, on the next page, is a page from a newsletter from the orthodontic office of a Dr. Kim Wass of Ames, Iowa. This publication is directed at employees and clients and their families. Because

Figure 1.22 Newsletter Excerpt Promoting Goodwill and Company Image

MOUTHGUARDS FOR SAFETY

We now carry safety mouthguards made especially for the needs of those who wear braces. They are made by a company called Ormco who also makes some of the braces we use.

The Ormco Sportsguard has several features that go beyond other mouthguards. Its custom fit can be re-formed up to four times in warm water, which is ideal for the changing teeth of those who wear braces. The center is also gel filled for added protection in cushioning the teeth.

The cost to purchase one of these Sportsguards is $12.00, which is basically our cost from Ormco. We just wish to make them available to our patients who desire maximum protection for their teeth during physical sporting activities.

COMPUTER UPDATE

Computers and programs are constantly changing and we are doing our best to stay up to date. Recently, we updated our program used during new patient exams and patient consultations. It now enables us to actually show our patients how their teeth can improve and change with short "movies" demonstrating simulated tooth movement or arch changes. It also contains many pictures of different stages of orthodontic treatment and many of the appliances that are used.

We hope these visual aids will help in communicating with our patients.

AFTER SCHOOL APPOINTMENTS

Many parents do not approve of their children being required to miss any school for orthodontic appointments. The problem is, the majority of our patients go to school. We have arranged our appointment schedule to accommodate as many people as we can. Our early morning and after school times are reserved for appliance adjustments and progress checkups, which are the majority of appointments during orthodontic treatment.

To provide more of these "prime" times for checkups, appointments that require more time need to be scheduled during school hours. This may happen approximately five or six times during the course of a two-year treatment. Loose braces or broken appliances sometimes cannot be repaired during regular appointments and often need to be rescheduled for a longer time during school hours.

Some patients request exceptions to these rules, but they must be denied because it would infringe on the rights of other patients. Thank you for your consideration and understanding of this problem. We will continue to try our best to accommodate everyone!

DATES OUR OFFICE WILL BE CLOSED FOR THE HOLIDAYS

November 24 & 25

December 23, 26, & 30

January 2, 1995

the publication is family-oriented, the newsletter, *Across the Smiles*, features a variety of professional and personal news: In addition to what is shown in Figure 1.22, it might contain announcements of prizewinners for excellent oral hygiene as well as for baby and spouse contests; information on a career in orthodontics; or even a recipe for "Scott's Five Alarm Chili." The page shown in Figure 1.22 focuses on problems and solutions that are at once professional and personal concerns.

Corporate Newspapers. Newspaper production, like newsletter writing, is beyond the scope of this text. Larger corporations, however, commonly publish newspapers, spreading good news about the company to employees and other audiences. Northwest Airlines, for example, has *Passages*, UPS has *International Update*, and 3M has *Stemwinder*; these, along with other corporate communication, help enhance corporate image. Building company image from within is a very important aspect of organizational culture. A large number of corporate publications, including booklets and magazines as well as newspapers, are devoted to this task.

RESPONSE SHEET

INTERCULTURAL COMMUNICATION

COMMUNICATING PARTIES: OCCASION:
CULTURAL MEMBERSHIP(S) OF EACH PARTY:

◆ TYPE OF INTERCULTURAL COMMUNICATION

What type of intercultural communication informs this particular occasion?

- communication between subcultures within an organization
- communication between employees within the same organization who are part of the same subculture but have distinct cultural backgrounds
- communication between employees who are part of the same multinational corporation but who are working at different sites
- communication between two organizations within the same country
- communication between two organizations from different countries

Name the cultures or subcultures involved and identify some of their main characteristics.

◆ CROSS-CULTURAL FACTORS

What are the cross-cultural factors important to this situation?

Diverse distinguishing traits (gender, race, age, ethnicity, etc.)

Company practices

Power structures and status (class)

Explain how or why these factors are important to communication between the parties.

◆ INTERNATIONAL CONSIDERATIONS

What international differences, if any, are important to the situation? [Research is often necessary to identify and understand international differences.]

Attitude toward authority

Willingness to take risks

Importance of individualism

Nature of social and gender-based expectations

Explain how or why the differences you've identified are important to communication between the parties.

◆ GOALS AND CRITERIA

What are the goals of this communication? How will the parties know if they are successful in reaching these goals?

ACTIVITIES, EXERCISES, AND ASSIGNMENTS

◆ IN-CLASS ACTIVITIES

1. Please refer to Figure 1.1, the Northwest Airlines letter in Japanese, for the following activity.
   a. Northwest Airlines is a major carrier between the United States and Japan. The strategic plan at Northwest includes the goal that the airline attract more business travelers. Do you think that this letter, written in Japanese about Northwest's environmental approach, helps to achieve this goal? Explain.
   b. How, in your opinion, does this letter contribute to Northwest's corporate image?
2. Smokey McKinney, who teaches business communication and Indian studies and who has received a Kansas Humanities Board grant to study the Potowatomie language, relates the comparison between Native American oral accounts and corporate stories shown in Figure 1.23.
   a. McKinney emphasizes the role oral tradition plays in "learning the ropes" in a particular culture. Discuss that role. Then think about the various cultures and subcultures to which you belong. Discuss the extent to which McKinney's account jibes with your experience.
   b. As this chapter indicates, conforming to company stylesheets and following corporate codes of ethics are two ways employees become a part of their organization's culture. In your opinion, how does this type of "acculturation" compare with the storytelling McKinney talks about?
3. Imagine that you have to define organizational culture to young (junior high school age) listeners at a career day. You decide that telling your listeners stories would be one way of getting the definition across. Discuss with classmates possible stories that you might include to help young listeners understand organizational culture. Together with several classmates, compose a 10-minute talk for the career-day listeners. Present your talk to other groups for their feedback.
4. Review the Skills and Strategies box "Establishing Goals and Criteria" (page 7). Discuss what goals and criteria you might have as a class during this course. To what extent is your class a group with its own organizational culture?

◆ INDIVIDUAL AND GROUP EXERCISES

1. At the beginning of this chapter, William J. Corbett (Vice President for Communications of the American Institute of Certified Public Accountants) was quoted

Figure 1.23 Narrative Accounts

Joseph Bruchac tells a Pawnee tale about Trickster Coyote, who cheats Rock. When Rock relentlessly pursues him, Coyote finds no help from other animals, whom he has likewise tricked. Coyote finally manages to trick some nighthawks into breaking Rock into little pieces, but when they find out Coyote has lied to them, they put all the pieces back together. Rock rolls on, eventually flattening Coyote.

Black Elk tells a Lakota tale about High Horse, a young Teton Sioux man, who desperately pursues the hand of a young woman. Because her father opposes the courtship, High Horse attempts to steal her away. The attempt fails. After he is almost caught in her tepee, High Horse is shamed into hitting the warpath, where he ends up stealing 100 Crow horses. He returns "a real man and worth something" in the eyes of the young lady's father.

Neither Bruchac nor Black Elk interprets his story. But from the narratives, young listeners have no trouble drawing lessons about youth, growth, love, family and community life. Through the telling and retelling of traditional tales, the young people learn about the culture that is "the People" (the name by which most Indian tribes know themselves).

Corporations have stories as well. Stories at the Hach Company invariably include how CEO Kitty Hach's devotion to airplanes has influenced the corporation's culture. Growing up with a barnstorming father, Kitty Hach (pronounced Kitty Hawk) developed a love of flying, which has become an integral part of Hach Company. Not an aerospace firm, Hach produces chemicals and computer chips. However, while bigger companies fly commercial planes, Hach sends its representatives on its private Beechcraft flown by the company pilot.

IBM has a favorite story about Lucille Burger, the "90-pound security supervisor who dared to challenge Thomas Watson, Sr., the intimidating Chairman of the Board." Burger turned Watson away from a certain secure area, choosing to stand by the rules of the company rather than bow to its personage. Initially surprised, Watson approved.

Like Indian oral accounts, these corporate stories are usually not interpreted, but simply retold again and again. Knowledge of the company tales separates insider from outsider. The lore of the corporation is found in stories told next to coffee machines, in restrooms, and at company social events.

as saying, "The shared values among employees, the heroes they create and stories they tell, the structure on which an organization centers—all these elements create a dynamic mix called corporate culture."

a. Review the stories we have told about several organizations. Beginning with the accounts of ABC/DEF, Inc., and Apple Valley Transit Authority, identify the various subcultures that you see in these stories. Use the Response Sheet on intercultural communication to help you in this identification. Pay special attention to the communication among subcultures.

b. Select one of the aforementioned organizations and compare and contrast its communication problems with those experienced between SNAP Hardware and Ramirez Rope. Use the Response Sheet on intercultural communication to help you get started.

c. If you had to make recommendations for improving communication in the organization you selected, what would they be?

2. Please refer to Figure 1.24 (below and on page 30) in completing this exercise. Figure 1.24 is a press release distributed by OptImage at a multimedia trade show.

a. Note all the technical terminology that the OptImage release contains. Compare and contrast the language here with that used in the 3M press release (Figure 1.21). Discuss how language at the multimedia trade show might be a barrier to those not involved in computer culture. Compare and contrast the language barrier here with that experienced by SNAP Hardware and Ramirez Rope.

b. Discuss how the press release addresses the 5Ws and an H. Discuss how the OptImage release fulfills expectations for how press releases in general should be written.

c. Discuss how both the OptImage release and the 3M release contribute to each company's corporate image.

Figure 1.24 OptImage Press Release

For Further Information Contact:
Laura Stillions, OptImage (515) 555-7000
Sarah Kavanagh, McLean Public Relations (415) 555-8800

SEE OPTIMAGE AT THE SANDS MULTIMEDIA PAVILION—Booth #M7145

OptImage Previews Multimedia Authoring Tool For Interactive TV

COMDEX/Fall (November 14, 1994)—At this week's COMDEX/Fall trade show and conference, OptImage is previewing tools for interactive TV authoring. Multimedia producers will be able to see how an application for interactive TV or video-on-demand is authored. In addition, OptImage is showing an application running over an interactive network via television set-top decoders based on the Microware DAVID system and created with OptImage tools.

OptImage's authoring tool, MediaMogul, the leading CD-i authoring tool on the market, has been extended to allow producers to create applications for DAVID-based interactive television systems. Because these systems use the same operating system as CD-i, OS-9, MediaMogul gives producers two output avenues for their applications: one for network broadcast; a second for output to disc for playback on CD-i players.

Gail Wellington, vice president of marketing and sales at OptImage, elaborates, "MediaMogul, the first authoring tool for the DAVID architecture, is an ideal tool for the interactive television market. First, MediaMogul has a proven track record—hundreds of interactive multimedia titles have been created with it. Second, it was developed specifically for the non-programmer—title designers and broadcast engineers can use MediaMogul without having to involve programmers or other technical resources. And third, it's available now."

-more-

◆ OUT-OF-CLASS ASSIGNMENTS

1. Develop a code of ethics for working in collaborative groups in your class. This code will set forth criteria for evaluating students' contributions to team projects and collaborative activities throughout the semester. (You might want to consult the performance review discussion on accountabilities and measures, pages 573–575, before you begin.) Analyze the code by listing its components and evaluating whether your colleagues will, from reading the code, understand what actions are acceptable and unacceptable in various situations. Write a memo that contains both the code itself and your analysis of the code.
2. Imagine that you work for SNAP Hardware. After NAFTA's passage, SNAP hired a bilingual Vice President of Operations and managed to salvage its relationship with Ramirez Rope. Their joint venture involves Ramirez supplying cotton and polypropylene braided rope to SNAP as part of SNAP's attachment hardware line. SNAP and Ramirez would like to announce their venture at an upcoming trade show in Chicago in a press release that will not only appear at the trade show but also be sent out to the editors of the business sections of regional daily newspapers. Write this press release. Feel free to generate any necessary additional information.

CASE

CENSORSHIP, CULTURAL VALUES, AND CODES OF ETHICS

CASE BY JUDY HAMILTON

Background. Your small community library has received 17 requests in the last four months for Herrnstein and Murray's book *The Bell Curve: Intelligence and Class Structure in American Life* (Free Press, 1994). At present, the library does

Figure 1.24 OptImage Press Release *(continued)*

Interactive TV authoring, page 2

Producers can begin creating interactive TV applications now using MediaMogul. The new extension to MediaMogul, script2net, which is expected to be available late this year, adds network broadcast capabilities, giving producers a complete production pathway—from asset generation and authoring to network broadcast. MediaMogul also includes built-in compatibility with the company's MPEG encoding tools.

MediaMogul is a full featured multimedia authoring package which makes it easy to combine video and audio assets—images, drawings, animation, full motion (MPEG) digital video, voice, music and sounds—into sequences and interactive branches that respond to user input. MediaMogul is available for a suggested retail price of $5000. Pricing for the MediaMogul extension for DAVID-based set-top decoders has not yet been announced. OptImage has also announced its intent to support other playback devices in addition to DAVID. Other OptImage authoring tools will be DAVID set-top compatible in the near future.

About OptImage

OptImage was formed to provide leading edge authoring solutions for developers of software titles for consumer and professional markets. OptImage's product line has grown to include additional multimedia tools such as audio and image conversion utilities, MPEG compression tools, CD recording software, disc building (including CD-ROM XA and Video CD) and emulation tools. The company offers a complete line of authoring tools for both the programmer and non-programming designer. Products are available for use in a variety of authoring environments including Macintosh, IBM PC and compatibles, SUN and Philips CD-i. For more information contact OptImage at 7185 Vista Drive, W. Des Moines, LA, 50266-9313, (515) 555-7000.

# # #

not own this book and, until the recent requests, had not considered purchasing it. A member of the Board of Trustees does not think that this volume should be in the library (or *at least*, if it were in the library, the book should not be categorized as "nonfiction"), because it bases its conclusions about the inability of minorities to take standardized tests, including IQ tests, on what some feel are highly suspect interpretations of statistical data. Also, the trustee is concerned about the public's opinion of expending public funds for material that might be considered offensive and misleading. Both the requesters and the Board member are adamant in their positions.

Task. Imagine that you are a member of this community and are drawn into the issue as both a community member and an outside consultant, because of your experience with a similar situation at a local high school, college, or university. (It is important that you create a scenario now to establish the nature of the community and your expertise. Research into your community and, perhaps, your personal experience will help you create this scenario.) You will be meeting with a committee to decide whether or not to acquire *The Bell Curve*. Your committee will produce a one-page memo to the general public reporting and explaining the committee's decision. Your committee is also to produce a similar—but perhaps not identical—memo to the Board of Trustees regarding this issue.

Committee Information. You will be meeting with the following people regarding the *Bell Curve* issue (you may want to work collaboratively with classmates who may play these roles):

1. a board member who is fiercely opposed to *The Bell Curve*, representing one cultural view that this book is offensive and that people do not need to be exposed to information that is so misleading or be forced to pay for it through tax dollars
2. one of the people requesting the book, who represents the cultural view that access to the book is a matter of freedom of speech as guaranteed by the First Amendment of the U.S. Constitution
3. a librarian who bases his or her decisions on a librarian's code of ethics, particularly the following:
    - Librarians must provide the highest level of service through appropriate and usefully organized collections, fair and equitable circulation and service policies, and skillful, accurate, unbiased, and courteous responses to all requests for assistance.
    - Librarians must resist all effort by groups or individuals to censor library materials.
    - Librarians must distinguish clearly in their actions and statements between their personal philosophies and attitudes and those of an institution or a professional body.
4. a second librarian who bases his or her decision on the collection development policy statement of this particular library, particularly on the following objectives:
    - Materials shall be provided that will increase the professional awareness and competency of individual staff members.
    - Materials shall meet high standards of quality in factual content and presentation.
    - Materials chosen shall have aesthetic, literary, or social value.
    - Materials shall be chosen to foster respect for minority groups, women, and ethnic groups, and shall realistically represent our pluralistic society, along with the roles and life styles open to both men and women in today's world.
5. a librarian who is familiar with local laws regarding the treatment of minorities

CHAPTER

2

Communication Processes in Organizations

OUTLINE

- Communication Style within a Corporate Framework: Kate Kramer and Certified Mail
- The Communication Process: Existing Views
- Communication Networks
- Management Styles
- Meetings
- The Composing Process within Organizations

CRITERIA FOR EXPLORING CHAPTER 2

What we cover in this chapter	What you will be able to do after reading this chapter
Communication styles within a corporate framework	Discuss relationships among individual and corporate factors in communication
Different models of the communication process	Discuss communication as an interaction of factors: writer, reader, occasion, and message
Communication networks	Discuss various channels, networks, and organizational relationships that affect strategies for communication within organizations
Management styles	Explain how different management styles can affect task and conflict management within an organization, and can influence strategies for interoffice communication
Meetings as corporate communication	Understand listening behaviors; discuss meetings as organizational communication
Composing process within organizations	Discuss how organizations influence a communicator's composing

Effective communicators know that they not only have to understand what factors are important to the communication process, but also have to consider how the structures of their particular organizations influence that process. Figures 2.1 and 2.2 indicate how organizational preferences can influence the writing process of individual communicators within a corporation.

CONTEXT

At Northwest Airlines, the communication process is highly influenced by Barbara Minto's *The Pyramid Principle: Logic in Writing and Thinking*. Because the official spokesperson and lead communicators for the organization like Minto's work, many Northwest employees keep a two-sided laminated card with Minto's "Problem-Definition Framework" and "Pyramid Principle" at their desks and use her worksheet—which graphically represents a top-down logical structure with a pyramid of empty boxes—in planning their documents. Communicators are thus encouraged to use both (1) a problem-solving approach and (2) deductive structure in thinking about their messages:

1. Situation
   Problem
   Tentative solution
   Complication

2. 

Figure 2.1, on the next page, shows such a problem-solving approach used by a communicator to help define a writing task: a report on gain-sharing—a benefits program featuring cash bonuses. Figure 2.2 (page 35) shows a draft of a top-down logical structure for that task.

1. What advantages can you see in having a single principle, such as Minto's "Problem-Solving Framework" or "Pyramid Principle," guide thinking about communication within an organization? Do you see any disadvantages?
2. What is attractive to you about having access to a worksheet that would provide a top-down diagram to help you in your composing?
3. How would your writing process change if you were to become an employee at a company such as Northwest that uses a particular approach to thinking about communication tasks?

Figure 2.1 Problem-Solving Approach to Defining a Communication Task

A Problem-Solving Approach

Situation:	*What's going on?* We are exploring various changes in the way we manage our employees as a company resource.
Problem:	*What is the problem?* We need to increase our productivity.
Complication:	*What factor(s) feed into this problem in this specific situation?* Our company human resources policies do not satisfactorily address the issue of increasing productivity.
Tentative solution:	*What do we want?* We want our employees to be as productive as possible, and we'd like a company policy or program that delivers this result. *What subject (policy) are we currently exploring?* Gain-sharing—a program that rewards increases in productivity with cash bonuses.
Situation:	*What's going on?* We'd like to introduce a gain-sharing program that will be the cornerstone of our human resource management philosophy.
Problem:	*What's the problem?* The effectiveness of gain-sharing programs varies a great deal.
Complication:	*What factor(s) feed into this problem in this specific situation?* We can't afford to adopt a plan that doesn't work for us long-term.
Tentative solution:	*What do we want?* A gain-sharing program that is tailored specifically to this organization, so that it produces long-term gains in productivity. *What subject are we currently exploring?* The factors that are involved in individually tailoring gain-sharing programs.
Primary question:	How can we tailor a gain-sharing plan so it works for us?
Secondary question(s):	What aspects of gain-sharing will help us determine what will work for us? What will our specific gain-sharing plan look like?
Preliminary stance:	Gain-sharing, if appropriately tailored, can help our company's financial standing.

Figures 2.1 and 2.2 are important because they show how communication can be structured according to a particular approach and suggest that individual communicators in a corporate environment need to understand several key factors:

- the communication process itself
- the structure of internal communication networks, both formal and informal
- the influence of contextual aspects—such as organizational climate and management style—on communication
- the interrelationship between personal style and corporate expectations in communication processes

COMMUNICATION STYLE WITHIN A CORPORATE FRAMEWORK: KATE KRAMER AND CERTIFIED MAIL

Kate Kramer is an administrative manager at an insurance company. Her office often sends correspondence and other communication by certified mail. Even so, Kate gets repeated questions about preparing certified mail receipts and domestic return receipts. As a manager, Kate could address the problem of repeated questions in a number of ways. She could continue to answer questions as they come up, as she has been doing. She could call a meeting about the problem. She could also write a directive like that shown in Figure 2.3, telling her employees what to do. (Kate, as we will see, discards this option.) In addition, Kate could write a set of instructions to post in the mail room to show her employees how to send certified mail (Figure 2.4 on page 36).

Instead of sending a directive, Kate chooses to bring up the subject of certified mail at a weekly staff meeting. At the meeting, she reveals that she will be posting the set of mailing instructions shown in Figure 2.4 throughout the building. The next day, she follows up by announcing the locations of these posted instructions in an e-mail message to all employees. As this chapter will illustrate, Kate's choice of how to handle this problem reflects her

Figure 2.2 Plan Using Top-Down Logical Structure

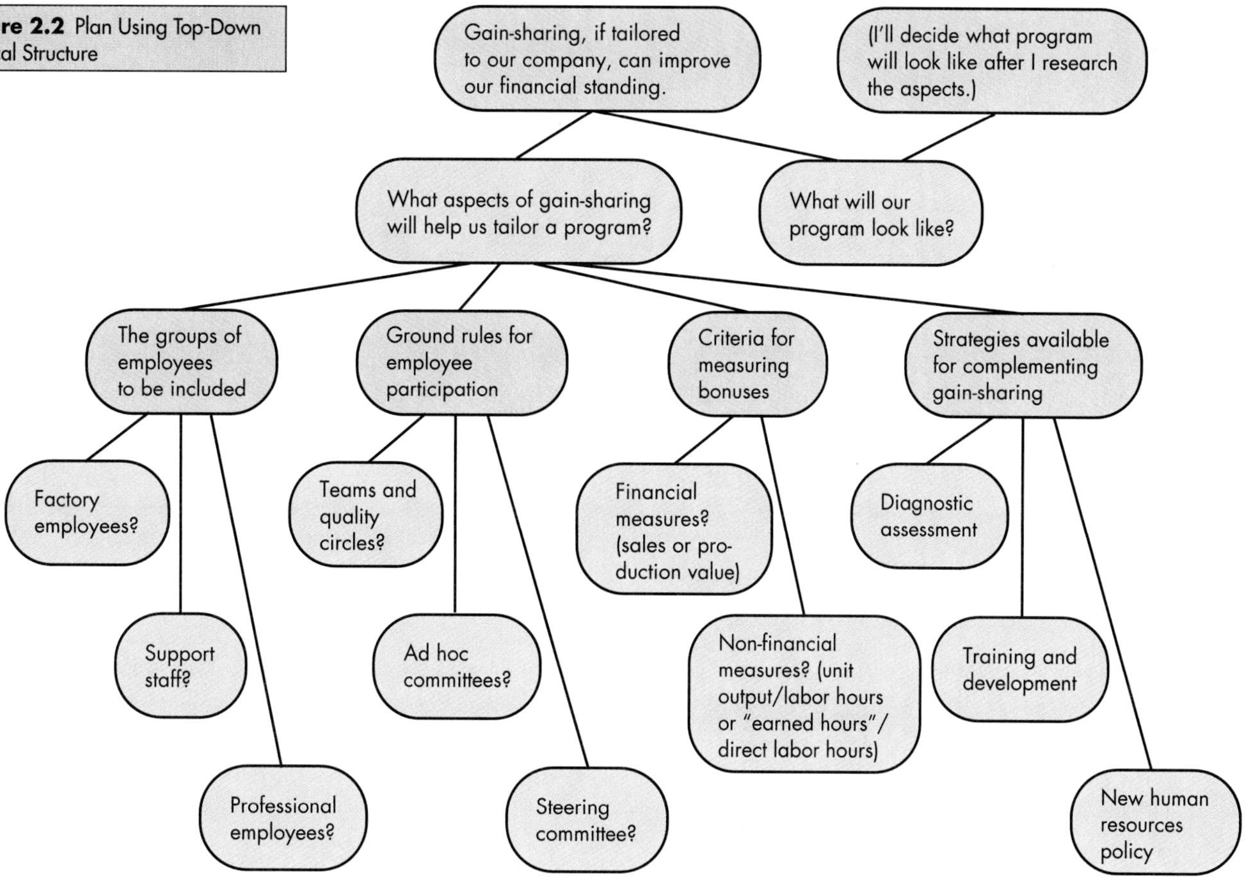

Figure 2.3 Directive Concerning Certified Mail

> Certified mail is necessary for all correspondence dealing with claims and other confidential issues. To send certified mail, you need to fill out both a certified mail receipt and a domestic return receipt.
>
> All necessary certified mail forms are located on the east wall of the mail room. In filling out these forms, please make sure the numbers and the addresses on both receipts match. Also make sure that the postage and fees are correct and that each receipt is affixed to its proper side of the envelope.

views about communication in general, her place in the communication network of the organization, and her personal management style.

THE COMMUNICATION PROCESS: EXISTING VIEWS

To communicate means to impart or to share something. It requires finding a common ground between a communicator's and an audience's understanding of information, situations, beliefs, approaches, and attitudes. The communication process provides a way to reach such common understandings.

You can describe the communication process in various ways, depending on whether you want to emphasize the *imparting* of information or the *sharing* of information, or if you want to emphasize the *assumptions* that underlie the act of communicating information.

Transmission Models

If you want to emphasize the *imparting* of information, you might use a model of the communication process that shows information being transmitted from a sender to a receiver (Figure 2.5 on next page).

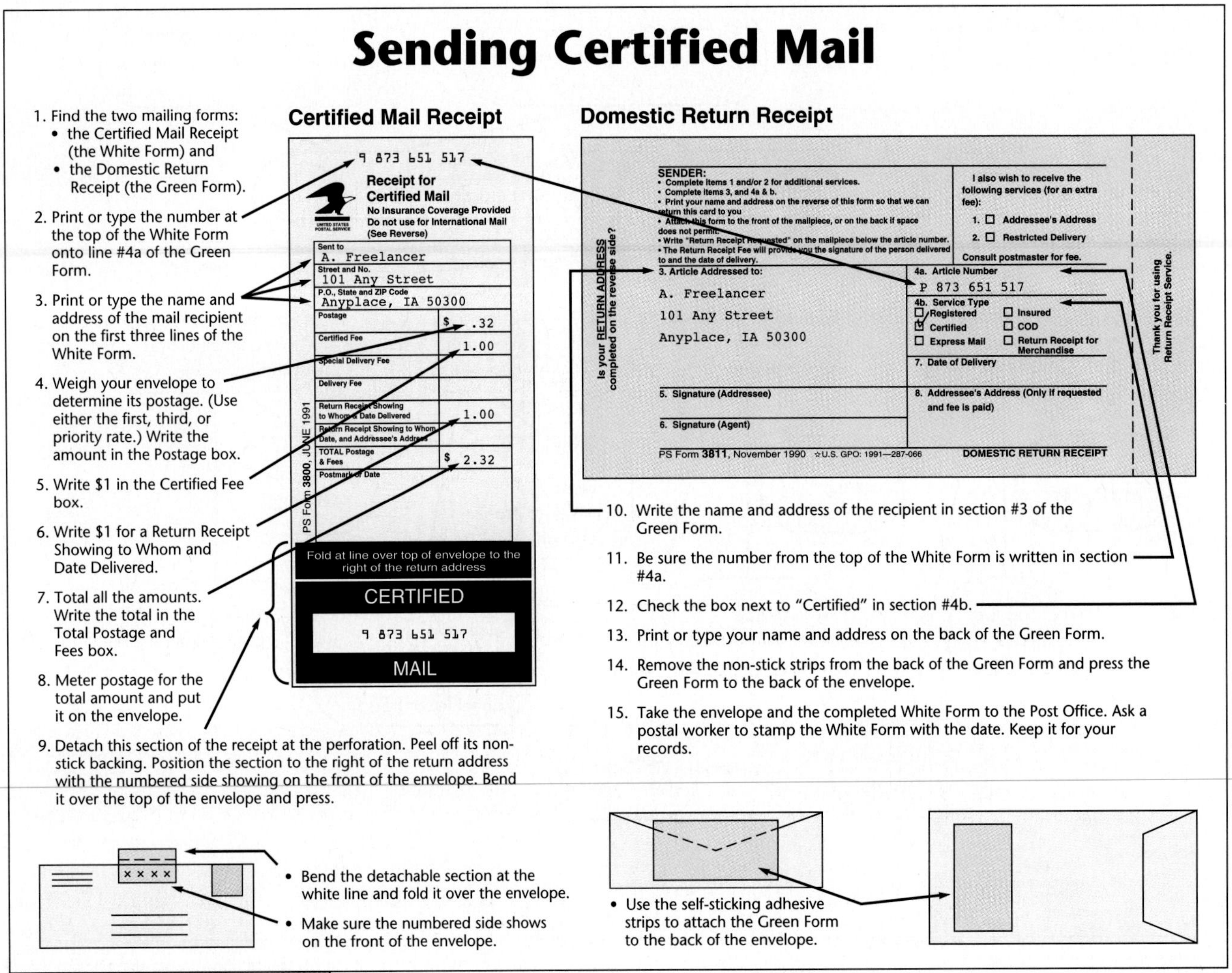

Figure 2.4 Set of Instructions Concerning Certified Mail

Transmission models of communication are linear: they show how messages move in one direction along a line or channel, with information traveling from the source that sends a message to an audience that receives the message. Transmission models assume that, in the absence of interference, or "noise," readers or listeners will interpret messages as the sender intends.

Using a transmission model, you might describe Kate's situation in the following way: Kate's job is to convey the proper way to send certified mail. If she writes a directive, she needs to make sure that it tells employees exactly what to do. If she writes instructions, she needs to make sure that they tell employees exactly how to do it. In any case, Kate's job is to write up (or encode) the information so that her employees will have no trouble reading her message and understanding (decoding) her exact meaning.

Figure 2.5 A Transmission Model of Communication

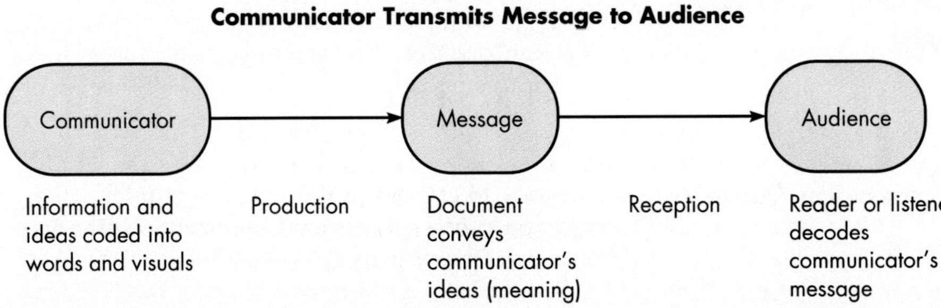

Street-corner negotiations like this one rely primarily on shared information, both verbal and nonverbal.

Reciprocal Models

If you want to emphasize the *sharing* of information, you might use a model of the communication process that shows information being shaped, exchanged, and interpreted by *each* participant in the situation. Such models are interactive, or reciprocal.

Reciprocal (interactive) models (Figure 2.6) tend to have simultaneous movements in a number of directions and to show that all participants contribute to making meaning. These models also recognize the roles, the occasion, the information itself, and the message (document) itself play in a communication. The *occasion* (the fact, event, state of affairs, or situation at the time of the communication) is particularly important because it serves as the immediate cause of the particular interaction between communicator, audience, and subject and provides the opportunity or impetus for composing the message.

Using a reciprocal model, you might interpret Kate's situation as an occasion for communication that grew out of the need to send certain types of correspondence by certified mail. The occasion is complicated by the fact that the procedure for sending certified mail is easy to forget, that Kate is approachable as a manager and has heretofore been willing to repeat the necessary instructions to each employee as needed, and that Kate has now decided to alter her usual practice of repeating instructions. It is also complicated by the fact that employees who have had to ask Kate to review the mailing procedure might resist the idea that she doesn't want to do so anymore, or they might feel bad that they have evidently annoyed Kate with their collective, repeated request. The employees' feelings will affect how they interpret Kate's message. Kate, therefore, not only has the information about certified mail to communicate, but also has the task of communicating her continued goodwill.

Figure 2.6 A Reciprocal Model of Communication

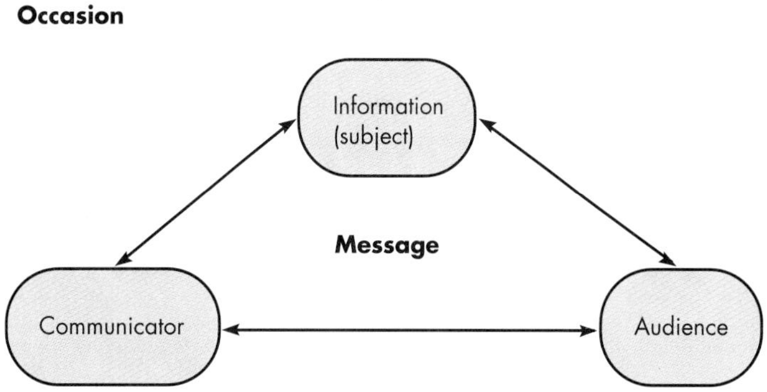

Meaning comes through interaction among the communicator, the information (subject), and the audience within a specific occasion for communication.

Models Highlighting Assumptions

If you want to focus instead on the *assumptions* that underlie the act of communicating information, you might use a model that identifies what both the communicator and the audience take for granted in communicating with each other.

Using an **assumptions-based model** of the communication process, you might emphasize what expectations both Kate and the employees share. Since Kate and her employees have traditionally used weekly staff meetings to discuss problems and tentative solutions to those problems (among other agenda items), Kate can take advantage of the expectations set by this established practice. Kate knows that if the certified mail instructions are discussed in this framework, they will probably be received as a solution to be tried in addressing a routine office problem. This expectation, in turn, helps reduce any negative reaction to Kate's change in how she gives advice for sending certified mail.

Communication experts have spent a good deal of effort trying to identify expectations or assumptions shared by communicator and audience. **Speech Act theorists,** for example, have offered a model specifically for conversations which features four maxims:

1. **Maxim of Quantity:** Provide enough information, but not too much.
2. **Maxim of Quality:** Be trustful, have evidence.
3. **Maxim of Relation:** Be relevant.
4. **Maxim of Manner:** Be orderly, clear, brief.

These maxims represent assumptions people share about how to talk with each other. For example, if you are like most people, you think it's a problem when someone talks on and on, tells lies, goes off on tangents, or incoherently jumps from topic to topic during a conversation. Speech Act theorists would say you think it's a problem because you have unconsciously assimilated cultural rules for conducting a conversation and now use these conventions to determine what's appropriate.

In observing the four maxims, you show that you want to cooperate with what's expected. You share the assumption that participants in a conversation want to obey the rules of speaking and expect others to do likewise. H.P. Grice calls this overarching assump-

Figure 2.7 Speech Act Maxims and Application Parallels in Business Communication

MAXIM	APPLICATION TO BUSINESS COMMUNICATION
Quantity	• In a short report, the writer forecasts "several recommendations." The reader expects more than one recommendation (but not a clutch of 20) to be presented. • In a letter requesting information from a financial aid office, the writer asks for information concerning aid for children of disabled veterans (CDVs). The writer expects the reader to provide a complete listing of CDV sources of aid, and not an abridged version showing only scholarships but omitting grants-in-aid.
Quality	• In a letter denying a reader's claim, the writer asserts that the carrier, not the company, is liable for shipping damages and provides the address of this shipper. The reader expects the writer's legal assessment to be correct and the carrier's address to be accurate. • In a letter from a financial aid office, the writer informs CDV students that they are eligible for full tuition credit. The student readers expect the information to be true and expect "full" to mean 100%, not 65% or "as much as we can manage, given the economy."
Relation	• In a letter making a claim against a company, the writer details a long history of past dissatisfaction with the company. The reader expects that at some point the writer will establish how this past dissatisfaction is connected to the current problem. • The person writing for information about CDV aid expects to receive information about aid available to *children* of disabled veterans, not concerning that available to veterans themselves.
Manner	• When listening to an oral presentation, a board of directors expects the speaker to be prepared, speak loudly and clearly enough to be understood, and to provide appropriate visual aids and handouts. In business messages in general, readers expect companies to be polite and service-oriented. • In a response telling about CDV financial aid, the reader expects a concisely annotated, easy-to-read list of available aid, not long paragraphs telling a story about the history of how the aid became available or a paragraph casually referring to the aid at various points.

tion **the *Cooperative Principle*.** Effective communicators understand that similar rules apply to oral presentations and written documents.

The conventions that business communicators use in their messages demonstrate the cooperative principle at work (Chapter 6). When writing formal reports, for example, writers know to include a title page. When reading formal reports, readers expect to see that title page and to use it to discover the subject, writer, and audience of the report. Communication conventions represent the common or expected way of handling a particular occasion for speaking or writing and a means of cooperating shared by communicator and audience.

The cooperative principle, however, does not mean communicators and audiences always agree. When you communicate in business, you cannot expect readers to always cooperate with what you want them to do. Nor can you expect to always be able to give readers exactly what they want. For example, you may have to deny a customer's request for a refund. But in doing so, you would still be able to cooperate with your client's general expectations about how business letters denying claims should be written. Similarly, your customer may resist your decision that you cannot give a refund, but he or she might still follow the cooperative principle by recognizing that you have appropriately addressed the request.

Figure 2.7 suggests how speech act rules can help identify what is taken for granted (assumed) in a business communication situation.[1]

Communication Problems and the Three Types of Models

Communicators and audiences both know that not all communication goes smoothly. Figure 2.8 identifies four common problem areas.

Problems at Global. As you might expect, problems in communication are seen differently in the three models we've discussed. For example, let's take the situation at Global Enterprises, an import-export firm. Global Enterprises had just adopted a smoke-free workplace policy. Global's Training and Development officer, Julie Thornberg, had to produce informational material about the new regulations.

Thornberg produced *An Informative Brochure Highlighting Global Enterprises' Commitment to a Drug-Free Workplace Environment*, which consisted of three interior sections:

- a policy statement summarizing the organization's commitment to a drug-free workplace
- a table detailing the characteristics and effects of common drugs of abuse (with tobacco products listed under nicotine; other drugs listed included heroin, cocaine, peyote, and LSD)

Figure 2.8 Problem Areas in Communication

OCCASION-BASED PROBLEMS	COMMUNICATOR-BASED PROBLEMS	TEXT-BASED PROBLEMS	AUDIENCE-BASED PROBLEMS
Time: The writer or the reader does not have sufficient time to devote to the message. *Technology:* The writer and/or the reader do not have adequate and/or compatible communication systems, including hardware, software, electronic networks. *Atmosphere:* The writer's or the reader's organizational climate is unfavorable (see page 46). *Money:* The writer does not have sufficient resources to present, convey, and/or distribute the message to the audience.	*Ideas:* The writer's main idea is unclear or ethically questionable. *Stance:* The writer's position and stake in the communication are unrealized or ambiguous. *Assumptions:* What the writer takes for granted is unrecognized, unidentified, or inaccurate. *Character:* The writer's credibility is uncertain and his or her expertise is in doubt.	*Organization:* The sequence of material is ineffective or illogical; the connection between ideas and evidence is not provided in the document. *Development:* The evidence is insufficient in quality or quantity. *Mechanics:* Basic errors appear: flawed syntax—fragments, unclear references, convoluted sentence structure; poor diction—ambiguity, wordiness, inappropriate word choice; grammatical and typographical mistakes. *Design:* The page design is cluttered, and has ineffective layout and/or inappropriate format.	*Feelings:* The reader or listener is angered, bored, or indifferent to the writer's ideas and the text. *Attitude:* The reader or listener comes to the text with a resistant stance. (Chapter 9 identifies possible causes of resistance.) *Expertise:* The reader or listener has insufficient background or training to understand the writer's ideas and the text. *Expectations:* The reader or listener does not share the same expectations as the communicator and interprets the message according to his or her own expectations.

- several paragraphs introducing a new drug awareness program to complement the substance abuse and rehabilitation programs already in place; several paragraphs reviewing details concerning the existing programs

The three exterior panels entailed a cover, a mailer, and information about available assistance.

Thornberg's materials received a mixed reception, especially in the public relations department. Employees who were smokers, upset that the policy had passed in the first place, were newly outraged that the pamphlet made no distinction between nicotine and drugs like heroin, cocaine, and LSD. Native American workers were incredulous that peyote was included on the list, because the drug does have legitimate use in Native American religious ceremonies. Other employees, especially nonsmokers or smokers who had "kicked the habit," were more positive. A common reaction was, "It's about time." Some even openly celebrated the fact that the company offered to help smokers and others "guilty" of substance abuse. Why did Thornberg's message receive such mixed reviews? What was wrong with the communication?

Examining Global's Problems with the Three Models. If you were using a transmission model to describe Thornberg's problems, you would think of the problems as **noise** preventing the message from getting through as intended. You would focus on Thornberg's writing of the document.

Occasion	You would consider how Thornberg could have spent more time researching the use of peyote and, as a consequence, omitted it from the table.
Communicator	You would point out that while Thornberg's stance was clear (a drug-free workplace is a good thing), her selection of detail was at times unfortunate.
Text	You would explore how Thornberg could redesign the pamphlet so nicotine would not appear in the same table as heroin, cocaine, peyote, and LSD.
Audience	You would examine how Thornberg could have used strategies so persuasive that all her readers, regardless of their *attitudes and beliefs*, would agree with her message.

As the emphasis on Thornberg indicates, transmission models take for granted that the kinds of noise experienced in a communication situation can most often be controlled by the communicator.

If you were using a reciprocal model, you would describe problems with Thornberg's message in terms of unsuccessful interactions. You would see the task of making meaning as shared and would, therefore, try to discover what the communicator and the audience shared and did not share in terms of technology, knowledge, expertise, conventions, and expectations. You would see that problems emerge when a match between Thornberg's intentions and the audience's expectations cannot be achieved, despite the efforts of both parties.

Occasion	You would examine the history of how the no-smoking policy came about to gauge the climate at Global regarding drug use in general and smoking in particular.
Communicator	You would explore Thornberg's intentions. (Thornberg's intentions might have been fine. She might have thought that some of her readers—especially smokers—might feel better about the policy if it were connected to other policies with which they more likely agreed.)
Text	You would study the way the text tries to deemphasize the no-smoking aspect of the new policy, by putting it in the same chart as heroin and other drugs, and to emphasize the drug-free workplace aspect in doing so. You would explore how else the material could have been presented so that the policy would be associated with something most readers would accept.
Audience	You would explore the various ways different groups of readers interpreted the pamphlet.

In a reciprocal model, the spotlight is not solely on Thornberg's choices, but expands to include the history of the situation, the writer's intentions, textual strategies, and readers' interpretations. Problems in communication could attach to any or all of these elements.

You would discover, for example, that the range of responses to Thornberg's message was typical of responses to previous attempts to restrict smoking in the company. That is, first smoking was restricted to hallways, employee offices, and the lounge. Then smoking was restricted to offices and hallways, then to individual offices, and then to parking ramps outside the building. Finally, smoking was entirely banned under the new policy. With each new restriction, the nonsmokers became increasingly happy and militant, and the smokers, increasingly unhappy and stressed out. Feeling harassed, smokers associated Thornberg's pamphlet with communications with which they had previously disagreed, and thus the earlier series of communications played an active role in how the pamphlet was received.

If you used an assumption-based model to explore the mixed reception to Thornberg's pamphlet, you would describe the problems as evidence of unidentified, unexamined, unshared, or even faulty assumptions held by the communicator, the audience, and/or the culture(s) to which each belongs.

Occasion	You would consider how assumptions tied to the occasion influenced the message (for example, since "smoking is hazardous to your health," everyone would naturally accept regulations designed to restrict its use; a drug-free workplace [no matter how defined] has the status of motherhood and apple pie).
Communicator	You would examine the writer's assumptions. (For example, Thornberg felt she could safely *assume* that readers would agree to ban legally prohibited drugs such as heroin, cocaine, and PCP. Thornberg thus incorrectly *assumed* she was increasing the likelihood of reader cooperation by making the ban on smoking [nicotine] part of the ban on 17 other named drugs that have long been legally and socially unacceptable.)
Text	You would explore the assumptions displayed in the text (for example, being addicted to nicotine is like being addicted to heroin, cocaine, LSD).
Audience	You would examine what assumptions various groups of readers shared and did not share with the writer. You would also explore related assumptions in the social context. (For example, smokers at Global commonly complained that while smoking used to be perfectly acceptable, smokers were now outcasts in their own departments: snubbed and even excluded from social functions. The assumption seemed to be, If you are a smoker, you are an undesirable person.)

Using an assumption-based model, you would target unshared or mistaken assumptions as the root of miscommunication between Thornberg and her audience. In doing so, you would also examine how cultural values contributed to communication problems.

COMMUNICATION NETWORKS

With any given communication model, you can describe a comprehensive and unlimited range of communication relationships. When you begin looking at communication within organizations, however, you notice *limits* on the types of communication relationships that recur within a company's structure. For example, in some hierarchical corporations, access to the company's chief executive officer (CEO) is severely restricted. At one major corporation, *limited access* to executive offices ran the gamut from a heliport atop headquarters and armed guards patrolling the hallways to a dictatorial management style and "a Byzantine approval process [that] made employees feel powerless."[2]

The limits on types of communication relationships within organizations can be described in terms of communication networks. Such networks include employees who communicate with each other on a regular basis about work-related matters. Knowing the communication relationships in an organization helps you know what normally happens in the organization, officially and unofficially, what is possible in the organization, and how information is processed. The first two of these topics will be discussed here; Chapter 3 covers in detail how information is processed with the aid of technology.

What Normally Happens: Formal and Informal Channels

Formal and informal channels of communication vary from organization to organization. **Formal channels** of communication can often be discovered by looking at the company's organizational chart (Figure 2.9, next page). An organizational chart typically assumes a hierarchical relationship between the divisions and positions shown. Within such a hierarchy, communication travels vertically between superior and subordinate, and horizontally between peers. For example, at OptImage, the primary use of the hierarchical chart is to determine who writes a performance review of whom (see Chapter 19). The head of training and support writes reviews for the four engineers in her section. In a horizontal relationship, the two managers in engineering services, who are jointly responsible for that section, do not review each other, but evaluate the employee(s) working under them.

Figure 2.9 OptImage Organizational Chart

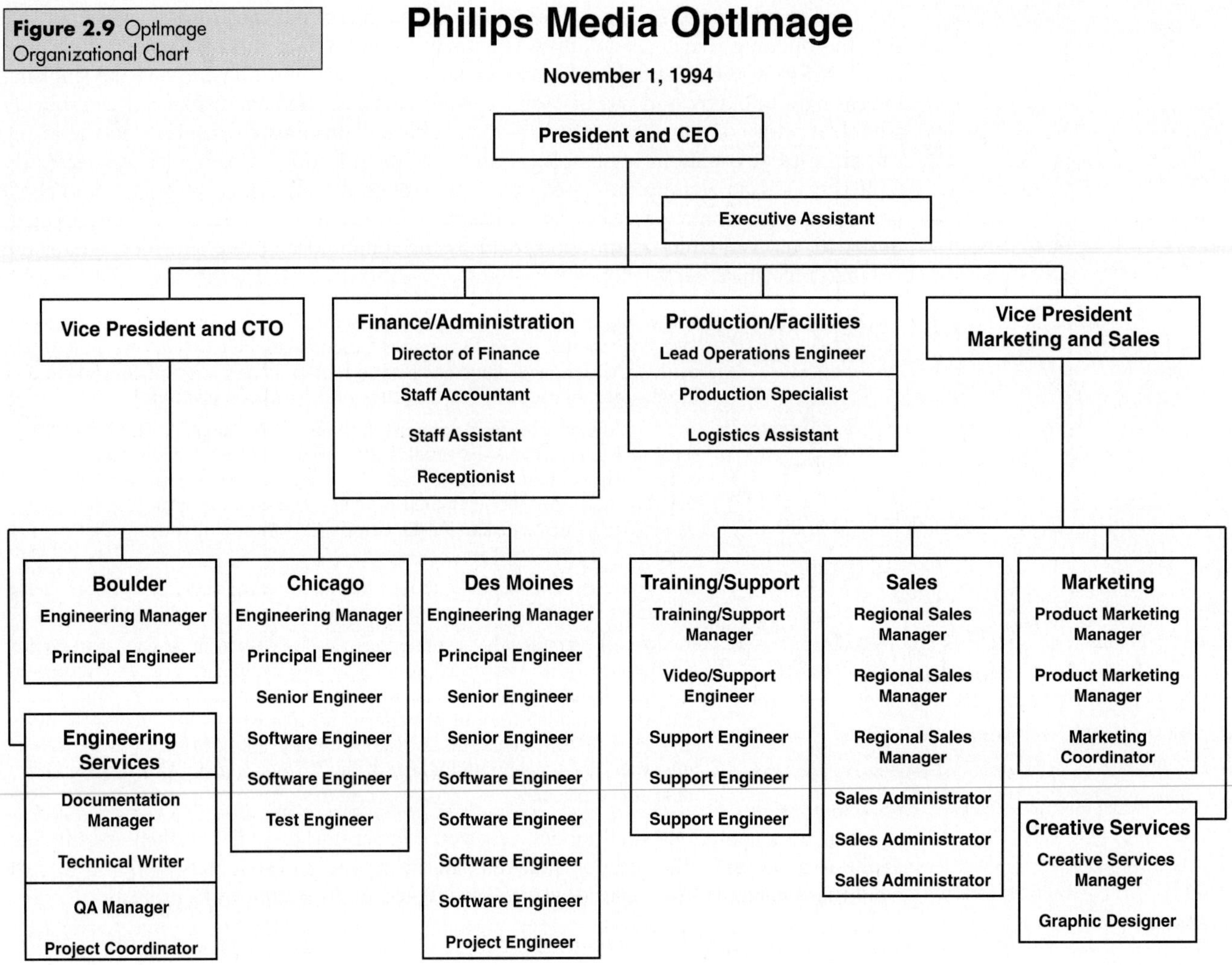

An organizational chart, while not foolproof in indicating how communication flows in a corporation, can indicate to clients and customers whom to contact about certain aspects of the corporation. For example, the organizational chart above indicates that marketing and sales are under separate command from engineering at OptImage. In addition, engineering is done at three different sites (Des Moines, Chicago, and Boulder) while marketing for the company is centralized. Thus, communication regarding engineering projects could probably be directed to each separate site, depending on the customer's location, but inquiries about marketing and sales would probably be best sent to the central office in Des Moines.

Organizational charts, however, do not tell the whole story regarding communication within an organization. Communication within OptImage, for example, is highly interactive, despite the official corporate hierarchy indicated by the organizational chart. The structure of the office space itself (Figure 2.10) is more indicative of the communication relationships than the organizational chart (Figure 2.9). OptImage has brand-new offices in Des Moines, with spaces partitioned by modular walls. Employees had direct input regarding the use of the space and the nature and location of their separate offices. The final office arrangement reflected the various communication networks in the company. For example, employees are located close to their managers. The secretarial and administrative assistant staff are located close to the people they support. In addition, employees who usually work together on team projects share the same office space. The four engineers using Macintosh computers share the space marked Engineering. (In the old office building, these same engineers had arranged their office space similarly and had arranged their work spaces themselves, rather than trust the job to the contractors. When the new building was built, they simply transferred the old arrangement to the new space.) Following a similar pattern, the

Figure 2.10 Map of OptImage Office Space

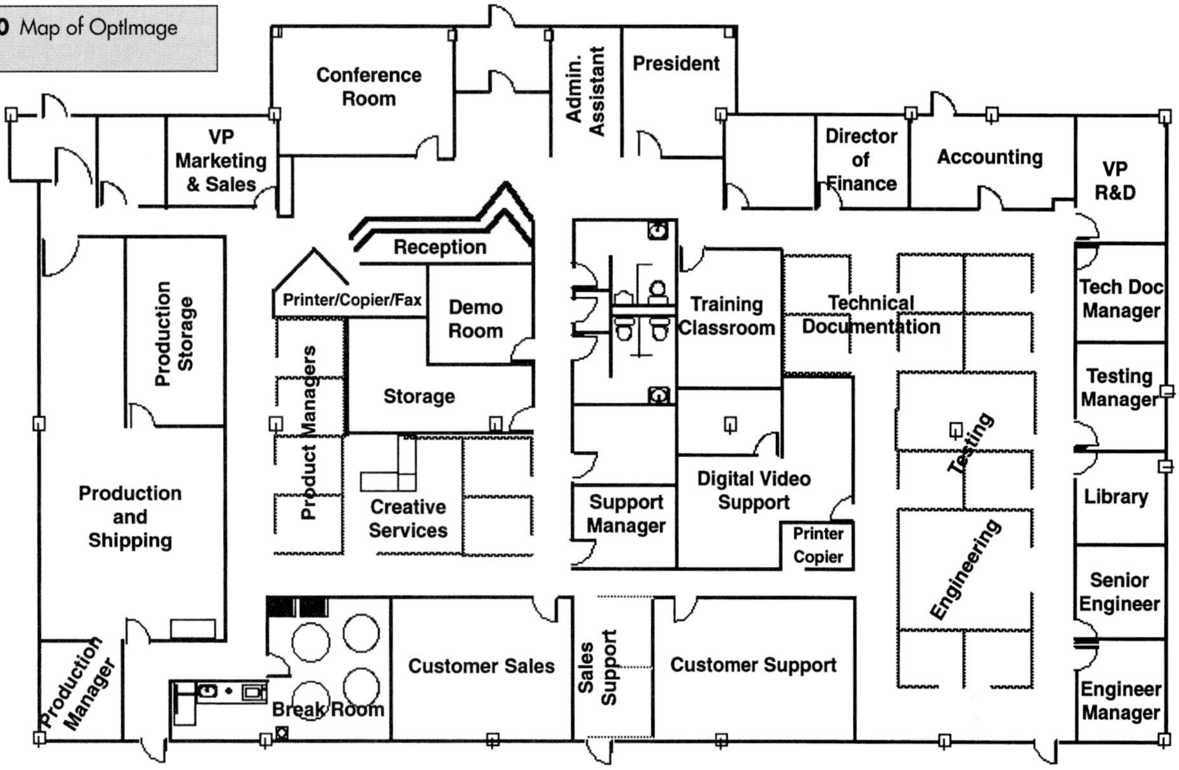

two employees in creative services share the same space, even though their official relationship is vertical.

Other communication at the company follows a similar pattern. Any employee can walk into the president's office to discuss company issues. Appropriately, the location of the President's office, closer to the main entrance than any other office, facilitates contact. The guest office allows visiting managers from other sites and corporations to have access to communications equipment and to have a space for meetings. In fact, having small meetings is an important use for the other single-person offices as well.

Informal channels ("grapevines," company-sanctioned social functions, personal contacts, and friendships) are also important to the communication within an organization. J. David Johnson, a corporate communication expert, remarks, "If three of the seven top officers in an organization have a regular golf match, this may result in a natural coalition that binds them together in ways that go far beyond their formal organizational relationships."[3] Most companies contain the kinds of informal channels presented in Figure 2.11 (next page). An employee may hold importance to a company well beyond her official rank if she is an active participant in such informal networks.

Whether formal or informal, communication can follow various patterns. For example, the normal communication at OptImage follows a "pinwheel" pattern, where every member talks to every other member directly (see Communication Spotlight I, pages 92–94). Communication at UPS follows a "chain" pattern, where organization members talk to immediate supervisors and subordinates—a "chain of command." Communication among team project members within either organization might follow a "circle" pattern, where all members have equal opportunities to talk with each other but may share information only with members in the same subculture. That is, certain software engineers might speak only to other software engineers on a project and leave direct talk with the marketing people to others.

What Is Possible: Boundaries and Aids

Communication channels set boundaries on what is possible in an organization. The flattened communication structure at OptImage makes it possible for everyone to talk to the company president. The "tall" hierarchical structure of communication at UPS (pages 3–5) discourages such direct contact, as does the sheer size and complexity of the company itself.

Figure 2.11 Informal Channels

INFORMAL NETWORKS	DEFINITION	VALUE	EXAMPLE
Conversation networks	Include employees who discuss work-related matters on a regular basis	Indicate to external audiences (customers, clients, organizations) the correct person to contact about company business: a specific problem or product and service Facilitate internal policies, procedures, and projects Helpful in trouble-shooting problems: gaps in the flow of information, the inefficient use of resources, and the failure to generate new ideas	Tell clients whom to contact at OptImage about engineering issues or marketing and sales information Indicate who is responsible for performance reviews in any given hierarchical structure Can help trace a breakdown in communication if there is a 3-week lag between the time a manager orders a report and the time the request itself is logged
Advice networks	Include the major players in an organization; also include employees that others depend on to help solve problems and provide information	Usually invisible to external audiences, but knowing who can provide information and support is very useful "insider knowledge" Provide informal mentoring and assistance among employees Helpful in analyzing "office politics," and a company's success or failure in problem-solving	Identify who should be "copied" in any given correspondence Enable strategically placed personnel to advance to management positions Identify the source and recipients of advice; help determine intentions and interpretations of advice and where a mismatch has occurred
Trust networks	Identify employees who share delicate political information and support each other in a crisis	Usually invisible to external audiences and to all but select internal audiences (e.g., those included in the network itself) Useful to tap in difficult or stressful situations, but usually accessible only to those in the network	Tell a manager whom to call on to help defuse a touchy situation Tell employees which other employees they can turn to when they suspect an ethics violation

On the positive side, a predictable pattern of communication relationships facilitates coordinated activity within an organization. For example, the fact that Northwest Airlines has an official program (COMPASS) for making suggestions for improvements encourages employees to make those suggestions, provides procedures for communicating those suggestions, and makes the improvements themselves possible.

Structured communication channels can also help employees make accurate predictions that help smooth day-to-day operations. UPS Prework Communications Meetings (Chapter 1) are an obvious example of a structured communication helping daily operations. Structured communication channels also make critical assistance available to employees (the intent of Global Enterprises' Employee Assistance Program). Communication channels also integrate diverse areas within the corporation. If the marketing and sales department at OptImage needs to talk with the engineering division about new products, specific channels facilitate this communication as well.

On the negative side, such structures can have adverse effects, since they can

- control the premises of discussion and the outcomes
- restrict the flow of information and access to it
- be used to manipulate others in service of the self-interests of a few

Potential difficulties growing out of these three effects are illustrated in the following group of scenarios, which dramatize possible problems.

ETHICS

WHO'S BEEN READING MY MAIL?

When Alana Shoars, the e-mail administrator for the Epson computer company, trained the company's 700 employees to use the company e-mail system, she assured them that their e-mail communications would be totally private. Later she discovered that her supervisor was intercepting and reading all e-mail messages. Shoars complained and was fired. She filed both a personal lawsuit and a class action suit on behalf of all the employees whose e-mail had been read. A lower court dismissed both cases, but the prosecuting attorney plans to press the suits all the way to the Supreme Court.

Opening another person's mail is commonly recognized as a violation of privacy. However, reading another person's e-mail is not always regarded as a violation. The Electronic Communications Privacy Act of 1986 (ECPA) specifically protects computer communications against interception and eavesdropping, but it does not legally protect employees from having their mail read by other company workers. For this reason, the issue of privacy in the workplace is an emerging area of concern in ethics research, case law, and company policy.

CONTEXT

Oberon Consolidated, Inc., is an intercontinental recycling firm. In Figure 2.12, Sandy Chapin, a vice president at Oberon, has written a report regarding an on-site office call. The report is for Chapin's eyes only (all names shown are pseudonyms). The meeting described is between Oberon representatives and Gates Maxwell, the president of INCON, an international recycling corporation. The purpose of the meeting is to see if Oberon and INCON can do business. The Gist process mentioned in this report is a manufacturing process used in recycling glass.

Base-Line Call Report. A call report is a written record of an important phone conversation or of business conducted during on-site visits. Figure 2.12 shows a call report for a visit between several business concerns regarding a possible joint project. For the purpose of our scenarios, the writer of this call report, a vice president of a corporation, represents a single channel of communication.

Problem Scenarios. Although the call report as it stands is very useful to Chapin and Oberon, the reports and the situation can be revised to demonstrate latent problems in communication structures.

Let's first explore a scenario that shows potential problems with *controlling the premises of discussion*. Imagine that Chapin does not consult with anyone regarding the conclusions about President Maxwell's response to the Gist process, which the Oberon company is promoting. Let's further say that Chapin is wrong in the assumption that Gist was the only process that Maxwell has found worth exploring. If Chapin has been overly optimistic about Maxwell's response, then a bad business decision could result. Oberon could spend a lot of time and money exploring possible connections with INCON when such business was doomed from the start. By imagining such a scenario, you can see the potential danger when one person, or one channel, is in sole control of the premises of discussion and the outcomes.

Second, let's explore a scenario that explores the issue of *restricted access*. R.W. Beaman's report cannot be copied for Oberon, because a third party, Pennsylvania Industries, is suspicious of sharing information and concerned with keeping certain information proprietary (the exclusive property of the company). In this case, restricted access to the report causes difficulties in communication, because Oberon has not had access to the report prior to the

Figure 2.12 Call Report for On-Site Meeting

Chapin mentions the Beaman report, which is evidently considered proprietary information by Pennsylvania Industries.

Chapin supplements the on-site observations.

Chapin suggests how much background can be assumed about INCON's knowledge of Gist.

Chapin records the main question growing out of the meeting. Chapin then states the meeting's outcome and action to be taken.

We were hospitably received by Gates, aged mid-40s, a strong voice, who brought us the R.W. Beaman engineering report to read on the recycling facility at Pittsburgh. Said it could not be copied because Pennsylvania Industries is part of the project and leery of having anything viewed/copied. We were given time to absorb this report before our discussions began.

INCON, wholly owned by the Maxwell family. A world of calm Anglo-Saxon money—an understated expanse of office. Persian carpets at intervals on the carpeted floors; portraits of the Maxwell parents participate from the wall of the Board Room. At one point, Gates' father joined our discussion. Though probably retired, he knows the business and plays a continuing role in the company—referred to as "Dad" by Gates, who defers to him in a pleasing filial way.

Gates had attended a recent London Symposium where Bill read his paper on the Gist process for recycling glass [Bill is an Oberon employee]. Unclear if he [Gates] attended the reading. Gates thought the papers were promises without commitment, except perhaps the Gist.

Because of recent escalation of wastepaper prices, Gates wants to know if the Gist process could provide a supplemental line which would permit INCON to use a combination of high and low priced raw material. If it can, they want to install this along with other new equipment.

Could the Gist machinery fit with the Pittsburgh project? Gates indicated there were other projects besides Pittsburgh in the offing. I said we would discuss issue with our engineers and revert.

meeting and cannot make a copy for future reference. Thus, Oberon must rely on Chapin's memory and understanding of a document that Chapin has viewed under severe time constraints. On the other hand, imagine what might happen if outside parties gained access to Chapin's report. The fact that access to these reports is normally restricted helps explain why Chapin feels safe in including personal detail about President Maxwell: because of the volume of professional business this vice president personally conducts, such detail helps Chapin remember a large number of clients. In this case, restricted access is desirable. If copies of the report were accidentally stapled to a revised prospectus sent to Maxwell, Maxwell might take exception to the characterization that his family represents "a world of calm Anglo-Saxon money," even though Chapin meant nothing derogatory by the remarks.

Third, let's consider the *issue of self-interest.* Imagine that Chapin shares a patent on a machine used in the Gist procedure. You can see that such an interest, especially given the fact that Chapin is a vice president at Oberon, has the potential to affect any proposal Oberon puts forth and to influence business decisions affecting a large number of people. Chapin and the scenarios we've just created are fictional. But by viewing Chapin as a communication channel, you can see potential drawbacks of structured communication networks within an organization.

MANAGEMENT STYLES

But the structure of networks tells only part of the story. The styles of people occupying any given spot in the network influences how communication works within an organization.

Kate Kramer, for example, has a management style that encourages employees to come in and discuss their problems. However, Kate had to draw the line at employees repeatedly coming in to discuss their problems with filling out certified mail forms. She balanced her need to interact with her employees with her need to accomplish her own work efficiently. In so doing, she did not abandon her role as a decision maker: she decided that instructions for sending certified mail should be posted throughout the building.

Experts in communication and in management have studied the way managers like Kate operate. Figure 2.13 suggests the relationship between a manager's personal needs, her management characteristics, and the communication structures and strategies that complement particular styles. Experts might classify Kate as driven by "achievement-affiliation," with enough dominance thrown in to guarantee that she does not abandon her role as decision maker. They also would observe that the choice of writing instructions, which call for employee participation, is consistent with Kate's needs and management style.

Organizational Climate

Organizational climate moderates the relationship between management style and the strategies managers use to exercise their influence. For example, if Kate were under pressure from the vice president of her division to meet certain production standards, she might have introduced penalties for any employee forgetting to follow the instructions. Of course, definitions of what makes a climate favorable or unfavorable vary with the person and even with the culture to which a person belongs.

Communication itself operates within the framework of favorable and unfavorable climates. Communicators may anticipate audience cooperation (a favorable climate for a message) or audience resistance (an unfavorable climate for a message). Chapters 8 through 10 go into extensive detail regarding how to adjust communication to meet the conditions.

Directives

Directives are communication tools that help managers get work done. Most directives are brief and focus on what is to be done. Unlike instructions, they do not include detailed explanations. A simple directive might read, "Please sign the attached form and return it to this office by June 15, so that we can process your request for reimbursement."

Directives often cover who, what, where, when, why, and how (the 5 Ws and an H). Figure 2.14 shows a directive that emphasizes benefits to the employees as the reason for the message. This emphasis on employee benefit suggests, but does not guarantee, a favorable organizational climate.

MEETINGS

Meetings provide opportunities for communication within an organization. OptImage, for example, has weekly Friday morning meetings of the top engineering managers from each of the three offices. Because the managers are located in Chicago, Boulder, and Des Moines,

Figure 2.13 Personal Needs, Management Styles, and Complementary Communication Practices

PERSONAL NEEDS	MANAGEMENT CHARACTERISTICS	COMPLEMENTARY COMMUNICATION VENUES AND STRATEGIES
Dominance—the need to control one's environment; to influence or direct the behavior of others by suggesting, persuading, or commanding; to be in charge	Stresses control, influence, persuasion, or authority. (As a sole motivator of subordinates, dominance is ineffective.)	Top-down channels or chain-of-command networks; communication strategies that emphasize the power and authority of the communicator
Achievement—the need to do one's best, to be successful as an individual, to accomplish tasks that require skill and effort	Seeks tasks that require personal expertise, skill, and effort. (In terms of management, an achievement orientation discourages the delegation of tasks and authority.)	Top-down channels or wheel networks, where the primary expert is at the hub; communication strategies that emphasize the quality and integrity of the document
Affiliation—the need to draw near and enjoyably cooperate or reciprocate with an ally, to participate in a friendly group	Values teamwork and cooperation and prefers not to work alone. (Although affiliative managers help build morale, they may consider tasks to be less important than people.)	Horizontal (or bottom-up channels); wheel or chain networks where everyone talks with everyone else; informal advice and trust networks; communication strategies that emphasize the needs or feelings of the communicator and audience
Dominance-Achievement	Controls and drives tasks without regard for teamwork and interaction; gives orders and rarely delegates. (This approach is valued in many "bottom-line" organizations.)	Top-down channels; communication strategies that emphasize the communicator's credibility and the document's integrity
Dominance-Affiliation	Assigns actual task achievement to subordinates but gives them strong direction and accountability. (A style with a very political feel that can be effective if not abused.)	Wheel networks or chain networks; communication strategies that emphasize the integrity of the document and the needs or feelings of the communicator and audience
Achievement-Affiliation	Gives a task to be performed and interpersonal relationships among those who are to perform it equal weight. (This approach is highly participatory and can be very effective if the manager does not abdicate the role of head decision maker.)	Balance of formal (wheel or chain) networks and informal networks; communication strategies that emphasize the needs or feelings of the communicator and audience, with one of these needs being a quality document
Dominance-Achievement-Affiliation	Balances influence, task orientation, and teamwork. (This rare style might be ideal.)	Balances input from various channels; features a variety of networks; uses multiple strategies

Figure 2.14 Company Directive

Please announce to division employees that when the new *Company Spirit* catalog is introduced in November, the items in this flier will be incorporated into the new catalog.

Ordering instructions in this flier are the same as for the current catalog. The flier is being released prior to the new catalog to give employees a jump on their Christmas shopping.

Who ["understood you" as reader and the employees and your audience]; What [catalog items]; Where [in this flier; in the catalog]; When [next fall]; How [ordering procedures]; Why [to give employees a head start on shopping]

the meeting is set up as a conference call. As a follow-up to the conference call, the managers send e-mail project summaries to the main office in Des Moines. These project summaries, which have a companywide distribution, are on the regular agenda of daily Monday morning meetings of top-level management at Des Moines headquarters. The Monday agenda also regularly includes weekly sales figures, support problems, and customer relations issues. The Friday and Monday meetings ensure regular communication within the organization, help the company keep track of its progress, and provide a means for solving any problems that might emerge.

MULTICULTURAL

PLANNING FOR MULTICULTURAL MANAGEMENT

The high cost of training managers in a U.S. company to be better multicultural communicators is offset by long-term benefits. Trainers recognize the four factors below as especially important:

Factors	Communication
Power Distance: the extent to which power is unequally distributed, and centralized, autocratic leadership is accepted • Highest power distance cultures: Philippines, Venezuela, Mexico • Lowest power distance cultures: Israel, Denmark, Austria • United States is somewhat low	Power distance directly affects the nature of the communication (autocratic, etc.) and audience selection (exclusion, inclusion)
Individualism vs. Collectivism: the extent to which people define themselves as individuals or groups • Most individualistic cultures: United States, Australia, Great Britain • Most collective cultures: Saudi Arabia, Venezuela, Colombia, Peru • United States is the most individualistic	Degree of individualism or collectivism directly affects communication style (the extent of collaboration and affiliation) and audience selection (individuals or groups)
Uncertainty Avoidance: the extent to which people feel threatened by ambiguous situations or risk taking • Highest uncertainty avoidance: Japan, Portugal, Greece • Lowest uncertainty avoidance: Singapore, Hong Kong, Denmark • United States is fairly low	Uncertainty avoidance affects audience motivation to act on a communication
Masculinity vs. Femininity: The extent to which dominant values emphasize assertiveness and materialism ("masculine") versus people, concern for others, and quality of life ("feminine") • Most masculine cultures: Japan, Austria, Switzerland, Italy • Most feminine cultures: Sweden, Norway, Netherlands, Denmark • United States is somewhat masculine	Degree of masculinity or femininity affects the pursuit and nature of goals put forward in communication

At the same time, meetings can make accomplishing business more difficult. At OptImage, for example, reading the summaries, which total 15 to 20 pages each week, takes time, and the meetings themselves also require blocking out Friday and Monday mornings for that purpose. The time factor explains why middle managers, who used to attend the Monday meetings, are just as happy that they are now excluded. Of course, at OptImage these managers can "crash" the Monday meeting if the posted summaries raise issues of concern, but they now have the extra time to get their other work done. Being excluded from meetings at other organizations might, however, mean not having a voice in company affairs.

Listening

To make the most of meetings, you need to understand both how to listen and how to compose effective agendas and minutes. Figure 2.15 presents dos and don'ts of good listening. Essentially, you become a good listener by reversing bad listening behavior: being active and engaged, openminded, attentive, and willing to exchange ideas.[4]

Agenda and Minutes

An administrator of a large department was famous for leaving notes in his employees' mailboxes: "I want to see you in my office." Employees joked that they couldn't escape the feeling that they were elementary school students being called into the principal's office for some infringement of the rules, although the administrator usually had only routine business to discuss. "Why doesn't he just add a phrase telling us what he wants to see us about?"

What the employees essentially wanted was an *agenda* to establish:

- context information, including the time, date, and location of the meeting, as well as the personnel or groups in attendance
- items for discussion

An agenda contributes to the pace of a meeting and helps ensure that certain business is conducted. When posted outside the meeting room, an agenda serves notice that the space is reserved at a particular time.

The question of who sets the agenda relates to the organizational structure and the types of communication networks within the company. If communication is top-down and

TECHNOLOGY

MEETINGS AND COMPUTER DECISION MAKING

By introducing a small computer network into meeting rooms, companies can cut meeting time and therefore expense while also reducing the posturing and bias often associated with group decision making.

The network system is simple: in front of each chair in the meeting room are a keyboard and a screen, and at the head of the table is a giant monitor. The participants enter the room, read the agenda sheet, and type their ideas about the day's issues into their terminal—anonymously. Everything typed appears on the giant monitor. No one knows who has said what. The ideas can be ranked and voted on on-line, decisions can be made quickly, and everyone leaves with a printed transcript of what has transpired.

In addition, the anonymity of the system can free up those attending the meeting from the bonds of the traditional company hierarchy. Employees who might have been hesitant to give input that disagreed with their superiors feel free to participate. Women and minorities, whose input may have been ignored under the old system, can give input on issues with less chance that their ideas will be automatically marginalized.

The advent of computerized workplaces has radically changed traditional communication patterns.

involves chain-of-command networks, then the agenda is most likely set by top-level management or the "ranking official" in charge. However, alternative arrangements might see the agenda being set collaboratively by committees or teams, or—in rare instances—by the people attending the meeting *after the meeting has convened*. Figure 2.16 (next page) shows a sample agenda.

Figure 2.15 Listening Guidelines

DON'T	DO
• Avoid listening if the subject is complex or difficult.	• Devote time and effort to trying to understand what the speaker is saying.
• Remain close-minded, denying the relevance or benefit of the speaker's ideas.	• Maintain an openminded attitude, willing to entertain the speaker's point of view.
• Be opinionated when arguing (outwardly or inwardly) with the speaker.	• Present your differences with the speaker calmly, and look for shared elements in your beliefs.
• Avoid eye contact while listening (in some cultures; in other cultures, this would be a sign of respect).	• Maintain eye contact with the speaker if appropriate, and assume that the speaker has good intentions.
• Demonstrate a lack of interest in the speaker's subject or become preoccupied with something else when listening.	• Take notes and nod in agreement where appropriate.
• Concentrate on the speaker's mannerisms or delivery or even on outside noise rather than on the message.	• Be prepared to ask relevant questions at the conclusion of the speaker's talk.

Figure 2.16 Agenda

AGENDA
HOSPITAL PLANNING COMMITTEE
ROOM 120
FRIDAY, APRIL 22, 1994, 1:00 P.M.

1. Approval of Minutes
2. Update on Objectives
3. Old Business: Software Format
4. New Business:
   - Report Outline
   - Recommendations
   - Title
5. Announcements

Figure 2.17 Detailed Minutes Organized around Main Points

Contextual details are included in the minutes.

The writer puts the subject of the meeting up front.

He has details regarding routine agenda items.

The writer uses marginal "call-outs" to subdivide his minutes. He organizes his minutes around main topics.

The writer calls attention to shared agreements by putting them in italics.

The writer includes enough detail here that there will be no confusion as to tasks and assignments.

The minute taker provides his name for the record.

HOSPITAL PLANNING COMMITTEE
ROOM 120
FRIDAY, APRIL 22, 1994, 1:00 P.M.

The Hospital Planning Committee meeting for the analysis of waste disposal for the Carver expansion project.

PRESENT Donisius Ladi, Traci Redman, Bill Lefevre

ABSENT Susan Reese-Graebener

MINUTES Approved, with a correction for the due date of the report: the report is **due May 14,** not May 24.

RECORD <u>Objective</u>

To create a working outline of the report and to consider conclusions and recommendations.

<u>Unfinished Business</u>

Bill said they were all on IBM in his division, so if we want his support staff to participate, we'll have to convert our Mac format to Word Perfect 5.1. Susan is on IBM. Traci said that would not be a problem. She also has a DOS mounter on her terminal and could read IBM disks. Donisius' terminal cannot read IBM disks. Conclusion: *We will use IBM format and Traci will get Donisius the mounter.*

Graphics: Bill said that his support staff is debating the advantages/disadvantages of two presentation software programs. Since we've decided that they will for sure be involved in the project, it might be an idea to *let them go with their strength.* Agreed.

<u>New Business</u>

Report Outline: Bill developed a working outline that covers the body of the report. The outline has sections for present waste disposal and future waste disposal needs once the new wings are built. The committee divided the outline into four parts. *Each group member will work on text for one part and finish a draft for the next meeting.*

Waste Types and Handling: Traci

Inadequacies of Disposal: Donisius

Government Policies: Susan

Waste Volume Change: Bill

Recommendations: Donisius stated that PVC pipe is best to prevent corrosion. Bill mentioned the design changes that would be necessary to accommodate PVC pipe. *More research needed.*

Title: Tabled Until Recommended Alternative Is Decided

NEWS Traci will be gone on Friday, May 6.

The next meeting will be Tuesday, April 26, 1994, at 8:00 a.m. in Room 200. *Donisius will do the agenda.*

The meeting was adjourned at 1:50 p.m.

William D. Lefevre,
Acting Secretary

Minutes are a formal record of the communication in a meeting. Minutes have components similar to an agenda's, except that minutes usually include the name and signature of the person taking the notes. Minutes are an important business record. Sometimes minutes are even revised for use in other company documents. They can, for example, be included as appendices to reports.

Figure 2.17 is a good set of minutes: (1) it is detailed enough for participants and nonparticipants alike to reconstruct the discussion, and (2) instead of focusing on procedural matters (for example, who spoke and for how long), it is organized around main points. (Figure 6.8 in Chapter 6 shows another excellent set of minutes.)

THE COMPOSING PROCESS WITHIN ORGANIZATIONS

As you may recall from introductory communication courses, the process of composing a message has a number of identifiable characteristics. The monologue in Figure 2.18 re-creates an employee's thinking after unsuccessfully trying to use the company's on-line directory to look up a phone number. (This lack of success is the *occasion* for writing.) The employee's thinking eventually leads to several communications: an article for the company newspaper on using the system, a laminated card with instructions to be posted at computer terminals, and an on-line HELP file.

Figure 2.18 Monologue Representing the Composing Process

Clarifying a topic or defining a problem (first paragraph)

Finding a purpose or goal for exploring the topic or problem (second paragraph)

Establishing a focus (third paragraph)

Generating a topic and purpose (fourth paragraph)

Considering purpose and audience (fifth paragraph)

Discovering information (sixth paragraph)

Considering arrangement and genre (type of writing) (seventh paragraph)

Considering design issues and genre; discovering information (eighth paragraph)

Considering audience (ninth paragraph)

This is frustrating. I must not be spelling her name right or something. What is the problem? Am I the only person who doesn't know how to use this thing?

I really need a set of instructions telling me how to use this system. I need to find out how this works and then write it up on an index card or something so I don't forget.

Maybe I'm going about this wrong. Maybe I need to know if there are other ways of looking up a person's number if I don't know their name. How many ways can I search for a number using the on-line directory? I wonder.

Maybe I could make the argument that the on-line system is being under-utilized. My reason for doing this could be to show the potential of the system.

No, scratch that. My purpose could be to convince employees of the benefits of the system *if they only knew how to use it.*

Well, how can I learn to use this puppy so that I can tell others? I could check to see if there is a user manual someplace or I could find someone who actually uses the system successfully. Maybe Joanna knows.

Actually, depending on how easy the system is to use, I could write up a set of instructions with the steps listed. . . .

Or screen dumps. That's it. A set of instructions illustrated with screen dumps. Well, if I use screen dumps, it would be an easy matter to put the instructions on-line—a Help file maybe. I'd have to get some engineering help for that.

Then I'd have to think of some way of advertising the stuff was there so people would know about it. . . . Yeah. Maybe I should write some of this down before I forget it.

You can see several aspects of the composing process in this monologue:

- There seem to be certain identifiable steps associated with thinking that result in composing. These steps include generating and clarifying topics, finding a purpose or defining a goal, establishing a focus, discovering information, considering audience, considering arrangement and genre, and considering design. (We have already covered setting of goals or criteria in Chapter 1, and we cover many of these other subjects in subsequent chapters.)
- Even though there are identifiable steps, these steps are recurring; that is, they can be repeated in the same or a different order. "Considering audience," for example, can occur more than once and at any point in the writing process.
- Although the steps in the composing process can be repeated in varying order, there does seem to be some kind of overall "pecking order." Topic generation and clarification, for example, take place before consideration of a focus and of arrangement. Questions concerning style such as "What tone of voice shall I adopt?" are not represented anywhere in the monologue. These questions evidently become important later, at least for the monologist.
- The composing process features both reconsideration and anticipation *throughout*. Reconsideration, or revision, occurs even at early stages. For example, the monologist both anticipates what the arrangement or genre is going to be like (a list) and reconsiders her options later (a card with a set of instructions; an on-line HELP).
- Because communicators can shuttle freely backward and forward while composing, they can forget or lose ideas and information. The monologist does well to start taking notes. Keeping a file or notebook for ideas and information is a good idea.

SKILLS & STRATEGIES

NAMING YOUR SUBJECT

Naming your subject is basic to composing any given communication. Communicators routinely ask *what* and *so what?* What am I talking about? What is my main point? What is the significance of what I'm trying to say? And why should my audience be interested?

In business communication, naming your subject takes on new dimensions. Memos, for example, have subject lines that address some or all of the above questions. An internal memo from a manager in marketing and sales to division employees about sending catalogs to international markets might use one of these subject lines:

- Sending Catalogs to International Markets (What is the memo about? *Sending catalogs to international markets.*)
- Our Need for an International Catalog (What is the main point? *Our company needs such a catalog.*)
- Increasing Our Markets through an International Catalog (What is the significance of the subject? *It will increase our markets.*)
- Procedures for Submitting Copy for the International Catalog (Why should my audience be interested? *The reader needs to follow certain procedures for submitting catalog copy.*)

But some subject lines are more effective than others. Effective subject lines name the subject and provide readers with a reason or a framework for reading about that subject. They are specific, concise, and to the point.

Sample Subject Lines	Analysis
Gain-Sharing	This subject heading names the subject but does not provide clues about why the writer is covering the topic or how the topic is important to the reader. This heading is *too general. It does not distinguish this message* from any number of other possible messages on gain-sharing.
Meeting about Gain-Sharing	This subject line provides the reader with a reason for reading, but says little about why the subject is to be discussed. It *omits pertinent contextual information.* (In some cases, not naming the purpose of the meeting might be a strategic choice.)
A Department Meeting to Discuss the Strategy of Gain-Sharing as a Means of Developing Human Resources on a Long-Term Basis	This subject line provides the reader with a reason for reading and establishes why the subject is to be discussed, but is *wordy and cumbersome.*
Meeting to Discuss Gain-Sharing as a Long-Term Company Strategy	This subject line provides the reader with a reason for reading and establishes why the subject is to be discussed. Although it is at a *maximum length* for a subject line (10 words), it is clear and to the point.

You may have a composing style that operates quite independently of the composing process itself. For example, you might revise as you go, or get the outline down first, or do initial drafts in longhand and use the word processor for later drafts.

In any case, if you are composing within an organizational setting, your company may very well have influenced your composing. For example, if you were a rank-and-file employee working for Northwest Airlines and you had a suggestion to make, you would structure your approach to the problem with the on-line directory according to a COMPASS form. The form would short-circuit any extensive consideration of organization that you might normally have followed in your composing by prompting you to arrange your ideas into three main groups: the idea or subject itself, the situation as you see it, and the solution or course of action (Figure 2.19).

As suggested by Figures 2.1 and 2.2, working for a company like Northwest would also influence your composing process if you were asked to write a report on a subject. To help you understand the impact of company preferences on composing, Figures 2.20 to 2.24 (pages 54–56) show how a writer would approach the subject of the on-line directory using three different **heuristics,** or methods of discovery.

First, Figure 2.20 (page 54) shows a writer using the common journalistic heuristic of who, what, where, when, why, and how (the 5Ws and an H) to think about the on-line directory. You might be expected to use such a heuristic if you worked for a newspaper or magazine, or if you contributed to a corporate newsletter or other such publications. In general, the journalistic heuristic encourages the communicator to discover certain types of information about a subject. You'll notice that the writer discovers several "whys" in the process of jotting down notes.

Figure 2.19 Form That Structures Employee Suggestions for Addressing Problems

NORTHWEST COMPASS
IDEA SYSTEM

Company Ownership Motivates People to Achieve Success & Savings

STOP BEFORE YOU FILL OUT THIS FORM... HAVE YOU TRIED ENTERING YOUR IDEA VIA THE EMPLOYEE ACCESS SYSTEM (EAS)? IF NOT, SEE EASY TO FOLLOW INSTRUCTIONS ON BACK.

Idea subject: *On-line directory information*	
If possible, estimate: Annual dollars saved: $	Annual new revenue generated: $
Your employee number (leave blank if submitting anonymously):	
If group submission, list employee numbers in the following spaces:	

State the situation as you see it:

The on-line directory is difficult to use – or at least it's not transparent. When I don't know the name – or the exact spelling – I can't locate the number, especially after the paper directory has been phased out.

State your solution/course of action: (Advise if you have more documentation)

Get instructions posted – perhaps on laminated card? Perhaps Passages could have articles about this subject.
An on-line HELP file?

1. After completion of this form, please submit it to your department for processing through the Employee Access System (EAS).
2. To track your idea you will need to access the automated system (see instructions on the back of this form).
3. When submitting ideas in the future, please use the automated system. It's easy... It's fun... It's paperless!

The information provided is your contribution to Northwest Airlines, Inc. and the exclusive rights to this information are maintained by Northwest Airlines, Inc.

While the journalistic heuristic governs how communicators for print media develop their topics and even discover subjects worthy of consideration, other heuristics adopted by certain types of organizations similarly affect composing. For example, Stephen Toulmin's structure for arguments has been used in a range of institutions and organizations for communicating about diverse areas including law, medicine, science, aesthetics, sports, and politics.[5] Toulmin's structure encourages communicators to think about their subjects as an argument to be made with a *claim* that is supported in various ways:

- with situational information (*data*)
- with a logical bridge (*warrant*) connecting the data to the claim and establishing the communicator's right to link the evidence (data) to the assertion (*claim*)
- with information that further justifies the communicator's right to make the claim (*backing*)

The claim can also be qualified and hedged (with a *reservation*) to allow for extenuating circumstances. Figure 2.21 (page 54) shows how Toulmin's structure can be applied to the issue of the on-line directory.

Because the Toulmin sequence (which can also be called a line of argument) begins with data or information and moves toward the claim, it can be regarded as basically bottom-up,

Figure 2.20 Notes Using the 5Ws and an H

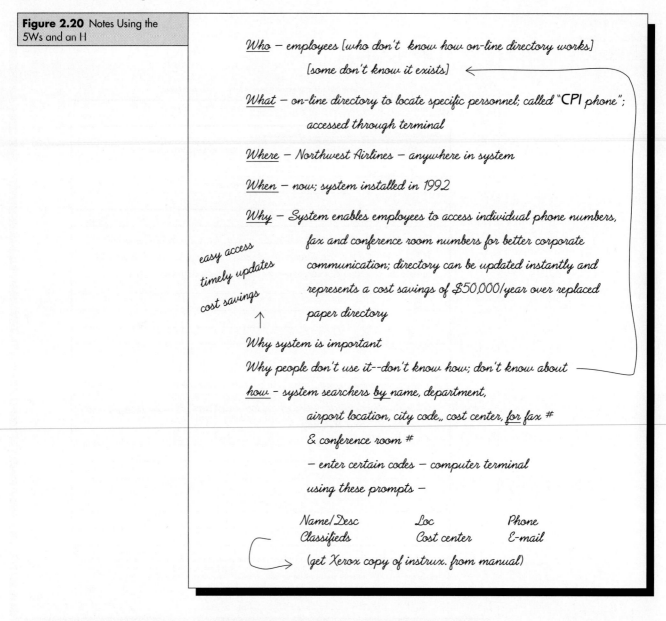

Who – employees [who don't know how on-line directory works]
[some don't know it exists]

What – on-line directory to locate specific personnel; called "CPI phone"; accessed through terminal

Where – Northwest Airlines – anywhere in system

When – now; system installed in 1992

Why – System enables employees to access individual phone numbers, fax and conference room numbers for better corporate communication; directory can be updated instantly and represents a cost savings of $50,000/year over replaced paper directory

easy access
timely updates
cost savings
↑
Why system is important

Why people don't use it--don't know how; don't know about

how - system searchers *by* name, department, airport location, city code,, cost center, *for* fax # & conference room #
– enter certain codes – computer terminal
using these prompts –

Name/Desc	Loc	Phone
Classifieds	Cost center	E-mail

(get Xerox copy of instrux. from manual)

Figure 2.21 Example of Toulmin Logic Applied to a Business Occasion

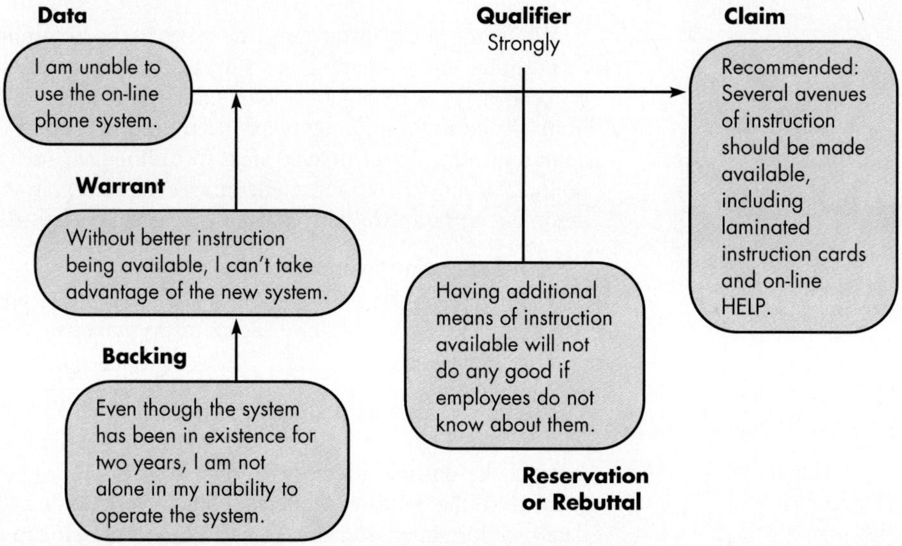
Data
I am unable to use the on-line phone system.
Qualifier
Strongly
Claim
Recommended: Several avenues of instruction should be made available, including laminated instruction cards and on-line HELP.
Warrant
Without better instruction being available, I can't take advantage of the new system.
Backing
Even though the system has been in existence for two years, I am not alone in my inability to operate the system.
Having additional means of instruction available will not do any good if employees do not know about them.
Reservation or Rebuttal

or inductive. Of course, this basic movement does not preclude the possibility of the communicator beginning with the claim and working backward to discover supporting evidence.

Figures 2.22 to 2.24, which also deal with the on-line directory, show heuristics that feature both the problem-solving framework and the top-down approach shown earlier in connection with Minto's work (Figures 2.1 and 2.2). You'll notice that these approaches combine to encourage the communicator to think about the subject as a problem that can be broken down into smaller and smaller chunks.

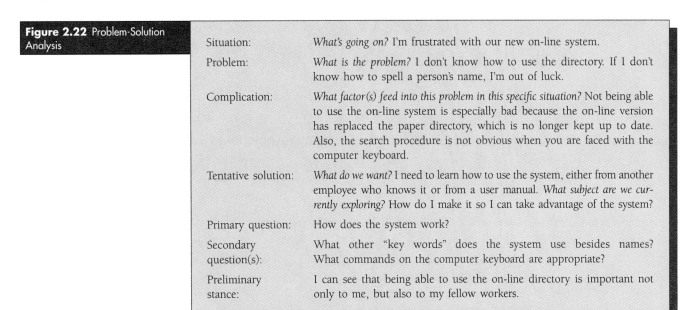

Figure 2.22 Problem-Solution Analysis

Situation:	*What's going on?* I'm frustrated with our new on-line system.
Problem:	*What is the problem?* I don't know how to use the directory. If I don't know how to spell a person's name, I'm out of luck.
Complication:	*What factor(s) feed into this problem in this specific situation?* Not being able to use the on-line system is especially bad because the on-line version has replaced the paper directory, which is no longer kept up to date. Also, the search procedure is not obvious when you are faced with the computer keyboard.
Tentative solution:	*What do we want?* I need to learn how to use the system, either from another employee who knows it or from a user manual. *What subject are we currently exploring?* How do I make it so I can take advantage of the system?
Primary question:	How does the system work?
Secondary question(s):	What other "key words" does the system use besides names? What commands on the computer keyboard are appropriate?
Preliminary stance:	I can see that being able to use the on-line directory is important not only to me, but also to my fellow workers.

Figure 2.23 Initial Worksheet

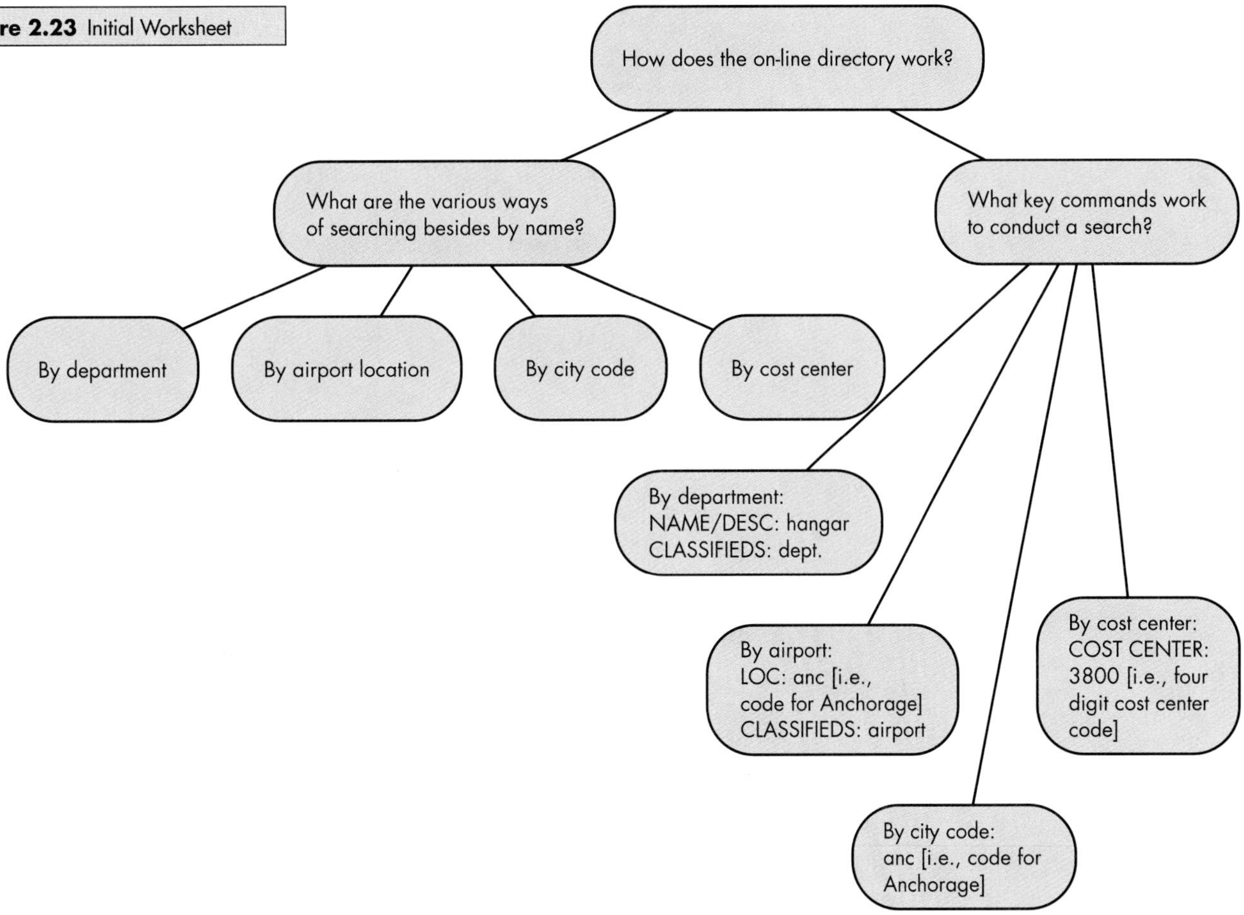

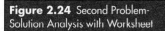

Figure 2.24 Second Problem-Solution Analysis with Worksheet

Situation:	*What's going on?* I now know the system, but a surprising number of other employees don't.
Problem:	*What is the problem?* Current methods of advertising the system's use don't seem to be working.
Complication:	*What factor(s) feed into this problem in this specific situation?* We can't depend on the mere existence of CPI phone or the corresponding absence of the paper directory to motivate employees to seek out appropriate help.
Tentative solution:	*What do we want?* We need new ways of publicizing the on-line system to help and encourage its use.
Primary question:	What ways can we use to promote the system?
Preliminary stance:	The on-line system is both helpful and necessary to corporate communication.

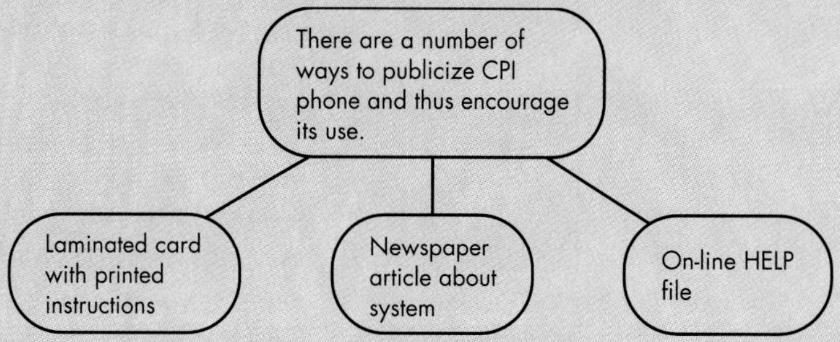
There are a number of ways to publicize CPI phone and thus encourage its use.
Laminated card with printed instructions
Newspaper article about system
On-line HELP file

Any organization that officially adopts one or more of these heuristics influences how its communicators think about the subjects of their messages: as a topic to be investigated, as an argument to be made, as a problem to be solved. Heuristics favored by an organization also influence how communicators for that organization develop information, evidence, or support for their messages (see Chapter 7).

Companies influence the composing process in other ways as well. For the monologist (Figure 2.18), issues of style become important later in the composing process. However, in organizations with precise stylesheets, stylistic considerations are important early on. (Communication Spotlights II and III on pages 216 and 309 present information on how revision works in an organizational setting.)

Organizations influence composing because they find it in their best interest to do so. They have discovered that having a writing policy fosters both unity and productivity. A writing policy, such as that adopted by a major corporation based in Baltimore and excerpted in Figure 2.25, establishes a cultural norm: "a common use of language that allows writers and readers to communicate the corporate message effectively."[6] This policy statement states what constitutes effective writing for that particular organization.

Figure 2.25 Writing Policy at a Major Baltimore-Based Corporation

"Use the ABCs of effective writing: Accuracy, brevity, clarity.
Write to communicate, not to impress."

1. Consider your audience. Write with the reader's needs in mind.
2. Use short paragraphs.
3. Use short, declarative sentences (15 to 25 words at most). Avoid overusing conjunctions such as "and."
4. Use short, concrete, specific words.
5. Use a brief example to illustrate a point, if this will be helpful. Indent an example. Designate it clearly by using the term "Example."
6. Instructions should be written at the 6th to 8th grade level.
7. Avoid jargon and acronyms.
8. Tone—writing should be positive, honest and clear. Use the active voice.
9. Clean up the details. Spelling, punctuation and grammar reflect the image of your organization.

RESPONSE SHEET

COMMUNICATION MODELS AND PROBLEMS

OCCASION:
COMMUNICATOR(S): AUDIENCE(S):
SUBJECT: MESSAGE:

◆ DESCRIPTION OF COMMUNICATION DIFFICULTIES

Identify and describe the occasion-based, communicator-based, text-based, and audience-based difficulties associated with a particular communication situation.

◆ ANALYSIS OF OCCASION-BASED PROBLEMS

What model or models (transmission, reciprocal, or assumption-based) best help(s) you understand the occasion-based difficulties of this particular communication situation? Explain.

- time factors
- technology
- atmosphere
- money
- other:

Analyze the described occasion-based problems using one or more communication models.

◆ ANALYSIS OF COMMUNICATOR-BASED PROBLEMS

What model or models (transmission, reciprocal, or assumption-based) best help(s) you understand the communicator-based difficulties of this particular communication situation? Explain.

- ideas
- stance
- assumptions
- character
- other:

Analyze the described communicator-based problems using one or more communication models.

◆ ANALYSIS OF TEXT-BASED PROBLEMS

What model or models (transmission, reciprocal, or assumption-based) best help(s) you understand the text-based difficulties of this particular communication situation? Explain.

- organization
- character
- mechanics
- design
- other:

Analyze the described text-based problems using one or more communication models.

◆ ANALYSIS OF AUDIENCE-BASED PROBLEMS

What model or models (transmission, reciprocal, or assumption-based) best help(s) you understand the audience-based difficulties of this particular communication situation? Explain.

- feelings
- design
- expertise
- expectations
- other:

Analyze the described audience-based problems using one or more communication models.

ACTIVITIES, EXERCISES, AND ASSIGNMENTS

◆ IN-CLASS ACTIVITIES

1. Please review Figures 2.1 and 2.2, the problem-solving approach and the example of top-down structure, for the following activity.

   a. Figure 2.1 shows the writer going through the problem-solving sequence twice before getting to the primary and secondary questions that pertain to the specific task: writing a report on a gain-sharing program tailored to the organization. Why do you think repeating the sequence was necessary to this communicator? Can you imagine an occasion for communicating that might have even more sequences? Explain.

   b. How, in your opinion, does the composing aid of a top-down graphic (Figure 2.2) help the communicator? How does the use of a particular approach to thinking about communication tasks in an organization define, reflect, or contribute to the company's corporate culture?

2. In the opening of the chapter we used Kate's certified mail situation to explain the differences between transmission, reciprocal, and assumption-based models of communication. Later, we used Thornberg's Global Enterprises pamphlet to demonstrate how the three different models explored communication problems. Discuss how the three models help explain communication occasions in business using examples from your own experiences. Then, working together with several classmates, pose a specific communication problem using the three different models. Use the Response Sheet on communication models and problems to help guide your analysis. Be prepared to present your problem and analysis to the rest of the class.

3. Remembering the situation at OptImage, discuss the communication channels or networks within an organization, using your own examples. Remember to distinguish between formal and informal channels of communication, and to consider both the advantages and disadvantages of communication structures.

◆ INDIVIDUAL AND GROUP EXERCISES

1. Please refer to Figure 2.26 to complete this exercise. Figure 2.26 represents a policy statement regarding reimbursement for miscellaneous expenses incurred on company trips.

   a. Assume that employees in your department are constantly becoming confused regarding when they need to file receipts for reimbursement and when they do not. Write a short set of instructions that clarifies the procedures for filing for expenses.

   b. Assume that in spite of the policy regarding ground transportation, several employees in your department were seen taking a taxi from the headquarters building to the airport. Discuss how you, as a manager, would handle the situation. Now write a directive regarding the taxi issue. (If you personally would not have written a directive regarding this matter, assume that you were asked to do so by your immediate supervisor.)

2. Work together with several peers to devise a **document cycling plan** (revision procedure) that would work for you as a member of a collaborative team. Be sure that you stipulate procedural expectations concerning how drafts should be formatted and submitted, etc. Then, on the basis of your discussion, write a revision policy statement for your group. (Figure 2.25 is a writing policy statement, but could be used as a model for your revision policy statement.)

3. Review Figure 2.25. Then revise the directive shown in Figure 2.27 so that it meets the Baltimore-based company's standard of effective writing. The directive is from top-level managers to middle management and concerns the formation of quality circles in each department.

   Your revision should maintain the basic organization of the example: the first paragraph deals with context for the request, the second deals with rationale for introducing quality circles into the organizational

Figure 2.26 Policy Statement Regarding Miscellaneous Expenses

- Receipts for parking are required if the total charge is $5 or more.
- Receipts for registration are required. You may prepay registration fees by processing a voucher or receive reimbursement on a travel expense voucher <u>after</u> you return.
- Telephone and fax charges. Indicate on the hotel bill which calls are for business purposes. If you are requesting reimbursement for calls charged to your home telephone, a highlighted copy of your phone bill must be attached.
- Ground transportation. Receipts are not required for taxis, shuttles, or subways. Reimbursement will be made for transportation to and from the destination airport and your hotel and to and from any business meetings at the destination. Taxis used for dinner arrangements are not reimbursable. A taxi should not be used for transportation from corporate headquarters to the airport. Five Oaks Charters, 555-6788, operates a shuttle to the airport.
- Tolls. Receipts are not required.
- Shipping and mailing charges. When goods must be shipped while in travel status, a postage or shipping receipt is required.
- Gratuities. Reasonable tips for cabs, skycaps, bellhops, etc., will be reimbursed. No receipt is required.

Figure 2.27 Material for Directive to Establish Quality Circles

> The art and architecture of change works through a different medium than the management of the ongoing, routinized side of an organization's affairs. Most of the rational, analytic tools measure *what already is* (or make forecasts as a logical extrapolation from data on what is). But change efforts have to *mobilize people around what is not yet known,* not yet experienced.
>
> For this reason, we need to concentrate on the symbolic or conceptual aspects of the change process—on new understandings, on the communication of those, and then on the inevitable reformulations as events move forward.
>
> To be able to operate integratively, to bring other people in, to bridge multiple realities, and to reconceptualize our organization to take into account these realities growing out of our commitment to innovation and change, we need to form Quality of Worklife Groups or quality circles in every department. These quality circles will be charged with outlining how the new Mission Statement for our organization, recently approved by the Board of Directors, entitled "Mission Statement 2000," and available on the Company Network in the Master Plan file, can be launched in their respective departments. The membership of these circles should be established by June 8, and meetings should begin immediately thereafter.

structure, and the third gives particulars. While you should maintain this sequence, you do not have to end up with three paragraphs. You should also feel free to make other changes that would bring the writing in line with the writing policy expressed in Figure 2.25.

◆ OUT-OF-CLASS ASSIGNMENTS

1. Take notes during a conference call with colleagues, during an on-site meeting at a company, or at an organizational or community meeting that you choose to attend. Convert your notes into minutes that will serve as an accurate record of the call, event, or meeting.
2. Imagine that the HELP program devised for your company's on-line directory, similar to that described earlier in this chapter (pages 51–56), is too complicated to be practical. Imagine further that you are employed by one of the following companies:
    - Northwest Airlines
    - UPS
    - OptImage
    - a company with which you are personally acquainted (provide a brief scenario)

    How would you bring the problem to the attention of company officials? For example, would you choose a face-to-face meeting, a telephone conversation, an e-mail message, a complaint/suggestion form, a memo, a formal letter, or perhaps a combination of methods?

    Write a memo to your teacher that briefly describes (a) the communication channels and networks at the company for which you work, (b) your plan for bringing the problem to official attention, and (c) the reasons justifying your planned procedure(s). Pay special attention to how you word your subject heading for the memo (see the Skills and Strategies box, page 52).
3. Together with several of your colleagues, establish a 12-point writing policy for your company. (For the purposes of this exercise, you may consider your business communication class to be your company.) Remember that a writing policy is different from a stylesheet. A writing policy, as shown in Figure 2.25, is like a directive: it tells employees what to do. A stylesheet (as shown in Figure 1.14) is like a set of instructions: it tells employees how to do it.

CASE

AMERICAN SURGICAL PRODUCTS, INC.

CASE BY ANDREA BREEMER FRANTZ

Background. American Surgical Products, Inc. (ASPI), is a $1.5 billion company that manufactures and markets surgical instruments and supplies. Since 1964, the company has been headed by Daniel Bauer, a brilliant entrepreneur and former medical student at Johns Hopkins. Bauer built the corporation into the nation's leading private medical supplier in 12 years. Profits have steadily increased since 1976, with a five-year stock price high of $142.50 in the late 1980s. The company's stock price has since plummeted, however (to $25.50), because of a number of factors.

- In 1990, ASPI marketed a new balloon-tipped catheter for angioplasty procedures. The new synthetic material used to create the tip of the catheter caused unexpected allergic reactions in some patients. ASPI was forced to recall the instruments and pay $245,000 in damages. The company has filed suit against the manufacturer of the synthetic material that caused the allergic reaction, but the case has not yet gone to trial.
- Late in 1990, the Vice President of Operations, Jack White, prematurely promised a new patient data analysis computer system to 400 hospitals for test marketing. The software experienced several setbacks in the development stage before it was finally released in April 1993. By then, many of the test market hospitals had lost interest and ASPI was left holding $500,000 of computer software and hardware. By February 1994, White was still researching alternative test sites while ASPI's strongest competitor, Johnson Medical Supplies Unlimited, had already market-tested a smaller sample of hospitals and had begun a formal sales campaign.
- In June 1994, CEO Bauer's youngest son, Frank, a commercial airline pilot, tested positive for marijuana use in a routine drug test. Though such tests are normally not made public, a national news magazine featured Frank's dismissal in a story on airline safety and pointed to the irony of the elder Bauer's billion-dollar medical supplies corporation.

Board members at ASPI fumed at the magazine's innuendo and released a public statement condemning the magazine's "yellow journalism."

- Health-care reform wrangling in Washington, D.C., and skittish market predictions have caused stocks in all health-related corporations to fluctuate wildly.

The ASPI Board of Directors seeks to put a positive spin on the overall situation in an effort to bolster shareholder confidence in their investments. As a result, the Board has drawn up an innovative 10-year plan:

- adoption of a new company logo that illustrates the "future" vision of American Surgical Products, Inc.
- a dramatic restructuring of the company management hierarchy that offers a more balanced distribution of power and benefits throughout the organization
- an electronic discussion board designed to engage all shareholders in company management and product development issues
- an unprecedented campaign to introduce 200 major new products by the year 2000
- international expansion of research and development departments in Canada, Mexico, Japan, and India
- an investors' incentive program that offers special discounts to investors who purchase 500 or more shares for new portfolios and additional breaks for large shareholders
- a gain-sharing program that rewards employees with cash bonuses for increased productivity

Task. As a member of the marketing team for ASPI, you have been charged with informing shareholders regarding the Board's plan. In composing your message, you have to decide whether (and how) to acknowledge some of the company's recent problems while encouraging a "team" effort at building for the future. You also have to decide what channel or channels of communication to use in presenting this message to shareholders. The vice president, for example, has suggested that the message should appear in the annual report and should inspire readers to read and analyze both the report and the plan. You can see the logic of the vice president's suggestion but are worried that the message might be overlooked because of the quantity of other information contained in the 40-page report.

Complication. After reading a draft of your message, the Director of Personnel suggests that the message would go a long way in boosting *employee morale* as well as shareholder confidence. Although you realize that these two groups differ in their interests, you also agree with the director's point. You now must decide how best to present this information to an internal audience: what channels to use and what points in the Board's plan to emphasize.

CHAPTER

3

Communicating with Technology

OUTLINE

Geist Software E-Mail Exchange

Electronic Communication Technologies

Issues Relating to Communicating with Electronic Technologies

Technology's Impact on Business Communication

CRITERIA FOR EXPLORING CHAPTER 3

What we cover in this chapter	What you will be able to do after reading this chapter
A workplace e-mail exchange to solve a problem	Recognize the benefits and potential problems of e-mail
Electronic communication technologies	Recognize uses of telephone systems, fax equipment, and networked computer systems
Issues that affect communicating with electronic technology	Appropriately respond to information overload, anonymity, lack of interpersonal contact, and organizational values in using technologies
Technology's impact on business communication	Identify workplace situations in which technology changes the nature of the communication

E

lectronic communication—voice mail, teleconferencing, e mail (electronic mail), electronic databases, electronic forms, electronic networks—is increasingly common in businesses. While technology may change the speed with which a message is generated and received, the amount of information available, and the number of people involved in generating and receiving a message, the technology doesn't change the quality of the message itself.

A poorly organized memo isn't improved simply because it is electronic rather than handwritten. A carelessly developed report isn't necessarily better because it is constructed with **groupware** rather than in face-to-face meetings. Groupware is software that helps groups manage their interactions, information, and plans. Effective communicators still need to consider the purpose, audience, and occasion of a message, regardless of the way the message is generated or transmitted.

CONTEXT

The story Tom Peters—syndicated columnist, author, and consultant on achieving excellence in business—tells in Figure 3.1, "Quick and Thick Ideas Rarely Produce Results," raises questions about the appropriate—or inappropriate—use of groupware. Using groupware, a well-known accounting firm, KPMG Peat Marwick, was able to produce a winning proposal over a weekend, written by team members in four different cities. Peters is not terribly impressed with the achievement and asks whether technology can substitute for time and effort.

1. Do you think Peters is objecting to the software that the KPMG Peat Marwick team used, to the way they used the software, or to their composing process?
2. What parts of the writing process (as explained in Chapter 2) may have been shortchanged by the KPMG Peat Marwick team?
3. Despite Peters' important objections, how do you think groupware might be able to help an organization?

In this chapter, you'll learn about the following aspects of communication networks and technologies:

- uses of e-mail in the workplace
- features of current electronic technologies
- issues relating to electronic technologies

GEIST SOFTWARE E-MAIL EXCHANGE

When employees at Geist Software work on a team project, they communicate regularly in order for the project to be successful. In addition to daily conversations, formal weekly meetings, and formal monthly project reports, teams depend heavily on their e-mail exchanges to transmit information, express opinions, ask questions, suggest alternatives—in other words, to carry on a conversation.

The selected e-mail messages in Figures 3.2 through 3.11 (pages 64–68) were sent over a five-day period among team members who were working on a project to develop DataGraph, an expensive new product that creates graphs from data. This five-member team was near the end of nearly six months on the development project:

Steve Hoffman. As a project director, Steve was responsible for the general management of the project, which included determining budgets, schedules, and personnel.

Harry Schmidt. As a software developer, Harry was responsible for designing the software program and supervising the programmers.

Kate Molitor. As a documentation specialist, Kate was responsible for creating the on-line help for the software as well as writing and designing the user manual and all the promotional materials.

Figure 3.1 Technology Cannot Make Up for Poorly Conceived Content

What does Peters suggest contributes to the quality of an effective document?

What does Peters suggest about the relationship of planning time and document quality?

What aspects of this situation—the occasion—does Peters suggest are indefensible?

Who does Peters seem to believe is responsible for the situation he describes?

What organizational pressures might have contributed to this situation?

What do you think Peters would say is the purpose of his comments?

Quick and thick ideas rarely produce results

Tom Peters

I fervently believe in electronic networking, using so-called groupware (for example, Lotus Notes), to create value through pooled knowledge. Lord knows, I believe in customer responsiveness. Still, I was repelled by a recent *Computerworld* article, "KMPG Turns to FirstClass Groupware."

One Friday at 3 P.M., the accounting-consulting firm KPMG Peat Marwick got a request from an insurance company to submit a bid for a "major technology overhaul," according to the magazine. Over the weekend four partners in four different cities prepared a "thick" proposal, complete with "graphics and diagrams," using the firm's new Knowledge Manager system. They delivered the document to the client at noon Monday and won the business, outbidding EDS, IBM and Coopers & Lybrand.

But wait . . . I call it the But-Will-You-Brag-About-It-to-Your-Grandkids? test. Suppose one of the four KPMG partners is 36. Twenty-four years from now, at age 60, will he thumb through a stack of 100 proposals and reports he worked on, stop at the one prepared over the hectic weekend, and exclaim, "Wow! A grand slam! A brand-new approach that led the insurance industry in a whole new direction!" I doubt it.

Call me a skeptic. Call me anything you want, and you'll not convince me that anything genuinely new, nifty and worth bragging about can be created in a groupware weekend in cyberspace.

Computerworld reports that a normal response time in this case would have been three to five business days. Well, a pox on both parties' houses: That is, I roundly condemn the insurance company that asked for a serious proposal in five days' time—and the consultants who accommodated the request. How stupid!

Writing 2,500 words about, say, your new service or product is not that hard. (You could do it in a weekend.) Writing 500 words is a lot harder. And writing three words about it—e.g., ad copy that turns the world upside down (Nike's "Just Do It")—is pure, unadulterated agony that could take months.

I'm hardly surprised, and even less impressed, that KPMG could create a "thick" proposal, replete with "graphics and diagrams" (doubtless in all the colors of the rainbow), in 60 hours.

Look, I've been in the proposal and report writing business for 28 years. There are a handful of my "products" I'm really proud of that made a difference; and a chest-full that are professional but blah—and not worth the Tylenol it took to produce them.

The great ones did invariably involve collaboration (which surely would have been easier with Notes or FirstClass). But they took time. Time to dance with the problem. Time to put the whole mess aside and let it gestate. Time to turn 10,000 "easy" words into 1,000 provocative, precise words.

"But we had no choice," the KPMGers might well rebut. "The deadline was absurd. So what? We were up against the likes of EDS. Doing the job over the weekend, with more creativity than the other guys, was a big win."

Don't be so sure. I have no idea how it will turn out. But I'd bet that the result for both parties—insurer, KPMG—will be unremarkable.

So, amen: Groupware yourself to the hilt. I'm all for it. But use the technology to do something with pizzazz, not just to become a lightning-fast drone.

Tara Reed and Rob Booker. As programmers, Tara and Rob were responsible for writing the computer program for the new software, based on the specifications established by Steve and Harry.

Steve, Harry, Kate, Tara, and Rob had been working together as a cooperative team, with each member involved in project decision making. This meant, for example, that Kate had made productive suggestions about the way the software could be made more user friendly. Now that the team was nearing the end of the project and Kate was ready to make decisions about the final production of the manual, she solicited input from other members of the team. These selected e-mail messages provide a window into the project team's ongoing conversation about producing the manual for DataGraph.

The e-mail exchange among Kate, Steve, Harry, Tara, and Rob saved them time and increased the information they had for discussion and decision making. This particular conversation about the manual was only one of many conversations on several topics. In other e-mail conversations, they considered other aspects of the project, including technical details of the computer program, marketing the software to a specialized audience, the usability of the manual, and various human factors problems such as making sure that the graphs were displayed on a background of contrasting color on the computer monitor. The e-mail exchange enabled the team to efficiently continue the conversations of their weekly face-to-face meetings. They could ask questions and provide information as ideas or questions occurred to them without interrupting their work.

Figure 3.2 Geist Software E-Mail: Kate to the Team

Most e-mail headings are similar to this one, identifying the sender and receiver(s) by both name and e-mail address, the date, and the subject. Anonymous messages aren't practical on a project team.

Because Kate knew her audience well, she used an informal tone in her message.

In some companies, Kate, as the documentation specialist, would make all these production decisions by herself or with other documentation specialists. However, Geist Software is organized around multidisciplinary teams. Thus, the purpose of Kate's message was to summarize the information she'd collected so that the team could discuss what they wanted to do and make an informed decision.

Even though the e-mail system at Geist Software offers almost no formatting capabilities, Kate made information more accessible to readers by using ALL-CAP headings and spacing between paragraphs. (See Chapter 12 on design.)

E-Mail

From Kate Molitor.GEIST@mac_link
Date 10 Aug 199- 14:36:05
Subject: manual production
To: "Steve Hoffman" <Steve Hoffman@GEIST>, "Harry Schmidt" <Harry Schmidt.GEIST@mac_link>, "Tara Reed" <Tara Reed@GEIST>, "Rob Booker" <Rob Booker@GEIST>

Based on your request at this morning's meeting about producing the manual, I've collected some preliminary information from three printers--one local, two out of state.

Now we need to make some more decisions. The low quantity we're printing makes some of our decisions for us (sorry, autobind is out--it's too pricey), but all the rest of the decisions are up to us.

BINDING
Three-ring binders are an option, but we need to stick to a standard size (8.5"x5.5" OR 8.5"x11") to be under budget.

Spiral binding may be the way to go. But even with that we need to decide on either continuous spiral (like your old school notebooks) or Wire-O (it's a neater, easier-to-use spiral), which, obviously, I favor over continuous spiral. (By the way, if you want to see an example of each of these, just stop by my office.)

If we got spiral binding, we have the option of making the cover of the manual cover the spiral bind also. Such a cover would basically mask the spiral bind and give the manual a cleaner look when it's sitting on the shelf.

SIZE
Standard size for three-ring binders (8.5"x5.5" OR 8.5"x11") is one option, but if we go with the spiral bind, options include 7"x9" or 8.5"x7".

PRINTERS
We have three to choose from right now. When we get pricing details it may be easier to decide, but right now we could begin weighing working with the one local company over working with one of the other two that are out of state.

That's all I'll give you for now. We'll need to continue making decisions as the software nears completion. Please let me know what you think of options so far.

--Kate

Figure 3.3 Geist Software E-Mail: Harry to Kate and the Team

Because this was a response to Kate's message, the subject line read "re: manual production." If Harry had been creating an original message rather than responding, there would be no "re."

Harry's practice of using no capital letters is part of the e-mail culture. It's a practice used by many e-mail correspondents.

E-Mail

From Harry Schmidt.GEIST@mac_link
Date 10 Aug 199- 15:16:03
Subject: re: manual production
To: "Steve Hoffman" <Steve Hoffman@GEIST>, "Tara Reed" <Tara Reed@GEIST>, "Rob Booker" <Rob Booker@GEIST>, "Kate Molitor" <Kate Molitor.GEIST@mac_link>

what do we need to give the printers for them to produce the manual? do we need to send them hard copy or what?

Figure 3.4 Geist Software E-Mail: Kate to Harry and the Team

Kate not only responded to Harry's question, but she anticipated his unasked questions about the process and benefits of various systems or approaches. Her purpose was to provide a rationale as to why such a system was important for their manual.

By the end of the day on August 10, the team had received and discussed quite a lot of information. Although there was not the interpersonal contact that would occur in another meeting, these people saw each other several times every day.

E-Mail

From Kate Molitor.GEIST@mac_link
Date 10 Aug 199- 16:32:15
Subject: Docutech
To: "Steve Hoffman" <Steve Hoffman@GEIST>, "Harry Schmidt" <Harry Schmidt.GEIST@mac_link>, "Tara Reed" <Tara Reed@GEIST>, "Rob Booker" <Rob Booker@GEIST>

Harry--

Good questions. We got the same answer from each of them. They all recommend using a system called Docutech. It sounds pretty cool. We just send them a disk copy of the manual (PostScript version) and they pop it into the machine. The Docutech equipment is able to read the disk and create first-generation images for each of the manuals it prints rather than second-generation copies the way a regular photocopier would have to if we gave them a camera-ready version.

--Kate

Figure 3.5 Geist Software E-Mail: Steve to Harry

Steve had a twofold purpose in sending Harry a message that didn't go to the rest of the group: to check about Docutech without publicly questioning Kate and to check on the schedule without publicly embarrassing Harry.

An additional benefit was reducing information overload that occurs when people receive information they don't need.

E-Mail

From Steve Hoffman.GEIST
Date 11 Aug 199- 8:17:37
Subject: Background
To: "Harry Schmidt" <Harry Schmidt.GEIST@mac_link>

Harry:

Can you give me any more information about this Docutech system that Kate seems sold on?

By the way, I notice we slipped in meeting last month's timeline for finishing on schedule. Can we pick up the time we've lost and still meet our original deadline?

Steve

Figure 3.6 Geist Software E-Mail: Harry to Steve

Harry's response confirmed Kate's recommendation to use Docutech. She will probably never know that Steve questioned her recommendation.

E-Mail

From Harry Schmidt.GEIST@mac_link
Date 11 Aug 1994 10:48:57
Subject: re: Background
To: "Steve Hoffman" <Steve Hoffman@GEIST>

i had never heard of docutech, but since Kate mentioned it yesterday, i've seen an article about the docutech system. its first-generation capabilities seem exactly what we need.

don't worry about the schedule. rob and tara are willing to put in the overtime to meet the deadline if they have to.

Figure 3.7 Geist Software E-Mail: Kate to Tara and Rob

This message from Kate went only to Tara and Rob, so it's another example of team members not overloading each other with unnecessary information. Kate asked Tara and Rob for help, knowing that this was outside their responsibilities. Sending the memo just to Tara and Rob also gave them a chance to say "no" more privately.

E-Mail

From Kate Molitor.GEIST@mac_link
Date 11 Aug 199- 15:17:53
Subject: re: Budget
To: "Tara Reed" <Tara Reed@GEIST>, "Rob Booker"
<Rob Booker@GEIST>

Tara and Rob--

Could you help me prepare the PostScript file including all the screen dumps so it's ready for the printer to put right into Docutech?

--Kate

Figure 3.8 Geist Software E-Mail: Tara and Rob to the Team

Information overload occurs when people receive too many messages. Tara and Rob controlled their incoming messages by deciding to respond when they had time rather than immediately after the message arrived.

Tara and Rob were working overtime, and they didn't respond to Kate's request until after 8:30 P.M.

Tara thought that attaching their opinion about the binding to their agreement to help would give more weight to their opinion.

E-Mail

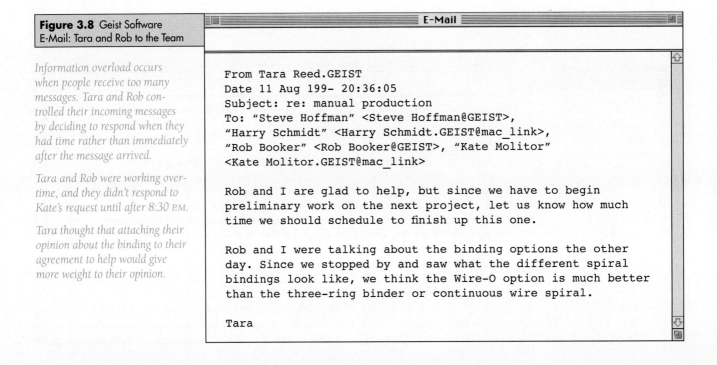

From Tara Reed.GEIST
Date 11 Aug 199- 20:36:05
Subject: re: manual production
To: "Steve Hoffman" <Steve Hoffman@GEIST>,
"Harry Schmidt" <Harry Schmidt.GEIST@mac_link>,
"Rob Booker" <Rob Booker@GEIST>, "Kate Molitor"
<Kate Molitor.GEIST@mac_link>

Rob and I are glad to help, but since we have to begin preliminary work on the next project, let us know how much time we should schedule to finish up this one.

Rob and I were talking about the binding options the other day. Since we stopped by and saw what the different spiral bindings look like, we think the Wire-O option is much better than the three-ring binder or continuous wire spiral.

Tara

Figure 3.9 Geist Software E-Mail: Harry to the Team

As in any productive problem-solving discussion, Harry's purpose was to raise alternative concerns that had not yet been considered.

Harry's concern with what cover to select for the long-term use was appropriate for the entire team to discuss.

E-Mail

From Harry Schmidt.GEIST@mac_link
Date 12 Aug 199- 8:14:39
Subject: re: re: manual production
To: "Steve Hoffman" <Steve Hoffman@GEIST>, "Tara Reed" <Tara Reed.GEIST>, "Rob Booker" <Rob Booker@GEIST>, "Kate Molitor" <Kate Molitor.GEIST@mac_link>

fine with me about the wire-o spiral bind, but what about the cover? the manual may look nice on the shelf, but after it's used for a few months, it may look pretty ratty because the top and bottom of the wire binding get beat up. is there anything we can do about that?

Figure 3.10 Geist Software E-Mail: Steve to the Team

As project director, Steve was responsible for the overall success (or failure) of the software and manual. Although he'd focused on budget in previous e-mail messages and during the team's regular meetings, he realized that image was important.

Even though Steve could have directed Kate to make certain decisions about the manual, he used e-mail to reinforce Geist's corporate culture, which encouraged team input.

E-Mail

From Steve Hoffman.GEIST
Date 13 Aug 199- 8:46:23
Subject: re: manual production
To: "Harry Schmidt" <Harry Schmidt.GEIST@mac_link>, "Tara Reed" <Tara Reed@GEIST>, "Rob Booker" <Rob Booker@GEIST>, "Kate Molitor" <Kate Molitor.GEIST@mac_link>

I haven't heard mention of the image of the software and manual. Buyers who spend $2,500 for software are going to expect something pretty slick for the manual. Besides that, given the complexity of the software, they're going to be using the manual a lot and not leave it sitting on the shelf. While we really have to keep this under budget, what can we do to account for buyers' expectations?

Steve

Figure 3.11 Geist Software E-Mail: Kate to the Team

Kate took her own information, the weeklong e-mail discussion, and feedback from other team members during meetings and came up with recommendations for the manual.

It was appropriate for Kate to send this message to the entire team.

E-Mail

From Kate Molitor.GEIST@mac_link
Date 14 Aug 199- 8:17:26
Subject: re: manual production
To: "Steve Hoffman" <Steve Hoffman@GEIST>, "Harry Schmidt" <Harry Schmidt.GEIST@mac_link>, "Tara Reed" <Tara Reed@GEIST>, "Rob Booker" <Rob Booker@GEIST>

Based on our conversations in the hallway, our meetings, and e-mail exchanges, this is my recommendation for producing the DataGraph manual.

Like Steve keeps telling us, price is an obvious factor. The option I'm recommending keeps the per-manual price at $5.60.

(Figure 3.11 continued on page 68)

Figure 3.11 Geist Software E-Mail: Kate to the Team (continued)

Kate's purpose was to provide a rationale for each recommendation, making a conscious attempt to respond to each of the concerns that had been voiced by other members of the team.

If Kate had first presented this information during a meeting, she would have had to write a short report, or team members would have had to take notes. By using e-mail, she gave the team an informal (but well-supported) summary of her recommendations so they could review them for discussion at the next meeting.

E-Mail

```
This is not the lowest price, but it accounts for all of the
factors we've said we'd like included in the manual.

For this price, we get high usability and high image. My
recommended option is to go with higher quality paper for two
reasons. It's going to look and feel nicer than the less
expensive paper PLUS it will last longer and be less likely
to tear or bleed through.

The binding should be functional and look good at an
affordable price. I recommend we go with the Wire-O bind with
the cover over the spiral. Harry's concern about wear and
tear is valid, but if we choose a sturdy paperboard cover,
this problem can be outweighed by the professional look of
the manual.

Using a second color will help users to identify key parts of
the graphics, focus on special terms, and locate main
sections more easily. I recommend blue. It's less expensive
than other colors and gives us nice screen variations. A
second color increases the per-manual price by only $1.46
(included in the $5.60 price). I think it's worth it.

Local printer prices are comparable with the national firms
who submitted bids, so I think we may as well go local. This
means that we will want to go with a 7"x9" page size since
that's what their equipment is set up to handle.

Naturally, I'm open to discussing any and all of this at
Monday's scheduled meeting. Now's the time to make these
decisions because I want to sign the contract and set up a
production schedule so we can roll when the software is done
(which Harry has promised for next week).

--Kate
```

ELECTRONIC COMMUNICATION TECHNOLOGIES

While formal networks are reflected visibly in a company's organizational chart, informal networks are invisible but nonetheless influential. When you work in an organization, you are automatically part of both its formal communication network and its informal networks, some of which are electronic. Clearly, the formal communication channels of Geist's DataGraph development team (their weekly meetings and formal monthly reports) were supplemented with informal electronic communication that was critical to their success.

When you need to communicate with someone—whether a co-worker in the office down the hall or a client across the country—you have a wide choice of technologies. This chapter focuses on frequently used electronic technologies that make communication easier or faster, or more efficient: telephone systems, fax (facsimile) equipment, and computer systems. When you're considering what technology to use, you can ask yourself the questions about purpose, audience, occasion, and message in Figure 3.12.

Once you have answered some of these questions for a particular occasion, you will have information for making a decision whether to jot down a handwritten note, pick up the phone, send a fax, or send e-mail. For example, when Kate, the documentation specialist on the Geist team, wanted to let other members on the team know the information she'd collected from printing firms, she made her decision to use e-mail based on these factors:

- *audience expectations*: The team members expected Kate to use the most efficient technology—in this case, e-mail.

Figure 3.12 Questions to Help Select Appropriate Technology

QUESTIONS	EXAMPLES
Purpose Does the content of the message require a particular technology? Does the need to document the message require particular technology?	For messages that need to be documented and need to be easily accessible, computerized records are the most practical. A computer-generated document could be mailed or faxed.
Audience Does the audience expect you to use a particular technology, believing it makes messages easier to understand and respond to?	To save time, many professionals prefer that short questions be asked over the telephone or via e-mail.
Does a particular technology make it easier to reach the audience?	In some companies, not everyone has easy access to a computer terminal, so paper copies of widely distributed messages are necessary.
Occasion Is the technology appropriate for the occasion or organization?	By convention, certain kinds of messages—thank you notes, for example—are handwritten. Similarly, in some organizations, meeting minutes are regularly available electronically, but seldom printed on paper and distributed.
How important is the ease of generating, sending, and receiving the message? Is a particular technology easier to use?	A basic, easily created computer-generated slide show displayed on a laptop computer may increase the clarity and effectiveness of a sales call.
How fast is fast enough? This week? Tomorrow? Within the hour?	You can send an e-mail message or fax as quickly as you can make a telephone call and have the added benefit of a copy of the communication.
Message Does the complexity or length of the message make one technology more suitable than another?	Many communicators tend to use computer technology for complex and lengthy messages.
How does the technology change the message—the tone I convey, the perceptions of the reader?	An identical message that's handwritten on a sheet of note paper, typed (or laser printed) on letterhead, or sent via e-mail will convey different impressions to the reader. For example, written notes are informal and personal, laser printing appears more "finished," and e-mail is informal and immediate.

- *convenience*: The least intrusive way to convey the information to team members was via e-mail because team members could read messages when they wanted to. The easiest approach for Kate was to turn her computer notes (taken when she was talking with printer vendors) into an e-mail message.
- *speed*: Members of the team wanted the information quickly. With e-mail they had the information almost immediately after Kate sent it.

Business professionals have their choice of a broad range of tools to communicate their everyday work. They can select the most appropriate electronic tool (or combination of tools) based on the purpose, audience, occasion, and message. Figure 3.13 (page 70) identifies some common applications for electronic tools.

Telephone Systems

The most common network in businesses is the telephone system. Whenever you begin a new job, you should learn the capabilities of your company's telephone system. Among the basic things you'll probably need to learn are how to transfer calls, put calls on hold, and arrange conference calls.

A telephone call is often the first point of contact with a company, so the impression created by that initial call is important for cultivating a positive image. You should be courteous and attentive to the other person (not chewing gum, eating, constantly responding to call waiting interruptions, or talking to someone else while you're on the phone). Your professionalism should show in what you say as well as in how you say it. You should listen carefully and respond clearly and directly. Even if the other person is belligerent or hostile, you should stay calm and polite. Even if you've been answering calls for six hours, you shouldn't mumble or slur your words, sound bored, or answer a call with "Yo. Help ya?"

Everyone's time is valuable and limited, so people appreciate efficiency in telephone conversations. Your calls should have a clear purpose; you should be sure that you're calling

Figure 3.13 Selected Current Electronic Applications

	PURPOSE	WORKPLACE APPLICATIONS
Telephone systems for calls, messages, and simple transactions	Telephone systems enable two-way voice communication. Most businesses have voice mail that allows speakers to distribute the same message to multiple receivers, calls to be directed to particular offices or people, callers to leave messages, and business to be transacted entirely electronically.	U.S. West has a voice mail system that gives callers a number of options, depending on the occasion—for example, leave a message for the person called, listen to and make changes to the message, leave a message for another person, transfer out of voice mail to speak to a human operator.
Fax (facsimile) equipment	Fax equipment enables an exact replica of a document to be transmitted over phone lines as quickly as a phone call.	OptImage prefers faxed orders from customers rather than phoned orders since the details are written by the customers and there is less error.
Electronic scanners	Scanners have a variety of purposes, from recording prices at grocery store checkouts to helping track inventory to recording documents and graphics.	Many medical office managers use a scanner to input patients' previous records so that the electronic files are complete.
Computer networks • Electronic messages (e-mail) • Electronic distribution	People in different offices, buildings, cities, states, or countries can communicate via e-mail. Computer networks enable print communication traditionally mailed to everyone on a distribution list to be sent by e-mail.	OptImage confirms many orders by fax or e-mail, which is faster and more convenient than phone or snail mail. At UPS, many announcements, memos, meeting minutes, and benefits updates are distributed electronically so that all UPS employees can read messages online.
• Teleconferencing	Telephone systems and computer networks enable groups of individuals in two or more locations to conduct two-way voice and video conversations and meetings to discuss any issues on their agenda.	Special meeting rooms with camera, audio, and computer connections at Xerox PARC (Palo Alto Research Center) enable professionals at different sites to conduct meetings despite the physical distance.
• Distance learning	Distance learning enables small or large groups in one location to learn about a subject from an instructor in another location.	Business management programs such as the one at Eastern Michigan University provide training for executives who want to stay current but can't leave their jobs for extended periods to attend classes.
• Electronic data collection	Easy-to-use electronic databases give users access to large quantities of shared information.	Employees at 3M who want to know more about a subject can access electronic databases that are part of the company's library information service.
• Electronic submissions	Computer networks enable people to electronically make bank deposits and submit tax forms, proposals, bids, reports, and other kinds of documents.	When employees at Northwest submit ideas for improving productivity and efficiency, many do so electronically.
• Electronic publication	Electronic publication makes newsletters and journals available on-line rather than as paper copies.	Readers may subscribe to on-line publications through some companies and professional organizations.

the appropriate person, and you should have a plan, knowing what you want to say, perhaps even having notes to refer to. In general, you should place your own calls. The person you're calling may be annoyed to answer a call only to hear, "Please hold for a call from Mr. Gibbs." Having a secretary place your call makes it seem as if your time is more valuable than the time of the person you're calling. It conveys a sense of superiority (whether intentional or not) that may annoy or alienate the other person.

Most businesses have telephone systems that incorporate a wide range of services. Figure 3.14 presents 12 typical services offered by U.S. West.

Figure 3.14 Selected Telephone Services Available to Businesses

TELEPHONE COMPANY SERVICES	EXPLANATIONS
Business Voice Messaging Service (BVMS)	Routes and processes calls. When a line is busy or unanswered, BVMS provides a recorded greeting and stores messages. Provides pre-recorded messages for frequently requested, routine information.
Central Office Automatic Call Distribution (CO-ACD)	Distributes large volumes of incoming calls equally among a designated group of answering positions. CO-ACD can provide real-time and historic reports on agent and group performance.
Centrex Plus	Provides a family of basic services such as audible message waiting, automatic callback, call forwarding, call hold, call park, call pickup, call transfer, call waiting, consultation hold, direct inward and outward dialing, distinctive ringing, executive busy override, intercept, line restrictions, and three-way calling. A large number of options can be added such as multilocation networking.
Station Message Detail Recording	Provides data on individual telephone calls that originate from a business: date, time, duration, extension from which calls originated, dialed digits, carrier selected. Provides data for reports about costs, usage, and traffic.
Custom Local Area Signaling Services (CLASS)	Provides services such as caller identification, continuous redial, call trace, last call return, priority call, selective call forwarding, call rejection.
Market Expansion Line (MEL)	Enables a business to have a local identity without having a physical location in the area. Callers dial a local telephone number, and the calls are automatically forwarded to another location.
Integrated Services Digital Network (ISDN) Services	Offers voice, video, and data delivery for applications such as telecommuting, image transfer, video conferencing, data networking, and distance learning. Provides opportunities for "borderless" communications and virtual offices.
Traffic Data Report Service	Offers a summary of traffic on selected individual lines or multiline groups. Provides regular reports to help track call activity, system use, and management of resources.
Fiber Optic Commercial Video Service	Provides one- or two-way video service that enables each location to originate video/audio channels and view all other locations simultaneously. Enables distance consultation and conferencing, distance learning, and legal functions (for example, video depositions).
Broadcast and Wideband Video Services	Broadcast Video Service sends a video/audio message, useful not only for commercial broadcasts but also for internal company announcements. Wideband Video Service is a one-way service, useful for surveillance and monitoring public safety.
Northern Telecom VISIT Video	Offers both Macintosh and Windows-based conferencing systems with desk-to-desk and face-to-face video conferencing, high-speed file transfer, and shared screen work space for collaboration on documents, drawings, and presentations.
PictureTel Video Conferencing Systems	Sets up video conference rooms with dial-up lines for multiple meeting sites.

Facsimile Equipment

Fax (facsimile) equipment enables you to send exact replicas of documents and visuals via telephone lines. With the advent of fax modems, you can send documents directly from one computer to another, without ever printing a hard (paper) copy. When you're sending a computer printout or typewritten document, you need to make sure the printer ribbon is dark. When you're sending a handwritten fax, you need to make sure to use a pen with dark ink. Fax machines are especially useful when you need to send a legal document because the copy is an exact replica. They're also useful for placing purchase orders and making financial transactions.

Fax machines that use thermal paper have some disadvantages if you need to keep the faxed document for your files. Messages on coated paper degenerate over time, and the image gets lighter and lighter. Because this paper is heat sensitive, you also have to be careful not to set a hot cup of coffee on top of a faxed document or to leave the fax on a radiator or in the hot sun. You'll end up with a black page (or at least a black circle where your coffee mug was set down). Plain paper fax machines are considerably more expensive but don't have the problems of the heat-sensitive, curling paper.

Computers and Computer Networks

In the early 1990s, more than two-thirds of the administrative, managerial, and technical workers in the United States were using computers on their jobs.[1] The numbers are even higher today. The chances are very good that once you are in the workforce, you will use computer technology every day.

A few examples will show the range of specific computer applications companies are developing to expand and improve their communications. Multinational corporations such as IBM, AT&T, Sprint, and MCI are putting global networks in place to link offices of corporations around the world. IBM, for example, has a 90-country fiber-optics network for international communication. Intel's CEO uses his personal computer to interview people at distant locations as well as to project himself and his slide shows on a large screen at distant sites.

The following examples illustrate very different kinds of businesses that are using computers to strengthen their communication. For example, Fannie Mae (the Federal National Mortgage Association), the nation's largest buyer of home mortgages, operates with a network of more than 2,000 personal computers.[2] Teams of financial, marketing, and computer experts are linked, breaking down the centralized departments that previously slowed down communication and decision making. *Business Week* reported that the $10 million investment in computers paid for itself in less than a year in increased communication and productivity.

Less dramatic but equally impressive is Progressive Insurance's system for customers who need to file auto accident claims. The customer calls a toll-free number and is automatically switched to the nearest claims official, who enters the accident information immediately into a database. The new system has decreased the amount of time that passes before a company representative arrives to estimate damages. The system has also improved communication by eliminating excessive paperwork, and even lowered premium rates.[3]

In retail sales, Frank's Nursery and Crafts, Inc., uses wireless scanners and a satellite network.[4] The employees use scanners to read the Universal Product Code labels on merchandise to immediately communicate reorders to headquarters when any item is out of

SKILLS & STRATEGIES

OVERCOMING COMPUTER ANXIETY

If you're a novice computer user, you might gain some reassurance from advice offered by Ann Hill Duin, an expert in training people to use computer technology:

- Take it slow. Don't be overwhelmed by how much there is to learn. Just tackle a few new skills at a time. Begin with creating a new file, entering text, and saving your file. Then learn how to reopen the file you've already created and add, delete, and move text.
- Explore and experiment. Don't be too hesitant to try a command. Computers are almost completely user-proof.
- Plan. Don't jump into drafting your document too quickly. You need to do the same kind of thoughtful planning when you write on a computer as you do when you write by hand or with a typewriter.
- Collaborate. Work with a partner to learn the capabilities of the hardware and software. Ask for help from more knowledgeable users.
- Keep documents simple. Don't get carried away with the formatting features of your computer. A document that has too many type variations (typeface, style, size) or too many typographic features (boxes and bullets and shading) is difficult to read.
- Label your drafts. As you revise a document, label each draft with a succeeding number so you can track your progress and check back to get something from an earlier version if you need to.
- Focus on the substance, not the appearance. Don't be seduced by the slick appearance of laser printing. Your writing doesn't get better just because it looks nicer.
- Be flexible. Don't get too attached to one hardware system or one software program. There are more similarities than differences if you need to shift from WordPerfect to Microsoft Word or from an IBM to a Macintosh.

College, workplace, and community libraries have CD-ROMs. Available resources range from catalog merchandise to citation indexes.

stock, eliminating paperwork and cutting the time spent replenishing inventories by 75 percent. Frank's also installed a satellite system connecting the stores directly to Visa, which has improved customer relations by reducing long credit card approval lines. Employees spend the time formerly used to maintain inventory on increased product training, which enables them to communicate with customers more effectively about products.

And L.L. Bean, well-known retail store and catalog, has recently joined a computerized shopping service. Customers can use a CD-ROM to select a particular catalog (the screen shows 25 catalogs viewers can choose from, including Spiegel, JCPenney, L.L. Bean, Target, and Service Merchandise). Once a particular catalog is selected, viewers can choose to see a short movie ad or move directly to the pages of the catalog, which they can leaf through one at a time to select merchandise. Once they choose an item to order, they select an icon to bring up an order form that can be completed and mailed or faxed to the company (see Figure 3.15).

Internet. Although many companies do not yet use computers, the number of companies who include computer technology as part of their communication network is rapidly increasing. One way of gauging this increase is to monitor companies using the **Internet**, an informal computer network that enables hundreds of thousands of individuals and companies to exchange messages and data files. *The Wall Street Journal* has reported a meteoric increase in the number of companies registered on the Internet (Figure 3.16, page 74).

The value of an Internet connection varies from company to company, but *The Wall Street Journal* has reported the following kinds of Internet activities:[5]

- Companies such as Read Rite and Matsushita Electric Industrial are offering interactive electronic brochures to potential customers.
- Macmillan Publishing editors and authors do book editing via Internet.
- Law firms and securities firms use Internet to send drafts of legal documents.

Figure 3.15 The Merchant, a CD-ROM: Pages from L.L. Bean's On-Line Catalog

Users select the merchant they want by selecting the logo of the company.

Users can choose to begin by viewing a movie advertisement or go directly to the catalog pages.

Since the purpose of the on-line catalog is to generate orders, placing an order is literally as simple as selecting a button.

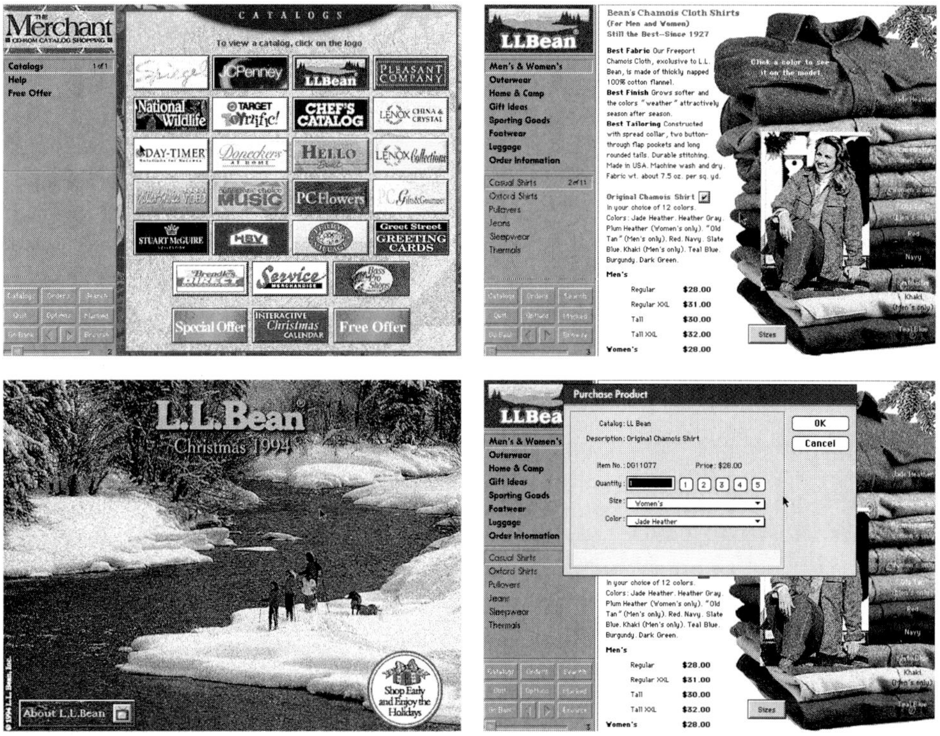

Figure 3.16 Increases in Companies Registered on the Internet

	1990	1991	1992	1993	1994
Financial services	3	17	46	125	281
Law	0	4	10	38	114
Advertising	0	1	1	7	21
Publishing	1	8	27	96	212
Entertainment	0	1	2	4	16
Venture capital	0	0	1	11	23
TOTAL*	93	1,044	3,054	8,412	18,425

*Includes other categories.

- Employment agencies offer detailed graphic and sound information about available jobs and candidates.
- Investment firms access information from databases through the Internet to learn what their competitors are doing.

Workplace professionals and students who have access to the Internet can also join specialized networks called **listservs,** electronic bulletin boards, and **usernet** groups, where individuals with similar interests have access to each other's on-line postings of questions, comments, and responses focused on specific topics. Figure 3.17 identifies some of the lists and groups that are useful to business professionals. As these few examples indicate, you can join a conversation about many areas of business and business communication.

Software is also available from Internet by using **FTP (File Transfer Protocol).** You can access games, computer utilities like virus checkers and file compressors, programming systems, text editors, Internet browsers—virtually anything you might need—free for the downloading.

Although you may initially find Internet confusing, it's a rich source of all types of information, well worth the time it takes to learn how to cruise it.

Types of Hardware. The equipment—the actual computer—is the hardware. There are three broad categories—mainframes, PCs, and dumb terminals—each suitable for different purposes in business communication.

ETHICS

WHO OWNS THE CLOCK ON THE INTERNET?

For many employees, access to the Internet is an attractive employment perk as well as an increasingly necessary corporate communication channel. Internet e-mail addresses are becoming common on business cards and letterheads. However, unlike paper-based communications, e-mail is usually monitored only by the individual user and perhaps the systems operator. Most workers understand that receiving personal mail at the office is inappropriate, but there is sometimes a fine line between personal and business e-mail use. For example, if an employee uses a company computer to routinely scan the World Wide Web (WWW) for industry trends, who is to say whether that employee's browsing will pay off for the company?

While some companies have policies that address worker interaction with the Internet, many companies do not. In addition, browsing the Internet is hard to police. The worker looks at the screen and taps keys—even if chatting about a non-work-related topic. Employees may also be tempted to sign on to non-business-related electronic bulletin boards or develop e-mail relationships that may not contribute to their productivity.

Public relations manager Allan Charnish estimates that he would save 22 days of work annually by not "answering, looking at, sending or responding to" e-mail. Even though computer-mediated communication is generally touted as instantaneous, time spent on-line can add up quickly. With more companies on-line and actively encouraging employees to use on-line tools, the use of e-mail and other Internet features raises important ethical questions about how employees spend time in the workplace.

Figure 3.17 Electronic Lists and Groups

NAME OF LIST OR GROUP	ELECTRONIC ADDRESS
Business newsbriefs	clari.biz.briefs*
Business earnings, profits, losses	clari.biz.earnings
U.S. economic news	clari.biz.economy
Business features stories	clari.biz.features
Interest rates, currencies	clari.biz.finance
News affecting financial markets	clari.biz.market.news
New York Stock Exchange reports	clari.biz.market.report.usa.nyse
Multi-level marketing	alt.business.multi-level
Business libraries list	bit.listserv.buslib-1
Japanese business and economics network	bit.listserv.japan
Organizational effectiveness	comp.org.eff.news
Desktop publishing	listserv@yalem.ycc.yale.edu
Editing and copyediting	listserv@cornell.edu
Copyright issues	listserv@cni.org
Indexing	listserv@binggvmb.cc.binghamton.edu

*All clari.biz groups require the use of the newsreader at newshost.cc.utexas.edu

For information on getting started, consult these sources:

Harley Hahn and Rick Stout (1994), *The Internet: Complete Reference*, Osbourne McGraw-Hill, Berkeley, Calif.

Brendan P. Kehoe (1994), *Zen and the Art of Internet: A Beginner's Guide*, 3rd ed., PTR Prentice Hall, Englewood Cliffs, N.J. This reference is also available on-line at http://cs.indiana.edu/docproject/zen/zen_1.0.html)

Mainframe computers are sophisticated systems used by large organizations for storing and manipulating extensive databases (for example, accounts payable, payroll, personnel, scheduling). These computers usually have a network of terminals linked to the mainframe so that people in various locations can obtain information for their work. Mainframe computers and their terminals can also be connected to the Internet or similar international networks.

PCs are personal computers that come in three physical sizes—desktop, laptop, and notebook. PCs can stand alone or be networked, that is, connected with a "server." Two main types of PCs are IBM systems (and IBM clones) and Apple Macintosh systems. PCs can also be connected to a mainframe computer, to each other, or to the Internet or similar international networks.

Dumb terminals are computers designed to complete a limited task, like the CD-ROM readers in a library. They can't perform any other functions. They may be stand-alone terminals, or they may be linked to a mainframe, which feeds them data.

Unfortunately, many computer systems are not compatible, so they can't be linked together. Information created on one can't necessarily be "read" on another. There are ways to "translate" work done on one type of hardware so that it can be understood and used by another type of hardware, but the conversion takes a little time and adds another task to someone's busy schedule. However, computer manufacturers recognize the limitations on effectiveness and efficiency when computers can't communicate. As a result, some of the largest hardware manufacturers such as IBM and Apple are forming joint ventures.

TECHNOLOGY

". . . NOW INSERT DISK C IN DRIVE A"

Much of what happens in today's business world happens on computers. But some use Word on the Macintosh while others use WordPerfect on IBM clones. The result is that everyone spends far too much time converting files from one format to another.

Many businesspeople spend large portions of their business day "inserting disk C in drive A." The answer? Standard General Markup Language, or SGML, an international system for marking files (documents) that allows them to be read by different computer systems using various kinds of software.

SGML is based on a simple idea. When documents are created on any system, they can be "marked up" with SGML codes. A marked-up memo, for example, might look like this:

<memo>
<header>
<recipient>Business Communication students </recipient>
<author> Your Instructor </author>
<date> December 5, 19— </date>
<body>
<para> This memo is marked up with SGML formatting.
</body>
</memo>

Any system equipped with an SGML reader would read these codes, know this is a memo, and convert it to the proper format:

To: Business Communication students
From: Your Instructor
Date: December 5, 19—
This memo is marked up with SGML formatting.

In SGML, documents can be moved quickly and easily between systems that can read SGML. No content, formatting, or time is lost in the transition. In addition, SGML can help preserve documents for future use. Documents marked up with SGML will always be accessible, even if the system they were created on becomes obsolete.

Because SGML makes computer documents easily transferable and improves their longevity, organizations such as the Securities and Exchange Commission, Shell Oil, Boeing Aerospace, and Hewlett-Packard have adopted it as a standard. These organizations have taken steps to improve the flexibility of their communication systems.

Types of Software. You will have access to many different types of computer software typically used in business. One of your challenges will be knowing what software to use for a particular audience, purpose, communicator role, or occasion. As shown in Figure 3.18, certain communication problems can be solved by using software.

In addition to word processing and spreadsheet programs, four types of software are particularly important for business communicators to know about and be able to use:

- groupware
- database management software
- project planning software
- multimedia software

Groupware. Groupware is becoming increasingly important to business communication because it allows you to collaborate with physically distant people. Well-designed groupware appears to aid productivity, even in very small companies. You can expect that in many organizations, part of your work will involve communicating electronically with colleagues. You may pool information about prospective clients exploring similar problems.

Some kinds of groupware make it possible for a team to move past restrictions imposed by social or political pressures in an organization. For example, Cigna Corporation employees are experimenting with ways to use their network's anonymous approach to brainstorming. Small groups of employees sit around a horseshoe-shaped table, typing into their networked PCs. Each person receives a printout of the comments from the others, without knowing who said what—no one knows which idea was suggested by the boss or which was suggested by the newest person hired by the company.[6]

Groupware also enables you to expand your resources and to draw on the expertise of others in the organization who may be able to help you answer a question or resolve a problem. For example, when Eastman Kodak is working on a new camera project, the computer links Kodak's headquarters in Rochester, N.Y., with its factories and toolmakers in Germany, France, and Mexico. This way designers, toolmakers, engineers, and vendors can all see and discuss an animated version of each part of the new camera system.[7]

One of the most widely used programs for collaborative interaction is Lotus Notes. This software helps people "access, track, share, and organize important data."[8] For example, people who use Lotus Notes or a similar groupware product can communicate easily with each other and can gain convenient access to databases to retrieve useful information. Ann Palermo, a technology consultant at International Data Corporation, conducted an investi-

Figure 3.18 Communication Problems Solved with Software

COMMUNICATION PROBLEM	SOFTWARE SOLUTION
You need to generate, revise, and store and print documents.	***Word processing software*** such as Microsoft Word or WordPerfect enables you to generate text. Most sophisticated word processors include spellcheckers, thesauruses, style checkers, and indexing capabilities as well as built-in graphics programs.
You need to organize numeric data in order to complete computations or transformations.	***Spreadsheet software*** such as Lotus 1-2-3 or Microsoft Excel enables you to enter numeric data and manipulate it. You can customize the software's formulas for specific purposes. Spreadsheets are useful for forecasting and decision making.
You need to create tables, graphs, diagrams, drawings, and other visuals.	***Drawing and graphing software*** such as Claris Draw, Lotus Freelance, or Adobe Illustrator enables you to create graphs and figures of various kinds that can be placed directly into documents.
You need to produce high-quality documents without the expense of outside designers and typesetters.	***Desktop publishing software*** such as Aldus PageMaker or Ventura Publishing enables you to keep the design of reports, flyers, manuals, and brochures in house.
You need to collaborate to share ideas and expertise, coordinate schedules, work on projects, prepare documents.	***Groupware*** such as Lotus Notes or CE Software's TeamVision allows you to collaborate with physically distant groups, sharing schedules, databases, mail, memos, and reports.
You need to organize and have easy access to large amounts of data that can be shared with colleagues.	***Database management software*** such as Microsoft's Access lets you obtain, organize, transform, and display information so that it can be shared and used in a variety of documents and oral presentations.
You need to (1) do complex, long-range project planning, (2) be able to track every aspect of the project, and (3) quickly obtain up-to-date information about the project.	***Project planning or project management software*** such as Microsoft Project lets you track and update deadlines, resources, and costs. Changes made in one area are reflected in other areas. Most planning packages enable you to generate information for reports at various stages in the process.
You need to create presentations with transparencies or slides and coordinated handout materials.	***Presentation software*** such as Aldus Persuasion or Microsoft PowerPoint enables you to create transparency masters, slide shows, and handout materials.
You need to create a presentation that attracts the audience through multiple senses.	Persuasion or PowerPoint in conjunction with QuickTime videoclips lets you integrate slides, clip art, video clips, and sound into simple multimedia presentations.
You need to input the information from paper documents and pictures into a computer.	***Imaging software*** enables you to scan paper documents or pictures so they are digitized in the computer and can be imported into the current document.

gation of the impact of Lotus Notes on productivity. Even with conservative calculations of productivity, she estimated that companies receive an average of 179 percent return on their investment in the third year after installation.[9] Figure 3.19 (page 78) shows three of the many functions for which groupware such as Lotus Notes can be used.

Price Waterhouse, the accounting firm, helps its 34,000 Los Angeles employees stay in touch using Lotus Notes, groupware that lets them dial into the company network from any telephone. This convenience frees employees who spend a great deal of time on the road from waiting for information to be sent via fax or messenger service.

Database Management. **Database management software** is vital to business communication because it gives users access to huge amounts of information that would otherwise be overwhelming or inaccessible. Such software lets you obtain, organize, and display a myriad of information so that it can be used in a variety of documents and oral presentations. (See Chapter 11.) Figure 3.20 (page 78) shows three screens from a widely used database management program, Microsoft Access.

Figure 3.19 Lotus Notes: An Example of Groupware

Users can adapt groupware such as Lotus Notes to meet the specific needs of their team or group.

Users can focus on a particular purpose and locate relevant information quickly.

Users can reconfigure the same information for different occasions.

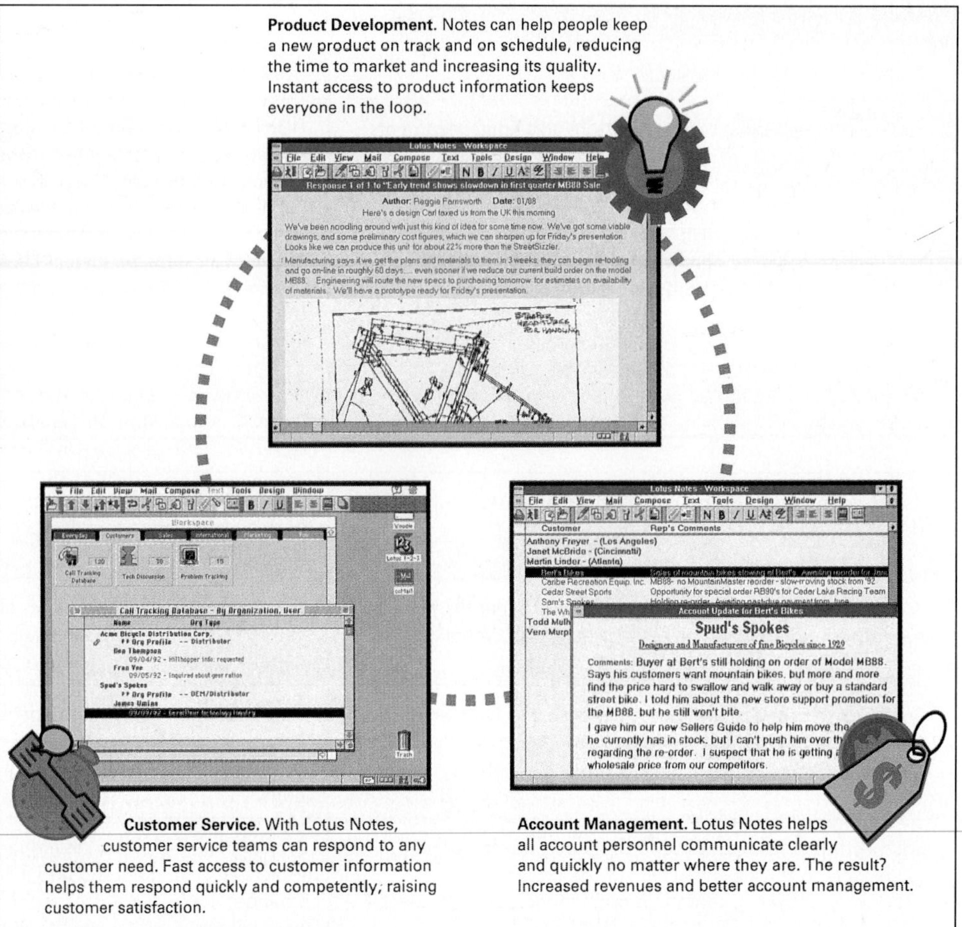
Product Development. Notes can help people keep a new product on track and on schedule, reducing the time to market and increasing its quality. Instant access to product information keeps everyone in the loop.
Spud's Spokes
Customer Service. With Lotus Notes, customer service teams can respond to any customer need. Fast access to customer information helps them respond quickly and competently, raising customer satisfaction.
Account Management. Lotus Notes helps all account personnel communicate clearly and quickly no matter where they are. The result? Increased revenues and better account management.

Access to a database can change the way people do their job. For example, the database used by the 4,000 employees at Silicon Graphics provides a large variety of materials, including company press releases, hundreds of ads, snippets of animation, and video clips of executives' presentations. Database management software lets employees know what information is available so they can draw on it to create new ads and presentations.[10]

Access to a database can also make the communication in a job easier. At Watson Mountaineering, the shipping coordinator, Jon Addison, uses a database management system that coordinates information about customers' orders and current inventory levels. When Jon enters information about an order, including quantity and price, the information automatically influences other databases in the system, adjusting stock levels and the customer's

Figure 3.20 Database Management Software

Users locate information using database management software.

Users can organize and calculate information to help identify patterns in the data.

Users display information in graphs, tables, and charts, depending on the purpose and audience.

Users can generate summaries, trends, and distributions for reports.

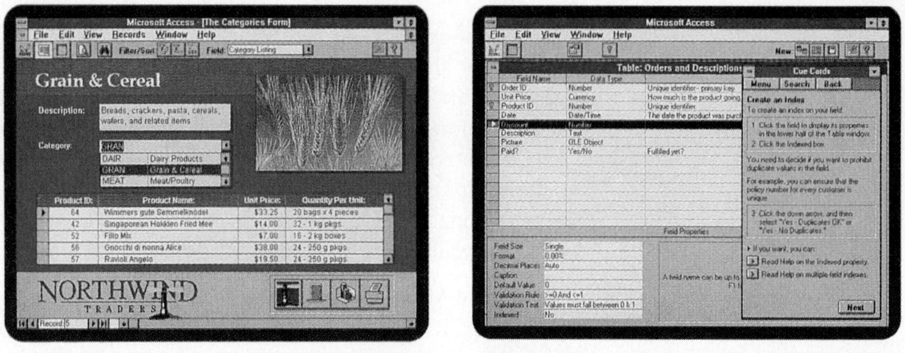

Make a database form work hard while making it easy to use. Just link or embed objects, like product pictures and graphs. And create buttons to trigger everything from simple macros to sophisticated functions you define.

With graphical examples and comprehensive instructions provided by Cue Cards, you can learn to use Microsoft Access as you build and work with your database. It's like having a database tutor on call 24 hours a day.

MULTICULTURAL

INTERNATIONAL ICONOGRAPHY

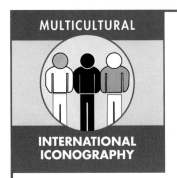

The word "icon" comes from the ancient Greek *eikon*, meaning likeness or image. Icons are an efficient way to communicate information. They are used, for example, in computer programs in place of text because one icon can represent a complete idea, such as the trash can icon on a Macintosh. In *Writing Effective Software Documentation*, Williams and Beason remark, "It's helpful to the readers to include [icons] in your text. They catch the eye and lead readers to the relevant material instantly."

Icons, however, are culture-bound. Their meanings may change from one culture to another. Icons such as street signs and symbols for airports, rest rooms, camping sites, and subway stations are not always universally understood, despite the common belief that certain symbols are common across cultures.

Dave Kansas, writing in *The Wall Street Journal*, points out that one of the most culture-bound computer icons is the hand. Ms. Howlett of Microsoft Corporation agrees. "As it turns out, hand positions mean a great many different things around the world. . . . It seems that a hand gesture benign in the U.S. means something horrible elsewhere, so we try to be careful with our hand images."

year-to-date account. At any time, Jon is able to tell division managers the status of orders and inventory. Using the same software, Jon pulls information for his monthly reports. For example, he typically includes a list of customers for the previous month, shipping expenses using two major carriers, and geographic buying patterns. Such information makes his reports interesting and useful to his manager.

Project Planning. Another very important kind of software for business communication is **project planning software** that lets you keep track of and update deadlines, resources, and costs. (See Chapter 7.) Information that influences other areas (for example, changing a deadline may change the cost) automatically changes the related areas. Figure 3.21 shows a computer screen with a business project planning system, MacProject II.

In her job as a construction supervisor, Sally Jacobs would be lost without project planning software, which lets her identify the steps for each job, construct a schedule, assign resources (equipment, personnel), and estimate costs. Of course, she would need to do the same tasks whether she used project planning software or not. The software simply makes her job much easier and reduces the time it takes her to get information when she needs it.

For Sally, the big value of the software comes when there are changes in her original plan. For example, when a shipment of lumber is delayed because of weather, Sally enters the information about the length of the delay. The software automatically adjusts the schedule, reassigns resources for optimal utility, and calculates any financial overruns or cash flow

Figure 3.21 Project Management Software

Users can keep track of the big picture as well as the details of a project so they can make and communicate changes based on the most recent information.

Team leaders and managers can use project planning software to accomplish ongoing communication tasks that are part of a project—daily shift meetings to give status changes, weekly updates, monthly progress reports, and so on.

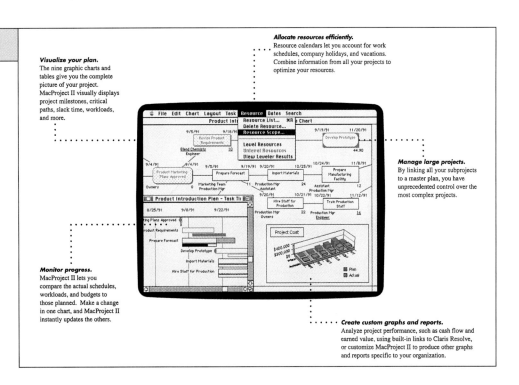

Visualize your plan. The nine graphic charts and tables give you the complete picture of your project. MacProject II visually displays project milestones, critical paths, slack time, workloads, and more.

Allocate resources efficiently. Resource calendars let you account for work schedules, company holidays, and vacations. Combine information from all your projects to optimize your resources.

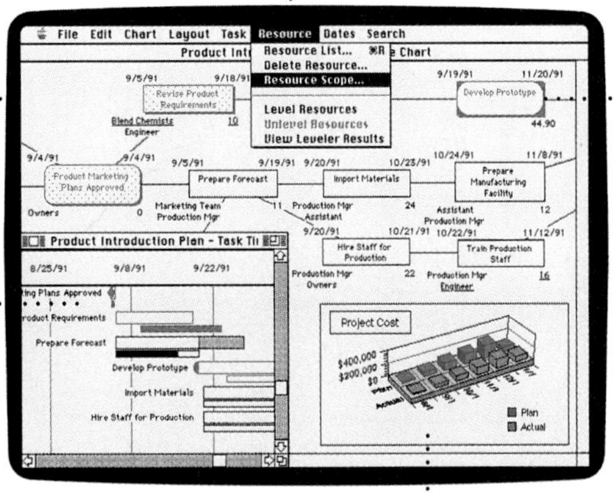

Manage large projects. By linking all your subprojects to a master plan, you have unprecedented control over the most complex projects.

Monitor progress. MacProject II lets you compare the actual schedules, workloads, and budgets to those planned. Make a change in one chart, and MacProject II instantly updates the others.

Create custom graphs and reports. Analyze project performance, such as cash flow and earned value, using built-in links to Claris Resolve, or customize MacProject II to produce other graphs and reports specific to your organization.

problems. With the updated information, Sally can quickly inform employees and suppliers of changes that affect their part of the project.

Multimedia Software. **Multimedia** presentations integrate slides, clip art, video clips, and sound (voice, music, sound effects) to create appealing business presentations. Authoring software makes it possible for people who have the time (and financial resources) to create what are often highly impressive and effective presentations. Learning the process of creating a very simple multimedia presentation is not much more difficult than learning to use a sophisticated word processing program such as Microsoft Word or Word Perfect. Multimedia presentations are widely used in sales and marketing presentations, in conference presentations, and at important meetings. Given the impact and effectiveness of multimedia presentations, workplace professionals can increase their value to a company by learning the rudiments of designing simple multimedia presentations.[11]

In an article explaining the uses of multimedia, Joseph Schorr, an expert in designing such presentations, described three presentations that he could create if he were the economic development director for a tiny fictional town in Arizona.[12]

Schorr's first presentation, a basic multimedia presentation to the city council, is something that, given the available equipment and some training, you could probably do by yourself. Such a project is within the ability of most novices who learn to use software such as Aldus Persuasion or Microsoft PowerPoint in conjunction with QuickTime videoclips. Schorr describes such a basic multimedia presentation for his fictional Arizona town as "a straightforward business presentation that had just enough pizzazz to make the city council sit up and vote yes." For this basic presentation, he would create "charts indicating proposed capital improvement, a graph with projected tourism revenues, and a few video clips of tourism professionals testifying to the validity" of his plan.

Schorr explains that creating a more complex multimedia presentation is beyond the capabilities of novice users. If you worked for a company that wanted a more complex multimedia presentation—perhaps for the annual stockholders' meeting or for a trade show booth—you would need to hire an expert in multimedia productions who knew how to use a full-blown multimedia authoring system. For his fictional Arizona town, Schorr describes "an interactive display for a booth that would include scans of color photos, a musical score, recorded narration, and an animated map." For this presentation, he would "include an interactive button that would allow viewers to access information on local history, recreational opportunities, restaurants, and lodging."

The third level of multimedia project that Schorr describes requires advanced skills. Such presentations are typically completed by companies specializing in multimedia production (with production prices ranging from $10,000 to $100,000). A company might use such a

Businesses have discovered multimedia software to be effective for getting people's attention and for presenting concepts. Here multimedia entices two children to explore human physiology in a retail store.

production for a special exhibit that would be seen by thousands of visitors. For his fictional Arizona town, Schorr's third multimedia presentation "could be a self-running, interactive information kiosk for the [town's] Visitor's Center that would showcase the town's most salable attributes." He would include "scans of color photos, a musical score, . . . animated maps and video sequences that featured nearby archaeological digs, Old West points of interest, public transportation options, and a special events calendar."[13]

ISSUES RELATING TO COMMUNICATING WITH ELECTRONIC TECHNOLOGIES

Knowing about electronic technologies for communication is important, but knowing the issues surrounding the use of these techologies will help ensure that you use them appropriately and productively. The changes resulting from the increasing use of electronic techologies have provoked heated discussions about issues affecting communication: information overload, anonymity, lack of interpersonal contact, and reshaped hierarchies. These issues merit ongoing discussion even though there are no immediate answers, simple or otherwise.

Information Overload

Some organizations create electronic distribution lists and indiscriminately send messages to everyone on those lists, which can create **information overload.** For example, the assistant department manager in one organization took a four-day weekend. When he returned to work on Tuesday morning, there were over 400 electronic messages in his in box. Most of these messages didn't require his input or action but rather were routine messages sent companywide. Figure 3.22 illustrates this problem.

Electronic networks make sending messages so easy that sometimes there's too much information, which results in such information overload. For example, in the e-mail exchange of the project team at Geist Software that you read at the beginning of the chapter, team members avoided information overload by purposely sending these messages only to those who needed the information. The issue of information overload raises questions that you should consider as you use e-mail:

- Does the recipient need the information?
- Do recipients begin to ignore all messages if many of them are irrelevant?

Figure 3.22 Problems from Information Overload

"At least 80 percent of the E-mail I get is a waste of time to even open," says Tom Steding, vice-president, strategic marketing, at 3Com Corp., Santa Clara, Calif., the world's leading maker of Ethernet networking systems. He's not alone. Executives, managers and knowledge workers at firms with sophisticated information systems are drowning in an info-flood—a daily deluge of E-mail, voice mail and faxes.

Forced to spend three hours of each 12-hour workday handling about 150 messages, Steding says, "The volume of E-mail is so high, it's become devalued. Sending an E-mail is no longer sufficient to ensure communication. You've got to go see them nose-to-nose. It's like the old way, except back then you didn't have to send E-mail first. We're going backwards."

The Information Revolution was supposed to save time and eliminate drudgery. What's gone wrong? Are we doomed to suffer from info-overload from here to eternity? Or do we just need better tools for sifting info-wheat from info-chaff?

If such tools can be invented, they'll have to be aligned with the fundamental properties of information itself. Claude Shannon, the father of communications theory and the fellow who coined the term "bit" (binary unit), once said, "Information is news that makes a difference. If it doesn't make a difference, it isn't information." A radio traffic report about a car crash up ahead is information if you can still change your route. But if you are already stuck in the backup, the message is a useless bunch of bits.

By Shannon's definition, most of the messages coursing through corporate networks aren't worthy of the name "information." Junk messages clog E-mailboxes, obscure useful information and force workers to waste hours each day simply trying to keep up with the flow.

Some observers blame the "group list" feature found on today's E-mail systems. "Group lists are an incredibly efficient tool for disseminating information when it's relevant to everyone in the group," says Don Wood, director of marketing for Milpitas, Calif.-based Octel Communications, a leading voice-mail systems supplier. "But the abuse of group lists causes a huge waste of time. Virtually all the junk I get comes from being on so many group lists."

- Is selecting only certain messages to read or installing a "filter" to prevent receiving messages from selected individuals or groups an appropriate solution to information overload?

Anonymity

Electronic networks sometimes protect a person's identity, making it possible to offer anonymous comments about plans, projects, or personnel. When anonymity is possible in network communication, business professionals need to explore these questions:

- Do writers generate messages differently if they know the messages will be anonymous?
- Do readers react differently to messages when they know who sent them?
- Do some purposes and occasions make anonymity acceptable, even preferable?

Anonymity can be a problem because knowing the source of information is an important part of making sense of that information (see the discussion of the cooperative principle, pages 38–39). The issue of anonymity came up in a story about a fictionalized company that is a composite of actual *Fortune* 1000 companies (see Figure 3.23).

Anonymity also can be beneficial, as in Cigna Corporation's anonymous brainstorming. Such anonymity can be particularly advantageous on teams with members from different levels in the organizational hierarchy because it reduces potential intimidation. Anonymity enables people to post comments that will be judged on their merits rather than on the rank or authority of the person making them. This is one reason why effective writing is a vital skill. Similarly, anonymity can allow members to offer criticism without fear of retaliation. Another potential benefit of anonymity is the freedom that shy or insecure individuals may feel to join a conversation so that attention is focused on the content, not on personalities. In order for an electronic network to have an anonymous option that works without the problems, users have to explicitly or tacitly agree not to abuse the cloak of anonymity.

Figure 3.23 Problems of Anonymity

XYZ Corp. (not its real name) has a problem that is driving top management crazy. A rogue piece of software has appeared that lets employees send electronic mail messages anonymously. There's been a rash of sexually suggestive—and even obscene—e-mail sent to several female employees. Unpopular managers have received insulting e-mail appraisals of their style and performance.

More ominously, several messages have been broadcast detailing serious problems with several of XYZ's key projects. These were setbacks that had previously been the secret of top management but, thanks to XYZ's global network, have now been instantly distributed worldwide to launch hundreds of e-mail inquiries and thousands of water-cooler conversations.

Like kerosene poured on a fire, this act of e-mail anonymity has ignited once smoldering resentments into openly burning issues. While half the company is thrilled that anonymity has caused these problems to surface for corporate-wide discussions, the other half is furious that the leakers can't be found and punished.

Ultimately, XYZ's top management pulled the plug on its global e-mail system, rewrote the network software to assure that all messages can be tracked at least two ways and issued an edict that absolutely forbids anonymous messages. The traffic that now flows on XYZ's network is excruciatingly polite.

Lack of Interpersonal Contact

In some businesses, electronic networks are reducing the frequency of face-to-face meetings, saving time in the short run but reducing the opportunities for building interpersonal relationships that enable organizations to function smoothly. The introduction of electronic communication as a primary vehicle for communication can change group dynamics and raises this question:

> What should be the balance of time and attention members of a group give to completing their task versus maintaining their groupness?

Groups that conduct a large portion of their work via an electronic network need to be especially careful not to ignore the importance of face-to-face interaction. The value of the interpersonal aspects of communication is so important that some researchers spend as much time looking for ways to improve on-line interpersonal interaction as they do investigating ways to improve on-line task performance. The lack of interpersonal contact caused managers at a leading high-tech firm to reduce the use of electronic mail despite its advantages in coordinating complex projects (Figure 3.24). The problems that developed as a result of the loss of face-to-face communication weren't worth the gain in efficiency.

When e-mail is effective on long-term projects, it's usually because the e-mail is only part of the communication, as you read about with the Geist project team (Figures 3.2 to 3.11). In addition to their e-mail, the team had regular weekly meetings, ongoing discussions in the lab and corridors, and occasional social activities. Their e-mail reduced meeting time and provided an efficient conduit for posing questions and exchanging information, but it didn't replace face-to-face interaction.

Figure 3.24 Problems When Face-to-Face Interaction Is Reduced

Since these managers did such an excellent job resolving most of their problems on electronic mail, they did away with regularly scheduled meetings, agreeing to meet only when confronted with problems too tough to handle over the network. What they discovered, however, was that when they got together to discuss their most intractable, controversial problems, the resulting meeting proved intense and unpleasant. Precisely because they have already used the network to reach easy consensus on other issues, debating the unresolved, tough issues in person turned their personal meetings into combat zones. After unanimously agreeing to hold the network responsible for their difficulties, the managers chose to go back to regularly scheduled meetings—albeit with less frequency than before.

Organizational Values

When you send a message over an electronic network, you convey information, but you also convey the organization's values toward people. An organization's values—partly conveyed by its attitudes toward dissemination of information, anonymity, and interpersonal interaction—may be magnified in its electronic communication. Discussing organizational values in relation to communication technology raises these questions:

- How does the organization feel about employee autonomy? About confidentiality? About traditional lines of authority?
- Do employees in companies really want or need to have access to all the information that they can obtain through e-mail and Internet?
- When people get information, should they always act on it?

Electronic networks are changing traditional hierarchies in organizations where employees can directly contact anyone else in the organization, regardless of rank or position. This widespread access can create problems, as shown in Figure 3.25, which describes a good idea gone bad when a company ignored its promises of autonomy, breached confidentiality, and overstepped authority. As a result, employees no longer trusted the electronic network as a forum for open, honest communication.

Figure 3.25 Technology as a Reflection of Organizational Values

One huge multidivision company I worked with spent tens of millions of dollars creating a superb management information network. Up-to-the-moment summaries of key sales and distribution figures became available at the touch of a button. Bidding to become a more "flexible" organization, this company also encouraged its divisions to become more autonomous. Top management insisted that it wanted to "push responsibility down, into the organization" and delegate key decisions to that field.

Understandably, this excellent new information network enabled top managers to retrieve data just as easily as the division managers. The technology made it possible for top management to peer over the division's shoulder as it tried to get work done: *"Saw the weekly sales figures, Tom. Apparently that promotion didn't work so well. What are you going to do?"*

As far as the divisional line managers were concerned, the network quickly became a medium for top management meddling. The network effectively became a tool that undermined trust because top management couldn't resist acting upon available information. Consequently, some of the division managers began "gaming" their numbers. Division managers now know that any initiatives they take have to be either coordinated with top management or done "off the net." So much for autonomy.

Individual employees' decisions about whether to take advantage of a network's capabilities will be determined in part by the way corporate values are conveyed in use of that technology. For example, a company that trusts middle managers to work productively without constant supervision shouldn't suddenly begin such supervision just because it is technologically feasible. Similarly, a company that ignores anonymous criticism shouldn't suddenly give credence to such comments just because they arrive electronically. Organizations should have clear policies in place regarding the use of technology so they don't find their unexamined values unpleasantly played out in situations such as the one in Figure 3.25.

TECHNOLOGY'S IMPACT ON BUSINESS COMMUNICATION

Given the potential problems with communication technology, why would anyone bother? The answer is simple: The benefits generally outweigh the problems. Despite the potential misuse and abuse, technology brings tremendous capabilities and benefits. Figure 3.26, an article from *The Wall Street Journal*, explores the topics we've just been discussing about technology: (1) information overload, (2) anonymity and authority, (3) lack of interpersonal relationships, and (4) organizational hierarchies and authority.

Figure 3.26 Computers and Workplace Culture

COMPUTER LINKS ERODE HIERARCHICAL NATURE OF WORKPLACE CULTURE

By John R. Wilke
Staff Reporter of The Wall Street Journal

Employees of Chemical Banking Corp. had been shaken by workforce cuts, reorganizations and a pending merger. Rumors often raced through the ranks, sapping productivity and morale.

But Bruce Hasenyager found a way to squelch the gossip in the bank's corporate-systems division: The senior vice president let employees post anonymous questions on an electronic-bulletin board, accessible to anyone who was on the office computer network. Then he responded to the questions on-line.

"It became a powerful tool for building trust." Mr. Hasenyager says: "We could kill off the crazy rumors. When it was whispered around the water cooler that part of our group's work might be contracted out to IBM, I had a way to tell everyone at once that it was baloney."

But Chemical's electronic water cooler soon spun out of control. When Mr. Hasenyager resigned last year, following the completion of Chemical's merger with Manufacturers Hanover Trust, his successor became uncomfortable with this unruly forum. After barbed criticism of management began appearing on the system, the new executive pulled the plug.

Computer networks—and the sticky management issues they present—are spreading across the workplace. In the first wave of desktop computerization, workers generally used their machines to perform tasks in isolation, such as writing, creating a financial spreadsheet or designing graphics or products. But as more and more office computers are tied together in networks—using cables or phone lines, "servers" that store data and direct traffic, and a new class of software called groupware—the nature of personal computing is changing. And office life is changing along with it.

Electronic mail is probably the simplest and most familiar form of groupware, in which notes are zapped across a network between two desktop PCs. More sophisticated groupware programs connect many people together at the same time, often functioning like a suite of electronic conference rooms where many conversations can take place at the same time. The programs can also collect these silent conversations and create an electronic transcript. And they are not limited to words. Some groupware programs can sift, sort and transmit scanned images, sound and even video.

Equal Access

Because they enable hundreds of workers to share information simultaneously, groupware networks can give lowly office workers intelligence previously available only to their bosses. Networks also can give the rank-and-file new access: the ability to join in on-line discussions with senior executives. In these interactions, people are judged more by what they say than by their rank on the corporate ladder.

"The cultural effect is enormous," says Bill Wilson, a manager at Johnson & Higgins, a New York insurance brokerage firm that links its professional staff with new network software. "It's helping to dissolve the old corporate hierarchy."

Studies by the Massachusetts Institute of Technology and others show that groupware can make design and sales teams more efficient, save time, and bring companies closer to customers and suppliers. Lotus Development Corp. President Jim Manzi says his company's Notes software for networks creates "electronic keiretsu"—high-tech versions of integrated Japanese business groups. Sales of Notes doubled this year, to $100 million.

"Bozo Filters"

But the proliferation of networks can also bring unintended tensions. In a corporate culture where information is already jealously guarded, some companies are finding employees unwilling to share their best work in network discussions. Managers like the ones at Chemical often feel the need to control what goes out across the network. And software such as Notes can raise the stakes by recording when someone fails to meet a commitment—such as finishing a report on time—and then make this failure plain to hundreds of colleagues.

Another problem with networks and groupware can be information overload. To help sift through it all, software makers are working on "agents," new types of programs that roam the network to look for information their keeper couldn't otherwise find. Some networks even offer a novel way to hold down unwanted information: "bozo filters" that can be activated secretly by a network user to block out messages from the people he or she really doesn't want to hear from.

The promise and perils of networks are coming into focus as more and more workplaces get wired. Forrester Research, of Cambridge, Mass., forecasts that 22 million office PCs—or nearly half of those in the U.S.—will be networked by the end of next year, up 54% from 1992. That pace is reflected in the surging sales and stock prices of network equipment and software makers such as Cisco Systems Inc., 3Com Corp., Cabletron Systems Inc., Novell Inc., Lotus and others.

Like the telephone, groupware isn't very useful unless the people you need to reach are using it. But when small groups within a company link up, the network often spreads rapidly to other parts of the organization, a process First Boston Corp. analyst Paul Johnson calls "the kudzu effect," alluding to the prolific vine. At Chase Manhattan Bank, it spread rapidly after its introduction in 1991 and now links 5,200 bankers world-wide. "It's becoming a team memory, or corporate nervous system," says Craig Goldman, the chief information officer.

Style Amplifier

This new electronic landscape can foster an egalitarian sense of empowerment among employees. Or it can be a tool of authoritarian managers, leading to loss of workplace privacy. For better or worse, "it's a powerful means of amplifying the style and character of a company and its managers," Mr. Hasenyager says.

At MTV Networks, groupware became a new weapon for the affiliate sales force. When the Viacom Inc. unit was battling last summer against rival Turner Broadcasting System Inc.'s Cartoon Channel, trying to get cable operators to carry MTV's new Comedy Central network instead, salesmen in some areas were meeting unexpected resistance. Then a saleswoman in Chicago discovered that a cable system in her territory had been offered a special two-year, rock-bottom price by Cartoon Channel.

She typed this intelligence into a groupware network that tracks most day-to-day activity of the sales force. Others noticed that another salesman in Florida had also heard something about a new, more aggressive deal from the competition. "Suddenly it clicked: we'd figured out their game," says Kris Bagwell, the young MTV salesman who helped design the new network. Top MTV executives were told of the tactic and were able to counterattack by changing their own pricing and terms, saving several pending deals, according to Mr. Bagwell.

Monitoring Tool

He says groupware gives management a better tool to follow what is going on in the field. "Let's say we need to know about every sales call last month on a Cox system where Nickelodeon was discussed," he says. "Or we need to know what people were hearing about Comedy Central's local ad sales in the Southeast last quarter. With a couple of mouse clicks, you can drill in and find what you need."

At Coopers & Lybrand's Atlanta office, William Jennings, director of fraud-investigation services, used groupware to win a contract that he says he wouldn't have known about otherwise. Using a system that electronically clips and categorizes news wires, he came across a report of a food-service company in Hawaii that had an inventory-theft problem, apparently covered up by fraud. He quickly turned to an in-house Notes database and discovered that people in Coopers & Lybrand's Los Angeles office knew people at the victimized company.

After on-line consultations, he decided to offer Coopers & Lybrand's services to ferret out the fraud. Clicking into another groupware database, which cross-indexed the background and skills of 900 auditors, he searched for someone with prior law-enforcement experience, a C.P.A., and familiarity with food-service inventories. "We found him in Dallas, and put him on a plane the next day. Coopers got the contract, and the client got the right man for the job."

Salute When You Say That

In some organizations, networks and groupware breach the lines of command. At Wright-Patterson Air Force base in Ohio, which uses network software made by Quality Decision Management, of Taunton, Mass., "rank doesn't really matter when you're on-line," says Lt. Col. Donald Potter. "An enlisted man could send a message to a colonel." Five years ago, he says, "there wouldn't have been an easy way for a sergeant to share an idea with a colonel short of making a formal appointment to go see him in his office."

At Johnson & Higgins, the insurance firm, groupware lets managers identify talent that they might not otherwise have known about, says John Deitchman, a senior vice president. When Mary Jo Dirkes, a young employee in Chicago, posted a particularly well-crafted memo on the network about the firm's efforts in workers' compensation, she got kudos from top management in New York and broadened responsibilities. In the past, Mr. Deitchman says, "I wouldn't have thought of going to her for help because she's relatively new and hadn't developed the traditional network of personal contacts in the firm."

The network also altered the chain of command in Ms. Dirkes's office. She now gets requests for help from around the firm via the network. When a client in Ohio needed someone with experience in cutting workplace injuries in plastics factories, Ms. Dirkes clicked into a groupware database to find an expert that could help. "Before, people would have called or sent a memo to my boss, then he'd assign it to me," she says. "Now I do it on my own."

How does her boss feel about this? "I'm essentially out of the loop—and that's the way I want it," says her supervisor, David North. "Problems now get resolved at the lowest practical level, freeing me to work on more-pressing policy and strategy issues."

But some employees are leery of the idea that everyone knows what everyone else is doing. "It's a double-edged sword," says Mr. Bagwell, the MTV salesman. "It helps you do your job, and everyone can see if you're working hard and making sales. But if you aren't, that becomes obvious, too. Your manager can see right away whether you're making three calls a day or eight."

Donald Shea, a Coopers & Lybrand partner, says that when the Lotus Notes system was first installed this summer, "there was some concern about Big Brother. Yes, it's easier for me to keep track of how everyone is doing. But the whole point is to become more open."

He says the system also lets him track people who help make a sale even if they don't get the commission. "I can record assists, just like a hockey coach. Before Notes, it was difficult to capture that level of detail, and a lot of good work went unrecognized."

Managing Relationships

Lynda M. Applegate, a Harvard Business School professor who has studied the organization effect of groupware, says that with the new technology, "instead of managing data, computers are being used, in effect, to manage networks of relationships between people."

With groupware, she says, companies must decide who can share with whom, or who has the authority to change, add to or approve a document written by a coworker. And someone has to decide who has access to the network, and what information is better kept private.

But at some organizations, knowledge is power, and sharing doesn't come easily. This became clear at Price Waterhouse, which uses Notes to connect 18,000 professionals. In an MIT study of an unnamed company—which others confirm was the big accounting firm—Prof. Wanda Orlikowsky found evidence that some junior employees wouldn't share information on the network because of the firm's intensely competitive culture.

Exclusivity Is Power

As one explained to Prof. Orlikowsky: "The corporate psychology makes the use of Notes difficult, particularly in the consultant career path, which creates a backstabbing, aggressive environment." Another said: "I'm trying to develop an area of expertise that makes me stand out. If I shared that with you, you'd get the credit and not me. . . . Power in this firm is client base and technical ability. Now if you put this information in a Notes database, you lose power." Price Waterhouse says it is happy with Notes.

Some employees balk at the added structure that networks can enforce. When groupware is used to manage projects, for example, it can be set up to specify who in a work group must get what done, and when. Then it can record whether a task was handled satisfactorily.

Sometimes the process got in the way, or was inflexible if an employee decided to skip a step or try something unplanned, "so we added ways to override the system when circumstances required it," says Charles Riley, a senior vice president at Young & Rubicam Inc., the New York advertising firm.

In a pilot project in the firm's San Francisco office, in which Notes was used to coordinate advertising for Chevron Corp. from the initial marketing concept into production, "some people felt there was too much reliance on the computer, and not enough face-to-face communications," he says. "Others were still writing paper memos to each other, though the same information was on the network," or holding meetings over things that had already been decided on-line.

When groupware isn't designed for the way people really work, it can cause a backlash. The Coordinator, a first-generation groupware product from Action Technologies Inc., elicited this reaction. Michael Schrage, of MIT's Center for Coordination Science, calls it a "social spreadsheet" because of its inflexibility and the way that it rigidly categorized interoffice communications.

"In oral conversation, there are all kinds of qualifiers or cues that are implicit and well understood," says Patricia Seybold, of the Seybold Office Computing Group in Boston. "But in groupware, you don't see these cues, and much of what is implicit in the everyday give-and-take of the workplace—in other words, 'let's do lunch,' when you don't really mean it—has to be made explicit."

Thomas White, Action's chief executive, says of the Coordinator, "we learned our lesson in a big way." The program has since been sold to another company, and Action has been successful with other groupware products.

Esther Dyson, an industry consultant, says managers must think carefully about how their company interacts before embracing groupware, lest they simply automate relationships that didn't work to begin with. "Everyone says groupware creates a flatter, more democratic organization. But that really only happens if the organization is ready for it."

RESPONSE SHEET

USING TECHNOLOGY

WRITER(S): AUDIENCE(S):
OCCASION FOR WRITING: DOCUMENT:
WHAT PROBLEM/ISSUE IS THE WRITER (AM I) TRYING TO ADDRESS IN THIS DOCUMENT OR PRESENTATION?

◆ APPROPRIATE TECHNOLOGY

What technology have I selected?

What is the purpose of using this technology?

- Speed?
- Access?
- Convenience?

Do I, as the writer, prefer a particular technology because of factors such as the complexity or length of the message?

Is the technology appropriate for the occasion? For the organization?

Do the expectations of the reader suggest the use of a particular technology because of factors such as believing the message is easier to understand and respond to?

Does the type of message suggest the use of a particular technology?

Does the need to document the message require particular technology?

How does the technology change the message—the tone I convey, the perceptions of the reader?

◆ TECHNOLOGY ISSUES

Will this message contribute to information overload?

Is anonymity a factor in this message?

Would interpersonal, face-to-face communication be more appropriate?

Are organizational values reflected in the technology?

ACTIVITIES, EXERCISES, AND ASSIGNMENTS

◆ IN-CLASS ACTIVITIES

1. Refer to Figure 3.1 to answer the following questions.
   a. Discuss whether you agree with Tom Peters's position about the importance of taking time to explore and reflect on a major problem before jumping in and proposing a solution.
   b. Discuss whether you think the problem is with groupware that encourages collaborative interaction or with people who don't understand the necessity of planning, regardless of the technology.
   c. Discuss how an organization might encourage employees to balance the time needed for exploration and reflection with the temptation to move right to the action.
2. Imagine that you, manager of the marketing department, have a conservative division manager who has resisted installing e-mail for the departments in his division. Finally, he's said, "I'll give you no more than five minutes" at the next department managers' meeting to make the case for installing e-mail throughout the division. Work with a small group to write the outline for your presentation. Use the questions on the Response Sheet (page 86) to help formulate your remarks.
3. Reread the Ethics sidebar "Who owns the clock on the Internet?" (page 74). Decide what you think about using a company's Internet connection for any of these purposes:
   a. Sending a message to your sister who works for another company to see if she can go hiking this weekend
   b. Sending a message to your sister who works for another company to see if the revision she's been doing of her company's grievance procedures is done because you'd like to read it to see if it would be appropriate for your company
   c. Searching a library database to see if you can find a particular article to help you write a paper for your management class
   d. Searching a library database to see if you can find a particular article to help you prepare a presentation your manager asked you to do for a group of international visitors coming in next week
4. Refer to Figure 3.23, which describes the problem one company had with anonymity in their computer network. Respond to the questions about anonymity that are posed in the text (page 82). Then discuss with other members of the class whether you agree or disagree with the decision of XYZ Corp. to track all messages two ways and to absolutely forbid anonymous messages.

◆ INDIVIDUAL AND GROUP EXERCISES

1. Refer to Figure 3.17. If you have access to the Internet, log on to a listserv. Check with the computer consultant in your department or in the technology center at your school to learn how. Listen in on the conversation, and then add your own comments.
2. Innovations in communication technology are representative of what *Business Week* says are "sweeping changes in management and organizational structure that are redefining how work gets done." A recent special report in *Business Week* explained that new technologies account for huge gains in productivity. Figure 3.27 (page 88) highlights four new technologies that are helping to improve productivity. Work in groups of four to complete the following tasks.
   a. Review the four terms and definitions in Figure 3.27.
   b. Have each person in the group select one of the four terms to explore in greater detail. Locate one or more articles that include understandable discussion and examples of one of the terms: (1) graphical user interfaces, (2) networking software and groupware, (3) electronic databases, or (4) imaging software. Start with general business publications such as *The Wall Street Journal, Fortune,* and *Business Week*. Check general computer publications such as *Computerworld* if you want more technical information. Summarize the discussion and examples for your group.
   c. As a group, answer the following questions:
      (1) Why are GUIs—graphical user interfaces—important for making computer technology accessible to nonexpert audiences?
      (2) In what ways do collaboration and teamwork change with networking software?
      (3) How does expanding the availability of data change the way decisions are made in business?
      (4) How do imaging capabilities change the notion of a "paper trail"?
   d. Prepare a brief oral presentation for the class in which you summarize the results of your library investigation and your group discussion.

◆ OUT-OF-CLASS ASSIGNMENTS

1. Work with a small group to design interview questions and/or a survey to learn about the electronic communication in a particular company. Use the Response Sheet (page 86) to help formulate your questions. Your purpose is to identify the kinds of electronic communication as well as the extent to which that communication is used. After you have designed your questions and survey, arrange to conduct an interview. Once you have the information, prepare a 5-minute oral presentation for the class in which you present your findings. Make a chart or table to display the various kinds of electronic communication used in the organization.
2. Select a new software package you are interested in using—for example, word processing, presentation, graphics, spreadsheet, project management. Locate reviews and articles about that software in computer magazines. If you have a computer store nearby, obtain

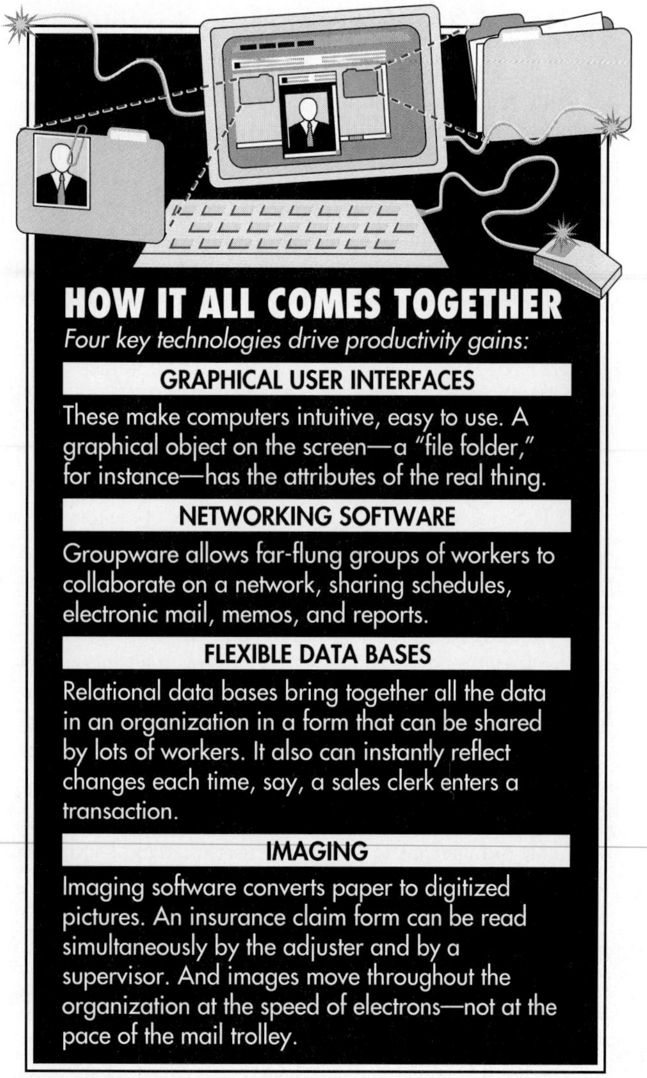
HOW IT ALL COMES TOGETHER
Four key technologies drive productivity gains:
GRAPHICAL USER INTERFACES
These make computers intuitive, easy to use. A graphical object on the screen—a "file folder," for instance—has the attributes of the real thing.
NETWORKING SOFTWARE
Groupware allows far-flung groups of workers to collaborate on a network, sharing schedules, electronic mail, memos, and reports.
FLEXIBLE DATA BASES
Relational data bases bring together all the data in an organization in a form that can be shared by lots of workers. It also can instantly reflect changes each time, say, a sales clerk enters a transaction.
IMAGING
Imaging software converts paper to digitized pictures. An insurance claim form can be read simultaneously by the adjuster and by a supervisor. And images move throughout the organization at the speed of electrons—not at the pace of the mail trolley.

Figure 3.27 Technologies That Drive Productivity

a brochure describing the software. Decide what features and criteria are important. Create a table that shows the positive and negative aspects of the software you're analyzing.

Name of Software:

Manufacturer:

Price:

Hardware Needed:

Strengths/ Appeals/ Advantages	Weaknesses/ Problems/ Disadvantages

CASE

HOTEL OR SHELTER?

Case by Andrea Breemer Frantz

Background. It has been three months since the January 16, 1995, killer earthquake in Kobe, Japan. Despite concerted efforts by international relief agencies and volunteer groups, many of Kobe's communication and transportation systems are still not in use. Aftershocks have hampered repair and caused further damage to makeshift systems set up for interim use. Phone lines have proven unreliable, as has electronic mail; highway and rail access are still limited to only a handful of routes in and out of the city. However, as aftershocks continue to rumble, the port city residents are emerging from mourning and beginning to rebuild.

You are a communication director for an international chain of hotels based in the U.S. The chain, owned by Florida real estate investors, has two hotels in Japan, one in Tokyo and one in Kobe. The Hatari Hotel in Kobe was only minimally damaged by the earthquake. The extent of the damage was limited to hairline cracks in the strong foundation and some water damage caused by a burst pipe in the basement. In general, owners, employees, and those residing in the hotel at the time were relieved at the minimal damage and the fact that no lives were lost there.

Immediately following the disaster, the manager of the Hatari, Ayisha Sumino, opened the hotel's doors to the homeless and allowed over 500 people to stay in vacant rooms, lobbies, and conference rooms. Though the hotel did not have the facilities to nurse the injured and referred those victims to seek help from the nearby Red Cross station, Sumino, along with numerous hotel employees, provided beds, cots, sheets, blankets, kitchen facilities, and moral support to many homeless families for weeks. In a cover story on the disaster, *Newsweek* magazine highlighted the manager's effort as "evidence of heroism born of tragedy." In a particularly poignant sidebar to the same story, Sumino was again commended when he helped to locate and reunite 7-year-old Rikihiro Toshitami and his mother, the only quake survivors of the Toshitami family, which owned the restaurant across the street from the Hatari.

Prior to the earthquake, the Hatari Hotel had been losing money. Though most of the problem appeared to be associated with ineffective marketing strategies for the area, a team of consultants from the U.S. went to Kobe to investigate possible mismanagement. The only mismanagement the consulting team could detect was that Sumino was unaware of low morale and a fairly significant increase in employee theft.

Although the majority of the homeless people who originally took refuge in the Hatari after the earthquake have gone to stay with relatives, the hotel still houses approximately 100 victims free of charge. Because the Hatari is one of the few hotels in the area in good enough condition to house people, the owners believe that now is the time to capitalize on reporters and officials who need places to stay. For every night that the Hatari continues to house the homeless instead of paying customers, however, the hotel loses profits that could ultimately put the Hatari in the black again.

Task. As communication director, you have been charged with two tasks. First, you must determine how to most effectively contact the manager, Sumino. The channel you employ is problematized by the message, the cultural differences between sender and receiver (low-context U.S. culture versus high-context Japanese culture; see the Communication Spotlight for Part V, pages 520–526), and the extenuating circumstances of the *Oh Jishin* (The Great Earthquake). You are considering sending a telegram due to the relative unreliability of other channels, but are unsure of this choice because of the potential multicultural difficulties that might emerge if your message is restricted in length. On the other hand, e-mail and telephone contact have been less than reliable, and overseas postal delivery will take a great deal of time. After you have discovered the best communication channel available, send a memo to the chain's owners (Clifford Margolin, Sam Smithson, and Alva Bridge) advising them of the best channel(s) given your circumstances. Second, you need to communicate with Sumino about getting the Hatari back "on-line."

Complication. After communicating with the owners, you realize that you are facing a very complex task with regard to your message. The owners are divided in their priorities. Smithson is content to have the Hatari house earthquake victims for the goodwill (and the good publicity) the action generates. Bridge primarily wants you to discover the precise date when the Hatari will begin charging for *all* rooms again. And Margolin wants to know "if we're running a business or a nonprofit relief agency." At the same time, the Hatari has enjoyed a good amount of positive attention for Sumino's relief efforts. To wantonly displace the homeless again will not reflect well on the hotel. In addition, you realize that there are *cultural implications* involved. How can you most effectively address the priorities represented by the owners and avoid offending Sumino, his staff, the city of Kobe, and perhaps even ultimately the American public? You realize that you need to plan not just a message, but an entire communication strategy taking into consideration internal as well as external audiences. Since things could get dicey, you decide to write a memo *for the record* to your immediate supervisor regarding the situation, your concerns, and your planned communication strategy.

ROLES AND RESPONSIBILITIES FOR TEAMS AND GROUPS

When you're part of a workplace team, you have to fulfill your role as a member of the organization and your role as a member of your team. You will be a more productive team member if you understand the roles and responsibilities that influence traditional teams, nonhierarchical teams, and communication networks.

Traditional Teams

Traditional workplace teams have a hierarchical structure, much like a pyramid, with clear lines of authority. The team leader is at the top and the team members are underneath. For example, UPS warehouse crews have a team leader who oversees the operation, enforces the rules, and resolves any interpersonal disagreements. Their primary responsibility is completing a well-defined task. (See the Communication Spotlight about team structure, pages 589–592.)

Even if a team's task is solving problems or creating new ideas rather than performing specific tasks, many organizations expect teams to have a leader who generally provides two kinds of support:

- Leaders can provide *interpersonal support* that focuses on feelings and attitudes, making sure that team members work in a positive atmosphere and feel part of the group.
- Leaders can provide *task support* that focuses on addressing the work to be done, so the leader helps by doing things such as defining the problem, coordinating activities, and providing evaluation.

Figure 1 Task Functions of Team Members

TASK FUNCTIONS	FUNCTION
1. Initiator-contributor	Recommends novel ideas about the problem at hand, new ways to approach the problem, or possible solutions not yet considered.
2. Information seeker	Emphasizes getting the facts by calling for background information from others.
3. Opinion seeker	Asks for more qualitative types of data, such as attitudes, values, and feelings.
4. Information giver	Provides data for forming decisions, including facts that derive from expertise.
5. Opinion giver	Provides opinions, values, and feelings.
6. Elaborator	Gives additional information—examples, rephrasings, implications—about points made by others.
7. Coordinator	Shows the relevance of each idea and its relationship to the overall problem.
8. Orienter	Refocuses discussion of the topic whenever necessary.
9. Evaluator-critic	Appraises the quality of the group's efforts in terms of logic, practicality, or method.
10. Energizer	Stimulates the group to continue working when discussion flags.
11. Procedural technician	Cares for operational details such as the materials, machinery, and so on.
12. Recorder	Provides a secretarial function.

While interpersonal and task functions are both important, these leadership functions aren't necessarily performed by the same person. Leadership can shift within a team, with more than one person assuming the responsibilities. In fact, interpersonal and task functions extend to members of the entire team. Benne and Sheats, who studied ways that team members interact, developed a catalog of interpersonal and task functions assumed by team members. Figure 1 identifies some of these task functions. If you're on a team that's having difficulty getting its tasks done, you can check to make sure these functions are being carried out by someone on the team.

Because there's not a one-to-one correlation between functions and team members, the functions may shift among members, depending on factors such as time availability, knowledge of the task, commitment to the project, personality, and so on. For example, on a five-person team that planned, wrote, and designed new policy booklets for health-insurance customers, everyone functioned at various times as an information giver and information seeker. Other roles, however, were assumed by different individuals. Carla typically acted as the orienter and coordinator. Virginia acted as the energizer and evaluator. Brian acted as the initiator-contributor. Joann acted as the opinion seeker and occasionally as orienter. Warren acted as the elaborator.

Figure 2 identifies interpersonal functions that team members often assume. Just as with task functions, there's not necessarily a one-to-one correlation between each interpersonal function and a person. On the five-person team planning new policy booklets, everyone functioned at various times as an encourager and harmonizer. In addition, Carla often acted as the gatekeeper and standard setter. Virginia often acted as the harmonizer and group observer. Brian, Joann, and Warren acted as followers willing to compromise. If you're on a team that's having difficulty getting along, you can check to make sure these functions are being performed by someone on the team.

Nonhierarchical Teams

Sometimes leadership on a team is shared so completely that there is no identifiable team leader. There are, in fact, specific circumstances in which a team doesn't need a leader.

If a small team is comprised of independent, professional individuals who have little need for group rewards, they will probably function well without a leader. If the team members have ability, experience, training, and knowledge, they probably don't need a task-oriented leader, but they may need a leader to provide interpersonal support.

Similarly, if a team provides its own feedback concerning an unambiguous and familiar task, it does not need a leader to help with task relationships but may need interpersonal support. And if the team members find the task intrinsically satisfying, they probably won't need interpersonal support, but they may need task support.

Figure 2 Interpersonal Functions of Team Members

INTERPERSONAL FUNCTIONS	FUNCTION
1. Encourager	Rewards others through agreement, warmth, and praise.
2. Harmonizer	Mediates conflicts among group's members.
3. Compromiser	Shifts his or her own position on an issue in order to reduce conflict in the group.
4. Gatekeeper and expediter	Smooths communication by setting up procedures and ensuring equal participation from members.
5. Standard setter	Expresses, or calls for discussion of, standards for evaluating the quality of the group process.
6. Group observer	Informally points out the positive and negative aspects of the group's dynamics and calls for change if necessary.
7. Follower	Accepts the ideas offered by others and serves as an audience for the group.

Finally, if an established, closely knit team has access to organizational rewards not within a leader's control (such as corporate bonus incentives) and has a superior who is physically distant (perhaps in another building), the team has little need for a leader to strengthen either interpersonal or task relationships. If the team members have explicit plans, clear procedures, and highly specified functions, they probably don't need task leadership, but they may need interpersonal support.

The following questions can help you assess whether a particular team would probably work more effectively with a leader or whether it could be productive without one.

- *Is the team large?* A three-person team may not need a leader. A five-person team sometimes needs a leader. A 13-person team almost always does. A 20-person team certainly does.
- *Is the broad objective of the team tactical?* Experts who study workplace teams describe a tactical team as having a clear sense of who does what, and setting a clear set of performance standards.
- *Does the task require management or administration?* If the task is complex and requires some oversight, then a leader is probably a good idea.
- *Does the team need someone to coordinate or negotiate the interpersonal relationships?* If a team has conflicts, a leader can be useful in helping to establish good working relationships among the members.

Webs and Networks

All team members, leaders included, form a web of individuals working for a common purpose. These webs tend to have "shapes" that describe the patterns of communication within the team. Different patterns not only influence the problem-solving efficiency of a team but also influence individual satisfaction.[1]

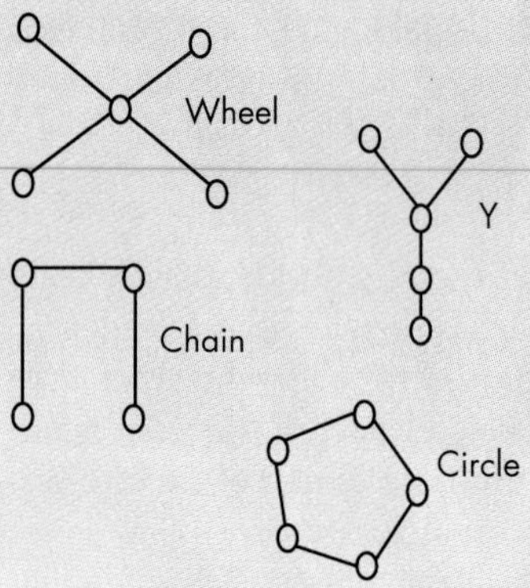

- If a team's pattern is shaped like a wheel, a central member talks with each of the other members on the team, but none of these other people talk with each other.
- If a team's pattern is shaped like a Y, a central member talks with or can get information to everyone on the team, even though not all members on the team talk with each other.
- If a team's pattern is shaped like a chain, the communication is linear, with each person talking to one or two members. No central person knows what everyone is doing.
- If a team's pattern is shaped like a circle, everyone talks to two other members, but no central person knows what everyone is doing.

Teams whose communication webs are shaped like a wheel or a Y tend to work well for simple tasks when the leader is in the pivotal position, making sure that everyone knows what everyone else is doing. For example, a wheel or Y structure might be used by a team composed of members from different departments who were asked to assess employee reactions to the company cafeteria's new low-fat meal options at lunch; one person might coordinate the input from people in different departments.

Teams whose communication webs are shaped like a chain or a circle tend not to work so effectively, since there's no common communication link. In fact, because these teams have no intersection, they often become dysfunctional—that is, they're unable to perform effectively or accomplish their task.

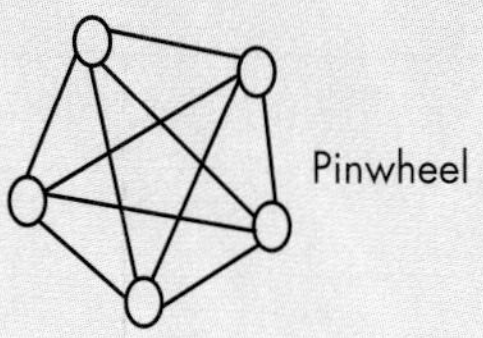

- In striking contrast to the chain or the circle, if a team's pattern is shaped like a pinwheel, everyone talks to everyone else on the team.

Teams whose communication web is shaped like a pinwheel—whether there is a designated leader or not—tend to be effective for solving complex tasks. For example, the team that planned, wrote, and designed new policy booklets for health-insurance customers couldn't have done an effective job without regular communication among the entire group. Even though one person mediated most of the substantive conflicts and another smoothed interpersonal disagreements by encouraging equal participation, each person in the group was linked with each other person.

In an organization, a large network (Figure 3) is formed by communication links among various smaller webs—formal teams working on defined projects and informal work groups who share observations and act as resources and sounding boards for each other.[2] This large network doesn't look anything like the formal organization chart. It's messy and flexible, changing as projects change and as people's needs change.

In these informal and constantly shifting networks, some people are nonparticipants (1 and 2 in Figure 3) who have little or no interaction with other people in the organization, but most people are linked to others in the organization. The person who is most important in the network functions as a liaison—a person with links to each team or work group in the network (3 in Figure 3). This person controls the flow of information and influences opinions and decisions. Through the liaison, each team or work group has the opportunity for input and feedback from the other groups.

These links characterize the interaction of the organization. Two aspects of the links between the teams and work groups are crucial:

- The *substance of the interaction*: This is the content of your interaction, the interpretation of that content, and attitudes and emotions associated with the content.
- The *form of the interaction*: This is the means by which you transmit your content, your selection of the recipient, and the relationship among people involved.

For example, the team that planned new policy booklets needed to communicate with other corporate groups, one of which was responsible for training account administrators whose responsibility was explaining all the changes to insurance carriers. These trainers needed to know how much of the document would be changed so they could schedule time for revising their training sessions. The interaction with the trainers could have been influenced in any numbers of ways: Should Carla have identified only the changes that had been approved to date and said nothing about parts of the booklet that were still under discussion? Should Carla have mentioned strongly divided opinions on the team about the way the exceptions should be handled? Decisions such as these influence interaction.

ACTIVITIES AND QUESTIONS FOR DISCUSSION

1. Refer to Figures 1 and 2 to use as self-assessment tools to determine how you functioned on the last team you were on. Go through the 19 items and decide whether that role described your interaction on the team.
2. Refer to the following questions to assess the last team you were on.
   - How was the group organized? What shape were the webs?
   - What kind of leadership was appropriate? Comfortable?
   - Who had the authority to establish the document's purpose? Who had the authority to establish the priorities for key points?
   - Who had the authority to make decisions?
   - What roles did various members of the team assume?
   - How did these roles influence the functioning of the team?

Explain in what ways the team was successful and unsuccessful. Given the information you have just read in this Communication Spotlight, what might you or other members of the team have done differently?

Figure 3 Informal Network Formed by Many Webs

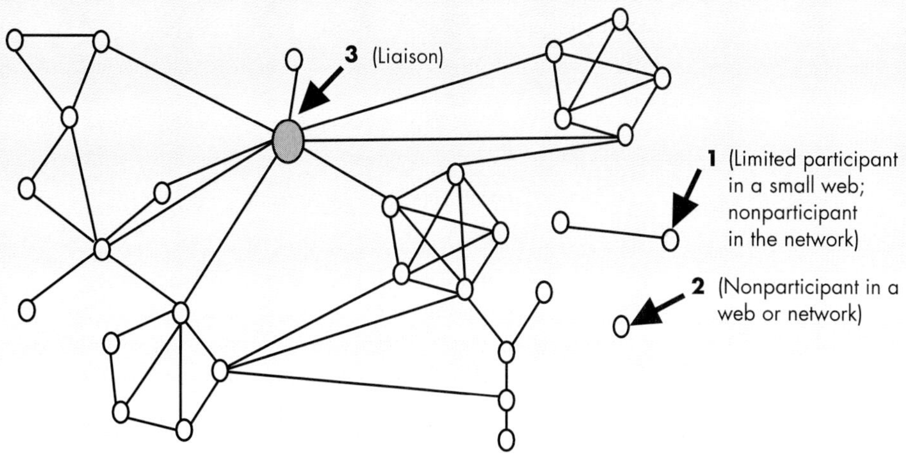

ESTABLISHING GUIDELINES AND STANDARDS

Question What is a good document?

Answer It depends.

It depends on how well the document addresses its audience, purpose, and occasion as well as on the message itself.

- Is the document adapted to the intended audience?
- Is the document appropriate for the purpose?
- Is the document suitable for the occasion?
- Is the document's message accurate and useful?

A document isn't inherently acceptable or unacceptable, effective or ineffective. For example, a Northwest Airlines press release about its on-time arrival record is appropriate for travel agents reading a business newsletter but of little use to Northwest ground crews working to develop an even more efficient way to service arriving planes. Conversely, a report documenting the results of a survey and focus groups about operations with selected Northwest ground crews is appropriate for ground crews themselves and for Northwest managers but of little interest to travel agents wanting information about group rates.

Guidelines and standards to assess documents help workplace professionals in a number of ways. On the most basic level, guidelines and standards can help you assess the accuracy of the message itself. They also give you a way to assess whether a document is meeting the needs of its audience and fulfilling its purpose. Finally, guidelines and standards help you assess conformity to text conventions, ranging from commas to headings, as well as conformity to corporate practices, ranging from ways of identifying yourself as a writer to handling proprietary information.

Sources of Style Manuals

When you join an organization, you can turn to a number of sources for information to help you assess the effectiveness of your documents. An important source is your own awareness of elements that help define a professional document. But the organization will probably also have published style manuals, computerized style checkers, and corporate style manuals.

One place to begin assessing a document is to examine the elements that influence every document: audience, purpose, occasion, and message. The questions in Figure 1 can help you plan and then assess your documents. The first column focuses on questions you need to ask during planning and drafting. The second column focuses on questions you can ask to assess the relation among the elements of your document.

Another place to get help in assessing documents is from published style manuals, three of which are listed here:

- *The Chicago Manual of Style*, published by the University of Chicago Press (the style manual used for this textbook)
- *MLA Style Manual*, published by the Modern Language Association
- *The New York Times Manual of Style and Usage*

Style manuals provide information about stylistic, grammatical, and mechanical conventions, but they seldom provide information about *why* a specific convention is appropriate for a particular audience, purpose, or occasion. Thus, when you're using a style manual, you need to ask yourself whether a convention or rule is appropriate for your document.

Figure 1 Factors to Consider in Global Revision

	FIRST...USE QUESTIONS TO HELP YOU PLAN YOUR DOCUMENT.	THEN...USE QUESTIONS TO HELP YOU ASSESS YOUR DOCUMENT.
Is your document adapted for the audience?	Who is your audience? How accurate is your perception of the audience? What does your audience expect? What does the audience need to know? What factors influence the audience's understanding of the information? How will you know if the information is appropriate for this audience?	How is content adapted to audience? Is the information/argument logical and easy for the audience to follow? How are the details/examples adapted to the audience? Why is the genre appropriate for the audience? How are visuals/document design adapted to the audience?
Is your document appropriate for the purpose?	What are the purposes of your document? What do you expect the document to accomplish? Will the audience be receptive or resistant to your purpose? How will their response affect the way you present the information? How will you know if you have accomplished your purpose?	How does content support the purpose? How does the information/argument support the purpose? How do the details/examples support the purpose? Why is the genre appropriate for the purpose? How are visuals/document design appropriate for the purpose?
Is your document suitable for the occasion?	How will the occasion be affected by the document? How has the occasion affected the document? How does the occasion affect the audience's receptivity or resistance to the document? What will change or happen as a result of the document?	How is the content suitable for the occasion? How are details/examples suitable for the occasion? Why is the genre suitable for the occasion? How are the visuals/document design suitable for the occasion?
Is your document's message accurate, complete, and persuasive?	What key points do you want to convey? How have you determined that these are the most important points? How will you know if you have conveyed these key points to the audience? Is the audience likely to be receptive or resistant to the message? What information or argument will help persuade the audience?	Why is the content complete and accurate? In what ways does the presentation conform to conventions? Is the information coherent, suitable, and persuasive for the occasion? Are the details/examples sufficient to reinforce the points? Why is the genre suitable to convey the message? How do the visuals/document design reinforce the message?

One increasingly popular form of a style manual is a computerized style checker that analyzes sentences for certain predetermined features such as passive voice. While computerized style checkers can signal potential problems in a document, the information isn't of much value unless the writer knows what to do with it. For example, imagine that a computerized style checker—say the one that came with the Microsoft Word software used to type the manuscript for this textbook—provides information that says this paragraph has 16 percent passive constructions. A writer would need to know the following things to make use of this information:

- what a passive construction is
- how to change passive constructions to active voice if a change were appropriate
- whether passive constructions are appropriate or inappropriate for this audience, purpose, occasion, and message

The point is that stylistic, grammatical, and mechanical conventions can be misused if you don't know what the convention is, whether it's appropriate, and how to use it in relation to a particular audience, purpose, or occasion. Simply put, style manuals usually concentrate on topics that have a "right" or a "wrong," even though the "right" may only apply in certain situations or may be one of several equally correct possibilities. Workplace professionals

Figure 2 Excerpt from OptImage Stylebook, Chapter on Lists

This second page of the chapter details the kinds of lists that are discussed and establishes the overriding purposes for lists.

Types of Lists

Basically, we have six types of lists:

- in-text
- bulleted
- subelement
- keyword
- numbered
- combination

Each of these has at least two subtypes, and each of the subtypes has its particular format. However, all lists have two fundamental, interrelated purposes.

First, all lists should help the reader chunk information appropriately.

Second, all lists should maintain the hierarchies that govern the organization of a manual from the broadest to the narrowest scope.

The following sections describe the types of lists we use and when to use them. Hopefully, the chunking and hierarching of the sections will help you to understand our system of lists.

need to learn when rules are absolutes (for example, no errors in agreement or parallelism or modifier placement) and when conventions are appropriate only in certain circumstances (for example, using bulleted versus numbered lists or using active versus passive voice).

Finally, individual companies often produce their own style manuals so that their employees have easy access to the conventions preferred in their particular organization. Frequently, corporate styleguides include information unique to an organization. For example, OptImage's style manual includes a 50-page chapter about lists since the software manuals they produce contain six different kinds of lists (Figure 2).

Applying Guidelines and Standards

So far you've been reading about general guidelines and standards, but to be useful, they need to be applied to a particular document. Imagine, for example, that Cy Malone is updating a procedures manual to persuade office managers to implement a new travel voucher policy. When he finishes his initial draft of the update and is ready to revise it, he asks himself the questions in Figure 1. Three particular questions help him accomplish his purpose (see Figure 3).

The three changes identified in Figure 3—a brief introductory explanation, a flow chart, and a sample of the new voucher—strengthen the manual by adapting it to the audience, making it more appropriate for the purpose, and making it more suitable to the occasion.

Editing and Reviewing

When a document that you plan and write is completed, it needs a final round of editing and reviewing. Even though editing and reviewing have been built in all the way through the process, a final check reduces the number of errors that slip through. In the workplace, editing and reviewing involve a number of steps that are frequently referred to as levels of

Figure 3 Questions That Lead to Changes to a Draft

GENERAL QUESTIONS (FROM FIGURE 1)	QUESTIONS ADAPTED TO THE PROCEDURES MANUAL	REVISION TO THE DRAFT OF THE PROCEDURES MANUAL
Is the information/argument logical and easy for the audience to follow?	What would make the information easier for users of this manual to follow?	Add a brief explanation to introduce readers to the procedural change.
How do the visuals/document design reinforce the message?	What visual would reinforce the message in this manual?	Incorporate a flow chart showing readers the overall sequence of the revised procedure.
Are the details/examples sufficient to reinforce the points?	What details or examples help reinforce the points in this manual?	Include a sample of the new voucher correctly completed so readers have a model.

edit and review cycles. Editing improves a document's accuracy as well as its appropriateness and appeal to readers. Review cycles confirm editing decisions and ensure that the document conforms to corporate standards.

Your willingness to revise what you write distinguishes you from novice writers who are either unaware of the benefits of revision or don't know how to go about it. In some companies, though—ranging from Alcoa to 3M to UPS—you have no choice about revision. It's one of the processes built into the organization in the formal review cycles.

Formal systems for reviewing documents differ from organization to organization, but generally the goal is for revision to improve document quality. Susan Kleimann, an expert in designing and revising professional documents and director of the Document Design Center in Washington, D.C., investigated revision cycles used in the federal government's General Accounting Office (GAO). She identified an approval process—"the chain of people who must read and approve the document." These people review successive versions of a document as it is revised. One example she gives illustrates the complexity of reviewing important documents in large organizations. She reported on a three-person GAO team who drafted a document that was reviewed by the organization's director, the assistant director, the office of report review, and five additional staff members. Copies of the draft—with comments from all the reviewers—were returned to the writing team, who prepared a second draft. The entire review process was repeated before the document was approved for its final version.

You seldom have control over the review cycles that your documents must go through in an organization—the cycles are typically part of department or organizational policy. You do, however, have some control over the amount of revision you might need to do on a document. The following guidelines should help you write documents that need less revision.

- Be familiar with the organization's *general standards* for effective documents. Check your document to make sure it complies with those standards before starting it on a review cycle.
- Role play your reviewers and conduct a mock review of the document—both of segments as you draft the document and of the document in its entirety—before you send it through the review process. What will the following reviewers look for: other members of your team? Division director? Technical experts? Editors? Designers? Legal adviser?

ACTIVITIES AND QUESTIONS FOR DISCUSSION

1. Contact a large local organization to find out about the approval process that their documents must go through. Work with a small group to design interview questions that you can ask, and conduct the interview. (See Chapter 11 for information about interviewing.) Compile the interview information into a memo that reports on the review process that the organization uses.
2. What are the advantages of having multiple reviewers for important documents? Why, for example, would a document need to be reviewed by an organization's director and assistant director, the office of report review, and five additional staff members? Would one or two people be sufficient?

PART II
THE WRITING PROCESS

CHAPTER

4

Planning Business Documents by Considering Audience

OUTLINE

Why Audience Analysis Matters: The Bellencamp Story

Factors Basic to Audience Analysis

Understanding How Audience Analysis Affects Writing Strategies

You-attitude

Reader Use

Readability

CRITERIA FOR EXPLORING CHAPTER 4

What we cover in this chapter	What you will be able to do after reading this chapter
Why audience analysis matters	Discuss how audience analysis helps writers avoid problems with readers
Factors basic to audience analysis	Explain the role reader characteristics, writer-reader relationships, environment and stance, and reader type play in understanding your audience
The relationship between audience analysis and writing strategies	Plan writing strategies appropriate to different audiences
You-attitude	Consider your reader in your pronoun use, positive wording, and strategies emphasizing reader benefit
Reader use	Select arrangement, details, format, and style to help readers
Readability	Write documents that are readable by considering document-based, reader-based, and context-based aspects of readability

Effective communicators know that readers make a difference. For example, you recognize that a memo to your boss asking for a day off will be worded differently from a casual note to a friend about the same day off. Figure 4.1, however, suggests that simply knowing that different readers have different needs and expectations doesn't guarantee you'll be able to write a document that gets the response from the reader that you want or expect.

CONTEXT

Rita, administrative secretary for a 24-person government office, has sent a memo to coffee drinkers about a new coffee service. Her purpose was twofold: (1) to sell people on the advantage of the new service and (2) to inform them how much each will have to pay for this service. Being aware of differences in her audience (the other support staff, 9 paralegals, and 10 attorneys), she has enlisted help from Bob, the attorney responsible for administrative functions, including supervising paralegals.

Even though Rita is aware of her audiences, the memo doesn't elicit the expected responses. Bob and Rita both receive unanticipated questions about the cost of participating and the procedure for stopping service if it doesn't work out. On July 25, they also received complaints when the coffee machine wasn't there.

Figure 4.1 Interoffice Memo

The writer mentions two different dates for delivery.

The writer provides extensive detail about varying prices for cases of coffee.

Three pots—cleaned by "they"—are part of the service. (Evidently, people in this office spent a great deal of time making coffee.)

Information is given about start-up contributions. Then, readers learn that they will be expected to make future contributions.

Readers are invited to comment.

July 24, 19--

TO COFFEE DRINKERS

From: Rita

RE: New machine

Bob and I have decided to go with a 3 month trial of a new machine for our coffee. They will either be bringing it Thursday July 25, or the following Thursday. The way I understand it, we will be getting the first 3 months of coffee at a discount of $17/case (42 packets) instead of $20/case. They are also throwing in a free case. After three months, the price will go back to $20/case. We are under no obligation to keep it. They will also come in and clean the three pots that come with it.

This machine will make a pot in 3½ minutes compared to ½ hour. It will also save trips to the store when it is "your turn" to buy the coffee. If I could please get everyone to contribute approximately $2.00 to get us started I would appreciate it. Please give the money to either Bob or me. Then, after we get our first case, I will be asking each one for their share after that.

If you have any questions or comments about this machine, please talk to Bob or me. Thanks a lot.

rh

1. Why do you think the memo failed to elicit the expected response?
2. What changes would you recommend that Rita make in her memo?
3. In what ways do you think Rita recognizes that she's writing to more than one audience? What strategies does Rita use to appeal to support staff? To paralegals? To attorneys?

The unexpected confusion generated by Rita's memo suggests that Rita needs to know about the following aspects of writing to different audiences:

- factors basic to audience analysis
- the relationship between audience analysis and writing strategies
- the principle of you-attitude, reader use, and readability

WHY AUDIENCE ANALYSIS MATTERS: THE BELLENCAMP STORY

The story we will tell you about the Bellencamp memo in Figure 4.2 will show what happens when you do not use your knowledge about your readers to make effective writing decisions. In this case, the writer, John Bellencamp, had access both to demographic data about the people who would be reading his memo and to information about each reader's specific performance for the publishing house. However, he did not use that knowledge to his best advantage.

Although Bellencamp uses traditional strategies in addressing his readers, such as complimenting the reader and stressing reader benefit, his message does not inspire author compliance. The memo fails for several reasons. One reason is that Bellencamp does not pay attention to what he knows about his audience. He knows that his authors in general have been missing their deadlines, but he ignores the fact that certain authors, including Wright, have been on schedule. Another reason for the memo's failure is that Bellencamp doesn't provide information that the reader needs. Wright does not need, for example, to be told about the importance of meeting deadlines, since she currently meets and, indeed, improves upon hers. She might need to know, however, if her latest revisions have been received and approved.

Bellencamp also does not account for reader motivation. Wright will not be motivated by the compliment that she is a "Special Author." The "Special Author" subject line rings hollow because Bellencamp does not acknowledge her exceptional performance. Also, Wright will not be motivated by a "pep talk" to keep on schedule. She is already doing so without Bellencamp's encouragement. And surely Wright will not be motivated by the fact that others are behind schedule and thereby may be adversely affecting the success of *her* book.

Bellencamp's message also comes at a bad time. Wright is neck-deep in correcting page proofs, the final draft version of her manuscript. The demanding nature of this task is in part responsible for Wright's having neither the time nor the inclination to respond to Bellencamp directly. Instead, Wright's response is included in a letter to her editor about the galleys (Figure 4.3). Wright resists Bellencamp's message, although she does not directly write him.

The sarcastic tone and overt "dig" in the second-to-last paragraph of Wright's letter clearly show that Wright is unhappy about the memo. It is also clear that Wright's relationship to Bellencamp is distant enough that she does not consider possible good points in the memo. A friend or colleague of Bellencamp might have looked for a positive interpretation, thinking, "It's good that John is concerned with the trouble the New York office is having and that he's trying to do something about it. It's appropriate that John contact all authors about a problem that, indeed, affects all authors." Wright has no such charitable interpretation.

C O N T E X T

Division Director John Bellencamp has been frustrated by the number of schedule delays recently experienced by his publishing company. Some authors have been late with their manuscripts, causing expensive delays in production and palpable tension among publishing house employees. Bellencamp knows he has a talented crop of authors, and he does not want to alienate them. At the same time, he knows that tardiness is not only costing the company money, but also affecting the potential sales and profits. Bellencamp thus pens a memo to his authors in an attempt to improve the situation.

Figure 4.2 Memo Trying to Enlist Reader Support

Bellencamp uses an interoffice memo format to imply the readers' membership in the company.

He uses specific author's name to decrease the "form letter" effect.

He compliments his audience as "special."

He makes indirect reference to reader benefit: sales of the authors' texts.

He calls attention to the readers' interest in (or benefit from) compliance.

He acknowledges the readers' past contributions while renewing the urgency of his request.

INTEROFFICE MEMO
RAFFERTY PUBLISHING

17 November 19--

TO: J.J. Wright

FROM: John Bellencamp *JB*

SUBJECT: A Special Request to Special People—Our Authors

We have very ambitious plans to grow our company over the next few years. Important to this growth plan is the maximization of sales potential for each text we publish.

We are planning for success but we need your help! We can construct our schedules and adhere to them, and we can coordinate our outside suppliers—compositors, printers, binders—to work within these schedules. In essence, we have a "handle" on the New York performance requirements.

A key element in meeting schedules is the cooperation you must provide, starting with manuscript completion and continuing through proofing, indexing, and supplement preparation. Without your attention to all of these, our schedules become in jeopardy—and the sales of your book may suffer.

I would like to enlist your support throughout the duration of the production process you are currently experiencing to do your utmost to improve upon, or at least keep to, the requested dates provided by our editorial people.

The time sacrifices you have already made are considerable, I realize, and the prospect of additional sacrifices may not be well received. However, the demands of the current college marketplace are such that early publication of all components of any new product is becoming essential to its success.

Thank you for your help.

Figure 4.3 Letter with Author's Response to Bellencamp Memo

Dear Barb:

I have several questions about the galleys you sent for correction on November 1.

1. Where is the illustration on page 66 going to be inserted? My original draft had it inserted at point "A" (see my marginal notations), but the galleys seem to have it positioned two paragraphs after that.
2. Have we reached a definitive agreement on whether or not we are going to hyphenate point-of-view? The previous galleys I sent omitted the hyphens, but now hyphens seem to have been inserted, pp. 55 ff.
3. The example of the brochure that I wanted to include on p. 78 has been completely revised, and I'm including a copy of the new version both with this letter and with the galleys themselves. Do you have any comments on the new version? I realize this will entail more copy-editing on your part, but I think the quality of the revised brochure speaks for itself.

Did you know about the memo John Bellencamp sent to me dated November 17? I've enclosed a copy for your reference. I'm wondering at this point what "page" John is on, since I thought we were on-time with our publication schedule. If John really wants to "grow" his company, he might consider taking a few diction and proofreading lessons from his "special people." (Sorry, I couldn't resist that dig.)

Please fill me in if I've missed something. The page-proofs you were expecting back will be in the mail by November 20. Then we both can have a good Thanksgiving.

Cordially,

Wright, however, is close enough in her relationship to Barb to make a complaint about the memo. She is also confident enough in Barb to use conventions to signal what Barb should do. Wright uses a convention when she places the complaint in the second-to-last paragraph, which usually does not contain action items. Wright thus indicates that Barb really doesn't have to take action. Barb's reply (Figure 4.4) indicates she has understood Wright's intentions: Barb cooperates with the message.

Bellencamp's memo shows that ignoring your audience can cause real problems. These range from abstract problems, such as bad feelings and tarnished company image, to concrete consequences, such as Barb's added task of sending out letters of assurance to her authors.

A number of other lessons can also be learned:

- Writer-reader relationships influence how a message is interpreted.
- The content of a message needs to be appropriate to the reader being addressed.
- A reader's motivations for reading a document can influence how it is received.

Figure 4.4 Editor's Response to Author's Letter Containing a Complaint

Dear J.J.

Your proofs arrived December 2. Thank you!

1. Unless you have a serious objection, the figure will be inserted on page 66 as shown in the galley proofs. This was the decision of the art department.
2. "Point of view" will not be hyphenated. Our copy editor will do a global change on the manuscript to make sure that we are consistent on this one.
3. The revised brochure you sent is indeed a good one. Perhaps we could use both and have you comment on the advantages of the second over the first? (We can still do this type of change at this point, but will hesitate to do similar changes after this set of proofs is in.)

I understand that you received a memo, dated November 17, from our division director, John Bellencamp. In the memo, he alludes to your adherence to production schedules, etc., etc. Some authors have been concerned that they were singled out for a reprimand for not meeting schedules. You were wondering what "page" John was on.

I'm certainly aware that you have met (and improved on) your schedule for completion of manuscript, revisions, and that you will continue to be on schedule throughout the production process. I want to reassure you that the letter was sent to <u>all</u> authors under contract for 19— titles, regardless of their performance to date in meeting schedules.

I hope that this letter will serve to clear up any misunderstandings you personally have had regarding the letter. As I hope I've said enough times while we have been working together, I couldn't ask for a better, more cooperative author. If you like my suggestion for handling the brochures, please send me the additional copy articulating the advantages by January 1.

Sincerely,

- The information in a message must meet the reader's needs.
- Conventions for writing may be adopted or adapted for an audience.
- Concrete factors, such as impending deadlines and time available, can influence the level of attention a reader can pay to a writer's concerns.
- Readers may either resist or cooperate with the writer's message.

These lessons show that when you plan business communications, you must pay careful attention to your audience.

FACTORS BASIC TO AUDIENCE ANALYSIS

When analyzing audiences, you consider various factors:

Characteristics of the audience	• factors that can be discovered by consulting secondary sources or databases (demographic data, geographic data, purchasing behavior) • factors that are inferred by directly interviewing or surveying audiences
The writer-reader relationship	• status of and distance between writer and reader • interpersonal aspects
The message itself	• information needed (excluded, included) • conventions used/not used
The occasion for communicating	• type of reader • the reader's stance: resistant or cooperative

Factors Tied to Reader Characteristics

To know your audience, you need to be able to create a profile of your reader's characteristics. These characteristics fall into two basic categories:

- factors that can be discovered by consulting databases (demographic data, geographic data, purchasing behavior)
- factors that are inferred or derived from interviewing or surveying audiences

Data-based factors include concrete facts about an audience's age, income, and marital status. Inferred factors involve your perception of the audience's attitudes and beliefs.

Much of the audience research in business communication has been connected with marketing a company's goods and services or promoting corporate image. Figure 4.5 suggests how databases have been used to target particular audiences with appropriate content and media choices.

Purchasing behavior often tells marketing experts what kinds of products to develop, promote, and advertise in a particular geographic area.

MULTICULTURAL

TARGET AUDIENCES, DEMOGRAPHICS, AND LANGUAGE CHOICE

According to the U.S. Census Bureau, there are over 31 million people who speak a language other than English at home. The table below provides numbers for the languages which at least 300,000 people speak at home. The figures do not indicate how many people read and write in these languages, but the numbers clearly give us some idea about which languages aside from English are in common use in the United States.

LANGUAGES SPOKEN AT HOME IN THE UNITED STATES BY PEOPLE OVER AGE 5

LANGUAGE	NUMBER	LANGUAGE	NUMBER
Spanish	17,339,000	Korean	626,000
French	1,703,000	Vietnamese	507,000
German	1,547,000	Portuguese	430,000
Italian	1,309,000	Japanese	428,000
Chinese	1,249,000	Greek	388,000
Tagalog	843,000	Arabic	335,000
Polish	723,000	Hindi, Urdu, etc.	331,000

This data is useful to business communicators in several ways:

- in identifying markets when writing advertising scripts for radio and television
- for deciding on marketing strategies for ethnically related products like cosmetics, music, videos, food, sports events
- for deciding how to design forms and applications, especially for government documents that concern recent immigrants
- in trying to determine ethnic and cultural market trends

Figure 4.5 Audience Research Using Secondary Sources and Databases

TYPE OF RESEARCH	OCCASION	TARGET AUDIENCE	RESULTS
Demographic: U.S. Census Bureau	Advertising for Nestlé's Taster's Choice coffee	Singles, who make up 39% of the 183.6 million U.S. adult population	The now famous romance between single neighbors in a TV commercial sets trend for industry advertising to singles
Demographic: U.S. Census Bureau	Product design and subsequent marketing for Black and Decker power tools	Working women and single mothers, whose numbers have increased significantly in the 1990s	New line of lightweight power tools with smaller hand grips; mainstream advertising
Daytime demographic: U.S. Census Bureau's ZIP Business Patterns	Choosing site location for Kenny Rogers' Roasters, a restaurant franchise, in Chicago	Corporate office park employees	Thriving restaurant using radio spots and billboards to advertise to commuters on their way to work
Demographic and geographic data	Advertising Kay-Bee Toys	Families living within a 10-minute drive of a Kay-Bee store and having children aged 4–14	*Goodtimes* magazine with feature stories and advertising that cuts through the ad clutter of mainstream media
Purchasing behavior: charge account records	Christmas catalog for Bloomingdales	Customers who have recently bought a men's suit	An additional postcard enclosed advertising a sale on men's shirts and accessories
Purchasing behavior: charge account records	Recruiting for Gallaudet University, a school for the hearing-impaired in Washington, D.C.	Customers who recently purchased hearing aids	A mailing list that only cost $520 that got the institution directly in touch with potential students and supporters

ETHICS

ETHICAL ISSUES IN USING MAILING LISTS

In *The Naked Consumer*, Erik Larson details many of the ethical issues that arise in the collection and use of mailing lists. He also provides examples of how these lists have been used improperly and unethically. For example, Larson details how mass mailings of advertisements can actually lead to discrimination. Some companies compile mailing lists based on ethnicity as determined by people's names and addresses. Companies can then send offers to people of selected ethnic groups and exclude members of other groups. In addition, companies often practice financial discrimination, sending offers for certain goods and services only to those people thought most likely to spend the most money on them.

Poorly controlled mass mailings can also cause distress. Mass mailings of "psychoactive" junk mail prey upon the psychological or physical problems of particular people. Companies may target for promotional material the elderly, people who are overweight, and the relatives of people who have died, who may feel pressured into buying goods or services they might otherwise have ignored. Mailings can also unintentionally hurt recipients, as in the case of parents who have recently lost a child but who continue to receive advertisements for diapers or toys.

Mass mailings can also be deceptive. Some businesses now attempt to disguise their mass mailings as something else. Mailings arrive in envelopes designed to look like they're from the IRS or other government agencies. Mailings appear as personal letters from friends or associates. For example, one advertising campaign targeted at the elderly used stick-on note paper with apparently handwritten notes to promote products. Many recipients mistook the notes, which were signed only with an initial, to be messages from friends or relatives recommending the product.

The extent to which mass mailings are used, the manner in which names are gathered and distributed, and the design of the mailings themselves can determine whether the advertisements benefit or damage the consumers to whom they are addressed. Mass mailings may indeed decrease the costs of goods and services by allowing businesses to reach the customers most likely to buy. Unfortunately, they can also hurt those same customers by encouraging them to buy products they don't need or can't afford, or by excluding them from an opportunity to investigate products that they actually need.

Data-based audience research can draw from a range of sources, including the U.S. Census, credit card purchasing records, lists of license plate numbers in a store parking lot, hospital admission records, mailing lists of catalog customers, Department of Transportation maps noting travel and traffic patterns, and so forth.

Value-based research, which uses personal interviews and surveys to determine values and lifestyle preferences, has become increasingly important to business communication strategy. Figure 4.6 shows how such research has been used in marketing company products.

Even if you are not in marketing, knowing data-based and value-based facets of your audience is important. Knowing the facts that reveal a reader's educational background, for example, may tell you whether your audience has a practical understanding of a subject,

Figure 4.6 Audience Research Using Personal Interviews and Surveys

TYPE OF RESEARCH	OCCASION	TARGET AUDIENCE	RESULTS
Value Structuring (VALS)—personal interviews	Advertising for three home health care products by Timex: a blood pressure monitor, a digital electronic scale, and a thermometer	"Boomers" at high end of market valuing health products	A print campaign that featured an "upscale-looking" couple who had just walked off the tennis court
Value Structuring (VALS)—personal interviews	Advertising for Stolichnaya vodka	Consumers who were discovered to value individuality, authenticity, and quality	A print ad showing an ice-cold bottle of Stolichnaya as the center of its own universe
Lifestyle analysis	Advertising for Domino's Pizza	Consumers who were discovered to have a particular "media psyche" that included watching Sunday TV football games	A TV spot about midway through the second quarter of the televised football game promising a pizza at the door in 30 minutes
Combination of demographic, geographic, and lifestyle analysis (MarketMetrics software)	Advertising for Kraft Velveeta Shells dinners at a large East Coast chain	Consumers who had certain incomes, lived within a certain radius of the store, and had certain lifestyles	Changed the flavors of the dinners available at each store according to database information; sales jumped 23%

TECHNOLOGY

COMMUNICATING TO *LARGE* AUDIENCES

Computers have made it much easier for firms to market their products to various audiences. In the past, firms needed help in fitting any raw data they had (on income, race, education level, geographic location, etc.) to the needs of the particular marketing scheme they were employing. Because the fees charged by the companies that tailored the data were so enormous, only marketing departments at big firms could afford to pay for this service. But today, even companies with very modest budgets can afford to analyze and even map their marketing areas in house. Sophisticated databases and mapping programs can now run on any IBM or Macintosh equipped with a CD-ROM drive.

In addition, the new demographic systems can handle more data and focus it more accurately than traditional methods. Many of these new systems use the U.S. Census as their database. Now, for $2,000, companies can take this census data and use it to get a more focused and accurate demographic analysis than $50,000 would have gotten them before. (Previously, the data could be narrowed only to a "census tract." Now, firms can refine data themselves to focus on a single city block.)

Once the data has been focused, many of these new demographic systems can work in conjunction with either internal or external mapping software to produce region maps and travel routes for salespeople. In the future, demographic software will be linked to the information superhighway, allowing companies to get the latest possible regional information almost instantaneously.

such as that of a high school-educated factory worker who uses a CAM (computer-aided mechanical) system at work, or a theoretical understanding, such as that possessed by an engineer who designs such systems. Audience background tells you whether a sales letter promoting office furniture should emphasize practical details, such as the five-point base of the typist chair, or should emphasize more abstract concerns, such as the ergonomics of a chair's design.

Facts about education also suggest how well the audience will be able to handle difficult, abstract material. In general, the more educated or skilled the reader, the more abstract the writer can be. However, the *type* of education a reader has also plays a role. For instance, a person with an M.A. in theoretical linguistics may be more excited by abstract information concerning speech development in children than an M.S.W. (Masters of Social Work), who would be interested in concrete casework and a child's "failure to thrive" as indicated by poor language skills—even though both readers have degrees at a similar "master's" level.

If you know the educational and professional background of your audience, you can make a good guess about their expertise. Both education and experience play a role in whether the reader can be considered expert or nonexpert in the issue you're addressing. For example, a chief executive officer (CEO) of a manufacturing firm who reads a proposal about adopting certain accounting software may be an expert on the company's marketing needs, but a nonexpert on accounting and on the system requirements for the software itself. An accountant for the same firm might be an expert on the accounting functions the software should handle, but might be a nonexpert regarding company long-term plans for budgetary investment.

Your knowledge of a reader's values and beliefs is also important to communicating in business. Your reader, for example, might be highly interested in knowing about additional health benefits but might be bored by the prospect of reading a detailed budget narrative. Knowing audience attitudes helps you tell whether the reader will resist or cooperate with your message.

Of course, you can work to develop certain audience attitudes. For example, Northwest Airlines, an employee-owned company, has a program called COMPASS (Company Ownership Motivates People to Achieve Success and Savings), geared toward developing a participatory attitude among its employees. COMPASS is supported in company communications, such as a brochure describing how to look for and submit ideas "to build a new, stronger Northwest that captures the spirit of innovation by encouraging the free expression of ideas, ensuring prompt action and recognizing the value of all employee contributions." The brochure is supplemented by an idea form that can be folded to fit into an employee's pocket, available for immediate use when an idea occurs (Figures 4.7 and 4.8, page 106). "Winning ideas" are reported in *Passages*, the newspaper published by Northwest and sent to all employees. Northwest's COMPASS program demonstrates how communication can cultivate a particular attitude in an audience or "public," a group with common characteristics or a shared bond.

Company
Ownership
Motivates
People to
Achieve
Success &
Savings

NORTHWEST
COMPASS
IDEA SYSTEM

Office Vision for COMPASS Idea System is: IDEAHUB

— Frequently Called Numbers —

1-612-727-7752	COMPASS Idea System
1-800-424-4692	Employee Assistance Program
1-800-NWA-BENS	Employee Benefits
1-612-726-3774	Employee Benefits (MSP)
1-800-NWA-CASH	NWA Federal Credit Union
1-800-NWA-NREV	Reservations - Non-Rev
1-612-726-NREV	Reservations - Non-Rev (MSP)
1-800-457-8667	Newsline (Use on-line if possible)
1-612-727-9600	Newsline (MSP)

FORM NO. 4728 4/94

NORTHWEST
COMPASS
IDEA SYSTEM

IDEA FORM

STOP BEFORE YOU FILL OUT THIS FORM . . . HAVE YOU TRIED ENTERING YOUR IDEA VIA THE EMPLOYEE ACCESS SYSTEM (EAS)? IF NOT, SEE EASY TO FOLLOW INSTRUCTIONS INSIDE.

Idea Subject:

Employee Number:

State the situation as you see it:

Figure 4.7 Northwest Idea Form, Side 1 (Folds in Fourths, So Upper Left Is the Cover)

State your solution/course of action:

1. After completion of this form, please submit it to your department for processing through the Employee Access System (EAS).
2. To track your idea you will need to access the automated system (see instructions on the following page).
3. When submitting ideas in the future, please try using the automated system. ***It's easy... It's fun... It's paperless!***

The information provided is your contribution to Northwest Airlines, Inc., and the exclusive rights to this information are maintained by Northwest Airlines, Inc.

How To Submit An Idea By Computer

You can submit your idea through the Employee Access System (EAS), the same way you check into job openings, pass travel and phone information.

1. Type: **SI:IBM ACCESS** if you're using a Westinghouse 1642 or 840 Terminal
2. Type: **ACCESS** if your screen reads: "XXXXXXXX IS AVAILABLE FOR LOGON"
3. Press the **TRANSMIT, ENTER** or **RETURN** key
4. Follow the INSTRUCTIONS on the SCREEN

ALWAYS READ THE HELPFUL MESSAGES AT THE BOTTOM OF THE SCREEN.
If you need further assistance, call the Help Desk at x6-6955 (1-800-328-2283).

A Good Idea . . .

Offers a solution .... focuses on a problem or opportunity within the employee's department that reduces costs, increases revenue, improves customer service, improves processes, increases safety, etc.

Is clear and detailed ...... enables the evaluator to take action.

Is capable of producing definite benefits .... specific and measurable results.

Figure 4.8 Northwest Idea Form, Side 2

Factors Tied to the Writer-Reader Relationship

You should consider three interrelated factors that define the **writer-reader relationship** when planning a communication:

- relative status
- distance
- interpersonal relations

The **relative status** between the writer and reader depends on job duties, rank, and personal credibility. John Bellencamp as a Division Director may, for example, outrank Barb King as a Developmental Editor in the company hierarchy, but Barb may overrule any of John's decisions concerning Wright's manuscript. Despite his rank, Bellencamp may never regain his credibility in Wright's eyes. Knowing the status of your reader in a particular communication situation helps you make a range of decisions, from who your primary reader should be to how the document should be organized and worded.

The emotional or physical distance between you and your reader will also affect your document planning. You may feel close to the CEO because you have a good working relationship, while you may feel distanced from a colleague with whom you have trouble collaborating. You may form close relationships with peers based on your work together on a number of on-site projects and write friendly memos as a result. Despite the marvels of modern technology, you might find your relationships less rewarding with those you know only via e-mail and fax. The distance you feel with such colleagues will probably lead you to be more formal in your correspondence.

It probably goes without saying that interpersonal relationships also affect how you communicate. If you don't like your reader, your message will either reflect your dislike or compensate for it in some obvious ways. A decidedly formal tone or exceedingly polite approach between colleagues, for example, can be a good indication of dislike.

Factors Tied to the Message

The message itself affects your planning for audience in terms of

- the nature of the information needed by the reader
- the conventions that can be appropriately drawn upon in the message and understood by the reader

Readers need particular *information* depending on their expertise or company role. When evaluating your reader's expertise, you need to consider both the reader's acquaintance with the subject and the situation. For example, you might want a colleague to read and provide feedback for a proposal that you have written—a request for new office equipment, your third in five years. Your colleague might be an expert on equipment specifications but not know anything about the political climate surrounding the proposal. You would, therefore, be wise to get a second opinion from a reader who knows company politics. Readers' different expertise would be a factor in a large number of writing choices, ranging from what definitions to provide to what specific detail should be included.

The reader's position within the company is also important. A CEO might be interested in a holistic assessment of the situation whereas the construction manager might need to focus on project specifications. In a different sense, a project manager might need only a brief list of the materials involved in a project, while a subcontractor might need an exact description of the finish on the brick and the color of the mortar.

As you plan your message, you also should consider the *appropriateness of the conventions* you will be using. (Chapter 6 discusses conventions in detail.) Wright, for example, goes against convention by lodging her complaint against Bellencamp within a letter of inquiry to her editor, but correctly uses convention when she places that complaint in the second-to-last paragraph. She feels free to adapt or adopt writing conventions because she is confident of her reader's knowledge and response, as well as her warm personal relationship with her developmental editor.

Factors Tied to the Occasion

You have a number of occasion-based factors to consider when planning your documents for a particular audience, including the type(s) of readers you are addressing and the reader's stance, whether resistant or cooperative, toward the subject of your message.

Audiences can be placed in different categories depending on the occasion. Figure 4.9 (page 108) suggests that a major difference between types of readers is how they are expected to *act upon* the contents of a document.

Figure 4.9 Types of Audiences in a Particular Occasion for Communicating

TYPE OF AUDIENCE	DEFINITION/EXAMPLE
Initial audience	Those people, such as an immediate supervisor, to whom a document is first directed and who, in a hierarchical corporation, pass the document on to the primary readers. *Example:* An administrative assistant who might pass a report on New York production problems on to Bellencamp.
Primary audience	Those people directly addressed by the communicator and expected to act upon the information. *Example:* Bellencamp's "Special People," the authors, are expected to act by improving their compliance with deadlines and schedules. Barb, as the primary reader of Wright's letter, must somehow respond to Wright's complaint about Bellencamp. Wright, as the primary reader of Barb's memo, is expected to act according to the numbered guidelines regarding the proofs.
Secondary audiences	People who have an interest in the communication and sometimes act on its contents. *Example:* Barb is an unwilling secondary reader of Bellencamp's memo. Although she is not addressed in the memo, she is interested in and affected by what the memo has to say. She is interested in the memo because she, like Bellencamp, needs her authors to follow production schedules. She is also affected by the memo because she must now smooth the ruffled feathers of the authors under her wing.
Other audiences	People who are outside the immediate occasion but still retain an interest in the communication or in any decisions based on it. *Example:* In the Bellencamp situation, the employees of the New York office who want the schedule problem solved might be in this category. Wright, as an author in good standing, should have been such a reader of Bellencamp's memo as well.

In addition to knowing the type(s) of audiences you are addressing, knowing a reader's or listener's **stance** toward your information is helpful: will the audience resist or cooperate with the message? The reader's stance tells you whether to present your recommendation to buy new computers up front or to save the recommendation until later. It tells you whether you are writing a message that should use good news or bad news conventions (see Chapter 6).

Formal presentations assume psychological distance between the speaker and the primary audience, which is generally expected to have a cooperative stance towards the message.

UNDERSTANDING HOW AUDIENCE ANALYSIS AFFECTS WRITING STRATEGIES

Your analysis of your audience directly affects document planning. The examples in Figures 4.10 to 4.13 are constructed with different audiences in mind, but address the same topic: the touchpad on a particular computer keyboard. The different audiences dictate a number of differences in the excerpts:

- how the reader is identified or acknowledged
- what assumptions or predictions the writer can make about the reader's knowledge and interests
- what details the writer chooses to include or exclude
- what factors, among those details included, the writer chooses to emphasize
- how the writer chooses to present those details (in words, pictures, graphs)
- what **diction** (wording) the writer selects

The annotations of Figures 4.10 through 4.13 should help you to spot these differences. The audience for the first excerpt is any general user reading about the product; for the second excerpt, a sales associate; for the third, an "educated nonexpert," who would read information about such systems in a published account such as a *Business Week* article; and for the fourth, an engineer/user. The touchpad discussed in each of these excerpts is a rectangular pad on the computer keyboard that works like a mouse.

Figure 4.10, addressed to a general user, includes even the most elemental detail (that the small blinking spot on the screen is the cursor). It also includes a figure that pictures not only the keyboard, but the entire system as well, so the reader is properly oriented. Because the reader could have any level of expertise, the writer assumes very little about the reader's knowledge and background.

Assumptions change with a different audience. Figure 4.11 addresses sales personnel and uses nontechnical vocabulary, describing cursor movement in the most common of terms: sliding or jumping. The writer also provides an illustration to help the reader understand the product. The writer emphasizes appropriate details by mentioning sales factors: the faster and easier operation. The language is even "salesy," representing a shift in tone from the previous example.

Figure 4.12 (page 110) differs from the previous figures, not so much because of the reader's level of expertise as the reader's reason for being interested in the subject. As a nonexpert (and in this case, a nonuser), the reader is interested in the touchpad as a technological advance rather than as a piece of equipment for immediate use. The descriptive details reflect this broader context. The touchpad is described as one of many additions to a CRT keyboard. The use of the touchpad, pictured in the figure, is representative. Other uses are possible.

In Figure 4.13 (page 110), the writer is able to assume both the engineer/user's familiarity with certain semitechnical terms and the user's ability to act without detailed instructions. The writer is also confident that the reader understands applications such as the benefits of having a time delay and doesn't need them explained in detail.

Figure 4.10 Excerpt Describing the Product from a Manual Addressed to General Users

The writer provides a figure that shows the whole system, not just the keyboard, as the context. The writer compares the arrow keys ("old" technology) and the touchpad (new technology). The writer uses the caption to reinforce the location and description of keys and touchpad. The writer describes details of touchpad operation. The writer connects procedures for operation and the movement of the cursor.

The <u>touchpad</u>, the rectangular framed area located on the right side of the keyboard of your Apollo DN300 desktop system (see fig. 1), is used to move the cursor (the small blinking spot on the screen which shows where you are on the screen's "page").

Although you can also move the cursor with the arrow keys ←|→, which are found near the bottom of the group of keys to the left side of the keyboard (also see fig. 1), the touchpad is a time-saver. Whereas the arrow keys will only move the cursor in a straight line, the touchpad allows you to move the cursor directly from one point on the screen to any other point.

The touchpad is operated by sliding a pointed object (finger, pen cap) along the surface or by touching any point on the pad surface. The cursor slides or jumps on the screen in a motion that corresponds to the movement of the pointer.

Apollo DN 300 desktop system. The arrow keys are located in the group of dark-colored keys to the left of the keyboard; the <u>touchpad</u> is the dark rectangular area on the right side of the keyboard.

Figure 4.11 Excerpt from a Memo with a Product Description for Sales Personnel

The writer acknowledges the reader's identity as someone in sales with the phrase "your customer," and then emphasizes the selling points (helpful, fast, accurate) and provides the exact product name/number.

The writer provides explanation of what the arrow keys are and a figure that shows the touchpad.

Your customer will find the touchpad portion of the keyboard a real help for fast, accurate design. The arrow keys ←|→ can move the cursor, but these keys allow only straight-line movement. With the touchpad (see fig. 1), the user can immediately reach any point on the screen, either by sliding or "jumping" to the desired point.

The design process is faster and easier with the touchpad feature of the Mentor Graphics IDEA 1000 Computer-Aided Engineering Workstation.

The <u>touchpad</u> is the dark square area to the right of the keyboard.

Figure 4.12 Excerpt from an Article Describing the Product to Educated Nonexperts

The writer identifies the reader as someone interested in CRT keyboards.

The writer provides a description to fulfill the expectation of defining terms in a description.

The writer acknowledges the reader's education when describing how the touchpad works.

The figure enables the reader to visualize a particular application of the function.

One of the more interesting additions to the CRT keyboard appears on the Apollo DOMAIN systems. Computer users are familiar with cursor movement by arrow or function keys, which move the cursor in a straight line, up/down, left/right.

The touchpad, however, as the name implies, operates by the touch from a pointer—a pen cap, even a finger (see fig. 1).

The touchpad moves the cursor immediately to any point on the screen by a sliding action or with a jump, exactly corresponding to the movement of the pointer on the pad. This makes any sort of screen work considerably faster and easier for the user.

Touchpad in use on a Mentor Graphics Apollo-based Computer Aided Engineering Workstation.

Figure 4.13 Excerpt from a Product Description in a Booklet Addressed to an Engineer/User

The writer recognizes the reader's knowledge by using a term such as "pixel."

The writer assumes the readers will be able to enter the command without instruction.

The writer depends on the engineer to recognize the use of a time delay.

Touchpad. The touchpad, on the right side of the keyboard, moves the cursor directly from pixel location to pixel location on the screen. Use of the touchpad facilitates design work, as it allows the user quick access to any point on the screen. The touchpad functions in three modes, activated by the command TPM (Touch_Pad_Mode):

- *absolute*—the cursor moves exactly as the pointer (finger or pen cap) moves on the touchpad (use TPM-a)
- *relative*—the cursor moves as it would with a roller ball, relative to the movement of the pointer (TPM-r)
- *absolute/relative*—operates as relative does but with a time delay (TPM-ar)

Caution: Touching the pad while running diagnostics or utilities will cause the program to abort.

In these examples, note the correlation between the type of document (manual, memo, article, booklet) and type of reader. Different types of documents (**genres**) have different functions. A user's manual functions differently from a magazine article. Readers, for example, use a manual to find out how to operate hardware and use an article to discover the latest trends in computer technology. Adapting to your audience involves considering the appropriateness of the genre (type of communication) you select.

YOU-ATTITUDE

You-attitude, a convention for addressing audiences in business communication, influences how you plan to word your message and to approach your topic. You-attitude involves being both polite and cooperative. Several writing strategies are associated with this concept:

- specialized pronoun use
- preference for positive wording
- emphasis on reader benefit

Pronoun Use

In focusing on the reader, you-attitude features the use of the pronoun "you" whenever appropriate. Figure 4.14 demonstrates how sentences can be revised to include "you."

There are exceptions to the liberal use of "you." These include (1) certain types of documents, including application letters and formal reports, (2) any occasion for writing that contains negative information, and (3) various commonsense stylistic constraints.

Application letters demonstrate "you" attitude by emphasizing reader benefit (discussed shortly) rather than the pronoun "you." For example, instead of stating that "you will be getting a good employee if you hire me," a sentence would emphasize those qualifications that the company most wants to see in an applicant. An applicant for a construction engineering position might say, "My past experience in construction includes a position at the

Figure 4.14 Sentences Revised for "You"

INITIAL	REVISED
The tool, with a curved blade at one end and a sharp point at the other, was designed for scraping old paint from round surfaces.	You can use this tool to scrape off paint from round surfaces, such as chair legs.
To process claim #2045 for a complete replacement of toaster model A890, we need both a dated sales receipt and a copy of the invoice.	You can assist us in processing your claim for a new toaster by providing a dated sales receipt and a copy of your invoice.
We are offering a discount of 25% on all orders received by October 1.	Take advantage of our 25% discount by ordering before October 1. [This sentence has an "implied you."]
The order will be processed within 60 days.	You should receive your Magnifique stemware in time for the Christmas holidays. [This assumes that December 25 will occur within 60 days.]
Argus, Inc., is pleased to announce its new spring line of sports clothing for women.	Celebrate Spring by stopping by Argus, Inc., where you will discover a new line of sportswear that has been designed especially for you. [This sentence has both an "implied you" and an explicit you.]

State Department of Transportation (DOT). As a transportation aide, I inspected various types of road construction, ensuring that the contractors followed DOT specifications. Correct asphalt temperature and aggregate size, amount of asphalt used, and correct slope of the new grade were some of the components I had inspected." Such a discussion omits "you."

Some *formal reports* do not use "you," since they are frequently written in third person. For example, the following sentence from a report omits personal pronouns altogether when referring to the writers (Comp-U-Safe) and the readers (Hahne Accounting): "In this report, Comp-U-Safe reviews the present situation for terminal operators at Hahne Accounting and offers suggestions and solutions to create an ergonomic environment. The goal shared by Comp-U-Safe, Hahne Accounting, and terminal operators is increased safety and productivity in the workplace."

Negative messages avoid using "you" because it sounds accusatory: "You owe us $250 for your surgery" sounds accusatory whereas "The $250 fee for minor elective plastic surgery is the patient's responsibility" sounds merely like a statement of fact. And "you" is not used in *stylistic* situations where it causes awkward syntax (sentence structure) or where it makes for a repetitious or comic effect. The sentence "As you know, you can count on your cable company for all your programming needs" probably overuses "you" and overstates the case at the same time.

Figure 4.15 shows one situation where using the pronoun "you" is probably not the best approach. The excerpt is taken from the rough draft of a background section of a proposal to revise accounting procedures at an expanding business. The use of "you" is inappropriate in Figure 4.15 for at least two reasons: (1) proposals, like many reports, are usually

Figure 4.15 Excerpt Using "You" in an Inappropriate Situation

A sense of accusation is caused by the use of you. The message becomes "you are to blame for the current mess."

The last sentence seems to add insult to injury: "Even your use of new technology hasn't helped."

Your company books for the past six months have been examined and have shown that your Accounts Payable procedures remain inconsistent, and that you are currently running six-weeks behind in your Accounts Receivable records, which started with a three-week backlog at the outset of the period. Your procedures are outdated, causing the current inefficiencies and shortfall.

You established your Accounts Payable procedures in 1980 when you only had two accountants on staff. The small size of the staff allowed for a lot of the procedures to be simply "understood" rather than codified. Since 1980, your accounting staff has increased in size by an average of 40% per year, with the greatest growth being experienced in the last two years when you hired four additional accountants. Even so, the workload in your Accounting Department has been heavy and your employees have not had time to codify and record procedures, integrating old understandings with new practices. Also, their use of computer accounting packages has nothing to insure regularized procedures.

Figure 4.16 Avoiding You-attitude in Negotiating Blame in a Background Section of a Proposal

The writer begins by overviewing the current situation.

The writer hastens to avoid placing blame for the situation on employees and explains why current procedures were acceptable at one time, implying that growth has been the primary factor in creating the current situation.

An examination of company books for the past six months reveals that Accounts Payable procedures remain inconsistent, and that Accounts Receivable records, which started with a three-week backlog at the outset of the period, are currently running six weeks behind. Neither the nature of the procedures nor the increased backlog, however, is attributable to current staff or management.

Accounts Payable procedures were established in 1980 when only two accountants were on staff. The small size of the staff allowed for a lot of the procedures to be simply "understood" rather than codified. Since 1980, the accounting staff increased in size by an average of 40% per year, with the greatest growth being experienced in the last two years when four additional accountants were hired. Even so, the workload in Accounting has been heavy and there has been precious little time to codify and record procedures, integrating old understandings with new practices. Also, subsequent use of computer accounting packages has done nothing to insure regularized procedures.

written in third person, and (2) this background section is dealing with negative information (problems with the current accounting system), and using "you" here sounds accusatory.

In the revision of this section of the proposal draft (Figure 4.16), the writer uses third person and tries to avoid assigning blame, while still establishing that there is a problem. The writer uses a historical approach to indicate that the current problem has arisen from the company's extensive growth and not from employee incompetence or inadequacies in company policy.

Positive Wording

You-attitude recommends using a positive approach when at all possible. Figure 4.17 illustrates how phrasing can be revised to emphasize the positive.

Although positive wording is characteristic of business discourse, this does not mean that negative elements are disguised or misrepresented in an effort to be positive. Instead, business writing has a number of conventions for conveying negative information in a positive, courteous, and ethical manner (see Chapter 9).

Figure 4.17 Revisions for Positive Wording

ORIGINAL	REVISION
We can't send you your order now because we won't have the items in stock until March 1.	Although items #6979 and #7000 are temporarily out-of-stock, you can expect to receive them by March 5.
Due to the numerous problems with your proposal, we have decided to reject it. It didn't measure up to the rest of the proposals that we received.	The proposals we received for the Court Avenue project were without a doubt among the most creative we've seen. We have informed the finalists of their oral presentation dates. Thank you for being a part of this competitive field. [The letter does not set a date for the reader.]
You must have ignored the fabric care instructions attached in plain sight to the neckline facing.	As noted on the fabric care label, dry cleaning is recommended for this garment.
Your merchandise is obviously shoddy and defective.	Ninety percent of the July 10th shipment had broken or missing parts.

Reader Benefit

Reader benefit emphasizes what the reader will gain in a particular situation. This emphasis can be concrete, as in the statement "You will save 40% if you act now," or abstract, as demonstrated by the situation in Figures 4.18 through 4.20.

The "Six C's of Women's Giving" in Figure 4.18 actually articulate six abstract benefits readers receive when they donate money to the campaign: the donor's ability to expedite change, to foster creativity, to form commitments, to become involved, to gain control through collaboration, and to make a difference. The brochure includes additional abstract benefits on its other panels. In Figure 4.19 (page 114), the panel suggests that donors, in giving, share in certain admirable characteristics of women philanthropists nationwide.

Figure 4.18 Brochure Panels Emphasizing Abstract Reader Benefit

Motivations and Rewards
(The Six C's of Women's Giving)

Change Women give to expedite change, rather than to preserve the status quo.

"I really want to see social change. I want to see the systems change with my money."

Creation Women donors enjoy setting a creative process in motion with their gifts and watching it unfold.

"I don't have children, so that in philanthropy I'm looking for a way to give something to the future the way parents give through their children."

Connection Giving may be just the beginning of a woman donor's relationship with her institution or cause, followed by increasing commitment to serve and give.

"(A gift) is like a child, and you have a lifelong commitment and responsibilities to that child."

Commitment to Volunteerism For many women, volunteer work precedes a financial gift.

"I've been involved with the Girl Scouts for a long time. I've given time but never money and we're always trying to figure out how to raise money. . ."

Collaboration Women generally work very effectively with others to solve problems.

"It feels better giving with other women, because we have control of where the money goes."

Celebration Giving should be fun, with creative giving opportunities and celebrations.

"Giving money is fun when you can make things happen with it."

Women truly want to change the world and make it a better place. Their giving reflects a duty to give back and a concern for others.

"The end result is that I was there and I was involved, and I made a difference."

CONTEXT

Kay Kirkman, Director of Development at Iowa State University, sent three mailings to a total of 10,000 women to promote a "Plaza of Heroines" campaign, which solicits funds to build a courtyard for a renovated campus building. Figure 4.18 shows the second of the three mailings with information about women philanthropists designed to show reader benefit. One-third of the 10,000 women received a starter brochure giving information about the campaign; one-third, this brochure about the national network of women philanthropists; and one third, a brochure that combined characteristics of the first two mailings.

Finally, this brochure appeals to the abstract benefit of membership in an avant-garde group (Figure 4.20, page 115). Through its appeals to abstract benefits, the brochure develops the sense that philanthropy itself is an expression of a woman's independence and leadership.

The effectiveness of the women philanthropists brochure's benefits strategy is seen in the response (Figure 4.21, page 115). At this point, it seems important to mention that an 11% return on such a mailing is considered quite good. The 11% was attained even with a high percentage (20%) of incorrect addresses. More important, the figures indicate that the mailing with the brochure on women philanthropists, which emphasized reader benefit, netted both the most donors and the most money.

READER USE

Reader use is a concept that assumes that documents will be used by readers in some way. If you, as a reader, receive a memo concerning a meeting, you use that notice to discover when and where the meeting will be held. You also use the memo to know who has called the meeting and perhaps who has been asked to attend. If the memo includes an agenda, you use it to understand what the meeting is about and decide if you want to attend.

Writers make planning decisions based on anticipated reader use. To anticipate use, you need a mental picture of your reader. After you form a mental picture of your reader, you can make a number of decisions:

- what order to use in presenting information
- what informational detail to include and exclude
- what design and format to select

Figure 4.19 Brochure Panel Suggesting Abstract Benefits Involving Character

One additional abstract benefit is personal satisfaction. (The donor thus is characterized as one who derives satisfaction from "giving back to society.")

The benefit is dramatized through a direct comment.

Another additional abstract benefit is the ability to work toward a common goal. (The donor is thus characterized as someone who sees the larger picture and works toward the common good.)

The benefit is again dramatized through a direct comment.

THE NATIONAL NETWORK ON WOMEN AS PHILANTHROPISTS

Extensive personal interviews, focus groups, and discussions with more than 100 women philanthropists throughout the United States have been conducted by the National Network on Women as Philanthropists, based in Madison, Wisconsin. Here are a few characteristics of women as donors that have emerged from their research, along with comments from the women philanthropists themselves:

- Female donors derive satisfaction from the opportunity to give back to society. They want to help provide others with the opportunities they have had.

"To me it also means giving back to this world and really giving from my heart. Giving to what is meaningful that reflects my values."

- Women donors understand that they need not be extremely wealthy to be philanthropists. They are aware of the power of combining forces and money for a common goal.

"The idea that you don't have to be a member of a family with a great fortune to be a philanthropist has a particular appeal, because it makes you think about the strength of numbers that may be able to accomplish something, and that you, as an individual of more limited means, can have an impact on the larger issues."

Organizational Sequencing

A writer draws on various conventions when organizing a document. Reader use affects the choice of such conventions. For example, if readers are using your document to learn your opinion, then you arrange your material **deductively**, placing the main point at the beginning. However, if readers are using your document to discover how you came to adopt a particular position, then you arrange the material **inductively:** the main point appears after you have presented the information that supports your position.

Just as reader use can help you decide how to structure messages overall, it can aid you in sequencing information *within* sections of a document. For example, when writing instructions and procedures, you want to sequence the steps the reader is to follow in the order in which the reader is to act. Figure 4.22 (page 116), an excerpt from an internal grievance procedure concerning employee performance reviews, describes the steps *in order* for amending a performance review.

Reader use also helps you take into account what the reader is actually going to be doing in response to a document. If you were writing a request for information on a product, you would group all questions about cost together instead of scattering them throughout the message. Such grouping anticipates that the reader will find it easier to research everything to do with cost in a single procedure, rather than having to go back to sources about financial information two or three times to address two or three different issues.

Figure 4.20 Brochure Panel Appealing to the Abstract Benefit of Select Group Membership

Donors are credited with being activists, rather than with simply having money to give away, as the "Lady Bountiful" image implies.

Demographics support the idea that a woman's wealth is her own to give and control.

Demographics are also cited to support the leadership offered by women in business and industry.

Women are breaking away from the "Lady Bountiful" image and presenting a new and stronger voice in their philanthropy. In part, that's because of changing demographics:

- 60% of the wealth in the U.S. is owned by women.
- More than 40% of the Americans classified as top wealth holders are women.
- More people are now employed by women-owned businesses than by Fortune 500 companies.
- 43.6% of all executive, administrative, and managerial positions in the U.S. are held by women.

Figure 4.21 Response Rates for Different Combinations of Mailings

GROUPS	% OF DONORS	AMOUNT OF DONATION
Group Receiving Informational Brochure Alone	11%	$xxx
Group Receiving a "Combined Brochure"	+7% Increase in Donors	+16% Increase in Amount of $xxx
Group Receiving Informational Brochure Plus **Brochure on Women Philanthropists**	+11% Increase in Donors	+18% Increase in Amount of $xxx

Figure 4.23 (page 116) shows the writer grouping particular types of information together to help the reader respond. In this example, the writer's groupings involve logistics, content, and format. The writer, having requested to be registered regardless, is obviously interested in attending the seminar even though she has yet to be informed of all the

Figure 4.22 Excerpt Showing Internal Sequencing

This excerpt comes after an introductory section which explains the entire performance review process at the company and which describes the amendment procedure, establishing what is acceptable as rationale and supporting evidence. The sequence represented in steps 1–3 here, of course, reflects the sequence which employees follow.

If you wish to amend your performance review, you need to take the following steps:

1. Review the performance evaluation as a whole with your immediate supervisor.
2. Target areas of concern and discuss possible modifications. (For a listing of acceptable rationale for making modifications, consult Section 2a).
3. Upon reaching an agreement with your immediate supervisor regarding modifications, submit evidence that your supervisor could use to amend the review. (For a summary of the type of evidence you could offer to substantiate modifications, see Section 2b.)
4. If an agreement with your immediate supervisor cannot be reached, you should then make an appointment with the director of your division to discuss your situation.

Figure 4.23 Draft Showing Sequencing Based on the Reader's Task in Dealing with the Document

Opening: a single primary topic

First list: basic information regarding seminar logistics

Second list: seminar content

Penultimate paragraph: a special interest

Last paragraph: participation and response

I am writing to request information about your seminar covering the CPA exam in late October.
I would like to know about seminar logistics:

- the location for the seminar in October, as well as information about lodging arrangements
- the schedule for the October seminar

I'd also like to know if the seminar will cover information about the following topics:

- specific test dates for the CPA exam
- locations where the exam will be given in Idaho
- listing of the parts to the exam and the subject matter tested in each
- suggested review material for the exam

I am especially interested in any information you have concerning the recent changes that are being made to the format of the CPA exam.

Please add me to the list of those attending the seminar. And please send me information concerning the seminar's location and the schedule before September 15, so that I can make appropriate travel arrangements.

details. The writer clusters types of information according to the reader's task: sending information that is immediately available (seminar location and time schedule). The letter defers asking about information that might not yet be available (details about seminar content).

Detail Selection

Reader use is also important in planning what information to include or to exclude in a document. Figure 4.24 shows a writer unsuccessfully grappling with the task of appropriately selecting information.

CONTEXT

Figure 4.24 is part of a financial planning report draft. The excerpt is the writer's first attempt at writing a section establishing the client's current financial situation.

This draft fails on a number of accounts. First, it includes information that is not particular to the specific client. Correspondingly, it omits any details regarding the client's particular financial situation. Moreover, it indirectly insults the reader by implying that equities, corporate bonds, and options will necessarily confuse him. But, perhaps most important, *the reader has absolutely no use for the information.* The client, in seeking advice for financial planning, already knows that his traditional investments are generating a low return and that he needs to expand his portfolio. He already knows that he does not want to handle the portfolio himself, even if he does understand the choices available. And he already knows that he should seek advice from a financial planner and has indeed done so. Because

Figure 4.24 Draft of an Opening Paragraph of a Report

In today's economy, people are facing low interest rates and therefore are unable to earn a good return from savings accounts and certificates of deposit. For this reason, people are turning to alternative investments in order to receive a higher return. Some of these alternative investments are equities, corporate bonds, and stock options. These alternative investments are much more complex than more traditional forms of investing (savings accounts and CDs). It is their complex nature that often confuses the individual investor and leads him to seek the advice of a financial planner.

there is no way the reader can use the information, it should have been excluded from the report. Instead, the writer should have given his overall assessment of the client's financial condition, followed with specifics.

Unlike the financial planner, the writers of the concluding section to a proposal for adapting a computer system (Figure 4.25) have reader use in mind. They want the reader to use their report to select their recommended alternative. To promote this use, the writers summarize only their recommended alternative in the conclusion and then give details that will enable its adoption.

Document Design and Format Selection

The design and format of a document often facilitate reader use. Figure 4.26 demonstrates the connection between format decisions and reader use.

A revision to the brochure panel would have to include information that tells what filling out the pre-registration form will accomplish, as well as how a participant may order a different number of forms for each respective conference.

Selection of Style

Closely related to such format decisions are stylistic decisions based on reader use. For example, Figures 4.27 and 4.28 (page 118) show an initial draft of instructions to vacation resort staff about what to do during a tornado warning. Figure 4.27 is the first page of the

Figure 4.25 Conclusion Recommending an Alternative

The writers repeat their recommendation of the third alternative.

The writers repeat the important points of the third alternative.

The writers make a specific recommendation concerning a computer company and facilitate contact with an address and phone number.

CONCLUSION

F.R.N. Consultants has reviewed three possible solutions to the problems facing the *Sun Daily Journal.* We feel that the third alternative is the most efficient way for the paper to update its current computer system without interrupting production. Therefore, F.R.N. Consultants suggests the acquisition of 80 new computers, 4 new printers, and new software including Microsoft and Venture AdPro packages at a total cost of $178,000 including training costs and consultants' fees.

For the software packages, F.R.N. recommends the following vendor:

Everglades MicroProducts, Inc.
770 St. Pierre Street
Sun, FL 33152
(305) 555-4323

F.R.N. also recommends H.M. Delacroix of its own staff as an excellent consultant. Mr. Delacroix can be reached at (305) 555-9000, ext. 456.

Figure 4.26 Brochure Form Involving Reader Use

The example on the right is from an otherwise well-designed brochure. This segment, however, needs a better design to accommodate reader use.

Rather than emphasize the form's use to the reader, this segment merely tells the reader what the form does not do: register the sender for the conference. It does not specify the writer's use for the information.

The design of the form restricts the reader to ordering the same number of forms for each conference. Thus it does not account for this alternative reader use.

TAKE THE CHALLENGE

Career Conference for young women in grades 6-12.

Pre-registration Form

This is a pre-registration form. Sending this form in does not register you for the conference.

Please print neatly.

I would like ______ registration forms for the following conference:

______ Conference I (6-9)
Sat., October 9, 1994

______ Conference II (9-12)
Thurs., October 21, 1994

Name: ______________________________
Address: ______________________________
City: ______________________________
State: ____________________ Zip: __________
Phone: ______________________________
School: ______________________________

Return pre-registration form to:

Conference Pre-registration

Program for Women in Science and Engineering
210 Melbourne Hall
State University
City, State 50000

Figure 4.27 Initial Version of Emergency Instructions, Page 1

STORM EVACUATION PROCEDURES:

In the event of a T.2. CONDITION (TORNADO WARNING), and once the decision has been made to begin evacuation of all guests to safe areas of the Resort, these are the procedures. Security and the M.O.D. will assign employees to these areas of safety and make sure that any restricted areas in the lower levels are unlocked for guests and employees to access.

SPECIFIC PROCEDURES FOR EVACUATION:

1. SWITCHBOARD: After all departments have been called, Switchboard will then begin calling all townhouse units to warn them of the storm and direct them to the basements of their units.
2. FRONT DESK: These employees will be responsible for calling all hotel rooms to warn them of the storm and direct them to safety.
3. GROUNDS AND MAINTENANCE: These employees are directed to go to the other areas (beach, tennis courts, north pool, launderette, mini-golf) where calling may not be possible and verbally inform guests that there has been a warning and direct them to areas of safety. Continue to do this as long as safety permits.

Figure 4.28 Second Page of Initial Version of Instructions

PRIMARY AREAS OF SAFETY INCLUDE THE FOLLOWING:

MAIN COMPLEX:

1. D LEVEL: THE TUNNEL, AND THE EMPLOYEE AREA.
2. C LEVEL: THE QUEEN ROOM KITCHENETTE, THE FITNESS ROOM, AND SALES OFFICES.
3. B LEVEL: THE EMPLOYEE CAFETERIA.
4. WEST WING: HALLWAY OF THE 100 LEVEL.
5. EAST WING: 400 LEVEL HALLWAY, WEST OF SUNRISE COVE OFFICES.

Other areas of safety will include the Lakeshares Marketing Office basement, and the Boat House on the beach. Be aware that inner hallways and doorways away from any windows may also be utilized.

emergency instructions issued to all personnel and variously posted on bulletin boards or taped on desks. Unfortunately, the information about areas of safety was located on a second page (Figure 4.28). The writer has overlooked the fact that staff will be consulting these instructions during an emergency. In other words, staff members will want information that they can use quickly, at a glance. Reading through prose instructions takes time, even if that prose is in a list.

The revision in Figure 4.29 considers reader use. The writer changes the format (using bulleted lists to facilitate quick reading) and the style (using imperative or "command" verbs and adding specific details, most notably the precise contacts and phone numbers) to facilitate appropriate action. The writer also instructs the staff to include a location-appropriate map of the safe areas. The reformatted, one-page instructions (Figure 4.29) make it easier for readers to follow the procedures and, in so doing, to cooperate with the writer's safety plan.

READABILITY

The term **readability** has a commonsense meaning (how easy a document is to read) and a technical meaning (what score a document receives upon the application of a readability formula). Although we do touch on **readability formulas**, we focus on the broader issues that make a document that is easy to read.

Readability involves a number of factors:

- document-based features
- reader expectations and attitudes
- contextual factors

Document-Based Features

Stylistic features, such as sentence length, are frequently used as measures of readability. The Flesch Readability Index and the Gunning Fog Index are two common "readability formulas" that depend on quantitative factors: these formulas determine word length and sentence length. Computer software for these formulas is available. The assumption underpinning these measures is the shorter, the better. The formulas would show, for example, that the revised versions in Figure 4.30 are easier to read than the originals.

Figure 4.29 Revision of Emergency Instructions

T.2. CONDITION (TORNADO WARNING)

STORM EVACUATION PROCEDURES:

SECURITY

- **Unlock lower levels of hotel.**
- **Alert townhouse units** and direct occupants to the basements of their units:
  Unit I: 555-8821
  Unit II: 555-2188

SWITCHBOARD

- **Alert hotel safety contacts:**
  A-Level: Roberts, ext. 3011
  B-Level: Green, ext. 5022
  C-Level: MacCleary, ext. 9012
  West Wing: Rodriguez, ext. 7734
  East Wing: Jenson-Chartes, ext. 8226

FRONT DESK

- **Alert hotel guests** and direct to lower levels.

GROUNDS AND MAINTENANCE

- **Alert guests at** beach, tennis courts, north pool, launderette, mini-golf and direct them to areas of safety.

AREAS OF SAFETY

[Staff: Insert Map Appropriate to Location of Posting Here.]

Figure 4.30 Sentences Revised for Brevity and Shorter Words

ORIGINAL	REVISED
The preponderance of the evidence indicates that the proposal by Brinkman and Associates represents the most favorable approach.	The facts show that Brinkman and Associates' proposal is best.
The profitability of sales in the real estate industry was precipitated by an upward tendency in figures achieved by the Gross National Product.	Increased profits in real estate sales followed a rise in the GNP.
Although the question of whether or not to incorporate television advertising into the promotion package for Sportsgoods, Inc., depends on information yet to be gathered about audience demographics, the incorporation of such advertising is now being studied.	The decision to use TV advertising for Sportsgoods, Inc., rests on demographic data now being gathered about our target audience.

While readability formulas provide the ratio between word length and sentence length, they do not consider other important factors that affect whether information is accessible and understandable. The formulas don't consider the design of the document, the use of visuals, the readers' familiarity with the subject matter, and the readers' motivation to use the document.

The drawback of formulas as the sole measure of readability is evident, if you consider some strategies used to increase the connectedness (coherence) of a document. Explicit transitions, topic announcements, and keyed repetition enhance the coherence (and thus the readability) of a document. They are also strategies that add length. A readability formula would judge passages with transitions such as "for example" or "in addition to the availability of personnel" as less readable than passages excluding those phrases, even though their inclusion actually might add to the document's readability.

Readability formulas also do not consider the reader's familiarity with vocabulary. "Amortization" is not a difficult word for an accountant; "demographic trends" is not a difficult phrase for a marketing expert. But both terms would be considered difficult by such formulas. What readability formulas can do is call attention to overly verbose constructions and help keep the text simple.

Figure 4.31 Initial Letter Sent in October

The opening provides a history but says nothing about the type of response currently expected of the reader.

The second paragraph states the request, but providing a response date here buries it in the letter and makes it less accessible.

The request does not present what is wanted in a systematic fashion.

The emphasis in the close is partially on address correction and omits any specific date for responding.

Illinois State Water Survey
WATER RESOURCES BUILDING URBANA, IL
217-555-2219
October 18, 19--

Dear Water Customer:

The State Water Survey is initiating a statewide inventory of total water use, with plans for a publication during the summer of 19—. The industrial use of water in Illinois has been periodically inventoried by the State Water Survey for many years. That measure of success attained thus far in this undertaking lies principally with response we have received from you and your associates in the past.

We most earnestly request your cooperation in providing us with figures on the total amount of water pumped for your system during 19—. We need this information no later than March 1 so that it can be included in the publication. All information will be considered confidential and will be used only in developing a summary of water used by industry in Illinois.

The data desired are the total gallons pumped from a lake, reservoir, river and/or each well. Combined well pumpage is acceptable if not available per well. Please include pumpage from all sources. In addition, for the ground water systems, we would like to receive water levels and pumping rates if available. If you do not have your own raw water source, we would appreciate knowing from whom you do get your water.

For your convenience, a printed reply form and pre-addressed, stamped envelope is enclosed. Please make name or address corrections that may be appropriate. Thank you for an early reply.

Very truly yours,
James R. Kirk
Illinois Water Use Inventory

JRK/gj
Enclosures

Figure 4.32 Revised Letter Sent in December

Main question moved up front.

The use for the requested information stated in one-sentence paragraph.

Information needed put in list for easy access.

Background information placed in second-to-last paragraph: this placement indicates that the reader does not need to "take action" on this particular information.

Dates given to facilitate compliance.

Enhanced signature block provides information about writer and specific phone number.

Postscript handles information that is secondary to the main purpose of the letter.

Illinois State Water Survey
WATER RESOURCES BUILDING URBANA, IL
217-555-2219
December 29, 19--

Dear Water Customer:

How much water did your facility use in 19--?

The State Water Survey is initiating a statewide inventory of total water use, with plans for a summary report during the summer of 19--.

There is space on the printed reply form for the information we need:

- the total gallons you pump from a lake, reservoir, river, and/or each well (combined well pumpage is acceptable if figures for each well aren't available)
- water levels and pumping rates for ground water systems
- where you get your water, if you don't have your own raw water source

All information will be considered confidential and will be published only in a summary of water used by industry in Illinois.

As you probably know, the State Water Survey has periodically inventoried industrial water use in Illinois for many years. These inventories owe their success to the cooperation you've given us in the past. Your response now will help make the summer of 19— summary as complete and useful as possible.

Please fill out the enclosed reply form as early in 19— as possible and return it to us in the stamped, self-addressed envelope by February 16, earlier if you can. If we get your response by February 16, we'll be able to produce an accurate summary report.

Thank you for your help.

Very truly yours,
ILLINOIS STATE WATER SURVEY
James R. Kirk
Project Leader
Illinois Water Use Inventory
Phone: (217) 555-0328

JRK:mji

P.S. If the name or address on the reply form is no longer correct, please indicate the necessary changes so that we may bring our records up to date.

In addition to style, document design, organization, and detail selection are all document-based features contributing to readability. For example, the original and revised letters in Figures 4.31 and 4.32 suggest the range of such document-based features.

A number of changes contribute to the increased readability of the document:

- *ordering and placement of information* (moving the main question up front, and relegating certain information to the next-to-last paragraph and to a postscript)
- *format* (listing data needed)
- *inclusion of certain detail* (having a clear statement of use, unambiguous deadline dates, and a specific phone number)

Reader Expectations and Attitudes

CONTEXT

Figures 4.31 and 4.32 (page 120) show two letters sent by the Illinois Water Survey two months apart. The first letter failed to elicit a significant response, prompting the writing of the second letter, which was more successful.

Readers have certain expectations about how a document should work. These expectations can influence the document's readability. For example, Figure 4.33 shows the draft of a response to a complaint from a customer about the lack of zest in a particular hot sauce. The writer is an employee in the complaint department. The initial reader, a co-worker who was asked to review the draft and provide feedback, reveals expectations about how negative responses should work as a type of writing. These expectations surface in the reader's comments, included at the left.

Prior expectations based on business conventions (Chapter 6) influence the reader's suggestions about

- how to begin the message (use a **buffer**) and how to form the recommended buffer (use information that represents a shared understanding between writer and reader)
- how to present the information (use you-attitude with positive wording)
- how to sequence information (cover the explanation for the refusal before presenting the refusal itself)

The reader concludes that the document is "hard to read" because it does not meet these expectations.

Reader *attitudes* can also influence the readability of a document. For example, you might find a document difficult to read because it uses language that you personally consider sexist, racist, or offensive because it differs from your own set of values and beliefs. A woman might feel excluded by terms such as "chairman" or "manpower." Similarly, a member of a minority group might feel put down by certain references, as in the sentence: "Dr. Robert

Figure 4.33 Edited Draft Indicating Reader's Expectations

COMMENTS BY INITIAL READER OF DRAFT	DRAFT OF RESPONSE TO A COMPLAINT ABOUT "NOT SO HOT" HOT SAUCE
You need "you" instead of "we" here. I don't think the reader cares if we stay in business. Your enthusiasm here won't be shared by the reader, so this won't work as a buffer. Drop your refusal down so it appears after the explanation.	We appreciate your interest and your pleasure in our products. Customers like you keep us in business! It seems that, unlike you, your restaurant's patron is the exception to the rule. For this reason, we cannot grant your refund of $10.22.
Since we aren't going to grant the refund, we don't really "do everything." Omit or revise this. Ditto for all the "nots."	As you know, we try to do everything to please our customers. We were guaranteed that a "very hot" reaction would occur with the majority of the population, and we cannot be held responsible for an individual customer's individual taste buds. We do not claim to refund money, in any case. However, because we are up to a challenge, I have enclosed a voucher for $1.00 to be used with any of our products. I have also enclosed a product brochure which has the testing data I've quoted below.
This data should function as an explanation. Put it in second paragraph; refusal in third.	Before we sell a product, we test it with several trained panelists for various attributes (like "hotness"). With this product, "#10 super-white hot sauce," 100 panelists tested this product and 100 of them judged our product as "extremely hot" on a scale from 1 to 5 with 1 being not hot and 5 being extremely hot. We cannot take responsibility for the reactions of every customer, however.
But not hot in the sense of angry? I really find this letter hard to read.	If we can be of further assistance please contact us immediately. We strive to keep our customers happy and hot!

Green, a black pediatrician, and Dr. William Styles, a neurosurgeon, have been appointed to the board of directors." The fact that Dr. Green's race is mentioned and Dr. Styles's is not may insinuate that Dr. Styles was appointed on the basis of merit but Dr. Green was appointed solely on the basis of race.

Such reader alienation is addressed in guidelines that provide alternative wording. Specifically, "chairman" is easily replaced by words such as "chair" and "manpower" is usually replaceable by "personnel," "workforce," or "human resources." Guidelines such as those found in company stylesheets also offer advice concerning the inclusion and exclusion of detail. In Dr. Green's case, the reference to race is gratuitous and should be omitted.

Context-Based Aspect

Writers must also recognize the *contextual* aspect of readability. Certain corporations, for example, might use a particular format for internal memos. If this format has been used a long time and readers are thus familiar with it, they might find a differently formatted version of the same document hard to read simply because it's different. In fact, studies have shown that readers will sometimes find the familiar document easier to read even when the revised document is actually "better" in its design, organization, and style. Such studies do not suggest that businesses are mistaken in revising their long-held corporate documents; rather, they suggest the need for document testing, which helps you revise documents with your audience in mind (Communication Spotlight for Part VI, page 593).

SKILLS & STRATEGIES

AVOIDING LANGUAGE THAT IS OFFENSIVE TO YOUR AUDIENCE

Robert Hughes [*Time*, February 1992] notes that a corporation's future in today's globalized economy rests with people "who can think and act with informed grace across ethnic, cultural, and linguistic lines." You can have good linguistic manners by avoiding offensive language.

Perhaps the most obvious way to avoid language that is sexist, for example, is to use pronouns carefully. Although many find it awkward, the double pronoun *he/she, his/her* is now commonly used to achieve nonsexist language. Other options exist:

- Eliminate the pronoun. (*Example:* The independent contractor shall furnish ~~his~~ professional consulting services and advice as specified by purchase orders. Or: The investor has in fact reaped more than a dollar of deductions for each dollar invested, often moving ~~himself~~ to a lower tax bracket.)
- Make sentences plural. (*Example:* ~~Each employee completes his time sheet at the end of his shift.~~ All employees complete their time sheets at the end of their shifts.)
- Address the reader directly. (*Example*: Complete your time sheet at the end of your shift.)
- Use the educational title or "Ms." when addressing a woman, until you are told differently. (*Example:* I would like you to meet Dr. Jones, Mr. Smith and ~~Debbie Miss Mrs.~~ Dr. [if appropriate] or Ms. Johnson.)
- Use vocabulary adaptations, such as CEO or Head instead of Chairman.

You can also pay special attention to language that respects diversity. Language used in business should be inclusive rather than exclusive:

- Check the way people are labeled. (*Examples:* ~~the handicapped~~ people with disabilities; ~~AIDS victim~~ people with AIDS; ~~man~~ human)
- Research how to refer to cultural groups. Either "Black," "Afro-American," or "people of color" may be preferred by your audience. "Hispanic" encompasses members of Hispanic cultures from both Europe and Latin America, "Latino" applies only to the latter, and a term that acknowledges a person's country of origin, such as "Peruvian," might be preferred. "Native American," "American Indian," or reference to the specific nation, such as "Cherokee," might be preferred.
- Avoid referring to people as deaf or blind or crippled in business communications; use "hearing impaired" or "visually impaired" or, only if necessary, "the accountant, who uses a wheelchair."
- Be careful of other language bias: ~~sexual preference~~ sexual orientation; ~~homosexual agenda~~ homosexual goals; ~~special rights~~ civil rights.

RESPONSE SHEET

ANALYZING AN AUDIENCE

WRITER(S): AUDIENCE(S):
OCCASION FOR WRITING: DOCUMENT:
WHAT PROBLEM/ISSUE IS THE WRITER TRYING TO ADDRESS IN THIS DOCUMENT?

◆ TYPES OF READERS

Who is the primary audience for this document?

Who is the secondary audience?

Other readers?

What is significant about the education of each audience?

About the professional experience?

About attitude or disposition?

◆ DATA ABOUT TARGET AUDIENCES

What significant demographic information does the writer have about the readers?

Geographic information?

What significant information does the writer (do I) have about their purchasing behavior?

About their preferences and values?

◆ AUDIENCE AND WRITING STRATEGIES

How is the audience identified or acknowledged in the text?

What assumptions or predictions can the writer make about the reader's knowledge and interests?

What detail should the writer choose to include or exclude?

What factors, among those details included, should the writer choose to emphasize about the main subject?

How should the writer choose to present that detail (in words, pictures, graphs)?

What diction should the writer select?

RESPONSE SHEET

YOU-ATTITUDE, READER USE, AND READABILITY

WRITER(S):	AUDIENCE(S):
OCCASION FOR WRITING:	DOCUMENT:

WHAT PROBLEM/ISSUE IS THE WRITER TRYING TO ADDRESS IN THIS DOCUMENT?

◆ YOU-ATTITUDE

To what extent is you-attitude appropriate for use in this document? (Remember, application letters, formal reports, negative messages, and stylistic constraints limit the use of "you.")

How does the writer incorporate the pronoun "you" in the document?

To what extent does the writer remember to use positive wording?

How does the writer include reader benefit?

How can the writer improve in this area? (Make suggestions directly on the draft.)

◆ READER USE

What has the writer done to accommodate reader use in the text's *organization*?

Has the writer chosen inductive or deductive arrangement appropriately? Explain.

What has the writer done to accommodate reader use in the *selection of detail*? In the choice of *format*? In the choice of *style*?

How can the writer make improvements in each of these areas to accommodate reader use? (Make suggestions directly on the draft.)

◆ READABILITY

How successful is the writer in using *document-based strategies* for readability?

- More specifically, how does the format promote readability?
- The organization?
- The detail or development?
- The style?

How successful is the writer in using *reader-based strategies* to enhance readability?

- More specifically, how does the writer address the reader's expectations concerning the document?
- How does the writer account for reader attitudes?
- Does the writer have to compensate for any specific aspect tied to reader motivation? Explain.

What are some *contextual factors* that might influence the readability of this document for this audience?

How successful is the writer in accounting for these factors?

How can the writer make improvements in each of these areas influencing the readability of a document? (Make suggestions directly on the draft.)

ACTIVITIES, EXERCISES, AND ASSIGNMENTS

◆ IN-CLASS ACTIVITIES

1. Please refer to Figure 4.1 (Interoffice Memo) for the following activity.

   a. Discuss the following questions in terms of what you have learned in this chapter about you-attitude, reader use, and readability in particular.

   - What trouble spots do the annotations for Rita's coffee memo signal?
   - What other factors diminish the effectiveness of Rita's memo?
   - What information that readers might need is missing?
   - What extraneous information is given?

   b. Revise Rita's memo so that it does a better job of addressing the audience and following the principles of you-attitude, reader use, and readability covered in this chapter. Use the Response Sheets on analyzing audience and on you-attitude, reader use, and readability to help your revision.

2. Discuss how data-based and value-based factors about your audience(s) might affect your decisions as a writer. Be sure to have in mind a specific document as well as specific factors and particular audience(s). Feel free to use details from your experience. In addition, consider how your decisions as a writer might also involve ethical issues about databases (see the Ethics box, page 104).

3. Assume that you are giving a 15-minute training session/seminar to interested employees on revising company documents to increase attention to you-attitude and reader use. Because the session will be short, you plan to supplement your presentation with a one- or two-page handout that demonstrates your points and that employees can take with them after the session is over. Plan your session, complete with handouts. Be prepared to present your information to a small group of classmates.

◆ INDIVIDUAL AND GROUP EXERCISES

1. Please refer to the letter in Figure 4.34 in completing this exercise.

   a. In your own words, briefly describe the situation as you understand it in Figure 4.34. Who is the writer, who is the reader, and what is the occasion?

   b. Please comment specifically on the strategies for you-attitude (specialized pronoun use, preference for positive wording, emphasis on reader benefit) attempted in Figure 4.34.

   c. Using the Response Sheet on you-attitude, reader use, and readability, revise the letter for effectiveness.

2. Please use the information in Figure 4.35 to complete this exercise.

   a. Assume that you have three different audiences for the above information: (1) children between the ages of 6 and 12 who collect such cards, (2) the parents of these children, and (3) professional collectors. Use the Response Sheet on analyzing audiences to help you analyze each of these three audiences. Discuss how these different audiences would affect your writing about the masterprints. Specifically, indicate

   - how the reader would be identified or acknowledged in your materials
   - what assumptions or predictions you could make about the reader's knowledge and interests
   - what details you would choose to include or exclude
   - what factors, among the details included, you would choose to emphasize about the main subject
   - how you would choose to present those details (in words, pictures, graphs)
   - what diction you would select

   b. Write a promotional paragraph about the masterprint offer targeted at one of the three named audiences. Describe or construct any visuals you would include. (You may find it necessary to *add information* to that given in the exercise or

Figure 4.34 Letter Excerpt with Attempted You-attitude

I received a letter on September 1 from your collection agency requiring payment for July's CD of the month. This letter states that payment for the amount of $19.95 should be received by you prior to September 15 or appropriate action will be taken.

I agree that even big companies like you can be concerned about getting payment for a CD. I agree that you have a right to direct unpaid bills to a collection agency, and if they are not paid, legal action should be administered.

I am a preferred customer in your club and always prompt with my payments. I send a notice to you each time that I choose not to receive the CD of the month. I was unable to send in a notice for July. I was in New York during the month of July.

Unfortunately, I did not receive the CD for the month of July. Since your records indicate that it was sent to my address, I must presume that it was either lost in the mail or stolen from my mailbox. Since I did not receive the compact disc, I should not be required to pay for it.

I hope you understand our unfortunate situation that exists. Please credit my account before September 15, and I will gladly continue membership with your club. I am sorry about the missing CD, and if I ever receive it, I will be sure to return it to you as soon as possible.

Figure 4.35 Information about Trading Card Offer

A trading card company is introducing a new line of trading cards. The line features all new artwork for the premiere edition. The company would like to offer a set of three specific masterprints from the new trading card series. Each masterprint is 7″ × 12″ and highlights the special talents of the artist Sandy Beaman. The company is offering the full-color masterprints for $4.99 each plus $1.50 shipping and handling. The offer will be good for two months. The home office for the card company is in Falls Church, VA 22046. The cards feature "superhero" fantasy characters. These heroes, both male and female, are also featured in a popular Saturday morning cartoon show. Comic books produced by this same company have proven to gain in value over time. Trading cards in general also have a chance of appreciating in value over time.

delete information that you feel is inappropriate to a particular audience.)

c. Revise your paragraph to address each of the other named audiences.

d. Compare your versions with those created by other class members.

3. Please use Figure 4.36 in completing this revision task.

a. Use the Response Sheets on analyzing audience and on you-attitude, reader use and readability to analyze the writing situation for Figure 4.36 for audience-based concerns. Your audience is the management of T.R.G., Inc., a small, locally owned specialty house involved in the manufacture and sale of souvenirs in Miami, Florida. In completing this assignment, you may need to generate additional information about your readers.

b. Revise the excerpt in Figure 4.36, remembering to account for various factors influenced by audience:

- how the reader is identified or acknowledged in the document
- what assumptions or predictions you can make about the readers knowledge and interests
- what details you choose to include or exclude
- what factors, among the details included, you choose to emphasize about the main subject
- how you choose to present those details (in words, pictures, graphs)
- what diction you select

CONTEXT

The excerpt in Figure 4.36 is from a draft of a proposal to change the hiring policies at a particular restaurant chain. Mistakes in grammar and so forth are currently unmarked, but the mistakes were in the original draft and should be corrected.

Figure 4.36 Excerpt of Draft of Proposal Section in Need of Revision

Proposed Solutions and Recommendations

We will firstly concentrate on proposing new hiring policies for your company, T.R.G., Inc. The managers that do the hiring at your retail site in the center of the city need to be more assertive in finding new and competent employees. To attract the right employees to your downtown site, the managers of your downtown site needs to look around the community a lot more. You must advertise job openings in and around the area by placing help wanted ads in the local media and newspapers and T.V. You must also use Spanish-language local media and newspapers and radio stations in and around the area. As far as the hiring policy after the applicant fills out an application, the interviewing procedure, your company needs to have multiple interviews with different interviewers each time. As established in our background section, you have one interview. We recommend two separate interviews at least a week apart with the second interview being more personal so as to find out what the person expects from the job. This will allow you to find out if they fit into your company.

Seeing that people learn at different rates, you need to adopt a employee input system where the employee has input for when he or she feels comfortable working alone so they will learn correctly instead of being forced to say they are ready. Our next recommendation then is concerned with the training techniques used by both your retail and manufacturing site. The trainee should be trained by different people each time so as to get a feel of how the other employees work. As stated in the needs section of this report, quality control is an issue at the manufacturing site in the research park, and customer service needs to be better at your downtown retail site. This needs to be taken care of during training and to be a part of the training.

We recommend a new wage schedule for your company. According to our research of surrounding employment opportunities, to be competitive in the job market you must pay a starting wage of up to 20% more that minimum wage. Also, raises based on good job performance within the first year will also be needed. As shown by the graph on page three, you don't pay enough, according to data we have collected.

◆ OUT-OF-CLASS ASSIGNMENTS

1. Assume that you are setting up a tutoring service for students in a business communication course. Recent research on students in such courses has concluded that demographic as well as academic factors play a role in a student's performance:
   - As the age of the students increased, so did the grades earned.
   - Part-time students did better than full-time students.
   - Women's course performance surpassed men's at all levels.
   - Weak performance in first-year writing courses predicted a weak performance in business writing courses.
   - There was a direct correlation between a student's overall grade point average (GPA) and performance in business writing courses (a high GPA overall predicted good performance).

   Using the Response Sheet for analyzing an audience, analyze the audience likely to need tutoring in a business communication course. Write a memo describing how you would account for the characteristics of this audience in a business message. Write an open letter to these students informing them of your tutoring program.
2. From personal interviews, you have discovered that the students you were writing to about the tutoring program in the previous assignment value three main things:
   - getting a good job
   - having a convenient academic and work schedule
   - being treated with respect

   Revise your open letter so that it takes these aspects into account.
3. Research into audiences interested in the Olympic Games has discovered that
   - Olympic viewing is less segmented by age, gender, race, education, occupation, and income than either regular television or regular sports viewing.
   - The Olympics were valued as an opportunity for gathering socially and were considered worthwhile because they demonstrated "Americanness."

   Imagine that you are part of a team of consultants to a small advertising firm which has subcontracted to do some local advertising for the Olympics. Together with several other students, write a memo to this firm, using the Response Sheet on analyzing an audience as a starting point. Your memo's main purpose is to outline differences between how the Olympics should be promoted and how regular sports events should be promoted. Be sure to include some of the research information cited above as context in an introductory background paragraph.

CASE

HAMILTON CONSTRUCTION

CASE BY ANDREA BREEMER FRANTZ

Background. You are co-owner of a medium-sized construction company based in Baton Rouge, Louisiana, called Hamilton Construction. Hamilton has been in business for 23 years and specializes in commercial building. Your two partners, Rob Juarez and Greg Lacombe, are mechanical and construction engineers, respectively. You have always been in charge of personnel and served as the legal/communication expert in negotiating and writing contracts as well as maintaining all communication with clients throughout the construction process.

About a year ago an investor, Al Willig, approached you about putting in a bid for a construction project in Cartagena, Colombia. Willig explained that he, two other investors from the New Orleans area, and three business people in Cartagena, Colombia, were interested in beginning a gourmet coffee shop chain which they hoped they could develop nationwide. Willig explained that he was interested in hiring a local (Baton Rouge) construction company to build a small airport at the edge of one of the bean fields outside Cartagena, for easy loading and delivery access. Willig told you that he was soliciting bids from four construction companies, of which yours was the smallest. Willig also explained that if the airport was done to everyone's satisfaction, there might be more business for the construction company in building the three coffee shops already planned for Baton Rouge, Lafayette, and Lake Charles.

Initially, you and your partners were skeptical, primarily because you didn't see yourselves as an international company. The logistics of splitting off a team for an extended stay in Colombia seemed unmanageable, and you expected any bid you would put in for such a job would be easily beaten by the larger firms. However, after Willig flew you, Rob, and Greg to Cartagena to meet with his other partners, you were so impressed with the people, their product, and their plans that you submitted a bid, even though you expected to be underbid by your competitors.

To your surprise, Willig called you three months later to accept your bid. You, Rob, Willig, and one of the Colombian partners, Joaquin, met and negotiated the contract, which dictated that your construction team would begin work in November and would use local distributors for materials and supplies. You also agreed to hire six local manual laborers as a show of international cooperation on the project.

Task. Now you face the task of establishing yourself at the Colombian work site. You understand that conditions at the construction site itself are rather primitive by U.S. standards, but are viewed as more than acceptable by the Colombians with whom you will be working. You do not want to offend your foreign partners, nor do you want to look particularly squeamish or inflexible, but you believe that you will have to arrange for various amenities at the site (modern latrine facilities, air-conditioned office trailer, etc.) and for accommodations for your workers that are more in line with the expectations of the 12 U.S. employees who will be making the trip south. You must choose how to broach the issue, keeping in mind that your approach should reflect an understanding of your multicultural audience. You decide to write one memo to all parties, setting forth your concerns. Your goal is to have the site "ready" in advance of the U.S. employees' scheduled arrival. (Since the Colombian partners are fluent in English, you have no need for a Spanish translation.)

Complication. Today was a bad news day. First, Rob, who was originally among the employees scheduled to make the trip south, broke his leg in a work-related accident and now must be replaced. Unfortunately, Rob was to be not only a key manager at the site, but also the main liaison between the Spanish-speaking Colombian laborers and the U.S. personnel. No other manager at Hamilton speaks Spanish fluently enough to serve in the same capacity. However, Greg is more than willing to go to Colombia to manage the work, and one of the carpenters scheduled to make the trip knows a smattering of Spanish, Cajun, and French. In addition, you learn that the unexpected need for on-site "amenities" may add $5,000 to $10,000 to the cost of the project. Although you'd like to add this overhead cost to your project bid rather than to absorb it, you can also see the wisdom of chalking the added expense up to the "cost of doing business." You decide that you should send a separate memo to each of the interested parties, advising each about what it needs to know regarding these developments.

CHAPTER

5

Planning Business Documents by Considering Purpose

OUTLINE

Why Purpose Is Important: The Cannes Dew Story

Characteristics of Purpose

Types of Purposes

Appeals and Purposes

CRITERIA FOR EXPLORING CHAPTER 5

What we cover in this chapter	What you will be able to do after reading this chapter
Why purpose matters	Discuss how purpose influences a communicator's choice and use of information
Characteristics of purpose	Recognize how main ideas, reader expectations, range of presentation, and generic constraints embody purposes
Different types of purposes	Discover and write operational, convention-driven, primary and secondary, and reader-based purposes
Major appeals and writers' purposes	Describe the connection between appeals, purposes, and basic writing principles; use the appeals as a writing strategy to achieve your purpose

Effective communicators know that they write or speak to achieve particular purposes. A communicator's purpose may be to inform, to explain, to persuade, to collaborate, or to interact with the audience in some other way. A direct statement of purpose does not always appear within a message, but communicators always need to give their audiences a clear sense of why the message was composed in the first place (so the reader/listener doesn't say "so what?") and *why* certain strategies are being used within that message. Figure 5.1 raises a number of questions concerning *why*.

CONTEXT

The following message is a letter written by a client corporation to a landscape services firm. The writer's overall purpose is to get a full refund for what she sees as Expertcare's unsatisfactory service. (The letter makes more sense if you know that Eire and Ireland are synonymous and that green symbolizes things Irish.)

Figure 5.1 Example Raising Questions about Writer Purposes

Why does the writer use a "subject" line within letter format? Why draw attention to the account number?

Why does the writer select this rather dramatic, yet somewhat cryptic opening? Why does the writer detail the gradual color change?

Why does the writer report on past thinking about the problem?

Why does the writer cite the guarantee, when the reader undoubtedly has a copy? Why too does the writer include both receipt and agreement?

Why does the writer select the phrase "its refund"?

Why does the writer use a somewhat humorous close? Why include a specific extension number?

July 17, 19--
Wesley Schoeneman
Expertcare Landscape Services
8345 Market Street
Presidio, CA

SUBJECT: Account No. 447814

The corporate lawn of Eire Enterprises is dying.

On May 3, 19—, Expertcare applied a fertilizer mixture to our lawn. Over the last two months, we have noticed a gradual color change in the 20 acres of lawn surrounding our corporate headquarters. The lawn has degenerated from a lush green to a pale green to the present light brown.

At first we thought that this change was due to the dry weather we had experienced in the first two weeks of June. However, since that time we have had adequate rainfall, yet the lawn has shown no signs of recovery.

Paragraph 5.1b of your guarantee states, "If not satisfied with the quality of Expertcare's nursery stock or services, the customer is entitled to a full refund." The cost of the May third application was $5,000 (20 acres @ $225 per acre). A copy of the receipt and our signed service agreement with you is enclosed.

Given your money-back guarantee, Eire Enterprises requests its refund of $5,000. We request this payment by August 1 to facilitate the repair or replacement of our turf.

After all, what is Eire without its green?

Sincerely,

Jessica Miller
Vice President
Eire Enterprises

805-555-9879, ext. 564

Encl.

1. Why do you think it's important that readers figure out answers to questions such as those raised in the annotations to Figure 5.1?
2. How would you answer the *why* questions in the annotations? What additional questions do you have about Miller's reasons for writing the letter as she has?
3. How many purposes and subpurposes does Miller have? (Identify any that you see.) How does she promote each of these purposes?

Audiences expect communicators to have reasons for what they do within a message. Writers like Miller know how important purpose is in planning a presentation or document:

- the characteristics of purpose
- the various types of purposes
- the relationship between appeals and purposes

WHY PURPOSE IS IMPORTANT: THE CANNES DEW STORY

Purpose helps a communicator shape information in a message. Consider the Cannes Dew story. Kate McDonnell works in the personnel department of Cannes Dew, a small confectionary firm. One morning, she discovers information about the **Americans with Disabilities Act (ADA)** taped to her computer terminal when she arrives at work (Figure 5.2).

Scrawled across the bottom of the posted information is "Kate, see me. Kelley." Because the information is presented out of context and its purpose is not revealed in the note, Kate does not know why Kelley Gaines, the Director of Personnel, has called her attention to the ADA at this time or why Kelley refers to the question of whether AIDS is a disability under the Act. On her way to Kelley's office, Kate runs into Jerry Fischer, another department employee, who has received a similar note.

As it turns out, Kelley wants Kate to redesign Cannes Dew's application form. After the ADA passed in 1990, the company redesigned its form so that it no longer asked whether applicants had "any physical defects or handicaps that might preclude them from performing certain types of work." The revision helped Cannes Dew meet the new standards of hiring described in the Act, but did not aid the company in making the "reasonable accommodations" required by the Act. Now Kelley would like the application form redesigned again so that the company has notice, when possible, of an applicant's disability, or, more accurately, notice of the accommodations necessary to employ a particular applicant. Such notice will help the company plan for these accommodations. Figure 5.3 (next page) demonstrates Kate's adaptation of Kelley's ADA information for that purpose. Kate's version is to be part of a special box on the application form.

Kate does not include specific reference to the AIDS issue, because such reference does not fit her purpose. She does add the example about communicable diseases to alert applicants with AIDS to the fact that

Disabilities do not prevent employees from being highly productive.

Figure 5.2 Information Presented without a Given Context or Revealed Purpose

The Americans with Disabilities Act (ADA) was passed in 1990. The Act covers "individuals with disabilities." Disability is defined under the Act the same way disability is defined under the Rehabilitation Act: "Disability means, with respect to an individual—(A) a physical or mental impairment that substantially limits one or more of the major life activities of such individual; (B) a record of such an impairment; or (C) being regarded as having such an impairment."

The Act prohibits discrimination "in regard to job applications procedures [or] the hiring" of applicants. The Act prohibits discrimination during recruitment. Discrimination is defined as treating a qualified handicapped individual differently solely on the basis of her condition.

Employers cannot use "qualification standards, employment tests or other selection criteria that screen out or tend to screen out an individual with a disability . . . , on the basis of a disability unless the standard, test, or other selection criterion as used by the covered entity is shown to be job related for the position in question and is consistent with business necessity."

One of the key provisions of the Act is "reasonable accomodations." Generally, the Act broadly defines accommodation as the necessary changes in the job or workplace which enable an applicant to work. An accommodation is reasonable as long as it does not "impose an undue hardship on the operation of the business." Undue hardship means that the accommodation would be unreasonable in terms of financial costs or workplace changes. Undue hardship is determined on a case by case basis.

Nowhere in the Act is HIV or AIDS mandated as a disability. However, there is strong precedent for doing so from the Rehabilitation Act. In addition, the ADA does not have a laundry list of impairments that are "disabilities," so the fact that HIV or AIDS is not mentioned does not automatically exclude it from being a disability.

the company considers such diseases to be covered under the Act. [Publisher's Note: We are in no way under the impression that AIDS is communicable through food products.] She also adds other examples to help applicants with other disabilities understand the information they are being asked to provide. In short, Kate's purpose affects how the information is shaped.

Kelley asks Jerry Fischer to use the information for a different purpose. Up to this point, Jerry has handled virtually all of the initial interviewing of prospective applicants for Cannes Dew. Recently, Jerry has also been asked to train other personnel to conduct interviews. Kelley wants Jerry to draw up a list of interviewing procedures that take ADA into account. Jerry's purpose, which is quite different from Kate's, affects how he approaches his material. Kelley's information provides Jerry with a starting point, rather than actual text to use in his document. Figure 5.4 shows the guidelines Jerry composes to ensure that those interviewing potential employees for Cannes Dew are sensitive to the ADA.[1]

Jerry draws upon his considerable interviewing experience, as well as his experience as a disabled Vietnam veteran, in picturing for the reader typical interviewing aspects covered

Figure 5.3 ADA Information Presented within the Context of an Application Form

Kate focuses on an accommodation that matches the use the company will make of the information.

Kate includes phrases in parentheses to further define what the Act means by a disabled individual.

Kate lists examples that imply the types of accommodations the company can make.

The Americans with Disabilities Act of 1990 requires that we, as an employer, not discriminate against individuals with handicaps. Moreover, the Act requires us to make reasonable accommodations for otherwise qualified disabled individuals. So that we may accommodate a disabled employee, we must know that an individual cannot perform the essential functions of a job.

If you (A) have a physical or mental impairment that substantially limits one or more major life activities (employment/work is considered a major life activity); (B) have a record of such impairment (that is, you have a history of or have been misclassified as having a disability); or (C) have been regarded as having a disability, you qualify as a disabled individual under the Act.

If you do qualify, then please briefly discuss the physical or mental job-related functions at which you would be limited or which you would be unable to perform. Examples include being unable to lift heavy objects, to work for periods of time such as exceeding two hours in length, or to work in tight or enclosed spaces. Examples also include having a communicable disease and, therefore, being unable to perform certain tasks, such as handling food.

We require no further information, nor will we inquire through an interview what your exact condition is.

Figure 5.4 ADA Information Used in Guidelines for Interviewing

Jerry opens with advice that attends to the issue of discrimination: the job functions must be clearly defined before interviewing begins, and the questions must be the same for all applicants.

Jerry's dos and don'ts address situations that arise with different disabilities. Jerry uses these situations rather than a prose text to define what a disability is.

Jerry's guidelines similarly describe what discrimination is, giving nondiscriminatory behavior in the dos and discriminatory behavior in the don'ts.

Like Kate, Jerry tries to encourage participation with a reassuring close.

ADA ETIQUETTE:
DOS AND DON'TS OF INTERVIEWING PROSPECTIVE APPLICANTS IN ACCORDANCE WITH THE 1990 ACT

- Do clearly define the essential functions of a position in preparing for an interview.
- Do ask the same questions of all applicants.
- In shaking hands at the opening of an interview, do accept what a disabled person has to offer—hand, hook, etc.
- Do sit down when talking to wheelchair users.
- Do look at the applicant and not the translator when interviewing hearing-impaired candidates.
- Do let the **applicant** bring up any disabilities and necessary accommodations. You can ask candidates to relate their history to you, as an opening for them to volunteer information.
- Do use appropriate vocabulary (disabled, not handicapped; hearing-impaired, not deaf; subject to seizures, not stricken by seizures; multiply disabled, not deformed). Both "visually impaired" and "blind" are appropriate.
- Don't be overly protective of disabled prospects. And don't pat them on the shoulder. (You can ask—once—"is there anything you need?")
- Don't ask how the applicant will get to work.
- Don't lean on anybody's wheelchair. Don't touch or distract guide dogs.
- Don't ask about an applicant's health. After making a conditional offer, you can ask the candidate to take a routine medical examination, provided that every applicant is required to do so.
- Don't write anything down during an interview that you wouldn't want a jury to look at. In other words, if ADA doesn't permit evaluating an applicant on certain types of information, you should not be asking about or taking notes on such information, even if the applicant brings the information up him/herself.
- Don't call people without disabilities "normal."

Just relax. Remember that people with disabilities have strengths and weaknesses just like everybody else.

by the ADA. Jerry's guidelines actually show how not to "discriminate." They also define, through example, what "disability" means. Although Jerry's use of the ADA information contrasts with Kate's, both writers let their respective purposes tell them what to include in a document and how to include it.

Kelley's initial note to both Kate and Jerry was also purpose-driven. Kelley's purpose was to provide the raw, legal information upon which Kate and Jerry could build their messages. Kelley thus worked less on shaping the information than on making sure it was correct. Her purpose thus also helped her choose what information to present and how to present it.

CHARACTERISTICS OF PURPOSE

The Cannes Dew story shows that purposes help you to decide how to incorporate information into a document. Although you may choose from a large number of purposes when writing, all purposes

- tie closely to the main idea of the document
- include a consideration of reader characteristics
- can be presented in a variety of ways (i.e., they may be general or specific, explicit or implicit)

Ties to the Main Idea

Communications of almost every kind have a main idea. Your purpose is tied to this main idea. In previous writing courses, you may have had the main idea statement described as having a subject and a predicate.

SUBJECT	PREDICATE
The proposal	should be adopted.

Another way to describe a main idea is that it commonly includes (1) a topic and (2) the writer's attitude toward or thinking about that topic. The statement of a main idea also frequently sets up (3) some expectation of how the document will proceed.

TOPIC	WRITER'S ATTITUDE	FORECAST
The proposal	should be adopted	for three reasons.

The phrase "for three reasons" sets up the expectation that the document will cite three reasons.

A writer's purpose incorporates the main idea.

PURPOSE	MAIN IDEA
I am writing this document in order to *persuade* my audience that	the proposal should be adopted for three reasons.

In simple terms, a purpose is what you, as a writer, intend that your documents do or achieve. Business presentations and documents, like other forms of communication, always have a purpose. That purpose, whether explicitly stated or implied within the message, helps you to make writing choices.

When the writer has an overtly persuasive purpose, the main idea can be described in terms of claims and evidence. Simply put, a **claim** is what the writer asserts is true, valid, or factual. Evidence is the basis or grounds for asserting something is true or valid or a fact.

PURPOSE	CLAIM	EVIDENCE
I assert, maintain, argue, intend to prove, believe	the proposal should be adopted	for three reasons.

Even though claims are most often linked to constructing oral or written arguments, they play an important part in knowing how to plan business communications. Asking "What am I trying to achieve?" is an important first step in planning a business message. Answering this question helps you to decide, among other things, whether your audience will cooperate with your message or resist it. In turn, knowing your reader's attitude tells you how to structure your message, because there are definite conventions in business communication for addressing either a cooperative or a resistant reader (see Chapters 8, 9, and 10). Asking yourself "How will I be able to prove my claim to my reader?" helps you decide what information to look for and, later, helps you to select which detail to include or exclude. Of course, you would include information that best supports your claim.

The Inclusion of Audience

Purpose characteristically includes audience. If your purpose is to inform, you assume that someone needs to be informed; if to persuade, that someone needs to be persuaded. The sentence "In this business communication [oral or written message], I want to persuade [action] someone [audience] of something [subject]" is a good reflection of the concept of purpose. Your purpose tells what you want your audience to do and why.

WRITER'S PURPOSE (INCLUDING THE AUDIENCE)	ACTION/RESPONSE EXPECTED OF AUDIENCE	REASON (RATIONALE) FOR THE ACTION/RESPONSE
I am writing this message to persuade my audience that	the proposal should be adopted	for three reasons.

Your audience is the final judge of whether your information or evidence is sufficient and whether your ideas or claims are justified, and whether you have fulfilled your purposes.

Presentation of Purposes

You have a choice about how to present your purposes to your audience. Purposes may be *general* or *specific*. The purpose "I am writing this document to persuade my audience to do something" is a very general purpose. A more specific purpose would be "As a local resident interested in sports programs, I am writing this proposal to convince the Parks Department to build a roller hockey rink."

As a rule, the more specific your purpose, the more effective your presentation or document will be. Figure 5.5 also suggests how specific purposes help communicators plan. The more experienced you become, the more internalized planning for purpose becomes. In any case, if you are struggling with getting your thoughts together, explicit purpose statements like those in Figure 5.5 will often help clarify an approach.

When it comes to writing the actual document, you can present your purposes *explicitly* or *implicitly*. An **explicit purpose** is stated in the text; an **implicit purpose** is suggested rather than directly stated in the document.

EXPLICITLY STATED PURPOSE	IMPLICITLY PRESENTED PURPOSE
I am writing this letter to thank project volunteers for their efforts and to provide a feeling of goodwill that will encourage their future participation in other such projects.	Thank you so much for your help with the Willow Tree Youth Network Symposium this fall. Largely due to the efforts of volunteers such as yourself, the program was a huge success. You have created a special place for yourself in the lives of these disadvantaged youngsters.

You might also have purposes that are important to your planning and composing but that never appear, either explicitly or implicitly, in your message. For example, in *Writing for the Computer Industry*, Kristin R. Woolever and Helen M. Loeb identify common objectives for computer documentation in terms of two sets of overarching purposes:

- company-driven objectives—to inform customers, to market products, to enhance corporate image, to state legal limitations for product, and to save company money
- audience-driven objectives—to make a decision about a product, to operate or maintain a product, and to program or analyze a product.[2]

Figure 5.5 General to Specific Purposes as Aids to Planning

PURPOSE STATEMENTS: GENERAL TO SPECIFIC	WHAT THE COMMUNICATOR PLANS ON THE BASIS OF SUCH A PURPOSE STATEMENT
If you have a general purpose of addressing the complaints of an audience,	you know that the reader has had certain complaints. In planning, you know you'll probably have to review the conventions for dealing with a negative situation before you begin to write, and in turn, you'll know what types of information you'll need.
If you have the more specific purpose of dealing with the problem of refunds for state fair concertgoers who have not received their money back for a rock group's canceled performance,	you now know that you represent the state fair, that the reader's complaints involve money, and that the readers want a refund. In planning, you now know to check the state fair calendar, find out which group canceled, find out what the cost of the tickets was, and determine what conditions were tied to their purchase.
If you, as the entertainment arrangements chair of the state fair, have the even more specific purpose of informing state fair goers who have not received their money back for the Beach Boys concert on Thursday evening of their options,	you now know that because you are representing the state fair in an official capacity, you must be concerned with corporate image; you can also make a guess about the general type of audience you will be addressing (assuming rock bands have certain types of fans) and plan how best to address them; and because you probably already know the cost of the tickets and the conditions of their purchase, you can begin to explore the options open to you in addressing the refund problem.
If you, as the entertainment arrangements chair of the state fair, have the even more specific purpose of informing state fair goers who have not received their money back for the Beach Boys concert on Thursday evening that they can either apply for a rain check for a Sunday evening concert or ask for their money back,	you additionally know that you should probably discover which option, if any, the fair board would prefer that you recommend or push.
If you, as the entertainment arrangements chair of the state fair, have the even more specific purpose of both (1) informing state fair goers who have not received their money back for the Beach Boys concert on Thursday evening that they can either apply for a rain check for a concert Sunday afternoon or evening or ask for their money back and (2) persuading them to attend either of the Sunday concerts that have seating available,	you additionally know that you have two purposes and that you should stress the attractiveness of the Sunday concert option.

Documentation written according to these objectives might fulfill both types of purposes without specifically mentioning them. A manual written by teachers to help students operate computer lab interactive software and a sales package designed by a computer firm to persuade architects to purchase a new graphics program would have separate purposes (stated or implied), yet both might share Woolever and Loeb's overarching purposes. Such purposes serve as criteria for composing and evaluating messages.

TYPES OF PURPOSES

To be an effective communicator, you should be familiar with different types of purposes. Although these different types often combine and overlap in practice, they can be described separately:

- purposes tied to the communicator (**operational purposes**)
- purposes tied to the message (**convention-driven purposes**)
- purposes tied to the occasion (primary and secondary purposes)
- purposes tied to the audience (reader-based purposes)

Purposes Tied to the Communicator

Purposes tied to the communicator are the kind usually associated with the concept of purpose. This type emphasizes the *writer* in the statement "*I* want to _____ in this business document." Writer-based or *operational* purposes involve a writer's specific goals or reasons for writing a particular document.

By convention, operational purposes rarely appear explicitly in the finished version of short business messages, such as letters, but regularly appear in other documents, including reports. Reports often have separate purpose statements or introductory sections that state what the writer wants to accomplish. In Figure 5.6, part of the opening section to a feasibility report, the writers' operational purpose is explicitly stated.

Figure 5.6 Introductory Section to a Report Stating the Writers' Operational Purpose

Because the plans are complicated and pose a range of alternatives, the writers must discuss the merits of each plan in detail.

> The purpose of this report is to discuss the relative merits of three plans for renovating the lower level of our offices at Parkview West. The three plans pose a range of alternatives that involve choices in facility use, floor plan and design, and cost.

Purposes Tied to the Message

Purposes that are tied to the message are determined by the type of document in which they appear. These *convention-driven* purposes emphasize the *document* in the statement "I want this *document* to ______." For example, advertising is a type of writing that characteristically has a persuasive purpose. Advertising documents, whether sales letters, brochures, posters, or other promotional documents, would therefore have persuasion as their convention-driven purpose.[3] (Chapter 6 discusses conventions in detail.)

A view of the complete opening paragraph of the Parkview West report reveals a convention-driven purpose associated with feasibility studies as a type of writing (Figure 5.7). This purpose, which is to determine which alternative is most feasible, is implicit.

Figure 5.7 The Purpose Section of a Report with an Implicit Convention-Driven Purpose

The writers establish their convention-driven purpose by referring to the task of assessing feasibility.

> The purpose of this report is to discuss the relative merits of three plans for renovating the lower level of our offices at Parkview West. The three plans pose a range of alternatives that involve choices in facility use, floor plan and design, and cost. In exploring these options, the report establishes evaluative criteria and research methods before presenting the alternatives in detail and assessing them point-by-point in terms of their feasibility.

Traditionally, feasibility reports have the purpose of determining which option is best. In this case, readers are cued to the implicit convention-driven purpose by the term "feasibility." They are aware of the *operational* purpose because it is explicitly stated. Figure 5.7 demonstrates, then, that a document may have both operational and convention-driven purposes and that these purposes may be explicitly or implicitly stated. You'll discover that business messages commonly have multiple purposes.

Purposes Tied to the Occasion

You will find two basic kinds of purposes tied to occasion:

- primary and secondary purposes within the document itself
- purposes determined or allowed by the context

When multiple purposes within a communication are of equal value, each purpose receives similar attention. There is a balance of the information devoted to accomplishing each purpose. When one purpose is more important than the other(s), however, purposes are ranked hierarchically, with some being **primary** and others **secondary.** Another look at the Parkview West excerpt (Figure 5.8) reveals which purpose is primary and which is secondary.

Figure 5.8 Parkview West Excerpt with Annotations Noting Purposes as Primary or Secondary

The writer discusses the merits of the alternatives to choose between them.

> The purpose of this report is to discuss the relative merits of three plans for renovating the lower level of our offices at Parkview West. The three plans pose a range of alternatives that involve choices in facility use, floor plan and design, and cost. In exploring these options, the report establishes evaluation criteria and research methods before presenting the alternatives in detail and assessing them point-by-point in terms of their feasibility.

Figure 5.9 How Varying the Primary and Secondary Purposes of a Document Affects Its Development

PRIMARY AND SECONDARY PURPOSES	HOW THE DEVELOPMENT WILL PROCEED
If the primary purpose is to determine which option is most feasible and the secondary purpose is to discuss relative merits in order to discover which option is best, then . . .	the merits of each option should be discussed in terms of criteria related to the option's feasibility.
If the primary purpose is to describe the merits of each option and the secondary purpose is to show the range of options available to Parkview West, then . . .	the merits of each option will be discussed in terms of their distinctive features and will show, secondarily, the variety available through the options.
If the primary purpose is to demonstrate the variety of architectural planning done by one firm (assuming that the options were designed by the same firm) and the secondary purpose is to describe the merits of each option, then . . .	the merits of each alternative plan will be discussed to showcase the differences in the plans available and, secondarily, to show the respective strengths of each option.

Primary purposes usually control the development of the document. As Figure 5.9 suggests, setting up different primary and secondary purposes for the Parkview West example results in changes in the document's development.

The *occasion* for writing helps determine which purpose is primary and which is secondary. For example, if the occasion for the Parkview West report involves the early stages of planning a project, then knowing the merits of each option seems to be a logical first step. The occasion thus suggests that describing the merits of each option should be the primary purpose rather than deciding which option is best. If the occasion, however, is a report submitted in the latter stages of the planning process after bids have been received, then knowing which option is best makes sense as a primary concern.

Context also dictates occasional purposes. Certain corporations, for example, may restrict the types of purposes appropriate to a particular kind of document. For example, a company may require that its documents avoid making political statements. In this context, you could not expect to write a story for the company newsletter with the purpose of backing either a conservative or a liberal candidate for national office.

Purposes Tied to the Audience

Audiences come to documents with their own sets of purposes. Influenced by their own agenda, readers sometimes misinterpret the purpose of a document or even construct a purpose for the document that runs counter to the writer's intentions. For example, your reader might bring to a brochure about a pest control product the purpose of "understanding how X-Terminate works to control carpenter ants." (Perhaps her purpose includes looking for an environmentally sound product.) Suppose you wrote the brochure with the aim of "selling X-Terminate." In so doing, you might forgo a complete description of the product that

TECHNOLOGY

E-MAIL IS GREAT, BUT NOT FOR EVERYTHING...

When e-mail systems were first developed in the late sixties, they were called electronic *messaging* systems, and that's how they were used: to send short, practical messages. In businesses today, electronic *mail* is becoming a substitute for traditional "snail" mail and is used for a variety of internal and external communication. However, e-mail is still inappropriate for some purposes:

- negotiating contracts: E-mail is not yet governed by the same breach-of-promise laws that control traditional communication. Messages are also easy to forge.
- internal personnel memos: Sensitive documents may be read by dozens of others, possibly damaging relationships within the organization.

Technology does exist that could expand the purposes for which e-mail is appropriate. Digital signature systems allow users to "sign" their e-mail, reducing the risk of forgery (although anyone who can access a user's account could use the signature). Security systems can limit account access to the user and minimize the risk of confidential documents becoming less than confidential.

But users should be aware that they're operating at their own risk if they are using e-mail to send contracts or other classified documents. The use of e-mail is evolving, but for some purposes, businesspeople are still better off with pen and paper.

ETHICS

SHOULD I BE POLITE OR RIGHT? KNOWING YOUR PURPOSE FOR COMMUNICATING

Roger Boisjoly, a Morton Thiokol employee, had several choices after he realized the potential for a disaster with NASA's shuttle *Challenger*:

- ignore the situation entirely
- report the situation, but downplay the danger by using polite, ambiguous terms
- report the situation, but rely on engineering jargon and doublespeak to conceal the potential degree of danger
- explicitly communicate his findings and his opinions

Boisjoly chose the last option and wrote a "company private" interoffice letter on July 31, 1985, six months before the *Challenger* disaster.

> This letter is written to insure that management is fully aware of the seriousness of the current o-ring erosion problem. . . . The result would be a catastrophe of the highest order—loss of human life. (Quoted in Elliot, Katz, and Lynch, 1993)

Because the shuttle exploded, Boisjoly's "company private" letter became public as evidence in the Rogers Commission investigation. The occasion thus transformed Boisjoly's original purposes of making management aware of the seriousness of the o-ring problem and of documenting his stand to one of making the entire nation aware of an internal problem which had tragic consequences when the *Challenger* exploded. (See Whistleblowers comment, page 12, to learn the personal consequences to Boisjoly of his action).

would include environmental concerns and highlight only its distinctive pest-control features. Your reader in turn might find simple "highlights" inappropriate to her purpose. She might also reach the unfortunate conclusion that your purpose is to gloss over the fact that X-Terminate harms the environment.

Purpose also involves *reader expectations*. Readers bring to texts expectations about what purposes are associated with certain types of documents and how these types work to promote these purposes. Such expectations help the reader predict what the writer's primary purpose is and how the document itself will work.

For example, company executives may expect short reports to have an informational purpose. If you were to file a short trip report to them that detailed facts about Japanese quality circles, these readers would assume that you were simply informing them about what you saw. If, instead, you were really trying to persuade them to adopt the circle system at the company's American site, your recommendation might be lost on your readers. Because of expectations set up by the context and tied to the type of document, your readers would not be looking for a document that was meant to persuade. If they did recognize your intent, however, you might be asked to file a proposal rather than a short report to present the recommendation "appropriately."

APPEALS AND PURPOSES

An appeal is a way of effecting your purposes. Appeals influence your audience to believe or act in a certain way. The famous Greek philosopher and rhetorician Aristotle, who discussed appeals in terms of persuasive purposes, identified three main appeals:

1. appeals to the character of the speaker or writer
2. appeals to the emotions and values of the audience
3. appeals to the internal consistency and logic of the communication

Colin Powell enhanced his credibility with his calm reporting of details during the Kuwait crisis.

Although Aristotle discussed these appeals as ways of making an argument, they can be used to help writers fulfill a number of other purposes as well.

The relationship between appeals and purposes is represented in Figure 5.10. As the figure suggests, you can make your appeals work to promote your purposes not only by selecting appropriate content, but also by choosing the appropriate stylistic options. These stylistic measures include characteristics basic to effective business communication:

- accuracy and correctness, which become a way of showing the credibility of the writer
- accessibility and courtesy, which accommodate the feelings of the reader

Figure 5.10 Relationship between Appeals and Purposes

PURPOSE	APPEALS	HOW TO MAKE THE APPEALS WORK
I want to persuade the owners of Autoworks to use my advertising agency to promote their dealership's sales and services.	To persuade the owners of Autoworks to use my agency to promote their dealership, I will have to convince them (1) that I'm a competent and trustworthy person, (2) that they need and will benefit from my services, and (3) that my general analysis of the market and specific advertising plan make sense and have merit.	In order to show the owners of Autoworks (1) that I am a competent and trustworthy person, I will have to give evidence of my past expertise in the area of advertising. I will also have to create a picture of myself as a writer and a tone that establishes my suitability for the task. I will also have to write a document that is accurate and correct to establish my credibility and trustworthiness on this project. In order to show the owners of Autoworks (2) that they need and will benefit from my services, I will have to dramatize how much they will benefit from it. I will also have to write a document that is accessible and courteous to my readers. I will have to get them to identify with the type of image I can provide them. In order to show (3) that my general analysis of the market and specific advertising plan make sense and have merit, I will have to include factual and logically presented detail. I will also have to write a document that is clear, comprehensive, and concise in order to ensure the integrity of my message.

- clarity, comprehensiveness, and conciseness, which become ways of ensuring the integrity of the message

These measures complement the writer's selection of detail and use of other strategies, such as dramatizing reader benefit (see Chapter 4).

Appeal to the Communicator's Character

The appeal of the writer or speaker's character reflects special concern for credibility and trustworthiness. It involves asking, "How can I present myself effectively, so that my audience will believe in me?" Figure 5.11 summarizes the connection between purpose and an appeal to character.

Using *details* that directly or indirectly call attention to your *expertise and reputation* can help you fulfill your purposes, because if readers trust you, they are more likely to cooperate with you. Simply listing your job title on a cover sheet under your signature, for example, might be a modest first step in indicating your expertise. Similarly, you could establish your expertise by including information about your past experiences in a cover letter to a report or attaching to a proposal your resume emphasizing your qualifications to address the problems in the proposal.

In Figure 5.12 (page 140), the writer, Dave Tedlock, balances being confident with being overconfident. He wants to develop credibility through demonstrable expertise without appearing to show off. Tedlock also balances the pursuit of his primary purpose—to persuade readers to adopt Tedlock Advertising—with an acknowledgment of the readers'

Figure 5.11 The Appeal to a Communicator's Character to Promote Purpose

THE APPEAL TO A COMMUNICATOR'S CHARACTER	HOW TO MAKE THE APPEAL WORK	GENERAL LIST OF STRATEGIES USEFUL IN MAKING THE APPEAL TO THE COMMUNICATOR'S CHARACTER
In order to fulfill my purpose of persuading the owners of Autoworks to use my agency to promote their dealership, I will have to convince them that I'm a competent and trustworthy person.	In order to show the owners of Autoworks that I am a competent and trustworthy person, I will have to give evidence of my past expertise in the area of advertising. I will also have to adopt a persona and tone that establish my appropriateness for the task. I will also have to write a document that is accurate and correct to establish my credibility and trustworthiness on this project.	• include details that show the writer to be intelligent and to have a good reputation • make sure the text is accurate and mechanically correct, demonstrating the writer's believability and trustworthiness • create a persona that suggests the writer is competent, intelligent, and of good character • use tone to show the writer has appropriate concern about and control over the information included

Figure 5.12 Follow-Up Letter Balancing Various Appeals to the Writer's Character

In his first paragraph, Tedlock acknowledges the first tension that needs balancing. He closes the first paragraph with a sales statement which indirectly identifies his primary purpose—to convince readers to adopt Tedlock Advertising.

Tedlock establishes his firm's expertise in terms of past successes.

Tedlock establishes his personal expertise by showing additional experience.

Tedlock offers proof of what he can achieve for a specific agency.

Tedlock nicely calls attention to the balance in his approach to the reader.

TEDLOCK
ADVERTISING & PUBLIC RELATIONS

February 4, 1993

Rick Watson, Director of Marketing
Marketing Department
3365 N. Campbell, Suite 121
Tucson, AZ 85719

Dear Rick and UMC/UPI Marketing Program Members:

Thank you for giving us the opportunity to share some of our thinking with you. While we understand your need to solicit proposals from Phoenix firms, we want to emphasize our belief that, when it comes to gaining favorable publicity for clients, no Phoenix firm knows the local media as we, and other Tucson firms, do.

Please note that our agency's relevant health care experience includes work for:

- Desert Hills (its RTC & two hospitals)
- Foothills Women's Center (OB/GYN group practice)
- National Medical Enterprises (80 psychiatric hospitals nationwide)
- Tucson Psychiatric Institute

Individually, our experience includes work for:

- Phoenix General Hospital
- Northwest Hospital
- Intergroup

We're particularly proud to offer proof that our creative ideas and public relations work produce measurable results. Our "Be An Air Freshener" campaign produced outstanding results for Pima County Department of Environmental Quality. In half the time, with less than half the budget, our campaign's measured level of awareness was higher than the previous campaign.

In completing this proposal, we've been torn between wanting to impress you with our creativity and needing to get to know you much better before making detailed recommendations. The balanced approach we've taken here should persuade you to see us in person, and we're looking forward to talking with you at length.

Sincerely yours,

Dave Tedlock
President & Creative Director

CONTEXT

Dave Tedlock of Tedlock Marketing, Advertising, and Public Relations in Tucson is writing a follow-up letter to a proposal presentation he made to a local business group. In addition to establishing his expertise without showing off, he balances the task of persuading the group to adopt Tedlock Advertising as a consultant with that of recognizing the group's reasons for not being able to make such an adoption at this point. Tedlock must also balance the task of showing general expertise with that of selling group members on what he can specifically do for them. And he must balance informational and persuasive purposes.

purpose of finding an agency that represents the most feasible solution to their advertising needs. Tedlock establishes himself as an evenhanded and fair-minded and thus trustworthy businessperson by mentioning the problem of location (the potential client must consider in-town agencies in Phoenix before committing to an out-of-town firm in Tucson).

Accuracy in a business message also demonstrates the communicator's credibility and trustworthiness. For example, if your communication is inaccurate, the reader or listener may conclude (1) that you do not know your subject and are not a "credible" source, or (2) that you cannot be trusted to give the straight story and thus are not trustworthy. The annotations for Figure 5.13 point to potential consequences of inaccuracy. The end result of inaccuracy is that the reader will reject your message, making it impossible for you to fulfill your purposes.

The potential inaccuracies shown in Figure 5.13 include not only possible mistakes in the information actually presented, but also possible omissions in the information necessary to the reader. An incorrect address would be a mistake in the information presented. Omitted information might include the fact that the seminar is particularly useful to the nontraditional student. If readers are either directly or indirectly misled, the writer's credibility suffers. In addition, there are potential legal consequences. If, for example, the writer has made a mistake concerning the test date and the reader misses the exam and consequently loses a job, the reader could sue the writer for damages.

Figure 5.13 Letter with Annotations Suggesting Potential Consequences of Inaccuracy

What if only certain applicants find the seminar beneficial?

What if the test dates are really November 11–12 and May 3–5?

What if exams are administered in a different location on one of the dates?

What if a major part of the test is excluded from the list? What if financial reporting takes only 2½ hours? How would that change its relative importance? The reader's study plans? Travel plans?

What if the address is incorrect? If the 800 number is for seminar organizers only?

What if the October seminar has openings or the February one has only a few left?

What if there is a specific deadline for receipt of the application, the payment, or both?

What if the writer personally cannot be reached at this number?

Dear Ms. Kaufman:

Thank you for your recent interest in the seminar presented by the AICPA. Participants find the information provided at the seminar to be extremely beneficial.

Regarding your requests, I am providing you the following information:

- The upcoming test dates are November 3–5, 19-- and May 11–12, 19--.
- All exams are administered at the Waverly Center.
- Specific parts of the exam include:
  - Business Law (3 hours)
  - Auditing (4½ hours)
  - Accounting & Reporting (3½ hours)
  - Financial Reporting (4½ hours)
- Review material can be obtained by contacting:

  The Complete Examination Review
  Neman & Graves Co.
  1500 Main Street
  Boston, MA 02108
  1-800-555-TEST

I have checked into your interest in attending the seminar presented this October. Unfortunately, the October seminar has been filled. However, we are now taking applications for our seminar to be held February 5. Considering you are planning to sit for the exam in May of 19--, the February seminar would be ideal for you. This seminar is being held in Memorial Auditorium in York, which would minimize your travel.

To assist you in applying for our February seminar, I have enclosed the appropriate forms. To register, please return the bottom portion of the application along with your payment.

Once again I would like to extend my appreciation for your interest. If you need any additional information, feel free to contact me at (804) 555-4763.

Sincerely,

Correctness, which traditionally includes such concerns as spelling and grammar, enhances a writer's credibility. Figure 5.14, a letter sent to the parent of a prospective student by an admissions office and mailed out with an unfortunate number of mistakes, creates a very poor impression of the writer and the institution itself. In fact, the person who provided us with this example could hardly believe that the message came from the Director of Admissions, since the errors were so basic and numerous.

The presence of mechanical miscues is particularly ironic in Figure 5.14, given the claim for academic excellence that the Admissions Director makes at the outset. Writers in any type of institution or business are held accountable for such mistakes by their readers. When your correspondence contains miscues, your credibility suffers and chances increase that your purposes will remain unmet. Certainly, the Admissions Director was unsuccessful in his bid to attract this particular student.

Figure 5.14 Miscues That Hurt the Communicator's Trustworthiness and Credibility

The typos call into question the claim that the institution is "one of the finest academic colleges in the country."

Capitalizations are inconsistent and inaccurate.

The reader has quite a few reasons to doubt that his daughter will be "learning" anything at a university whose Admissions Director sends such correspondence.

Dear Mr. Bennett:

In selecting Major State University, you are considering one of the finest academic colleges in the country. MSU **studends** have a certain **advange** in gaining employment after they graduate. As you might know, our Computer **s**cience department is **inthe** top ten in the country. It is even up to your tough Ivy League standards.

Besides our high **scholast satndards**, MSU offers many civic and cultural activities for your daughter Andrea. She will have over 2,000 student organizations to choose from. Andrea will find the dormitory a great place to make lasting friends. The students at MSU are very friendly and helpful. Also **consulors** are available to help her with her problems.

Going to college at MSU, your daughter will **learnin** a highly academic atmosphere. Along with learning she will be among friends. MSU is a **student oriented** college. MSU is always delighted to have students like your daughter attend. We hope she will put us at the top of her college list.

Sincerely Yours,

H.M. Smith
Admissions **d**irector

The effective use of *persona* and *tone* also work to establish your credibility and promote your purposes. A **persona** is the picture you create of yourself in a communication. Developing a trustworthy persona enhances your reputation and, by extension, the image of the company you represent. Figure 5.15, an excerpt from an internal memo addressed "to all employees" from "the personnel office," establishes a strong persona. The "take-charge" personality established in this excerpt matches the memo's purpose, which is to present information about a newly established change in policy. Although this no-nonsense persona cannot be ascribed to any one person, since the memo is officially from the personnel office, it encourages the sense that the decision should be respected by the reader.

Figure 5.16 is also from a group (the League of Women Voters) but is signed by the president of the organization. The letter establishes a persona of someone who is receptive to the reader's opinions. The writer's receptive persona matches her purpose of eliciting the reader's participation and support. This match between persona and purpose increases the chance that the writer's purpose will be fulfilled.

Tone, the stylistic attitude of the writer, often carries the burden of establishing the writer's credibility. Writers usually depend on a courteous tone to establish credibility. Consider, for example, Figures 5.17 through 5.19, three collection letters from the office of Dr. Kim Wass, an orthodontist with a busy practice in a small midwestern community. The letters, while all reasonable and courteous, do differ in approach. The first two use a direct approach, appropriate to a routine and a direct request, respectively. The last message uses an indirect approach, appropriate to a negative message. The collection sequence moving from routine request to negative message is established by convention (see Chapter 9).

Figure 5.15 Excerpt Showing Persona of a Writer Who Is in Charge

The writer creates a persona at the outset of someone who should not be questioned and who handles possible concerns firmly and directly (note underlining and CAPS).

Effective September 1, 19-- (August payroll deduction) the High Option medical program will be discontinued. All employees currently enrolled in the High Option program will be transferred to the LYF 600 program. There will be no loss of coverage as a result of this change. THE CHANGE DOES NOT AFFECT MERIT SYSTEM EMPLOYEES ENROLLED IN THE FOREFRONT MEDICAL PROGRAM.

This action was taken by the Annuities and Insurance Committee, with the approval of the Chief Executive Officer, after several years of careful consideration. Levels of coverage, enrollment trends, and premium increases were all thoroughly reviewed before reaching this decision.

Figure 5.16 Excerpt with the Persona of a Writer Who Is Receptive to a Reader's Opinions

By heading the letter with questions, the writer immediately establishes herself as a listener.

The salutation "Dear Friend," and the fact that the writer waits to introduce her subject until after she has touched base with the reader's opinions adds to the picture of receptiveness.

League of Women Voters
Washington, D.C. 20036

Were you satisfied with your choices for President in the last election?

Are you satisfied with the current American system of nominating and electing Presidents?

Dear Friend,

If you answered "no" to either of these questions, we in the League of Women Voters would like to talk to you.

We want to talk to you about a matter of major importance to all Americans concerned about democratic and responsive government. And, we want to seek your opinion about this important matter.

That matter is the American system of nominating candidates for the Presidency, conducting Presidential campaigns, and determining Presidential elections.

Figure 5.17 First Notice

This letter uses a neutral tone to present the context and a very polite tone to request the amount still due on the account. This is a routine request for payment.

It has been an office policy that the orthodontic account be on schedule at the time appliances are removed.

Since we are approaching the time when Sandy will have appliances removed, we would appreciate the current and past due balance paid.

Would it be possible to pay $150 on the account by the removal date, July 20, or make some arrangements with our office? Please call me. Thank you.

Figure 5.18 Past Due 60 Days

This letter, signed by the financial coordinator, uses a reasonable, neutral tone throughout. The offer to make alternative arrangements encourages reader cooperation.

> Our records show that you now have a balance of $150 for orthodontic treatment and that no payment has been received since June 15, 19--.
>
> If we do not hear from you to the contrary, we will assume that this balance will be brought up to date this month, and that future payments will be made on schedule as per our agreement. If other arrangements need to be made, please call us immediately.
>
> Please remember that a payment of $75.00 is due each month regardless of appointment scheduling.

Figure 5.19 Past Due 90 Days

This letter, also signed by the business manager, uses a reasonable but decidedly persuasive tone throughout. This is the patient's past due 90 days notice.

> I regret the necessity of writing to you regarding the past due balance on Terry's contract. As you know, when we began treatment on November 14, 19--, you agreed to an original contract amount of $1700, a down-payment of $200, and 20 monthly payments of $75.
>
> A review of Terry's account shows a balance of $300, of which $225 is past due. You need to pay at least the past due amount immediately.
>
> If there's some reason why you cannot send $225 at once, please call me and let's discuss the matter. Terry's treatment is of paramount importance to us both, of course; but you need to settle your financial obligation as well.
>
> I look forward to hearing from you soon.

The neutral tone of the opening to Figure 5.17, combined with the very polite request at the end of the letter, encourages a good opinion of the writer, which in turn should encourage reader cooperation.

Sometimes, however, patients find themselves in arrears. Figure 5.18 shows a letter sent out when the account is 60 days past due. The reasonable tone used here by the writer argues for the reasonableness of the request and maintains the writer's professional credibility. In Figures 5.17 through 5.19, the writer establishes credibility by using a tone appropriate to each situation, and the tone itself varies from message to message. In addition, the writer's correct use of collection conventions suggests the writer's expertise.

Even a tightly controlled tone, as found in the persuasive request in Figure 5.20, can add to the credibility of the writer, if that tone is appropriate to the situation. This request follows weeks of negotiations and many polite and courteous requests, all ignored by Sherri, the letter's recipient. The writer has repeatedly tried to get Sherri, the manager of his apartment complex, to correct a problem in his unit. Sherri has yet to fulfill her promises to correct the problem.

Figure 5.20 avoids an emotional tone, even though it's quite apparent that the writer is thoroughly angry. The letter's tone, which is stern and uncompromising, complements the demand for immediate redress and the threat of legal action. The writer enhances his credibility by stylistically "controlling his temper" and thus increases his chances of finally getting the problem solved.

Sometimes, however, using an emotional tone is appropriate in business writing. An emotional tone is most effective when it enhances the writer's credibility. For example, Figure 5.21 (page 144) highlights the emotionally charged vocabulary in bold while showing the more

Figure 5.20 Excerpt from Persuasive Request Showing a Tightly Controlled Tone

The formal punctuation (a colon instead of a comma) indicates that even though the writer knows the reader well, this is a business message. The letter continues formally, using legal language to underpin the threatened course of action.

> Dear Sherri:
>
> This letter constitutes formal notice under State Code 562A.2(1) and (2) of your noncompliance with our rental agreement and State Code 562A.15 (1)(b) and (d). If the following breaches are not remedied within fourteen (14) days of receipt of this notice, I intend to exercise my legal right to terminate the agreement as of January 31, 19-- and to recover all damages to which I am legally entitled, including attorney frees, moving costs, temporary housing, rental differential, injunctive relief, etc. I have formally advised you of these problems, both verbally and in writing, on several occasions, but you have done nothing to correct them. The problems have been confirmed in writing by the resident apartment complex manager, John Craft, and a maintenance operator from PPM checked the premises on November 3, 19--, and identified the source of the noise problem as a sanitary drainage pipe.

Figure 5.21 Excerpt with Emotional Tone

The writers use highly charged words such as ***critical, crucial, exhaustive,*** *and* ***essential*** *to enhance their points.*

The writers also emphasize their concern by citing "a complete battery of" tests and by repeating a reference to the workers' safety and invoking the workers' importance to their families as they "return home."

> Boadin and Group, a company devised to take care of the **critical** (special) clothing needs of highway construction workers, creates clothing that improves upon the visibility, comfort, thermal comfort, mobility, and the **crucial** (adjective omitted) overall safety of these workers. In order to achieve a fully functional garment for these workers, we run **exhaustive** (a series of) tests on the current clothing that they wear, before deciding on garment specifications that **are so important to enhancing** their safety (that are important to their safety).
>
> We propose to help your city road crews in two ways. First we will perform **a complete battery of** (a number of) tests that will yield criteria for designing and evaluating the clothing that is **essential** (that will) to keep your workers comfortable and safe. Then we will design and, after additional user testing, construct a line of clothing that, **when secured by the city, will help these workers return safely to their homes at the end of their workday** (make that line of clothing available to the city).

objective language that the writer could have chosen in parentheses. Because the writers are dealing, literally, with a life-and-death situation when it comes to the safety of highway construction workers, they appropriately include emotional language in describing both the problem and the solution, and, in so doing, add to their credibility as citizens concerned for the health and safety of others in their community. Of course, such a subjective description of the real dangers faced by highway construction workers also appeals to the emotions and values of the reader. A disciplined use of a subjective tone can, then, be an effective way of accomplishing your purposes.

Appeal to the Audience's Emotions and Values

An appeal to the audience's emotions and values means asking such questions as: How can I make the reader open to my message? How can I best engage my readers' emotions and imagination? How can I appeal to my readers' values and interests?[4] Figure 5.22 reviews the connection between purpose and the appeal to a reader's emotions and values.

When you use *details* to dramatize the information included in your message, you create a picture that allows readers to put themselves into the situation or to experience the feelings and emotions of a particular event or action. Figure 5.23 dramatizes the benefits of using a computer in a small feeder operation that fattens swine for market. The writer, Gary Armstrong, poses a question in this internal memo that draws the reader, his employer, into the situation and invites the employer to share in the difficulty of addressing some of the complex problems that Armstrong as an employee has had to face. Armstrong figures feed-ration formulas. Because ingredient prices fluctuate on a daily basis, Gary is asking his employer at this point to invest in a computer system with appropriate software to make his job more manageable and the fledgling business more profitable. By instilling in the

Figure 5.22 The Appeal to a Reader's Emotions and Values to Promote a Writer's Purposes

THE APPEAL TO AN AUDIENCE'S EMOTIONS AND VALUES	HOW TO MAKE THE APPEAL WORK	GENERAL LIST OF STRATEGIES USEFUL IN MAKING THE APPEAL TO THE AUDIENCE'S EMOTIONS AND VALUES
In order to *fulfill my purpose of persuading the owners of Autoworks to use my agency to promote their dealership,* I will have to convince them that they need and will benefit from my services.	In order to show the owners of Autoworks that they need and will benefit from my services, I will have to dramatize how much they need my help and, in turn, how much they will benefit from it. I will have to get them to identify with the type of image I can provide them. I will also have to write a document that is accessible and courteous to my readers.	• Use details that dramatize the situation so that readers can picture or feel a personal involvement in what the writer is discussing. • Make sure the text is accessible and courteous, demonstrating the writer's sensitivity to the feelings of the reader. • Provide identification between what the writer and the reader value; include details that show the writer and reader share certain responses.

Figure 5.23 Writer Dramatizing the Problem behind His Request by Using Details

The writer, who does the calculations and who is respected for his skill in doing so, has previously established the "impossibility" of calculating everything by hand.

He cites facts that the employer knows, defines a representative problem, then asks a question inviting the employer to walk in Armstrong's shoes.

The cost of the computer will be paid for in a short period of time when the computer is utilized to provide information that is nearly impossible to obtain by hand calculations. With this computer system, Growfast, Inc. will be able not only to keep track of its accounts and stock, but also to show what daily changes in our ration formula can be made to account for the price fluctuations in various foodstuffs.

For example, it's not at all uncommon for Growfast, Inc. to use a ration that has ten different feedstuffs with ten different protein values and ten different (and fluctuating) prices.

The computer could increase profits by figuring the complicated least-cost ration formulas on a daily basis. Or would you like to provide a 16% protein ration that would meet all the daily nutrient needs of our stock while accounting for such fluctuations in feedstuff prices as occurred between Wednesday and Thursday of last week?

The picture and text in this promotion create a dramatic emotional appeal.

MULTICULTURAL

THE IMPACT OF CULTURAL CONCEPTS ON COMMUNICATION GOALS AND PURPOSES

Purposes influencing communication are governed by cultural practice. Propriety (right action) has exerted a great deal of influence on Eastern communication. Propriety originates in the Chinese philosophy of Confucianism. Confucianism specifies that right conduct results from four positive aspects of human nature: *li* (propriety), *ren* (humanism), *yi* (righteousness), and *chih* (wisdom).

Of these four virtues, propriety is the highest ideal because it ensures harmony and unity in human relationships. The emphasis on maintaining harmony and unity makes communication in Eastern cultures oriented more toward accommodation than confrontation. Discourse features such as overpoliteness, implicitness, indirectness, and modesty are thus commonly found in Chinese, Korean, and Japanese messages.

While the highest goal of communication in the Eastern cultures is to achieve propriety, the highest goal of communication in the West is to achieve the practical cooperation from others that is necessary for self-realization (or company profit and success). The emphasis on clarity, directness, and assertiveness in Western communication reflects the influence of the concept of self-realization. These features appeal to the communicator's credibility and enable the writer to achieve individual or corporate self-realization.

Often, these two "highest" goals are in opposition and can be the source of tension in multicultural transactions.

reader a type of empathy for what it means to be in his situation, Armstrong increases the chances that his employer will comply with his request.

In Figure 5.24, the writers dramatize the attractions of a convention site by using concrete detail to help the reader anticipate the excitement of being there. Creating excitement helps to fulfill the writer's purpose of getting the reader to attend. In their dramatization, the writers select attractions that involve both culture and consumerism and that appeal to the sports-minded and the education-minded. In so doing, they appeal to a readership with a wide range of values and interests.

Accessibility, in terms of both designs and word choice, helps you fulfill your purposes by making sure the reader understands and appreciates what you have to say. Designing for accessibility entails a significant number of strategies that will be covered in detail in Chapter 12.

Careful word choice also can make a document accessible. By avoiding jargon, clichés, and "pompous" language, writers help make a document approachable. Figure 5.25 shows a writer using acronyms, a type of jargon, to discuss recycling procedures. In so doing, the writer makes the document less accessible—and more frustrating—to those readers who do not know what the acronyms mean.

The acronyms are ineffective in this excerpt because they have not been previously identified. If the acronyms had been previously identified, they might actually have enhanced accessibility by relieving the reader from having to read through a long name or complicated title. Note that the use of bold face in this excerpt *does* enhance the accessibility of the information about the drop-off times.

Courtesy, as the word implies, means treating the reader with respect. In business communication, respect is often displayed through careful phrasing. Contrasting the phrasing of

Figure 5.24 Dramatization of Site Attractions for Potential Conventioneers

The writers lead into the body of the letter with a statement about "perfect location" and proceed to dramatize how perfect that location is.

The writers focus on the reader's room and board needs first.

The writers then focus on the entertainment available. They even facilitate the reader's participation in these activities with the SKI number.

The convention hotel at 1881 Curtiss Street is the perfect location for a meeting. For a single, you get a private bedroom and a separate luxurious living room, complete with wet bar, refrigerator, and coffee maker. The double has the same arrangement, with a queen-size sleeper couch. Included in the room rate is a complimentary cooked-to-order breakfast every morning and complimentary cocktails for two full hours every evening. Convention room rates are $95 for a single and $145 for a double, plus 11.8% tax. The Airport Commuter leaves every 15 minutes from the airport (outside doors 2, 6, and 10) and costs $5, or you may take a taxi for $10–12.

The downtown location is within easy walking distance of historic Larimer Square, the Tabor Center, the 16th Street Mall, the U.S. Mint, the Capitol, the Denver Art Museum, and an endless number of shops. Skiing in the Rockies is an hour away by car, or you may want to ride the Budweiser Ski Train, which runs on Saturdays and Sundays, and departs from Union Station, also a short distance from the hotel. For reservations on the Ski Train, call (303)-555-I-SKI. Along with the stimulating sessions at our meeting we have scheduled a tour of the Executive Development Center, adjacent to the hotel.

Figure 5.25 Excerpt Illustrating Issues of Accessibility

Usable latex paint in quantities of at least one-half gallon can be dropped at the RRP **May 7 between 8 a.m. and noon.**

If you have questions about products, make a list of those products and their amounts. (TCD participants will be limited to 25 gallons or 220 pounds of hazardous materials per household.)

If RRP hasn't been previously identified in the document, the location is inaccessible to the reader. If TCD has not been identified, knowledge concerning who is bound by these limitations is inaccessible.

original and revised paragraphs denying credit (Figure 5.26) nicely dramatizes the courtesy provided by carefully selected words. Using a courteous approach such as that shown in the revised phrasing in Figure 5.26 encourages a positive and secure writer-reader relationship.

Avoiding sexist, racist, or other exclusionary language is another important way to demonstrate courtesy. Corporations commonly have explicit policies regarding sexist and other politically sensitive language and codify these policies as part of company stylesheets.

Identification is also a strategy that appeals to the reader's emotions and values. Identification involves forging a link between what the reader values and what the writer has to say. For example, the logo in Figure 5.27, incorporated in various messages from elementary school personnel to parents, promotes identification in that it pictures what the readers are sure to value: happy, smiling children's faces. Both reader and writer value happy children. Thus, a link is made between what the reader values and what the writer wants, in this case a correct estimate of school enrollment. Using a memo headed by the logo, the writer reminds parents to return their child's registration card by Friday, May 13. Returning the registration cards guarantees both that children will be able to attend their chosen elementary school and that the school will be able to plan accurately for enrollment and staffing.

Identification can also establish less obvious connections between writer and reader. Figure 5.28 (page 148), also featuring a visual, establishes a link between Native American culture and readers who may or may not share that heritage. At first glance, the artwork might appear simply to feature a stylization of American Indian figures. A closer look, however, reveals that the stylized figures are doing a "Three Stooges" move, with fingers to the eyeballs. There is also a remarkable similarity between the upturned mouth of the totemlike head topping the artwork and that of a Greek mask of comedy, commonly represented with its tragic counterpart on American theater playbills. The classic traditions of both cultures thus merge in the artistic image. The Indian (Ioway) artist Lance Foster, by incorporating these non-Indian elements so cleverly in his portrayal, has drawn from the comic heritage of both writer and reader to forge a link that complements the idea of the symposium, that "all of us" share in this type of humor.[5] In his clever use of images, Foster has also proven to be a "trickster" himself.

Figure 5.26 Excerpts Showing Revision to Include a Courteous Approach

ORIGINAL PARAGRAPH	REVISED PARAGRAPH
After researching your credit rating, we discovered that you do not take home enough money to qualify for a $12,000 loan based only on your signature without collateral. You were therefore not approved for the loan you requested.	We have carefully reviewed your loan application. To receive an unsecured loan for any amount over $10,000, you must earn at least $21,000 a year in annual income. At this time, you qualify for an unsecured loan of $5,000.

Figure 5.27 Logo Promoting Identification

Figure 5.28 Identification through Artwork by Lance Foster

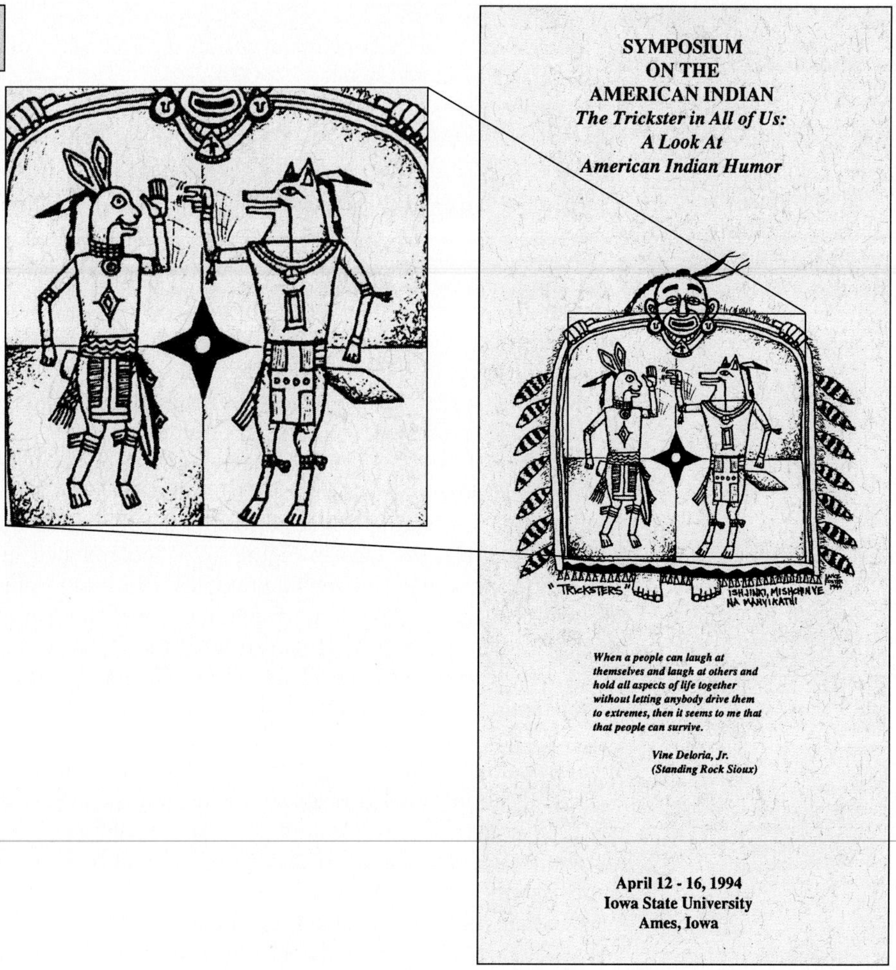

Appeal to the Integrity of the Communication

You appeal to the **integrity** of a communication when asking: How can I make the document internally consistent and logical? How can I find the best reasons and support them with the best evidence? Different types of documents will, of course, require different lines of argument and different kinds of evidence.

But in any kind of communication, the principles of clarity, comprehensiveness, and conciseness are particularly appropriate to this appeal. This appeal, historically associated with logical thought, promotes the writer's purposes by presenting information in such a way that it appears watertight and immune to attack. Readers are thus encouraged to cooperate with the communicator's message because its information appears unassailable. Figure 5.29 introduces the basis of this appeal.

Figure 5.29 The Appeal to the Integrity of a Document to Help Fulfill the Writer's Purposes

THE APPEAL TO THE INTEGRITY OF THE COMMUNICATION	HOW TO MAKE THE APPEAL WORK	GENERAL LIST OF STRATEGIES USEFUL IN MAKING THE APPEAL TO THE INTEGRITY OF THE DOCUMENT
In order to persuade the owners of Autoworks to use my advertising agency to promote their dealership, I will have to convince them that my general analysis of the market and specific advertising plan make sense and have merit.	To show the owners that my general analysis of the market and specific advertising plan make sense and have merit, I will have to include sound supportive detail. I will also have to write a document that is clear, comprehensive, and concise to insure the integrity of my message.	• Include information that is sound and makes sense. • Make sure the text is clear, comprehensive, and concise.

Information that is *sound* and *logically presented* supports the integrity of your message. Figure 5.30 suggests several important ways of establishing the soundness of information in communication.

Clarity requires sound logic as well as precise diction. For example, the sentence, "Due to my previous satisfaction with your company, I feel the need to inform you of my unhappiness with one of your company policies" is unclear because the writer's thinking is unclear. Part of the confusion lies in an odd cause-and-effect relationship set up by the sentence: essentially, the writer is saying, "Due to my satisfaction, I am unhappy." Perhaps the time element needs clarification; that is, maybe the writer's past satisfaction contrasts with her present unhappiness. Or maybe the writer is using the past satisfaction as a factor that gives her confidence to express the complaint. At any rate, the writer needs to make the statement clearer, as in "While I have previously been very satisfied with your company's products and service, I feel I must advise you of my unhappiness with . . ."

Figure 5.31 (page 150) is also unclear on several counts. The status of the document, the writer's expectations, the reasons for the writer's request, and the relevance of certain detail are all unclear.

Comprehensiveness adds integrity to a document, thus supporting the writer's purposes. The amount of detail that you need to be comprehensive depends on both your purposes and the reader's familiarity with the subject. This does not mean, however, that you are free to exclude detail just because the reader is familiar with the situation. For example, the following excerpt is a problem statement from a proposal to redesign the professional development program at a U.S. Army Intelligence School.

> *Statement of the Problem*
>
> Maintenance Training Department must increase common leadership training and solve training problems currently existing in professional development.

The writer of the problem statement might be tempted to stop here, since the reader knows what's involved in "common leadership training" and what the "problems" in the courses have been. In fact, *comprehensiveness* in this case does not demand that the writer explain what "common leadership training" is, since he and the reader share the same

Figure 5.30 Strategies for Establishing the Soundness of Information in a Communication

STRATEGY	REASONING BEHIND THE STRATEGY
Define controversial or ambiguous terms.	When you define terms, you help your reader understand exactly what you mean and promote the idea that you are making sense.
Attend to the facts.	When you claim only what could be confirmed by a disinterested third party looking at the same evidence, then you are operating within the realm of fact rather than fantasy or fiction and building a reputation for trustworthiness.
Distinguish between conclusions that are inferences or interpretations and those that are facts. This is another way to encourage the idea that you know what you are talking about.	If you write that "the briefings for new employees were poorly attended because the personnel we have been hiring lately are an apathetic group," you cannot present this information as a fact. What proof could you offer that apathy was the reason for their nonattendance? It might be easier to prove, and closer to the truth, that "the briefings were poorly attended because of a lack of publicity."
Pay attention to logical relationships.	If you are careful to avoid logical fallacies, you will demonstrate the intelligence important to the reputation of a communicator. We discuss how to avoid logical fallacies in Chapter 11. See also the Skills and Strategies box, page 151.
Demonstrate concern for telling the truth.	When you studiously avoid misrepresenting material and relate only that information which you personally can vouch for, then you are producing a document that will have the type of integrity that works to fulfill your purposes.

Figure 5.31 Letter Demonstrating a Lack of Clarity

The company letterhead coupled with the informal salutation and punctuation (comma instead of colon) make it unclear whether this is a personal or a business letter.

The writer asks for parts here and service later, making it unclear whether he expects both or only one to be free.

The last paragraph implies that the service is necessary because of the age of the speakers; the first, because of a specific problem with the speakers. The reason for the request is thus muddied.

It's unclear how the trip to Canada figures in. Also, it's unclear if the stereo is used in the business or in the home.

HAWKINS MERCHANTILE
17th and Market
In the Heart of Downtown Dyersville
Dyersville, IL 46380

June 22, 19--

Dear John,

Recently, I was listening to my pair of Klipsch Heresy speakers. There was a slight "pop," and afterwards the speakers didn't produce any bass. Since the warranty covers parts, I would like you to replace the woofers free of charge.

My amplifier, the SAE model A-7, was driving the speakers. The speakers were connected to the amplifier with Monster Cable. The tape deck is an Optonica X-100. According to the meters on my amplifier, the speakers were only putting out 10 watts RMS per channel.

Since my speakers are only 4 months old (copy of the receipt enclosed), I would like to send them to you for service provided by the warranty. Please respond by July 2, since I will be leaving for Canada at that time.

Sincerely,

Mark Smith
President

Encl.

military definition, which applies across situations. However, the writer would be wise to include a description of the training problems themselves, since such a description would serve as grounds for the proposed redesign. Including more detail about the problems would promote the writer's purposes. Also, articulating the problems ensures that writer and reader have the same view of the problem.

Figure 5.32 introduces another aspect of comprehensiveness. The writer is responding to a college student who has asked a home-town auto repair shop if repairs to his car can be made in time for a job-interview trip that he is going to make. Figure 5.32 shows that a writer can be too comprehensive or, at least, can include too much detail.

Conciseness in a business document involves large concerns, such as organization and format, and local concerns, such as phrasing and diction. Figure 5.33 lacks conciseness on a number of fronts. The memo is a follow-up to a meeting between the writer and the person orchestrating an advertising campaign for a new line of products. The writer's purpose is to note changes he wants made to some of the agreements reached at the recent meeting.

In a revision (Figure 5.34), the writer recognizes the need to reorganize, rephrase, and reformat to achieve a concise presentation, so that he attains his purpose of directing new changes in the advertising campaign. The writer directly states the topic up front, regroups material to eliminate repetition, and uses shorter paragraphs.

You revise for clarity, comprehensiveness, and conciseness in the late stages of planning and drafting a document.

Figure 5.32 Excerpt Raising Issues Involving Comprehensiveness

In the interest of being comprehensive, this service-oriented writer offers the reader two alternatives. Since the reader should not drive his car, option two is obviously the better option. The writer should, therefore, probably include only option two in the letter, even though it would entail being less comprehensive.

In repairing the exhaust system or fuel line of a car, quite a bit of time is involved. This is due to the fact that these parts must be ordered from our suppliers in Chicago. Because deliveries take 3-5 days, it is not likely that the parts can be here and repairs completed by April 7. I can, however, offer you the following alternatives:

1. We can inspect your car and begin repairs as soon as the parts arrive, with no guarantee of their completion by April 7.

2. We can repair your car for you while you are away. We can provide you with a dependable loaner car to use while we make the repairs.

To ensure that no further damage is done and that the fumes you describe do not pose a threat to your safety, you should refrain from driving your car any distance until it can be repaired.

Figure 5.33 Letter in Need of Revision for Conciseness

The phrases "each component building on its predecessor" and "straight-across advertising" are redundant.

The writer unnecessarily covers the discussion of possible changes in three separate paragraphs.

The comment about company image is self-evident, and the racing angle contradicts the earlier statement about keeping a space theme.

SUBJECT: Thoughts Concerning Our Tentative Agreements Reached Monday

Regarding the advertising campaign we discussed in New York, would it be feasible to convert the original 30-second product introduction spots into a comprehensive, professional series? I'm thinking of sets of three 15-second commercials, with each component building on its predecessor. I'm thinking that I need more than just straight-across advertising to successfully compete in the market I want to reach. I still want to keep the high-technology space theme, since it conforms with our fashions so well. This, I of course realize, will change portions of the campaign we discussed, and the same time schedule still applies. I plan on being on the coast most of next week and would like to meet with you and discuss with you this in further detail. What days would be best for you?

I also feel we need to think about having a single spokesperson to represent our image in our broadcast commercials. This also differs from the previous plan we discussed in New York. I'd like you to be thinking of some personalities who could best represent our new line, and we'll discuss this next week also.

I'm also considering an auto racing angle as part of our promotional strategy. Have you ever done commercial spots involving racing teams? I'm still trying to work out how all of this would fit together. I still want to keep with the high-technology space theme. I'd appreciate any ideas you might have on this subject.

I feel these changes will best represent the image our company wishes to portray to the public. Please try to find some time to put some thought into what I've mentioned, and I'll contact you Monday to confirm my schedule for next week.

Figure 5.34 Letter Revised for Conciseness

The writer states the topic in the subject heading and opening sentence.

He groups the changes together and thus eliminates repetition.

He connects the racing angle with the space theme angle, so the reader does not have to wonder about contradiction.

SUBJECT: SOME CHANGES IN OUR TENTATIVE AGREEMENT REACHED MONDAY

I've been considering some changes to our New York plan.

In terms of format, I'd like to convert the original 30-second product introduction spots into a comprehensive professional series, involving sets of three 15-second commercials.

I'm also considering employing a *single* spokesperson to represent us in broadcast commercials.

I still want to keep with the high-technology space theme and the same time schedule. However, I'm toying with adding an auto racing angle to our promotional strategy—with futuristic vehicles, of course.

I plan on being on the coast most of next week and would like to meet with you to discuss these changes in further detail. What days would be best for you?

I'll contact you Monday with my schedule. I'm open to any input and hope you might have feedback at that early date.

Appeals, Purposes, and Planning

Business communicators fulfill their purposes by promoting their credibility, accommodating the feelings of their audiences, and ensuring the integrity of their messages. You can include these areas in your planning by remembering to ask questions about appeals as you draft (Figure 5.35).

Figure 5.35 Questions to Ask Concerning Appeals When Planning a Document

How can I assure the reader of my good character in this communication?

- What details can I include that show my character and expertise?
- How can I ensure my text is accurate and mechanically correct to demonstrate my believability and trustworthiness?
- What persona should I use to demonstrate my competence and character in this situation?
- What tone can I use to show appropriate concern for and control over my information?

What can I do in this communication to acknowledge and identify with my reader's feelings and values?

- What details can I use to dramatize the situation so that readers can picture or feel a personal involvement in what I am discussing?
- How can I make sure the text is accessible and courteous?
- How can I show or suggest that I value the same ideals as my audience—that is, how can I demonstrate that I identify with my audience?

What can I do in this communication to ensure its integrity?

- How can I make sure that my information is sound and makes sense?
- How can I make sure the communication is clear, comprehensive, and concise?

SKILLS & STRATEGIES

THE USE AND ABUSE OF PASSIVE VOICE

Professional writers often use active voice instead of passive voice to achieve conciseness. You construct passive voice with a form of the verb "to be" plus "by." Of the two sentences "The CEO was blamed for low morale by the employees" and "The employees blamed the CEO for low morale," the first, which is two words longer, is in passive voice.

Most stylesheets recommend against the use of passive voice, with the goal of eliminating *wordiness.* But wordiness can come not only from passive constructions, but also from a weak vocabulary and certain habits in phrasing:

. . .The main value ~~that~~ a Rabbit Diesel ~~has to offer~~ *offers* is the incredible mileage. According to *Road and Track* ~~magazine, a reputable authority~~, the Volkswagen, equipped with ~~an~~ optional five-speed transmission, ~~achieved an overall~~ *averaged* forty-three miles-per-gallon ~~mileage rating~~. With a ~~recorded~~ high of sixty ~~m.p.g.~~ and a ~~recorded~~ low of forty ~~m.p.g., this Rabbit Diesel has excellent advantages.~~

One trade off, however, for superior mileage is ~~the lack of neck-breaking speed of~~ *slow* acceleration ~~. The Volkswagen Diesel is slow. It has a 0.60 m.p.h. time of~~ *from 0 to 60 in* 22.9 seconds. This time can be ~~cut down~~ *assisted* considerably ~~with the addition of~~ *by* turbo-charging. ~~It's~~ a process of rerouting *and using* ~~the~~ discharged exhaust ~~and using it~~ for combustion ~~purposes~~. However, ~~this process~~ *turbo-charging* is not yet available on the Rabbit Diesel. Aesthetically, the V.W. is ~~a~~ practical ~~means of transportation~~. The car's ~~exterior is styled for four adult-sized people. Consequently,~~ *interior accommodates four adults.* the ~~shape of the body~~ *exterior* is boxy, rather like a stagecoach.

In the example, the use of linking verbs, prepositional phrases, the "it is" transformation, and redundant wording all contribute to wordiness. Passive voice is not the culprit.

Moreover, passive voice can correctly be used when the *agent or person doing the action* is not significant in the sentence. For example, in the sentence "The motion was raised and seconded," the agent is not stated. The focus is on the motion itself, and not on who might have enabled a vote on the issue by taking the parliamentary action of moving the motion. You do not have to support a motion to bring it up for a vote. A problem does occur, however, when the agent is significant but purposely omitted. For example, in the sentence "The product was found to be effective in eliminating termites," who found the product effective *is* important. Did the inventor of the product find it effective? The research and development team testing it? The federal agency regulating the product? The company marketing it? The union representing the employees producing the product? The consumers using it? In this case, a full passive construction might read, "The product was found to be effective by ninety-five percent of the customers using it." The active construction would read: "Ninety-five percent of the customers found the product effective." The active voice is preferable here because the agent is important and the active sentence is less wordy.

Passive voice is also a consideration in *paragraph emphasis.* Consistent paragraph emphasis can be maintained by having one grammatical subject and one verb tense per paragraph. Sometimes eliminating passive voice can help you maintain a single emphasis. The revision below enables the paragraph to have one emphasis (the doctor) rather than three (the lab specimen, the patient, the tests).

ORIGINAL	REVISION
The laboratory specimen was analyzed by the doctor. It was found to contain pre-cancerous cells. The patient was advised by the doctor to undergo other tests. These tests were to determine if the pre-cancerous cells here indicated the probability of the patient having cancer elsewhere in his body.	After finding pre-cancerous cells in the specimen, the doctor advised the patient to undergo other tests to determine the probability of existent cancerous growth.

Sometimes, however, passive voice can correctly be used to preserve paragraph emphasis, as a paragraph adapted from a 1993 Brad Edmondson editorial in *American Demographics* demonstrates:

> Consumers do need some control over sensitive information like credit and medical records. But they already have the option of getting off direct-mail lists. Consumers *should be given* easier access to this option *by* marketers.

In this example, passive voice helps the writer maintain *consumers* as the main emphasis of the paragraph. The active sentence "Marketers should give consumers easier access to this option" is shorter, but loses the advantage of its reduced length because readers must work to process the new subject, "marketers," introduced at the end of the paragraph.

RESPONSE SHEET

ESTABLISHING A PURPOSE

WRITER(S): AUDIENCE(S):
OCCASION FOR WRITING: DOCUMENT:
WHAT PROBLEM/ISSUE IS THE WRITER (AM I) TRYING TO ADDRESS IN THIS DOCUMENT?

◆ OVERALL PURPOSE STATEMENT

In this business message, the writer wants to [persuade/inform/etc.(?)] someone [what audience?] of something [what subject?].

◆ OPERATIONAL PURPOSE(S)

What does the *writer* want to achieve? (List various operational purposes.)

◆ CONVENTION-DRIVEN PURPOSE(S)

What purpose(s) are usually associated with the type of business document the writer is writing? (List various convention-driven purposes.)

◆ OCCASION-DRIVEN PURPOSES

Primary and Secondary Purposes: Of the purposes listed above, which are the most important, in rank order? (Rank order the purposes by numbering them in the margin.)

Does the development of the information in the document reflect the priorities set up by this ordering of purposes? Explain.

Purposes Allowed by the Context: How will the contextual constraints influence what the writer tries to do in this document?

◆ READER-BASED CONSIDERATIONS

How are the writer's purposes affected by reader expectations?

◆ PRESENTATION OF PURPOSES

Comment on how the writer presents the purposes in the document. Should the purposes be more specific? Should some explicit purposes be made implicit, or vice versa?

RESPONSE SHEET

APPEALS AND PURPOSES

WRITER(S): AUDIENCE(S):
OCCASION FOR WRITING: DOCUMENT:
WHAT PROBLEM/ISSUE IS THE WRITER (AM I) TRYING TO ADDRESS IN THIS DOCUMENT?

◆ APPEAL TO THE WRITER'S CHARACTER

How can the writer enhance (his, her) credibility in this document? What information can the writer include to enhance this credibility?

How does the writer address concerns for accuracy and correctness? How can the document's accuracy and correctness be improved?

What persona is established in this document? How does that persona enhance writer credibility?

What is the tone used in this document? How does that enhance writer credibility? How can the use of tone be made more appropriate?

◆ APPEAL TO THE READER'S EMOTIONS AND VALUES

How does the writer *dramatize* the content of the document to enhance its reader appeal?

How does the writer make the document accessible to the reader? What improvements are possible?

How does the writer display courtesy in the document? Improvements?

How can the writer effect improvement in this area? (Make suggestions on draft.)

◆ APPEAL TO THE INTEGRITY OF THE DOCUMENT

How does the writer attend to the soundness of the information in the communication?

How does the writer effect clarity in the document?

Is the document comprehensive? Explain.

How does the writer show concern for conciseness?

How can the writer effect improvement in this area? (Make suggestions on draft.)

ACTIVITIES, EXERCISES, AND ASSIGNMENTS

◆ IN-CLASS ACTIVITIES

1. Please refer to Figure 5.1, the Eire Enterprises letter, for the following activity.
   a. Discuss the questions raised in the annotations to Figure 5.1 in terms of what you have learned in this chapter about purposes and appeals.
   b. Identify the various types of purposes that you see in the Eire letter that correspond to those discussed in this chapter.
   c. Compare your answers to parts a and b with your answers to similar questions asked at the beginning of this chapter (page 130).
2. Recalling the Cannes Dew story, discuss several ways purposes might influence a communicator's presentation and use of information. To answer this question, you might create an illustration based on the subject in which you have the most expertise.
3. Imagine that you have to give a short oral presentation for an in-service training session on the three major appeals communicators can use to help fulfill their purposes. In this presentation, you know that you should define each appeal and name various writing strategies associated with each appeal. In so doing, you should also describe each strategy in terms of a specific example, either one of your own making or one that you have obtained or received from a business organization. Finally, you should summarize how knowing these appeals and strategies is helpful in planning a business message. Be prepared to present your discussion to the rest of the class.

◆ INDIVIDUAL GROUP EXERCISES

1. Please refer to the two-part Figure 5.36 in completing this exercise.
   a. Identify various purposes you see in the letter.
   b. Identify and discuss any appeals that you find in the letter. How successfully does each appeal support the writer's purpose(s)?
   c. What details in the letter are extraneous?
   d. In your opinion, does the letter raise any ethical issues? Explain.
   e. Together with several fellow students, revise the letter so that it better fulfills its purposes.
2. Please refer to the letter in Figure 5.37 (page 156) in completing this exercise.

CONTEXT

Figure 5.36 shows a two-page letter written by an insurance agent to his clients. (Any mechanical errors noted in **bold** were miscues in the original document.) The document raises questions about the writer's purpose(s).

Figure 5.36a AIDS Letter, Page 1.

Dear Clients:

The fear of AIDS is **begining** to **effect** every part of our society. It has become a major concern of the life and health insurance companies. Those who have been with me for some time know that I have notified you as new coverages became available, so you could take advantage of them if you wished. It's also my duty to notify you when reality isn't so pleasant and suggest some possible actions.

It would be a tragedy if any of us came down with AIDS! That's scary enough. My clients who are doctors at our fine clinics are also worried about the tests that are used to check for AIDS. The life and health insurance companies are **begining** to use blood tests to check for AIDS before they approve the applications. They are the best tests currently available at a reasonable cost. What our doctors are worried about are "false positives." These are when the tests inaccurately suggest the presence of the AIDS virus where none actually exists. A positive reaction to the AIDS tests, whether it is accurate or "false," will force a rejection of the application. The insurance companies will try to maintain complete confidentiality of records of refusal. But our doctors are worried that records may be stolen by the types of people who are "computer hackers" or leaked accidentally. Then other companies would probably not accept coverage. They also worry that job discrimination (legal or illegal) may be the result for us—or for our children.

Alliance Insurance, Inc. is a midwestern company primarily serving middle-class clients. Fewer cases of AIDS have been discovered in our population—so far. Alliance has been slower to begin testing blood samples for AIDS on the life and health applications than companies based on the Coasts. Many companies begin tests at life insurance applications above $100,000 coverage. Some request blood tests for <u>all</u> applications. Alliance is still just testing on applications at or above $250,000. The trend is for testing on smaller life insurance policies and health insurance policies. These trends suggest that Alliance may go to lower **minimus** in early-to-mid 19—. <u>Within a year or two, probably all life and health insurance applications for all companies will include the blood tests for AIDS.</u>

ALLIANCE INSURANCE, INC.

Figure 5.36b AIDS Letter, Page 2

AIDS Message, page 2

As your agent, I encourage you to set up programs on all children and adults who do not have sufficient coverage, before the AIDS blood tests are mandatory. For children, **premiumus** of about $6 per month for about 15 years will establish a $5000 whole life program. This includes "Guaranteed Insurability" which will allow them to purchase $5000 more coverage six times between ages 25 and 40 without proof of good health. For adults we have decreasing and level term packages, as well as universal and whole life policies. We also have good health insurance programs which will generally not yet require testing.

Cost is always a factor. That's why I suggest we sit down now and work out an affordable program for your family's budget.

For your convenience I've enclosed the tearoff sheet below and a stamped, return envelope. Please send it back whether or not you are interested in life coverages. Then I can show those who really care about you that I did try to help.

Sincerely yours,

A.J. Hammel
Your Alliance Agent

AJH/jrd

- -

Due to the agency letter we are aware about the concern for AIDS and the limitations of the testing for it by the insurance industry. At the present time:

_____ We would like to meet with you to review our life and health insurance needs. Please call us at ________. The best time to reach us is ________.

________________ ________________ ________________

Signed Signed Date

Incidentally, we now have the "earthquake coverage" available for homes and rental properties. Call if you're interested.

UPDATE: We just received notice that as of December 1, we must attach a supplemental AIDS questionnaire to all health insurance applications. I doubt that similar items are far behind, probably within the next 3 to 6 months, for life insurance.

Figure 5.37 Letter Requesting Monetary Compensation

CONTEXT

Figure 5.37 shows a letter written by Monika Balint asking secure compensation for lost luggage. Monika is a successful competitor in the 800 meters and has spent a great deal of time traveling to international track meets.

Dear Mr. Mulineck:

On the flight SR 125 of January 14, 19--, from Zurich to New York City my two pieces of luggage, containing several valuable items, disappeared. After having waited 20 minutes at the already silent carousel I contacted the airport officials and reported my loss to the International Air employees.

The employees investigated immediately, but without any prompt success. I was then told to fill out some forms and sent home with the promise that I would be notified of its arrival. On January 17, 19--, International Air called and notified me that my luggage was not found. I was told to file a formal report and claim to your office for proper compensation.

I hereby list you the rather valuable items lost with my suitcases, which were also insured at International Air in Budapest, Hungary:

Mid 19th century hand made Thailand rug	*$2000.-*
2 business suits (Gian Franco Ferre)	*$600.-*
Cashmere sweater (Pierre Cardin)	*$300.-*
4 pairs of leather shoes (Bally)	*$700.-*
Miscellaneous (Polo, Liz Claiborne shirts)	*$400.-*
2 suitcases	*$400.-*
Overall value of approximately	*$4400.-*

My loss of belongings is quite significant personally as well as financially; the rug from Thailand, for instance, was a Christmas present from a close friend. I have enclosed the insurance papers and the International Air luggage numbers and am kindly asking you to compensate me as soon as possible.

I have traveled International Air for the last five years and have always been pleased with your services. I would like to continue traveling with your company in the future as well.

Thank you for your cooperation.

Sincerely,

Monika Balint
Tel. (212) 555-6126

Encl. 2

a. Please comment specifically on the strategies Monica used to establish her credibility in this letter (on details showing her expertise as well as the document's accuracy, correctness, persona, and tone).

b. Please comment specifically on the strategies for appealing to the reader in this letter (on its dramatization, accessibility, courtesy, and identification).

c. Please comment specifically on strategies contributing to the integrity of this letter (on its soundness, clarity, comprehensiveness, and conciseness).

3. Please use the information in Figure 5.38 to complete this exercise.

a. Write two different versions of the information in Figure 5.38 using separate purposes. To do so, you might start with a very general purpose of informing or persuading, before generating a more specific purpose. You may have to add information to ensure that your versions make sense.

b. Explain how the different purposes you have chosen affect your presentation and the reader's understanding of the information.

c. Compare your versions with those of other students in your class. Discuss similarities and differences in your approaches.

4. Please use Figure 5.39 in completing this task. This letter is a rough draft of a response to a complaint filed by Mr. Taylor regarding service at your company.

a. How would you react if you received such a letter? Identify areas in need of improvement in this letter. (Use one or both of the Response Sheets at the end of this chapter to aid you.)

b. Revise the letter, focusing on clarity, comprehensiveness, and correctness, and on reader-centered appeals.

Figure 5.38 Information Presented without a Specified Purpose

Freeman-Ruiz, a brokerage firm, currently maintains a hard-copy filing system for client information. Client files are separated into two groups. The first group, containing information entered within the last 1 to 10 years, is filed in the records division of the main office. The second group, consisting of information older than 10 years, is stored in archives in the basement of the main office. Both groups are arranged alphabetically according to client last name. It is estimated that between both filing areas, the company has over 250,000 files.

To access files, an account executive either fills out a written request (Client Files Request Form 6-A) or simply e-mails a request to the records division (JRMab.@freemanruiz.recdiv.c). Requests are usually fulfilled within 2 days of their receipt at the division office. Accessing older files involves a two-step process. An account executive must first get an approval slip (Records Form FLCK-1) from the records division affirming that the file is not there. Then, the account executive attaches to that approval slip a written request (Client Files Request Form 6-B) for the older file in question and sends that request through in-house mail to archives. Such requests are usually filled within 10 days of receipt.

Freeman-Ruiz has a strict policy of keeping the information within a file organized. Account executives are responsible for the "housekeeping" of their individual client files. Files are routinely updated every 3 months.

Figure 5.39 Rough Draft of Letter in Need of Extensive Revision

RE: The order letter sent to you last week.

Dear Mr. Taylor,

I appreciate your letter saying that you and your co-workers have received discourteous treatment from one of our departments. Your letter also stated that extra supplies were sent. We strive to meet the needs of our customers.

As a valued client, we strive to serve your needs. We apologize for any discourteous treatment that you or your co-workers may have received from the from one of our departments. Our office etiquette training program to better serve our customers has been established for the past two months.

I have personally reviewed your order. You stated you were sent and charged for extra supplies that you did not order. Your letter also requested a full refund. When we receive phone orders, our operators read back the order to verify the order. This extra step is to correct any mistakes in processing your order.

It is the client's responsibility to verify the order when it is read back to you by our operator. A representative of your firm verified the order when it was read back to him. Your company ordered the extra office supplies shipped with that order. Since the extra supplies were returned unopened, we will credit your account for this amount. The company will be responsible for the shipping costs of the extra supplies. The policy does not cover a refund on shipping if supplies are returned.

We hold the high regard of its clients, partly due to the high quality of the products we sell but largely because of the courteous, client centered image we have projected during our many years of business. We want to keep your company as a customer and we are willing to deduct 10% from an order. If you have any comments, please feel free to contact us at our new toll free number. As times change, your needs change and we change to meet the needs of our clients.

Sincerely,

◆ OUT-OF-CLASS ASSIGNMENTS

1. Select a workplace document or a business message written for a previous class assignment that you believe could be improved in terms of purpose. Use the Response Sheet on establishing a purpose to aid your analysis of the document. Then revise the document so that the reader has a clearer idea of what the document/writer is trying to accomplish, and why various strategies are used in the document.
2. Select a business communication that annoyed you because it used an inappropriate tone with its audience. Write a one-paragraph assessment of the problems with the existing document. Revise the document to eliminate the problems you have identified. When you turn in the assignment, include (a) the original document, (b) your assessment of the document's problems with tone, and (c) the revised document.
3. Imagine that you, too, work at Cannes Dew and discover information about the Americans with Disabilities Act (ADA) taped to your computer terminal when you arrive at work (Figure 5.2). Imagine further that Kelley Gaines wants you to consider this information when you write an "open letter to potential employees" about the company to be handed out at job fairs on college campuses. The letter is to have two primary purposes: to recruit personnel who might be included under the ADA and to promote Cannes Dew's corporate image as a company concerned with diversity in its hiring practices and its workforce. You may want to generate additional information to make your open letter effective. Use both the Response Sheet on establishing a purpose and the Response Sheet on appeals and purposes to help you draft your letter.

CASE

BOOKER PAPER COMPANY

CASE BY ANDREA BREEMER FRANTZ

Background. You are the personnel director for Booker Paper Company, a relatively small paper processing plant located in Waters, Washington. The plant employs approximately 275 people in chemical processing, machine operation, and transportation and is an important source of jobs in the small town. Important details about the plant's history include:

- Founded in 1964, it experienced growth for the first 11 years, adding 50 new employees, a loading dock, and a new office facility.
- In the mid 1970s, the area experienced severe economic decline. In 1975, the plant manager made the difficult decision to lay off 30 percent of Booker's workforce and cut back operations. Waters residents were furious, particularly because the layoff came shortly before Christmas. Booker management worked hard to assuage the community's anger by initiating a job placement and counseling program for those workers willing to relocate and retrain; however, the plant manager was socially ostracized by Waters residents and eventually left the community.
- In direct response to the demoralizing layoff, employees voted to join the union in 1976.
- In 1978, the company began once again to add employees and increase production.
- In 1979, there was a brief threat of a union strike because of possible loss of health insurance benefits, but management averted the strike by maintaining health benefits and dumping a plan to renovate the office structure at the plant.
- By 1984, Booker had recovered the 30 percent employee loss suffered in 1975, and by 1987 had again increased ranks by another 10 percent.
- In 1989, Booker experienced financial difficulties when two long-standing contracts expired and were not renewed. Once again, Booker was forced to cut back its workforce, this time by nearly 20 percent, a significant loss of jobs for the community. Union members called a strike, which lasted for three months and required arbitration.

During the strike, the plant's office facility received two bomb threats. The city mayor, Alice Mayo, sharply rebuked plant management for "damaging community morale by treating employees shabbily . . . without thought or consideration for the lives disrupted by such erratic personnel decisions." Shortly after the mayor's comments, the company president, James Booker, Jr., fired the plant manager and two plant foremen in a move to "restructure the organization to avoid further personnel problems." Union workers returned to the plant with the guarantee that no more jobs would be lost and no benefits cut. However, in annual personnel reviews, Booker Paper employees reflected an all-time low in morale and productivity, and operational meetings continued to be fraught with tension.

Booker then hired Sam Carver-Smith, a specialist in community relations and human resources, to manage the plant. Carver-Smith hired two new foremen: Grover Farney, employed by Booker since 1968, and Union Davis, a relatively new employee who managed to escape the layoff. Both Davis and Farney commanded obvious respect from their coworkers. Since 1990, Booker's employee ranks and productivity have increased slowly. Employees generally acknowledged that the team of Farney, Davis, and Carver-Smith is people-oriented and interested in building the company. However, given Booker's history, morale is tenuous and productivity fluctuates.

Last night, the president and the management team signed an important contract to develop a recycling unit as an addition to the plant. The deal was kept secret from Booker employees to avoid further morale problems if agreement could not be reached on contract terms. The plan

- adds permanent positions to the plant
- increases security in existing contracts, ensuring more job security and a likely wage increase for current employees
- necessitates temporarily (up to a year) adding a graveyard shift to the plant (10 P.M. to 6 A.M.) and rotating employee schedules once every three weeks

One potential problem management sees with the new scheduling is that Booker employs at least 20 people who are single parents, most of them with small children. For these people, working graveyard for one week out of every month will be difficult, and perhaps impossible.

Task. The management team has asked you, the personnel director, to determine how and when to communicate the expansion and added-shift decision to Booker employees. James Booker, Jr., has asked you to consider the fact that rumor travels quickly in the plant and employee morale will suffer if workers hear the news on the street rather than from you and the management team. You must *plan* one document or several documents that address the following purposes:

- to help employees feel positive about this change
- to inform employees fully about the long-term and short-term changes (or face possible repercussions from union workers)
- to reflect a community-relations orientation as well as an internal human relations appeal, in the likely event the story is picked up by the local press
- to acknowledge (carefully) that the decision making has largely taken place behind closed doors
- to consider the concerns of single parents, who may face hardship with the scheduling changes
- to protect manager Carver-Smith and foremen Farney and Davis from criticism because they have been so instrumental in building employee faith in management

Your planned message or messages need to address all these purposes in a timely fashion.

Write a memo to Booker for review that outlines your planned communication(s). Remember, if you are planning more than one communication to address these purposes, the likelihood is that all of the various parties involved will eventually see each communication.

Complication. Booker reveals that two of the single parents, Bryan Aller and Margo Busch, who face possible hardship with the scheduling change, are the most likely to be tapped by their supervisors for promotion. These two individuals have a great deal of seniority and have been in line for promotion for a long time. Both have had a history in the company of encouraging dissent. Both were vocal about their anger at being passed over for promotion when Davis and Farney were promoted; however, little came of it because Davis and Farney were so popular. Since the hiring, however, Busch has assumed a key spokesperson role with the union.

Your communication materials must now address an additional purpose: to prevent public conflict with Aller and Busch. Amend your plans and reveal your revised plans in a separate memo to Booker.

CHAPTER

6

Conventions in Correspondence: Common Strategies for Organization and Development, and Ways to Adapt Them

OUTLINE

Major Factors Influencing the Use of Conventions: Nick Sanger's Choice

Why Knowing about Conventions Matters

Conventional Organizational Strategies

Common Strategies for Development

Issues Involving the Use of Conventions

CRITERIA FOR EXPLORING CHAPTER 6

What we cover in this chapter	What you will be able to do after reading this chapter
Choices in dealing with conventions	Demonstrate how both using and changing conventions can be appropriate to communication
Major factors that influence textual conventions	Explain how the writer, reader, and occasion affect the use of conventions
Why knowing about conventions matters	Understand how writing decisions, reader use, and the writer-reader relationship relate to conventions
Conventional organizational strategies	Arrange information inductively and deductively, appropriate to the main idea and the situation
Conventional strategies for development	Use both general and specific ways of presenting information involving traditional organizational patterns and sequences
When and how to use or to adapt conventions	Appropriately depart from conventions, describe unsuccessful ways of departing from conventions, and tailor use of conventions to specific situations

Effective communicators know that they have to consider both the past and the present when they write. They consider the past by knowing how similar occasions for speaking or writing have usually been handled in the past. They consider the present by altering past practice that has been codified in conventions to fit a specific writer, reader, or message in the present. Figure 6.1 shows a writer mixing both conventional and unconventional strategies in a single message.

CONTEXT

Figure 6.1 shows page 1 of a four-page sales letter offering student readers the chance to apply for a credit card. The message is conventional enough that the reader can recognize it immediately as a business letter, but, as the opening of the message itself suggests, the writer's idea of a "perfect corporate information letter" is anything but traditional.

Figure 6.1 Credit Card Solicitation, Page 1 (of 4)

With the salutation "Joe Student" the writer signals the unconventional nature of the document that follows.

The writer directly establishes that this letter will depart from convention. In fact, what the letter does is actually follow convention, at least in part, highlighting the specifics present in any credit card application solicitation.

The writer emphasizes his rebellious spirit with a deliberately ungrammatical phrase, "don't got it."

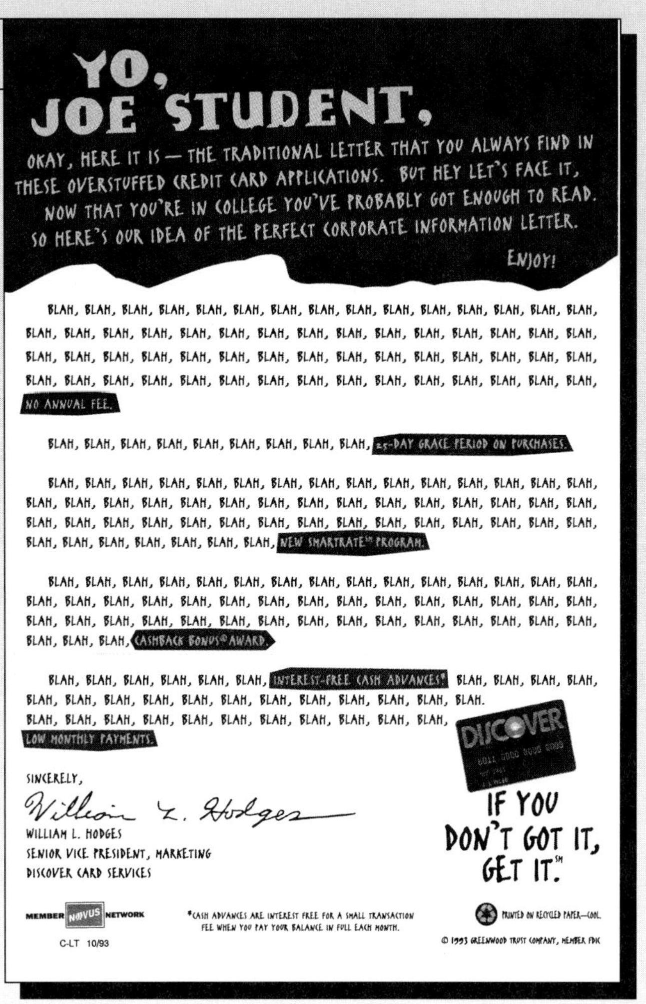

YO,
JOE STUDENT,

OKAY, HERE IT IS — THE TRADITIONAL LETTER THAT YOU ALWAYS FIND IN THESE OVERSTUFFED CREDIT CARD APPLICATIONS. BUT HEY LET'S FACE IT, NOW THAT YOU'RE IN COLLEGE YOU'VE PROBABLY GOT ENOUGH TO READ. SO HERE'S OUR IDEA OF THE PERFECT CORPORATE INFORMATION LETTER.

ENJOY!

BLAH, NO ANNUAL FEE.

BLAH, BLAH, BLAH, BLAH, BLAH, BLAH, BLAH, BLAH, BLAH, 25-DAY GRACE PERIOD ON PURCHASES.

BLAH, NEW SMARTRATE℠ PROGRAM.

BLAH, CASHBACK BONUS® AWARD.

BLAH, BLAH, BLAH, BLAH, BLAH, BLAH, INTEREST-FREE CASH ADVANCES* BLAH, BLAH, BLAH, BLAH, BLAH, BLAH, BLAH, BLAH, BLAH, BLAH, BLAH, BLAH, BLAH, BLAH, BLAH, BLAH. BLAH, BLAH, BLAH, BLAH, BLAH, BLAH, BLAH, BLAH, BLAH, BLAH, BLAH, LOW MONTHLY PAYMENTS.

SINCERELY,

William L. Hodges

WILLIAM L. HODGES
SENIOR VICE PRESIDENT, MARKETING
DISCOVER CARD SERVICES

IF YOU DON'T GOT IT, GET IT.℠

MEMBER NOVUS NETWORK

C-LT 10/93

*CASH ADVANCES ARE INTEREST FREE FOR A SMALL TRANSACTION FEE WHEN YOU PAY YOUR BALANCE IN FULL EACH MONTH.

PRINTED ON RECYCLED PAPER—COOL.

© 1993 GREENWOOD TRUST COMPANY, MEMBER FDIC

1. How do you know that this is a letter rather than, say, a short story? Why do you think the writer chose to mix traditional elements that tell you this is a letter with unconventional elements, like "blah, blah," in this business message?
2. What makes this a "perfect corporate information letter"?
3. What factors in the letter encourage you to believe that the writer is departing from convention on purpose? Why is it important that the writer establishes that he knows what he is doing, even though part of what he is doing is quite unusual?

The reason William Hodges' "blah, blah" letter works is that you recognize enough of the traditional elements in the letter to realize what is different in the writer's approach this time. A writer like Hodges knows

- how certain conventional strategies basic to writing in general affect the arrangement and development of business messages
- how to adopt, alter, or abandon traditional strategies to fit the occasion, the writer, and the audience

MAJOR FACTORS INFLUENCING THE USE OF CONVENTIONS: NICK SANGER'S CHOICE

The occasion, writer, and audience all influence the use of conventions. Writing rejection letters, for example, is an *occasion* for writing. It shares similarities with other situations where unfavorable news about people must be conveyed. Other occasions for unfavorable news include declining a request for a refund, giving negative performance reviews, and terminating employment.

Nick Sanger, personnel director for a medium-sized pharmaceutical firm, recently had occasion to write a letter rejecting job applicants. Sanger's experience with this task demonstrates how the occasion, writer, and reader can interact to influence choices involving conventions. After hiring a particularly outstanding applicant for Assistant Director of Marketing for the Western Division, Sanger had to send letters to the 40 applicants who were rejected for the position. Three of the rejected applicants were in-house candidates.

Sanger is acquainted with established ways of handling such unfavorable news. These conventions, which are similar to those used in any message that anticipates reader resistance, include a specific sequence for presenting information:

- opening: contains detail that buffers or softens the impending bad news
- body: states the reason for the bad news, then the bad news itself
- close: attempts to convey a helpful and friendly attitude

Sanger uses this conventional structure to draft a rejection letter (Figure 6.2) that he intends to send to all rejected applicants.

Sanger has written a letter that he could send to all 40 rejected applicants. But he realizes that three of the applicants are in-house. He has two different *audiences*. Although sending the conventional letter of rejection to the three in-house applicants would match the occasion, it would not necessarily match the writer-reader relationship between Sanger and the in-house applicants.

Figure 6.2 Conventional Letter of Rejection

Opening: Sanger uses a "thank you" as a buffer or soft opening.

Body: He provides reasons before giving the "bad news."

Close: Sanger concludes with a positive assessment.

Thank you for your application to be the Assistant Director of Marketing for the Western Division.

Yours was among 41 applications for the position that were, without exception, highly competitive.

Upon careful consideration of all the applicants, the selection committee has decided to hire a candidate with both excellent advertising experience in the competitive Eastern seaboard market and several years of managerial experience.

We feel that your credentials are impressive and that you should have no difficulty in securing a position that best matches your considerable qualifications. We wish you the very best in your job search.

Figure 6.3 Unconventional Letter of Rejection

Opening: Sanger's buffer is based on his personal knowledge of the applicant.

Body: He presents the decision and immediately gives reasons for it.

Close: He positively assesses the applicant's future.

We both know that you have been anxiously awaiting the selection committee's decision concerning the Assistant Directorship that you applied for.

The decision has just reached my desk, and I regret having to inform you that another applicant was selected for the position. This applicant was selected for her unique combination of marketing and managerial experience.

You will be gratified to know that the committee was extremely impressed by your qualifications and your credentials were highly competitive within the rather large pool of 41 applicants.

I'm confident that you will have no trouble moving into a directorship in the near future and, selfishly speaking, I hope we will be the ones able to offer you such a position. Your contributions to the company have been outstanding, and we would hate to lose you to another firm.

Please give me a call or drop in if you would like to discuss possible future openings.

Conventions for conducting interviews differ depending on the occasion, whether it involves applying for a job or discovering information about an employee's performance on the job.

Although there would be nothing really "wrong" in sending the conventional letter to in-house candidates, Sanger exercises his privilege as the *writer* in this situation to compose a second, more personal letter (Figure 6.3). By writing this letter, Sanger hopes to maintain his good relationships with the rejected internal applicants and to encourage their continued presence in the company.

Sanger's decision to depart from convention in the alternative letter suggests that what has been appropriate to past situations, defined in this case by the convention for handling bad news, might not always be the most effective approach to a present communication.

WHY KNOWING ABOUT CONVENTIONS MATTERS

A **communication convention** is an established way of approaching an occasion for speaking or writing. Conventions are strategies that have been found to be successful over time. When written down or codified, they provide guidelines for communication and represent a shared agreement between communicator and informed audience concerning what the listener or reader can expect. Conventions serve a number of important purposes:

- aiding communicator decisions
- facilitating reader use
- establishing a secure writer-reader relationship
- defining the communication context

Aiding Communicator Decisions

One important reason for knowing about conventions is that they help you decide what and how to write. Conventions serve as a *heuristic*, or planning strategy, that prompts you to consider aspects appropriate to the occasion and to your specific readers.

Conventions serve as a heuristic no matter what type of writing you are doing. For example, you are probably familiar with the journalistic convention of including information about *who, what, where, when, why,* and *how* in every news story. This convention prompts you to ask and write about each of these six elements when covering such a story. Similarly, you might be acquainted with the "five-paragraph theme" from a first-year English course. The five-paragraph theme convention tells you to include your thesis in paragraph one, to develop three supporting examples or argumentative proofs in each of the next three paragraphs, and to have a concluding statement or assessment in the last paragraph. Although following such a formula does not guarantee good writing, it does help you consider what to include and where to include it.

Business communication, as you are discovering, is a type of writing, or *genre*, that has many conventions. These conventions involve overall approaches, such as you-attitude (Chapter 4), as well as specific expectations tied to the type of message you are writing (as discussed in Chapters 8, 9, and 10). Knowing these conventions helps you to generate and manage your information. For example, if you are composing a formal report, convention tells you that such reports contain introductory sections that establish the report's purpose, scope, assumptions, and methods. Simply knowing this about reports reminds you to collect information on these areas and helps you to place that information appropriately in the finished document.

Facilitating Reader Use

Selecting the appropriate conventions also facilitates reader use. Conventional strategies, such as deductive (top-down) and inductive (bottom-up) organizational patterns, for example, aid different uses.

Let's take a situation where a board of directors is trying to decide whom to promote to a managerial position. If the board prefers not to evaluate the candidates for the position themselves but rather to rely on the opinions of the candidates' immediate supervisors, then deductive organization would be appropriate. A deductively arranged evaluation submitted to this board would identify the supervisor's position up front. If board members then cared to look at the reasons for a supervisor's decision, they could do so, but they would not have to read through the entire document to discover what the supervisor thought.

Similarly, if a different board consisted of members who wanted to come to a decision independent of that of the supervisors providing evaluations, then inductive organization would be more appropriate. An inductively arranged evaluation submitted to this board would provide reasons for the supervisor's assessment of the candidate before a final evaluation was given. If board members wanted to make up their own minds, they could simply weigh the evidence presented in the first part of the message, reach a conclusion before reading the supervisor's final evaluation, and then compare their assessment with that of the supervisor and other board members. (Additional information about deductive and inductive organization appears later in this chapter.)

Establishing a Secure Writer-Reader Relationship

Conventions also establish what linguists call a secure writer-reader relationship. A secure relationship is one in which the reader understands what the writer intended. It is not necessarily "secure" in the sense that good friendships are secure or that long-standing relationships are stable. Experts point out that the closer the match between the writer's intention and the reader's interpretation, the better the chance that the document will have a shared "**exchange value**" between writer and reader.[1] Conventions help make this match.

MULTICULTURAL

DIFFERENCES IN CONVENTION USE BETWEEN NATIVE AND NONNATIVE SPEAKERS OF ENGLISH

Companies that have branch offices in other countries routinely face differences in the way native and nonnative speakers of English approach conventional components of business writing.

Brenda R. Sims and Steven Guice examined 214 business letters written by native speakers (NS) and nonnative speakers (NNS) looking for cultural differences. Sims and Guice discovered significant differences in four distinct categories.

Sims and Guice also found that nonnative speakers and native speakers differed in the way they handled standard letter elements: salutations, closings, tone, and detail. They concluded that nonnative speakers apparently misunderstood native readers' expectations and the context in which letters would be received. Native speakers of English face similar difficulties, in reverse, when communicating in English to a nonnative speaker audience.

Four Categories of Difference in Native Speaker and Nonnative Speaker Business Letters

Characteristics Contrasting with U.S. Business Correspondence	NS	NNS
exaggerated politeness (such as "I humbly request you to take into consideration my ardent desire to continue my studies")	18%	44%
unnecessary professional information (such as detailed employment and educational information)	21%	64%
unnecessary personal information (such as "I am a Korean woman . . .")	20%	51%
inappropriate requests (such as "I would appreciate it very much if you would excuse me from this standard requirement")	24%	43%

Conventions tell us what direction(s) to take in meeting others' expectations.

For example, Nick Sanger knew that a business message containing "bad news" conventionally begins with a statement that tries to establish some common ground between writer and reader. Thus, if you use such a statement at the beginning of a message, the reader who knows the "bad news" convention also knows, upon reading the opening, that you intend to convey bad news of some sort in the letter. There is, therefore, less chance that the informed reader, anticipating bad news, will misinterpret your decision. But what of the reader who does not know this business-specific convention? Because readers not knowing the convention depend solely on what the text says, you need to be very careful in how you word the next-to-last paragraph, which contains the bad news, so that they understand its meaning. There is more of a chance of a misunderstanding with readers who do not know the convention, because these readers would not be able to use the conventional common-ground opening as a cue for how to interpret the details that appear later in the letter.

As you use conventions, you both signal your own intentions and meet your readers' expectations. This helps you to establish understanding between you and your audience. When you use conventions, you invoke the Cooperative Principle, which assumes that communicators and their audiences share an interest in making a communication work (Chapter 2). You appeal to a set of expectations held not only by you and your reader on this occasion, but also by past communicators in similar situations.

Defining the Communication Context

Conventions help define the communication context and, in so doing, identify the setting for the message. Certain conventions are important across situations. For instance, it is important to have a main idea in almost every type of writing. Other conventions are specific to a particular context or group. These conventions help define the communication context.

You may already be familiar with conventions for handling negative information in other types of writing. You might know, for example, that in a mystery story, the occasion for writing—a murder—usually appears up front. You also might know to expect to wade through a pile of evidence before discovering the "bad news"—that the kindly grandmother did the dastardly deed by short-circuiting the wiring in the bathroom. Conventions associated with mystery stories also tell you that some of the evidence presented along the way will be "red herrings," or clues planted to divert you from discovering "who dunnit." In short, conventions associated with mystery stories tell you to set boundaries concerning what the writer can and cannot do.

TECHNOLOGY

INTERNET CONVENTIONS

While traditional forms of communication are governed by conventions, electronic correspondence on the Internet is so new that conventions haven't been firmly established. There are, for example, virtually no legal consequences for "flaming," sending messages filled with profanity or even racist remarks. Flaming is perfectly legal on the Net, even though it would be unacceptable in any other form of communication.

Flaming is often directed at new users ("newbies") on the Internet. Newbies tend to assume that their Internet correspondence is governed by the same conventions and ethics that shelter them when they write letters or talk on the phone. They soon find out they're wrong. Let there be any slip-up, such as posting a "dumb" question to a newsgroup, and the newbie's computer mailbox fills with insulting, often hateful and profane messages from irate "old-timers."

In any other form of communication, these abusive correspondences would be considered harassment. But the Internet is new. The very qualities that make it a unique and useful communication tool also make it prone to abuse: people who would otherwise have no contact can correspond in seconds, and they feel shielded by the miles, the impersonal feeling of computer communication, and the lack of enforceable rules. As a result, messages dripping with bile that would never be delivered in person or by post are quickly written and zapped off to far-flung locales without a second thought.

Business communication conventions also set parameters for communications and expectations for audiences. For example, business writing, like mystery stories, conventionally waits to present its bad news. A letter from a customer complaining to a contractor about faulty wiring waits to state the opinion that the contractor's electrician "did it" until the evidence implicating the electrician is presented. However, other conventions in the message, beginning with the occasion for writing and including elements like format and design, tell readers that they are not reading a mystery story but are reading a business letter trying to identify the causes of a problem as support for filing a claim against the party responsible. "Red herrings" are definitely not allowed. Knowing conventions helps you identify the context for the communication, which, in turn, helps you form expectations for writing, reading, and understanding the message.

CONVENTIONAL ORGANIZATIONAL STRATEGIES

In addition to suggesting how to handle particular occasions (such as the task of presenting bad news), conventions also tell you how to organize information. Conventional strategies for organizing presentations and documents have a long history. Most conventional arrangements have roots in classical Greece. Aristotle, for example, presented deductive arrangement and inductive arrangement as the two major kinds of *logical proof.* A proof is a means of arguing a point.[2]

Deductive and inductive sequences, which are the focus of this section, differ in their placement of the main idea. Deductive, or **top-down,** arrangement places the main idea up front; inductive waits until later. As our discussion shows, this simple difference has a number of implications for writer and reader alike. Although many types of writing, or *genres,* may arrange material either deductively or inductively, business communication assigns the use of deductive and inductive arrangements to specific occasions for writing. Figure 6.4 summarizes the conventional organization sequence for two types of business messages.

Those familiar with business communication conventions, therefore, know to put the main idea up front in most occasions that involve reader cooperation and to place the main idea later in the message when faced with occasions entailing reader resistance.

Figure 6.4 Chart Summarizing Organizational Conventions

OCCASION	OPENING	BODY	CLOSE
Message assuming reader cooperation	Main idea or good news statement	Support for main idea or details of good news	Action or complimentary close
Message assuming reader resistance	Neutral, buffered, or common ground statement	Explanation for bad news followed by the bad news itself	Action or complimentary close

Deductive Sequences

CONTEXT

In Figure 6.5 (next page), the chair of an Arrangements Committee for an annual corporate sales meeting is contacting several resorts to get comparative information about facilities and costs. On the basis of the responses, the writer will then make arrangements with the resort best able to meet company needs.

Following business writing convention, Figure 6.5 uses a deductive sequence for requesting information about resort facilities. Since the request involves potential business for the reader, the letter is a message that can assume reader cooperation.

Besides being in line with conventional use, selecting deductive organization in this case provides a context for Tanaka's responses to later portions of the document. Tanaka, for example, knows that the "group rate" he quotes (in answer to bullet one, paragraph two) should be one that is appropriate to a group of 150 (noted in paragraph one).

By convention, deductive organization appears in three main categories of business documents that contain information that the reader will readily accept:

- **routine or neutral messages** (direct requests, orders, announcements)
- **positive messages** (positive replies, credit approvals, order acknowledgments)
- **goodwill messages** (congratulations, greetings, condolences, thank-yous)

Although conventionally used in such messages, deductive organization can sometimes also be used to present information that a reader may resist, as discussed in Chapter 10 under persuasive requests.

Figure 6.5 Letter with Deductive Organization

In top-down fashion, the writer names the subject of the letter in the first paragraph.

The writer details the type of information she needs in the body of the letter.

The writer facilitates any necessary additional contact in the final paragraph.

Dear Mr. Tanaka:

I am writing on behalf of the DeAngelo Corporation requesting information about your resort for an upcoming company event being held the week of July 20–25, 19—. We would like for the event to be an appreciation trip and getaway for 150 employees.

I would appreciate the following information to assist me in planning the event:

- the cost of individual rooms including the group rate
- the availability of meeting rooms
- the types of recreational activities provided at the resort
- the nature of the restaurants and other dining facilities
- information on transportation to the airport and local sites

Our group will need a large banquet hall and three or four small meeting rooms. We would also like a continental breakfast to be provided throughout the week concluding with an evening banquet on July 24.

If you have any questions regarding the event or our request, please call me at (319) 555-5671 between 9 a.m.–5 p.m. Monday through Friday. I look forward to receiving information about the Yacht Club Resort.

Sincerely,

Inductive Organization

The structure for Figure 6.6 follows business convention by using an inductive approach to present bad news. Since the letter denies the reader's previously submitted claim, it is certain to contain information that a reader will resist.

Several occasions in business communication conventionally require the inductive arrangement:

- **negative messages** (negative responses, credit refusals, rejections of job applications, back orders)
- **persuasive messages** (collections, persuasive requests)
- **sales documents** (sales letters, promotional material)

Chapters 9 and 10 cover these types of messages in detail.

CONTEXT

In Figure 6.6, the writer responds to a customer who wants to avoid being billed for goods that he claims not to have ordered. The writer makes it clear that the reader is nevertheless responsible for the amount due.

COMMON STRATEGIES FOR DEVELOPMENT

Just as there are conventional ways of arranging presentations and documents overall, so too are there conventions for arranging individual parts of documents and managing information within those parts. The way you develop the body of any given communication is

Figure 6.6 Letter of Response with Inductive Structure

The writer opens with the subject of the letter, but not with the main idea regarding that subject.

The writer explains the situation, but still does not reveal the main idea.

The writer explains the reasons underlying his refusal, and then states the refusal, which is the main idea of the message.

The writer provides additional information that serves to "sandwich" the refusal.

In a positive move, the writer facilitates further contact.

Dear Mr. McKinney:

Thank you for your letter of April 6 regarding invoice #67878. I understand that you were surprised to receive the compact disc *The Scorpions, the Best of Rockers 'n Ballads*, along with the shipping invoice billing you for the disc.

Because of the large selection of compact discs CDC offers each month, we place a date on the top of our notification cards. The cards are to be received by us on or before the specified date so that we can fill members' orders as quickly as possible. This allows us to offer members new and exciting compact discs each month in a timely fashion. If the notification card isn't received by us on or before the specified date, we assume that the featured selection has been ordered. The member is then sent the selection along with a billing invoice.

As we've indicated in the *CDC Membership Guide* issued with your membership, members must return their notification cards on or before the date printed at the top of the cards to avoid billing. A careful review of our March records indicates that we received your notification card on March 18, three days after the specified date of March 15. Therefore, we sent and billed you for the featured selection, *Scorpions, the Best of Rockers 'n Ballads* (catalog number 207964). Given these circumstances, we cannot accept the return of the disc or credit your account for the $19.45 charge.

In the event that you have lost yours, we are enclosing the *CDC Membership Guide*. Following the guidelines in the *Guide* will enable you to be successful with your selections of quality music in the future.

If you have any questions about information in the *Guide*, please feel free to contact me at our toll free number: 1-800-CDC-DISC.

Sincerely,

determined in part by your choice of inductive or deductive arrangement. If you choose an inductive arrangement, for example, the main idea of the message will be found in the body or sometimes at the end. This placement affects how you place other information in the document.

The arrangement of central portions of the document is also influenced by rhetorical convention. We will discuss patterns of organization that have been in use for a long time. Some are traditionally considered "logical patterns"; others we call "developmental patterns."

Common Logical Patterns

You may recognize the **logical patterns** listed in Figure 6.7 from previous writing classes. These patterns often appear in both expository and creative writing, as well as in a wide range of more specific genres. In business communication, these patterns commonly appear as strategies for organizing parts of messages.

A document often contains several of these patterns. For example, if you write an analytical report based on identifying and analyzing alternatives for the expansion of corporate headquarters, you will probably use *cause and effect* to identify the problem, *definition* and *division into parts* to discuss the aspects of the problem (cramped quarters, filing cabinets in washrooms, etc.), *description* and *narration* to explain the history of the problem, and *comparison* to analyze the advantages and disadvantages of several solutions (including renting space in other buildings, reducing inventory and production, and so forth). Figure 6.8 demonstrates how even a short business document can have a number of these logical patterns.

Developmental Patterns

The developmental patterns we show are used to manage information within parts of a document. Although these patterns are used in other genres to structure entire documents, they conventionally appear in business documents as strategies to sequence supporting information or evidence and to effect connections between units of information.

Figure 6.7 Logical Patterns of Development Seen in Business Messages

LOGICAL PATTERNS	DEFINITION	EXAMPLE / APPLICATION
description	provides details that create an image	the section of an annual report that presents information about the company's new product line
definition	identifies differentiating feature(s) as well as a broader category	the paragraph in a claim adjustment letter that explains what is and is not covered in an insurance policy
partition	identifies parts or components	the components of a toner cartridge shown in a detailed-view drawing in a maintenance manual
classification	groups into identified categories	a marketing brochure that identifies types of personal computers
exemplification	uses an example to illustrate or demonstrate a point	the section of a response letter that gives examples of different activities available at a resort
comparison	presents the similarities and differences; presents pro and con arguments	a memo that distinguishes between the old way and new way of filing travel vouchers
narration	tells a story	the opening section of a promotional video that provides a brief history of the company
process	identifies a sequence	the steps in conducting an inventory shown in an instructional chart within a new-employee orientation guide
cause and effect	identifies the impetus and the result(s); identifies a problem and its solution(s)	the sections in a formal proposal showing the need to adopt a new flextime policy because of difficulties with the present system

Figure 6.8 Document with Several Logical Patterns

*The first paragraph combines **narrative** and **cause/effect**.*

*The second paragraph has a **classification** of the kinds of business.*

*Numbers 1–3 represent a **partition**. There is also an implicit **comparison** in number 2 between what the old and expanded versions are like. Number 3 addresses a **partition** of duties.*

*The detailing of the duties themselves is primarily **descriptive**.*

*The format stipulations provide a **definition**.*

*Overall the minutes provide a **narrative** of what happened at the meeting.*

MINUTES OF COMPUTER GRANT WRITING COMMITTEE
FRIDAY, FEBRUARY 19, 19--
3:00 P.M., MEDIA LAB 1

Present: Andrews, Cantor, Sheerer, Sun; Absent: None

The meeting was held from 3:00-4:00 p.m. in the computer room instead of the conference room, because each team member needed to be able to access the Forum file for finalizing the format of the resumes.

There were three areas of business discussed at the meeting: ancillary materials, performance appraisal issues, and task definition.

1. Rules for appended resumes, based on Sheerer's format, stipulated that they should be in 12-point, Palatino, with bold for the major heads and default margins. Each team member agreed to have final copy ready by Feb. 25 to share with other members. We also decided that the mathematical calculations for costs would be included in Appendix C.
2. Evaluation criteria were revised and expanded upon by Cantor and Andrews to account for the new specifications received Feb. 15 regarding the Hodge grant and to include review by an outside consultant to be named later.
3. Responsibilities for parts of the final proposal were divided as follows:

   Charlie Sun: Write, revise, and expand these sections: present system, problems with present system, and conclusion.

   Jane Sheerer: Collaborate with Andrews on these sections: possible solutions and objectives of proposed solutions. Write section: "write program."

   Beth Andrews: Collaborate with Sheerer on these sections: possible solutions and objectives of proposed solutions. Write these sections: install and purchase, resources needed.

   B.J. Cantor: Write training system section, with input from Kumar, Personnel Division.

Drafts of all assigned sections will be available to team members by e-mail on or before 8:00 a.m., February 25. The next meeting will be held on February 25, Andrews' office, 4:00 p.m.

Strategies Involving Sequencing. The following strategies for sequencing information help you to order your information and also consider the nature of the details that make up that information:

- chronological order
- least to most important
- specific to general
- general to specific

When using *chronological order,* you are using a time sequence. Chronological order is basic to telling about an event in creative writing genres like short stories and novels. In business writing, chronological order is important to organizing parts of documents, such as the history section of a proposal, or to lists in messages of any type. Figure 6.9 shows chronological order in a list from a letter providing information about company internships. The list follows chronological order in that a definite time sequence is involved: an applicant must apply to the program (points 1 and 2) before she participates in the program

Figure 6.9 Excerpt Showing Chronological Sequence

Some details of our program are as follows:

1. To qualify for the program, you must submit an application to the regional office in your area.
2. Experience or academic training in the hotel industry is preferred but not required.
3. The internship program lasts twelve weeks.
4. Each week interns are assigned to different departments with specific tasks to be observed, learned, and performed.
5. Interns are trained from the same manual as that used for any new employees in the company.
6. Interns are tested at the end of the program after learning front-of-house procedures and back-of-house operations.
7. Resorts Southwest subsequently hires 90% of its interns for full-time positions.

(points 3 through 5). The participant must participate in the program (points 3 through 5) before she is tested (point 6). And the participant must be tested (point 6) before she is hired (point 7).

Figure 6.9 also involves a time sequence in a different respect. The details from one point serve as necessary *prior knowledge* for the details given in the next point. Knowing the information in point 3, for instance, helps "explain" the information in point 4. That is, we know from reading point 3 that interns have twelve weeks; this knowledge helps the reader determine, upon reading point 4, that interns will be assigned to at least twelve different departments (twelve weeks, each week a different department). In short, the information in point 3 must be known before it can help the reader fully understand the information being conveyed in point 4.

CONTEXT

The writer has been asked to research alternative valet systems for renting ski equipment at a resort. Valet systems not only allow equipment such as skis, boots, and poles to be rented by the day or week, but also provide the means for guests to check their personal equipment when not on the slopes. The paragraphs in Figure 6.10, excerpted from her report, come after the writer has presented her purpose, background, criteria, and methods. The job of this excerpted section is simply to identify the alternatives, describing them in terms of criteria that will later on be used for analysis, as in a cost-benefit analysis.

When using a *least to most important* sequence, you must make a value judgment. You evaluate your information and determine its relative worth or significance. Not surprisingly, business communication has conventions for when to use this sequence. In messages that are highly persuasive in nature, such as persuasive requests, proposals, and feasibility studies, business communicators put their most important argument last.[3] In reports, the material that is most significant to the concluding recommendation appears last.

In Figure 6.10, the writer is moving from what she thinks is the least important to the most important alternative. Because she is writing an analytical report that will contain a concluding recommendation, the writer places the most feasible option last. Readers familiar with business convention will at this point expect Alternative #3 to play a major role in the writer's recommendations at the end of the report. Readers unfamiliar with the convention will probably discover the significance of the sequence later, when they reach the analytical sections of the report. Because the writer in Figure 6.10 is submitting an internal report and thus knows her readers personally, she has reason to be confident that they will recognize the significance of her conventional placement of the third alternative.

The reason the presentation in Figure 6.10 is least to most does not have much to do with the fact that the costs are from least to most expensive, although least to most expensive would be a valid pattern. The pattern is from least to most important in that the third alternative, as the most feasible, plays a major role in the report's recommendation.

When using a *specific to general* sequence, you arrange details from most specific to least specific. As in other genres, the choice in business communication whether to move from specific to general or, conversely, from general to specific rests primarily with the nature of

Figure 6.10 Excerpt Using Least to Most Important Sequence

The alternatives below represent the range of choices suggested by my research:

Alternative #1: Present system with more record keeping

My first suggestion is the least expensive route. We keep the present system *[the present system has been previously described in the background section]* of using paper slips as claim checks and adopt a new record-keeping procedure. We use a logbook to record guests' names and the date they check the skis. This record provides proof of ownership of the equipment, even if the claim tickets are lost.

The financial cost of this alternative is minimal, around $500. This price includes the logbook, additional paper materials, and training. We would use current personnel in the Ski Valet area to do the additional paperwork.

Alternative #2: Use current storage procedures with a computer

The second alternative uses the current means of storage but has a computer keep the records. All guests' names would be recorded in the computer along with the number given to them. Although we would still use the paper slips as a means of claim by the guest, we would have a more accurate record with this system.

The system costs around $10,000 to implement, with an additional amount each month for upkeep. This cost includes the computer terminal and installation, training, and funds for an increase in personnel to run the computer.

Alternative #3: Replace current system with a new storage system

Replacing our current system with a new lock-and-key storage system is the most costly choice and constitutes the most changes. It also increases security above the other two alternatives. In this system the current storage system is replaced with a more technologically advanced system. The new system consists of portable storage racks with a key lock for each pair of skis. The key is removable and will be given to the guest when the skis are placed in the storage rack. The keys need to be purchased. Due to the cost of the keys, it would be to our advantage to keep better records. We would use a logbook with a list of all key numbers in which we are able to write in the guest's name.

The cost of the system is $30,000. This includes all the new equipment, installation, training, and logbooks.

Figure 6.11 Excerpt Using Specific to General Sequence

The exact percentage (the 150% in the first subsection) is more specific than the "significant increase" mentioned later.

The concept of a "corporate image" is abstract in itself, and the idea of "enhancing" this abstract quality makes this piece of information much more abstract than either the idea of achieving an exact percentage or even of promoting an increase in productivity.

Additional Benefits

Additional benefits to Goodman and Associates include a potential increase in clientele, increased productivity, and an enhanced corporate image.

Increase in clientele

Because the fiber optics system would allow our clientele to have their calls received on the first attempt, Goodman and Associates could increase the number of customers served per hour by 30, or 150% (see Appendix C for mathematical calculations). The added speed of service would also allow a corresponding ability to increase the size of the total number of customers served.

Increase in productivity

With the fast connection provided by fiber optics, time can be saved when placing calls as well. While the time savings here might seem minimal at first, it in fact has the potential of increasing the productivity of our sales staff significantly when measured over the time frame of a fiscal year and multiplied by the number of sales personnel we have on board.

Enchanced corporate image

With all the other benefits mentioned previously, the fiber optics system will provide Goodman with the opportunity to communicate a sophisticated and efficient corporate image.

your material. Figure 6.11, which shows a section of a proposal, suggests the additional benefits that a company will enjoy if it installs the proposed fiber optic telephone system. These benefits start with the specific and move to the general. This sequence is a wise one in this case, because the material becomes more and more abstract as the writer proceeds. Moving from specific to general thus complements the strategy of going from least difficult to most difficult. Presenting the reader with the least difficult information first is generally a good idea.

CONTEXT

The writer in Figure 6.11 has just finished outlining the direct benefits of installing a fiber optic telephone system in soon-to-be-renovated corporate offices. She now moves on to discuss additional benefits.

The writer in Figure 6.11 finds it better to present specific factors that the audience can readily see first before arguing for something the audience cannot readily see, "a sophisticated and efficient" corporate image.

Figure 6.12 uses a *general to specific* sequence that is presented in a list. The choice of sequence here, as in Figure 6.11, also relates to the content. The 26 percent drop is dramatic in itself, and, because of its specificity, attracts reader attention. The fact that readers are likely to get "excited" about this detail makes its placement appropriate. In sum, the writer in Figure 6.12 evidently knows that the specific decrease in productivity is her most persuasive argument. She thus chooses to order her list from general to specific, so her most persuasive item appears last.

Lists, as shown in Figures 6.9 and 6.12, are a conventional way of formatting internal sequences and clusters of informational items within business documents. Strategies for constructing effective lists can be found in Appendix C.

Strategies Focusing on Connections. In addition to strategies for sequencing and presenting information, you also have available a number of strategies for helping readers see the connections between different parts of your text:

- transitions
- prepositions and pronouns
- topic announcements
- keyed repetition
- given-new structures
- format conventions

Transitions are important to many types of writing. Transitions link information in a document and reinforce whatever organizational pattern you're using. For example, if you are using a cause-and-effect pattern, standard transitions such as "because" or "since" and

Figure 6.12 Excerpt Using General to Specific Sequence

These two alternative work options, Flextime and Job Sharing, would help to eliminate three major problems currently existing within the company:

- low employee morale
- excessive absenteeism in the form of tardiness, sick leave, and time off for personal appointments
- a 26% drop in productivity over the last 6 months.

SKILLS & STRATEGIES

CONVENTIONS AND LISTS

Lists are conventionally used to present certain types of information:

- step-by-step instructions (e.g., how to operate a fax machine)
- components in an object or a system (e.g., the parts of a bar code scanner)
- features or characteristics (e.g., design specifications for a newsletter)
- options for consideration (e.g., the alternatives presented in a feasibility study)
- restrictions or cautions (e.g., procedures to follow when filing a grievance)

Lists also have three conventional designs.

- ***keywords***—presenting the items or terms without numbers or bullets
- ***bulleted list***—presenting the items or terms preceded by a bullet
- ***numbered list***—presenting the items or terms preceded by a number

Company stylesheets (see Chapter 1, page 12) often determine which design convention business writers select.

Regardless of the information type or the design convention, lists are traditionally *parallel* in grammatical construction and in format. In the revisions below, the writer is careful to make each item in the list parallel—or precisely alike in form (but not content)—to other items in the same group.

Original Construction	**Revisions**
We feel that National's new hometown Visa and MasterCard are better than the others. Here's why. • All decisions are made locally. • waiver of annual fee • offering a low 15.96% annual percentage rate for financing	We feel that National's new hometown Visa and MasterCard are better than the others. Here's why: [colon introduces list because "Here's why" is a complete sentence.] • Local Credit Decisions • Waiver of Annual Fee • Low 15.96% Annual Percentage Rate Financing
	OR • All decisions are made locally. • The annual membership fee is waived for the first year. • The annual percentage rate for financing is a low 15.96%.
[This last list needs to be introduced differently; e.g., "We feel that National's new hometown Visa and MasterCard are better than the others because we're . . .". Note: With this introduction, a colon does not apear before the list because the introductory clause ending in "because we're" is grammatically incomplete.]	**OR** • making all decisions locally • waiving the annual fee • offering a low 15.96% annual percentage rate for financing

transitional sequences such as "if-then" reinforce the connections in your material. The transitional words used in Figure 6.13 (*thus, in addition,* and *for example*) establish virtually the same relationship regardless of the type of document you are writing. *Thus,* for example, usually establishes a cause-effect relationship whenever it is used. It also establishes that the information following *thus* is a direct result of the foregoing. For example, if you write, "The bids are to be submitted on September 4; thus, cost estimate figures for your part of the project are due August 20," you are saying that the August 20 deadline was set in response to the September 4 deadline. Evidently, you want a few weeks to study the cost estimates before submitting a bid containing those figures. A complete list of transitions can be found in Appendix C.

Prepositions often function as transitions, showing temporal (time) as well as spatial relationships. *After* and *during* would be examples of prepositions showing temporal relationships. *Beside* and *under* would be examples showing spatial relationships. *Pronouns* with clear antecedents (see Appendix C) necessarily establish connectedness because they refer to material contained earlier in the document. The key to effective pronoun use lies in the clarity of the antecedents. If the antecedent is unclear, then the pronoun causes confusion rather than connectedness. For example, consider the description: "John Baxter, owner of Pet Specialties, keeps an iguana in his house. He greets company with a dry hiss." Because "he" could refer to either the iguana or John Baxter, it is unclear which party hisses at guests.

Although business communication makes use of these conventional strategies for establishing connections, it also characteristically uses strategies that are tied to the particular document being written. These are called **text-specific strategies.** Figure 6.13 shows how text-specific strategies such as topic announcements, repetition of key terms, given-new structures, and format are used to make connections in a business message.

In Figure 6.13, the writer *announces the topic* of her proposal in the first sentence. She follows a similar practice of announcing the topic of each subsequent paragraph by making the topic the subject of the first sentence. Announcing a topic up front also entails using headings and subheadings (to be discussed shortly). Announcing a topic helps readers know what the document is about, so they can anticipate what's going to be discussed. Figure 6.13 also uses the repetition of key terms such as "difficulties" and "hiring" to establish connectedness.

Repetition of key terms involves either the identical repetition of words or the use of synonyms. Although the practice of substituting synonyms can be confusing if overdone, planned repetitions can aid the reader to see relationships within a text. In addition, Figure 6.13 makes use of **given-new structures** to link new information to information readers already know. In the sentence "Although Paul liked winter, he did not like ice storms," the fact that Paul liked winter is considered old information, and the fact that he did not like ice storms, new information. In Figure 6.13, the new information, "references," is tagged on to the given information, "prospective employee" and "application." When "references" is used again, it becomes old information.

Format is also used in documents to establish connections, and the extensive use of formatting distinguishes business communication from many other types of writing. Titles, subject lines, headings, and subheadings are just a few of the format features that enhance connectedness. In Figure 6.13, for example, the writer uses the subject line to establish the subject or focus of the message. The topics being discussed in connection to this subject are indicated by the headings in the memo itself. Establishing an effective set of headings and subheadings is important to almost any type of business message and is crucial to longer documents. When you use headings and subheadings, you help the reader in three important ways:

- establish expectations concerning what is to follow
- reveal the organizational structure of your document
- indicate how different sections of the document are related to each other logically (their connectedness) and hierarchically (their relative importance)

Writing effective headings and subheadings is not as easy as it may first seem. Strategies for doing so are found in Appendix C.

CONTEXT

The excerpt in Figure 6.13, from the first page of a short proposal (memo format), argues for new hiring policies and an updated training program for new employees. Written by the center's director, the memo (and the study it uses) addresses parents' complaints about certain staff members. The conventional transitional words and phrases are indicated in italics. The text-specific strategies are noted in **bold.**

Figure 6.13 Message Annotated for Text-Specific Strategies for Coherence

The writer sets forth the main subjects of the memo. The writer later establishes coherence by directly repeating these subjects.

The mention of difficulties is echoed in the paragraph, providing coherence through repetition.

The writer's headings aid coherence.

The word "references," which is new information in its initial use, is repeated as "old" information in the next, providing coherence.

Use of the words "two weeks" echoes their use previously.

Date: December 9, 19--
To: Board of Directors, Wednesday's Children
From: Mindy Ramos, Center Director
Subj: Proposal for **New Hiring Policies** and **Training Program**

Background

Wednesday's Children, which strives to offer the best in child care in the Key West Area, is having **difficulties** maintaining an efficient and effective staff of caregivers. We have *thus* decided to examine our present **hiring policies** and **training** practices to see if a revision of *these* policies and practices will address the budgetary and public relations **difficulties** we are currently experiencing. A summary of *these* **difficulties** can be found in John Gutierrez' letter of November 15 (Attachment A).

Present Policies

Presently, the **hiring policies** at Wednesday's Children include only a "Help Wanted" sign in the front window and word of mouth to spread the fact that our center needs help. *After* the prospective employee has filled out an application, we check the listed **references** by phone. If the **references** are positive, we *then* conduct a structured interview and hire on-the-spot if the applicant looks promising.

As far as **training** is concerned, the current training program for new employees includes an initial period of approximately **two weeks,** when the employee "learns the ropes" from another caregiver in the assigned room. *After* **two weeks,** the employee is ready to be left alone to do the work assigned to him or her. *In addition,* the employee is *then* considered available to serve in any other assigned area. Caregivers trained in the infant room, *for example,* are free, without further **training,** to move to the toddler room if the need arises.

ISSUES INVOLVING THE USE OF CONVENTIONS

When you use communication conventions, you are tapping into the history of how various occasions for speaking and writing have been handled in the past. You benefit from using conventions, whether your audience is familiar with a particular strategy or not. If your audience is familiar with the convention, you have the distinct advantage of sharing your listener's or reader's expectations about how the communication is to proceed. If your audience is not familiar with it, you are still taking advantage of the expertise of other communicators who have successfully faced similar situations.

But there are also times when *not* using a convention can be effective. Departures from convention allow you to tailor a document specifically to the occasion, purpose, and audience. Variations on traditional practice can even be more effective than standard practice in certain situations. When you use conventions, therefore, you are always faced with the issue of whether or not to proceed with "business as usual."

Departing from Convention

When departing from convention, you purposely and purposefully use strategies that run counter to standard practice. The key terms here are "purposely" and "purposefully." Sometimes communicators can depart from a convention simply because they are unaware of it. Other times communicators can be aware of a convention, depart from it on purpose, and still be ineffective because their departure serves no real purpose. Figure 6.14 is a letter that departs from convention in a number of respects. While it is unclear whether the departures are on purpose, it is clear that they are ineffective.

The writer of the letter in Figure 6.14 may have been able to avoid such ineffective departures from convention by looking more carefully at the occasion for writing, her audience, and herself as a writer:

- *occasion*. The writer's main goal seems to be to persuade the reader to attend the city council meeting and, once there, to support Davidson's position that curbside pickup of recyclables is both unnecessary and expensive. The writer should thus have realized that a persuasive request was her best option for writing. Knowing this would have helped her organize the information deductively, with the main request up front and with the details supporting that request in the body of that letter. Knowing this would also have helped her select and organize the supporting details around her two points: (1) curbside pickup of recyclables is unnecessary, and (2) curbside pickup is expensive.
- *audience*. The writer seems well aware that her readers are probably concerned about recycling. (She is even careful to use paper with a recycling label at the top.) Keeping the audience better in mind throughout the letter might have helped the writer to structure her points of support. Perhaps, for example, she could have adjusted her points so that they better matched audience concerns: (1) the current options for recycling in Janesville represent close to the optimum achievable when various trade-offs are analyzed, and (2) the addition of the glass-only recycling pickup represents a sound and proven (two carriers are already doing it) initial investment of funds. Restructuring her points this way would have allowed the writer the added advantage of arguing for positives rather than negatives.
- *writer*. The writer indirectly acknowledges her precarious position as a person with vested interests in the outcome in several rather clumsy attempts at building her credibility. Her company hauls garbage the old-fashioned way and would incur significant costs or losses if the proposed curbside pickup of recyclables were effected. Recognizing this, the writer estab-

CONTEXT

The letter in Figure 6.14 was sent by a private York County sanitation service, Davidson's Pickup, to its customers in the city of Janesville. The Resource Recovery Center mentioned in the letter is Janesville's city-owned operation that recycles metal and glass and burns everything else, including paper and plastic, to fuel the Janesville power plant.

The occasion: A new collection system has been proposed to the city by a rival sanitation service: customers would separate metal and glass recoverable items into color-coded bins to be placed curbside on collection day. The rival vehicles collecting these recyclables would be truck-drawn trailers with large receptacles for metals, plastics, glass, and paper, respectively. What's left, or the "garbage," would be collected separately.

Significance: If the proposed system were adopted, Davidson would either have to invest in new trailer equipment or be left with hauling garbage only.

Writer's stance: Davidson is proposing that customers simply start separating out their glass and that they oppose the more elaborate proposal at an upcoming city council meeting.

Note: Unfortunately, the grammatical miscues in this example were in the final draft of the Davidson letter.

Figure 6.14 Ineffective Departures from Both Specific and General Conventions

Since the occasion calls for a persuasive request, the writer departs from convention by structuring this letter like a negative message, with a buffered opening. The writer also ineffectively departs from convention by

- *introducing the "good news," that the RRC is already recycling metals, as "bad news"*
- *placing the "good news" about Davidson's glass recycling plan in the "old news" position and placing the information about the two noncollecting haulers in the "new news" position, thereby violating the old/new convention*
- *providing too much detail about an impending fee hike of $10 per ton and **not** providing enough detail about the million dollar figure*
- *combining the answers to unrelated and unstated questions into one paragraph*
- *having miscues in grammar, spelling, and format*
- *placing the request dead last*

*Printed on recycled paper

Dear Customer,

Emphasis on recycling has reached us from many sources in recent months. While recycling is the most effective way to conserve resources in most counties, York County has a unique situation with the Resource Recovery Center (RRC), which uses 75% of the incoming refuse as fuel.

I believe very little information has been provided to the residents being served by the RRC concerning it's functions. With the completion of the Beck Study and their recommendations of updates to the RRC and recycling drop boxes throughout the county, I feel I must share some points of interest. *The RRC Plant automatically "pulls out" approximately 92% of the food cans from the waste during processing.* The metals are then sent for recycling. Plastics and paper are burned for fuel. Plastic is especially good fuel, and *for each ton of plastic used, two ton of coal are saved.* Water is also conserved because jugs and cans don't need to be rinsed. Glass cannot be saved if it's put in the garbage, and needs to be kept separate and recycles. We are presently working on a system whereby we can collect the glass on the same route as the garbage, but keep it separate for recycling. Two other York County garbage haulers already pick up glass on their routes, and when ours is completed, there will only be two haulers who are not collecting glass yet. Quality paper, such as computer printouts, and cardboard should also be recycled, but usually neither of these are collected at a home, or left at a drop box.

The proposed drop boxes and operating costs is estimated at $1/3 million *per year.* This amount is to be added to the cost of the RRC update, and will be added to dump fees and/or taxes. If we can concentrate on removing glass, which is our only problem (not being currently recycled), we can avoid this being added to our already escalating garbage rates. (Our dump fees are scheduled for another $10 per ton increase on 7-1-19—.

I feel that with the present system, the drop boxes are not necessary. If York County residents feel that drop off recycling is the only way to go, there are currently 3 drop off sites in Janesville for plastic, and two for glass. If, in 3 or 4 years, we do not meet our waste reduction expectations, the issue can be re-addressed. Meanwhile, we will have saved $1 million.

In answer to other questions that often arise: Davidson's is not connected with the city of Janesville. We dump our loads at RRC and pay the fee that they set. RRC does not *need* the plastic, and are not competing for it. Burning plastic for fuel, and saving coal, water, and transportation fuels is simply more resource conservative. Emmissions at the city power plant are well below standards, even when burning plastic. I am not trying to evade the recycling issue, but simply [to] conserve as many resources as possible by integrating reccling with our present system. many experts agree with this opinion (philosophy). I am enclosing a copy of an article by a former EPA Assitant Administrator for Solid Waste who expresses such an opinion.

There is a public forum scheduled for this Wednesday (Nov. 18th.) at 7:00 p.m. at the public library. It would be helpful to our council to know what the residents want with regard to recycling. Please let them know: 1. If you think that when glass is picked up at residences that drop boxes are a duplication of the service of the RRC. 2. If you would use drop boxes if they are placed in 3 additional locations in Janesville.

As indicated by this spoof of formal family portraits, the Simpsons thrive on undermining expectations about the conventional all-American family. Departures from convention are not always as successful in business messages.

lishes herself as an authority (she knows information about the RRC operation that has not been widely distributed, she has a modest plan for improving recycling, she is "not trying to evade the recycling issue," and she includes an enclosure by an EPA official that supports the view that you can have too much of a good thing, even if that good thing is recycling.

However, the writer's indirect organization, sometimes puzzling inclusion and exclusion of detail, and flagrant mechanical miscues, along with an overall defensiveness in tone, all work to undermine the reader's faith in the writer and her opinions.

The writer might have more skillfully built her credibility by arguing the reasonableness of her proposal and reminding the customers of the good service Davidson has provided in the past. The reader might then have found the writer more persuasive.

An analysis of occasion, audience, and writer would have helped the writer decide whether departing from convention was appropriate to this situation, and, if so, what kind of departures would be most effective.

Figure 6.15 (page 176) is more purposeful in its departures from convention. As the annotations suggest, the writer departs from a number of expectations specific to negative messages.

In Figure 6.15 the "bad news" that Helen is no longer on the staff of *Poet and Critic* is conveyed implicitly in the very first paragraph with the phrase "I'm starting out this fall with a staff of one." In later paragraphs, the writer moves to compliments that reinforce the collegial relationship that already exists between writer and reader. The writer's departure from convention in this case makes the message sound less like a form letter and

Figure 6.15 Negative Message Which Departs from Convention

Instead of containing a buffer, the opening sentence contains the bad news. The opening paragraph cites the reason for the writer's bad news decision.

Instead of containing the explanation and the decision, the body contains a compliment, which might have served as a buffer had it appeared in the opening.

Poet
& Critic

August 27, 19--

Dear Helen,

As the new editor of *Poet & Critic,* I'm starting out this fall with a staff of one. This seems a practical way to begin, especially considering our new alliance with the ISA Press and the Press's assumption of many of the tasks that were previously delegated.

I'm sure that everyone associated with *P & C* appreciates the excellent work you've done over the years. Your energy and support have been essential to the well-being of the magazine.

I'll do my best to keep you posted on the progress of *P & C* as I work to build upon the gains you've helped make.

Sincerely,

Neal Bowers
Editor

CONTEXT

In Figure 6.15 above, the writer and the reader are department colleagues. The writer is trying to present the reader with the "bad news" that the reader has lost her unpaid but enjoyable position as an occasional copy editor for a locally published literary magazine.

enhances the feeling that the writer and reader share a secure writer-reader relationship in a linguistic as well as a collegial sense.

When departing from convention, you also must consider that unconventional strategies might be recognized by some of your readers and not by others. They also might appeal to some readers and not to others.

Figure 6.16 contains a number of departures from convention. Even with all its departures, this letter succeeded in drawing a large number of book orders. One reason for its success as a marketing tool is that the writers let the letter's context, the audience and purpose, guide their departures. The letter was sent to a narrow audience consisting of graduate students in English. The jargon is that of the audience, not the writers. The claim of special literacy is one carefully calculated to make the targeted audience of English students read further. The short length of the message, the breezy tone, even the negative apology, all seem calculated to appeal to these graduate students.

If Figure 6.16 had been addressed to a different audience, it might not have been successful. A different audience, for example, might not have recognized certain departures, such as boasting in the first sentence and the apology in the second sentence, where the letter refers to itself negatively as an intrusion. Furthermore, a different audience might not have recognized certain jargonized vocabulary, such as "tautology" or "epistolarily," or the use of a cinematic allusion to Humphrey Bogart at the end.[4] In short, a different audience might have found the letter puzzling instead of clever, irritating instead of amusing.

If you can adapt conventions or create original ways of presenting information, you can many times enhance the effectiveness of your messages, showing particular consideration

Figure 6.16 Sales Letter Flouting Conventions

CONTEXT

Figure 6.16 is a sales letter from a local bookstore that was mailed to selected graduate students at a Big Ten university. Addressed to this particular audience, it was an unqualified (and unconventional) success.

Dear Navigator of the Deep Tautology,

This might be the most literate piece of "junk" mail that you have ever received. Please forgive the intrusion, but we wouldn't have bothered you unless we were fairly certain that you would be interested in the books that we have for sale.

Attached is a selection of fiction, poetry, literary criticism and works of and about philosophy. Some of the authors you will encounter in this list are Pushkin, Sartre, Petronius, Byron, Shelley, and Goethe. All of these books are being offered at a substantial price reduction—some for as low as $1.00. All are original hardcover publisher's editions. All are unconditionally guaranteed to be to your satisfaction or your money will be refunded without question.

Here are some of the features of our company: There is no minimum purchase required; there is no obligation to buy anything in the future; should you choose not to respond to this solicitation, we will not bother you again; all orders are shipped within four days of receipt; everything is done by human beings (the same two human beings hacking out this literate junk mail); there is not a final in this course.

Thank you for your time. Here's looking at you, kid.

Epistolarily yours,

ETHICS

PROMISES, PROMISES: IS DECEPTION WORTH THE COST?

Listerine is a sore throat remedy. Volvos survive crashes better than the competitor's cars. Greyhound Lines' new *Trips* computerized reservation and ticketing system makes travel more convenient. Wrong! Deceptive advertising, whether a false claim in ad copy, a misleading picture, or a false promise in a prospectus, violates the implicit cooperative agreement between writers and readers, and that violation of communication convention can be costly. In the case of the Greyhound Lines prospectus, scathing coverage on the front page of *The Wall Street Journal* chronicled questionable business practices (like executives selling stock for high profits right before the highly touted *Trips* system collapsed).

Fierce competition for business—whether for mouthwash, car, or stock sales—can tempt writers to overstate, or promise more than the product can deliver. When writers succumb and produce deceptive advertising or distribute misleading information, the Federal Trade Commission (FTC) can mandate corrective advertising. Such retractions are costly not only in terms of diminished consumer confidence and increased advertising dollars but also in terms of lawsuit settlements.

of your audience and fulfilling your purposes. The key is to keep in mind the occasion, communicator, and audience.

Ineffective Departures from Convention

As Figures 6.15 and 6.16 suggest, departures from convention can increase your effectiveness as a communicator, if they are purposeful and are addressed to an appropriate audience. However, in your attempts to be innovative, you should avoid certain types of departures no matter what, because they are nearly always unsuccessful and jeopardize the writer-reader relationship:

- **violating** (purposely but quietly disobeying a convention in an effort to disguise your own purposes or to somehow mislead the reader)[5]
- **opting out** (openly demonstrating an unjustified or petulant unwillingness to follow conventions)
- **clashing** (putting yourself in a position so that the material in your document must disobey one communication principle to follow another, resulting in a clash between the two principles)

Violating. When you violate a convention, you purposely disobey certain communication principles, thinking that the reader will fail to recognize what you are doing. The net effect if readers recognize your violations is severe damage to your credibility as a writer.

For example, under the guise of you-attitude, the letter from a loan institution in Figure 6.17 conceals the writer's self-serving agenda. The writer purposely withholds some of the information necessary for the reader to make a sound financial decision.

CONTEXT

As you may know, when you take out a large loan from a bank, there is sometimes a penalty for paying off the loan early. The writer of the memo in Figure 6.17 seems to be doing the reader a favor by offering to cancel this prepayment penalty. However, another factor you must always consider is the interest rate. It may be to a borrower's advantage to *not* pay off a loan if the interest rate is low. When the interest rate on an "old" loan is 8% and the interest rate on new loans is 10.5%, it is to the bank's and not the customer's advantage to have the old loan paid off. The writer of this memo does not mention interest rate as a factor. This silence is at the root of the violation in this message.

Figure 6.17 Letter "Violating" Business Convention

RE: LOAN 44083

During the past few months, we have had several requests from our borrowers asking if they would be allowed to pay off their loan without any prepayment penalty being charged.

In these times with our economy being in a recession, the uncertainty of employment, and the volatility of rates, we understand your concerns and why a "debt free" home would be comforting.

City Loan Incorporated encourages you to call or visit our office about paying your loan off. For a limited time, we are offering you a cash discount with no prepayment penalty.

It is not only a happy occasion when a mortgage loan is paid off, but it allows you peace of mind and your family greater financial freedom.

Call today for details on your cash discount.

Because the loan the recipient of the letter has is five percentage points below the current rate, the loan company rather than the customer stands to benefit from the prepayment encouraged in Figure 6.17. Thus, the letter not only insults the reader's intelligence, but also challenges the writer's trustworthiness. Moreover, the writer also risks his credibility by giving customers unsound advice. The customer would probably be better off to keep the low-interest loan and direct current income into higher-yielding investments.

Opting Out. When you opt out, you explicitly demonstrate an unwillingness to follow a certain convention. The net effect is usually to hurt the reader's feelings. For example, in Figure 6.18, the writer elects not to use a "good news" arrangement, even though she has good news for the reader.

The overall effect of this letter is negative, even though the news being conveyed is positive. The good news is buried in the second paragraph. The student will be exempted from actually taking the course. He is to register for the class, but his summer work will substitute for the regular assignments. The first paragraph delays the good news by stating the regulation and providing information about the Foreign Study Program, irrelevant to the student's case. The memo "succeeds" only in making the student feel bad about making a valid request and getting the exemption.

CONTEXT

Chemical Engineering 300, in which students are given credit for visiting a major corporation, is supposed to be a required course for all students with the reader's major. The good news in Figure 6.18 is that the reader is being granted an exemption from taking this course. However, the writer, an adviser who has had a long-standing objection to such exemptions, openly refuses to consider the exemption good news.

Clashing. Clashing occurs when you must violate one convention to fulfill another. The common effect of such a clash between two conventions or principles is damage to the integrity of your document. In Figure 6.19, for example, the writer is promoting a candidate but is unable to emphasize reader benefits—a business writing principle—without calling into question his own credibility, essential to the success of any message.

Since apparently, in Figure 6.19, the main—and we begin to suspect the only—thing that qualifies the candidate for the position is her gender, the writer has a difficult time exploring the benefits of voting for her without sacrificing his ethical responsibility as a writer to present accurate qualifications. At the same time, the writer has a hard time preserving his own credibility, despite his many qualifications, due to the very fact that he is supporting such a poorly qualified candidate.

Figure 6.18 Excerpt of Memo "Opting Out" of Convention

After consulting with the faculty, we have affirmed our policy that Chem. E. 300 is required for graduation for all students except those who participate in the Foreign Study Program. In their case, they participate in similar visits as part of the program.

Because a University activity in which you have an important function conflicts with the Chem. E. 300 trip, you will not be required to go. However, you should register for the course spring quarter and submit to Dr. Smith a written report describing in detail your summer work experience and your visits to Monsanto in St. Louis. Please give an evaluation of the importance to chemical engineering students of plant trips such as this.

Figure 6.19 Excerpt of Letter with "Clashing"

Dear Fellow Voter:

I am writing this letter to solicit your support in the September 13 election for the Board of Directors of Area XI. I am a history instructor at the community college and also serve on the Executive Board representing the IHEAUU. Individuals from our local group have, with some success, actively attempted to elect pro-education candidates to the board for the last four years. This year we are making a concerted effort on behalf of candidates that we support.

In your district, I, we are asking you to vote for Jean Wills from Collins. We view her as a capable person, and we are anxious to elect at least one woman to an all-male, nine-person board. No woman has served on the board in its ten-year history, and this may be one reason that we are in trouble with the federal government because of discriminatory pay practices. We feel that Jean can make a real contribution to the board, and we urge you to vote for her on September 13.

If you have any questions about Jean or would like to ask about any other matter, please call me collect in the evening at 555-5000. I really feel that the education "ball game" is often being won or lost on the level of local board elections, and since our election coincides with your local election, please cast another pro-education vote by supporting Jean Wills for the Area XI Board of Directors.

The writer establishes his credentials to speak. He then talks about the candidate's qualifications. The only qualification the writer cites that is particular to the candidate is her gender.

The writer returns to his own authority to speak in the close.

The writer facilitates action by noting that the local election will be held at the same time, so voting will be convenient.

CONTEXT

Figure 6.19 is supporting a particular candidate for the board of directors of an education district, Area XI. The acronym IHEAUU stands for a national political action group known to the reader.

Factors to Remember When Departing from Convention

Figures 6.17, 6.18, and 6.19 dramatized how certain departures from convention can be disastrous to the writer's credibility, to the reader's feelings, and to the integrity of a document. Your ability to distinguish violating, opting out, and clashing from *effective* departures from convention increases your ability to spot ineffective attempts at innovation in your own speaking and writing.

Figure 6.20 suggests some basic guidelines for working with conventions in your business message. Perhaps a good overarching guideline for you to remember is that effective departures from convention observe the cooperative principle (Chapter 2). While writers can depart from certain conventions of organizations and development, they are not free to ignore fundamental rules of communication that preserve a secure writer-reader relationship.

Figure 6.20 Guidelines for Departing from Conventions

DO	AVOID
Depart from conventions when you can do so purposely and purposefully.	Purposely but quietly disobeying a convention in an effort to disguise your own purposes or to somehow mislead or conceal facts from the reader.
Depart from conventions when doing so will enhance your relationship with your reader.	Openly demonstrating an unjustified or petulant unwillingness to follow conventions.
Depart from conventions when the occasion is appropriate and the message will benefit from a nontraditional approach.	Putting yourself in a position in which the material in your document must disobey one communication principle in order to follow another, resulting in a clash between the two principles.

RESPONSE SHEET

CONVENTIONS IN CORRESPONDENCE

WRITER(S): AUDIENCE(S):
OCCASION FOR WRITING: DOCUMENT:
WHAT IS THE WRITER'S MAIN PURPOSE IN WRITING THIS DOCUMENT?
WHAT IS THE READER'S PRIMARY USE OF THE DOCUMENT GOING TO BE?

◆ CONVENTIONAL ORGANIZATIONAL STRATEGIES:

Should the overall structure of the writer's document be inductive or deductive? Explain.

◆ CONVENTIONAL STRATEGIES FOR DEVELOPMENT

What sections, parts, or paragraphs will/does the document contain?

What strategies for development should/does the writer employ in these various parts? (Where possible, note the strategy on the writer's planning document and then label the part that will/does employ that strategy.)

- description
- division into parts (includes partition)
- exemplification
- cause and effect (includes problem/solution)
- comparison (includes similarities/differences, pro/con)
- definition
- classification
- narration
- process

Check for the following strategies for internal sequencing of information. Label or suggest appropriate uses.

- chronological order
- least to most important
- specific to general
- general to specific

Check for the following strategies for presenting information if appropriate. Label or suggest appropriate uses.

- lists
- headings and subheadings

Check for the following strategies for establishing connectedness. Label or suggest appropriate uses.

- transitions
- topic announcements
- given/new structures
- prepositions and pronouns
- keyed repetition
- format conventions

◆ DEPARTING FROM CONVENTIONS

Does this particular writing situation lend itself to departures from certain conventions? Explain.

Does the present document unsuccessfully depart from conventions? Explain.

ACTIVITIES, EXERCISES, AND ASSIGNMENTS

◆ IN-CLASS ACTIVITIES

1. Please refer to Figure 6.1 (Credit Card Solicitation) for the following activity.
   a. Discuss the following questions in terms of what you have learned in this chapter about following and departing from conventions:
      - What elements does this letter have in common with other business letters of this type (check your "junk mail")? What unusual elements do you see?
      - What type(s) of information are covered as a "Blah"? What type(s) of information are covered in actual words and phrases?
      - How do you think the writer made the choice of using either "Blah" or "actual detail"?

   b. Please read Figures 6.21a, b, and c. These figures are also part of the "Blah" example. Now answer the following questions in terms of the additional pages:
      - Again, what type(s) of information are covered in the conventional way? What type(s) in the unconventional way (as a "Blah")?
      - Do you see any significant differences between the various pages? Explain.
      - How, in your opinion, are the writer's choices purposeful?
      - If you as a student received this message, would you find the departures from convention effective? Explain.

2. Chapter 2 introduced you to Toulmin's structure for arguments that appeared inductive, and to a Minto-inspired top-down framework that was primarily deductive. In this chapter, you learned that Aristotle regarded inductive and deductive arrangement as two types of "logical proofs" (or patterns for presenting evidence). Therefore, it looks as if inductive and deductive arrangement can variously help you to plan your messages. Discuss how several conventional patterns of organization and development covered in this chapter can help you plan a message.

3. Imagine that you have just joined a conservative firm as a professional writer. You want to be able to depart from standard company practice in some of your messages, but need to argue about the effectiveness of occasional departures from convention with your immediate supervisor. You set up a meeting with your supervisor. To prepare for such a meeting, construct a list of several ways communicators can make sure that

Figure 6.21a Second Page of the "Blah" Example

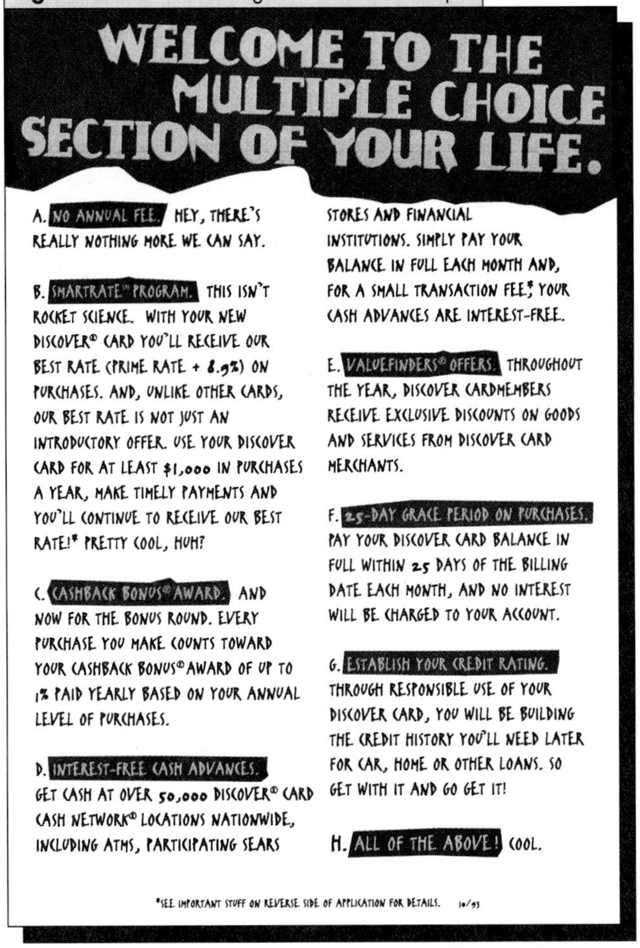

WELCOME TO THE MULTIPLE CHOICE SECTION OF YOUR LIFE.
A. NO ANNUAL FEE. HEY, THERE'S REALLY NOTHING MORE WE CAN SAY.
B. SMARTRATE℠ PROGRAM. THIS ISN'T ROCKET SCIENCE. WITH YOUR NEW DISCOVER® CARD YOU'LL RECEIVE OUR BEST RATE (PRIME RATE + 8.9%) ON PURCHASES. AND, UNLIKE OTHER CARDS, OUR BEST RATE IS NOT JUST AN INTRODUCTORY OFFER. USE YOUR DISCOVER CARD FOR AT LEAST $1,000 IN PURCHASES A YEAR, MAKE TIMELY PAYMENTS AND YOU'LL CONTINUE TO RECEIVE OUR BEST RATE!* PRETTY COOL, HUH?
C. CASHBACK BONUS® AWARD. AND NOW FOR THE BONUS ROUND. EVERY PURCHASE YOU MAKE COUNTS TOWARD YOUR CASHBACK BONUS® AWARD OF UP TO 1% PAID YEARLY BASED ON YOUR ANNUAL LEVEL OF PURCHASES.
D. INTEREST-FREE CASH ADVANCES. GET CASH AT OVER 50,000 DISCOVER® CARD CASH NETWORK® LOCATIONS NATIONWIDE, INCLUDING ATMS, PARTICIPATING SEARS STORES AND FINANCIAL INSTITUTIONS. SIMPLY PAY YOUR BALANCE IN FULL EACH MONTH AND, FOR A SMALL TRANSACTION FEE,* YOUR CASH ADVANCES ARE INTEREST-FREE.
E. VALUEFINDERS® OFFERS. THROUGHOUT THE YEAR, DISCOVER CARDMEMBERS RECEIVE EXCLUSIVE DISCOUNTS ON GOODS AND SERVICES FROM DISCOVER CARD MERCHANTS.
F. 25-DAY GRACE PERIOD ON PURCHASES. PAY YOUR DISCOVER CARD BALANCE IN FULL WITHIN 25 DAYS OF THE BILLING DATE EACH MONTH, AND NO INTEREST WILL BE CHARGED TO YOUR ACCOUNT.
G. ESTABLISH YOUR CREDIT RATING. THROUGH RESPONSIBLE USE OF YOUR DISCOVER CARD, YOU WILL BE BUILDING THE CREDIT HISTORY YOU'LL NEED LATER FOR CAR, HOME OR OTHER LOANS. SO GET WITH IT AND GO GET IT!
H. ALL OF THE ABOVE! COOL.
*SEE IMPORTANT STUFF ON REVERSE SIDE OF APPLICATION FOR DETAILS. 10/93

Figure 6.21b Third Page of the "Blah" Example

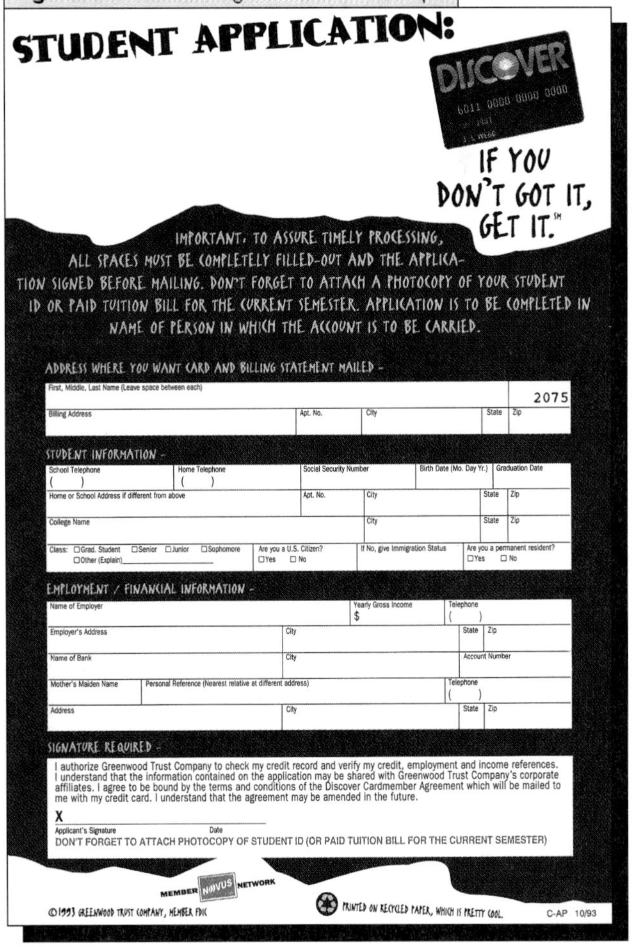

STUDENT APPLICATION:
DISCOVER
IF YOU DON'T GOT IT, GET IT.℠
IMPORTANT: TO ASSURE TIMELY PROCESSING, ALL SPACES MUST BE COMPLETELY FILLED-OUT AND THE APPLICATION SIGNED BEFORE MAILING. DON'T FORGET TO ATTACH A PHOTOCOPY OF YOUR STUDENT ID OR PAID TUITION BILL FOR THE CURRENT SEMESTER. APPLICATION IS TO BE COMPLETED IN NAME OF PERSON IN WHICH THE ACCOUNT IS TO BE CARRIED.
ADDRESS WHERE YOU WANT CARD AND BILLING STATEMENT MAILED -
First, Middle, Last Name (Leave space between each)
2075
Billing Address
Apt. No.
City
State
Zip
STUDENT INFORMATION -
School Telephone ( )
Home Telephone ( )
Social Security Number
Birth Date (Mo. Day Yr.)
Graduation Date
Home or School Address if different from above
Apt. No.
City
State
Zip
College Name
City
State
Zip
Class: ☐Grad. Student ☐Senior ☐Junior ☐Sophomore ☐Other (Explain)
Are you a U.S. Citizen? ☐Yes ☐No
If No, give Immigration Status
Are you a permanent resident? ☐Yes ☐No
EMPLOYMENT / FINANCIAL INFORMATION -
Name of Employer
Yearly Gross Income $
Telephone ( )
Employer's Address
City
State
Zip
Name of Bank
City
Account Number
Mother's Maiden Name
Personal Reference (Nearest relative at different address)
Telephone ( )
Address
City
State
Zip
SIGNATURE REQUIRED -
I authorize Greenwood Trust Company to check my credit record and verify my credit, employment and income references. I understand that the information contained on the application may be shared with Greenwood Trust Company's corporate affiliates. I agree to be bound by the terms and conditions of the Discover Cardmember Agreement which will be mailed to me with my credit card. I understand that the agreement may be amended in the future.
X
Applicant's Signature
Date
DON'T FORGET TO ATTACH PHOTOCOPY OF STUDENT ID (OR PAID TUITION BILL FOR THE CURRENT SEMESTER)
MEMBER NOVUS NETWORK
©1993 GREENWOOD TRUST COMPANY, MEMBER FDIC
PRINTED ON RECYCLED PAPER, WHICH IS PRETTY COOL.
C-AP 10/93

Figure 6.21c Fourth Page of the "Blah" Example

IMPORTANT STUFF.

Annual Percentage Rate For Purchases	Variable Rate Information	Grace Period For Payment Of Balances For Purchases	Method Of Computing The Balance For Purchases	Annual Fees	Minimum Periodic Finance Charge
As of October 1, 1993, your Annual Percentage Rate is 14.9% for first year; for each subsequent year your Annual Percentage Rate is determined by total purchases in previous year: $1,000 or more –14.9% (Best Rate); $500 to $999.99 –16.9% (Better Rate); less than $500 –19.8% (Standard Rate) (18% for residents of ME, NC and WI).*	Your Annual Percentage Rate may vary. The rate is determined for each billing period by the highest Prime Rate reported in *The Wall Street Journal* on the last business day of the previous month plus a fixed amount of percentage points as follows: Initial year and Best Rate – Prime Rate plus 8.9 percentage points; Better Rate – Prime Rate plus 10.9 percentage points (but not exceeding Standard Rate); Standard Rate –19.8% when the Prime Rate is lower than 10.9% and Prime Rate plus 8.9 percentage points, when the Prime Rate is 10.9% or more (18% for residents of ME, NC and WI).*	25 days.	Two-cycle average daily balance (including new purchases).	None	$.50

*Better and Best Rates have a 12.9% minimum, and for residents of ME, NC and WI, 18% maximum. Failure to make required payments converts you from Better or Best Rate to Standard Rate.

Annual percentage rate for cash advances: As of October 1, 1993, 19.8%; this rate may vary, i.e., 19.8% when the Prime Rate is lower than 10.9%, and Prime Rate plus 8.9 percentage points when the Prime Rate is 10.9% or more; for residents of ME, NC and WI, 18%. Transaction Fee Finance Charge for each cash advance: $500 or less – 2.5%; $500.01 to $1000 – 2.0%; $1,000.01 or more – 1.5%, with a minimum of $2.00 and no maximum. Late payment fee: $15 for payment more than 20 days overdue. Over-the-credit-limit fee: None.

I understand this account is only for personal, family and household purposes. It is not for business or commercial purposes. The applicant, if married, may apply for a separate account. Finance charges will not exceed those permitted by law.

ALL ACCOUNT TERMS AND CHARGES DISCLOSED HEREIN ARE ACCURATE AS OF THE PRINTING DATE, BUT ARE SUBJECT TO CHANGE. TO FIND OUT WHAT MAY HAVE CHANGED AFTER THE PRINTING DATE, WRITE TO US AT: P.O. BOX 15410, WILMINGTON, DE 19886-0820.

A consumer credit report may be ordered in connection with this application, or subsequently in connection with the update, renewal or extension of credit. Upon your request, you will be informed whether or not a consumer credit report was ordered, and if it was, you will be given the name and address of the consumer reporting agency that furnished the report. The Discover Card is issued by Greenwood Trust Company, Member FDIC.

I understand that the joint cardmember accepts individual and joint liability for all charges to this Discover Card. I also understand that if I have previously applied for, and either have received or am waiting to receive my Discover Card, I should not reapply at this time.

ILLINOIS RESIDENTS: Residents of Illinois may contact the Illinois Commissioner of Banks and Trust Companies for comparative information on interest rates, charges, fees and grace period. Write: State of Illinois — CIP, P.O. Box 10181, Springfield, Illinois 62791, or call 1-800-634-5452.

OHIO RESIDENTS: The Ohio laws against discrimination require that all creditors make credit equally available to all creditworthy customers, and that credit reporting agencies maintain separate credit histories on each individual upon request. The Ohio Civil Rights Commission administers compliance with this law.

WISCONSIN RESIDENTS: No agreement, court order, or individual statement applying to marital property will adversely affect a creditor's interests unless prior to the time credit is granted the creditor is furnished with a copy of the agreement, court order, or statement or has actual knowledge of the adverse provision. You must indicate the name and address of your spouse below.

Spouse's name ______________________________

Spouse's address ______________________________

the departures from convention are effective, and construct a number of examples of effective departures (complete with a rundown of the occasion, communicator, and audience) to prove your point.

◆ INDIVIDUAL AND GROUP EXERCISES

1. Please refer to Figure 6.22, an excerpt from a letter containing both bad and good news, in completing this exercise. The paragraphs are excerpted from a letter that denies the reader's request for a company visit but offers to have company personnel visit the school instead.

   a. After reading the excerpt, identify the various "logical" patterns that you find.

   b. Locate and discuss several strategies designed to increase the connectedness of the letter.

   c. Comment on the overall pattern presented by these three paragraphs. Especially note how the bad and the good information are placed. Do you think the placement of information in this excerpt is effective? Why or why not?

2. Please refer to Figure 6.23 (page 184), which shows ineffective departures from convention, in completing this exercise.

   a. Locate and label miscues and instances of departing from convention.

CONTEXT

The memo in Figure 6.23 was posted in a research lab where everyone, except the administrative assistant, has at least a master's degree in some area of biology. The only place the lab workers had smoked in the past was the basement table area (the "break" area). The new law did not change the situation.

   b. Locate and label instances of opting out, clashing, or violating.

   c. Analyze what the writer was trying to do when writing this message, and evaluate the writer's success or lack of success.

3. Please return to Figure 6.23 and complete the following tasks:

   a. Revise the letter so that it contains no departures from convention whatsoever.

   b. Revise the letter a second time so that it contains several instances of successful departures from convention. As best you can, name or describe the convention(s) you are departing from and explain your purpose in doing so.

Figure 6.22 Excerpt from Letter with Both Bad and Good News

> The design and implementation of information systems have been crucial to the success of our company. As a result, the company prides itself on updating and maintaining our information systems with the newest and most effective technology.
>
> Currently, our information systems personnel have undertaken two types of projects. One is an extensive project involving our whole integrated system. This project addresses issues in emergency support and backup. A second project involves the improvement of the ES/9000 - 720 mainframe computer. This project addresses issues of personnel access and security. Taken together, these projects make it impossible for our systems specialists to provide your class with the kind of educational company tour that you have requested and that we would like to provide.
>
> Our systems specialists would enjoy visiting your class, however, and sharing information regarding our different approaches to system design. The IEF CASE tool, for example, is quickly becoming the tool of choice among system analysts. Our team has found IEF to be a very reliable and efficient method of designing integrated information systems and would be glad to demonstrate its capabilities. The knowledge you gain about IEF by applying it in the classroom will prove very helpful during your search for employment upon graduation.

4. Please refer to Figure 6.14, the letter about garbage collection and recycling, to complete the following tasks:
   a. Revise the letter so that it avoids ineffective departures from convention and becomes a request that will convince readers to attend the council meeting.
   b. Discuss whether or not any departure from convention would be effective for this situation. If you think so, describe what you have in mind. If not, state why such departures should be avoided here.

◆ OUT-OF-CLASS ASSIGNMENTS

1. Select a document that you believe departs from conventions effectively. Annotate and highlight this document to identify the places where the departures from conventions occur. Make sure the annotations include information about each convention and the effectiveness of departing from it.
2. Select a document you have written or one that you have received that you think could be improved by strengthening its use of conventional strategies for organization and development. Revise the document using the strategies you learned in this chapter. Use the Response Sheet on conventions in correspondence as a first step toward this revision. After finishing the revision, annotate and highlight the document to identify the changes you have made.
3. Imagine that you work as a professional writer at a company that is experiencing "the best of times and the worst of times." The good news is that the company has just hired two new full-time employees to help with composing the firm's business communication and three new office personnel to help with data entry, word processing, and general clerical work. In hiring these five new employees, the company has essentially doubled the staff assigned to your particular division. The bad news is that because of the jump in the number of employees, the three "old" communicators and two "old" staff members feel that the close-knit nature of the office has been sacrificed to the new efficiency. The new members, for their part, are having difficulties following long-standing procedures that the old members know but that have not been written down. Taking the initiative, you decide to call an informal meeting to discuss these and other problems, to establish a good working relationship between the groups, and to enhance general morale. Write the memo that informs employees in your expanded division of the meeting and that persuades all to participate. Feel free to add detail of your own making. In drafting the memo, pay particular attention to how you adopt or adapt conventions that you are familiar with that pertain to this message. Use the Response Sheet on conventions in correspondence to aid you in considering conventions.

CASE

CROSS POINTE CONSULTANTS

CASE BY ANDREA BREEMER FRANTZ

Background. You are a business consultant for Cross Pointe Consultants, a moderate-sized consulting firm based in New York City, which specializes in finance management, investments and mergers, and organizational restructuring. Cross Pointe's first task is to convince a prospective client of what Cross Pointe may offer to a specific business situation or culture. This step normally involves a series of meetings with the client's upper management, followed by or interspersed with several social gatherings including other staff members. Cross Pointe's team leader then offers a formal proposal that specifically outlines the situation, the client's needs, and how Cross Pointe can meet those needs in an extended study or program.

Once Cross Pointe is hired, team leaders assign the appropriate specialists to the client's case. For example, a national

Figure 6.23 Letter with Ineffective Departures from Convention

> Effective 1 July 19—, smoking is restricted in any "facility which is open to the public," in any "public building owned by or under the control of this state." This means that all office and research areas and headquarters are off limits to smoking.
>
> We "may permit smoking by persons seated at tables provided for the purpose of consuming food or beverages," "where the words 'smoking permitted' are posted." Accordingly, the basement table area (exclusive of the research lab area) is designated as our smoking area, and will be used for our "break" area. Open air areas are not covered by this new law. Safety in the presence of flammables and toxicants, and animal health, will determine whether smoking may occur in work areas not accessible to the public.
>
> There is no reason that any Commission employee should flaunt or ignore so simple a law. The law does provide that any "person smoking in (this) facility in violation of this Act," having been informed "that smoking is prohibited by law," "shall pay a civil fine of five dollars for the first violation and 10 to 100 dollars for each subsequent violation."
>
> Thank you for your cooperation and compliance.

transportation conglomerate asked Cross Pointe's input in a recent merger deal. Cross Pointe's team leader assigned specialists in human resource management, finance and investments, engineering, and communication, and also hired a freelance consultant in transportation management to evaluate the proposed merger. The team spent five months familiarizing themselves with the organizational hierarchies and management styles of those involved, evaluated the technological capabilities, and conducted a complete financial review. Cross Pointe finally concluded that it was not in its client's best interest to move ahead with the merger, largely because the financial problems that had plagued the company over the last year were expected to improve dramatically in the next year. Cross Pointe also recommended that the client instead consider a re-evaluation of management style which would bolster worker productivity and efficiency.

Cross Pointe has recently been approached by Weber & Associates (W&A), a landscape design firm widely known for its highly unusual and artistic designs. Critics noted, for example, that W&A's design for a water and rose park seemed to "defy the laws of nature . . . and spark the postmodern imagination." Weber's designs reflect artistic passion and flair, and are particularly coveted by celebrities. W&A has been touted as one of the premier landscape design firms in the country and has recently been experimenting with some international markets. Sabine Weber has acknowledged that despite the firm's strong desire to break into the European market, it is having trouble finding a foothold, and has had difficulties making the contacts necessary to create a strong European client base.

Weiss Architecture, based in Manhattan, has offered Weber a partial merger deal for the European market only. Weiss, an old and reputable firm, has cultivated a strong European client base since the late 1960s. The firm is run by Thomas Volker, a German immigrant. Volker initially flirted with Bauhaus designs, but shortly after he came to America he reconfigured his style to emulate an interesting marriage of ornate form with traditional function. His designs became the signature for the architectural firm.

Despite the surface appearance of a very attractive offer for a partial merger, W&A is leery. Thus, Sabine Weber has decided to consider a number of consulting firms in the New York area, in an effort to find a team that may help direct her landscape design firm to the right decision. "I'm an artist first," says Weber, "and a businessperson somewhere else down on the list."

Cross Pointe has been asked to compete for W&A's business and must show how it offers the best consulting for Weber's needs. The procedural conventions for such a "pitch" would involve

- studying Weber's management structure, goals, financial stability
- interviewing key people in the organization about their perception of the problems and possibilities of the merger
- writing a proposal (see Chapter 15) using a standard background-needs-idea (plan)-benefits-implementation structure that examines what the client's situation is, what the client wants, and how to get from where the client is to where he or she wants to be
- promoting the proposal in a formal oral presentation to Weber's management team by using the appropriate visual displays and highlighting the specific expertise that Cross Pointe would expect to employ for a lengthier study.

However, W&A is made up of an unusual group of people. Sabine Weber is known as the consummate artist, and historically has had difficulty accepting criticism from her own clients. She has little patience with formality, and insists on casual dress in the office and at whatever private functions she may attend. Her nickname among colleagues is Maverick, which, she noted in a recent interview, suits her fine. Her landscape designers and architects are of similar ilk. Many of her employees have been accused by clients of being moody or excitable. Weber launched a libel lawsuit three years ago when a high-profile client accused two of her employees of "being stoned" while on the job because the two chose to lie under a poplar tree for two hours staring and pointing into its branches overhead. Weber argued that such behavior was perfectly normal and natural for any true artist in her field and that she was surprised they'd only done it for two hours. The case was settled out of court.

Task. Cross Pointe is in heavy competition for W&A's business, and because the culture of the landscape design firm is unusual, team leader Jacob Blume has asked you to carefully consider Cross Pointe's pitch. Because you are young and innovative, Blume believes you may lend an important perspective on the proposal team. "Maybe standard research procedures, a conventional proposal, and a formal presentation aren't the right appeal with these folks," he said.

You are asked to evaluate the situation and write a memo to Blume detailing what conventions Cross Pointe should and should not employ as it appeals to W&A. If you recommend against following a certain convention, you have been asked to articulate a general plan of action for your departures from convention. (You might scan the conventions for proposal writing in Chapter 15, but your main task here is not to make specific recommendations for how to write the proposal itself. You are concerned with the general approach the proposal will be taking to examine what the client's situation is, what the client wants, and how to get from where the client is to where he or she wants to be.)

Complication. Cross Pointe's CEO, Ashley Sosnouski, has overheard rumors of Blume's and your plan to consider something unconventional in your approach to securing the W&A account. Write a memo to Sosnouski concerning your plans and your reasons for pursuing an unconventional approach.

CHAPTER

7

Planning Business Messages

OUTLINE

Expert Planning: Hsing-luen's Story

Defining Tasks, Planning Documents, and Structuring Arguments

Collaborative Planning

Visual Tools for Organizing Business Messages

CRITERIA FOR EXPLORING CHAPTER 7

What we cover in this chapter	What you will be able to do after reading this chapter
Expert planning	Identify and adopt expert planning behaviors
Nature of the task, approaches to planning, and development of claims and arguments	Define tasks; use schema-driven, knowledge-driven, and constructive planning in appropriate situations; develop claims and lines of argument
Collaborative planning	Work with others to consider critical factors such as purpose, audience, occasion, and various conventions
Visual tools for organizing	Use visual tools to organize business messages

Expert communicators do a lot of planning—sometimes in their heads, sometimes on paper, sometimes alone, sometimes with others. Expert planners consider not only content but also other factors such as the purpose, audience, organization, and design. Novice communicators, on the other hand, tend to do little planning—and what planning they do usually focuses on content. Figure 7.1 shows representative excerpts from the planning sessions of two pairs of business communication students, with one pair approaching their task much like experts and the other approaching the task like novices.

CONTEXT

In the short excerpts from each team's second planning session shown in Figure 7.1, both teams discuss their plans to design and write an information sheet about solar hot water heaters that sales representatives will use with customers. Rick and Maggie prepared for their meeting by defining the purposes of the document they were producing. In contrast, Josh and Pete did not do any advance planning for their meeting.

Figure 7.1 Two Collaborative Planning Excerpts

How would you describe Rick and Maggie's opening concerns?

Beyond the content of the information sheet, what do Rick and Maggie consider in planning?

What tells you that Rick and Maggie have come prepared to this planning meeting?

How do Rick and Maggie deal with conflict?

How effective are Rick and Maggie's explanations?

How do Josh and Pete begin?

Beyond the content of the information sheet, what do Josh and Pete consider in their planning?

What tells you that Josh and Pete have come unprepared to this planning meeting?

Rick	. . . I see our purpose as setting up an information sheet that is more brief. . . . Who said it had to be a bunch of paragraphs?
Maggie	Mmuh.
Rick	Why do we have to limit ourselves to that type of thinking? Why can't this be organized into three columns: one for commercial, one for homeowners, one for small businesses?
Maggie	. . . I don't think you can organize like that. You just can say somewhere that this can be used for commercial, home, or whatever.
Rick	Mmuh.
Maggie	It's gonna serve the same purposes for all three of them: it's gonna give you heating. That's all the system does. . . . And you can say that this—these are what its benefits are. Say, "It's effective. It's cost-saving. . . ." We don't have to break it down into different components.
Rick	Well, see, what I was saying is more of a design issue. . . . I think we may be limiting our effectiveness with this sheet by limiting ourselves to . . . a series of paragraphs, which is what the old sheet looks like. Okay? What if we made the whole sheet . . . more graphic . . .?

Pete	We can make it a marketing tool. . . . Also—and also an information sheet.
Josh	Right.
Pete	Just that an ordinary person can understand.
Josh	Oh, yeah. Definitely.
Pete	Okay. So we see that—and we need—I think we need . . . maybe just a title and a couple of headings. . . . Maybe a sentence under the heading.
Josh	Yeah. Like one sectional paragraph or something.
Pete	Yeah. One paragraph under one—under the heading.

1. What pre-meeting planning might have helped Josh and Pete? What effect did Josh and Pete's lack of preparation have on this segment of their planning meeting? How did Rick and Maggie's pre-meeting planning seem to help them?
2. Given the topics Josh and Pete discussed (the information sheet as a marketing tool, the use of a title and headings), what could they have added to their conversation to make their planning more productive?
3. What could Josh and Pete learn from Maggie and Rick's session?

Expert planners know that learning about planning develops the following skills that improve business messages:

- defining tasks and structuring arguments
- participating in collaborative planning
- using tools for organizing information

EXPERT PLANNING: HSING-LUEN'S STORY

Hsing-luen Ching is a marketing project leader for a United States company, Worldwide Entertainment Corporation (WEC). She grew up in Shanghai in the People's Republic of China and went to the high school affiliated with Shanghai International Studies University, which acquainted her with North Americans and their language. By the time she graduated from a university in the United States with an undergraduate double major in marketing and professional communication, she was culturally and linguistically bilingual.

WEC hired Hsing-luen because of her fluency in Mandarin and her ability to translate cultural conventions. She is a valuable project leader for WEC, as it expands its musical CD market in the People's Republic of China. Because Hsing-luen knows Chinese business strategies, she is able to give her company an edge. Just as important, Hsing-luen is adept at planning professional documents and oral presentations.

As Hsing-luen organizes her day's work on a particular Monday, she needs to complete three tasks: a meeting reminder memo to WEC staff members, an oral description of her latest project for the monthly meeting of other project leaders, and the first draft of a proposal for a new project. One of the first things she does is match the type of planning she needs to do with the nature of the task (Figure 7.2). Knowing the task and her various audiences and purposes helps Hsing-luen make decisions about her documents based on readers' familiarity with the content of each message and their familiarity with Chinese culture.

Hsing-luen draws up initial plans of the memo right away and then spends the afternoon completing the project description. However, as expected, planning for the proposal

Figure 7.2 Expert Planner Matches Type of Planning to Task

HSING-LUEN'S SUMMARY OF THE TASK	THE TYPE OF PLANNING APPROPRIATE TO THE TASK
Memo: I need to remind department members about a change in time for the weekly staff meeting, to note a revision of the agenda to include the just-awarded contract and to explain changes in individual and team responsibilities made necessary by this contract.	A standard format exists for departmental memos and for the sequence of information on an agenda. Therefore, I can draw on familiar, standard formats and organizational conventions to quickly organize my information and meet my readers' expectations. *In my planning, I'll use a conventional memo format to help me select and organize the information.*
Oral Project Description: I need to plan a brief oral presentation for the monthly meeting with other project leaders. I'll describe the process I developed to monitor magazine, poster, and radio marketing efforts in China.	Because I designed and implemented this project to monitor Chinese media myself, I won't have any trouble digging up and organizing the content. I'll just have to consider my purpose and audience: Do I want this oral presentation to do more than simply describe the progress of our monitoring efforts? Do leaders of other projects need an overview of the long-range marketing efforts, the current problems of monitoring media in China, or any solutions being tried? *In my planning, I'll use an outline to help me organize information that I already know so that the audience can understand it.*
Proposal: I need to argue that WEC create an innovative plan for marketing CDs (especially folk and pop music) in China. This proposal will go to my supervisor, then to the division manager, and then to the vice president. Lots of revision is ahead, that's for sure.	I'm definitely going to have to spend a lot of time up front analyzing all the factors involved (purpose, audience, occasion) and dealing with the message itself (content, organization, design). This will take some time. I can't depend entirely on the standard organization of proposals. I don't have the content under control at the outset either. I have to consider the economic and political purposes of the proposal and my readers' limited background about Chinese culture, not to mention the complexities of the content itself. *In my planning, I'll construct an argument to help me persuade an audience that is not only unfamiliar with the information but also slightly resistant.*

is more complicated and takes a great deal of time. The next morning, Hsing-luen decides that she has a better chance of convincing her readers—managers at Worldwide Entertainment—about the merits of her proposal if she plans to explain the challenges of negotiating and marketing in China before discussing why traditional U.S. marketing approaches are unlikely to work.

In fleshing out her plans, she decides to explain that oral messages are given and interpreted differently in China than in the United States: North Americans tend to use a deductive approach, saying what they want up front, whereas Chinese are more likely to use an inductive approach, saying what they *really* want toward the end of a conversation. She also decides that her readers need a point-by-point discussion of how her plan meets Eastern cultural expectations. Well into her second day, she marks out large chunks in her daily planner to reserve time for continued work on the project.

Chinese businesspeople generally plan a point-by-point discussion of all of the details before they plan the main idea of a presentation.

On the basis of what Hsing-luen knows, she develops planning strategies for each occasion. She acts as an expert planner in four ways:

1. She does a great deal of preliminary planning and is willing to revise her plans when necessary.
2. She considers more than content in her planning. She starts with occasion, purpose, and audience.
3. She does not make the mistake of jumping right into a task without developing a plan first.
4. She matches the type of planning to the task.

Hsing-luen bases her decisions on the type of document or presentation, her knowledge of the subject matter, and the complexity of the situation.

DEFINING TASKS, PLANNING DOCUMENTS, AND STRUCTURING ARGUMENTS

Hsing-luen begins her planning by considering four factors:

- the nature of her planning
- claims she wanted to make
- the line of argument she wanted to use
- the components of each argument

The Nature of Planning

Whenever you start a project, you need to define the task. Tasks can be defined by purpose and audience as well as by the nature of the occasion and the message itself. For example, you can ask yourself or a collaborator the following questions during your planning:

- *Purpose.* What need does this document or oral presentation fulfill?
- *Audience.* Who needs this document or oral presentation? What are the attitudes, abilities, and expectations of this audience?
- *Occasion.* Why is this document or oral presentation useful or necessary?
- *Message.* What arguments will persuade the audience to act on the purpose and agree with the key points?

Sometimes planning the task is neither difficult nor complicated. For example, Hsing-luen's memo and project description were easy to plan because she already knew the conventional organization and standard formats. Planning the project description was also easy because she was already familiar with the content, which she had organized previously and kept on file. She was able to draw on her prior knowledge about audience, purpose, and occasion to complete these tasks quickly and efficiently.

At other times, such as writing a project proposal, planning is complex. That's when knowing about different approaches to planning is helpful:

- **Schema-driven planning** enables you to draw on familiar, standard formats and organizational conventions such as memos, oral project reports, and press releases. Hsing-luen uses schema-driven planning for her staff memo.

- **Knowledge-driven planning** enables you to draw on your extensive knowledge of content, which has already been organized and is readily available. Hsing-luen uses knowledge-driven planning for her project description.
- **Constructive planning** enables you to consider the complex relationships among audience, purpose, occasion, message, organization, and design. Hsing-luen uses constructive planning to draft her proposal.

The type of planning you choose to use depends on which elements you already know from the outset and which you need to explore as you start your planning.

Schema-Driven Planning. *Schemata* (singular, *schema*) are images, expectations, or patterns that people carry in their heads. For example, if you have reservations for dinner at a fancy restaurant, your schema for "nice restaurant" makes you expect valet parking, linen napkins, a wine list, good service, and high prices. If, on the other hand, you have dinner at a fast-food restaurant, your schema makes you expect drive-up windows, paper napkins, soft drinks in paper cups, fast service, and low prices.

Many kinds of business messages have widely recognized schemata you can use: you don't have to make decisions about a range of factors, because they're already determined by the occasion. For example, meeting announcement memos typically include a brief statement of the meeting purpose and then the date, time, and place of the meeting. An agenda listing the sequence of topics for discussion is often attached. Knowing this about meeting announcements helped Hsing-luen quickly organize her memo.

Figure 7.3 shows how a memo schema helped Howland Kirk inform his department about an upcoming visit from the internal auditors. Howland used the who-what-when-where-why-how sequence common in memo writing (and newspaper articles). Using such familiar planning strategies will help you produce routine messages with little effort.

Figure 7.3 Schema-Driven Planning to Organize a Memo

who—an internal team

what—to conduct periodic audit

when—beginning May 24

where—using the small conference room as their office

why—shifting to a new system at the end of the fiscal year

how—make computer and paper files available with 24 hours' notice

May 17, 199--

TO: Marketing Department
FROM: Howland Kirk HK
SUBJECT: Audit

A team of the company's internal auditors will be in our department to conduct the periodic audit for two or three days beginning May 24. They will be using the small conference room as their office.

Because we'll be shifting to a new accounting system at the end of the fiscal year, this is a good time to make sure our records are in order.

You will need to make your computer and paper files available to the team members. They will try to give you at least 24 hours' notice about any files they need.

Knowledge-Driven Planning. In knowledge-driven planning, communicators depend on their extensive store of information about the subject. When you have a well-organized storehouse of information, as Hsing-luen does when planning her oral project description, you can adapt that content to a specific purpose and audience and decide the most effective organization.

One effective way for organizing your store of information is to use an outline. Outlines allow you to rearrange points, delete irrelevant ones, add new ones, and note where support may be needed. They also allow you to decide on the number, type, and location of supporting details. Although outlines are structured—with their Roman numerals, capital letters, and parallelism—they can be adapted to meet the needs of the task you're completing. An outline should free you to examine the overall structure of your plan and to try various arrangements of large amounts of information. Outlines, like blueprints, are easier to change than the finished product.

Figure 7.4 shows the outline for an article to help small business owners adapt print documents to the computer screen. The writer, Karen Massetti Miller, the managing editor

Figure 7.4 Topical Outline to Help Knowledge-driven Planning

Miller considers her audience's prior knowledge: she starts with issues and difficulties related to screen design and then jumps right into the differences between what the readers know (paper) and what they don't know (screen). Afterward, Miller uses key questions as a bridge to connect potentially new terminology to ideas the readers will understand.

All the items in each section are parallel in importance and grammatical structure.

Road Signs for the Information Highway: Adapting Printed Documents to the Computer Screen

I. Introduction: Adapting design techniques to the screen

II. Differences between paper and screen
   A. Screen size
   B. Screen orientation
   C. Character definition

III. Elements of effective screen design
   A. Screen layout: Where is information located on the screen?
      1. Information to include on the screen
      2. Need for consistency
      3. Establishing a visual hierarchy
   B. Screen density: How condensed is information on the screen?
      1. Line length
      2. Typeface
      3. Line spacing
   C. Document features: How accessible is information?
      1. Pull-down menus
      2. Scroll bar
   D. Design weaknesses: What might give users difficulty?
      1. Navigation between screens
      2. Typeface
   E. Suggestions for redesign: An example

IV. Guidelines for professionals
   A. Guidelines for screen layouts
   B. Guidelines for screen density

of a regional feature magazine, developed an outline to organize her information. Initially, she defined terms and differentiated paper and computer screen design before focusing on effective screen design. By reviewing the outline, she ensured that she covered the critical elements of screen design with the same level of detail. The outline (minus the Roman numerals, letters, and numbers) later provided the headings and subheadings for her article—another advantage of using traditional outlines.

Constructive Planning. When a task is particularly complex, like Hsing-luen's proposal, schema-driven and knowledge-driven planning may be insufficient. A simple strategy such as who-what-when-where-why-how won't work, and devices such as outlines to organize the information are insufficient. In such situations, you need to use constructive planning. Like Hsing-luen when she plans the draft of her proposal, you need to consider how the purpose, audience, and occasion affect the construction of your plan.

Most constructive planning involves developing an argument, which is the focus of the following section. Any argument you develop is based on your careful analysis of the audience—which claims and appeals will be most effective.

Claims in Argument

All business documents are in some way persuasive. Even if your general purpose for a document or oral presentation is "to inform" or "to explain" rather than "to persuade," you will still be making an argument. In her memo, for example, Hsing-luen informs her colleagues that the new contract will have an impact on individual and team responsibilities. Because the item is on the agenda, the implicit message is that colleagues should come prepared to discuss changes in these responsibilities. Hsing-luen doesn't need to explicitly persuade her readers to come prepared; the agenda item—"changes in individual and team responsibilities"—is enough of a cue to persuade colleagues to come prepared to discuss the issue.

An effective argument gets readers to see a situation as you see it. For example, a memo announcing new federal safety standards from OSHA fulfills the statutory requirement to inform employees about the changes. The same memo *persuades* employees to follow these new standards.

Regardless of the line of argument you plan, there are certain elements common to all of them (see Chapter 2):

- a *claim* that identifies what you're trying to establish
- *support* for the claim
- a *warrant* that states the underlying assumption you make, which is sometimes taken for granted and thus left unstated

When you plan an argument, you have to decide what kind of *claim* you're going to make and what kind of appeals can be used to support that claim. The easiest way to think about claims (sometimes called propositions or positions) is to separate them into three broad categories: claims of fact, claims of value, and claims of policy.[1]

Claims of fact assert that something has existed, exists, or will exist—whether a policy, a practice, an object, an organism, a belief, or a system. For example, you might claim that employees with children take more sick days for child-related illnesses than for their own illnesses. Your plan to use claims of fact will be strengthened if you follow these general guidelines:

1. Clearly state your claim.
2. Define terms that may be unfamiliar or controversial.
3. Select reliable evidence from recognized and accepted sources.
4. Distinguish between accurate, verifiable facts and potentially slanted or biased interpretations of those facts.

Sometimes business communicators neglect to plan effective arguments for claims of fact because they presume that everyone "knows the facts." But people frequently disagree about facts for a variety of reasons: they aren't familiar with the support, they have such a strong stake in an opposing view that they refuse to acknowledge the support, or the facts change. For example, the claim that employees with children take more sick days for child-related illnesses might be challenged by arguing that the sample of employees was not representative or that the person providing the information had a stake in making the assertion. (See Figure 7.5.)

Figure 7.5 Claims of Fact

TYPE OF CLAIM	DEFINITION OF CLAIM	SUPPORT FOR CLAIM	EXAMPLE OF STARTING POINT FOR CLAIM OF FACT
Claim of fact	Claims of fact assert that something has existed, exists, or will exist.	• examples • statistics • testimony • observation	Employees in businesses that offer on-site child care with sick-child facilities use fewer personal days and take fewer sick days.

Claims of value attempt to establish that something is desirable or undesirable. For example, you might claim that employees who utilize the services of on-site pediatric nurses who provide sick-child care are more focused on their own work. Using a claim of value, you must consider what criteria will be used to assess the argument. Your plan to use claims of value will be strengthened if you follow these general guidelines:

1. Establish that the value you're presenting should be important to all readers or listeners.
2. Argue that accepting this value has clear benefits (and the obvious problems if it is rejected).
3. Use strong, vivid support—examples, testimony, anecdotes, statistics.
4. Include instances of respected individuals agreeing with your values and support.

MULTICULTURAL

CONSIDERATIONS IN INTERNATIONAL DOCUMENTATION

International communication involves considerations that range from the general, such as the audience's values and beliefs, to the specific, such as page size, translation information, legal and regulatory issues, document distribution, and on-line distribution.

Kathy Spencer and Peggy Yates, experts in international document standards, remind business communicators that in preparing international documents, professional communicators should follow these guidelines:

- *Avoid uniquely North American examples.* State what something is rather than what it is called in your part of the world. For example, "stock exchange index" is an international term, while "the Dow" is an American term and "the FTSE 100," British.
- *Be aware of cultural sensitivities.* Avoid religion, race, sex, politics, and stereotypes in documentation. Be aware that some words or terms common in English may be offensive in other cultures. For example, people of some cultures find the term "left hand" offensive. "On the left" or "left side" should thus be used instead.
- *Avoid humor.* Humor is often culture specific. What is funny to you may not be readily understood in another culture. Worse, it may be offensive.
- *Use consistent terminology and style.* Using consistent terminology and style enhances understanding and assists the translator of the material.
- *Avoid jargon, slang, and idioms.* Jargon, slang, and idioms are difficult to understand for nonnative speakers. Consider using terminology that everyone can understand or find in a reputable dictionary.
- *Limit use of acronyms.* Some acronyms are generally recognized worldwide, such as IBM. Others are not recognized internationally and may even have different meanings, depending on where they are used. Acronyms should be spelled out the first time they appear in a document unless they are recognized only in acronym form.

Your success in using a claim of value may hinge as much on the reader or listener's acceptance of the standards or criteria you pose as on the value itself. Claims of value may be rejected by readers or listeners because of strong personal views—whether political, religious, social, moral, or economic—that have little to do with the logic of your claim or the strength of your support. For example, your argument that employees who utilize services of on-site sick-child care are more focused on their work might be criticized by opponents who argue that it's wrong to take a sick child away from home—regardless of the nursing care the company provides. (See Figure 7.6.)

Figure 7.6 Claims of Value

TYPE OF CLAIM	DEFINITION OF CLAIM	SUPPORT FOR CLAIM	EXAMPLE OF STARTING POINT FOR CLAIM OF VALUE
Claim of value	Claims of value make a judgment. They attempt to establish that something is desirable or undesirable.	• accepted standards • testimony • examples • anecdotes	Businesses that offer on-site child care with sick-child facilities are more appealing to employees than businesses that don't.

Claims of policy argue for or against particular practices. For example, you might claim that a portion of the personnel and financial support for on-site sick-child care should be supported by employees. Of course, in order to accept the claim that a new policy is necessary, readers and listeners must first accept that there's a problem that your plan for a new policy corrects. Your plan to use claims of policy will be strengthened if you follow these general guidelines:

1. State a clear proposal for the new policy.
2. Establish a need for a new policy.
3. Acknowledge and respond to opposing views.
4. Identify the benefits of your new policy.
5. Provide strong support and logical reasons. (See Figure 7.7 on page 194.)

Claims of policy may be rejected for a number of reasons—lack of established need for the policy, insufficient evidence that the policy change responds to existing needs, conflict with existing policies or statutes, conflicting precedents. For example, union critics of your claim that employees should partially support on-site sick-child care might argue that such

Figure 7.7 Claims of Policy

TYPE OF CLAIM	DEFINITION OF CLAIM	SUPPORT FOR CLAIM	EXAMPLE OF STARTING POINT FOR CLAIM OF POLICY
Claim of policy	Claims of policy establish a need and propose a new policy to fulfill that need.	• examples • statistics • testimony • observation	Businesses should establish on-site child care with sick-child facilities for their employees. Underlying claim of fact: Personal days and sick days are often used to care for children. Underlying claim of value: Businesses whose benefits include personal days and sick days are appealing to employees.

a contribution by employees would violate provisions in the current union-management contract.

Although readers and listeners may accept your claim that a problem exists, they might disagree with the way your message responds to the problem. Thus, it is vital that you plan arguments that your audience will find persuasive. If you're arguing for on-site sick-child care to management, you could use statistics to show how the program will help the bottom line—an appeal to reason. If you're arguing for on-site sick-child care to parents, you can tell about the benefits for the family—an appeal to emotion.

Line of Argument

Just as you tailor your appeals and claims to your audience, you also plan arguments to support those appeals and claims. Arguments can be built on any of the four traditional case structures explained in Figures 7.8 through 7.11. These traditional lines of argument—need-plan, comparative advantage, criteria-goals, and net benefit—are conventions available to communicators as basic arguments.

A **need-plan line of argument** (sometimes called a **problem-solution line of argument**; see Figure 7.8) is appropriate when you wish to persuade your readers or listeners that a change of some sort is necessary. This line of argument depends on convincing your reader that the problem is directly caused by or related to current policies, practices, or systems. If the problem is inherent in the system, your argument, based on a claim of policy, is that the only way to eliminate the problem is to change the system.

Figure 7.8 Need-Plan Line of Argument

TYPE OF ARGUMENT	DEFINITION OF ARGUMENT	SEQUENCE FOR A NEED-PLAN LINE OF ARGUMENT
Need-plan	A compelling need or problem—caused by an inherent flaw in the current policy, practice, or system—is solved by the proposed plan.	1. Establish a need or problem. A. Identify the existing need or problem caused by some inherent flaw in the current policy, practice, or system—even an error of omission. B. Establish that the need or problem is serious (for example, in terms of personnel, time, money, reputation, and so on). C. Identify separate aspects of the need or problem. 2. Present an argument that your plan solves the need or problem. A. Present the overall plan. B. Show how plan is practical and workable. C. Show how each aspect of need or problem is addressed by the plan. D. Identify any additional benefits of the plan and reassure the reader that no additional problems will result from the change.

Kerrie Elliott used a need-plan line of argument when she planned a proposal urging her employer to install new payroll software. The union contract at her company specified that employees be given a printout with their payroll check on the status of individual and corporate contributions to various options beyond the standard deductions for taxes and FICA: retirement, stock purchases, credit union, and so on. The company's current software had no way of providing all of the necessary information on the payroll printout. Kerrie used appeals to reason (efficiency and legal compliance) in planning her need-plan line of argument: There was a compelling need (providing information specified in the union contract); the problem was caused by an inherent flaw in the current system (the software is inadequate); and her plan would solve the problem (new software will enable the payroll department to provide the appropriate information).

Related to a need-plan argument, a **comparative-advantage line of argument** (Figure 7.9) is appropriate if your purpose is to persuade your readers or listeners to modify an existing policy or practice. This line of argument acknowledges that the current policy, practice, or system may not cause a serious problem; however, your claim of value is that the proposed alternative offers clear advantages over present practices.

Jason Hathaway used a comparative-advantage line of argument in planning his marketing presentation to a corporate client that wanted its employees in three locations—Boston, Chicago, and San Diego—to be able to have meetings without traveling to one of the sites. Jason wanted to persuade this client to use video teleconferencing with interactive desk pads. Jason began by reviewing the company's ideal telecommunication goal: to provide fast, efficient, cost-effective communication (supported by claims of fact and appeals to reason). He presented a plan for video teleconferencing with interactive desk pads and explained why this system would accomplish the goals far better than the current practice of conference calls interspersed with cross-country trips. Not only would Jason's plan allow visual contact to capture the subtlety of body language, but the interactive desk pads would enable teleconference participants to see and write immediate responses to blueprints and technical drawings, a capability impossible with the company's current technology. Jason pointed out that the current system worked, but the proposed system not only worked better but also offered capabilities impossible with the current system.

Figure 7.9 Comparative Advantage Line of Argument

TYPE OF ARGUMENT	DEFINITION OF ARGUMENT	SEQUENCE FOR A COMPARATIVE-ADVANTAGE LINE OF ARGUMENT
Comparative advantage	The proposed plan not only achieves the goal but has more advantages than the current approach.	1. Present the goal of the current policy, practice, or system. 2. Present a plan to accomplish this goal. 3. Explain why this plan is superior to current policy, practice, or system. A. Establish that the advantages of the plan are measurable (for example, increased impact, reduced risk, greater appeal, longer duration of benefit, and so on). B. Establish that the advantages of the plan are significant in overcoming the limitations of the current approach (for example, cost, speed, and efficiency). C. Counter potential objections to possible disadvantages.

A **criteria-goals line of argument** (Figure 7.10 on page 196) is appropriate if your purpose is to persuade your readers or listeners first to accept your criteria for accomplishing the agreed-on goal and then to accept your plan. Your argument is that once the criteria are established for your claim of policy, your plan meets them better than the current policy, practice, or system.

Katherine Stevens used a criteria-goals line of argument when she planned a short memo to her manager, the director of Human Resources, recommending a testing program for job candidates. Katherine began with a restatement of the current goal: to hire the best available candidate for each position. She used a current posting for a company newsletter editor as an example when she posed a list of criteria that considerably expanded the current

Figure 7.10 Criteria-Goals Line of Argument

TYPE OF ARGUMENT	DEFINITION OF ARGUMENT	SEQUENCE FOR A CRITERIA-GOALS LINE OF ARGUMENT
Criteria-goals	The criteria to determine if the goal has been reached are established first; then the plan that fulfills those criteria is presented.	1. Establish the goal of the present policy, practice, or system. 2. Propose criteria for assessing whether the goal is met. 3. Present a plan to accomplish the goal. 4. Show how the plan fulfills the criteria. 5. Establish the advantages of the plan.

criteria. Among other things, she included these criteria: "demonstrates ability to work on a Macintosh platform," "demonstrates expert or near-expert skill in using Pagemaker," "demonstrates ability to rewrite news releases and fact sheets into high-interest articles." Katherine pointed out that the current candidate application and review process depended entirely on third-party recommendations and each candidate's statement of experience. She proposed a plan that would have candidates actually complete representative tasks, thereby demonstrating their skills in the necessary areas. In concluding her criteria-goals line of argument, Katherine pointed out that the plan would reduce the chances of hiring a highly recommended person who really didn't have the necessary skills.

A **net benefit line of argument** (Figure 7.11) is appropriate if your purpose is to persuade your readers or listeners to accept a plan with a better cost-benefit ratio than the current policy, practice, or system. In this line of argument, you are working under the assumption that readers or listeners already agree that problems exist and that changes should be made; your argument is that your plan creates the greatest benefits, both tangible and intangible, with the fewest problems.

Wyndell Jefferson used a net benefit line of argument when he planned a feasibility report to identify and evaluate the options his department had for retrofitting a manufacturing line. Wyndell identified the problems with leaving the manufacturing line unchanged (reduced competitive advantage, equipment breakdowns, retraining of workers, potential OSHA fines for safety risks) and the benefits of leaving the line as it is (no capital expenditure; no retraining of workers). Once he was convinced that he had a strong case for the net benefit of changing the current manufacturing line, he did a cost-benefit analysis of each of the retrofit plans and identified criteria for assessing each option (appeal to reason). Then he established the competitive advantages of each option, considering capital expenditures, worker safety, worker retraining, and equipment durability and maintenance. With this information, he rank-ordered the options in his feasibility report according to his net benefit analysis.

Figure 7.11 Net Benefit Line of Argument

TYPE OF ARGUMENT	DEFINITION OF ARGUMENT	SEQUENCE FOR A NET BENEFIT LINE OF ARGUMENT
Net benefit	The limitations (that is, costs) and benefits of the proposed plan are identified so that the approach with the fewest costs and greatest benefits (that is, net benefits) can be adopted.	1. Identify the net benefits of the current policy, practice, or system. A. Establish costs. B. Establish benefits, both tangible and intangible. 2. Identify the net benefits of the proposed policy, practice, or system. A. Establish costs. B. Establish benefits, both tangible and intangible. 3. Establish cost-benefit ratios that show the comparative net benefits of the proposed plan.

Like other conventions in communication, these lines of argument are used because they're effective. However, they don't have to be followed slavishly. They can and should be adapted to meet the needs of the particular audience, purpose, and occasion.

Components of Argument

Regardless of how you develop your line of argument, you need to consider the ways in which the audience, purpose, and occasion shape the nature of your argument.

Writer-centered components include **stance placement** and **stakeholding.** (Of course, part of effective communication is to recognize the readers' stake as well.) A communicator's *stance,* often equated with a thesis or position statement, may be located at the beginning or end of a message, depending on the receptivity or resistance of the audience.

If a communicator states a strong or controversial position too early, the audience may not respond positively to the message. For example, if a writer is composing a proposal and places the stance that "McPherson Realty should adopt an entirely new system of handling clients" up front, readers—especially resistant readers—may immediately question the writer's thinking or even his right to make such a statement. However, if the writer delays the placement of the stance until after the problems with McPherson's current way of handling clients have been explored, readers may entertain the writer's solution and more receptively acknowledge the writer's authority to speak on the subject.

Business communication has various conventions about where to place the thesis in a document or an oral presentation. Persuasive requests traditionally place the stance up front, whereas bad news messages traditionally defer placement; this convention holds true even though both message types characteristically face resistant readers.

In every interaction, communicators and audience each hold certain *stakes* in the issue at hand. That is, they have something to gain (and, by extension, something to lose) in every communication. When you're planning a document or an oral presentation, you need to decide what your stakes are, what your audience's stakes might be, and how to present the different points of view. For example, in job application letters, the writer's stake in the situation is obvious: the writer's prospective employment is at stake. The readers' stake is equally clear. They want to hire the best possible person for the position.

In other documents, the writer's stake is not as transparent. In Figure 7.12 (on the next page), we cannot identify the writer's stake by pointing to the type of document or to a particular comment within the text itself. Understanding the stakeholding in Figure 7.12 requires more background about the occasion, UPS's Prework Communications Meetings.

ETHICS

DO COMPANIES REALLY LIVE UP TO CORPORATE MISSION STATEMENTS?

Seven people died in 1982 after they took Tylenol that had been laced with cyanide. The parent company, Johnson and Johnson, immediately responded with a massive campaign designed to protect the public from further harm. It recalled the product and shifted advertising from sales to warnings and updates on its responses to the crisis. Instead of glossing over the situation and evading responsibility, Johnson and Johnson dealt openly with the media. It instituted an open-information policy that included answering as many questions as possible and sharing information as it became available.

These actions were based on a crisis management plan that was the direct result of the Johnson and Johnson Credo. Johnson and Johnson insiders, industry analysts, ethics scholars, and corporate image specialists all agree that this crisis management plan resulted in the support of the media, the FDA, and, most important, the customers. Within three months, Extra Strength Tylenol had regained 98 percent of the market share.

The role of the company Credo in the Tylenol crisis shows that it's wise to plan ahead. Johnson and Johnson's management didn't have to build a crisis management response from the ground up. The foundation, the Credo, was already in place. Instead of denying responsibility for the poisoning (investigations cleared the company of any wrongdoing), Johnson and Johnson acted out its Credo and placed the safety of the public first and its profits second and earned the respect—and the business—of the public.

Planning possible responses to media in advance contributed to Johnson & Johnson's timely and successful handling of the Tylenol crisis, which involved fatal product tampering.

CONTEXT

In 1993, UPS had a good year, with total revenues of $17.8 billion and a profit of $810 million. Management wanted to present this information to all company employees *before* they learned about it by reading their local newspapers or listening to the TV news. Having this news come from the company accomplishes two things: (1) the company will be seen by employees as the provider of job-related information, and (2) the employees will feel like insiders because they have information not yet available to the general public.

Local managers were given the PCM outline and Management Background sheets, so that the company could tell its own employees about its 1993 finances. Corporate headquarters wanted to put its own interpretation on the information rather than have employees learn about the profits without a context to help explain the figures. Figure 7.12 presents the outline local managers received.

Figure 7.12 Company Stake in Effective, Timely Communication in This Excerpt from an Outline for UPS Prework Communications Meeting

The date of use, before the publication of the information in national newspapers, is critical.

What stance does UPS reveal by focusing on 1993 expenditures rather than on revenues?

How does the company want employees to perceive the company's expenditures?

What stake does UPS reveal by the sequence of the key points?

Why do you think critical terms—even those that are quite simple such as revenue dollars for people or operating expenses or profit or reinvestment—are defined and explained?

What does UPS imply about the importance of making a profit?

Prework Communications Meeting

OUTLINE

SUBJECT: 1993 Financial Results

FOR: All Work Groups

DATE OF USE: March 31

VISUAL: Poster: How Our 1993 Dollar Was Used

Introduction

UPS's financial results are now calculated and will become public shortly. In a company as large as UPS, it is sometimes difficult to draw the connection between the hard work we do in our operation and the bottom line impact on our company. 1993 was a successful year for UPS. Total revenues were $17.8 billion. One way to look at the financial health of our company in a simple way is to look at how we spent our 1993 revenue dollar.

Key Points

- UPS spent 60 cents of every revenue dollar on people—wages and benefits, including holiday pay, Social Security taxes and vacations.
- 35 1/2 cents went to other operating expenses—paid for use and upkeep of vehicles, aircraft and buildings, and for supplies, services and taxes.
- This left 4 1/2 cents as profit—dividend and reinvested portions combined—$810 million. Profits are what's left over after a company pays its costs.
- 1.6 cents of profit used for dividends to shareowners.
- 2.9 cents of profit, or $525 million, reinvested for:
  - airplanes, vehicles, facilities
  - all a part of $1.1 billion in total reinvestment
- Most of profit reinvested—to support business and build future business.
- A healthy profit is necessary for any company to support fair compensation.
- Companies with little or no profit have difficulty competing.
- UPS has remained a profitable company despite strong competition, a tribute to all UPSers' contributions to providing excellent service and efficiency.

Every workday of the year, as we saw in Chapter 1, the manager of every UPS office in the country holds a 3-minute Prework Communications Meeting (PCM) to update employees with information affecting their job—weather conditions, safety information, changes in UPS policies and practices, local or companywide UPS news, and so on. About half of the PCMs are about local concerns; the other half are about companywide issues and information. To prepare for the companywide PCMs, every manager is provided with two documents:

1. A one-page outline with an introductory paragraph and a list of key points suggests the topics to be covered in the PCM (Figure 7.12).
2. The Management Background (usually one or two pages) discusses the details of the points in the outline so that managers can easily answer employees' questions or provide additional information about topics that employees are particularly interested in.

Understanding what's at stake in the message in Figure 7.12, the outline for a UPS Prework Communications Meeting, requires an understanding of the occasion that prompted this particular PCM.

As Figure 7.12 shows, UPS clearly had a stake in having employees see the corporate profit in a positive light, especially since a negative view might affect collective bargaining: UPS wanted to reinforce the image of a corporation concerned about the equitable treatment of its employees. The PCM provided simple definitions and explanations that would enable virtually anyone—even employees with no financial sophistication—to understand that about two-thirds of the profit was reinvested in resources such as facilities, vehicles, and airplanes that would make work more pleasant and efficient. The other one-third of profit went to stockholders, some of whom were also employees holding 401(k) plans.

Once you understand your stake or agenda (and your audience's) in a message, you can plan your line of argument more easily, even if your stance and stake remain implicit in the final communication.

Message-centered components are the structural elements of an argument. Stephen Toulmin's six components of argument can be used in creating this structure.

In Figure 7.12, UPS made an informal argument in the PCM outline, taking the position that the company's profits were being reinvested in ways that would benefit the employees. In more formal arguments, traditional or classical strategies establish a position and create an argument designed to appeal to the rational side of a reader's or listener's nature. Business communicators typically use formal arguments to justify a claim. Thus, planning a formal argument allows you to test your ideas critically. Toulmin, known for his analysis of the uses of argument, asserts that argument involves six interrelated components:

- claim
- grounds (evidence)
- warrant (logical bridge)
- backing
- qualifiers
- rebuttal[2]

We have already discussed claims of fact, value, and policy earlier in the chapter, so now we can move on to discussing the **grounds** for a claim, the evidence upon which a claim is based. Grounds for a claim are often claims of fact, supported by statistics, quotations, and so on. The graph in Figure 7.13 (on page 200), for example, contains data that could act as grounds for the claim that a particular corporation should consider adopting a proposed flexible benefit plan. (Graphs will be discussed at greater length in Chapter 13.)

This graph implies several different conclusions that could support different claims. One implication is that if the corporation does not adopt the flexible plan to be proposed, the company will fall even farther behind the times. In short, the company must adopt the plan to remain competitive. Another implication is that such a benefit plan has already proven successful at a growing number of companies, and the company addressed in the proposal should therefore be confident about adopting a flexible plan tailored to on-site needs.

The **warrant** serves as a logical bridge between the grounds and the claim. Principles or assumptions can serve as warrants connecting the grounds and the claim. For example, if you were to claim that company profits for the past year had been inadequate and, as grounds for that claim, you cited a 5 percent increase in sales, your warrant for making that claim might be the assumption that an 8 percent increase in sales is necessary before profits can be considered "adequate," based on industrywide performance.

Facts can also serve as warrants. Suppose again, for example, you claimed that company profits for the past year had been inadequate and as grounds for that claim you again cited a 5 percent increase in sales. Your warrant for making that claim might be a published internal memo establishing a 7 percent increase in sales as the target for that year. That 7 percent figure and the memo itself would be facts providing the connection between your

Figure 7.13 Graph Serving as Grounds for a Claim

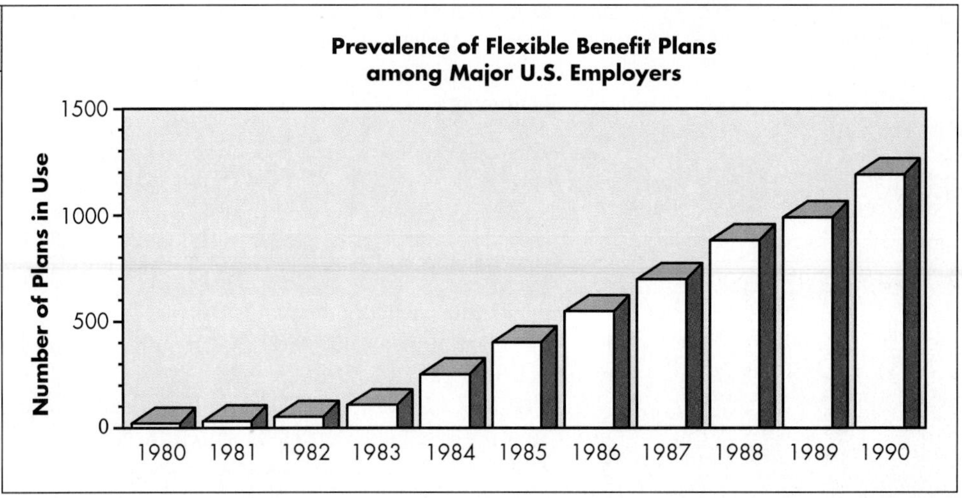

grounds and your claim. Such connections show your audience that your evidence is appropriate and adequate to justify your claim.

Backing is information offered when additional support for the warrant is required. Backing supports the writer or speaker's assertion that what is being argued is safe or valid. For example, if the claim that a 5 percent increase in sales was inadequate were based on the assumption that an 8 percent increase is necessary, then backing for that warrant might include statistics that showed industrywide rates of increase in companies of a certain size.

Qualifiers indicate the strength of the relationship between the evidence and the claim. Writers qualify their arguments to counter possible objections from resistant readers or listeners. In general, a strong claim or argument is appropriately qualified if it shows that you recognize exceptions to your argument. Qualifiers include words such as "probably" or "certainly." If you were to qualify your claim that a 5 percent increase in sales was inadequate, you might say that the increase was *probably* inadequate, given general expectations of the industry, or was *certainly* inadequate in comparison to the published target increase of 7 percent.

A **rebuttal** counters actual or potential opposing arguments, usually arguing that the grounds are not legitimate. For example, a rebuttal might involve the writer or speaker's presenting the argument that a 5 percent increase is acceptable, even given the 7 percent goal, because of a recession or a major change in the market.

A plan to include photos of children helps create a persuasive, reader-centered message for parents and grandparents who are considering a particular day-care facility.

As you plan complex business messages, you can use the components Toulmin identified to construct your argument. Specifically, you need to identify the *claim;* the *grounds* for that claim; the *warrant,* that is, the assumptions that connect the claim and the grounds; the *backing* and the *qualifiers;* and any *rebuttal* relevant to the claim. Figure 7.14 shows how you could develop a logical argument using one of the claims presented earlier in the chapter. If you leave out one or more of the components as you read through the argument, you'll see that it doesn't hold together.

Reader-centered components emphasize finding a *common ground* shared by writer or speaker and the audience. **Rogerian strategies** of argument stress this common ground by recognizing the importance of receptive attitudes and a willingness to listen coupled with a cooperative, nonconfrontational style

Figure 7.14 Toulmin Argument

COMPONENTS OF TOULMIN ARGUMENT	EXAMPLE OF TOULMIN ARGUMENT WITH APPEALS TO REASON
Claim	Businesses that offer on-site child care with sick-child facilities spend less in training and retraining employees than businesses that don't.
Grounds	The U.S. Department of Labor reports that employees in businesses that offer on-site child care with sick-child facilities have lower employee turnover than businesses that don't offer such facilities.
Warrant	Employees prefer to work in a stable environment that has a low turnover rate and good benefits—and employee turnover is costly.
Backing	Lack of day care is a main reason for turnover, especially for women. A study by the U.S. Department of Health and Human Services as well as a Carnegie Foundation report on early childhood development both endorse on-site child care with sick-child facilities.
Qualifiers	On-site child care with sick-child facilities will probably need to exclude children with communicable or chronic diseases.
Rebuttal	Opponents might argue that the U.S. Department of Labor report is flawed because it only gives data about selected businesses. The rebuttal can argue that those surveyed were randomly selected to represent businesses around the country, considering factors such as size and type of business, employee demographics, and geographic location.

as factors in persuasion. Carefully reasoned logical arguments may not be effective in situations where the readers' or listeners' values or beliefs seem threatened. Straight facts, no matter how well researched, may not be convincing in plans where the audience holds a definite stake in having the argument go a certain way.

The success of Rogerian argument depends on reducing the readers' or listeners' feelings of being threatened. These feelings make readers and listeners resistant to any new ideas. Communicators who use Rogerian argument attempt to reduce readers' or listeners' fears by establishing a shared understanding with their audience about what is important. In doing so, they try to facilitate change by striving for mutual understanding and cooperation with the audience.[3]

To work toward mutual understanding, you need to follow these steps, which can sometimes overlap:

- Define the problem.
- Assure resistant readers or listeners that you understand their point of view and establish the circumstances under which you agree that their point of view could be valid.
- Convince resistant readers or listeners that you share similar values and goals with them.
- Establish your own position and show resistant readers or listeners how your position could benefit them.
- Establish points on which you and your audience can agree.

Figure 7.15 on page 202 illustrates the structure for an argument for a new community sports complex.

In the excerpt in Figure 7.16 (page 202), the writers use the opening of a recommendation report to establish the sense that they share an understanding of the situation with their readers. While this recommendation report was written for the management of Keyes Manufacturing, the key ideas came from both employees and managers, so the goals can be seen as shared. Finding such common ground becomes a large part of your planning if you are using a reader-centered approach to present your line of argument.

Appeals, of course, are themselves writer-centered, message-centered, and audience-centered. Sometimes it works well to match the type of appeal you are using with an emphasis on the corresponding argumentative component. For instance, if you are using a writer-centered appeal, making certain that your stance is explicit might be one way of enhancing your credibility as a communicator. Or, if you are using an appeal centered on creating identification with the reader, emphasizing Rogerian strategies of argument would be a complementary way of taking into account your reader's feelings and beliefs.

Figure 7.15 Rogerian Argument

COMPONENTS OF ROGERIAN ARGUMENT	EXAMPLE OF ROGERIAN ARGUMENT
Define the problem.	The city council is divided about the issue of building a new community sports complex.
Assure resistant readers or listeners that you understand their point of view.	Citizens in favor of the new community sports complex assure opponents that they understand the two main concerns: (1) current underutilization of some school and community recreation center facilities, indicating that there's little need for a new sports complex, and (2) the thinly stretched city budget which cannot afford a $7-million-dollar sports facility.
Establish the circumstances under which you agree that their point of view could be valid.	Citizens in favor of the new community sports complex argue that if all the school and community recreation center facilities were well staffed and in good repair, the concern would be valid. They also point out that there will be little noticeable influence on the city budget because of federal support as well as a new bond issue.
Convince resistant readers or listeners that you share similar values and goals with them.	All members of the community want to provide opportunities for citizens of all ages to participate in a variety of year-round sports activities.
Establish your own position.	The proposed new community sports complex should be built.
Show resistant readers or listeners how your position could benefit them.	Everyone in the community will benefit from the opportunity to participate in year-round sports activities. Cooperative programs between the schools and the sports center will also be a benefit.
Establish points on which you and your audience can agree.	Everyone agrees on the community health benefits and the financial feasibility.

Figure 7.16 Report Opening That Establishes Common Ground Shared between Writers and Readers

The report opens with the idea that the recommendation discussed in the report is common to the writers, the employees, and management alike.

The contents of the appendix mentioned here suggest that employees have had input into the recommendation being discussed and, thus, are somehow invested in the solution.

> This report recommends opening an employee investment office at Keyes Manufacturing. The idea was initiated by employees of Keyes but has been endorsed and promoted by upper management.
>
> The first section of this report discusses the problem—the low rate of return that employees have been receiving in personal savings accounts and CDs. An analysis of current investment services in the community shows few opportunities for small investors.
>
> When the problem came to the attention of management, the idea of having employees take part in the corporate investment program was born. The main discussion in the report presents the results of focus groups and surveys exploring the advantages and disadvantages of opening an employee investment office that gives employees that opportunity to invest in various mutual funds and bond funds. The first appendix presents findings from surveys answered by employees in order to determine whether they want such an office. The second appendix presents representative responses from focus groups.

COLLABORATIVE PLANNING

You probably feel at this point that there is an overwhelming array of important approaches to consider as you plan your business messages. Workplace professionals often plan some (or even all) of their messages with colleagues. As much as 87 percent of the planning and preparation of workplace documents and presentations is in some way collaborative.[4]

In your own experience as a communicator, you may have found it helpful to talk through your ideas with a fellow student. Collaborative interaction assumes that our collective efforts will be more effective than our individual efforts. **Collaborative planning** is a team strategy that focuses on concerns beyond content. The elements most frequently considered by expert writers—purpose, audience, occasion, and a variety of conventions—are the focus of their planning whether individual or collaborative. The advantage of collaborative planning is that all communicators—expert or otherwise—are reminded to consider these important elements of planning.

The excerpt from a collaborative planning session in Figure 7.17 shows how a pair of business communication students, Andrew and Susan, asked each other questions. Their collaborative planning at this stage focused on defining the purpose of their document. Susan suggested that perhaps one possible plan would be to offer a solution to customers' unfavorable reactions to the inadequate and confusing product information they receive; Andrew reinforced her plan and built on it. Susan then built on Andrew's reaction, generating a purpose that he agreed to.[5]

The interaction between Andrew and Susan in Figure 7.17 is typical of successful collaborative planning sessions. Through such give-and-take, planners address the critical areas of purpose, audience, occasion, and various conventions. Because collaboration is the norm in many organizations, you will more than likely participate in such conversations.

Such question-and-answer conversations provide a strong start to a productive collaborative planning session, but they may not be enough. The following four specific verbal moves enable collaborators to clarify their thoughts more effectively than they could alone. These four verbal moves—usually used in combination—are some of the most productive you can use during planning conversations: prompt, contribute, direct, and challenge.

Prompt. Collaborators ask and respond to questions that urge clarification and synthesis of a plan. Prompts include acknowledgments, reinforcing comments, and questions that urge clarification and elaboration, encouraging the planner to say more. Simple prompts include comments such as "Tell me more" and "What else could you consider?" More provocative prompts include comments such as "What's your stand?" or "Okay, try to convince me how your recommendation solves the problem."

Contribute. Collaborators contribute and respond to new ideas as well as to modifications and elaborations of a plan. Contributions, from new ideas to modifications and elaborations of plans, can include facts, observations, suggestions, summaries, syntheses, or reflections. In general, supporters can expect their contributions to be better received if they build on the writer

Figure 7.17 Excerpt from a Collaborative Planning Session with a Collaborative Pair

Andrew questions the purpose.	Andrew	We need a purpose for this memo. What is our purpose? The purpose is to—
Susan poses one possible purpose.	Susan	—to point out that perhaps this is a—*perhaps* . . . this is a solution to the bad statistics that we've been receiving about customer reactions; perhaps this would help make those statistics look a little bit better.
Andrew develops Susan's ideas.	Andrew	So, perhaps improve the, uh, the effectiveness of the information we're sending out.
Susan relates Andrew's idea about purpose to their task.	Susan	Yes. Perhaps increase, the increase . . . OK. So what we're going to do is write a memo to suggest that *this* seems to be the problem—
	Andrew	Right.

SKILLS & STRATEGIES

HOW TO BE A CONSTRUCTIVE CONTRIBUTOR

Before you even begin . . .

- Let colleagues know you're glad to help.
- Arrange a time so you and your colleagues won't be interrupted.
- Confirm or clarify your role—as a consultant, not a regular project member.

At the beginning . . .

- Confirm what it is your colleagues want to know or learn.
- Make sure you and your colleagues are defining terms and concepts the same way.
- Learn about the context of the problem.

As ongoing practices . . .

- Be an active listener.
- Be alert for nonverbal cues.
- Build in checkpoints to confirm that your colleagues understand what you're explaining.
- Check that you're responding to your colleagues' needs.

As an effective communicator . . .

- Consider the sociopolitical context in which your colleagues are working and in which the information will be used.
- Adapt the information to your audience (or the audience your colleagues will be addressing).

or speaker's plan rather than charge in to redefine the content and purpose of the document or presentation. Rather than devalue the planner's work, an effective supporter can use it as the foundation for revision.

Direct. Collaborators both suggest and respond to directions for specific changes. Collaborators direct changes by adding, changing, or deleting. Sometimes suggesting additions, modifications, or deletions isn't enough. Some writers and speakers appreciate straightforward directions about how to make a recommended change. However, few professionals like to be ordered around, so directions are usually more effective if accompanied by explanations.

Challenge. Collaborators offer and respond to challenges about the plans for content and other rhetorical elements. Challenges that focus on the content, purpose, audience, organization, and design can be highly productive. Such conflict should focus on the substance of the planning (rather than on interpersonal issues or procedures). When collaborators challenge a single approach and pose alternatives, they have the opportunity to consider a range of possibilities, some of which may be more effective than the original approach. Collaborators can also act as the reader's eyes, challenging undeveloped parts of a draft. (See the Communication Spotlight, pages 212–215, for the role of constructive conflict in collaboration.)

VISUAL TOOLS FOR ORGANIZING BUSINESS MESSAGES

Whether you're planning your document or oral presentation individually or as part of a collaborative team, your task will be easier if you use appropriate tools to organize your information. The tools discussed in this section of the chapter have a visual component—they not only help you organize information, but they also help you *see* that organization during planning:

- locating gaps in information—Warnier-Orr diagrams
- identifying the sequence of information—flow charts
- organizing information so that it's manageable—Gantt and PERT charts

Warnier-Orr Diagrams

While traditional outlines can be useful, they have limitations because of their rigid hierarchical format. **Warnier-Orr diagrams** try to maintain the benefits of outlines while gaining flexibility by rearranging traditional outlines into columns. Unlike a traditional outline that indents points and subpoints to show hierarchical relationships, a Warnier-Orr diagram separates each level into its own column, aligning first-, second-, and third-level elements. When the planner examines a Warnier-Orr diagram horizontally—that is, scanning across the columns—the focus is primarily on both organization and completeness of the content. However, when the planner examines a Warnier-Orr diagram vertically—that is, scanning down each column—the focus is primarily on the logical flow of ideas.

Figure 7.18 shows an example of a Warnier-Orr diagram for a report. Presenting the plan in columns reveals two critical problems with the plan for this report: missing content and inconsistent organization. The information gleaned from analysis of this Warnier-Orr diagram lets the planner know that major changes are necessary in the plans for the report. Specifically, important content and key points are missing and the organization of the report is flawed and needs to be revised.

Flow Charts

Tables, graphs, flow charts, and other visuals, discussed in Chapter 13, can be used for planning. For example, Figure 7.19 on page 206 shows how a writer used a **flow chart** in planning a segment of a manual. Specifically, she was planning to revise a segment that dealt with a confusing process about filing claim forms with an insurance company. She created a flow chart, which not only identified all the parts of the process that readers needed to know but helped her determine whether any information about the process was missing.

Project Management Tools

You can certainly keep track of a project by hand, manually creating the schedules and charts. Today, however, planning for major projects is usually done with software designed for general business professionals that is relatively easy to use.[6] Most project planning software provides Gantt charts and Program Evaluation and Review Technique (PERT) charts.

A **Gantt chart** identifies each of the tasks in a project and provides a visual representation of the schedule for those tasks (start date, duration, end date), usually in the form of bars (Figure 7.20 on page 206). When you are responsible for planning a project, you can use a Gantt chart to identify each task and subtask—all the activities that need to be done in order for the project to be completed—as well as the personnel who will complete these activities. Gantt charts can include the scheduled start date for each task, actual start date,

Figure 7.18 Warnier-Orr Diagram Revealing Flaw in Organization and Missing Content

COLUMN 1 (I, II, ETC.)	COLUMN 2 (A, B, ETC.)	COLUMN 3 (1, 2, ETC.)
I. Introduction	A. Current fixed benefit plan is inadequate. B. A flexible plan would better meet employee needs.	• benefits static • company growing with increasing diversity
II. Problems exist with Cuoco & Associates' current plan.	A. Changing demographics aren't addressed. B. Fixed benefit plan wastes money and other resources. C. Fixed benefit plan contributes to low morale and, thus, low productivity. D. Cuoco & Associates is disadvantaged without a flexible benefit plan.	• more women, more minorities, more part-time workers • many unused benefits; waste of resources • no employee input into benefits, thus low motivation and high turnover • losing potential employees
III. A flexible benefit plan meets employee needs.	A. Flexible benefit plan allows employees to choose from selection of benefits. B. Flexible benefit plan helps meet several goals and objectives.	• employee choice of benefits with predetermined credits based on employee status • use of resources; lower turnover; cost containment; motivation; competition
IV. Costs must be considered.	A. An appropriate consultation firm will determine a successful or unsuccessful plan. B. Administrative costs are a major consideration. C. Communication between management and employees would be essential.	• responsible for designing and implementing flexible benefit plan • enrollment costs; reporting; hires; status changes; insurance carriers • group and individual meetings; counseling
V. Special features about a flexible plan need to be addressed.	A. A method for allocating credits must be determined. B. Medical and dental options need to be determined. C. A method to handle unused credits must be determined and then developed.	• credits based on status • medical plan • dental plan • life insurance • child care • unused credits • individual benefit changes
VI. Several benefits are associated with a flexible benefit plan.	A. A flexible benefit plan helps contain costs. B. A flexible benefit plan eliminates unused benefits. C. Employees choose the benefits they receive. D. Cuoco & Associates will have a strategic advantage in recruiting and retaining employees.	• cost containment • reduction in expenses • employee involvement • competitive edge in hiring

Problem 1: You can discover the problem of missing content by reading down column 1.

The major topics in column 1 identify only the current problem and describe a possible alternative. Even though the report is supposed to deal with the feasibility of implementing a flexible benefit plan, no major heading in column 1 focuses on whether the proposal can be implemented or whether it addresses the problem.

Problem 2: You can discover the organizational problems by reading across the columns for each major topic.

Organizational Problem 1: Section III, column 2, identifies two categories of employee needs that are met with a flexible benefit plan:
(1) employee choice
(2) other goals and objectives
Then column 3 elaborates employee choice and identifies several of the additional goals and objectives:
(a) use of resources
(b) lower turnover
(c) cost containment
(d) motivation
(e) competition
Readers might logically expect that the report would address all five of these factors as major topics. Instead, the diagram shows that, of these five factors, only cost is considered as a major topic. The other topics are discussed in section VI, column 3.

Organizational Problem 2: Section V, column 2, indicates that the report deals with allocation of credits, medical and dental options, and unused credits. However, column 3 shows that the report also discusses life insurance, child care, and individual benefit changes, which do not fit into the categories identified in column 2.

Figure 7.19 Visual Used in Document Planning

The writer used the flow chart to plan all the parts of the process she needed to include in a revised segment of the manual.

The flow chart enabled her to plan the information so that it was manageable once she started drafting the text.

Because the flow chart identified all the parts of the process, the writer was able to identify places where information was missing.

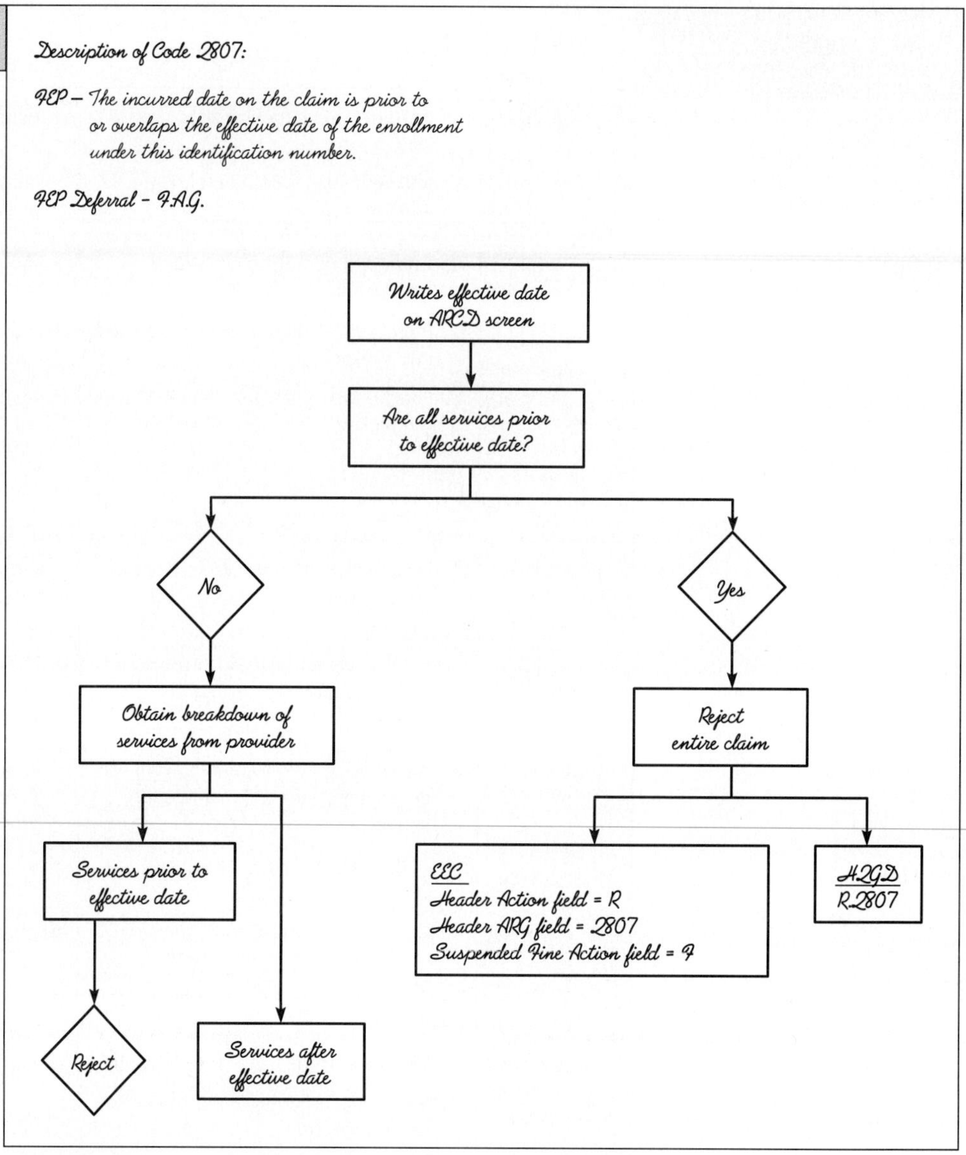

Figure 7.20 Gantt Chart

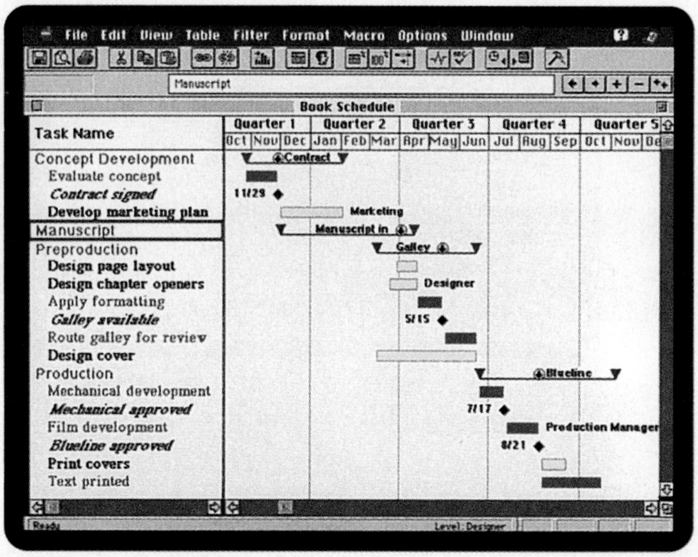

TECHNOLOGY

PROJECTS BY COMPUTER

A company's workload is divided into projects that superiors assign to subordinates, until even the smallest details have been delegated. But for a typical manager, who may at any given time be in charge of three or four (or maybe even 10 or 12) unrelated projects, keeping track of everything can be a logistical nightmare. This nightmare can be simplified by using any of the excellent project management software packages on the market.

Although there are minor variations among software packages, the principles of operation remain the same. The manager simply enters information about a project into the computer: the tasks that need to be accomplished, when they need to be completed (and the order in which they must be completed to allow other tasks to be accomplished), who will accomplish the tasks, the amount of time each task requires, and basic accounting information (costs, budget constraints, etc.). Entering the information forces the manager to think through the entire project. After the entire project has been entered, the software takes over, organizing the data, generating schedule sheets, and reminding the manager of the next task on the list.

Many packages can handle more sophisticated duties as well. For example, many allow scheduling of individual employees. Using the task data, the computer "red flags" overworked (or underused) employees, allows for employee vacations, accounts for part-timers, etc. The computer also points out time conflicts, cost overruns, and other problems. When combined with an office e-mail system, the software can also automatically remind employees of deadlines and keep bosses informed of the project's progress. In addition, many of the programs can produce timetables (such as Gantt charts) and flow charts (such as PERT charts) suitable for presentations and progress reports.

scheduled end date, and actual end date. Gantt charts show the percentage of each task that has been completed. Project planners thus have an immediate visual overview of whether a project is on schedule or slipping.

Program Evaluation and Review Technique (PERT) depicts the interrelationships of tasks in a project. In addition to identifying the activities necessary to complete each task, a PERT chart identifies the sequence necessary to complete the activities. PERT charts are basically flow charts that show the sequence of operations in a process. You can represent each individual operation, called an activity, with a straight line with an arrow at one end to show the direction of movement through the process. You can indicate the beginnings and ends of activities (called events or nodes) with circles or some other consistent geometric shape (Figure 7.21). A PERT chart is useful for identifying the complex links that are part of virtually all major projects. If a deadline is missed or resources are reduced, for example, the other parts of the project automatically affected are shown in the PERT chart.

Whatever tools or strategies you use, planning itself is critical to the success of all your documents and oral presentations, since it is the single biggest factor distinsguishing novice writers from expert writers.

Figure 7.21 PERT Chart

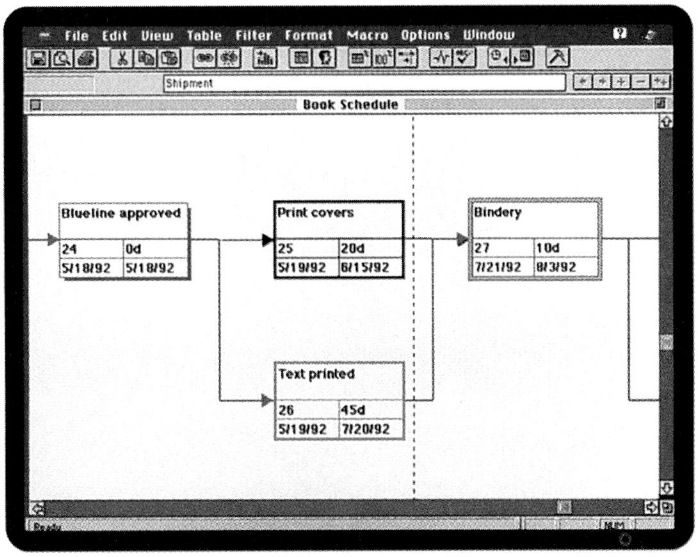

RESPONSE SHEET

PLANNING BUSINESS MESSAGES

COMMUNICATOR(S): AUDIENCE(S):
OCCASION FOR WRITING: DOCUMENT:
WHAT PROBLEM/ISSUE AM I TRYING TO ADDRESS IN THIS DOCUMENT?

◆ PURPOSE

What is the purpose of my document or oral presentation?

◆ NATURE OF THE TASK

What factors concerning the occasion and the message are important to defining the task?

- *Occasion.* What occasion does this document or oral presentation address? How does the occasion affect planning factors such as audience, purpose, content, key points, arguments, organization, details, visuals, and design?
- *Key Points/Supporting Information.* What key points need to be made? What supporting information is needed? Where will I get this information?
- *Arguments.* What arguments will best persuade the audience to act on the purpose and agree with the key points?

◆ TYPES OF PLANNING

What type of planning best matches my writing task?

- *schema-driven planning* that enables me to draw on familiar, standard formats and organizational conventions
- *knowledge-driven planning* that enables me to draw on an extensive knowledge of content that has already been organized and is accessible
- *constructive planning* that enables me to consider the complex relationships among a document or presentation's occasion, content, purpose, audience, organization, design

Explain your choice.

◆ LINE OF ARGUMENT

What type(s) of claim(s) will I be making in the document or oral presentation?

Briefly, what is the claim? What types of support are available?

What is the line of argument?

◆ ARGUMENTATIVE COMPONENTS

What is my stance? What plans should I make for the presentation of that stance?

What stakeholding is involved in my document or presentation?

How do/should Toulmin's six components of argument (claim, grounds, warrant, backing, qualifiers, rebuttal) figure into my plans?

How should I establish common ground with the reader (Rogerian argument)?

◆ PLANNING STRATEGIES AND TOOLS

Who is my collaborative planning partner?

What type(s) of planning tools will be useful as I plan my document or oral presentation?

What project planning software can I use to help me plan more efficiently?

ACTIVITIES, EXERCISES, AND ASSIGNMENTS

◆ IN-CLASS ACTIVITIES

1. To answer these questions, please refer to the transcript excerpts from the collaborative planning sessions presented in Figure 7.1. Read the following comment that Rick made during an individual interview with a researcher after he and Maggie completed their report and then comments made by Josh and Pete in separate interviews. How do you think their attitudes about planning and their approaches to planning affected their interactions? How might they have affected their success?

   Rick: . . . We both came to all three meetings really prepared to argue our points. We had written our thoughts and formulated our opinions and were ready when we walked in. I don't think we were abrupt or harsh; we were just both very opinionated about our work. I think due to our dedication to the class and the assignment, we were excited to hear the other's work so we were both very critical, in a good way.

   Josh: . . . I do not like to plan. I prefer to sit down and work out the problems as I go. I find that planning and producing can be combined into one process with results similar to a separate planning session. . . . I get impatient and sometimes just want to rush things through.

   Pete: I am not a good planner at all. I am not used to it, and I do not like it. When I write, and I know this is bad, I like to plan in my head as I go along. I always think of planning as wasting my time. . . .

2. Think of a proposal you'd like to make (for example, getting pizza delivery to more places or eliminating downtown parking meters to increase the appeal of local business). Using Toulmin's six components of argument, give a brief oral outline of an argument you would use as the basis for your proposal.

3. Refer to the section "Conflict: What to Encourage, What to Discourage" in the Communication Spotlight (pages 212–215). Discuss what kind of conflict you think might occur during a productive collaborative planning session. How could the planners discourage unproductive conflict?

◆ INDIVIDUAL AND GROUP EXERCISES

1. The following note (Figure 7.22) was sent by elementary school teachers to the parents of third-grade students in a modest-sized midwestern town located in an intensely agricultural area. The town itself is host to a major land-grant university. Your task is to read the short note carefully and then identify the elements that the teachers considered during planning in order to create or imply shared goals between themselves and the parents.
   a. Who are the stakeholders? How does the way they relate to the subject help define what's at stake?
   b. What is the teachers' stake?
   c. What is the parents' stake?
   d. Could those shared goals be addressed more effectively?

2. Review Figure 7.20, the Warnier-Orr diagram that outlined a feasibility report about a new flexible benefit plan for a company, Cuoco & Associates. Carefully reread the annotations to determine the problems.
   a. Transform the Warnier-Orr diagram into an outline. Make any changes that you think are necessary so that the sequence is logical and complete.
   b. Compare your outline with those completed by others in the class. Each individual or team should give a brief explanation and rationale for the changes made. What are the similarities and differences among the different versions?

Figure 7.22 Note Teachers Sent to Parents of Third-Grade Students

Dear Parent,

This year the Human Body component of the Science Curriculum focuses on cells, tissues, organs, and some systems. In addition to our study of the musculo-skeletal system, students will be studying the immune system. Additionally, an introductory lesson on human reproduction will be covered by Caren Bates, the school nurse.

Sincerely,

Mrs. Mully
Mrs. Tibben

◆ OUT-OF-CLASS ASSIGNMENTS

1. Select a major project that you will be working on this term. Complete the Response Sheet to help you review your planning options. Use at least three of the tools presented in this chapter to begin your planning. The following examples show you how these tools can be used together:

   Planning example 1: A project for a formal proposal for a new inventory control system might use a pair of *flow charts* to compare the existing inventory control process with the proposed one, use a *Warnier-Orr diagram* to outline the major components of the proposal, and use a *Gantt chart* to identify the tasks necessary to implement the proposal. The flow charts and the Gantt chart could be included in the final proposal.

   Planning example 2: A project for an oral presentation about a new internal training program might use a PERT chart to show the complex process of creating the video script and then producing the video.

2. Make an appointment with the director of corporate communications at a local company. Using the information you have learned in this chapter about planning, develop a series of questions to ask how this company plans individual documents and presentations as well as major projects. What planning tools does the company use? How does it develop its schedules? What computer software does it use?

3. Locate information about project planning or project management software to compile for a review that will include a comparative table as well as recommendations of software that would be appropriate for different occasions, users, projects, budgets, and so on. Make sure to include a range of available software. Begin by reading reviews of software published in computer magazines. Also check manufacturer and distributor information available at computer stores and centers. Identify an audience that would need this information. Write a review adapted in content, detail, format, and examples for this particular audience.

CASE

THE WYMARK ADMISSIONS DILEMMA

CASE BY ANDREA BREEMER FRANTZ

Background Information. You are a junior at a private residential liberal arts college located in a sparsely populated area of the state. The school, Wymark, has an enrollment cap of 2,500 students, and has been acknowledged annually in *Consumer Reports Guide to Colleges and Universities* as one of the "best buys in American higher education." In addition, the following information is common knowledge:

- Wymark offers 38 majors and 20 pre-professional programs in six schools: Business; Communications and Arts; Education; Engineering; Science; and Social Science, Philosophy and Religion.
- Wymark boasts a faculty-student ratio of 1 to 12. Eighty percent of the faculty possess terminal degrees in their fields (Ph.D., or the equivalent in a given discipline—e.g., M.F.A. in the fine arts or Ed.D. in education).
- The college is accredited by the Commission on Institutions of Higher Education and the North Central Association of Colleges and Schools. All academic programs are approved by the state's Department of Education.
- Wymark's accounting program has the highest number of students in the state (fifth highest in the nation) who pass the CPA exam the first time they take it. The creative writing department has seen many of its graduates publish extensively, especially in fiction and screenwriting. This is in part credited to faculty member Jan Bilmer, who, after being blackballed by Hollywood because of a series of profoundly disturbing—though brilliant—film noir scripts, retired to assume a successful teaching career in his home state.
- Currently, Wymark's most popular second major (behind creative writing and accounting) is political science. This is not so much because of the curriculum or the faculty, but because of the students who are currently majoring in it (the best and the brightest on campus, an extremely vocal, almost glamorous group). The Political Science Club has organized "alternative" spring breaks in affiliation with Habitat for Humanity and the Jesuit Domestic Volunteer Corps. This band of approximately 40 students was recently featured in *Newsweek* as part of a story on the "anti-80's attitude whiplash."
- Wymark also assumes the attitude, "If you want a good private education, you will pay for it." Tuition at Wymark is $18,200 and is expected to reach $20,000 by next year. Financial assistance, however, generally does not meet students' financial need as determined by the FAFSA form.
- Wymark's athletic teams have been notoriously unsuccessful for over a decade. Its football, baseball, basketball, and tennis teams all finished at the bottom of their conferences last year. Women's volleyball finished third last season, but the team lost two key starting players to graduation and expects a lower finish this year. Despite a strong intramural program, Wymark's athletics are a bit of an embarrassment.
- Wymark is generally regarded as a "liberal oasis" in the area. Students are often activists for the more liberal-leaning candidates and take a strong interest in politics. The small community in which Wymark is located, Farrington, is wealthy and largely conservative.
- Students, who generally mistrust administrators at Wymark, are angry about the high price tag they pay and consequently question administrative moves on such issues as funding for faculty positions, co-curricular financial support, and recruitment. In the latter case, many students argue that Wymark has focused too much on finding wealthy, slightly above-average students who can foot the bill, over students from less economically advantaged families who might enhance the academic environment and cultural diversity on campus.

Wymark has been experiencing a drop-off in the number of new student applications it receives annually. Through some marketing research, the College Relations Director has discovered that the first three "standard mailers"—which include a general information tri-fold pamphlet; an eight-page pictorial viewbook that highlights the six schools; and a college catalog with an application—somehow are falling short of meeting what the prospective students want to know about college life. Said one young woman in an interview with Wymark's telemarketing firm, "Yes, the publications are attractive, but they just give me the numbers and the names of the majors or courses. I don't have any idea what student life is like or how the students see their experiences."

In response to what appears to be a gap between administrative needs in terms of "selling" the college and prospective students' expectations, the offices of College Relations and Admissions have formed a 12-student task force to identify the following:

- What do prospective students specifically want and need to know about colleges before they apply? What are students' main criteria for choosing a college to apply to? Whom does the college primarily want to target for mail campaigns?
- What sorts of Wymark student experiences are relevant to prospective students? How might those experiences and insights be best communicated to prospective students?
- What might be the most effective approaches to designing a publication that best meets these informational needs and wants?

The directors of Admissions and College Relations chose members of the task force who would represent a variety of majors and interests. All classes are represented, and there are seven women and five men. You were chosen in part because of your abilities and insight into the "Wymark experience."

Task. Clearly, this task force has its work cut out for it. It will be asked to complete a number of objectives as a group, culminating (probably) in creating the document Admissions and College Relations will use to bolster applications and better reach student clientele.

First, however, your task group has decided to begin by creating research tools to gain more insight about aspects of student life which adequately reflect the nature of Wymark's campus and the residential experience. With fellow task force members, decide (1) the type of information you need and (2) how best to discover or obtain this information. For example, you might decide to design a one-page questionnaire that will help your task force narrow down the aspects of student life to highlight on the promotional materials it eventually develops. This questionnaire would need to encourage prompt and thorough response from readers, and the answers it yields should help steer the task force toward people to interview or scenes to photograph. A variety of research tools are possible. Your task force should both choose the tools and then design them.

Complication. The Director of Admissions has just learned that the budget both for producing research tools and for producing final promotional materials has been cut in half. The Director has therefore asked the task force to submit a memo that names in rank order the research tools that the task force intends to use, estimates the cost of each instrument, and justifies the choice of each instrument. Even if your task force had anticipated using only one instrument, you need to justify its use and also show that using only one tool will be sufficient to your task.

CONFLICT: WHAT TO ENCOURAGE, WHAT TO DISCOURAGE

To become a more effective collaborator and team member, you'll need to manage various kinds of conflict that arise as you work with others. Some kinds of conflict damage the interaction of a group or team. Another kind of conflict can be productive, actually improving the quality of the decisions, the quality of the document or presentation, and the attitudes the group members have about their work together. You can learn to reduce or eliminate unproductive conflict and to encourage, and sometimes even provoke, productive conflict.

Initial agreements with other team members about what you're all trying to accomplish can reduce unproductive conflict. Figure 1 suggests early decisions that can make your group's work together more productive.

If you can agree on the goals and the procedures you will follow as a group, your collaboration will be much more productive.

Figure 1 Suggestions for Determining the Focus

Determining Your Team Focus

- Agree on the task you're trying to accomplish, including the specific products (often called deliverables in the workplace).
- Agree on the purpose(s) or objective(s).
- Determine the audience for your deliverable(s).
- Agree to spend as much time considering purpose, audience, organization, development and design as you spend considering content.

Affective Conflicts

Affective conflicts are interpersonal disagreements that often impede collaborative interaction, slowing down or derailing teams. Your attitudes and biases, your personality, and your values all influence the way you approach your participation on a team. Affective conflicts can result from differences in actions or perceptions related to factors about which people usually hold strong opinions: ethical standards, race or ethnicity, religion, social actions, economic choices, interpersonal behaviors, and so on.

Figure 2 suggests ways to avoid affective conflict. Some of the suggestions are simply common sense; others require that you actively observe yourself and others, monitoring actions and words that might be offensive or embarrassing.

Procedural Conflicts

Procedural conflicts arise from misunderstandings about the way a team functions—when to meet, how long to meet, where to meet, how to resolve disagreements, who's going to be the leader, how roles are to be determined, and so on. Consider these problems that could be avoided. Before you schedule an 8:00 A.M. meeting, you need to know that one team member on flextime always arrives after 8:30 because of his child care responsibilities. Before

Figure 2 Suggestions to Avoid Affective Conflict

Suggestions to Avoid Affective Conflict

- Acknowledge your own biases and prejudices and make an effort not to be negatively influenced by them.
- Consider whether responding to a particular bias or comment will improve the function of the team. If not, let it slide.
- Monitor your own behavior to eliminate actions or words that could offend or insult anyone or that could be construed as prejudicial.
- Procedural conflict that gets out of control can lead to affective conflict, so monitor and control procedural problems so they don't become destructive.
- Be aware that particularly sensitive areas (and ones protected by federal and sometimes state statutes) include gender, race, ethnicity, national origin, religion, age, sexual preference, physical appearance, and disabilities, which may not be visible. Unintentional offhand comments and jokes are frequent culprits in starting affective conflict.
- If you observe unprofessional behavior directed at someone else on your team, speak privately to the person displaying the unprofessional behavior and point out how the behavior obstructs team efforts. The person may not know that the actions or words offend, embarrass, or hurt another team member.
- If a team member offends you or is prejudicial in some way, speak to that person privately. The person may not know that the actions or words offend, embarrass, or hurt you.

you presume that silence means consensus, you need to know that one team member's response to criticism is to retreat into silence. Before you think that another team member is nodding off because of boredom, you need to know that she has chronic fatigue syndrome. Before you schedule the distribution of an information survey, you need to know if someone arranged with the support staff to print, copy, and distribute the questionnaire. If you find that the ground rules aren't working, be flexible enough to change them appropriately.

Discussing procedures can strengthen a group's cohesiveness—their feeling of "groupness" and their commitment to the task. Most team members resent what they perceive as unilateral decisions, even if your intent is for the good of the project, so make sure to keep team members informed about what you're planning. Sometimes just asking questions about procedures makes people aware of potential problems that can be easily resolved by preliminary discussions. Figure 3 offers suggestions that experienced collaborators use to help avoid or at least reduce procedural conflict.

Figure 3 Suggestions to Avoid Procedural Conflict

Suggestions to Avoid Procedural Conflict

Procedures dealing with a group or team's operation

- Determine details of meetings: time, place, duration.
- Create an agenda with input from everyone on the team.
- Determine scheduling and deadlines.
- Agree on the amount/kind of preparation each person will have done for each meeting.

Procedures dealing with a group or team's interaction

- Determine the responsibilities and roles that each individual will assume.
- Agree to encourage substantive conflict and to minimize affective and procedural conflict.
- Decide on decision-making process, including ways to negotiate alternatives for resolving disagreements.
- Decide on how the group process and product will be evaluated and monitored.

Substantive Conflicts

The agreements—the consensuses—that let a team move forward are critical to successful collaboration. However, this consensus should not come too quickly. Deferring consensus can give collaborators time to identify and consider opposing points of view. They may also need time to generate and critically examine issues and ideas.

To defer consensus, you can engage in **substantive conflict.** Substantive conflict, which focuses on the issues and ideas of your collaborative work, includes two specific types of interaction:

- *Considering alternatives.* When one person suggests, "Let's do this approach," another team member might respond, "Yes, your approach is a possibility, but let's consider other approaches, too."
- *Voicing explicit disagreements.* When one person suggests, "Let's try this idea," the other might respond, "No," "I don't think that will work," or "I disagree," and then usually offers alternatives or reasons for the disagreement.

Conflicts involving substance focus on the content of the project, people's perceptions about the task, the purpose of the project, the audience, and a variety of textual and visual conventions. For example, substantive conflict on a project about revising an in-house document about solar hot water heaters could include decisions about whether to present technical details in text or diagrams, whether to include pricing, and whether to create a brochure or a flier. Team members who neglect these concerns risk decreasing their team's effectiveness. Members who discuss the substance of the project increase the probability that all the collaborators on a team will have the same general interpretation of their task.

Figure 4 lists several suggestions to help you engage in substantive conflict without alienating or annoying other team members or getting sidetracked from the goal.

Agreements emerging from discussions with substantive conflict can increase team commitment and product quality. Collaborators who agree to engage in substantive conflict know that criticisms aren't personal attacks, but rather they're ways to bring potential problems into the open and explore alternatives.

Figure 4 Suggestions to Help Collaborators Engage in Substantive Conflict

Suggestions for Engaging in Substantive Conflict

- Don't mistake an objection to your ideas as an attack on your character, personality, or intellect.
- Ask questions that focus on potential problems between various elements: for example, "How can we use the design to help show our purpose?" "How can we explain these examples so the readers will be able to understand them?"
- Ask your collaborators for elaborations, clarifications, and explanations of statements . . . and be prepared to offer elaborations, clarifications, and explanations of your own statements.
- Ask for reasons to support arguments . . . and work on developing and supporting well-formed arguments of your own.
- Try never to settle on one solution or decision without first having considered some alternatives.
- Assume the role of devil's advocate.
- When you disagree with something, say so...and support your disagreement with a reason and, if possible, an alternative that will work.
- If other collaborators don't generate substantive conflict by raising alternatives and voicing disagreements about your ideas, bring up alternatives and possible objections yourself.

ACTIVITIES AND QUESTIONS FOR DISCUSSION

1. Tape-record a collaborative session of a group or team that you're part of. Listen to 10 minutes of the tape to complete these two tables about the different kinds of conflict that you hear. If you hear no instances of a particular kind of conflict, write 0 in that cell. You'll discover that you sometimes disagree with team members about the kind of conflict you're hearing when you replay the conversation.

   a. Count the number of instances of each kind of conflict that you hear on the tape of your group or team.

KIND OF CONFLICT	SUBSTANTIVE CONFLICT	PROCEDURAL CONFLICT	AFFECTIVE CONFLICT
Total number of instances			

   b. Identify your own role in substantive conflict, procedural conflict, and affective conflict that you hear on the tape of your group or team.

KIND OF CONFLICT	SUBSTANTIVE CONFLICT	PROCEDURAL CONFLICT	AFFECTIVE CONFLICT
Number of instances you initiated			
Number of instances in which you were involved			
Number of instances you resolved			

   c. What can you say about your own contributions to productive and unproductive conflict?

   d. What could you do to strengthen your own contributions to productive, substantive conflict? What could you do to diminish unproductive conflict?

2. If there is an absence of substantive conflict on the tape of your group or team, does that mean that the collaborators have simply come up with the best approach or product the first time? What else might the absence of such conflict mean?

3. If there is an absence of affective conflict on the tape of your group or team, does that mean the collaborators have successfully avoided or overcome any personal biases or prejudices? What else might the absence of such conflict mean? What are the ramifications for the process and product that result from your collaborative effort?

4. If there is an absence of procedural conflict on the tape of your group or team, does that mean the collaborators have worked out and agreed on the way to approach all procedural issues? Can you see ways that such procedural conflict might still be going on? What should you do about it? What else might the absence of such conflict mean? What are the ramifications for the process and product that result from your collaborative effort?

DETECTING, DIAGNOSING, AND REVISING: BAILING OUT OF REVISION

Imagine that you've spent two weeks working on a feasibility report for a new approach to software development. The draft is done, and you've given a copy to your supervisor for comments and suggestions. One of the really hard parts of writing—revisions—is about to begin . . . and sometimes you get stuck. Knowing the places you can get stuck during revision, the reasons why you get stuck, and ways to get out of your dilemma can help you become a better writer.

People who seek and use feedback about their documents do a better job of revising than people who don't. Getting the feedback isn't much of a problem: you simply ask colleagues and supervisors to read and respond to your document. However, you're likely to get more useful feedback if you tell them what kind of help you need—for example, whether you want them to verify accuracy, check logic, strengthen coherence, and so on.

The revision we're talking about is more than cleaning up spelling and punctuation errors, which is called **local revision.** We're talking about **global revision**, which means checking and revising for the following kinds of things:

- clear purpose
- appropriate adaptation for the audience
- logical organization
- effective examples
- appealing, usable design

Cleaning up mechanical and grammatical errors can improve the superficial features of a document, but you need to do global revision first.

Barbara Sitko, an expert in writing strategies, explains that in order to revise a document you first have to *see that a problem exists* and then *know how to eliminate that problem.*[1] She provides a decision tree that shows the steps you go through during revision and the places where you can seek additional help—or bail out. At each decision point, you have choices, as shown in Figure 1.

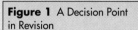

Figure 1 A Decision Point in Revision

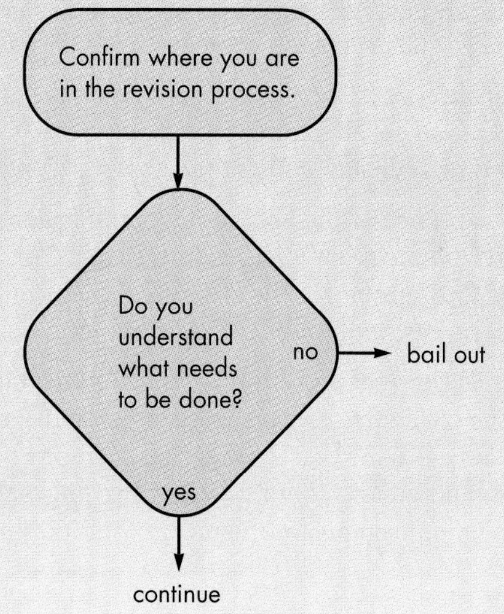

Figure 2 shows six decision points that Sitko identifies as leading up to revision.[2] Knowing the options you have and ways to respond when you're stuck may keep you from bailing out.

You'll be able to see how this process works by looking at Ellen Muncie as she revised a feasibility report for implementing the Safety Training Observation Program (STOP) in the molecular screening lab at her company. When initially outlining her feasibility report, Ellen used the sequence shown in Figure 3a on page 218. Ellen completed this preliminary out-

Exploring Feedback: Writers Meet Readers

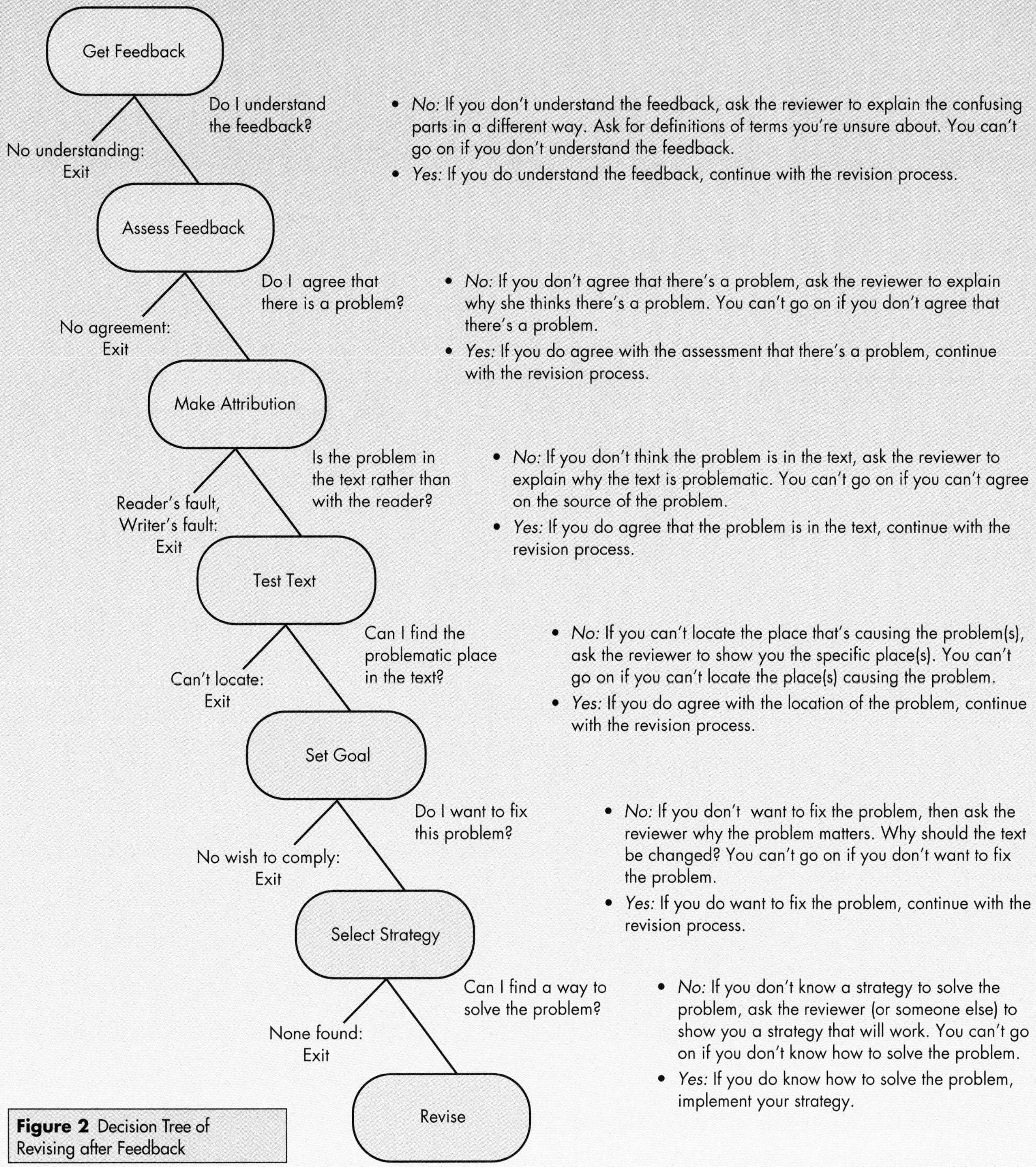
Get Feedback
Do I understand the feedback?
No understanding: Exit
• No: If you don't understand the feedback, ask the reviewer to explain the confusing parts in a different way. Ask for definitions of terms you're unsure about. You can't go on if you don't understand the feedback.
• Yes: If you do understand the feedback, continue with the revision process.
Assess Feedback
Do I agree that there is a problem?
No agreement: Exit
• No: If you don't agree that there's a problem, ask the reviewer to explain why she thinks there's a problem. You can't go on if you don't agree that there's a problem.
• Yes: If you do agree with the assessment that there's a problem, continue with the revision process.
Make Attribution
Is the problem in the text rather than with the reader?
Reader's fault, Writer's fault: Exit
• No: If you don't think the problem is in the text, ask the reviewer to explain why the text is problematic. You can't go on if you can't agree on the source of the problem.
• Yes: If you do agree that the problem is in the text, continue with the revision process.
Test Text
Can I find the problematic place in the text?
Can't locate: Exit
• No: If you can't locate the place that's causing the problem(s), ask the reviewer to show you the specific place(s). You can't go on if you can't locate the place(s) causing the problem.
• Yes: If you do agree with the location of the problem, continue with the revision process.
Set Goal
Do I want to fix this problem?
No wish to comply: Exit
• No: If you don't want to fix the problem, then ask the reviewer why the problem matters. Why should the text be changed? You can't go on if you don't want to fix the problem.
• Yes: If you do want to fix the problem, continue with the revision process.
Select Strategy
Can I find a way to solve the problem?
None found: Exit
• No: If you don't know a strategy to solve the problem, ask the reviewer (or someone else) to show you a strategy that will work. You can't go on if you don't know how to solve the problem.
• Yes: If you do know how to solve the problem, implement your strategy.
Revise

Figure 2 Decision Tree of Revising after Feedback

line and sent it by e-mail to her supervisor, Charles Anderson, asking for comments. Her supervisor's comments are shown as the annotations to Figure 3 on page 218. Before Ellen began the revision of the outline, she made sure that she understood and agreed with the feedback, located the specific problems, and had ideas about ways to fix them. On the basis of her interpretation of the feedback, Ellen revised the outline (Figure 3b).

Upon receiving the initial feedback, Ellen realized that she couldn't move forward without identifying and discussing criteria for selecting a safety training program. She passed the criteria on to Charles for his comments (Figure 4a, page 218). Ellen had been concentrating so hard on the effectiveness and appropriateness of the program that ease of learning and cost had simply slipped her mind. While she was embarrassed that she had

Figure 3 Draft and Revised Version of a Report's Outline

Charles read the draft outline and then commented . . .

- *How will you establish STOP as an effective safety program if you don't identify criteria for making recommendations?*
- *You weaken your credibility by not identifying the sources of your information.*
- *You need to provide readers with information for decision making—which you can't do if you don't evaluate STOP.*

3a. Early Draft of Report Outline

E-Mail

1.0 Introduction
2.0 Background of STOP
3.0 Objectives of STOP
4.0 STOP Training
5.0 Effectiveness of STOP
6.0 Benefits of STOP
7.0 Feasibility of Implementing STOP
8.0 Conclusions

3b. Revised Version of Report Outline

1.0 Introduction
2.0 Criteria for Implementing a Safety Program
3.0 Method of Obtaining Information
4.0 Background of STOP
5.0 Objectives of STOP
6.0 Evaluation of STOP
7.0 Conclusions
8.0 Recommendations

Figure 4 Draft and Revised Criteria for Selecting a Safety Training Program

Charles read the initial list of criteria Ellen proposed and then asked . . .

- *How will you convince a committee that this program is feasible if cost isn't considered?*

4a. Early List of Criteria

E-Mail

Criteria
A. Flexibility
B. Adaptability
C. Effectiveness

4b. Revised List of Criteria

Criteria
A. Flexibility
B. Adaptability
C. Ease of learning
D. Cost efficiency
E. Effectiveness

forgotten two obvious criteria, she was thankful that the omission was corrected before many people saw a draft of the report. The revision was easy (Figure 4b).

Ellen drafted the criteria section of the report, which Charles read and returned with comments (Figure 5). However, unlike the earlier suggestions, which had seemed obvious and sensible, this time they weren't clear, so Ellen sent Charles an e-mail message asking for clarification: "What exactly do you mean by preview?" "How detailed should the reasons be?" "By balance do you mean that each criterion should be about the same length?" "By transitions do you mean numbers? Should I use numerals or words?"

Without answers, Ellen would have struggled. With the answers, she could go ahead with the revision (Figure 6). Once Ellen and Charles agreed on the criteria, the rest of the document was relatively easy for Ellen to construct.

When you're revising a document, you may sometimes feel like bailing out—a decision that is sometimes appropriate. An example of an appropriate decision to bail out was made by Lena Hill, a capital budgeting analyst. The state legislature had mandated that the Bureau of the Budget where Lena worked establish a formula for maintenance and utility costs for the various kinds of state building. The mandate was far too vague, and there was no agreement about criteria, no information available about how the formula should be constructed, no computer capability for estimating maintenance and utility costs, and no collected data to use as evidence. Lena figured out what needed to be done, but when she asked herself to identify the source of the problem, it wasn't in the text. She bailed out because the task was too large and too abstract because the legislature hadn't established clear boundaries or criteria.

Remember, when you get stuck, you can bail out. But before you do, pause and ask for help. Consider whether you can get the information you need to proceed. Rather than give up in frustration, make an informed decision.

Figure 5 Draft of the Criteria Section

Charles read this draft and then commented . . .

- *Add a preview.*
- *Provide reasons for the criteria.*
- *Balance the amount of detail you provide for each criterion.*
- *Provide transitions so readers can keep track of how many criteria you have.*

E-Mail

Criteria for Implementing a Safety Program

A safety program must be flexible. Safety hazards encountered in the laboratory are constantly changing.

A program needs to be adaptable. The structure of the Molecular Screening Lab is very complex. Three biology laboratories combined with storage and work rooms comprise the entire Molecular Screening Lab. Also, a wide variety of equipment and chemicals make the lab extremely susceptible to accidents.

A program should provide training that is easy for employees to learn and use.

A safety program must be cost efficient. The monetary benefits must outweigh the cost of implementing a program.

A safety program must be effective. Not only must the program train employees, but it needs to change their behavior. Safety is a long-term issue.

Figure 6 Revision of the Criteria Section

CRITERIA FOR IMPLEMENTING A SAFETY PROGRAM

Any safety program selected for the Molecular Screening Lab needs to meet five criteria:

1. A safety program must be *flexible.* Safety hazards encountered in the laboratory are constantly changing. Therefore, a safety program that can be updated to meet the needs of new situations is crucial for a safe working environment.
2. A program needs to be *adaptable.* The Molecular Screening Lab is very complex: three laboratories plus workrooms and storage facilities. The wide variety of equipment and chemicals make the lab extremely susceptible to accidents. Any safety program must be adaptable to the different areas of the lab.
3. A program should provide *training* that is easy for employees to learn and use. Because the Molecular Screening Lab is a complex working environment, everyone involved in the lab must be able to comprehend and use safety procedures.
4. A safety program must be cost *efficient.* The monetary benefits must outweigh the cost of implementing a program. Since the Molecular Biology Lab is on a restricted budget, the program must prove beneficial to justify spending limited funds.
5. A safety program must be *effective.* Not only must the program train employees, but it needs to change their long-term attitudes and behaviors to create a safe working environment. Any program must reduce the number of accidents in the laboratory by 50%.

ACTIVITIES AND QUESTIONS FOR DISCUSSION

1. Recall a situation in which you started to revise a document and then stopped. Using the information from Figure 2, explain what you now see as the probable reasons that you stopped revising that particular document. Did you bail out prematurely? How could you have pursued revision?
2. The points in Figure 2 are not intended to convey the idea that revision is always a good idea. Describe a situation in which you know how to fix a problem in your document but decide not to.
3. Look at a recent document you have completed that could be improved. Write a revision plan based on the feedback you received on the paper. Use Sitko's process as a guideline to indicate how you'll go about revising the document.

PART III
WRITING BUSINESS CORRESPONDENCE

CHAPTER

8

Letters, Memos, and Other Documents That Assume Audience Cooperation: Routine, Positive, and Goodwill Messages

OUTLINE

Aspects of Audience Cooperation: Street Resurfacing in American City

Audience Cooperation

Routine or Neutral Messages

Positive Messages

Goodwill Messages

Document Webs and Series

CRITERIA FOR EXPLORING CHAPTER 8

What we cover in this chapter	What you will be able to do after reading this chapter
Reader cooperation	Recognize strategies and occasions for writing that assume reader cooperation
Routine or neutral business messages	Write effective routine messages, inquiries, and direct requests
Positive messages	Write positive replies, credit approvals, order acknowledgments
Goodwill messages	Write greetings, invitations, condolences, thank-yous, and other such messages for a business setting
Document series	Describe the interconnectedness and reciprocity of daily business correspondence

Effective communicators recognize that they can assume audience cooperation when composing certain types of messages. That is, their audience will not automatically resist the main idea and content in such messages. This is not to say that readers will always take the action suggested by the communicator. For example, the welcome letter in Figure 8.1 encourages readers to fill out an enclosed questionnaire and return it to the office before the scheduled appointment. Readers may see the importance of making the best use of the appointment time and may therefore complete the questionnaire at home, but may, because of time constraints, not mail the questionnaire in advance as requested. They may, instead, have to bring it in with them to the appointment.

CONTEXT

Dr. Kim J. Wass's orthodontic office mails the welcoming letter shown in Figure 8.1 to parents after they make an appointment for their child's initial visit. Adults seeking orthodontic treatment receive a similar letter. In this case, Dr. Wass was one of two orthodontists recommended to the parents by their regular dentist.

Accompanying Dr. Wass's welcome letter are a health questionnaire, an informational sheet for those patients with orthodontic insurance coverage, a postpaid envelope for return of the questionnaire (and the insurance sheet if appropriate), a promotional brochure produced by Dr. Wass's office, and another brochure published by the Association of Orthodontists, St. Louis, Missouri.

Figure 8.1 Letter of Welcome

Dear Mr. and Mrs. Edwards:

Welcome to our office! Thank you for selecting us to serve your orthodontic needs. We are dedicated to helping you receive the finest orthodontic treatment possible.

We have enclosed our health questionnaire for you to complete. This information will introduce you to us before Amanda's first visit and will allow us to spend the maximum amount of your appointment time addressing your orthodontic concerns. It is important that you return it to us by Amanda's appointment, which is on Wednesday, October 27, 19-- at 10:45 A.M. A stamped envelope is enclosed for your convenience.

We have also enclosed two brochures for you to read. One helps you better understand our dental specialty of orthodontics and the other provides you with information about our office.

If you have questions that I may answer prior to Amanda's first appointment, please feel free to contact me at 555-2152 (or outside-of-town 1-800-555-2244). We are looking forward to meeting you.

Sincerely,

1. To what extent do you think this letter of welcome is a goodwill message, designed primarily to create a positive writer-reader relationship? To what extent is it a routine message, designed to take care of necessary business?
2. Is the writer correct in assuming reader cooperation in this letter of welcome? That is, is the reader likely to do what the letter requests?
3. What strategies does the writer use to make the reader feel welcome? In your opinion, are the enclosures one of these strategies, or do the enclosures serve a different function? Explain.

The fact that Dr. Wass's office routinely sends out the letter of welcome (Figure 8.1) and the enclosures to all patients after they schedule an initial appointment suggests that Dr. Wass's staff is familiar with

- aspects of reader cooperation
- routine, positive, and goodwill messages

ASPECTS OF AUDIENCE COOPERATION: STREET RESURFACING IN AMERICAN CITY

Like other municipalities across the nation, American City faced the annual task of resurfacing designated streets during the spring of 1994. During the first week in May, the city sent a routine message (Figure 8.2) to its residents notifying them of the city's resurfacing plans.

Because street resurfacing is an annual (some might say continual) event and because residents generally appreciate such resurfacing once it's completed, Art Smith, the city Construction Supervisor and writer of the message, could reasonably expect reader cooperation with this routine message. (In addition, there aren't too many motorists who would argue with a pavement milling machine or a steamroller.) He appropriately chose a deductive organizational plan, with crucial information included in the body of the message and photocopies provided for critical city personnel. However, despite anticipated reader cooperation, Smith's letter still contained persuasive elements. For example, the fact that "American City is requiring that College Avenue, West Street, and State Avenue be finished before the students return for fall classes" showed that Smith was aware of the increased traffic returning students brought and had strategically planned for it. This strategy enhanced Smith's credibility. In addition, the promise of on-street parking, the assurance of advance notice of total street closures, the admission that the work will mean some "inconvenience," and the sending of photocopies (c.c.) to emergency and support services all worked to reassure residents that their safety and feelings were important.

Smith's letter, although vital to the smooth running of this municipality, was, like the bulk of routine messages in government and business, not intrinsically interesting. Motorists using the affected streets would, of course, see Smith's letter as an important "fair warning." And Smith's letter that May did spark a lot of interest from four residents on Park Avenue. Seven years previously, the city had also resurfaced Park Avenue. The resurfacing had created a slight rise around a drainage opening that had steadily increased as seams in the asphalt had ridged up. Residents who owned houses close to the opening had experienced huge puddles in their driveway entrances during subsequent winters, because rainwater and snow melt could no longer drain 15 feet north to the raised grate, but had to travel 400 feet around the corner to the south. When snow blocked this flow, miniature lakes formed on the avenue. Needless to say, these residents contacted Smith to ensure that this problem would be addressed.

Figure 8.2 Street Resurfacing Letter of Notice

The writer puts the routine announcement up front.

The writer's list provides detailed information regarding the announced resurfacing project.

The writer continues by stating procedures and then policies regarding the resurfacing project.

The writer stipulates further conditions in the next two paragraphs, giving residents notice of what to expect.

The writer invites further contact in the interest of maintaining goodwill.

Dear Resident:

American City has selected the following streets for resurfacing this construction season:

1. College Avenue, West Street to 400 feet west of Westwood Drive
2. West Street, Sheridan Avenue to Hillcrest Avenue
3. State Avenue, Arbor Street to Lincoln Way
4. Jefferson Avenue, Lincoln Way to Washington Street
5. Jefferson Avenue, 5th Street to 6th Street
6. Ridgewood Avenue, 6th Street to 9th Street
7. Park Avenue, Ridgewood Avenue to Brookridge Avenue
8. 28th Street, Dale Avenue to Hoover Avenue.

The work will be done in two phases, the first being concrete repair work and the second being asphalt repair work. The first phase will be done over the next five-week period; phase two will follow. American City is requiring that College Avenue, West Street and State Avenue be finished before the students return for fall classes.

Concrete repairs have been identified for the Contractor with marking paint. If your driveway is to be blocked by these repairs, you will receive advance notice. The duration of this blockage is generally three to five days. On-street parking should be available each evening for those residents with blocked driveways.

The asphalt repair work will begin by removing the existing surface with a milling machine. Limited access will be available during this stage. Total street closure will be necessary on the day the street surface is restored with hot asphalt. Advance notice of this closure will be delivered to all households. It is expected that the inconvenience of this work will last about five working days.

If you have concerns and/or need further information, please feel free to contact me at 555-5722.

Thank you,

Art Smith
Construction Supervisor

cc: Gerry Berg, Municipal Engineer; Police Department; Fire Department; 911; Municipal Transit Authority; Post Office

At the end of September, Smith sent the message shown in Figure 8.3 to those Park Avenue residents.

When several Park Avenue residents called to confirm that the "adjustments" included eliminating the rise around the drainage grate, Smith informed them that although the street was originally designed to drain to the south, the engineers on site would try to lower the grate so that overflow drainage to the north would be possible, as was the case before the previous resurfacing. Although Smith's news was not entirely good, he maintained goodwill by having "done his homework" and by taking the residents' concerns seriously.

Figure 8.3 Follow-Up Notice of Specific Street Work

Again, Smith uses a direct plan to inform residents of impending work. This message fulfills the promise made in Figure 8.2 that residents would be given prior notice of specific work.

Re: Park Avenue Resurfacing Between Brookridge Avenue and Ridgewood Avenue

On Wednesday, September 28th, the City contractor will begin removing the existing asphalt surface with a milling machine. This operation along with manhole casting adjustments will continue through the week. Local traffic will be allowed but will be subject to occasional delays.

Asphalt surface restoration will take place after all clean-up and fixture adjustment has been completed. You will be notified prior to the actual day of closure.

If you have any questions, please call me at 555-5722.

cc: Gerry Berg, Municipal Engineer; Chris Church, Street Supervisor; Doug Masterson, Utility Maintenance Supervisor; Fire Department; Police Department; 911; Municipal Transit Authority

AUDIENCE COOPERATION

As suggested in the discussion of the cooperative principle in Chapter 2, cooperation between communicators and audience routinely governs business communication.

Messages that assume reader cooperation anticipate a nonresident stance from the audience. This anticipated cooperation lets the writer assume a business-as-usual stance toward problems, as in Art Smith's correspondence (Figure 8.3). Smith cannot reengineer the street. He does, however, ask city crews to eliminate the rise around the grate, which seems to have contributed to the residents' drainage problem. When assuming audience cooperation, a business-as-usual attitude persists, even if, for some reason, the audience cannot cooperate exactly as expected. For example, the writer may directly request the reader's attendance at a business function. The reader might wish to attend but be unable to do so due to a schedule conflict. Even though the writer's request does not result in the reader's attendance, the reader is not really resisting the request so much as finding it impossible to comply. If schedules did not conflict, the reader would probably cooperate and attend the function.

Strategies to Encourage Audience Cooperation

You can use explicit cues to encourage audience cooperation:

1. a clear and direct statement of the main idea at the outset (deductive organization)
2. indication of confidence in the reader's positive response
3. all information necessary to explain the action(s) indicated, included with the message

MULTICULTURAL

CULTURAL DIFFERENCES IN BUSINESS LETTERS

Studying both the form and content of business letters of request of English, French, and Japanese writers, Susan Jenkins and John Hinds found that the letters had similar components but were different in how the content was handled in each component, as demonstrated by these openings:

- American English letters opened with the point of view of the reader: "We have a client who is interested in purchasing good-quality, tall-back dining room chairs with tie-on seat cushions. We have seen some of your excellent products and believe that you may have something in your line to fill this need."
- French letters tended to take the point of view of the writer: "We acknowledge receipt of your check for $43.71 that you sent in payment of your subscription to our magazine. 'Aujourd'hui.' We thank you for it."
- Japanese opened with detail that reflected a cultural sense of what was appropriate to include in such letters: "In Japan, fall has deepened, and the trees have begun turning colors. We believe that you, as exchange students, are busy studying every day."

These findings indicate that writers in international business must understand that although American, French, and Japanese letters share many of the same conventional components, these elements are expressed differently from culture to culture.

Tour guides must take care to make their presentations direct, clear, and specific. Humor must be low-key and appropriate.

4. clear, specific action statements at the close to specify the action(s) the writer wants the reader to take
5. information included with the message, in the form of enclosures, etc., that enables the reader to act or to understand the course of action in detail
6. humor

Clear and direct statements of the main idea aid audience cooperation by avoiding any misunderstanding about what the reader is to know or do. Figure 8.4 suggests how unclear opening statements can lead to confusion on the reader's part and shows how the writer can, through revision, establish the relevance of the information and, in so doing, avoid frustrating the reader's desire to cooperate. The revision strategies used to improve the opening statements in Figure 8.4 might also be used to make statements within the body of a letter more specific and complete, as shown in Figure 8.5.

Indicating that you have *confidence in the reader's positive response* also encourages cooperation. Simply using "please" and "thank you" within a letter makes a statement sound less like a demand and more like a request. Communicating in a positive manner creates the impression that courtesy will be sufficient to ensure the wanted action—that threats are not necessary.

Figure 8.4 Clarifying the Main Idea in a Message That Anticipates Reader Cooperation

ORIGINAL STATEMENT	POSSIBLE CONFUSION	REVISION
Would you please provide us with information about your company?	Companies have a lot of information about themselves and their products. Because this question specifies neither the nature of nor the use for the information, the respondent doesn't have much of a clue as to what information to send.	Would you please provide us with information regarding what measures your company has employed in response to EEO guidelines during the past six months? [*Subsequent paragraphs would establish the writers' authority to ask for the material, the nature and scope of the measures the reader should report, and how the writer plans to use the information.*]
Last summer my family took its annual vacation tour of the Northeast, and we were again impressed with the rich history of the area. The buildings in Deerfield's historic district were especially impressive for their architecture and authenticity.	Members of the Deerfield Chamber of Commerce receiving this letter have no idea what the letter is about from reading this opening paragraph. Only after wading through several paragraphs do they learn that the writer wants information on how the paint schemes for the various historical buildings were chosen.	A member of Chalk Beach's Restoration Society, I am interested in how the lovely color schemes for the buildings in your historic district were determined and authenticated. [*The letter goes on to describe the specific concerns the Chalk Beach society has regarding historic preservation and restoration efforts and closes by expressing appreciation for Deerfield's historic district.*]

Figure 8.5 Revision for Clarity and Completeness to Aid Reader Cooperation

ORIGINAL STATEMENT	POSSIBLE CONFUSION	REVISION
Please make the changes noted below in my special order of building supplies and deliver the materials to the above address as soon as possible.	Since companies characteristically file orders by order number and since this customer might have more than one special order, the reader does not immediately know which order is involved. The reader also does not know what "as soon as possible" might mean. Does it mean that the writer needs the supplies by a specific date or that the reader should respond at his or her convenience?	Please make the changes in the size and quantity of green board noted below to order #24356A placed on February 1. [*A subsequent list would then detail the changes. The close would then specify delivery instructions.*] Please deliver the materials to the above address by Wednesday, February 15.

Figure 8.6 Request Letter That Facilitates Reader Cooperation

The writer provides the exact series number and specific preferences in the first paragraph.

She specifies the type of information needed regarding the materials.

The writer's "use" in paragraph 2 provides the information needed to determine eligibility for the discount implicitly requested here.

The writer indents the address for easy access and details four additional ways to make contact.

Dear Mr. Folger:

Please send me information on your latest toy models, series 4526. I am especially interested in your futuristic solar-powered vehicles.

Because I will be using these models as educational support materials for my sixth-grade science students, I am interested both in the nature of the vehicles you have available and in the cost of individual kits as well as of the series as a whole.

I am also interested in any educator's discounts that may apply.

To be able to view the materials so that I can make a decision regarding their adoption by our deadline, I will need to receive them by March 1.

Please send the information to my school address:

Kathy Harvey
Wanamaker Elementary School
R.R. 4
Louisville, Kentucky 40205

Please contact me if you anticipate a delay in granting my request: 502-555-6666 (Office) or 502-555-9834 (Home). My office phone has voice mail. My e-mail address is S2.KRH@wesel.edu.

Sincerely,

Providing *crucial information* (see Figure 8.6) is another way to facilitate audience cooperation. Such information might include invoice numbers, cost figures, specific dates and addresses, specifications, and so forth.

Specific action statements at the close of the message are another way you can help readers cooperate. For example, this specific and to-the-point closing with a request for information provides clear action the reader should take:

> Please write me or call me at (410) 555-5950 before August 3 to set up an interview regarding your participation in City Center days.

The letter in Figure 8.7 does a good job of motivating the reader to take action and attend a career conference. Although the original draft effectively sandwiches factual information necessary to attending the conference between details that persuade the reader to participate, the revisions to that letter (shown in the figure and annotated in bold) provide a clearer statement of the action the reader is to take.

Figure 8.7 Draft with Revisions to Encourage Action

The writer establishes the letter's context, states conference goals, and includes an additional selling point of the conference.

She conveys information necessary to attendance.

*She **decides to save mention of the brochure until the action paragraph, since the brochure aids action.** She incorporates another selling point.*

The writer adds a clear action and a deadline for that action.

*She again invites the reader to look at the brochure, and **reminds the reader of the action to be taken** as a way of facilitating further contact.*

Dear Ms. Molstad:

Thank you for your interest in the career conference "Taking the Road Less Traveled." Our career conference gives young women the opportunity to interact with professional women in the science, engineering, and technical fields. There are also student guides assisting with the career conference that also serve as valuable resources for the young women visiting the campus.

The conferences are held four times a year: two in the fall and two in the spring. The conference is open twice for girls in sixth-ninth grade and twice for girls in ninth-twelfth grade.

~~I am enclosing a brochure that includes a registration form for the conferences for next fall when your daughter will be able to attend.~~ You may attend the conference with your daughter and can go to a few of the speaker sessions. There are also special "resource" sessions for parents and educators that you may attend while your daughter is on a tour.

Lunch will be served and the cost is included in your $15 registration fee per registrant. Both you and your daughter will have to register for this conference and pay the fee.

The enclosed brochure outlines the day's events and gives more detailed information on the conference. ***Add:*** *It also includes a registration form which should be filled out and mailed before February 15 if you are to attend the conference.*

If you have any more questions please feel free to contact me at (515) 555-9964. Again thank you for your interest, and I ~~hope to see you and your daughter next year~~ *look forward to receiving your registration form in the mail.*

Sincerely,

Lorri Paul
Program Assistant

Providing *appropriate enclosures* is yet another way to facilitate cooperation. Figure 8.8 on page 226 is a flier sent as seasonal greetings to past customers of a copy house. The flier, accompanied by a sales letter encouraging further business, has slots that hold two enclosures: a business card and a Rolodex entry. The coupons at the bottom of the flier, the business card, and the Rolodex card all encourage reader cooperation by offering a financial incentive and making it easy for the reader to contact the company.

Humor, if used appropriately, can also encourage audience cooperation. But humor in workplace correspondence is "like quicksand: If you're in it, you'd better be effective or you're dead."[1] Humor can be used to perk up information that anticipates reader cooperation, as in this instruction manual for a complex book-publishing program. In an *example of a numbered list*, the writer spoofs the language of income tax forms:

> **3.** If line 32 less the difference of lines 73 and 74 on Schedule C is greater than line 36 plus line 17 of Schedule A and you are under 65 years of age, go to step 1, where you will be in a loop until you are 65.
>
> *****
>
> **5.** Enter the root-mean-square of line 14.

But when in doubt, leave it out. For example, one American businessman used humor—apparently to good effect—at the beginning of a speech to a group of Japanese businessmen. Upon returning home, however, a Japanese-speaking employee looked at the videotape of the presentation and provided this interpretation of the translator's comments:

> Ladies and gentlemen, the speaker is thanking you for inviting him to address you. He is honored. At this moment he is telling a joke. Many Westerners do this to begin presentations. The joke is about a horse and a boy and a pile of dung. It does not translate well. I will tell you when he has finished the story. Then, if you will be so kind as to laugh and applaud, I'm sure he will soon get to the matter at hand.

Strategies to encourage reader participation can be used both in documents that assume audience cooperation and in those that anticipate audience resistance. In Chapters 9 and 10, we focus on strategies used in business messages to encourage audience participation in messages that anticipate resistant audiences.

Figure 8.8 Flier with Business Card and Rolodex Entry Included

Business card, Rolodex card, and coupons encourage further contact

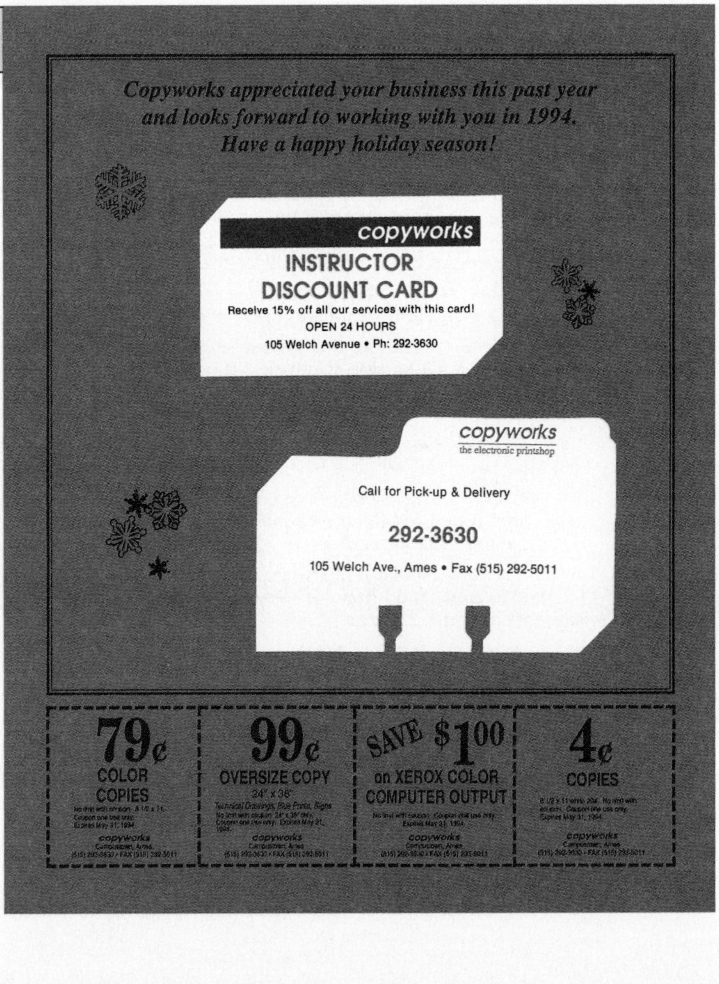

SKILLS & STRATEGIES

MAINTAINING CROSS-CULTURAL GOODWILL

Communicating goodwill differs from culture to culture. The following dos and don'ts should help you avoid insulting a foreign colleague when you are actually trying to make a good impression. Because individuals may or may not share in the stereotypical qualities identified with their particular culture, the advice offered in the following table is far from foolproof.

Dos (Based on Stereotypical Qualities)	Don'ts (Based on Stereotypical Qualities)
Provide plenty of background information when working with Germans. They have a saying "You have to start with Charlemagne," which means they require detail and a historical perspective before making decisions.	Don't suggest casually to a German individual, "Let's get together for lunch sometime," unless you mean it. Taking the comment literally, the German is apt to take out a calendar to schedule a time.
Remember to use formal titles with the French until you've known them for a long period of time. The quick familiarity of Americans can be offensive to them.	Don't ask a French person, "Where do you live?" or "What do you do?" It's similar to asking an American, "How much money do you make?"
Realize that in Latin countries, it isn't what you do that counts, but to whom you're related. While Americans tend to rank each other by occupation, Latin Americans want to know who your father is. In Germany, on the other hand, credentials are what matter. It's where you went to school that counts.	Don't make the mistake of not knowing whether a person you're working with in Czechoslovakia or Poland is aligned with the old communist system or the new generation of free enterprise. Values, goals, and expectations between the two groups are apt to be very different.
Remember that the Japanese are interested in long-term relationships that generally are based on trust, friendship, service, and quality, rather than price.	Don't stand more than a foot away from a business associate in Saudi Arabia. Too much distance is a sign of rejection.
Feel free to make physical contact—a pat on the back, a long handshake, or a kiss on the cheek—with your associates in Europe and Latin America. These gestures are almost always acceptable in a business setting. However, in India and Pakistan, no type of touching is acceptable. People simply bow.	Don't cross your legs or expose the heel of your foot during a business meeting in the Middle East. This gives the signal to your hosts that they're worthy of being stepped on.
Offer a gift when invited to a Japanese home. Gifts must not be lavish, but in good taste and nicely wrapped. Don't use white wrapping paper, however. It's a sign of death.	Don't hold up your hand, palm outward, in Africa. Such a gesture is considered rude and inappropriate.

Messages That Assume Audience Cooperation

A good proportion of daily business communication consists of messages that assume reader cooperation. Such messages traditionally fall into three basic categories:

- routine or neutral messages
- positive messages
- goodwill messages

These messages, although run-of-the-mill, often contain a surprising variety of purposes and appeals, and a mix of both informational and persuasive elements. We focus on these types of messages in this chapter.

ROUTINE OR NEUTRAL MESSAGES

Routine or neutral messages assume audience cooperation and conduct necessary business for an individual or a corporation. These messages are arranged deductively and include announcements, reminders, and simple transmittals. Inquiries and even direct requests can also assume audience cooperation. Orders are one type of direct request that anticipates such cooperation.

Announcements, Reminders, and Simple Transmittals

Announcements, reminders, and simple transmittals help ensure the smooth running of a business. Part of the "grease" that lubricates normal operating procedure is employee or customer pride, so many of these routine messages have implicit public relations or persuasive elements.

Figure 8.9, for example, shows a routine office *announcement* or bulletin at 3M. The bulletin, meant for posting, has two purposes: it provides information and promotes company image.

Figure 8.9 3M Bulletin for Posting

3M News Bulletin

3M AGAIN NAMED ONE OF BEST COMPANIES FOR WORKING MOTHERS 09/13/94

3M has been named one of the 100 Best Companies for Working Mothers for the seventh consecutive year. The annual recognition is given by Working Mother magazine. The 1994 "best companies" list appears in the magazine's October issue.

Companies on the list are selected and ranked on the basis of competitive pay, opportunities for women to advance, support for child care and family-friendly benefits.

Employee Communications
3M Corporate Marketing and Public Affairs

3M Center, Building 225-IS-15
St. Paul, MN 55144-1000
612 555 9745

Printed on recycled paper

Figure 8.10 Reminder (with Informational Brochure)

Main idea stated up front, followed by relevant/explanatory details.

Alternative action (the primary action is keeping the appointment), plus goodwill close.

Dear Holly

We would like to remind you that you are scheduled for the following appointment(s):

Date	Time	Physician	Phone
09/29/94	0100P	Samuel Blount	201-555-4394

If for any reason these appointment(s) are not convenient, please call the department at the number listed above and a new appointment will be scheduled.

Thank you for your consideration.

Figure 8.10 demonstrates how a routine *reminder* can include a public relations component. The letter is from a local clinic reminding the reader of her appointment with a dermatologist and follows a typical pattern for a routine message. Accompanying this reminder was an eight-page brochure from the department of dermatology with a welcome, a review of various policies and procedures, a listing of the professional staff, and a map showing how to find the clinic. In addition to providing relevant information, this brochure creates a positive image for this particular medical department and for the clinic as a whole.

Simple **transmittals** also aid routine business operation. A transmittal is basically a cover sheet that conveys a document from writer to reader and provides any necessary contextual details. For example, Figure 8.11 provides the context for an attached two-page management briefing.

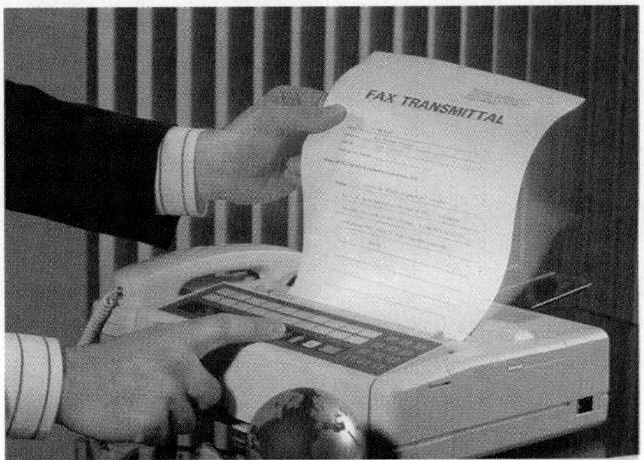

Transmittals ensure that the fax recipient knows how many pages are coming, so that the chances of incomplete information are minimized.

At times, even simple transmittals have persuasive elements. For example, Figure 8.12 shows a transmittal from a law office that has, appropriately enough, legal implications. By signing the receipt and release as requested, the reader, a privately employed medical caseworker, implicitly agrees that she will not file any more claims against the estate. The fact that the release is separate from the check, and not part of the check itself, strongly implies (and reinforces) that recipient's willingness to cooperate. (If the attorneys had anticipated reader resistance, they would have made the release part of the check, so Ms. Johnson could not cash the check without signing the release.)

Figure 8.13 further demonstrates how routine transmittals can be persuasive. The transmittal itself conveys a booklet about how to handle annoying phone calls. The fact that the writer has opted to handle this negative situation in a business-as-usual fashion

Figure 8.11 Memo of Transmittal

To: Region and District Human Resources Managers
From: Jack Kelley
Subj: Management Briefing: Intrastate Deregulation Update

Enclosed is a Management Briefing update regarding legislation before Congress that would preempt states from regulating express carriers' rates and services.

Please duplicate and distribute the Management Briefing to all management people.

If you have any questions regarding this Management Briefing, please contact John Smith in Corporate Public Affairs at ATLAS 555-4220.

pc: Region and District Managers
Corporate Department Managers
Region and District Labor Relations Managers
Region Internal Communications Managers
District Internal Communications Supervisors

Figure 8.12 Letter of Transmittal from a Law Office

Dear Ms. Johnson:

Enclosed is a check in the amount of $2,073.20 payable to you by the Estate of Gretchen A. Pfennig, Deceased, in full and final payment of your claim against the estate. Please sign and date the enclosed Receipt and Release and return it to me in the self-addressed envelope provided for your convenience.

Do not hesitate to contact me if you have any questions, comments, or concerns. Thank you.

Figure 8.13 Letter of Transmittal from a Telephone Company

The reader has clear action he can take to address the problem. The fact that this action might be "valuable" aids cooperation.

The reader is given a clear condition for alternative action. The enclosure of the authorization encourages cooperation.

Dear Mr. Klein:

Enclosed is a pamphlet covering how to handle annoying telephone calls. At the back of this booklet you will find space for your use in keeping a date and time record of annoyance calls as they are received. The information record might give you valuable clues to the identity of the caller and help both the telephone company and the police (if necessary).

Upon completing this log for one week, if you are still receiving calls and wish additional assistance from U.S. WEST Communications, please call our Call Identification Center at 1-800-555-3386 (local Denver customers call 555-7765). Included is a Customer Authorization Letter that the center may have you complete. I am sending it to you now to prevent unnecessary delays in resolving your problem.

Sincerely,

encourages the reader to handle it in like manner. If the calls persist, however, the situation becomes more than a routine matter. The writer is prepared to handle that escalation as well, and the reader can be equally prepared by completing the enclosed authorization. Overall, the prompt and graduated response represented by this transmittal and its separate enclosures works not only to address the readers' concerns, but also to promote company image.

CONTEXT

The writer in Figure 8.14 (page 230) is an agriculture student and family farmer who is writing to a regional farm equipment outlet regarding new field equipment. Such equipment is necessary for new types of conservation tillage being used in the Midwest corn belt.

Inquiries and Direct Requests

Both inquiries and direct requests ask the reader to provide information.

Inquiries seek that information by asking questions. You have various options for presenting these questions. For example, you can state the questions explicitly in list form or pose them implicitly within a paragraph. Inquiries assume that the reader has the information the writer needs and is willing to provide it. An inquiry has three basic parts:

- an opening that contains any necessary information about the context for asking the questions

Figure 8.14 Letter of Inquiry with Explicit Questions

The writer presents a context having public (a publication) and private (his problems) sources.

He compliments the company on the specific product that is the subject of the inquiry, and then lists explicit questions regarding the product.

He covers cost in a separate paragraph, enabling the reader to extol the product separately from its cost in a subsequent response.

He requests additional information, and facilitates action with a return address at the top of the letter.

Dear Mr. Carver:

I recently came across an advertisement for Lentz tillage equipment in *The Farm Journal*. After a frustrating fall of continual corn stalk plugs, uneven soil distribution, and abundant down-time, I am searching for a solution to primary tillage.

The Lentz Residue-Master chisel plow intrigues me as a well-designed and built piece of equipment. There is a good possibility that it would work well in my operation.

I do have a few questions about the machine:

1. How much room is available for trash clearance?
2. What is the working depth?
3. What is the horsepower requirement for a 12 foot model?
4. Are walking tandem axles available?

I would also like an estimate concerning my final cost of a 12-foot model including walking tandem axles (if available).

If you have a brochure on the Residue-Master alone, please enclose it.

I definitely need to make a change before spring field work and would, therefore, appreciate a response by the end of February. I feel that Lentz Equipment has the product to help me. Thanks for your time and cooperation.

Sincerely,

Mike Gerdts

CONTEXT

The writer in Figure 8.15, a university student, is the director of The Maintenance Shop, a popular gathering place where local, regional, and national entertainers perform. Part of the writer's job is to secure that entertainment. In the letter, he is writing a talent agency concerning a number of its bands.

- a body that presents questions, with explanations when appropriate
- an action close

Figure 8.14 shows these traditional features.

In Figure 8.15, the writer chooses to construct questions as prose within paragraphs. Questions are both implicitly and explicitly stated.

Writers sometimes have to provide explanations to help the reader answer their questions. For example, if you ask "Does your resort facility provide child care?" you should follow the question with a brief explanation of how old your children are and of any special needs that they might have: "I have a son, age 8, and a daughter, age 7 months. Due to frequent ear infections, my son cannot participate in any pool activities." This information helps the reader discuss the child care appropriately. The resort, for instance, may not have infant care, but may offer structured activities for children over 5.

Figure 8.15 Letter of Inquiry with Both Implicit and Explicit Queries

The writer opens with his primary question.

He puts his questions about band information and cost in prose format.

He encourages his reader to accept by citing previous performers who have appeared and who are also clients of the agency being addressed.

He considers the performers' needs if they choose to perform, compliments the agency, and facilitates action by providing a date and phone number.

Dear Mr. Maahs:

Would you please let me know if any of your progressive bands will be touring in the Midwest in the Fall of 19--? I have recently become the director of the Maintenance Shop, a pub in Ames, Iowa. I would like to schedule as much progressive talent as possible.

A description of each band's musical material would be appreciated. Would you also include the costs for each band, along with any other special details?

The Maintenance Shop seats roughly 200, and has a 20 foot by 40 foot stage. Some bands that have appeared here in the past include: The Young Fresh Fellows, Scruffy the Cat, and The Hoodoo Gurus.

Nightly accommodations are available at several motels in the Ames area. Two very popular motels are the Holiday Inn and the Best Western Starlite Village. I have enclosed information from the Ames Chamber of Commerce which includes a complete list of accommodations, restaurants, and so forth.

Alternative Music Productions has a fine reputation, and I am looking forward to seeing some of your bands this fall in the Maintenance Shop. Please contact me before March 3, 19--, or call me at 515-555-4246.

Sincerely,

John C. Grimm
Maintenance Shop Director

Encl.

Direct requests, like inquiries, can ask for routine information and action. Writers of direct requests tend to provide some justification for the request, even though they assume reader cooperation. Occasions for direct requests include:

- requests that are internal to an organization and that reflect the writer's certainty that the reader can provide what is being requested
- requests for products and services (orders for goods or services are direct requests)
- requests for credit or for letters of recommendation
- requests for the reader's participation (invitations, when structured as a direct request, emphasize reader benefit)
- routine claims and other requests for adjustment (see Chapter 9, pages 265–269)

Direct requests, like other messages that anticipate reader cooperation, conventionally follow a deductive arrangement:

- main idea or subject of request up front
- any necessary details, explanation, or justification
- a courteous close plus request for specific action

Figure 8.16 uses a conventional direct request arrangement. In this case, the direct request reads very much like an inquiry with implicit questions. In other direct requests, the need to justify the writer's request for the information or merchandise is more pronounced.

Direct requests differ from persuasive requests in that direct requests assume reader cooperation while persuasive requests anticipate reader resistance (see Chapter 10). For example, a request that local landlords attend a luncheon to hear a guest speaker discussing the implications of a new zoning ordinance would probably be structured as a direct request, since landlords are now subject to the ordinance and its implications, regardless of whether they attend or not. Organizers of the luncheon could anticipate reader cooperation, especially if the ordinance had benefited the landlords in some way, such as reducing the number of parking slots that they needed to provide for apartment complexes. However, even if the rezoning somehow entailed adverse effects, such as downzoning an area from commercial to low-density residential (which would permit fewer units and would require fewer occupants), the landlords' cooperation could be anticipated, because it's in their best interest to know what is now required. However, a request that landlords do something of their own free will to increase the lighting in their parking lots would probably be structured as a

CONTEXT

The writer in Figure 8.16 is part of a committee gathering information from a number of resorts and convention centers regarding accommodations and convention facilities. The committee will then use the information gathered in deciding where to hold the first gathering in what is to be an annual event.

Figure 8.16 Direct Request

The writer uses an attention line in lieu of a salutation.

She mentions that the meeting is the "first annual," implying other meetings and hence other business to come. She then makes her request.

She lists the type of information requested, and suggests that the information sent by the reader will play a role in UST's decisions.

She facilitates a response. The address here is especially important because it differs from the one on the letterhead. She also gives a deadline for the response.

Attention: Reservations Department

Universal Systems Technology, Inc. (UST) is planning its first annual user-group gathering for any corporation which has purchased development management systems from UST in the past year. We are requesting information about Carriage Gate's conference facilities in order to pursue the possibility of having this user-group meeting at the Carriage Gate Convention Center.

We will need the following information:

1. group rates for hotel accommodations
2. conference room sizes and rates
3. electrical specifications for computer use
4. options for catered banquets

We plan to hold the three-day gathering in July or August of 19--, but these plans have not been finalized. The dates selected will depend in part on the availability and selection of appropriate facilities.

We are currently in the process of moving to our new location at Bridgeport Research Park; therefore, please send your information to our new address:

Universal Systems Technology, Inc.
1616 North Parkway, Suite 555
Bridgeport Research Park

Your response would be most helpful if received before our planning committee meets on February 20.

Sincerely,

Ann M. Henricks
Arrangements Chair, UST

Figure 8.17 Structuring Inquiries and Direct Requests

INQUIRIES/DIRECT REQUESTS

CONTEXT OPENING

BODY [OPTIONS IN MAKING THE REQUEST, in providing details, explanation, or justification]

Option: explicit questions, listed

Would you mind answering the following questions?

1. Is the dance instruction adjusted for ability, or are the classes divided according to age?
2. Can participants select instructors, or are the instructors assigned?

Option: explicit questions, grouped

What features does model X4000 share with the older model X2500? What features are unique to the X4000?

If Vector Research does offer a warranty on this model, what exactly is covered? Will there be any cost to me to purchase this warranty?

Option: implicit questions, listed

The following information about your facility would be helpful:

- the capacity and layout of your banquet rooms
- the types of rate packages available for 100-member groups

Option: explanation/question

I am working on a camera-ready 200% positive layout with drilling locations marked by standard "donuts." Can you give me an estimate of what it would cost me for these boards in quantities of 100?

What are your day care center's polices on illness, and do these policies differ according to age group? We have a 6-month-old and a 4-year-old.

Option: explanation or justification/request

I found the abstracts of the papers presented at last year's conference very interesting and would like to have the complete *Proceedings*. Please send me order information.

As the new owner of a large home in the recently established historic district, I would also like a concise review regarding the improvements I can and cannot make to my home's exterior facade.

ACTION CLOSE

persuasive request, since compliance with such a request would be voluntary and probably also costly. In other words, landlords would probably resist the request.

Figure 8.17 helps summarize the conventional ways of structuring inquiries and direct requests. The figure shows various *options* of how to phrase requests for information within the body of these types of message. The options featuring implied questions and explanation/justification (both shaded in figure) are most common to direct requests.

POSITIVE MESSAGES

Positive messages convey good news to the reader. They include positive responses, credit approvals, and order acknowledgments.

Positive Responses

Positive responses answer inquiries or direct requests. These responses commonly have a context opening, a body with answers or requested information, and either an action or a goodwill close.

TECHNOLOGY

HOW TO STAY HOME, SAVE MONEY, AND CONDUCT BUSINESS LONG-DISTANCE

Teleconferencing, audioconferencing, and videoconferencing are revolutionizing the way people routinely communicate in business. And nothing offers a business a bigger and quicker return on an investment than teleconferencing. That is, for a few thousand dollars, a company can save thousands of dollars in trip expenses and hundreds of working hours.

Today, businesses and their clients can buy teleconferencing setups, usually consisting simply of a monitor (or a PC), a camera, and a phone line. Suddenly, meeting with clients means only a trip down the hall to the conference room. No time or money is lost to traveling, and the burden of getting the job done isn't all placed on one jet-lagged employee far from home. Anyone in the company who wants to can participate in the meeting, because the teleconferencing systems allow everyone to see and hear what's going on, as well as be seen and heard at the other end of the line. The whole meeting can be over in a few hours, and problem solving is not held hostage to airline schedules and travel budgets.

In Figure 8.18 the writer answers an inquiry included earlier in this chapter (Figure 8.15). The sequence of points covered in the response is in part determined by the sequence in the writer's inquiry.

In Figure 8.19 on page 234, the writer groups her answers according to topic area. Here the sequence of points covered is influenced both by the structure of the reader's inquiry and by the subject matter itself. The listed questions address the reader's previously stated concerns; the remaining paragraphs give detail the writer thinks necessary to include about the subject. The initial paragraph in this response establishes a context which emphasizes reader benefit.

Like inquiries, positive responses can include explanations. In Figure 8.19, for example, point number 3 explains what is included in the $50 cost.

Figure 8.20 (page 235) helps summarize the conventional ways of organizing a response deductively. It shows *options* for structuring the information in the body of such a letter.

Credit Approvals

Credit approvals, which like other positive messages follow a deductive pattern, often contain a review of the underlying conditions for granting credit and an explanation of credit terms, as in Figure 8.21 (page 235). (Here, the Carters are taking advantage of an all-time low in home loan interest rates.)

Figure 8.18 Positive Response to Request for Bookings

The writer notes the context in an indirect way up front, along with the good news about the bands.

He offers background about each band's music and cost, and the bar's percentage.

He chooses to separate a description of the band's music from cost factors for the next two bands, because they share cost and percentage information. He then clusters the shared information.

He also clusters the information that applies to all three bands.

He requests confirmation and facilitates that action with a response date and phone number. He closes with a "sales" detail.

Dear Mr. Grimm:

Thank you for your interest in Alternative Music Productions and for your information about Ames, Iowa. Three of our bands, Scruffy the Cat, Husker Du, and the Woodentops, will all be touring in your area of the Midwest this fall.

I am sure you are familiar with Scruffy the Cat, as they have already played at the Maintenance Shop. They will be playing in Peoria, Illinois on September 21, and in Lincoln, Nebraska on the 24th, so a possible Ames date would be the 22nd or 23rd. Tickets for Scruffy the Cat are $6.00 each, with 20% kept by the bar or arena.

Husker Du is a thrash band from Minneapolis, Minnesota, and they will be in your area in late October. The 25th of October would be the most convenient date for an appearance at the Maintenance Shop.

The Woodentops are from London, England, and they play bouncy, light dance music with a reggae influence. Even though you might not consider The Woodentops progressive, considering that reggae has been around for a while, they have an excellent sound and have proven to be real crowd-pleasers. They will be in Iowa City on November 3rd and have open dates until November 25th. November 4th would be a good date for The Woodentops to play at your bar.

The prices for both Husker Du and The Woodentops depend on the seating capacity of the bar. Because the Maintenance Shop only seats 200, ticket prices for each band would be $12.00 per ticket. Of the $12.00, 15% would be kept by the bar or arena.

The three bands I have listed all prefer to stay in national chain motels, so the accommodations you mentioned in your letter would be acceptable.

Alternative Music Productions is happy to serve you, and we are looking forward to scheduling these concerts for the Maintenance Shop. You can call me at 212-555-7811 before March 10th to confirm the exact dates, times, accommodations, and financial arrangements for Scruffy the Cat, Husker Du, and The Woodentops.

We also have several jazz and folk artists who will be touring this fall, so if you should have any interest in this type of music, please let me know.

Sincerely,

CONTEXT The writer of this letter (Figure 8.19) is responding to an inquiry written by a student majoring in marketing who had requested information about an upcoming seminar held by a metropolitan chamber of commerce. The writer, a member of the professional organization sponsoring the seminar, is the local arrangements chair.

Figure 8.19 Positive Response to Request for Information

The writer's opening establishes the context for the response to follow, personalizes that context for the reader, and promotes the event that was the subject of the reader's inquiry.

The writer lists answers to the reader's specific questions in the order in which they appeared in the inquiry.

She includes additional information, divided into two paragraphs according to subject.

She facilitates further contact and reminds the reader of the action she is to take (registering).

Dear Ms. Ehr:

Thank you for your recent letter expressing an interest in the Eleventh Annual Student Professionals Seminar. This seminar is an excellent opportunity for individuals, especially marketing and advertising students such as yourself, to learn more about the professional world of advertising and to make important business contacts for the future.

Regarding your questions:

1. The seminar is scheduled for March 26, 19-- at the University Park Inn on University and 52nd. The theme for the seminar is "The Advertising Revelation: Before You Go into the Lion's Den."
2. The luncheon guest speaker is Wendy Peterson, Senior Vice President of Burnett & Co., Chicago. She will present her agency's work on the city airport authority campaign and discuss where she sees advertising headed in the future.
3. The cost for the seminar is $50 for students. This includes a continental breakfast and the luncheon, information packets, and planned activities.

The enclosed brochure details the seminar schedule of events, which begin at 8:00 A.M. and continue until 5:00 P.M.

I have also enclosed a registration form with your brochure. The deadline for registration is March 3.

Please call me at 1-800-555-1000, ext. 804 if you have questions or need more information. I'm sure that you'll find the seminar to be a rewarding experience and I look forward to receiving your registration.

Sincerely,

Credit approvals also commonly encourage prompt payment (a persuasive function) and mention reader benefits (a public relations function). Because Birmingham Savings Bank uses a legally separate mortgage company for its home loans, it has included these aspects in a separate follow-up letter (Figure 8.22, on page 236), which readers receive after the conditions listed in the initial letter (Figure 8.21) are met.

Order Acknowledgments

Order acknowledgments, like credit approvals, often repeat or clarify the terms of agreement between writer and reader. Although both orders and order acknowledgments commonly appear as standardized or computerized forms, orders can also be verified with either memos or letters, as shown in Figure 8.23, on page 236.

GOODWILL MESSAGES

Goodwill itself is important to all business communication and is an aspect of you-attitude. *Goodwill messages*, however, are those documents designed for the primary purpose of establishing or maintaining good writer-reader relationships. They include public relations messages or greetings, as well as welcome messages, invitations, congratulations, and thank-yous.

Goodwill messages are

- necessarily timely
- often handwritten
- commonly addressed to the client's, colleague's, or employee's home

Public Relations Messages or Greetings

Figure 8.24, on page 237, is a personal message that performs a public relations function for the writer. The business aspect of this figure becomes clear when you know that both the writer, Chester, and the reader, Michael, are attorneys. Michael remarked after reading the message, "Well, if I need to refer anyone to an attorney in Chicago, I can give them Chet's number now that I have it."

Figure 8.25, on page 237, introduces another way of enhancing goodwill: L.L. Bean sends Christmas cards to its frequent customers. Included with this card is a fold-out strip with

Figure 8.20 Structuring Positive Responses

POSITIVE RESPONSE

CONTEXT OPENING

ANSWERS

Explicit answers: listed

Here are answers to your questions:

1. Dance instruction is arranged according to ability and age, with beginning, intermediate, and advanced classes for elementary, junior high, high school and adult students.
2. Yes, you can select your instructor, provided the section you're interested in isn't full.

Explicit answers: grouped

The Center's illness policy, which is designed to protect your children from becoming sick when in care, applies equally to each age group.

Answers with explanation

This guaranty is offered to you at no cost and covers all parts and labor for one year from date-of-purchase. The only cost you could incur would be the shipping charges, if your receiver ever had to be shipped to us for repair. Even then, we would pay for return shipment.

OR

We will be able to deliver your initial order in 2 weeks. Since we keep your master layout and drilling tape on file, subsequent reorders can be completed within 10 days.

ADDITIONAL INFORMATION [unrequested]

Information which is necessary

In addition, please note that your children will need a complete physical examination performed by your doctor within 1 month of enrollment at Center Services.

Information of interest

Another Milwaukee attraction you might be interested in is located just 2 blocks from Raintree. For only a $3.00 admission, you can explore the natural and local history of Wisconsin at the Downtown Museum.

CLOSE

Figure 8.21 Credit Approval of Home Mortgage

Initial statement of good news

Statement of credit terms

Conditions

Goodwill close

Dear Mr. and Mrs. Carter:

We are pleased to offer you a commitment for a fixed rate first mortgage loan as follows:

Principal Balance:	$80,000.00	Monthly Payment: $918.59
Interest Rate:	6.750%	Amortization Term: 10 years
Closing Costs:	Origination fee of 0.75% and all other actual costs incurred	

Commitment expiration date: November 12, 1993
Secured Property: 1208 Grove, Pleasant Valley Estates

We are currently waiting for an updated abstract, and title opinion from Smith Law Firm. Our closing department will contact you when all necessary documentation has been received. Thank you for selecting Birmingham Savings Bank, FSB, for your financing needs.

Sincerely,

BIRMINGHAM SAVINGS BANK, FSB

Courtney Rasmussen
Vice President

Figure 8.22 Follow-Up Encouraging Prompt Payment and Suggesting Reader Benefit

Subject line after salutation provides context for letter.

The enclosure provides information useful if the readers decide to accelerate their payments.

The letter reviews the reader's obligations, and facilitates prompt payment with the use of coupons. (Accelerated payments benefit the readers by reducing the amount of interest paid.) The close indirectly cites reader benefit in that two companies are providing services for the clients.

Dear Mr. and Mrs. Carter:

Subject: Mortgage Loan # 60-0132904
Property Address: 1208 Grove, Pleasant Valley Estates

Welcome to Birmingham Mortgages, Inc. We are pleased to have this opportunity to service your mortgage for our affiliate bank, Birmingham Savings Bank. Your first payment is due December 1, 1993. For your convenience, an amortization schedule is enclosed. The breakdown of your total monthly payment is as follows:

PRINCIPAL AND INTEREST:	$918.59
ESCROW:	.00
TOTAL MONTHLY PAYMENT:	$918.59

Subsequent payments are due on or before the first day of each month.

You will receive a coupon book within the next few weeks. Please review it to make sure all information is correct. If you have any questions concerning your loan or you wish to prepay principal or make payments in advance, please contact our Customer Service Department at 555-5234 or 1-800-555-1287. We will be happy to discuss your account with you.

Birmingham Savings Bank and Birmingham Mortgages, Inc. are working together to provide the professional service you expect.

Sincerely,

Deborah Williams
Loan Servicing
Encl.

Figure 8.23 Order Acknowledgment

The subject line notes the sequential number the company has assigned to the order and indirectly acknowledges the order. The opening sentence directly acknowledges the order.

The details confirm the order specifically.

The close notes terms and includes goodwill.

FROM: Van der May Bros.
P.O. Box 2001
Lyon, N.Y. 11702
1-800-555-9595

SHIP TO: R. P. Hyatt

SUBJECT: ORDER NUMBER 93-0280-8688

Thank you for your order.

Qnty	Shp	Stock #	Description	Price
3	A	9992	Holland Bulb Booster	3.95
25	D	5034	Giant Yellow Daffodils	4.50
20	E	5509	Darwin Hybrid Tulips	4.50
8	F	5560	Red Riding Hood	4.50
10	F	5564	Narcissus Jack Snipe	4.50
1	A	9989	Early Order Bonus Daff.	.00
			Total	$21.95
			Shipping, Handling	5.50
			Total of Order	$27.45
			Your VISA will be billed for	$27.45

Your order will be shipped at the proper planting time. If you require a specific shipping date, please contact our customer service department.

Please refer to your Order #93-0280-8688 if you contact us.

"Favorite Holiday Recipes from your friends at L.L. Bean." Such public relations messages and greetings acknowledge a positive past relationship between communicator and audience and implicitly look forward to a continuation of goodwill.

Welcome Messages and Invitations

Both welcome messages and invitations attempt to establish or enhance the relationship between the communicator and the audience.

Welcome messages, like Dr. Wass's letter of welcome (Figure 8.1), set the stage for a positive communicator-audience relationship. Often these letters go so far as to assume that relationship by including sales information about company products and services (Figure 8.26 on page 238).

As noted previously, *invitations*, when structured as direct requests, emphasize reader benefit. The invitation to an office party shown in Figure 8.27 on page 238, issued via e-mail, is not structured as a direct request but still mentions benefits: beverages and edibles supplied by a fun-loving host.

Figure 8.24 Public Relations Message Based on Goodwill

LAW OFFICES OF CHESTER S. HOFFMAN, P.C.
120 MADISON DRIVE—SUITE 210
CHICAGO, ILLINOIS 60603-1800
312-555-9222
FAX 312-555-3900

July 25, 19--

Michael Chen
135 S. Fifth Ave.
Rutherford, NJ 07073

Dear Michael:

I just wanted to drop you a brief letter to say how much I enjoyed seeing you at our 30th Class Reunion. You looked super, and I enjoyed getting caught up with all the events in your interesting life since I saw you last. I hadn't expected a great time, but I had one. I can't wait for the next get-together. It was nice to see how well *everyone* else in our class has done, too.

I'm glad you came. It wouldn't have been the same for me otherwise. I look forward to seeing you again soon. If you come to or through Chicago, give me a call! Best personal regards.

Very truly yours,

THE LAW OFFICES OF
CHESTER S. HOFFMAN, P.C.

Chester S. Hoffman

Figure 8.25 Christmas Card Goodwill Enclosure

Favorite Holiday Recipes from your friends at L.L.Bean

Baked Chicken with Apples

Serves 4

⅓ cup raisins	2 tbsp. dry vermouth	2 tbsp. lemon juice
4 lb. broiler/fryer, cut up	½ cup heavy cream	½ tsp. cinnamon
1½ lb. apples (peeled, cored & sliced)	4 tbsp. butter	
	salt & pepper	

Soak raisins in warm water for 1 hour. Heat half the butter in skillet & brown the chicken pieces on all sides. Remove chicken from skillet, then set aside. Add remaining butter and apple slices to skillet and brown lightly. Place half the apples in the bottom of a casserole dish, and arrange chicken on top. Mix lemon juice, vermouth, salt and pepper, cinnamon and drained raisins. Add remaining apples around the chicken, and pour the raisin mixture over the chicken and apples.

Cover and bake for about 1 hour. Stir in the cream and return to the oven to heat through for 5 minutes.

Cooking time: 1 hour, 15 minutes.

Temperature: 325 degrees

Kim J. Talbot

L.L.Bean®

Wild Rice and Mushroom Stuffing

4 tbsp. butter	2 cups chicken or vegetable stock	½ cup diced red pepper
3 cloves garlic, minced	1 tbsp. chopped parsley	½ cup diced green pepper
1 onion, chopped	¼ tsp. thyme	1 large carrot, diced
⅓ cup brown rice	Pepper to taste	½ cup slivered almonds
⅓ cup dry wild rice		

In a one-quart pot, melt butter. Saute garlic, onion and mushrooms. Add rice and cook, stirring, until rice browns. Pour in chicken stock. Add parsley, thyme and pepper. Cover pot and bring to a boil. Reduce heat and simmer for 25 to 35 minutes more. Let stand covered for 10 minutes. Sprinkle on top. For turkey stuffing, double the recipe (for a 12- to 14-lb. bird.)

A delicious side dish or tasty stuffing… a favorite, no matter how it's served.

Linda Herling

L.L.Bean®

Invitations can also have a sales function. In such messages, the reader benefit may entail new products, convenient services, a free gift, or the opportunity to win a $50 gift certificate.

Figure 8.26 Welcome

The letter opens with a friendly tone that encourages goodwill. The implied reference to Mr. Rogers' Neighborhood suggests the nature of the store's specialty merchandise.

The letter assumes audience cooperation with its reference to credit (credit implies buying merchandise).

The letter details some of the attractive features of its merchandise before inviting the reader in for a neighborly cup of coffee.

Welcome to the neighborhood! You may not have Mr. Rogers living next door, but you have Calliope Music and Books just down the street.

When you finish moving in, why don't you drop by our store in the Mountain View Mall, 3000 Pine Crest Avenue? We honor MasterCard and Visa, and also have credit accounts available.

You will notice from the enclosed flyer that Calliope merchandise is currently on sale for 20% off. You will find that, true to our namesake, we have a large selection of children's poetry books. You will also find sheet music for the beginning orchestra member, and, occasionally, a half-size or three-quarter-size violin, viola, or cello for sale on consignment to meet the needs of your young musician.

Come join us for a leisurely cup of coffee in our reading room. We look forward to being your neighbor.

Figure 8.27 E-Mail Invitation to Office Party with Clip Art

Neil Nakadate	**TechMail**	**Mon, 05 Sep 94**
Party, Saturday, September 17, 1994; 7:00 PM		**Neil Nakadate, Page 1**

Date: Mon, 05 Sep 94 19:45:46
From: neiln (Neil Nakadate)
To:
Subject: Party, Saturday, September 17, 1994; 7:00 PM
Fcc: Savebox

The trouble with this superhighway stuff is that from time to time glitches appear in otherwise flawless text, typically at unopportun 

, if you know what I mean.

In any case, this is an attempt on my part to venture into the brave new world of inform

without a single backward glance at archaic methods of sending messa

As for the party, the host will provide beer, some pop, and a few choice edibles. Please contribute a comestible of your own device, worthy of the occasion. Whatever occasion you think it is.

For my part, it's good to know that it's easy to enter the internet comfort zone, where it's not what you know or even how well you say it, but how fast you

Well, so much for scribal fluency. Hope to see you. (Regrets only)

903 Steele Ave.

Congratulations and Thank-Yous

Both congratulations and thank-yous acknowledge a job well done. Both anticipate a continued positive relationship between communicator and audience.

Congratulations in business are appropriate when a colleague or a department has notable professional success. To avoid sounding insincere, congratulations should avoid overdramatization ("We are just thrilled to pieces to award you . . ." or "We are overwhelmed by the magnitude of your accomplishment . . .") and should cite specific detail that shows the writer is in fact familiar with the reader's accomplishment. (See Figure 8.28.)

Thank-yous sent to customers typically recognize significant purchases and sometimes contain resale information, such as announcements of future sales. Thank-yous also recognize client effort. For example, the orthodontic assistants at Dr. Wass's office routinely send thank-yous to patients who have just had their braces installed (Figure 8.29). Since this procedure often takes about an hour and a half, the thank-you recognizes what is often a "heroic" effort on the part of the younger patients, ages nine to twelve: sitting still and keeping their mouths open (without talking).

Figure 8.28 Congratulations

The good news is up front.

The explanation includes detail showing that the writer has taken interest in why the award was made.

The close is enthusiastic.

Congratulations on being selected Employee of the Month!

You have worked extremely hard to give our customers the type of efficient and friendly service they deserve. One customer remarked on the evaluation card:

"Our server, Lee S., took special pains to be helpful and polite. This was especially important because Grandma is unfortunately embarrassed by her inability to read the menu due to failing eyesight. Lee handled the situation beautifully."

Hats off, Lee!

Figure 8.29 Thank-You to Patient

Notice the handwritten additions that personalize the note and enhance goodwill.

James,

Congratulations on receiving your new appliances! I also wanted to let you know how much I appreciated your patience and cooperation during your recent appointment.

Thank you for being such a super patient!

Should you have any questions or problems, please do not hesitate to contact our office. I'll look forward to seeing you again soon.

Hope you are getting used to all of your appliances! - Kelly.

Dr. Wass and Staff

ETHICS

WHAT HIDDEN AGENDA? PRACTICAL CONCERNS BEHIND POSITIVE MESSAGES

"Welcome, new customer!" seems like a straightforward positive message, but is it? When businesses make the investment in goodwill communications, the main agenda may be hidden by the apparent positive message. For example, a thank-you letter may cloak the primary purpose of offering further goods or services. "Every aspect of client contact has come to be seen as an opportunity for marketing," and many companies "teach their professional staff how to write with marketing implications in mind." Writers, however, must balance the ethics of piggybacking messages with the practical concerns of maximizing each customer contact.

Marketing isn't inherently unethical, but positive messages that cloak marketing programs might violate Grice's maxim that communication should be clear and truthful. When readers receive positive messages, they don't necessarily expect a hidden agenda. If, however, they expect goodwill messages to have a persuasive component, then the ethical tension created by the discrepancy between apparent and hidden purposes disappears.

DOCUMENT WEBS AND SERIES

Earlier (page 227) we identified three categories of messages that anticipate audience cooperation. However, this three-bullet list does not indicate the actual complexity and variety of business messages that assume audience cooperation. Such messages often form a web of documents, complete with multimedia support, connected to a single occasion for communication. Figure 8.30 provides three representative examples.

With the explosion of communication materials, a single message is often only a small part of the materials anticipating audience cooperation that relate to a single communication occasion in business. Figure 8.31 attempts to visualize the web of cooperative messages and communication venues that can be associated with a single occasion for communication.

In addition to incorporating a range of messages, such document clusters can also represent a sequence of exchanges between different parties. For example, Figures 8.32 to 8.34 (pages 242–244) are a series of letters among the Nature Conservancy, 3M, and the Minnesota Department of Natural Resources. All assume reader cooperation (for obvious reasons). Figure 8.33 shows a thank-you letter from the Nature Conservancy (Minnesota Chapter) for 3M's donation. With its thank-you, the Conservancy encloses sections of its report that mention the 3M contribution. (The enclosures are not shown here.) Figure 8.33 is a good news letter from the Minnesota Chapter of the Nature Conservancy to the Minnesota Department of Natural Resources that formally conveys the 3M Nature Conservancy donation to the state.

Figure 8.30 Examples of Web of Business Materials Anticipating Audience Cooperation

OCCASION	ASSOCIATED DOCUMENTS/MEDIA THAT ANTICIPATE AUDIENCE COOPERATION
Materials Associated with a Single Task or Event: Update of Computer-Based Training (CBT) for Service Skills (Version 2.0) at UPS	• Memo Briefing Management on Background of Update for Prework Communications Meeting • Memo Outlining Agenda of Meeting • Management Informational Sheet Explaining CBT and Identifying Potential Users • 9-page Booklet That Serves as a Training Guide for Service Skills, Version 2.0 • Service Skills Software
Materials Associated with a Process or Procedure: *Starting* Orthodontic Treatment at Dr. Wass's Office [*First Three Weeks*]	• Introductory Package Including Welcome Letter [Figure 8.1] • 4-page Office Newsletter • "Tickets" Recording Appointments and "School Passes" to Get Back into Class after an Appointment • Policies and Procedures Flier (Informed Consent Form) • 3-page Consultation Report • Supporting Software Explaining Treatment Plan • Glossy 17-page "Orthodontic Handbook" Entitled "The Smile of Your Life" • A Half-Sheet Describing "Spacers," a Preliminary to Installing Braces • Video Explaining Routine Care of Teeth with Braces • Thank-You Note to Patient from Orthodontic Assistant in Charge of Installing Braces
Internal Documents Building Corporate Image: Routine Monthly Employee Communication Materials at 3M	• Electronic Flier with 3M News • News Bulletins for Posting • 32-Page Glossy 3M International Ambassador Magazine (this month on 3M's China Region) • 3M Stemwinder (a 16-page newspaper for employees in specific areas, such as the Twin Cities)

Figure 8.31 Multiple Messages Assuming Audience Cooperation Associated with a Single Communication Occasion

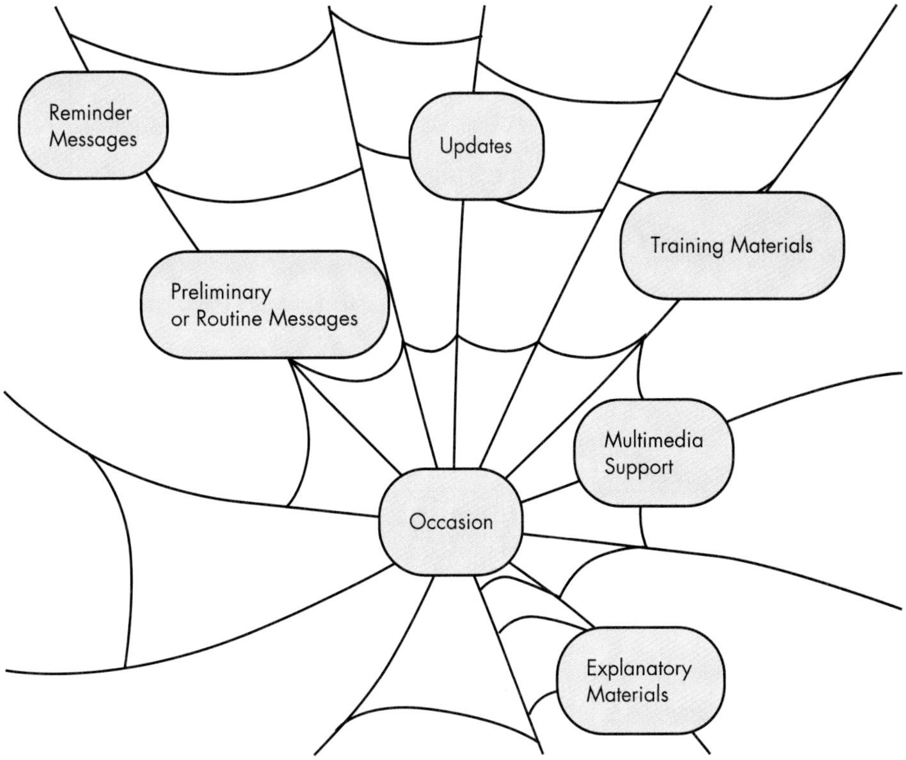

Crystal Bay figured largely in 3M's donation to The Nature Conservancy (see Figures 8.32–8.34 on pages 242–244).

CONTEXT The Nature Conservancy is a nonprofit organization "dead serious about hanging on to nature's precarious balance." The Conservancy uses monetary donations to buy land for nature preserves and often operates on a matching funds basis. That is, if it gets a large donation, wealthy contributors match the value of that donation to the Conservancy in cash. The letters in Figures 8.32, 8.33, and 8.34 mark a large donation by 3M, which has made its pledge in the form of land instead of cash. The Conservancy can both use the land (in this case, donate it to the Minnesota Department of Natural Resources) and also ask other contributors to its Trade Lands and Last Great Places campaigns for contributions that match the 3M offer.

Figure 8.32 shows 3M's positive response to a call for support from the Nature Conservancy.

Figure 8.32 Positive Response from 3M

The good news is up front.

Contingencies (these also very positive) follow.

An explanatory paragraph is followed by a goodwill paragraph that implies further action.

L.D. DeSimone
Chairman of the Board and
Chief Executive Officer

3M

January 22, 1993

Mr. John Sawhill
President & Chief Executive Officer
The Nature Conservancy
1815 North Lynn Street
Arlington, Virginia 22209

Dear Mr. Sawhill:

I am pleased to inform you that 3M has accepted your invitation to be a partner in the Capital Campaign to raise funds for your Last Great Places Campaign. We have agreed to raise one million dollars through the gift of Trade Lands to be made over a period of the next five years. Our pledge will be in Trade Lands only or equivalent values and will not be a cash donation.

In addition to the pledge of one million dollars in Trade Lands, we would also, at the same time, donate environmentally significant properties with an estimated value of one and one-half million dollars, thus making 3M's total contribution to your Last Great Places Campaign at a projected two and one-half million dollars.

I have enclosed a brief outline of both the Trade Lands and environmentally significant lands which 3M has identified for donation to The Nature Conservancy.

We look forward to working with you and your staff in this endeavor.

Sincerely,

L. DeSimone

L. DeSimone
Chairman of the Board and
Chief Executive Officer

Enclosure
c: David Braun - The Nature Conservancy - Texas
John Cornwell - 3M CM/PA - 225-1S-15
Nelson T. French - The Nature Conservancy - Minneapolis, MN
Kate A. Herrod - The Nature Conservancy - Arlington, VA
Charles E. Kiester - 3M - 220-13E-30
Mark Scott - The Nature Conservancy - West Virginia
James W. Stoker - 3M Real Estate - 42-8W-06
Russ Van Herik - The Nature Conservancy - Pennsylvania
Anne Walton - The Nature Conservancy - Arlington, VA

3M General Offices
3M Center Building 220-14W
St. Paul, Minnesota 55144-1000
612/736 0478

Figure 8.33 Thank-You Letter from the Nature Conservancy's Minnesota Chapter

The opening paragraph not only thanks the donor but shows how the donor has benefited from the donation (positive publicity).

An explanation that dramatizes the effects of the donation follows.

The second-to-last paragraph contains "resale" information.

Note again the handwritten addition that adds to the goodwill.

The Nature Conservancy

MINNESOTA CHAPTER

December 1, 1993

James W. Stoker
3-M Real Estate
900 Bush Avenue Box 33331
St. Paul MN 55133

Dear Jim,

Thank you for 3M's generous support of The Nature Conservancy's fiscal year 1993. Attached please find the Minnesota Chapter's Annual Report on the use of your gift and the important accomplishments it afforded us in 1993.

Last year, the Chapter made unprecedented gains in conservation. The largest land acquisition in our Chapter's history took place in the Aspen Parklands ecoregion. A strong financial year prevailed with a 15 percent increase in operations and a nine percent increase in membership. Last fall, after two years of intensive negotiating and partnership building with the Lake County, the City of Silver Bay, the Department of Natural Resources, and the Minnesota Parks and Trails Council, some 4,000 acres were added to Tettegouche State Park. Numerous volunteers helped to keep our preserves maintained, participated in office projects, restoration projects, and educational activities. It is through their contributions that your funds are further leveraged. With this report, we salute their gifts of time and talent as well.

But this report also represents an important change for the Conservancy. A change from a preserve management focus to landscape-based conservation that includes entire human communities, covering a much larger protection area. On the pages of this report you will see how the Chapter is beginning to employ this new focus. We hope you'll continue your support of our efforts to be even more effective conservators by building the necessary partnerships to accomplish these goals.

On behalf of future generations of Minnesotans, thank you for your support of our 1993 year!

Sincerely,

What a wonderful year. I look forward to working with you more in 1994

Nelson T. French
State Director

Enclosure

NTF/tlt

The Nature Conservancy • Minnesota Chapter • Box 110
1313 SE 5th Street • Minneapolis, Minnesota 55414-1588 • (612) 331-0750

printed on recycled paper

Figure 8.34 Good News Letter about the 3M Donation Written by the Nature Conservancy (Minnesota Chapter) to Minnesota's Department of Natural Resources

The Nature Conservancy
MINNESOTA CHAPTER

December 27, 1993

Mr. Rodney Sando
Commissioner
Minnesota Department of Natural Resources
500 Lafayette Road
St. Paul, MN 55155

Dear Rod:

I am writing to formally indicate our interest in donating approximately 338.9 acres, known as Crystal Bay, in Lake County to the State of Minnesota for conservation purposes. Crystal Bay is one of the tracts of land donated to The Nature Conservancy by the 3M Company in March, 1993, as part of the Conservancy's Last Great Places campaign.

Over the past several months representatives from The Nature Conservancy, Lake County, and the Department of Natural Resources Division of Parks and Recreation have been discussing possible protection strategies for these tracts of land with local citizens and elected officials. Discussions have most centered around the possibility of adding Crystal Bay to Tettegouche State Park.

I would like this donation to be considered as a donation through the RIM Critical Habitat Matching Fund program in the event that it becomes an addition to the Outdoor Recreation System as part of an expanded Tettegouche State Park.

We are pleased to make this donation of land to the citizens of the State of Minnesota. We are also pleased that 3M Company has made this tremendous resource and opportunity available for the enjoyment of current and future generations.

Sincerely,

Nelson T. French
State Director

Enclosures

cc: Roger Holmes, Division of Fish & Wildlife
Bill Morrissey, Division of Parks & Recreation

The Nature Conservancy • Minnesota Chapter • Box 110
1313 SE 5th Street • Minneapolis, Minnesota 55414-1588 • (612) 331-0750

printed on recycled paper

RESPONSE SHEET

INQUIRIES/DIRECT REQUESTS

WRITER(S): AUDIENCE(S):
OCCASION FOR WRITING: DOCUMENT:
WHAT PROBLEM/ISSUE IS THE WRITER TRYING TO ADDRESS IN THIS DOCUMENT?

◆ OPENING

Does the writer use a direct opening? Does the writer provide a context for the questions to be asked? If not, recommend an opening which the writer could use. If so, edit the opening to make it more effective.

◆ QUESTION

List the primary questions the writer has.

List any secondary questions.

Comment on the order in which the questions are presented. (Are the questions grouped according to subject? Do cost factors appear last?) Any recommended changes?

Comment on the details used to phrase the questions or to itemize the request. Are the details sufficiently specific?

Comment on the "explanations" offered by the writer. (Are they necessary to answering the questions asked? Are they sufficient?) Any recommended changes?

Comment on the "justifications" offered by the writer. Do they provide an appropriate and sufficient rationale for the writer's request? Any recommended changes?

◆ CLOSE

Comment on the letter's close. (Does it contain a deadline for receiving the requested information? Does it somehow compliment or otherwise mention the company?) Again, any recommended changes?

RESPONSE SHEET

POSITIVE RESPONSE

WRITER(S):	AUDIENCE(S):
OCCASION FOR WRITING:	DOCUMENT:
WHAT PROBLEM/ISSUE IS THE WRITER TRYING TO ADDRESS IN THIS DOCUMENT?	

◆ OPENING

Review the opening paragraph. From reading the opening, try to recreate the letter that the writer is responding to. What is the context for this response?

◆ QUESTIONS

To what primary question is the author responding?

List the secondary questions which the writer is answering.

Comment on the order in which the answers are presented. (Are the questions grouped according to subject? Do cost factors appear last?) Any recommended changes?

Comment on any "explanations" offered by the writer. (Are they necessary to explaining the answers given? Are they sufficient?) Any recommended changes?

Is there any additional information which the writer should include? Are there any additional questions which the writer should address (that may not have been included in the inquiry)?

◆ CLOSE

What "action," if any, does the writer want the reader to take? How does the writer facilitate that action? (Or, how could the writer facilitate that action?)

ACTIVITIES, EXERCISES, AND ASSIGNMENTS

◆ IN-CLASS ACTIVITIES

1. Please refer to Figure 8.1, the orthodontist's letter, for the following activity.
   a. After reviewing the letter, list the strategies the writer uses to encourage and facilitate reader cooperation.
   b. Even though the writer can assume reader cooperation (the parents, after all, have made the initial appointment upon the recommendation of their regular dentist and are evidently in need of orthodontic services for their daughter), comment on any strategies that you see in the letter that seem to have the persuasive purpose of selling the parents on the services. Discuss possible reasons why the writer has used the persuasive strategies that you find.
2. Working in a group, discuss how each of the five strategies below encourages reader cooperation:
   - a clear and direct statement of the main idea at the outset
   - indication of confidence in the reader's positive response
   - information included within the message that is necessary to the action(s) indicated
   - clear, specific action statements at the close that specify the action(s) the writer wants the reader to take
   - information included in addition to the message, in the form of enclosures, etc., that enables the reader to act or to understand the course of action in detail

   Using specific examples from documents that you or members of your group have received, or that you or members of your group have written, prepare a chart that lists each of the five strategies in the left-hand column and includes several examples of each strategy (taken from your sample documents) in the right-hand column. Be prepared to present your chart to the rest of the class.

◆ INDIVIDUAL AND GROUP EXERCISES

1. Please refer to Figure 8.35 in completing this exercise. Figure 8.35 is routinely enclosed with all 1099 tax forms sent out by a large corporation.
   a. Remembering the business-as-usual approach taken to problems or potential problems by Art Smith (pages 222–223), comment on the effectiveness of the notice (Figure 8.35) as a routine message.
   b. To what extent can the message be regarded as a goodwill gesture? In your opinion, what difference does it make, if any, whether the reader sees the message as a routine or a goodwill message?
2. Please refer to the direct request in Figure 8.36 in completing this exercise.

CONTEXT

The writer of this direct request (Figure 8.36) is the administrative assistant for a project manager, who is in charge of coordinating various aspects of a construction project. The manager asked the administrative assistant to request information from several suppliers concerning the availability and cost of various building materials, including—as is the case in this letter—insulation.

   a. Review the opening of this direct request. Does it effectively establish the subject and any necessary context?
   b. Review the body of the letter. Comment on the justification and details offered in these paragraphs.
   c. Review the close of the letter. Suggest any necessary improvements.

Figure 8.35 Tax Enclosure

Enclosed is your 1099 form for tax year 1995. If you have any questions, please call our Hotline at 1-800-555-4569 between the hours of 9:00 A.M. and 3:30 P.M. Pacific Standard Time.

Thank you.

Figure 8.36 Letter Requesting Information

Dear Product Manager:

I am writing to request information on your Certainteed Insulation products. I will be using the insulation for both crawl space and attic projects.

General Contractor is a home-building business new to the central Missouri area. We are currently looking for suppliers that offer high quality products and excellent service.

We currently are using other insulation products that perform well and are cost effective, but are sometimes hard to obtain. We require the highest quality products to go into our homes in order to build a reputation for quality.

I would like some information regarding your line of insulation and its pricing. I would like to remind you that our company prefers to work with reliable firms for extended periods of time.

Sincerely,

3. Please again use Figure 8.36 to complete this revision exercise.

   a. Using your previous discussion, revise the direct request so that the project manager is sure to get adequate information.

   b. Using the Response Sheet on inquiries/direct requests as a starting point, revise the letter again so that it is written as an inquiry rather than as a direct request.

   c. What are some similarities and differences that you see between asking for information using a direct request format and asking for information by writing an inquiry?

4. Please use Figure 8.37 in completing this task.

CONTEXT

The writer, a local concrete contractor, knows that this letter (Figure 8.37) is a good news message and, accordingly, uses a deductive approach. The "error" mentioned in the first paragraph was to overestimate the cost of the work. The price originally quoted for the work is the "normal price" handwritten in red in the margin. The letter, in presenting a bill for the work, actually announces a savings of $83.27.

   a. Comment on the selection of a good news arrangement for this letter. Comment on the strategy for announcing the "error" in the first paragraph. Comment on the apology in the last paragraph.

   b. Discuss the use of the handwritten detail in the margin of this letter.

   c. Discuss the attention to reader benefit.

   d. Comment on the nature and function of the enclosure, which explains "Procedures to Consider for Prolonging the Life and Service of Concrete Services" (enclosure not shown here). To what extent does such an enclosure promote a positive writer-reader relationship?

   e. Revise the letter, making any improvements that you think necessary.

◆ OUT-OF-CLASS ASSIGNMENTS

1. Using the Response Sheet on positive responses as a guide, write a response to the administrative assistant's request for information (Figure 8.36). (Respond to the letter *as is*, without adding or inferring information and needs.)

2. Select a product or service that you need. Outline your specific needs, making sure to identify the criteria that would make the product or service acceptable. Write a direct request for information to determine if this company's product or service will fulfill your needs.

3. Contact a local business or nonprofit organization, or a local student group or organization. Explain that as a class project, you will be working with a small group of students to write a series of documents for an organization. Arrange an interview with the manager or an-

Figure 8.37 Letter Concerning Charges for Concrete Work

Bob, I was in error with my guess for the concrete work we completed for you at your residence. The final charges for the concrete work we completed for you are actually as follows:

		Normal Price
CITY SIDEWALK, 60 sq. ft., 4 inch		
CITY SIDEWALK, 36 sq. ft., 6 inch	$96.00	126.00
DRIVEWAY, 88 sq. ft., 4 inch, cut	72.00	90.00
APPROACH, 54 sq. ft., 6 inch	176.00	184.80
CURB/GUTTER, 15 feet, cedar, cut, 8 inch x 18 inch	135.00	135.00
TAX	105.00	127.50
	29.20	
TOTAL DUE	$613.20	696.47

Of course, as per our bid, the above work was completed utilizing a 4000 pound, crushed hard rock, air-entrained concrete mix. When properly maintained, the *"4000 pound per square inch"* mix provides a very durable concrete surface. The *"crushed hard aggregate"* helps prevent popouts and subsequent rust spotting, whereas *"air-entrainment"* helps deter surface scaling in freeze-thaw cycles.

You should enjoy many long years of service from this work we have completed. We have included a listing of rules you might wish to consider as you maintain and enjoy this concrete work.

Thank you for the opportunity to be of service to you. I am sorry for the "crooked sidewalk lines." If you have any questions, please feel free to call me at 515/555-1285.

Sincerely,

Enclosure

Paid # 1214 9/25/87

other appropriate person to discuss the organization's communication needs. Based on what you learn during the interview, create or revise a series of routine, positive, and/or goodwill messages for the organization. You will need to learn about the occasion, audience, and purpose of each document as well as to determine what specific content must be included. Ask if the business or organization has examples that it views as positive or negative models. (*Alternative:* Instead of interviewing an actual organization, you may be asked by your teacher to work in groups, with each group assuming the identity of a separate organization. After creating a scenario concerning "your organization," you should interview other groups in the class about their organization's communication needs, and write the document series as described above for one of the groups you interviewed.)

CASE

WORCHESTER FAMILY CLINIC (WFC)

CASE BY ANDREA BREEMER FRANTZ

Background. Though the Worchester Family Clinic has been in existence for only 15 years, it has gained a solid reputation all over the state of Massachusetts as a progressive health system. The medical facility is particularly tailored to meet the needs of families in four different areas:

- *Obstetrics.* This area offers five doctors (two men and three women) who specialize in obstetrics, two of whom are well known for their success with difficult or high-risk pregnancies. In addition, a midwife, contracted by the clinic, offers alternative birth counseling to women and couples who are interested. The midwife consults with the obstetricians in case of emergencies.
- *Pediatrics.* The clinic offers eight highly regarded pediatricians, four of whom also specialize in pediatric areas of internal medicine and cancer treatment. Two WFC pediatricians were recently cited by the American Medical Association as "Gold Medal Practitioners." The pediatrics wing of the clinic also offers a large playroom for children.
- *Social work.* As one of its most special services, WFC has a social work wing with five counselors who specialize in educating young and often socioeconomically disadvantaged parents. The program offers new parent counseling and skills training, home visits, federal aid counseling (e.g., filling out welfare or food stamp applications), and health and nutrition programs.
- *Fertility.* The newest addition to the clinic is the fertility wing, which opened in January 1989. The fertility center employs two embryologists and two fertility specialists and is one of the few to offer the new ICSI (intracytoplasmic sperm injection) procedure to infertile couples. WFC's fertility success rate, 30.2 percent with women under 40 years of age, is considered an above-average rating nationwide.

Over its first 15 years, WFC has enjoyed a great deal of public praise for its efforts to combine medical care with social and emotional development in its clients. In a recent survey of patients who had used one or more of WFC's services over the last five years, an above-average response of over 800 patients (92 percent) indicated "complete satisfaction." When asked about adding services, 73 percent indicated a desire for more complete women's health services and 60 percent indicated a desire for child care at the clinic while parents are visiting with physicians.

Two months ago, WFC received an anonymous $4.5 million gift. There are rumors that the gift came from the estate of Estelle Farnsworth, a Smith College Board of Trustees member and billionaire businesswoman; however, the estate executor will not acknowledge the gift, noting only that Farnsworth's wishes were that her estate's distribution be kept secret. The $4.5 million gift put WFC well over its goal for raising $8 million to build a new wing and add a new service to the growing clinic.

After market analysis, WFC officials have decided to add four more doctors and a new women's health wing to the clinic. This section of the clinic will offer all areas of reproductive health services for women, cancer tests including pap smears and mammograms, pregnancy tests, and abortion counseling and procedures. This section of the clinic will also offer limited child care services and a day care information database which all WFC patients may access when they come to the clinic. This database will provide up-to-date information about licensed day care providers in the entire state of Massachusetts as well as specific descriptions of each day care center and its primary contact person (including capacity, daily and weekly rates, and facilities).

Task. As the public relations coordinator for WFC, you oversee all publications and press releases. You must create a document to be sent to all current and former patients of the clinic announcing the $4.5 million gift and the decision to build the women's health wing and child care services. The purpose behind the letter is twofold. First, through the announcement, you hope to encourage those women who already use the clinic for other needs to also use the women's health wing for annual exams, for tests, and as a source of information. Second, you will ask those who use the clinic's services to be patient through the construction period and the ensuing disarray which always comes with building.

Though you are clearly communicating good news to patients, you must be aware of the fact that not all patients will approve of the addition, particularly because the plan includes adding abortion counseling and procedures. Because abortion is one of the most socially divisive issues of our time, your challenge is to communicate the positive WFC expansion in a way which does not anger pro-life clients (of which, you are sure, WFC has many).

Complication. Shortly after the mailing, you received a voice mail message from a very concerned Father Frank O'Malley, who was shown WFC's promotional material on the new women's health wing by a parishioner. O'Malley commented that "to mask abortion behind the admittedly attractive child care service [was] unethical."

The WFC Board has asked you to address the ethical issue that the clinic is trying to "mask" the fact that it performs abortion services by emphasizing other services that are more universally attractive. Your task at this point is to write a message to the board informing it of how you intend to proceed. (Writing to Father O'Malley himself would require skills learned in Chapter 9, "Letters and Memos That Anticipate Audience Resistance.")

CHAPTER

9

Letters and Memos That Anticipate Audience Resistance: Negative Messages

OUTLINE

The Nature of Reader Resistance: Responses to Jamison Cable

Reasons for Audience Resistance

Overcoming Audience Resistance

Composing Negative Messages

Adjusting Common Structures

CRITERIA FOR EXPLORING CHAPTER 9

What we cover in this chapter	What you will be able to do after reading this chapter
The Nature of Audience Resistance	Describe how audience resistance influences the interpretation of messages
Reader Resistance	Discuss common causes for reader resistance
Overcoming Reader Resistance	Use strategies to counter common causes of reader resistance
Composing Negative Business Messages	Write effective messages with negative information: negative responses, bad news in internal messages, bad news about orders, claims and complaints, and negative adjustments
Adjusting Conventions for Negative Messages	Explore various ways of adapting conventional structures to address concerns of audience, purpose, and occasion

An effective communicator knows that audiences bring their own agendas to a communication. These agendas may cause the listener or reader to disagree with the communicator or to be skeptical of what the communicator has to say. In short, these agendas contribute to the audience's resistance to the message. Figure 9.1 is an electronic communication that anticipates reader resistance.

CONTEXT

Figure 9.1 appeared over Coastland Travel and Ferry Services' electronic employee newswire. It discusses an increase in the amount certain employees will have to pay for ferry passes and travel packages for their families. Increases in passes and packages for union employees are to be discussed at the next Labor Advisory Council meeting. Although Coastland is an employee-owned company and the increases are financially justified, the writer anticipates that the audience will resist the message, because it contains bad news.

Figure 9.1 Coastland Electronic Bad News Message

EMPLOYEE NEWSWIRE PLEASE POST PROMPTLY

SPECIAL EDITION
JULY 5, 1995

PASS CHARGES UNDER REVIEW

At the requestion of the Labor Advisory Council, Coastland Travel and Ferry Services has suspended consideration of increases in vacation packages and ferry pass charges for families of Coastland employees who participated in the Labor Agreements. Senior management will discuss the matter with the Council at its August meeting before considering any increases.

In a letter to the Labor Advisory Council, C.J. Van Slyke, Director of Employee Relations, said—

Coastland's pass program is one of the most generous in the travel industry. There are no limits on the number of family passes available. In comparison, Sassafras Seashore 'n Ship Company limits its ferry passes for relatives to 5 one-way trips per year and Starlight Holiday Lines only offers one reduced cruise package a season for family members.

In addition, Coastland's pass charges have not increased in the past five years. Pass privileges and vacation packages to all contract employees and union leaders were improved during the recent negotiations. What we must decide together is the best way to continue providing a generous program while covering program costs and protecting the interests and priority status of our revenue passengers.

An increase in pass travel for Coastland management personnel and other employees who did not participate in the labor agreements will take effect August 1. These employees will see an increase in service charges for dependent children and spouses. The new service charges are as follows:

	Current, as of 7/1/95	Service charge effective 8/1/95
Contiguous Island Fares	$15.00	$25.00
Two-Day Packages	$125.00	$150.00
Three-Day Packages	$170.00	$200.00
Seven-Day Packages	$350.00	$400.00

Employees may access additional information using Coastland's net home page under Pas and Pac.

End special newswire

1. What can you say about the possible agendas that the employees of this employee-owned company will bring to this memo?
2. What facts in the memo do you think most readers will resist? What facts encourage reader cooperation?
3. How does the writer attempt to reduce reader resistance to this message? How does the writer attempt to reduce reader resistance to subsequent messages on this same topic?

The writer of the memo in Figure 9.1, on page 251, knows he faces reader resistance because of the negative nature of what he has to say. Such a communicator knows

- how to recognize occasions that entail reader resistance
- how to structure specific kinds of messages that face reader resistance, including negative messages (this chapter) and persuasive messages and promotional documents (Chapter 10)

THE NATURE OF READER RESISTANCE: RESPONSE TO JAMISON CABLE

It seems like common sense to point out that readers will resist information that they don't like. Because few readers like rate increases, the writers at Jamison Cable faced a difficult situation. Their cable TV customers needed to be informed of increases not only in subscription rates, but also in the cost of auxiliary materials, like outlets. They tried to address the situation in a letter intended to convince subscribers that an impending rate increase was reasonable and justifiable because of a U.S. court ruling involving copyright and the need to pay actors' residuals. The goal of the letter (Figure 9.2) was to maintain customers' goodwill, despite the bad news.

Company spokespeople often have to own up to company mistakes while still trying to preserve a positive corporate image, as was the case with Exxon officials after the Valdez oil spill.

While the intent of the letter was good and the reasons for the rate hike were truthful and justifiable, readers responded to the letter negatively. Jamison's switchboard lit up with scores of complaints and hundreds of cancellations per day. The readers' dramatic resistance to Jamison's letter was due, in part, to its bad news. But the writers at Jamison were actually operating at a double disadvantage. Not only did they have to convey bad news, but they also had to do so in the context of readers' negative past experiences with the company.

An audience's experiences profoundly affect how messages are interpreted, and the experiences of Jamison's customers had, unfortunately, been negative. Jamison had made a lot of promises to the city and its citizens in order to get cable rights there; the promises

Figure 9.2 Message Trying to Deal with Anticipated Audience Resistance

In the three years since Jamison Cable was awarded a license by the city of Sandville, there has been no overall change in prices. Now, I am writing to let you know of a rate increase for many of our services, that will be effective with your next bill, January 1. This first increase is necessary to meet certain expenses beyond Jamison Cable's control and to continue to provide the high quality of service and programming you enjoy today.

The details of this rate increase are as follows:

Copyright Assessment: The Federal Copyright Royalty Tribunal (CRT) in Washington more than doubled its royalties charged to Jamison for re-broadcast of "superstations." Despite appeals to the CRT and pending lawsuits filed by Jamison Cable, this higher expense has not changed. The city of Sandville has approved the "pass-through" of these costs to subscribers. Jamison retains none of this revenue, but pays it directly to the CRT.

Premium Rates:

a. Jamison Cable's premium rates will rise to $10.50 on an a la carte basis. This will become the **non-package** rate for premium services.

b. **Package discounts** will be adjusted. This will contribute to a slight increase in the total package prices.

c. The $.95 discount for our **Economy Package** (1 premium service) will be eliminated.

Auxiliary Items

a. **Remote Control:** This feature will increase $.50, from $3.00 to $3.50.

b. **Additional Outlets:** Additional outlets monthly service charge will now be $7.95, instead of the current $4.95.

c. **Jam Magazine:** The subscription price for this monthly guide to Jamison Cable programming will be $1.50 instead of $1.00. Newsstand price is $2.00.

To understand how Jamison Cable's new rates will affect your January bill, please refer to the reverse side of this letter. Remember, package subscribers receive valuable discounts and, therefore, will not be impacted as much by the rate change compared to a la carte subscribers.

In February, your bill will reflect an additional amount due for city license fees. This "pass-through" is approved by the city of Sandville and is paid directly to the city.

Over the last three years, Jamison Cable has brought Sandville the highest quality cable service available today. I would like to thank you personally for your valued patronage and add that we look forward to serving you in the future.

had for the most part remained unkept. In addition, Jamison was guilty of unanswered service calls, delays in installation, and service outages. Under the circumstances, a negative reaction to Jamison's message was predictable. The statement about "high quality of service" in the first paragraph, in fact, was like a red flag waved in the faces of the already dissatisfied readers. Although Jamison had been trying to rehabilitate its image at the time of the letter, the dramatic resistance demonstrated that Jamison had yet to overcome its past.

REASONS FOR AUDIENCE RESISTANCE

As the Jamison Cable experience suggests, audiences may resist a message because it contains bad news and because of a negative past history with the communicator or the company. Audiences may also resist a document for a number of other reasons:

- the "age" of the information
- the alteration of a traditional practice or a call for change
- organizational hierarchy
- group membership considerations
- mismatch in expectations concerning the writer's or reader's expertise

Any or all of these are factors that contribute to the agenda, or personal needs and desires, that the reader brings to a presentation or document.

Old and New Information

Audiences resist messages that contain information that is either too old or completely new. For example, if a student receives a notice at midterm about disruptions to use of recreational facilities, and if these disruptions have already been happening since the beginning of the semester, the student is likely to become impatient with what is old news and to be doubly resistant to news about further disruptions.

In Figure 9.3, the writers use old information, even though it was originally negative (about not being able to smoke in the office building), to preface new information which also is negative (about not being able to smoke in the parking garage either). In doing so, the writers apparently believe that old information, no matter its nature, helps pave the way for new information. The message was, in fact, welcomed by nonsmokers and accepted as inevitable by smokers.

Figure 9.3 Writers Using Old Information to Preface New Information

The writers anticipate reader resistance and establish their authority to speak by noting their official titles and ranks.

The lead reminds the reader of the "old news." The "new bad news" then appears and emphasizes the positive, saying where smoking is still allowed. The "new bad news" is thus sandwiched between the old and the positive information.

To: Corporate Center Employees
From: Greg Gardiner, M.D. Medical, G-8, x76149
Dani Kennedy, Human Resources, S-3, x75045
Subject: SMOKING IN OUR PARKING RAMPS

Several years ago, we instituted our smoke-free work environment. However, at this time, smoking was allowed within the confined spaces such as the enclosed stairwells and lobby areas servicing the elevators in our parking ramps. This memo is to alert you to a change in this policy. Effective immediately, smoking will no longer be permitted in these areas of our parking ramps. Smoking will be allowed once you have exited the building to the outside or on the way to your car in the open space.

As many of you have recently heard, the Environmental Protection Agency has indicated that second hand smoke has been rated as a Class I carcinogen, which is the most serious rating they give to cancer causing substances. Therefore, for the health and safety of all of us, smoking will be banned in these areas.

GG/DK: rsm

Audiences may also resist completely new information simply because they have not had time to consider its ramifications. Figure 9.4 on page 254 contains an appeal in every paragraph as part of the writer's strategy to get the reader to attend a political function. One reason the writer uses so many appeals in this invitation is that the memo's information, although not bad news, is new and unexpected to the reader.

The letter's initial emphasis on good news and subsequent compliments and thank-yous seem designed to counter any resistance the reader might have to the information in the message. Even though the information is all good news, it is also new news, so the writer seems compelled to repeatedly encourage reader participation. Because of the rather insistent nature of the writer's efforts, staff members may even get the impression that attendance at the party is a "command performance," which is not the case.

CONTEXT

The excerpt in Figure 9.4 is from an internal memo of invitation to a political function. Even though the memo is being sent well in advance to members of the political candidate's staff and even though readers are being treated with complimentary tickets to a gathering at an exclusive hotel, the writer anticipates some resistance, because the party being announced is an addition to the staff calendar. News about the party is therefore new information.

Figure 9.4 Invitation Attempting to Overcome Reader's Potential Resistance to New Information

The writer begins with the good news about the complimentary tickets and the exclusive setting for the party.

The writer thanks and compliments the reader.

The writer attempts to make the event's program appealing before asking for the reader's participation.

Please find enclosed two complimentary tickets to the party we are having Friday evening, October 10, 19--. It will be at the Lion's Head Inn.

This is one small way for me to express my appreciation for all the excellent work you have done—work which has given me a strong record on which to run for re-election.

I am traveling the state every weekend now, and it gives me a chance to talk about what I consider to be one of my primary accomplishments: assembling an outstanding staff which is doing distinguished work. I am proud of your work.

And I think that you will enjoy the party. Senator Smith will be our special guest. You will enjoy his humor and his thoughtful ideas on where our country should be heading.

So, please join us on October 10th if you can.

And thank you again for your very effective work on behalf of the citizens of this state.

Traditional Practice versus Change

Audiences also resist change itself, because they may find it confusing or threatening. For example, students informed about a change in school curriculum might immediately resist, because they feel uneasy about enrolling in unanticipated courses or fear a delay in their own graduation.

Because of this natural resistance to change, communicators often need to reassure their audiences of the reasons for the change and the benefits that will likely result. The writer in Figure 9.5, for example, balances his news about the change itself (involving a new ZIP code) with various reassurances regarding the necessity for the change, the one-time nature of the change, and the benefits of the new ZIP code.

Even though the writer above seems to ignore a few conventions of business writing in this letter (he apologizes mid-letter and does not, in the closing paragraph, specify the exact dates of the transition period), he *does* show his sensitivity to the reader's resistance to

TECHNOLOGY

WHERE'S THE SUPERHIGHWAY GOING?

By the year 2000, more than two-thirds of American workers will have daily access to ISDN (Integrated Services Digital Network) or a similar technology that permits simultaneous voice and data transmissions and interactive graphics. Scott Cunningham and Alan Porter, experts in forecasting the future of such developments, have predicted that recent technological advances such as videoconferencing with ISDN will probably have a number of negative effects:

1. More information about more people will be relatively easily available, reducing privacy. Safeguards to ensure individual rights—of both employees and customers or clients—will be needed.
2. Data tampering will be relatively easy, whether the data is numeric or textual, audio or video, internal or external to the company. Safeguards will be needed to ensure the accuracy.
3. Computer crime and sabotage will increase. Companies will need to increase internal security to protect against everything from computer viruses to embezzlement.
4. Access to information available on massive databases—collected, for example, by banks or insurance companies—may be available only to those able to pay. Thus, poor companies (or countries) may have limited access to information.
5. People with limited communication technology skills will have limited employment opportunities. The poor and poorly educated may be shut out of many jobs.
6. The pace of change will increase because people will hear about new developments more quickly. Fax machines, e-mail, and teleconferencing get information to people more quickly, sometimes increasing pressure and reducing time to think about a problem.
7. Electronic transfers of enormous amounts of money ($114 trillion in 1990) can destabilize all but the largest national economies. International transfers are poorly regulated.
8. Fewer face-to-face interactions due to telecommunication may reduce the quality of people's workplace social lives.

Figure 9.5 Letter Outlining a Change

The writer begins with what should be "good news" for most readers: their town is flourishing.

He bases the change to be announced on this "good news." The change is announced as a general fact for "some" before it is established as a reality for the reader.

The writer gives the reader the new ZIP and basically assures the reader that this is a one-time adjustment. He also hints at the "efficiency" which will be gained with the new ZIP: a reader benefit.

The writer then sympathizes with the reader and reassures the reader of the need for the change.

*The writer highlights the reader's expected actions in **bold**.*

He reassures the readers of continued service during the transition.

United States Postal Service

Hawkeye District
1165 2nd Avenue
Des Moines, IA 50318-9998

Dear Postal Customer:

Over the past several years we in Ames have enjoyed exceptional growth and progress. That growth now requires a readjustment to local mail delivery zones. As part of this readjustment, it will be necessary to change the mailing address for some residences and businesses in the 50010 ZIP Code area. Your address is included in that change.

A new ZIP Code (50014) has been created for your address. A new ZIP Code is a rare occurrence in the life of a postal customer. It becomes necessary only when a delivery area has grown too large to maintain efficient distribution of the mail.

Effective July 1, 1993 the last line of your official address should be changed to read:
AMES IOWA 50014

I realize that change can sometimes be difficult, and I apologize for any inconvenience that this one may cause. Be assured that the change is the result of months of delivery pattern analysis, and reflects the best alternative to provide the most efficient mail service possible.

There are two things you will need to do:

As soon as possible, **please notify your correspondents** (utility companies, magazine publishers, friends, etc.) of the new ZIP Code for your address. Tell them that the change is effective July 1, 1993.

When you reorder checks and stationery, please make sure the new ZIP Code is reflected on those documents. (Note: Feel free to use your existing checks and letterhead until it's time to reorder. The Postal Service will continue to deliver to your old or new address during the transition period.) It is important, however, to convert to your new address as soon as possible.

Thank you for your cooperation,

David L. Massarini

David L. Massarini, Postmaster
Ames, Iowa 50010-9998
(515) 232-1113

CONTEXT

In Figure 9.5, the Postmaster of Ames is faced with announcing a change that will directly affect his audience on a more or less daily basis and that involve action on their part as well. The change involves a change in the ZIP code for half of the addresses in the town of 45,000. (This letter was sent to postal customers months prior to the change.)

change. He associates need for the change with something good (a flourishing community) and establishes the change itself as something unique (a rare occurrence). He also refers twice to the main benefit of the change to the reader (increased efficiency of mail delivery). He further reduces resistance by highlighting and detailing the actions readers must take in order for the change to benefit them. Finally, he reassures readers of continued service. In fact, the writer's vagueness regarding the dates for the transition period might also be reassuring in that readers who take the appropriate action are not doing so "under the gun" of a cutoff date, but rather are operating within a relaxed transitional time frame. The effective date for the change itself is clearly given (July 1, 1993).

An audience's natural resistance to change is so great that messages addressing change usually have conventional sections or aspects that address this resistance. These include contextual background, needs or reasons for change, the change itself, benefits of the change, and a call for action. If we look again at the Postmaster's letter (Figure 9.5), we can see these parts represented here in a short business message.

- first paragraph: background/need/change
- second paragraph: change/benefit
- third paragraph (centered in bold): the change
- fourth paragraph: appeal to reader's feelings/need/benefit
- remaining paragraphs: call to action, action detailed, close

Organizational Hierarchy

As indicated in Chapter 2, audiences expect the flow of information to follow certain organizational channels. If certain types of information come from middle management rather than from the CEO, for example, audiences might resist that information simply because they do not perceive the communicator as having the proper standing to speak on the subject.

Figure 9.6 shows two versions of a report's conclusion. Each represents adjustments based on the hierarchical rank of the audience. The writer includes information to his project team that he later excludes from his memo to the Vice President. More specifically, the writer excludes recommendations in the second version because he does not have the *standing* to make a recommendation to the VP, but he does have that standing when addressing the team for which he was asked to do the investigation.

The writer feels confident in revealing tentative answers and decisions to team colleagues because, as equals, they share jointly in the site selection process. Correspondingly, the writer observes proper procedure by avoiding recommendations in the memo to the Vice President. The Vice President would have resisted any tentative recommendations, since the Vice President's role is to act upon recommendations submitted by the entire team. Moreover, both the Vice President and team members would have resisted any recommendations made to upper management that had not first been discussed with the team as a whole.

CONTEXT

The writer in Figure 9.6, an employee of a civilian construction firm, traveled to a military base (Site A) to discover information about the base's suitability as a lab site. As a member of the project team that will eventually recommend which of three sites should be selected, the writer is filing a trip report following his visit to each site. Lt. Stewart is the writer's contact at Site A. Figure 9.6 shows two versions of the report's conclusion for Site A addressed to the project team and the VP, respectively.

Group Membership and Shared Goals

If you assume the reader shares your goals and your assumption is incorrect, readers are likely to resist what you have to say. For example, if you hear a speech at a political rally that assumes that, as a member of the same political party, you share the speaker's philosophy that military intervention in Third World countries is justified "for humanitarian reasons" and you do not believe that such intervention is ever justified, you might resist the speaker's message, even though it might contain some ideas that you would otherwise have accepted.

Figure 9.6 Conclusion Drafted for Fellow Team Members and for the Vice President

Conclusion of trip report memo with recommendations or answers included for fellow members of the project team	**Conclusion without recommendations or answers in trip report memo to Vice President**
Remaining Questions • Lt. Stewart wanted to know our test configuration (closed loop or open air). Although I haven't decided on the configuration yet, I believe the answer to this question will determine the site we use. Site A is more appropriate for the former and Site B for the latter. • Lt. Stewart also wanted to know if a PRF tracker were available. I tentatively answered yes, but I left this open, since an exact description of what he had in mind was unavailable at the time of my visit.	*Remaining Questions* • Will the project team use a closed loop or open air test configuration? • What site is most appropriate to each respective configuration? • Do we have a PRF tracker available?

Figure 9.7 Letter Assuming Group Membership

Dear Resident:

With summer approaching quickly, we are entering the busy apartment leasing season. We ask that you pause to consider your housing needs for next fall.

We are experiencing a very heavy demand from grad students and professionals for housing next year, and many would like to take care of their accommodations soon.

The rents for next year will be $15.00 higher. However, if you sign a lease by May 26th, your increase will only be $10.00.

We would appreciate it if you would let us know your plans by May 26th, even if you will not be re-signing your lease. For your convenience, please call our office so that we can prepare your lease in advance. We do hope that we can continue to provide for your housing needs in the coming year.

If you have any questions, please feel free to contact us.

Thank you for your cooperation.

The letter from an apartment management agency in Figure 9.7 assumes (wrongly) that the reader will share the writer's concern that the agency will be facing heavy demands for leases. Although the writer probably intended the details about the heavy demand for apartments to "buffer" the information about the rate increase, the strategy failed here because readers did not see that they shared in the agency's problem. Furthermore, because the opening does not serve as an effective buffer, the placement of the bad news about the rate increase in the middle of the letter could be interpreted as an attempt at burying the real purpose of the letter. In fact, because goals are not shared, the reference to heavy demand could almost be interpreted as a "threat" or an attempt to coerce readers into silently

Figure 9.8 Example Involving Expertise

CONTEXT

The excerpt in Figure 9.8 is from the Summary Review Form regarding a proposal to the U.S. Department of Agriculture that was not approved. The criticism here ("Recommendations for Strengthening Item D") focuses on the expertise of the two principal investors. It questions whether they have the qualifications to implement part of a plan that requires expertise in speech communication.

D. PERSONNEL

Capabilities of the proposers and of key personnel to be affiliated with project, such as:

- Designated project personnel are qualified to carry out a successful project.
- Personnel associated with project are sufficient to achieve stated objectives and outcomes.

Commendable Features of Item D.

Recommendations for Strengthening Item D.

Oral & visual coommunication expertise merits more attention. Page 7 suggests that the principal investigators might be those experts. Courses taught, etc. by Hopkins & Green don't immediately evidence that expertise. Valuable interaction with other communication faculty at State needs to happen for project quality and credibility accepting the rent increase. In such a context, readers responding quickly to the agency's suggestion to sign leases soon would not necessarily feel smart for saving $5.00 per month, but rather resentful at being threatened.

Expertise

Readers may also resist a message because it does not match their level of expertise. Audiences may become impatient with a message and resist what the communicator has to say if the material is either too difficult or too easy. Similarly, readers may resist the writer's message because they do not believe the writer has the qualifications or expertise to provide the information.

OVERCOMING AUDIENCE RESISTANCE

Implicit in our discussion of audience resistance are recommendations for overcoming such resistance:

- Build or preserve a positive history with the audience.
- Find ways of softening bad news or of finding positive aspects of a negative situation.
- Pay attention to the "age" of your information. In general, present old news before new news, and be especially alert when handling information that is either too old or too new.
- Recognize that change itself is often threatening. Doing so will help you realize that even if what you are proposing is a change for the better, audiences will probably be resistant.
- Know the established channels of communication in your office and be aware of hierarchical relationships within an organization. Enlist the support of authority when appropriate.
- Analyze the interests of members within a group before you assume and appeal to shared goals.
- Remember that an audience's area and level of expertise helps you predict how the audience will respond to your communication.

Communicators often have to draw on strategies to defuse resistant or even hostile audiences. Here, proponents of downzoning try to convince their neighbors of its advantages in a town meeting.

In short, you can overcome reader resistance by paying attention to who your reader is, and to how she is situated in terms of time, place, experience, and expectations. Figure 9.9 shows that the writer can consider one or more of these strategies in a single document.

In her letter, the writer in Figure 9.9 has considered

- *History.* The excerpt has a good chance of identifying goals shared by both the writer and reader because the writer and reader belong to the same professional organization from which the mailing list was obtained. In other words, writer and reader share a common history, and because they remain in the organization, it is probable that this history is on balance a positive one.
- *Showing the positive in a negative situation.* The positive here is that most teachers of basic writing find in writing the "constant joy of discovery"; this positive claim precedes the negative realization that most of the students involved probably do not share in this joy.
- *Old-new sequence.* The old news about the contrasting disposition of teachers and students is followed later in the letter by new news about the journal; in addition, old news about the journal itself, its founding, and so forth, precedes the new news about the new board and the journal's new status as a "refereed" journal.
- *Practice versus change.* The change from a "nonrefereed journal" to a "refereed" one means that articles being published in the journal will have to pass muster with outside readers before they make it into print. That such practice increases the status of the journal in the profession—and also that the new board is prestigious—is good news. Nevertheless, it also represents a change, so the writer reassures her readers that they will be receiving not only a quality publication, but also one that will continue to be responsive to their needs. In addition, the opening promise of a bonus offer is intended to offset the threat represented by the changes indicated.
- *Channels, hierarchy.* The letter is signed by the editor of the journal, certainly the appropriate person to make assurances. In addition, because the editor is well known in the profession, her status helps her credibility here.

Figure 9.9 Excerpt Using Various Strategies to Counter Resistance

Special BONUS Offer
Expires October 31, 19--

"There is in writing the constant joy of discovery."

H.L. Mencken

Dear Colleague:

For most of us the above statement is true. But is it true for the basic writing students we teach? Probably not.

Our goal as teachers of basic writers is to help these writers, students with little experience in writing academic discourse, to become fluent and competent in their writing and in doing so to experience the "joy of discovery."

Accomplishing this important goal is not an easy task. The *Journal of Basic Writing* is a critical resource that will provide you with fresh ideas as well as the latest thinking on the teaching of basic writing. *JBW* was founded by Mina Shaughnessy and her colleagues at The City University of New York in 1975. Its purpose is to provide a forum dedicated to improving the teaching of basic writing. Since its inception, the *Journal of Basic Writing* has served as the principal means for communicating new advances in the teaching of basic writing.

. . . [letter proceeds to list major topics covered by the journal] . . .

Recently, the *Journal of Basic Writing* has been revitalized. A new and prestigious editorial board of outstanding scholars and teachers has been appointed. In addition, *JBW* is now a refereed journal. It is our intention to carry on the best traditions while promoting new thought and discussion in the hope of providing teachers of basic writers with knowledge and techniques that will enable us to do more effective jobs in the classroom.

CONTEXT

The excerpt in Figure 9.9 is from a letter whose primary purpose is to invite the reader to subscribe to a professional journal. The writer appears to expect resistance on a number of grounds, including the cost of a new subscription, the change in status from nonsubscriber to subscriber, the changes that have been made with the journal itself, and so forth.

- *Shared interests and goals.* The fact that the writer and reader belong to the same organization and are engaged in the same enterprise strongly argues for shared goals. In addition, the fact that the writer opens by invoking an educated reader (one familiar with Mencken; see Chapter 10 on implied readers) both identifies a high level of formal training on the reader's part and suggests that this reader will be impressed with, rather than intimidated by, the journal's having a prestigious board and refereed scholarship.
- *Expertise.* The reader's expertise in teaching basic writing is fundamental to the writer's subject and appeal.

Because the writer has used various strategies to counter anticipated reader resistance, she has an excellent chance of being successful in her communication.

COMPOSING NEGATIVE MESSAGES

Negative messages convey information that the audience will likely resist. Occasions for writing negative messages can be grouped into three broad categories:

1. writer-centered situations when a writer must give a negative response to a routine request that often requires his or her personal attention or participation
2. reader-centered occurrences when a reader's direct request for information, goods, or services or persuasive request for action, adjustment, or funding meets with a negative reply
3. message-centered occasions when negative information must be conveyed about an organization's operations, performance, or products

Figure 9.10 (on page 260) notes examples from each category and suggests the goals of each. Most of the examples listed in Figure 9.10 characteristically use an inductive or indirect plan.

Conventional Organizational Components

Using a conventional organizational plan is one strategy for addressing reader resistance. When you write a negative message, you have a choice between using an inductive and using a deductive approach.

Indirect Approach for Presenting Negative Information. The more common plan for meeting reader resistance in a negative message is an **indirect** or **inductive approach:**

- opening: contains detail that "buffers" or softens the impending bad news
- body: has the reasons for the bad news, followed by the bad news itself
- close: uses phrasing that attempts to convey a helpful and friendly attitude

Figure 9.10 Occasions for Negative Messages

OCCASIONS FOR NEGATIVE MESSAGE	EXAMPLES OF MESSAGES FITTING SUCH AN OCCASION	GOALS OR WHAT THE MESSAGE DOES
Occasions when the writer must respond negatively to a routine request that often requires his or her personal attention or participation.	• expressing inability to honor routine requests • declining invitations and requests for favors • refusing to write letters of recommendation	Preserves the integrity of the writer with a tactful refusal and an offer of an alternative if appropriate. Avoids insincere expressions of regret, impersonal clichés, and negative personal judgments.
Occasions when the writer or organization needs to address a reader's correspondence (inquiry, direct request, order, persuasive request) with information that will be negative for the reader and that most often involves the company's answers or actions	• responding to an inquiry with negative answers • providing negative information about an order placed by the reader (back orders and orders that are unclear, inappropriate, or unfillable) • refusing to grant requested credit or to allow a claim, complaint, or adjustment	Shows sensitivity to the feelings and beliefs of the reader. Emphasizes areas of agreement and maintains a confident and supportive tone. Emphasizes what the firm is doing rather than what it isn't doing. Provides reasons that anticipate the decision. Avoids blaming or criticizing the reader. Avoids any sense that the decision is tentative or subject to change.
Occasions when the organization must convey negative information about itself	• conveying bad news about goods and services (rate hikes, recalls, controversial products or unpopular services) • revealing bad news about operations (changes in policy or procedure) • providing negative information about company performance (loss of contracts, shortfalls); reporting bad news internally about company performance	Emphasizes the logical or reasonable nature of the company's decision; provides rational and candid reasons for the company's negative performance. Stresses reader benefit of the decision; works to rebuild customer confidence. Thoroughly explains any problems that the reader needs to understand and can perhaps help correct (as with unclear or inappropriate orders). Avoids any hint of "cover-up" or of helplessness.

Successful communicators and mediators manage to overcome sources of audience resistance to new ideas as in this management–labor negotiation meeting.

In Chapter 6, Nick Sanger used this conventional structure to draft a rejection letter (Figure 6.2, page 162) that was sent to unsuccessful out-of-house applicants.

When you construct the *opening* for a negative message using an indirect plan, you need to be aware of a number of conventional dos and don'ts. Figure 9.11 gives conventional advice about how to structure a *buffer*, the device in the opening paragraph of a negative message that attempts to soften bad news.

A number of conventions govern the *body* of negative messages as well. These conventions can be seen as a series of guidelines:

- Explain why you have made your negative decision before stating what the decision is.
- Make sure that your explanation is specific and relates to the reader's particular situation.
- Use only your strongest reasons in your explanation. Avoid hiding behind company policy and blaming or criticizing others; accept responsibility for the decision.
- Structure the explanation so that it leads logically to the decision. That is, the reader should be able to reach the same decision that you have reached based on the explanation.
- Remember "you" attitude: use positive wording and tone, refer to reader benefit if possible, and try to create some type of reader identification. (Remember, though, that using the pronoun "you" in negative messages is not a good idea because it sounds accusatory.)
- Place the decision in the same paragraph as the explanation. The decision can be explicitly stated or implied, but in any case it must be clear and unequivocal.

Figure 9.11 Advice for Constructing Buffers for Negative Messages

CONSTRUCTING BUFFERS WHEN USING AN INDIRECT PLAN FOR NEGATIVE MESSAGES	
DON'T	DO
Don't apologize. If you have valid reasons for disappointing the reader, apology is not only unnecessary, but also distracting.	Do find some common ground or point of agreement to mention. Do demonstrate that you understand the reader's needs. *[**Example:** We share your concern that personal care products be as safe as possible.]*
Don't say no. If you say no at the beginning, the reader might not read your reasons for saying no with an open mind. By the same token, don't put the negative news in the subject line of a memo. Simply state the topic but not the negative action regarding the topic.	Do thank the reader when appropriate. Do express your willingness to cooperate or help where possible. *[**Examples:** (1) Thank you for your application to be the Assistant Director of Marketing for the Western Division. (2) Job Services of New York is here to provide you with updated job listings and with assistance in job placement.]*
Don't sound like you're lecturing the reader or imply that the reader has failed in some way. If you blame the reader, you forfeit the chance of creating good will.	Do assure your reader that you have been fair in dealing with the situation or complaint. Do praise the reader when appropriate. *[**Examples:** (1) We submitted the sample of fixative that you sent us to our lab for a complete pigment analysis. (2) Your attention to detail in your letter of March 5 regarding Chamber of Commerce fiscal matters is commendable.]*
Don't waste time. If you spend time with irrelevant phrases or unnecessary detail, your reader may lose patience at the outset.	Do start with any good news that you may have. Do provide a brief chronology of events when necessary. Do refer to enclosures if appropriate. *[**Examples:** (1) We have located the problem with your Kiefer Original timepiece. (2) Over the past several years we in Ames have enjoyed exceptional growth and progress. That growth now requires a readjustment to local mail delivery zones.]*
Don't mislead the reader. Even though you are using an indirect plan for presenting your information, remember that indirection (starting with something other than the bad news) is not the same as misdirection (using positive or neutral information in the opening to mislead the reader about the primary purpose of the message).	Do consider using resale in your opening when including favorable discussion of the company or product is appropriate. *[**Example:** With 1.75 MB capacity, our new line of formatted diskettes provides .25 MB more capacity than older 3.5″ formatted disks and delivers the same high quality expected by workplace professionals nationwide.]*

- When constructing the decision, try to minimize its negative impact: avoid "no" and "not," subordinate the bad news in your sentence, limit the space devoted to the bad news, and "sandwich" the decision between the explanation and an additional reason for refusal when appropriate.

Sometimes the body of a negative message poses alternatives for the reader to consider. Alternatives usually appear in the paragraph following the explanation and decision, and offer different ways of addressing the reader's problem. For example, a company might agree to repair rather than replace a malfunctioning unit. The customer would thus get a unit

ETHICS

CAN BAD NEWS BE GOOD NEWS? PHRASING NEGATIVE MESSAGES

How far should writers go in buffering bad news? When should a writer just "tell it like it is"? How can you know when it is ethical to use buffers and positive statements of negative messages?

Kim Sydow Campbell writes that explanations that accompany negative messages have two distinct purposes: first, to deny the request; and second, to maintain the reader's goodwill by being polite. Both purposes have to do with the ethical notion of self-interest. In a negative message situation, it is unlikely that both the writer's and the reader's self-interests will be the same. For example, when a businessperson must tell an applicant that someone else got the job, the writer's self-interests might include wanting to protect the applicant's feelings or simply wanting to be finished with an unpleasant task. On the other hand, the applicant's self-interests might include needing to know the real reason for not getting the job or the real chances of future employment. In this situation, is it ethical to be polite instead of direct?

Ethical dilemmas like deciding whether or not to follow conventions and buffer a negative message are complex. They can be approached with an analysis of your interests and of your ethical framework.

SKILLS & STRATEGIES

HOW TO SAY NO

Business communicators can't "just say no." When conveying negative information, business communicators characteristically use certain *vocabulary*—positive words and phrases—and avoid "you" and other personalized language.

Instead of saying	Say
I don't think I should have to remind you that the deadline for getting me this information was last Monday.	Information about personal achievements had to be in by Monday, October 10, to be published in the November issue.
We cannot automatically transfer funds from your savings to your checking account to cover your bad checks.	The automatic transfer of funds between various types of accounts is outside the capacity of our current computer system and our current procedures for managing accounts.
No, I cannot write you a letter of recommendation without knowing about your recent work in this area of specialization.	Please provide me with a current resume so that I can consider your request for a letter of recommendation.
You must realize that a person with your credit history is a poor risk for a loan of any amount over $50.00.	You qualify for an unsecured loan of $50.00.
Jeffreys Inc. has no choice but to reject your claim.	Because the damage your mixer incurred was due to unusual use, your request for a complete refund has been denied.

In addition, business communicators traditionally *subordinate* negative information in a sentence.

Instead of writing	Write
We no longer carry porcelain fittings.	Although we no longer carry porcelain fittings, you can find a line of lovely brass fittings on page 33 of the enclosed catalog.

Business communicators also *limit the space* devoted to negative information in a message and, correspondingly, reserve space for emphasizing the positive. For example, characteristically only one line in a negative message is devoted to the bad news. The rest of the message is devoted to a positive opening and close and to neutral explanations.

Instead of saying	Say
We cannot reimburse you for damage that occurred during storage.	Listed below is the name and number of the person to contact at Parker Moving and Storage regarding your claim.

Business communicators also frequently *"sandwich"* negative information in between information that is neutral or positive. For example, a performance appraisal might read: "John has made great strides in planning visuals for his oral presentations. Although he still nervously clears his throat and says 'you know' a lot, he maintains good eye contact and holds the attention of his audience by interspersing his presentation with anecdotes and interesting detail."

that works, although not a new one. When you offer an alternative, you often need to get the customer's approval. For example, if you are offering to repair rather than to replace equipment, the customer should be asked to approve the repairs. You would request such approval in an action close.

You may choose to *close* a negative message with either an action close or a positive (goodwill) close. An action close is especially appropriate to negative messages that specify alternative actions that a reader can take, since it suggests how the reader can proceed. For example, a writer might detail how the reader must act to initiate necessary repairs:

> All you need to do to take advantage of this offer to repair your stereo speaker is to sign the enclosed work order and return it to us by October 30 in the envelope provided.

Figure 9.12 Problems with the Positive Close in a Negative Message

COMMON PROBLEMS IN USING A POSITIVE CLOSE FOR A NEGATIVE MESSAGE	WHY THE STRATEGY BECOMES A PROBLEM WHEN WRITING A NEGATIVE MESSAGE
Wanting to sound cooperative: "If we can be of any further help, please let us know."	Since you have probably not provided the type of help the reader has asked for, this close might elicit the response, "With help like you give, who needs hindrance?"
Wanting to facilitate further contact: "Please feel free to contact me if you have any further questions," or "If there is anything we can do to help you find an alternative way to address this problem, please let us know."	Since you should have answered all the questions, anticipated all the objections, and addressed all needs that the reader may have had in the body of your letter, this close might unnecessarily reopen what should be a settled issue.
Wanting to use resale: "We are proud to offer you a 10% discount on your next purchase of any of our high quality products."	Since you may have just received a complaint about the quality of one of those very products, your reader might find this offer silly at best.
Wanting to establish common ground: "We hope you understand why we had to refuse your claim."	Since you should have provided a sound explanation for your decision in the message, this close undercuts your previous work and suggests doubts (with the word "hope") about the explanation's effectiveness. This close has the added problem of repeating the bad news itself ("refuse your claim").
Wanting to create a good impression (the impression that you're fair and concerned): "Although we firmly believe that our decision is a fair one, we are very sorry for any inconvenience that you may have experienced."	Since you are not granting the reader's request, making an apology at this point leaves the impression that you are, in spite of everything, doing the wrong thing and that you are still somehow liable for the problem. If your decision is, indeed, a fair one, you should have nothing to apologize for. This close has the added problem of putting the decision in a subordinate clause—thus minimizing its fairness.

A positive close ends the message in an upbeat manner and may include subtle and appropriate sales information. As you write a positive close for a negative message, you need to be alert to some common problems. Figure 9.12 shows a few of the difficulties writers face when trying to follow general principles that might work well in closing other correspondence but actually backfire when used in negative messages. Yet even with all the difficulties positive closes for negative messages pose, they are a good strategy because they promote goodwill.

Direct Approach for Presenting Negative Information. Although it is more common to use an inductive or indirect plan for negative messages, a **deductive** or **direct plan** is appropriate to certain situations. Negative messages that use a deductive approach state the bad news at the outset but share other conventions basic to presenting negative information. Figure 9.13 suggests factors that indicate you should consider using a deductive approach.

Figure 9.14 (page 264), which uses an indirect approach, meets at least three of the four criteria mentioned in Figure 9.13: the message is internal to the corporation, readers have a positive relationship with the writer, and the writer, as an employee, shares in the bad news regarding benefits packages. Also, the bad news is quite mild for at least a portion of the audience.

Figure 9.13 Indicators That a Direct Approach Could Be Used in a Negative Message

OCCASION	COMMUNICATOR	AUDIENCE	MESSAGE
The bad news is and will remain internal to the corporation. The communication is informal.	The writer shares in the consequences of the bad news.	The reader has a positive previous relationship with the writer.	The bad news is mild and does not involve personnel matters.

Figure 9.14 Internal Memo about Discontinued Coverage and Increased Cost

RE: I. Discontinuance of the Bankers Life High Option Medical Plan
II. Premium Change for the Bankers Life PAT 500 Medical Plan

I. Effective September 1, 19-- (August payroll deduction), the Bankers Life High Option medical program will be discontinued. All employees currently enrolled in the High Option program will be transferred to the Bankers Life PAT 500 Program. There will be no loss of coverage as a result of this change. The change does not affect company employees enrolled in the BLUE CROSS/BLUE SHIELD MEDICAL PROGRAM.

This action was taken by the Annuities and Insurance Committee, with the approval of the President, after several years of careful consideration. Levels of coverage, enrollment trends and premium increases were all thoroughly reviewed before reaching this decision.

II. Effective September 1, 19xx (August payroll deduction), the cost of the Bankers Life PAT 500 medical program will be as follows:*

Vested Employees	Total Premium	Corp. Cost	Employee Cost
Old Rate PAT 500 Family	$82.53	$48.93	$33.60
*New Rate PAT 500 Family	$91.67	$62.00	$29.67
Part-Time Employees	Total Premium	Corp. Cost	Employee Cost
Old Rate PAT 500 Family	$82.53	$6.00	$76.53
*New Rate PAT 500 Family	$91.67	$6.00	$85.67

Any adjustments for employees who have paid premiums in advance will be taken care of on an individual basis.

Retirees and eligible disabled employees currently enrolled in the Bankers Life medical programs will receive separate notices outlining the effects of these changes as they apply to those specific groups.

PAT 500 ID cards and benefit booklets will be sent to those whose High Option coverage has been discontinued.

THE PRE-EXISTING CONDITION LIMITATION ON PAT 500 HAS BEEN ELIMINATED EFFECTIVE SEPTEMBER 1, 19--.

If you have any questions concerning these changes, please call the Personnel Office at 555-7860.

CONTEXT

Figure 9.14 is an excerpt from a personnel director's memo to all employees regarding a cancellation of certain benefits packages and an increase in the cost of others. This occasion is complicated by the fact that the cost increases are borne differently by the two primary audiences. For vested employees, some increases are accompanied by a compensatory increase in the employer's contributions (not necessarily bad news). For part-time employees, the increases directly result in a rise in the employee's cost. The impact of the cost increase on retirees and eligible disabled employees, although not specified in this memo, is an implied part of the bad news.

Negative Responses

Negative responses reply to a previous communication with information that the audience will resist. Figure 9.15 shows such a response which follows an inductive plan.

Negative responses can also use a deductive or direct approach. Consider an e-mail message that begins "The letter from Joe is somewhat confusing in that he managed to misconstrue my proposal significantly" and continues by outlining the main reasons Joe's reaction to the writer's proposal is faulty. A direct approach is appropriate because the e-mail message is informal and internal and, in this case, the writer and reader share a positive relationship.

CONTEXT

The letter shown in Figure 9.15 responds to the parents of a child tested for admission into Pegasus, a program for talented and gifted young children. Before knowing the results of the test, the parents decided to lodge a persuasive request asking for a retest for their child, based on certain problems they perceived with the testing procedure that they ascribed, in part, to the person giving the test. The director of the program refuses their request in this letter.

Bad News about Orders

Companies may have to convey bad news about orders for several reasons:

- The product is on back order, is out of stock, or is unavailable.
- The order itself is unclear, is inappropriate, or necessitates a substitution.

When you convey bad news about orders, your job is to maintain the attention and interest of the customer, while facilitating any corrections or changes necessary in the order itself. After reading your message, readers should feel that you will give them what they want, if at all possible. Figure 9.16 summarizes conventional advice about how to present negative information about orders, in addition to the inductive/deductive conventions discussed previously.

This conventional advice is good for both oral and written communication about orders. Figure 9.17 on page 266 shows a writer notifying the reader that an order substitution must be made. Because the substitute part is more expensive than the one originally requested, the writer opts for an inductive arrangement, with an action close soliciting the customer's approval of the changes.

Figure 9.15 Negative Response with an Inductive or Indirect Arrangement

The writer demonstrates that she understands the reader's needs in her buffered opening.

She establishes the credibility of the test, and, acknowledging that those unfamiliar with the test might have questions, explains that the procedure itself is tied to standardization and to test guidelines. The mention of a test manual indirectly establishes the expertise of the tester.

These elements are alluded to again just before the refusal. The letter ends on a positive note.

In two weeks, we will be providing all families with test results and information regarding their children's possible placement into the Pegasus program. In the meantime, I would like to respond to some of the concerns you expressed about the test your daughter took on April 12.

Melissa was given a standardized test, the Stanford-Binet test of intelligence, 1972, Form L-M. This is the most widely respected test of intelligence for young children. The validity and reliability of this instrument are essentially beyond reproach. We have used this instrument successfully for the past six years for the purpose of screening children to enter the Pegasus preschool program. The concerns you raise regarding the semantics of the test have been mentioned by some parents in the past. Because the Stanford-Binet is a standardized test, each question must be asked verbatim as indicated in the test manual. We are not permitted to offer variations or probe with any child to assist in answering questions. To do so would violate the standardized rules of the test and, therefore, make the test results invalid.

Since our program does not itself provide testing services and since Fatima is the only trained tester available to me at this time, I cannot accommodate your request to have Melissa retested. Private testing can be arranged using the services of psychologists in the Queen City area. These services are listed in the Yellow Pages. To be used in this year's placement, alternative test scores from certified testers must be received in our office by April 15.

We thank you for your interest in the Pegasus program. We are always pleased to hear from parents who are interested in providing exciting learning experiences for their children.

Sincerely,

Figure 9.16 Conventions Concerning Negative Information about Orders

RECOMMENDED STRATEGIES	STRATEGIES TO AVOID
Do welcome a new customer or acknowledge the receipt of a specific order in the buffer.	Avoid a flashy sales opening or expressions of delight at receiving the order.
Do emphasize what the company is doing or what the company does have.	Avoid such phrases as "we cannot send," "the warehouse is out of stock."
Do explain why an order is unclear. Do provide information that will help the reader clarify the order (product numbers, specific descriptions, aids for determining sizes).	Avoid blaming or shaming the reader with phrases such as "you did not specify size or color," "you forgot to list the style number."
Do explain why an item is out of stock. Do provide positive reasons for the item's popularity.	Avoid apologies and regrets.
Do explain the policy that makes the order inappropriate (required minimums, deposits, and forms of payment).	Avoid simply stating company policy or blaming "powers beyond your control."
Do explain the situation and emphasize its benefits.	Avoid sounding tentative ("We hope you'll be satisfied with this alternative.").
Do explain why orders cannot be filled. Do suggest another source that can provide the ordered item or service, if your company no longer carries the item.	Avoid the sense that only "second-rate" companies now carry the product or provide the service requested by the reader.

Claim Letters and Complaints

Typically, customers or clients write **claim letters** to request that a company take specific action or make a financial adjustment. **Complaints** generally cite problems with policies and procedures. In either case, the customer or client is generally dissatisfied and wants to be compensated in some way.

Claims and complaints follow two common structures: a deductive, "direct request" pattern and an inductive, problem-solving approach. The deductive pattern features argumentative components in each part of the letter:

- a direct opening, stating the claim (or complaint)
- an explanation of circumstances, providing the grounds for the claim (or complaint)
- an inclusion of the warrant, explaining why you expect the company to act upon the claim or solve the problem, given the circumstances you have just described (warrants can include

CONTEXT

A comparator is a digital electronic device that compares two voltage levels: a fixed value and a linear amp. When the amp becomes equal to the fixed value, the comparator switches from off to on to protect the equipment from excess voltage (like a circuit breaker). The letter in Figure 9.17 is in response to an order for replacement parts on a certain model of equipment. The part ordered is not recommended for use in the model specified, and it's unclear how the part ordered came to be used in the reader's equipment.

Figure 9.17 Negative Message Indicating an Order Substitution

Tri-State Electrical recognizes the importance of replacing parts like those you ordered on March 15 for the Model X45s at your remote sites. We test all our parts to make sure they meet all safety requirements recommended by the federal government and update our replacement parts with newer and better models.

For your convenience, each electronic part you order from us has specifications for the maximum voltage and current levels printed on the outside. The 74131-10 model comparators that you ordered have a maximum voltage level of 10 volts and a current maximum of 3 amperes. These comparators work well with a 6 volt battery and copper or aluminum wiring. If the 10 volt maximum level is exceeded, the excess voltage is converted into heat energy causing the integrated circuits inside the comparators to burn up.

Because your model uses a 12 volt battery with copper wiring, we recommend that you order the 74131-15 comparator, which has a maximum voltage level of 15 volts, instead of the 74131-10. We believe that you will find the 74131-15 superior in both performance and safety. These comparators cost $2.75 each or $2.60 each if ordered in bulk. These prices are good until the end of the fiscal year on June 30.

If you wish to revise your order in favor of the 74131-15, please check YES on the enclosed card and return it to us by June 30. You will receive your new comparators within 10 days of our receipt of your response. Please feel free to call us with any questions that you might have at 1-800-555-9889.

Sincerely,

Donald L. Freerksen

The writer establishes common ground—both he and reader see the importance of replacing parts. This buffer also indirectly establishes a motivation for the reader to replace parts, regardless of the substitution revealed later.

The second paragraph explains correct use and the consequences of incorrect use. It serves as grounds for the substitution and provides motivation to accept the substitution.

The writer implies the bad news rather than stating it. The less expensive cost of the originally ordered part is not mentioned. The close facilitates the reader's action.

quotes from warranties, contracts, or leases, personal assurances from sales representatives, appeals to the company's corporate image or mission statement, etc.)

- an action close, reinforcing the claim (or complaint) statement

Figure 9.18 shows a claim letter written to an automobile dealership and using a direct pattern. The writer places the bad news regarding his new Daytona up front. His choice of a direct plan here seems appropriate given his positive past relationship with the dealership. (Chapter 10 discusses the use of humor in messages that anticipate reader resistance.)

Claim letters using a direct pattern assume that the reader will be swayed primarily by logic: given the facts, the reader will objectively reach the same conclusion that the writer has reached. Figure 9.19 helps summarize the deductive or direct request pattern for structuring a claim or complaint.

Claims and complaints can also use an indirect, problem-solving approach. With this approach, the writer assumes that a reader's feelings and beliefs will play a large role in accepting the solution the writer has proposed. Used in many persuasive messages, this approach to negative messages tries to establish common ground and to anticipate and address a reader's fears or other negative reactions:

- an indirect opening, establishing common ground
- an explanation of circumstances, providing a description or definition of the problem
- a description of the solution to the problem
- a section showing that advantages outweigh disadvantages
- a summary of any additional benefits
- an action close, reinforcing the proposed solution

Figure 9.20 on page 268 shows a memo expressing a complaint using a problem-solving approach. Even though the memo is internal, the writer has selected an indirect approach because the readers might interpret the bad news as serious and upsetting, and because the job performance of specific personnel might be at issue. You will notice that the subject line

CONTEXT

The letter in Figure 9.18 is addressed to the service manager (John) of a hometown auto dealership where the writer, a student at an out-of-state college, bought a Daytona. The writer wants some needed repairs done by this dealer rather than by an automotive repair shop where he is going to school. He has had difficulty reaching the manager by phone during normal business hours due to a heavy class and work schedule.

Figure 9.18 Claim Letter with Direct Organization

The writer states the problem.

The explanation describes the circumstances and tries to inject some humor. (In so doing, the writer implies the reader will recognize the "trial and error" word play and understand that error in this case might involve a head-on crash.) The explanation also designates a cause.

After presenting two warrants that connect the problem to the dealership (a warranty and the technician's past expertise), the writer states the "decision" and closes with an appeal.

Dear John:

My Daytona has been running a bit strange lately. From a dead stop, acceleration is poor and the engine is very rough.

I've noticed the symptoms gradually getting worse over the past few months. Passing other cars on the highway has become a real trial (fortunately, no error yet). I thought it was the turbocharger acting up again, but I had a mechanically inclined friend take a look at the engine, and he determined that one or more of the fuel injectors are probably bad.

Since the car is only two years old, and the fuel injectors fall under the "engine" category, the repairs I need should be covered under the original 5 year/50,000 mile warranty. I'd like to have your service department do the work (rather than a local car repair place) because your technicians know the car quite well.

Please call or write me and let me know when I should come up to have the injectors replaced. My schedule is pretty tight, and I'd like to have the work done on a Friday afternoon so that I don't have to miss any classes or work. If that's not possible, I'll be glad to play phone tag with your service department to schedule an alternative time.

Thanks for all your support, John. I look forward to hearing from you within the week so that we can take care of what could be a dangerous situation without further delay.

Sincerely,

Figure 9.19 Deductive Pattern for Claim or Complaint

CLAIM OR COMPLAINT: DIRECT REQUEST PATTERN

Direct Opening

- The barrel on my new Ithaca-SKB 12-gauge shotgun has developed two small bulges on it after firing only 25 shells.
- Recently, I was listening to my pair of Klipsch Heresy speakers, when there was a slight "pop" and the bass disappeared. I would like your store to replace the woofers free of charge.

Explanation: Circumstances

- Two months ago, I scheduled the editors' dinner to be held on Saturday, September 18, at six o'clock in the evening. At that time, I gave your sales office an approximate guest count of 65. On Friday, September 17, I confirmed that number. However, on the night of the banquet, three editors were unavoidably detained and were unable to attend. I was unable to notify your sales staff as to the unexpected change, but I did speak to Ed Baker and informed him that the three dinners would not be needed.
- On May 3, 19--, Schoenrock Lawns, Inc., applied a fertilizer mixture to our corporate lawn at Eire Enterprises, 1710 Gaelic Avenue. Over the last 2 months, I have noticed a gradual change from lush green to pale green to light brown. At first, I thought that the change was due to the dry weather we had experienced the first weeks in June. However, since that time, we have had adequate rainfall, yet the lawn has not shown any signs of recovery.

Warrant

- Upon receiving the bill, I discovered I had been charged for three surplus dinners. Since I did notify Ed Baker of the change in attendees, and since he said that Ale 'n Ribs would use the dinners elsewhere, I request a refund of $32.85 (3 dinners at $10.95 each).
- As stated in paragraph 5-1b of the guarantee, ". . . if the customer is not satisfied with the quality of Granville Corporation's workmanship or services, a full refund will be granted." Thus, National is entitled to a refund of $527.00 (invoice and receipt enclosed).

Action Close

- We are planning a fireworks display for Labor Day weekend and will be ordering the fireworks for that occasion by July 31. We need your refund for the defective displays by July 20, so we can budget our new order accordingly.
- Please send us the adjustment by August 1, so that we can schedule fall planting. After all, what is Eire Enterprises without a plush green lawn?

CONTEXT The writer in Figure 9.20, the office manager for Heartland Development, is in the awkward position of having to point out problems with a much-anticipated and long-worked-for plan for office reorganization. The writer's position is made more difficult by the fact that she does not want to alienate either those involved in planning the reorganization or the administrators, staff, and secretaries now working to implement the new system. Although she is addressing the administrators in this document, she knows her comments will filter down to the rest of the staff and secretaries as the new procedures are evaluated and possibly changed. A carbon copy of the memo was sent to the team in charge of planning the reorganization.

Figure 9.20a Complaint Memo Using a Problem-Solving Approach, Page 1

The writer uses a neutral subject line and begins with a common ground opening.

She presents more buffering with historical details before stating the problem.

She provides two examples. The first involves a problem that she is willing to concede might lessen with time. This open-minded approach strengthens her claim attached to the second problem that a "just-in-time" approach causes problems that won't go away. She also avoids specifics regarding the sensitive and personal issue of hard feelings mentioned above. (Her criterion of "just-in-time" as a foundation is a warrant.)

SUBJECT: Secretarial Help in the Heartland Development Office

Successful interaction with support personnel is crucial to having a pleasant and efficient office. Prior to the administrative reorganization undertaken in 19xx, staff employees in the development office took their work to secretaries with specifically assigned tasks. For example, Ms. Walker might have been involved exclusively in transcription and dictation while Mr. Gallagher might have handled word processing assignments. Administrators had specific secretaries to serve as receptionists and office assistants. Under reorganization, all secretaries now form a general secretarial pool available to administrators and staff alike. Although this reorganization was intended to balance out work loads and to enable "just-in-time" project completion, the situation, in fact, has led to confusion, frustration, and even a few hard feelings.

The confusion has entailed a number of staff members still following the old system, secretaries not used to handling duties that were once the exclusive province of someone else, and administrators assuming that a certain secretary is still screening their calls. These problems will probably lessen as everyone has more experience with the new procedures. The frustration, however, might not be as easily finessed. Although the new system was supposed to enable a "just-in-time" approach to handling secretarial work, it has encouraged secretaries to list their projects, adjusted for number and difficulty, but not always adjusted for timely completion. Depending on when he or she was initially approached, one secretary might have three projects due in one week, while another secretary might have projects that are primarily long-term. In addition, since the secretaries are now "booking" projects as they come in, it is difficult to schedule in unforeseen office work and to accommodate the ebb and flow of daily client and employee contact.

As a result, secretaries have become frustrated with unscheduled work and with projects that take longer than expected, staff members have been frustrated when an unexpected task cannot be undertaken, and administrators have been frustrated with the growing number of complaints and with the fact that they cannot automatically have top priority on certain types of projects important to the functioning of the company as a whole. Since "just-in-time" secretarial work is one foundation of the administrative reorganization, the frustration with problems associated with it promises to continue, even after the system has been implemented for a period of time.

Cont.

Figure 9.20b Complaint Memo Using a Problem-Solving Approach, Page 2

The writer strategically places her proposed solution at the top of the second page of the memo.

She lists the benefits of her solution and concludes with an additional benefit. She then specifies an action.

To solve these difficulties with secretarial help, I suggest that we modify our procedures in two ways:

- Certain secretaries can be assigned to handle office traffic, general phone calls, emergency typing, and the like.
- Specific secretaries can be assigned to the Director and the Assistant Director of Development.

These modifications would still take advantage of the secretarial pool concept for certain types of work while providing the means for handling unforeseen and unpredictable tasks. The modifications would also allow top administrators to give priority to assignments that benefit the organization as a whole. Finally, the suggested modifications can be easily accommodated within our fledgling reorganization plan.

Please contact me at ext. 4576, so that we can discuss setting up a possible meeting about these proposed modifications and their implementation.

states the topic but not the negative decision or opinion about the topic. Using a neutral subject line is a good idea for memos containing negative information: it encourages the reader to read through your document instead of just throwing it down in disgust.

Besides being a good example of an indirect, problem-solving approach to negative messages, Figure 9.20 demonstrates how problem occasions can sometimes be transformed into problem-solving occasions. The writer could have sent a "bad news" message to her superiors stating that the reorganization plan was not working. She could have conveyed her decision that the old system should be reinstated. Instead, she addresses the situation by

Figure 9.21 Problem-Solving Pattern for Claim or Complaint

CLAIM OR COMPLAINT: INDIRECT, PROBLEM-SOLVING PATTERN

Opening: Common ground

- With the newly announced budget constraints, all of us here at Writers' Group are feeling the crunch.
- Successfully mainstreaming our juvenile offenders into the community is very important. Such mainstreaming not only results in more productive youth and, eventually, citizens, but it also enriches the experience of community members as a whole.

Problem definition

- As the policy now stands, only full-time employees are granted free access to the exercise facilities. This has meant that the machines are underutilized (5 or 6 are commonly empty at any given hour). In addition, special classes in karate, aerobics, and self-defense techniques often have low enrollments. Four such classes have been canceled in the past six months due to insufficient numbers.
- Currently, Gear employees must take their children to privately-owned day care providers. Unfortunately, the waiting lists to get into these centers are often long. At one facility, parents need to give 10-months advanced notice plus 2-months deposit, if they want a child placed in infant care. Moreover, these centers have health policies which often necessitate parents taking time off work to care for their sick child. Finally, the costs for all types of care, especially infant care, are high. Infant care runs between $375 and $500 per month; toddler and preschool rates are slightly less, but still substantial.

Suggested solution

- We suggest that a sign-out procedure be implemented so that PALS knows where its employees are when they leave the premises during working hours (8-5).
- A solution to this situation would be to grant sales agents $100 in petty cash.

Advantages/disadvantages/benefits

- To be sure, offering flextime to all employees will initially cause a few scheduling headaches. Furthermore, established workplace teams might be broken up or find meeting difficult because team members no longer work identical hours. However, the experience of other corporations using flextime shows that initial difficulties in scheduling work themselves out within two months to the satisfaction of those involved. Moreover, because established workplace teams have a smaller window of opportunity for planning and joint discussion, work sessions and meetings tend to be more efficient. [Added benefit] In addition, employees who have never had the opportunity to work together before because they have been on separate shifts now form new and productive collaborative relationships.

Action Close

- It would be most helpful to have this benefit in place by the start of the fiscal year, 19—.
- We would like to schedule a conference with you about our proposed policy before the next union meeting, January 12. Our number is: 555-7289, ext. 500.

proposing a solution that represents a compromise between abandoning the new system altogether and sticking with the new system, unmodified, for a period of time.

Figure 9.21 summarizes the inductive (indirect) problem-solving pattern for structuring a claim or complaint.

Negative Claim Adjustments

Negative adjustments are written when you have to deny a reader's request or claim. Often the key to writing a negative adjustment is to challenge, explicitly or implicitly, either the evidence upon which the claim is based or the warrant(s) used to show the connection between what happened and what the reader expects to happen as a result. Such challenges are often inductively arranged as explanations and can use several strategies.

- Challenges can redefine the situation so that the connection between the reader's problem and the writer's responsibilities (the warrant) is denied and the claim becomes invalid.

Sample Situation	Challenge
Newburg & Company claims that Working World should repair or replace the lighting fixtures in the Newburg offices [the claim]. The fixtures have not been giving off enough light [grounds]. Newburg assumes a connection [the warrant] between their insufficient lighting and Working World, since Working World supplied Newburg with the fixtures.	Working World redefines the situation so that the insufficient lighting is not due to the fixtures themselves, but is due to the design of Newburg's offices. Working World asserts that the fixtures work well but are too few and poorly placed. In short, although Working World may be responsible for the fixtures, it is not responsible for the office design. Therefore, there is no connection between Newburg's insufficient lighting and Working World's area of responsibility [denial of warrant]. Working World will, therefore, neither repair nor replace Newburg's lighting fixtures, which would be sufficient under different circumstances.

- Challenges can also question the claim itself, showing that grounds or evidence, although sound, does not logically support the claim.

Sample Situation	Challenge
Melissa Meyer complains to Watchman's clock repair shop that, despite the repairs that Watchman's did on her anniversary clock, it still does not work [the claim]. Melissa wants a full refund of the $75.00 that the repairs cost. She reasons that since Watchman's was responsible for restoring the clock to working order and since Watchman's repairs failed [the warrant], she deserves her money back.	Watchman's examines the clock and states that the clock *does* work. Watchman's then suggests that Melissa check how she has balanced the clock, since anniversary clocks must be perfectly level to work correctly. Watchman's denies the claim, stating that if Melissa follows the correct setup procedure, the clock will work.

- Challenges can also deny the grounds for the claim by showing how the evidence given as supporting the claim, although it may be sound, does not support the claim being made.

Sample Situation	Challenge
Gerry Rondel complains that she has been unfairly evaluated by her boss, Arthur Perkins, on her performance appraisal [claim]. In the appraisal, Perkins has criticized her dictation skills, remarking that letters he has dictated to her come to his desk for signature full of omissions and inaccuracies in proofreading. Gerry admits to the errors, but states that the evaluation is unfair, because Arthur speaks so quickly that she finds taking dictation for him difficult [grounds].	Linda points out that there might be some connection between Perkins' speaking fast and Gerry's inability to take accurate dictation, but she doesn't see a connection between his speaking fast and the proofreading errors in the typed letters [challenge to grounds for claim]. After a moment Gerry agrees to this point. Linda then also reveals that the other secretaries working with Perkins have not had a problem with his speaking speed [challenge to grounds for claim]. After some discussion, both Gerry and Linda conclude that Gerry's problems probably do not support the claim about an unfair evaluation at this time. However, Linda agrees to a request to sit in on a dictation session to get a better picture of the situation, so that Gerry (and perhaps Perkins) can improve.

Figure 9.22 shows a negative claim adjustment that denies the claim by challenging the warrant or connection between the reader's problem, refrigerator odor, and the writer's responsibilities as landlord.

Negative claim adjustments usually use an inductive arrangement. Figure 9.23 shows both buffered and unbuffered openings before summarizing the other components of a negative adjustment. The overall pattern shown in Figure 9.23 works for negative messages in general.

Figure 9.22 Negative Claim Adjustment

The buffer names a point of agreement: successful repair.

The explanation suggests the cause of the remaining odor, linking that to circumstances within the reader's control.

The writer makes it clear that getting rid of the odor is the reader's responsibility, thus challenging the warrant.

I am pleased that the repairs we completed for you last week were successful and that your refrigerator is once again working well. St. George Properties strives for a quick response to tenant complaints.

The odor you detect is undoubtedly a result of the food which spoiled when the refrigerator failed during your two-week absence. When repairing your refrigerator, our maintenance person completely scrubbed it inside and out with vinegar. We noticed a considerable improvement and believed that, with time and several boxes of baking soda, all offensive odors would eventually disappear.

As your landlord, we are obligated to supply, in good working condition, the major appliances which were in place upon leasing the apartment. This obligation was fulfilled when your refrigerator was promptly repaired and returned.

Food spoilage is covered under most renter's insurance, and any collateral effects, such as the odors you have been noticing, are the renter's responsibility.

I would recommend that you continue to absorb odors with baking soda. Most odors will disappear given more time.

Figure 9.23 Negative Adjustments Using the Overall Pattern for Negative Messages

NEGATIVE ADJUSTMENT: NEGATIVE MESSAGE PATTERN

Opening: Buffered or unbuffered

- I am glad that you approve of the department's efforts to reconstruct Carver Avenue. The project will provide you with a new and smooth roadway for many years.
- Thank you for bringing your concerns about your Magicwand dishwasher to our attention. Certainly, having a dishwasher which bumps through the rinse cycle must be disconcerting.
- Bright-light Electric's approved rate increase went into effect on January 1. Your bill of $60.90 reflects this approved $2 increase.

Explanation: Reasons for denial

- Since banquets such as yours are important to the Royale, we maintain an excellent staff to better serve you. To do so, the sales office must have a guaranteed number of guests attending any given dinner. As stated when you placed your reservations, this number is requested 48 hours in advance. The advanced-notice procedure has made possible the reasonable prices customers currently enjoy.
- Maplewood has an ordinance which states that the city owns the land 10 feet on either side of a roadway. This land can be used for road expansion or other improvements. Owners of property damaged outside this easement were compensated. The three oak trees that were removed were within the city's easement. Enclosed is a survey of your lot indicating the position of the trees and the construction.

Decision (indirect plan)

- As stated on page 21 of your owner's guide, only the cost of routine maintenance, defined in paragraph 2, is covered by the warranty.
- It is unfortunate that three of your editors were unable to attend the dinner; yet, I am unable to adjust your bill as requested.

Alternative compromise (optional)

- We suggest that you contact the shipper, A.J. Trucking at 303 Walnut, Denver, CO 80010. (303) 555-8990. We have had excellent response with this firm.
- We can offer you a 20% discount on your next order, if placed by June 1. Please use the enclosed order form or phone 1-800-555-0989.

Positive close: Action, if appropriate

- To take advantage of this offer, please return the enclosed card by May 1.

MULTICULTURAL

THE NON-WESTERN NEGATIVE FACE

Politeness theorists Penelope Brown and Stephen Levinson define *face* as the public self-image every member of a society wants to claim for himself. They argue that politeness originates in our desires for "negative face" and "positive face." Negative face refers to one's want to be unimpeded by others and to one's claim for freedom of action. Positive face has to do with one's want to be appreciated and approved by others.

LuMing Robert Mao, however, argues that the concept of negative face does not apply to Chinese and Japanese politeness behaviors. To Chinese and Japanese, "face is not the accommodation of individual 'wants' or 'desires' but the harmony of individual conduct with the views and judgment of the community."

Face work in Japanese and Chinese cultures manifests itself in the strategies used to convey negative messages. As it is regarded rude and face-threatening not to honor requests, Chinese and Japanese avoid saying *no* directly to refuse requests. To maintain social harmony, Chinese typically say things such as "possible," "maybe," and "I will consider it," to indicate noncompliance. Japanese avoid saying *no* through ambiguous and vague answers, silence, counterquestions, delaying responses, and apologies.

ADJUSTING COMMON STRUCTURES

As indicated in Chapter 6, you might depart from conventional structures to fit the writer, reader, or occasion. In Nick Sanger's case, for example (pages 162–163), Sanger adjusted according to his feeling that he should change the letter of rejection to reflect his closer relationship with in-house candidates.

You can also adapt conventions for negative messages to fit the reader. For example, when Gene Kennedy informed Rachel Johnson that her academic department would no longer be able to help her market her credentials, he went against convention when presenting the bad news: "So, in spite of your generous offer to pay for the service, I'm afraid we won't be able to handle your dossier." As Rachel's former adviser and major professor, Gene felt he knew her well enough to express personal regret at not being able to provide the dossier services she had requested: "I'm sorry we can't handle your credentials any longer, but please let me know how your search works out. I'm still at my old number."

Finally, you can also adapt negative message conventions to fit the occasion. Figure 9.24 shows a letter that begins with a conventional buffer, but then departs from convention when it omits any type of explicit explanation for the bad news. The situation does not lend itself to an explanation, and the writer chooses instead to motivate the reader to accept the alternative. By emphasizing reasons why the reader should accept the alternative, Figure 9.24 comes close to being a persuasive request; however, the response is still structured as a negative message. (A thorough discussion of persuasive requests appears in the next chapter.)

CONTEXT

The writer in Figure 9.24 is responding to a letter requesting a Professional Images, Unlimited credit card free of charge. The writer must tell the reader that, while the card itself is indeed free, it is free to members only. Membership involves a one-time enrollment fee plus a yearly maintenance fee.

Figure 9.24 Negative Response Using an Indirect Plan without any Explicit Explanation

The writer uses a thank-you and sales information as a buffer.

He mentions the services offered to members of Professional Images. Because of the number and the nature of the services, the reader should get the idea that all of this can't be offered free of charge. Even if the reader doesn't pick up on this "warning," the detail works to sell membership.

The bad news of the cost is softened by information about the benefits of the credit card and sandwiched between this and the information that membership is a one-time expense, besides a nominal maintenance fee. The action close facilitates enrollment.

Thank you for your recent letter concerning the Professional Images, Unlimited, credit card. We are excited about the opportunities that Professional Images can provide to young professionals such as yourself who are just starting out in their chosen careers as well as to those professionals who are already well-established in their fields.

Your membership in Professional Images includes a wide range of career networking, educational, and financial services. Our computerized data base provides you with a direct link to corporations nationwide looking for prospective employees with your credentials. Through Professional Images, you can also learn about graduate education and advanced training programs in your area of expertise and can receive all the information necessary to apply for scholarships, grants, and loans to attend these programs. Our members also enjoy many special discounts on professional titles and trade publications.

In addition, our members have the opportunity to build a valuable credit history by applying for a Professional Images credit card, which is good in a significant number of retail outlets nationwide. Although this credit card is free of charge to Professional Images members, there is a one-time cost of $75 for new member enrollment, with a $15 records maintenance fee upon each anniversary of your enrollment. There are no other charges.

We believe that Professional Images is a career networking service that will provide you with unlimited opportunities for an unlimited period of time. To enroll, please complete and return the enclosed membership form with your payment or phone 1-800-PROIMGE.

Sincerely,

RESPONSE SHEET

READER RESISTANCE AND NEGATIVE MESSAGES

WRITER(S):	AUDIENCE(S):
OCCASION FOR WRITING:	DOCUMENT:

WHAT PROBLEM/ISSUE IS THE WRITER TRYING TO ADDRESS IN THIS DOCUMENT?

◆ READER RESISTANCE

What will be/is the main source of resistance that the reader will have to the message? What might be/are other sources of resistance?

What are some ways that the writer could/does manage to overcome reader resistance?

◆ NEGATIVE MESSAGES

Does/should the writer use an indirect or a direct approach in conveying the negative information in this message?

What else does/should the writer consider when handling the negative information in this message?

◆ BUFFERED OPENING

What strategies for constructing a buffer does the writer use?

- establish common ground or point of agreement
- express thank you or willingness to cooperate
- provide assurances or praise
- refer to good news, chronology of events, or enclosures
- present resale information

How can the writer make improvements in the buffer? (Make suggestions on the draft.)

◆ EXPLANATION AND DECISION

Does the explanation appear before the decision? Is the explanation specific? Does it relate to the reader's particular situation? Explain.

Are the reasons offered in the explanation equally strong? Does the writer include a reason that needs to be strengthened or eliminated because it is weak?

Does the writer avoid hiding behind company policy and criticizing others? If company policy is cited, is the policy fully and carefully explained?

Does the explanation anticipate or lead directly into the decision?

How well does the writer use you-attitude but avoid the use of the pronoun "you"?

(Make suggestions directly on the draft that might improve this section.)

◆ CLOSE

Comment on the writer's close. If a positive close, does it avoid strategies that are a problem when used in negative messages?

If the writer has offered an alternative, does the close facilitate the reader's response to that alternative?

(Make suggestions directly on the draft that might improve this section.)

ACTIVITIES, EXERCISES, AND ASSIGNMENTS

◆ IN-CLASS ACTIVITIES

1. Please refer to Figure 9.1, the Coastland internal electronic communication about passes and packages, for the following activity.

   a. Even though this electronic communication is internal and the communicators are in the "same boat" as their audience (fellow employees of an employee-owned organization), the communication uses an indirect approach to convey negative information. Discuss the appropriateness of an indirect approach in this situation.

   b. Discuss what you consider the strengths and weaknesses of the communication as it is now written.

   c. Compare and contrast the Coastland message (Figure 9.1) with the internal memo about a cancellation of and change in health benefits (Figure 9.14).

   d. Suggest how you would change the Coastland communication if you had chosen to use a direct approach. Suggest how you would change the benefits memo if you had chosen to use an indirect approach.

2. This chapter discusses reasons why audiences might be resistant to your message, and strategies you can use to overcome their resistance. Working in groups, create a table that names a specific occasion for audience resistance and suggests a common strategy for overcoming that resistance. Then, using examples from your own experience, tell or show how a communicator could work to overcome the anticipated resistance.

Specific Occasion for Resistance	Strategy to Overcome That Resistance	Example of Overcoming Audience Resistance

3. Imagine that you have just been promoted from a lead writer position to a managerial position within a claims department. You decide it would be a good idea to hold a meeting to present successful ways of answering claims. You decide further to focus on *challenges* that a communicator can use to refuse claims. You prepare notes for making a 10-minute "background talk" and a handout showing sample claims and successful challenges to those claims. (Hold your meeting and present your talk; classmates can play the role of co-workers attending the meeting.)

◆ INDIVIDUAL AND GROUP EXERCISES

1. The following are buffers taken from Figure 9.11.

   We share your concern that personal care products be as safe as possible.

   Job Services of New York is here to provide you with updated job listings and with assistance in job placement.

   We submitted the sample of fixative that you sent us to our lab for a complete pigment analysis.

   Your attention to detail in your letter of March 5 regarding Chamber of Commerce fiscal matters is commendable.

   We have located the problem with your Kiefer Original timepiece.

   With 1.75 MB capacity, our new line of formatted diskettes provides .25 MB more capacity than older 3.5″ formatted disks and delivers the same high quality expected by workplace professionals nationwide.

   a. Collaborating with several classmates, discuss the strategy each buffer employs. Brainstorm your expectations about the negative information that is likely to follow each buffer.

   b. Select one of the buffers and write a negative message that might follow.

2. Please refer to the letter in Figure 9.25 in completing this exercise.

Figure 9.25 A Negative Response in Need of Revision

Dear Ms. Nelson:

I have received your request for information concerning arrangements for a visit to Wild River by the Pioneer Canoe Club and would like to answer your questions and provide you with information to help plan your trip.

Here are specific answers to some of your questions:

1. Permits are assigned when you check-in as a group.
2. A variety of fish can be caught in the river, including Northern, Walleye, and Bass.
3. Groceries may be purchased on site to supply your needs.
4. A variety of wildlife can be found in the Wild River region as detailed in the enclosed brochure.

I have enclosed a brochure with information concerning the river and surrounding area. Although your group has expressed an interest in a fall trip, it is our recommendation that you schedule your trip in the spring. The overuse of a natural wildlife area for recreational purposes needs to be guarded against. The weather and fishing would better suit the needs of your group during the spring months. If you have additional questions or concerns, please feel free to write or call us for information. We encourage your visit to Wild River and look forward to hearing from you to confirm your visit.

Sincerely,

CONTEXT

The purpose of the letter in Figure 9.25 is to inform the reader that her group will not be granted a permit to take a canoe trip at a wildlife refuge during the fall. The letter writer also wants to suggest a spring trip as an alternative.

a. Discuss the ways this letter successfully uses conventional strategies for writing negative messages.

b. Discuss any problems with the way the message is written. Where does it send mixed messages? Explain.

c. Suggest changes that the writer could make to the message that would improve it as a conventional negative message.

d. Suggest any unconventional strategies that the writer could use to improve this negative response.

e. Revise the letter so that it relates the writer's intentions more effectively.

3. Refer to the letter sent by Jamison Cable (Figure 9.2). This letter caused problems for the company because of the cancellations it provoked.

a. On the basis of information you've learned in this chapter about writing negative messages, identify what you see as the main problems in the way the rate hike is presented to the customers (especially considering the negative past history many customers have had).

b. Revise the letter so that it accomplishes its purpose of informing customers about the rate hike without alienating them.

◆ OUT-OF-CLASS ASSIGNMENTS

1. Select a business communication that annoyed you because it conveyed negative information poorly. Write a one-paragraph assessment of the reasons for your resistance to the document and the major weaknesses in how the document was written. Use the Response Sheet on reader resistance and negative messages to aid your assessment. Now revise the document to eliminate the problems you have identified. When you turn in the assignment, include (a) the original document, (b) your assessment of the document's problems with tone, and (c) the revised document.

2. Please use Figure 9.26 for this assignment.

CONTEXT

Wood Products, Inc. is a paper pulp brokerage. Like Oberon Consolidated, Inc. (Chapter 2), Wood Products commonly keeps detailed records of its telephone conversations. Bill Sandburg, mentioned in the report, is a Vice President at National Paper Board Co., a bulk milling company possibly interested in a joint venture with Wood Products. At this point, however, Sandburg is not at all sold on the rather technical proposal submitted to him by Wood Products. Kastner, a Controller at National, is relaying the bad news.

a. Assume that you have to take the information in this report and write a memo to all Wood Products employees about the failure of Wood Products' initial proposal to National. Together with several of your classmates, discuss whether you will be using an indirect or a direct plan and how you will present the negative information. Use the Response Sheet on reader resistance and negative messages to aid your discussion. Then, either collectively or individually, write the memo. Feel free to add information if necessary.

b. Now assume that you are Kastner and must write a negative message to Wood Products explaining the bad news that National is not interested in Wood Products' proposal. Together with several of your classmates, discuss whether you will be using an indirect or direct plan and how you will present the negative information. Use the Response Sheet on reader resistance and negative messages to aid your discussion. Then, either collectively or individually, write the letter.

Figure 9.26 Call Report Containing Unbuffered Negative Information

Kastner called saying that Sandburg had gone over everything we had sent, including the samples of refined material and the paper. Commented that he [Sandburg] would not have recognized the idea described in our proposal as having any relation to the paper. Unfortunately.

Result: Sandburg is not interested in our proposal. He feels that there has to be a better way. Stated "this is not a hot item for them."

Reasons:

1) Volume. The Federal Government is pushing for bulk mills to have up to 20% recycled content. Soon this will be put into law and this will push the numbers up. A unit of 100/200 TPD is not appropriate. A 500 TPD unit, as described in our proposal, is exorbitant in price. There are other processes they are looking at which are more appropriate.

2) Maintenance. Sandburg feels our process is more maintenance involved than other processes.

3) Effluent. There is the problem of disposal of liquor [liquid], which must be done in a prescribed manner. At National it is burned in boilers.

4) Compatibility. The proposed idea would not run in conjunction with theirs. It would have to be a separate process, and not an on-line process.

Conclusion: Kastner says this is a door closed. He also said you don't know about corporations. They close a door, then down the road open it.

I said we will get further cost and process info on 500 TPD units and pass it on to him.

CASE

A NEW FRANCHISE FOR MAJOR LEAGUE BASEBALL

CASE BY ANDREA BREEMER FRANTZ

Background. It is once again time for the Major League Baseball Commission to consider league expansion. To be named a new baseball franchise "home," cities must draw up attractive packages which outline the specific benefits they offer Major League Baseball. In the past, the commission has relied upon several key criteria to determine which cities to add as franchise sites:

- *Sponsorship.* The potential owner(s) must be able to afford the league entry fee of $150 million and also possess other assets and cash reserves for operation expenses. Sometimes, a team of investors is less attractive than a sole owner because of the potential for partnership collapse; however, it is becoming increasingly difficult to entice the superwealthy into long-term investment in sports teams because of players' strikes.
- *Population base.* A new franchise city must have a viable population base to lend support to the team and enough financial stability to maintain upkeep of facilities. Franchise cities must offer enough of a cosmopolitan appeal to draw crowds from out of town; must have enough hotel accommodations, restaurants, and businesses to attract tourists and baseball fans; and must boast a population of at least 1 million unless there is a large neighboring city or powerful tourist draw.
- *Television market.* Because Major League Baseball relies heavily on television advertising revenues, any city which offers an established local broadcasting network is particularly attractive (e.g., Chicago's WGN baseball coverage, and Atlanta's TBS).
- *Existing stadium or potential for new stadium.* Stadiums frequently create a specific persona for a ball club. (Think of the tradition that would be lost if the Boston Red Sox were no longer housed in Fenway Park, the home of the Big Green Monster.) Baseball teams require a "home," and successful proposals will guarantee an existing or new stadium to house the franchise.
- *History of athletic support.* The commission will carefully scrutinize a city's potential to create a secure environment for a major league team.

Of course, each of the proposals from the prospective cities includes specific information unique to the area, and certain locations may appeal on the basis of relative distance from competing teams or a specific cultural or climatological appeal. All of the proposal packages sent to the commission are designed by professionals who are well aware of how to "sell" their particular area. The following cities have applied for a National League franchise this year.

- Indianapolis, Indiana
- New Orleans, Louisiana
- Monterrey, Mexico

Task. You are a part of the five-member panel that will decide which of the applicants will be awarded the new franchise in the National League. You must decide, on the basis of the information provided, which city will receive the franchise. You may research the cities beyond what is provided here to make your decision. In using such research, you need to cite outside source(s) *and* set up the criteria (e.g., climate, international flavor) by which you judge the information.

Once you have determined which city will be awarded the franchise, you need to inform the nonfranchise cities that they were not selected. Remember, although you are informing your readers of their status, you are also convincing them of the viability of your decision-making process and rationale. Your audience consists of powerful people who have expended a great deal of energy creating proposal packages. You owe them the courtesy of being thorough (your message will probably extend past one page). You may design and format your message in a way you think most appropriate to the occasion.

Complication. Completely *after the fact* but *before* you mail the messages, you discover that one of the sponsors of a losing proposal went to school with you. Although you were not good friends—which explains why you did not recognize his/her name (she may have submitted the proposal under her married name, or he may now be using initials instead of his first name)—you feel that you have to at least *consider* editing your message to acknowledge this personal connection. Decide whether and how you would edit your message. If you decide *not* to edit but to send the same message to everyone, write a memo to your instructor explaining that decision. If you decide to edit the message to acknowledge the personal connection, do so, and submit the revised message along with your original version.

City Information

- ***Indianapolis, Indiana (Committee Chair, Brian J. McDonough)***
  Sponsorship. The proposal details a partnership as primary sponsor for the new franchise. Partners include R. J. Ford, retired stockbroker; Kenneth McGuire, judge; and Andrea Schoell, stockbroker. The partnership is worth an estimated $1 billion.
  Population base. 1,424,050.
  Television market. Current local stations include WTPN, WNOW, and WTSN. WTPN and WNOW are local to Indianapolis and cover a limited regional area around the city. WTSN is a TNT affiliate. At present, the committee is only in the discussion stages of negotiating bids from the stations to cover baseball games.
  Existing stadium. As a short-term solution to the issue of a stadium, the committee has guaranteed that the Colts' football stadium could be converted to a baseball field.
  History of athletic support. Indianapolis has a strong history of athletic support, with one professional football team, the Indianapolis Colts, and one professional basketball team, the Indiana Pacers. Indianapolis annually hosts the most prestigious and best-attended stock car race, the Indianapolis 500.
- ***New Orleans, Louisiana (Committee Chair, Daniel Mills)***
  Sponsorship. The proposal details a married couple as primary sponsors for a new franchise. Freida and Bill Monholtz, co-founders of Holtz Brewery and Holtz Vineyards, are estimated to be worth approximately $240 million.
  Population base. 1,302,697.
  Television market. Current local stations include KSPZ and KKLO. These are local to New Orleans and cover a limited regional area.
  Existing stadium. Presently, the committee is researching whether the Superdome (currently used for New Orleans

Saints games) can feasibly be converted for baseball.
History of athletic support. At present New Orleans supports a professional football team, the New Orleans Saints, as well as a triple-A baseball team, the New Orleans Zephyrs. New Orleans is considered a city with good potential for athletic support.

- ***Monterrey, Mexico (Committee Chair, J.T. Santiago)***
Sponsorship. The proposal details a single individual as primary sponsor for a new franchise. F. Ramirez, a businessperson and commercial airline owner, is estimated to be worth $440 million.
Population base. 3,385,000.
Television market. Monterrey offers four local television stations and is also the base for one of Mexico's national television corporations. ESPN and Prime Network (Texas) have already agreed to cover baseball in Monterrey if offered a franchise.
Existing stadium. Monterrey officials have already begun work on a baseball stadium, which they expect will be finished by autumn next year.
History of athletic support. American support for professional sports based in Mexico is as yet untested. Because of Monterrey's location near the border, it has proven a popular American vacation spot and offers adequate hotel and restaurant facilities. The committee argues that baseball tourism will primarily come from the U.S. desert southwest.

CHAPTER

10

Documents That Anticipate Audience Resistance: Persuasive Messages, Sales Messages, and Promotional Packages

OUTLINE

Selecting the Main Selling Point: Tedlock Advertising

Persuasive Messages

Sales Messages

Promotional Packages

CRITERIA FOR EXPLORING CHAPTER 10

What we cover in this chapter	What you will be able to do after reading this chapter
The Main Selling Point	Discuss what factors influence the selection of a main selling point for sales and promotional materials
Persuasive Messages	Write persuasive requests, claims, collections, problem-solving messages
Sales Messages	Create effective sales letters and direct mailings
Promotional Packages	Discuss and outline effective product, policy, and press packages

Effective communicators recognize that trying to persuade audiences to think or do something is hard work, even if readers or listeners will reap tangible benefits from complying with a communicator's request. The writer of Figure 10.1 anticipates reader resistance, even though it advertises a good time for participants.

CONTEXT

A six-panel brochure invites potential patrons of a full participation dinner theater to escape into a fantasy world of danger, romance, mystery, and intrigue. Figure 10.1 shows two interior brochure panels promoting this particular theater offering. Although dinner theaters appeal to fantasy, they are in reality a serious business venture and must attract a sufficient number of clients to remain a money-making enterprise. Managers for this enterprise have a product to sell: food, fun, and self-fulfillment through participation in the performance.

Figure 10.1 Interior Panels of a Promotional Dinner Theater Brochure

THE MYSTERY OF
THE MALTESE FALCON

A Role-Playing Audience Participation Dinner Drama

The year is 1938. Storm clouds gather over Europe as Hitler invades Czechoslovakia. In the United States, people are recovering from the Great Depression. San Francisco is a wide-open town, where hard-boiled detectives swill gin and smugglers operate at Half-Moon Bay.

Lovers sway to the big bands at the Rose Bowl Dance Hall in Larkspur. International spies hold forbidden *rendez-vous* in China-town. And the grand dames of Burlingame society are making plans for their annual social season.

You are cordially invited to the Astor Fall Cotillion, where secretaries rub shoulders with debutantes, cat burglars survey their prey, and bubble dancers mix with high society nobs. Money talks, and sometimes it whispers "murder."

The dinner will be held in costume, and guests play the parts of detectives, society matrons, servants, entertainers, federal agents, and international spies, each with his or her own secrets and motivations.

Each guest receives a role packet with some background information on the pre-war era, a summary of historical events of 1938, a dictionary of detective slang, a list of all the other characters, and any documents needed (such as stage money, magazines, or a 1938 newspaper), as well as a detailed description of the character's background, goals, and resources.

There are numerous plots unfolding simultaneously, and each guest may be involved in one or more of these plots. The roles are arranged in order of difficulty, from simple parts which require little experience to major roles which involve considerable acting expertise. There are over forty role-playing parts.

The Astor Fall Cotillion will open at 6:00 PM, at which time a half-hour orientation will be held to hand out props and stage money and to explain the rules. The drama itself begins at 6:30 PM. A dinner buffet will be served at 7:00 PM.

NO MURDERS ARE ALLOWED
BEFORE 8:30 PM

The drama will continue until about 9:15 PM. At that time, a cast party will be held to complete the event, with awards and prizes for those Guests voted to have best played their roles. Everyone will then find out what the others were doing and understand what was *really* going on.

1. How does the writer attract readers and engage their interest?
2. How would you describe the intended audience for this brochure? Explain.
3. Why might the writer anticipate reader resistance to the message in the brochure? What sources of resistance would the reader have to address in the information? What strategies does the writer use to overcome reader resistance?

Dinner theaters can invoke the mystery and intrigue of such movies as *Murder on the Orient Express.*

The brochure's writer invites members of the audience to become part of the drama even before attending the dinner theater and thus demonstrates knowledge basic to writing

- persuasive messages
- sales messages
- promotional packages

SKILLS & STRATEGIES

DESIGNING A BROCHURE WITH THE MAIN SELLING POINT IN MIND

In selecting and organizing information for brochures such as those included in promotional packages, you need to keep in mind several conventions:

- Brochures generally have one main idea or selling point that serves as an overarching theme. Only material that most strongly supports the theme should be selected. (For more details about brochures, see Chapter 17.)
- Brochures usually reinforce their main idea or selling point visually with a symbol or graphic that is repeated throughout the document. For example, a brochure advertising the Olympics might repeat the Olympic rings in various renditions or might continue one rendition across various panels with the help of line extensions or other such devices.

The three lines below might extend across several folds:

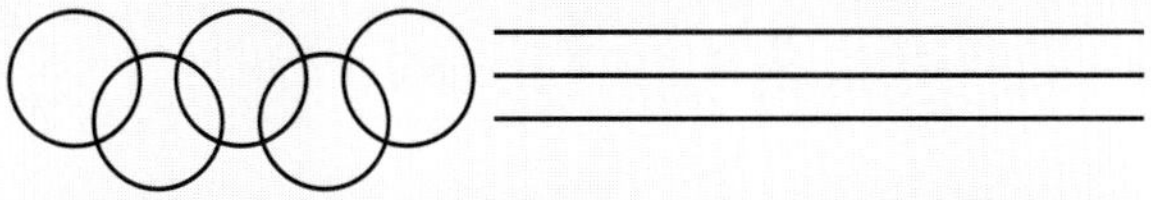

(For further information on design and visuals, see Chapters 12 and 13.) Other brochures might contain a select cluster of images that relates to the main theme, such as an apple, an open book, and a sharpened pencil in a brochure about school issues; or a dog dragging his master by a leash in one panel and—in a subsequent panel—the same dog at a perfect sit next to his master, in a brochure about dog obedience training. (When using visual clusters in brochures, you need to remember, however, that "less is more.")

- Brochures also have conventional sites for various types of material. Context information appears on the front cover, which operates much like a title page. Mailing information appears on the "back." (The type of fold you use determines which panel ends up being the back panel.) Response information appears on a panel that can be detached from the brochure without affecting the message of the remainder. The body of the message is then distributed among the remaining panels. (See Appendix A for more information on brochures.)

SELECTING THE MAIN SELLING POINT: TEDLOCK ADVERTISING

In 1989, Dave Tedlock founded Tedlock Advertising and Public Relations in Tucson, Arizona. In designing materials to promote his fledgling business, Tedlock considered what services would be attractive to potential clients, what he himself could offer, and how his skills matched clients' needs. Tedlock also considered how his business could help clients make money, or save money, time, and effort—important appeals in promoting any service or product. All of these considerations helped Tedlock determine his main selling point. Figure 10.2 shows an initial brochure designed by Tedlock and featuring his main selling point: his talents, supported by a diverse background.

The choice of Tedlock's talent as a main selling point was definitely appropriate to the situation. Like many entrepreneurs, Tedlock brought to his new business both educational experience and professional expertise. Although he could not claim a proven track record for his newly formed company, Tedlock could cite his own past accomplishments with other organizations.

By 1994, however, Tedlock's promotional materials *could* claim past success as a main selling point for the firm. Tedlock's brochure now features "Success is Sweet" as a main selling point for his services in marketing research, advertising, media buying, public relations, and promoting specialty items. His promotional materials include the brochure (Figure 10.3a and Figure 10.3b, page 284) and a separate publication noting "14 Reasons for Choos-

Figure 10.2 Initial Brochure for Tedlock Advertising

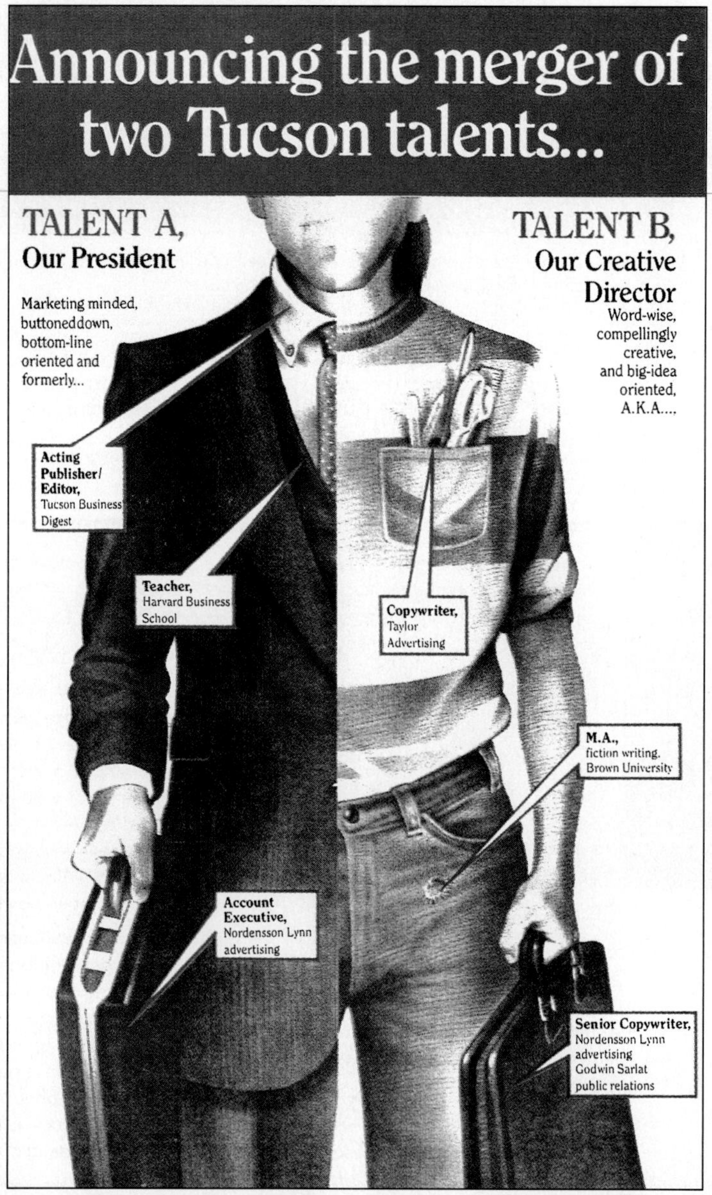

Drawing rendered by John Edwards

Figure 10.3a Current Interior Brochure Panels for Tedlock's Business

Success is Sweet.

Dave Tedlock opened Tedlock Marketing, Advertising and Public Relations in February of 1989. According to the *Arizona Daily Star,* the Tucson economy had just hit the worst of times. However, Tedlock grew steadily over the next few years, becoming one of only three Tucson advertising agencies to be accepted for membership in the American Association of Advertising Agencies (nationally, only 3 of every 10 agencies which apply are accepted for membership). *That's success.*

In a time when employment in advertising agencies and public relations firms has dropped by over 50%, Tedlock has become a leader in the field. *That's success.* More importantly, the clients the agency has served have their own success stories:

Pima County Department of Environmental Quality Clean Air Campaign

For the two years prior to hiring Tedlock, PDEQ paid another firm to create and execute its Clean Air Campaign, "Spare the Air." The results: at the end of two years, a 61% recognition level. Tedlock's "Be An Air Freshener" campaign was far more effective. "Be An Air Freshener" earned a 62% recognition level in half the time, with less than half the budget. *That's success.*

La Hacienda—Miss Teen USA Fashion Show & Auction

In 1994 when the staff at La Hacienda needed to raise money for their foster care program they turned to Tedlock. In just four months, Tedlock helped create and execute the Miss Teen USA Fashion Show & Auction. Tedlock's work on this first-ever fundraiser produced outstanding results. The event: • attracted over 400 participants • was covered by the *Arizona Daily Star, Tucson Citizen,* KVOA/NBC Channel 4 and KOLD/Channel 13 • produced a $15,000+ profit • generated an additional $15,000 gift • created a statewide PSA on foster parenting which features Charlotte Lopez, Miss Teen USA. *That's success.*

Pecan Shell Products, Inc.

To launch its new barbecue briquets Pecan Shell Products, Inc. retained Tedlock in 1994. Tedlock created a marketing plan, logo, bag design and executed product kickoffs in Tucson and Phoenix. The result—stories about Natural Pecan Shell Barbeque Briquets have appeared in the *Arizona Daily Star, Arizona Republic,* KTVK/Channel 3, Phoenix and on KOLD/Channel 13, Tucson. *That's success.*

ing an A.A.A.A. Agency," published by the American Association for Advertising Agencies Inc. of New York, to which Tedlock's firm now belongs. Because Tedlock can now claim success both for himself and for his clients, he shifted his main selling point from his personal talents to his agency's track record. His claims to success invite new clients to share in his successes.

PERSUASIVE MESSAGES

Promotional documents such as Tedlock's brochures clearly have persuasion as their primary purpose. Although all professional documents have a line of argument and most have "to persuade" as one of their purposes, there are also documents in business communication that are specifically labeled persuasive messages. *Persuasive messages*, like negative messages, can use either an inductive (indirect) or a deductive (direct) approach.

Persuasive messages anticipate reader resistance. An important distinguishing feature of persuasive messages is that their primary goal is specifically to overcome a reader's objections. In doing so, they stress that the benefits of what is being proposed or requested outweigh the sources of reader resistance, such as time required, cost, unfamiliarity, the influence of past history or practice, or general resistance to change (see Chapter 9, pages 253–258).

Occasions for persuasive messages include two broad categories: (1) requests for information, action, adjustment, or funding, and (2) efforts to change people's actions. We discuss

Figure 10.3b Current Interior Brochure Panels for Tedlock's Business

7 secrets to our success.

1. Outstanding Service

By listening carefully, working hard, communicating well and following through, we provide outstanding service. Please, ask our clients about our service. We'll be glad you did. So will you.

2. Computer-Aided Design & Production

A state-of-the-art computer network and peripherals, plus special training make our computer-aided graphic design and production capability second to none in this market. From word processing to layout and design, from illustration to scanning and visual enhancements, our clients get the best that technology can deliver. The result: our clients are better informed, get shorter turnaround times and save money.

3. Business-Like Performance

We combine outstanding creative services and professional business practices. For example, our computerized billing program, ADMAN, provides you with billing that is double checked and extremely accurate. And because we pay our vendors so promptly, they give us (and therefore you) excellent service.

4. Selective, Integrated Services

Do you need to conduct market research, launch an intensive public relations effort, advertise or do all three? Because you can get marketing, advertising and public relations from a single source—our firm—you can get exactly what you need, no more, no less. Integrating these services adds muscle to your marketing. And getting them in one place can save you time and money. Another money saver: we'll recommend the services we believe you need, not just what we have to sell.

5. Resources

As a member of the American Association of Advertising Agencies, we have access to over 200 databases as well as the professional services of a research staff. When it comes to resources, the planning and budgeting we do isn't seat-of-the-pants—it's state-of-the-art.

6. Knowledge

We know our business. In marketing, our innovative approaches include, for example, conducting a customer satisfaction survey of the clients of a major law firm. In advertising, experience has taught us some surprising lessons about television versus the Tucson Shopper. And in public relations, we know there's no substitute for our experience with local reporters and editors.

7. Big Ideas

Thomas Edison said genius is 1% inspiration and 99% perspiration. We agree. We sweat a lot (but never in front of you) to come up with all those great ideas that keep our clients asking for more. Let us show you a few samples of our work that are relevant to your needs.

persuasive requests and fund-raising letters as examples of the first category and a collection series as an example of the second. Before discussing these particular messages, we outline a second distinctive feature of persuasive messages in general: the use of the implied reader.

The Implied Reader

Writers find the strategic use of implied readers especially appropriate in situations that involve reader resistance. An implied reader is different from a *real reader*, who is an actual person who exists outside the writing situation. A real reader is the reader that pollsters have in mind when they do demographic surveys to determine specific characteristics of a target audience. An **implied** (or **invoked**) **reader** is an abstraction (sometimes the image of an ideal reader) shaped by the writer and implied within the document. The implied reader is a role that a real reader is invited to play, even though the characteristics of that role may not fit the real reader's attitudes and reactions perfectly.

Writers do not use implied readers because they lack demographic information about their audience. Quite the contrary. Writers need to know quite a bit about their real readers to be able to create an appropriate and attractive role for them to play as implied readers. For example, consider the role invited by the following sentences: "There's a very important reason for you to look at global investing now: *diversification*. Adding a global component to your domestic equity portfolio can be a *smart move*." Not every real reader would find the role of global-investor-with-a-diversified-portfolio immediately compelling.

Figure 10.4 Techniques for Working an Implied Reader into a Document

Direct references, collective references, and demonstratives all attribute qualities to the implied reader, but do so differently. In addition, each uses different types of pronouns as referents.

Questions and comparisons allude to knowledge needed by or possessed by the implied reader.

Negations and overjustifications involve objections or doubts attributed to the implied reader. Negations and overjustifications are particularly appropriate when you anticipate strong reader resistance.

DEVICE	DEFINITION, EXAMPLE, EXPLANATION
Direct references	Refer to specific qualities the implied reader is supposed to possess, or address the implied reader as "you." [*Example: A persuasive request that opens with "Dear Friend of Homeless Children" directly establishes the implied reader as a friend among other "caring people" concerned about the homeless. The reference thus attributes specific qualities to the reader with such a salutation.*]
Collective references	Indirectly attribute a quality to a reader using the pronouns "we" and "our." [*Example: A persuasive request for support from a State Capital Funding Project that opens with "WE HAVE A COMMON GOAL . . . maintaining the excellence of state and local services in our city."*]
Demonstratives	Use "this," "that," or "those" to attribute qualities to an implied reader. [*Example: A promotional letter for a trade publication that suggests the implied reader is one of "those": "Those who take advantage of government programs, available credit, and current market information to buy out their neighbors will keep on expanding."*]
Questions	Pose rhetorical questions that originate neither with a writer's persona (or self-image presented in the text) nor with a specified actual reader. [*Example: A promotional letter that asks, "What accounts for the success of The Business Handbook?" immediately after announcing the Handbook's forthcoming second edition.*] (Because the writer presumably knows the answer to this question, the question signals an implied reader. The question arises from this implied reader's curiosity about the book's apparent success and attributes interest in such matters to this reader.)
Comparisons	Use comparisons or analogies to signal an implied reader. [*Example: An advertisement that states that Zud works better than Ajax to clean sinks.*] (Because the second term of a comparison is usually assumed to be better known than the first, a comparison helps paint a picture of the implied reader's world. In this case the comparison implies that the implied reader knows how Ajax works.)
Negations	Counter an implied reader's objections or preconceptions. [*Example: A fund raising letter that states, "Your sponsorship gifts will only be used to meet the needs of your sponsored child."*] (Such a statement attempts to counter an objection implicitly attributed to the implied reader: that perhaps some of the donated funds will be used for administrative or other purposes and will not directly benefit the needy child.
Overjustifications	Refer to and allay the implied reader's apprehensions or prejudices. [*Example: A cover letter for a survey that opens with melodramatic wording and uses capitalization for emphasis: "I know that you must gasp in despair when you get a request to fill out YET ANOTHER questionnaire."*] (It is an overstatement to anticipate that a questionnaire would result in a "gasp of despair" from any reader. To deal with this implied reader's anticipated [over]reaction, the author promises that the questionnaire will be short and includes a self-addressed, stamped envelope.)

For example, a real reader who was facing foreclosure or who was struggling to pay this semester's college tuition might reject the role right away—it doesn't fit. Even real readers who had cash to invest but who preferred investing in land and gold rather than in stocks and bonds or who made a practice of donating their discretionary funds to charity might refuse the role. Real readers with a domestic equity portfolio and with money to spend, however, might be willing to play along and, in so doing, become persuaded that the writer's particular global fund is the one to try. To use implied readers effectively, you need to consider the real audience and make the role you imagine for the implied reader truly attractive to that audience.

You can probably see the advantage of creating a cooperative reader within your document if you anticipate that the real reader will be resistant to your message. Although you may use many techniques to construct an implied reader, you should be aware of those

Figure 10.5 Excerpt Creating a Caring and Generous Implied Reader

This excerpt attributes qualities through direct reference and comparison ("like").

> . . . until Soh-ra can have a permanent family, she will receive care through our agency from people who love her. That can happen only because people like you care and contribute the money that makes it possible to meet her needs every day. Her food, clothing, shelter, medical treatment and the staff who care for her are all gifts made possible by you and people like you.

particularly appropriate to business writing, especially to writing persuasive requests. In Figure 10.4 (page 285), seven common devices for creating an implied reader are named, defined, and (as necessary) explained.

In using implied readers, writers *attribute qualities* to the audience that would be desirable in their real readers on a particular occasion and for a specific message. For example, if you as a writer were writing materials to solicit donations to support homeless children, you would create an implied reader that possessed the caring requisite to giving to such a fund. Consider, for example, Figure 10.5, excerpted from an appeal by Holt International Children's Services. The chance that the reader will play the role written here is increased by the nature of the real audience. The mailing list for this appeal consists of people who have had past contact with Holt International or a history of giving to similar causes, such as the Heart Connection (an organization enhancing the lives of children living with cancer) or Habitat for Humanity International (an organization providing low-cost family homes in low-income neighborhoods).

In using implied readers, writers also *allude to knowledge and positions* that their audience must have to cooperate with the message. For example, the cover of a direct mailing from the National Rifle Association of America (NRA) states: "Sarah Brady and Handgun Control, Inc. **don't** want you to open this letter." The reference to Sarah Brady in this statement works like a comparison to establish what the audience knows (who Sarah Brady is and what her connection is to gun control) and what the audience's attitude is ("I'm *not* in agreement with Sarah Brady and Handgun Control, Inc., and therefore I *am* going to open this letter"). This cover eliminates real readers who may be on NRA's extensive mailing list even though they *do* believe in gun control. The statement on the envelope also defines the context necessary for the remaining readers—loyal gun rights advocates—to play along.

Finally, using implied readers allows writers to *counter anticipated objections or doubts*. For example, when a sales message promoting a computer software package reads,

> No, you do not have to be a computer whiz to use RoboHELP. Even novice programmers can easily build Help files from scratch.

the writer is countering a potential objection by readers that the advanced tool designed for constructing "elegant Help files" is just too sophisticated to be practical for anyone except an expert. The statement allays any doubts the real reader might have about being able to use the software easily and effectively.

Persuasive Requests

Persuasive requests usually use an inductive approach that is traditionally called the AIDA plan of organization. The **AIDA plan (Attention, Interest, Desire, Action)** incorporates many of the same functions as the claim-warrant-grounds sequence of an argument:

- The *attention* section establishes that the subject of the message is in itself either useful or interesting or both. (When the attention section contains the claim, the message straddles the fence between an inductive and a deductive approach; see Figure 10.10 on page 290.)
- The *interest* section establishes the subject's relevance to the reader. In connecting the subject and the reader, it functions like a warrant.
- The *desire* section enhances the reader's sense of need and willingness to take action. It presents grounds for the claim.
- The *action* section urges and facilitates the reader's response. It makes the claim or reinforces any earlier claim.

Figure 10.6 shows a persuasive request using the AIDA plan.

You can use the AIDA pattern when writing informal persuasive requests that are internal to the corporation or a particular department and that deal with social events. Figure 10.7 (page 288) shows an internal notice encouraging employees to be members of a planning

CONTEXT

Acting in his capacity as a public relations consultant, the writer in Figure 10.6, Dave Tedlock, is requesting that a local television station broadcast a story that informs the public about mental health information available through the Tucson Psychiatric Institute. Sandy Tedlock, an attorney in private practice, who voluntarily edited the informational booklet to be mentioned in the public service announcement, is willing to discuss the booklet's availability and benefits on camera. Since networks are required by the FCC to devote a percentage of their broadcast day to public service stories and announcements, the resistance Dave anticipates does not really involve the request for air time itself. Instead, Tedlock is concerned that the station manager will not find this particular service worthy of mention. In this request, Tedlock attempts to influence a reader's behavior.

Figure 10.6 Persuasive Request Using AIDA

Dave uses an implied reader who "cares about the kids" as an ***attention*** *getter. The mention of* ***free*** *information is also an attention getter. In this case, the attention getter provides the warrant as well: caring people like the reader are interested in telling about the information the writer has to offer.*

Dave increases ***interest*** *in the request by establishing the expertise of the available spokesperson. Having an expert spokesperson also makes the TV person's job easier and adds to her willingness to fulfill the request.* ***Interest*** *is thus combined with an element of* ***desire.***

Dave then enhances the need to get this information to the children and thus introduces a different aspect of ***desire.***

Dave returns to the expertise factor and thus reinforces ***desire.***

The close mentions the ***action*** *to be taken for the first time and does so implicitly as part of a thank-you. The close compliments the reader, since the writer assumes the reader (as a caring person) will be doing some sort of story.*

TEDLOCK
ADVERTISING & PUBLIC RELATIONS

February 3, 1993

Patty Weiss
KVOA-TV
P.O. Box 5188
Tucson, AZ 85703

Dear Patty:

We know how much you care about the kids of Pima County. Here's a chance for them to get valuable information for free. The enclosed booklet, Where Do I Stand?—A Guide to Separation and Divorce for Children and Teenagers, is available **free** at Tucson Psychiatric Institute.

Sandra Tedlock, the editor, is available to go on camera and talk about the book and about kids and divorce. She's appeared on television before and on talk radio shows and does well on camera, giving short answers.

Where Do I Stand? is unique. The law in Pima County is different from other counties and other states. No other book explains divorce law in Pima County to kids. Getting this information to kids is important, because:

- During divorce, parents don't necessarily fully understand the law themselves, so explaining it to their children can be difficult.
- Given the stress parents are under, they may not communicate very well with their children about divorce and the law.
- Children and teenagers need to be empowered by having this information available for their own reference.
- By giving parents a way to explain the law to their children, the booklet **also** encourages parents to share their feelings with their children.

Tedlock is one of only a dozen or so lawyers who are members of the American Academy of Matrimonial Lawyers. She has also been certified by the State Bar of Arizona as a specialist in domestic relations law, and she is the former chair of the Family Law Section of the State Bar of Arizona.

Thanks again for whatever kind of story you can do!

Sincerely yours,

Dave Tedlock

DT:sj
Enclosure

Figure 10.7 Informal Persuasive Request to an Internal Audience Using AIDA

*The header is an **attention** getter. The first paragraph contains an appeal to an implied reader who would have an **interest** in the event. The appeal plus the implied group membership serves as a **warrant**. The **desire** to participate is implied by the idea that the committee is the party. The close indicates what **action** should (and should not) be taken.*

We Need Your Corpses (or Bodies)

The Halloween Committee Meets Tonight for the First Time This Year. You, as an esteemed member of the Professional Writing Staff, are encouraged to attend.

Meet the rest of us at Dugan's Deli at 6:30 p.m. (Monday, October 7) for a Beer, a Few Big Laughs, and a Bit of Haggling over Setting Up This Year's Howl.

So Be Part of the Month-Long Social Event That Precedes the Big Party. Be a Member of the Halloween Committee. We Cherish and Celebrate New Members. We Don't Eat Them.

Now Stop Hunting For Grammar Errors on This Memo and Plan to Meet Us at Dugan's Tonight.

ETHICS

CHEERS OR JEERS—THE ETHICS OF JUNK MAIL APPEALS

"I will choose what enters me, what becomes flesh of my flesh. Without choice, no politics, no ethics lives. I am not your cornfield, not your uranium mine, not your calf for fattening, not your cow for milking. You may not use me as your factory. Priests and legislators do not hold shares in my womb or my mind. This is my body. If I give it to you I want it back. My life is a non-negotiable demand." —Marge Piercy

"As President, Bill Clinton is the sworn defender of the United States Constitution. But he recently said:

We can't be so fixated about our desire to preserve the rights of ordinary Americans to legitimately own handguns and rifles that we are unable to think about reality.

The reality here is that Bill Clinton wants to rip the Second Amendment right out of the Constitution."

"Please consider giving the shelter, the diapers, the food, the caring arms that will reach out to homeless children. That's what your gift can do this Christmas."

"[We do not] know, any of us (yet), just how our lives and survival may rely on the survival of hackberry trees and piping plovers, Indiana bats, wild orchids, golden-cheeked warblers, needle-and-thread grass, an insignificant little fish called the Panaca Big Spring spinedace (*Lepidomeda mollispinis prantensis*), or most of the tens of thousands of other rare living things now thriving on the lands we care for.

But you and I both know we *must* treasure that diversity of nature—and *we're losing ground.*"

If you are a pro-choice, anti-Clinton, and anti–gun control person whose heartstrings are tugged by homeless children and endangered species, you are apt to be cheering after you read the above paragraphs. If, however, you are a pro-life, pro-Clinton, and pro–gun control person who believes charities spend most of their money on administration and feels equally turned off by environmentalists, then you are more likely to be jeering than cheering.

What are the ethical issues raised by using heartstrings to loosen purse strings? When fund-raisers test different approaches, they sometimes test the effectiveness of the appeal rather than the quality of the information. For example, in one campaign, the appeal featured one hungry child and suggested that funds would feed hungry children, when in reality the organization makes grants to other organizations. Another test campaign centered on a suicide note left by an impoverished 12-year-old and included the phrase "one less mouth to feed." The solicitation neglected to mention that the youth died over a decade ago.

Charities might argue that emotional appeals are ethical because an appeal's success allows the organization to fulfill its intent, which ultimately is to feed hungry children. The success of fund-raising is measured in cash, not in the ethics of the approach. Although Kenneth Anderson would rather that the ethics of an appeal be measured by society's willingness to take responsibility for the conditions that make the appeal for cash necessary, the consensus is that direct mail works. For example, the NRA has a huge building in Washington, D.C., funded by member contributions, from which to launch its lobbying efforts.

committee for an annual social event. Like Figure 10.6, Figure 10.7 uses an implied reader in the attention portion of the request.

Fund-Raising Letters

Fund-raising letters, considered by some to be sales messages and by others to be persuasive requests, often make use of an implied reader. Implied readers are particularly appropriate to this type of letter because a basic strategy behind such letters is vicarious participation. Just as readers can assume roles implied for them by writers, so too can readers making donations assume roles working on projects that they never personally see or actually spend time completing.

Figure 10.8 (pages 289–290) shows excerpts from a four-page fund-raising letter that invites readers to help support a cause. Part of a direct-mail package (see pages 294–296), the letter uses a strong emotional appeal to encourage the reader's investment in the problem and an implied reader to invoke participation in the solution.

CONTEXT

As noted in Chapter 8, The Nature Conservancy is a nonprofit organization which uses monetary donations to buy land for nature preserves and often operates on a matching funds basis. Shown in Figure 10.8 are pages 1 and 4 (page 290) of a fund-raising letter about sandhill cranes. The final appeal in this letter can be found in the fine print at the bottom of page 4 (not shown): "The most recent Nature Conservancy financial report filed with the Department of State may be obtained by writing to: New York State, Department of State, Office of Charities Registration, Albany, New York 12231, or The Nature Conservancy, 1800 North Kent Street, Arlington, Virginia 22209. If you like to read financial statements, this one is a beauty. We're rather vain about it. Do ask." This appeal directly establishes the integrity of the writer, who can demonstrate fiscal responsibility. It also appeals to the reader to share group membership with the many others who have already donated.

Figure 10.8a Page 1 from a Fund-Raising Letter with Implied Reader

*The salutation offers the implied reader the role of "investor." (The ogling bird is the **attention** getter.) The phrase "catches your throat" implies a reader that is moved by the sight of cranes in the wild.*

*The letter establishes **interest** on the basis of past success.*

The letter anticipates a conservative implied reader who might object to more militant approaches to preserving the environment.

*Pages 2 and 3 (not shown) increase the reader's **desire** to "invest" with an invitation to visit other impressively described Conservancy sites and to receive an attractive magazine published by the organization.*

*The last paragraph (Figure 10.8b, page 290) directly states the **action:** go to the mailbox and send a check. The implied reader does so and is thus now a "wise fellow investor in nest eggs." The crane theme informs the entire direct mail package pictured on the next page.*

Nancy C. Mackinnon
Membership Director

The Nature Conservancy

1800 North Kent Street
Arlington, Virginia 22209

Dear Investor:

The bug-eyed bird on our envelope who's ogling you with such distemper has a point. He's a native American sandhill crane and you may be sitting on top of one of his nesting sites.

As he sees it, every time our human species has drained a marsh, and plowed it or built a city on it, since 1492 or so—there went the neighborhood. It's enough to make you both a bit edgy.

So give us $10 for his nest egg and we'll see that a nice, soggy spot—just the kind he and his mate need to fashion a nest and put an egg in it—is reserved for the two of them, undisturbed, for keeps. Only $10. (Watch those cranes come in to land, just once, and you're paid back. Catches at your throat.) Then the cranes can relax, and so can you. A bit.

How will we reserve that incubator with your $10?
Not by campaigning or picketing or suing.

We'll just BUY the nesting ground.

That's the unique and expensive and effective way The Nature Conservancy goes about its nonprofit business. We're as dead serious about hanging on to nature's precarious balance as the more visible and vocal conservation groups. But our thing is to let money do our talking.

And we buy a whopping lot of land: starting with 60 acres of New York's Mianus River Gorge in 1951 (now 395 acres), we have protected 2,000,000 acres—about the area of Rhode Island and Delaware. The plots are spotted coast to coast and from Canada deep into the Caribbean, 3,157 of them sized from a quarter of an acre to hundreds of square miles.

All of it is prime real estate, if you're a crane or a bass or a sweet pepperbush or a redwood. Or a toad or a turtle.

Collections

Collection letters try to change the behavior of the reader, urging payment when payment has not been forthcoming. In so doing, they may find it useful to create an implied reader who, for example, is "more than willing" to pay the bill. Collection letters usually appear in a series, and their nature and the appeals they use depend on what stage they address.

Figure 10.8b Page 4 from a Fund-Raising Letter with Implied Reader

– 4 –

Enclose a check for $10 in the return envelope (more, if you can spare it). NOTE that it's tax-deductible. Mail the form. Go.

Thank you, and welcome!, dear wise fellow investor in nest eggs. For your fanfare, listen for the wondrous stentorian call of that sandhill crane.*

Sincerely,

Nancy C Mackinnon

Nancy C. Mackinnon
Membership Director

*We borrowed his picture from Country Journal magazine where he illustrated an article about the International Crane Foundation of Baraboo, Wisconsin. The photo is by brave Cary Wolinsky. And we don't actually know if the crane is as upset as he looks. Maybe he's smiling? Certainly he will if, when he leaves the Foundation, his first motel stop has been reserved with your $10.

A collection series moves from showing confidence that the reader will pay to emphasizing the consequences of nonpayment. A collection series thus represents a range of message types (Figure 10.9). The routine request and direct request both assume reader cooperation, while the persuasive request and the negative message assume reader resistance. Even though the series itself contains different types of messages, as a whole it represents a single persuasive strategy aimed at collecting the money owed while maintaining goodwill with the customer.

Figure 10.10 shows a collection letter that suggests an alternative payment arrangement. Even though the letter is a persuasive request, it contains a lot of

Figure 10.9 Collection Series Showing Range of Message Types

ROUTINE REQUEST	DIRECT REQUEST	PERSUASIVE REQUEST	NEGATIVE MESSAGE
The original bill. →	The second notice requesting payment or a reminder that the bill is past due. (Form letters or copies of the original bill are often used at this stage.) →	Letters that follow the second notice, starting with personalized letters urging payment and offering to negotiate a new payment schedule and ending with an urgent notice conveying the seriousness of nonpayment. →	Letter threatening legal action or informing the reader of other consequences in effect due to nonpayment: no further credit given, access to services restricted or denied, etc.

Figure 10.10 Collection Letter (Persuasive Request) Suggesting an Alternative Payment Schedule

A history of correspondence allows the use of the first name and leads into the reminder of the fee due.

The second paragraph appeals to the reader's sense of fair play. "I'm sure you'll agree" is a direct reference to an implied reader who will agree.

Dear Mary:

You have received a number of notices during the past several weeks from us regarding the materials fee for the arts workshop you took this summer. The fee, which amounts to $65.00, is past due.

Certainly, being a part of the arts community is personally rewarding, and I'm sure you'll agree that participation is at its best when all members of the community share not only their talents but also their responsibilities.

If you are finding it difficult at this time to pay the full amount of the cost of the materials that you used this summer, may we suggest that you contact us regarding a revised payment schedule? Please call us this week between 9:00 a.m. and 5:00 p.m. at 555-ARTS to discuss our options.

Sincerely,

Figure 10.11 Persuasive Requests Using the Overall Pattern for Persuasive Messages

PERSUASIVE REQUESTS: AIDA PATTERN FOR PERSUASIVE MESSAGES

Attention opening: Establishes that subject is of interest, importance, or both

- It's that time again! It has already been a year since Roosevelt had its first formal exhibition of student talent. Thanks to many volunteers, we were able to present a professional showing of work by each of Roosevelt's student artists. The purpose of this memo is to fill you in on exhibition details and ask for volunteers to help ready the work for display.
- Beware. You are about to be robbed. In the coming months, right before our eyes, long-distance telephone companies plan to commit one of the biggest, boldest consumer ripoffs in history. Their "take"? *More than $6.5 billion.*
- Should Colonel Oliver North be jailed or given a medal of honor? Do you want to tell your own Congressman and the Congressmen and Senators on the TV hearings what you think?

Interest section: Shows the connection between the subject and the reader

- For years liberal groups and the welfare lobby have successfully pushed self-serving government programs and wasteful social spending. As a result, taxpayers like you are being robbed blind to keep our bloated government afloat. I'm sure you would rather have $1,488 for yourself and your family than see it squandered by some government bureaucrat.
- All the camps are planned by professionals, and all our staff go through two weeks of intensive staff training. Some camps last three days, others six, and all are overnight. Whichever camp you choose, you can rest assured that your child will be learning and having fun. The facilities at both the 4-H Center and Pine Bluff consist of sleeping cabins with electricity and nearby bathrooms. Meals are planned by a dietician and delivered to the sites.

Desire section: Enhances reader's willingness and need to take action

- How can you help? Volunteers are needed to help ready the work for display. No experience is needed! We need people to measure, cut, label, tape, glue, and hang artwork. All materials will be provided (including a brand new Logan mat cutter).
- There are some items that are not within the Physical Plant's guidelines of custodial duties. These items include watering plants, moving material on desks or windowsills for dusting, relocating furniture for individual needs, or cleaning, dusting, or vacuuming personal items, including area rugs. If cleaning is desired where personal items do not allow access, your removal of these items will allow the cleaning to take place.

Action close: Reinforces claim and facilitates action

- As your means permit, please share your blessings with a student this year. A response card and postage paid envelope are enclosed for your convenience. We will continue to make awards as resources become available, so by sending a gift today you may significantly affect a student's future.
- The following dates and times [refers to tear-off form at bottom of memo] have been arranged as work sessions. If you are able to come for any of these times, please sign your name(s) in the appropriate space and return by FRIDAY, JANUARY 7. Thank you in advance for your willingness to participate. Your help will insure a successful project.

buffering. For example, the first sentence, which serves as an attention getter, both buffers and forecasts the bad news, which immediately follows. The letter actually straddles the line between inductive and deductive organization, since there is a modest attempt to establish common ground (a shared history) but, at the same time, no attempt to exclude the bad news from appearing up front in the opening paragraph. (The collection letters from Dr. Wass's office, Chapter 5, Figures 5.17 through 5.19, represent further examples of letters that can appear in a collection series.)

Figure 10.11 summarizes the standard components of persuasive requests. The pattern represented in Figure 10.11 is used in persuasive messages that use an indirect plan.

SALES MESSAGES

Attempts to influence a buyer's *purchasing behavior* are most often called sales messages, rather than persuasive requests, although the two types of messages share many characteristics. Sales letters also conventionally use the AIDA plan of organization. In examining sales messages, we cover both sales letters and direct mailings.

A distinguishing feature of sales messages is that their main idea emphasizes the main selling point of the goods or services being promoted in the communication. As the Tedlock Advertising brochures indicate (Figures 10.2 and 10.3), this main selling point is tied to a primary claim that the communicator can support at a particular point in time about the goods or services being promoted. Several questions can help you to determine the main selling point:

- What is special about the product or service? What are its distinctive features?
- What makes these special features special? (How does the product or service compare with others? How does the product or service relate to what has happened in the past? Does it represent new thinking, new knowledge, or innovative technology? Does the solution it offers differ significantly from other solutions in the past? Is the solution a marked improvement?)
- For whom will these features be special? What are these potential buyers or users really looking for? In other words, what do potential clients need, what do they want, and how does the product or service address their needs and wants?
- What are the major benefits of the product or service? How do these match up with the needs and wants of the potential clientele?

Sales Letters

Sales letters characteristically have dramatic attention getters and appeal to a range of needs. The use of an implied reader suggests in itself a number of alternatives for gaining the attention of your audience. Other devices for gaining attention range from incorporating narrative

Figure 10.12 Attention-Getting Openings for Sales Letters (and Persuasive Requests)

STRATEGY	EXAMPLE
Ask a question. Pose a puzzle.	In England, *Granta* is read by more people than any other literary magazine in the history of the 20th century, but its editors don't like literature.
Cite statistics or data.	According to recent surveys, the No. 1 concern of university alumni today is *career networking.*
Create an analogy.	If I did it, you can do it, too! You can create a beautiful home and the elegant lifestyle to go with it. I grew up the oldest child in a family of eight with very modest means . . . [account continues for two paragraphs; the letter eventually connects (through analogy) the writer's experience with that projected for the reader].
Emphasize a problem, need, benefit, or solution.	As you may know, the new tax law will phase out deductions for consumer loan interest, except for interest secured by a home mortgage, such as a home equity loan. I want to invite you to apply for an American Federal Homeowner's Equity Loan—at a *special introductory rate of only 5.9%* through April 30, 19xx.
Forecast important information to come.	No beating around the bush. We'd love you to try your own personal subscription to the *Chronicle.* And here's an exceptional offer to persuade you to do so.
Include interesting details or facts.	The bug-eyed bird on our envelope who's ogling you with such distemper has a point. He's the native American sandhill crane and you may be sitting on top of one of his nesting sites.
Provide a free sampler or the opportunity to obtain one.	We've made our list and checked it twice, and you're on it! Your gift from us is a designer notepad. Just order $25.00 worth of gift items, and the notepad is yours.
Quote memorable phrases, statements, or passages.	"The arts are the universal language of mankind." Jane Alexander, head of the National Endowment for the Arts "Do students respond positively to shared inquiry? More than positively. I would say gloriously." Larry Yoder, Lenoir-Rhyne College
Tell a story or relate an anecdote.	In January 1982, in Los Angeles, Tommy Lasorda, who previously knew nothing about Valpo, enthusiastically accepted my invitation to speak at a Valparaiso University Award Dinner honoring Bill Buhler, a Valpo alumnus, a trainer for the Los Angeles Dodgers, and the dean of all trainers in the major leagues. [The next two paragraphs finish the narrative.]

to constructing an analogy, from citing statistics to relating an anecdote, from asking a question to quoting a memorable statement, from simply using good specific detail to providing a sample of the product. Figure 10.12 summarizes some of these effective attention-getting devices.

Within the body of your message, you can appeal to a variety of reader needs. The psychologist Abraham Maslow outlined a well-known hierarchy of needs, ranging from basic physiological needs to abstract needs involving self-actualization. Figure 10.13 identifies Maslow's needs in descending order and shows examples of these needs as they might be addressed in sales documents. Appealing to these needs is one way to appeal to the feelings and the beliefs of the reader (see Chapter 4). Audience analysis is important in determining which needs and interests are most likely to be important to particular readers.

Figure 10.14 (page 294) shows a sales letter using the AIDA pattern with a dramatic attention getter and an implicit appeal to the basic human need for affordable shelter.

Humor in Sales Messages

Humor can be an attention getter or can be used to maintain reader interest in sales messages.

But use of humor in any business message can be a risky strategy. What is funny varies from culture to culture and from audience to audience. In addition, jokes that may work in informal messages might call into question the credibility of the communicator in formal

Figure 10.13 Maslow's Hierarchy of Needs in the Body of Sales and Promotional Documents

MASLOW'S NEEDS	EXAMPLES OF POSSIBLE APPLICATIONS
Self-actualization: creativity, fulfillment, self-realization, vocation, wisdom	You'll be inspired by stories in our "On the Line" section about the unsung Americans who are making social change every day across this country . . . restoring the environment . . . revising the labor movement . . . resisting U.S. intervention abroad. . . . [This also has an appeal to esteem, social values, and safety and security issues.] CBD Weekly Release gives you the means to respond quickly to new contract opportunities. You can plot sales strategies before your competition even knows the contract exists.
Esteem and status: recognition in community, respect, self-worth, uniqueness	Specifically, to be eligible to use the Energy Star logo for marketing purposes, manufacturers must produce PCs and monitors that consume less than 30 watts each in the standby mode. The program was expanded in 1993 to include printers. [This also, with its concern for the environment, has an appeal to survival.] I'm delighted to inform you of a special honor! [opener] An Associate membership in The National Museum of Women in the Arts has been reserved in your name. Yes, an Associate Membership in the first—and only—major museum in the world dedicated to celebrating the stunning achievements of women artists, past, present, and future.
Social values: affection, friendship, ties to group	Bicyclists of all ages and skill levels are encouraged to participate. This is a community-wide, family-oriented event. A special registration fee will be offered to families. Our goal is to be a socially responsible company. One that supports the same worthy causes you do.
Safety and security: personal confidence, protection from enemies, stability	Living Choices is a rider that allows you to receive all or a portion of your life insurance benefits before your death if you are diagnosed with a terminal illness and have a life expectancy of 12 months or less. This is important to you because medical care has increased dramatically in cost. These expenses associated with care required during terminal illness can wipe out a family's assets in a very short period of time. [This also has an appeal to basic survival of the beneficiary's family.] As a Chase Gold Visa card member, you'll enjoy an initial credit line of up to $10,000. How's that for buying power? [In addition to appealing to personal confidence, this also has an appeal to status and esteem.]
Basic survival: air, food, water, sleep, shelter	Choose the directory that's right for you and join us in making a choice for the environment. [This also has an appeal to group membership.] Each day they [children helped by the Children's Defense Fund] face crime, parental drug addiction, hunger and a hundred other obstacles that come with growing up poor in America. [This also has an appeal to safety and security of the children.]

Figure 10.14 Sales Letter Using AIDA

Dear [insert owner's name here]:

YOUR PROPERTY TAXES ARE GOING UP!

The Tax Assessor has raised your property value! So you'll be paying more tax in 1994. We can change that. Here's why:

- **Experience Counts!**
  With us, you benefit from 23 years of success in tax appeals—more than any other firm. Since 1970 we've been developing the most knowledgeable, experienced staff in Arizona. If there's a way to get a reduction on your property valuation—**and your tax**—we'll know what it is.
- **Local Market Knowledge**
  Unlike many firms, we're headquartered in Tucson. So we know the local real estate market from first-hand experience. And market knowledge is a key to the most effective tax appeal, and the lowest possible taxes.
- **Detailed Analysis of Your Property**
  Usually the assessor values your property on a generic basis. We do the exact opposite. To get you the biggest possible tax savings, we study your property in detail—the way only a local, highly experienced firm can.
- **Market-Wise Data Base**
  Through our mainframe computer data base and analysis, we've compiled the most comprehensive real estate valuation information available anywhere. Our system gives us essential evidence in getting you the lowest possible valuation.
- **Number One For a Reason**
  We're #1 in the total dollar value of property taxes appealed. We're #1 because we get what you and all other property owners want—*results.*

For details about our company and your property taxes, see the latest copy of our newsletter, *Property Lines.* You'll want to choose our firm for five key reasons: experience, local market knowledge, detailed analyses, state-of-the-art data bases, and proven results.

Our fee is based on how much money we save you—that's a great incentive for us, and another savings for you.

For details on how we can lower your taxes, call us today.

TO SAVE CALL 555-6270 or 1-800-555-9635.

1994 appeals must be filed by December 31, 1993!

There are no extensions!

So call us now, in Tucson at 555-6270 or toll free, 1-800-555-9635. We'll assign a specialist to begin working on your property tax appeal immediately.

documents. Humor is also expected in certain situations, like the opening of an after-dinner speech at a business convention, but unexpected—and sometimes downright dangerous—in others, like a letter denying credit.

Figure 10.15 shows a news release excerpt that attempts to use humor in announcing a reduction in the price of airline tickets. The success of the humor in this release depends almost entirely on who is reading the message.

Direct Mail

Persuasive messages and sales messages can be conveyed not only in single letters, but also in direct-mail packages. **Direct-mail packages** consist of unsolicited sales materials sent out to consumers on computerized mailing lists. These packages have several standard components:

- the outside envelope, which can feature attention getters or even sales information
- the sales letter
- supplementary material, which might feature a brochure, a free sample, a small gift
- response material, which includes the means for ordering or subscribing and a return envelope (sometimes the outside envelope can be converted into a return mailer)

Figure 10.16 on page 296 describes the contents of two direct-mail packages that are soliciting membership in national charitable organizations, the National Museum of Women and the Nature Conservancy (excerpts of the fund-raising letter for this package were shown in Figure 10.8).

Figure 10.15 News Release Excerpt on Price Reduction That Uses Humor

NORTHWEST
AIRLINES

NEWSrelease

Northwest Airlines, Inc. 612 726-2331
5101 Northwest Drive
St. Paul, MN 55111-3034

FOR IMMEDIATE RELEASE January 5, 1993

DON'T CRY DADDY—
NORTHWEST HAS SPECIAL "ELVIS FARES"
TO MEMPHIS

MEMPHIS, Tenn. — (Jan. 5) — It's not "One Broken Heart for Sale" but rather airline tickets to Memphis. Fans will think they've found their "Good Luck Charm" when they take advantage of special "Elvis Fares" Northwest is offering to celebrate Elvis's 59th birthday on Jan. 8. Even a "Poor Boy" can "Follow His Dream" for as little as $39 round-trip to Memphis from cities throughout the United States.

Whether they live at home or the "Heartbreak Hotel," passengers must take the early Saturday morning flights to Memphis on Jan. 8 and "Return to Sender" later that day. Tickets can be purchased in advance or "Until It's Time for You to Go." All "Hound Dogs" should be placed in a kennel. "Don't Ask Me Why," but tickets are non-refundable.

"Passengers just 'Can't Help Falling in Love' with these fares," said Michael E. Levine, executive vice president—marketing. "'Suspicious Minds' will end up 'Crying in the Chapel' if they pass up this King-sized travel bargain."

(more)

WORLDWIDE RELIABILITY KLM NORTHWEST

"'Hard Hearted Women,' 'U.S. Males' and 'Kissin' Cousins' will be flocking to Graceland for Elvis' birthday," said, Carolyn Mears, sales director for Graceland. "Visitors usually get 'All Shook Up' with the city's other music-oriented attractions such as Sun Studios where Elvis recorded early hits like 'That's Alright Mama' and 'Blue Moon Kentucky,' and Beale Street, birthplace of the Blues."

Northwest, the official airline of Graceland, and its regional airline partners, together with KLM Royal Dutch Airlines form the world's first global airline alliance and the third largest airline system, serving more than 380 cities in 81 countries on six continents.

###

(For more information contact Northwest Media Relations at 612-555-2331.)

TECHNOLOGY

INTERNET ADS—A BIG NO-NO?

The Internet, which connects well over 5 million users across the globe, seems like a natural place for market expansion, since it allows advertisers access to over 5 million intelligent people with disposable income. But the Internet is also a realm governed only by a loose set of user-defined customs, one of which is an extreme hatred of advertising. An Arizona lawyer who posted an ad for his services, for example, received thousands of hate messages, hundreds of crank phone calls, and several death threats. (He also received numerous queries about his services, however, and says that he'll advertise on the Internet again.)

Even though old-timers tend to see the Internet as their private domain, which it *was* back when the Internet was first put together by universities and the government, the number of new users on the Internet is growing rapidly (15 percent per month by some accounts). The Internet is increasingly being run by businesses that need advertising to recoup their expenses for on-line services, like Prodigy and America On-Line, or by companies that are in the business of installing fiber optic cables for the very purpose of expanding the information highway. The Internet is no longer a private club, and it seems inevitable that advertising will expand despite the howls of protest from some long-time users. It seems equally inevitable that users will adjust to the change.

MULTICULTURAL

THE IMPORTANCE OF BEING "POP" IN INTERNATIONAL MARKETING

In addition to the "four P's" (product, price, place, and promotion), "pop," or quick response to the customer, is a fifth key marketing tool for success in business sales. It's the action-right-now quality that wins contracts and sells products all over the world. It's the tone that pervades a company and gives the prospective client the feeling that a firm really cares about solving his or her problems. It's answering the mail, today!

Kim Dae-Waon, the political and economic editor and deputy managing editor of *Cholla Ilbo,* the local newspaper of Chonju, Korea, visited the United States in 1989. Commenting on "pop," Kim revealed a common Korean viewpoint that when a businessperson from his country calls a company in the United States, often to purchase something, the U.S. company is not always as responsive as it could be. "Even in your restaurants," he said, "no one seems to care. There is just not a feeling of urgency or responsiveness in America."

Direct-mail packages are also used to sell goods and services. An interesting development in such packages is the use of cellophane wraps to display samples of the goods being marketed and to contain sales materials, which are stuffed in scattered fashion inside the wrap. Consider, for example, the direct mail package for Easy Home Repair (Figure 10.17), a modular collection of informational cards that instruct readers how to do different home maintenance tasks. Easy Home Repair, like Book-of-the-Month Club, sends you a collection of cards per month if you sign up.

In direct-mail packages, the main selling point is complemented by an overall theme for the package itself. This theme can be expressed in a variety of ways. For example, the Nature Conservancy package pictures its own logo—a green oak leaf—on the envelope, on the letterhead of the two enclosed letters, and on the application form. The enclosed bumper sticker is the oak leaf logo also. In addition, for this particular campaign, the sandhill crane, which appears on the envelope, provides the thematic focus and is featured in the various enclosures (Figure 10.18).

The main theme for a direct-mail package provides the same type of unity that the main selling point provides for a single persuasive or sales message.

Direct mailings are a natural part of fund-raising efforts. A direct mailing from Amnesty International USA, an organization "helping prisoners and others threatened with torture or death," uses various strategies to drive home its theme that a basic need for survival drives its cause. The package, described in Figure 10.19 on page 298, uses fundamental materials and colors to distinguish itself from its cousins promoting merchandise and other products.

Direct mail is a cross between sales letters and promotional packages, which we discuss next. Whether sent singly or as a package, the objective of promotional and sales documents is to reduce reader resistance while maintaining goodwill.

Figure 10.16 Direct-Mail Packages Soliciting Membership

COMPONENT	EXAMPLE
National Museum of Women: Outside envelope	Sophisticated peach color, 4″ x 6″, with fancy lettering for addressee and a scriptlike "R.S.V.P." in corner
Sales letter	Eight pages inviting membership in the National Museum of Women
Supplements	A formal card of invitation with fancy lettering and R.S.V.P.
Response	Enrollment form and postpaid return envelope
Nature Conservancy: Outside envelope	White with clear window for address, picture of bird's head, printing stating "do not fold; bumper sticker enclosed," and "RELAX! both of you. (A $10.00 nest egg will do it.)"
Sales letter	Four-page letter (printed and folded on one sheet of paper) inviting membership in the Nature Conservancy
Supplements	A second letter that pictures wild animals and is addressed to the "Skeptical Investor," and a bumper sticker
Response	Membership application card, postpaid envelope

Figure 10.17 Cellophane Wrap Direct-Mail Package Advertising Product

COMPONENT	EXAMPLE
Easy Home Repair: Cellophane wrap serves as outside envelope	Sample home repair cards can be seen through the wrap. A "Personal Claim Label" doubles as the address label. The reverse has an "Open Immediately" sticker and shows a bingo card.
Sales letters	Two pages inviting readers to sign up to receive repair cards each month. Sales letter is attached as the bottom half of a "claim certificate." A second sales letter to those who have decided *not* to claim their "welcome" package.
Supplements	12 sample cards (double as gift); bingo game; flier advertising free gifts as part of the welcome package.
Response	"Claim certificate" detached from two-page sales letter functions as order form; postpaid return envelope.

Figure 10.18 Direct-Mail Package Text Using Sandhill Crane as Thematic Focus

NATURE CONSERVANCY ENCLOSURES	CRANE THEME
Primary promotional letter	*Opening sentence:* "The bug-eyed bird on our envelope who's ogling you with such distemper has a point. He's a native American sandhill crane and you may be sitting on top of one of his nesting sites." (*The reference to the crane continues throughout the letter.*)
Secondary promotional enclosure	*Opening sentence:* "If putting a landing pad under a crane's egg, as Ms. Mackinnon's letter [the primary letter] urges, seems too dank an investment for your $10, the other side of this note illustrates some different fauna which can use all the acreage we can buy for them."
Membership application form	*Blurb at top of form:* "O.K., I'm good for $10. Buy another spot of rocky or soggy or inaccessible land and reserve it for nest eggs and such, for keeps, for me."

PROMOTIONAL PACKAGES

Although promotional packages can fulfill a range of purposes, we focus on three:

- to promote goods and services
- to promote company image
- to promote a particular action or behavior

Although there is some predictability in the purposes of these packages, they feature a wide array of components, depending on the communication situation. In other words, there does not seem to be a set of standard components for these packages.

Promoting Goods and Services

Like direct mail, promotional packages can persuade audiences to use particular goods and services. For example, Chapter 8 opens with a welcome message from Dr. Wass's orthodontic office. As noted in the context box, the message is actually part of a package containing

- a health questionnaire
- an informational sheet for those patients with orthodontic insurance coverage
- a postpaid envelope for the return of the questionnaire (and the sheet)
- a promotional brochure produced by Dr. Wass's office
- a brochure about orthodontics produced by the American Association of Orthodontists, St. Louis, Missouri

Although the package contains many messages that are routine or goodwill messages, the purpose of the package *as a whole* is to convince clients that they have chosen the right specialist for addressing their orthodontic needs.

While Dr. Wass's package was directed to an external audience, other packages can have internal audiences as well. For example, for its package introducing a three-day package

Figure 10.19 Amnesty International Direct-Mail Package

AMNESTY INTERNATIONAL PACKAGE	THEMATIC COMPONENTS
Outside envelope	Standard business-size envelope of plain-brown [recycled] paper, with a window for the receiver's address and the brief note in black letters "Free personalized address labels enclosed. . . ." This cover in its minimal presentation and unpretentious offer of address labels reinforces the basic nature of the appeal inside.
Fund-raising letter	Four pages, black print on plain-cream stationery, starting with bad news. The direct approach and "plain English" of the opening encourage the sense that the situation is so serious that it would be inappropriate to buffer the "severe crisis" the organization faces. The message includes selected graphic detail of atrocities endured by prisoners of conscience as well as a testimonial from a prisoner eventually set free.
Supplements	1. A small "message of hope" card to be signed by the reader, with the Amnesty International logo (a candle surrounded by barbed wire) on the front and the message "Do not be discouraged. We know you are alive." 2. A small bumper sticker in black, white, and gold with the Amnesty International logo. 3. The promised address labels, with the logo and the recipient's name and address.
Response	Donation form and postpaid return envelope. (Modest elements of red, white, and blue add a patriotic touch that complements the black and white of the logo.)

delivery service, UPS developed materials for both internal and external audiences (Figure 10.20). Of course, because these materials were designed for different audiences, they did not appear in the same mailing, but they constitute a package nevertheless, because they are all consciously designed to support each other as they promote the same service.

Promoting a Particular Action or Behavior

Promotional packages, many published by organizations and institutions, can also promote particular actions or behaviors. The U.S. Department of Education's campaign against drug use provides an easily accessible example of such a package. This package has two

Figure 10.20 Promotional Package to Internal and External Audiences for New UPS Service

UPS PACKAGE INTRODUCING 3-DAY SELECT	
INTERNAL AUDIENCES	EXTERNAL AUDIENCES
• employee training booklet for all employees • a service briefing booklet for managers • a service explanation "posting" for employees containing general rules and regulations for transporting 3-Day Select packages	• a customer service brochure • a "guide" to 3-Day Select for customers using the service • a "posting" advertising the 3-Day Select Service to potential shippers • a fold-out mailing (with envelope) advertising the service to potential customers

primary external audiences: children and parents. Instead of a company logo, the package has a mascot—Ricky Raccoon—to provide continuity among the materials:

- a booklet "Growing Up Drug Free: A Parent's Guide to Prevention"
- a brochure targeted at middle school and high school students that explains the warning signs of possible involvement with drugs or alcohol; it also explains how and where to get help if a friend exhibits any of these signs
- a four-page pamphlet targeted at elementary school children encouraging them to say no to drugs, with a drug-free certificate suitable for framing that verifies a child is a "drug-free kid"
- various ancillary materials, ranging from a drug-free rap song to bumper stickers, book covers, and bookmarks, all featuring Ricky Raccoon "just saying no"

Walking the narrow line between promoting goods and services and promoting a particular action or behavior are packages that promote a particular investment behavior. The promotional package produced by the Overseas Private Investment Corporation (OPIC), a U.S. government agency, is a good example. This package contains

- a program handbook
- a current annual report
- a brochure advertising a current investment mission to Central Asia
- two four-page regional reports (e.g., for Africa and for Central and Eastern Europe)
- a copy of a recent news article detailing OPIC activity
- preliminary application forms for financing and for political risk investment insurance

Because OPIC is encouraging American business investment in areas that have been underdeveloped and/or unstable—politically and economically—the agency must overcome the natural resistance of business to making a high-risk or low-profit investment. OPIC thus provides risk insurance (which reimburses corporate losses in case of disasters, like a political revolution that would nationalize business and industry). It provides other services to corporate investors as well.

Promoting Company Image

Press packages, which share many of the goals of other types of promotional packages, have as their primary goal promoting a company's image. The 3M promotional package focuses on innovativeness, which is a *Fortune* criterion for excellence. The 3M package contains

- an annual report to share owners
- a second glossy brochure promoting 3M innovative technologies
- a *Fortune* 500 offprint (a selected portion of a document published separately by the original publisher) of a *Fortune* article on "stretch targets," which explains how 3M employs stretch targets, "which require big, athletic leaps of progress"
- a second offprint from *Fortune,* which rated 3M as one of three most admired U.S. companies for long-term investment value and total return on investment
- an offprint from *Business Week*, which had a cover story on 3M: "Masters of Innovation"
- an offprint from *R&D: Research and Development* profiling 3M
- an offprint from the *Journal of Business Strategy*, which featured an article about 3M entitled "Three Roads to Innovation"
- three separate fact sheets, about 3M's diverse product lines, its research programs, and its financial success

Each piece of information in the 3M package directly relates to the innovation theme, creating a clear, dramatic, and unified image for the company.

RESPONSE SHEET

READER RESISTANCE, PERSUASIVE MESSAGES, SALES MESSAGES, PROMOTIONAL PACKAGES

COMMUNICATOR(S): AUDIENCE(S):
OCCASION: DOCUMENT:
WHAT PROBLEM/ISSUE IS THE WRITER TRYING TO ADDRESS IN THIS DOCUMENT?

◆ READER RESISTANCE

What will be/is the main source of resistance that the reader will have to the message?

What might be/are other sources of resistance?

What are some ways that the writer could/does manage to overcome reader resistance?

◆ PERSUASIVE AND SALES MESSAGES

Does/should the writer use the AIDA plan of organization? Explain.

Does/should the writer make use of an implied reader? Explain.

◆ ATTENTION OPENING

What strategies for getting the reader's attention does the writer use?

- ask a question or pose a puzzle
- cite statistics or data
- create an analogy
- emphasize a problem, need, benefit, or solution
- forecast important information to come
- include interesting details or facts
- provide a free sample or that opportunity
- quote memorable phrases or statements
- tell a story or relate an anecdote

How can the writer make improvements in the opening? (Make suggestions on the draft.)

◆ INTEREST

How does the interest section establish the subject's relevance to the reader? Explain. (Make suggestions directly on the draft that might improve this section.)

◆ DESIRE

How does the desire section enhance the reader's sense of need and willingness to take action? (Make suggestions directly on the draft that might improve this section.)

◆ ACTION

Comment on the writer's close. Does the close facilitate the reader's response? (Make suggestions directly on the draft that might improve this section.)

◆ MAIN SELLING POINT

If this is a sales letter, what is the writer's main selling point?

Comment on how the writer reinforces the main selling point in each section of the message. (Make suggestions for improvement directly on the draft.)

ACTIVITIES, EXERCISES, AND ASSIGNMENTS

◆ IN-CLASS ACTIVITIES

1. Please refer to Figure 10.1, the dinner theater brochure, for the following activity.
   a. After reviewing the brochure, discuss whether you think the brochure's purpose is primarily to make a persuasive request (to get into the swing and be a participant-guest) or to sell a product (the dinner theater experience). What difference, if any, does the purpose of the message make in this case?
   b. Discuss the degree to which the writer uses an implied reader in this brochure. For example, did you recognize the reference to the "Maltese Falcon"?
2. Review what Chapters 2 and 7 have to say about *heuristics*, or tools for discovery in composing oral and written communication. Then imagine that you, as a lead writer for your company, have been asked to give a brief talk (5 to 10 minutes) to new members of your marketing and sales staff about how to use the AIDA pattern as a heuristic for composing persuasive requests or sales letters. Plan the talk, and then be prepared to present it to a small group within your class.

◆ INDIVIDUAL AND GROUP ASSIGNMENTS

1. Working in teams, gather together the junk mail several people receive for two weeks, making sure to keep separate piles for each recipient.
   a. What can you tell about the recipients for each of the stacks of junk mail that you have collected? What kind of audience profile can you build from looking at the junk mail each person receives?
   b. Look at the letters accompanying the junk mail. To what extent do these letters employ implied readers? Explain.
2. Review the components of the direct-mail packages noted in Figures 10.16 and 10.17.
   a. Discuss the main selling point suggested by the components listed in Figure 10.21.
   b. Discuss the unifying theme.
   c. Do you think that direct-mail packages make use of an implied reader? Explain.
3. Figure 10.21 describes (1) two direct-mail packages selling magazine subscriptions to *Granta* literary magazine and to *Martha Stewart Living*, an upscale magazine

Figure 10.21 Direct-Mail Packages Selling Various Subscriptions

COMPONENT	EXAMPLE
Granta: Outside envelope	Garish gold with clear window for address and the messages "Save 55% off the bookshop price!" and "Interested in a thought-provoking magazine about writers and writing? You are? Then you can THROW AWAY THIS ENVELOPE because GRANTA, Britain's best selling literary magazine, is edited by people who don't like literature."
Sales letter	Four-page letter (printed and folded on one sheet of paper) with pictures and graphics inviting subscription.
Supplements	Color brochure.
Response	Order form and postpaid return envelope.
Martha Stewart Living: Outside envelope	Colored envelope with clear window for address and featuring pink, gray, and green and picturing a woman and the text "Shake before opening. Free Burpee basil seeds inside!" and "Come home with Martha Stewart."
Sales letter	Six-page letter (printed and folded on one sheet of paper plus an inserted page) inviting a subscription.
Supplements	A color brochure picturing and discussing material from issues of the magazine. A second, one-page letter serving as a personal invitation. The Burpee herb seeds.
Response	Membership application card, postpaid envelope.
Wildlife: Outside envelope replaced by cellophane wrap	Cellophane wrap reveals sample wildlife cards. "Gift Package Validation Label" serves as address label; on reverse, "open early" seal promises an extra bonus.
Sales letter	Gift claim certificate forms top of two-page sales letter which congratulates the reader for winning a game pouch; the letter tells the reader, "To discover the value of your Free Gift Package, simply tear open the enclosed Instant-Value-Game Pouch." After concerning itself with reader benefit, the second part of the message "sells" the wildlife cards.
Supplements	The sample wildlife cards themselves, the game pouch, a second letter that is to be opened only if the reader has decided not to claim the free gift package and that assures readers that there's no catch to the offer.
Response	The gift certificate serves as a response card and comes with a postpaid envelope.

for homeowners, and (2) a cellophane package marketing nature cards (like the home repair cards, Figure 10.17).

a. Discuss the main selling point suggested by the components.

b. Discuss the unifying theme. Why, for example, should the *Martha Stewart Living* direct-mail package enclose Burpee herb seeds?

c. Do you think that direct-mail packages make use of an implied reader? Explain.

4. Please use Figure 10.22 in completing this revision exercise.

a. Discuss the strategies the writer uses in writing this persuasive request. Identify those strategies that you think most effective and least effective.

b. Revise the letter so that it has an improved chance of achieving its objective.

◆ OUT-OF-CLASS ASSIGNMENTS

1. Contact a local company to arrange an interview with the manager of the department handling collections. The purpose of the interview is to gather information about the approach that the company uses in planning a sequence of collection letters. Work with a small group of classmates to design a series of questions. (Use the Response Sheet on interviews, page 337, to help you get started.)

a. As your group plans for the interview, consider questions such as these:
- How do you balance collecting the money owed against maintaining good customer relations?
- What alternatives do you offer for payment plans?
- How important is the exact wording of collection letters?
- Do you ever use humor in an attempt to encourage payment?

b. Modify these questions to fit your specific purposes. Design additional questions suitable for the particular company. Ask the person you're interviewing to show you examples that illustrate each point.

c. Ask if you can have a series of the collection letters. If you receive a set, analyze them to see how they fulfill the company's goals and meet the more general criteria explained in this chapter.

d. Write a detailed memo from your group to the rest of the class explaining the results of your interview and, if you obtained a set of collection letters, the ways in which the letters support the company's goals.

2. Select a product or service or an idea or image that you wish to promote.

a. Using the Response Sheet on persuasive, sales, and promotional messages as a start, design a persuasive message (persuasive request or fund-raising letter) or sales letter that promotes the idea or item to a specified audience.

b. Suggest what you would include in a direct-mail or promotional package promoting your "item." What would be your main selling point? What would be your unifying theme?

c. In a message to the marketing director of your company, provide details about your promotional plans in an effort to persuade the director to support your ideas.

Figure 10.22 Persuasive Request in Need of Revision

Dear Mr. Reynolds:

This letter is in reference to proposals submitted to your Department by Toronto Heavy Equipment and one other firm on December 9, 19-- for twelve Random Crack Router Machines.

I believe the decision has been made to recommend to your Highway Department's Commissioners that the low bidder, the other firm, should receive the contract.

There are factors other than price that the Commissioners should consider in approving the purchase of the cheaper product. Toronto's Crack Router is a product tried and tested by users across the United States and Canada. The names of users were provided to you as references to verify our product's dependability. One of the units was used by your department on a rental basis during the summer and fall of 19--. It was found superior to routers in your fleet, which were supplied from the company who is the low bidder in this instance.

Now, this company has cost reduced its machines effecting a lower bid price in its proposal to you. There was a demonstration of the modified unit made to Department personnel. But there is no apparent evidence of extensive filed testing with this cheapened unit. Nor does literature seem to be readily available providing specifications as required in your proposal documents.

It would seem that the Department is about to purchase some $85,000.00 worth of untried equipment. Are the users in the Department comfortable with this prospect? At the least, prudence might suggest that dividing the order between two suppliers would reduce the potential risk.

It is not possible for a representative of Toronto to travel to Omaha in the near future to express our protest. However, I believe it is reasonable to request that this letter be presented to the Department Commissioners in order that they reach their decision with all the facts at hand.

Sincerely,

TORONTO HEAVY EQUIPMENT

Harold Pierce
Contract Administration

CASE

PROMOTING TRUST IN FINANCIAL TRUST

CASE BY JUDY HAMILTON

Background. Financial Trust is a banking institution with a complete range of financial services. Operating out of Towson, Maryland, Financial Trust faces stiff competition for customers, especially from the larger banking institutions based in nearby Baltimore.

Members of the bank's trust department have the responsibility of writing the promotional material about Financial Trust's personal trust services. These services include investment accounts, living trusts, conservatorships, estate administration, testamentary trusts, financial planning, and tax preparation and planning. (You may find it beneficial to do preliminary research regarding such services.)

The services have some built-in selling points:

- freedom from the responsibility of managing one's money in a complex marketplace
- advantages of pre-death tax planning
- personalized service from well-trained officers
- records provided for tax and reporting purposes
- regular communication regarding accounts

Since the larger competing institutions can say the same thing about their trust services, however, the department's promotional committee is also faced with the task of building trust in and creating a stronger profile for Financial Trust as an institution.

Task. Because you have extensive course work in professional communication, you have been appointed head of the committee charged with designing a series of promotional materials for the trust services of Financial Trust. In designing this series, you and your committee will have to decide what type of promotional campaign you want to wage: internal communication to current customers, external sales letters, brochures, promotional package, direct-mail package, or some combination of these options. While cost is not a paramount concern in producing these materials, you do not have a blank check either.

Complication. Your task is complicated by the heterogeneous nature of the committee working with you (classmates may want to play these roles):

1. a member of the marketing department who subscribes to the value of "truth in advertising," but also recognizes that the nature of advertising is to enhance the desirability of products and services through selective claims and appropriate persuasive strategies
2. a member of the marketing department who subscribes to the value of "fluffing" information and of using emotional appeals for effect
3. a member of the trust department who is opposed to fluffing on the grounds that there is the potential for legal action based on the public's understanding of such terms as "best possible investment" and "expertise"; this member is fond of citing a case against First Alabama where legal action taken by an investor resulted in damages awarded based on a trust department's misleading literature
4. a member of the trust department who upholds the bank's code of conduct, which, in part, states:
   - We must recognize that our first duty to the bank and its customers is to act in all matters in a manner that merits public trust and confidence.
   - Extreme care must be exercised to avoid any statements that could be interpreted as the giving of legal advice. The customers should always be encouraged to consult with their own attorneys and consultant.
5. a member of the trust department who upholds the following recommendations for advertisements found in the bank's trust division policy manual:

   Advertisements related to the Trust Division

   - should be dignified
   - should not imply that legal services will be rendered
   - should have no reflections, expressed or implied, upon other trust institutions or individuals
   - should neither overstate nor overemphasize the qualifications of the Trust Division
   - should be helpful to the trust industry as a whole

NEGOTIATION ON WORKPLACE TEAMS

Because certain kinds of team conflicts are counterproductive, you need to learn specific strategies to manage disagreements. One of the most successful strategies is negotiation.

When conflicts between two individuals on a team begin interfering with the effectiveness and efficiency of the team, it's time for another member of the team or an agreed-upon third party outside of the team to step in as a facilitator. A facilitator can help negotiate a serious, seemingly unresolvable disagreement by using the following process.

- Help both sides reduce their emotional reactions by giving all the people involved an opportunity to articulate their feelings. People who are calm tend to be more willing to listen to opposing views.
- Encourage both sides to clearly present their views and offer alternative solutions. Encourage people to find terms that don't provoke a reaction from either side.
- Provide opportunities for graceful retreat. People don't like to be embarrassed. Face-saving is important.
- Try to open constructive communication between the opposing sides. Give everyone a chance to talk. Help people understand what the other side is saying.
- Plan a meeting site that is neutral. Consider other factors people will react to: time of the meeting, length of the meeting, other people who should attend.[1]

A situation to consider: These five steps came in handy for Sandra Duke when she helped team members Janet Pearso and Matt Southby negotiate a dispute that seemed to be headed for a standoff. They all worked for a company that produced consumer appliances: washing machines, dishwashers, refrigerators, and so on. One of the production and paint lines in the manufacturing plant was getting two industrial robots to take over finishing processes that involved hazardous chemicals. The team had been assigned the task of making recommendations about retraining, cross training, and layoffs for the four people on the production line who would no longer be needed in the paint shop. Sandra, Janet, and Matt needed to write their report so that the division manager could take their position into account when he made his decision.

Janet and Matt stood on different sides of the issue. Janet thought employees should be retrained or cross-trained regardless of the cost. Matt thought that since all four employees were young, it was kinder in the long run to lay them off since the jobs they'd be retraining for would eventually be taken over by robots—part of the long-range plan that would probably be implemented within the next five years. And he happened to know that one of the company's competitors had five positions open for which these workers were qualified.

Head-on arguing occurs when people present firm, unyielding positions. They simply reiterate their arguments, refuse to budge from their positions, and ignore other points of view. Let's look at three reasons why head-on arguing probably won't work to help Janet and Matt resolve their disagreement:

- *Not moving*. Because head-on arguing over positions usually creates a stalemate, the discussion tends to repeat itself, but it doesn't move forward.
- *Digging in*. Head-on arguing solidifies each person's static position. The more people argue about and defend their positions, the more firmly committed to those positions they'll get.
- *Listening less*. The more that people with firmly established positions argue, the less likely they are to be able to listen to a reasonable solution.

Head-on arguing becomes a battle of wills: who will give in first rather than who has the more reasonable position. Experts in negotiation like Roger Fisher, William Ury, and Bruce Patton describe positional bargaining—that is, bargaining in which people take clearly defined positions—as either "**soft**" or "**hard**" (Figure 1). Whether you tend to take a "**soft**" position or a "**hard**" one, such an approach usually leaves everyone feeling uncomfortable—and there's no assurance that the decision reached is the most appropriate.

Figure 1 Positional Bargaining

SOFT BARGAINING	HARD BARGAINING
Participants are friends.	Participants are adversaries.
The goal is agreement.	The goal is victory.
Make concessions to cultivate the relationship.	Demand concessions as a condition of the relationship.
Be soft on the people and the problem.	Be hard on the problem and the people.
Trust others.	Distrust others.
Change your position easily.	Dig in your position.
Make offers.	Make threats.
Disclose your bottom line.	Mislead as to your bottom line.
Accept one-sided losses to reach agreement.	Demand one-sided gains as the price of agreement.
Search for the single answer: the one they will accept.	Search for the single answer: the one you will accept.
Insist on agreement.	Insist on your position.
Try to avoid a contest of wills.	Try to win a contest of wills.
Yield to pressure.	Apply pressure.

Soft and hard bargaining lead to "win-lose" situations rather than "win-win" situations because neither takes a cooperative, collaborative approach. Soft and hard bargaining can also be aggravated by affective conflicts (stemming from attitudes and personality) and procedural conflicts (stemming from differences of opinion about approaches to the task). (See the Communication Spotlight for Part II, pages 212–215, to review ways to avoid affective and procedural conflicts and to promote cooperative, productive conflict.)

The situation continued: Janet and Matt dug in for the long haul. They had a deadline, but that didn't seem to matter to them. A six-year working relationship and their friendship were at stake. They both took a hard position.

Sandra knew she needed to help them move off center. She used the skills and strategies she had learned in a management training course that had focused on *negotiation on the merits* or *principal negotiation*, a strategy developed by the Harvard Negotiation Project.

Negotiation on the merits depends on four basic points that enable people on opposing sides to move away from positional bargaining.[2]

- *People:* Separate the people from the problem.
- *Interests:* Focus on interests, not positions.
- *Options:* Generate a variety of possibilities before deciding what to do.
- *Criteria:* Insist that the result be based on some objective standard.

In their book *Getting to Yes*, Fisher, Ury, and Patton explain that these four points need to be discussed during the analysis and diagnosis stage of negotiation, again during the planning and idea-generating stage, and finally during the discussion and agreement stage. During the *analysis and diagnosis stage* of negotiation, the parties involved define the problem and then determine its causes. During the *planning and idea-generating stage*, the parties decide how to approach the problem, agree on criteria for an effective solution, and develop several alternatives to resolve the problem. During the *discussion and agreement stage*, the parties explore the strengths and weaknesses of each alternative and apply the criteria so that they can agree on an appropriate resolution.

The situation: Sandra knew that she first needed to help Janet and Matt define the problem and agree on its causes. Then she could facilitate their discussions about how to approach the problem. Once they had an approach, Sandra could get them to agree on criteria for an effective solution, and then develop a series of alternatives to resolve the problem. Sandra knew that she had to encourage them to explore the strengths and weaknesses of each alternative before they could apply the criteria in order to narrow down their choices. Finally, they would need to agree on an appropriate resolution.

Separate the People from the Problem

Separating the people from the problem helps reduce problems caused by emotions and egos. You want people to attack the problem, not each other. The following suggests strategies that negotiators can use to help separate the people from the problems.

- *Individual differences.* Respect people's backgrounds, opinions, and experiences. Don't underestimate the value of making people feel good about themselves.
- *Perceptions.* Try to understand the other person's perception about the problem. Discuss each other's perceptions. Don't view the other person or that person's position in the worst possible light.
- *Emotions.* Acknowledge people's emotions. Give people a chance to vent frustrations. Don't react to emotional outbursts.
- *Communication.* Use active listening strategies. Talk to explain, not to argue. Express your own views and reactions rather than describing the other person's.

The situation: As she reviewed ways she might facilitate the negotiation between Janet and Matt, Sandra—who was on the committee as the representative from the Human Resources Department—reviewed some information about her teammates.

Janet was on the committee because she was a production and finishing line supervisor of the line receiving the robots. Because she was completing a degree in industrial management, she had been invited to serve as an employee liaison with the company's Human Resources Department, a role she'd enjoyed for the past year. She worked with the production crew every day, but she also understood management concerns. She believed that cross training she'd received when she worked for another company had moved her out of a dead-end job and given her career options.

Matt was also on the committee because he was a production and finishing line supervisor, but not of the line receiving the robots. In a previous supervisory job in another company, Matt had seen the effects of line automation. More than half of the workers he'd supervised had been laid off over a three-year period; workers were spared only if they had the background or the ability to learn to operate the programmable robots and become mini-managers for the robots on a line.

Focus on Interests, Not Positions

At the heart of every unresolved problem is a conflict of interests—the underlying basic needs, concerns, and fears people feel. For example, Janet and Matt said they were disagreeing about retraining, cross training, or laying off workers. It's also likely that they were disagreeing about economic security and a sense of control over one's life. Janet believed that economic security and a sense of control can come from having more skills and job options. Matt believed that economic security and a sense of control can come from getting on with things.

They also disagreed about some fundamental gender issues. Janet saw training as an important career opportunity, especially for women. Matt commented that he didn't think women in these line jobs were interested in careers, just extra income. Janet and Matt did, however, share a common concern for the employees involved.

The following strategies help negotiators focus on interests, not positions.

- *Learn interests.* What are shared interests (for example, control of one's life)? What are conflicting interests (i.e., control of the project)?
- *Establish reasons.* Why does the other person hold his or her position? Why doesn't the other person hold your position? Provide specific details to support your explanations.
- *Be firm.* Be forthright in presenting your interests. Show why your interests matter.

The situation: Sandra explained to Janet and Matt that she wanted the three of them to focus on interests, not positions. She described interests as the reasons that motivated each of them. She said that their *positions* were simply fixed, unmoving points. What she wanted to hear about was their *interests*—their underlying motivations, their needs, concerns, and fears.

In explaining her interests, Janet said that she didn't want anyone to be unemployed. She thought additional training was a safeguard for employment security—not a guarantee, but certainly a help. She had an interest in helping people advance. She also wanted them to have a sense of community, to realize that their contribution to the company was important.

Matt was equally clear in expressing his interests. He didn't want anyone to be unemployed, nor did he want his workers to have the worry of inevitable unemployment hanging over their heads. He had an interest in helping people locate positions with long-term job security. He also wanted them to have some sense of control over what happened to them rather than being at the mercy of management.

Generate Alternatives

Generating a variety of alternatives before deciding what to do increases the range of options people can consider. These strategies help negotiators create an atmosphere in which alternatives are possible.

- *Inventing versus judging*. Separate creativity from criticism. Brainstorm solutions, deferring judgment until after all the ideas are presented. Try to brainstorm with the people who disagree with you.
- *Options*. Come up with more alternatives (rather than fewer). Examine the problem from multiple perspectives. Rank-order your alternatives from strongest to weakest.
- *Gains*. Adopt a win-win attitude rather than a win-lose attitude. Identify shared interests—things you'll both agree with. Identify complementary interests.
- *Decision making*. Make reasonable efforts to help the person with the opposing view make the decision you want.

Fisher, Ury, and Patton recommend an effective sequence of actions to help negotiators generate alternatives: (1) identify the problem, (2) analyze the situation, (3) pose possible approaches to solve the problem, and (4) generate alternatives to solve the problem. This sequence keeps people focused on the problems rather than their emotionally charged positions.

The situation: Sandra encouraged Janet and Matt to come up with a list of alternatives that would address their problem. Sandra encouraged them to move through these specific steps:

- Discuss and agree on the definition of the problem.
- Analyze the problem by listing its causes, identifying barriers to resolving it and resources available to help resolve it.
- Brainstorm—and defer judgment on—a list of approaches. Develop the promising ideas. Set aside the inadequate ideas.
- Check the links between the problem and the possible solutions. Decide how each alternative addresses the underlying interests expressed by each person. Rank-order lists of alternatives.

By using this negotiating approach, Sandra encouraged Janet and Matt to develop at least three solutions that addressed their interests rather than reiterating their original positions without listening to any other ideas.

One of the solutions that Janet and Matt developed was to arrange a meeting with the workers involved. Workers could be given a choice: (1) Make a commitment to a retraining program within the company or (2) resign if they preferred to take a job elsewhere. This would enable the training to be given only to employees who were committed to improving job skills and continuing with this company.

Establish Criteria

Establishing criteria for decision making reduces the chances that a decision will be made simply because one of the people is stubborn or can outlast the other(s). The following suggests strategies to help establish criteria for making decisions during a negotiation.

- *Fair standards*. Establish standards for developing criteria. Use some impartial external source—for example, government standards, fair market value, professional organization standards, legal standards, cost limits.
- *Fair procedures*. Establish procedures for developing criteria—for example, the childhood practice of dividing cake or candy ("one cuts, the other chooses"), depending on an independent arbitrator, "last best offer."
- *Rationale*. Use the criteria for negotiating the decision. Keep asking people for the rationale behind their decisions. Ask people to explain the principles they're using.
- *Decision making*. Attempt to help the person with the opposing view come to the decision you want.

The situation: With Sandra's encouragement, Janet and Matt agreed to establish criteria for making a decision so that their team could write the report. They agreed that the decision should meet this single criterion:

- The decision should help employees in both the short term and the long term.

They also agreed on two other points:

- A unilateral decision, without consulting the employees, was undesirable.
- They would recommend that all line employees, including those not immediately affected by this change, should be informed about the reasons for the decision.

The four principles briefly discussed in this section don't guarantee successful negotiations. However, if you separate the people from the problem, focus on interests rather than positions, generate alternatives, and establish criteria, you have a better chance of success than if you simply stake out a position and insist on it.

ACTIVITIES AND QUESTIONS FOR DISCUSSION

1. Think about a professional, personal, or work-related disagreement you have had. Explain which of the principles presented in this section might have helped resolve the disagreement.
2. Throughout this section, you have read about the ongoing disagreement Janet and Matt had about their decision retraining, cross-training, or laying off workers. Generate at least two additional alternatives that would fairly address the interests that Janet and Matt expressed.
3. The three criteria for assessing the alternatives that Janet and Matt established reflected their interests. What criteria would you have established for assessing the alternatives?

Communication Spotlight: Revision

USING GLOBAL REVISION TO STRENGTHEN BUSINESS DOCUMENTS

Inexperienced writers often think of revision simply as catching and correcting errors—finding spelling mistakes, eliminating comma problems, rewriting a few awkward sentences, changing a sentence fragment or two. And, in fact, local revision focuses on just such errors.

Global revision, however, is quite different. Global revision is a way for writers to re-envision—actually re-see—a document so that it is better adapted to a specific audience, more appropriate for a specific purpose, and more suitable for a specific occasion. Global revision focuses on eliminating problems that affect an entire document—for example, inappropriate organization, a series of examples that are not adapted for the audience, or a design of the document that makes information difficult to access.

One characteristic that distinguishes inexperienced writers from more experienced writers is their approach to revision. Inexperienced writers tend to concentrate on local revision, going from word to word and sentence to sentence in an effort to correct errors. In contrast, more experienced writers usually begin their revision efforts by focusing on elements that influence the entire document—content, organization, line of argument, supporting examples, genre, approach and tone, visuals, and document design. Once experienced writers are satisfied with the global revision of a document, they turn their attention to local revision.

There's no single best way to begin global revision, but one useful approach is to consider audience, purpose, and occasion. You can ask questions about these categories as you draft and revise your own documents. You can also ask these questions when you are invited to review documents written by colleagues.

For people who must provide detailed answers over the phone to non-experts, information manuals must be clear and answers must be easy and quick to find.

Reviewing an example of global revision will enable you to understand the complexity of such revision. This example focuses on Elizabeth Running Hey, who works for The Principal Financial Group as a pension training specialist. Elizabeth was assigned to work on a global revision of the 37-page loan section of the *Pension DC Administration Manual*, which includes procedural and background information about the company's defined contribution pension products.

The in-house *Pension DC Administration Manual* was used daily by administrators at The Principal Financial Group who required instructions or needed to answer a customer question. Pension administrators had commented that they sometimes had difficulty locating information in the loan section, and the explanations and examples weren't very easy to understand.

Figure 1 (page 310) shows an excerpt of the loan section of the manual that Elizabeth had to redesign and the marginal comments that she made as she read it. This excerpt explains handling loan payments that exceed the amount that's due. Elizabeth recognized that this section of the manual contained information that was technically correct, but she could see why it was difficult for pension administrators to use the manual easily, quickly, and accurately.

When Elizabeth began this project, she did what any professional would: she spent time making initial assessment notes about the loan section of the manual and talking with administrators who used the manual. In part of her initial assessment, she said

> The loan section of this manual needs a complete overhaul. Some of the information is no longer pertinent; other important information is

Figure 1 Excerpt from The Principal Financial Group *Pension DC Administration Manual—before* Revision (page 19-1-12, issued 11/11/92)

The information isn't chunked into segments that users can easily locate.

Where's the hierarchy? Users can't see any main or subordinate points.

Where are the steps? Users can't distinguish the steps in the process. How are they supposed to know what to do?

Users can't tell the difference between the main steps and the explanations and details that elaborate those steps.

Payment Amount Exceeds

Go ahead and process the payment amount based on the amortization schedule provided it's not an exact multiple of the payment amount. (See statement below regarding the system's capability to handle multiple payments.) The excess amount should be processed as a principal only payment. The principal only transaction will produce a new amortization schedule. You will need to mail this to the customer since the final payment has now changed. (The amortization schedule produced as a result of a principal only payment will keep the payment amount the same, but will change the loan's duration and final payment amount.)

Unfortunately, it's common that we continue to receive loan payments for members after the loan balance has been paid in full. It's also common that we don't receive the correct amount for the final payment.

Our processors are to refund any amount which exceeds a loan's final payment amount. Loan payments which we continue to receive after a loan is paid in full must also be refunded. If the customer continues to send payment amounts which differ from the payment amount on your amortization schedule, see your assistant manager.

missing. The biggest problem is the organization. Chunking and hierarchies aren't readily apparent.

Elizabeth responded to her initial concerns about audience, purpose, and occasion, which led to a plan of necessary changes. Her plan guided the global changes in organization, content, and design so that the information was more accessible and usable (see Figure 2).

The process that Elizabeth used in her assessment and global revision of the loan section of the *Pension DC Administration Manual* is similar to the process you can use when you need to globally revise a document, whether a one-page memo or a 300-page manual. After her preliminary assessment, Elizabeth listed the 32 major topics covered in the loan section and spent time grouping and regrouping these topics until she was comfortable with the way they were chunked. She knew that reorganizing information would make it easier for readers to understand.

Sometimes writers know all the information necessary to revise a document. More often, though, they need to draw on expertise from others. At The Principal Financial Group, a subject matter expert (SME) is assigned to projects so there's always someone available to answer questions about content accuracy.

Figure 2 Factors Elizabeth Considered in Global Revision

GLOBAL REVISION CATEGORY	ELIZABETH'S ASSESSMENT TO GUIDE GLOBAL REVISION
Adapted for the audience	Reorganize information so that it's more accessible and easier for users to follow. Redesign the document using Information Mapping, which is an organizational technique that helps the audience to see the relationship among various chunks of information.
Appropriate for the purpose	Use more concrete examples to help users complete the process quickly and accurately.
Suitable for the occasion	Add information about loan balancing. Check information with Bill Nelson for accuracy.

Figure 3 E-Mail about Revising the *Pension DC Administration Manual:* Elizabeth to Bill

During the early stages of planning, Elizabeth asked Bill his opinion about a new topic that she believed users needed. Of course, she had already done a good deal of work before she contacted him. Based on her assessment of the loan section and her talks with pension administrators using the manual, she was sure this content addition was a good idea.

E-Mail

Date: Wednesday, March 16, 19–, 10:15am CT
To: NELSON.BILL
Cc: MCKINESS.SARAH
From: RUNNING.HEY.ELIZABET
Subject: LOAN SECTION

Brad,
I'm ready to begin working on the Loan section of the DC Admin Manual. I'd like to add information regarding loan balancing since admins must balance loans before sending a 5500 job to the Gov't Reporting Unit. Do you think we should include information on this topic?

At this time can you think of any changes that need to be made?

Is it possible to get a copy of your most recent loan class handout?

Thanks, Elizabeth Running Hey, Pension Training, T-7, ext. 79261

Once Elizabeth understood the scope of the project, she sent an e-mail message (Figure 3) to Bill Nelson, the SME assigned to her project, asking his opinion about her idea to add information about loan balancing to the manual as well as seeking his general recommendations. She knew that establishing and maintaining an open and congenial relationship with the SME was critical since he not only had to verify the accuracy of her information and provide any missing information but also had to sign off on the revision once it was completed.

Elizabeth received an almost immediate response (Figure 4), which provided the information she needed to continue with her reorganization of the manual and to set up a meeting. She was less sure how to handle Bill's negative reaction to her question about adding information on loan balancing to the manual.

The response from Bill represents a typical snag in global revisions—a change you're sure will work isn't accepted by someone with veto authority. Global revision isn't a clean, simple, one-time-around process. Instead, it often requires several cycles of revising and checking until all parties involved agree with proposed changes.

Once Elizabeth completed her assessment of the manual and received preliminary feedback from Bill, she confirmed her initial opinion that she needed to make global changes

Figure 4 E-Mail about Revising the *Pension DC Administration Manual:* Bill to Elizabeth

Bill Nelson was not enthusiastic about Elizabeth's proposed addition to the manual. He didn't think that the occasion necessitated additional information about loan balancing.

E-Mail

Date: Wednesday, March 16 19–, 10:28am CT
To: RUNNING.HEY.ELIZABET
From: NELSON.BILL
Subject: LOAN SECTION
In-Reply-to: The letter of Wednesday, 16 March 19–, 10:15 am

since the support teams have the responsibility for balancing any loans accums, i hate to see us put much info on loan balancing in the manual. i'd like to see the emphasis on loan balancing be in the support manuals.

i really like the idea of you reorganizing the loan section. please set up a meeting and we can talk about needed changes.

Figure 5 Excerpt from The Principal Financial Group *Pension DC Administration Manual—after* Revision (page 19-9-2, draft 5/94)

Organization: The three steps and their related actions are separated so that pension administrators can easily follow them.

Content: A procedural label is added so that users know they need to follow a sequence of steps.

Design: The Information Mapping format—the narrow column for the heading, the definition of the task, the chunked and labeled rows and columns—anticipates readers' needs.

PAYMENT AMOUNT EXCEEDS

The following procedures explain how to process a loan payment if it exceeds the correct payment amount.

STEP	ACTION
1	Process loan payment based on the amount shown on amortization schedule. (If payment is exact multiple of amortization payment, see related info in this section.)
2	Apply excess amount as principal only.
3	Mail resulting new amortization schedule to customer. (The payment amount remains the same; duration of loan and/or final payment changes.)

Refund any amount that exceeds loan final payment amount. If the customer continues to send payment amounts that differ from the payment amount on your amortization schedule, see your assistant manager.

in content, organization, and design. She proposed a tentative outline to serve as a jumping off point for discussions about the revision with Bill and other stakeholders. These discussions provoked her investigation of new topics that needed to be included. For example, an examination of the procedure for balancing loans was a topic that Elizabeth believed was needed, so she added it (despite Bill's voiced objections) in order to see how other reviewers would react. In the workplace, making decisions about global revisions of documents that have numerous stakeholders may involve negotiations.

As the global revision of the loan section progressed, Elizabeth made important decisions about content and organization:

- add new information about loan balancing
- reorganize major sections to chunk related topics

She also made a decision to redesign the loan section using the format specified for all documents in The Principal Financial Group. This format is called **Information Mapping**, a flexible design that depends on chunking, labeling, and structuring information so that it is appealing and accessible to readers.

While you may not work for an organization that requires all its documents to be based on Information Mapping, you may need to design a document using some of the same principles: chunk related information, accurately and clearly label each chunk of information, place information on a page so that each chunk is easy to locate.

Once a revision of the loan section was completed, Elizabeth conducted both user testing and editorial review to evaluate whether the global changes were effective. The feedback she received from the testing gave her information for the final revision of the new version of the loan section of the manual. While you may choose to complete a global revision without doing any kind of document testing, you increase your chances of producing an effective document if you—like Elizabeth—test whether your revision works.

When Elizabeth neared the end of the project, she used the results from user testing to help shape her decision about the most effective way to present the complex information that had been difficult for users. For example, she decided to add tables in long subsections of the loan section. Tables would solve two problems that users had experienced during testing of the revised version: the need for advance organizers and retrievability of information.

Figure 5 shows a small segment of the loan section of the *Pension DC Administration Manual* as it looked after Elizabeth completed the revision. (Compare with Figure 1.) In this revision, you can see examples of all three categories of revisions that Elizabeth implemented to make the document more accessible and usable for the audience, appropriate for the purpose, and suitable for the occasion: organization, content, and design.

ACTIVITIES AND QUESTIONS FOR DISCUSSION

1. Select a document that you have drafted but not yet completed for this class or another class. Go through the document to assess (1) adaptation for the audience, (2) appropriateness for the purpose, (3) suitability for the occasion. Assess what global changes are necessary so that the document meets professional standards.
2. Select a document that you found unclear, confusing, or inappropriate in content, organization, and/or manner of presentation. Revise this document so that it is adapted to the audience, appropriate for the purpose, and suitable for the occasion.

PART IV
DESIGNING
BUSINESS
DOCUMENTS

CHAPTER

11

Collecting and Interpreting Information

OUTLINE

How Pamphlet, Inc., Collected and Interpreted Information

Locating and Selecting Sources of Information

Interpreting Information

CRITERIA FOR EXPLORING CHAPTER 11

What we cover in this chapter	What you will be able to do after reading this chapter
The value and limitations of various sources of information	Use a variety of sources to collect information
Constraints in interpreting information	Analyze information and avoid distortion caused by errors in logic; recognize fallacious logic in others' writing

Experienced communicators know that every document and oral presentation they prepare rests on the foundation of information they collect and interpret. If this foundation is inadequate, the resulting document or presentation will also be inadequate and will thus reflect badly on you and your organization. Figure 11.1 shows the importance of the collection and interpretation of information—and ramifications of communicators not planning this part of their work seriously.

CONTEXT

Every year teams of students in an agribusiness senior projects class work with client companies to propose solutions to actual problems. The excerpt in Figure 11.1 from an assessment of students in the course identifies problems in collecting and interpreting information that resulted from one team's insufficient planning. These students were investigating whether ISO 9000 (a set of voluntary standards and guidelines for quality management) should be adopted by the client company, especially since one of this company's major competitors recently adopted these standards. Unfortunately, while the students knew the general topic, they didn't develop key questions they needed to investigate, so their research efforts were inadequate. Their recommendations were eventually presented to the client in a formal oral presentation and in a written report, but because of the students' careless collection and interpretation of information, their work wasn't taken seriously.

Figure 11.1 Neglecting Skills for Collecting and Interpreting Information

Team members knew the general topic, but didn't formulate key questions to guide their research.

By neglecting to do a careful database search, the writers did not have current information.

In not arranging in advance for the interview, the writers created an unprofessional impression.

The writers potentially biased their interpretation by relying on one person to guide their search.

The writers prematurely established their position about the situation even before they collected all the information.

The team of students investigating the adoption of the ISO 9000 standards made the following decisions in their collection and interpretation of information:

- Used only the university's computerized catalog to locate information. Did not do a search of any database.
- Did not use their prepared questions for the on-site interview with their client because they let the interviewee manage the interview.
- Did not dress professionally for a meeting with the client.
- Did not call ahead to arrange a time for an informational interview; the team simply showed up at the client's office door expecting to see him.
- Did not make prior arrangements for informational telephone interviews.
- Did not have the name of the person they were going to interview at one company; called and asked for the "plant manager."
- Relied on a single person—a cooperative and friendly researcher in their university department—to provide the majority of materials for their investigation as well as to provide leads for people to interview.
- Overgeneralized the information they learned about ISO 9000 in one company from one interview to form the basis for their recommendation.
- Made a team decision about their recommendation early in the project—and then spent the rest of the term looking for information to support their decision.

1. How do you think the students' failure to prepare and collect information affected their report?
2. What changes would you recommend that (a) the students make the next time they approach a project and (b) the client make the next time he works with a student team?
3. How do you think the students' failure to sufficiently plan before they collected information affected their client's impression of their work?

The students needed to plan key questions so that they could make sure that the information they collected was relevant to their line of argument (Chapter 7). More specifically, they needed to know about three critical aspects of collecting and interpreting information:

- defining the task, which includes assessing factors ranging from identifying necessary skills to determining outcomes appropriate for the occasion, purpose, and audience
- using sources of information, including library resources, databases, e-mail, interviews, focus groups, government documents, and surveys
- avoiding errors in logic when interpreting information

HOW PAMPHLET, INC., COLLECTED AND INTERPRETED INFORMATION

When Pamphlet, Inc., took the job of redesigning the First National Bank's customer pamphlet about terms and conditions of accounts, the members of the design team knew they'd need more than the current 12-panel pamphlet as a source of information. During their planning, the team members agreed that they had to appeal to the wide range of the bank's new customers and provide them with accessible, easy-to-understand information. This planning helped the team use its knowledge of the occasion, audience, and purpose to select the range of sources:

- First National Bank's current 12-panel customer pamphlet
- correspondence from the First National Bank establishing what they want for the new customer pamphlet
- interviews with the First National Bank Customer Service Manager and the two New Account Representatives who open new accounts for customers
- interviews with 10 new First National Bank customers immediately after they opened an account
- federal regulations stipulating the information that must be included in a customer pamphlet
- selection of customer pamphlets from competing banks

During their planning, team members decided they had several tasks. First they needed information to help assess problems with the current pamphlet. Not only did they do their own expert analysis of the pamphlet, but they also needed to learn the perspectives of both the bank and the bank's customers. The team needed to fulfill all statutory requirements and to see how competing banks handled similar customer information.

Another task was the responsibility to draft a preliminary report to the First National Bank Customer Service Manager. During this drafting stage, the team had several brief telephone conversations with the bank's Customer Service Manager and the New Account Representatives to clarify interpretations of information about legal requirements and definitions of terms.

A third task was completing a preliminary report that discussed three main problems of the current customer pamphlet:

- confusing information about service fees and rates presented in long, complex sentences
- unfamiliar terms that remained undefined or had confusing explanations
- an unappealing format with information that was difficult to locate

On the basis of the information they collected and analyzed, the Pamphlet, Inc., team recommended three changes:

- placing information about service fees and rates in easy-to-read tables
- defining unfamiliar terms and, whenever possible, substituting less complex terms
- designing an appealing, accessible format so that information would be easy to locate

Once the Customer Service Manager approved the general approach suggested by these changes, the Pamphlet, Inc., team redesigned the customer pamphlet.

Government regulations require that banks include a lot of technical information in any kind of public documents. Because many readers find such information difficult to understand, bank employees must work not only to collect the appropriate information, but also to provide a clear interpretation of it for their audience.

When the redesign was completed, the team needed three additional kinds of information:

- feedback from user testing of the redesigned customer pamphlet to determine if actual customers interpreted the new pamphlet as expected
- results from a focus group made up of the same 10 new First National Bank customers examining the redesigned pamphlet to assess their reactions to the differences between the old and new designs
- feedback from a group meeting with the First National Bank Customer Service Manager and the two New Account Representatives to report consolidated results and gain approval for final changes in the design based on feedback from the user test and the focus group

Armed with feedback from the user testing and the focus group as well as the final suggestions from the Customer Service Manager and New Account Representatives, the Pamphlet, Inc., team made final changes to the design. They submitted a report to outline the proposed changes and included a mockup of the revised design. Two weeks later, Pamphlet, Inc., received a letter from First National Bank, which showed that the time and effort they had put into gathering relevant information had paid off:

> We feel that the outline you have created covers all of the FDIC regulations we are required to release to our customers in a brief, easy-to-understand format. We also think presenting the service charges in an informal table makes complicated information more accessible.

LOCATING AND SELECTING SOURCES OF INFORMATION

Part of planning carries over into collecting information. To make the general elements of occasion, purpose, audience, and message usable, you need to define the task so that it guides you in collecting appropriate and useful information. After you have defined your task for your document or oral presentation, you need to draw on information that you already know or information that you have to somehow obtain. This chapter is about ways to obtain and interpret information you need. Figure 11.2 shows the assessment you can make during planning and then the preliminary searches you can make. Your planning questions can guide your search.

You can begin by first looking for information at "home"—that is, in your own organization. Well-run organizations keep accessible records that might include information about finances, personnel, manufacturing, marketing, or shipping. However, sometimes easily accessible information from company records isn't enough.

For example, David Clark, a financial planner for Financial Management Systems, has been asked to write a series of articles for one of the company's monthly newsletters targeted to middle-income clients who are interested in tax-deferred investments. One of the articles in this series will focus on Keogh plans, an underused and misunderstood tax-deferred investment strategy for self-employed people. His purpose is not only to explain Keogh plans but also to answer client questions about why Keogh plans might be part of a good long-term investment strategy.

Figure 11.2 Planning and Preliminary Searches for Information

PLANNING	PRELIMINARY SEARCHES
Gather information about the topic of the interview. • What do you already know? • What do you need to know?	Conduct searches of resources to obtain (1) definitions, pronunciations, and brief histories of the key terms and concepts you're interested in learning more about (2) information about the various positions or points of view held about these terms or concepts (3) an understanding about the arguments that are used to defend one position or another Once you've done a careful review of available information, prepare a list of areas you still need to know about. These topics can become one or more specific questions you need to answer as you collect and interpret information.

Because of his professional expertise, David knows the technical aspects of Keogh plans. On the basis of his preliminary planning, however, he knows that he needs to gather Keogh success stories and information about problems that his middle-income clients need to be aware of. In order to locate this information for his Keogh article, David turns to seven sources for collecting information that are discussed in this chapter:

- traditional library resources
- computerized databases
- e-mail
- Internet
- interviews
- focus groups
- surveys

Library Resources

Regardless of the kind of document or presentation you're preparing, you may need information that's available in a library. But given the vast library resources that are available, knowing how and where to begin is often a problem. For example, the Library of Congress has over 20 million books. In addition to books, libraries can have many of the more than 141,000 different periodicals currently listed in *The Serials Directory: An International Reference Book*, which lists both print and electronic periodical publications. With these vast resources, you need strategies to sort and select the information: a road map to any library.

In the workplace, you may have access to three different kinds of libraries, all with professional librarians who are usually very willing to help anyone who asks for assistance:

- *Company libraries*: If you work for a large organization, it probably has a corporate library that subscribes to relevant professional periodicals and databases, maintains a collection of books related to the company's business, and can obtain specialized materials (ranging from patent information to information from this morning's wire service). Some departments, like R&D or engineering in very large organizations, maintain their own satellite libraries.
- *College and university libraries*: Many companies maintain a cooperative arrangement with local college libraries that lets employees use the library facilities, including interlibrary loan. This gives company employees access to books, periodicals, and electronic services.
- *Public libraries*: If you live in a large city, your public library will have a useful reference section and many business books and periodicals, though it won't be likely to have specialized ones related only to your company's business. Small public libraries may have limited resources, but many do belong to an interlibrary loan network so you can get what you need if you know what you want.

Large businesses often have their own information services. For example, the Information Services division of 3M Corporation, headquartered in St. Paul, Minnesota, has 75 professionals dedicated to providing information to 3M employees. Barbara Peterson, Director of Information Services for 3M, explained in a recent interview[1] that Information Services has four distinct responsibilities (see Figure 11.3). You may work for an organization with such resources, so you need to be familiar with available services.

Unlike a public or college library that is available so people can locate their own answers, a corporate library typically provides the answers. For example, 3M employees who request in-depth information surveys from Information Services estimate that, on the average, receiving this information saves them 28 to 29 hours per project.

Although the search process is individualized for every 3M client who requests help, one example illustrates the general approach Information Services uses: A 3M marketing expert who was interested in the personal voice communication industry needed details about the major players, demographics, and global market growth of this technology. One of the librarians at Information Services spent a great deal of time interviewing this client in order to provide just the resources she needed. The information from the reference interview helped shape a focused search about personal voice communication technology. The client was provided with the following information:

- a search of previously published articles listed in 10 to 15 different databases
- articles from ongoing monitoring of current journals, magazines, and newspapers
- wire service stories from 3M Information Service's Wire Watch, which constantly monitors wire services and selects information such as competitors' product announcements and partnership ventures related to specific projects
- a search of patents to provide information that may give a competitive advantage by revealing competitors' management and marketing strategies

Figure 11.3 3M Information Services

RESPONSIBILITIES OF CORPORATE LIBRARIAN	EXPLANATION
1. responding to three kinds of inquiries: (a) answering fact-based questions, (b) identifying publications related to a particular topic, (c) monitoring ongoing developments with SDI (selective dissemination of information)	Fact-based questions range from locating potential consultants for a new project to identifying regulatory requirements that may affect the development of a new product. Publications related to a particular topic come from sources as far-ranging as state-of-the-art information from patent applications to newspaper articles, all of which help 3M professionals build on what is already known as they prepare research proposals or oral presentations. SDI (selective dissemination of information) enables searches to be tailored to individuals' needs for information. For example, 3M Information Services can monitor what is being published in the field of "competitive intelligence," providing ongoing information from both wire services and journals.
2. providing access to materials	Providing 3M professionals with easy access to traditional library materials means purchasing or having access to all the resources that might be needed, which range from journals to Internet.
3. organizing and maintaining a system that helps 3M tap into the knowledge that has been developed internally in R&D	3M's Information Services organizes internal research and development information—research proposals, laboratory notebooks, research reports—so that it is available and useful to others in the company. Information Services also maintains an on-line database of skills of 3M scientists and engineers, so that when an expert is needed, project teams have a good chance of locating one from among the eight thousand 3M technical employees.
4. helping 3M professionals use and manage information	Ongoing education provided by Information Services helps 3M employees use and manage information effectively. 3M employees learn strategies for sharing information, which makes these employees more self-sufficient.

Reference Resources. You can often find what you need in the reference section of a library—whether corporate, college, or public.

- *Annotated bibliographies*: summaries of books and articles on a variety of specialized topics in business. The following are two representative resources:
  ~*Marketing Ethics: A Selected Annotated Bibliography of Articles*
  ~*The Social Dimensions of International Business: An Annotated Bibliography*
- *References*: compact, organized one-volume reference works, usually presenting information in tables, charts, diagrams, graphs, and glossaries.
- *Specialized dictionaries*: precise, current meanings of specialized, often technical, terms.
- *Specialized encyclopedias*: overview, summary, and discussion of basic facts and theories about a subject; sometimes statistical data, historical background, and bibliographic references.
- *Business and industry guides:* information about companies' locations, structures, officers, services, financial conditions. The following are representative resources:
  ~*Standard & Poor's Register of Corporations, Directors, Executives*
  ~*Thomas Register of American Manufacturers*
  ~*Dun & Bradstreet's Million Dollar Directory*
  ~*Dun & Bradstreet's Middle Market Directory*
- *Career guides:* information about career opportunities. Here are some representative resources:
  ~*Career, the Annual Guide to Business Opportunities*
  ~*The College Placement Annual*
  ~*Who's Hiring Who: Job Directory*
- *Available resources:* reference volumes that identify other sources of information about business. The following are representative resources:
  ~*Daniells' Business Reference Sources*
  ~*Coman's Sources of Business Information*
  ~*Encyclopedia of Business Information Sources, Klein's Guide to American Directories*

Card Catalog. A card catalog—whether drawers of 3″ × 5″ cards or a computerized file accessed by a computer screen and keyboard—is a file of all the library's books and audiovisual holdings such as paintings, films, records, and audio and video tapes. Sometimes a card catalog also lists bound periodicals—a year's issues of a particular journal bound into a single volume. You use a card catalog to determine if the library has books, bound periodicals, or audiovisual materials that you need.

Each item in a college library is assigned an individual number according to the Library of Congress classification system. (Public libraries use the Dewey decimal system.) This Library of Congress system divides books into 20 categories, each identified by a letter followed by specific numbers. The broad letter categories represent major subject areas. The broad categories are further subdivided until each book has an individual number—the *call number*—unique to that specific item. This call number is one of the crucial pieces of information that appear on a card or screen. Every book (or other holding) is cross-referenced by at least three catalog cards (or screens, if the catalog is electronic):

- a card or screen with the book's *title*
- one or more cards or screens with the book's *subject*
- a card or screen with the book's *author*

Sometimes you'll find all three types of cards filed together; at other times you'll find a separate file for subject cards.

Each screen has the same basic information. For example, if David Clark wanted to locate a book about Keogh plans, expecting to find a chapter about potential problems, he could look up "Keogh plan" in the electronic catalog. If he knew a specific author who wrote about Keogh plans or a specific book title, he also could locate a book by looking up the title or the author. This standard information appears on each card or screen:

- identification: complete title, authors and/or editors
- call number: location of the book on the library shelves
- publication: publisher, place of publication, copyright date
- physical information: number of pages of front (prefatory) matter, number of pages, height of book
- supplements: bibliography, index
- cross-references: other card catalog entries for the same book
- library information: order or acquisition date, Library of Congress number

David Clark used an on-line (computerized) catalog to locate resources about Keogh plans. As with a traditional card catalog, he searched for information by *author* or *title*. However, computerized catalogs have a powerful feature that enables users to search by *keyword*, which is the option David decided to use. This option incorporates both a subject search and a search for related terms. Figures 11.4a, b, and c show a series of three computer screens of information that appeared when David conducted his computerized search. This online catalog enabled David to conduct a thorough search much more quickly and efficiently than he could have completed using a traditional card catalog.

Figure 11.4a Computerized Card Catalog Screen: Entries Located by Key Word Search

This is the first screen of information that David received when he entered "Keogh" as his keyword.

Given his interest in locating information about potential problems, David decided that the second entry, "Your Complete Guide to IRAs and Keoghs," looked promising, so he pushed 2 in order to see the individual record about this entry.

```
Search Request:   K=KEOGH PLANS          Library Catalog
Search Results:   2 Entries Found          Keyword Index
--------------------------------------------------------------------
   DATE  TITLE                                      AUTHOR
1  1989  The Dow Jones-Irwin guide to Keoghs
                                                    Cheeks, James
2  1982  Your complete guide to IRAs and Keoghs :
                                                    Egan, Jack
--------------------------------------------------------------------
STArt over       Type number to display record
HELp
OTHer options
NEXT COMMAND:
```

Figure 11.4b Computerized Card Catalog Screen: Basic Information about One Entry

This screen shows basic information about the entry (the same information that would be on a 3″ × 5″ catalog card)—full title and editors (or authors), publisher, description (that is, length, dimensions, illustrations), subjects included, notes.

The information about the book doesn't all fit on one screen, so David moved to another one to get more information. He pressed the F8 key to move to the next screen.

Reading the subjects in a source helps a writer decide if it may be helpful.

```
Search Request: K = KEOGH PLANS              Library Catalog
BOOK – Record 2 of 2 Entries Found                 Long View
----------------------------------------------------------------
Author:         Egan, Jack.

Title:          Your complete guide to IRAs and Keoghs : the
                simple, safe, tax-deferred way to future
                financial security / Jack Egan.

Edition:        1st ed.

Publisher:      New York : Harper & Row, c1982.

Description:    viii, 246 p. : ill. ; 22 cm.

Subjects:       Individual retirement accounts—Handbooks,
                manuals, etc.
                Keogh plans—Handbooks, manuals, etc.

Notes:          Includes index.
----------------------------------------------------------------
STArt over          BRIef view        <F8> FORward page
HELp                INDex             <F5> PREvious record
OTHer options

NEXT COMMAND:
```

Figure 11.4c Computerized Card Catalog Screen: Continued Information about One Entry

The third screen gives the library location, provides the call number so the book can be located in the stacks, and identifies the status: checked out or not.

Checking a source's status can save a lot of time.

```
Search Request: K = KEOGH PLANS              Library Catalog
BOOK – Record 2 of 2 Entries Found                 Long View
----------------------------------------------------------------
Title:          Your complete guide to IRAs and Keoghs : the
                simple, safe, . . .

Notes:          Bibliography: p. 239–241.
----------------------------------------------------------------
LOCATION:            CALL NUMBER          STATUS:
PARKS LIBRARY        HG1660.U5 E36 1982   Not checked out
General Collection
----------------------------------------------------------------
STArt over          BRIef view        <F7> BAck page
HELp                INDex             <F5> PREvious record
OTHer options

NEXT COMMAND:
```

Because David wanted more information about Keogh plans, he decided to use the **Library of Congress Guide to Subject Headings.** This guide identifies alternative labels and related areas of study for the questions or terms you are investigating. Such information provides suggestions for related keywords to check. Figure 11.5 on page 322 reproduces a section of the guide David Clark used during his research.

Periodical and Newspaper Indexes. You can use periodical and newspaper indexes to locate articles in magazines, journals, and newspapers. If you're investigating an unfamiliar field, a good first step is to learn what periodicals publish material in the fields you're interested in. Both *Ayer Directory: Newspapers, Magazines, and Trade Publications* and *Ulrich's*

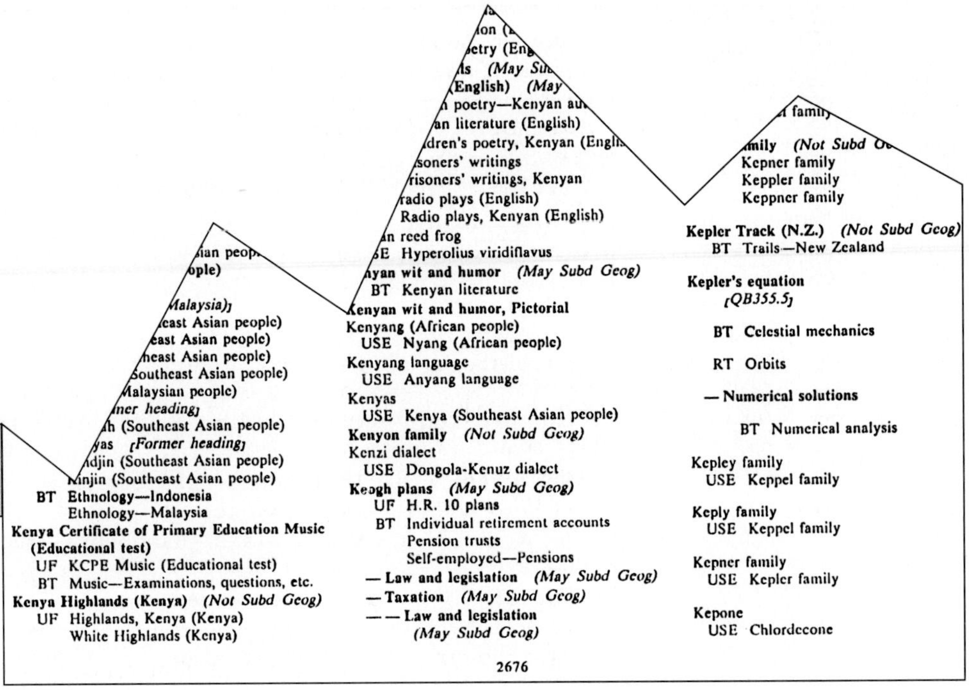
ian peo
ople)
Malaysia)]
east Asian people)
east Asian people)
heast Asian people)
Southeast Asian people)
Malaysian people)
ner heading]
h (Southeast Asian people)
yas [Former heading]
djin (Southeast Asian people)
njin (Southeast Asian people)
BT Ethnology—Indonesia
Ethnology—Malaysia
Kenya Certificate of Primary Education Music (Educational test)
UF KCPE Music (Educational test)
BT Music—Examinations, questions, etc.
Kenya Highlands (Kenya) (Not Subd Geog)
UF Highlands, Kenya (Kenya)
White Highlands (Kenya)
on (
etry (En
s (May Su
English) (May
poetry—Kenyan au
n literature (English)
dren's poetry, Kenyan (Engl
soners' writings
risoners' writings, Kenyan
radio plays (English)
Radio plays, Kenyan (English)
n reed frog
E Hyperolius viridiflavus
yan wit and humor (May Subd Geog)
BT Kenyan literature
Kenyan wit and humor, Pictorial
Kenyang (African people)
USE Nyang (African people)
Kenyang language
USE Anyang language
Kenyas
USE Kenya (Southeast Asian people)
Kenyon family (Not Subd Geog)
Kenzi dialect
USE Dongola-Kenuz dialect
Keogh plans (May Subd Geog)
UF H.R. 10 plans
BT Individual retirement accounts
Pension trusts
Self-employed—Pensions
— Law and legislation (May Subd Geog)
— Taxation (May Subd Geog)
— — Law and legislation (May Subd Geog)
family
mily (Not Subd G
Kepner family
Keppler family
Keppner family
Kepler Track (N.Z.) (Not Subd Geog)
BT Trails—New Zealand
Kepler's equation
[QB355.5]
BT Celestial mechanics
RT Orbits
— Numerical solutions
BT Numerical analysis
Kepley family
USE Keppel family
Keply family
USE Keppel family
Kepner family
USE Kepler family
Kepone
USE Chlordecone
2676

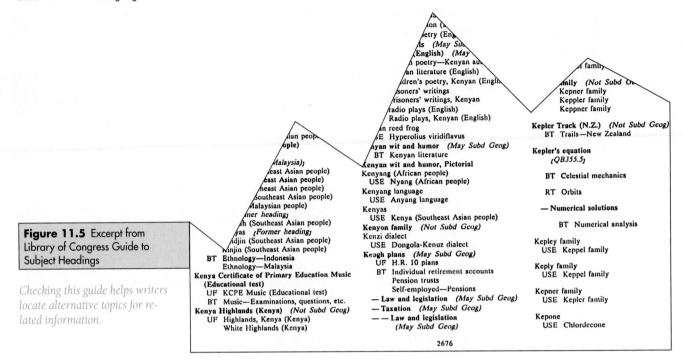

Figure 11.5 Excerpt from Library of Congress Guide to Subject Headings

Checking this guide helps writers locate alternative topics for related information.

International Periodicals Directory: A Classified Guide to Current Periodicals, Foreign and Domestic (with its supplements) are helpful resources to locate relevant periodicals. The following periodical indexes are particularly useful in business:

Accountants' Index

Business Index

Business Journals of the United States

Business Periodicals Index

Index of Economic Journals

Index to Legal Periodicals

Trade, Industrial, and Professional Periodicals of the United States

You will find two broad categories of periodicals: trade magazines and professional journals. *Trade magazines* are usually published for commercial purposes. Sometimes they are published by a professional society in conjunction with an independent publisher, but more often they are published solely by an independent publisher as a for-profit venture. Trade magazines typically accept advertising, post job listings, and offer a broad range of articles that may go through an editorial review but not a strict peer review. Some trade magazines accept product announcements written to look like articles, even though the company has a vested interest. Moreover, trade magazines sometimes accept advertising in the form of articles so that readers sometimes cannot easily differentiate the articles from the ads.

In contrast, *professional journals* are usually published by a professional society, sometimes in conjunction with an independent publisher because of the enormous expense of publication. Professional journals seldom accept advertising and nearly always have strict standards for publishing articles. These standards are maintained because the articles submitted for consideration are reviewed both by the journal's editor and by experts in the field. You will find that professional journals publish more research information and more scholarly information than trade magazines, whose primary purpose is to provide up-to-date information about industry trends, products, practices, and services and to sell the products advertised.

Depending only on trade magazines for information means that you may not have much depth or breadth to your investigation. It may also mean that your material is potentially biased if the articles were written by a company with a vested interest in a product or service. However, while professional journals can add the theoretical or conceptual depth and

SKILLS & STRATEGIES

SELECTING THE RIGHT KIND OF DATABASE

As you begin a database search, you need to review available electronic databases so that you can efficiently gather the kind of information you need.

1. *Reference databases* of two types provide references to other sources of information.
   a. *Bibliographic databases* refer users to citations of published works.
      i. *On-line databases* are accessed on a computer through a telephone connection. Tapes of database records are available by subscription from a database vendor (for example, Dialog). Most people use databases available in libraries. Charges vary from database to database and vendor to vendor. Some vendors have a flat fee. Others have an annual fee plus a per minute connect-time charge. Still others have additional charges for telecommunication links, printing, per citation charges, postage (for mailing a printout), and so on.
      ii. *Compact Disk Read Only Memory* (CD-ROM) databases are accessed with a CD-ROM player and a personal computer. You gain access to CD-ROM databases through a subscription. The cost varies according to the database, vendor, number of backfiles, number of annual updates, and number of users. One CD can hold the equivalent of 275,000 pages of text.
   b. *Referral databases* refer users to other sources for more information.
2. *Source databases* provide on-line users with original information—for example, the results of survey data, results of experimental studies, complete texts of documents.

breadth your investigation may need, they don't necessarily focus on explaining the latest product release you might be interested in or on improving a particular company's competitive position.

Two of the most widely used newspaper indexes are the *New York Times Index* and *The Wall Street Journal Index*. In locating information for his series of articles about tax-deferred investments in general and Keogh plans in particular, David Clark checked several of these indexes to identify the success stories and potential problems he was looking for.

Abstract Indexes. You can use abstract indexes to identify the author, subject, and title references of relevant articles, as well as to read an abstract of each article. Abstract indexes can save you a great deal of time because you can skim the abstracts to determine if articles are relevant before reading them in their entirety. For example, if you have identified the titles of 25 ten-page articles that *might* be relevant to your research, you have 250 pages to read. If you started by reading 25 abstracts, you could select the relevant articles and thus save time, effort, and copying costs.

Computerized Databases

Computer databases permit you to conduct a resource search that is usually far more exhaustive than what you could find manually in an equivalent amount of time. Because available information is increasing at an astounding rate, you need to use computerized databases to access current information. You usually have two broad options for searches:

- CD-ROM databases, which usually charge no fee, so that you can conduct the search yourself using the directions that most libraries provide
- on-line databases, which usually charge by the minute, so that these searches are usually conducted by a research librarian trained to conduct them

Whether you're doing a CD-ROM search yourself or working with a librarian to conduct an on-line search, the general strategies in Figure 11.6 (page 324) will help you plan a focused database search that is time- and cost-effective.

In his database search, David Clark included the following terms: *Keogh plan, self-employed pensions, tax-deferred investments*. He limited his search to the five previous years of books and articles written in English. He requested that the search, which he did not want to exceed $50.00, provide a printout of the summaries so that he could make a decision about which materials would be helpful.

E-Mail

You can request and receive information using e-mail. For example, Denise Steele Stricker, Coordinator of *Newswire* for Northwest Airlines, obtains some of the information she needs for a companywide newsletter from the e-mail information sent to her by other people at Northwest Airlines. Five days a week, she works against her daily 5:00 p.m. deadline to put together *Newswire*, the Monday-through-Friday on-line news for all 46,000 full-time

Figure 11.6 Database Search Strategies

SEARCH STRATEGIES	EXAMPLES
Identify your questions. Look in the database's thesaurus.	What are synonyms for your terms? What alternative terms are used to refer to the topic? For example, if your topic is computer printers, you'll also need to check laser printers and inkjet printers.
Combine the key terms to reflect your questions.	Do you want to search for "usability *and* testing" or "usability *or* testing"? The first combination would give you all citations that contain both the words usability and testing. The second combination would give you all the citations with only usability, only testing, and both usability and testing.
Specify the time frame for your search.	Do you want information from only the current year? from the past five years? ten years? everything that's available?
Specify the type of materials you want to know about.	Do you want only books? articles? audiovisual materials? presentations?
Specify the language(s) in which the information can be presented.	Do you want materials only in English? also in French? in German? Russian? Japanese?
Specify the print format.	How do you want to receive the information? An on-line screen is expensive but available immediately. An off-line printout is usually less expensive but takes longer. What information do you want included in the printout? titles? full citations? complete records with the abstracts?
Specify a price limit.	Who is paying for the search? What is the budget for the search? \$10? \$25? \$50? \$100? \$500?

employees of Northwest Airlines (NWA). Each edition of *Newswire* is approximately four screens (or the equivalent of two pages) and always includes these components:

- an easy-to-read table with the previous day's on-time performance, cancellations, and luggage handling performance of NWA
  example: Denise generally gets this information from the computerized compilation of NWA's daily performance statistics that she receives by e-mail.
- a lead story about some policy or practice of NWA, often a version of a press release about some accomplishment
  example: Denise generally gets this information from press releases she receives from NWA's Media Relations Department.
- industry news about national and international concerns such as earnings and cutbacks
  example: Denise generally gets this information from regional and national newspaper and magazine clipping files compiled daily by the student interns in NWA's Media Relations Department.
- a bulletin board column with NWA-specific announcements
  example: Denise generally gets this information from e-mail messages sent to her by other people at NWA.

The e-mail messages for *Newswire* may come from colleagues in departments as diverse as ground operations, benefits, media, or health care.

Receiving information via e-mail has distinct advantages. First, the person who needs information can send a nearly instantaneous request to one person or a group of people, saving the time and expense of printing and mailing a request. Second, the person providing the requested information can also respond nearly instantaneously. Third, information received on e-mail doesn't have to be typed into a document, since it's already in the computer. Fourth, receiving information by e-mail makes it easy to create an archive of the information. Once the information is in the computer, the receiver can easily keep files of messages organized—essentially a series of electronic file folders to organize and store the information received by e-mail.

Internet

Internet allows access to traditional libraries anywhere in the world. You can "travel" (for example, via Gopher or Telnet) to nearly any library in the world and search its card catalog. Entire books and journals are also available over Internet. Increasingly, publishers are publishing works in both traditional and electronic formats. You can read *USA Today* and *Business Communications Review*, for example, either in hard copy in the library or electronically on the World Wide Web. An increasing number of publications are available online, including *The Nasdaq Financial Executive Journal* and *The Internet Business Journal*.

In addition to having access to traditional sources like books and periodicals, if you use Internet, you can access data sources that offer the latest possible information on the stock exchange, Nielsen ratings, sports scores, business statistics, technical reports—virtually whatever information you need, constantly updated by the supplying agencies. The latest political speeches, Supreme Court rulings, and international news can be accessed, sometimes only minutes after the fact.

Informational Interviews

Frequently, the information you need to complete a task, whether a letter to a disgruntled customer or a rationale for a budget item, is only available by asking another person. As a result, effective professionals develop informational interviewing skills. **Informational interviews** may be conducted in person, by telephone, or by mail. More recently, such interviews are being conducted electronically using an organization's in-house e-mail system for internal interviews and on Internet or a similar network for external interviews.

Such interviews may be very brief and informal—three or four minutes standing in the doorway of a colleague's cubicle as you ask whether the RFQ (request for quotation) needs to be sent to more than three vendors. Or these interviews may be lengthy and formal—like the hour that David Clark spent with the in-house expert on tax-deferred retirement plans. David was particularly interested in asking about ways in which changes in laws regulating Keogh plans affect the information he plans to present to clients in his newsletter article.

Figures 11.7, 11.8 (page 326), and 11.9 (page 327) suggest ways to plan and conduct successful interviews. Figure 11.7 encourages you to collect background information about the person you're interviewing and the company that person works for and suggests ways to approach the person. Planning an interview increases the likelihood of success.

Preparing for an informational interview has two advantages. (1) You'll feel more confident if you know the relevant background of the person you're interviewing. You should do such background work before beginning to frame the specific questions you'll ask during

Figure 11.7 Preparing for an Informational Interview

PLANNING AREA	PREPARATION OF THE INTERVIEW
Gather information about the person you're interviewing and the organization the person works for. • What is the person's job title? • What has this person or organization done or accomplished in relation to the topic you're investigating? • What areas or topics do you expect this particular person to be able to tell you about?	In advance of the interview, send for and carefully read the information packet about the organization that's available from the PR department of virtually every company. Conduct a library search of current periodicals and books to identify and read (1) articles, chapters, or books about the person you're interviewing and (2) articles, chapters, or books written by that person Go through your list of questions to identify and refine those appropriate for the person you're interviewing. Use informal information networks.
Approach the person you want to interview. • What should you know before you contact the person? • How should you contact the person? • What's the best time and place for the interview?	Essential courtesies include knowing the title of the person you're interviewing and learning to pronounce that person's name. Be able to say in one or two sentences why you want the interview. By telephone or letter, arrange an interview at a time and place convenient for the person you're interviewing. Decide on the duration of the interview. If you want to tape-record the interview, ask in advance. Generally avoid interviews early Monday morning or late on any afternoon. Usually you go to the person's place of employment. The day before the interview, call again to confirm the details.

Figure 11.8 Guidelines for Questions to Ask in an Informational Interview

GUIDELINES FOR INTERVIEW QUESTIONS	AVOID ASKING QUESTIONS THIS WAY . . .	INSTEAD, ASK THIS WAY . . .
Create questions whose responses require a definition or an explanation rather than a simple yes or no.	Are employees' working conditions improved by offering flex-time options?	In what ways are employees' working conditions improved by offering flex-time options?
If you must ask a yes/no question to establish a position, follow it with a question requiring some explanation.	Has there been an increase in the past five years in companies using flex-time options?	What has contributed to the increase (or decrease) in the past five years in companies using flex-time options?
Ask questions that require a focused response, not a broad, rambling discussion.	What do you think of management attitudes about flex-time options?	What specific strategies might work to persuade management to offer flex-time as an option for all employees?
Ask a single question at a time, not combined (complex) questions that require multiple answers.	Describe the factors responsible for the slow acceptance of flex-time options in this organization and the work to counter these negative factors.	Describe the factors responsible for the slow acceptance of flex-time options in this organization. Then ask: What is being done to counter these negative factors?
Use terminology that narrows the area of response.	How do flex-time options compare with other nontraditional options?	How do flex-time options compare with job sharing and extended work days?
Prepare questions to tactfully redirect a respondent who has begun to ramble.	If we could get back to the subject, I'd like to ask you to focus on the ways in which flex-time options have been improved.	I'd be interested to hear more of the ways in which flex-time options have been improved.
Research other interviews in the field to avoid asking what have become cliché questions. Instead, find a new angle so that the respondent will be interested in what you ask and will know you have done your homework.	What are the advantages of flex-time options?	How do you think the advantages of flex-time options could be used to extend employee cross-training programs?
Refer specifically to the respondent's published work.	I liked your recent article about flex-time options.	Your article in last month's Personnel Journal effectively supports the importance of flex-time options in rapid-growth companies.
Prepare questions the respondent might perceive as hostile so that the respondent is not offended but, instead, answers.	How can you carry out objective research about flex-time options when your work is funded by the American Management Association?	I understand that your research is funded by the American Management Association. Does that make it difficult for you to conduct your research objectively?

the interview. You'll be far less likely to make foolish, preventable mistakes (like asking the person if he can recommend a good book on the subject you're asking about—only to find out that he has written one of the most widely cited books about the subject). (2) The person you're interviewing will be far more likely to answer your questions if you demonstrate that you cared enough about the occasion to be well prepared.

Once you've collected the necessary background information, you have to prepare the actual questions. Trying a shoot-from-the-hip, I'll-think-of-the-questions-when-I'm-in-the-room approach is not only unprofessional; it's foolish. Top-notch interviewers keep the person they're interviewing focused and get good answers because they're prepared. Figure 11.8 identifies several guidelines to increase the chances that you'll be able to do the same thing.

You need to write your main questions as well as optional follow-up questions that might be appropriate, depending on the answers you get. By writing the questions, you can check that you're actually asking what you want to know. For example, have you made sure that you and the person you're interviewing are defining key terms the same way? Have you asked about assumptions you've made?

Figure 11.9 Effectively Managing an Informational Interview

INTERVIEW MANAGEMENT	INTERVIEW STRATEGY
What basic courtesies should you observe?	Arrive or call on time, and do not exceed the agreed-on length. Even if you have already explained on the phone or in writing, begin by explaining the purpose of the interview, the approximate amount of time you'll take, and the use you'll make of the information.
What questions should you ask?	Prepare your questions in writing to check their wording and double-check their sequence. Write possible follow-up questions (though some follow-up questions can't be anticipated in advance). Practice asking your questions aloud.
What should you wear?	Dress professionally for the organization you're visiting.
What should you bring to the interview?	Bring your questions in a folder or notebook, typed out with plenty of space for answers after each question. Bring two or three pens. If you're using a laptop computer to take notes, make sure its batteries are fully charged. Do not assume there will be an available electrical outlet. If you're using a tape recorder, bring tapes and extra batteries. Make sure to ask permission to tape.
How should you monitor interview behaviors?	Give the person time to respond to your questions. Don't interrupt unless the person strays off track or becomes too long-winded. Convey interest through your tone of voice, facial expressions, and body language. Note the person's body language as a signal to how well the interview is going. Consider asking the person to prepare responses to statistical questions prior to or after the interview itself.
What should you do after the interview?	Write a thank-you letter acknowledging your appreciation for the person's time and assistance. Mention one or two things the person said that were particularly helpful or interesting. Send a copy of the finished article, so the person can make sure the information has been used accurately and ethically.

Informational interviews require careful preparation and adaptation to the occasion if they are going to provide useful information.

Writing the questions also lets you review them to make sure the sequence is logical. Changing the order in which you ask a series of questions may result in different answers, because it's not just the questions that trigger a response—it's also the occasion, which includes the information that the interviewee has just explained. Finally, if you have written the questions, you can ask someone else to review them. Because listeners may not interpret questions the way you intend them, you need to check that at least one other person reacts to the questions the way you expect.

While *what* you ask is important, *how* you ask it is also important. Managing an effective informational interview means following basic courtesies as well as considering organizational conventions such as appropriate attire. You also need to be familiar with ways to make sure the interview moves smoothly.

Focus groups often provide crucial information about how a product will be received by the public.

Equally important is the manner in which you ask the questions—what communication experts call **paralanguage.** Paralanguage refers to your volume, articulation and pronunciation, rate and pauses, pitch, emphasis, and so on. A question might be construed as acceptable or rude depending on your delivery. Similarly, a comment might be perceived as serious or sarcastic depending on your delivery.

In arranging for the interview, you want to convey a sense of professional integrity—ask permission to tape; bring well-researched, well-designed questions; convey interest; express your appreciation for the person's time. Figure 11.9 encourages professional strategies that contribute to successful interviews.

Focus Groups

While e-mail and interviews provide information from one person at a time, **focus groups** compile the opinions of small groups of people into a single data set. These groups, if well designed and carefully run, can provide communicators with detailed feedback from representative opinion holders. Focus groups are run by a trained leader, usually from outside the organization, who is skilled in getting people to provide helpful commentary. A group leader may begin with specific questions but knows the problems and issues well enough to be able to ask appropriate follow-up questions and encourage productive discussion, which can then be turned into suggestions for revision.

Figure 11.10 shows how information from focus groups forms a strong part of a corporate report. In the focus groups, managers and employees were encouraged to express opinions about a range of topics related to employee communication. These opinions were tape-recorded and transcribed. Segments from these transcripts are used liberally throughout the report. As a result, the "voices" of the managers and employees who participated in the focus groups are a central part of the report.

Surveys

While focus groups compile the opinions of small groups of people into a single data set, surveys compile the opinions of many people into a single data set that can be used to substantiate a position. Like informational interviews, surveys may be conducted in person, by

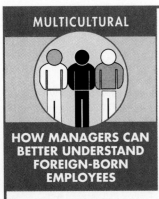

MULTICULTURAL

HOW MANAGERS CAN BETTER UNDERSTAND FOREIGN-BORN EMPLOYEES

Communicating with employees for whom English is a second language can at times be difficult. Sondra Thiederman, president of San Diego–based Cross-Cultural Communication, offers tips about how to communicate with someone with limited English skills.

These tips will help you communicate with people for whom English is a second language:

- Construct your sentences carefully and precisely.
- Don't shout.
- Emphasize key words.
- Let the worker read your lips.
- Use visual aids.
- Use handouts and nonverbal signals (cautiously).
- Repeat and recap frequently.
- Take care not to patronize.

These tips will help you assess how well you've been understood:

- Watch for nonverbal signs that indicate confusion or embarrassment.
- Notice a lack of interruptions.
- Notice employees' efforts to change the subject.
- Notice inappropriate laughter.
- Be alert to the *yes* that means "Yes, I hear your question" not "Yes, I understand."
- Be alert to a positive response to a negative question or vice versa.
- Have the listener repeat what you have said.

These tips will help you understand people who are learning English:

- Share the responsibility for poor communication.
- Repeat what the speaker has said.
- Read the speaker's lips.
- Give the speaker plenty of time to communicate.
- Listen to all that the speaker has to say before assuming that you don't understand.
- Remember to listen and expect to understand.

CONTEXT

Northwest Airlines Corporate Communications prepared a report, "An Assessment of Employee Communications within Ground Operations." Figure 11.10 shows part of the information in this report. This information was obtained from focus groups made up of managers as well as focus groups consisting of employees in each of five major Northwest Airlines locations around the country. The report itself included dozens of comments made by both managers and employees during the focus group sessions.

Figure 11.10 Excerpts from a Northwest Airlines Internal Report That Uses Information from Focus Groups

The writers in NWA Corporate Communications clearly identify the purpose of the report, the sources of information they used, and the extensive data that was collected from these sources.

AN ASSESSMENT OF EMPLOYEE COMMUNICATIONS WITHIN GROUND OPERATIONS

BACKGROUND/PURPOSE

The purpose of this study was to better understand the present employee communications issues, barriers and opportunities within Ground Operations that would lead to the development of a plan that would strengthen the quality and effectiveness of the organization's employee communications.

This study was conducted during November 1993 and included the following components:

- one-on-one interviews with three key executives within Ground Operations
- five focus groups with a total of 75 station managers
- five focus groups with 90 employees in the following markets: Seattle, Minneapolis–St. Paul, Detroit, Boston and Orlando
- a written survey of 275 employees in domestic markets outside the five noted above

More than 22 hours of discussion took place, yielding in excess of 400 pages of transcripts. Notes from these meetings along with careful review of the transcripts provided the basis for the findings that appear in this report.

Because of the strong range of feelings expressed during the course of this study, several of the actual comments made have been reported in this study. Respondents are not identified. These comments are important in helping to communicate the concern and depth of feeling of those who participated and are, therefore, an integral part of this report.

I think one of the biggest problems we have as a company is we turn our voice mail on at 9:00 and off at 5:00, when we should be turning it off at 9:00 and on at 5:00. (Manager, p. 10)

One of the things I've noticed about *Passages* [the twice-a-month company newspaper distributed to all NWA employees] and have enjoyed a lot is reading about the marketing strategies and financial strategies and the reasoning behind it. (Employee, p. 10)

I think the company needs to make an attempt to let the ticket agent and the rep service worker know that their job is every bit as important as the pilot's and the maintenance worker's. (Manager, p. 17)

Northwest can help me communicate by involving me in the decision-making process. (Manager, p. 19)

Listen to us. Act on what we're saying. Don't read more into it and don't pussyfoot around. But listen to us. (Employee, p. 20)

Our best asset is probably *Newswire* [the daily on-line newsletter for all NWA employees], if you have a place you can view the printouts. (Employee, p. 25)

Quotations from focus group comments selected from throughout the report.

telephone, by mail, or with e-mail. When you use "snail mail" (U.S. mail) or e-mail, you need to give people a due date for returning the completed survey.

In order for survey data to be representative, you need to construct the survey items so that you address all your key questions, select the test group, and compile the results. The questions you design for the survey should reflect the key questions you are trying to answer as you collect information from various sources. There are many different types of surveys, but most are based on the six different types of questions defined in Figure 11.11 (page 330). Each type of question has definite advantages and disadvantages. Figure 11.12 (page 331) presents specific examples of several types of questions.

INTERPRETING INFORMATION

Defining the task and collecting information is only half your battle. The other half is making sure that you interpret and present the information as accurately as possible. This section of the chapter focuses on issues associated with recognizing your stance, recognizing the importance of question structure, eliminating errors in logic, and assessing your argument.

Figure 11.11 Types of Questions for Surveys

TYPE OF QUESTION	DEFINITIONS/APPLICATIONS	LIMITATIONS
Dual alternatives	• Respondents choose one of only two choices: yes/no, positive/negative, true/false. • Dual alternatives adequately address simple issues.	• Dual alternatives unrealistically limit range of responses for complex situations.
Multiple choice questions	• Respondents select from several alternatives to indicate preferences or opinions. • Multiple choice questions are appropriate if all reasonable alternatives can be identified.	• Multiple choice questions may not offer an answer with which respondents agree.
Rank-ordered items	• Respondents rank-order a series of items according to preference, frequency of use, or some other criterion.	• Distortion may occur if the mean (arithmetic average) differs significantly from the mode (most frequently occurring number; see page 332). • Respondents usually have difficulty rank-ordering a series of similar items, so they may assign an arbitrary order.
Likert scales	• Likert scales provide a method for respondents to express their opinion by rating items either numerically or verbally on a continuum.	• Tabulation may give distorted results if the mean and mode are significantly different. • If a scale has a middle choice (as occurs when the scale has an odd number of choices), respondents choose it a disproportionately large percentage of the time. Thus, scales are most effective if they have an even number of choices (usually four or six).
Completions	• Completions ask respondents to provide information, both fact and opinion, either in fill-in or open-ended responses.	• Answers are simple to tabulate if the responses are quantitative (for example, age, frequency, amount). But opinion questions present problems in tabulation if respondents give a variety of answers.
Essays or open-ended questions	• Open-ended questions give respondents the opportunity to fully express themselves, presenting both facts and opinions.	• Open-ended questions can generate vague responses that are difficult to tabulate and don't provide much information.

Recognizing Your Stance

Nearly everyone agrees that there's no such thing as a completely objective document, oral presentation, or visual. During initial planning (see Chapter 7), you identify your position, point of view, perspective—your stance. This stance affects the information you choose to collect. It also affects your interpretation of that information.

A team you read about near the beginning of this chapter, the one that worked for Pamphlet, Inc., spent a considerable amount of time in the early stages of their project defining their task. Later in their project, this definition helped them make decisions as they discussed and constructively disagreed with each other about the information they'd collected. Once the team had collected preliminary information (for example, the existing pamphlet as well as interviews with bank officials), they disagreed about how to interpret this information in light of customer needs.

Most of their disagreements centered on the information in the existing 12-panel pamphlet, much of which was mandated by the Federal Deposit Insurance Corporation (FDIC). The team disagreed about the sources of the problems:

- Was the pamphlet difficult to understand because the content was complex or because the design was poor?

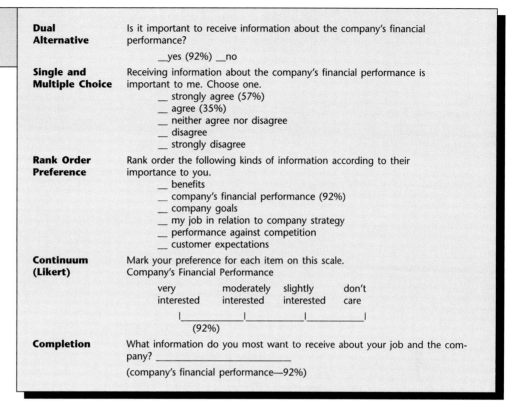

Figure 11.12 Variations of Survey Questions That Could Produce the Same Response but with Different Implications

The type of question a survey asks really does make a difference.

Knowing that 92% of respondents think it's important to receive information about a company's financial performance isn't enough. You need to know what question was asked. Dual alternatives, for example, could elicit far more positive responses than completions.

Dual Alternative	Is it important to receive information about the company's financial performance? _yes (92%) _no
Single and Multiple Choice	Receiving information about the company's financial performance is important to me. Choose one. _ strongly agree (57%) _ agree (35%) _ neither agree nor disagree _ disagree _ strongly disagree
Rank Order Preference	Rank order the following kinds of information according to their importance to you. _ benefits _ company's financial performance (92%) _ company goals _ my job in relation to company strategy _ performance against competition _ customer expectations
Continuum (Likert)	Mark your preference for each item on this scale. Company's Financial Performance very interested / moderately interested / slightly interested / don't care |_______|_______|_______| (92%)
Completion	What information do you most want to receive about your job and the company? ____________ (company's financial performance—92%)

- How much prior knowledge did customers need in order to understand the mandated information?
- Which information would customers perceive as important?

The team's disagreements in interpreting their information made it necessary for them to collect additional information in order to accomplish their task. On the basis of interviews and user tests with bank customers, the team finally agreed about their interpretation of the information and drafted a report that proposed a new design for the bank's customer pamphlet.

TECHNOLOGY

NUMBER CRUNCHING

Computers can help us with our math just as easily as they can help us create written documents. Using any of a number of increasingly sophisticated spreadsheet packages on the market, even novice number crunchers can easily make calculations, determine statistical probabilities, and create charts and graphs.

A spreadsheet is essentially rows and columns of boxes that contain data or formulas. The user enters her data into the sheet (one number per box), then selects other boxes in the sheet to display the results. She selects the display box, picks a formula from a menu (anything from a simple sum to sophisticated statistical calculations) and highlights the numbers she wishes to be calculated by the formula, and the result is displayed automatically. If she goes back and changes any of the original data, the result is automatically recalculated. Most spreadsheet programs can perform these functions:

- create full-color (even 3-D) line graphs, bar graphs, and pie charts
- add clip art, company logos, and other art
- incorporate the images into presentation software or business reports.

But the applications of spreadsheets don't end at doing math and creating displays. Because spreadsheets allow users to recalculate entire complicated formulas by changing a single number (and without having to re-do all the math), they have come to be used for modeling and forecasting. Thus, businesspeople can change projected sales figures for a given month and instantly see how the change might affect their bottom line.

For example, some top-of-the-line spreadsheets include "sliders," which allow users to input a range for a given value (for example, $100,000–$200,000 for a monthly sales figure) and then calculate output for each value in the range automatically.

The Pamphlet, Inc., team found it difficult to identify a single, simple position without a great deal of discussion. Everyone on the team interpreted the information through individual filters of experience. Similarly, you will find it impossible to be objective in interpreting information, but you *can* be fair. That is, you can articulate your stance as well as identify factors that might bias your audience.

Recognizing the Importance of Question Structure

The types of questions you ask in a survey, an interview, or a focus group really do make a difference. The Northwest Airlines report (Figure 11.10 on page 329) presented survey results that said 92 percent of employees stated that it's important to receive information about the company's financial performance. However, this percentage doesn't mean much unless you know the type of question and the specific wording. It is possible to have the same answer to several different versions of a question, as you can see in Figure 11.12 (page 331). However, a 92 percent response to a dual alternative question is not nearly as impressive as a 92 percent response to a completion question. The explanation is simple: When 92 percent of the respondents give the same answer selected from an unlimited number of unprompted choices, it's more persuasive than when 92 percent give the same response out of only two possible choices.

As you see in Figure 11.12, the way that results are reported influences the way they're interpreted. Reporting averages is common in business documents: "the average worker . . . ," "the average number of safety violations . . . ," "the average cost of a maintenance agreement. . . ." However, unless you specify what you mean by *average*, readers or listeners may interpret what you mean in a different way from what you intend. Wording that may lead readers to an erroneous interpretation raises ethical concerns. For example, the scale used as part of the answer to a question about average salary (Figure 11.13) provides a fair and reasonable response; there is no attempt to distort or manipulate the information. But the "average" in the answer may not be what the potential entry-level employee interprets when reading this excerpt from a recruitment brochure.

The term average has three different meanings, *mean*, *median*, and *mode*, all of which are **measures of central tendency:**

mean—the arithmetical average
median—the middle term
mode—the most frequently occurring

As Figure 11.14 shows, there are different ways to calculate answers to the question, "What's the average salary in the Corporate Communication Department at XYZ Computer Corporation?" Three different choices—$36,600 or $34,000 or $29,000—are correct. The first is the mean, the second the median, the third the mode. To avoid confusion and misunderstanding when stating an average, you should specify which measure of central tendency you're using.

Assessing Errors in Logic

The credibility of every document or oral presentation you prepare depends on the logic and integrity of the information (see the material in Chapter 5 about appeals to character). One way you can ensure the integrity of your information is to obtain it from recognized authorities in the field. Evidence loses its effectiveness if the expert's qualifications are suspect or if the expert has a vested interest in a particular position. Once you have established the authority of your information, you can examine it to make sure there are not errors in logic as you interpret and present it.

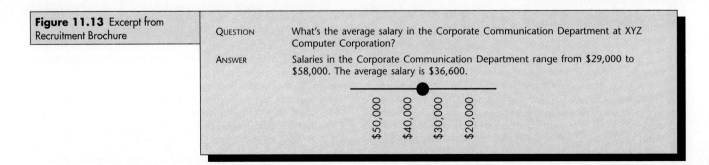

Figure 11.13 Excerpt from Recruitment Brochure

QUESTION What's the average salary in the Corporate Communication Department at XYZ Computer Corporation?

ANSWER Salaries in the Corporate Communication Department range from $29,000 to $58,000. The average salary is $36,600.

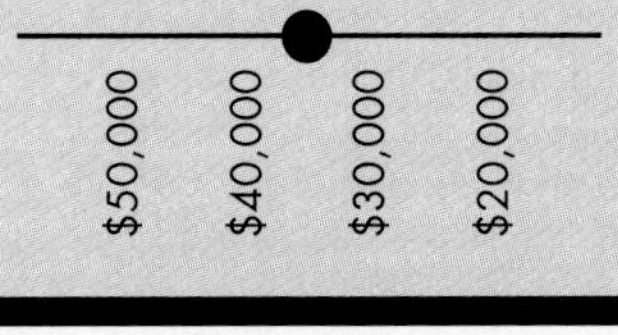

Figure 11.14 Measures of Central Tendency: Mean, Median, and Mode

Mean, median, and mode are all used to indicate "average." A writer could unintentionally mislead readers by not specifying which way an average was calculated. Information might be mathematically accurate but not communicate clearly.

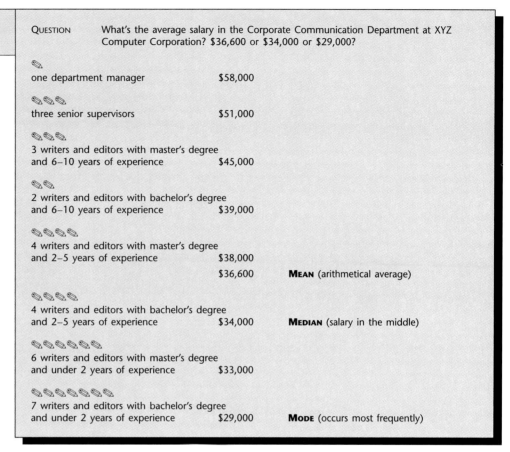

QUESTION What's the average salary in the Corporate Communication Department at XYZ Computer Corporation? $36,600 or $34,000 or $29,000?

one department manager	$58,000	
three senior supervisors	$51,000	
3 writers and editors with master's degree and 6–10 years of experience	$45,000	
2 writers and editors with bachelor's degree and 6–10 years of experience	$39,000	
4 writers and editors with master's degree and 2–5 years of experience	$38,000	
	$36,600	**MEAN** (arithmetical average)
4 writers and editors with bachelor's degree and 2–5 years of experience	$34,000	**MEDIAN** (salary in the middle)
6 writers and editors with master's degree and under 2 years of experience	$33,000	
7 writers and editors with bachelor's degree and under 2 years of experience	$29,000	**MODE** (occurs most frequently)

There are dozens of types of errors in logic (commonly called **fallacies**) and an equal number of ways to classify them. The fallacies discussed here are those most likely to interfere with the interpretation of information in business documents and oral presentations. We have separated these errors in interpreting information into five categories:

- fallacies that establish erroneous assumptions
- fallacies that divert attention and overgeneralize
- fallacies that decontextualize and oversimplify
- fallacies that draw incorrect inferences
- fallacies that misrepresent causal relationships

Fallacies That Establish Erroneous Assumptions. A writer or speaker can mislead an audience about the people, issues, or alternatives involved in a decision. Whether purposefully or accidentally, you affect the accuracy and credibility of your document or oral presentation by establishing erroneous assumptions. Figure 11.15 (page 334) presents three of these fallacies that lead the audience away from central issues of the argument.

Fallacies That Divert Attention and Overgeneralize. Information can be misinterpreted simply because a writer or speaker distracts the audience's attention or encourages them to overgeneralize the situation. These errors may occur when you jump to conclusions or have not examined enough cases to justify a generalization. Figure 11.16 (page 334) identifies four common examples.

Fallacies That Decontextualize and Oversimplify. You will sometimes need to use statistics, quotations, or visuals to support your points. If your supporting information is superficially accurate but in some way incomplete, out of context, oversimplified, or distorted, readers can be misled. Out of context, even facts can be misleading. Figure 11.17 on page 335 summarizes errors in logic that result from decontextualizing and oversimplifying.

Figure 11.15 Fallacies That Establish Erroneous Assumptions

FALLACIES THAT ESTABLISH ERRONEOUS ASSUMPTIONS	EXAMPLE	ANALYSIS
Ad hominem *Ad hominem* (Latin for "against the man") means attacks against the person making the argument rather than against the argument itself.	We should not include ComTech as one of our vendors because we suspect the regional sales rep who handles our account might be HIV-positive.	A person's physical condition—being HIV-positive or having any other disease—has nothing to do with the quality of the product that ComTech sells or with the sales rep's ability to handle the account in a professional manner.
Begging the question The writer assumes that the question being argued has already been proven. Circular reasoning is an extreme example of begging the question.	A report criticized the failure of a company to hire as full-time employees students who had completed its internship program.	The writer ignores the point that the purpose of an internship is to establish whether a student is a good match for the position and the company. It's not a guarantee of employment.
False dichotomy Posing an "either-or" situation misleads readers to believe that only two alternatives exist—even though there may be other possibilities.	Our department has an important decision to make—choosing between two short training courses, one offered by an in-house trainer and the other offered by an outside consultant.	There are other training possibilities—for example, a long course rather than a short course, a self-paced course, a short course followed by individual support. Falsely offering only two choices misrepresents the situation.

Figure 11.16 Fallacies That Divert Attention and Overgeneralize

FALLACIES THAT OVERGENERALIZE	EXAMPLE	ANALYSIS
False analogy The writer argues that because situation X was treated a particular way, situation Z should be treated the same way—with no proof that X and Z are connected.	We have always used three-panel direct-mail fliers to announce new software. We should do the same thing now and forget about proposals to make demonstration disks available.	Just because previous software has been announced in three-panel direct-mail fliers is not necessarily a good reason that new software should be announced in the same way.
Straw man Two positions are presented. The weaker or less relevant position is attacked so the remaining position is left to be accepted.	The committee should reject the Harding plan, which advocates cumulative sick leave.	Rejecting the Harding plan leaves a more controversial plan that proposes a sick leave bank from which employees could draw in an emergency.
Non sequitur A non sequitur (Latin for "it does not follow") makes claims that are irrelevant to the point being argued.	This employee evaluation system has been adopted by the Human Resources departments in 50 major corporations. Therefore, we should be willing to try it in our 75-person company.	Just because a system is widely used by large organizations does not mean that it's appropriate for small organizations.
Slippery Slope The writer argues, usually simplistically, that taking the first step will inevitably lead to a second, usually undesirable step.	If we approve company-paid fitness checkups, soon we'll be paying for every little personal thing that anyone asks for—a vacation in Tahiti to improve fitness, a new mountain bike to improve fitness, a company swimming pool to improve fitness.	Company-paid checkups give employees a baseline to work from in order to plan a regular program of fitness. There is no direct link between fitness checkups and requests for vacations, bikes, or pools.

Fallacies That Draw Incorrect Inferences. You frequently draw inferences based on the information you collect. These inferences will be faulty if you make hasty generalizations, assume irrelevant functions, or fall victim to fallacies of composition and division. You need to check that your information is representative of the general condition or situation that you're discussing. Figure 11.18 summarizes errors in logic that result from drawing incorrect inferences.

Figure 11.17 Fallacies That Decontextualize and Oversimplify

FALLACIES THAT DECONTEXTUALIZE AND OVERSIMPLIFY	EXAMPLE	ANALYSIS
Omitted or incomplete information Omitted or incomplete information affects the accuracy and credibility of a document.	The primary reason for recommending Carlyle copiers to replace the outdated Canon printers in the accounting office is that Carlyle printers have a significantly lower price for toner cartridges—less than 50% of the current copier's discounted price.	Although toner cartridges for Carlyle printers are significantly lower in price—less than 50% of Canon's discounted price—the messy and time-consuming process of using these cartridges must be weighed against the convenience of competitors' higher-priced cartridges.
Out-of-context information The omission of relevant background or contextual information gives readers a distorted view.	Many of 3M's new, successful marketing products come from entrepreneurial efforts—like Post-it brand notes.	In most technical areas at 3M, employees can devote 15% of their time to personal projects. A few entrepreneurial projects have turned into successful products—like Post-it brand notes.
Oversimplification of information Oversimplification distorts by reducing a complex occasion to simple issues and ignoring relevant details.	A newspaper ad by the management at Firestone Tires explained that the negotiating package on the bargaining table offered Cost of Living Allowance (COLA) wage payments linked to offsetting improvements in productivity.	The company proposed that COLA payments be linked to offsetting improvements in productivity, but required productivity levels to increase in each period according to standards set by the company. (From a responding union ad)
Visual distortion of information Visual distortion misleads readers by presenting data that manipulates or omits critical information. (See Chapter 13.)	The graph presents employment figures for the state, showing that the percentage of unemployed workers is dropping.	The graph doesn't include workers who have been unemployed more than 12 months. While short-term unemployment may be dropping, chronic unemployment is not.

Figure 11.18 Inferential Fallacies

FALLACIES IN DRAWING INFERENCES	EXAMPLE	ANALYSIS
Hasty generalizations A particular case or situation is mistakenly assumed to be typical or representative of a broader time period or a larger group.	Annual reviews include a 15-minute observation of every employee in which the manager unobtrusively notes characteristics of the employee's behavior.	A 15-minute observation out of what is typically a 2,400-minute workweek is an observation of only 0.6% of the time an employee is at work, hardly enough on which to base an evaluation.
Irrelevant functions Something is criticized for not having a characteristic it was never intended to have.	This new, larger hard drive in my computer is inadequate because my files are still disorganized.	A larger hard drive enables a user to install more (or larger) software applications and to store more files, but it does nothing to organize those files.
Fallacy of composition and division Characteristics of individual components are attributed to the whole, or characteristics of the whole are attributed to each of the individual components.	I've always owned an ExcelloVax vacuum cleaner. Even though they're very expensive, they've always been excellent. If I buy another ExcelloVax vacuum, I'm sure I'll be satisfied.	For 40 years, ExcelloVax ranked among the top in the industry. Now the product name has been sold to a company that is using the name on one of its models that has only moderate efficiency. The ExcelloVax name recognition enables the company to continue to charge high prices.

Fallacies That Misrepresent Causal Relationships. Business documents frequently discuss cause-and-effect relationships. Readers can be misled by a condition that is not a sufficient cause and by false causal relationships (traditionally called the fallacy of *post hoc, ergo propter hoc*), as summarized in Figure 11.19 on page 336.

Knowing these fallacies—recognizing them in your own drafts as well as in documents others write—will help you accurately interpret the information you collect. Documents that avoid fallacies are more effective and create a more positive image.

Figure 11.19 Causal Fallacies

FALLACIES IN CAUSAL RELATIONSHIPS	EXAMPLE	ANALYSIS
Condition not a sufficient cause One cause by itself cannot produce an effect.	When Enrico Juarez joined the company soccer team, they started winning. His South American training is the reason.	At the same time, the team also started having longer practices and received new equipment, both of which probably contributed to its success.
Post hoc ergo propter hoc One event following another does not necessarily mean that the first event causes the second.	A small business finally was able to provide health insurance for its 12 employees. When seven employees filed claims within the first six months of the policy, the owner said that having medical coverage caused his employees to get sick.	The increased medical coverage didn't cause employee illness. Instead, the coverage probably made it possible for them to report and get treatment for conditions that they might previously have ignored.

ETHICS

DATA MASSAGE: THE ETHICS OF GRAPHICS DISPLAYS

In addressing practical ethics, expert Herbert Michaelson points out a "subtle conflict between an author's self-interest and the obligation to provide adequate information for readers."

Sometimes writers misrepresent information by manipulating (or massaging) data. For example, the first time a field test engineer looks at test data for an instrument prototype, her spreadsheet might show quite a variance in the data. She can "correct" the raw data statistically to control for variance and, lo and behold, the next graph she produces may show that the prototype performed well during the test. The manipulation allows the test results to be shown in the best possible light and contributes to continued support for the project. However, even though such manipulation is technically permissible, it might not be the most ethical course of action, especially if only the "massaged" data is included in the final report.

In addition to massaging data, there are several other ways to visually misrepresent data:

- omitting data points that skew results
- manipulating the *X* and *Y* axes
- using units of measurement that present the data in a more favorable light.

In each case, readers are deceived, and the integrity of the document is diminished.

Misleading graphic elements may also cause readers to overlook weaknesses of a product or a plan. Using graphics to distract readers from text that contains undesirable information is an ethically questionable practice.

RESPONSE SHEET

INFORMATIONAL INTERVIEWS

WRITER(S): **AUDIENCE(S):**
OCCASION FOR COMMUNICATING:
END PRESENTATION/DOCUMENT:
WHAT PROBLEM/ISSUE AM I TRYING TO ADDRESS IN THIS PRESENTATION/DOCUMENT?

◆ PLANNING

What do I already know about the topic of the interview?

What do I need to know?

Who am I going to interview? What professional information do I know about the interviewee (job title, appropriate experience, expertise)?

What information do I have about the interviewee's corporation?

What contact information do I need (time needed, time scheduled, method of contact, method of recording information)?

◆ QUESTIONS

What questions am I going to ask the interviewee? How do my questions avoid a yes/no response? (If a question needs a yes/no response, how do I follow it to require some explanation?)

Do I vary the type of question I ask (multiple choice, direct questions, open-ended questions, hypothetical questions) according to the topic?

How do I focus my questions to solicit a directed, rather than a rambling, response? Do I avoid broad questions (with absolute words like all, always, each, every, never, only, none)?

Do my questions ask about one point at a time? How do I avoid asking marathon questions that require multiple answers?

What questions do I have on hand to redirect a respondent who has begun to ramble?

According to my research, what questions are clichéd questions about this topic? How do I avoid asking such questions and take a fresh approach?

What do I do to avoid sounding hostile when asking difficult questions?

What is my concluding cue?

◆ OVERALL CONCERNS

Have I identified my assumptions? How will I be able to tell if my interviewee shares these assumptions?

Have I prepared questions to make sure that the interviewee and I share the same definition of key terms?

Is the sequence I've chosen for my questions logical? (See Chapter 7.) What logic governs the sequence?

How will a different order for my questions possibly change the responses of the interviewee?

Have I asked someone else to review my questions before I go out for my interview?

◆ INTERVIEW MANAGEMENT

What basic courtesies am I prepared to observe?

Have I practiced asking my questions aloud?

How should I dress for the interview, considering the interviewee and the organization involved?

What should I bring to the interview? (Do I have fresh batteries and extra tapes?)

How can I plan to allow the interviewee plenty of time for my questions?

What have I planned as a follow-up?

ACTIVITIES, EXERCISES, AND ASSIGNMENTS

◆ IN-CLASS ACTIVITIES

1. Imagine that you are one of the students on the team (Figure 11.1) investigating the ISO 9000 standards for a client company. Write a memo to the other team members that recommends a plan to help the team do a better job of collecting and then interpreting information. Use the following questions as a guide.

   a. What key questions could the team consider as the focus of its inquiry?

   b. What are possible sources of information about ISO 9000? (You may need to collect some information to answer this question.) What sources may you need to revisit later in the process?

   c. Imagine that your team's report needs to be submitted to the client in 10 weeks. Given this schedule, what sequence do you recommend for collecting information from your sources—that is, what will you do first, second, and so on?

   d. At what point in the process do you think the team should plan to shape its recommendation?

2. a. Review the search strategies in Figure 11.6, and then work in a small group to brainstorm alternative key terms for one of these subjects (or select a subject of your own):

   - TQM
   - flex-time
   - aseptic beer production
   - groupware
   - CPM (critical path method)
   - multimedia

   What are the advantages of having a list of alternative key terms?

   b. Review Figure 11.8. Then, using the same subject that you selected to answer question 2a, work with your group to write three questions you'd like to ask during an informational interview. Explain your rationale for the way you word each question.

3. Re-read the Skills and Strategies box, "Selecting the Right Kind of Database." Then visit the library and learn what kinds of databases are available that are relevant to your profession or discipline. Make a list of the names and descriptions of databases that would be useful to you.

4. Work in a group of four to review the fallacies discussed in the chapter. Collectively select one fallacy from each of the following categories to review. Then work together to select examples and discuss why each example is a problem. Present your examples and explanations to the class.

   a. a fallacy that decontextualizes or oversimplifies

   b. a fallacy that draws incorrect inferences

   c. a fallacy that misrepresents causal relationships

   d. a fallacy that diverts attention and overgeneralizes (*Hint*: Editorials in college newspapers are great sources for this.)

◆ INDIVIDUAL AND GROUP EXERCISES

1. Locate the reference section of your library and spend some time there browsing. Locate five business reference books that you've never used. (You may select these reference books yourself, or your instructor may suggest specific ones to check.)

   a. Record information about each book:

   - bibliographic information for each of these five books
   - type of information in each book
   - audience for the reference book
   - features that make this reference book easy to use
   - at least two situations in which you might use each book (something like this: "You might use this book if you wanted to find out about. . . .")

   b. Contribute your information to a whole-class reference list that everyone collaboratively prepares so that all members in the class have a list of your library's reference books related to business.

2. On the basis of the information in this chapter, and especially in Figure 11.8, revise the following informational interview questions posed to a company's human resources manager. Use the Response Sheet to help you plan.

   a. Is your company's benefits policy clearly explained?

   b. Has there been any increase in the past five years in companies using user-friendly, accessible benefits package information?

   c. What do you think of management attitudes about revising the employee benefits booklet?

   d. Describe the factors responsible for the slow acceptance of making benefit information available in a direct and timely manner.

   e. What are the advantages of providing employees with clear benefits information?

3. Each of the following situations has a problem with logic. Work with a small group in class to assess the logical problems in each situation. Be prepared to explain your analysis of each situation to the class, identify the kind of error, and suggest a way to eliminate the problem.

   a. Sauer Mining Company has announced that because women miners at its Midland Mine have consistently lower accident rates than male miners, the company is going to operate a mine with only women miners.

   b. The Northwest Sales Division of Chi Industries, Inc., consistently has the highest quarterly repeat sales of all the company's sales groups. Therefore, the Northwest Division must have the best employees.

   c. Because 77 percent of the students who pass the Jordon Training Program are hired by a company and retain their jobs for more than six months, the program is considered a success.

d. A store installed bar code scanners at the beginning of January. When January sales were lower than December sales, the manager argued that since the scanners were installed in December and the sales dropped the next month, the scanners were responsible for the reduced sales.

e. Graphics artists who use the best desktop publishing software are going to produce excellent drawings.

f. One company announced that its new hiring and leave practices resulted in increased productivity and higher sales. Specifically, the company said that three factors—hiring of "mommy track" employees, approval of a family leave policy, and hiring of a number of minority-group employees and promoting them to management—resulted in higher sales. The company ignored the fact that at the same time there was an increase in the tariff on the product the company produces.

g. A company wrote a simple harassment policy. It stated, "No inappropriate language or gesture shall be tolerated."

h. What are these speakers forgetting to consider?

- I won't ever work for a boss who is ___. (Fill in the blank: a "woman," "anyone under 30," and so on.)
- I don't want to work for ___. (Fill in the blank: "an organization with a negative national image but good local divisions," and so on.)

i. A union representing company employees offered a seminar on sexual harassment issues. In the next six months, there was a 50 percent increase in sexual harassment charges against company personnel. During the same six months, there was national news coverage of a sexual misconduct case involving a public official. At about the same time, one of the employees in the company successfully prosecuted a fellow supervisor for sexual assault. A manager was overheard to say that the union, with its seminar, had set up a situation which encouraged harassment and that is why there had been an increase in claims.

◆ OUT-OF-CLASS ASSIGNMENTS

1. Locate at least two published interviews with a business professional in two different issues of a widely read weekly business magazine. Imagine that you are a consultant asked to analyze the questions that the interviewer asked in an effort to strengthen the interviews done for this magazine. Use the guidelines for composing interview questions discussed in this chapter to help you assess the type and structure of the questions, their sequence, and their content. Write a brief recommendation report presenting your analysis. Provide specific examples identifying things that should remain unchanged and recommending ways the interviewer could improve questioning strategies. (Make sure to provide appropriate citations for the articles you review.)

2. Select a business topic that interests you—anything from paternity leave to foreign investments in American companies. Imagine that you are preparing an annotated bibliography of eight entries about your subject for a professional magazine or journal of your choice.

An annotated bibliography is a list of useful, current sources about a specific topic. Each entry in an annotated bibliography includes a citation that identifies where the article or book chapter is located and a short paragraph (usually only a few sentences) that provides key information about the article or chapter's content and usefulness. To locate possible articles and chapters for your annotated bibliography, use traditional library resources as well as computerized databases.

Your annotated bibliography should look like an article for the publication you have selected. Your article should have an introductory section of two or three paragraphs, explaining why the subject is of particular interest or importance to readers of the publication you have selected. Then the annotated bibliography entries should follow. The entry for each article should include (1) a complete bibliographic citation (see Appendix B for formats) and (2) a brief annotation (150–200 words) that identifies the content of that article, the article's intended audience, your opinion about the accuracy or bias of the article, and your opinion about the helpfulness or interest of the article.

CASE

ENERGY COMMISSION RECOMMENDATION

CASE BY ANDREA BREEMER FRANTZ

Background. You have recently been appointed to a special task force connected with the U.S. Department of Energy and the U.S. Department of Education, which have joined forces to allocate special funds recently set aside by Congress to educate large energy users about conservation. The energy education program is designed to target five states with high-profile campaigns to encourage energy conservation, environmental awareness, and community involvement. The *1993 Annual Energy Review* has provided you with the following data regarding energy consumption:

Rank	State	Trillion Btu
1	Texas	9,915.1
2	California	7,092.3
3	Ohio	3,732.6
4	New York	3,616.0
5	Pennsylvania	3,597.0
6	Louisiana	3,557.5
7	Illinois	3,487.3
8	Florida	3,066.4
9	Michigan	2,784.1
10	Indiana	2,407.8
11	New Jersey	2,401.0
12	Georgia	2,094.7
13	N. Carolina	2,018.9
14	Washington	1,991.2

(cont.)

Rank	State	Trillion Btu
15	Virginia	1,853.3
16	Tennessee	1,792.7
17	Alabama	1,653.2
18	Kentucky	1,532.4
19	Missouri	1,499.2
20	Wisconsin	1,404.3
21	Massachusetts	1,369.5
22	Minnesota	1,369.1
23	Oklahoma	1,302.0
24	S. Carolina	1,224.3
25	Maryland	1,203.7
26	Kansas	1,013.5
27	Mississippi	967.5
28	Colorado	958.9
29	Arizona	944.5
30	Oregon	942.4
31	Iowa	926.7
32	Arkansas	796.0
33	W. Virginia	794.2
34	Connecticut	761.7
35	Alaska	611.5
36	New Mexico	584.3
37	Utah	556.8
38	Nebraska	505.8
39	Wyoming	422.3
40	Nevada	411.5
41	Idaho	386.6
42	Maine	370.3
43	Montana	340.5
44	N. Dakota	327.2
45	Hawaii	263.1
46	Rhode Island	246.8
47	New Hampshire	244.1
48	Delaware	240.6
49	S. Dakota	204.9
50	Vermont	139.9

In addition, you have the following data issued by the Bureau of the Census:

State Populations, 1993 and 1990

State	1993	1990
California	31,210,750	29,760,021
New York	18,197,154	17,990,455
Texas	18,031,484	16,986,510
Florida	13,678,914	12,937,926
Pennsylvania	12,048,271	11,881,643
Illinois	11,687,336	11,430,602
Ohio	11,091,301	10,847,115
Michigan	9,477,545	9,295,297
New Jersey	7,879,164	7,730,188
N. Carolina	6,945,180	6,628,637
Georgia	6,917,140	6,478,216
Virginia	6,490,634	6,187,358
Massachusetts	6,012,268	6,016,425
Indiana	5,712,779	5,554,159
Washington	5,255,276	4,866,692
Missouri	5,233,849	5,117,073
Tennessee	5,098,798	4,877,185
Wisconsin	5,037,928	4,891,769
Maryland	4,964,898	4,781,468
Minnesota	4,517,416	4,375,099
Louisiana	4,295,477	4,219,973
Alabama	4,186,806	4,040,587
Arizona	3,936,142	3,665,228
Kentucky	3,788,808	3,685,296
South Carolina	3,642,718	3,486,703
Colorado	3,565,959	3,294,394
Connecticut	3,277,316	3,287,116
Oklahoma	3,231,464	3,145,585
Oregon	3,031,867	2,842,321
Iowa	2,814,064	2,776,755
Mississippi	2,642,748	2,573,216
Kansas	2,530,746	2,477,574
Arkansas	2,424,418	2,350,725
Utah	1,859,582	1,722,850
West Virginia	1,820,137	1,793,477
New Mexico	1,616,483	1,515,069
Nebraska	1,607,199	1,578,385
Nevada	1,388,910	1,201,833
Maine	1,239,448	1,227,928
Hawaii	1,171,592	1,108,229
New Hampshire	1,125,310	1,109,252
Idaho	1,099,096	1,006,749
Rhode Island	1,000,012	1,003,464
Montana	839,422	799,065
South Dakota	715,392	696,004
Delaware	700,269	666,168
North Dakota	634,935	638,800

State Populations, 1993 and 1990 (cont.)

State	1993	1990
Arkansas	599,151	550,043
Vermont	575,691	562,758
Wyoming	470,242	453,588

Task. Using the figures from the two tables, and whatever other specific information about each state's natural resources you uncover through your own research, carefully analyze the importance of the data in terms of the special funds to be allocated and determine from your analysis which five states to target for the Commission's energy conservation campaign. Your report will go to the Commission Chair, J. P. Turow, and should clearly outline the specific criteria you used in making your decision. Though you do not know Turow, you have heard he is a stickler for *support* and *clarity* in recommendation reports.

Complication. Turow just contacted you and said that (1) some attempt should be made for *geographical distribution* in the selection of states to receive the funds and you should consider this one of your key criteria, and that (2) the program can accommodate six target states, instead of the original five. Revise your report accordingly.

CHAPTER

12

Designing Pages and Documents

OUTLINE

Designing a Conference Program: How Susan Foley Transformed Text

Functions and Principles of Design

Applying Design Principles to Business Documents

Redesigning Documents

CRITERIA FOR EXPLORING CHAPTER 12

What we cover in this chapter	What you will be able to do after reading this chapter
The basics of page design to make plain text appealing and usable	Design text for specific purposes and audiences
Functions and principles of design	Appreciate functions of design: to attract readers, conform to conventions, and aid comprehension
Applications of design principles to business documents	Use standard principles: chunking related information with grids and white space; labeling chunks with headings; creating visual coherence through typography and integrated designs; and establishing emphasis through font styles and typographic devices such as lists, boxes, shading, and color
Reader resistance caused by various design problems	Redesign pages to avoid design problems

All of us have had the experience of struggling through documents whose designs are unappealing and perhaps even inaccessible. The lack of appeal and accessibility comes from many possible factors such as dense text, lack of white space, inappropriate font choices, and problems in chunking (grouping) information. As you'll learn in Figure 12.1, there may be other factors that also contribute to an unappealing design. For example, the federal Securities and Exchange Commission (SEC) closely regulates the information that must be included in a prospectus, so brokerage houses and investment firms are compelled to include a great deal of information in a compressed space.

CONTEXT

Waddell & Reed, Inc., is an investment firm that includes United Funds, Inc., as one of its collection of mutual funds. Like all mutual funds, the United Funds has a prospectus that defines the expenses, provides organizational and financial details about the fund, summarizes performance information, and so on. Figure 12.1 reproduces a page from the United Funds prospectus, a document that potential investors should read but many probably don't.

Figure 12.1 Page from United Funds, Inc., Prospectus

Choices that make the document appropriately formal—for example, the fully justified (lined-up) margins and relatively long lines—make it difficult to read.

The use of BOLD ALL CAPS calls attention to the topic heading so readers can anticipate the content.

RISK FACTORS OF HIGH-YIELD INVESTING

The market for high-yield, high-risk debt securities is relatively new and much of its growth paralleled a long economic expansion, during which this market involved a significant increase in the use of high-yield debt securities to fund highly leveraged corporate acquisitions and restructurings. Thereafter, this market was affected by a relatively high percentage of defaults with respect to high-yield securities as compared with higher rated securities. An economic downturn or increase in interest rates is likely to have a greater negative effect on this market, the value of high-yield debt securities in a Fund's portfolio, a Fund's net asset value and the ability of the bonds' issuers to repay principal and interest, meet projected business goals and obtain additional financing than on higher rated securities. An investment in a Fund which invests in high-yield debt securities may be considered more speculative than investment in shares of a fund which invests primarily in higher rated debt securities.

Prices of high-yield debt securities may be more sensitive to adverse economic changes or corporate developments than higher rated investments. Debt securities with longer maturities, which may have higher yields, may increase or decrease in value more than debt securities with shorter maturities. Market prices of high-yield debt securities structured as zero coupon or pay-in-kind securities are affected to a greater extent by interest rate changes and may be more volatile than securities which pay interest periodically and in cash. Where it deems it appropriate and in the best interests of Fund shareholders, a Fund may incur additional expenses to seek recovery on a debt security on which the issuer has defaulted and to pursue litigation to protect the interests of security holders of its portfolio companies.

In the past, the prices of high-yield debt securities have declined substantially reflecting an expectation that many issuers of high-yield securities may or will experience financial difficulties. At various times, yields on high-yield debt securities have risen dramatically. These higher yields reflect the risk such securities may lose a substantial portion of their value as a result of their issuer's financial restructuring or default. Moreover, a further economic downturn or an increase in interest rates could have a further negative effect on the high-yield debt securities and on the market value of the high-yield debt securities held by a Fund.

Because the market for lower rated securities may be thinner and less active than for higher rated securities, there may be market price volatility for these securities and limited liquidity in the resale market. Unrated securities are usually not as attractive to as many buyers as rated securities are, a factor which may make unrated securities less marketable. These factors may have the effect of limiting the availability of the securities for purchase by a Fund and may also limit the ability of a Fund to sell such securities at their fair value either to meet redemption requests or in response to changes in the economy or the financial markets. Adverse publicity and investor perceptions, whether or not based on

12

1. What does this prospectus do to make the information accessible to readers?
2. What changes could make this page of the prospectus more appealing and accessible—without deleting any content or exceeding one page?
3. In what ways does the *design* of this prospectus reinforce the necessity of careful investment decisions?

Elements that influence the ease or difficulty in reading the United Funds prospectus are discussed in this chapter:

- basic functions and principles of design
- application of these principles to business documents
- the effect of redesign on readers

DESIGNING A CONFERENCE PROGRAM: HOW SUSAN FOLEY TRANSFORMED TEXT

When Susan Foley agreed to serve as assistant program chair for a regional conference, she thought it would be a good chance to meet colleagues from other companies, since her primary responsibility would be to greet and register the presenters when they arrived. But a month before the conference, the program chair was in a serious auto accident. Susan had to take over as chair, using information about the speakers and sessions sent by e-mail (see the excerpt in Figure 12.2a) to design a conference program.

Susan's first step was to list each individual segment of the program in order to identify each item of information for the program booklet. A portion of the list is shown in Figure 12.2b.

Susan's next move was to create groups or chunks of related information. As shown in Figure 12.2c, she identified the time slots for the presentations and then added indentations and adjusted the line spacing (called **leading** and pronounced *leding*) to make the chunking obvious.

Once the chunks were established, Susan drew upon design conventions (see Chapter 6). She italicized presentation and book titles, increased the size of the type, and put headings in boldface (Figure 12.2d).

Having finished the preliminary program design, Susan decided to emphasize the opening address. She highlighted the regular sessions to make it easier for readers to differentiate among the presentations in each time slot. She also made slight adjustments so that the text adhered to design conventions that discourage the sloppiness of an "**orphan**," a single word left alone on a line (Figure 12.2e on page 346).

If one of the early versions of the schedule (Figure 12.2a, 12.2b, or even 12.2c) had appeared in the conference program instead of the final version, professionals attending the conference might have formed negative judgments about the conference organizers, and they might even have formed unwarranted negative opinions about the presenters. In following design conventions, Susan created a program that met the expectations of her audience and thus avoided reader resistance.

Figure 12.2a Plain Text in an Undifferentiated Block

This excerpt cannot be used as a conference program because the text is neither appealing nor accessible. The text is differentiated only by the presence of upper- and lowercase letters. The text provides virtually no cues to help readers remember it.

Opening Address, 1:00 Mary M. Lay: Collaborative Writing in Industry and the Classroom: Bridges and Connections (Co-editor of Collaborative Writing in Industry and Practice) Session A, 2:15–3:30 Panel A1, The Rhetorical Elements of Electronic Mail, Rockie Lyons Beaman Panel A2, English as an International Language in Business Settings, Carol Leininger Panel A3, The Politics of Collaborative Writing, Barbara Mirel Session B, 3:45–5:00 Panel B1, Contextualizing Technology: Choice of Media and Corporate Culture, Craig Hansen Panel B2, Managing a Culturally Diverse Workforce, Jean Bush-Bacelis Panel B3, Collaboration via Multimedia: Implications for Business Communication, Ann Hill Duin

Figure 12.2b List That Identifies Individual Items

The list separates items so that they can be examined and then chunked into groups of related information.

Opening Address, 1:00
Mary M. Lay: Collaborative Writing in Industry and the Classroom: Bridges and Connections (Co-editor of *Collaborative Writing in Industry and Practice*)
Session A, 2:15–3:30
Panel A1, The Rhetorical Elements of Electronic Mail, Rockie Lyons Beaman
Panel A2, English as an International Language in Business Settings, Carol Leininger
Panel A3, The Politics of Collaborative Writing, Barbara Mirel
Session B, 3:45–5:00
Panel B1, Contextualizing Technology: Choice of Media and Corporate Culture, Craig Hansen
Panel B2, Managing a Culturally Diverse Workforce, Jean Bush-Bacelis
Panel B3, Collaboration via Multimedia: Implications for Business Communication, Ann Hill Duin

Figure 12.2c Text That Chunks Information by Using White Space and Indentation

Indentations help create a hierarchy—a time period as the main point and specific presentations chunked together as the subordinate points.

Increased leading separates one panel session from another.

Opening Address, 1:00
    Mary M. Lay: Collaborative Writing in Industry and the Classroom: Bridges and Connections (Co-editor of *Collaborative Writing in Industry and Practice*)

Session A, 2:15–3:30
    Panel A1, The Rhetorical Elements of Electronic Mail, Rockie Lyons Beaman

    Panel A2, English as an International Language in Business Settings, Carol Leininger

    Panel A3, The Politics of Collaborative Writing, Barbara Mirel

Session B, 3:45–5:00
    Panel B1, Contextualizing Technology: Choice of Media and Corporate Culture, Craig Hansen

    Panel B2, Managing a Culturally Diverse Workforce, Jean Bush-Bacelis

    Panel B3, Collaboration via Multimedia: Implications for Business Communication, Ann Hill Duin

Figure 12.2d Text Incorporating Conventions

The main time blocks are emphasized and distinguished from the individual sessions by increasing their size and by boldfacing each session.

The titles of all the presentations, both the opening address and the panel presentations, are italicized.

Opening Address, 1:00

Mary M. Lay: *Collaborative Writing in Industry and the Classroom: Bridges and Connections* (Co-editor of *Collaborative Writing in Industry and Practice*)

Session A, 2:15–3:30

Panel A1, *The Rhetorical Elements of Electronic Mail*, Rockie Lyons Beaman

Panel A2, *English as an International Language in Business Settings*, Carol Leininger

Panel A3, *The Politics of Collaborative Writing*, Barbara Mirel

Session B, 3:45–5:00

Panel B1, *Contextualizing Technology: Choice of Media and Corporate Culture*, Craig Hansen

Panel B2, *Managing a Culturally Diverse Workforce*, Jean Bush-Bacelis

Panel B3, *Collaboration via Multimedia: Implications for Business Communication*, Ann Hill Duin

Figure 12.2e Text That Emphasizes Differences for Readers by Using Boxes, Shading, and Bullets

The opening address is given special prominence by placing the information in a shaded box.

The choices in each time block are distinguished by bullets.

Line endings are adjusted so there is no orphan.

Opening Address, 1:00

Mary M. Lay: *Collaborative Writing in Industry and the Classroom: Bridges and Connections* (Co-editor of *Collaborative Writing in Industry and Practice*)

Session A, 2:15–3:30

- Panel A1, *The Rhetorical Elements of Electronic Mail,* Rockie Lyons Beaman
- Panel A2, *English as an International Language in Business Settings,* Carol Leininger
- Panel A3, *The Politics of Collaborative Writing,* Barbara Mirel

Session B, 3:45–5:00

- Panel B1, *Contextualizing Technology: Choice of Media and Corporate Culture,* Craig Hansen
- Panel B2, *Managing a Culturally Diverse Workforce,* Jean Bush-Bacelis
- Panel B3, *Collaboration via Multimedia: Implications for Business Communication,* Ann Hill Duin

APPLYING FUNCTIONS AND PRINCIPLES OF DESIGN

As may be apparent from Susan Foley's experience, the way you present your information influences readers' reactions to the message. In designing a document—whether a single-page flier or memo or a multipage report or instruction manual—you need to consider three kinds of elements:[1]

- **textual elements**: letters, numbers, and symbols—that is, the characters that form the words in the body of the document as well as the headings, labels, page numbers
- **spatial elements**: spaces between textual elements (like page breaks) as well as the size and location of textual and graphic elements
- **graphic elements**: punctuation marks, typographic devices such as bullets and icons, geometric forms on charts and diagrams, visual displays such as graphs, and logos

Figure 12.3, an excerpt from a brochure for Working Assets (a long-distance telephone company), shows how these elements are part of every document you write.

Your goal is to incorporate textual, spatial, and graphic elements so that readers are encouraged to cooperate. An effective design performs these functions:

- helps *communicators* organize information
- attracts an *audience* and aids comprehension

Figure 12.3 Textual, Spatial, and Graphic Elements at Work in a Text

Spatial Elements

- *Spacing makes words easy to differentiate from each other.*
- *Variations in line endings as well as space between lines make information easy to read.*
- *Bullets are aligned, showing the equal importance of the points.*
- *Spacing between sections helps chunk related information.*

Top Quality Service

Working Assets gives you the same high quality sound and service you get from other long distance carriers:

- Easy "dial 1" calling
- 24-hour operators
- Free calling cards with an easy-to-remember number—your area code, home phone number, plus four digits
- Direct international calling
- Friendly customer service

You Help the Environment

Working Assets is the only long distance company that prints its bills on unbleached, 100% post-consumer recycled paper. If every phone company in America did this, over a million trees a year would be saved!

We also print with soy-based ink whenever possible to minimize toxins in the environment and the workplace. And we plant 17 trees for every ton of paper we use. So when you choose Working Assets, you help the environment.

Textual Elements

- *Differences in the size, style, and weight of the type distinguish the headings.*
- *Headings separate each section of the text.*

Graphic Elements

- *A high-recognition logo is used as part of each section heading.*
- *A single rule (line) separates the heading from the text.*
- *Bullets identify the five service features.*
- *Punctuation follows conventions (with the :) and aids readers in interpreting information (with the !).*

Figure 12.4 Functions of Design in Relation to Elements of Business Communication

FUNCTIONS OF DESIGN			
Helps a *communicator* organize information and reinforce specific purposes	Attracts *audience* attention and aids audience comprehension	Creates a coherent *message* and identifies hierarchical relationships	Uses conventions associated with the genre and *occasion*

- creates a coherent *message* and identifies hierarchies
- uses conventions of design associated with specific *genres* and *occasions*

Figure 12.4 matches these functions with the basic elements of business communication that you already know.

Achieving these functions takes some effort. In order to implement them in your own professional documents, you'll need to keep the following four basic principles in mind:

- chunking or grouping related information
- labeling parts and their relationships
- creating visual coherence
- establishing emphasis by visually calling attention to important distinctions

Look at what happens when these basic principles are violated. Figure 12.5 presents all the information you would need to order any of the computer supplies listed. The information is even chunked—insofar as each product is listed separately. Unfortunately, the categories of information aren't labeled, nor are there any cues (typographic or spatial) to help readers use the information. In fact, unless the product quality, on-time delivery, and prices are

Figure 12.5 Information to Order Computer Printer Supplies and Accessories

1710012-001: Black Toner Cartridge (3,500 prints) Carton (4) @ $65.00

808R63-2021-000: Legal-Size Paper Tray (250 sheet capacity) (8.5″ × 14″ /216mm × 356mm) Requires optional paper feeder tray, part number 808R63-9004-700. Single @ $79.00; Multiple (2–3) @ $68.00; Multiple (4+) @ $60.00

808R63-2022-000: A4-Size Paper Tray (250 sheet capacity) (8.3″ × 11.7″ /210mm × 297mm) Requires optional paper feeder tray, part number 808R63-9004-700. Single @ $69.00; Multiple (2–3) @ $59.00; Multiple (4+) @ $50.00

808R63-2023-000: Letter-Size Paper Tray (250 sheet capacity) (8.5″ × 11″ /216mm × 279mm) Requires optional paper feeder tray, part number 808R63-9004-700. Single @ $69.00; Multiple (2–3) @ $59.00; Multiple (4+) @ $50.00

808R63-2025-000: Envelope Tray (20 envelope capacity) Requires optional lower paper feeder tray, part number 808R63-9004-700. Single @ $89.00; Multiple (2–3) @ $79.00; Multiple (4+) @ $70.00

808R63-2026-000: Executive-Size Paper Tray (250 sheet capacity) (7.25″ × 10.5″ /184mm × 267mm) Requires optional paper feeder tray, part number 808R63-9004-700. Single @ $79.00; Multiple (2–3) @ $68.00; Multiple (4+) @ $60.00

TECHNOLOGY

DESKTOP PUBLISHING

In the recent past, companies that wanted their own letterhead, envelopes, stationery, newsletters, advertisements, and other publications had to either have an in-house artist or hire an outside artist to create the materials and ready them for printing. Now, with desktop publishing (DTP) software, nearly anyone can produce these documents.

Already, three different types of DTP software are on the market and are in heavy use. The lowest-level DTP software is actually high-end word processing that can accommodate both text and pictures and has low-level capabilities for wrapping text around images, drawing pictures, and adding borders, headings, and so on. Low-end DTP software can manipulate images: changing colors, dragging and resizing existing pictures, and creating new pictures.

A high-end package can do all of what the low-end packages do but offers far more precision and variety in selecting colors and in making tiny changes in font and image sizes. High-end software also includes additional features that simply aren't available in cheaper packages (like wrapping text within an image or color blending).

Whatever the specific needs of the company, in the hands of a competent user, any DTP software can create camera-ready copy and save the cost of hiring artists to create publications.

Figure 12.6 Excerpt from *QMS Supplies and Accessories Catalog*

Each column is clearly labeled with a heading, so readers can identify the major categories of information.

The choice of fonts—sans serif for the headings and serif for the main text—emphasizes the categories of information.

The quantities and prices are chunked so readers can distinguish the options.

Part Number	**Description**	**Quantity**	**Price**
1710012-001	**Black Toner Cartridge** *(3,500 prints)*	Carton (4)	$65.00
808R63-2021-000	**Legal-Size Paper Tray** *(250 sheet capacity) (8.5″ × 14″ /216mm × 356mm) Requires optional paper feeder tray, part number 808R63-9004-700.*	Multiple (4+) Multiple (2–3) Single	$60.00 $68.00 $79.00
808R63-2022-000	**A4-Size Paper Tray** *(250 sheet capacity) (8.3″ × 11.7″ /210mm × 297mm) Requires optional paper feeder tray, part number 808R63-9004-700.*	Multiple (4+) Multiple (2–3) Single	$50.00 $59.00 $69.00
808R63-2023-000	**Letter-Size Paper Tray** *(250 sheet capacity) (8.5″ × 11″ /216mm × 279mm) Requires optional paper feeder tray, part number 808R63-9004-700.*	Multiple (4+) Multiple (2–3) Single	$50.00 $59.00 $69.00
808R63-2025-000	**Envelope Tray** *(20 envelope capacity) Requires optional lower paper feeder tray, part number 808R63-9004-700.*	Multiple (4+) Multiple (2–3) Single	$70.00 $79.00 $89.00
808R63-2026-000	**Executive-Size Paper Tray** *(250 sheet capacity) (7.25″ × 10.5″ /184mm × 267mm) Requires optional paper feeder tray, part number 808R63-9004-700.*	Multiple (4+) Multiple (2–3) Single	$60.00 $68.00 $79.00

The information is easy to read because each product is a distinct chunk, separated from the other products by horizontal white space.

The differences in font styles—boldface, italics—emphasize the different types of information in each entry.

Coherence is achieved by consistency of font choices, sizes, and styles in each product entry. For example, the product title is always boldfaced; the specifications for the product are always in italics.

dramatically better than competitors' products, most buyers would go elsewhere just to avoid the annoyance of using this catalog.

The application of these four principles—chunking, labeling, creating coherence, and establishing emphasis—is illustrated in Figure 12.6, an excerpt from the actual computer supply catalog. The designers of the catalog knew that information about their products needed to be accessible.

APPLYING DESIGN PRINCIPLES TO BUSINESS DOCUMENTS

Effective design means applying strategies for chunking information, labeling, creating a coherent design, and emphasizing appropriate information.

Chunking Information

You can **chunk** or group related information by creating **grids,** which help you organize textual and graphic information on a page, and **white space,** which is blank space on a page, with no textual or graphic material. Figure 12.7 shows how chunking helps fulfill design functions.

Grids. A "grid" is a pattern of columns and rows (separated by white space) that helps you organize information on a page. For most documents, you'll use a one-column, two-column, or three-column grid like the thumbnail sketches presented in Figure 12.8. Each column forms a chunk of related information. Effective communicators nearly always have a mental image of the grid they want to use for a document. For complex design tasks, communicators often create thumbnail sketches to help them visualize the design.

Grids also have rows, as shown in Figure 12.9. The combination of columns and rows forms sections or quadrants, to which readers give unequal attention. Most Americans begin reading in the upper left-hand section of a page, so that's a good place for important infor-

Figure 12.7 Chunking Strategies That Affect Design

CHUNKING STRATEGIES	ORGANIZING INFORMATION (COMMUNICATOR)	ATTRACTING ATTENTION; AIDING COMPREHENSION (AUDIENCE)	ESTABLISHING RELATIONSHIPS (MESSAGE)	USING CONVENTIONS (OCCASION)
• grids • white space	During their planning, communicators use grids and white space to help chunk related information.	Effective use of grids and white space attracts the audience and makes information easier to locate and understand.	When related information in a message is chunked, readers can more easily identify the key points and recognize related ideas.	Various genres have an identifiable "look" because they use grids and white space in conventional ways.

Figure 12.8 Thumbnail Sketches for Page Design: One-Column, Two-Column, and Three-Column Grids Separated by White Space

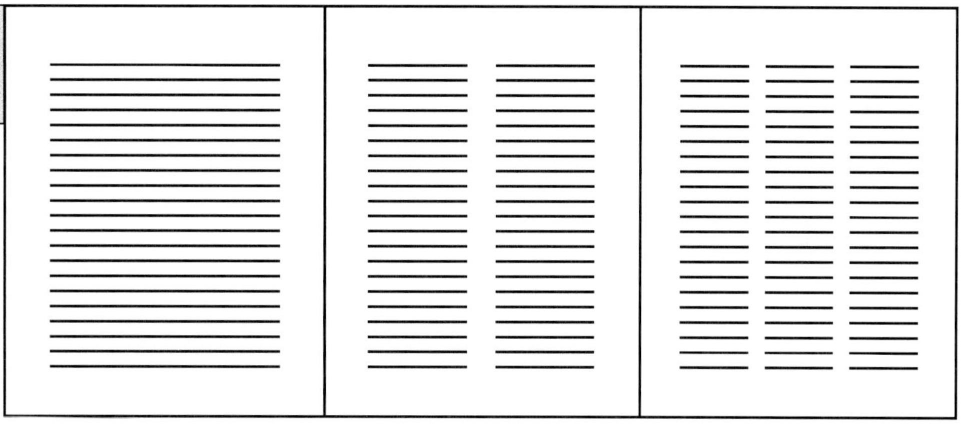

Figure 12.9 Thumbnail Sketches of Grids

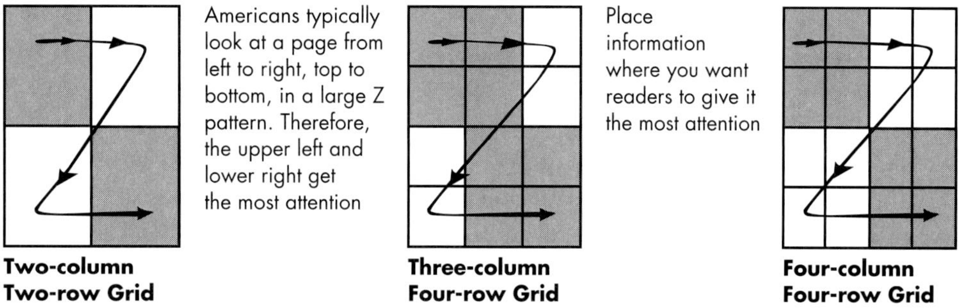
Americans typically look at a page from left to right, top to bottom, in a large Z pattern. Therefore, the upper left and lower right get the most attention
Place information where you want readers to give it the most attention
Two-column Two-row Grid
Three-column Four-row Grid
Four-column Four-row Grid

mation. Similarly, most Americans finish on the lower right section of a page, so that's another good place for important information.

You make your choice about which grid to use on the basis of the occasion and the conventions of the genre as well as the expectations of the audience and the purpose of the document. Readers expect certain kinds of documents to look a particular way. For example, by convention, one-column grids are typically used for correspondence, press releases, manuals, reports, and proposals. Two-column grids are often used for information brochures, articles in professional journals and trade magazines, and package inserts. Two- and three-column grids are often used for newsletters, specifications, and single-sheet flyers.

Readers typically want to locate and read information quickly. A three-column newsletter format addresses readers' needs by incorporating a design layout with prominent headings and short line length. Figure 12.10 on page 350 shows the front pages of two newsletters that are well designed but make different use of their three-column grids.

You can also use grids to help reinforce your purpose. A two-column grid may use columns of unequal widths: the narrower column can be used for marginal headings that not only label the chunks of information but provide an at-a-glance review of what's on the page, as shown in Figure 12.11 on page 351.

Figure 12.10 Different Newsletters with the Same Grid

Despite major differences in their appearance, the front pages of these two newsletters have a number of similarities:

- *prominent mastheads that draw readers' attention*
- *three-column grids with short lines that are easy to read*
- *photographs that create interest and appeal but aren't intended to convey important content*
- *a major article and a column with less important information*

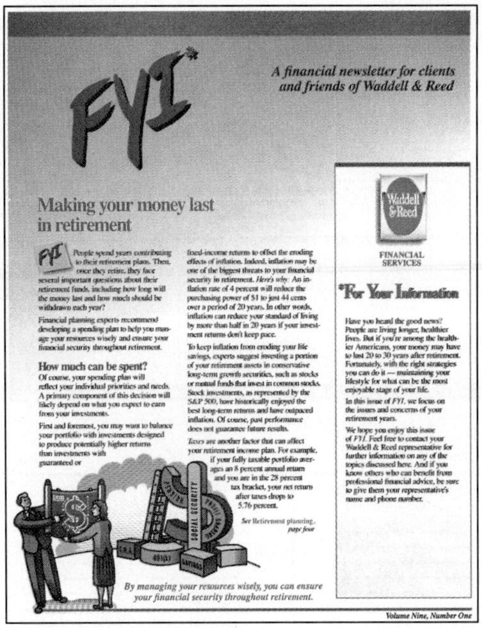

FYI*

A financial newsletter for clients and friends of Waddell & Reed

Making your money last in retirement

How much can be spent?

Waddell & Reed

FINANCIAL SERVICES

For Your Information

By managing your resources wisely, you can ensure your financial security throughout retirement.

See Retirement planning, page four

Volume Nine, Number One

Report of Earnings and Activities 1996 First Quarter/Three Months

Quarterly

Heinz Expands Operations in Eastern Europe With Russian Factory, Czech Acquisition, And Increased Investment in Hungary

H. J. Heinz Company added to its roster of international affiliates with the opening of a factory in Russia, and the acquisition of an infant formula and dairy products company in the Czech Republic. The same week it announced the Czech acquisition, Heinz substantially increased its stake in a Hungarian food processor.

According to Heinz Chairman, President and CEO Anthony J.F. O'Reilly, "These investments have transformed our manufacturing capabilities in the region, enabling Heinz to market high quality baby cereals, formulas, foods and juices to Russia, Hungary, the Czech Republic, Slovakia and Poland. Our total sales in Eastern Europe should be in excess of $100 million in the next twelve months."

Russia

Heinz C.I.S., based in Moscow, opened a newly constructed baby food factory in Stavropol. The plant, which officially began operations in October, will be featured in the next issue of *Quarterly*.

PMV/Zabreh

Heinz now holds a majority interest in PMV/Zabreh, a producer of infant formulas and dairy products located in Zabreh, Moravia, Czech Republic. The other shareholders of PMV/Zabreh, a publicly traded company, include local management, an association of regional farmers, various investment funds and individual investors.

PMV/Zabreh holds leading market shares in the Czech and Slovak Republics for infant formula sold through pharmacies under the Sunar and Feminar brand names. It also makes Sunarka, a dried milk and cereal product, and the Eligo line of powdered milks. Additionally, the company sells butter and liquid and powdered milk to bakeries.

(Continued on page 9)

Total Heinz sales in Eastern Europe should be in excess of $100 million in the next 12 months.

Double-Digit Growth Cited in Secondary Public Offering 4

Ketchup Sign Lights Up City Skyline 6

Ribbon Cuttings At Three Locations 8

White Space. The grids on pages are composed of spaces with ink and spaces without ink; white space is the space that is blank—no print or visuals. White space makes documents more attractive and easier to read. Although there are no absolute rules concerning the use of white space, readers have strong expectations about conventions for certain documents. Violating these conventions can annoy or confuse your readers.

Designers make decisions about grids and white space based on the language they are using and the culture they are addressing.

The four designs in Figure 12.12 use white space in different ways. **Justification** (alignment of the margins) affects a document's formality, appeal, and reading ease. For example, readers usually see annual reports as formal documents. The formality is reinforced by justified left and right margins (that is, both are aligned). While some readers like the neat, clean appearance of fully justified text, many readers consider such text intimidating. And, on a practical level, many readers prefer documents with ragged right margins. Thus, it makes sense that documents such as manuals, press releases, and newsletters use ragged right margins—both because the documents are less formal and because most readers find texts with ragged right margins easier to read.

Another use of white space in these four designs (Figure 12.12) relates to line length, which also affects readers' perceptions of formality, appeal, and ease of reading. A document with shorter lines (and, thus, more white space) gives the impression of being informal, appealing, and easy to read. In contrast, a document with very long lines (and, thus, less white space) gives the impression of being formal, intimidating, and difficult to read. However, readers are frequently annoyed by lines that are too short (just a few words long). Readers usually perceive one-column documents with "average" line length (typically 5 to 6 inches) as appealing and easy to read.

Another use of white space in these four designs (Figure 12.12) appears in the spacing between lines of type, called *leading*. You make a decision about leading every time you decide whether to single-space or double-space a paper. Although readers have strong individual preferences, most generally find long documents appealing and easy to read if the leading is about 150 percent to 200 percent the height of the letter *x* (that is, one-and-a-half spacing or

CONTEXT

The *Guide to Billing* shown in Figure 12.11 was written by Blue Cross and Blue Shield of Iowa (BCBSI) for medical facilities (doctor's offices, clinics) that need to know how to bill patients. The manual is used by office managers and support staff such as secretaries and billing clerks, who need to understand the overall billing process as well as know the specific details needed to process a claim.

Figure 12.11 Page from a Manual Based on a Two-Column Grid

Readers use this manual for reference, so the marginal labels make it easy to scan a page to locate needed information.

Readers often use the information to answer on-the-job questions that need immediate responses. The small chunks make it fast and easy to read and use the information.

The supporting visuals are embedded in the text so that readers can see examples of cards they may need to identify.

Callouts (arrows pointing to specific sections) draw readers' attention to key features.

Readers can check the section label in the footer (strip at the bottom of each page) that identifies the information on that page and the date the information became effective.

BlueCross BlueShield of Iowa

Guide to Billing the HCFA-1500

Different Features on ID Cards

A variety of different features may appear on ID cards. Some groups have their name or logo printed on the front of the card, such as the example shown below. Other cards may show special benefit features, such as preventive service benefits. You do not need to submit this information on the claim form.

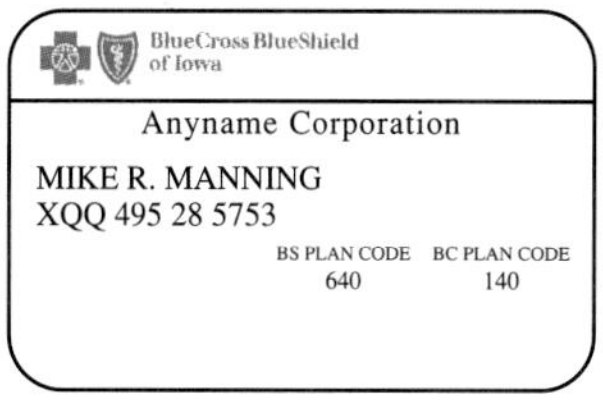

BCBSI Primary to Medicare

There are situations when Blue Cross and Blue Shield of Iowa coverage is primary to Medicare, known as "Medicare Secondary Payer (MSP)."

Example of ID Card for MSP Insureds

The identification card for insureds with Blue Cross and Blue Shield of Iowa coverage primary over Medicare will either have TEFRA or OBRA written on the same line as the identification number (see the example below).

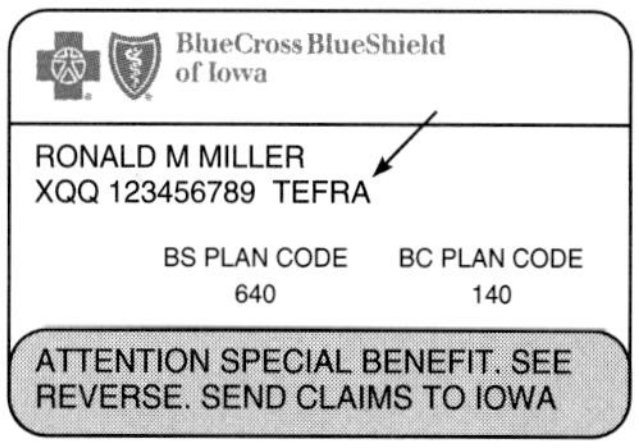

TEFRA indicates the Medicare beneficiary over age 65 has elected BCBSI as primary over Medicare. OBRA is written on a card when a disabled beneficiary has elected BCBSI as primary over Medicare.

MSP Claim Submission

Submit claims for patients carrying these identification cards to BCBSI first and then to Medicare for consideration of additional benefits.

Spring 1993 Insured's Identification 4

Figure 12.12 Thumbnail Sketches of Conventional Grids and White Space for Common Business Documents

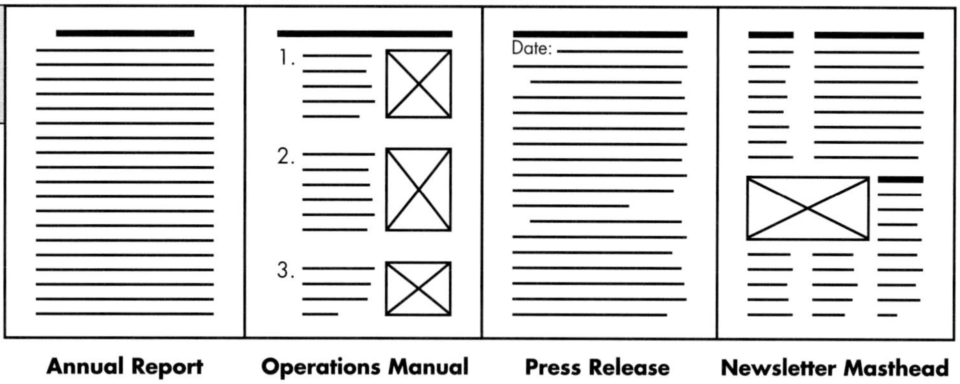

double spacing) in whatever typeface you're using. All typewriters and word-processing software give you the option of adjusting the spacing—the leading—between lines.

Information should be chunked—with an appropriate grid and adequate white space—so that it attracts readers to the document, reinforces conventions, and makes the information easy to locate, understand, and recall. The example in Figure 12.13 is a page from a newsletter designed for busy professionals who need accurate information quickly. The designer of the newsletter used chunking strategies that responded to reader needs. For example, the two-column grid and ragged right margins make the information accessible. The three articles on the page are chunked not only by the grid and white space, but also by design strategies: screened box, bulleted list, and flow chart. The dramatic differences in the presentation of each article make the separate chunks easier to remember.

CONTEXT

The page in Figure 12.13, from a newsletter for Real Estate Tax Services of Arizona, Inc. (RETS), was created by Tedlock Advertising for all RETS members. This particular page focuses on three issues dealing with property tax assessments: (1) taxing business owners who lease property and thus have a "possessory interest," (2) identifying legislative concerns about assessment, and (3) reviewing the process and schedule for assessment appeals.

Labeling the Chunks

Chunks of information by themselves aren't very appealing, so readers benefit from another basic design principle—the use of headings and subheadings to *label parts of a document and the relationship among those parts*. Headings not only identify the conventional sections of a document (for example, background, recommendations, sources cited), but also group the information in labeled, manageable chunks. Headings also help to convey your hierarchy of information—that is, the relative importance of various chunks of information. Finally, headings signal new topics, thus providing abbreviated transitions between sections. Figure 12.14 shows how labeling helps fulfill the design functions.

The hierarchy of information can be signaled by characteristics of the labels you use—type style (for example, **bold**, *italics*, SMALL CAPS) and type placement (for example, centered, left justified, indented, separated, or run-in). Level-1 headings are the main headings (equivalent to the Roman numerals in an outline). Level-2 and level-3 are two levels of subordinate headings.

Figure 12.13 Chunking Influenced by Purpose and Audience

Textual Elements
Headings help readers immediately identify the topic of each article so they can decide whether or not to read it.

Spatial Elements
The white space in the margins, reinforced with the graduated color, forms a border that chunks these three articles together. The cohesive design reinforces the related purposes of these articles.

Graphic Elements
The flow chart helps readers understand and remember the appeals process and critical dates.

The screened box distinguishes one chunk of information.

The bullets help chunk information.

The color highlights the flow chart, which has particularly important information for readers about dates.

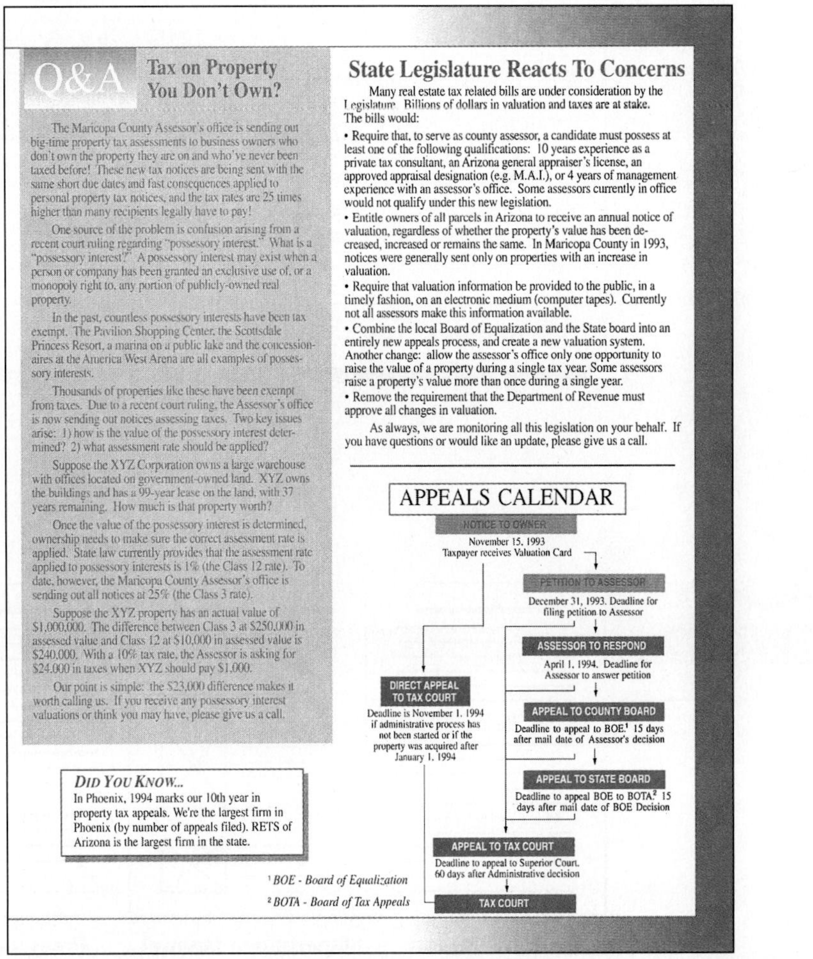

Q&A **Tax on Property You Don't Own?**

The Maricopa County Assessor's office is sending out big-time property tax assessments to business owners who don't own the property they are on and who've never been taxed before! These new tax notices are being sent with the same short due dates and fast consequences applied to personal property tax notices, and the tax rates are 25 times higher than many recipients legally have to pay!

One source of the problem is confusion arising from a recent court ruling regarding "possessory interest." What is a "possessory interest?" A possessory interest may exist when a person or company has been granted an exclusive use of, or a monopoly right to, any portion of publicly-owned real property.

In the past, countless possessory interests have been tax exempt. The Pavilion Shopping Center, the Scottsdale Princess Resort, a marina on a public lake and the concessionaires at the America West Arena are all examples of possessory interests.

Thousands of properties like these have been exempt from taxes. Due to a recent court ruling, the Assessor's office is now sending out notices assessing taxes. Two key issues arise: 1) how is the value of the possessory interest determined? 2) what assessment rate should be applied?

Suppose the XYZ Corporation owns a large warehouse with offices located on government-owned land. XYZ owns the buildings and has a 99-year lease on the land, with 37 years remaining. How much is that property worth?

Once the value of the possessory interest is determined, ownership needs to make sure the correct assessment rate is applied. State law currently provides that the assessment rate applied to possessory interests is 1% (the Class 12 rate). To date, however, the Maricopa County Assessor's office is sending out all notices at 25% (the Class 3 rate).

Suppose the XYZ property has an actual value of $1,000,000. The difference between Class 3 at $250,000 in assessed value and Class 12 at $10,000 in assessed value is $240,000. With a 10% tax rate, the Assessor is asking for $24,000 in taxes when XYZ should pay $1,000.

Our point is simple: the $23,000 difference makes it worth calling us. If you receive any possessory interest valuations or think you may have, please give us a call.

DID YOU KNOW...
In Phoenix, 1994 marks our 10th year in property tax appeals. We're the largest firm in Phoenix (by number of appeals filed). RETS of Arizona is the largest firm in the state.

State Legislature Reacts To Concerns

Many real estate tax related bills are under consideration by the Legislature. Billions of dollars in valuation and taxes are at stake. The bills would:

• Require that, to serve as county assessor, a candidate must possess at least one of the following qualifications: 10 years experience as a private tax consultant, an Arizona general appraiser's license, an approved appraisal designation (e.g. M.A.I.), or 4 years of management experience with an assessor's office. Some assessors currently in office would not qualify under this new legislation.
• Entitle owners of all parcels in Arizona to receive an annual notice of valuation, regardless of whether the property's value has been decreased, increased or remains the same. In Maricopa County in 1993, notices were generally sent only on properties with an increase in valuation.
• Require that valuation information be provided to the public, in a timely fashion, on an electronic medium (computer tapes). Currently not all assessors make this information available.
• Combine the local Board of Equalization and the State board into an entirely new appeals process, and create a new valuation system. Another change: allow the assessor's office only one opportunity to raise the value of a property during a single tax year. Some assessors raise a property's value more than once during a single year.
• Remove the requirement that the Department of Revenue must approve all changes in valuation.

As always, we are monitoring all this legislation on your behalf. If you have questions or would like an update, please give us a call.

APPEALS CALENDAR

NOTICE TO OWNER
November 15, 1993
Taxpayer receives Valuation Card

PETITION TO ASSESSOR
December 31, 1993. Deadline for filing petition to Assessor

ASSESSOR TO RESPOND
April 1, 1994. Deadline for Assessor to answer petition

DIRECT APPEAL TO TAX COURT
Deadline is November 1, 1994 if administrative process has not been started or if the property was acquired after January 1, 1994

APPEAL TO COUNTY BOARD
Deadline to appeal to BOE.[1] 15 days after mail date of Assessor's decision

APPEAL TO STATE BOARD
Deadline to appeal BOE to BOTA.[2] 15 days after mail date of BOE Decision

APPEAL TO TAX COURT
Deadline to appeal to Superior Court. 60 days after Administrative decision

TAX COURT

[1] *BOE - Board of Equalization*
[2] *BOTA - Board of Tax Appeals*

Figure 12.14 Labeling Strategies That Affect Design

LABELING STRATEGIES	ORGANIZING INFORMATION (COMMUNICATOR)	ATTRACTING ATTENTION; AIDING COMPREHENSION (AUDIENCE)	ESTABLISHING RELATIONSHIPS (MESSAGE)	USING CONVENTIONS (OCCASION)
• headings • subheadings	Headings and subheadings help a communicator plan and then "advertise" a clear, logical sequence of information.	Effective headings and subheadings make documents appear appealing and accessible.	Headings and subheadings identify a document's hierarchy so the information is easy to locate and understand.	Headings and subheadings identify document sections, signal new topics, and reinforce transitions.

Figure 12.15 Type Style and Placement of Labels to Indicate Hierarchy

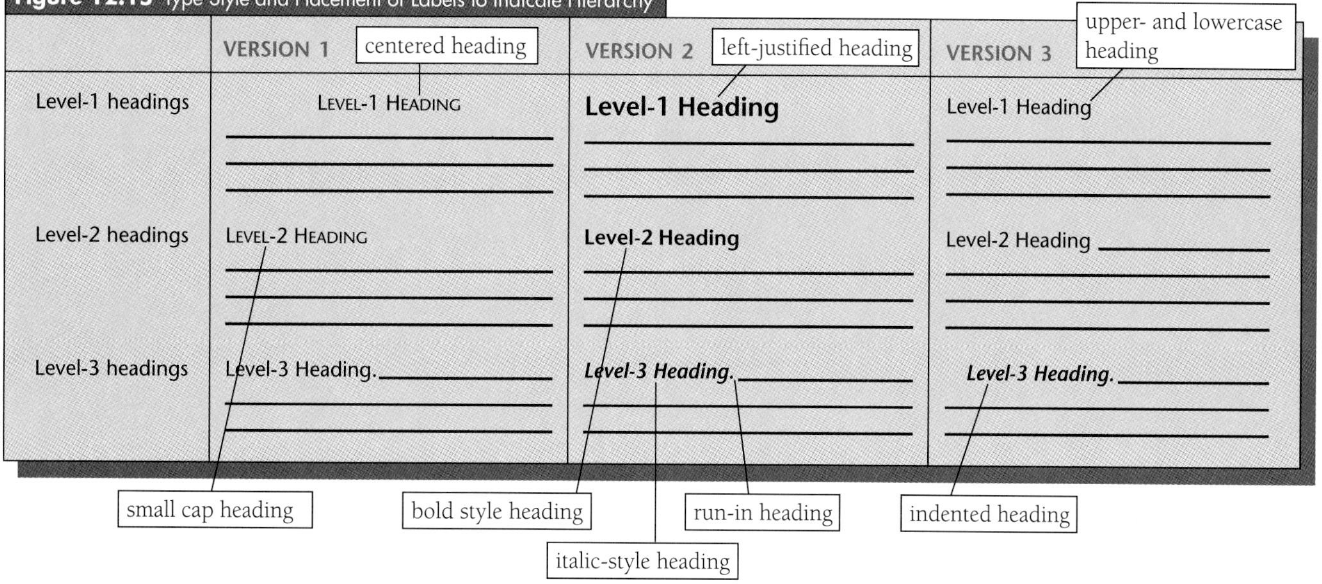

Figure 12.15 identifies three different ways you might label your headings. The most important consideration in deciding about type style and placement for headings is to be consistent within a single document.

If you look back at Figure 12.6 on page 348, you'll see that the four-column grid from the computer supplies catalog makes it easy for readers to understand the relationships because each column is clearly labeled: part number, description, quantity options, and prices for each product. Similarly, Figure 12.11, which reproduces a page from a BCBSI manual, labels the chunks of information so office workers can easily locate answers to their questions as they complete billing forms.

Labels help readers locate information they need—for example, with headings, subheadings, introductions to lists, and identified rows and columns in tables. Figure 12.16 (on the next page) is a page from an administration manual used daily to locate answers to questions quickly. Every page in this manual has a topic heading—*Loans: Takeover Loans* on this page. The two-column grid provides a narrow left-hand column for headings so that readers can quickly scan this column to locate information.

Creating Visual Coherence

A third basic design principle is to *create visual coherence*—that is, a document in which readers can visually identify the parts as a single document or a document in which the parts look as if they belong together. If you look at Figure 12.2d (the conference program),

CONTEXT

The *Pension DC Administration Manual* at The Principal Financial Group is an internal document used by pension administrators when they require instructions to complete a procedure or to answer a customer question. The manual, which is used daily and updated bimonthly, includes procedure and background information on pension products. The administrators are already familiar with the acronyms and jargon.

Figure 12.16 Labeling Influenced by Purpose and Audience

Textual Elements
Readers can distinguish hierarchy by the type style of the headings. Level-1 headings are signaled by BOLD SMALL CAPS. *Level-2 headings are signaled by plain text.*

Spatial Elements
Readers can distinguish hierarchy by the placement of the headings. Level-1 headings are left justified. Level-2 headings are indented.

Graphic Elements
The labels on the action chart make it easy for readers to identify the "steps" and related "actions."

Pension DC Administration Manual

Page 19-10-3
Issued 00-00-00

Loans: Takeover Loans

JTS JOB

Build JTS job for building of loan screen, deposit year and plan year accumulators. The job is built as EE level upkp/verify; the sub-job is Misc changes/coding. Be sure to include the following information on the note screen or in the job folder:

- ID number(s),
- Takeover Loan Checklist,
- instructions to "build loan screens," and
- notation the loans are "takeover."

Include the amortization schedule in the job and make sure you mark the last payment made on the amortization schedule. Also show which payments made represent payments for the current plan year and deposit year.

MULTIPLE TAKEOVER LOANS

Many takeover customers have members who have more than one loan outstanding. We limit recordkeeping services to one loan per member to our existing customers. Explain alternatives for providing loan recordkeeping services when more than one loan per member is outstanding.

Alternative 1

Pay off the member's multiple loans and create a new loan. The following tables describes the procedure:

STEP	ACTION
1	Add member's current outstanding loan balances.
2	Ask customer to establish new loan documentation (Promissory Note and Irrevocable Pledge and Assignment) based on total balance. A new, current interest rate must be given as well.
3	Request PC-generated amortization schedule from support unit. If customer agrees, base amortization schedule payment amount on sum of payments currently withheld. The new loan's origination date should be effective date of new loan documents.
4	Submit JTS job to support unit as outlined previously in this section. Include copy of PC-produced amortization schedule.

Figure 12.3 (the sales brochure), Figure 12.13 (the newsletter), or Figure 12.16 (the manual), you can see that a primary way you can achieve visual coherence is to be consistent in your choice of fonts for variations in both typefaces and type sizes. For example, in the excerpt from the Working Assets brochure (Figure 12.3), each chunk of information is introduced by a heading and a horizontal rule (line). Figure 12.17 suggests how visual coherence can help fulfill the design functions.

Typeface. **Typeface** (also called **type font**) can affect readers' attitudes and reactions to a document as well as their ability to read and understand a document easily and quickly. Because of the desktop publishing revolution, you should know some basic information

Figure 12.17 Visual Coherence Strategies That Affect Design

VISUAL COHERENCE STRATEGIES	ORGANIZING INFORMATION (COMMUNICATORS)	ATTRACTING ATTENTION; AIDING COMPREHENSION (AUDIENCE)	ESTABLISHING RELATIONSHIPS (MESSAGE)	USING CONVENTIONS (OCCASION)
• typeface • font size	Writers use typefaces and font sizes to signal primary and subordinate points.	Effective use of fonts helps create documents that are appealing and accessible because they are consistent and coherent.	Effective use of typefaces and font sizes helps identify the hierarchy of the ideas in a document.	Certain font characteristics are conventionally associated with particular occasions and genres.

about typefaces so that you can make informed decisions when you're designing your documents. Typefaces can be broadly categorized in three ways:

- serif fonts such as Bookman or Times Roman (often referred to simply as Times)
- sans serif fonts such as Geneva or Helvetica
- specialty fonts such as *Zapf Chancery* or **London**

SKILLS & STRATEGIES

USING SERIF AND SANS SERIF TYPEFACES

Serifs are the tiny fine lines usually found at the tops or bottoms of letters. A *serif* font refers to a typeface that has serifs. A *sans serif* font refers to a typeface without serifs (*sans* meaning "without"). Each type of font has specific uses.

Below are examples of lowercase and uppercase versions of some letters in serif and sans serif typefaces: *a* (which sits on the line), *p* (which has a descender that falls below the line), and *t* (which has an ascender that rises above the line).

serif font—10-point Times
serif font—10-point Bookman
serif font—10-point New York

International understanding in a global economy
International understanding in a global economy
International understanding in a global economy

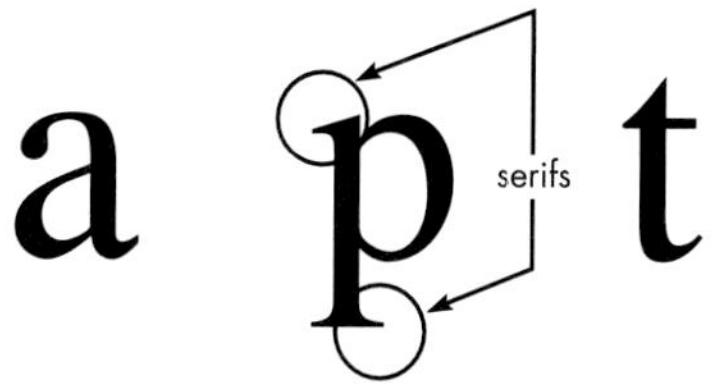

sans serif font—10-point Helvetica
sans serif font—10-point Geneva
sans serif font—10-point Avant Garde

International understanding in a global economy
International understanding in a global economy
International understanding in a global economy

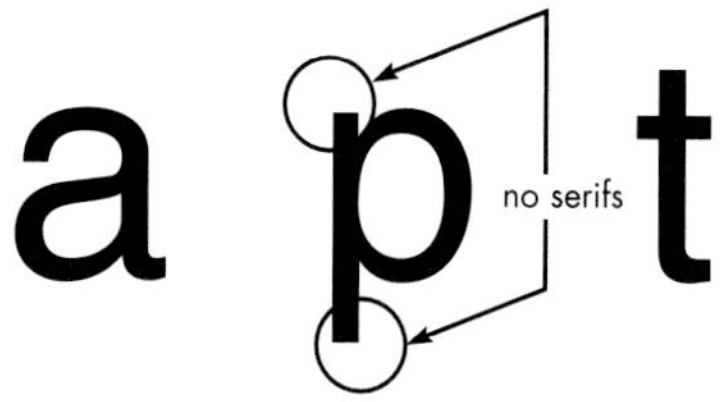

Sans serif fonts, because of their clean, sharp lines that have a neat, appealing appearance, are appropriate for short documents—notices, memos, letters, short reports. But because letters in sans serif fonts don't have many distinguishing features, some people think they are slightly more difficult to read than serif fonts. Thus, long documents—reports, proposals, articles—tend to use serif fonts because of a common belief that they're easier to read for an extended period of time so readers won't tire as quickly.

Adult readers typically read serif or sans serif fonts with equal ease, though many people have distinct preferences. Your selection of font or typeface should be influenced both by the type of document and your sense of readers' reactions. Most specialty typefaces are inappropriate for business documents, tend to be difficult to read, and discourage readers from reading further. You should generally select conventional serif or sans serif fonts.

You can see the impact of fonts on ease of reading and document image by examining three versions of the same excerpt from an OptImage *Project LifeCycle Overview*, an internal document describing the steps for project development. Figure 12.18 shows the same paragraph in a specialty font, a sans serif font, and the serif font in which it was originally published. The specialty font, **Chicago,** is annoying to read for more than a few words at a time. The sans serif font, Geneva, would be acceptable, providing a clear, contemporary image; however, for lengthy documents (and the *Project LifeCycle Overview* is 35 pages long), some readers prefer serif fonts. The serif font, **Times,** is a conventional one that readers usually find easy to read.

Figure 12.18 Three Font Variations for a Document Excerpt

This is a specialty font called **Chicago.** *While this font is distinctive—even dramatic—readers typically find it very difficult to read. Fonts such as this should be restricted to use in headings.*

2.2
QA Manager

The QA Manager is responsible for overseeing that the Project conforms to the established policy. This includes reviewing internal documentation such as Engineering Requirements Specification and Design documentation for completeness and verifying that phase requirements are properly met. The following is a list of some of the QA Manager's responsibilities during the Project LifeCycle.

This is a widely used sans serif font called Geneva. *This would be an appropriate font for virtually any short business document.*

2.2
QA Manager

The QA Manager is responsible for overseeing that the Project conforms to the established policy. This includes reviewing internal documentation such as Engineering Requirements Specification and Design documentation for completeness and verifying that phase requirements are properly met. The following is a list of some of the QA Manager's responsibilities during the Project LifeCycle.

This is a widely used serif font called Times. *This font was used in the original OptImage document. This would be an appropriate font for any short or long business document.*

2.2
QA Manager

The QA Manager is responsible for overseeing that the Project conforms to the established policy. This includes reviewing internal documentation such as Engineering Requirements Specification and Design documentation for completeness and verifying that phase requirements are properly met. The following is a list of some of the QA Manager's responsibilities during the Project LifeCycle.

Type Size. You can affect readers' attitudes about reading a particular document, as well as their comprehension of it, by changing the size of the type. Although tiny type reduces the number of pages in a document, it also makes the document difficult for readers to use. However, a font size larger than 12 points often has a "primer" look and reminds people of their elementary school reading. (Exceptions to this, of course, are materials for visually impaired readers.) Type sizes that range between 8 and 12 points are usually appropriate for business documents. Headings are often larger. The type used for transparencies should be larger still: 18-point or 24-point type works well for making transparencies to accompany oral presentations.

You can vary type size to capture readers' attention. This warning, printed in 24-point Times, is intended to caution readers.

WARNING! Dangerous Radiation!

ETHICS

CONSIDERING FINE PRINT? THE ETHICS OF SLEIGHT-OF-HAND TEXT

Ever read the back of a credit card bill or the teeny print at the bottom of an ad? The choice to use fine print may be made for financial reasons: to save on printing and paper costs. However, fine print can also disguise unattractive information (such as the penalty for late payment on a credit card bill or the extra charge for a monitor in a computer ad).

Readers need access to accurate information to make informed decisions. To meet this need, the government requires disclosure of requirements for interest rates, fees, and penalties in financial documents and ads. However, even though the required text must be there, it doesn't have to be easy to read. In fact, recent court rulings support the use of fine print and place the responsibility for deciphering the text squarely on the reader's shoulders.

How can business communicators use fine print? Miles A. Tinker, who researched the effects of fine print, line length, and space between lines, concluded that legibility diminishes with type less than 9 points (this text is in an 8-point font), especially when small print is in long lines of closely spaced text. Print between 7 points and 9 points can be legible in short lines spaced somewhat apart.

As you decide whether and how to use fine print, consider these factors:

- readers' needs
- purposes for including information
- the letter and spirit of applicable regulations
- the cost to your organization of various sizes and arrangements of the information
- the cost to your readers of illegible information
- the cost to your business of loss of credibility

When you balance these considerations, you may discover that fine print has its place when you need to include reference information or supplemental details, but not when you are presenting information crucial to the message.

Remember your audience as you decide on font and type size.

The warning would not be nearly as effective if it were printed in 9-point Times.

WARNING! Dangerous Radiation!

Although readers are usually comfortable with 10-point, 11-point, or 12-point type, the typeface itself influences the size. For example, as you can see in the Skills box (on page 355), all 10-point type is *not* the same size. Small type enables you to fit more into a space; however, if the type size is too small, the material will be difficult to read. Slightly larger type can make material more accessible and appealing.

Choices in fonts, sizes, and styles not only contribute to a document's coherence but also influence the image of the document. Figure 12.19 (on page 358) reproduces the response to a fan letter that goes a long way in creating a positive image, both for the child who received the letter and for the parents, who also read it.

Establishing Emphasis

A fourth basic design principle is to *establish emphasis* by calling readers' attention to features or distinctions in your text. In Figure 12.6, the excerpt from the computer supply catalog, for example, the headings for each column are emphasized in specific ways—separated from the descriptions with a rule (line), the bold sans serif headings contrast with the serif font of the information itself. Similarly, in Figure 12.16, the page from The Principal Financial Group administration manual, the bold small caps headings are separated from the text in a narrow vertical column. Figure 12.20 (page 358) shows how emphasis can help fulfill the design functions.

Style Choices. The style of the type you select can influence readers. ALL CAPS, SMALL CAPS, **boldface,** and *italics* each have value in helping to establish emphasis. You might want to emphasize terms or phrases for any of these reasons:

- headings or subheadings
- new or unfamiliar terms
- key points
- critical or central questions

Regardless of the kind of document you're planning, you should apply all of these style choices with restraint (see Figure 12.21 on page 359). Individual pages that use more than three or four variations of typeface, type size, or style may look cluttered, and readers will probably be distracted.

Figure 12.19 Creating Visual Coherence for Purpose and Audience

Textual Elements
The primer size font is appealing to and appropriate for the young reader.

Spatial Elements
The ragged right margin not only makes the letter easier to read, but it also appears friendlier and less formal.

Graphic Elements
The Nike logo reminds the reader that Michael wears Nikes . . . and indirectly suggests to a young reader—not yet aware that corporate logos always appear in the letterhead of a sponsoring organization—that maybe fans loyal to Michael do too.

NIKE

Dear Michael Jordan Fan,

Thank you for your letter and interest in Michael Jordan. It is always nice to hear from true Air Jordan fans like yourself. As one of the most exciting, high-flying pro basketball players today, Michael has been very busy traveling around the country and is not able to write to you personally.

However, to show his appreciation of your support, Michael is sending you an autographed photo for your collection. We hope you enjoy this very special momento.

As you know, Michael is committed to doing his best at everything he pursues. We hope that you share this same commitment to excellence in pursuing your goals. Both Michael and NIKE wish you the best of luck in all your future endeavors!

NIKE, Inc. One Bowerman Drive Beaverton, OR 97005-6453 Telephone: (503) 671-6453 Fax: (503) 671-6300

CONTEXT

The letter in Figure 12.19 was mailed to an 8-year-old boy who had written a fan letter to Michael Jordan. The letter is sensitive to the audience—a child learning to read—because of the type style and size as well as the margins.

Figure 12.20 Emphasis Strategies That Affect Design

EMPHASIS STRATEGIES	ORGANIZING INFORMATION (COMMUNICATOR)	ATTRACTING ATTENTION; AIDING COMPREHENSION (AUDIENCE)	ESTABLISHING RELATIONSHIPS (MESSAGE)	USING CONVENTIONS (OCCASION)
• type styles—ALL CAPS, SMALL CAPS, **bold**, *italic* • typographic devices—lists, boxes, color	Emphasizing headings and key terms gives communicators a way to check that their sequence of information is logical and that all new information has been defined or explained.	Emphasizing headings and key terms increases the attention the audience gives to important and/or unfamiliar information.	Emphasizing certain terms distinguishes primary from subordinate information, familiar from unfamiliar information.	Certain ways of achieving emphasis are conventionally associated with particular occasions and genres.

Typographic Devices. Information can be visually distinguished by several devices including numbered and bulleted lists, boxes, and color. Carefully selected devices can highlight critical information and reinforce the points you want to make. Figure 12.22 summarizes guidelines and applications for using these devices.

Sometimes readers need to have attention drawn to specific parts of a document. Figure 12.23 (on page 360) shows how several stylistic and typographic devices are used to empha-

Figure 12.21 Style Choices

STYLE	HINTS ABOUT USE	EXAMPLES
ALL CAPS	• Emphasize a single word or a short phrase with ALL CAPS. • CONSIDER THAT USE OF ALL CAPS FOR EXTENDED SECTIONS OF A DOCUMENT VIRTUALLY GUARANTEES THAT READERS WILL SKIM OR EVEN SKIP THAT SECTION BECAUSE READERS AREN'T ABLE TO PROCESS WORDS WHEN ALL THE LETTERS ARE THE SAME HEIGHT. AS A RESULT, READING IS SLOWER.	• title of your document if the title is short • headings if they're short • labels for warnings, cautions, dangers
SMALL CAPS	• Use SMALL CAPS rather than ALL CAPS, if you have a choice. The distinction between the letters makes SMALL CAPS much easier to read than ALL CAPS.	
Boldface	• Use to emphasize key terms and phrases. • Use for headings to differentiate from the body of the text. • Use to signal something important. • Avoid overuse because frequency diminishes the impact.	• title of your document • key terms or phrases • headings • labels for warnings, cautions, dangers
Underlining *Italics*	• Use to emphasize key terms and phrases. • Use to identify titles of books you refer to. • Avoid overuse because frequency diminishes the impact.	• key terms or phrases • foreign terms • book titles • special sections of the document

Figure 12.22 Typographic Devices

DEVICES	HINTS ABOUT USE	EXAMPLES
Numbered and bulleted lists	• Use a numbered list when the sequence or chronology of items is important. • Use a numbered list when the priority of items is important or when the total count of items is important. • Use a bulleted list when all items in the list are equivalent.	• Instructions, promotional materials, memos, letters, reports, and proposals
Boxes	• Use boxes when you want to emphasize or separate material. • Surround box by white space so that the text does not run into the box. • Relate boxed information directly to the text or use as supplemental information, as in sidebars in magazines, newspapers, and newsletters.	Boxes can be used effectively to help readers in a number of ways: • identifying major headings • highlighting definitions of key terms • signaling sidebars • separating formulas or equations
Color	• Clarify or highlight information. • Create visual interest, highlight section headings, identify examples, and emphasize important points.	

size key information, making it accessible and understandable to the readers. This page from a computer manual is near the beginning of a chapter introducing a new procedure for recording and previewing audio and video clips. The design emphasizes information with headings, italics, font changes, marginal labels, icon diagrams, and bullets.

CONTEXT

Figure 12.23 shows a page from a beta release of the *Delta Vc Manual* for software created by OptImage. The beta release is a test version of the manual sent to major customers, who will use the manual with the software and identify places where the manual is confusing, incomplete, or incorrect. Once suggestions come back from these major customers, the manual will be revised.

Figure 12.23 Establishing Emphasis for Purpose and Audience

Textual Elements
The heading helps readers identify this major chunk of information.

Italics differentiate terms that represent windows on the computer screen.

Spatial Elements
White space helps differentiate the various buttons.

Graphic Elements
Small iconic diagrams help readers know exactly what they'll see on the screen.

Bullets mark the encoding parameters for readers.

◆◆◆ Using mpegStudio

Beta Release

Recording and previewing

All recording and previewing of audio and/or video is initiated from the `Control` window, based on parameters set in the `Source` and `Parameters` windows.

These three windows are accessed by selecting either `Record` or `Preview` from the `Sessions` menu. Each window in turn has a button panel to access the other windows (Figure 1-1).

Source window button

Parameters window button

Control window button

Encoding Parameter Settings

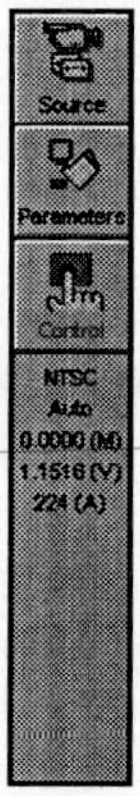

***Figure 1-1:** Button panel in Record/Preview windows*

The current encoding parameters are displayed at the bottom of the button panel:

- Video Standard: `NTSC`, `NTSC 4.43`, or `PAL`
- Video Source Type: `Video` or `Film`
- Timecode: `Control Track`, `MTC`, `LTC`, or `Auto`
- Multiplex Bitrate in Mbits/second
- Video Bitrate in Mbits/second

1-5

REDESIGNING DOCUMENTS

Audiences get used to familiar designs, recognizing everything from the monthly telephone bill to the IRS forms that are due every April. Thus, when a document is redesigned—even when the design is a major improvement, readers are often confused and sometimes annoyed because the format no longer matches their expectations. Readers may resist the unfamiliar new version simply because it is unfamiliar.

UPS decided that its Delivery Service Bill should be designed so that customers could more easily locate and understand call information. After the statement was redesigned, UPS created the brochure in Figure 12.24 to explain the design changes. This brochure anticipates and defuses possible customer resistance by explaining what has been changed—and how the changes benefit UPS customers.

MULTICULTURAL

CULTURAL ASSOCIATIONS OF COLOR

Colors have cultural associations that come from religion, literature, and graphic arts. Because the symbolic meaning of color varies from culture to culture, ignorance about color associations may create unintended meanings. The following are some examples of cultural associations of color:

Culture	Red	Yellow	Green	Blue
Europe and North America	Danger	Caution Cowardice	Safety Sourness Growth and rebirth	Masculinity Sweetness Calm Authority
Japan	Anger Danger	Grace Nobility Childish gaiety	Future Youth Energy	Villainy
China	Joy Celebrations Power	Honor Royalty	No special associations	No special associations
Arabic countries	No special associations	Happiness Prosperity	Fertility Strength	Virtue Faith Truth

Figure 12.24 Brochure Explaining Redesigned Service Delivery Bill to Customers

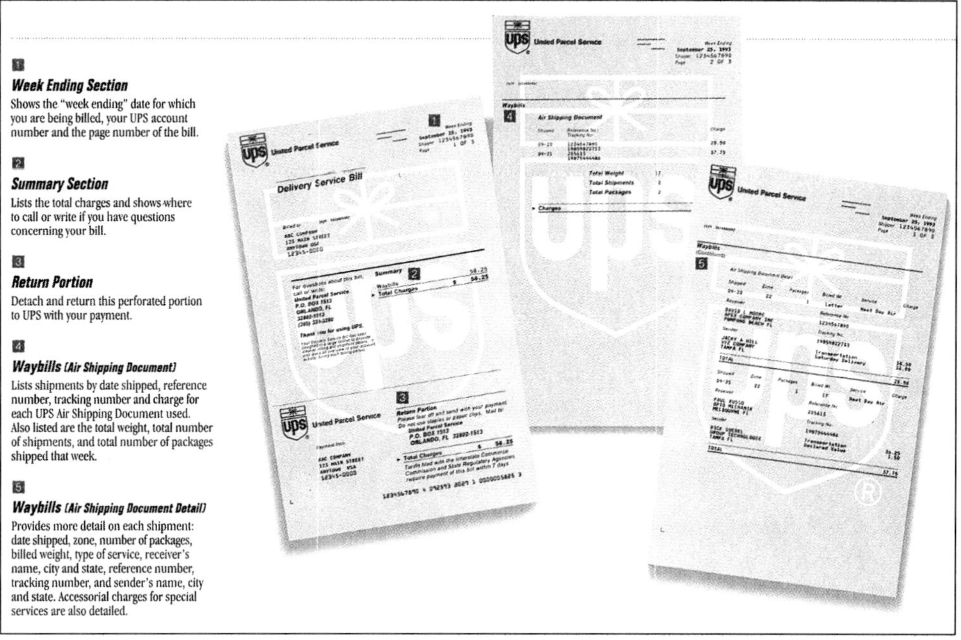
1
Week Ending Section
Shows the "week ending" date for which you are being billed, your UPS account number and the page number of the bill.
2
Summary Section
Lists the total charges and shows where to call or write if you have questions concerning your bill.
3
Return Portion
Detach and return this perforated portion to UPS with your payment.
4
Waybills (Air Shipping Document)
Lists shipments by date shipped, reference number, tracking number and charge for each UPS Air Shipping Document used. Also listed are the total weight, total number of shipments, and total number of packages shipped that week.
5
Waybills (Air Shipping Document Detail)
Provides more detail on each shipment: date shipped, zone, number of packages, billed weight, type of service, receiver's name, city and state, reference number, tracking number, and sender's name, city and state. Accessorial charges for special services are also detailed.
United Parcel Service
Delivery Service Bill

- *chunking and labeling*
  - —*separates billing information (charges) from identifying information (waybill)*
  - —*clearly labels all sections*
  - —*separates total due*
  - —*separates shipping details*
- *graphic devices*
  - —*uses rules (lines) of different lengths to chunk information*
  - —*uses arrowheads to draw attention to charges*
  - —*uses UPS logo as page screen*
- *white space*
  - —*separates shipping details and charges with horizontal space*
  - —*uses ragged right margin*
- *type style*
  - —*uses* ***italic bold****, ALL CAP, and* **boldface** *to signal key information*

RESPONSE SHEET

DESIGNING PAGES AND DOCUMENTS

COMMUNICATORS:	AUDIENCE(S):
OCCASION FOR WRITING:	DOCUMENT:

HOW CAN THE PAGE AND DOCUMENT DESIGN HELP ME ACCOMPLISH MY PURPOSE ON THIS OCCASION, WITH THIS AUDIENCE?

◆ DESIGN ELEMENTS

What are the textual elements in my document? How can I use them effectively?

What are the spatial elements in my document? How can I use them effectively?

What are the graphic elements in my document? How can I use them effectively?

◆ CHUNKING INFORMATION

What *chunking* strategies can I use to organize information, attract attention, establish relationships and hierarchies, and follow the conventions of the document?

- What grid should I use for this occasion, purpose, and audience?
- How should I use white space on each page?

◆ LABELING THE CHUNKS

What *labeling* strategies can I use to organize information, attract attention, establish relationships and hierarchies, and follow the conventions of the document?

- What headings and subheadings should I use to identify the content?
- How should I signal the levels of the headings: placement, font size, font style?

◆ CREATING COHERENCE AND HIERARCHIES

What *coherence* strategies can I use to organize information, attract attention, establish relationships and hierarchies, and follow the conventions of the document?

- What font types and sizes are appropriate?

◆ EMPHASIZING APPROPRIATE INFORMATION

What *emphasis* strategies can I use to organize information, attract attention, establish relationships and hierarchies, and follow the conventions of the document?

- What font styles are appropriate?

ACTIVITIES, EXERCISES, AND ASSIGNMENTS

◆ IN-CLASS ACTIVITIES

1. Refer to Figure 12.1 and then discuss the following questions in terms of what you have learned in this chapter about designing information.
   a. Legal regulations mandate the inclusion of all the information in the prospectus. What problems arise when you have a great deal of complex information that must be included in a relatively limited space for an audience that may be unfamiliar with the information?
   b. What design principles will be useful in making this information more accessible?
2. Re-read the Ethics box, entitled "Considering Fine Print? The Ethics of Sleight-of-Hand Text." Then locate a business message that uses very small print. Discuss with a small group whether the use of very small print is justified in the example. Share your group's opinion with the class.
3. Apply what you've learned in this chapter to explain why you agree or disagree with the position of a newly hired employee who was annoyed that she was expected to use her word-processing software and laser printer to produce professional documents. She wanted to write drafts and turn them over to a secretary, whom she expected to design and format her documents. She said, "My job is to provide the information. I don't much care about making it look pretty. That's someone else's job. Anyone who really needs this information is going to read it no matter how it looks."
4. Designing documents that are appealing, accessible, understandable, and memorable almost always takes a writer more time. Have half the class support the manager who said, "This extra time is justified for all external documents, but I don't want anyone wasting that kind of time for internal documents." Have the other half of the class oppose the manager's position. Work in teams to prepare for an informal debate about this issue.

◆ INDIVIDUAL AND GROUP EXERCISES

1. Work in small groups to design oversize thumbnail sketches of the first page of any three of the following kinds of documents:
   - resume
   - newsletter to employees
   - memo to staff
   - article in a professional journal
   - business letter
   - budget page in a proposal
   - trip report
   - ad for computer software
   - ad for seminar to upgrade professional skills
   - announcement for annual company picnic
   - catalog of available products
   - set of instructions to office staff
   - page from benefits booklet
   - package insert with medication

   Discuss what characterizes the design of each type of document; what makes it recognizable. Make the sketches large enough that people in the class can easily see them, but do not label the sketches. When each group is done, the rest of the class can try to identify each type of document. The "guessers" should say why they think a sketch fits a particular type of document. Discuss why people can often identify these documents simply by seeing a sketch of the first page.
2. Working with a small group of classmates, examine the page in Figure 12.25 on page 364. Identify ways in which the page follows and violates the design principles you've learned. Use the Response Sheet to help review the document. Redesign the page so that the information is more appealing and accessible. Annotate the revised page to explain why you made the design changes.

◆ OUT-OF-CLASS ASSIGNMENTS

1. Refer to Figure 12.6, 12.11, or 12.18 in this chapter. Create another version of one of these documents. Explain why your revision works.
2. Work with a small group and arrange a meeting with an actual client who needs a short document redesigned—brochure, flier, ad, announcement. After interviewing the client to learn about the occasion, purpose, and audience of the document (and why it needs to be redesigned), offer to provide two redesign options. Prepare the new designs and a one-page explanation that explains how each version addresses the client's concerns. After a meeting with the client to get reactions to your designs, make a final recommendation to the client and submit it along with a cover letter that presents your recommendation and provides a rationale.

CASE

THOMPSON APPLIANCES—A DESIGN FOR SAFETY INSTRUCTIONS

CASE BY ANDREA BREEMER FRANTZ

Background. You are a technical writer for a moderate-sized national appliance company. This company is well known for its sturdy, dependable kitchen appliances (for example, stoves, refrigerators, dishwashers, and garbage disposals) and last year enjoyed its largest jump in sales in its 34-year history. Based in Morgantown, West Virginia, Thompson Appliances was founded by Keith and Suzi Thompson, who led the company from a local, one-room appliance and repair shop to a 42-store nationwide chain. Though Keith and Suzi Thompson recently retired to Garnavillo, Florida, their sons, Burke and Frasier, currently own and manage the growing company.

Figure 12.25 Letter from SBA

U.S. SMALL BUSINESS ADMINISTRATION
WASHINGTON, D.C. 20416

Dear PASS Participant:

Enclosed you will find a copy of your company's profile which has been listed in the Small Business Administration's (SBA) Procurement Automated Source System (PASS) for at least one year. Please take a few minutes to review the profile and make any changes you believe are appropriate so that we are able to keep the information on your company current and useful.

Within the past year, the PASS system was enhanced to accommodate several new information fields which were designed to allow you to provide a wider range of important information on your company. These new fields include Security Clearance of Site and Key Personnel, Contract Performance Data, FAX number, Bonding by Aggregate Total, U.S. Citizenship Indicator, and Metric Capability. A new "Special Equipment" text field has been added so that you can specifically list any special equipment or facilities. Two existing fields have also been replaced: Number of Employees has been changed to Average Number of Employees (over the last 12 months) and Sales has been changed to Average Gross Revenue (for the last 3 years). These two fields are critical to us in determining your status as a small business.

When you review your company's profile, please be sure that you have accurately completed all sections. SBA's regulations now allow for your registration in PASS to be accepted as an official representation of your firm's status as a small, minority or women-owned business. Pay particular attention also to the statement of your company's capabilities. Your company will be listed in PASS under the goods, services, and products that you describe in this section. Then, please sign the profile and return it to the address listed at the top of the form, rather than to the SBA in Washington, DC.

It is important to note that if you do not respond, we regret that your firm's profile will be dropped from the PASS data base. We are making every effort to keep the information in PASS as up to date and as useful as possible.

More than 950 government procurement offices and commercial contractors now rely on PASS to help them identify small businesses for contracting opportunities and there are approximately 220,000 firms listed in PASS. Although there is an increasing number of users of PASS, it is not a universal Federal source list and is meant only for those firms which are seriously interested in selling goods and services to the Federal government and its prime contractors. Registration in PASS does not provide a guarantee of new business.

Thanks for your participation in PASS!

Sincerely,

Thomas A. Dumaresq
Acting Associate Administrator
for Government Contracting

Enclosure

When they assumed control of the company late in 1993, Burke and Frasier Thompson announced that their primary goal was to maintain the strong family image of Thompson Appliances. Thompson's then launched a national advertising campaign for their new line of deluxe, frost-free refrigerators. The television and print campaign featured a real-life couple who from 1964 to 1982 had adopted 12 children of various races and ages.

Wilma Blanke, the mother of the family, spoke in the ad about the many important events that had taken place in their kitchen over the years. In her inimitable Southern drawl, Wilma's voice served in the television ad as the background to a series of black-and-white and color photographs of family members in the kitchen: "We've shared tears and laughter. We've had arguments, fixed up Christmas dinners, and . . . oh, we've made *enormous* messes. Why just last year, Janet and I sat up half the night makin' those little mint candies for her high school graduation party that we held right here." The camera then focused on Wilma in her kitchen next to the Thompson refrigerator, which was covered with magnets holding hand-drawn pictures, photographs, lists, and coupons. "And this Thompson fridge," she said with a smile as she leaned against it, "has seen it all." The slogan "this Thompson fridge has seen it all" quickly caught on, and the ad campaign boosted sales 27 percent over the previous year. Among the most important benefits to the ad campaign in the Thompson brothers' minds, though, was the fact that the campaign reflected the sort of traditional family values and realism they believed Thompson Appliances should stand for.

Last week tragedy struck. In Oberlin, Ohio, the Forrester family had just purchased a new home and were in the process of moving in when they discovered their 2½-year-old daughter, Leah, missing. They searched everywhere and called the police. A massive search ensued, and for three days volunteers combed the area to no avail. On the fourth day, as the Forresters prepared to move the refrigerator (a Thompson deluxe frost-free) from the enclosed back porch where they had stored it, they discovered that Leah had crawled into the appliance and had smothered. Movers had inexplicably removed the shelves and placed them in a box next to the refrigerator, so the small child could easily fit inside. The local news station echoed the nationwide slogan "this fridge has seen it all," which now took on an ironic and even somewhat sinister meaning.

Though the incident was tragic, clearly Leah Forrester's death was accidental. However, the Thompson brothers were emotional about the accident and sent cards and flowers to the Forrester family. The Thompsons then began to examine the owner's manual that accompanies the sale of any new Thompson appliance. Though the manual offered step-by-step directions for removing and replacing the reversible door, nowhere did the manual offer any safety instructions regarding how to store or dispose of the appliance.

Task. In response to this oversight, Burke and Frasier Thompson have challenged you, a technical writer for the company, to create an instructional brochure that outlines specific safety instructions for storing and disposing of Thompson refrigerators. This brochure will accompany all owner's manuals. The design of the brochure should

- specifically target new appliance owners with small children
- outline specific steps to help prevent similar tragedies
- emphasize family values, the *key* to Thompson's image

Complication. After you have been working on the brochure's design for several weeks, Suzi Thompson approaches you with the possibility of making the material in the brochure directly accessible to small children. Although you do not think that the entire brochure could be targeted to small children, you do think that components—perhaps inserts or detachable panels—could be made accessible to this age group, especially to children age 5 and older. You incorporate Suzi's suggestion into your final design.

CHAPTER

13

Designing and Incorporating Visuals

OUTLINE

Choosing Visuals to Convey Image and Content: The Story of a Municipal Booklet

Adapting Visuals to Audience Needs

Functions of Visuals

Use and Misuse of Visuals

CRITERIA FOR EXPLORING CHAPTER 13

What we cover in this chapter	What you will be able to do after reading this chapter
Features and functions of visuals in a document	Recognize and appropriately use visuals
Audience, purpose, occasion, and conventions to help adapt visuals for various audiences	Be able to select appropriate visuals for various audiences
Visuals as ways to accomplish specific functions	Use visuals to accomplish a number of functions in documents and oral presentations
Use and misuse of visuals	Avoid misuses that manipulate or obscure meaning

Effective communicators know that some information is appropriately and effectively communicated visually with devices that range from tables and graphs to charts, diagrams, and drawings. For example, Figure 13.1 displays the front panel of a promotional brochure mailed to business professionals and researchers in the United States who might be interested in attending a five-day institute. The institute was to focus on the economic and social complexities of doing business in 1990s Africa. This drawing not only attracts readers but also reinforces the key ideas of the brochure.

CONTEXT

When the 11″ x 17″ promotional brochure shown in Figure 13.1 arrived, the dramatic portrait was the first thing readers saw. The entire brochure had been folded in half and then folded again in thirds for mailing. Readers discovered that one side of the brochure was a single-panel poster advertising the institute. The other side had six panels, created by the folds. Of the three outside panels, one displayed the dramatic visual shown in the figure, one was for the mailing label, and one listed the committee members who had planned the institute. The three inside panels contained details about the five-day institute program.

Figure 13.1 Cover Panel for a Promotional Piece

What is your initial reaction to this visual that depicts an ancient tribal mask and the portrait of a modern African woman?

How does the visual provide a context for the institute?

What might be the reason for using a computer rendering of the portrait of a modern African woman rather than a photograph or a drawing?

Why do you think institute organizers chose to use a dramatic visual for the cover of the brochure?

What do you predict are some of the presentation topics included in the institute?

1. The institute organizers received a great deal of positive feedback about this brochure. Why do you think the brochure was successful in gathering so much attention?
2. What changes might you recommend in the visual on the front of the brochure if you were targeting a different segment of business owners?
3. In what ways does the visual reinforce the theme of the institute?

You can use visuals in documents and oral presentations more effectively if you know about the following factors:

- adapting visuals to audience needs
- functions of various kinds of visuals
- use and misuse of visuals

CHOOSING VISUALS TO CONVEY IMAGE AND CONTENT: THE STORY OF A MUNICIPAL BOOKLET

Sean Cory, Brenda Harvey, and Janelle Hoover, a student business communication team, were particularly concerned with the effective use of visuals. Their team agreed to revise a 22-page information booklet published by the City of Ames about the municipal Resource Recovery System for the city's garbage and recycling. Sean, Brenda, and Janelle wanted to improve the public's image of the Resource Recovery System and to encourage residents to use its facilities. They needed to adapt a great deal of complex information to make it accessible to a nonexpert audience with a variety of educational backgrounds—members of the general public who would read the booklet. They agreed to select and incorporate visuals to *clarify* or *reinforce* the text so that there would be a strong link between the words and the images.

Sean, Brenda, and Janelle agreed that one way to help the audience understand the information was to make sure key points in the text were reinforced and explained by visuals. By using visuals effectively (summarized in Figure 13.2), the team helped the audience in five different ways:

- established a positive image
- provided an overview
- reinforced the familiar
- explained the unfamiliar
- organized numeric data

Sean, Brenda, and Janelle accomplished their first goal of creating a positive image by printing the booklet on recycled paper and providing facts about the 1,800 tons of tin cans that are in the Ames garbage every year: "... 97% of the ferrous [metal] materials in the waste stream are recovered [and recycled]." They established a positive visual image that readers would notice from the moment they picked up the booklet. By using a satellite color photo of Earth on the cover of the booklet, they conveyed the image of an environmentally sensitive and ecologically responsible community. They accomplished their second goal of providing an overview by designing a flow chart on a two-page foldout that identified the categories of garbage sent to the landfill, recycled, or burned in the city's power plant.

To reinforce familiar information, their third goal, the team reviewed the 20-year history of the facility in the booklet's introduction and included a photograph of the well-maintained physical facility, a familiar sight to area residents. The photograph showed the physical facility as seen by anyone driving on one of the city's busiest commercial streets.

Sean, Brenda, and Janelle addressed the fourth goal—explaining the unfamiliar recovery process to their readers—by arranging the information sequentially, describing the way that garbage moved through the recovery process. The details of the process were important because other recycling options were available to residents. Sean, Brenda, and Janelle thought readers needed the details in order to make an informed decision about participating in this recycling effort, so they identified and described the equipment, explained its function, and included simplified line drawings to help readers visualize the equipment in operation.

One of the major purposes of the booklet was to remind residents that about 80 percent of their garbage was recovered: 74.5 percent burned as refuse-derived fuel (RDF) and 5.3 percent recycled. The text in the booklet provided part of the information: "The Ames Power Plant annually burns about 35,000 tons of RDF [refuse derived fuel], which provides about 10% of the utility plant's annual fuel requirements." The team's fifth goal was accomplished in part with a simple pie graph with four colored wedges (using the same colors as in the foldout flow chart) that effectively organized the numeric data so readers could easily see what happened to their garbage.

By incorporating visual information into the verbal presentation, Sean, Brenda, and Janelle established a positive image of the facility, reinforced the familiar sight of the physical plant, organized numeric data in an easy-to-read pie graph, explained unfamiliar equipment and processes with simple line diagrams, and provided an overview by using a flow chart. Their visuals were suitable for their audience and were also effectively integrated into the booklet.

Figure 13.2 Visuals in the Resource Recovery System Booklet

TYPE OF VISUAL	PLACEMENT AND FUNCTION	THUMBNAIL SKETCH
Satellite color photo of Earth	• booklet cover • to reinforce the idea that sound environmental practices affect the entire planet	
Color photo of exterior of the Resource Recovery System's facility	• opening section of booklet dealing with history of the Resource Recovery System, p. 2 • to show the physical plant and reinforce the idea that the facility is attractive and well maintained	
Colored pie graph titled "Garbage in Ames—What Does It Become?"	• section explaining the tipping floor where trucks dump the garbage, p. 4 • in general, to show what happens to the garbage that's delivered to the Resource Recovery System; specifically, to highlight that 74.5% of the garbage is turned into fuel for the power plant	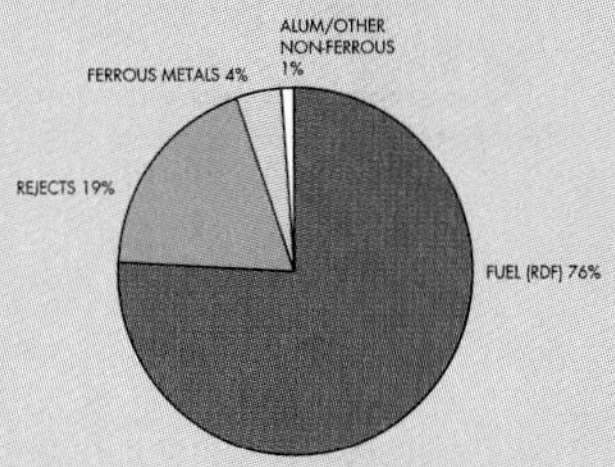
Series of five diagrams	• sections explaining equipment used (1) shedder, p. 5 (2) disk screen, p. 6 (3) electromagnet, p. 7 (4) air classification system, p. 9 (5) storage bin, p. 12 • to illustrate the physical structure and function of equipment that would be unfamiliar to most readers	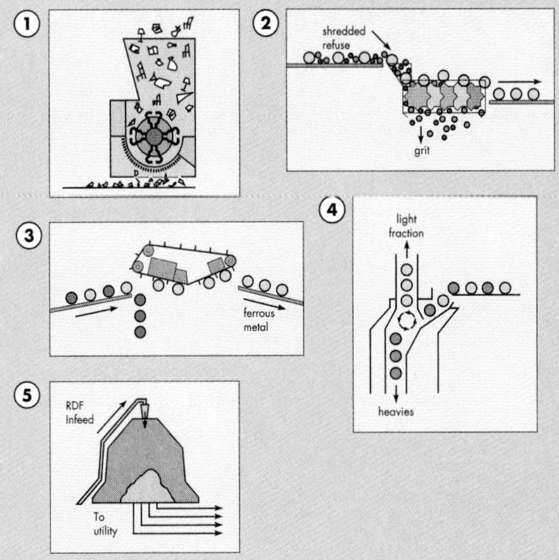
Flow chart	• two-page foldout showing flow of garbage as it moves through the recovery process, pp. 10–11 • to illustrate the sequence of steps in the process	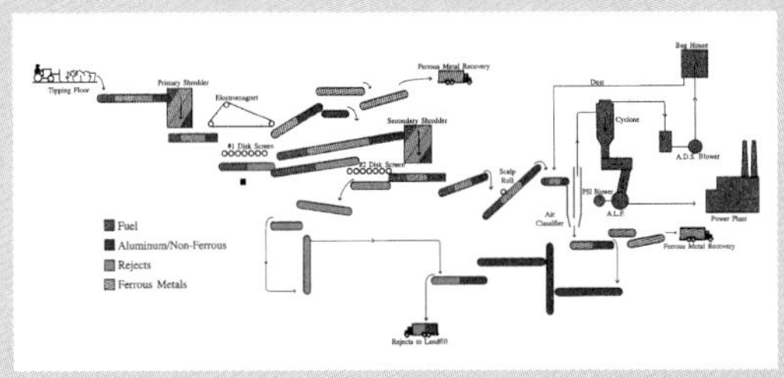

ADAPTING VISUALS TO AUDIENCE NEEDS

Your choice about using visuals should be influenced by whether your audience expects, or even depends on, visuals to help them understand the information. In general, an audience can locate key information in well-designed tables or charts more quickly than in well-organized paragraphs. When Brian Gibson was given the job of explaining health benefits offered to hourly employees, he decided employees would quickly understand a summary

MULTICULTURAL

GRAPHICS FOR INTERNATIONAL DOCUMENTS

Graphics enhance our capability to communicate across barriers of language and culture. In interlingual documents, graphics can be used to accomplish several goals:

- Reduce the size and number of editions of documents. Multiple translations can fit in a single document if only labels and brief annotations need to be translated.
- Reduce translation. Translation of technical documents is expensive. Sometimes fees can be as high as 60 cents per word. If a company needs to translate documents into three or four languages, the cost of translation may exceed the cost of originating the documents. Even though we cannot say everything visually, we can still reduce dependence on verbal language and lessen the possibility of erroneous translation.
- Ease learning. It is often easier to see and understand than to see, translate, and then understand because visual images are less ambiguous and more memorable.
- Improve comprehension. Those who read in a second language rely more heavily on graphics than those who read their first language because the understanding imparted by the graphic helps readers translate the text.
- Take advantage of an already existing body of recognizable symbols. Signs like those used in international airports are almost universal language. Using international signs and graphics can help us direct readers through our documents.

of the information presented in a two-column chart of coverage categories and specific benefits.

Readers with strong spatial skills can understand trends and relationships more readily in graphs than in paragraphs—assuming, of course, that they know the conventions used in the graphs. And some members of your audience can visualize the appearance of people, objects, or places more accurately from drawings, maps, and photographs than from verbal descriptions.

The decision to use visuals can also be determined by the occasion and purpose. Thus, visuals are appropriate when they're needed to complete a task, such as setting up computer hardware. They're also appropriate when fast, accurate comprehension or easy reference is important. Brian Gibson wanted hourly employees to use the summary chart as a convenient reference, so he put it on the back of the company HMO membership card that all employees carried in their wallets.

As you plan your document or oral presentation, you need to consider whether your audience will feel that information will be clearer and more easily understood in words or in images, or both—and balance your use of verbal and visual information accordingly. When Brian Gibson was planning the brochure to explain health care benefits, he wanted employees to understand the coverage without needing to ask for help from Human Resources personnel. So Brian presented examples of benefits in a series of paragraphs, but after each paragraph he summarized the coverage in an easy-to-read table. The tables not only aided reader comprehension, but they also helped separate the chunks of text so the brochure didn't look intimidating even though it contained complex information.

Once you've decided to include a visual, you need to plan the most effective way to adapt the information to your audience. Decisions about occasion, purpose, conventions, added features, and tone and image are particularly important in planning how to adapt visuals for a particular audience. Answers to the questions in Figure 13.3 can help you plan your use of visuals.

Although concepts such as tone and image are difficult to define, they definitely influence an audience's reaction to a document or an oral presentation. For example, a brochure that uses a *font like this* and snapshots has a far less formal tone than one that uses a font like this and professional boardroom photos. A user's manual that includes humor and a breezy, light writing style conveys a more relaxed image than a manual that sticks strictly to business and never varies from simple, conventional sentences.

Just as you learned to adapt verbal information to various audiences, you need to adapt visual information to the audience by considering the overall occasion and purpose of the visual, special features that the audience will need or expect, appropriate conventions, and the tone or image of the document or presentation.

FUNCTIONS OF VISUALS

Now that we have discussed considerations in selecting visuals in business communication, we explore how visuals of all types—tables, graphs, drawings, diagrams, charts, maps, and

Figure 13.3 Questions for Adapting Visuals

AREAS FOR DECISIONS	QUESTIONS FOR ADAPTING VISUALS TO THE AUDIENCE
Occasion	• What makes the visuals appropriate for this occasion? • What kinds of visuals will readers expect or accept on this occasion?
Purpose	• If I use a visual, what do I want it to accomplish for this audience? • How do I want the audience to get the primary information—from the text or from the visuals? • How will the visual help *introduce* or *illustrate* a concept?
Conventions	• What kind of visual is appropriate for displaying the particular kind of information I have? • How do I know that readers are familiar with the visual conventions I'm using? What adaptations may I have to make to accommodate their familiarity?
Added features	• How can added features (color, 3-D, human interest) make the information in the visual more accessible or comprehensible? • What added features might make the visual more appealing or interesting? • What added features might distort or detract from the key information?
Tone and image	• Given the occasion, what tone or image do I want to convey in the document or oral presentation as a whole? • What tone or image should each specific visual convey?

photographs—can communicate ideas and information to an audience. Specifically, we consider the *functions* that visuals serve in documents and oral presentations:

- organize numeric or verbal data
- identify chronology or sequence
- identify relationships
- show appearance or structure
- identify location
- create visual appeal

Figure 13.4 (page 372) indicates that each of these functions can be fulfilled in more than one way. However, one particular kind of visual may be more appropriate for presenting information to some audiences. Some visuals can also serve more than one function.

SKILLS & STRATEGIES

CONVENTIONS FOR CREATING VISUALS

1. Place visuals as close as possible following the reference to the visual in the text. If a visual requires an entire page, place it on the page facing the text reference and discussion.
2. Accurately label each visual. Include complete identification, title, and caption.

Example
Table 1: Fatigue of Office Workers Using VDTs
Worker fatigue was compared using three different models of video display terminals during a two-week period.

3. Include dimensions and units of measure.
4. Whenever possible, spell out words instead of using abbreviations. If abbreviations are included, use standard ones and include a key.
5. Surround the visual with white space to separate it from the text of the document.
6. Include a complete textual reference. Do not assume that readers will check a visual unless you refer to it. Your reference should include the number and title. Textual references can be accomplished in several ways:
   - . . . as illustrated in Figure 2.
   - . . . (see Table 3).
   - The effectiveness of TQM for the department is presented in Figure 4.
   - Table 5 shows the rapid increase of gas prices during a five-year period.
7. If a document has more than five visuals, include a List of Figures or List of Tables at the beginning of the document.
8. Identify the source of the data as well as the graphic designer.
9. In the text, specify the interpretation you want readers to consider when examining a visual. Without information to identify the significance of a visual, readers may not understand its purpose.

Figure 13.4 Primary Functions of Selected Types of Print Visuals

	ORGANIZE AND DISPLAY VERBAL OR NUMERIC DATA	IDENTIFY SEQUENCE OR CHRONOLOGY	IDENTIFY TRENDS OR RELATIONSHIPS	SHOW APPEARANCE	IDENTIFY LOCATION	CREATE APPEAL
Tables	•		•			
Line graphs	•	•	•			
Bar graphs, histograms, and Pareto diagrams	•		•			
Pie graphs	•		•			
Pictorial graphs	•		•			
Scatter graphs	•		•			
Classification charts						
Organizational charts		•				
Block component charts						
Flow charts		•				
Milestone charts		•				
Diagrams			•	•		
Schematics					•	
Blueprints				•	•	
Phantom, cutaway, and exploded drawings				•		
Action drawings		•				
Realistic drawings				•	•	•
Cartoons or cartoon strip				•		•
Photographs				•	•	•
Maps				•	•	

Although each function displayed in Figure 13.4 can be fulfilled by several kinds of visuals, the following discussion focuses just on these you are most likely to use in preparing business documents and presentations.

Organizing Data

The most common way to organize information for readers is to present it in a table, with each row and column displaying some portion of the information (Figure 13.5). You might use a table when you need information organized so that the audience can more easily understand the categories and the relationships among them.

Many people mistakenly believe that tables simply organize information. However, tables also interpret information. When you select the categories for the rows and columns and choose their sequence, you are, in fact, influencing not only how easy (or difficult) a table

Figure 13.5 Definition of a Table

VISUAL	SKETCH	DESCRIPTION AND FUNCTION	EXAMPLE
Table	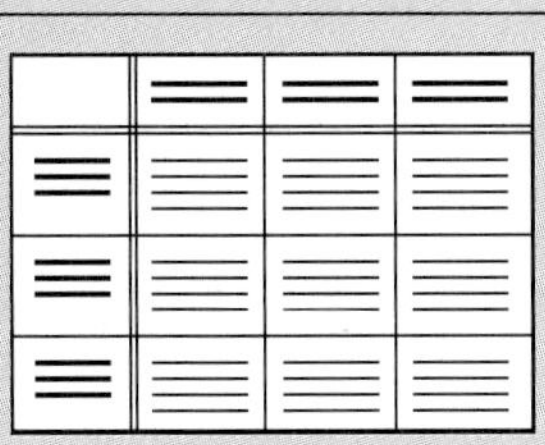	*Description:* displays verbal or numeric information in rows and columns *Function:* to organize numeric or verbal data; to identify trends or relationships; to identify components or parts	To present costs of health insurance policies from five companies for basic and extended coverage for individuals and families

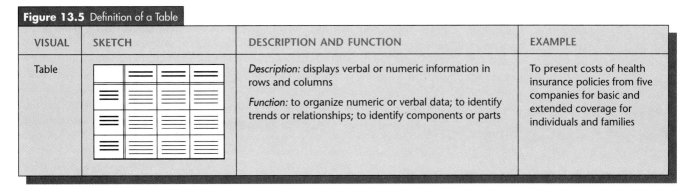

Figure 13.6 Column Labels Shape Audience Perceptions

	A.M. Productivity	**P.M. Productivity**
Line A		
Line B		
Line C		
Line D		

	Workers Under 45	**Workers 45 and Over**
Line A		
Line B		
Line C		
Line D		

	Men Workers	**Women Workers**
Line A		
Line B		
Line C		
Line D		

	Mon/Fri Productivity	**Tues/Thurs Productivity**
Line A		
Line B		
Line C		
Line D		

is to read but also what interpretations the audience will likely form. For example, the four table templates in Figure 13.6 can all be used to organize the same data about the productivity of four manufacturing lines, but readers form different impressions about the nature of the data and the focus of the inquiry because the information is organized differently in each case.

Because tabular data are open to multiple interpretations, readers appreciate accompanying text that explicitly discusses your interpretation. You can tell the audience what you want them to pay attention to in the table—otherwise they may attend to some other aspect of the data. Figure 13.7 presents a verbal table (words rather than numbers) from a brochure

Figure 13.7 Example of a Verbal Table

Because there is little text accompanying the table, it bears the brunt of persuading readers that this new award structure is appealing.

By emphasizing the number of air miles a passenger has collected, the table makes it easy for readers to determine if they qualify for an award.

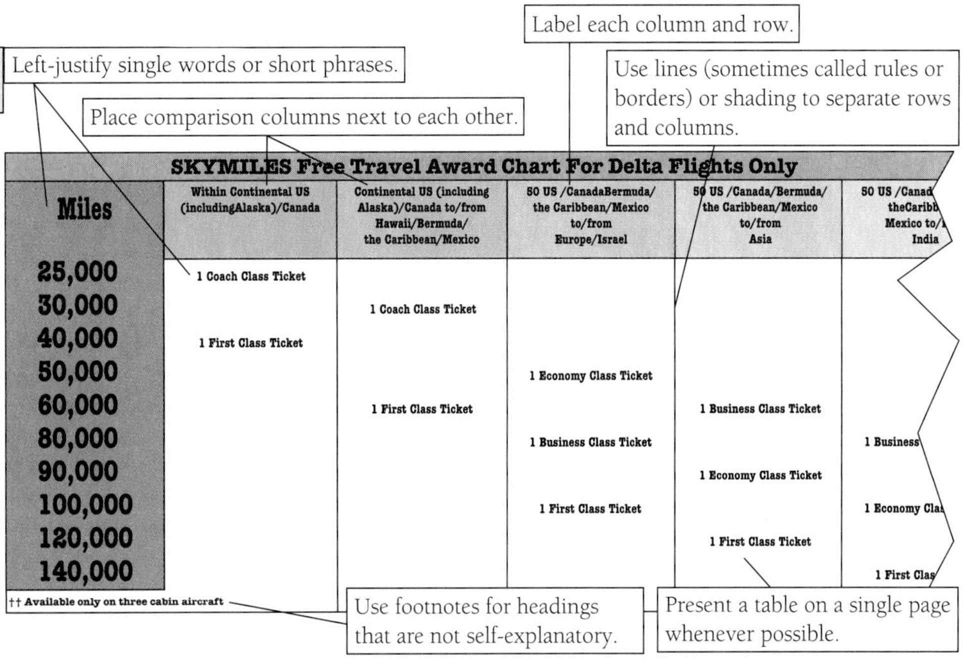

that an airline mailed to all its frequent flier customers to announce a change in the award structure. The table is designed to convince readers that the new award structure is appealing. It also makes checking for current award status easy for readers.

Both informal and formal tables are common ways to organize information in business documents and presentations. Short, **informal tables** are embedded in the text. Because such tables depend on the surrounding discussion for identification and context, they are usually not numbered or titled. Informal tables are usually separated from the text by white space but without rules (lines) marking the borders, rows, and columns, as the following informal table shows:

	Size	**Labels**	**Rules**
Informal table	3 rows x 3 columns or smaller	No number or title	No rules
Formal tables	Usually larger than 3 rows x 3 columns	Number and title	Rules

Formal tables, on the other hand, are distinct from the text, have a table number and title, and are usually separated not only by white space but also by rules marking the borders, rows, and columns. Figure 13.8 organizes information about the prices of five common prescribed drugs charged by independent and chain pharmacies in one state.

Identifying Chronology

One of the most common uses of visuals is to present information chronologically. Line graphs, flow charts, and milestone charts are widely used ways to show chronology or sequence (Figure 13.9). When the duration of events, the time between events, or the order in which they occur is particularly important, you should select one of these visuals.

Line graphs show the relationship between pairs of values displayed on the horizontal and vertical axes on a grid. Line graphs usually show changes in quantity over a period of time. They are particularly helpful in three broad ways: organizing both numeric and verbal data, identifying chronology or sequence, and identifying trends or relationships.

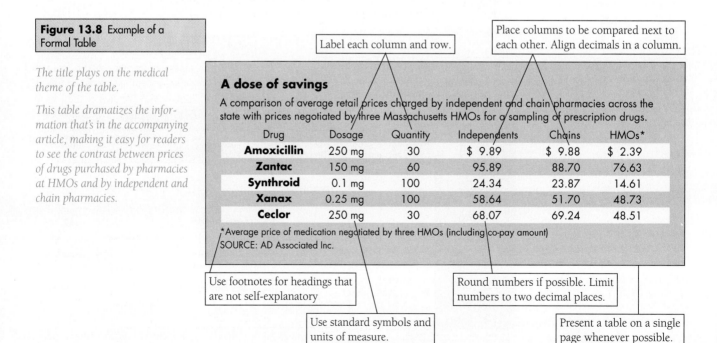

Figure 13.8 Example of a Formal Table

The title plays on the medical theme of the table.

This table dramatizes the information that's in the accompanying article, making it easy for readers to see the contrast between prices of drugs purchased by pharmacies at HMOs and by independent and chain pharmacies.

Label each column and row.

Place columns to be compared next to each other. Align decimals in a column.

A dose of savings

A comparison of average retail prices charged by independent and chain pharmacies across the state with prices negotiated by three Massachusetts HMOs for a sampling of prescription drugs.

Drug	Dosage	Quantity	Independents	Chains	HMOs*
Amoxicillin	250 mg	30	$ 9.89	$ 9.88	$ 2.39
Zantac	150 mg	60	95.89	88.70	76.63
Synthroid	0.1 mg	100	24.34	23.87	14.61
Xanax	0.25 mg	100	58.64	51.70	48.73
Ceclor	250 mg	30	68.07	69.24	48.51

*Average price of medication negotiated by three HMOs (including co-pay amount)
SOURCE: AD Associated Inc.

Use footnotes for headings that are not self-explanatory

Round numbers if possible. Limit numbers to two decimal places.

Use standard symbols and units of measure.

Present a table on a single page whenever possible.

Figure 13.9 Definition of Visuals to Identify Chronology or Sequence

VISUAL	SKETCH	DESCRIPTION AND FUNCTION	EXAMPLE
Line graphs	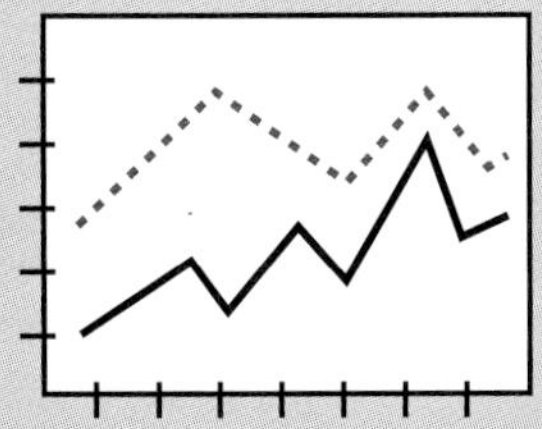	*Description:* show the relationship between pairs of values displayed on the horizontal axis and another value, usually time, displayed on the vertical axis *Function:* to organize numeric or verbal data; to identify chronology or sequence; to identify trends or relationships	To show changes in percentage of unemployment during a 12-month period
Flow charts	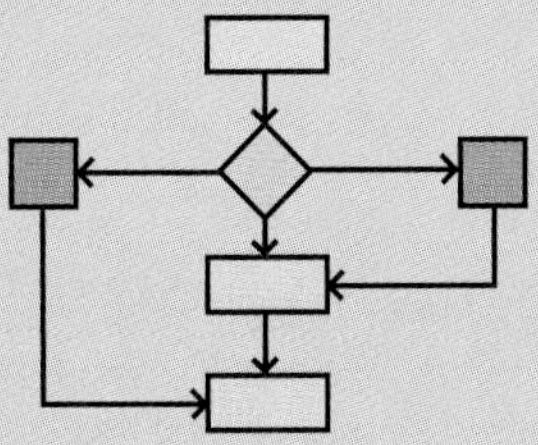	*Description:* depict a sequence of steps in a process, usually using arrows to indicate the direction or movement of the process *Function:* to identify chronology or sequence; to identify components or parts	To show sequence of processing a purchase order
Milestone charts *(Also see Gantt charts in this chapter.)*	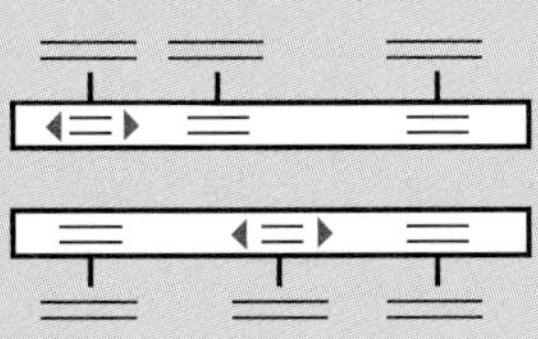	*Description:* identify the sequence of a major project and highlight the critical points (the milestones) in the project *Function:* to identify chronology or sequence; to identify components or parts	To preview stages in an 18-month project to plan and implement a new employee wellness program

Figure 13.10 shows the retention of membership in a professional organization over a 10-year period. This line graph was published in one of the organization's newsletters sent monthly to the organization's leaders.

Flow charts depict a sequence of steps in a process, usually using arrows to indicate the direction or movement of the process. Flow charts are particularly effective for showing processes that have decision points and recursive (nonlinear) segments. Illustrated in

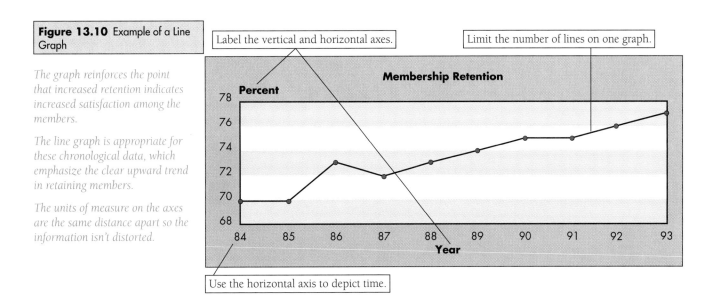

Figure 13.10 Example of a Line Graph

The graph reinforces the point that increased retention indicates increased satisfaction among the members.

The line graph is appropriate for these chronological data, which emphasize the clear upward trend in retaining members.

The units of measure on the axes are the same distance apart so the information isn't distorted.

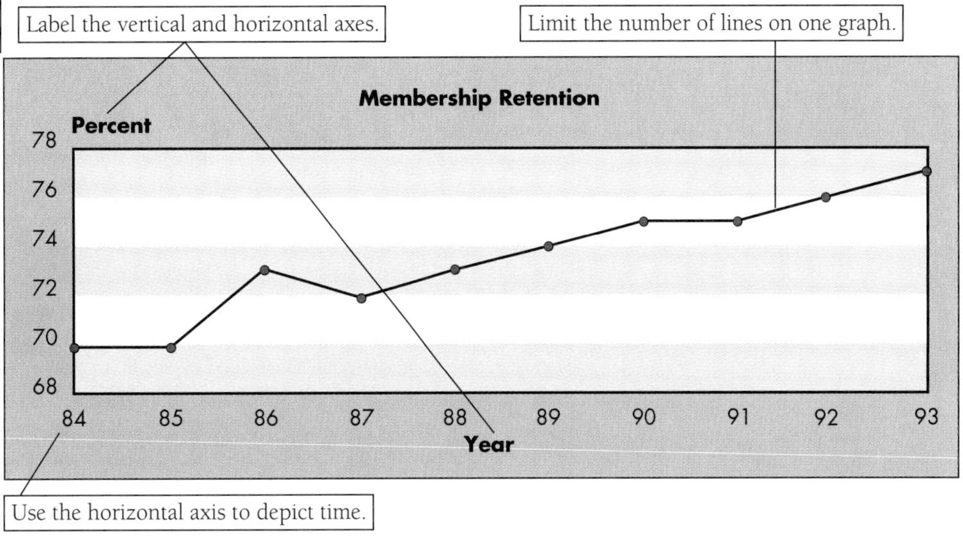

Figure 13.11 Example of a Flow Chart

The writer/designer made the process easy to understand by identifying three ways to move through the chart.

The writer's parenthetical comments ("what to do" and "how to do it") make the jargon accessible.

The text at the bottom of the flow chart indicates both positive and negative outcomes.

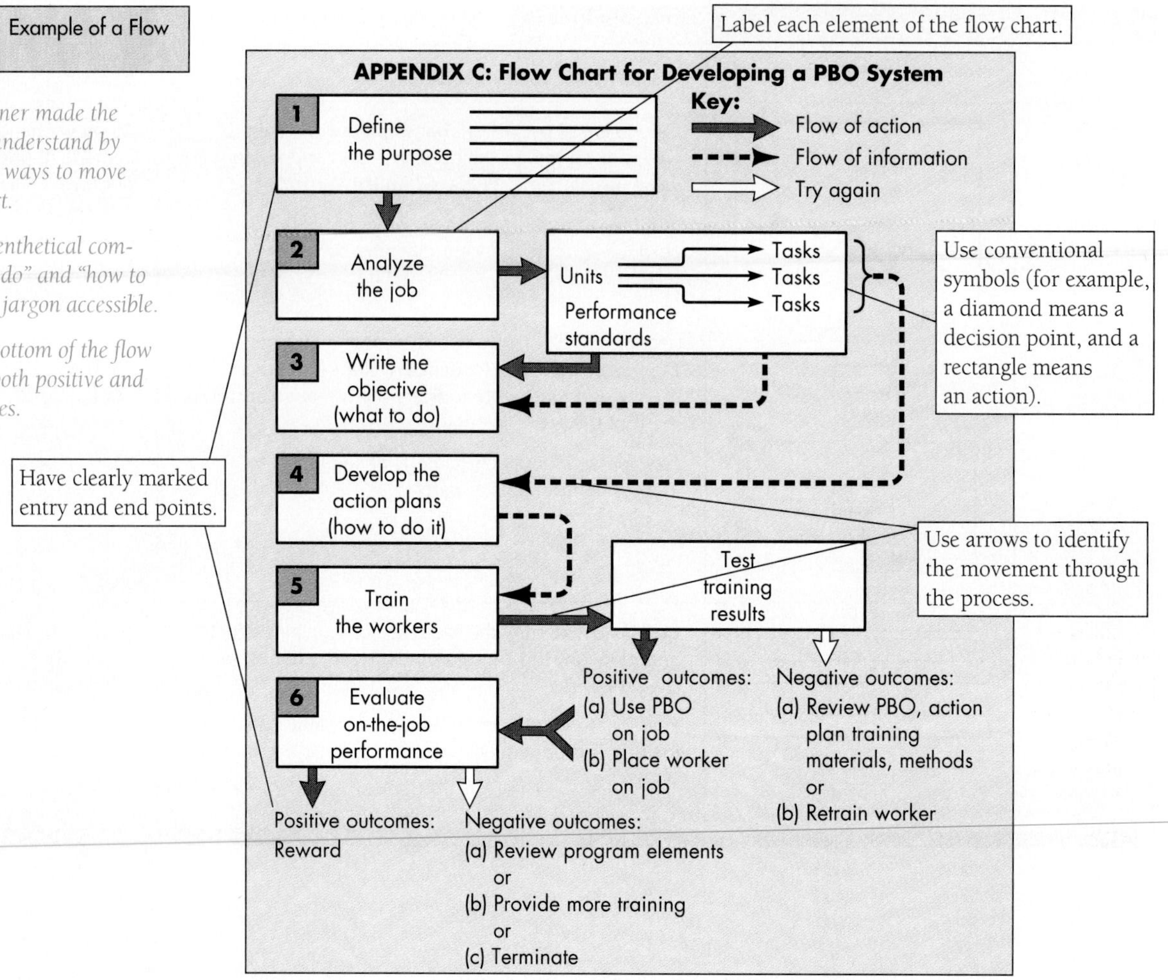

Figure 13.12 Example of a Milestone Chart

A milestone chart enables you to track the relationship between the project tasks and the schedule.

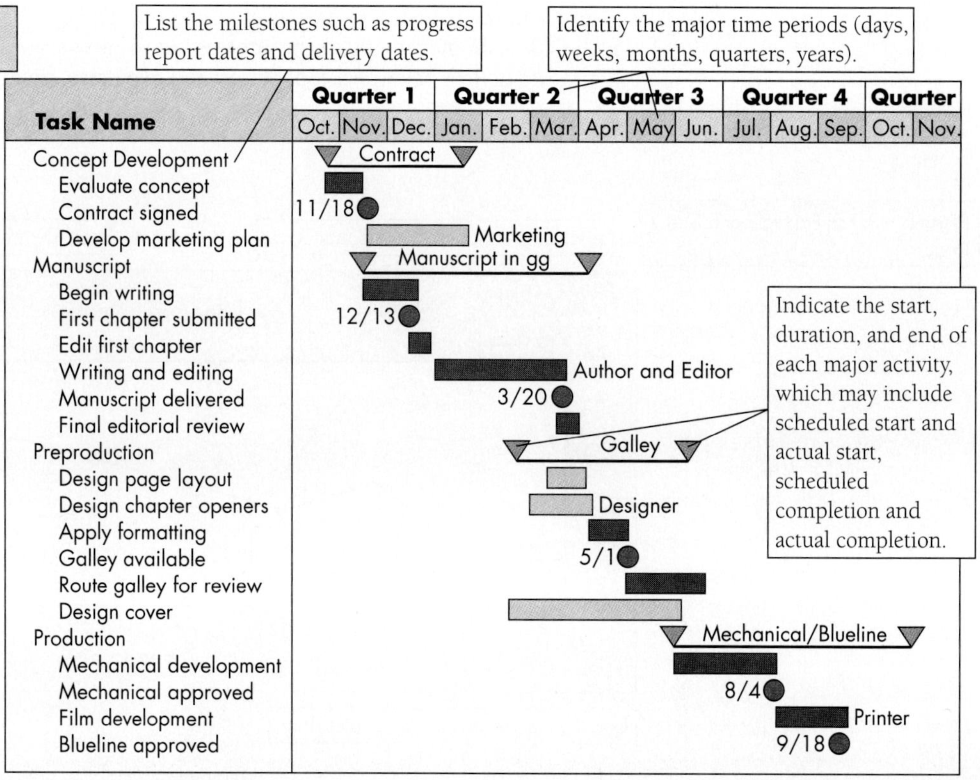

Figure 13.11 is the sequence of actions for developing a performance by objective (PBO) system. The flow chart has three kinds of arrows: flow of action arrows, flow of information arrows, and repetition arrows.

Milestone charts identify the sequence of a project and highlight the critical points (the milestones) in that project. Some milestone charts track the critical path of a project; that is, they indicate not only who did what when, but they identify the path the process takes. Milestone charts are also common in project proposals, as Figure 13.12 shows.

Identifying Relationships

Graphs are well suited to identify relationships. Some of the most frequently used types—pictorial, pie, scatter, and bar graphs—are presented in Figure 13.13. Even though these three kinds of graphs look very different, they are all especially useful when you want the audience to understand the relationship between two variables.

Figure 13.13 Definition of Visuals to Identify Relationships

VISUAL	THUMBNAIL SKETCH	DESCRIPTION AND FUNCTION	EXAMPLE
Pictorial graphs	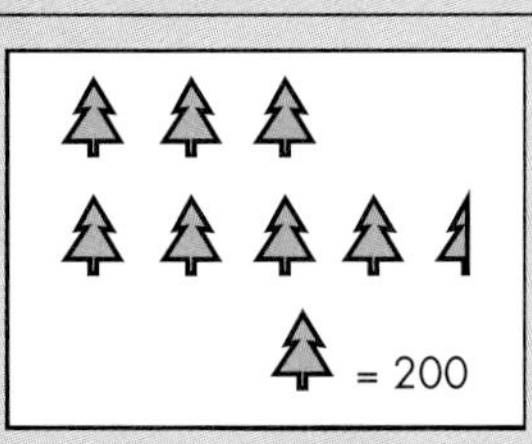	*Description:* Use symbols to make up each bar. Each symbol represents a specific number of people or objects.	To depict the increase in employees willing to report sexual harassment.
Pie graphs	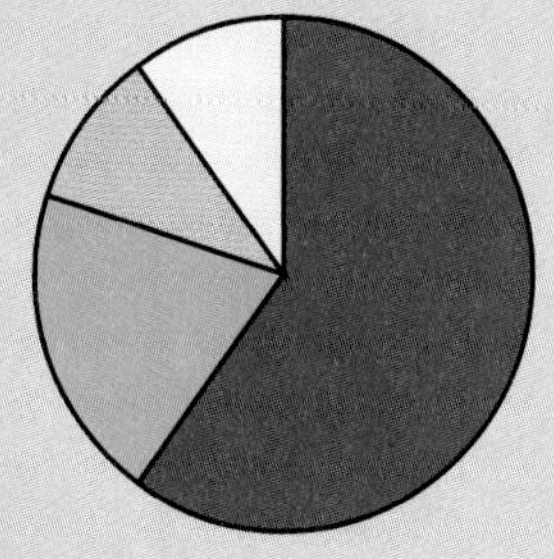	*Description:* 100 percent graphs in which each percent represents 3.6° of the circle. *Function:* To organize numeric or verbal data; to identify components or parts.	To show the percentages of time devoted to various tasks during the work day.
Scatter graphs	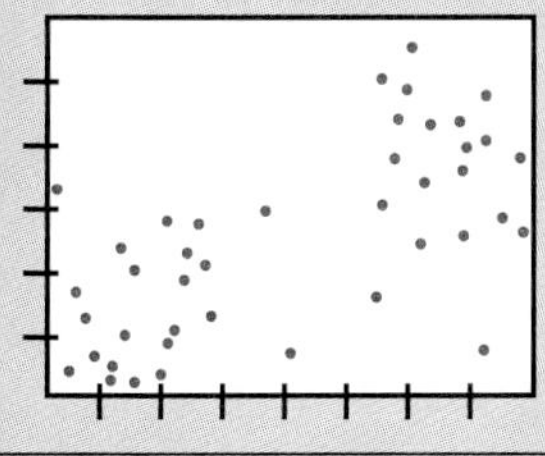	*Description:* Plot the individual points, each one representing the intersection of the two variables on the *X* and *Y* axes.	To display relationship between the accuracy of sales representatives' reports and their participation in on-site training
Bar graphs	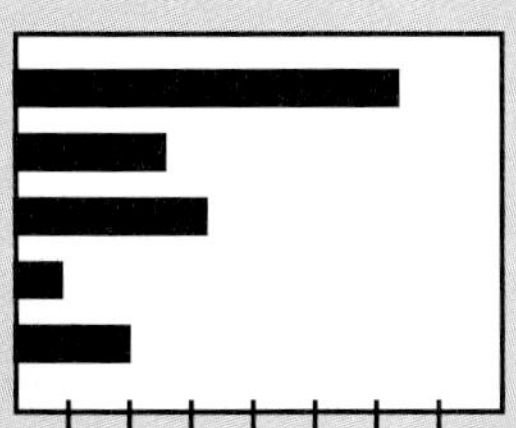 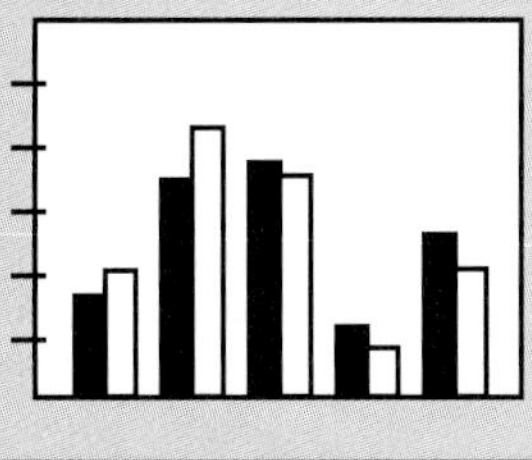	*Description:* Show comparisons, trends, and distributions. The values are represented by vertical or horizontal bars, with each bar representing a separate quantity. Bar graphs are especially appropriate when the data consist of distinct units.	To display relationship between building air quality and employee sick time taken

Figure 13.14 Simple Information Difficult to Get from a Pictorial Graph

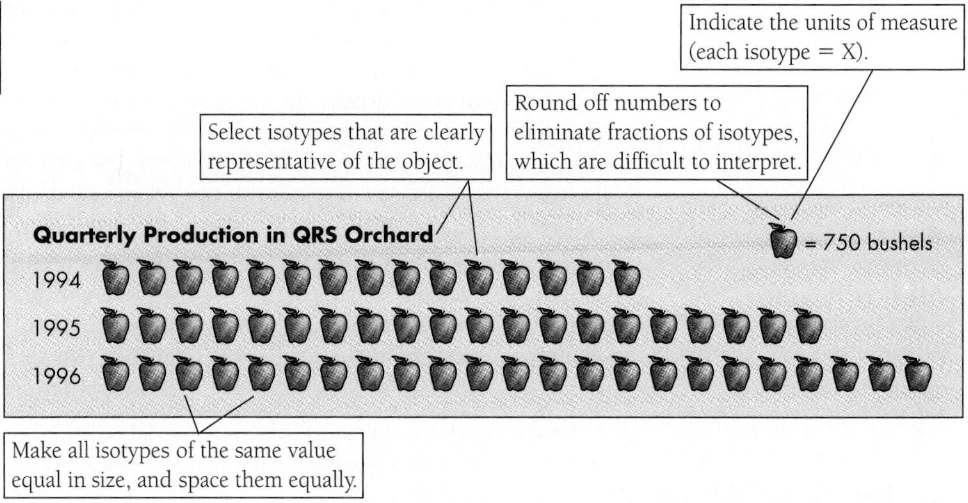
Indicate the units of measure (each isotype = X).
Round off numbers to eliminate fractions of isotypes, which are difficult to interpret.
Select isotypes that are clearly representative of the object.
Quarterly Production in QRS Orchard
= 750 bushels
1994
1995
1996
Make all isotypes of the same value equal in size, and space them equally.

This apple orchard produced approximately 11,000 bushels in 1994, 15,000 in 1995, and 17,000 in 1996.

Such information, especially with the need for partial isotypes, is difficult to process in a pictorial graph.

Figure 13.15 Single Isotypes to Represent Magnitudes in a Pictorial Graph

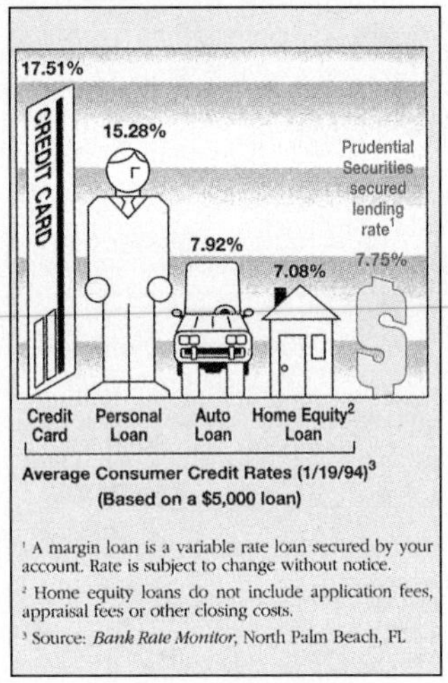
17.51%
CREDIT CARD
15.28%
Prudential Securities secured lending rate[1]
7.92%
7.08%
7.75%
Credit Card
Personal Loan
Auto Loan
Home Equity[2] Loan
Average Consumer Credit Rates (1/19/94)[3]
(Based on a $5,000 loan)
[1] A margin loan is a variable rate loan secured by your account. Rate is subject to change without notice.
[2] Home equity loans do not include application fees, appraisal fees or other closing costs.
[3] Source: Bank Rate Monitor, North Palm Beach, FL

The drawings are visually appealing. However, there is no way that these drawings can accurately represent the loan rate they are intended to depict.

The variations in the height of these isotypes provide readers with only a very general impression of the relative differences in the rates.

Pictorial graphs, which are a kind of bar graph, use symbols to make up each bar. These graphs are usually used with nonexpert audiences who only want the most general image of the data or in presentations before audiences who appreciate the entertainment value of such visuals.

Each symbol (called an **isotype**) represents a specific number of people or objects. Pictorial graphs are visually appealing, but they are inappropriate for depicting fractions or for displaying complex data. For example, Figure 13.14 displays relatively simple information (annual apple orchard production for three years), but determining the actual production is difficult.

Pictorial graphs can use single isotypes of different sizes to represent the relative quantity or magnitude of each object or concept, as shown in Figure 13.15. Such a graph is appropriate for attracting reader attention, but it should not be used to present complex or technical data. Figure 13.15 shows the average consumer rates consumers pay for common kinds of credit: credit cards, personal loans, auto loans, and home equity loans. If you use single isotypes to represent different values, the size of the isotypes should be proportional to the numbers they're depicting.

Pie graphs, also called pie diagrams, pie charts, percent graphs, or divided circle graphs, emphasize the relation of the parts to the whole, as in Figure 13.16. Pie graphs, which often display money or time relationships, should follow the conventions indicated on the figure, though they're frequently violated by designers more concerned with impact than with clarity or convention.

Scatter graphs display the unconnected, individual data points of two variables. The pattern formed by these points shows whether there is any relationship between the two variables, one on each axis. If the points are scattered randomly on the grid formed by the two axes, then there is no relationship. If, however, there is a positive correlation, the points

TECHNOLOGY

BUSINESS GRAPHICS

Non-artists can install software on their desktop computers that can make them look like professional artists. Gone are all the confusing tool bars and terminology. In their place are stencils of common shapes—not just circles and rectangles, but flow chart symbols, maps, and office furniture, among others, all of which can be easily grabbed with the mouse and dropped into a document. These shapes can be rotated, enlarged, decreased, and colored. Shapes can be connected to other shapes with lines that behave like rubber bands, keeping the shapes linked even when they are moved nearer or further apart. In addition, the programs come with thousands of pieces of "clip art," professionally drawn images of everything from airplanes to four-leaf clovers that can be easily dropped into documents and sized and oriented to fit.

occur in a pattern from the lower left of the grid to the upper right. On the other hand, if there is a negative correlation, the points occur in a pattern from the upper left of the grid to the lower right. Figure 13.17 shows a positive correlation between a country's wealth and the number of telephone lines in that country.

Bar graphs (sometimes called column graphs) show comparisons, trends, and distributions. Each vertical or horizontal bar represents a separate quantity. Like the line graphs discussed earlier in this chapter, bar graphs are constructed from a series of values plotted on two axes, but the values are represented by vertical or horizontal bars instead of points joined by a line. Because each bar represents a distinct quantity, bar graphs are especially

Figure 13.16 Example of a Pie Graph

While pie graphs do attract readers' attention, they have disadvantages. One disadvantage is that comparison of the areas is difficult. Another disadvantage is that readers have trouble distinguishing between wedges when the percentages are close.

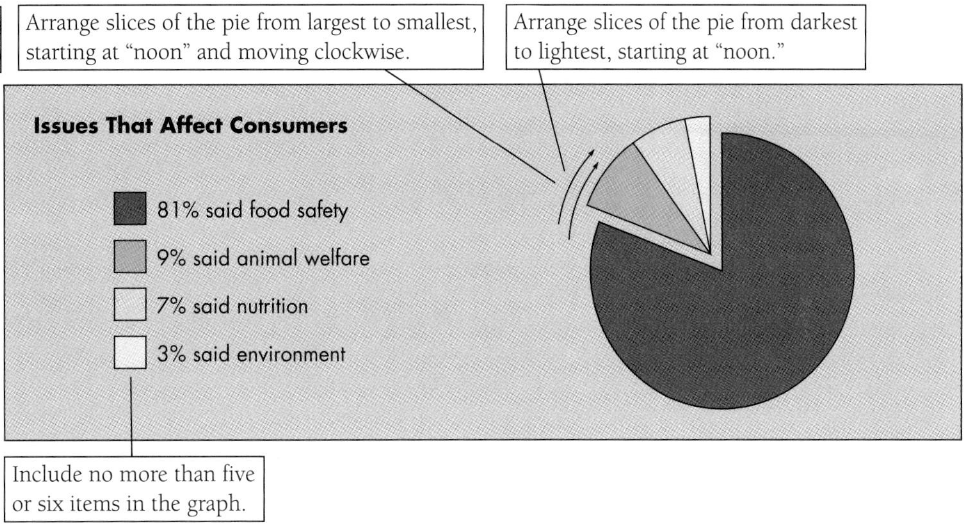

Figure 13.17 Example of a Scatter Graph

The subtle color and shading in this graph are appealing.

The clustering of the emerging economies and the developed economies reinforces the discussion in the accompanying article that investment in a telephone company that is focusing on emerging economies has tremendous growth potential.

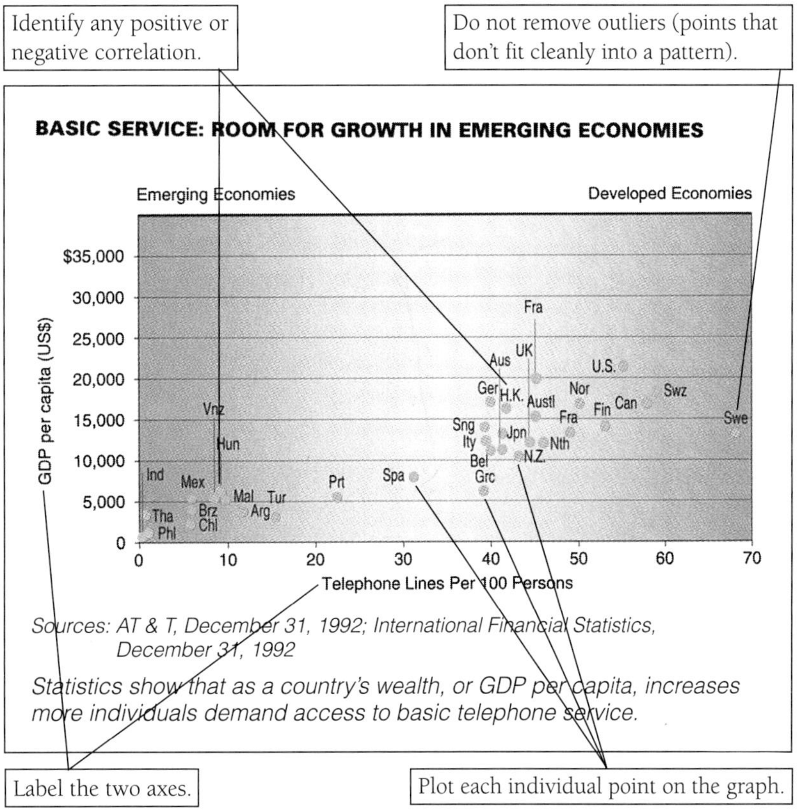

Figure 13.18 Definition of Types of Bar Graphs

VISUAL	SKETCH	DESCRIPTION	EXAMPLE
Simple bar graphs	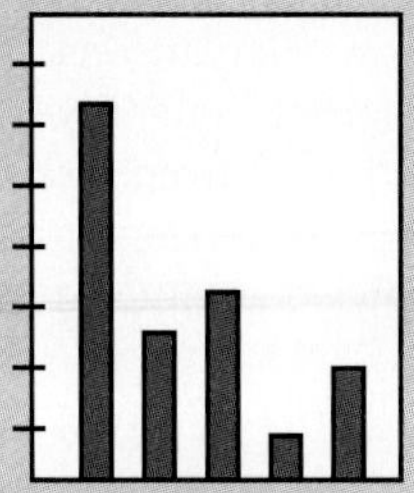	*Description:* Show the relationship between two categories of information, with the height of a bar depicting the quantity of the variable.	To show the average number of service calls for five brands of photocopiers during a one-year period
Subdivided bar graphs	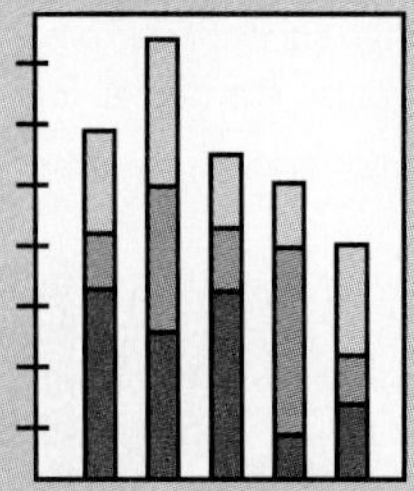	*Description:* Each bar represents some whole and is separated into components that contribute to the whole.	To compare the total number of men and women in management in each decade since 1930
Subdivided 100 percent bar graphs	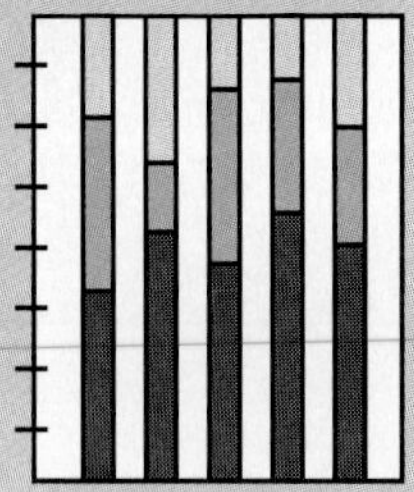	*Description:* Each bar represents some whole that has been extended to 100 percent so the components can be compared easily.	To show the market share of manual, semiautomatic, and automatic cameras every ten years since 1955
Multiple bar graphs	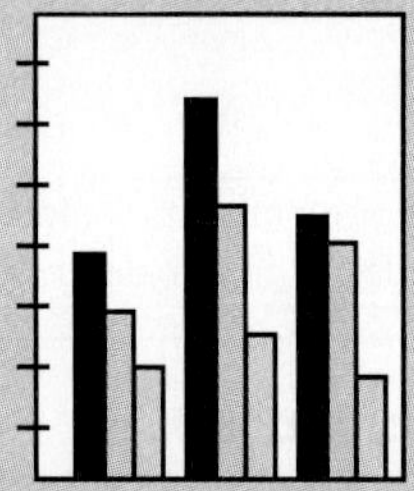	*Description:* Use two or more bars to compare the magnitudes within each variable as well as overall.	To compare the exports to and imports from Japan every ten years since 1950
Sliding bar graphs	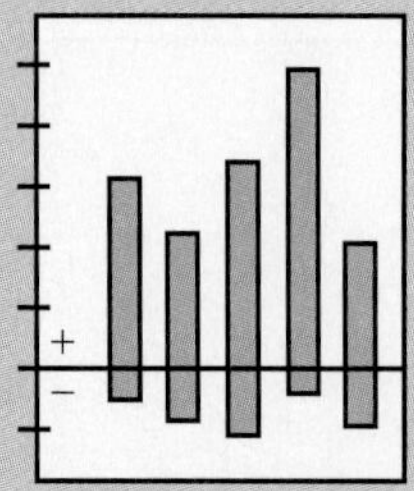	*Description:* Display variables that slide along either side of an axis with a central point.	To display changes in the inventory levels held by OEMs (original equipment manufacturers) of large home appliances

appropriate when the data consist of distinct units, such as tons of recycled paper each month or megawatts of hydroelectric power used each year. Figure 13.18 illustrates several common types of bar graphs.

The **simple bar graph** in Figure 13.19 shows the increasing share in the market for meat that poultry has gained since 1965—and a projection for the market share in the year 2000. Because readers can easily compare the height of the various bars, a simple bar graph is useful for emphasizing the magnitude of whatever variable is displayed. Note that Figures 13.19, 13.20, 13.21, and 13.22 illustrate four variations of information about the same general subject.

Figure 13.19 Example of a Simple Bar Graph

The bars, all representing the same type of information, stress the relative magnitude among items.

The writer/designer chose to end the Y axis at 50 percent, thus making the percentage of market share initially appear larger than it actually is upon closer inspection.

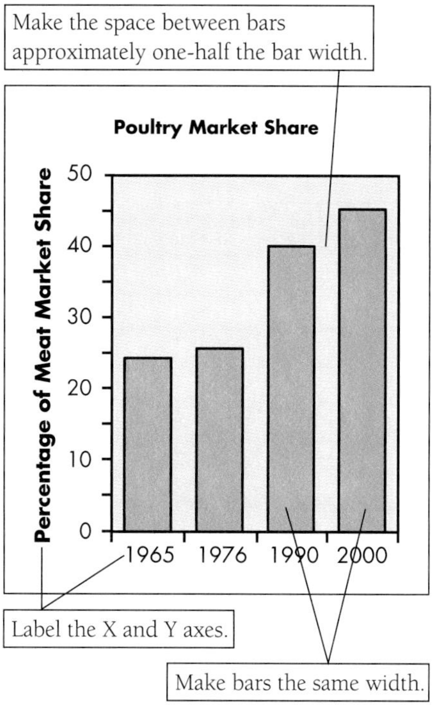
Make the space between bars approximately one-half the bar width.
Poultry Market Share
Percentage of Meat Market Share
50
40
30
20
10
0
1965
1976
1990
2000
Label the X and Y axes.
Make bars the same width.

Figure 13.20 Example of a Subdivided Bar Graph

The advantage of a subdivided bar graph is that the magnitude of each bar can be compared.

Although it is easy to compare the overall magnitudes of these bars, the individual segments of each bar are not so easily compared.

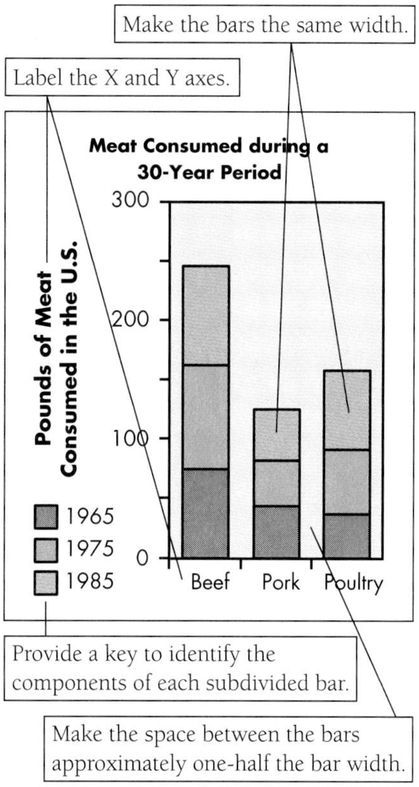
Make the bars the same width.
Label the X and Y axes.
Meat Consumed during a 30-Year Period
Pounds of Meat Consumed in the U.S.
300
200
100
0
1965
1975
1985
Beef
Pork
Poultry
Provide a key to identify the components of each subdivided bar.
Make the space between the bars approximately one-half the bar width.

In a **subdivided bar graph,** sometimes called a stacked bar graph (see Figure 13.20), each bar is subdivided to represent the magnitude of different components, in this case the number of pounds of different kinds of meat consumed at the ends of different years. Parts are differentiated by shading or crosshatching. While readers can still determine the magnitude of each variable, there is equal attention given to the components.

Figure 13.21 Example of a 100 Percent Subdivided Bar Graph

The advantage of a 100 percent subdivided bar graph is that the components can be compared relatively easily, but the magnitude of the individual bars is lost.

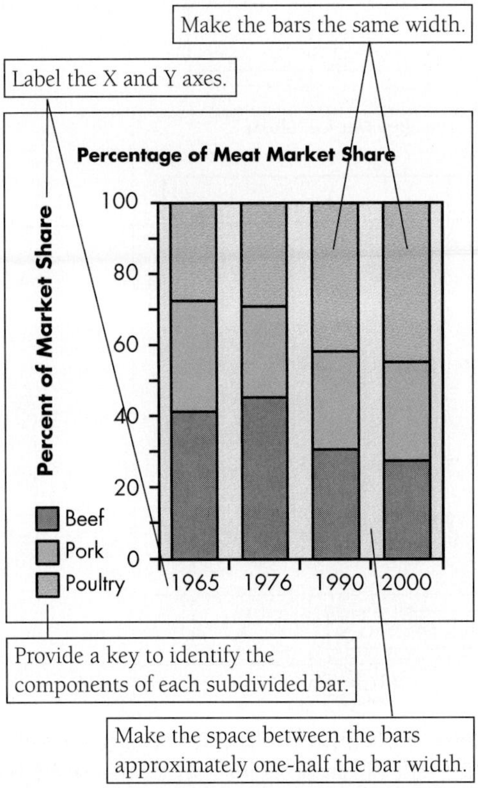
Make the bars the same width.
Label the X and Y axes.
Percentage of Meat Market Share
Percent of Market Share
100
80
60
40
20
0
Beef
Pork
Poultry
1965
1976
1990
2000
Provide a key to identify the components of each subdivided bar.
Make the space between the bars approximately one-half the bar width.

Figure 13.22 Example of a Multiple Bar Graph

The advantage of a multiple bar graph is that the distinctions among the individual components (bars) are immediately apparent. However, the magnitude of the whole is lost since readers can't easily visualize how much the "whole" would be if the bars were stacked on top of each other.

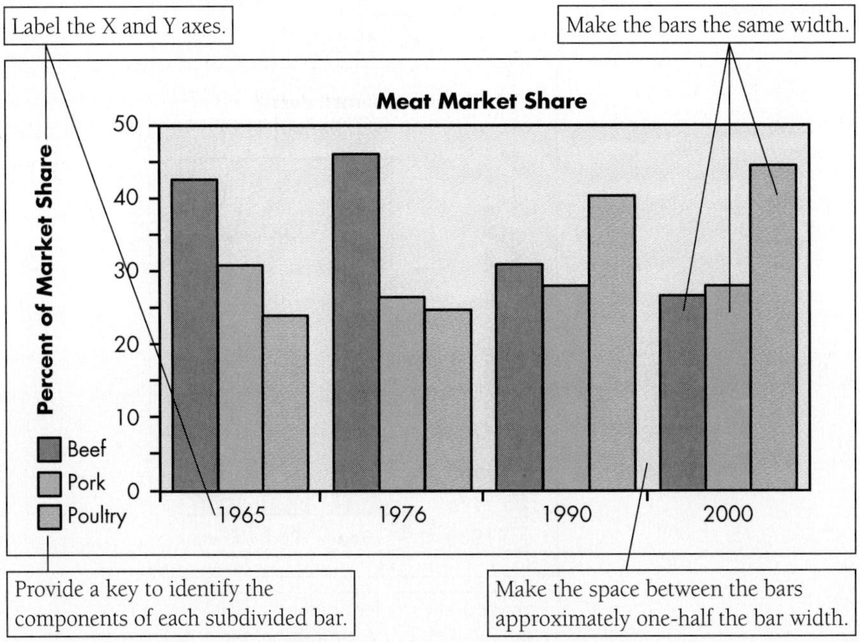
Label the X and Y axes.
Make the bars the same width.
Meat Market Share
Percent of Market Share
50
40
30
20
10
0
Beef
Pork
Poultry
1965
1976
1990
2000
Provide a key to identify the components of each subdivided bar.
Make the space between the bars approximately one-half the bar width.

While Figure 13.20 displays pounds of consumption of three kinds of meat in three separate years, Figures 13.21 and 13.22 show the market share represented by the numbers of pounds in those same years. In a **subdivided 100 percent bar graph** (Figure 13.21), each bar extends to 100 percent; the components are divided by percentages. The information conveyed in the lightest-colored bars in Figure 13.22 is identical to the information in Figure 13.19. While the magnitude of the whole is lost in a subdivided 100 percent bar graph, readers are able to compare the relative proportion of the components that make up each bar. However, the precise relationships among these components are difficult to determine.

Figure 13.23 Example of a Sliding Bar Graph

The +/− scale on the vertical axis of this sliding bar graph reinforces the dramatic fluctuations, both positive and negative, in the price of finished goods over a 12-month period.

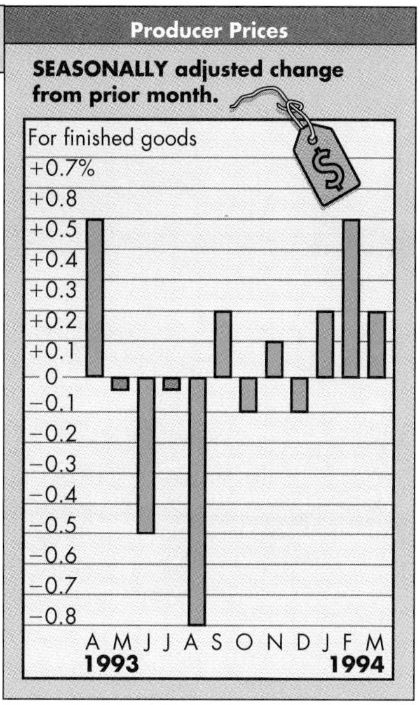

A **multiple bar graph** groups bars to present the magnitudes of related variables. Figure 13.22 compares the percentage of market share held by three different kinds of meat. Readers are able to readily compare the magnitudes of the individual parts even though a sense of the whole is lost because the components are not stacked as they are in subdivided or 100 percent subdivided bar graphs.

The bars in the **sliding bar graph** move along an axis that is usually marked in opposing values (active/passive, hot/cold) that extend on either side of a central point, such as values on a temperature scale. The sliding bar graph in Figure 13.23 reflects the percentage of seasonally adjusted change in the price of finished goods from the previous month. Graphs of seasonally adjusted prices such as this example are common in the business sections of daily newspapers.

Showing Appearance

Visuals of objects, mechanisms, or organisms can depict exterior or interior views. Figure 13.24 identifies two commonly used visuals that show appearance.

Figure 13.24 Definitions of Visuals That Show Appearance

VISUAL	SKETCH	DESCRIPTION AND FUNCTION	EXAMPLE
Cartoons		*Description:* depict an artist's interpretation of people, objects or situations *Function:* to identify chronology or sequence; to show appearance or structure	To represent the narrator for a training video in a nuclear power plant, providing a contrast to the technical complexity of the content
Photographs	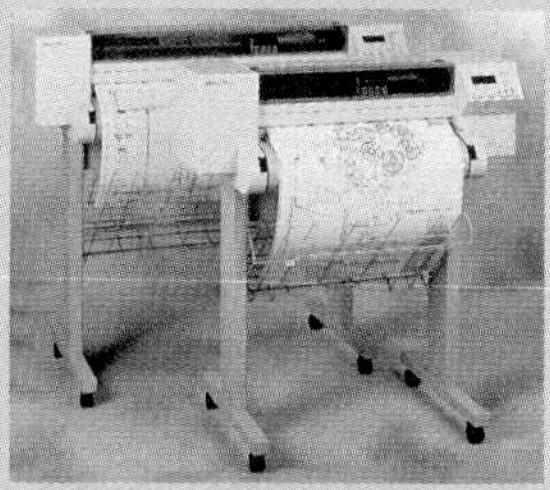	*Description:* depict the actual appearance of an object or organism *Function:* to show appearance or structure; to identify location	To show the appearance of a fax machine on a promotional brochure.

Figure 13.25 Example of a Cartoon Drawing

The cartoonlike drawing is colorful and appealing to readers.

The drawing—simple, even childlike—is especially appropriate given the brochure's focus on children.

Serious messages don't always have to be accompanied by serious visuals.

The background depicts a doctor's office, reinforcing the point about health.

Decide whether you want a cartoon or a caricature (an exaggerated cartoon).

Focus the drawings on the features you want to emphasize.

Consider details that reinforce your points.

Sometimes cartoons or cartoonlike drawings are effective because they catch readers' attention and are less intimidating than other visuals. Figure 13.25 is from a brochure published by Ben & Jerry's, an ice cream company that encourages the social and political involvement of its investors, employees, and customers. This brochure has a series of five drawing panels (the first depicted here) that encourages people to join Ben & Jerry's Children's Defense Fund Action List.

Photographs are extremely realistic, showing the actual appearance of an object, a mechanism, or an organism. However, a photograph is not always appropriate, because it might show too much detail. For this reason, callouts (small arrows superimposed on a photo)

Figure 13.26 Example of a Photograph

The photo helps readers better understand the process discussed in the text.

The use of color attracts attention and adds realistic details.

The cropping of this photograph focuses attention on the main piece of equipment.

This specially equipped revolving door at the airport serving Myrtle Beach, South Carolina, uses concealed electromagnetic locks, supplied by our Exit Device Division, to provide easy access for people with disabilities and to prevent entry when the airport is closed. In addition, the division's emergency-exit pushbars are used on bordering doors. To help the airport meet new Federal Aviation Administration security requirements, the division also supplied a security-control console and card-access system to monitor and operate all doors throughout the facility.

Figure 13.27 Selected Types of Maps

VISUAL	SKETCH	DESCRIPTION	EXAMPLE
Population Maps		*Description:* usually display population density, but can also display population by ethnic, racial, or economic strata	To display population density by age and income in a suburban area being considered for a new shopping mall
Surface feature maps	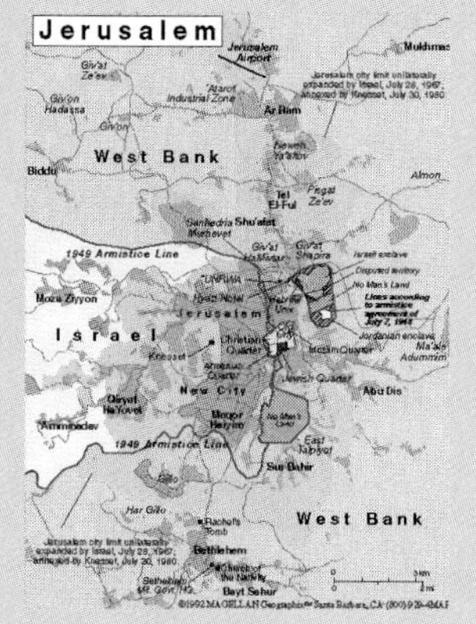	*Description:* can display a variety of geographic features: rivers, lakes, and wetlands; elevations; areas of erosion; areas of hazardous waste; vegetation; forest and timberland	To identify a wetland area protected from new construction

are used to draw attention to main features. When a photo is printed, its appearance can also be altered so that the primary subject is visually more prominent than the background, thus giving emphasis not possible in a normally printed photo. Figure 13.26 shows a photo taken from the annual report of 3M.

Identifying Location

Maps display geographic information (although we speak of charts, not maps, for air or water). To most people, maps mean road guides. But maps can also display topographic, demographic, agricultural, meteorological, and geological data. Maps show features of a particular area, such as land elevation, rock formations, vegetation, animal habitats, crop production, population density, or traffic patterns. Statistical maps can depict quantities at specific points or within specified boundaries. Data can be presented on maps in a number of ways: dots, shading, lines, repetitive symbols, or superimposed graphs. Figure 13.27 identifies two common maps used in business communication.

A **population map** is a visual representation of demographic information. Such maps provide useful information for decisions about target audiences, expansion of businesses, and provision of services. The map in Figure 13.28 (page 386) displays the percentage of population age 3 and older who are enrolled in private schools. The government officials in the 25 towns represented on this map need such information in order to plan town and school budgets for the upcoming year.

A **surface feature map** displays geologic and geographic characteristics of a particular area. Highway maps are probably the most widely known kind of surface feature map.

Figure 13.29 (page 386) displays a surface feature map and the textual content in which the map was presented. When a large earthquake hit the greater Los Angeles area, many companies donated food and other needed goods and services. Several months later, one of these companies, H.J. Heinz, informed stockholders in the quarterly newsletter that the company had supported victims of the earthquake.

Figure 13.28 Example of a Population Map

The color-coded legend accompanying this population map makes it easy for readers to determine which towns have the highest density of children enrolled in private schools.

Other than color coding, the map includes only essential information: the name of each town and the percentage of students enrolled in private schools.

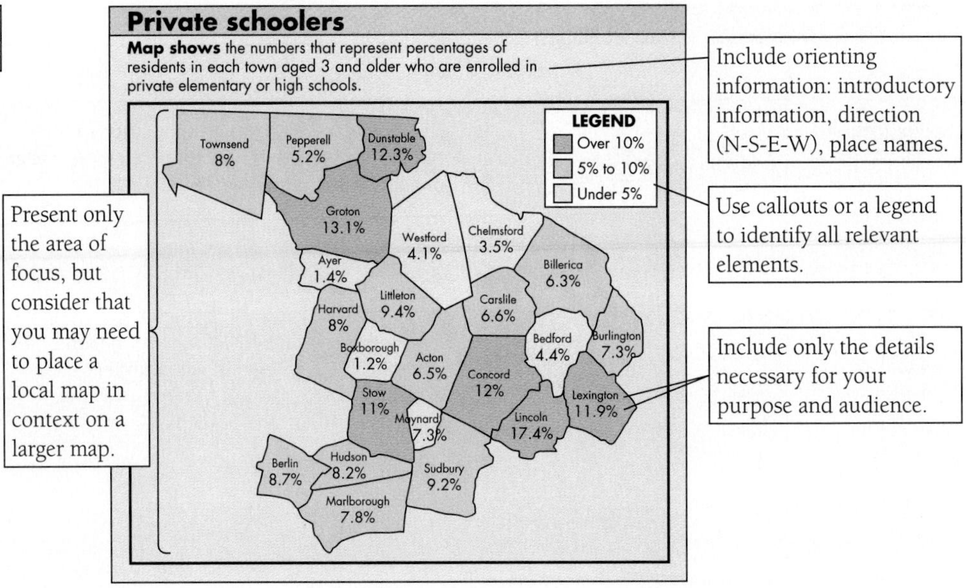

Figure 13.29 Example of a Surface Feature Map

This surface feature map reminds readers/viewers of the widespread area covered by the earthquake.

The inset of the map locates the area in the region.

The main portion of the map helps readers understand the severity of the earthquake by indicating the fault lines as well as the cities.

HEINZ AFFILIATES AID EARTHQUAKE VICTIMS... Heinz U.S.A. and Weight Watchers Food Company responded to hunger relief efforts in the Los Angeles area following the recent California earthquake.

The donation wheels rolled into motion the same day as the earthquake. Heinz donated more than 4,000 cases of baby juice, instant baby cereal, soups and broth, chili macaroni, tomato juice, pickles, vegetarian beans, vegetable purees, single-serve jellies, and Weight Watchers brand puddings, cookies, and other products. The bulk of the donation came from Heinz U.S.A.'s West Coast and Pittsburgh locations. The contribution was made directly to Second Harvest, the nationwide network of food banks responsible for directing relief supplies in the wake of the devastation.

Additionally, Weight Watchers Food Company participated in *Family Circle* magazine's "Open Your Hearts" program, which presented relief packages to quake victims.

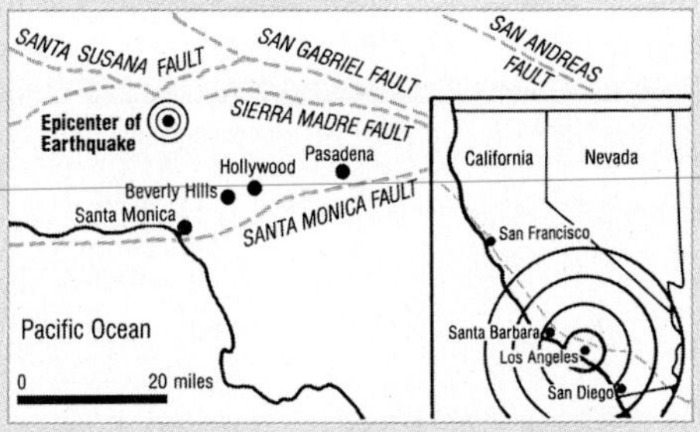

More than 2,000 units of Weight Watchers brand Smart Snackers items, ranging from oatbran pretzels to chocolate chip cookies, were included in gift bags distributed by Feed The Children, an international relief organization.

Creating Appeal

Even though decorative visuals fulfill varied functions in business documents and presentations, their overall purpose is to increase the appeal of the information and to increase reader or listener motivation, as shown in Figure 13.30.

While decorative visuals are aesthetically appealing, they may also have some thematic connection to the information. Some of the visuals also function as thematic tags, cueing readers about the content of the article or signaling a particularly important point. Sometimes the figure is whimsical, adding humor.

USE AND MISUSE OF VISUALS

Communicators have long known that many members of their audience respond more strongly to visuals than they do to the text document or oral presentation. This section of the chapter begins by focusing on manipulation (not always a bad thing) and distortion of a visual image (always a bad thing). We conclude with a discussion comparing "chartjunk" with visuals that have design appeal.

Manipulation and Distortion

Visuals are as susceptible to manipulation and distortion as any other form of communication. Sometimes manipulation is appropriate and intended entirely to aid readers in understanding the information. For example, a writer might be able to help readers interpret information by changing the sequence of columns in a table or adjusting the scale in a graph.

Figure 13.30 Selected Types of Visuals to Create Appeal

VISUAL	SKETCH	DESCRIPTION AND FUNCTION	EXAMPLE
Drawings		*Description:* attract attention; reinforce theme, tone, or key issue(s) of the document or oral presentation *Functions:* • grab attention—for example, a holographic image on a report cover • give readers mental breathers—for example, illustrated section dividers in long reports • provide humor—for example, cartoon figure on a series of overhead transparencies • provide aesthetic appeal—for example, decorative borders on announcements • provide coherence—for example, a visual device repeated throughout the document	To show potential buyers the attractive appearance of a new running shoe by using it as the background for the ad copy in a marketing brochure
Cartoons or cartoon strips			To amuse readers with caricatures of stereotypical managers in an article about management styles
Photographs			To show readers whom the article is about with a photograph of the company CEO being interviewed

However, communicators need to be especially careful to represent tabular and graphic information in a way that does not encourage a distorted interpretation by readers. We address three potential problems:

- changing scales
- changing baseline
- ignoring dimensions

Changing the Scales. The two graphs displayed in Figure 13.31 (page 388) show the impact of manipulating one of the axes on a graph. You should avoid the manipulation of information, like that illustrated in the left-hand graph in Figure 13.31, unless the intended audience is able to understand the context and correctly interpret the information. This left-hand graph could easily be read as a dramatic increase in the ratio of growth by people who don't understand the way the *Y* axis has been manipulated. When viewed in the context of a *Y* axis that begins at zero, the fluctuations are negligible. *Time* magazine may have used this graph to dramatize its point, but with such a complex topic, the information was certainly open to misinterpretation.

Changing the Baseline. Changing the baseline on an axis (in this case, the *Y* axis of Figure 13.32, version A, on page 388) can influence the way readers interpret the information. A quick look at version A makes it look as if poultry is predicted to capture nearly all of the meat market share by the year 2000. Changing the baseline changes the impression that is created. All four versions (Figure 13.32) are accurate, but each needs a label on the scale so that readers are reminded of the minimum and maximum of the axis. Readers also probably need to see other meats' market shares in relation to poultry in order to form an accurate impression.

Figure 13.31 Graphs That Distort Numeric Information

These two graphs display the same information; unbelievably, both are accurate.

The graph on the left, in an effort to show dramatic monthly fluctuations, begins the Y axis at .924. As a result, the line covers nearly all of the graph. Because the increments on the Y axis cover such a small segment of the range, the changes appear to be very large.

The graph on the right uses a Y axis that begins at zero and accurately depicts the very slight changes in the ratio of growth—between .925 and .942.

It borders on the unethical (and certainly the grossly misleading) to use the graph on the left without clearly establishing that it covers only 0.018 on a scale that typically ranges from 0 to 1.0.

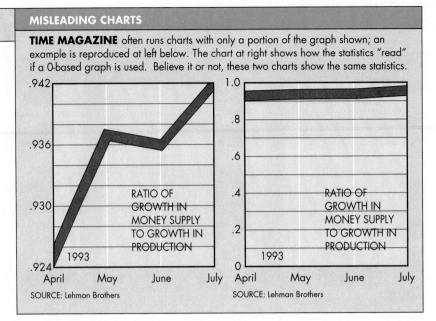

MISLEADING CHARTS

TIME MAGAZINE often runs charts with only a portion of the graph shown; an example is reproduced at left below. The chart at right shows how the statistics "read" if a 0-based graph is used. Believe it or not, these two charts show the same statistics.

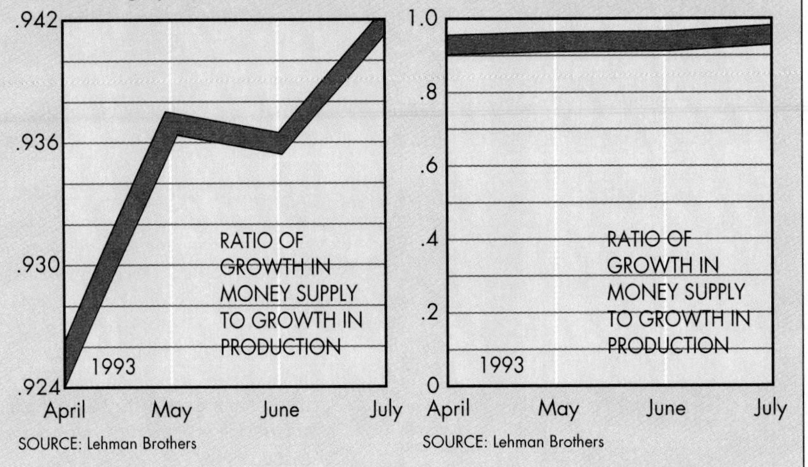

Ignoring Dimensions. Graphs can be used to depict increases or decreases in the quantity of something, whether seed corn production in Iowa, computer sales to homeowners, or employees using corporate day care. For example, in Figure 13.33 the isotype displaying the 1995 guard is twice as tall as the isotype depicting the 1985 guard, supposedly indicating the doubling of the number of guards in the ten-year period. Unfortu-

Figure 13.32 Four Versions of a Bar Graph with Varying Scales on the *Y* Axis

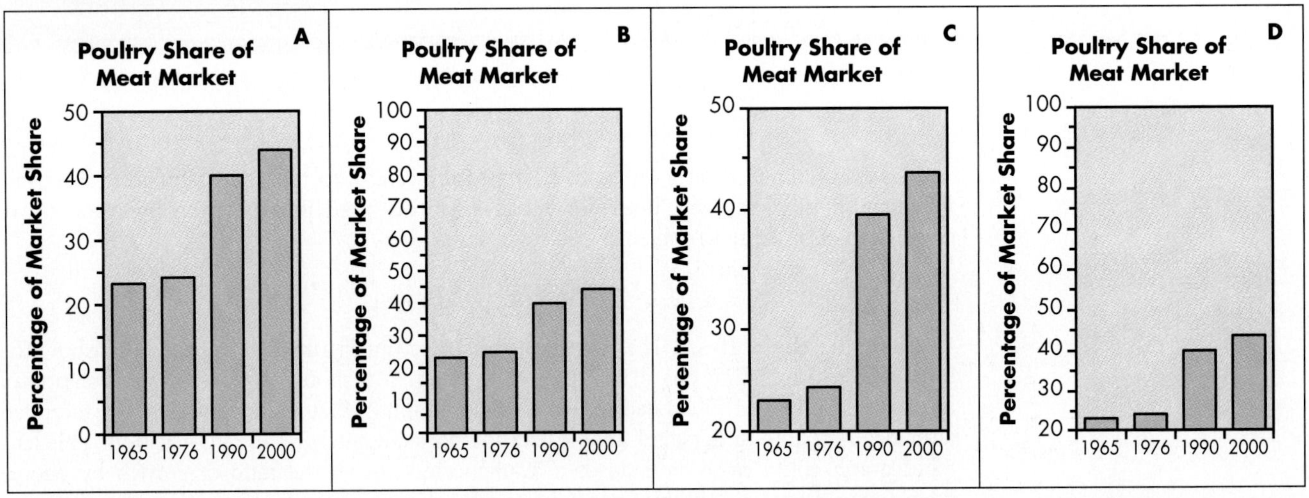

Figure 13.33 Distortion by Ignoring Area and Volume

Increased Security. Over a 10-year period, the number of security guards used by private corporations has doubled.

ETHICS

THOU SHALT NOT PIRATE: THE ETHICS OF SOFTLIFTING

The estimated annual cost of softlifting—software piracy by individuals—exceeds $1.2 billion. Software piracy by corporations adds to this cost. The federal government is trying to curb such violations, particularly in China, where piracy is condoned. In 1993, softlifting in China cost U.S. software manufacturers an estimated $800 million. International trade regulations establish clear legal boundaries and penalties for businesses that copy software.

Because piracy regulators seldom go after individuals, the ethical boundaries for personal softlifting can seem fuzzier. Nevertheless, unauthorized copying of software is illegal. Even when your company indicates that you should copy software for doing work at home, softlifting is a crime. Until three grades of unauthorized use—innocent copying, unfair use, and criminal piracy—are recognized and prohibited, individuals face ethical dilemmas when it comes to copying software. Software vendors could help by writing more realistic license agreements that limit and clarify definitions of what constitutes individual and corporate piracy.

nately, the area occupied by the 1995 isotype is approximately four times larger than that occupied by the 1985 isotype, and the volume is eight times larger. When you want to use isotypes to create a general impression of a change or to appeal to nonexperts, the isotypes should accurately reflect changes in area and volume as well as in height.

Chartjunk versus Design Appeal

As the availability of computer graphing programs has increased, so has the frequency of **chartjunk**, a term coined by Edward Tufte.[1] Chartjunk includes features added to a visual that don't add content or aid understanding. Further, chartjunk may obscure information or distract readers so that they miss the point of the visual. One of the easiest places to spot chartjunk is on graphs that should be straightforward displays of quantitative information. Chartjunk on graphs has a number of characteristics: unnecessary depth to bars, unnecessary tick marks and axis numbers, unnecessary borders surrounding the visual, and inappropriate font styles. Figure 13.34 illustrates these characteristics, and Figure 13.35 (page 390) illustrates the same graph free of chartjunk. (Review Chapter 12, where design appeal was discussed in depth.)

While chartjunk can be distracting and sometimes even misleading, there are times when readers can be helped by added art that reinforces or clarifies information in the graph.

Figure 13.34 Graph with Distracting Chartjunk

Chartjunk tends to obscure the information on a graph so that readers may pay more attention to the design than to the information. In this sample graph, the most inappropriate element is the depth that has been added to the bars.

Depth carries meaning; it's not just a design feature added with a computer graphic program. For example, a simple bar signals a <u>*quantity*</u> *(36 in the case of the first bar), but the depth adds* <u>*volume*</u>*, which may change the meaning.*

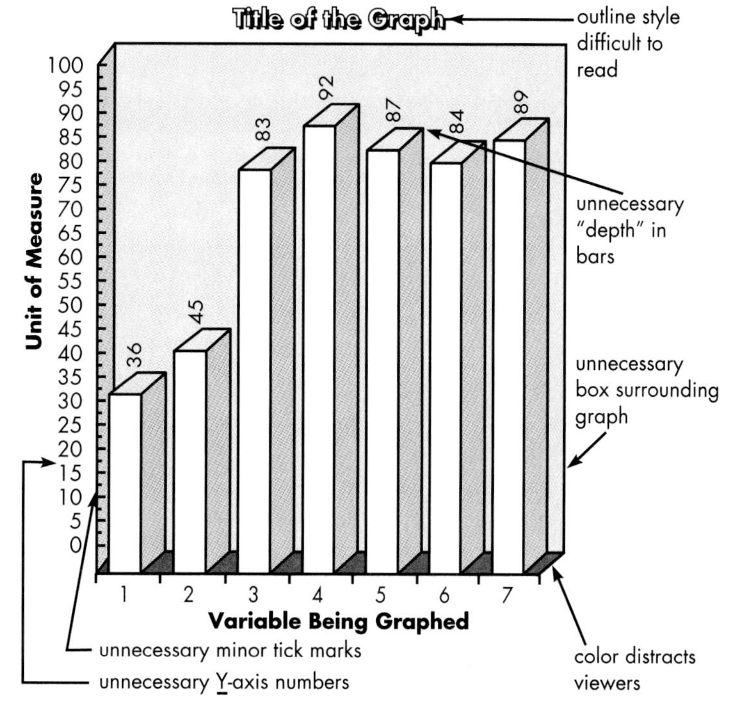

Figure 13.36 provides just such an example. Not only does this multiple bar graph capture readers' attention with the use of cigarettes for bars, but the amount of smoke reinforces the main point of the graph.

The line graph in Figure 13.37 shows another example of a graph that violates the conventions of uncluttered visuals, but does so effectively. This line graph shows changes in Americans' diets over a 30-year period.

When you're preparing a document or an oral presentation, you naturally consider the audience, purpose, and occasion for the text. This chapter has suggested ways in which you need to consider these same factors in relation to the visuals that are part of documents and presentations.

Figure 13.35 Graph without Chartjunk

In deciding what added features to include in a graph, a writer/designer has to ask whether an added feature will enable readers to access and understand the information more easily.

Most readers will find the information in this graph easier to understand without the unnecessary elements (depth, tick marks, axis numbers, borders, and font style).

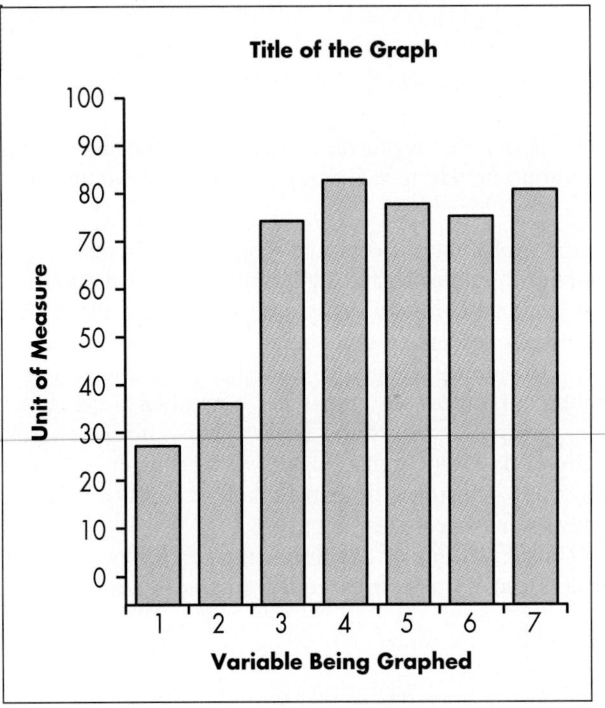

Figure 13.36 Graph with Added Art that Attracts Rather Than Distracts

This graph has a straightforward title and a clear explanatory sentence that directs readers' interpretation.

The greatest amount of smoke is coming from the cigarettes that represent the highest percentages for women and for men.

Given the subject of the graph and common associations with smoke ("where there's smoke . . . ," "a smoking gun . . . ," polluting smokestacks . . .), the use of cigarettes for bars not only attracts readers but reinforces the idea of the risks of smoking.

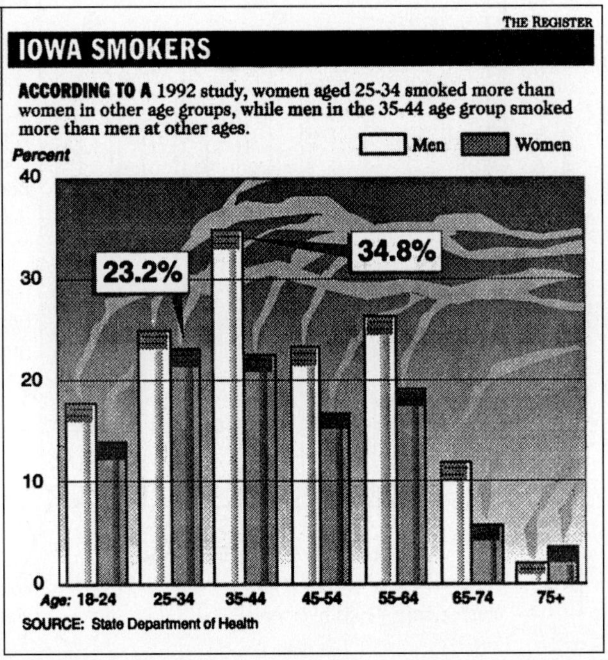

Figure 13.37 Example of a Line Graph

The topic of the change is indicated in the graph's title.

The lines are distinguished by color, shading (light to dark), and, most dramatically, by silhouettes that identify the sources of three kinds of meat: poultry, beef, and pork.

The graph clearly organizes the data, making it easy for readers to see the upward trend of poultry consumption, the downward trend of beef consumption, and the relatively steady rate of pork consumption.

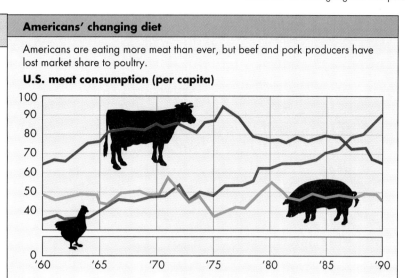

Americans' changing diet

Americans are eating more meat than ever, but beef and pork producers have lost market share to poultry.

U.S. meat consumption (per capita)

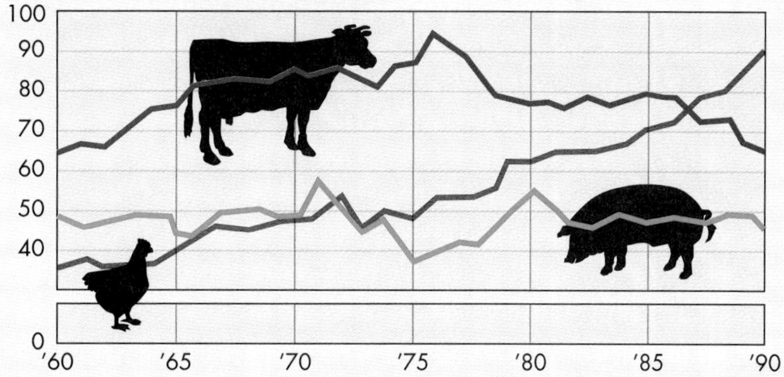

RESPONSE SHEET

DESIGNING AND INCORPORATING VISUALS

COMMUNICATOR(S):	AUDIENCE(S):
OCCASION FOR VISUAL:	TYPE OF VISUAL:
WHAT PURPOSE AM I TRYING TO CONVEY IN THIS VISUAL?	

◆ DECISIONS ABOUT USING VISUALS

What do I want the visual to accomplish?

What kind of visual is appropriate for the occasion?

What features will make the information more accessible? More understandable?

What image do I expect the visual to convey?

◆ DETERMINING THE FUNCTIONS OF VISUALS FOR A DOCUMENT OR PRESENTATION

Organizing Data

Do I want to display verbal or numeric data? How should I organize the table?

Identifying Chronology

Do I want to display a chronology or sequence? What kind of graph or chart should I use?

Identifying Relationships

Do I want to display trends or relationships? What kind of graph should I use?

Identifying Components

Do I want to display parts that comprise objects, mechanisms, or organizations? What kind of graph, drawing, or chart should I use?

Showing Appearance

Do I want to display physical features? What kind of drawing or photograph should I use?

Identifying Location

Do I want to show where something is located? What kind of map should I use?

Creating Appeal

Do I want to increase audience motivation or add decoration to the document? What kind of drawing, cartoon, or photograph should I use?

◆ AVOIDING MISUSE AND DISTORTION

How have I eliminated possible sources of confusion in visuals?

- Do I manipulate the scales in graphs?
- Do I address changes due to inflation and population growth?
- Do I inappropriately change the baseline?
- Do I ignore dimensions?

Have I eliminated chartjunk that distracts or distorts?

ACTIVITIES, EXERCISES, AND ASSIGNMENTS

◆ IN-CLASS ACTIVITIES

1. Please refer to Figure 13.1 for the following activity. The institute was designed, at least in part, for individuals interested in legal, economic, environmental, and workforce issues in Africa.
   - In what ways does this visual reflect these business interests of the institute?
   - Do you agree or disagree that this visual works well to convey the theme of the institute: old myths and new realities?
2. Imagine that you work for H.J. Heinz and have been asked to write the text for the 30-second caption that will be read aloud to accompany the slide of the surface feature map in Figure 13.29. Create the text for Figure 13.29 for these different situations:
   a. in a slide presentation for the annual stockholders' meeting
   b. in a slide presentation for elementary school children
   c. in a slide presentation for new employee orientation
3. Discuss with your classmates whether you think decorative visuals are appropriate in professional publications. Brainstorm two lists—one including situations in which the use of such visuals would probably be appropriate for the occasion, purpose, and audience and another list in which they probably wouldn't be appropriate.

◆ INDIVIDUAL AND GROUP EXERCISES

1. How could the two different ways shown in Figure 13.38 for presenting the same data about the productivity of four different manufacturing lines influence readers? What assumptions has the designer of each table made about the nature of the data? When would version A be appropriate? When would version B be appropriate?
2. Use the text and graph in Figure 13.39 as the basis for this exercise, which you can complete individually or in a small group.
   a. Read the short article and identify its main point(s).
   b. Examine the graph and identify its main point.
   c. Decide if this modified pie graph is technically accurate. Does the area in each slice of the apple accurately reflect the indicated percentage (taking the curve of the apple as well as the bite into consideration)? Does the accuracy matter?
   d. Discuss whether the main point of the graph and the main point of the article reinforce each other. Explain your position. Given the source of the article and graph (the regular newsletter to clients of a major investment company), what is the unarticulated agenda of the graph? Is the choice of size simply decorative, a way to get readers' attention?
   e. Explain whether you believe the graph and the overall design of the article need to be revised or whether they are effective as they are. What conventions does the visual follow? Which are violated?

◆ OUT-OF-CLASS ASSIGNMENTS

1. Locate a visual in a business document that you believe masks or distorts the basic information. Using the questions in Figure 13.40 to guide your assessment, write a one to two-page evaluation of the visual. Refer

Figure 13.38 Different Ways of Presenting Data

	Mon/Fri Productivity	Tues/Thurs Productivity
Line A		
Line B		
Line C		
Line D		

Version A

	Monday Productivity	Tuesday Productivity	Wednesday Productivity	Thursday Productivity	Friday Productivity
Line A					
Line B					
Line C					
Line D					

Version B

Figure 13.39 Short Article with Graph for Exercise 2

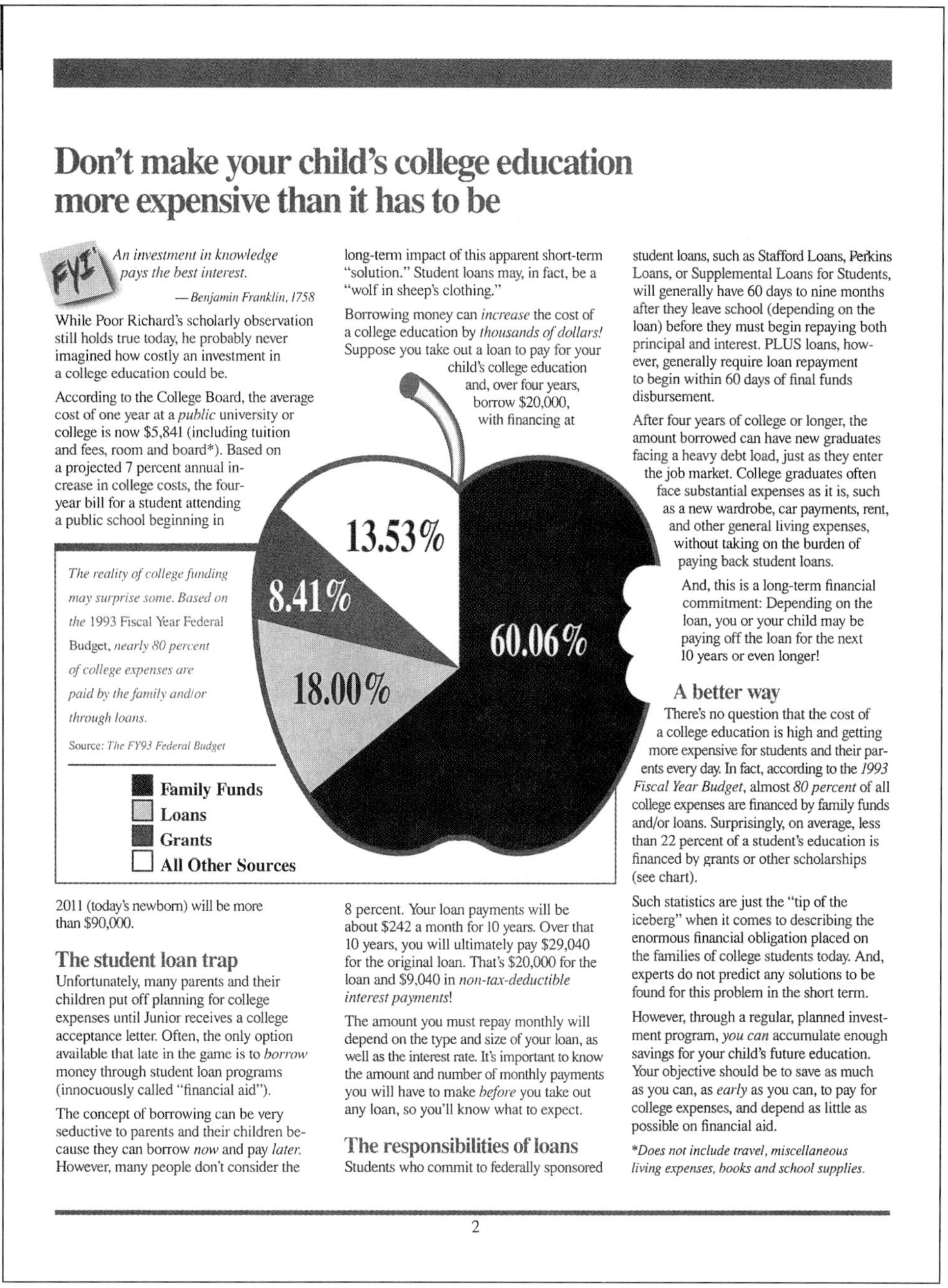

Don't make your child's college education more expensive than it has to be

FYI

An investment in knowledge pays the best interest.

—Benjamin Franklin, 1758

While Poor Richard's scholarly observation still holds true today, he probably never imagined how costly an investment in a college education could be.

According to the College Board, the average cost of one year at a *public* university or college is now $5,841 (including tuition and fees, room and board*). Based on a projected 7 percent annual increase in college costs, the four-year bill for a student attending a public school beginning in 2011 (today's newborn) will be more than $90,000.

The reality of college funding may surprise some. Based on the 1993 Fiscal Year Federal Budget, *nearly 80 percent of college expenses are paid by the family and/or through loans.*

Source: *The FY93 Federal Budget*

The student loan trap

Unfortunately, many parents and their children put off planning for college expenses until Junior receives a college acceptance letter. Often, the only option available that late in the game is to *borrow* money through student loan programs (innocuously called "financial aid").

The concept of borrowing can be very seductive to parents and their children because they can borrow *now* and pay *later.* However, many people don't consider the long-term impact of this apparent short-term "solution." Student loans may, in fact, be a "wolf in sheep's clothing."

Borrowing money can *increase* the cost of a college education by *thousands of dollars!* Suppose you take out a loan to pay for your child's college education and, over four years, borrow $20,000, with financing at 8 percent. Your loan payments will be about $242 a month for 10 years. Over that 10 years, you will ultimately pay $29,040 for the original loan. That's $20,000 for the loan and $9,040 in *non-tax-deductible interest payments!*

The amount you must repay monthly will depend on the type and size of your loan, as well as the interest rate. It's important to know the amount and number of monthly payments you will have to make *before* you take out any loan, so you'll know what to expect.

The responsibilities of loans

Students who commit to federally sponsored student loans, such as Stafford Loans, Perkins Loans, or Supplemental Loans for Students, will generally have 60 days to nine months after they leave school (depending on the loan) before they must begin repaying both principal and interest. PLUS loans, however, generally require loan repayment to begin within 60 days of final funds disbursement.

After four years of college or longer, the amount borrowed can have new graduates facing a heavy debt load, just as they enter the job market. College graduates often face substantial expenses as it is, such as a new wardrobe, car payments, rent, and other general living expenses, without taking on the burden of paying back student loans.

And, this is a long-term financial commitment: Depending on the loan, you or your child may be paying off the loan for the next 10 years or even longer!

A better way

There's no question that the cost of a college education is high and getting more expensive for students and their parents every day. In fact, according to the *1993 Fiscal Year Budget*, almost *80 percent* of all college expenses are financed by family funds and/or loans. Surprisingly, on average, less than 22 percent of a student's education is financed by grants or other scholarships (see chart).

Such statistics are just the "tip of the iceberg" when it comes to describing the enormous financial obligation placed on the families of college students today. And, experts do not predict any solutions to be found for this problem in the short term.

However, through a regular, planned investment program, *you can* accumulate enough savings for your child's future education. Your objective should be to save as much as you can, as *early* as you can, to pay for college expenses, and depend as little as possible on financial aid.

**Does not include travel, miscellaneous living expenses, books and school supplies.*

2

to the Response Sheet for useful questions. Include the visual with the assignment when you submit it. Remember to include a citation that documents the source of the visual.

2. Select a business document that you believe could be improved by the addition of a visual. Design the visual following the general practices and guidelines presented in this chapter. Include the original text as well as the redesigned text with the incorporated visual when you submit the assignment. Remember to document your source.

3. Select a visual that you think is badly designed or distorts information. Following the general practices and guidelines presented in this chapter, redesign the visual so that it is accurate and appealing. Include the original as well as the redesigned version, with the visual incorporated appropriately on the page of the document when you submit the assignment. Remember to document your source.

Figure 13.40 Questions for Assessing Visuals

Occasion

- Why is the visual appropriate for the occasion of the document?

Purpose

- In what way(s) does the visual accomplish its purpose?
- Why is the visual effective for the content it's presenting?

Audience

- How is the visual adapted for and appealing to the audience?
- What makes the visual easy to understand and interpret?

Conventions

- What conventions are followed for this type of visual—for example, accurate label (e.g., "Figure 11.3"), descriptive title, clear caption, keys, labeled axes, page placement, and so on?
- How is the visual coordinated with the accompanying discussion in the document?

Accuracy

- Explain whether the information in the visual is complete and accurate.
- What distortion or chartjunk interferes with interpretation of the visual?

CASE

ROCK SPRINGS ART GALLERY/HISTORICAL MUSEUM

CASE BY ANDREA BREEMER FRANTZ

Background. You are a member of the Rock Springs, Wyoming, Long-Range City Planning committee. The city council recently formed this committee to address areas of development (economic, social, political, environmental, educational) to be implemented before the year 2000. A major concern is how to bolster the economy and increase tourism. In a recent questionnaire, residents uniformly agreed that Rock Springs has a great deal to offer tourists, particularly those attracted to Yellowstone National Park. However, tourism has historically taken a back seat to other forms of economic and community development, such as Project Main Street (a project designed to enhance the downtown business district through storefront competitions; small, low-interest loans for renovations; and a series of citywide festivals held in the downtown district) and community action programs. Responses suggested that the local approach to bolstering the economy had run its course: Rock Springs residents now are interested in focusing on how to use the city's downtown improvements to bolster out-of-town interest.

One idea that came up was to create a local art gallery/historical museum to showcase the American Western culture unique to Wyoming and specifically the Rock Springs/Green River area. The committee agreed that a gallery should emphasize the geographical importance of the area, its natural resources, and the history of change, both industrial and social. Committee members concluded that the gallery would need to house art not only by Wyoming residents, but also by artists who focus on Western subjects.

Naturally, the city does not have the funds necessary to implement the plan immediately, though you all agree it *is* a good idea. Three committee members, yourself included, have been asked to research possible grant sources for funding the art gallery/historical museum project. According to research another subcommittee has done, initial start-up costs vary according to the level of investment you want to commit to. The following are the rough estimates for three levels of quality:

Low-end investment	Includes using a building already in place, one staff member, and low-cost renovations and artifacts (e.g., inexpensive art shows)	$175,000 start-up $60,000 annual budget
Moderate investment	Includes buying an existing building and renovating, 2–3 staff members, and moderately priced art shows and artifacts	$400,000 start-up $150,000 annual budget
High-end investment	Includes building a new facility, 5–6 staff members, moderate- to high-cost artifacts and shows	$1.5 million start-up $300,000 annual budget

Task. Your task is to carefully research as many different foundations and grant sources as you can to provide a viable list of possibilities to the committee (a viable list from you would likely include ten sources). You are faced with determining specific criteria appropriate to the project in order to narrow the scope of your research.

Once you have gathered the data, create a brief report which incorporates the information in tabular form so that committee members will be able to quickly and efficiently assess their prospects and begin work on a proposal. The table should provide specific information about the foundation (e.g., deadlines for submission, chief criteria, presentation requirements, and so on) that is relevant to your needs.

Complication. Committee Chair Herbert Wells has called just after you've completed your report and asked you to please rank-order what you believe to be the most likely prospects for funding your project. You should use your own criteria for ranking your data. However, Herbert has said you will probably need to explain your rationale for how you ranked them.

You are well aware that these committee meetings frequently drag on far too long, and people are sometimes resentful of Herbert's tendency to add tasks to the agenda at the last minute. Therefore, your challenge is to keep your explanation brief but thorough. You may consider altering the tabular data you have already compiled and presenting them instead of a visual data display that incorporates a rating system of your own creation.

DEVELOPING PRODUCTIVE TEAM SKILLS

When you work on a team, the group may not have an official "writer" as a member. Instead, you and your colleagues may be entirely responsible for planning and preparing team documents.

Learning to be a good team member on a productive team takes some effort. Walden Miller, Manager of Technical Documentation at OptImage,[1] a CD-i (Compact Disc-interactive) firm that uses teams to create many of its manuals and other publications, offers practical suggestions that will help you be a more effective and productive team member and, thus, better equipped to prepare necessary documents and presentations: tuning in, listening, asking questions, sharing, and reflecting.

Tuning In

Tuning in begins with what Walden Miller calls having an "inner focus" about the project—"knowing what you know and what you don't know." The importance of being receptive to the ideas of others is emphasized by Walden Miller: "It is important to be openminded about other people's ideas, to trust what other people [in the group] know. You need to be able to defend your own views and be very willing to listen and to understand what someone else knows. It's important to be able to disagree strongly with your collaborators and expect to be disagreed with."

Tuning in also means being able to keep on track: team members may agree to restrict what is addressed in each meeting so that the work is manageable. Walden Miller says that teams he's on often "limit our agenda to, say, two items, so we can get those two things solved." Team members need to judge which suggestions are worth pursuing and which should be dropped as impractical. Team members also need to be able to tune out distractions—ranging from noise in the next office to worries about the upcoming meeting for a different project.

To tune in to the ideas of your collaborators, consider the general guidelines in Figure 1, which suggest practical ways that you can improve the likelihood of participating in productive team meetings.

A good manager can help team members stay tuned in by judging how long the team can work productively at any given time. Walden Miller explains that "too much new information at one time is counterproductive to a group's success because people need time to mull it over." A good leader can make everyone more productive by monitoring the focus and attentiveness of the team.

Figure 1 Guidelines for Tuning In

- Always come prepared for any collaborative meeting, which means gathering necessary information and having something to contribute to the collaboration.
- Be able to articulate the purpose of your collaborative work. What's the task? What's the process? What's the goal? How can you get all of the collaborators in your group to represent or interpret the task, process, and goals in the same way?
- Be articulate in expressing your views. Don't assume body language or silence will sufficiently (or accurately) convey your views.
- Be cooperative and supportive rather than competitive and antagonistic.
- Be direct in stating your own opinions . . . but don't trample on the ideas of other collaborators.

Listening

You can learn a great deal if you are an **active listener**, one who is attentive, involved, and interested. An active listener pays attention to the content (what other people say as well as what they don't say) and to the manner of expression (tone of voice, pacing, and inflection). In commenting about the importance of give-and-take on teams, Walden Miller said, "I think listening and questioning—the give and take of a meeting—are extremely important. Listening to the content is extremely important. I think it's equally important to pay attention to the flow of the conversation, trying to understand where the words are going."

Active listening means that you focus on the speaker, even if you disagree with what the speaker is saying. You give plenty of nonverbal cues that you're listening: direct eye contact, relaxed body language, acknowledgments that you're paying attention. While a person is speaking, you absorb and organize what is being said, without making value judgments. And you periodically paraphrase the other person's views and ask if your summary is an accurate representation of what's being said.

It's difficult to be a productive participant on a team if you aren't listening to the other team members, so active listening sometimes means asking questions when you're confused. An added benefit of active listening is that if you actively listen to other team members, they're more likely to listen to you.

Asking Questions

The other half of listening is asking good questions and making productive contributions. Questions can help you assess what you already know as well as what you need to know:

- Ask questions that require comments or discussion rather than questions that ask for yes/no responses.
- Ask questions that focus attention on a range of elements important to the project.

Figure 2 Questions to Help Collaborators Deal with Content and Other Concerns

Purpose
- What are the purposes of this document (or oral presentation)?
- What main point(s) do we want to make?
- How will the audience react to the purpose and points?

Audience
- Who is the intended audience? Why is this the appropriate audience?
- What will a reader expect to read (learn, do)?
- What problems, conflicts, inconsistencies, or gaps might a reader see?

Occasion
- What external factors may impinge on preparing this document or oral presentation?
- What genre is appropriate for this occasion?
- What will be resolved by this document or oral presentation?

Message
- What critical information needs to be included in this document?
- What else should we consider including or excluding?
- What sources will be used?

Conventions of Organization and Support
- How can we organize the content to achieve our purpose?
- What evidence can we use to support the purpose and appeal to the audience?
- What examples (anecdotal, statistical, visual, and so on) should we use?

Conventions of Document Design
- How can design features be used to convey our main point(s)?
- What design features will the audience expect? What will they respond to?
- How can we balance verbal and visual information?

The questions in Figure 2 (page 399) are the kinds that experienced writers ask themselves (and each other) on virtually any complex project they work on.

Although the questions in Figure 2 are listed in separate categories, you may find it useful to combine questions: How will the *examples* reinforce our *message*? How will the *design* help the *audience* understand the *message*? What *organization* is most effective for helping accomplish the *purpose*?

You need to ask questions early in the process to establish the scope and purpose of a document. At any stage in the process, you and your colleagues can help each other elaborate important ideas and eliminate inconsistent or contradictory ideas. And all along the way, you need to ask questions like these: Is this information necessary? Will it be distracting to the audience?

Asking questions increases the likelihood that you won't let things slip by at meetings. If asking questions doesn't work, you can address concerns in other ways—resolve or dismiss the concern, agree to explore it further, or agree to postpone consideration of the item. In other words, you shouldn't ignore points that need to be discussed.

Walden Miller encourages good questions to get at important information. He says, "You have to pay attention enough to ask good questions. It's extremely hard to ask good questions. That's the key to collaboration. Timing is extremely important for questions. You have to ask good questions early enough in the process to use the information from the answers."

Sharing

Effective, successful collaborators share information and insights. Your team members will expect you to provide detailed and accurate information unless some prior agreement restricts such sharing (usually for reasons of confidentiality). As part of your procedural agreements, you and other team members can establish a regular process and schedule to exchange information.

Getting comfortable enough to share information isn't automatic. Team members need to trust each other and respect the experience each member adds to the team. Walden Miller explains that

> to strengthen individual team-building skills, most important is being willing to put forth ideas in a nonconfrontational manner and to actively seek out opposing views, especially if you tend to show that openness is there. It's okay to have strong views and to have strong opposition, but you must be willing to listen to the opposition, must be willing to give ground as well as stand firm. It's to everyone's benefit if a team has players that are willing to give in and then come back at a later point, that know when to compromise, and know when to pull things out.

You can help create an atmosphere for sharing information by taking time to learn what expertise each person brings to the team. Additionally, you can share your own assumptions, information, and insights. This sharing needs to lead to action. A productive team agrees on action items and commitments to deliver on them.

Reflecting

The workplace is usually busy, sometimes even frenetic, in its pace. Everyone wants everything done yesterday. Yet, we know that people do a better job if they have time to reflect, to mull over the ideas they've heard. Walden Miller, in talking about the intensity of a design team, says that "reflection matters immensely."

- *On a daily basis:* "I usually spend the first hour of every morning figuring out what I need, trying to figure out where I am."
- *On a project basis:* "So much of it [team project management] is just sitting back and thinking about what I'm doing. You don't need to have a computer or the document you're working on . . . You tend to think about the process."

A good collaborator carefully considers ideas and opinions from other people. Planning a specific time for reflection is difficult when time is scarce—when deadlines slip, when your day is filled with back-to-back responsibilities, when you barely have time to eat lunch—but it is nonetheless an important part of the collaborative process.

You need to sift through the information you've collected and assess its value, decide what information to use and what to discard, and then pinpoint areas of confusion that should be clarified and areas of disagreement that should be resolved. Your reflection may also show that you need to go back to your colleagues or team for additional information or clarification. More decisions may be needed. In short, without reflection, you won't be able to effectively use the information you gain through collaboration.

Working Together

A successful team depends on members' fulfilling several responsibilities. The following list of practical suggestions will help you be a more productive member of any team:

- Prepare *your* agenda or a brief, preliminary plan before the meeting so you'll be prepared to make a contribution.
- Be receptive to suggestions that may help you improve your ideas. Respond to comments and contributions.
- Be flexible so you can improve your ideas.
- Give thoughtful responses to questions. Respond to challenges.
- Listen actively. Ask for explanations and clarifications.
- Offer comments that help everyone think about the strengths and weaknesses of ideas on the table. Offer relevant contributions.
- Encourage exploration by asking probing questions. Challenge other members on the team to encourage creative thinking.
- Be interested, attentive, and engaged.

The decision to tune in, listen, ask questions, share, and reflect may result in big benefits. Members of highly productive teams often have long-term commitments to each other. Janis Foreman, an expert in management teams, has explained that a team's successful prior history is one of the main factors in predicting the same team's future success.[2] And at OptImage, Walden Miller explains that "productive team members are rewarded by putting them on design teams again. Design teams are considered the elite jobs; it's a bonus for a good team to work together again."

ACTIVITIES AND QUESTIONS FOR DISCUSSION

1. As a reflective exercise about your own collaborative skills, spend some time thinking about previous collaborative or team experiences you've had. Then respond to these questions:

   a. Review the five guidelines for tuning in that are presented in Figure 1. Comment on which ones you have typically followed, which ones you have occasionally followed, and which ones you have avoided. What advice can you give yourself about tuning in more completely in future collaborations?

   b. Review the questions in Figure 2. Which ones are you likely to be comfortable asking during a team meeting? Which ones would you like to add to those you typically ask?

2. Arrange to interview a workplace professional who spends a portion of his or her time working collaboratively or on a team. When you interview this person, ask about the person's attitudes and perceptions about the importance of these skills for collaborators:

   - tuning in
   - listening
   - asking questions
   - sharing
   - reflecting

ELIMINATING PROBLEMS IN TEAM-WRITTEN DOCUMENTS

Revision becomes critical when problems in collaboration lead to problems in writing. These are typical collaborative problems that can result in writing problems:

- *Failure to create a group plan*: Team members presume that the task is so obvious and/or simple that they don't need to create a plan.
- *Failure to allow time for reading and revising drafts*: Team members misjudge the scope or complexity of the task, so there is time only to complete the draft and little time to coordinate the sections completed by members of the team.

These lapses can cause a number of writing problems. The examples that follow illustrate specific problems that result from lapses in collaborative processes. The first example shows collaborators who include unnecessary repetition. The second shows how problems in collaboration result in an incoherent document.

Failure to Create a Group Plan

Failure to establish a group plan can cause collaborators to produce a document with problems, including unnecessary repetition. That's what happened with Theresa Humpal and Deborah Fauser, employees at the local Perkins Restaurant who were also taking a business communication course. Both noticed that skim milk was frequently requested by customers even though it wasn't on the menu. As one of their class projects, they prepared a collaborative feasibility report for their team managers at Perkins about adding skim milk to the menu.

Theresa and Deborah violated a basic guideline for effective collaboration: they didn't discuss each other's areas of responsibility for the report nor did they create a joint outline of the report's contents. As a result, they weren't entirely clear about what should be covered in each section. Even though they selected sections of the report to write individually, they didn't decide what they'd actually include in each section.

Their final document (from which the excerpts in Figure 1 are taken) contained repetition that could have been avoided if they had viewed themselves as collaborators with complementary responsibilities rather than as two individuals working separately toward the same goal. Unfortunately, Theresa and Deborah worked on their own parts of the project, preparing each one as if it were an independent, stand-alone section. They prepared a memo of transmittal and a report that included five short, independent sections—with a great deal of unnecessary repetition, as you'll see in the excerpts in Figure 1.

If Theresa and Deborah had had a detailed working plan for their project, they would have saved themselves time and increased the chances of producing a more effective report. This plan could have included a collaboratively constructed outline and ongoing discussions about what to include in each section. Much of the revision could have been avoided if they had planned together from the beginning.

Failure to Allow Time for Reading and Revising

A second major problem that occurs with groups is not planning enough time to complete the project. The unfortunate reality is that while groups often produce better products than individuals, the effort is often more time consuming.

Jason McAlexander, Carrie Matlock, and Rachel Woods worked together on a workplace project for their business communication course. They decided to propose the installation of a computer system to a local company where they all were employed. The individual segments of their proposal worked adequately by themselves, but when the pieces were put

Figure 1 Excerpts from a Repetitious Report

In the memo of transmittal to the management team at Perkins Restaurant:

. . . By adding skim milk to the menu, we would expand the existing "Lite and Healthy" menu. This menu was developed in response to customer preferences for healthier alternatives when eating out. Because of the growing concern for low fat and low cholesterol food items, adding skim milk would not only increase sales, but it would also better Perkins' public image. . . .

In the introduction to the report:

. . . In the past, Perkins has offered "Lite and Healthy" items on the national menu—items with decreased cholesterol and fat contents. By including skim milk on the menu, we would be continuing Perkins' desire to achieve complete customer satisfaction by responding to their requests. . . .

In the background section of the report:

. . . Perkins employees are trained to notice when a customer is not satisfied and whenever possible to respond to the customer's needs and requests. One of the major requests is for the addition of skim milk onto the menu. . . .

In the needs section of the report:

. . . ~~Because of their concern for customer satisfaction, Perkins Restaurants have added special menu items for the health conscious. These "Lite and Healthy" menu items are marked with a green circle to indicate low fat and cholesterol content.~~ . . .

. . . ~~Many customers would like to see the "Lite and Healthy" menu expanded to include~~ [S]kim milk [is] a request made [in writing] every month by 10 to 15 customers. This does not include the number of oral requests the service staff encounters during its shift. . . .

In the proposed solution section of the report:

. . . Considering this information [about heart and weight problems], we feel there is a great need for Perkins to place skim milk on the menu. ~~Consistent with Perkins' concern for people's health as shown by the "Lite and Healthy" menu items, skim milk would be a welcome addition. Because customers are the source of Perkins' business, the company should act on customers' requests, which would show Perkins' concern for their customers.~~ . . .

In the caption to accompany Figure 1 (circle graph showing percentages of customer requests separated by subject):

. . . There are three main requests per month that Perkins receives: comments about general service, comments about menu items, and requests for skim milk. Th[is]e ~~above~~ graph shows that skim milk is the most popular request among customers. ~~Because of the concern for customer satisfaction and their requests, we would like to propose the implementation of skim milk into the menu at the Perkins Restaurants.~~ . . .

Collaborators may sometimes work through complex plans and problems in informal settings.

together, they didn't work. Unfortunately, the team simply did not plan time for each member to review the document and suggest necessary changes. Part of the result, as you can read in Figure 2 (page 404), was a transmittal memo that was not logical or coherent.

Jason, Carrie, and Rachel could have solved a good part of their problem by doing some **backward planning:** marking the project's due date and then listing all the tasks, personnel, and time needed to complete the project, who would perform what tasks, and the amount of time each task would take. Included in their tasks should have been time for each team member to review and revise. Such a schedule would have let team members know when they needed to start each task in order to complete the project on time.

Figure 2 Excerpts from a Memo That's Not Sufficiently Logical or Coherent

What's the connection between tracking shop worker activities and acknowledging an increase in clientele? The link is assumed but not articulated.

What's the connection between a decrease in worker output and difficulty in tracking shop worker activities? The link is assumed but not articulated.

What's the connection between the information in paragraphs 1 and 2 and the information about time and employee power?

DATE November 4, 19—
TO Jim Zeivers, Chief Executive Officer
FROM Jason McAlexander, Personnel Manager
Carrie Matlock, Plant Manager
Rachel Woods, Computer Programmer
SUBJECT Computer System Proposal

In response to your inquiry about the proposal for the MAS 90 software computer system to keep track of shop worker activities, we have enclosed the feasibility report about this system.

Since IF&G has increased its clientele, additional help is necessary to help meet demands. This need for additional workers became apparent when the decreased output from the shop area was examined. Accompanying this increase in the work force is an increase in the difficulty keeping track of the work done by these additional workers.

We propose installing the MAS 90 software computer system, including their PC accounting and Job Shop Module. The latter will help to keep track of employees' work on various tasks and help the company to estimate the amount of time and employee power needed to complete certain tasks. This will, in turn, help the management to find redundant activities, find those who are unmotivated to get their jobs done, and ultimately increase shop output.

We thank you for your consideration in this matter. Please contact us if you have any questions.

Revision on a Team

Collaborators who plan together generally create higher-quality products. Planning may reduce the amount of revision if, at the beginning of their work together, team members discuss and agree on their purpose, audience, occasion, and message.

Among the things team members should discuss is how the revision will be handled. A number of factors can appear in numerous combinations:

- Who will do the revisions?
- What kind of feedback is expected?
- Will the emphasis be global or local?
- What revision cycle will be used?

Which factors come into play will be determined by the schedule and organizational expectations. For example, in an organization that mandates a multi-level review process (team members, supervisors, managers, directors), you may have to build three to four weeks for review and revision into a nine-week project. In a three-week class project, you may have to build in a week for review by everyone on the team.

ACTIVITIES AND QUESTIONS FOR DISCUSSION

1. Recall a collaborative project you have worked on, a project that didn't go smoothly or produce a particularly effective product. Reflect on possible causes for the problems with the project. Write a memo to your instructor suggesting ways that you could avoid similar problems in the future.
2. Refer to Figure 2. Working with a small group, revise this transmittal memo so that the unarticulated assumptions are expressed. You may need to make up details in order to create a logical, coherent memo.

PART V
PREPARING REPORTS, PROPOSALS, MANUALS, AND PRESENTATIONS

CHAPTER

14

Functions and Structures of Reports

OUTLINE

Reports to Reinforce a Healthy Business Relationship

Purposes of Reports

Functions of Conventional Components

A Sample Report

CRITERIA FOR EXPLORING CHAPTER 14

What we cover in this chapter	What you will be able to do after reading this chapter
Occasions that affect business reports and the influence of those reports on business relationships	Recognize complex occasions that affect business reports and the importance of reports for business
Purposes of reports	Use reports to document, investigate, and evaluate information
Functions of conventional components of reports	Structure reports to orient, inform, persuade, and provide details for them
A sample formal report	Recognize purposes and components in a sample report

Reports communicate a range of information—from straightforward, implicitly persuasive accounts for receptive audiences to complex, explicitly persuasive arguments for resistant audiences. Like other kinds of business communication, all reports are in some way persuasive, even though the persuasive elements may not be the primary purpose. The reports in this chapter are implicitly persuasive for audiences that are, by and large, receptive. Even though a report's explicit purpose may be to document a current corporate practice, its underlying purpose could be to convince readers that the practice is sound and to promote a positive company image.

CONTEXT

The report excerpt in Figure 14.1 answers basic questions about 3M's Pollution Prevention Pays (3P) program. The report includes information unfamiliar to outside readers who want to understand the role of the 3P program. The report is written in a manner simple enough for schoolchildren who request information from the company but complex enough for interested adult readers. The examples help receptive readers understand the importance of the 3P program to 3M.

Figure 14.1 Beginning of a 3M Information Report

Reports provide readers with the background necessary to understand the information in the report. Does this background seem appropriate for an internal or an external audience?

Reports have explicit and implicit purposes. What does the explicit purpose of this report seem to be? What implicit purposes might 3M have for writing this report?

Reports explain unfamiliar concepts. What do the level of detail and the nature of the explanations convey about the writer's perception of readers' ability to understand complex information?

Reports present readers with detailed information. How does the embedded table help readers make an informed decision about the value of the 3P program?

3P Background

3M is one of the nation's leading blue-chip companies. It also is one of the world's premier new-product companies, developing and manufacturing more than 60,000 quality products for business, industry, government and consumers around the globe—57 nations in all. 3M employs over 88,000 men and women, all of whom are encouraged to explore new ideas and share what they learn with fellow employees. This philosophy carries over to environmental responsibility and is the basis of the internationally known 3M Pollution Prevention Pays (3P) program.

The 3M Pollution Prevention Pays (3P) Program

The 3M Pollution Prevention Pays (3P) program, an industrial environmental conservation initiative begun in 1975, has been recognized the world over for its achievements. It has been widely praised by environmental organizations and environmental officials of many governments, including the United Nations; it has been copied by many companies and it has received numerous environmental achievement awards.

The 3P idea is to prevent pollution at the source in products and manufacturing processes rather than remove pollution after it is created. The idea itself is not new.

However, the concept of applying pollution prevention on a companywide basis, through a globally organized effort and recording the results, had not been done before. The dramatic results demonstrate the environmental and financial impact of such efforts and argue for government-sponsored support mechanisms by industrial nations.

Yearly Pollution Prevented

Pollutant	United States	International
air pollutants	140,000 tons	14,000 tons
water pollutants	16,300 tons	1,400 tons
wastewater	1 billion gallons	700 billion gallons
sludge/solid waste	416,000 tons	16,600 tons

These figures represent first-year savings only. Projected over a period of several years, the prevented pollution becomes significant, indeed. In addition, the prevented pollution has resulted in a savings of $573 million for 3M ($470 million from U.S. Operations and $103 million from International Operations).

1. Explain how the writer of this excerpt documents information so that it's accessible to the nonexpert audience.
2. How would you change this excerpt if you were writing it for a different audience—say, new 3M employees or people in public relations who wanted to promote the program?
3. What kinds of information do you think that the writer of this report needed to collect and understand in order to prepare this report?

The 3M report in Figure 14.1 introduces two factors that are important to reports:

- routine purposes of reports
- components of reports

REPORTS TO REINFORCE A HEALTHY BUSINESS RELATIONSHIP

Jeremiah Thompson was an international sales representative for Corometrics, a Connecticut-based medical supply company specializing in neonatal units (facilities and equipment for newborn infants) as well as disposable hospital supplies. He traveled frequently—making trips from six to twelve weeks long—and was on the road for as many as 20 weeks a year covering markets in Asia, Africa, and Australia. He regularly wrote reports, which were his primary tool for communicating with Corometrics' managers—keeping them informed about his progress and problems and persuading them to accept his recommendations. Because his trips were so long, his reports served multiple purposes:

- documenting the events of the trip
- investigating problems with Corometrics distribution in each country
- evaluating the options that were best for his company such as expanding the product line it made available or changing the distributor in a country

His reports were arguments for the recommendations about the complex occasions that he encountered. He usually organized a series of reports by country, so on one trip he might write five reports—one each for Israel, Kuwait, Egypt, Lebanon, and Saudi Arabia.

At the end of one of his trips to Saudi Arabia, Jeremiah (Jerry) sat in the Riyadh airport, waiting for his flight to Abu Dhabi. He pulled out the notes he'd made, ready to organize them. He knew the purpose of the trip—to assess and reinforce previously established business connections and to establish new contacts. He also had details about his contacts, client questions, problems that he'd helped to resolve, and information that might affect Corometrics' future business in Saudi Arabia. He also knew what actions he wanted to recommend. Jerry used an inductive organizational pattern for his report because he wanted to lay the groundwork for his recommendation before presenting it.

Portable computers help professionals who are on the road for long trips keep track of their ideas and progress so they can more easily prepare reports.

The segment of the report reproduced in Figure 14.2 (page 408) presents Jerry's discussion about Louis Bathish, General Manager of the Arabian Health Care Supply Corporation (AHCSC). While the initial purpose of Jerry's trip report was to document the events of his trip to Saudi Arabia, he also wanted to persuade Corometrics' managers that they needed to accept his end-of-report recommendation to change Saudi Arabian distributors. These managers were generally receptive to Jerry's ideas but unfamiliar with the foreign markets Jerry was responsible for expanding. The excerpt in Figure 14.2 is part of the evidence that Jerry used to support this recommendation.

The report continued for several pages beyond the excerpt in Figure 14.2, summarizing the understandings reached between Jerry and Louis Bathish as a representative of AHCSC. Then Jerry made his recommendation to Corometrics' managers: "I recommend we offer AHCSC distribution rights in Saudi Arabia as soon as AHCSC establishes its Medical Electronics

ETHICS

THE ETHICS IN CORPORATE VOICE: ANNUAL REPORTS SPEAK ABOUT MORE THAN MONEY

The days when a corporation's worth was described solely in terms of pages and pages of financial data are gone. Annual reports now discuss more than the bottom line; they also adopt a voice that is refreshingly blunt about company operations and open about future plans.

John F. Budd of the Omega Group, a public relations firm that tracks annual reports, points out that some CEOs are "building credibility by being clear and candid." This move toward clarity and candor reflects a shift from an emphasis on expediency and efficiency. It suggests increased ethical concern for the reader's needs. In some cases, businesspeople like Ben Cohen (Ben and Jerry's Homemade, Inc.) use their annual report not only to articulate financial and traditional corporate information, but also to express the corporation's ethical approach to employees and stockholders. Annual reports also express a company's activist positions on ethical issues involving the environment, politics, and other social issues. In fact the Ben and Jerry's Homemade annual report contains a "social audit," which has been called "a form of investigative journalism, with the company investigating itself."

Figure 14.2 Trip Report Excerpt

Organization of information: Jerry arranged the details in this section of the report to help his readers, Corometrics managers in the United States eager to assess AHCSC as a potential distributor for Corometrics.

Prior history: Jerry reminded his readers that Corometrics already had a connection with one of AHCSC's suppliers.

Expansion plans: To help readers understand whether AHCSC would be an appropriate distributor, Jerry reviewed Mr. Bathish's expansion plans for the hospital supplies section of the company.

Current practices: Jerry needed to investigate AHCSC's current business to show Corometrics' managers how the company's products would fit into AHCSC's current mix and that there would be no conflict of interest.

Competition: There was little competition, so Corometrics might get a strong foothold in the Middle Eastern market. Another company Corometrics already approved (Atom) considered AHCSC an appropriate distributor.

Competition: Jerry provided readers with additional information about the competitive position of AHCSC and about Bathish's stated interest in representing Corometrics.

Criteria: Jerry established conditions for action.

Categories of discussion: Jerry informed readers about the main categories of his conversations with Mr. Bathish.

Summary of evaluation: He summarized his evaluation but still didn't give his recommendation.

Meeting with AHCSC

The next day I met with Mr. Louis Bathish, General Manager of the Arabian Health Care Supply Corporation (AHCSC), a member of the Olayan Group. Mr. Bathish is an American of Arabic descent and a graduate of Pomona College and the California Institute of Technology. He is knowledgeable and experienced (several years in sales and marketing with Abbott and American Hospital Supply Corporation in the United States in the medical supply business, particularly for laboratory equipment and supplies).

AHCSC's current business is more than 95% hospital supplies from companies such as Becton-Dickinson, Seamless, Kimberly-Clark, Smith Kline, as well as products supplied by an associate company, General Medical International Services in Richmond, Virginia. (I've made two presentations to GMIS.)

Mr. Bathish took responsibility for AHCSC's operation six months ago and is still building the first phase of the business: hospital supplies. He is actively recruiting to increase his sales force to include another sales representative and three district managers (he already has four sales representatives) and to open branch offices in Jidda and Riyadh. To date, AHCSC represents only two equipment companies: Fukuda (for electrocardiographs) and Atom (our distributor in Japan). Atom is not directly promoting its products in the Middle East but rather is working through Mitsui trading company. Mr. Bathish believes that AHCSC may be able to sell some Atom incubators.

Mr. Bathish said he had received a strong recommendation from Muhammad Alyusf in New York to establish a Medical Electronics Division within AHCSC for the sale of Corometrics' products and three or four other noncompetitive, complementary product lines. He asked whether he could have the Corometrics line for all of the Arab world when he had such capability. I told him of our past activity in the area and our new capability for intensive support of our distributors in the Middle East. I told him we would be very interested in having a strong distributor in Saudi Arabia and of our dissatisfaction with what Isam has accomplished in the past three years. I also told him we would not appoint such an area distributor until the candidate (1) had performed well in Saudi Arabia and (2) could demonstrate the organization and capability for strong efforts in the other countries.

We also discussed in detail the personnel and test equipment necessary for sales and service, our demonstrator policy, the need for service kits or spares, and training we could provide.

Mr. Bathish then said he had decided to establish a Medical Electronics Division within AHCSC in three to six months. He is totally occupied with developing the disposables business for at least the next 90 days. He said after-sales service is the key in the Saudi market, so he first will hire an electronics service technician, build a well-equipped electromed service center in Dhahran, and offer hospitals service for existing medical electronics equipment. Then he will actively market new equipment.

This seems like an excellent approach to the Saudi market.

Division, orders demo equipment, and meets our other conditions." Jerry's report incorporated the conventional elements of a trip report, but it also assumed some of the functions of a recommendation report.

PURPOSES OF REPORTS

Jerry Thompson's report (Figure 14.2) fulfilled three purposes: he documented the events of his trip, investigated options for his company to consider, and evaluated situations in order to make recommendations. While Jerry's report integrated three purposes, his primary purpose evolved as he realized that Corometrics' current distributor was inadequate and that AHCSC would be a good replacement. The portion of the report you read in Figure 14.2 focused on his third purpose: building the background for his recommendation to offer AHCSC distribution rights in Saudi Arabia.

In general, business reports can be categorized into three broad purposes:

- *Reports that document progress, discussions, and actions* provide the audience with up-to-date information for background or decision making.
- *Reports that investigate available options* provide the audience with information for decision making.
- *Reports that evaluate personnel, objects, and practices* assess impact or recommend changes.

Business reports can be placed on a continuum as represented in Figure 14.3. At one end of the continuum are reports that presume reader cooperation, so they typically present straightforward accounts of verifiable information (discussed in this chapter). At the other end are reports that presume reader resistance, so they typically present persuasive feasibility analyses and proposals. In between are reports like the one Jerry Thompson wrote (Figure 14.2) that expect readers to be receptive to some of the information and potentially

Figure 14.3 Report Continuum

Reports whose purpose is to document, investigate, or evaluate can generally assume some degree of reader cooperation.

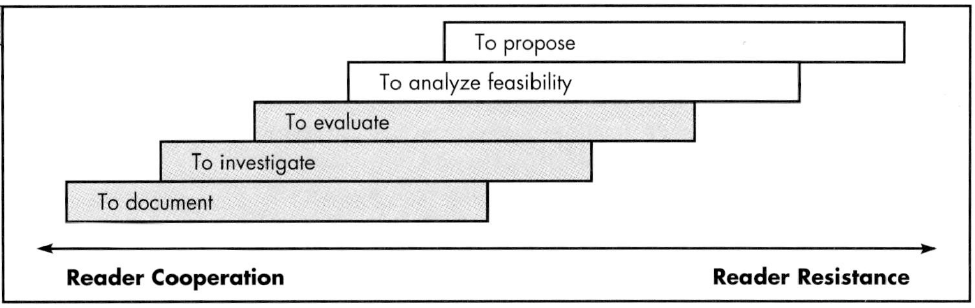

resistant to other information. Readers can be alternatively cooperative and resistant to different parts within the same report.

In addition to the continuum that indicates whether readers are cooperative or resistant, reports can be thought of on a continuum that moves from informal to formal (see Figure 14.4). Readers who are familiar with a report's content, expect little elaboration, and are close to the occasion typically expect informal reports. Readers who are unfamiliar with the content, expect elaboration, and are distant from the occasion typically expect formal reports. The most obvious distinctions between informal and formal reports have to do with treatment of audience, purpose, and occasion as well as tone, length, and conventional sections.

Documentary Reports

Documentary reports record progress, discussions, and decisions in an organization. These reports record and monitor ongoing activities and provide an account of completed activities and activities that still need to be done, as well. Typically, reports that document activities provide information and suggest implications. Less often such reports offer explicit conclusions or recommendations.

Figure 14.5 (page 410) is not an inclusive list of reports that document activities, but it presents conventions of documenting reports you are likely to use.

Figure 14.6 (page 410) presents two progress reports written by four students in a senior agronomy seminar. Their semester project was to research a problem and recommend solutions

Figure 14.4 Characteristics of Informal and Formal Reports

INFORMAL REPORTS TEND TO . . .	FORMAL REPORTS TEND TO . . .
• have an *audience* that is already familiar with the subject of the report and probably familiar to the report writer	• have an *audience* that is unfamiliar with the subject of the report and probably unfamiliar to the report writer
• respond to a *purpose* for which readers expect main points but may find elaborated explanations and details unnecessary or inappropriate	• respond to a *purpose* for which readers expect main points and also often need elaborated explanations and details in order to understand the points
• address an occasion in which the readers are already involved or about which they know a great deal	• address an *occasion* from which the readers are distant (whether politically or geographically) or about which they know little
• assume a relatively informal tone appropriate for a document addressed to a familiar audience	• assume a relatively formal tone appropriate for a document addressed to an unfamiliar audience
• be relatively short since background sections and detailed explanations are often omitted	• be long enough to include background sections and detailed explanations appropriate for the audience
• exclude all front matter or even be presented in a memo or letter (typically when audience needs minimal orienting information, background, or supplemental information)	• include front matter (title page, table of contents, and so on) possibly being accompanied by a letter of transmittal (typically when the audience needs orienting, background, and supplemental information)

Figure 14.5 Conventional Elements Addressed in Reports That Document Activities

TYPE OF DOCUMENTARY REPORTS	CONVENTIONS OF DOCUMENTARY REPORTS
Progress (status update) and periodic activity reports Document the status of a project or detail work accomplished during some period	1. Identify an activity or a project that's being reported on or the period of time in the report—for example, week, month, quarter 2. Provide background about the project, which may include the context or a long-term plan 3. Specify project tasks that are *completed, in process,* and *planned* 4. Identify necessary changes in schedule, personnel, and budget 5. Discuss implications of the necessary changes
Trip or conference reports Document the purpose and success (or failure) of a trip	1. Identify purpose and date of the trip 2. Provide background about the importance of the trip 3. Identify your role and tasks, including people contacted, and questions raised or resolved 4. Specify the information gained 5. Discuss impact of what was learned on the trip or at the conference

(a) Class Report
An informal report in a memo was appropriate for their instructor. Because the instructor knew a great deal about the topic and the occasion, the team didn't need to provide detailed information.

The team members defined the problem and explained the focus of their project.

They identified their client and then listed questions for which they needed answers in order to resolve the client's problem. This background section showed their instructor that they had an appropriate preliminary focus for their work.

(b) Client Report
In accordance with conventions, a cover page was appropriate for a document going to a client.

It was appropriate to identify the client by title, position, and organization.

It was also appropriate to identify the report writers by title, position, and organization. By convention, writers were listed in alphabetical order.

Figure 14.6a Page 1 of Documentary Report for a Class

October 11, 19--

To Alex Carson
From Perry Edmond, John Howard, Lori Samuels, and Aaron Walsh
Subject Progress Report: Agstar and ISO 9000

Project Problem

At the beginning of the semester, our group selected a problem for which Agstar Seed Company needed a solution.

Should Agstar adopt ISO 9000 standards, maintain their current quality control standards, or consider some other modification of what they have?

Background

Our client, Dr. David Baker, is Director of Agronomic Quality and Seed Technology for Agstar.

In preparing to investigate this problem, we developed three general questions:

- What are ISO 9000 standards and how do they differ from Agstar's current standards?
- How important are ISO 9000 standards to the seed industry, now and in the future?
- Is the adoption of ISO 9000 standards economically beneficial to Agstar? How would the adoption affect their competitive position in the United States? Abroad?

Figure 14.6b Title Page of Documentary Report for a Client

Agstar and ISO 9000:
Is Implementation Necessary?

Progress Report Submitted to
Dr. David Baker, Director
Agronomic Quality and Seed Technology
Agstar Seed Company

Submitted by
Perry Edmond, John Howard, Lori Samuels, and Aaron Walsh
Agronomy Consultants
Iowa State University

October 11, 19--

for an actual business client. Their problem was to investigate possible changes in Agstar Seed Company's quality control standards: Should the company adopt ISO 9000 standards, maintain its current quality control standards, or consider some other modification? Except for brief weekly meetings with their instructor, the students functioned as an independent consulting team working for their client.

(c) Class Report
In accordance with conventions for progress reports, the team listed the completed work.

In order to assess whether the students were approaching the project professionally—appropriate focus, depth, and so on—the instructor expected specific categories of information the team had obtained.

The report would have been better if the students had explained what they planned to do with the information they had collected.

Students needed to justify the people they chose to interview. They should have explained more about why Landeau was interviewed.

Figure 14.6c Page 2 of Documentary Report for a Class

Work Completed

We have collected a number of books about ISO 9000 standards—most obtained through interlibrary loan.

We have conducted two interviews:

(1) Dr. David Baker told us his concerns about ISO 9000 standards, suggested questions he needed answered, and summarized what he expected from our group. He also provided us with information:

- names of individuals and organizations to contact about ISO 9000 standards
- print material that he'd collected about ISO 9000 standards

Follow-up to the interview: We read the materials he provided, set our project goals, and started brainstorming approaches to the problem.

(2) Mr. Bob Landeau, Iowa Crop Improvement Association, was important to interview because of ICIA's involvement with overseas shipping of seeds and his familiarity with current export and standardization procedures. From this interview, we learned these main points:

- Mr. Landeau had a negative view of ISO 9000 and its possible impact on the seed industry. He seemed concerned with its economic effects on smaller seed companies. He cited one source as saying that ISO 9000 would cost $2,000,000 per production plant to implement and another $75,000 per year for upkeep.

Agstar
-2-

(d) Client Report
The team stated the problem for the client to give him a chance to correct any misconceptions or misunderstandings.

Baker would also have an opportunity to modify questions or add ones that the team missed.

The team wanted the client to see that they had been making progress.

Figure 14.6d Page 1 of Documentary Report for a Client

Project Problem

We have focused our work on the following problem:

Should Agstar adopt ISO 9000 standards, maintain their current quality control standards, or consider some other modification of what they have?

Background

In preparing to investigate this problem, we developed three general questions:

- What are ISO 9000 standards and how do they differ from Agstar's current standards?
- How important are ISO 9000 standards to the seed industry, now and in the future?
- Is the adoption of ISO 9000 standards economically beneficial to Agstar? How would the adoption affect their competitive position in the United States? Abroad?

Work Completed

We have collected a number of books and articles as well as a list of individuals and organizations to contact about ISO 9000 standards:

- copies of the report and OECD standards for corn
- the Pioneer Hi-Bred's proposal to the OECD
- names of people to contact at the Illinois Crop Improvement Agency who helped in the ISO 9000 certification/registration of a Pioneer production plant

Agstar

(e) Class Report
Pioneer Hi-Bred is a competitor of Agstar, so their experiences in implementing ISO 9000 standards would be useful information for Agstar.

The team members explained how they would use the information they obtained from Landeau as a way of informing their instructor that they understand the process they were engaged in.

Figure 14.6e Page 3 of Documentary Report for a Class

Work Completed, continued

- When we asked about Pioneer Hi-Bred International's conversion to ISO 9000 standards, Mr. Landeau said he saw no benefits to Pioneer in shipping seeds overseas. Pioneer believed their ISO 9000 registration enabled them to avoid traditional certification that seed companies use with a form from Crop Improvement Agencies such as ICIA. After submitting a proposal to OECD to certify their own ISO 9000 seed, Pioneer Hi-Bred was subsequently rejected and must still use their current standards in spite of ISO certification.

We obtained the following materials from Mr. Landeau:

- the Pioneer proposal to the OECD
- more current articles about ISO 9000 standards
- copies of export and OECD standards for corn
- names of people to contact at the Illinois Crop Improvement Agency who helped in the ISO 9000 certification/registration of a Pioneer production plant

Follow-up to the interview: We will contact the people Mr. Landeau recommended, review the articles relevant to Agstar, and see whether the Pioneer proposal is in any way similar to Agstar's situation. We are not yet sure of the financial impact ISO 9000 would have on Agstar.

Agstar
-3-

(f) Client Report
The team should have mentioned that Landeau had a vested interest in maintaining his point of view. If ISO 9000 were widely implemented and accepted, it could replace the traditional ICIA certification.

The team thought that the client would be interested in an assessment about how a competitor had fared in its implementation of ISO 9000 standards.

Figure 14.6f Page 2 of Documentary Report for a Client

Work Completed, continued

From our interview with Bob Landeau (Iowa Crop Improvement Association), we learned these points:

- He had a negative view of ISO 9000 and its possible impact on the seed industry. He seemed concerned with its economic effects on smaller seed companies. He cited one source as saying that ISO 9000 would cost $2,000,000 per production plant to implement and another $75,000 per year for upkeep.
- When we asked about Pioneer Hi-Bred International's conversion to ISO 9000 standards, Mr. Landeau said he saw no benefits to Pioneer in shipping seeds overseas. Pioneer believed that their ISO 9000 registration enabled them to avoid traditional certification that seed companies use with a form available from Crop Improvement Agencies, such as ICIA. After submitting a proposal to OECD to certify their own ISO 9000 seed, Pioneer Hi-Bred was subsequently rejected and must still use the current standards in spite of ISO certification.

Work in Process

Our current work falls into three categories:

- We are reading the collected print materials, looking at ways ISO 9000 standards might affect Agstar.
- We are checking into local and export standards and the ways in which these compare to ISO 9000.

Agstar
-2-

(g) Class Report
The team members identified recommendations they were considering as a way of letting their instructor know that they had plans to develop.

They provided their instructor with information about their responsibility in meeting course requirements.

The team showed that they were aware of the process of their project and the conventions of a progress report by separating work completed, work in process, and work planned.

(h) Client Report
The client and the instructor both expected to learn about the work the team anticipated completing, so this section is essentially the same in both reports.

The team members should have included more specific information about the next meeting with the client and the expected schedule for the rest of the project.

(i) Class Report
By drawing attention to their original questions, the team showed that they hadn't lost track of their goal and gave their instructor touchpoints to refresh his memory.

(j) Client Report
The team members appropriately indicated to both their instructor and their client that their work was progressing satisfactorily.

Figure 14.6g Page 4 of Documentary Report for a Class

Work in Process

Our investigative work falls into two main categories:

- We are reading the collected print materials—from interlibrary loan as well as from Baker and Landeau—specifically looking at ways ISO 9000 standards might affect Agstar.
- We are also checking into local and export standards and the ways in which these compare to ISO 9000.

We continue to meet as a group every Tuesday and Thursday, as we have all semester. We have discussed four possible courses of action for Agstar: total conversion, partial conversion, no conversion, and "wait and see." We are currently leaning toward recommending partial conversion. We believe an export plant in Indiana would be the ideal choice for this implementation.

Work Planned

We will continue to contact people about ISO 9000 to gather more opinions about conversion.

- ISO 9000 certification companies
- Illinois Crop Improvement Agency
- Pioneer plant manager in St. Joseph IL, who already converted to ISO 9000
- someone in Pioneer's Human Resources department who is knowledgeable about the conversion's effect on personnel

Agstar
-4-

Figure 14.6h Page 3 of Documentary Report for a Client

Work in Process, continued

- We continue our discussions about four possible courses of action for Agstar: total conversion, partial conversion, no conversion, and "wait and see." We are currently leaning toward recommending partial conversion. We believe an export plant in Indiana would be the ideal choice for this kind of quality control implementation.

Work Planned

We will continue to contact people about ISO 9000 to gather more opinions about conversion.

- ISO 9000 certification companies
- Illinois Crop Improvement Agency
- Pioneer: (1) plant manager in St. Joseph IL, who already converted to ISO 9000 and (2) someone in Pioneer's Human Resources department who is knowledgeable about the conversion's effect on personnel

We plan on another meeting with Dr. Baker to learn more about Agstar's size, export numbers, current quality control, and so on.

A review of our original questions shows that we still need some information:

- What are ISO 9000 standards and how do they differ from Agstar's current standards? *We have information about ISO 9000, but still need information about Agstar's current standards.*

Agstar
-3-

Figure 14.6i Page 5 of Documentary Report for a Class

Work Planned, continued

We will also contact Dr. Baker to learn more about Agstar's size, export numbers, current quality control, and so on.

A review of our original questions shows that we still need some information:

- What are ISO 9000 standards and how do they differ from Agstar's current standards? *We have information about ISO 9000, but still need information about Agstar's current standards.*
- How important are ISO 9000 standards to the seed industry, now and in the future? *Based on reading and our interview with Mr. Landeau, we can now answer this.*
- Is the adoption of ISO 9000 standards economically beneficial to Agstar? How would the adoption affect their competitive position in the United States? Abroad? *We still need information to answer all parts of this question.*

We are continuing to work toward our goal of making a recommendation about ISO 9000 for Agstar.

Agstar
-5-

Figure 14.6j Page 4 of Documentary Report for a Client

Work Planned, continued

- How important are ISO 9000 standards to the seed industry, now and in the future? *Based on reading and our interview with Mr. Landeau, we can now answer this.*
- Is the adoption of ISO 9000 standards economically beneficial to Agstar? How would the adoption affect their competitive position in the United States? Abroad? *We still need information to answer all parts of this question.*

We are continuing to work toward our goal of making a recommendation about ISO 9000 for Agstar.

Agstar
-4-

Figure 14.6a, c, e, g, and i was written for the seminar instructor, Alex Carson. He expected the report to conform to progress report conventions (Figure 14.5) and to convey a clear sense that the students understood and followed professional practice.

The students also needed to submit a progress report to their client (Figure 14.6b, d, f, h, and j). The content for the two reports was very similar. However, since the client was less familiar with the information (in fact, familiarizing the client with the information was one of the project's purposes) and more distant from the team, he received a formal report. To prepare the client report, the students modified the class report to include fewer details about the team's process and more information about their findings. To meet client expectations, they also needed to follow progress report conventions.

The primary purpose of the students' report to their client was to document their findings about ISO 9000 standards. Agstar was clear that the students only secondarily needed to investigate whether these standards would help or hinder Agstar's quality control for national and international markets.

Investigative Reports

Investigative reports identify and investigate components necessary to make critical decisions. These reports may, but don't necessarily, offer explicit conclusions or recommendations. Conclusions or recommendations are included depending on whether the writer was asked to simply investigate and report findings or to also make recommendations on those findings. Reports that are explicitly persuasive usually include recommendations. Whether conclusions or recommendations are included also depends on the audience. Some managers welcome recommendations; others don't. Figure 14.7 on the next page identifies conventions of two widely used types of investigative reports.

Figure 14.8 on the next page shows the sequence of events that led to the writing of an investigative report by Jeff White, an engineer at Sands Environmental Services, to Jim Andrews, president of Hansen Enterprises. This report announced Sands' stop of cleanup activities and proposed a new investigation of the site. The sequence started when Groundwater Service and Supply sampled the monitoring wells at the Four Corners area in Able, Iowa, and found *free product*—that is, they found petroleum product floating on top of the groundwater of the wells on land previously owned by Hansen Oil (and now owned by Kum & Go).

In accordance with state law, Hansen decided to hire Sands Environmental to remove the free product, which they believed had originated on their former property and for which they therefore thought they were responsible. Hansen's expenses for removing the free product would be reimbursed by the state. In beginning the job, Sands contracted with a lab to analyze the free product. The analysis determined that the free product was not gasoline but, instead, No. 2 fuel oil, which can be either diesel fuel or home heating oil. As a result of the analysis, Sands concluded that Hansen couldn't be responsible because the company hadn't dispensed any product other than gasoline in at least 35 years.

Sands engineer Jeff White then wrote the report (Figure 14.9 on page 415) from Sands to Hansen. Jeff recognized that the problem had to be addressed in stages. First he had to tell Hansen that, in his best professional judgment, they were not responsible for the free product. Jeff's analysis and recommendation in this report eliminated the rest of Sands' work for Hansen, but Jeff knew that the problem of the free product still had to be addressed. The next stage was to conduct another formal investigation to determine the source of the free product. As you'll read at the end of the report, Jeff was preparing a proposal to do just that.

The explicit purpose of Jeff White's report to Jim Andrews was to explain the investigation of the free product found on property for which Hansen Enterprises was responsible. However, a secondary purpose was to evaluate information from that investigation. In this report, Jeff focused on the investigative aspects of the situation because it was not Sands' contractual responsibility to evaluate the situation or make recommendations about further action to resolve the problem of free product at Four Corners.

Evaluative Reports

A third category of business reports evaluates objects or occasions. Such reports have the power to inform or influence readers or to recommend that readers accept a particular position, policy, or finding. **Evaluative reports** may also assess an organization's compliance (or noncompliance) with statutes or regulations. Evaluative reports typically provide essential information for readers who have to make decisions.

While evaluative reports nearly always include conclusions or recommendations, these reports do not necessarily attempt to explicitly persuade readers to adopt the conclusions

Figure 14.7 Conventional Elements Addressed in Reports That Investigate Information

TYPES OF REPORTS THAT INVESTIGATE	CONVENTIONS OF INVESTIGATIVE REPORTS
Analytical reports investigate a particular problem, question, or issue and sometimes offer recommendations	1. Identify problem, question, or issue that needs to be analyzed 2. Provide background about the importance of the problem, question, or issue 3. Identify the scope of the report, which includes the components of the problem, question, or issue as well as the criteria for analysis 4. Present the results, which includes establishing the relationship among components 5. Discuss recommendations based on the results
Product and document testing reports investigate accuracy and effectiveness of products and related documents	1. Identify the object or situation that's the subject of the report 2. Provide background about the context 3. Identify the scope of the testing situation 4. Specify the results, differentiating between observations and interpretations 5. Discuss implications of the results

or recommendations. Evaluative reports enable you to establish your position with an implicit argument that rests on the strength of the evidence rather than on the power of an explicit argument, as in a proposal.

Evaluative reports are useful to you as a business professional because they enable you to assess information important for decision making. Figure 14.10 (page 417) presents the conventions of three common evaluative reports.

Figure 14.11 on page 418 presents the first third of a year-end market report evaluating Corometrics Medical Systems' success in its Japanese market. The company is Corometrics Medical Systems (see Figure 14.2). The report writer, Jerry Thompson, evaluated five areas. Jerry organized the information from general to specific—beginning with an overview of the broadest issues (Japanese health care budget) and concluding with the most specific (pricing of Corometrics products). By using this organization, Jerry helped orient his readers to the problems in this international market.

The audience for this report, managers at Corometrics back in the United States, expected to learn initially about the overall issues so they would have a context for the information that followed. While the readers were not specifically resistant to Jerry's evaluation, they

Figure 14.8 Sequence of Events That Led to the Investigative Report Shown in Figure 14.9

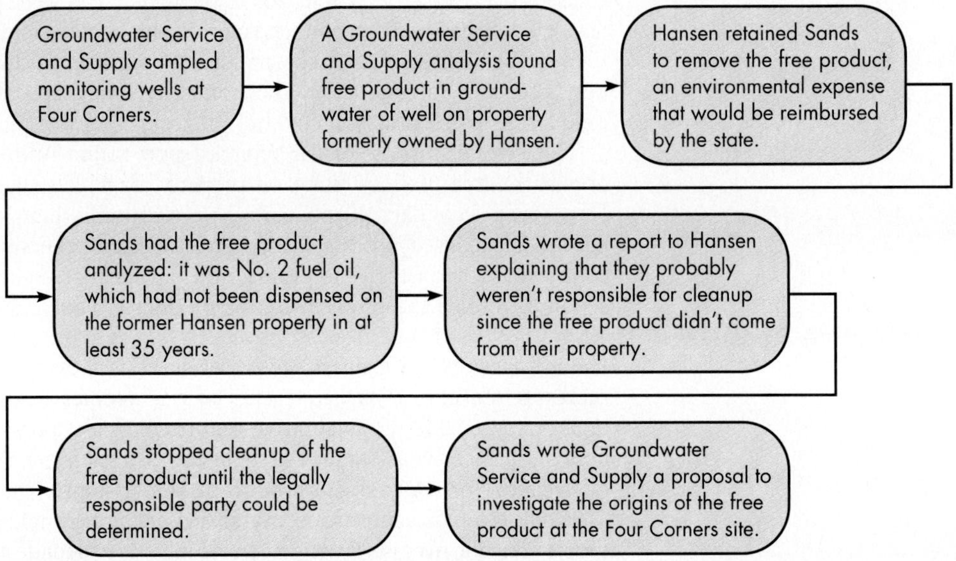
Groundwater Service and Supply sampled monitoring wells at Four Corners.
A Groundwater Service and Supply analysis found free product in groundwater of well on property formerly owned by Hansen.
Hansen retained Sands to remove the free product, an environmental expense that would be reimbursed by the state.
Sands had the free product analyzed: it was No. 2 fuel oil, which had not been dispensed on the former Hansen property in at least 35 years.
Sands wrote a report to Hansen explaining that they probably weren't responsible for cleanup since the free product didn't come from their property.
Sands stopped cleanup of the free product until the legally responsible party could be determined.
Sands wrote Groundwater Service and Supply a proposal to investigate the origins of the free product at the Four Corners site.

Figure 14.9 Example of a Report That Investigates Information

A letter report was appropriate for this occasion. Although the reader, Jim Andrews of Hansen Enterprises, was an outside client (thus necessitating a level of formality demonstrated in the formal salutation and the formal wording of the letter), he was also quite familiar with the problem at the Four Corners site (eliminating the need for a full-blown formal report).

In the report that he wrote from Sands to Hansen, Jeff White identified the problem that was being investigated and provided readers with important background information by reviewing the history of Sands' involvement.

In the first paragraph, Jeff informed readers about the scope of the report.

Jeff reviewed the occasion: he provided readers with background information about how the problem had been detected and work that had been done during the previous three months.

So that readers would understand the work done so far, Jeff specified the results of the investigation, including laboratory analyses, summaries of reports detailing products stored in the site in question, and a description of the movement of the free product through monitoring wells in the Four Corners area.

December 5, 19--
SANDS No. 8101
IDNR LUST No. 7LTL98
Registration No. 8605772

Jim Andrews, President
Hansen Enterprises
911 Main Street
Able, Iowa 50003

Subject: Report of Free Product at Four Corners Site in Able at Kum & Go Store (Hansen Oil site)

Dear Mr. Andrews:

Sands Environmental is pleased to submit a copy of this report concerning the free product found in the monitoring wells at the Kum & Go Store in Able. This report is in response to your request of November 30, 19--. It contains a brief history of the free product at the site, the results of the laboratory analysis of the free product, a discussion of possible sources of the free product, and some recommendations for corrective action.

Groundwater Service and Supply (GSS) of Ankeny encountered free product in three wells on the Kum & Go site when they performed interim monitoring on September 1, 19--. GSS checked and sampled all wells in the Able 4 Corners site and reported that only MW1, MW4, and MW5 on the Kum & Go site contained free product.

On September 20, Hansen Enterprises, which retains responsibility for "old" contamination at the Kum & Go site, contracted with Sands Environmental Services to perform weekly free product recovery by bailing. Sands personnel began the free product recovery on September 23, 19--. Free Product Reports have been submitted to the IDNR for September and October. The November report will be submitted by December 15.

Free product was found in a new well every few weeks until November 22, by which date the plume encompassed seven monitoring wells: MW5, MW4, MW1, MW6, MW7, MW8, and MW3. Hansen Enterprises stopped the free product recovery at that time because the increasing size and nature of the plume suggested that the source might not be the responsibility of Hansen Enterprises.

With the concurrence of Hansen Enterprises and Neil Sears of GAB Business Services, on November 16, 19--, Sands personnel collected a sample of the free product and sent it to ILFC Laboratories for an abbreviated forensic analysis. The laboratory analysis stated that the sample contained No. 2 fuel oil and that no other petroleum hydrocarbon products were detected. No. 2 fuel oil can be diesel or home heating oil, so the source could be a leaking residential or commercial UST. A copy of the laboratory analysis is enclosed with this letter.

Several pieces of evidence suggest that the free product probably originates at a location other than the Kum & Go site:

- Krause Gentle Corporation reported that they have had no releases of any fuel.
- According to Gary Ranger of Krause Gentle Corporation, Jim Andrews, and other available reports, the Kum & Go site has not stored or dispensed diesel or fuel oil.
- The free product is too thick and widespread to originate from old petroleum contamination held in the soil.
- Overall, the free product plume appears to have spread from west to east across the site.

These terms would all be familiar to the recipients of this letter report:

free product—any petroleum product such as fuel oil or gasoline floating on top of groundwater; detectable by using an oil water probe or by conducting a visual examination

IDNR—Iowa Department of Natural Resources

MW1, MW2, etc.—monitoring wells installed in a bore hole below the groundwater level so engineers can measure groundwater elevation, sample groundwater, and check for free product

plume—a trail of free product

ILFC—a laboratory, well known for its forensic analyses

UST—underground storage tank

AST—aboveground storage tank

LUST—leaking underground storage tank

were unfamiliar with the information and, therefore, unlikely to be receptive to recommendations until they had been convinced that the problems merited their attention. To reinforce his credibility, Jerry reviewed the political and economic influences on Corometrics' success in Japan.

The report is relatively informal, not because the reader was already familiar with the issues or the specific content but because of Jerry's place in the organization in relation to the reader. In Corometrics' structure—which was relatively flat instead of hierarchical—Jerry was directly below the corporate vice president to whom the report was submitted.

Figure 14.9 (Continued)

To avoid inappropriate political complications, Jeff was careful not to point fingers indicating guilt, but provided enough information to help readers start on the probable track.

In an appropriate move and a good business decision, Jeff recommended that the sources of the free product be found and stopped, but indicated that Hansen was unlikely to be responsible.

Jeff suggested to his audience that there was a process for addressing the problem, and he offered a reasonable and workable solution to solve the problem.

Aware of the value of continuing clients, Jeff closed with a reminder that Sands was available to help Hansen and other local businesses with their environmental problems.

A proposal to address the problem of free product at the Four Corners site was later submitted to Andrews, Ranger, Fulton, Wagner, and North. Copies of the proposal were forwarded to Rogers, Franklin, Ray, and Sears.

Jim Andrews
December 5, 19--
Page 2

According to the Groundwater Contour Maps in the Site Cleanup Reports submitted by Environmental Resource Services, groundwater flow is generally toward the north and the east. However, the watertable is relatively flat and is subject to local variations. The actual flow direction on a given property is difficult to determine and probably varies over time. Without further data, it is not possible to estimate the source of the free product from the direction of groundwater flow.

Free product that consists of fuel oil causes less groundwater contamination than does gasoline because fuel oil contains few soluble compounds that dissolve in the groundwater. Fuel oil typically migrates slowly and exists in a free state for a relatively long period of time. The soil particles absorb the fuel oil to form a persistent type of soil contamination that degrades slowly. The greatest danger represented by the product plume is from the migration of the free product into a basement, sanitary sewer, or other underground structure.

Sands Environmental recommends that the source of the free product be found and immediately stopped. The first action is to check all monitoring wells in the area for free product. Any known diesel USTs should be checked or tested. If no USTs containing diesel are in the immediate area, then property owners of the nearby residences should be contacted to determine if they might have home heating oil USTs or ASTs.

Sands Environmental further recommends that the free product be addressed by a temporary free product recovery system. Because of the large quantities of free product, hand bailing is not a good method of recovery. Soil vapor extraction would not work well because of the low volatility of the fuel oil. Only an active pumping system can effectively remove the free product.

The GSS monitoring report of October, 19--, shows that natural attenuation has significantly decreased the levels of groundwater contamination since the wells were checked two years ago. Once the free product recovery is completed, it is quite feasible that the contamination at the site can be addressed by natural attenuation and that only high risk monitoring will be required. Sands Environmental is preparing a proposal and budget to address the free product investigation and recovery.

As we have previously discussed, we are sending copies of this letter report directly to all interested parties. Please do not hesitate to call if you have any questions or comments. Thank you for the opportunity to address your environmental needs.

Sincerely,

Jeffrey H. White
Registered Groundwater Professional

cc: Murray Rogers
JF 8101
Keith Franklin, LUST Section of IDNR
Pat Ray, Williams & Company
Neil Sears, GAB Business Services
Gary Ranger, Krause Gentle Corporation
Tom Fulton, Fulton Standard
Marlin and Carolyn Wagner
Glenn North, Costa's General Stores

FUNCTIONS OF CONVENTIONAL COMPONENTS

The components of reports not only contribute to the purposes of informing and persuading readers but also help them move easily through a document. Reports have conventional components that perform the following functions:

- orienting readers (front matter)
- providing an introduction for readers
- persuading readers to accept the information
- including supplementary details for readers (end matter)

Figure 14.12 (page 419) provides a convenient summary of functions fulfilled by conventional components of informal and formal reports. Whether you choose components more appropriate for an informal or a formal report depends on the purpose, audience, occasion, and company conventions. For example, one company may require all internal, informal reports to be presented as a memo (see Appendix A). Another company may require such reports to be in a traditional report format with a title page.

Figure 14.10 Conventional Elements Addressed in Reports That Evaluate Information

TYPES OF EVALUATIVE REPORTS	CONVENTIONS OF EVALUATIVE REPORTS
Market (or product or service) reports evaluate projected market goals and assess whether the product or service has met those goals	1. Identify the market, product, or service that is being evaluated 2. Provide background about the market, product, or service, including market position and target population 3. Identify the scope and methodology of the evaluation—for example, surveys, interviews, or focus groups 4. Specify the results of the evaluation—that is, the opinions and perceptions revealed in the surveys, interviews, or focus groups 5. Discuss the implications of the results
Compliance reports evaluate regulations or statutes under consideration and then show how the organization has met the stipulations	1. Identify the regulation or statute under consideration 2. Provide background about the relevance or importance of the regulation or statute 3. Explain how the organization has complied with the stipulations of the regulation or statute 4. Explain areas of noncompliance that are being addressed 5. Discuss the impact of compliance (or noncompliance)
Recommendation reports evaluate a problem and offer recommendations to resolve the problem	1. Identify the problem that needs to be evaluated 2. Provide background about the importance of the problem—that is, why evaluating the problem matters 3. Provide information about the scope and nature of the problem 4. Specify recommendations that resolve the problem and provide rationales for those recommendations 5. Discuss the implications of the recommendations

This section of the chapter discusses the conventional components that help you orient readers, provide an introduction for them, persuade them, and include supplementary details for interested readers.

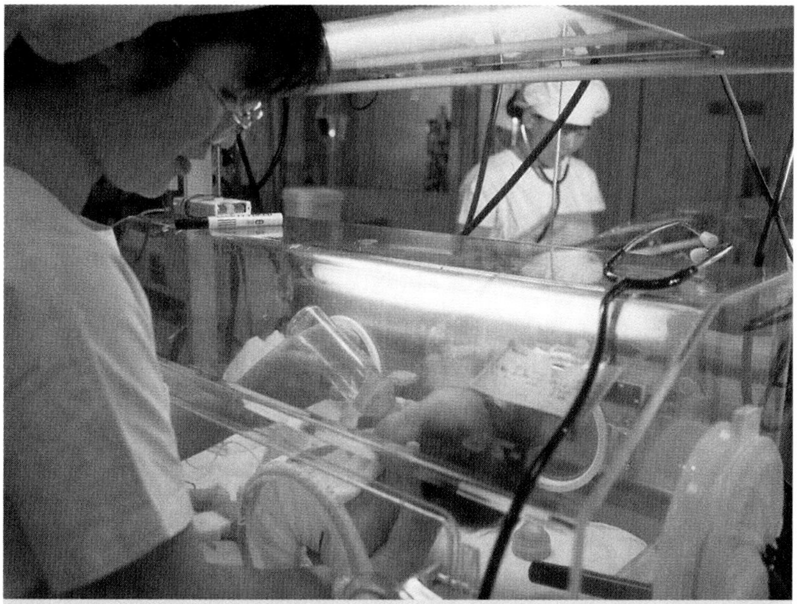

Professionals who travel internationally (like Jerry Thompson, who wrote the reports excerpted in Figures 14.2 and 14.11) often have to give their audiences at home a more thorough background about international markets in any reports or recommendations they make.

Orienting Readers of Reports

Orienting sections provide readers with information that identifies the topic of the report and helps them move easily through the report.

In memo or letter reports, this orienting information may be a subject line identifying the topic of the report. In a short, informal report, this orienting information may be an informative title. The more formal a report, the more orienting information a writer is likely to include. Formal reports assume a reader distant from the situation and unfamiliar with the content. Formal reports typically have the following initial components or front matter that precedes the main body of the report:

- letter of transmittal
- title and title page
- abstract or executive summary
- table of contents

Figure 14.11 Example of a Report That Evaluates Information

Jerry informs readers about the scope of the report in the subject line.

The purpose of the report is to candidly evaluate the current market for Corometrics products in Japan.

Jerry establishes his credibility and the source for information when he refers to his six trips to Japan during the previous 12 months.

Jerry reviews the organization of the report by previewing the list of five problems that act as headings for the rest of the report.

Jerry recognizes that the report's readers need to understand the complex political and economic influences that affect sales.

September 15, 19--

To: Bruce Renfrew
Phil Young
From: Jeremiah Thompson
Subject: Japan--Annual Review and Trip Report

Since September, 19--, I've visited Japan six times to manage, support and train our three distributors. Development and growth of our business in Japan is hampered by several problems, some of a general nature and some unique to our situation.

These include:

1) Japan health care budget
2) how medical equipment is purchased in Japan
3) competence of our distributors
4) stocking agreements with our distributors
5) pricing

Japan Health Care Budget

The current budget of Japan (for the period 1 April 19-- through 31 March 19--) provides for no increase at all for medical and health care expenditures and a decrease of 6% for social welfare expenditures. Some medical services come from the social welfare fund, especially for the aged.

Against this fixed budget there are (1) increasing costs for labor, essential materials and services, etc., and (2) rapidly increasing demand for medical and health services by the Japanese. Japan has one of the fastest aging populations in the world.

Thus, funds available for purchase of sophisticated medical equipment—especially new, innovative, relatively unproven products—for the moment at least, are severely restricted. Well established and successful American companies selling medical instrumentation in Japan are experiencing significant reductions in orders in 19-- vis-a-vis 19-- or even 19--, including:

Corometrics Medical Systems	−29%
Physio-Control	−21%
Hewlett-Packard	−23%
Squibb Medical Systems (monitoring products)	−88%

Our situation is further complicated by the Japanese method of paying providers a set amount for each particular service or procedure. The payment schedules are based on (1) established and thus older methods, and (2) what can be "Made in Japan." Thus, the reimbursement schedule for an I.V. Set is $1.64, but our distributor, Japan Medical Supply, sells a set with our cassette for $2.46, and loses money doing so because the cassette alone costs JMS $1.38 (f.o.b. Mt. View). Thus, both JMS and the hospital lose money whenever an OXIMETRIX pump is used.

JMS is planning to offer sets for our pumps for $1.56 in desperation to get business. Thus, JMS will lose even more, whereas the hospital would theoretically profit 8 cents.

A similar dilemma frustrates our Oximeter distributor, Tokai Irika, in selling the P7110 Opticath, as the reimbursement schedule is locked to the price of standard Swan-Ganz.

There is a Catch-22 to all this. If and when a cassette-type pump or opticath is manufactured in Japan, then the reimbursement schedule should go up for these products. But there goes much of our present competitive advantage of performance.

The 19-- budget is expected to provide only small increases in health and social welfare spending.

Letter or Memo of Transmittal. A **letter or memo of transmittal** accompanies virtually every formal report and unsolicited informal reports. In general, readers of a letter or memo of transmittal expect to learn some or all of the following information:

- the report's subject and purpose
- the process of preparing the report
- the key findings or recommendations
- ways the reader can contact the writer

The specific content and the level of detail in a letter or memo of transmittal depend upon the audience, purpose, and occasion. For example, if you are writing to a reader who is familiar with the content of the report, you need to provide less background information in the transmittal than you would if the reader is learning about this information for the first time. Similarly, if you have written your report in response to a request, you don't need to provide detailed explanations or justifications. If you've written an unsolicited report, however, you need to explain why you've written this document.

A sample letter of transmittal in Appendix A follows the conventional pattern of identifying the problem, reviewing the recommendation, and adding a courtesy closing.

TECHNOLOGY

AUTOMATIC STYLE

An important part of creating any document is choosing fonts, adjusting margins, setting tabs, and creating titles and headings. Thinking carefully about all of these elements and making sure they are consistent is crucial to creating effective documents. For this very reason, many of today's word processing programs, including WordPerfect and Microsoft Word, offer style settings that automatically format parts of documents to a user's specifications.

The programs allow users to specify formats on two levels: character level and paragraph level. At character level, users preset styles such as fonts, boldfacing, and underlining. If, for example, a user wants all of her level-one headings to be in 12-point bold Helvetica, she would save this setting, then simply select the style every time she created a heading. Should she later decide the headings would look better in 12-point bold Times, she would simply change the style setting, and all the headings would change automatically.

Paragraph-level formatting allows users to preset anything that affects the appearance of whole paragraphs, such as line spacing, margins, and indentations. Users can switch back and forth between settings with ease by simply highlighting a section and selecting the desired style. This is especially useful for documents such as newsletters and proposals that often involve multiple formats. Should the user decide a particular document would look better with, say, 1.5-inch rather than 1-inch margins, she can switch all the formats by simply changing the preset in the style.

Preset paragraph formatting can be especially useful for documents that must be created over and over again, such as memos and minutes from meetings, or for lengthy, multisection documents such as formal reports. The writer simply loads in the style and starts typing. No time is lost to formatting, and the format is perfect every time. The use of automatic style can improve both the professional appearance of documents and a user's productivity.

Figure 14.12 Summary of Conventional Components in Reports

FUNCTION	INFORMAL REPORTS	FORMAL REPORTS
Orienting readers	**Memo** Standard to/from/subject headings **Letter** Inside and return addresses Opening paragraph **Short report** Title (sometimes a title page) Sometimes a table of contents	Title page Letter of transmittal Abstract Table of contents List of figures
Providing an introduction	*Overview:* Includes some of these elements—subject and purpose, foregrounding topics of the report, boundaries or scope of the report, methods for collecting information, role of the writer, intended audience Present this *overview* in an introductory paragraph, whether in memo, letter, or short report Almost never have a background section	*Overview:* Includes some or all of these elements—subject and purpose, foregrounding topics of the report, boundaries or scope of the report, methods for collecting information, role of the writer, intended audience *Background:* Includes some or all of these elements—assumptions of the writer, historical background, definitions of unfamiliar terms Present *overview* and *background* in an introductory section that may be several paragraphs or pages long
Persuading readers	*Key points:* Use a well-structured argument to make each point *Evidence:* Include some or all of these elements—results, data, findings *Discussion and conclusions:* Include some or all of these elements—explanations, implications of results, or recommendations	*Key points:* Use a well-structured argument to make each point *Evidence:* Include some or all of these elements—results, data, findings *Discussion and conclusions:* Include some or all of these elements—explanations, implications of results, or recommendations
Including details for readers	Seldom use bibliography (or list of works cited) or appendixes	Frequently use bibliography (or list of works cited) or appendixes

Title and Title Page. All reports need a title, but only formal reports always have a title page. Short, less formal reports may occasionally include a title page if they're being circulated outside the immediate department or group. More frequently, in short, less formal reports the title page is placed at the top of the first page. If the report is being submitted to a person within the same organization, you need to include the following information on a title page:

- title of the report
- name of the writer as well as that person's title, position, and contact information such as telephone and fax numbers and e-mail address
- name of the person to whom the report is submitted as well as that person's title and position

If the report is being submitted to a person in a different organization, you also need to include the following information:

- the organization and address of the writer
- the organization and address of the person to whom the report is submitted

The format of a title page can vary from organization to organization. The generic models in Appendix A, however, will work for virtually any occasion.

The title of your report, whether on a title page or in the subject line, should provide readers with information about the topic and your position regarding the topic, as shown in Figure 14.13. Simply presenting the topic is insufficient. If you don't present a specific title, readers will construct a more specific version in their own minds and perhaps be disappointed if you don't follow through according to their expectations.

Figure 14.13 Examples of General versus Specific Titles

GENERAL REPORT TITLES	REPORT TITLES WITH A POSITION
• Daycare Facilities at Telecom	• Daycare Facilities at Telecom: A Factor in Improved Employee Attitudes and Reduced Absenteeism
• ISO 9000 Standards at Agstar	• Deferring the Implementation of ISO 9000 Standards at Agstar
• Ergonomic Workstations	• Cost Savings from Converting to Ergonomic Workstations

Abstracts and Executive Summaries. Most business professionals agree that an **abstract** or **executive summary** is the single most frequently read section of a report because it identifies the key points covered in the report. An abstract or executive summary includes the following points:

- the topic or goal and its importance
- the major findings, results, evidence
- a summary of the recommendations
- a conclusion that usually focuses on the impact of the recommendations

An abstract or an executive summary is virtually always included with a formal report. This component of the front matter is especially important if the report is complex or if readers are busy decision makers. A manager who has five formal reports to read each week is likely to turn to the abstract or the executive summary to learn the main points before deciding which one(s) to read more carefully.

Abstracts and executive summaries are virtually identical for short reports (under 10 pages). For short reports, both abstracts and executive summaries are approximately one paragraph long, but they may be as long as a page. However, as the length of a report increases, the abstract remains short. The abstract for a 10-page report is the same length as one for a 50-page report. However, an executive summary may be as long as 10 percent

MULTICULTURAL

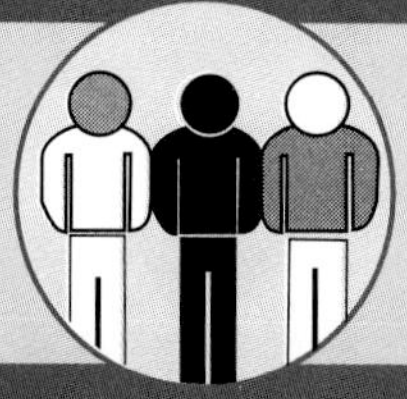

THE EFFECTS OF CULTURE ON REPORT WRITING

People in different cultures have different ideas about how reports should be organized. For example, John Mackin, who has lived in Japan for over 20 years and holds an executive position in a major Japanese company, observes that Japanese reports do not follow American-style logical development. Japanese report writers tend to skip intermediate steps of logical development and then seem to go "off point." To American readers, Japanese reports seem to have no structure: most of them are bottom-bottom, that is, "a collection of details with no introductory or conclusive matter to help the reader put details into context." In addition, John Hinds has conducted research that shows Japanese writing in general is extremely writer oriented. In Japanese, the person who is primarily responsible for effective communication is the reader, whereas in English the writer is held largely responsible for clarifying ideas and providing transitions between ideas and between paragraphs. Such differences in reader and writer responsibilities in communication certainly affect the structure of Japanese reports.

Different cultures also demand different types and quantity of detail. Germans consider historical facts and in-depth explanations so crucial that they tend to include information in a report that other cultures view as unnecessary. German reports stress content (the more the better) over form. French reports, on the other hand, tend toward abstract concepts and theories. In Latin American reports, it is not what is included but what is omitted. Latin Americans sometimes omit negative information altogether, and potential problems may not be reported and discussed.

of the length of a report. The executive summary for a 10-page report may be only one page, but an executive summary for a 50-page report may extend up to five pages.

Figure 14.14 shows an abstract for a short report that investigated problems a company was having with its product packaging and offered recommendations to correct those problems.

Table of contents. A table of contents identifies the topics in a document, the hierarchy of those topics, and their sequence. Minimally, you need to identify the main sections of a report, making sure that the headings in the report match the entries in the table of contents. Figure 14.15 on the next page shows two variations of a table of contents with only one level of heading. The left-hand version presents generic labels that don't provide the reader with any specific information. This form of a table of contents is useful when you're drafting a report—as a way to remind you to include each section. However, the right-hand version is what should be used in the report itself. The table of contents uses the same headings that appear in the report so readers can anticipate what's discussed. (Refer to Appendix A for additional discussion.)

Providing an Introduction for Readers

The introduction of a report provides overview and background sections. This introductory discussion establishes a common footing between the writer and reader, so that they have similar information about the purpose and occasion for interpreting the remainder of the report.

Figure 14.14 Example of an Abstract for a Short Report

The writer identifies the main problems that the investigation uncovered and presents them in order of importance for change.

The writer provides readers with a summary of the changes that are recommended in the report, beginning with immediate changes and concluding with long-term changes.

Abstract

A complete review of the product packaging for Web Form, Inc., has uncovered six major problems: (1) Packaging isn't always being built to print specifications. (2) Available packaging drawings are incorrect or incomplete. (3) There is no incoming inspection to detect inconsistencies when packaging is shipped from suppliers. (4) Packaging is not always appropriate for the products being packaged. (5) Packaging drawings are not accessible to anyone except the corporate packaging engineer. (6) There are no procedures for creating new packaging.

Problems dealing with nonconforming packaging, the need for incoming inspection, and the confusion in ordering can be addressed immediately. Updated, complete drawings and specifications will be sent to suppliers. Incoming inspection procedures will be implemented and enforced, and an additional inspector will be hired. The ordering procedures will be modified to assure that available packaging matches production output. Problems with redesign of packaging will require long-term efforts.

Figure 14.15 Table of Contents: General and Specific Versions

(Table of Contents for Draft Purposes)

Table of Contents

List of Figures ii
Statement of Problem 1
History of Problem 2
Discussion of Possible Solutions 4
Recommendations 9
Conclusions 11
Sources Cited 13
Appendixes 14

(Final Table of Contents)

Table of Contents

List of Figures ii
Warehousing Problem: High Cost/ Low Productivity 1
Warehousing, 1975–1995 2
Warehousing Solutions 8
Use JIT with Teams 10
Low Costs/High Productivity 12
Sources Cited 14
Appendixes 15

- An **overview** establishes the purpose and/or problem discussed in the report and may define the breadth, depth, and organization of coverage. This overview may also identify the role of the writer, the intended audience, and the occasion. An overview focuses readers' attention, in an attempt to establish consistent expectations among readers. In an informal report, the overview may be as brief as a subject line in a memo or letter. In a formal report, the overview may be several paragraphs.
- The **background** presents information necessary for readers to understand the scope and approach of the report. It may include assumptions about the topic, definitions, criteria for classifying or analyzing information, previous approaches to the problem, personnel, methodology, materials and equipment, or any other pertinent background information. In an informal report, the background may be as brief as parenthetical references in some sentences. In a formal report, the background may take an entire section of the report.

Virtually all reports, informal and formal, include an overview, but many informal reports omit the background. The further away readers are from the situation the report is about, the more likely they are to need background information, since they may be unfamiliar not only with the occasion that prompted the report but also with the subject matter of the report.

The introductory information is not a repeat of the abstract or executive summary. An abstract or executive summary is essentially a miniversion of the report—all the key points are presented. The introductory information of a report is concerned with telling readers about the purpose of a report and its evolution, not about the conclusions.

Overview. The overview of a report generally identifies the subject and purpose, establishes the significance of the subject, and often previews how the report is organized. Both informal and formal reports usually have overviews, though they're far more detailed in a formal report.

Writers of formal reports often spend several sentences—and sometimes even a few paragraphs—presenting introductory information so that readers unfamiliar with the situation can understand the report:

- subject and purpose
- topics of the report
- boundaries or scope of the report
- methods for collecting information
- role of the writer
- intended audience

The writer of the first sentence in Figure 14.16 succinctly identified the *subject and purpose* of this investigative report. In the second sentence, he clearly *foregrounded* the structure by listing the three sections in the report dealing with a new way of setting up tooling to do jobs in a machine shop. The writer's purpose statement was clear without his needing to say, "The purpose of this report is to examine preset tooling. . . ."

The writer of the excerpt in Figure 14.17 established the **boundaries** or **scope** of a recommendation report in which she argued for a number of changes: updated equipment, workstations redesigned ergonomically, and reconsideration of scheduling procedures. This segment of the overview informed readers about what the report covered, but it also identified potential influences not addressed in the report. Readers who understood the boundaries of the investigation could place reasonable limits on applying the report's recommendations.

The excerpt in Figure 14.18, included in a **methods statement**, summarized key sources of information for a report. The example is from an analytical report about changes in a large company's $8.5 million in contracts for photocopiers. Methods statements, especially in analytical reports, can justify a writer's procedures and choices. If readers accept the methods as responsible and appropriate, the writer's credibility is increased.

A statement that's often part of report overviews identifies the *role of the writer*. This information helps readers assess the credibility of the information and whether the writer had a vested interest. Figure 14.19 on the next page not only told readers who initiated the writing group, but also identified departments and individual responsibilities.

The overview of a report also typically identifies the *intended audience*. Explicitly identifying the audience and occasion, as shown in Figure 14.20 on the next page, is an effective way to help readers decide if a given report is one they're supposed to read. The team writing this report wanted the audience, the City Planning Commission, to apply the information broadly to a series of proposals they were considering.

Figure 14.16 Example of Purpose and Foregrounding Statements in an Overview

The writer identified the subject and purpose and then foregrounded the major sections.

> Preset tooling is one way to make our machine shop more competitive with other shops in the area by reducing the cost per hour to do a job. This report reviews the current methods operators use to set up their tools, defines preset tooling, and explains the cost reductions that are possible using preset tooling.

Figure 14.17 Example of a Statement Establishing the Scope of a Report

The writer identified the focus of the report, the sequence of information, and what wouldn't be included.

> Several factors are contributing to the increase in worker compensation claims for medical expenses and sick time due to carpal tunnel syndrome. Most of these claims appear related to the use of outmoded equipment, poor design of the work space, and inequitable scheduling of jobs. Other factors such as the general health of workers and the skill level of workers assigned to particular jobs are not discussed.

Figure 14.18 Example of a Statement Identifying Sources of Information

The writer summarized the sources of data so readers could assess whether the information was complete.

Mentioning Sandra Kline, an administrative assistant in marketing, and Ed Houghton, the assistant manager of purchasing, acknowledges their assistance and adds credibility.

> The data in this report have come from four sources:
>
> - survey results of current photocopier use completed by every department in our company (see Appendix C)
> - department records about past photocopier use (see Appendix D)
> - facilities reports about the number and location of photocopiers throughout the company (see Appendix E)
> - specifications from vendor literature, including lease price, price per copy, volume, maximum copy size, ease of operation, copy time, reduction/enlargement, plus additional features (see Appendix F)
>
> Internal company records were collected and organized by Sandra Kline. Vendor information was gathered with the help of Ed Houghton.

Figure 14.19 Example of a Statement Identifying the Role of a Report's Writer(s)

Telling readers the makeup and origin of the committee making the recommendations gave them the opportunity to assess the information.

The recommendations in this report were developed by a five-person committee of the Asbury Mobile-Home Park Tenants Association to identify ways that mobile-home owners can safeguard their substantial investment. The committee included three long-term residents and two recent residents of Asbury Mobile-Home Park. Although the committee as a whole assumes responsibility for the report, individuals are credited with compiling information for the following sections during the investigation. . . .

Figure 14.20 Example of a Statement Identifying the Audience and Occasion of a Report

Not only have the writers identified the audience, but they have also acknowledged the complex problem facing the audience—that is, the occasion.

We anticipate that the members of the City Planning Commission will find the information in this report useful as they consider the various proposals to develop the 55-acre site situated between Interstate 90 and State Highway 65.

Background. The background section of a report can provide readers with a richer, more detailed understanding of the situation and may include some or all of the following information:

- assumptions of the writer
- historical background
- definitions of unfamiliar terms

You decide what background information is critical or supplemental depending on the audience, purpose, and occasion of your report.

Although background details may be embedded in informal reports, such reports seldom have a separate background section. The decision to include a background section in a formal report is usually based on the usefulness of the information.

Readers are better able to understand a report if they know a writer's *assumptions* early on. A writer cannot assume that readers will be able to figure out the assumptions on which a report is based, even if readers are familiar with the situation and organizationally close to the writer. Sometimes assumptions simply establish common understandings, but other times a writer's assumptions call for the acceptance of situations that have not yet occurred, as in Figure 14.21. A writer can also influence readers' reactions by urging their acceptance of particular assumptions. The assumptions readers make—whether they're explicitly stated in the report itself, implied by the writer, or constructed entirely by the readers—will guide readers' interpretation of a report.

Having some familiarity with the *historical background* of a situation lets readers put a report's information in perspective. An important part of preparing a report is finding out how what has happened in the past relates to the situation being investigated. Especially in preparing formal reports, you need to ask yourself questions such as these: What is the company's long-term record? What historical barriers to solving the problem exist? Who has been involved in previous inquiries?

Figure 14.22 shows historical background that summarizes four decades of safety practices. Other historical sections may focus instead on the immediate past, drawing readers' attention to previous attempts to solve a persistent problem.

Figure 14.21 Example of Assumptions Stated in the Background Section

If readers miss the assumption in this background section, they can easily misunderstand the report.

When discussing the trends of young automobile buyers in today's market, this report assumes that gas prices and inflation will remain relatively stable during the next six years.

Figure 14.22 Example of History Identified in the Background Section

Readers will understand how the report's investigation of the company's safety practices fits into a long-term picture.

Historically, LuvStuff Toys, Inc., has been a leader in implementing safety features that are now accepted as standard in the toy manufacturing industry. Although we have a long and consistent history of initiating safety features, some milestones stand out. In the 1960s, we mandated the use of flame resistant and retardant fillings and coverings for all stuffed toys. In the 1970s, we responded to consumer concerns to remove all parts that could be accidentally aspirated. In the 1980s, we changed the way components were assembled so that all potentially dangerous wire, line, and other fasteners were eliminated. Now, in the 1990s, we have changed dyes in an effort to reduce potential allergic reactions.

Figure 14.23 Example of Definitions Stated in the Background Section

Because the information is included in the text of the report, readers will understand the critical features of flex time and job sharing when they need to. The writer will not have to depend on readers' turning to a glossary to make sure they share the same understanding of these terms.

Before examining scheduling alternatives, it is necessary to establish what this report includes under each of these concepts: flex time and job sharing.

Flex time: Employees work a full 8 hours, but the scheduling of those hours can be anywhere between 6 am–8 pm. In certain situations, the scheduling does not need to be the same each day.

Job sharing: Two people qualified to do the same job agree to split the job, each one assuming between 33% and 66% of the hours and responsibilities, totaling 100%. Each employee receives full health and dental benefits and the percentage of vacation time, sick time, and contributions to retirement equal to their percentage of the job.

Readers may need assistance if a report uses specialized terms. Sometimes a writer knows these terms are familiar to readers, so the terms don't need to be defined. At other times, though, specialized terms may be unfamiliar to readers and need *definitions*. If a document uses a large number of such terms, there is usually a glossary, mentioned at the outset of the report and included at the end. However, sometimes knowing a definition of a term mentioned in the text is critical to understanding the report, as shown in Figure 14.23.

Readers who don't understand key terms are unlikely to respond to a report the way a writer expected and may, in fact, entirely lose interest in reading the report. For example, if readers of the report in Figure 14.23 don't know the key terms about employee scheduling, they won't understand the key points the writer is making.

SKILLS & STRATEGIES

DOES YOUR DOCUMENT'S OUTLINE WORK?

Asking certain questions about both the organization and content of your outline will help you decide if the outline works:

Organization

- Are the main sections and subsections of your outline presented in some identifiable organizational pattern (chronological, causal, comparative, and so on)?
- Is this organizational pattern appropriate for the occasion? the audience? the content?
- Can a reader use the sequence of major headings to summarize the main points of the document or presentation?
- Do the major headings emphasize the major categories you want your audience to remember?
- Are the headings and subheadings parallel, both grammatically and logically?

Content

- Is all important information included in the appropriate places?
- Is all included information in a logical sequence?
- Is the level of detail appropriate? Are the types of details appropriate?
- Are there any undeveloped major sections?
- Are there any gaps of information?
- Are there any subsections unrelated to the whole?
- Is the information balanced—that is, less information for less important topics, more information for more important topics?

Persuading Readers

The central sections of a report usually make key points, provide supporting evidence, and include any necessary discussion.

- The **key points** identify conclusions or recommendations (often in order of importance). Whether these key points appear near the beginning of a report or near the end depends on whether the report is organized inductively or deductively. If a writer doesn't explicitly identify key points, readers will create their own—and even though they'll be based on the same information, they're likely to be different from the ones the writer wanted emphasized. In an informal report, key points may simply be listed, sometimes in a numbered or bulleted list. In a formal report, key points may be elaborated on in great detail, with explanations and examples, in a recommendations or conclusion section.
- The **evidence** or supporting information presents the results or findings. This section can include a preliminary summary followed by a more detailed presentation. An explanation of this evidence or supporting information helps readers interpret it. In an informal report, evidence may be presented briefly, sometimes with each key point it supports. In a formal report, evidence is sometimes presented in a separate section called the results or findings. Whether in an informal or a formal report, evidence needs to be verifiable. (See Chapter 7 for a discussion of structuring an argument and of the kinds of lines of argument.)
- A **discussion** explains or justifies the conclusions or recommendations on the basis of the evidence that is provided. In an informal report, the discussion may be as brief as a single paragraph. In a formal report, a lengthy discussion may be in a separate section; other times it will be integrated into a presentation of the key points and evidence. Whether in an informal or a formal report, the discussion not only needs to present a writer's rationale for decisions but also needs to anticipate readers' questions and concerns.

Because the key points, evidence, and discussion in any report you write will be in some way persuasive, you may use some or all of the interrelated components identified as parts of an effective argument: claim, evidence, warrant, backing, qualifiers, rebuttal.

Members of the Health Management Task Force at Westwood Associates faced the task of constructing a logical argument when charged with investigating the company's out-of-control health insurance and illness-related costs. The Task Force was appointed by the General Manager of Westwood Associates, Taylor Sheraton.

Mr. Sheraton wanted the Task Force, made up of management and labor representatives, to identify health-related problems in the company and to come up with some creative solution(s) for cost containment. Taylor Sheraton put no restrictions on the Task Force, but the Task Force recognized that he was expecting a cost-containment report that would suggest ways to reduce health insurance coverage, eliminate coverage on some conditions, increase the employee contributions to health insurance costs, and increase the time before new employees received coverage.

After lengthy discussions and extensive research, the Task Force decided that increasing wellness was the most cost-effective recommendation. To outline its argument, the Task Force completed a form like the one in Figure 14.24. This enabled the Task Force to view the sequence of its argument to determine if there were gaps or inconsistencies.

The Task Force used the information in Figure 14.24 to develop an argument for a wellness center and program for all Westwood employees. The Task Force determined that Mr. Sheraton would initially be skeptical because its plan was so different from what he'd anticipated; however, members of the Task Force believed that he was not inherently resistant. Because of expected skepticism, the Task Force thought carefully about how to organize the report so that Mr. Sheraton would recognize the powerful connection between wellness and cost containment before reading the recommendation to create a wellness center and program.

The Task Force presented a report to Taylor Sheraton that outlined the problems and explained how a successful wellness program could help employees avoid expensive illnesses or work-related injuries or at least minimize the effects. The Task Force substantiated its argument with evidence from other companies that had saved large amounts of money after implementing wellness programs.

Many companies now recognize the impact that employee wellness programs can have in reducing insurance costs. Pictures like these can help report writers convince their audiences of the soundness and applicability of ideas contained in investigative reports.

Figure 14.24 Argument Sequence

COMPONENTS OF ARGUMENT	SEQUENCE OF ARGUMENT IN A REPORT
Problem	Westwood Associates' health insurance and illness-related costs are out of control.
Claim	The most cost-effective approach to containing out-of-control health insurance and illness-related costs is increasing employee wellness.
Grounds (evidence)	The National Survey of Worksite Health Promotion Activities reported that wellness activities improved employee health.
Warrant	The National Survey of Worksite Health Promotion Activities accurately reflects the situation at Westwood—that is, healthy employees generally have reduced health-related costs, increased productivity, and improved morale.
Backing	Companies of all sizes have saved large amounts of money after implementing wellness programs, including cost savings in health care costs, insurance costs, worker compensation claims, and absenteeism.
Qualifiers	A wellness program will probably need to be introduced with a major PR campaign and then regularly reinforced, since such a program requires lifestyle changes rather than one-time changes.
Rebuttal	Opponents might argue that while the National Survey of Worksite Health Promotion Activities report indicates improvements, these changes might be attributable to other factors such as a better informed workforce, better health education programs in schools, and attention in the mass media to health-related issues. The rebuttal position can argue that those surveyed were randomly selected to represent businesses around the country, considering factors such as size, type and location of business as well as employee demographics.

The Task Force decided that an inductive argument would be the strongest approach. Therefore, once the Task Force convinced Mr. Sheraton of the connection between wellness and cost savings, the argument could move forward with its primary purpose: planning a wellness center and program. An excerpt from the beginning of the section "General Benefits of Worksite Wellness" shows how part of the argument appeared in the Task Force report (Figure 14.25 on the next page). The appeal to Mr. Sheraton's cost concerns was made by placing the reduced costs column next to the improved employee health column in the embedded table.

If your audience is neutral or receptive toward the subject of your report or the position you're taking, you can feel confident in organizing your argument deductively—that is, placing the claim first and following it with appropriate evidence. However, if your audience is skeptical or even mildly resistant, you may be better off organizing your argument inductively—that is, placing the warrant first, following it with appropriate evidence and backing, and then finally presenting your claim.

The overview, background, key points, evidence, and discussion can be combined and rearranged depending on the needs and receptivity of your readers, as shown in Figure 14.26 on the next page. For example, receptive readers will probably respond well to recommendations that are presented before the discussion of those recommendations (deductive arrangement). On the other hand, resistant readers may reject recommendations they already disagree with, not bothering to read any further. However, if the sequence of the information is rearranged so that the evidence for the change and the discussion containing the rationale for a change come before recommendations for change (inductive arrangement), a resistant reader may be convinced by the discussion.

Including Details for Readers

While the orienting, introductory, and persuasive sections may be sufficient in most reports, sometimes you may need to provide additional information:

- bibliography or works cited
- appendixes

Such information is most frequently found in formal reports. Occasionally, however, an informal report will use one of these components. This usually happens when the subject

Figure 14.25 Excerpt from Report Recommending Westwood Wellness Center and Program

Readers are presented with a modified version of the backing of the argument at the beginning of this section. This paragraph foregrounds the key points—improved health, reduced costs, increased productivity, and improved morale—which are the warrant of the argument.

The helpful embedded table reinforces the warrant—the key points the Task Force wants to emphasize.

The benefits are convincing, helping to persuade readers that wellness has distinct advantages.

Each key point is developed in its own section.

General Benefits of Worksite Wellness

Companies with wellness programs typically reduce health care costs, insurance costs, worker compensation claims, and absenteeism. Although most companies begin wellness programs to reduce health care costs, there are unexpected additional benefits. Employees experience improved health, reduced costs, increased productivity, and improved morale as shown in Table 1.

Table 1: Benefits of Worksite Wellness Activities

Topics	Improved Employee Health	Reduced Costs	Increased Productivity	Improved Morale
Nutrition	59.6%	5.8%	25.5%	20.7%
High blood pressure control	57.5	13.6	31.8	15.0
Physical fitness	53.5	4.7	26.0	37.4
Weight control	53.2	6.4	29.6	34.4
Health risk appraisal	47.1	14.3	24.2	14.2
Smoking control	40.9	7.9	16.4	9.0
Stress management	20.2	4.2	46.5	30.0
Back care	26.3	40.7	24.3	—
Off-job accident prevention	19.8	24.9	23.2	—

Source: National Survey of Worksite Health Promotion Activities, 1987

Improved Health. Employees who regularly participate in a wellness program are measurably healthier than . . .

-4-

Figure 14.26 Ways to Organize Information for Readers

POSSIBLE DEDUCTIVE SEQUENCE OF INFORMATION FOR RECEPTIVE OR NEUTRAL READERS	POSSIBLE INDUCTIVE SEQUENCE OF INFORMATION FOR RESISTANT READERS
• *Overview:* problem, writer's interest, audience, occasion	• *Overview:* problem, writer's interest, audience, occasion
• *Background:* assumptions, definitions, history, criteria for decision making, methodology, and so on	• *Background:* assumptions, definitions, history, criteria for decision making, methodology, and so on
• *Summary of Key Points:* recommendations or conclusions	• *Evidence:* results or findings, supporting information
• *Evidence:* results or findings, supporting information	• *Discussion:* explanations, justifications, and rationale for recommendations or conclusions
• *Discussion:* explanations, justifications, and rationale for recommendations or conclusions	• *Summary of Key Points:* recommendations or conclusions

is particularly complex for the audience or when an embedded explanation would detract from the appeal or flow of the report.

Bibliography or Works Cited. When you use information from any source, you must document that source, both in the text of the report and at the end of the report, using either a list of works cited or a bibliography:

- **works cited:** a list of sources that you specifically refer to in the report
- **bibliography:** a list of sources that you used to prepare the report, even if you don't refer to them directly

Refer to Appendix B for formats you can use when you prepare a list of works cited or a bibliography.

Appendixes. Appendixes (also correctly spelled "appendices") are sections at the end of a report that include information that is important but might distract readers or interrupt the flow of the discussion. The following materials are frequently included in an appendix:

- detailed visuals: diagrams, tables
- survey or questionnaire responses
- formulas
- personnel qualifications (resumes)
- definitions (glossaries)
- survey or questionnaire forms
- specifications
- budgets
- budget narratives
- sample materials

You can decide whether to include an appendix by asking yourself if the readers need that level of detail in order to understand your argument, regardless of whether you are preparing an informal or a formal report. If you decide to include an appendix at the end of a report, you need to refer to it in the text by saying something such as "The municipal zoning map in Appendix 7 shows that. . . ." or "As you can see from the design of the survey (Appendix B). . . ." Refer to Appendix A for information about presenting appendixes.

A SAMPLE REPORT

The analytical report in Figure 14.27 was written by Carl Chapman, a City of Ames employee invited by his supervisor to write a report investigating and documenting the differences among three benefits plans that were being considered by the City. Carl saw his

Figure 14.27 Sample Report

Carl knew that a number of people beyond his supervisor, to whom the report was directed, were likely to read his report, so he wanted to make his role clear.

Carl reviewed his purpose and established the focus of his investigation: the choice between Iowa Benefits and Legal Systems.

He provided a rationale for dropping consideration of the third company.

Carl identified the criteria on which he would base his conclusion; thus he foregrounded his report's content and organization.

These criteria formed the basis for the headings for his report.

Carl added to his credibility by quoting and paraphrasing from the proposals submitted by the companies.

Carl developed coherence, in part, by effective use of transitions.

Carl created an effective argument by discussing parallel points for each company. If he hadn't discussed parallel points, he would have little on which to base a comparison.

At the end of each section, Carl stated his conclusion drawn from the evidence he presented.

SELECTING A THIRD PARTY ADMINISTRATOR FOR THE FLEXIBLE BENEFITS PLAN

In response to your request for my thoughts on the final selection of an administrator, I offer these ideas on the choice between Iowa Benefits, Alliance General, and Legal Systems.

I feel the real selection is between Iowa Benefits and Legal Systems. The Alliance General proposal does not offer enough significant advantages to offset the comparable programs of Iowa Benefits as a locally owned and operated organization that seems to have a far more professional staff. Significant differences between the proposals and operating procedures of Iowa Benefits and Legal Systems, however, do warrant careful side-by-side consideration.

I believe that the comparison of these two plans should be done on the basis of four prominent areas that highlight the differences between the two plans:

1) staff resources and services offered (apart from the Flexible Benefit Plan)
2) cost of implementing the plan
3) operating methods
4) ability to maximize total tax savings for employees and employer

STAFF RESOURCES/SERVICES OFFERED

Iowa Benefits and Legal Systems are significantly different in size. Iowa Benefits is a small concern conveniently located in Ames. Its staff of a dozen people is probably sufficient to administer a Sec 125 plan. However, Iowa Benefits states in its proposal that the company does not take legal responsibility for our plan but ". . . will provide assistance as needed" (p. 12, Iowa Benefits proposal). Nor will they offer tax advice for employees although the enrollment counselors will advise each employee (p. 13). Iowa Benefits currently administers five clients comparable in size with the City (over 250 employees).

Legal Systems, on the other hand, is a much larger company centered in Minneapolis, Minnesota. Its operation is large enough to offer to take legal responsibility for our plan (p. 2, Legal Systems proposal). It will also offer tax advice for our employees (p. 3) in writing and through its "Flex-Line" service, a 1-800- telephone number conveniently accessible round-the-clock, 365 days a year. Legal Systems has enrolled 76 clients with over 200 employees, of which 24 have over 500 employees.

In this category, I believe Legal Systems is the more qualified provider. The advantage of Iowa Benefits' convenient local office does not outweigh Legal Systems' superior services: the ability to accept legal responsibility for the plan and to offer legal and tax advice, its Flex-Line for dealing with employees' questions and problems, and the extent of its experience with large clients.

COST OF IMPLEMENTATION

Iowa Benefits projects that implementation of its plan would cost the City $97,232 over the next five years. This is broken down to be $3,750 per year for enrollment and the balance to be a $3.50 fee per month per participating employee. Iowa Benefits recommends that the on-going administrative fees be paid by the employees so ". . . that the employee retains a greater understanding and appreciation of the benefit. . . ." (p. 4). Iowa Benefits projects that the City will realize a five-year FICA savings of $199,140.12. When the total costs (including the recommended employee-borne administrative cost) are subtracted from this savings, the net savings is projected to be $101,908.12. The Iowa Benefits proposal contains no guarantee that the FICA savings will exceed the costs, but indicated willingness to consider such a guarantee.

Under a similar cost structure, Legal Systems estimates that its plan would incur a five-year cost of $45,257 to the City. The proposal makes no mention of passing fees on to

Figure 14.27 (Continued)

Carl's document design—boldface small cap headings and a sans serif font (Geneva)—made this a visually attractive report for the audience.

Carl carefully built his argument by providing accurate financial details and then summarizing these details in an in-text table.

Because Carl finds Legal Systems superior, he moved beyond a straightforward comparison. Iowa Benefits simply didn't have an alternative for comparison.

Again, Carl summarized his position at the end of the section.

In case his audience missed the potential problems that might arise if Iowa Benefits were selected, Carl posed questions that he believed needed answers.

Carl effectively used a bulleted list to call attention to questions.

Carl strengthened his argument by reviewing the process and then drawing attention to the potential hardship on employees.

Carl was particularly careful in this section to draw attention to the employee point of view, referring to reduction of net income, interference with household budgets, and disruption of cash flow. Carl was intent on emphasizing that Iowa Benefits would be a distinct disadvantage to employees.

the employees; rather, it suggests that they be taken out of the City's FICA savings, which it estimates to be $196,211 over five years. This translates to a net savings to the city of $150,954.

	Legal Systems	Iowa Benefits
Est. 5-year FICA savings	$196,211.	$199,140.
Est. 5-year cost	$ 45,257.	$ 97,232.
Est. net savings to the City	$150,954.	$101,908.

Legal Systems also offers an alternate cost structure based on a savings guarantee. The first $2,000 in FICA savings would go to Legal Systems; the remaining FICA savings would be split on a fifty-fifty basis with the City. Using the same projected figures, this option would only provide $97,105 in savings to the City over the five-year period. But it is clear that Legal Systems has no doubt that the Flexible Benefit Plan's costs would NOT exceed any savings realized, and they are willing to guarantee it.

Cost and savings analysis clearly shows that Legal Systems' proposal projects $49,046 more in FICA savings over five years than Iowa Benefits' does. In order for Iowa Benefits' proposal to be cost competitive from the perspective of the City, the "loss" in savings would have to be offset by requiring employee contributions to the plan (thereby making it uncompetitive from an employee perspective). Several questions arise:

- Why does Iowa Benefits' proposal appear to be so much more costly?
- Are the additional costs of Iowa Benefits' plan accompanied by additional services provided to the City and/or City employees?
- Are decreased costs of Legal Systems' plan accompanied by fewer services provided or increased burdens on the City and/or its employees?

OPERATING METHOD

Iowa Benefits manages the reimbursement of employee funds paid into the Flexible Spending Account by (1) collecting and screening employees' requests for reimbursement, (2) verifying the requests with third party documentation of expenses (bills, statements, receipts, etc.), and (3) issuing paper checks to the City so the reimbursement may be included in the employee's next payroll check. The City is required to (1) transfer funds to the Flexible Spending Account at the beginning of each month and (2) receive checks from Iowa Benefits and distribute them with paychecks.

City employees are required to fund the Flexible Spending Account up front, pay the monthly $3.50 administrative surcharge, and submit claims to Iowa Benefits for reimbursement in order to pay the bills.

Legal Systems administers the plan utilizing the employers' existing computerized payroll system. The employee submits requests for reassignment of pay in the same manner as Iowa Benefits, except the request is made to the payroll department instead of the Third Party Administrator.

The City is required to handle the request for payment by entering it directly into the payroll computer, where it then shows up on the employee's next check, reassigned as a pre-tax expense.

The employee's responsibilities under this system include submitting claims as well as verification of eligibility for his/her own expenses, following Legal Systems' written guidelines or the advice of its staff via toll-free, round-the-clock "Flex-Line" service. The employees, under this plan, are NOT required to fund the Flexible Spending Account up front;

Benefits Plan - 2

task as identifying the features of each plan. Although he didn't need to, Carl added a recommendation based on the information he presented in this analytical report.

When Carl submitted his report, he attached a brief cover memo. However, Carl did not summarize his conclusion in the memo, because he knew his position supporting the larger, more qualified—but not local—company was not a popular one.

Figure 14.27 (Continued)

In his concluding section, Carl reinforced his argument by summarizing the attributes of each company. The visual impact alone is powerful. The content is even more convincing.

Carl clearly stated his conclusion supporting Legal Systems.

Because Carl knew there was strong support for the local company, he was careful to explain that if all things were equal, a local company should receive the contract. But when the local company is inadequate in a number of ways, the stronger company should receive the contract.

rather, because they are already in possession of their full wages with which to pay the bills, they simply declare the amount of the claim as tax exempt and are granted the "tax refund" in the next pay period.

In my estimation, Legal Systems' plan is preferable for the employees because it does not reduce their net paychecks from the outset or interfere with their household budgets. Under Iowa Benefits' plan, the employee's capital is reduced for weeks or even months by the initial funding of a Flexible Spending Account. The Iowa Benefits proposal is even less palatable for employees when the prospect of disrupted cash flow is coupled with the additional administrative expense which Iowa Benefits suggests they bear ($3.50/month or $42/year). I feel that any surcharge of this type will diminish employee participation in the program.

From the perspective of the City, the question is to what degree, if any, the FICA cost savings of approximately $49,000 offered by Legal Systems would be encroached upon by increased costs in the finance or payroll departments (e.g., need for training, possible need for additional personnel or computer hardware). It is difficult for me to say if entering claim information under Legal Systems' method is any more or less time-consuming than the handling of paperwork required by Iowa Benefits' method. In addition, further investigation into the verification procedure and liability for errors may be needed.

Maximization of Total Tax Savings to Employer and Employees

To determine the savings to the city and the employees, it may be useful to tally the positive attributes of each plan:

Iowa Benefits	Legal Systems
Small local concern	Legal responsibility
Local access for questions	Tax advice for employees
Less clerical work for City	Much greater experience
	Least costly to administer
	Less paperwork
	No employee admit cost
	No deduction from pay
	24-hour/365-day toll-free phone

I think that the sum of positive features of the Legal Systems method for administering Flex plans indicates that it is a better plan than the cumbersome paperwork-laden system that Iowa Benefits proposes.

I believe that patronizing a local business is appropriate and desirable when the product or service they offer is comparable to a competitive product or service. However, when the products or services offered by a competing outside concern are significantly cheaper or of higher value, that competitor should receive the business. In this case, the services offered by Legal Systems are measurably superior. Legal Systems should get the business.

Benefits Plan - 3

RESPONSE SHEET

PLANNING REPORTS

COMMUNICATOR(S): AUDIENCE(S):
OCCASION FOR WRITING: DOCUMENT:
WHAT TOPIC, ISSUE, OR PROBLEM AM I TRYING TO ADDRESS IN THIS REPORT?

◆ PURPOSE

What is the purpose of my report?

- Do I want to *document* the progress, discussions, or actions about a subject? Do I need to prepare a progress report or a trip report?
- Do I want to *investigate* available options to aid decision making? Do I need to prepare an analytical report or a report about product or document testing?
- Do I want to *evaluate* personnel, objects, or practices to encourage some action? Do I need to prepare a market report, compliance report, or recommendation report?

◆ OCCASION

Does the occasion point to a formal or an informal report?

- If formal, what features of a formal report do I need to include?
- If informal, what features of an informal report do I need to include?

◆ READERS

What do I know about my audience?

- Are the readers likely to be familiar or unfamiliar with the topic and issues involved?
- Do I anticipate cooperative or resistant readers?

◆ CONVENTIONAL COMPONENTS

How can I best orient the audience?

- Why would each of these elements be appropriate or inappropriate: (a) title page? (b) letter of transmittal? (c) abstract? (d) table of contents? (e) list of figures?

What will be the most effective introduction?

- What information should I include in an overview?
- What background information is necessary, given the occasion, purpose, and audience?

How can I persuade the audience to accept the information?

- What key points do I need to include? What line of argument (Chapter 7) should I use to present these points?
- What evidence should I include? What fallacies or errors in logic (Chapter 11) do I need to guard against?
- Is the sequence of my argument easy to follow? How have I defined the problem? established the claim, grounds, and warrants? provided backing? included qualifiers? provided a rebuttal?
- What do I need to explain in the discussion? What implications should I mention? What recommendations, if any, should I make?

What supplementary details does the audience need?

- Why would each of these elements be appropriate or inappropriate: (a) bibliography or works cited? (b) appendixes?

ACTIVITIES, EXERCISES, AND ASSIGNMENTS

◆ IN-CLASS ACTIVITIES

1. Refer to the 3M report excerpt in Figure 14.1 to answer these questions.

   a. The report is labeled as an informative report. In what ways is the report also evaluative?

   b. What about the organization of the report lets you know the writer assumed a receptive audience?

2. Refer to the letter report in Figure 14.9, which notes that copies of the report have been sent to a long list of people:

   Nelson: Seneca manager
   Bridson: director of the Department of Natural Resources LUST (leaking underground storage tanks) division
   Rounds: director of the insurance fund to cover environmental costs incurred during assessment and cleanup
   Searcy: adjuster who approves payment from the insurance fund
   Reynolds: representative of the current owners of the property where Kum & Go is located
   Fuller, the Weineths, and Norgart: owners of other gas stations located at Four Corners

   Explain why you think the writer decided to send a copy of the report to each of these individuals.

3. Read the Communication Spotlight for Part V, "Influences on Multicultural Teams," and then review two report excerpts you read in this chapter: the one Jerry Thompson wrote after a trip to Saudi Arabia (Figure 14.2) and the one he wrote after a trip to Japan (Figure 14.11). Recall that Jerry's managers at Corometrics (the audience for his reports) were not familiar with the Middle and Far Eastern countries where Jerry was doing business for the company.

   a. How do you think the managers' lack of familiarity with the countries Jerry was writing about affected the way Jerry wrote his reports? Explain any connection you see between the informal, narrative approach that Jerry used and the managers' lack of familiarity with the countries.

   b. What kinds of factors probably influenced Jerry's perception of the events in Saudi Arabia and Japan? How would Jerry's ability to speak some Arabic and some Japanese affect his business interactions?

◆ INDIVIDUAL AND GROUP EXERCISES

1. Refer to the report in Figure 14.27. Work in a small group to answer the following questions:

   a. Identify the occasion, audience, and purpose for the report.

   b. How are readers provided with information about the subject, purpose, scope, methodology, writer's role?

   c. What criteria are established for forming opinions about information in the rest of the report?

   d. What is your assessment of the overall effectiveness of the report?

2. The following list identifies the topics discussed in the report prepared by the Westwood Associates' Task Force about the wellness center and program, discussed in Figure 14.25.

   - Promotion of Westwood Wellness Center and Program
   - Budget of Westwood Wellness Center and Program
   - General Benefits of Worksite Wellness
   - Sources Cited
   - Improved Health Due to Workplace Wellness
   - Escalation of Health- and Illness-Related Costs at Westwood, 1985–1995
   - Improved Morale Due to Workplace Wellness
   - Plan for a Westwood Wellness Center and Program
   - Appendixes
   - On-Site Facilities and Staff of Westwood Wellness Center and Program
   - Reduced Costs Due to Workplace Wellness
   - Westwood Benefits of Worksite Wellness
   - The Problem: Spiraling Health- and Illness-Related Costs at Westwood
   - Increased Productivity Due to Workplace Wellness
   - Operation of Westwood Wellness Center and Program
   - Monitoring and Evaluating Westwood Wellness Center and Program

   Construct a table of contents for this report. Use level one and level-two headings. Identify which sections are the introduction, background, key points, and concluding discussion.

◆ ASSIGNMENTS

1. Locate a client who has a problem you can investigate and evaluate (much like the students who made recommendations to Agstar about their involvement in the ISO 9000 standards). Arrange interviews to help define the problem (refer to Chapter 11 to review informational interview strategies). Then begin your collection and analysis of data in preparation for the information (and perhaps recommendations) you're going to present to the client.

   a. *Week 1:* Prepare a memo from your group to your instructor that identifies the topic and client, explains why the project is interesting or important, identifies the sources you plan to use, and suggests a schedule for completing the report. If the project is collaborative, identify each person's role.

   b. *Week 2:* Prepare a 5-minute oral progress report for the class or client.

   c. *Week 3:* Prepare a 10-minute formal oral presentation about the project for the class or client.

   d. *Week 4:* Prepare a report that presents your recommendation to the client.

CASE

A NEW SOCIAL SERVICES PROGRAM

CASE BY ANDREA BREEMER FRANTZ

Background. Your boss, Renee O'Leary, Director of Youth Programs and Shelter Services (YPSS), has called you into her office.

"We got great news today," she says with a grin. "The state has just allocated an extra $100,000 for us. Confidentially, I think it's in response to the national award we got last month, but hey, I don't really care *why* we got it. My job is to spend it."

"That *is* great news," you agree enthusiastically.

Renee smiles again. "Since I'm going to be at the conference next week in Washington, D.C., I'm going to need some help figuring out where this money can best be spent, though."

"And that's where I come in, right?" You are Information Services Coordinator/Media Specialist for YPSS. However, for the last seven months you have also served unofficially as Assistant Director. Glen Cross, the real Assistant Director, has been on an extended leave of absence and will return at the end of this month.

Renee nods. "I just don't have the time to do all the research on our options and make an adjustment to the budget by the deadline—two weeks from tomorrow. We've got about three different program options, as far as I can see, but I need to have all budgeting information and pros and cons spelled out for me as soon as I return from D.C. What do you think? Can you draw together some research for me and write it up?"

You nod. Although you have a number of other projects that need your attention, you know Renee is right. If the money isn't spent, the program will lose it, which doesn't look good for future funding. And if the money is spent wisely, there are often options for matching grants and endowments. It will likely be important to show some sort of positive results fairly quickly in order to justify further funding. You enjoy working for Renee, and want to impress her. You would like to be promoted to Assistant Director within the next 15 months or so: Glen Cross plans to return to finish his major project (a small residential treatment center for emotionally disturbed children under 13), and then plans to leave the program permanently, though he has told no one but you this.

"Do you want me to make recommendations?" you ask.

Renee hesitates. "No, I'd better figure those out for myself. Why don't you just summarize the information for me, so I can make a decision pretty quickly. I'll only have a couple of days to write up the proposal and amendments to the budget after I get back."

Task. It is now five days later and you have accumulated the information Renee has requested. You are now ready to write the information up as requested. Information that you are drawing from for your message is provided in Figure 14.28.

Complication. Although Renee told you she does not want you to make recommendations, you know she's under some time constraints. You know you cannot make overt recommendations to her in your message, but toy with the idea of pointing to conclusions and possible options. This additional work may annoy Renee, but it also might help her out and show your initiative at the same time.

Figure 14.28 Data Sheet with Information Needed for Preparing Report for the "New Social Services Program" Case

RESEARCH FINDINGS

The Crisis Hotline Project

- This is a project YPSS has been considering for approximately 18 months, but has lacked adequate funding for.
- The program would involve setting up two toll-free telephone lines in a small, currently vacant backroom office in the main administrative offices for YPSS and would require training three part-time salaried employees who would recruit and train volunteers to operate the crisis lines. The crisis lines would be staffed 24 hours a day and primarily serve teenagers in crisis (i.e., potential runaways, abuse victims, intervention services, etc.) across the state.
- The project is a natural offshoot of the two runaway shelters YPSS offers in the county and the addictions recovery program, which is in its tenth successful year.
- It will take approximately 6–8 months to start the program (including hiring, training, and a promotional campaign), so any sort of tangible "results" would not be likely before 12–15 months, maybe longer.
- This project would require ongoing funding, which, of course, is not guaranteed.

Cost Estimates

Salaries	$36,000	Training/Recruitment	$8,000
Technical Services	$14,000	Miscellaneous	$5,000
Promotional Campaign	$15,000	**Total**	**$78,000**

ADDITION TO RUNAWAY SHELTER #1

- This is a project which has been proposed by the counseling staff at youth shelter #1 (called "Moore House") within the last three months. Again, because of finances, YPSS postponed any formal discussion of an addition.
- Because of the rising number of sexual abuse perpetrators referred to Moore House as temporary housing prior to court-appointed treatment programs, counselors at the youth shelter proposed that an additional dormer bedroom be built and a full-time night counselor position be funded. Regulations prohibit alleged perpetrators from being housed unattended with the other youths at the shelter. Consequently, alleged perpetrators have historically slept on the sofa bed within eyesight of the night counselor on duty, a practice which has become more and more difficult with the rising numbers of youth referred to Moore House.
- The dormer bedroom would have the capacity for four beds and a night attendant station separate from the night counselor office for the rest of the house.
- The initial building and outfitting will be a one-time cost. Maintaining the salary for the full-time night counselor position will be an annual, renewable cost (not guaranteed in the budget).
- The shelter addition would take approximately four weeks to build and the counselor position could be filled within that time as well.

Cost Estimates

Salary/Training	$24,000	Miscellaneous	$3,000
Building Costs	$60,000	**Total**	**$95,000**
Maintenance/Equipment	$8,000		

INDEPENDENT LIVING PROGRAM

- This project has not yet been formally proposed, though Renee, Glen, and others have brainstormed a little about it.
- The Independent Living Program is also a natural offshoot of the addictions recovery and foster care programs YPSS currently runs. It would support youths who have determined either through the court system or through YPSS not to return to their parents' homes and instead will live independently until they graduate from high school or turn 18. This program will supplement apartment living costs and continue counseling services, though the client will be required to have a 20 hour/week job to defray food and living costs.
- YPSS currently has on staff a woman who is interested and prepared to head the program, but she counsels for addiction/recovery now. Therefore, addiction/recovery would eventually need to replace her, but could shuffle current counselor loads for a time.
- YPSS would likely not be able to cover all costs for such a program; however, this is the likeliest of the three options to be awarded additional grants and matching funds through the federal government and local donors. One patron for YPSS has already hinted at a substantial (guesses are $100,000) gift for such a program.
- Clearly, this would require annual funding, and initial "results" would be unlikely before 2–3 years.

Cost Estimates

Salary	$35,000	Utilities	$40,000
Rental Costs	$40,000	Miscellaneous	$50,000
Food	unknown	**Total**	**$165,000***

*A great deal about the costs for initial start-up for this program is unknown and difficult for you to ascertain during this research project.

CHAPTER

15

Proposals and Feasibility Reports

OUTLINE

Connections between Proposals and Feasibility Studies: The Solar Industries Reports

Characteristics of Proposals and Feasibility Reports

Conventional Segments of Feasibility Reports

Proposal Components

Principles of Argument in Proposals and Feasibility Reports

How Proposals and Feasibility Reports Are Evaluated

Example of a Proposal

CRITERIA FOR EXPLORING CHAPTER 15

What we cover in this chapter	What you will be able to do after reading this chapter
Proposals and feasibility report relationships	Demonstrate how proposals and feasibility reports extend the same argument
Characteristics of proposals and feasibility reports	Describe similarities and differences between proposals and feasibility reports
Conventional elements of proposals	Construct background, needs, idea, benefits, additional benefits, implementation, and recommendation sections of proposals
Conventional elements of feasibility reports	Write criteria; establish and assess and recommend alternative
Line of argument in proposals and feasibility reports	Discuss how proposals and feasibility reports use persuasive strategies
Evaluation of proposals and feasibility studies	Address six major concerns of evaluators

Effective communicators know that proposals and feasibility reports are powerful documents that have the ability to persuade readers to fund a wide range of projects, to adopt a spectrum of policies and procedures, or to address specific problems in a certain way. Communicators also know that proposals and feasibility reports are written within a climate of reader resistance. Figure 15.1 shows a writer introducing a proposal with information that readers will resist.

CONTEXT

The excerpt in Figure 15.1 is an introductory section to a proposal dealing with ways to best value inventory. The writer wants to replace the current last-in, first-out (LIFO) system with a first-in, first-out (FIFO) system. The writer's task is complicated by the fact that the LIFO system was itself adopted in 1974 as a solution to a different set of inventory problems.

Figure 15.1 Proposal Excerpt Anticipating Reader Resistance

To establish the problem, the writer must admit to "bad news" or "problems" in the opening or forecast section of the proposal.

The writer faces resistance to the idea that LIFO has problems, as well as resistance to change itself and to a new interpretation of the appropriateness of LIFO to the company.

Purpose

This report has two purposes. The first purpose is to illustrate the problems that Delta Manufacturing has experienced by using the last-in, first-out (LIFO) method of valuing inventory. The second purpose is to illustrate how a switch from the LIFO method to the first-in, first-out (FIFO) method would eliminate these problems and be beneficial to the company.

Background

Delta adopted the LIFO method in 1974 to help counteract the effects of inflation on the income statement. In this period of high inflation, Delta's reported net income was artificially high because of the time lapse between when an inventory was produced and when it was sold. The aim of adopting the LIFO method was to compare the present sales price of an item with the present cost of manufacture to achieve a more accurate assessment of net income.

1. What strategies for overcoming reader resistance (see Chapter 9) does the writer employ in this short excerpt?
2. How do the strategies differ from those used in a letter or a memo? How are they the same?
3. What is the purpose of each section of the proposal excerpt in Figure 15.1?

Proposals and feasibility reports share certain features. Effective communicators know

- what characteristics these types of writing share
- how the conventional components of each compare and contrast
- how each report uses argumentative strategies
- how both have similar methods for evaluation

CONNECTIONS BETWEEN PROPOSALS AND FEASIBILITY STUDIES: THE SOLAR INDUSTRIES REPORTS

As consultant for Solar Industries, Loras Goedken faces the task of writing a feasibility report for one of his clients, farm owner Jim Mason. Mason had requested the report as a follow-up to a proposal Goedken had submitted earlier about implementing a solar grain drying system on Mason's farmstead.

As a first step toward writing the feasibility report, Loras looks at the implementation section of his proposal, which suggests several system options. Goedken's original purpose for including these options was to indicate that such systems are "easy" to implement because they can be adapted to site-specific specifications and owner preference. The thrust of the section (Figure 15.2, page 438) was to get Mason to use a solar grain drying system,

Figure 15.2 Implementation Section of Goedken's Proposal

Loras opens with a first alternative for implementation: free-standing collectors. He provides data that will be important in choosing the size of any collector.

He continues with a second alternative for implementation: mounting on existing farm structures. He "sells" this option by picturing it in a figure and explaining its mechanics.

Loras offers a third option: incorporating the system in new construction. He cites costs savings enjoyed by a client using this option.

Implementation

Employing free-standing collectors is one of the most basic applications of supplying supplemental solar heat to a corn dryer. The principle of the system is much like that of a solar collector for a home hot water heater. For the corn dryer, the solar collector can be of almost any height or width desired. The larger the collector, the greater the surface area it will have and the larger the total BTU temperature rise it will create. For each square foot of collector space added, the collector will gain an additional 1000-12000 BTU's per day.

The roofs and walls of agricultural buildings provide large flat surfaces that can readily be adapted for use as solar collectors also. The mechanics of this system (fig. 2) are such that the sun's rays, in striking the building's roof and facing wall, raise the temperature of these surfaces and warm the air beneath them. The heated air is then drawn out of the building's attic through a system of tubes and ducts by the bin fan. Blown into the stored grain, the solar heated air produces a temperature rise in the grain and dries it.

While it is true that the cost of modifying a building just for the purpose of providing supplemental solar heat may be economically prohibitive, it is also true that when buildings are constructed to include the modifications for providing solar heat, the incremental material and labor costs are quite justifiable economically. For example, one of our clients, Illinois farmer Mr. Dale Sass, included a 4,700 sq. ft. collector upon construction of a pole building. Costs for including the collector in the building were $4,028, or $0.86/sq. ft. At an annual cost of $421 (includes depreciation), the collector saved 1,330 gallons of LP gas valued at $483—a net savings of $62. In addition, the supplemental heat provided by such a system can be transported by air for use in a number of other farmstead applications, including preheating ventilating air for livestock buildings and heating a farm shop. Grain drying alone does not have to recoup the whole incremental investment.

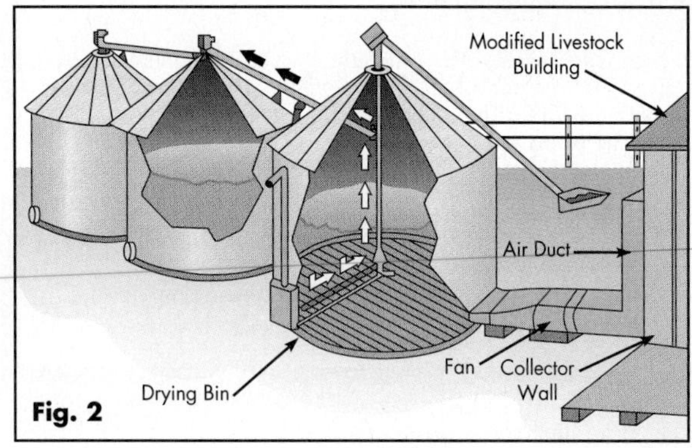

Fig. 2

such as that which Loras has proposed. In the proposal, then, Loras was more concerned with the adoption of a solar system than with how it would be set up on this particular site.

After examining this section of the proposal, Goedken decides to do a site-specific analysis of the three options outlined: using free-standing collectors, adapting current farm structures, and building a new structure which accommodates such a system from the start. He anticipates that his feasibility report will compare the advantages and disadvantages of each option before recommending one for use on Mason's farmstead. One of Goedken's first tasks will be to discuss criteria for evaluating the options with Mason. Knowing Mason's values and priorities will help Goedken analyze each option and recommend which one is best for this particular client.

CHARACTERISTICS OF PROPOSALS AND FEASIBILITY REPORTS

Of the lengthy messages covered in this book, proposals and feasibility reports anticipate the most reader resistance (Figure 15.3). The recommendation reports (see Chapter 14) that grow out of proposals and feasibility reports assume a history of prior argument(s)—oral or written—that has convinced readers of the need for and the feasibility of the recommendation.

Proposals and feasibility reports share several general characteristics:

- Both address a problem.
- Each can be solicited or unsolicited.
- Both are fundamentally persuasive.

Figure 15.3 Proposals and Feasibility Reports Anticipate Reader Resistance

Reports whose main purpose is to propose, as with proposals, and to analyze alternatives for change, as with feasibility reports, assume reader resistance.

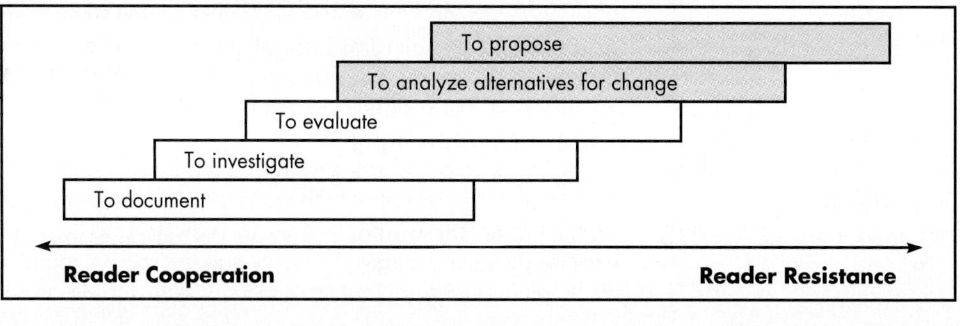

As the Solar Industries story suggests, one way of understanding proposals and feasibility reports is to see them as extensions of the same argument. A **proposal** argues that there is a *problem* and offers a *solution* to that problem. A **feasibility report** assumes that its audience agrees on the dimensions or definition of a problem and discusses the merits of a number of proposed solutions, settling on one as preferable for the specific situation.

People write different types of proposals to fulfill various purposes, including grant applications to address a problem or investigate a subject, marketing proposals to sell a product or service, and investigative proposals to explore a subject. While proposals characteristically balance discussion of problems and solution, feasibility reports focus on investigating solutions.

Proposals may be *solicited* or *unsolicited*. Solicited proposals are initiated by potential readers and often require a response to a formal **request for proposals (RFP)**—a document developed by businesses and agencies that want to contract out work. Solicited proposals may include an invitation to bid, a purchase request, or a **request for a price quotation (RFQ).** A grant could be considered a solicited proposal. An unsolicited proposal is initiated by the writer in response to a need or opportunity. Both solicited and unsolicited proposals can range from informal one-page memos to lengthy formal reports. If a proposal is written in response to an RFP, the writer follows any specifications regarding length and format outlined by the request.

Requests for proposals typically contain the following elements:

- *Proposal preparation instructions:* give a precise format for proposals, so consultants get an idea of how specific they must be. These instructions must be followed to the letter, because the requesting company uses the format as a common basis from which to compare all the submissions.
- *Statement of work (SOW):* describes the work to be performed.
- *System specification:* details the level of performance the company expects from the completed work, whether it be a computer system or a training program. Contractors should consider whether they can meet the demands before submitting a proposal.
- *Work breakdown structure:* gives a breakdown of what the company expects (or is willing) to invest in the project. Consultants should certainly take the company's cost breakdown into account when preparing a proposal.
- *Time schedule:* gives a (usually) precise schedule for both the submittal of the proposal (generally the requesting agency allows about a month for the proposals to be submitted) and the

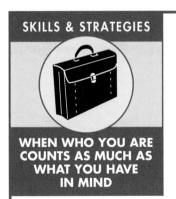

SKILLS & STRATEGIES

WHEN WHO YOU ARE COUNTS AS MUCH AS WHAT YOU HAVE IN MIND

Proposals submitted in highly competitive situations often have to spend as much time arguing for the writer's credibility as for the writer's ideas. For this reason, experts on proposal writing divide their idea section into two equally important slots:

- a "methods" section, which articulates ideas for how readers can reach their objectives (the writer's proposed plan for addressing the problems present in the situation)
- a qualifications/staffing section, which explains the qualifications of both the proposal writer and the organization's personnel for implementing the writer's ideas

Often in such an arrangement, the qualifications cited read very much like feasibility criteria (review Figure 15.15, page 448):

Generic methods for an R&D proposal	We will use the Army's specifications; we will design the missile this way; we will build it that way.
Generic qualifications: material assets	We have the facilities to build it, and our team has worked on similar projects before, producing result within budget.
Generic methods for a consulting proposal	We will analyze your business, those of your competitors, and the market; define the niche best for you; and devise an appropriate plan.
Generic qualifications: material assets (writer's experience becomes an asset)	We know your market, and we have done similar studies for similar organizations.

Such qualifications sections can also be supplemented by functional resumes appended to the proposal. The emphasis you give to your qualifications depends on the situation and may be stipulated in an RFP.

completion of various stages of the work. Potential consultants should consider whether they can realistically complete the work in the time frame allowed before submitting a proposal.

- *Contractual information:* describes the requirements for completion and basis for payment.

Several public resources list specific RFPs and identify proposal requirements, including *Catalog of Federal Domestic Assistance, Commerce Business Daily, Federal Grants and Contracts Weekly, Federal Register, Research Monitor News,* and *Research Monitor Profile.*

Feasibility reports are almost always solicited documents internal to an organization. Like proposals, feasibility reports can vary in length and format. Specifications for feasibility reports may be found in stylesheets specific to a particular business or institution.

Experts emphasize the *persuasive nature* of proposals by viewing the writer as a seller and the reader as a buyer. To make the "sale," the writer moves from a current situation, which the writer wants to change, to a desired result, which often entails a number of reader benefits (Figure 15.4).[1]

You can move from the current situation to the desired results with the help of objectives and methods. Objectives specify goals, such as a gender-neutral family leave policy that grants equal opportunities for men and women to participate in family care. Methods for developing such a policy might include surveying employees about what they would include in a revised policy, investigating alternative policies at comparable companies, and discovering any constraints management might see as governing any revised policy offered.

Feasibility reports are also persuasive. A feasibility report shows how *what the reader wants* can be reached in several ways and how *what the reader will receive* can be evaluated and compared according to established criteria. The argument in a feasibility report can thus be described as primarily a move from *what options the reader has* to *the best option the reader has*. When a feasibility report focuses only on the reader's best option, it is often called a recommendation report (see page 452).

Figure 15.4 The Basic Movement of a Proposal

CURRENT SITUATION	PROBLEMS OR NEEDS	DESIRED RESULT	BENEFIT
What the readers have is a gender-based family leave policy at their corporation. →	*What the readers want* is to develop a revised policy for family leave that will address the gender bias problem. →	*What the readers will receive* upon adoption of the proposed revision will be a policy that grants new-baby leave to both men and women and sick leave to both to take care of family members. →	Benefits might include increased opportunities for men to take on the care of family members and, conversely, for women to pursue careers immediately after childbirth.

CONVENTIONAL SEGMENTS OF PROPOSALS AND FEASIBILITY REPORTS

Proposals and feasibility reports share many of the same segments. Figure 15.5 names these components and notes (in bold) the main differences between the two types of writing.

When structured as a formal report, a proposal or a feasibility report may have certain introductory sections, including (1) a purpose section that states the subject and specifies aims or objectives; (2) methods and scope section(s) that present the method of inquiry or procedure and that set the boundaries of the discussion, present a task breakdown, and establish criteria; and (3) a section outlining the qualifications of the proposers (proposals often attach functional resumes of the proposers in an appendix). Proposals and feasibility reports may also have front and end matter common to reports (see Chapter 14).

PROPOSAL COMPONENTS

Although the sections of a proposal might vary, the seven components described in this section represent basic tasks that proposals must tackle.

Background

The background section in a proposal presents detail that will aid readers in understanding the specific situation informing the proposal itself. For example, the background section in Figure 15.1 explains that the LIFO system, which the proposer wants to replace, was instituted at Delta Manufacturing as the result of economic conditions in the 1970s.

Figure 15.5 Standard Components of Proposals and Feasibility Studies

PROPOSALS	FEASIBILITY REPORTS
• Background section: establishes any historical or contextual detail necessary for understanding the proposal	• Background section: establishes any historical detail necessary for understanding the feasibility report; **establishes criteria for evaluating alternatives (e.g., cost, personnel, ease of maintenance, facility use); establishes methods for researching factors important to feasibility**
• Needs section: dramatizes the problem addressed in the proposal	• Needs section: dramatizes the problem addressed in the feasibility report
• Idea section: details the writer's proposed solution(s) to address the problem (can include objectives, methods, and qualifications, if proposal is not structured as a report)	• **Idea section (overview of alternatives): introduces the writer's researched or proposed solutions to address the problem; evaluates these solutions according to criteria established in the background section**
• Benefits section: shows the benefits to be gained by addressing the problem as outlined in the needs section in the way proposed in the idea section	• **Assessment section: assessment of alternatives according to criteria;** often the assessment entails benefits and thus sometimes looks like an expanded benefits section of a proposal
• Additional benefits section: where appropriate, shows other benefits not directly tied to previously established needs	• (No comparable section in feasibility reports)
• Implementation section: optional on proposals; explains how to implement the proposal at the specific site involved (budget, schedule, personnel, facilities)	• Implementation section: optional on feasibility reports; explains how to implement the feasibility report at the specific site involved (budget, schedule, personnel facilities); sometimes implementation factors are included as criteria and therefore discussed as part of the assessment
• Recommendation: urges acceptance of the proposal and suggests action	• Recommendation: urges acceptance of the report and suggests action

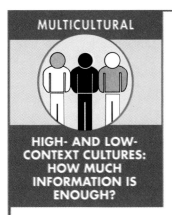

MULTICULTURAL

HIGH- AND LOW-CONTEXT CULTURES: HOW MUCH INFORMATION IS ENOUGH?

In proposals and feasibility reports, the background and needs sections provide context for understanding the problem the writer is to solve. But the quantity and quality of context needed varies from culture to culture.

In high-context cultures, meaning is communicated as much through the ongoing situation as through the content of a specific message. Japanese, Arab, and Mediterranean people, for example, have extensive information networks among family, friends, colleagues, and clients. As a result, for most transactions, they neither require nor expect much in-depth background information.

By contrast, in low-context cultures, meaning must be communicated principally through the content of a specific document, because context is an insufficient indicator of meaning. Low-context people include the Americans, Germans, Swiss, Scandinavians, and other Northern Europeans, who normally do not favor extensive, well-developed, informal information networks. As a result, the task of developing a context through writing flourishes in a low-context culture. Every contingency is anticipated because there is little guidance, other than the document itself, to ascertain what the parties mean. On the other hand, in a high-context culture, spelling out every contingency may be considered an insulting display of mistrust.

When communicating interculturally, professionals need to know the appropriate level of contexting in the foreign culture. This knowledge not only helps professionals make decisions regarding how much information to include in a document but also helps them decide whether a proposal, a report, and (subsequently) a written contract are needed in a given situation. The high-context Japanese culture, for example, considers a spoken agreement as binding as a written agreement.

Corresponding principles apply to high- and low-context organizations. Some high-context business organizations, for example, do not even ask for RFPs to start business projects, because much of the information included in proposals is communicated informally through relationships. Similarly, internal proposals in high-context corporate situations tend to have abbreviated background and needs sections, because the writer can assume that readers understand the issues and have already discussed the situation and the need for a solution among themselves. Indeed, it is common for high-context corporate managers to call for proposals when what they really want is a recommendation report. For all practical purposes, both the needs and the alternatives have already been sufficiently hashed out.

Figure 15.6 Introductory Excerpt with Questionable Background Elements

This report discusses the feasibility of implementing ergonomic adjustments in the workplace of Hahne Accounting, a medium-sized firm in the Pittsburgh area. The Ergo-Safe program shows that modest changes can be made in the existing workplace at Hahne, rather than a total restructuring of work site facilities.

The work environment has a direct effect on the performance of workers. The present work environment has not been changed for five years and the management wishes to become up-to-date on the current safety and production standards concerning, for example, visual display terminals (VDTs) and their users. Due to the fact that this is a complex system specialized for Hahne, there is concern towards a complete restructuring of the workspace, as opposed to adjustments in moderation. These adjustments should result in increased competency and safety for workers.

In this report, Ergo-Safe reviews the present situation for employees at Hahne and offers suggestions and solutions to create an ergonomic environment. The goal, which is shared by Ergo-Safe and Hahne employees in general, and VDT operators in particular, is increased safety and productivity in the work environment.

The phrase "a medium-sized firm in the Pittsburgh area" is silly, since the audience is Hahne employees. Since this audience includes "the management," the phrase is odd here.

The writers do not identify who has the "concern." If the writers have not done enough research to make this statement about shared goals, it could raise a red flag.

Many factors influence how this detail is presented. Chief among these are the audience(s) for the report and the necessary link(s) between what has happened up to the present and what is proposed for the future. If the audience for the Delta proposal had nothing to do with the original decision to use LIFO, then the writer could anticipate less resistance than if the audience had instituted LIFO as the best method of valuing inventory.

Proposals characteristically have multiple audiences. Appealing to diverse readers presents a special challenge when writers present historical facts about the company. If the readers are company managers, for example, they probably know the history of the firm. In fact, company managers and company employees alike may very well know the history of the situation better than the writer, especially if the writer is an outside consultant.

How, then, can a writer establish credibility to speak on company issues? Certainly, the task is made easier if writers can present an appropriate, informed, and relevant history of events, something which the writers in Figure 15.6 fail to do. The inappropriate wording and phrasing, and the yet-to-be-supported claim of shared goals, make the writers' presentation of background material in this excerpt potentially damaging to their credibility.

When writing a proposal or feasibility report, you must often present basic information that is already known to your readers. When doing so, you can preserve your credibility by specifying the significance of the included detail in the text, as shown in Figure 15.7. The statement of significance, which we have highlighted in bold, allows the reader to say, in effect, "Yes, I already know these figures, and the data in the appendix clearly support the writer's claim. The lack of maximum capacity is a good point and must be important to the writer's proposal. Perhaps the writer's proposal will show us how to reach capacity."

You also face the potentially dangerous task of identifying and possibly placing blame on your readers in your presentation of background. This issue of blame threatens a positive writer-reader relationship. Strategies for presenting negative information (Chapter 9) help you display the proper courtesy in background sections.

Needs

The **needs section** in a proposal establishes the fact that *what the reader currently has* is either inadequate, inappropriate, or characterized by a number of other problems in need of solution. The needs section of a proposal can be viewed as "reasons" for changing the current situation or as a rationale for making the proposal itself.

To make a proposal persuasive, you must somehow dramatize the needs or problems. Dramatizing needs involves *picturing* the problem for readers. Two excellent strategies for dramatizing are using direct observations or other data gathered at the site of the problem,

Figure 15.7 Excerpt Establishing Significance of Known Information

The GMBL Hotel has average annual sales compared to other hotels in the Houston airport area and other geographical areas of similar attributes in the U.S. (See Appendix A for detailed information.) This figure ranges between $13.5 million and $15.2 million per year, which results in a room occupancy rate of 65% to 75%. **This shows that none of these hotels, thus including GMBL Hotel, are at their maximum productivity.**

Figure 15.8 Dramatization of Needs through On-Site Data

The writers label the needs as problems and list them at the outset. Just naming these problems, however, is not enough. Numerical data create a picture of 75 people trying to use 20 terminals at the same time; a quote from a reporter dramatizes software problems; and a quote from an editor dramatizes the inadequacy of the system overall.

The writers summarize the previously dramatized problems and name two main failings observed on-site. A quote from an editor shows the frustration felt with current maintenance.

The writers use on-site observations of missed deadlines and poor attitude to conclude their presentation of needs.

Problems with Current Computer System

The *Journal's* computer system has three major problem areas: access, software capability, and maintenance.

Access. The *Journal* currently employs one minicomputer which is accessed by 20 remote terminals clustered in one area of the news room. All terminals are linked to a minicomputer used solely for creating and editing stories. Because the *Journal* employs approximately 60 reporters and 15 editors, access to the minicomputer via 20 terminals creates a problem, especially when the 4:30 deadline has to be met.

Software and system capability. There have also been problems with software. According to one reporter:

> *"The current software just doesn't meet our needs. We are not able to set up our articles in column format. This makes it nearly impossible to approximate story lengths."*

Editors seem to agree that the paper has simply outgrown the present system.

> *"With all of the technology out there and the graphic capabilities, there should be no reason why we're limited to a precious few format and visual options."*

The current minicomputer runs special purpose software, written specifically for the newspaper business. This software, provided by the same company (Halcyon Partners) that leases the computer system, does not seem adequate. It provides word processing capabilities without the ability to set up stories in column format. It also lacks graphic displays. Overall, reporters and editors are very disappointed with the computer's capabilities.

Maintenance. Currently the *Journal* relies on Halcyon Partners Inc. to come in and solve any problems that may occur. This reliance has proven frustrating. As one editor explained:

> *"When something happens to the minicomputer nothing gets done. By the time we get a call into Halcyon, and they get things fixed, everyone is complaining about how much extra time everything takes. It would be nice if someone here knew what was going on!"*

The frustration is compounded by the fact that once the minicomputer is "down," the entire network is affected. Network slow-downs and complete failures have caused missed deadlines and create a poor attitude toward the system among reporters and editors.

and using visuals and graphics. For example, the proposal excerpt in Figure 15.8 features on-site data, including direct quotes from employees, that help the reader picture the drawbacks in the current system.

Second, you may create a picture of needs graphically or visually. The graph in Figure 15.9 is part of a needs section from a proposal written by a consultant specializing in transportation and logistics. The purpose of the graph is to dramatize the cost savings of establishing a centrally located regional warehouse for a small California manufacturing firm with several retail outlets located throughout the western United States. Currently the firm, which is not centrally located, ships directly to each outlet. The writer chooses to include this graph early in the report in the needs section instead of later in a benefits section because she anticipates that her readers might be highly resistant to the notion that building or purchasing a regional warehouse is really cheaper in the long run than continuing to ship directly from the point of manufacture. The need established through the graph is thus

Figure 15.9 Dramatization of Needs through Graphics

The graph dramatizes needs by picturing a $60,000 difference in projected expenses.

Figure 1. Transportation Costs

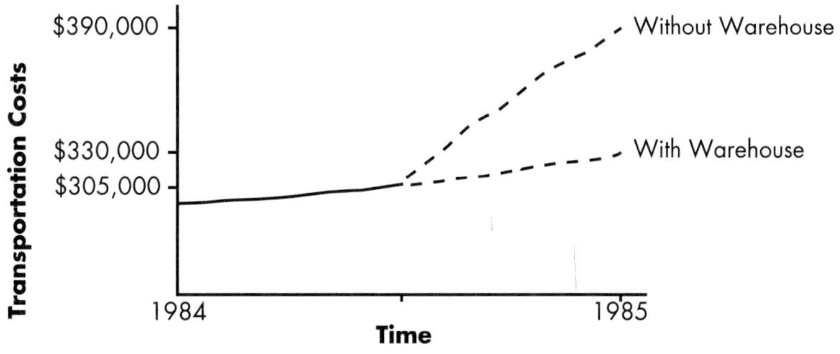

twofold: the need to save money on transportation costs *and* the need to consider what might be thought a radical solution.

Idea Section

The **idea section** of a proposal, often labeled "Plan" or "Proposed Solution," describes the writer's plan for addressing the current problem(s). Sometimes, this section incorporates the writer's credentials into the discussion of the proposed plan (for example, "This plan takes advantage of the leadership our firm has demonstrated in hypertext software . . ."). Like the needs section, the idea section can be made persuasive through dramatization. You can dramatize an idea with a detailed description, as seen in Figure 15.10.

Benefits

The **benefits section** of a proposal describes the results of adopting the proposed alternative or solution. An effective benefits section dramatizes the advantages of adopting the proposed project, product, or policy and articulates benefits that relate directly back to the previously established needs. A close relationship between benefits and needs not only contributes to the unity of the report, but also helps prevent the writer from either introducing new, undisclosed needs late in the report, or forgetting to show how the solution he or she proposed addresses each and every need previously identified.

The excerpt in Figure 15.11, which is an initial draft of a proposal for new equipment to handle hospital wastes, shows the difficulties writers can run into when benefits do not

Figure 15.10 Dramatization of Proposed Product

The writer introduces his idea in the context of research and naming the proposed equipment.

He describes the features of the proposed model as advantages.

He names an additional feature and uses a quote from marketing literature to flesh out the description. He dramatizes this feature using actual employees.

Proposed New Pager

After careful research with both our dealer, Mobile Page, Inc., and several others in the Denver area, we recommend that KGNG rent the Data Page. Besides being light and compact like most current pager models, the Data Page has several new features that make it superior:

1) It is whisper quiet.
2) It has a ten-digit lighted display, which makes it possible to send an encoded message. The display either gives the person a telephone number to call or a message which the receiver can decode.
3) It has a memory function which will store the message in case the reporter is busy.

In addition, the Data Page is easy to hook up to a phone. "The message sender uses a push-button phone or accessory. She punches the individual phone number of the beeper unit, then taps out the ten-digit signal, which is relayed to the beeper." In terms of our news operation, it would work in a similar way. For example, when a big story breaks, our news director Jan Henry would call a predetermined number to activate the Data Page worn by reporter Sue Smithson. When Sue's pager beeps, then Jan would push numbers on the phone to send out the appropriate message. Sue would see the message on her pager and then decode the message. After that, Sue would either call Jan at the station or, following her directive, get to the assignment.

Figure 15.11 Benefits Section Introducing Previously Unmentioned Needs

The writer focuses on the problem of meeting new state and federal regulations in the needs section. He singles out "infectious waste" and asserts that the volume of such waste to be incinerated or sterilized on-site will increase by 50%, a statistic supported by figures in an appendix.

After his proposed idea, the writer starts with a benefit that addresses the "need" to follow regulations. But he unwittingly introduces a series of additional needs—to reduce fines, to meet emission standards, and to reduce operational costs—which have not yet been discussed as problems.

NEEDS

Hospital administrators are currently questioning the ability of the hospital complex to handle wastes because regulations facing the hospital will be stricter when the new wings are open.

The hospital will have to manage directly more waste due to both state and federal regulations. Currently, the state regulations concerning the disposal of infectious, Type IV waste are in a state of flux. These regulations will require incineration or sterilization of more infectious waste in the near future. The enforcement of such regulations would mean a 50% increase in the amount of waste that would have to be incinerated or sterilized on-site (see Appendix B for complete breakdown). The hospital will also lose its existing exemption from EPA regulations when the new wings are open. The practice of sending certain infectious wastes to the landfill without incineration violates current EPA standards but has been "grandfathered in" as a permitted practice. The loss of this exemption will result in an additional 15% increase in waste the hospital will have to manage on-site.

[In the idea section, the writer then proposes a new pathological incinerator equipped with a secondary pyrolithic combustion chamber to solve the problem of increased waste.]

BENEFITS

Installation of the new incinerator will allow County General to meet all regulations and avoid fines because of violations. The new incinerator will also be capable of burning a greater amount of waste, while at the same time it will be able to meet emission standards. Emissions are reduced by the secondary pyrolithic combustion chamber which keeps flue gases and ash to a minimum. The incinerator will also require less fuel, thus reducing the high cost of operation.

ADDITIONAL BENEFITS

The new incinerator also has the potential for great waste-heat recovery. . . .

TECHNOLOGY

CREATING MANAGEABLE COMPUTER-GENERATED PRESENTATIONS

Computer-generated materials can be excellent tools for increasing the persuasiveness of business presentations. These materials come in especially handy when the presenter anticipates audience resistance, as in the oral presentation of ideas in a written proposal or in a feasibility report.

However, using elaborate materials can create problems for the presenter. Sometimes exciting and visually stimulating materials can actually distract from the message or be interpreted as "too slick" for the occasion. Also, preparation time is extensive, and multimedia presentations are often extraordinarily expensive. In any case, anyone considering computer-generated presentation materials needs to ask

- Which media would be effective? Illustrations and colors should highlight important concepts, provide appropriate entertainment, and serve to further the communicative interaction.
- How will the presentation be delivered or distributed? The media should complement the location.
- What technical expertise will be required? There should be a match between the materials and the presenter's expertise.
- How much will it cost? A one-time presentation that will result in a $10,000 sale is not going to support a $20,000 CD-ROM-based multimedia presentation. Similarly, devoting weeks to creating new visuals for a presentation may not be the most efficient investment of a presenter's time. On the other hand, if the presentation will be used many times or if the potential payoff is significant, a large investment might be worthwhile.

An additional issue of concern is that corporations generally like their presentations to have a consistent approach. New presentation materials need to be consistent with those of previous presentations and to complement the products, services, or information being presented.

match up with previously established needs. The needs introduced in the excerpt's benefits section all seem serious and worthy of detailed development earlier in the proposal. The very introduction of these new needs here may cause the reader to doubt the viability of the proposed solution, because the solution was offered before the needs were identified and because the writer has not shown through specific detail that he has researched these important aspects of the problem. The presentation greatly reduces the writers' credibility.

Additional Benefits

Because the benefits section is logically tied to the needs section, you may want to have a section that discusses additional benefits that are not directly tied to needs.

The additional benefit of waste-heat recovery mentioned in the hospital waste excerpt (Figure 15.11) is a good example of an additional benefit addressing no specific need. Similarly, a company may have an excellent corporate image and thus may not "need" to enhance it, but such enhancement never hurts. Therefore, one "additional benefit" might be that the proposed service nicely fulfills the already high expectations of company customers. In a different instance, a company may have adequate funding for advertising, and the proposed idea for a new marketing strategy may not change this budget significantly but may simply call for shifts in a few budget lines. In such a case, an "additional benefit" might be that no new money is needed to finance the new publicity campaign.

Implementation

The **implementation section** of a proposal pictures how the proposed policy, procedure, or innovation could be put into place. When writers choose to present more than one method of implementation, as Loras Goedken did in the implementation section of his proposal (Figure 15.2), the purpose is likely to stress the practicality of the idea.

You can also discuss implementation in terms of project schedules (Figure 15.12, page 446), which add to the reader's sense that the project is doable.

A bottom-line consideration for most proposals is cost. Most proposals include budgets and estimations of financial support necessary for the plan either in the body of the document or in the appendix. Although costs may include virtually anything that affects the plan's implementation, the following items are most typical:

- salaries and benefits
- equipment purchases
- meeting expenses
- printing
- operating expenses (telephone, electronic links, fax, photocopying)
- contractor and consultant fees

Figure 15.12 Schedule for Implementation

Schedule

The target day of completion for the proposed project is January 1, 19--. This date represents when the new plant will be able to begin production and all supporting operations. A 23-month schedule incorporating 6 phases has been developed to meet this deadline. As of November 1, 19--, this schedule had been approved by the following parties:

McAnich Construction	General Contractor
Genex Engineering Ltd.	Equipment Manufacturer
Theresa K. Thurston	V.P. - General Counsel
John F. Ford, Jr.	V.P. - Human Resources

The following timeline indicates the length of time each phase will require. This timeline is supplemented by a Phase-Activity Schedule.

Phases I–VI: Time Requirements

```
2 Mos.      4 Mos.      9 Mos.              3 Mos.    3 Mos.     2 Mos.
+------+------------------+--------------------------+----------+------------+-----------+
Phase I     Phase II    Phase III           Phase IV  Phase V    Phase VI
```

Phase-Activity Schedule

Phase	Beginning Date	Activities
Phase I	February 1, 1994	Land Procurement Legal Contracts Financing
Phase II	April 1, 1994	Site Preparation Sewer Installment Road Construction Foundation Poured
Phase III	August 1, 1994	Construction Electrical Plumbing Inspection
Phase IV	April 1, 1995	Equipment Installation Finished Area Drywall Equipment Testing
Phase V	July 1, 1995	Employee Training Office Area Completed
Phase VI	October 1, 1995	Additional Testing Small Batch Production Quality Sampling Production

- supplies and materials
- travel
- books and subscriptions

Proposals with a budget often include a **budget narrative**, which is a brief explanation and rationale for each category or for each line item in the budget. The budget narrative connects the expenses identified in the budget with the plan's implementation. You can use the budget narrative as a way to extend your argument by showing that your plan is not only workable but financially feasible.

The example in Figure 15.13 shows three excerpts from a budget narrative for a three-year project submitted to a federal agency. The excerpts show part of what was included in their respective sections of the budget narrative—travel, materials and supplies, and matching contributions. (The unexcerpted version "unpacked" the various entries in a design with more white space.) Although the budget narrative presumes that readers are familiar with the proposed plan, the explanations consciously repeat the language used earlier in presenting the objectives and solutions. This repetition reinforces the plan and increases the coherence of the entire proposal.

Recommendation

Recommendation sections often repeat the call to adopt the writer's solution. You can treat this section like an action close that recommends actions like letting bids, hiring certain consultants, and setting start-up dates. Figure 15.14 recommends a specific construction firm for a project as well as a completion date. The cost-sharing component of the proposal will be implicitly accepted if Jackson agrees to use the recommended firm. The recommendation here appears together with the implementation, a common occurrence in the concluding section of a proposal.

Figure 15.13 Excerpts from a Budget Narrative

The writer identifies expenses for each year involved in the proposal, because some budget items (e.g., salaries, benefits, travel, consultants' fees, overhead expenses) may be affected by inflation.

She separates administrative trips from conference trips. She relates budget items to the objectives specified in the plan.

The writer is careful to provide a breakdown of expenses, expected in budget narratives. The writer includes examples (50 @ $3) that show how the budget figures were reached.

The writer includes the "matching contributions" of her organization. (An organization may show its financial contribution to a project by calculating the value of elements such as secretarial time or figuring costs such as overhead, which may vary from as little as 10 percent to more than 60 percent of the total budget amount.)

TRAVEL

The travel budget includes an annual trip for two of the project directors to attend the funding agency's meeting each fall. Additionally, the budget includes support for all four principal investigators to present papers about this project at national conferences in the second and third year of the project. This budget covers the basic transportation, registration, hotel, and per diem expenses for meals. Each trip is estimated at $900 for the first year, and, to take inflation into account, $950 for the second year, and $1,000 for the third year. Each conference paper presented by principal investigators will be revised and submitted for publication.

Year 1	Year 2	Year 3
2 trips @ $900 = $1,800	2 trips @ $950 = $1,900	2 trips @ $1,000 = $2,000
	4 trips @ $950 = $3,800	4 trips @ $1,000 = $4,000
$1,800	*$5,700*	*$6,000*

MATERIALS AND SUPPLIES

The majority of the materials and supplies are for two parts of the project: (1) providing detailed accounts of the team training to build collaborative skills and (2) recording interviews with the team members for project evaluation.

Year 1	Year 2	Year 3
audio tapes (450 @ $1)	audio tapes (450 @ $1)	audio tapes (450 @ $1)
video tapes (50 @ $3)	video tapes (50 @ $3)	video tapes (50 @ $3)
photocopying $1,000	photocopying $3,000	photocopying $1,500
disks $100	disks $100	disks $100
office supplies $300	office supplies $500	office supplies $400
$2,000	*$4,200*	*$2,600*

The printing is specifically for (1) the manual developed for the training sessions, (2) the documentation for the hypertext, (3) information packets sent out upon request.

Year 1	Year 2	Year 3
manual $2,000	manual $0	manual $0
documentation $0	documentation $600	documentation $0
PR requests $0	PR requests $1,600	PR requests $1,600
$2,000	*$2,200*	*$1,600*

Example: Manual (100 pages × 400 = 40,000 pages × .04) + $1/binding = $2,000

Example: Documentation (25 pages × 400 = 10,000 × .04) + $.50/binding = $600

MATCHING CONTRIBUTIONS

Secretarial tasks will be supported by the proposing organization. A secretary will be assigned to devote 12.5% of worktime to this project.

Year 1	Year 2	Year 3
salary: $4,832	salary: $5,074	salary: $5,327
12-month benefits:	12-month benefits:	12-month benefits:
% of salary × 39.45% =	% of salary × 39.45% =	% of salary × 39.45% =
$1,906	$2,002	$2,102
$6,738	*$7,076*	*$7,429*

CONTEXT

The owners of a small business adjoining Jackson Bicycle Works have proposed that the fire wall conjoining their two businesses be repaired. Even though the fire wall is shared, the writers own the property actually cited in the Fire Marshal's report and thus propose paying 60% of repairs, with Jackson paying 40%. The situation is complicated by the fact that Jackson's owners live out of state.

Figure 15.14 Recommendation Section of a Proposal

The writers reinforce their credibility as being more than a neighboring business by using the phrase "concerned citizen." Since the work involved is minor, they recommend a contractor and imply that bids do not have to be let. They also show a rationale for deadline.

Recommendation

Our recommendation, both from the standpoint of a neighboring business as well as from that of a concerned citizen, is that Antiques Unlimited and Jackson Bicycle Works contract B.B. Smith Construction Company for the recommended repair work. The contact person at Smith would be:

Joyce Greenlaw, Assistant Manger
B.B. Smith Construction Company
1200 Railroad Avenue
Jackson, MS 39201

Greenlaw can also be reached at 601-555-9000.

We also recommend that the proposed work on the fire wall be completed by July 1, when the next round of city inspections is scheduled to begin.

CONVENTIONAL SEGMENTS OF FEASIBILITY REPORTS

Because feasibility reports can be seen as extensions of the arguments in proposals, it is not surprising that they share many of the same sections. We include here a detailed discussion of those sections unique to feasibility reports.

Criteria

The criteria set forth in a feasibility report allow writers to evaluate various solutions fairly on the basis of reader concerns. As shown in Figure 15.15, criteria often involve the material assets of the company, including personnel; the characteristics of the proposed product, procedure, or policy; issues of deployment; and future developments.

In selecting criteria, you should always include criteria that your readers have stipulated as important, even if these criteria do not point to significant differences between the options. Beyond this, you should focus on those criteria that identify significant differences in the alternatives and should not feel compelled to include every possible means of evaluation.

For example, in the feasibility report written by Scott Construction for the new headquarters for Celestial Seasonings (which was submitted after Scott reviewed Celestial's design criteria, which appear in Chapter 1, page 22), Scott transformed the goals set forth for the project in Celestial's overarching criteria for the assessment of the "Master Plan" alternative recommended in Scott's feasibility report. The goals were first divided into three categories in the Scott report:

- functional goals (e.g., a building that could accommodate 900 employees)
- form goals (e.g., a design that would "project an image of realistic fantasy: real places that are uplifting to the spirit")
- time goals (e.g., a schedule that would have the plant in operation by August 1986)

The Master Plan could thus be evaluated by setting criteria in line with the goals: for example, "Was the recommended alternative successful in 'projecting an image of realistic fantasy'? If so, how so?" All in all, the goals outlined in the first pages of the Scott report could be transformed into 32 criteria for evaluating the Master Plan.

Overview of Alternatives

Unlike proposals, feasibility reports do not have to describe an alternative in detail the first time it is presented. A feasibility report may simply provide a descriptive list of the alternatives first, and then analyze and detail these options in the assessment section.

Figure 15.15 Common Criteria in Feasibility Reports

CATEGORIES OF CRITERIA FOR ASSESSING SOLUTIONS	EXAMPLES OF CRITERIA	SPECIFIC EXCERPTS SHOWING DISCUSSION OF CRITERIA
Material assets	• availability or adaptability of personnel • availability and location of space • cost of purchase, installation, maintenance	"We have *personnel* on staff with appropriate experience. Mary Ashcroft has successfully developed posters and brochures for a wide range of in-house projects and would be able to spearhead publicity efforts."
Characteristics of proposed solution	• scope of coverage, physical dimensions, system requirements • performance specifications • ease of adoption or operation	"Since all employees are required to be to work 5 minutes early anyway, having cashiers count their drawers prior to clocking in could be *easily accomplished.* Cashiers would simply count their drawers in the 5 minutes prior to their shifts and initial the slip of paper provided with each drawer."
Deployment	• training required • compatibility with existing systems or current policies and procedures • lead time needed	"According to net income projections, the expenses required for the improvements outlined in this proposal are *well within the amounts currently budgeted* for repair and maintenance of the facility."
Future developments	• flexibility for expansion or contribution to employee development • legal or ethical implications • environmental impact	"The addition of the safety covers for all electrical outlets will make us *in compliance with all* recently passed federal and state *regulations.*"

If the alternatives to be presented are complex, however, the writer faces the task of providing a description of each alternative in an *overview of alternatives* that is complete enough to serve as a context for understanding the assessment to follow. In other words, readers must be able to picture the various alternatives as a whole before they can compare them according to specific criteria. For example, let's assume you are going to assess the feasibility of using (1) Claim Form A, designed and used by a large corporate insurance firm, (2) Claim Form B, used by a private health care facility, and (3) Claim Form C, which you designed. In this case, your *overview* should provide a specific description of each form and/or reference samples in an appendix, so that the reader will be better able to understand the comparisons being made in terms of criteria such as readability, completeness, appropriateness, and design costs.

Assessment

The **assessment section** in a feasibility study describes and compares the alternatives in detail according to the criteria set up earlier in the report. Assessments can follow different patterns, according to the way they're used (Figure 15.16). In a **partitioned pattern,** the assessment is divided between describing each alternative and comparing each alternative point-by-point by criteria (Figure 15.17, page 450).

In an **integrated pattern,** the assessment is either structured around the alternatives themselves or listed by criteria. Comparisons between alternatives are integrated into the discussion. In Figure 15.18 on the next page the alternatives drive the arrangement. This example discusses one alternative first before concentrating on the comparison of two other alternatives.

A criteria-driven integrated approach is especially useful when criteria are more or less self-evident in the alternatives, and when you know that the reader is going to key in on certain criteria when evaluating the proposal. In Figure 15.19 on the next page, the options of "promoting from within" and "hiring from outside" to fill a vacant managerial position are good examples of alternatives that readers will easily understand. Analysis of these alternatives suffices; no separate description is necessary.

In a **mixed pattern,** the assessment uses an integrated approach to discuss the alternatives in terms of one or more criteria and a partitioned approach to discuss the alternatives in terms of other criteria. A mixed approach allows you to discuss the more abstract criterion in a section of its own to help readers understand what you have in mind. Figure 15.20 (page 451), for example, slates the complex issue of corporate image for a separate section.

A mixed approach also enables you to cover simpler criteria first, before launching into more complex criteria that might entail a number of aspects. You might, for example, use an integrated approach to cover criteria such as "space available" first. You might then use a partitioned approach to discuss a more complex criterion, such as the "ability to attract

Figure 15.16 Assessment Patterns, Uses, and Examples

PATTERN	USE	EXAMPLES
Partitioned	Used to present complex alternatives	Present *alternatives* with a large number of variables, such as designs for a day care center that must meet various and numerous educational criteria, building and fire code criteria, company image criteria, and parental criteria; or *alternatives* which entail a degree of expertise to understand, such as options for engineering a security system; or *alternatives* of any kind that do not have clear-cut strengths and weaknesses
Integrated	Used to cover and then dismiss an alternative at the outset before concentrating on the remaining alternatives for serious consideration; also useful when the nature of the first alternative(s) presented can be easily kept in mind during later discussion of similarities and differences	*Dismiss* the *status quo* as an alternative at the outset before concentrating on whether to build a new practice arena or to renovate current facilities for that use; the *first alternative,* "promoting from within," can be easily kept in mind while going on to discuss the remaining alternative of "hiring from outside"
Mixed	Used when one criterion is either more abstract or more complicated than the others being used to assess feasibility; used when one criterion is more complex than others	Present an *abstract criterion,* such as corporate image, along with *concrete criteria,* such as cost; present a *complex criterion,* such as "ability to attract clients," along with *less complex criteria,* such as "availability of support personnel"

Figure 15.17 Partitioned Pattern for Assessment of Alternatives

Pattern:

Choices considered:

- *option A described in terms of criteria*
- *option B described in terms of criteria*
- *option C described in terms of criteria*

Point-by-point comparison:

- *options A, B, and C compared and contrasted in terms of first criterion*
- *options A, B, and C compared and contrasted in terms of second criterion*
- *options A, B, and C compared and contrasted in terms of third criterion*

Example:

We have three valid options for a revised system of employee review.

- First is a 6-month review cycle based on accountabilities and measures established at each half.
  - ~ 6-month cycle described in terms of legal implications
  - ~ 6-month cycle described in terms of personnel involved
  - ~ 6-month cycle described in terms of employee development
- Second is a project or task oriented review system with each task being monitored at its completion or on a regularly scheduled basis.
  - ~ task system described in terms of legal implications
  - ~ task system described in terms of personnel involved
  - ~ task system described in terms of employee development
- Third is a 3-year review sequence with a standing committee for evaluation purposes.
  - ~ 3-year sequence described in terms of legal implications
  - ~ 3-year sequence described in terms of personnel involved
  - ~ 3-year sequence described in terms of employee development

We can ascertain the relative strengths and weaknesses of each of these options with a point-by-point comparison.

- In comparing the legal implications of the 6-month cycle, the task system, and the 3-year sequence, we see no clear advantage being gained by any option. *[specific discussion of options in terms of legal implications follows]*
- In comparing the personnel involved in each option, we find the 6-month cycle is the least labor intensive, but the most personal; the task sequence is the most labor intensive, and can be either personal or company-oriented; the 3-year sequence is labor intensive for committee members and the most company-oriented. *[specific discussion of the options in terms of the two aspects of personnel involvement—labor and orientation—follows]*
- In comparing options in terms of employee development, we find the 3-year sequence most advantageous for developing individual employee strengths within the context of the company as a whole. *[specific discussion of options in terms of employee development follows]*

Figure 15.18 Integrated Pattern Featuring Alternatives

Pattern:

Description of alternative A in terms of criteria 1, 2, and 3

Description of alternatives B and C with their similarities and differences integrated into the discussion

Example:

<u>Staying in the present location</u> has disadvantages in terms of production capacity, access to markets, and cost.
[analysis of this alternative according to the three criteria follows]

<u>Leasing space at a different site</u> and <u>building an entirely new facility</u> address the problems of production capacity, market access, and cost differently.

- A description of alternatives B and C in terms of production capacity with the similarities and differences between them
- A description of alternatives B and C in terms of access with the similarities and differences between them
- A description of alternatives B and C in terms of initial and ongoing costs with the similarities and differences between them

Figure 15.19 Integrated Pattern Featuring Criteria

Pattern:

- *criterion 1: options A and B compared in terms of criterion 1*
- *criterion 2: options A and B compared in terms of 2*
- *criterion 3: options A and B compared in terms of 3*

Example:

- The potential impact on the morale of present employees of promoting from within versus hiring from outside can be approximated by analyzing survey and interview responses to these options. *[comparison of the alternatives in terms of the criterion of employee morale follows]*
- A cost comparison of promoting from within versus hiring from outside must consider not only the salaries involved, but also recruiting expenses. *[comparison of the alternatives in terms of comparative costs involving salary and recruiting follows]*
- Legal implications, especially in terms of affirmative action issues, complete the criteria for selecting whether to hire from within or without. *[comparison of the alternatives in terms of the criterion of legal implications follows]*

Figure 15.20 Mixed Pattern Using Both a Partitioned and a Criteria-Driven, Integrated Approach

Pattern:

- *choices*
  - *—option A discussed in terms of criteria 1, 2, and 3*
  - *—option B discussed in terms of criteria 1, 2, and 3*
  - *—option C discussed in terms of criteria 1, 2, and 3*
- *point-by-point comparison of A, B, and C according to criteria 1, 2, and 3*
- *criterion three—options A, B, and C compared in terms of criterion 4*

Example:

The three alternatives for proactive publicity can be compared in terms of cost, ability to convey specific information, and dissemination of corporate information (or "reach").

The poster with tear-off response cards is, including bulk rate postage permit, moderate in cost but limited in the amount of information presented. The poster has good dissemination of information when displayed in traffic areas.
[description of this alternative in terms of cost, information conveyed, and reach follows]

The brochure is average in cost for publicity expenditures and can convey a good amount of information, but cannot be easily posted and therefore depends on bulk production and mailing for any kind of good dissemination.
[description of this alternative in terms of cost, information conveyed, and reach follows]

The brochure which, when unfolded, converts into a poster is a bit above average in cost as a publicity item, can convey a good amount of information, and can be posted. When posted, it does not have tear-off response cards.

The poster, brochure, and brochure-poster represent three publicity options that all fall within a reasonable range of expenditure but that show significant differences in terms of ability to carry information and to reach target audiences.
[comparison of the alternatives in terms of range of expenditure and ability to carry information to target audiences follows]

It should also be pointed out that the poster, the brochure, and the brochure-poster contribute differently to the company's image.
[description of the alternatives in terms of corporate image follows]

Figure 15.21 Implementation Section for Feasibility Report

CELESTIAL SEASONINGS' FUTURE ACTIONS

	In order for this Master Plan to be further refined during Schematic Design and Design Development, a number of actions must be taken by Celestial Seasonings:
Phase I Program	Phase I program evaluation must be completed prior to the commencement of Schematic Design. It is anticipated that this activity will be completed during April 1984.
Site Information	Prior to the commencement of Schematic Design, it will be necessary to have updated, accurate topographic and soil analyses of the site. No date has presently been set for completion of this activity.
Agency Activity	During Schematic Design and Design Development, Celestial Seasonings will need to prepare and submit materials for revised Planned Unit Development (PUD) zone designation for the northern 51.2-acre triangular parcel. Initial zoning, annexation and PUD zone designation for the adjacent 40-acre parcel will also be required. This can either be done concurrently with the submittal of the revised PUD or later, prior to use of the 40-acre parcel.
	Also, Celestial Seasonings will need to develop necessary materials to obtain approvals from the Colorado Department of Highways (CDoH) and the Public Utilities Commission (PUC) for the design and implementation of the Gunbarrel Avenue extension from Spine Road to the Diagonal.

clients," that might entail a detailed market analysis of target audiences, an overview of the existing competition, and an outline of available marketing strategies. In short, using a mixed approach allows you to assess alternatives using criteria that differ in kind or complexity.

Implementation

Even though implementation sections are components shared by proposals and feasibility reports, there is a subtle shift in emphasis between the two types. The implementation section of a proposal pictures how the proposed policy, procedure, or innovation could be put into place in the future. The same section in a feasibility report states what should be done so that the plan being recommended can be implemented. This shift in emphasis reflects the underlying difference in the occasion for writing each type of document. The problem solving is in a more advanced stage in the feasibility report than in the proposal.

Figure 15.21 shows the implementation section of Scott Construction's feasibility report for Celestial Seasonings. Scott essentially puts the ball back into Celestial Seasonings' court, stating what Celestial must do to implement the recommended alternative. The title of the section, "Celestial Seasonings' Future Actions," reinforces this sense that ongoing commitment is necessary and more reports are forthcoming.

Figure 15.22 Standard Argumentative Elements in Proposals and Feasibility Reports

ARGUMENTATIVE COMPONENT	APPLICATION TO PROPOSALS AND FEASIBILITY REPORTS
Claim	The idea that is presented in the proposal or feasibility study as the appropriate or best way of addressing the situation outlined in the background and needs sections. A proposal typically has one claim; a feasibility report commonly features competing claims (the various alternatives assessed by the writer).
Grounds or evidence	The evidence of a problem that usually appears in the background and needs sections of a proposal or the introductory section of a feasibility study. The grounds often entail claims of fact. Thus, even though proposals and feasibility studies feature claims of policy and value, respectively, each has claims of fact to support the existence of a problem or the need for a change.
Warrant	The benefits, outlined in a proposal or feasibility study, that provide a justification—in terms of reader benefit—for addressing the problem in the way proposed. In a larger sense, background and needs sections provide the warrant for writing a proposal in the first place. The background and needs, however, do not provide the warrant for the idea presented within the proposal itself. Similarly, the existence of alternative ideas or claims might be seen as the warrant for writing a feasibility report in the first place. But each claim must be justified in the report.
Backing	Provides additional support that the idea is safe or valid. An implementation section can be thought of as backing, because it explains how the company can profitably (safely) pursue the writer's plan.
Modal qualifiers	Qualifiers that indicate the strength of the step taken from facts or information to claim. Proposals usually assume "certainly" as their modal qualifier; feasibility studies analyze the relative certainty of a number of options. Modality in a feasibility report is then expressed in the comparative appropriateness of each alternative.
Rebuttal	Appears in feasibility reports, where various alternatives are analyzed and several are set aside in favor of the one solution which seems most tenable.

PRINCIPLES OF ARGUMENT IN PROPOSALS AND FEASIBILITY REPORTS

Because both proposals and feasibility reports are persuasive in nature, they incorporate many principles basic to argumentation itself.

Argumentative Elements

You can create persuasive proposals and feasibility reports with the help of Toulmin's six argumentative elements—claim, grounds, warrant, backing, modality, rebuttal. Proposals usually feature the first four elements. It is not unusual for feasibility reports to have all six. Figure 15.22 shows how Toulmin's elements apply to these documents.

Figure 15.23 should help you picture how argumentative elements appear in proposals. This example *does not* represent the proposal in its entirety. The claim alone, when presented in the actual proposal, entailed two pages describing exactly the type of facility the writer had in mind.

Single-Option Feasibility Reports as Recommendation Reports

Feasibility reports that focus on showing the feasibility of a single alternative can be viewed as a type of **recommendation report.** They represent the "end of the line" of the proposal-feasibility argument and establish the reader's best option.

Figure 15.24 (page 454) is such a report in memo format. The memo summarizes the proposal and feasibility stages of the line of argument in the opening sentence: "After months of analysis [proposal stage] and the investigation of a wide variety of alternatives . . ." [feasibility report stage]. Previous oral discussion and written documents on this issue have established, for example, the needs arising out of the situation, the corresponding benefits of proposed changes, and the relative feasibility of the various options. As essentially the last document in a series, this recommendation report reinforces the idea that (1) proposals and feasibility reports extend the same line of argument and (2) more than one report can be issued on a single topic or project. A subsequent feasibility or recommendation report based on the results of the 6-month direct marketing test described in Figure 15.24, for example, would be a natural outgrowth of the situation.

Figure 15.23 Argumentative Elements in a Proposal's Line of Argument

Grounds:	There are no on-site child care facilities at Brown and Associates.
Implicit Warrant (Assumption):	*[It is within the scope of corporations to be concerned about child care facilities for their employees.]*
Grounds:	The nearest child care facilities for preschool children are located 3 and 6 miles, respectively, from corporate offices. There are no facilities available for children of school age.
Explicit Warrant:	Thus, parents cannot easily visit their little ones during the course of the workday.
Explicit Warrant:	This lack of accessibility is especially hard on nursing mothers who feel they must race to meet feeding schedules on their breaks. In addition, school-age children often become latch-key children.
Explicit Warrant: / modality expressed in verb "may be"	The lack of adult supervision for elementary school children in particular may be one cause for low productivity between the hours of 3:30 and 5:00 p.m. among employees with children home alone.
Implicit Warrant (Assumption):	*[Parents will naturally be concerned about their infant and older, unsupervised children, and these concerns will affect their performance on the job.]*
Grounds:	Absentee rates among employees who are parents with young children are running at 12%.
Explicit Warrant:	When surveyed, these employees stated that about 75% of their absences were due to child care difficulties.
Backing:	The lack of child care is thus costing Brown and Associates about $750 per month in wages paid for substitutes and about $900 per month in lost productivity.
Implicit Warrant (Assumption):	*[Brown and Associates cannot continue to shoulder these costs.]*
Claim:	Brown and Associates should establish a day care facility on-site which could handle care for preschoolers and after school programs for school-age children of employees.
Explicit Warrant:	With day care facilities on-site, parents would have immediate access to their preschoolers. . . .
Explicit Warrant:	With on-site facilities, availability of child care would be assured, thus reducing absences.
Backing:	A survey of employees showed that 75% of parents with preschoolers would be interested in visiting their children during lunch if an on-site facility were available.
Explicit Warrant:	Costs associated with lost productivity would also be reduced.
Backing:	Costs associated with lost productivity at Image Productions and at Grandy Manufacturing were reduced 50% after on-site day care facilities were installed.
Explicit Warrant:	An on-site child care facility is feasible.
Backing:	Costs associated with the establishment of an on-site child care facility would be recouped in three years.
Backing:	Recruiting of excellent employees would be enhanced, contributing to the overall effectiveness of the company.
Claim (roughly restated):	We, therefore, urge that the following steps be taken to establish an on-site facility at Brown and Associates.

HOW PROPOSALS AND FEASIBILITY REPORTS ARE EVALUATED

Readers evaluate proposals and feasibility reports according to any number of criteria, depending on the funding source or the site of implementation.

Demonstrating a **shared agreement** between writer and reader is frequently important in both proposals and feasibility reports. For proposals, writer and readers must agree on the questions to be answered and must share an understanding of the solution being proposed, the benefits involved, and the ways the writer and reader will work together as a team to implement the solution. For feasibility reports, a shared agreement between writer and reader about the criteria for evaluating solutions is crucial.

In Figure 15.25 (page 455), the writer presents criteria for evaluating several alternative safety training programs, including the Safety Training Observation Program (STOP), in a molecular screening lab. Because of on-site research she has done—interviewing fellow employees, checking company records, and researching the STOP program as it has been implemented at other sites—the writer can assume that the criteria she poses both address concerns of managers and employees alike and represent a shared understanding between

Figure 15.24 Report Recommending One Alternative

The exact percentages have been omitted from this figure at the request of the memo's author for reasons of confidentiality.

Southwest Silver and Such — Memorandum

DATE: July 30, 1994

TO: James Finnegan
John Wolf
Beverly Smithson

FROM: Val Green

After months of analysis and the investigation of a wide variety of alternatives, I recommend we proceed with a limited 6-month test of direct marketing of Southwest merchandise through our jewelry boxes and our crates and canisters. This test will be executed though the business structure of a partnership between Southwest and Black Canyon Alliance, Inc. (a Santa Fe based marketing firm whose principals have significant direct marketing experience).

The test calls for the insertion of "mini-catalogs" into jewelry boxes, crates, and canisters offering a variety of products, including art prints, wildlife T-shirts, hand-loomed rugs, leather goods, and jewelry items. This test is designed to use our existing inventories of specialty products with a wide cushion for large response rates. The beauty of this initial test as proposed is that Southwest's capital contribution to the partnership is used to purchase inventories we already own. We would sell the inventory to the partnership at a 10% mark-up. We also realize revenue by marking up the cost of inserting the catalogs into our jewelry boxes, and crates and canisters. And, of course, Southwest will ultimately make money as a 50% partner in the partnership.

Attached are complete financial projections for the business at various consumer response levels. A break-even response rate is projected at __%. Given that these mini-catalogs are being delivered directly to our consumers, I am confident that we will exceed this response rate and make money on this test. Concerns about an overwhelming consumer response are addressed by the fact that the delivery of the mini-catalog container inserts will be staggered over a long enough time frame for us to easily accommodate response rates upward of __%! Because Southwest has already committed to the purchase of a significant quantity of art prints and T-shirts, this proposed partnership/test is the ideal way to determine the viability of a direct marketing program, sell existing inventory, and create a channel of distribution for additional Southwest merchandise as it is produced by our licensees. (The ability to guarantee the purchase of a quantity of licensed products significantly facilitates Southwest's ability to secure such licenses.)

I spoke with our licensing agent, Adam Berger, about the alternative of licensing a catalog company to take over and run a Southwest direct marketing program without our involvement (paying us a royalty on sales). Adam said we would be far better off to conduct this initial test ourselves, by way of the partnership I propose, so that if the test is successful and we decide we want to license out our direct marketing business, we will have an existing track record and a database of customers to bring to the table. If licensing is ultimately chosen over partnership or in-house approach, we will thus be able to make the best deal with the best direct marketing company.

Under the circumstances, I believe the proposed structure is a super deal for Southwest which will cost us very little for a money-making "learningful" test of a potentially huge business. The capital call for the partnership is $85,000, approximately $77,000 of which will be paid back to Southwest for the purchase of our inventory, making the outlay of additional cash to conduct the test minimal, because of our existing inventory commitment. Black Canyon Alliance will also contribute $85,000, which spreads half of the risk of the test to them. The ROI on this test at a response rate of __% is 15.4% for the 6 month test. At a __% response rate the ROI is 146%! Please review the attached projections. If the test is approved, the next step will be to enter into a partnership agreement and proceed with the execution of the mini-catalog.

writer and users of how to evaluate each of the alternatives explored in the report. The "warrants" mentioned in the annotations represent justifications of the criteria being offered.

In addition to creating a general sense of shared agreement, you should also consider the six concerns listed in Figure 15.26 (page 456) and the strategies for addressing them. Although you can directly address these six general concerns, you usually cannot directly affect other concerns important to the evaluation of a proposal or feasibility report:

- the amount of money available
- any "hidden agenda" or proposal evaluators
- the credibility of other proposers
- previous success rate (while writers can improve their own success rates by getting grants themselves, they do not control the pool of applicants and, consequently, do not directly control how their rate measures up to that of others)

Remember that your proposal will usually be competing with other proposals. In highly competitive situations, you can almost expect to be turned down, especially the first or second time you seek support or approval. You should, therefore, be prepared to revise and resubmit your proposal as part of the proposal process.

ETHICS

ETHICS IN PROPOSAL WRITING: FUNDING OR FLEECING?

As the accompanying table attests, sometimes a surprising amount of funding is granted by government agencies to those promising to address some pretty amazing research questions or problems.

Research Funded by Successful Proposals to Government Agencies

Research Question or Subject	Funding Source	Award
What was the African climate during the last Ice Age?	National Science Foundation	$121,000
What are the major characteristics of primate teeth?	Internal Revenue Service	$25,000
Why do people fall in love?	National Science Foundation	$84,000,000
Why do rats clench their teeth?	Office of Naval Research	$500,000
Why are people rude on tennis courts?	National Endowment for the Humanities	$2,500
How long does it take to cook breakfast?	U.S. Department of Agriculture	$46,000
How do you feel about large trucks on the highway?	Federal Highway Administration	$222,000 and $297,633
Are sunfish that drink tequila more aggressive than sunfish that drink gin?	National Institute on Alcohol Abuse and Alcoholism	$102,000
Does runoff from open stacks of cow manure cause pollution?	Environmental Protection Agency	$38,174
Do college students, when watching television, differentiate fact from fiction?	Office of Education	$219,592

In *Academic Gamesmanship*, Pierre L. Van den Berghe remarks, tongue in cheek, that "in drafting a research proposal, the primary concern should be to write it in such a way as to appear worthwhile to the evaluators rather than to give a candid description of what you intend or hope to accomplish; hence the need for dishonesty."

Not only do such documents raise fiscal and ethical issues, but they also demonstrate that research and development labs are capable of inventing an astonishing array of "solutions" to problems. Consider, for example, the U.S. Army Research and Development Laboratory in Natick, Massachusetts, which has brought us both useful products such as Gore-Tex, freeze-dried foods, and instant coffee and some questionable inventions as well, such as air-conditioned underwear and Vietnam War–era combat boots with soles shaped like the footprints of Vietnamese peasants. "The boots," admitted a Natick spokesperson in retrospect, "had limited use."

Figure 15.25 Writer Criteria and Reader Expectations Linked in a Shared Understanding of Factors Important to Evaluation

The first criterion is followed by a warrant. (The need for updating was emphasized in the lab history.) The second has warrants based on observations and company records.

The third presents a warrant based on employee interviews; the fourth on management's concerns about cost.

The fifth has two warrants. The goal of changing behaviors and attitudes is derived from research on safety; the 50% figure, on the reduction rate at other sites.

CRITERIA FOR IMPLEMENTING A SAFETY PROGRAM

There are five criteria essential to evaluating the alternative safety training programs available to us.

First, a safety program must be flexible. Safety hazards encountered in the laboratory are constantly changing. Therefore, a safety program that can be updated to meet the needs of new situations is crucial to providing a safe working environment.

Second, a program needs to be adaptable. The structure of the Molecular Screening Lab is very complex. Three biology laboratories combined with storage and work rooms comprise the entire Molecular Screening Lab. Also, a wide variety of equipment and chemicals make the lab extremely susceptible to accidents. As a result, a program must adapt and provide safe working situations for the different areas of the lab.

In addition, a program should provide training that is easy for employees to learn and use. Because the Molecular Screening Lab is a very complex working environment, it is important that everyone involved in the lab be able to comprehend and use safety procedures.

Also, a safety program must be cost efficient. The monetary benefits must outweigh the cost of implementing a program. Since the Molecular Biology Lab is on a restricted budget, the program must prove beneficial to justify spending limited funds.

Finally, a safety program must be effective. Not only must the program train employees, but it needs to change their behavior. Safety is a long-term issue. Therefore, employees must change their attitudes and behaviors to create a safe working environment. In addition, after implementation, a program must reduce the number of accidents in the laboratory by 50%.

Figure 15.26 Concerns and Strategies Involved in Proposal or Feasibility Report Evaluation

CONCERN	STRATEGY
Demonstrating significance of problem or need	Background and needs sections are convincing in dramatizing the seriousness or significance of the problem.
Matching solution to problem	Articulated benefits address the previously outlined needs.
Specifying situational criteria	Proposal or study follows format stipulated in RFP, addresses any known criteria (e.g., necessary budget information researched), and adheres to given deadlines.
"Packaging" the proposal attractively	Oral and written presentation of materials is error-free and uses the best available visual support.
Observing the "politeness" principle	Discussion is positive (doesn't disparage others' ideas or work); is courteous; provides necessary definitions, table of contents, etc.
Appealing to communicator credibility and expertise	In addition to or in place of a qualifications section, functional resumes included with the proposal or feasibility report establish the writer's qualifications to comment on the problem, to propose the idea, and to complete the project; the roles of multiple investigators are clearly established; previous successes are indicated.

EXAMPLE OF A PROPOSAL

The competitive nature of writing proposals affects both their packaging and their presentation. The proposal in Figure 15.27 (on the next four pages) is framed like a letter but uses callouts, graphics, and headings and subheadings like a report. Its unique but professional presentation is one way the writer calls attention to her work. You will also note that the proposal does not slavishly fit information into set categories, such as "needs" and "proposed idea," but adjusts the coverage of such components to fit the situation. This proposal also includes discussion of the writer's qualifications in the idea portion (see the Skills and Strategies box, page 439).

CONTEXT

El Camino Associates is a consulting firm which specializes in systems management but which handles a wide range of organizational and management issues. Randy Sanchez, new to management at Frox, Inc., a recently established computer firm specializing in entertainment products, asked El Camino Associates to submit a proposal that will address efficiency problems at Frox. The writer for El Camino, Janet Renze, identifies Frox's needs in her background ("situation") section, states her idea or proposal in her "methodology" section, supplies aspects of feasibility in her "qualifications" section, and shows benefits under "benefits." Her "action close" implies Frox's recommended course of action: call us at El Camino to set up a meeting to discuss feasibility and costs.

Figure 15.27 Proposal Using Letter Format

El Camino Associates

315 Ellis Avenue
Mountain View, CA 94040

May 3, 1994

Randy Sanchez
Frox, Inc.
4500 Sandia Way
Sunnyvale, CA 94036

Dear Randy:

Thank you for this opportunity to present El Camino's proposal for a study to improve efficiency at Frox. We believe that this study would provide you with a plan for improving efficiency at Frox now, as well as one that would complement your projected needs.

The Situation at Frox, Inc.

In 1986, Frox, Inc., launched into the new world bridging home entertainment systems and personal computers with the Wondra system. The system's innovative product features—such as the patented one-button remote, jukebox sound feature, and lifelike screen resolution—all stunned competitors and quickly captured a large segment of high-end buyers.

% of Market Share for 3 Major Home Entertainment System Manufacturers

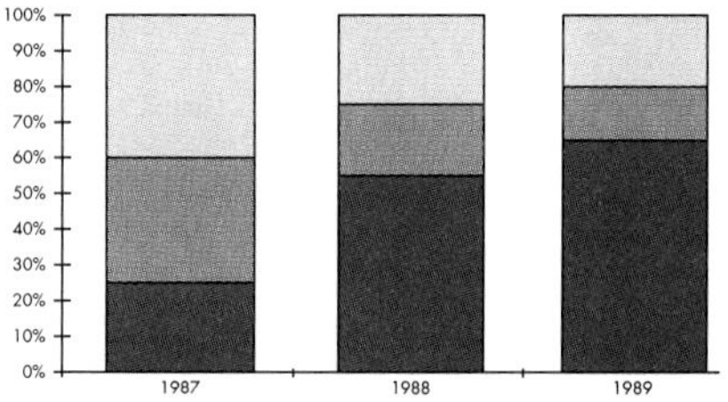

Proposal to Frox, Inc. *Page 1*

Figure 15.27 Proposal Using Letter Format (Continued)

El Camino Associates

The group of engineers and entrepreneurs that founded Frox pooled ideas and resources to develop an unparalleled interactive home entertainment system. But similar to many start-up companies, there was little internal, not to mention corporate, structure. All employees performed multiple roles in the company, driven by the concept of an exciting new product. Camaraderie and a common drive kept employees both motivated and focused. "Band-Aids" were the fix for problems as they arose.

When you joined Frox in 1989, the lack of structure was causing problems with many departments. Frox was still making products and progress, but the carefree management style that had been the rule would not work for the challenges in the rapidly changing high-tech marketplace. Too many people were doing their "own thing" and efficiency was a secondary concern to releasing new products. You devised a new organizational structure, and implemented new policies and procedures. Efficiency shot up, Frox enjoyed renewed success, and employees grew comfortable with these new procedures.

In 1992 and 1993, the Wondra system underwent a redesign to counter recent releases by competition. These new product enhancements necessitated hiring large numbers of engineers and programmers. The majority of available resources was, in fact, pumped into hiring and product development. Hiring of support personnel and computer procurement were delayed until January 1994 so that resources could be focused on the system redesign.

Professional Staff Hired vs. Support Staff, 1989-1993

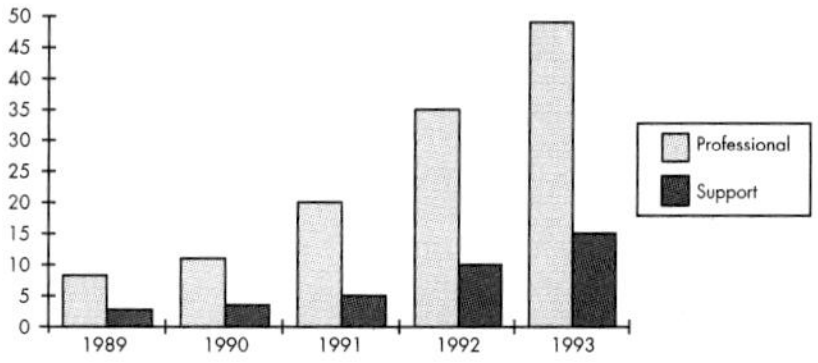

Proposal to Frox, Inc. *Page 2*

Figure 15.27 Proposal Using Letter Format (Continued)

El Camino Associates

Yet because of your current financial constraints, hiring new support staff and buying new computers is not possible. The current downtrend in research investments, which Frox depends on, has also taken its toll. For instance, the InterComp Foundation, which awarded Frox $750,000 in research grants last year, has decreased its award to $200,000 this year.

Percentage of InterComp Grant in Proportion to Total Budget

Frox can hold on until holiday buying pumps in much needed cash flow, but until then, inefficiencies need to be reduced.

To alleviate some of these problems, Frox is considering several options. These options include hiring temporary employees, leasing additional equipment, instituting flex-time, or some combination of the above.

Complicating your need to move quickly is the need to have a carefully developed plan. A quick fix now may not work into the long-term. The plan you need should answer questions such as:

Key Questions

- What resources can be evaluated to determine efficiency?
  - Professional staff
  - Support staff
  - Equipment shortages
- Considering these resources, which options will best increase efficiency?
  - Hiring temporary employees
  - Leasing equipment
  - Instituting flex-time
  - Devising a combination plan
- How will implementation of one of more of these options affect Frox now and in the future?

Proposal to Frox, Inc. *Page 3*

Figure 15.27 Proposal Using Letter Format (Continued)

El Camino Associates

What Frox Needs in This Engagement

To help answer these critical questions in a timely manner, you need a study methodology that will enable you to select the most effective options to increase efficiency. Factors that must be evaluated include employee satisfaction, your desire for minimal interruption, and costs of each option.

You need a firm that has intimate knowledge of your company. This will facilitate getting answers that you can use—solutions that will help preserve your family atmosphere, keep employees focused, and develop an orientation for both the short- and long-term goals of Frox.

You also need a firm you can work with, one that will compile information quickly, obtain results quickly, and provide reliable, realistic results.

After carefully considering your needs, we have devised a methodology that will not only identify immediate ways to increase efficiency, but a concrete plan for implementing the one that will maintain family atmosphere and future growth. You will know what option or options will lead your company to greater efficiency and higher productivity both now and down the line.

Methodology

During our initial meeting, you stressed your desire to forge a close working relationship with your consultant. To ensure you have a significant role in this engagement, El Camino will form a study team consisting of Frox representatives you designate and El Camino analysts. The members from El Camino will have areas of expertise in human resources, operations, and MIS. The team will make use of market forecasts, employment reports and other data to make recommendations. The team will have frequent contact during the engagement to address new concerns and questions.

Early in the engagement, we will have a kick-off meeting with all Frox employees to inform everyone of our involvement, alleviate any fears of extensive time requirements on their part, and to solicit questions about the engagement. As a result of this meeting, we hope to address concerns of all employees.

Proposal to Frox, Inc. *Page 4*

Figure 15.27 Proposal Using Letter Format (Continued)

El Camino Associates

To complete this engagement, we will conduct four major tasks so that you will be provided with the best possible plan. Specifically, we will:

- identify required personnel and equipment resources
- investigate potential plans and their feasibility
- determine short- and long-term effectiveness of each option
- select the most appropriate option and formulate a plan to implement the option or options.

Each of these is elaborated below.

Task #1. Identify Required Resources

What factors are involved in your current crunch? Is a shortage of people in general your biggest factor for inefficiency? Do you primarily need secretaries? Or clerks (to work on inventory, accounting, payroll)?

Would having more personal computers help increase efficiency? Or better software programs? How about your filing system? Is it the most effective one possible?

To answer these questions and to form a valid assessment of your situation we will:

- ♦ identify abilities and needs of professional staff
- ♦ identify abilities and needs of support staff
- ♦ identify equipment needs of all employees

By correctly identifying each of these three areas at this point, we will have the most current information possible, as well as information for making sound decisions later in the engagement.

Task #2. Investigate Potential Options and Their Feasibility

Once we identify your greatest needs, we will investigate potential options to increase efficiency at Frox. Our company will investigate "friendly" options—screened temps with above-average skills, easy-to-use equipment, and flex-time options. To do this we will:

- ♦ contact temporary agencies
- ♦ inquire about leasing additional hardware and software
- ♦ survey effects in companies that switch to flex-time
- ♦ consider combinations of options

This specific information will help us effectively match needs with resources to increase efficiency. After gathering this information we will also have a foundation for future decisions on which option or options to select.

Proposal to Frox, Inc. *Page 5*

Figure 15.27 Proposal Using Letter Format (Continued)

El Camino Associates

Task #3. Determine Short- and Long-Term Effectiveness of Options

The options we consider must fit criteria mentioned above, namely, working for both the short- and long-term.
To confirm that the recommended plan will work, we will:

- ♦ confirm market forecast
- ♦ determine if selected options facilitate growth

We will do this by comparing information from many different sources.

Task #4. Select the Most Appropriate Option and Formulate a Plan

The Frox–El Camino team will form a plan, based on all the information available, for which option or options should be implemented to best increase efficiency at Frox. You will know that this decision has been made logically and will work for you.

Qualifications of El Camino Associates

El Camino Associates has diverse capabilities to help you consider each option and to complete this engagement. Specifically:

- El Camino Associates can start immediately
- I know the Frox atmosphere
- we will avoid interruptions
- El Camino will plan for your immediate needs and consider your growing future

El Camino Associates Can Start Immediately

There is a break in our schedule, so we have staff available to perform this study. All our consultants are adept at performing studies against pressing deadlines, and will work with the necessary staff to provide you with a feasible plan, *as soon as possible.* We have experience in human resources and knowledge of many computer systems, especially in high-tech industries, so our learning curve will be short.

I Know the Frox Atmosphere

Since I have experience with the family atmosphere at Frox, I know how important it is for you to maintain. By working in human resources at Frox and helping bring people aboard, I developed an intimate knowledge of your organizational structure. After completing an MBA and working with a consulting company, I have experience with developing plans to increase efficiency. I have a special tie to the people at Frox, and want to help your company succeed. But I also have objectivity from time away and can therefore provide a fresh insight on your current situation.

Proposal to Frox, Inc. *Page 6*

Figure 15.27 Proposal Using Letter Format (Continued)

El Camino Associates

We Will Avoid Interruptions

My familiarity with Frox will facilitate identification of key people to meet with, thus *avoiding unnecessary interruptions.* By going directly to critical people within Frox—instead of interrupting multiple people or setting meetings that involve too many people—we can save time and disruptions. This will help your people stay on track now, as well as when the plan is implemented.

El Camino Will Plan for Your Immediate Needs, and Consider Your Future Growth

The management and corporate planning experience of El Camino consultants will help in focusing on options that address your *immediate and future needs.* El Camino has experience screening various options you are investigating, such as temporary employees. In addition, we have knowledge of current software and hardware releases that could help make better use of your time.

Benefits

The logical methodology we are proposing and the capable staff we will assign to this engagement will produce a sound, beneficial study. Following are the benefits we believe you will receive from our efforts.

Quick, Quality Results

Our team will devote all available resources to develop the best plan possible, in a time frame you can work with. El Camino consultants have the capability to work quickly to provide you with results you can have confidence in.

A Team That Will Work with You

El Camino has a knowledgeable and qualified staff ready to work with Frox and will consider your best interests at all times. That means letting Frox employees work with minimal interruptions, and finding options for increasing efficiency that will fit into your current overall structure.

A Plan That Will Work Now, As Well As into the Future

Because of the insights you will be presented with, you will be assured of a plan that will be helpful for both your short- and long-term needs. Whatever ideas are considered must allow Frox the ability to maintain operations now and expand in the future.

Proposal to Frox, Inc. *Page 7*

Figure 15.27 Proposal Using Letter Format (Continued)

El Camino Associates

Randy, thanks for your time. El Camino is ready to help and is looking forward to the chance to work with Frox, Inc. We have an understanding of your situation, knowledge of the high-tech industry, and resources available to complete this engagement. We would like to visit more in person to review our methodology and establish costs of the engagement. I will give you a call by Friday to set up a meeting.

Sincerely yours,

Janet L. Renze, Partner
El Camino Associates

Proposal to Frox, Inc. *Page 8*

RESPONSE SHEET

PROPOSALS

WRITER(S): AUDIENCE(S):
OCCASION FOR WRITING: DOCUMENT:
WHAT PROBLEM OR ISSUE IS THE WRITER TRYING TO ADDRESS IN THIS DOCUMENT?

◆ PROPOSAL SITUATION

What the readers have:

What the readers want:

What the readers will receive from the writer:

◆ REPORT FRAMEWORK CONSIDERATIONS

What framework sections are appropriate to this proposal? Describe.

- Purpose section—What is the subject; what are the writer's specific aims?
- Methods and scope sections—What was the writer's method of inquiry or procedure; what are the boundaries of the discussion, e.g., limitations, task breakdown, criteria?

◆ CONVENTIONAL COMPONENTS

How should/does the writer handle the conventional tasks of a proposal in writing about this subject? Explain.

- Does the proposal need a separate background section to establish historical or contextual detail necessary to understanding the proposal? Explain.
- How should/does the writer dramatize the problem that has initiated the proposal?
- How should/does the writer detail the proposed solution to address the problem?
- How should/does the writer show the benefits to be gained by addressing the problem as outlined in the idea section?

Do the writer's benefits "match" needs or problems covered in the needs section? How so?

- Would it be appropriate in this proposal to include additional benefits not directly tied to previously established needs? If so, name those additional benefits.
- Would it be appropriate to include an implementation section in this proposal? If so, what aspects should/does the writer cover (budget, schedule, personnel, facilities)?
- How should/does the writer urge acceptance of the proposal and facilitate action?

How can the writer make improvements in handling each of these tasks? (Make suggestions directly on the draft, if available.)

RESPONSE SHEET

FEASIBILITY REPORTS

WRITER(S): AUDIENCE(S):
OCCASION FOR WRITING: DOCUMENT:
WHAT PROBLEM OR ISSUE IS THE WRITER TRYING TO ADDRESS IN THIS DOCUMENT?

◆ FEASIBILITY REPORT SITUATION

What the readers have:

What the readers want:

What options the readers have for solution(s), or what they will receive:

What option is best in terms of what the reader will receive:

◆ REPORT FRAMEWORK CONSIDERATIONS

What framework sections are appropriate to this report? Describe.

- Purpose section—what is the subject; what are the writer's specific aims?
- Methods and scope sections—what was the writer's method of inquiry or procedure; what are the boundaries of the discussion, e.g., limitations, task breakdown, criteria?

◆ CONVENTIONAL COMPONENTS

How should/does the writer handle the conventional tasks of a feasibility report in writing about this subject? Explain.

- Does the report need to include any background material to establish historical or contextual detail? Explain.
- What criteria will be used to evaluate the alternatives to be presented in the report—e.g., material assets of the company; the characteristics of the proposed product, procedure, or policy; issues of deployment; and future developments?
- How should/does the writer dramatize the problem that has initiated the alternatives to be discussed in the feasibility report?
- How should/does the writer present the overview of alternatives?
- How should/does the writer assess the alternatives?
- Should/does the writer select a partitioned, an integrated, or a mixed approach? Explain.
- Are the benefits of each alternative tied to previously established needs? How so?
- Would it be (was it) appropriate to include an implementation section in this feasibility report? If so, what aspects should/does the writer cover (budget, schedule, personnel, facilities)?
- How should/does the writer urge acceptance of the recommendation(s) and facilitate action?

How can the writer make improvements in handling each of these tasks? (Make suggestions directly on the draft, if available.)

ACTIVITIES, EXERCISES, AND ASSIGNMENTS

◆ IN-CLASS ACTIVITIES

1. Please refer to Figure 15.1 for the following activity.

   a. On the basis of your own observations, compare and contrast the way proposals and the way letters and memos address reader resistance. Does Figure 15.1 dramatize any of these similarities or differences?

   b. Do you think the writer in Figure 15.1 is an insider or an outsider to Delta Manufacturing? Do you think the proposal was solicited or unsolicited? Discuss the differences the writer's and the proposal's status might make.

2. Imagine that several of your co-workers invariably submit recommendation reports, even when they have been requested to write either proposals or feasibility reports. Because you commonly do not make the same mistake, you have been asked to "brief" these co-workers on the similarities and differences between these conventional types of documents. Prepare your oral briefing. (You might review what Chapter 14 has to say about recommendation reports as a first step.) Be sure to include in your preparation presentation aids and handouts that you think would be helpful to your colleagues.

◆ INDIVIDUAL AND GROUP EXERCISES

1. You will have to do research in the library or your college's grant office to complete this exercise.

   a. Look up several funding sources that circulate guidelines for submitting proposals, and/or locate some specific RFPs.

   b. Collaboratively, discuss differences in formats and requirements among three different RFPs. Write a memo to your instructor that details these differences.

2. Please refer to Figure 15.28 to complete this exercise.

   a. Comment on the effectiveness of the presentation of needs in this excerpt. Does it show that the problem(s) definitely warrant attention? Explain.

   b. Remembering the discussion of the dangers of relating negative background material in the opening section of a

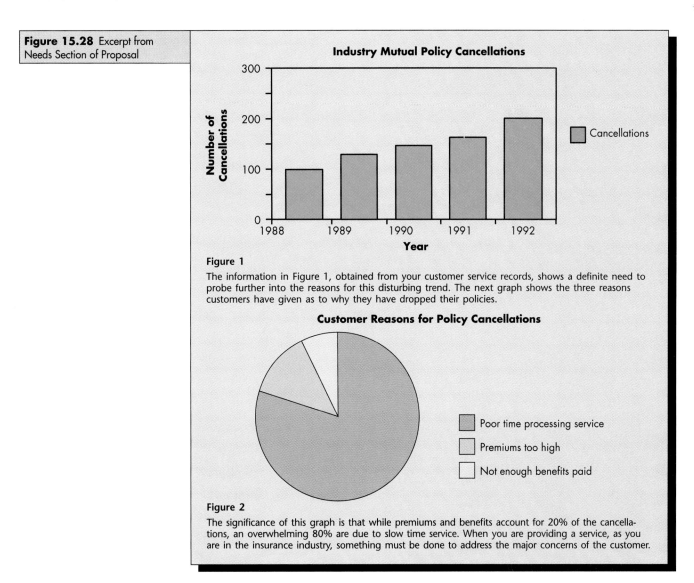

Figure 15.28 Excerpt from Needs Section of Proposal

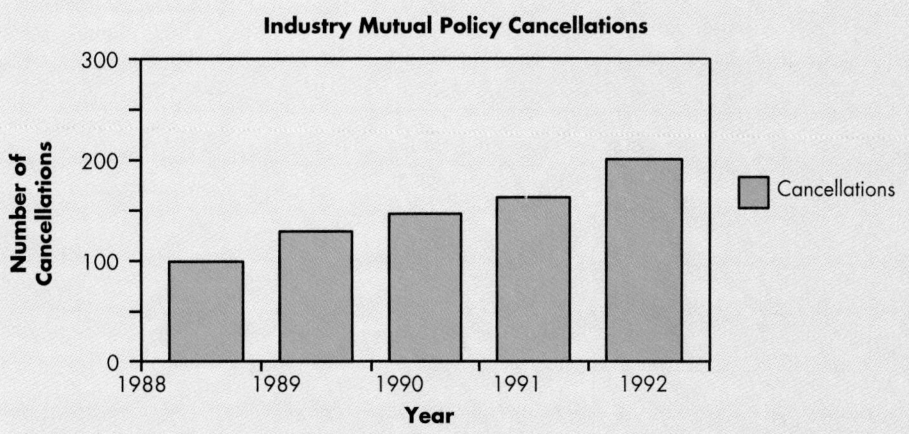

Figure 1

The information in Figure 1, obtained from your customer service records, shows a definite need to probe further into the reasons for this disturbing trend. The next graph shows the three reasons customers have given as to why they have dropped their policies.

Figure 2

The significance of this graph is that while premiums and benefits account for 20% of the cancellations, an overwhelming 80% are due to slow time service. When you are providing a service, as you are in the insurance industry, something must be done to address the major concerns of the customer.

proposal, comment on whether or not the writers are successful in presenting the insurance company's problem(s) without giving offense. (You might also review the use of "you" in negative messages when answering this question, page 111.)

c. The writers dramatize the *needs* both in text and in visual form. Comment on the mix of text and visuals here. Do you think it is effective? Explain.

d. Comment on how this material would be presented differently if used as background in a feasibility report.

3. Please refer to Figure 15.29 when completing this exercise.

   a. Figure 15.29 refers to itself several times as a proposal. Review the Response Sheets on proposals and on feasibility reports. Is the memo a proposal, a feasibility report, or a recommendation report, or does it straddle the fence between these types of documents? Explain.

   b. What difference does the type of document (proposal or feasibility report) make to the writer? To the readers?

4. Please review the needs section shown in Figure 15.28, making any necessary improvements.

5. Review Figure 15.29. Please decide what type of document you want to write and then revise the memo in Figure 15.29 accordingly.

◆ OUT-OF-CLASS ACTIVITIES

1. Identify a problem or need on your campus, in your workplace, or in your community which you have the knowledge or skills to analyze and for which you can then propose a solution. Problems might include inadequate library hours, insufficient workplace child care facilities, inadequate training for temporary employees, or inaccurate inventory records. Prepare a *proposal* with the necessary sections. Use the Response Sheet on proposals to help you.

2. Identify a problem or need on your campus, in your workplace, or in your community which you have the knowledge or skills to analyze and for which you can then propose a series of solutions. Problems might include selecting the most appropriate spreadsheet software, assessing options for employee medical coverage, determining the safest air-filtering system, or recommending departmental reorganization. Prepare a *feasibility report* with the necessary sections. Use the Response Sheet on feasibility reports to help you.

CASE

PIZZA PLACE POLICY

CASE BY ANDREA BREEMER FRANTZ

Background Information. You are a manager of a Pizza Place restaurant in Houston, Texas. Over the past two years, three of your employees have been robbed or assaulted while attempting to deliver pizzas in a particularly high-crime area of the city (Neighborhood Z). Neighborhood Z is one of the poorest areas of the city, supports a great deal of drug trafficking, and is the most ethnically diverse (supporting 23 percent Hispanics, 27 percent African Americans, 17 percent Asians, 29 percent Caucasians, and 4 percent unspecified). The Houston

Figure 15.29 Memo "Proposing" a Magazine Resource Center

June 25, 1993

To: Mike Bruder
Fr: Frank Racioppi
Re: Magazine Resource Center

One of the most critical resources for a Communications department is available information. Although the archives is an important resource for historical data, there is presently no resource for current material such as magazines and newspapers.

My proposal hopes to improve everyone's access to important information and make us more responsive to clients. What I propose is a Magazine Resource Center. This center--set up in the archives and administered by Fran Gasper--would store magazines and newspapers, along with compiling an information database.

Here's how it would work. Magazines would be supplied by specified Communications people. After reading the magazine, that "reader" would mark down on a Post-it note what articles could be useful to Communications people. Fran would then log in these article titles in a computer database and store the magazine in the archives.

The types of magazines include *Time, Newsweek, BusinessWeek, Health, Training* and *Fortune.* To retrieve information, Communications people could ask Fran to search her database for any publications with articles on a specific topic—value, for example. Also, people could browse through the resource center for articles not in the database they may find helpful.

Before starting this center, decisions would have to be made on what publications would be included, who the readers are and how the database is set up. Since there are many Communications people with subscriptions to publications, this center wouldn't entail purchasing UPS subscriptions and assigning readers.

If you have any questions about this proposal, or would like to discuss it in more detail, please let me know.

cc: John Bott
Jerry Johnson
Bill Perry

Police Department has attributed most of the crime in the area to warring gangs and struggles for control of the drug market.

Though Neighborhood Z has a rough reputation, community leaders have also attempted to address the area's problems through neighborhood development programs, community education opportunities, and a Crime Stoppers network of residents. These development programs have served to forge a bond among the area's residents, particularly families with small children and the elderly. Several groups of Neighborhood Z residents have been featured in local television and newspaper stories as they have defiantly held their ground against gangs and drug traffickers by setting up neighborhood watch systems, holding "take back the night" rallies, and sponsoring clothing and food drives.

The Pizza Place you manage is not located in Neighborhood Z. However, this high crime area does fall within the boundaries of where you deliver. Though you generally have had no problems delivering in the area, you have experienced three significant incidents in the last two years:

- Two years ago, a 21-year-old Houston University student, Damien, worked as a part-time delivery person for you and was robbed at knifepoint as he attempted to deliver a pizza to a home in Neighborhood Z. Damien was not injured, but he quit working at Pizza Place within two weeks of the incident.
- Four months ago, another employee, 18-year-old Curtis, was robbed and beaten as he attempted to deliver a pizza to approximately the same area. Curtis was briefly hospitalized and returned to work after approximately two weeks, though he refused to continue delivering in the area and shortly thereafter became a full-time cook for your restaurant.
- Last week, a 26-year-old female employee, Lin, was accosted in front of a house where she was about to deliver pizza. Three youths approached Lin asking for change, and when she yelled for help, one of the youths punched her in the abdomen and tried to rip the change purse from her waist. At that point, the resident of the house intervened, and the youths fled with the pizza, but no money. Lin has taken a leave of absence, but has assured you she will return to work.

Task. The last incident, involving Lin, prompted you to consult with corporate headquarters. Corporate executives responded by asking you to send them a message documenting the problem and your ideas for addressing the problem. The bottom line is, Should you continue to deliver in Neighborhood Z or not? Your answer to that question should be carefully detailed and justified, and you should be careful to develop a sound line of argument. Your message to these corporate executives may be in the form of a letter, a memo, or a report. It also may be framed as a proposal, a feasibility report, or a recommendation report, depending on which you think is most appropriate to the situation.

Complication. Your immediate supervisor, District Manager Pat Roberts, has told you that corporate headquarters will likely support any recommendation that comes through under a district manager's signature. Pat has also warned you that corporate executives might extract information from your document to use in press releases about Pizza Place's position regarding the incidents.

In addition, Pat feels that your document needs to include research about a number of pizza chains which have experienced similar situations. The following are the results of that research:

Pizza Chain	Delivery Problems	Solution	Results: 1988	Results: 1990	Results: 1992
Brando's (locations: Chicago, Des Plaines, and Ann Arbor)	In 1987: five assaults and 22 robberies (cumulative) reported by delivery personnel	Limit delivery hours and increase delivery personnel (two to each delivery)	Staffing costs: +37% Violent crime: −20% Natl. chain estimated losses for year: −4.2%	Staffing costs: +17% Violent crime: −2.3% Natl. chain estimated gains for year: +2.2%	Staffing costs: +5.6% Violent crime: no change Natl. chain estimated gains for year: +6.1%
Major League Pizza (locations: Chicago, Des Moines, Minneapolis)	In 1987: sixteen assaults, one murder, and 23 robberies (cumulative) reported by delivery personnel	Halt all deliveries—chain becomes dine-in and carryout only	Staffing costs: −2.5% Violent crime: −96% Natl. chain estimated losses for year: −8%	Staffing costs: −2% Violent crime: steady Natl. chain estimated losses for year: −2.3%	Staffing costs: steady Violent crime: −.6% Natl. chain estimated gains for year: +1.6%
Giorgio's (locations: Chicago, Minneapolis, Ann Arbor, and Kansas City)	In 1987: fifteen assaults, 34 robberies (cumulative) reported by delivery personnel	No change in delivery policy made	Staffing costs: steady Violent crime: +2.3% Natl. chain estimated gains for year: +2.3%	Staffing costs: +4% Violent crime: +2.6% Natl. chain estimated losses for year: −12%	Staffing costs: +3% Violent crime: steady Natl. chain estimated losses for year: −4%

You are pleased with the research, but you are not certain if it clearly supports one recommendation over another. Pat also points out that the data you have gathered feature Midwest locations and wonders if the results from the Midwest region can be applied without question to southern Texas. You now have to decide if additional research is necessary, or if this data will work. You also have to decide how you are going to present your recommendation, once it's made, to the Board of Directors for Pizza Place.

CHAPTER

16

Instructional Documents

OUTLINE

Instructions for a New Market

Types of Instructional Documents

Planning Instructional Documents

Using Conventional Elements in Instructional Documents

CRITERIA FOR EXPLORING CHAPTER 16

What we cover in this chapter	What you will be able to do after reading this chapter
Instructional documents that integrate informational, instructional, and persuasive elements	Write instructional documents that integrate informational, instructional, and persuasive elements
Basic types of instructional documents	Select instructional sheets, brochures, manuals, or reviews for a particular task, audience, and purpose
Planning instructional documents	Plan instructional documents by analyzing task and purpose, identifying the audience, and responding to the occasion and related constraints
Using conventional elements to create instructional documents	Orient readers, make information accessible, select appropriate alternative structures, and consider liability

Effective communicators know that instructional documents do more than provide information about *how to . . .* by simply listing steps in a sequence. Instructional documents need to be appealing so the intended audience is persuaded to read them, and accurate so users will make few errors. These documents also provide readers with reasons to read the documents; such documents protect both writers and readers from legal consequences. An example of such a legal safeguard is shown in the license agreement in Figure 16.1.

CONTEXT

Too often instructional documents sit on a shelf, ignored because readers have had too many bad experiences of being unable to locate the help they needed. The publishers of EasyFlow, a software program to aid designers in creating flow charts, decided that they'd follow conventions in instructional manuals, but they'd inject humor in an effort to get readers' attention.

Figure 16.1 Example of a License Agreement in a Software Manual

Is humor successful in getting readers' attention?

Does humor influence readers' receptivity to information about license agreements that they might want to ignore?

What risks are there to taking a humorous approach?

What is the effect here of plain language on readers who are accustomed to seeing legalese in such disclaimers?

What does the humor set up readers to expect in the manual itself?

BLOODTHIRSTY LICENSE AGREEMENT

This is where the bloodthirsty license agreement is supposed to go, explaining that EasyFlow is a copyrighted package, sternly warning you not to pirate copies of it and explaining, in detail, the gory consequences if you do.

We know that you are an honest person, and are not going to go around pirating copies of EasyFlow; this is just as well with us since we worked hard to perfect it and selling copies of it is our only method of making anything out of all the hard work. For your convenience EasyFlow is distributed on a non copy-protected diskette and you are free to do what you want with it (make backups, move from machine to machine, etc.) provided that any one copy is never in use by more than one person at a time. You are quite free to run EasyFlow on a network, as long as the number of people using EasyFlow at any given time is never greater than the number of copies you have.

If, on the other hand, you are one of those few people who do go around pirating copies of software you probably aren't going to pay much attention to a license agreement, bloodthirsty or not. Just keep your doors locked and look out for the HavenTree attack shark.

HONEST DISCLAIMER

We don't claim EasyFlow is good for anything—if you think it is, great, but it's up to you to decide. If EasyFlow messes up, it's you that's out the millions, not us. If you don't like this disclaimer: tough. We reserve the right to do the absolute minimum provided by the law, up to and including nothing.

This is basically the same disclaimer that comes with all software packages, but ours is in plain English and theirs is in legalese.

We really didn't want to include any disclaimer, but our lawyers insisted. We tried to ignore them but they threatened us with the attack shark (see license agreement above) at which point we relented.

1. How does this license agreement try to appeal to the audience so that they'll actually read it?
2. What changes would you recommend in tone or humor used in the license agreement?
3. After users read the license agreement, what expectations might they have for the rest of the manual accompanying the software? How would these expectations affect their willingness to read the manual itself?

To do a good job of preparing instructional materials used in business, you'll need to know this information:

- major types of instructional materials: instructional sheets, instructional brochures, manuals, and review cards
- factors to consider when planning instructional documents: task and purpose, audience and occasion, and related constraints

- factors to consider when using conventional elements in instructional documents: orienting readers, making information accessible, selecting alternative structures, and considering liability issues

INSTRUCTIONS FOR A NEW MARKET

After working for two years as assistant manager of the Hampshire Inn in Orlando, Florida, Rene Marcel was promoted to manager of the Hampshire Inn located less than a mile from Bradley International Airport outside of Hartford, Connecticut. One of the biggest differences between the two facilities was the hotel's clientele. In Orlando, most of the guests were families on vacation. In contrast, in Connecticut, more than 75 percent of the guests were business travelers on short trips.

In reviewing the Connecticut facility's operations, Rene noticed that the front desk staff and the switchboard operator received a great number of calls from hotel guests asking how to place credit card and 1-800 calls and what additional charges were added by the hotel for originating the phone calls. These questions perplexed Rene, since she knew that each room phone had an instruction card that was permanently in place over the touch pad, as shown in Figure 16.2.

When Rene reviewed the telephone instruction card, she realized that the questions guests were asking weren't answered on the card. What she didn't know was whether enough guests needed this information to merit changing the cards in the hotel she managed. She also needed to consider whether to recommend that other franchise holders change their cards as well.

Rene decided to survey guests to determine what telephone information and instructions they wanted the hotel to provide. Rather than leave the survey in the room, which would probably result in no more than a 10 percent return, she designed a survey that 100 percent of her guests could complete in less than one minute when checking in. She didn't need to ask about all the instructions that would be on the card, since she decided that most of what was already on the card was necessary (Figure 16.2). What she wanted to know was what additional instructions guests might want.

As soon as Rene reviewed the compiled results, she recognized that the current instruction card was inadequate for the business travelers who stayed at the Hampshire Inn. A high percentage of guests surveyed indicated that they would use most or all of the additional information and instructions (Figure 16.3).

The challenges Rene faced in redesigning the phone instruction card were similar to those that face anyone creating business documents that serve multiple functions. In this case, she needed to address an occasion with three different purposes:

- *Provide basic information.* Guests need hotel and room phone numbers as well as information about charges for hotel-originated calls.

Figure 16.2 Telephone Information Instruction Card

The information on the phone card anticipates the needs of many hotel guests: hotel and room phone numbers, and so on.

These instructions, however, do not anticipate that the highest percentage of hotel guests make credit card phone calls.

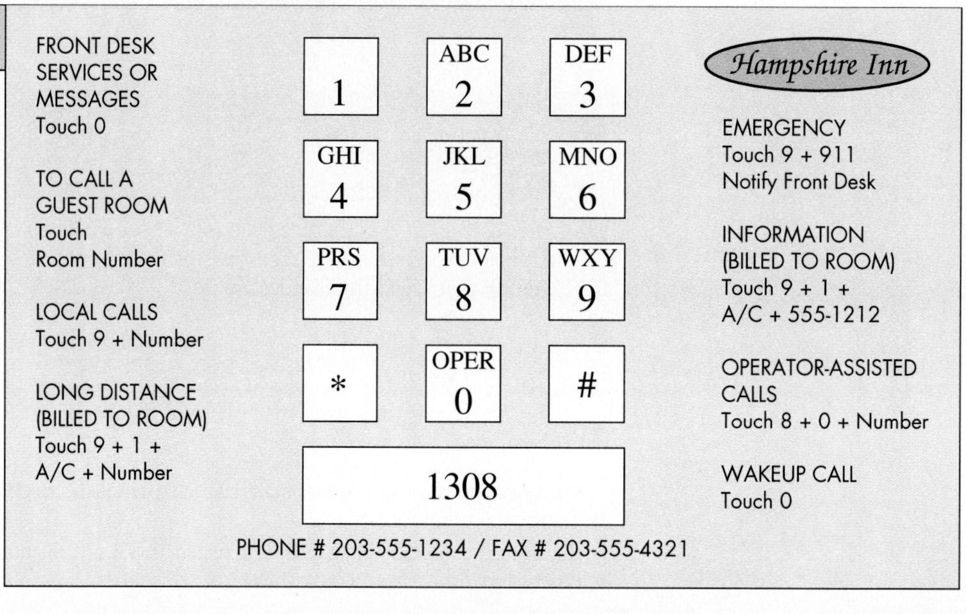

Figure 16.3 Survey Results about Telephone Information or Instruction Needs

PHONE INFORMATION THAT COULD BE PROVIDED	GUESTS REQUESTING INFORMATION (%)
Instructions to make a credit card call	100%
Information about charges for hotel-originated calls	98%
Instructions to reach alternative long-distance carriers	97%
Instructions to make a 1-800 call	91%
Instructions to use a modem	83%

- *Provide basic instructions.* Guests need instructions about local and long-distance calls billed to the room, credit card calls, and modem hookups.
- *Be persuasive.* Guests need to be persuaded to use the information and instructions provided rather than call the front desk or the operator.

Rene also had additional considerations. She was addressing a diverse audience: businesspeople, the majority of the guests; as well as tourists and families. Rene needed to provide information in response to anticipated questions from guests. She was dealing with an audience that was probably receptive: they would use the information to address their phone needs.

She didn't need to be concerned with a key element of most directions: sequence of steps. However, she did need to place the more important and frequently used instructions first. She also needed to be aware that the instruction card, like virtually all business documents, had a persuasive component. And she had serious constraints in format and design because all the instructions had to be understandable and accessible but still fit on the phone card that slipped over the touch pad. Once Rene decided that hotel guests needed additional instructions, she established a schedule to design the new card and then to test it.

TYPES OF INSTRUCTIONAL DOCUMENTS

Rene's instructions are characteristic of many instructional documents: they address readers who are receptive to the task but might be resistant to reading detailed instructional documents about that task. These instructional documents also have the multiple responsibility of providing users with background or decision-making information, informing them about how to do something, and persuading them that they want to do it. Four types of business documents address these receptive/resistant readers and focus on these objectives:

- informational and instructional sheets
- instructional brochures
- manuals
- review cards

Informational and Instructional Sheets

Many products and services come with one-page instructional sheets. In many cases, users are receptive to carrying out the task or process, but they may be less receptive to an information or instruction sheet. Instead, users often want to be able to complete the task intuitively. They're seldom interested in reasons behind a step in the process because they simply want to get the process over with.

For this reason, writers of such sheets often take a "minimalist" approach. You can ask yourself, What is the minimal amount of information that users need to do this task without getting into trouble? or, What is the minimal amount of information that users need to get out of trouble once they've made a mistake?

Figure 16.4 on page 470 shows an excerpt from an information sheet for completing an updated travel reimbursement form. New employees as well as long-term employees accustomed to completing the old form were making mistakes on the updated form, which not only asked for more information about the trip itself but had updated levels of mileage and per diem meal reimbursements. In an attempt to reduce mistakes, the office manager created an instruction sheet to accompany the new form.

Figure 16.4 Excerpts from Minimalist Information Sheet

Faster reimbursement acted as motivation for completing the form correctly.

The clearly labeled sections of the instruction sheet made it easy for users to locate information about completing the two most problematic sections of the form: meals and mileage.

Readers could reduce their chances of errors if they used the tables with critical information for completing the form.

Readers could calculate mileage, but needed to refer to the Office Procedures Guide for mileage estimates between major cities.

TRAVEL REIMBURSEMENT

All travel expenses not paid in advance (such as registration and airfare) are reimbursed by filing an Expense Reimbursement form. Completing this form correctly will speed reimbursement.

Meal Allowances

Meals are reimbursed up to the following maximum amounts:

	Out of State	In State	Foreign
Breakfast	$8	$5	Call travel office for per diem rates for each city
Lunch	$12	$7	
Dinner	$20	$14	
Total	**$40**	**$26**	**Variable**

Even if the traveler spends more than the maximum amount, expenditures above the maximum will not be reimbursed.

Mileage

Mileage for travel in a personal vehicle is reimbursed at the rate of $0.21/mile.

Mileage estimates for driving between major cities are found in the *Office Procedures Guide*. Your mileage can't exceed the estimates given in the *Office Procedures Guide* by more than 10%.

Mileage to and from the airport is standard:

Company → Airport = 42 miles @ $0.21/mile = $8.82
Round trip = $17.64

One way the manager could have approached the sheet would have been to do a step-by-step match: question 1 on the form with step 1 in the instructions, and so on. However, she decided to take a "minimalist" approach by providing information only about parts of the form in which people had been making mistakes.

The general goal in writing instruction sheets is to make the steps of the task so obvious that additional instructions aren't necessary. Procedures can be designed so that instructions are built in. For example, customers who call the AT&T customer helpline when they have trouble with their portable telephone find themselves responding to a series of questions by pushing 1 or pushing 2 on their touchpad. The entire process, which takes only a few minutes, is a do-it-yourself troubleshooting sequence that enables customers to solve a large percentage of telephone problems for themselves because of the carefully worded and sequenced instructions.

However, writing easy-to-use instructions isn't always possible. For example, when a company installed a new e-mail system to connect UNIX, DOS, and Macintosh operating systems, there wasn't one generic set of instructions that worked for everyone who wanted to be connected. Instead, each operating system had a separate set of instructions and the availability of a technician who could make the connections for people unsure how to proceed or for hardware that had unusual configurations.

When the occasion requires a brief, task-oriented instruction sheet, you need to keep in mind that readers want to focus more on the "how to" than on the "why." They want to complete the task, but they don't care much about background information or rationales. Figure 16.5 presents the instructions (in six languages) for installing a new Hewlett-Packard print cartridge in an inkjet printer. The six-step instructions are coordinated with six numbered drawings that use color to draw readers' attention to the action required in each step. The handling tips are clearly labeled so they're easy for readers to locate. The caution (and limitation of liability) is signaled by "**Caution!**" and an accompanying visual. In a very short amount of space, these instructions fulfill the general guidelines of accuracy, completeness, and accessibility.

Presenting the instructions in six languages does several things. It saves the company the logistical problem of publishing six different sets of instructions and then shipping only the packages with the appropriate language to the matching country. It also solves the problem of multinational users—for example, readers of Spanish working in the United States or readers of French working in Canada. The multiple-language instruction sheet also promotes the image of Hewlett-Packard as an international corporation. This image is reinforced by the list in another part of the instruction sheet of HP dealers in 26 countries outside the United States.

Figure 16.5 Simple Task Instruction Sheet in Six Languages

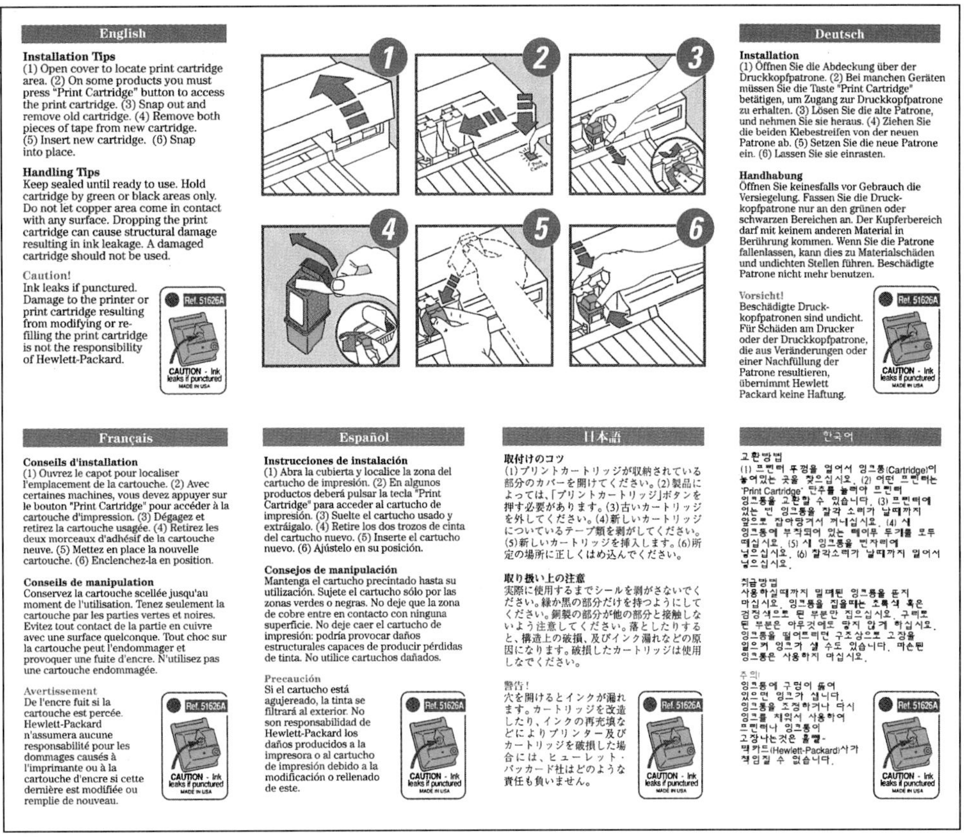

The numbers in the pictures not only coordinate with the verbal steps, but they eliminate any ambiguity about the sequence or direction of moving through the steps, a genuine concern when writing for multinational audiences.

The green and black drawing of the printer cartridge reflects its actual colors. The colored drawings help readers orient the cartridge correctly when installing it, which would be difficult without the color.

The handling tips are presented in the sequence readers are likely to use them.

*The last two handling tips are reinforced by the "**Caution!**" that follows.*

*The visual accompanying the "**Caution!**" draws readers' attention to the vulnerable place on the cartridge.*

Instructional Brochures

Readers often need more information about how and why to complete a process than can easily be provided on a one-page sheet. In fact, many readers are more likely to complete a process correctly if they know *why* the various actions are necessary. In some instructional brochures, the emphasis is on background information rather than on instruction. The rationale is that if readers understand the features of a product or the reasoning behind a process, they'll be more likely to follow instructions. For such occasions, brochures are appropriate. Brochures provide potentially resistant readers with background information and explanations about why they need to do certain things. Resistance may range from not backing up computer files to not taking necessary safety precautions when commuting.

A brochure works most effectively when it has a single point for an identified audience—for example, to encourage home remodelers to install a particular kind of insulation or to encourage patients to follow all orthodontic guidelines. Because a brochure is short—usually four or six panels and seldom more than eight panels—you need to be precise, accurate, and focused in the language and visuals you use in a brochure.

The widespread use of desktop publishing software makes creating elegant, effective brochures relatively easy. But it makes creating ugly, tacky brochures equally easy. To avoid creating ugly documents, you'll need to do more than make decisions about the purpose, audience, occasion, and message; you also need to decide about design features beyond the page grid and selection of visuals:

- Determine the dimensions of your completed brochure. What size paper do you want to use—conventional 8.5″ × 11″ or 8.5″ × 14″ or 11″ × 17″, or some less common size that will need to be trimmed because many printers typically carry only standard sizes? Do you want the brochure to fit in a business-size envelope? Do you want to hand it to people? What size best fulfills your purpose?
- Determine how many panels you need to convey your message. Decide how the brochure will be folded. How many panels will your audience be receptive to? What are the conventions for using a particular size for this occasion or for this message?

Figure 16.6 on page 472 is from an informational brochure that contains a powerful indirect message: follow the instructions from the orthodontist if you expect treatment to

Figure 16.6 Two Panels of a Six-Panel Instructional Brochure

The orthodontist, Dr. Wass, makes the assumption that patients who understand what they're supposed to do will be more cooperative and undergo more successful treatment.

Readers learn why the orthodontic process needs to be completed exactly as prescribed.

Readers learn some of the problems that might occur if the instructions are ignored.

Indirect instructions (for example, the importance of "frequently and properly" brushing teeth) are incorporated with the information.

Readers are given reasons that may explain unexpected incidents during the treatment.

Readers—both patients and their parents—are asked to read and sign an acknowledgment that they understand the information in the brochure.

RISKS AND LIMITATIONS OF ORTHODONTIC TREATMENT

Generally, excellent orthodontic results can only be achieved with informed and cooperative patients. While recognizing the benefits of a pleasing smile and healthy teeth, you should also be aware that orthodontic treatment, like any treatment of the body, has some risks and limitations. The risks are seldom serious enough to offset the advantages of treatment but you should consider the following information before deciding to begin orthodontic treatment.

Treatment Goals

The general purpose of interceptive (preliminary) treatment is to improve the most serious orthodontic problems that are present. Also jaw structural problems can be more successfully treated during periods of active growth. Since there are many deciduous (baby) teeth remaining, the goal of this treatment is not perfectly aligned teeth. Ideal alignment of all the permanent teeth can occur only after the permanent teeth have erupted. Additional treatment will most likely be necessary at that time with a full set of braces.

Tooth Decay/Gum Disease/Decalcification

Tooth decay, gum disease, and decalcification (permanent white spots) on the teeth can occur if your child eats foods containing excessive sugar and/or does not brush his/her teeth frequently and properly. These problems can occur in everyone, but the risk is greater while wearing braces.

Root Resorption

The length of the roots of some teeth may shorten during orthodontic treatment. Some patients are prone to this; most are not. Usually this is of no consequence, but on rare occasions it may become a threat to the longevity of the teeth involved.

Loss of Tooth Vitality

It is possible for the nerve of a tooth to die during orthodontic treatment, especially if the tooth has a large filling or was previously injured or impacted. Sometimes minor bumps can result in nerve damage that is unknown to you. An undetected nonvital tooth may develop a problem during orthodontic treatment requiring endodontic (root canal) treatment to maintain it.

Injury from Appliances

Sometimes orthodontic appliances may be accidentally swallowed or aspirated, or may irritate or damage the oral tissues. The appliances we use are designed to have a maximum amount of strength and a minimum amount of injury potential.

Discomfort

The mouth is very sensitive to changes and the introduction of any appliance means that your child should expect a period of adjustment.There may be some occasional discomfort associated with orthodontic treatment. This usually can be resolved by using a simple over-the-counter headache remedy.

work. The interior of the $8\frac{1}{2}'' \times 11''$ brochure presents three panels of information about orthodontic treatment (two are shown in Figure 16.6). Of the three exterior panels, one is a cover panel, a second panel asks the parent and the patient to sign to indicate they've read and understood the brochure, and the third panel (the back of the brochure) is blank.

Figure 16.7 is another brochure, but this one is more explicitly instructional than the one in Figure 16.6. The message from the American Automobile Association (AAA) is direct: follow the instructions if you expect to be safe. The eight panels of information (of which three are shown in Figure 16.7) provide instructions for motorists about avoiding a breakdown, getting to and from the car safely, deciding what to do if a vehicle breaks down,

MULTICULTURAL

USING SYMBOLS IN INTERNATIONAL DOCUMENTATION

Because of differences in traditions, customs, religions, and related cultural features of a society, extreme care must be exercised in selecting symbols in international documentation. For example, comparing people to animals or utilizing animals in cartoons or drawings to portray human beings may be quite unacceptable to Buddhists, who believe in reincarnation. A drawing that uses an animal to represent a person also runs the risk of being offensive to a Muslim. ("A beast is a beast and a man is a man. Allah says so.")

Similarly, professional communicators must be careful about using animal symbols in company logos. These too, can be "misinterpreted" and "mistranslated." For example, in India a U.S. company used an owl in a promotion. To an Indian, the owl is a symbol for bad luck. The company was not successful.

The layout of documents should match the reading patterns of the target market. A laundry detergent company marketing in the Middle East had all its visuals structured with pictures of soiled clothes on the left, its soap in the middle, and clean clothes on the right. Since many Middle Eastern languages are read from right to left, many potential customers interpreted the message to indicate that the soap actually soiled the clothes.

Communicators should also make sure that the symbols to be used are accurate and up to date. A number of years ago, McDonnell Douglas Corporation got an unexpected reaction to a brochure to be sent to potential aircraft customers in India. An old photo was used which depicted turbaned men who turned out to be Pakistani men, not Indians. Care must be taken in using symbols in international documentation, or audiences may get an unintended message.

Figure 16.7 Three Panels of an Eight-Panel Instructional Brochure

Readers are presumed to be receptive to the idea of safety but unfamiliar with simple measures to increase their own safety.

The seriousness of the message is balanced by the friendly tone of the brochure, prompted by the use of modified traffic signs and questions as headings.

Each piece of advice is signaled with the bullet •. Numbers are inappropriate because there is no sequence to these safety tips.

The purpose of the brochure—to promote safe behavior—is reinforced because each tip is presented in an imperative verb form: "Hold . . . ," "Check . . . ."

The brochure is a handy size—an 8.25″ × 14″ sheet folded into a 3.5″ × 8.25″ brochure—that fits into a glove compartment.

Detailed explanations are given for actions people might be likely to ignore—like not rolling down a window for a person from an unmarked law enforcement vehicle.

*The international ⊘ sign and a **BOLD, ALL-CAP** warning emphasize the caution not to stop to help a stranded motorist.*

← GETTING TO AND FROM YOUR VEHICLE SAFELY →

- Hold your keys as you approach your vehicle. Experts say you are most vulnerable when you are getting into or out of your vehicle.
- Check the passenger compartment before getting into the vehicle, even if you left the vehicle locked.
- Lock all doors and roll up windows when driving.
- Never pick up hitchhikers.
- Sound the horn in short blasts in dangerous situations.
- To help deter theft of your vehicle, consider having an alarm system installed.
- Always park in a central, well-lighted place, preferably where there are attendants on duty. Try to park so that you will approach the driver's side of the vehicle when you return.
- If you notice someone near your vehicle, walk toward a public place and seek help.

WHAT TO DO IF YOUR VEHICLE BREAKS DOWN?

- If your vehicle should break down on the highway, position the vehicle as far from the traveled roadway as possible.
- Turn on your four-way flashers.
- Open the vehicle's hood. Always exit the vehicle on the passenger side.
- Tie a light-colored cloth to the antenna or door handle to signal distress.
- Try to stay with the vehicle until uniformed law enforcement arrives. Do not leave the vehicle at night or during bad weather.
- Place a sign that says "Send Help" in a window so it is visible to other motorists.
- If a person should approach, crack a window and ask them to call law enforcement.
- If you must walk, write down your name, date, time you left, the direction you started going and what you are wearing. Law enforcement often find deserted vehicles and do not know where the driver is.
- If you must accept a ride with another motorist, leave the following information in your vehicle: Your name, name of the motorist with whom you are riding, the date and time you left, the plate number of the vehicle in which you are riding, a description of that vehicle and the direction you are going.
- Notify law enforcement of the location and circumstances in which you left your vehicle.
- Consider carrying these items: Pen/pencil, paper, "Send Help" signal, plastic bottle of water, CB radio or cellular phone and a flashlight. For winter weather consider a blanket, extra clothing, matches or lighter, coffee can, small snow shovel and non-perishable food items.
- Beware of individuals in civilian clothes driving unmarked cars who show what appears to be a law enforcement badge. Do NOT roll down your window or get out of the vehicle. Instead, request that a marked law enforcement vehicle be called.

To Give Help To A Stranded Motorist

- DO NOT STOP. Signal your intent that you will call for help; then notify law enforcement. Motorists are often leery of those offering assistance.

helping a stranded motorist, avoiding carjacking, and increasing overall safety. AAA not only provides this instructional brochure to its members but also provides it upon request to area businesses that are interested in promoting employee safety.

Manuals

Although there are numerous types of manuals, the discussion here focuses on procedures and policy manuals.

A **procedures manual** generally specifies ways to complete tasks, processes, or procedures, ranging from completing quarterly tax reports to qualifying a new vendor. A procedures manual (sometimes called an operations manual) includes some or all of the following sections:

- overview of the task, process, or procedure
- tutorial to teach users what to do
- step-by-step instructions for task, process, or procedure
- rationales or explanations of steps
- illustrations of selected steps
- warnings, cautions, and dangers
- glossary of key terms

Figure 16.8 (page 474) shows an excerpt from a manual that provides procedural and background information for in-house pension administrators at The Principal Financial Group. This *Pension DC Administration Manual* is used daily by administrators when they require instructions or need to answer customer questions.

This particular page from the manual explains how in-house pension administrators should deal with loan payments that are less than the amount due. Because the administrators at The Principal Financial Group want to do their job accurately and efficiently, they are receptive to explanations that provide options for permanently correcting the problem of underpayment. One of the options leads to step-by-step instructions that are designed so that the administrators can focus immediately on the actions they need to perform.

The writer of this manual made the assumption that users would be more likely to do their job well if they could anticipate why some of the problems arose and what some of the circumstances might be. This assumption explains why background information is included. For example, completing the task of assigning payment only to the principal doesn't require any more than a list of steps: "Identify it as principal only on the JTS screen," and so on. However, users are more likely to feel they are part of the organization if they know more information: "Since adding the new loan service, we've received frequent payments to apply only to the loan principal."

A **policy manual** is one of the few documents produced by an organization that are intended for everyone, from entry-level employees to upper-level management. A policy manual generally records the *what*, the *how*, and the *why* of the organization's decisions and actions, states the organization's management and operating philosophies, and provides a

Figure 16.8 Excerpt from a Procedures Manual

Marginal headings inform users about the two topics covered on this page.

Users can offer customers some control by posing options. People who have options are likely to be more cooperative.

The CAUTION is signaled in multiple ways: the use of the caution symbol △, the label CAUTION, and the shading of the boxed area.

Placing the caution before the relevant steps reduces the chance of error.

Users clearly understand the sequence of steps they need to follow because the number of steps and the actions are clearly labeled.

Examples of situations that frequently occur help readers see where they can use the procedures.

Comparisons between what users already know—the original amortization schedule—and what they don't know helps understanding.

Pension DC Administration Manual | **Page** 19-9-3 | **Issued** 00-00-00

Loans: Payments

PAYMENT AMOUNT IS LESS

If the customer sends the incorrect amount, ask that the payroll deduction amount be corrected to match the amortization schedule's payment amount. Give the customer the following options:

- receiving a refund for the partial payment and sending the full amount with the next remittance, or
- applying the partial payment as a principal only payment

If the customer indicates the amount you received is the amount sent on an ongoing basis, use the following procedures.

△ **CAUTION:** Don't process the loan payment until the terms of the loan have been changed.

STEP	ACTION
1	Request amortization schedule via the loan system. Base payment amount on amount payroll deducted.
2	Build job requesting terms of loan be changed to match new amortization schedule.
3	Review new amortization schedule. If acceptable, mail copy to customer to alert them to change of final payment.
4	Build job to have payment processed based on new amortization schedule.

PRINCIPAL ONLY PAYMENTS

Since adding the new loan service, we've received frequent payments to apply only to the loan principal. For example, a member who received an income tax return may want to apply the refund check to the loan.

If you receive a payment for principal only, identify it as principal only on the JTS note screen. When the principal only payment is processed, the system automatically produces a revised amortization schedule for you to send. This schedule is the same as the original amortization schedule with one exception: the number of payments required to pay the loan decreases.

Many companies work to develop a harmonious, yet diverse, workplace by explicitly stated policy manuals that deal with such topics as sexual harassment and on-site behavior.

framework for decision making. To help managers and employees put these philosophies into practice, many policy manuals identify employer and employee rights and responsibilities and establish ground rules for behavior. A policy manual typically includes these actions:

- organizational philosophy and goals
- image of the organization
- equal employment policy
- benefits, including health benefits, vacations, contributions to pensions and retirement, sick leave, personal leave, education
- employee reviews
- pay scales, overtime provisions
- harassment policy
- leave of absence policy
- disciplinary procedures
- grievance procedures
- information about termination of employment

A policy manual also usually includes a statement about the employer's right to revise the policies. Employees are often asked to sign and return a card or letter indicating they have received and read the policy manual. Acknowledging that they have read company policies holds employees responsible for upholding them.

Figure 16.9 presents an excerpt from a policy manual. This particular section focuses on defining sexual harassment. If reading this document helps employees know what sexual harassment is, they'll be better able to identify it and prevent it.

Figure 16.9 Excerpt from a Policy Manual

Defining key terms for readers reduces ambiguity. It also establishes legal criteria in case a situation cannot be settled with the organization's policy.

Providing examples of harassment helps employees put the abstract definitions into an understandable context of actions they may have seen or experienced.

If employees understand what's expected and accepted, they know what they should and shouldn't do in the workplace.

Definition of Sexual Harassment

. . . Sexual harassment, in its legal definition, includes unwelcome sexual advances, requests to engage in sexual conduct, and other physical and expressive behavior of a sexual nature where (1) submission to such conduct is made either explicitly or implicitly a term or condition of an individual's employment or education; (2) submission to or rejection of such conduct by an individual is used, or threatened or suggested to be used, as the basis for academic or employment decisions affecting the individual; or (3) such conduct has the purpose or effect of substantially interfering with an individual's academic or professional performance or creating an intimidating, hostile, or demeaning employment or academic environment. Determination as to whether the alleged conduct constitutes sexual harassment should take into consideration the totality of the circumstances, including the context in which the alleged incidents occurred.

. . . Under this policy, sexual harassment can be verbal, visual, or physical. It can be overt, as in the suggestion that a person could get a higher grade or a raise in salary by submitting to sexual advances. The suggestion or the advance need not be direct or explicit—it can be implied from the conduct, circumstances, and relationships of the persons involved. Sexual harassment can also consist of persistent, unwelcome attempts to change a professional or academic relationship to a personal one. It can range from unwelcome sexual flirtations and inappropriate put-downs of individual persons or classes of people to serious physical abuses such as sexual assault. Examples include, but are not limited to, unwelcome sexual advances; repeated sexually-oriented kidding, teasing, joking, or flirting; verbal abuse of a sexual nature; commentary about an individual's body, sexual prowess, or sexual deficiencies; derogatory or demeaning comments about women or men in general, whether sexual or not; leering, touching, pinching, or brushing against another's body; or displaying objects or pictures which are sexual in nature and which create a hostile or offensive work or living environment.

Reviews

Review cards, keyboard prompts, and frequent-user guides provide receptive users with quick and easy reminders to refresh their memory about key points to complete a task. Such reviews show up in a number of guises:

- frequent-user guidelines tucked into a pocket at the end of a manual
- overlays summarizing frequently used key commands and placed on a computer keyboard
- section of a manual labeled explicitly for frequent users

In a longer brochure or manual, this review section is usually placed after the step-by-step instructions so that new users won't be tempted to use the abbreviated instructions instead of the detailed ones. Some companies print frequent-user guides on plastic or cardboard that users can place near the equipment for easy reference.

Figures 16.10a, b, and c show three versions of instructions for double-sided copying on a photocopy machine. Figure 16.10a is an excerpt from the equipment manual—the primary information source. Figure 16.10b is the instructions on the reference cards attached to the

Figure 16.10a Manual Instructions

Users read this version when they need background information as well as step-by-step instructions.

- Duplex 1 and 2 mode -

1. Position the last page of the original on the exposure glass.

2. Select the appropriate mode by pressing the Duplex key.

3. Select the paper size, reproduction ratio and copy quantity.

   Maximum = 50

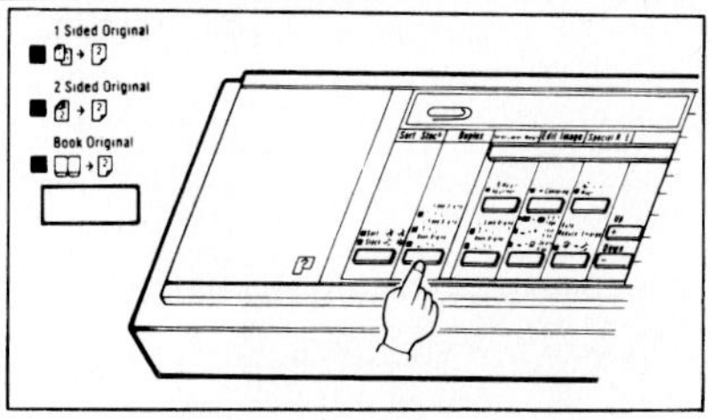

4. Press the Start key. The copies are delivered to the duplex tray.

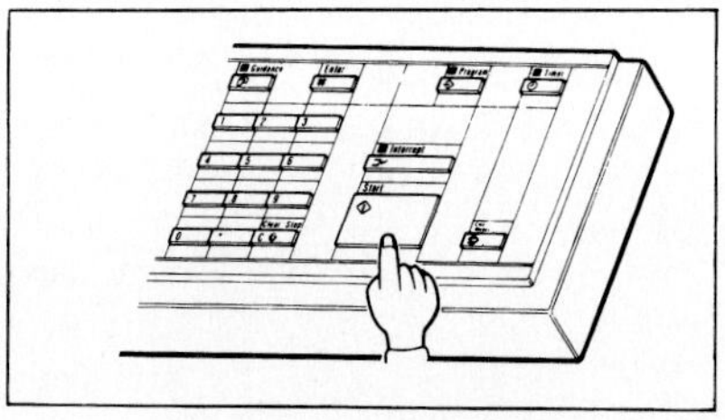

5. Place the next original on the exposure glass.
   Press the Start key.

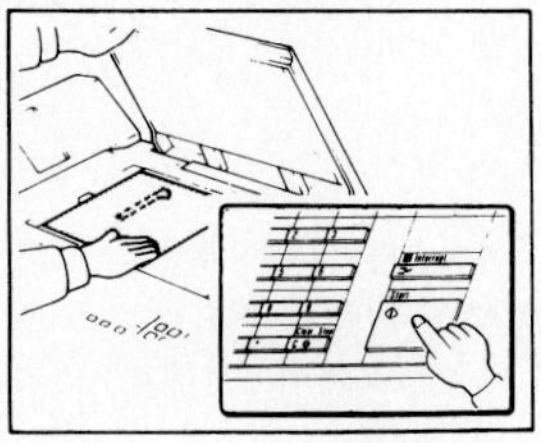

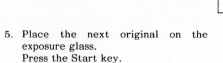

6. The finished duplex copies are delivered to the copy tray.

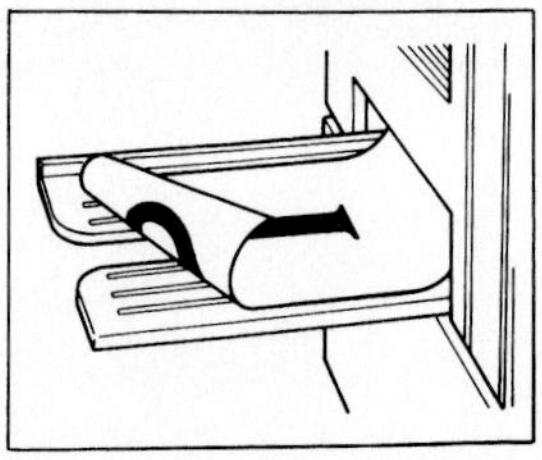

—29—

Figure 16.10b Review Instructions

Users read this version for a quick review of the steps to complete the task.

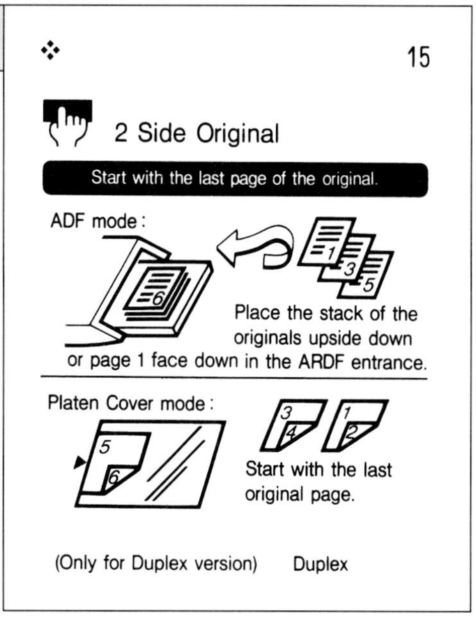

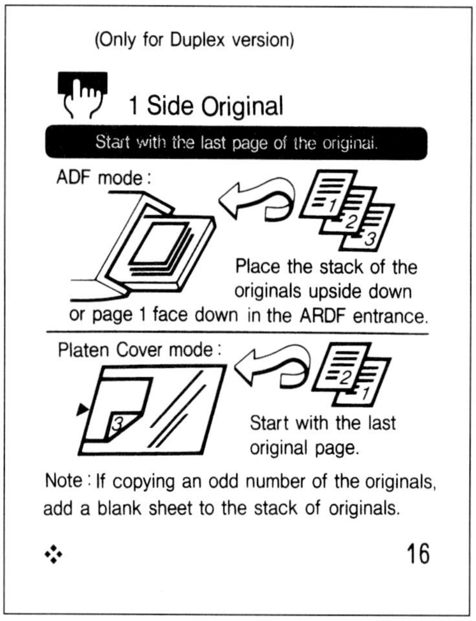

Figure 16.10c Icon Instructions

Users check these icons on the machine simply as a prompt about how to complete the task.

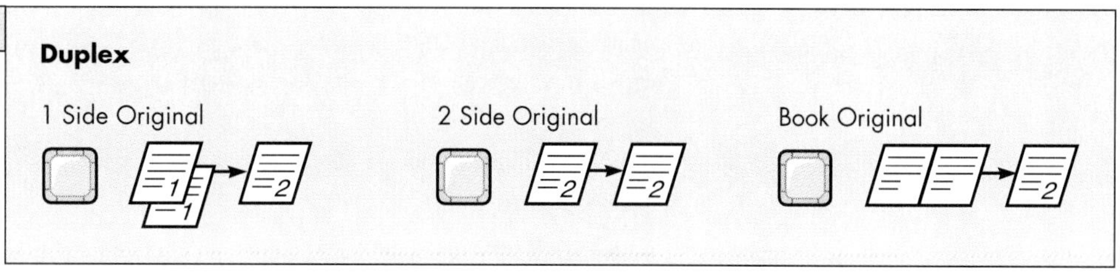

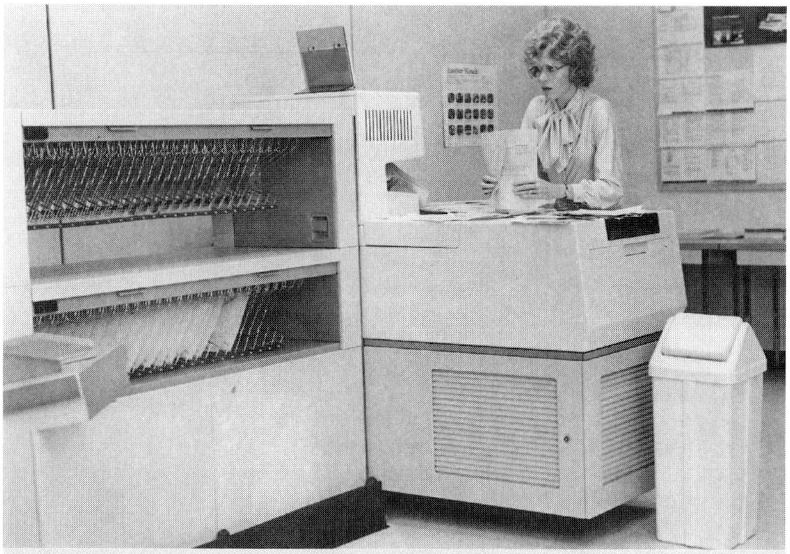

Effective review cards can reduce users' confusion and frustration in figuring out how to operate equipment.

copying machine. Figure 16.10c is the icon by the button a user pushes to activate double-sided copying. By itself, Figure 16.10c might be understandable to experienced users familiar with other photocopy machines, but it is actually intended as a prompt for people who have read the manual. Figure 16.10b is a shorter verbal explanation, also intended for users who have read the manual.

Whenever you're responsible for preparing instructional documents, you can ask if you also need to prepare a review sheet for frequent users. Ideally, a review sheet should provide the minimum amount of information that a user needs to get started.

PLANNING INSTRUCTIONAL DOCUMENTS

Instructional documents of all kinds—for example, instruction sheets, instructional brochures, manuals, and review cards—are among the most prevalent forms of professional communication. Like Rene, who needed to redesign the phone card, you can help persuade users to pay attention to instructional documents by representing each process completely and accurately.

Because instructional documents usually encourage the completion of a task, most writers begin their planning by analyzing the task users of the instructions will perform. Instructions are distinctive in that the task remains the same, regardless of the purpose, audience, or occasion. For example, the task of processing returned merchandise in a particular retail store is clearly established, but the way that process is presented might vary considerably. New sales associates just learning to process returns would need details about the task different from those directed at new store managers learning to complete monthly sales reports about the same returns.

Analyzing Task and Purpose in Composing Instructions

When you need to write instructional documents, you begin by analyzing the overall task users will perform. The task will have definable objectives that will be influenced by purpose, audience, and occasion. For example, if the purpose is to make information on a DOS disk accessible to a Macintosh user, the simple task is converting a computer file from a DOS-readable format to a Macintosh-readable format. This conversion task has a clear sequence of mechanical steps that don't change regardless of who's doing them or what's on the disk.

Regardless of the nature of the task, you'll want to ensure that no steps are omitted. Simply put, instructions need to be accurate and complete. A particularly effective way for you to keep track of all the steps is to construct a flow chart that presents the relationship among the steps.

Typically, a flow chart uses the basic symbols that are illustrated in Figure 16.11. These are the basic minimal elements:

- a clearly identified start and end
- arrows that indicate movement through the process
- decision points
- arrows that show loops for recycling through certain steps
- constraints that influence the process

A flow chart can depict a process with steps that occur simultaneously or, less frequently, steps that occur in no set order. More typically, flow charts depict steps that need to be completed in an established sequence.

Figure 16.11 Generic Model of Basic Flow Chart Symbols

Users know where to begin the task.

Users are reminded of possible constraints.

Users can be told either that these steps are completed simultaneously or that they must be completed but the order is not important.

Users can see by this sequence—something before and something following a single step—that the order is important.

Decision points—and their implications—are identified.

The end of the task is clearly signaled for users.

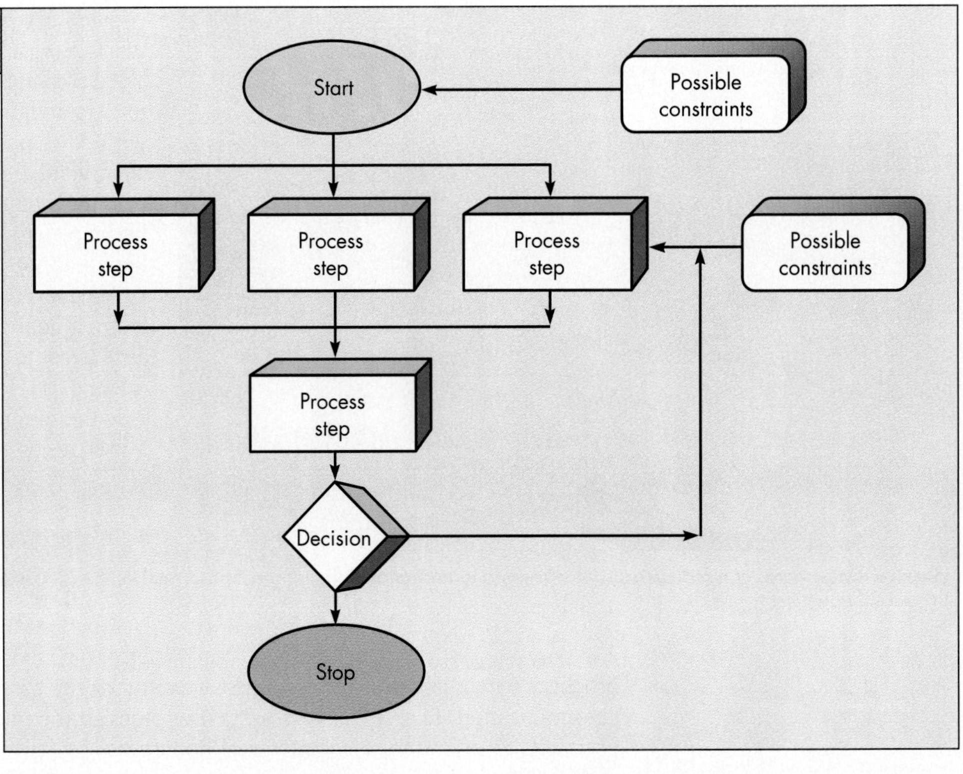

The flow chart acts as a preliminary outline of steps for instructional documents. But simply focusing on the steps and constraints of the task isn't enough. You need to ask yourself a series of questions about the nature of the task itself:

- What is the expected outcome? How will you know if this purpose has been achieved?
- What background information will help users complete this task?
- What is the most effective or appropriate way for users to accomplish the task?
- What constraints might affect users trying to complete the task?

The answers to these questions suggest information that may need to be included in the instructional documents. For example, the task might be helping customers complete a loan application for a new car. The task won't change, but how it's presented could be affected by the purpose, audience, and occasion. Should the instructions give step-by-step guidance or simply offer advice about the most frequently asked questions? Should the instructions presume first-time car buyers with a limited credit history or buyers with a strong credit history who are purchasing a second car? Should the instructions be intended for use at the dealership or at home?

Analyzing the Audience

In addition to being accurate and complete, instructions need to be accessible to the audience. You need to make sure that qualified, prepared users can complete the task accurately and efficiently. In order to adapt instructional materials to the appropriate users, you need to ask another series of questions:

- Who is intended to use these instructions? Who *shouldn't* be expected to use this product or complete this process?
- What knowledge, background skills, or experience is a user likely to have? What knowledge, skills, or experience *should* the user have?
- What is known about typical users' receptivity or resistance to the product or service?
- How much time will typical users take to complete the task? How might the occasion influence the completion?

Answers to these questions can influence both the actual content of the instructions and the amount of detail you include. For example, imagine that you're writing instructions for temporary office employees who will open and sort incoming mail and then respond to routine inquiries. In answering the preceding questions, you are reminded by the office manager not only that time is at a premium but that temporary employees assigned to this task are experienced workers with a great deal of prior knowledge about the task. So, as you plan the instructions, you decide to exclude discussion about rationale and focus simply on the sequence of steps. On the other hand, if employees are permanent and the inquiries are complex, you would expect to give much more rationale about how decisions should be made.

Analyzing your intended audience also gives you information so that you can restrict the task to qualified users. You can incorporate guidelines to identify the level of prior knowledge or experience users need to complete the task. You can include a sentence that warns users, "If you want to begin the process of *WXY*, then you should already know how to do *OPQ*." For example, "If you want to begin the process of cleaning out and reorganizing all the personnel files, then you should have completed the Windows tutorial on file management." Within the instructions themselves, you can caution users by saying, "Before you begin the next step, make sure you have arranged the necessary tools and have measured the appropriate quantities of materials." For example, "Before you invite employees to review their own personnel files, make sure you have a checklist of what *must* be in each file and what *is* in each file for them to use."

Responding to the Occasion

The occasion for a task users perform influences decisions you make about the content, organization, and design of instructional documents. You can ask yourself questions about the occasion for which the task will be completed:

- For what occasion will the instructions be used?
- What constraints will influence the completion of the task?

Responses to these questions affect your decisions about the overall approach to your audience, the purpose of the instructional documents, and the organization and design of the information.

Different occasions affect instructional documents for the same task, requiring writers to make decisions about the document's purpose, audience, organization, and design. Figure 16.12 shows how two different occasions affect the installation of a toner cartridge in a laser printer.

Figure 16.12 Developing Instructional Materials Based on the Occasion of Use

	LASER PRINTER USER IS INSTALLING A NEW TONER CARTRIDGE	LASER PRINTER USER NEEDS TO KNOW HOW TONER CARTRIDGE WORKS
Type of document	Instruction sheet that comes with a new cartridge.	Section of manual with instructions about the printer.
When used	Once, when user installs the cartridge.	Repeatedly—for first-time use, replacements, or troubleshooting.
Approach to audience	Provide users with steps and illustrations to help them change a cartridge.	Provide users with background to understand how a cartridge works and task information to change a cartridge.
Purpose of instructions	Enable users to change a printer cartridge quickly and efficiently.	Enable users to understand how a cartridge works, change a printer cartridge, troubleshoot minor problems that occur.
Organization of information	Provide list of numbered steps. Mark cautions and hints clearly.	Include troubleshooting charts to help identify problems and solutions related to cartridge use.
Design of information	Use a simple, functional design with headings and separated steps. Ink shouldn't bleed through on instruction sheet printed on both sides, but use inexpensive paper suitable for one-time use.	Use a design consistent with the entire manual. Pages in the manual should lie flat so readers don't have to hold manual open. Use coated stock suitable for repeated use in a bound manual.

Managing Constraints

Constraints are factors that limit, restrict, or influence the way a document is developed. Imagine this scenario: Walden Miller, Documentation Manager for OptImage, was just told that his department would be responsible for yet another new manual, the third new project this week, making a total of 23 projects his department was working on. In planning for this new project, Walden identified the constraints resulting from occasion that he had to consider. Some of his constraints were imposed by the time and money available for development of the manual while others were imposed by the way the manual would be used. Answering the questions in Figure 16.13 was one way for him to assess some of the factors that influenced the work schedule as well as the final document. Knowing information about these constraints helped Walden plan the manual and anticipate users' needs. If he had ignored these constraints that stemmed from the occasion, he wouldn't have had the information he needed to supervise the production of this manual.

Testing the Document

One of the most effective ways of determining potential trouble spots that might not be anticipated by you or other experts who know the process or task well is user testing. The Communication Spotlight for Part VI, on document testing, discusses the value of testing: improvement in product quality and customer satisfaction as well as reductions in support and training costs. Another reason for user testing is that it can help you identify potential trouble spots. Once you identify problems, you can change the text where the problem occurs. You can also add additional cautions or warnings that signal readers to pay special attention.

Well-planned and carefully tested instructional documents should enable readers to understand and perform the tasks, present no liability risk to the company, and engender goodwill because they make completing tasks easier.

Figure 16.13 Production and Use Constraints on Developing a Manual

PRODUCTION CONSTRAINTS IN DEVELOPING A MANUAL	END-USE CONSTRAINTS IN DEVELOPING A MANUAL
What's the budget for developing the manual?	What's the budget for purchasing the software for which the manual is written?
What equipment and materials (including software) do writers need to complete the project? Where are the equipment and materials located? Do the writers have ready access to them?	What equipment and materials (including software) do users need to complete the task? Where are the equipment and materials located? Do the users have ready access to them?
How much time is scheduled for the design, development, and production of the software? of the manual? How much time is available for testing? for revisions?	How much time is needed to complete the various tasks in the manual?
What safety precautions and/or regulatory restrictions must be considered and explained so that the users will adhere to them?	What safety precautions and/or regulatory restrictions must be considered and may restrict use?
What access do writers of the manual have to people who developed the software?	What access do users have to hotline or on-line help systems?
What is the environment in which the manual will be written?	What is the environment in which the software will be used?

USING CONVENTIONAL ELEMENTS IN INSTRUCTIONAL DOCUMENTS

Once you have analyzed the task users will perform, analyzed the audience, and assessed the occasion including the constraints, you can make decisions about ways to orient readers, select alternative structures for presenting instructional information, conform to legal standards, and test the document.

Orienting Readers

Instructional documents have a bad reputation, sometimes justified, for being inaccessible. Readers need to be able to keep track of where they are in long instructional documents. They also need to be able to easily and quickly locate information they need. A useful rule of thumb is that users should be able to access the same information in at least three ways in multipage brochures and manuals (other than just accidentally turning to the page). Readers can easily access information through conventions such as advance organizers to preview the process or policy, design elements, visual presentations, summaries, cross-references, glossaries, and indexes.

TECHNOLOGY

ON-LINE DOCUMENTATION

Nearly all new software available today includes on-line documentation, or indexed menus with instructions and exercises that are programmed right into the software to help users learn how to use it effectively.

On-line documentation is often presented as a *help menu*. Users pull down the menu with a mouse to access the particular information they need by either typing in key words (e.g., "tables" or "footnotes") or by working through a series of menus (hypertext links). Menus often start with a fairly general table of contents:

Getting Started
Creating a Document
Formatting
Reviewing Disk Options

Users select the subject that interests them, which takes them to a series of other, more specific menus until they find the needed information. Accessing instructional materials via these hypertext links is often quicker, easier, and more efficient than finding the same information in a book. Help menus thus increase productivity.

In addition, on-line documentation can be more flexible and user-friendly than traditional book documentation. Like books, on-line instructions often include step-by-step how-to instructions, but unlike a book, they can actually accomplish the task. For example, documentation in a spreadsheet program can "walk" users through creating a graph step by step ("Highlight your data," "Press F1," etc.). When the exercise is over, the graph is done. Book users would still have to apply what they'd learned from the book.

Someday, on-line documentation may also save paper, although it's not likely to happen soon. It's likely that computer users will continue to accumulate huge, creaking shelves full of dusty and unused computer books for many years. But on-line documentation is doubtless the real future of computer instructions: it's more efficient, better demonstrates procedures to users, and saves shelf space.

When conventions are ignored in instructions, the result may be an unusable instruction sheet or manual. For example, one small entrepreneurial company developed a software tool—a sophisticated product intended to help programmers write the code for business application software products. The tool was very powerful; the manual wasn't. The manual ignored virtually all the needs established by the occasion, audience, and purpose. Users naturally expected a table of contents, glossary, and index. These sections weren't included. Users expected an overview that introduced them to the features and functions of the tool. It wasn't included. They also expected step-by-step procedures that explained the software's operation and examples that explained its capabilities and options. These explanations weren't included.

Given the complexity of the software tool, users could have learned from a brief tutorial showing the software in operation and a troubleshooting guide to provide help when problems arose. These sections weren't included. Actually included in the manual were a summary of operating steps and a series of computer screens showing the software in various key operations. Each screen was annotated to show special features the tool provided. Unfortunately, while some of the most powerful features were illustrated, the basic ones weren't. When the software received a less-than-lukewarm review in a computer magazine, the software developer (and president of his own entrepreneurial company) was surprised to read, "This software doesn't live up to its advance billing. It's almost impossible for new users to figure out how to use it."

An important convention to orient readers is to provide **advance organizers** that preview information in a number of ways, including a title, a table of contents, purpose statements, goal statements, and lists of objectives. Readers not only benefit from having a preview of what will be covered in each section of the instructional document, but they formulate their expectations about the information in a document on the basis of this advance information. For example, a table of contents helps users identify main sections and subsections. Other kinds of advance organizers can be presented as brief paragraphs or as numbered or bulleted lists.

Design elements help orient readers by providing visual cues about what's important:

- Heading and subheadings indicate main and subordinate sections of the document.
- Bulleted or numbered lists indicate key sequences of items.
- Typographic cues (italics, boldfacing) signal important terms.
- Boxed or shaded sections of text indicate important chunks of information.

In instructional documents, it is important to orient readers by distinguishing the background, or "to learn," information from the action, or "to do," information. It is particularly important to visually highlight and draw readers' attention to dangers, warnings, and cautions.

Visuals can help orient readers and make information more appealing, accessible, and understandable. The decision about whether to include visuals must be balanced by space requirements and production costs.

To help you decide whether visuals are appropriate for a particular set of instructions, answer the questions in the following checklist. A yes to any of these questions suggests that visuals should be considered as a way to orient readers:

- Will visuals clarify the overall process for the user?
- Will they enable the user to clearly understand the goal or product?
- Will they help the user correctly identify parts, either physical parts or parts of the process?
- Will they help the user understand and implement individual steps?
- Will they emphasize safety and decrease the likelihood of accident, injury, or misdirection?

Visuals need to match the purpose, audience, and message. Figure 16.14a shows a portion of a document to help health care professionals know whether a beneficiary is qualified to receive Intermittent Medicare coverage. This information would be more effective presented in a flow chart, like the one in Figure 16.14b, that moves readers easily through the steps in the process. The writer, who also trained the office workers using this instructional document, knew that busy office workers tended to be more accurate when they could see the process as well as read about it.

Cross-references, both in the text itself and in the index, help orient readers by directing them to other relevant sections of the document. You can decide on the form that cross-references will take. You have several options:

- **abbreviated parenthetical references**
  example: xxxxxxx xxxxxx xxxxxxxxxx xxxxxx xxxxxxx xxxxxxxxxx xxxxxx xxxxxx xxxxxxxx xxxxx xxxxxxx xxxxxx xxxxxxxxxx xxxxxx xxxxxxx xxxxxxxx. (See pages 76–77.)
- **sentence parenthetical references**
  example: xxxxxxx xxxxxx xxxxxxxxxx xxxxxx xxxxxxx xxxxxxxxxx xxxxxx xxxxxx xxxxxxxx xxxxx xxxxxxx xxxxxx xxxxxxxxxx xxxxxx xxxxxxx. (For further information, refer to pages 76–77 in Section 4.)
- **in-text references**
  example: xxxxxxx xxxxxx xxxxxxxxxx xxxxxx xxxxxxx xxxxxxxxxx xxxxxx xxxxxx xxxxxxxx xxxxx xxxxxxx xxxxxx xxxxxxxxxx xxxxxx xxxxxxx. This process is discussed in detail in Section 4, pages 76–77.

Figure 16.14a Text: Inappropriate to the Purpose, Audience, and Message

This text does not have difficult concepts or language, but it is awkward to read.

Qualifying Criteria
Intermittent Care—Tier I

1. Does the beneficiary receive Medicare covered physical therapy, speech therapy, or continued occupational therapy?

   Yes — Intermittent qualifying criterion is met. Go to Part-Time Section.

   No — Go to question 2.

2. Does the beneficiary receive a Medicare covered skilled nurse visit at least once every 90 days?

   Yes — Go to question 3.

   No — Beneficiary does not qualify for the Medicare benefit.

3. Does the beneficiary receive Medicare covered skilled nurse visits 5, 6, 7 days per week?

   Yes — Go to question 4.

   No — The intermittent qualifying criterion is met. Go to Part-Time Section.

Figure 16.14b Flow Chart: More Appropriate to the Purpose, Audience, and Message

The flow chart identifies the steps in the process and indicates the sequence of these steps.

Intermittent and Part-Time Care Checklist

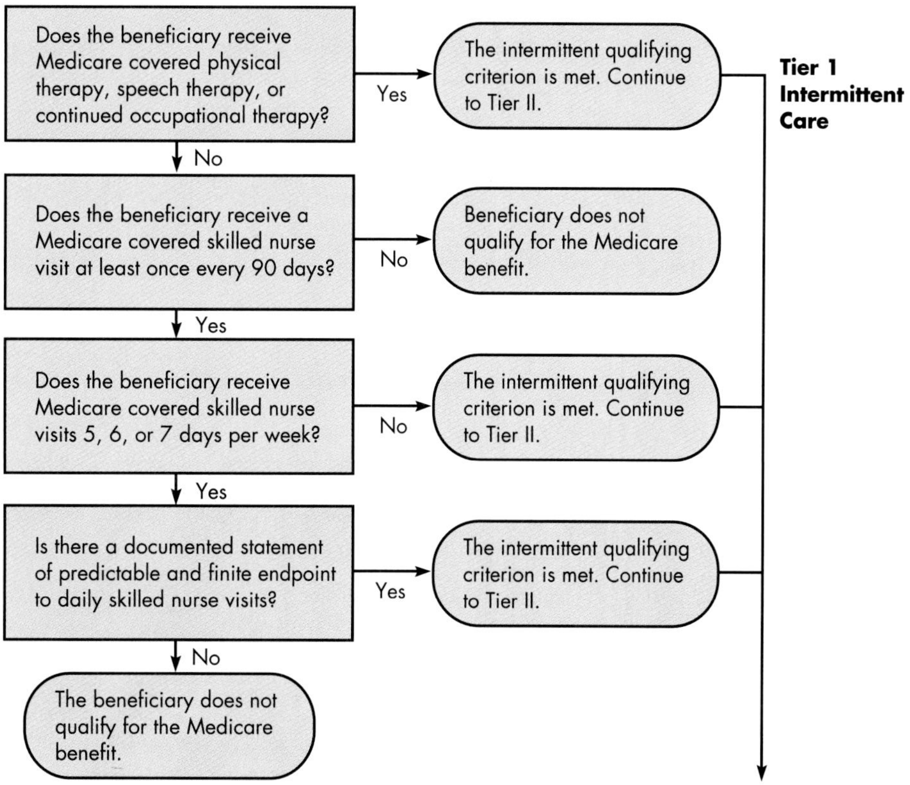

Providing readers with periodic **reviews** or **"You're here!" summaries** helps them stay oriented and keep track of the key information you have covered. With particularly complex processes, readers may need regular reviews in order to ensure that they're at the appropriate place in the process and have completed the task correctly up to this point. For example, if you're installing a fax-modem, you may appreciate frequent checks (perhaps screens that show where you should be in the process) as you move through the instructions. The amount of detail in a review may vary depending on the audience and the complexity of the information.

Glossaries orient readers by providing definitions (and sometimes examples) of key terms. Essentially a mini-dictionary, a glossary may be presented as an early section in a document or it may be in an appendix. It's a convenient way of making sure that readers know the way that you, as the writer of the instructional document, are defining terms. Most word-processing programs have a sort function or alphabetizing function that lets you enter terms on a glossary file or page as you think of them and then alphabetize them with no effort.

Indexes orient readers by alphabetically listing all of the concepts, terms, and processes with appropriate page numbers. Readers who can't locate a term in the index are not likely to use the section of the document where it occurs. Most sophisticated word-processing programs (for example, MS Word, WordPerfect) have a built-in indexing function that will enable you to easily index a document that you write using the software.

Selecting Alternative Structures

Explanatory information is usually presented to readers in paragraphs, and instructions are usually presented in numbered or bulleted lists. However, sometimes these aren't the most effective ways to present instructional information. Two useful alternatives are playscripts and structured writing.

Playscripts. **Playscripts** are a useful alternative for presenting processes involving a number of people who may not have regular contact with each other but who are equally important in completing a task. Playscripts are also useful for people who are likely to perform better if they understand how their part of the process contributes to the whole. As the name of this alternative implies, the people responsible for completing the task are listed—like the characters in a play—in order of performance and with a brief description of their role. The advantage of playscripts is that everyone involved knows everyone else's responsibilities. The players also know the ramifications of failing to complete their own part of the process.

Figure 16.15 presents an excerpt from an instructional document organized as a playscript. The writer was responsible for revising a set of instructions that hadn't worked very well, in part because the people involved hadn't understood how their part of the process fit into the whole. In fact, a number of them hadn't realized that their part mattered much at all, so work had been sloppy and incomplete. The writer's decision to use a playscript for the revision emphasized the importance of each person's role.

SKILLS & STRATEGIES

GUIDELINES FOR WRITING INSTRUCTIONAL MATERIAL ABOUT PRODUCTS

Juries sometimes award large settlements to consumers who can prove that a product warning label or manual was not clear or was misleading and, as a result, led to an accident in which material loss, injury, or death occurred.

Pamela S. Helyar, an expert in products liability, has identified ten guidelines for writing instructional materials about products:

- Describe the products' functions and limitations.
- Fully instruct users about all aspects of product ownership.
- Include clear, accurate, and tested instructions.
- Use words and graphics appropriate for the intended audience.
- Appropriately warn of product hazards.
- Offset claims of product safety in advertising with appropriate warnings.
- Present directions and warnings clearly.
- Meet government, industry, and company standards.
- Reach product users.
- Offer timely information to consumers of defects discovered after purchase.

Figure 16.15 Playscript as an Alternative Form of Instructional Document

Participants can see their role in relation to the entire process—the sequence, the timing, the importance to the whole.

The instructional sequence is clear, with each person's task separated but still placed in relation to the overall process.

The impact of not completing an action is clear to the participants.

TUITION ASSISTANCE APPLICATION PROCESSING	
ACTORS	ACTIONS
Department Clerk	1. Sort applications from mail and date-stamp. 2. Put in coordinator's mailbox.
Coordinator	3. Review applications and gather missing information (i.e., cost center, training plan). 4. Assign reimbursement levels and taxation. 5. Put applications in Director's signature folder.
Director	6. Approve and sign the applications.
Secretary	7. Return applications to Department Clerk.
Department Clerk	8. Enter information from applications into the Tuition Assistance log. (Remember to order an updated HR0059.1 report from Human Resources the first of each month.) 9. Separate forms and mail to applicants and supervisors. White copy is mailed to employee, yellow copy is mailed to supervisor, and pink copy is retained. 10. File pink copy into the Tuition Assistance pend book.
Secretary	11. On a monthly basis, key the Tuition Assistance log onto Filemaker files.

Structured Writing. **Structured writing** applies principles from psychology, reading, and document design to the organization and presentation of information. Among the principles are ones familiar to you, such as chunking and labeling, as well as ones perhaps less familiar, such as using a two-column page design and providing a goal or objective for each task or subtask.

A well-known form of structured writing is Information Mapping,® an approach developed by Robert Horn and used in a wide variety of businesses, ranging from airlines to insurance companies. The idea behind structured writing in general and Information Mapping in particular is that readers can comprehend information much more quickly when it is separated into logical chunks, correctly labeled, and easily accessible. (See the Communication Spotlight for Part III for additional discussion about Information Mapping.)

Figure 16.16 on page 486 shows a segment of structured writing to organize information and instructions in a manual that is intended for office managers. This manual is initially used for training as managers learn to follow these procedures. The two-column format makes it easy for readers to scan pages to locate the information they need.

Considering Liability

Companies are legally and morally responsible for providing notices of cautions, warnings, and dangers that signal potential risks in completing a task. Failing to provide reasonable and adequate notices of cautions, warnings, and dangers may expose customers to risk of accident, injury, and—in worse-case situations—death; and it may also result in damage to equipment; loss of time; loss of goodwill, reputation, and customers; and litigation.

Notices of cautions, warnings, and dangers should provide readers with information about things they *must do* as well as things they *must not do*. For example, forms frequently come with a caution that they will not be processed without a signature. Similarly, computer disks come with warnings not to place them on or near magnetic surfaces. And telemarketing guides warn callers to maintain a pleasant demeanor despite the reaction of the person they've called.

When you write instructions, you should make every effort to provide readers with information that enables them to complete the process accurately and efficiently, without undue delays and without risk of injury to themselves or damage to the equipment. This means you need to anticipate and address potential problems that users might have.

Figure 16.16 Structured Writing as an Alternative Form of Instructional Document

BlueCross BlueShield of Iowa

Guide to Billing the HCFA-15

Readers using structured documents become accustomed to having the purpose identified.

The purpose of this section is to help you identify a BCBSI insured.	This section provides you with information on how to identify a Blue Cross and Blue Shield of Iowa (BCBSI) insured and basic information to look for on an identification card. We'll also tell you when BCBSI is primary to Medicare and how to file these claims. Finally, we'll provide you with step-by-step instructions on how to use the Audio Access system to get basic patient and claim information.
Patient information you'll want to know when filing a claim.	As the insurance clerk, there is some information you will want to have from the patient to help you file claims correctly. 1) *Make a copy of the front and back of every patient's identification card* and keep this in his or her patient record. A copy of the card helps you understand the patient's coverage and where to submit claims. 2) *Ask the patient if he or she has other coverage.* Write down the name and address of the other insurance company so you can include that information on the claim form.
How to identify a patient who has BCBSI coverage.	Blue Cross and Blue Shield identification cards are nationally recognized and accepted by most physicians and hospitals across the United States. Although there are many different types of cards, some basic elements, identified on the example below, are found on all Blue Cross and Blue Shield cards.

The two-column format not only makes reviewing the key points or steps easier for readers, but it also simplifies scanning for a particular point.

Readers can tell at a glance what is expected because the steps are clearly identified.

Labeled visuals reduce the chance of users making mistakes.

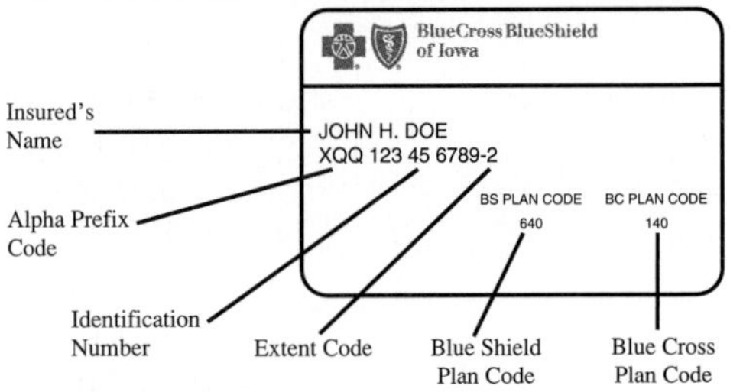

1994 Insured's Identification 1

ETHICS

WHAT ARE THE ETHICS OF WARNING?

When it comes to warning labels, communicators in business commonly consider legal implications. Ethical considerations, however, tend to be considered less often or not at all. Of course, the legal requirements of a situation can be viewed as one argument for an ethical position. Ethics expert John Bryan says, "acknowledging the role of law in a case actually helps to clarify the distinctions between secular law and moral reasoning" (p. 58). The law provides guidelines for writing warning labels as well as other text.

In order for warnings to meet legal standards, they should be accessible and appropriate to the user. Business consultant and researcher Kristin Woolever outlines legal responsibilities and states, "If a warning is present but not prominently displayed, it also fails to achieve its goal and the company could be liable" for resulting injuries.

You can call readers' attention to cautions and warnings with layout and typographic cues:

△ CAUTION Using paper of the wrong weight or surface finish in the copier may cause the feeder to jam.

△ CAUTION The scanner can read characters only in one direction. That is, it can read A, but it cannot read ∀. If you place a page upside down on the scanner, all you'll get is gibberish.

You can increase the likelihood that you have the user's attention by using typographical devices to signal the important information:

- standard symbols △
- **Boldface Items**
- **BOLD ALL-CAP ITEMS**
- **BOLD SMALL-CAP ITEMS**
- **bold shaded items**
- boxed items
- colored items
- bulleted items

However, such devices lose their effectiveness if they're used too often, so their use should be reserved to gain initial attention and to emphasize critical points.

Cautions and warnings should be placed in the instructional document at the place the reader will need the information. Instructional documents that place all the cautions and warnings in a single list increase the chances that readers will ignore them.

You can attempt to minimize liability by following these guidelines, all of which relate the task to the audience:[1]

- *Clarity*: The instructions need to be understandable by the intended users. The concepts, vocabulary, sentence structure, and visuals must make sense to the users.
- *Emphasis*: The way you word a caution or warning should make the proportional risk clear to users. A big risk should have attention drawn to it by wording and physical presentation. A small risk should have less attention drawn to it.
- *Availability*: Users should be able to easily locate instructional information and notices of cautions, warnings, or dangers. If a user is unlikely to refer to the written instructions when actually engaged in a process, then specific cautions, warnings, or dangers should appear on the equipment (or screen or form) as well as in the instruction sheet or manual.
- *Salience*: Users need to be able to see relevant cautions and warnings when they need them. The occasional practice of listing all cautions and warnings together at the beginning or end of a document results in users' seeing all of them as having equal status, with no link to the place where each is relevant.

Figure 16.17 Panel from Instructional Brochure Requiring Patient's Signature

Dr. Wass emphasizes to readers that the damages are possible but rarely occur.

Implicit in this message is that patients must follow the instructions they receive.

The brochure shifts to a more formal tone and vocabulary in this legal consent section.

A similar consent form is used for adult patients.

Refer to Figure 16.6 to read two other panels in this brochure.

And Finally . . . A Personal Comment

The overall intent of this pamphlet is to inform you of some of the possibilities that exist as potential problems for the patient undergoing orthodontic treatment. The problems or conditions mentioned here occur only occasionally or rarely. There may be other inherent risks not mentioned. The point is that you should be aware that there are some potential problems and hazards with orthodontic treatment just as there are with the treatment of any human condition. Your treatment depends on a close working relationship, and we will make every effort to discuss and explain the specifics of your treatment. Understanding and cooperation are absolutely essential to obtain the result we all seek.

I have read, understood, and have had all my questions answered regarding the risks and limitations of orthodontic treatment and hereby consent to treatment.

____
signature of parent

____
Date

I realize that in order to get my teeth straightened properly, I need to cooperate with Dr. Wass and his staff. I promise to follow their instructions, brush my teeth and braces thoroughly each day and avoid eating hard or sticky foods which might damage or loosen my braces.

____
signature of patient

In order to increase the likelihood of reader understanding and cooperation, some organizations require employees and customers to indicate that they've read important documents. For example, many employee orientation meetings require that new employees return a signed card, to indicate that they've read documents such as benefits options, the employee handbook, the policy manual, and so on. A similar practice is used by many doctors, including Dr. Wass, most of whose instructional brochure you read in Figure 16.6. On the last panel of the brochure (Figure 16.17), he provides a place for patients and their parents to sign, indicating that they've read and understood the information. This signature increases the chances that patients will be receptive and cooperate with the treatment plan.

RESPONSE SHEET

INSTRUCTIONAL DOCUMENTS

COMMUNICATOR(S):	AUDIENCE(S):
OCCASION FOR WRITING:	DOCUMENT:
WHAT TASK WILL THIS INSTRUCTIONAL DOCUMENT ADDRESS?	

◆ TYPES OF INSTRUCTIONAL DOCUMENTS

What type of instructional document do I need for this occasion, purpose, and audience?

- instructional sheet
- instructional brochure
- manual
- review card

◆ PLANNING INSTRUCTIONAL DOCUMENTS

What factors are important for defining the task users will perform?

- What is the expected outcome? How will you know if this purpose has been achieved?
- What background information will help users complete this task?
- What is the most effective or appropriate way for users to accomplish the task?
- What constraints might affect users trying to complete the task?

What factors are important for defining the audience?

- Who is intended to use these instructions? Who *shouldn't* be expected to use this product or complete this process?
- What knowledge, background skills, or experience is a user likely to have? What knowledge, skills, or experience *should* the user have?
- What is known about typical users' receptivity or resistance to the product or service?
- How much time will typical users take to complete the task? How might the occasion influence the completion?

What factors are important for defining the occasion and related constraints?

- In what context will the instructions be used?
- What distractions will influence the completion of the task users will perform?
- What support can users depend on?

◆ CONVENTIONAL ELEMENTS IN INSTRUCTIONAL DOCUMENTS

How can I use advance organizers, design elements, visuals, cross-references, reviews and summaries, glossaries, and indexes to orient the audience?

How can chunking, labeling, and using parallel structure help make information accessible?

◆ ALTERNATIVE STRUCTURES FOR INSTRUCTIONAL DOCUMENTS

Will the instructions be clearer or more likely to be followed if they are presented in one of the alternative structures—playscripts and structured writing?

◆ LIABILITY ISSUES IN INSTRUCTIONAL DOCUMENTS

What liability constraints do you need to address to protect users? What cautions, warnings, or dangers need to be included?

Have you minimized liability by following guidelines related to issues of clarity, emphasis, availability, salience?

ACTIVITIES, EXERCISES, AND ASSIGNMENTS

◆ IN-CLASS ACTIVITIES

1. One of the appealing things about the Bloodthirsty License Agreement in Figure 16.1 is its humor.

   a. List the factual information in this license agreement (minus the humor). Place your list side by side with the original and discuss possible reader reactions to each version.

   b. Locate a nonhumorous license agreement that accompanies software. Explain which agreement you think is more effective.

   c. Explain whether you think humor has a place in professional communication. What is the potential value of humor in workplace communication? What are the potential problems?

2. Review the discussion in the chapter about using flow charts to help analyze a task. Work with a small group and select a common task to analyze, one of those listed here or one the group agrees on.
   - changing from "grade" status to "pass/fail" status in a course
   - registering for courses using the automatic phone system
   - renewing a driver's license
   - sending a fax
   - retrieving voice mail messages
   - formatting a computer disk

   Have each person in the group complete an individual flow chart for the same process. Then compare the flow charts. Discuss what might account for the differences and how such differences might influence the preparation of instructions.

3. Re-read the Skills and Strategies box, "Guidelines for Writing Instructional Material about Products" (page 484). Locate a set of instructions and use these guidelines for evaluating whether you believe the instructions are reasonable and adequate for the purpose and audience. Discuss your analysis of the strengths and weaknesses of the instructions in a small group.

◆ INDIVIDUAL AND GROUP EXERCISES

1. Refer to the telephone instruction card in Figure 16.2. Work with a small group to complete the following tasks. First determine criteria for a successful instruction card. Then work with this same group to design an instruction card that you believe would work. Finally, display the cards designed by all the groups in the class and discuss the probable merits and possible problems of each.

2. Select an instructional document for analysis. It can be an instructional sheet, an instructional brochure, a section from a manual, or a review card. Use the Communication Spotlight for Part V, "Using Local Revision to Strengthen Business Documents" (pages 527–532), to help you in the analysis.

   a. Assess the following criteria as adequate or inadequate for evaluating this particular instructional document. Modify these criteria so that they are appropriate for the purpose, audience, and occasion of the document you're analyzing.

Orienting sections	• title and goal statement or objective • advance organizers • parts list, equipment list, materials list • index
Content	• clear, direct wording and consistent terminology • accurate, relevant details • clear, representative examples • appropriate justifications • legal protections: necessary warnings and cautions
Conventions	• accurate chronology, with time factors • logical chunking and labeling • parallel structure
Help sections	• tutorial section • cross-references • reviews and summaries • troubleshooting and maintenance • glossary
Design and visual elements	• appropriate visuals, especially for key parts and processes • accurate, understandable, labeled visuals with relevant text • an appealing, usable format

   b. Use the modified criteria to evaluate your instructional document. Imagine that this document is going to be revised. Write a memo to the person responsible for the revision in which you recommend the elements you'd keep the same and those you'd change. Make sure to give reasons for your recommendations.

3. Revise Figure 16.15 as a flow chart so that workers can see at a glance what they're supposed to do. Compare your revision with the original and explain which version you think is more appropriate given what you know about the occasion, purpose, and audience.

4. Individually locate an instructional document that you think is poorly written and designed.

   a. Work in small groups to share examples collected by the group, collectively agree on the problems, and collaboratively suggest ways each person's example could be improved. Use the questions in the Response Sheet and in the Communication Spotlight for Part V, "Using Local Revision to Strengthen Business Documents" (pages 527–532), to help you in the analysis.

   b. Select one of the examples as the basis for developing a detailed revision plan. Develop a plan that lists the changes needed and the reasons for the changes.

◆ OUT-OF-CLASS ASSIGNMENTS

1. You can choose one of three versions of this assignment to design, test, and revise instructions. First you

will analyze the context as well as the instructions themselves. Then you will plan and construct (or revise) instructions. You must create and implement a testing plan to ensure that the intended audience understands and can use the instructions. As part of your testing, include one or more subject matter experts to verify that the information is accurate. The instructions should also be appealing, accessible, and usable. The design should be consistent with organizational image and audience needs as well as with the purpose, audience, and occasion.

a. You may choose to revise an existing but inadequate portion of a policy manual or to construct an entirely new portion of a policy manual for an organization. Before writing (or revising) this portion of the manual, you will need to analyze the organizational context in which the policy will be used. You are not creating the policy; rather, you are recording organizational practice.

b. You may choose to revise an existing but inadequate set of instructions or to construct instructions for a task that some audience needs. These instructions should have a real audience, someone who really needs them to complete a task or procedure. The task should be completable in less than 10 minutes. The task might be complex, but it shouldn't take a long time to perform.

c. You may choose to construct instructions for a task needed by a specialized audience—for example, readers or users who either have or lack special knowledge, are visually impaired, are physically challenged, are very young, are very old, or have limited literacy. The task should be completable in less than 10 minutes.

What you turn in for whichever version (a, b, or c) you select:

- An explanation of the context: This is a discussion of the situation necessitating the instructions, including the characteristics of the users. (If you're revising existing instructions, include a copy of the original.)
- A detailed analysis of either the policy and the procedures for reporting a problem that violates the policy (for assignment a), or the task (for assignment b or c).
- The testing plan you designed and used: You need to include a list of your testing methods, a rationale for each method, the test procedures you used, the test results.
- The best-shot set of instructions with detailed annotations to show problems that turned up during testing.
- The final set of instructions with detailed annotations to identify your decisions and changes.

2. Select a process or task for which you have already prepared written instructions. Redesign these written instructions as either (a) an oral training session or (b) an on-line training session for the appropriate group of employees or customers. Consider the following adaptations:
   - what sequence of information will work best
   - what visual aids users will learn from
   - what handout materials users will need
   - what demonstrations will help users
   - what kind of practice users will need (and how much)
   - what questions users will ask
   - how users will be able to review new and/or difficult material

   Prepare the presentation outline and the necessary materials for this oral or on-line training session.

CASE

LAKE VIEW T-SHIRT CONTROVERSY

CASE BY ANDREA BREEMER FRANTZ

Background. Two longtime football rivals will again be facing each other on the playing field at Lake View's homecoming game with Walford College. Both schools are small liberal arts colleges and both have church affiliation. Lake View's enrollment is approximately 4,300, and Walford's is slightly smaller at approximately 3,200.

The rivalry between the schools is long-standing, but this year the rules of the "game" changed a little. Two Lake View male students sold 250 T-shirts in advance of the weekend's homecoming game. The shirts depicted caricatures of Lake View football players and Walford cheerleaders in sexually suggestive positions. Some fans found the caricatures and the accompanying slogan on the shirts offensive.

Several student groups and faculty members have written formal complaints about the T-shirts, claiming that the images perpetuated male-female stereotypes, encouraged male dominance over women, and even inspired harassment. Since the shirts have already been sold, there is little the college can do to recall them. In addition, the shirts themselves are a protected form of free speech. Peer pressure has effectively removed the T-shirts from open circulation on campus, and most who bought the shirts have said they don't feel comfortable wearing them now.

Lake View officials have determined that much of the problem with the shirts centers on the fact that the school has no clearly defined policy or code of ethics regarding sexual harassment among students. Currently, the Lake View faculty manual states, "Any faculty or staff member accused of sexual harassment and found guilty after due process will be terminated regardless of contract status." Nothing addresses student behavior on these issues.

Task. A task force including faculty, staff, administration, and student members has been formed to create a policy for student conduct regarding sexual harassment. As a leader of the Lake View student body, you have been chosen to serve on this task force. Each member's first task is to create a policy independent of the group, so that you will all have ideas to work from as you create a policy together. Then your group is to write a policy for student conduct regarding sexual harassment which serves to both define the concepts and address the problems that arise from them. (Class members may play specific roles—faculty, staff, and student members.)

Complication. After drawing up the policy, your task force is asked to present the policy in a series of meetings to student, faculty, and community groups. One of these meetings is even to involve Walford College. Your group, therefore, must design materials for making these various presentations. In doing so, you must consider whether an informal or a formal presentation would be most appropriate to the respective groups in presenting your policy decisions and rationale.

CHAPTER

17

Oral Presentations

OUTLINE

Presentation Preparation: The Perils of Ignoring Time

Active Listening: Engaging Your Audience

Purposes of Presentations

Preparing a Professional Presentation

Preparing Visuals and Other Support Materials

Evaluating Presentations

CRITERIA FOR EXPLORING CHAPTER 17

What we cover in this chapter	What you will be able to do after reading this chapter
Approaches to preparing a presentation	Understand the importance of preparing a schedule, gathering and organizing information, and practicing
Active listening to overcome listener resistance	Recognize and use strategies to engage listeners
Purposes of presentations	Select the appropriate type of presentation for the occasion, purpose, and audience
Preparing a presentation	Prepare and present presentations that are well organized, are interesting, and convey a professional image
Visuals and other support materials	Prepare support such as flip charts, transparencies, and handouts
Evaluating presentations	Engage in assessment of your own presentations and presentations of others

Effective communicators realize that oral presentations are as important as written business messages. A recent survey of more than 700 managers rated "the ability to communicate ideas and plans effectively in front of an audience" as *the* most important career skill. Twenty-five percent of these managers said they give presentations at least once a week.[1] Figure 17.1 pictures two professional situations in which you might expect to present information orally.

CONTEXT

The speakers in both these photos have to get their audiences to listen by reducing distractions and focusing on audience needs. The formal presentation engages listeners by stating a clear purpose; the informal presentation engages listeners by actively involving them in discussion. Both speakers make their points accessible and memorable by careful organization of information, effective examples, and appropriate pacing.

Figure 17.1 Different Types of Oral Presentations

1. What major distractions or problems do you think each speaker has to overcome in these two situations?
2. What different kinds of audiovisual support (for example, overhead transparencies, slides, computer displays, flip charts, posters, handout materials, and so on) might speakers use in each situation?
3. What differences do you see in the ways these speakers probably prepared for their presentations?

The skills used by the speakers in Figure 17.1 are critical to career success.

- recognizing the importance of scheduling
- encouraging active listening
- preparing oral presentations
- identifying various purposes of presentations
- preparing support materials
- evaluating presentations—your own and those given by others

PRESENTATION PREPARATION: THE PERILS OF IGNORING TIME

On the morning of September 1, EnviroFirm manager of community relations Lee Sommers received two calls. Both calls requested formal presentations from EnviroFirm, which was a growing recycling and energy conversion company.

1. The first invitation was to speak on the morning of October 20 at a regional symposium sponsored by the local community college about ecological, economic, and engineering issues involved in managing the waste problem since landfills all over the state were being closed.
2. The second was an invitation to be the monthly speaker for the local Chamber of Commerce dinner, also on October 20; as a nod of support to the symposium at the college, the

Chamber of Commerce wanted a presentation about how one local company was addressing the waste problems in line with concerns of local citizens, business, and government.

Both presentations were important opportunities for EnviroFirm to demonstrate its technical excellence and its sensitivity to community concerns. Although Lee was going to be out of town on October 20, he had recently expanded his one-person department to include two new employees.

Lee asked Beth Rollins, a staff researcher, to prepare the presentation for the regional symposium. He asked Barbara Sage, another staff researcher, to prepare for the Chamber of Commerce presentation. He sent each an e-mail message making his request and explaining that he knew few details about the times, places, facilities, and audience needs. He explained that he'd already given their names to the organizers of the symposium and the dinner. Lee then listed the names and phone numbers of the contact people so Barbara and Beth could confirm the arrangements and get the details themselves. He reminded them both that EnviroFirm had paid for the privilege of using the library at the local community college; the company also maintained an up-to-date file of articles about itself (and competitive companies) and subscribed to key professional journals and trade magazines. He also mentioned that the company had a slide file with more than 500 professional quality 35-mm slides that anyone in the company could draw from for a presentation. He said he'd like to read their presentation notes and see their visuals well in advance of the presentations. He also mentioned that he'd be glad to schedule a run-through of the presentations whenever they were ready.

The calendar that begins below indicates the major actions that Beth and Barbara took as they prepared their presentations, right up to the moment each was to speak. It seems that Beth experienced a number of mishaps, but that most things went smoothly for Barbara. As the brief history shows, Beth's difficulties and Barbara's success were no accident but could be explained by the kind of *planning* each worker undertook.

	Beth's Preparation	**Barbara's Preparation**
7 weeks to go		
September 1	Lee asks Beth to prepare a presentation as one of the speakers at the October 20 regional symposium being held at the community college.	Lee asks Barbara to prepare a presentation as an after-dinner speaker for the October 20 Chamber of Commerce dinner. When Barbara calls the Chamber of Commerce to confirm that she will be glad to make a presentation, she asks questions: • what time the dinner starts • when she'll begin speaking • how long she's expected to speak • how many people will attend • whether the Chamber has a carousel slide projector and screen • whether the podium has a microphone Barbara creates a schedule for preparing her 25-minute presentation.
September 2	Beth selects key words about the related environmental problems and then calls the community college reference librarian and asks him to conduct a search for relevant articles published in the past six months. He says the list will be ready on September 6. Beth asks Barbara if she'll save time to edit her paper. Barbara suggests that writing a paper isn't a good idea. She says she's had better luck working from an outline or notecards.	Barbara reviews the extensive file that EnviroFirm keeps of newspaper and magazine articles published about itself and competitive companies. She also checks for relevant articles in the past year's issues of journals and trade magazines the company keeps in its small on-site professional library/reading room.

(continued)

	Beth's Preparation	Barbara's Preparation
6 weeks to go		
September 5	Beth receives a call from the symposium director, who wants to confirm whether Beth is able to make the presentation. He asks if she'll need an overhead projector; she says yes. He asks if she can send a bioblurb that can be used to introduce her and a 100-word abstract of her presentation by September 20, so it can be included in the final program.	Barbara prepares a one-page outline of the main points she wants to cover and puts it on Lee's desk for comments. Barbara receives a call from the speaker coordinator for the Chamber of Commerce, who wants a bioblurb to introduce her and a 100-word abstract by September 22, so it can be included in the promotional mailing.
September 8	Beth receives a call from the library that her search list has been completed for several days. Does she still want it? She says yes; she'll be by to pick it up.	Barbara makes some of the changes Lee suggests but disagrees with others. She makes an appointment to go over these areas of disagreement.
September 9		Barbara and Lee discuss their points of disagreement and reach consensus. Barbara revises the outline and starts to fill in the details and examples.
5 weeks to go		
September 12	Lee asks Beth how she's coming; she says everything is on schedule. She says she'll have a copy of her paper ready next week. He says that writing out a paper isn't a good idea; she'd be better off working from an outline or notecards.	Barbara makes a two-column version of her presentation: one column for the outline, the other for listing the slides. She also creates a title and writes the abstract and her bioblurb. She puts them all on Lee's desk for his comments.
September 14	Beth stops by the college library to pick up the database search she ordered. She realizes that the printout has only the abstracts; she still has to look up the articles and photocopy them.	Barbara makes the changes Lee suggested to the title, abstract, and bioblurb and sends them to the Chamber of Commerce. Later she goes through the company's slides to select photographs to use.
September 16	Beth goes to the college library to locate the articles she needs. She finds some, but the library doesn't subscribe to all of the publications on the printout. She figures if the community college library doesn't subscribe, her company's smaller professional library is less likely to.	Barbara decides to help her audience understand and remember the information by involving them. She develops an 8-item questionnaire the audience can take and she can help them interpret during the presentation.
4 weeks to go		
September 20	Beth receives a call from the symposium director, who wants to know if Beth has mailed her abstract. Could she please fax it immediately. She writes it out, spellchecks it, and faxes it within the hour.	Barbara schedules about three hours when she's unlikely to be interrupted to use the presentation software on her computer to create the masters for her text slides. She leaves the slide masters on Lee's desk for his comments.
September 21	Lee asks Beth about her presentation. When she says she's working on the paper, he reminds her she'll be better off doing an outline. He suggests she stop by his office with the outline later in the week. He asks if she's up to speed using presentation software. He says if she needs help, she just needs to ask.	Barbara makes the content and design changes that Lee suggests and then sends the masters out to be made into slides.
3 weeks to go		
September 26	Beth works on her paper nearly all day, incorporating what she can from the database search. Lee asks again about her outline. She figures once she has the paper drafted, she can outline its main points for Lee.	Barbara picks up her slides and a carousel. She organizes and does a quick run-through to make sure they're right side up and in the correct sequence.

(continued)

3 weeks to go (continued)		
September 27	Beth works on her paper for most of the day. She is up to 12 pages. She's not sure how long she has to speak, but she figures it's better to have too much than too little and she can cut as she goes along if she has to.	Barbara practices her presentation out loud and with the slides—behind the closed door of her office with no one watching.
September 28	Lee says he wants to see whatever Beth has done so far—this afternoon! Beth reformats and spellchecks the 15 pages she has so far and puts them on Lee's desk.	Barbara practices her presentation out loud and with the slides—this time with a video camera running so she can look at the tape and do a self-evaluation.
September 29	Lee wants to see Beth immediately. He asks why she has concentrated exclusively on the environmental issues and ignored the economic and engineering aspects. He suggests a brief outline that balances the issues that need to be discussed.	Barbara tells Beth that if she wants her help—discussing the outline, designing the slides, practicing the presentation—she should let her know when so they make sure to schedule the time.
September 30	Beth thinks a lot about Lee's ideas, but can't come up with a plan for working with it. She's frustrated about how to proceed.	
2 weeks to go		
October 3	Beth works on the outline, trying to fit in the information she's already collected. She wonders how she'll remember what to say if it's not written out.	Barbara asks Lee if he can schedule a run-through on October 11, at 9 a.m. in room 217, one of the conference rooms.
October 5	Beth works on the slides for her presentation, listing the information that the slides should include.	Barbara prepares a one-page handout to distribute at the end of her presentation, which summarizes her key points.
1 week to go		
October 11	When Lee checks, Beth says everything's fine. He asks if she wants suggestions about slides she might use from the company's files. She says she knows what she wants the slides to be though she hasn't looked at the company's files yet.	Barbara shows up at 8:40 to set up the projector. At 9:00, she's ready to go. At 9:25 she's done and Lee and the three people who listened are asking questions, some tough ones that she didn't anticipate.
October 12	Beth receives a speaker badge and symposium program in the mail. The accompanying letter explains that the badge will let her park in the reserved lot next to the building where she'll be speaking.	Barbara makes a list of the questions she might be asked and practices answers to them. On the basis of the comments in yesterday's run-through, she revises her handout and includes a list of references.
October 14	Lee checks with Beth. He forcefully reiterates that he *really* wants to see a run-through of her complete presentation before he leaves on a trip next week. She says she'll be ready right after the weekend.	
3 days to go		
October 17	Lee checks how Beth is doing. She says she's really sorry, but she won't be ready for a run-through until tomorrow. She takes her slide masters in for overnight processing. Unfortunately, Lee is leaving this afternoon for his trip.	Lee checks how Barbara is doing. He says her nervousness is natural, but she's well prepared and should do a terrific job.
October 18	Beth picks up her slides. She remembers something about inserting slides into a carousel upside down and backwards; she hopes she gets them in right.	Barbara calls the Chamber of Commerce to recheck the time and place and to verify that she'll have a slide projector and microphone.

(continued)

	Beth's Preparation	Barbara's Preparation
3 days to go (continued)		
October 19	Beth wants to do a run-through of her presentation, but the conference room is booked, the slide projector is being used, and no one is free to watch her. She practices with no slides and no audience.	
The Day!		
October 20	Beth gets to the college at 9:45 a.m., but she can't get into the lot reserved for participants since she forgot her speaker badge. She has to park in the general visitors' lot and rush across campus for her 10:00 session. When she gets to the room, there is an overhead projector set up but no slide projector.	Barbara double-checks that she has her carousel and outline before she leaves her house. Because there won't be much traffic by that time, she leaves at 6:30 p.m.—for the 20-minute drive to the 7:00 dinner. She's scheduled to speak at 8:00.
1 week later		
October 27	Since Lee returned from his trip, he's received five phone calls from people who attended Beth's presentation, all of them negative. Even though he's disappointed, angry, and professionally embarrassed, he calls Beth in to ask her what happened. He has two items on his agenda: he tells Beth that her failure is a serious professional problem and that they need to prevent it from happening again.	Lee is back in town from his trip. He calls Barbara in to give her a copy of the letter he's just received from the Chamber of Commerce expressing appreciation for the excellent presentation that she made. Lee tells her that the congratulatory letter will go into her personnel file.

The elements of planning that helped make Barbara's presentation a success and Beth's a disaster are the focus of this chapter. We begin this chapter by encouraging the use of active listening. Then we identify purposes for presentations, suggest strategies for preparing a presentation and making a good impression, and review visuals that are appropriate for presentations. Finally, we provide criteria for assessing presentations, both those you give and those you listen to.

ACTIVE LISTENING: ENGAGING YOUR AUDIENCE

When you're giving a presentation in the workplace, as much as 30 percent of your audience may already be interested in the information you have to present. In an article in *Supervisory Management*, communications expert Floyd Wickman explains that you may expect another 30 percent to question whether you have anything to say that they'd be interested in. Another 30 percent probably won't even want to be there. A final 10 percent of your audience may not listen no matter what you do.[2]

That 70 percent of your workplace audience may be resistant is not the only problem you face as a speaker. In an article in *Training and Development*, Kittie Watson and Larry Barker, experts in listening, caution that additional problems occur if you accept any of the following assumptions:[3]

- When you start speaking, members of the audience start listening.
- If members of the audience are looking at you, they must be listening.
- Members of the audience will remember points you think are important.
- Members of the audience keep listening until you finish speaking.

You will find the suggestions in this section useful for overcoming listener resistance and for understanding what you face as a speaker. The suggestions will also help you actively engage your audience in your presentation.

Consider the Way People Listen

Getting an audience to listen means more than selecting relevant content, using understandable vocabulary, and/or preparing professional visuals: it also means considering the way that most people listen. Such consideration increases the likelihood that your audience will pay attention.

- If you reduce distractions, people are more likely to listen. The physical environment needs to be comfortable. You can check and adjust factors such as the temperature, lighting, air flow, chairs, and ambient noise from an air conditioner, a corridor conversation, or a jackhammer just outside an open window. You can also adjust distractions that *you* might cause: wearing inappropriate clothing for the situation, playing with your hair or dangling jewelry, jiggling change in your pocket, or displaying nervous mannerisms such as constantly clicking your retractable pen.
- When you begin the actual presentation, get the audience's attention. An engaging example can hook the audience. A dramatic visual on the screen can focus audience attention. Your goal is to get people to refocus their attention on you before you move to the substance of the presentation.
- People receive and process information differently. Some people get most of their information by listening; others get most of it by seeing; still others get most of their information by acting or practicing what you demonstrate. You can increase the likelihood that more people in your audience will understand and remember what you say if you reinforce your speaking with visuals and activities.

Reduce Distractions

Undistracted, attentive listeners who receive information through several senses are likely to comprehend and retain more information than listeners who are distracted or inattentive. For example, the administrative assistant James Thomas knew that his meeting with office staff to introduce the reorganization plan for the office would be important. As you can see in Figure 17.2, he made it easy for the audience to pay attention.

Focus on the Audience

An audience likes to have the sense that you're talking directly to it rather than giving a presentation that could be for anyone. The following suggestions help you adapt an oral presentation to a specific audience.

- If you show that you're glad to be giving the presentation, the audience is more likely to be receptive to your ideas.

  Example: Your invitation to make this presentation has given me the opportunity to return to the division where I did my first internship.
- If you know some specific points of information about the audience, you can make a relevant, audience-related comment in your opening.

  Example: Your division's safety record of only one injury per 1,800 employee hours is consistently lower than the national average.
- If you show that you know the audience's purpose for being there, they're more likely to pay attention.

  Example: You may be able to use the information presented this morning as you work toward your goal of having an accident-free workplace.

Figure 17.2 Take Steps to Help People Listen More Effectively

Reducing distractions increases the likelihood that the audience will pay attention.

Giving people a signal that you've started gives them a chance to focus their attention.

Providing more than one way to access the information increases people's opportunity to access the information.

In arranging for his presentation about the reorganization of the office staff, the administrative assistant James Thomas checked with the maintenance staff to fix the annoying buzz from one of the ceiling lights in the conference room and asked the grounds staff not to mow the lawn on that side of the building from 9 to 10 a.m. on Tuesday, when the meeting was planned. He also reminded himself to empty his pockets of keys and loose change before going to the meeting.

He decided to gain people's attention with a slide of the office staff that had been published as a photograph in an issue of the company newsletter—a picture of smiling, happy colleagues. He said one of his goals was to maintain the comfortable, friendly office environment; that wouldn't change. Then he moved to the purpose of his presentation, the office reorganization, which he said could make people not only happy but more efficient and productive.

As part of his planning, he developed a clear line of argument, showing how the current structure contributed to problems and how the reorganization would reduce these problems. He designed a series of transparencies that illustrated the new organization, and then he reinforced his talk and transparencies with a handout that showed people specifically how their own responsibilities would be adjusted.

- If you imagine some of the questions this particular audience may ask, you can incorporate your responses into the presentation.

  Example: A higher safety record will increase productivity and decrease insurance rates. But more important, a higher safety record will improve the working conditions, which will lead to more satisfied, committed employees.
- If you ask rhetorical questions during the presentation, you can proceed to answer them during the presentation.

  Example: Some of you may be asking, "How will you improve a safety record that's taken us five years to achieve?"

The higher the stakes, the more important it is for the audience to believe you are speaking directly to them. The national account representative in Figure 17.3 knew that the company where she was conducting an information session prior to a major sales presentation prided itself on the ability to increase earnings in a sluggish national economy. She also knew that the company was committed to supporting a large number of youth activities. Her opening remarks showed that she understood the commitment and goals of her audience.

Figure 17.3 Focus on the Audience

The occasion made it appropriate for the presenter to look for information in conventional sources such as business periodicals and less usual sources such as the company bulletin board.

After a national account representative scheduled an information presentation about a new telecommunications system for the corporate executives of a large potential account, she did her homework. She checked the past year's issues of publications such as the *New York Times*, *The Wall Street Journal*, *Business Week*, and *Fortune* for any articles about the company. She asked for copies of their annual report, their external newsletter for stockholders, and their internal newsletter for employees. And when she arrived for her presentation, she checked out the employee bulletin board as she walked down the hallway.

In her opening remarks, she included this comment: "I'm glad to be here with corporate executives who not only increased the company earnings 26.7 percent last quarter, but also sponsored the best girl's softball team in the city."

Encourage Audience Involvement

People tend to understand and remember information better when they are involved in a presentation than when they're passive recipients. Encouraging audience involvement also has the added benefit of keeping people's attention focused on what you're saying.

- You can involve members of the audience in an activity related directly to the points in your presentation. Members of the audience might solve a problem related to your topic, pose solutions to an ethical dilemma, or evaluate events on a videotape.
- You can invite audience members to help with a demonstration.
- You can encourage members of the audience to gather in small groups to discuss specific questions you ask during the presentation. After an appropriate period of time, bring everyone back together to share the opinions of each group.

The trainer in Figure 17.4 surprised the project managers in her workplace seminar by expecting their active involvement. They had expected to hear her give an expert opinion about what was wrong with their reports and how to improve them. Instead, they were asked to analyze the inadequate introduction to a report. The involvement helped them see

Figure 17.4 Encourage Audience Involvement

By encouraging audience involvement, the trainer helped participants see their dual role as readers with reactions and writers with responsibilities.

A trainer in corporate communications was invited to present a series of seminars to help project managers write more effective reports. During the first seminar, she explained that she was going to talk about writing reader-based reports, ones that responded to the questions and concerns of the readers rather than just telling what the writer had to say. Then she distributed copies of the one-page introduction to a report and asked the audience to work in groups of three or four for five minutes to identify strengths and weaknesses in the introduction. She asked the groups to list questions they wanted answers to that weren't in the introduction. She asked them to indicate whether they could identify what the rest of the report was going to include.

After five minutes, she asked for feedback from the groups and wrote their comments on a flip chart pad. She used their comments as the basis for the next section of her presentation about anticipating readers' needs and questions.

that their opinions as readers mattered but also helped them recognize the kind of information that readers need to know when they begin a new document.

Make Information Accessible and Memorable

Considering listeners' ability to absorb information as you plan your presentation increases the likelihood that they will be able to understand and remember what you've said.

- Typically, a person's short-term memory holds 5 to 7 chunks of information, a number that decreases as the complexity of the information increases. It's also a number that tends to decrease when information is presented orally. If you respect the limits of people's short-term memory—that is, the number of chunks of information they can remember at the same time—they'll recall more of your presentation.
- People like relevant stories and tend to remember stories long after they have forgotten individual pieces of information, so if the stories act as triggers or cues to your main points, they can serve a useful function. Brief anecdotes can illustrate your points (what *Time* magazine writers call "nuggets"). In general, you should avoid rambling "war stories" (stories about personal experiences) that have only superficial relevance.

The company safety officer in Figure 17.5 knew that employees resented mandatory safety seminars, but he also knew that they needed an easy way to remember the information, which might mean the difference between an accident-free environment and workplace injuries. When he prepared his presentation, he tried to make the information more accessible and memorable by respecting the limits of people's short-term memory.

Figure 17.5 Make Information Accessible and Memorable

The audience and occasion for this presentation required that the information be accessible so that listeners could understand it and memorable so that they could remember it.

A company safety officer had to arrange safety certification seminars for all employees as part of the company's safety program. In the introductory session for new employees and biannual update for current employees, he needed to review the procedures for handling a variety of hazardous and toxic substances, each with numerous steps for safe handling and disposal.

Rather than say, "You must learn all 27 hazardous and toxic substances in your work area," he chunked the substances into categories. This chunking enabled him to say, "You must learn the five categories of hazardous and toxic substances in your work area. Each category has between four and seven substances."

Later in the seminar, he found another segment he could make more accessible. Rather than say, "You must learn the twelve standard steps for emergency action if any misuse of hazardous and toxic substances occurs in your work area," he chunked these steps. Thus, he was able to say, "You must learn the three main stages for responding to any misuse of hazardous and toxic substances in your work area. Each stage has four steps."

Vary Pacing in a Presentation

Just as a monotonous tone of voice can tire listeners, an unvarying pace can also tire (and annoy) listeners. You vary your pace in presentations by changing the speed at which you present information as well as changing the type of activities listeners will be involved in.

- If you try to cram too much information into the time allotted for your presentation, you'll be forced to rush. It's convenient to know how much text (an outline or script, for example) can be covered in a set time period. For example, the script for a 20-minute presentation typically should not exceed 8 double-spaced pages.
- If you integrate difficult material with easy material, the audience will have an easier time keeping up with your argument.
- Lengthy presentations are generally more effective (as well as enjoyable) if there is some audience participation. For example, in a day-long session, you might begin with a formal presentation followed by small-group discussions. Select activities that encourage audience participation.

A benefits manager designed an evening-long presentation (Figure 17.6 on page 500) to include an engaging slide show and active involvement in small groups. He was particularly careful to adjust the pace so that participants wouldn't feel overwhelmed (or bored).

PURPOSES OF PRESENTATIONS

Presentations can be thought of on a continuum that moves from informal to formal, as explained in Figure 17.7 (on page 500). So, for example, an informal presentation that provides information might be a brief summary of potential new paper suppliers that you give

Figure 17.6 Vary the Pace

Variations in the mode of presentation as well as the content increase people's attention span and the amount of information they can absorb.

The benefits manager for a company's personnel office needed to arrange a three-hour evening program for about 60 employees who were considering early retirement.

The program started with the benefits manager giving a 30-minute formal presentation about the advantages and disadvantages of early retirement. Then he presented a short slide show of three different scenarios for early retirement. Each scenario emphasized two critical concerns: (1) financial issues such as investment income and taxes and (2) personal issues such as boredom and depression.

After the formal presentation, the audience was able to select any four of six small groups for 25-minute question-and-answer sessions about specific aspects of retirement—for example, medical coverage, taxes on investments, taking a part-time job, and so on. A representative from Human Resources attended each group to answer the questions about specific aspects of retirement. People moved from one small group session to another every 25 minutes.

For the final portion of the program, the entire group came back together briefly to learn about upcoming sessions dealing with retirement.

Figure 17.7 Characteristics of Informal and Formal Presentations

INFORMAL PRESENTATIONS TEND TO . . .	FORMAL PRESENTATIONS TEND TO . . .
• have an *audience* that is already familiar with the subject of the presentation and probably familiar with the presenter	• have an *audience* that is unfamiliar with the subject of the presentation and probably unfamiliar with the presenter
• respond to a *purpose* for which elaborated explanations and details may be unnecessary or inappropriate	• respond to a *purpose* for which elaborated explanations and details are often needed for understanding the main points
• address an *occasion* in which the audience is already involved or about which it knows a great deal	• address an *occasion* from which the audience is distant (whether politically or geographically) or which it knows little about
• assume a relatively informal tone appropriate for a presentation addressed to an audience familiar with the subject, presenter, and occasion	• assume a relatively formal tone appropriate for a presentation addressed to an audience unfamiliar with the subject, presenter, and occasion
• be relatively short, since background explanations are often omitted	• be long enough to include background explanations appropriate for the audience

during a weekly department meeting. A formal presentation that provides information might be a 20-minute prepared talk with slides that explains the results of an 18-month experiment with telecommuting that you give during a national conference.

Regardless of the level of formality, workplace presentations have four broad purposes, which generally occur in combination:

- providing background information
- moving to action
- demonstrating
- training

Background presentations provide listeners with verifiable information. However, presentations usually have some built-in bias. For example, a marketing representative for control systems software gave a presentation about options for inventory control at a conference. The presenter explained that inventory control systems that are tied into point-of-sale registers provide the most accurate and current accounting. Not surprisingly, her company sells software to operate such systems. Her presentation not only summarized various types of inventory control systems, but it also included persuasive elements (and potential bias) because the systems that she ranked highest were the systems her company sold.

Presentations designed to move listeners to action try to convince the audience about the advantages of engaging in particular actions. They can range from a sales pitch for brand X office equipment to a proposal for cross-training assembly workers in a manufacturing facility. A presenter who wants to convince listeners they should accept a proposition tries to establish common ground between her ideas and the ideas of the listeners. A presenter

ETHICS

ORAL PRESENTATIONS AS REFLECTIONS OF CORPORATE AND PERSONAL ETHICS

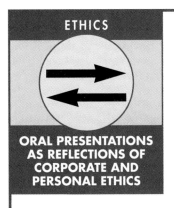

What happens when communicators give oral presentations that are in line with the corporation's code of ethics but in conflict with their own? In some instances, communicators deflect the issue in a statement like, "My company's position is X, and, as a representative of my company, my personal beliefs are irrelevant." However, at other times presenters may feel strongly enough about an ethical issue to distance themselves from the company's position. In these cases, presenters must realize that a public statement, whether an expression of a personal belief or a manifestation of a corporate ethical stance, has potentially a broad reception, including audiences far beyond those present.

Even presentations made by mid-level managers have the potential to attract media coverage, particularly if the issue is volatile or the implications for action depart from a previous corporate stance. For example, the controversy surrounding the discovery of contamination in bottled water marketed by Perrier was complicated when multiple divisions of the company issued contradicting statements in response to the initial discovery of the contamination. In part, the different versions reflected personal rather corporate stances.

The ante is upped when the oral presentation is a speech by a corporate CEO rather than, say, a middle manager. Because speeches are newsworthy, corporate CEO speeches represent a company's ethical stance in ways that other corporate communications do not.

may provide information about competing views, but she will also provide verifiable information and relevant evidence supporting her purpose. For example, department supervisors listening to a presentation about flex-time scheduling might be positively influenced by hearing information not only about increases in employee productivity and satisfaction but also about reductions in absenteeism and fewer abuses of sick leave.

Demonstrations show an audience how to do something, so the focus is on the process more than on the presenter. The audience observes the process, which may be defined and described by the action itself or by the presenter acting as a narrator. For example, explaining the process of operating and servicing a new, complex photocopy machine is done more effectively through a demonstration. While the office workers will probably want an introductory overview and a manual for reference, they will first want to *see* how the equipment functions rather than just hear about it. Demonstrations usually include verifiable information about the process and persuasive information to convince people that the approach is feasible. Frequently, demonstrations precede training sessions.

Training teaches participants how to do something, providing them with the opportunity to learn and practice a skill. Training sessions usually include background information (why the training is important) and action information, which involves persuading participants to approach the task in a particular way with a particular level of attention and accuracy. Demonstrations usually show participants how something is done before they have to do it themselves. Trainers not only have to teach concepts and techniques to the assembled group but also have to provide assistance and reassurance to individuals unsure of their own capabilities.

PREPARING A PROFESSIONAL PRESENTATION

If Beth had understood more about the process of preparing an effective presentation, she could have turned her good intentions and misdirected efforts into an effective presentation. The following guidelines about preparing presentations can be traced back nearly 2,500 years to the ancient Greeks, who taught these elements:[4]

- **invention**—discovering what to say about a subject
- **organization**—deciding how to effectively organize or arrange the information
- **style**—making appropriate choices and pleasing arrangements of words
- **memory**—learning the presentation
- **delivery**—using voice and body language to the best advantage

Discovering What to Say: Invention

The ancient Greeks developed an approach to help communicators discover what they want to say about a subject by encouraging them to identify what they already know and to discover what they need to know. In this approach, you first need to formulate a proposition (determine a topic and a position you take about that topic). Then you need to consider how to develop your proposition.

Propositions. If you're going to give a presentation, you need something to talk about—a question, a problem, an issue that the audience needs or wants to hear about. Virtually every subject you might need to speak about can be expressed as a **proposition:** a sentence that makes an assertion about the subject. Even the most apparently bland and straightforward subjects can be expressed as propositions that state positions, as these examples show:

Subject:	project to provide all managers with laptop computer
Proposition:	Data to date indicate that providing all managers with laptop computers will improve project supervision as well as productivity when managers are on road trips.

Questions for Invention. Once you have established a proposition, you can ask a number of questions to help you discover what you want to say about it. Think of what members of your audience want to know. As you put yourself in your audience's place, you can decide which of the following questions are relevant and collect information accordingly. Imagine that X is any subject you might speak about.

Definition	1. To what larger group does X belong? 2. What are the parts of X?
Comparison	3. How is X similar to related topics? 4. How is X different from related topics? 5. Does the intensity, frequency, or kind of X matter?
Relationship	6. What causes X to occur? What is the impact or the effect of X? 7. In what situation does X occur? What situation typically follows X? 8. What is the opposite of X? 9. What is X not?
Circumstance	10. What is possible and what is not possible in relation to X? 11. How can you tell if X has occurred or will occur?
Testimony	12. What do experts say about X? 13. Who supports X? 14. What statistics support (or discredit) X? 15. What are the laws regarding X? 16. What are the precedents or examples regarding X?

Answers to these questions can provide some of the information for virtually any presentation you may need to give, helping you focus your presentation so that it addresses audience needs and interests.

Deciding How to Arrange Information: Organization

It's not possible to provide fail-safe formulas for organizing every presentation, but a basic formula is that every presentation needs an introduction, some kind of central development in the body, and a conclusion, often followed by questions.

Introductions. The initial goal of an introduction is to make the audience receptive to your presentation. Your introduction should get the audience's attention, urge them to feel well disposed toward your cause, and encourage them to be compliant—that is, ready to be instructed or persuaded.[5] If your audience members are already receptive and engaged, your introduction can be quite brief. If they have a negative attitude, you will need to convince them that it is to their advantage to listen to you.

In addition to identifying the subject and purpose in an introduction, you also need to establish your credentials. Usually restraint and modesty in presenting qualifications are more effective than reciting a long list of experiences. Among the things that will help you establish your credibility are your qualifications to deal with this subject, the amount of time you spent on the investigation, the thoroughness of your investigation, and your familiarity with and fair responses to opposing views.

The introduction to a presentation is usually the last part that you prepare. The introduction grows out of the presentation you have developed using the strategies for invention. Depending on the occasion, purpose, and audience for the presentation, you can choose from among five types of common business presentation introductions shown in Figure 17.8.

Whether you are speaking in front of a receptive or a resistant audience, you can end the introduction with a preparatory statement of what's coming up in the presentation (the

Figure 17.8 Types of Introductions for Presentations

TYPE OF INTRODUCTION	EXAMPLES FROM BUSINESS SPEECHES
Inquisitive: This introduction takes the position that the subject is important and merits inquiry, that hearing about it will be interesting. Audience members are engaged as they discover how important the subject is.	I am here today because I believe that the ideas you are examining and JSCOPE's [Joint Services Conference on Professional Ethics] existence as a professional seminar are vitally important for the individual well being of the members of our Armed Services and for the overall *readiness* of all military forces. The question of military character and ethics is not an abstract topic for discussion. It is a *readiness issue.* It is a readiness issue because without ethical leadership in our Armed Forces, there can be no trust by subordinates in the orders of their superiors. There can be none of the special spirit or bonding that we consider essential to the teamwork required for combat. And there would be little confidence by the American people in the rightness of our actions. Without trust and confidence, there cannot be an effective military in America. *—John B. Dalton, Secretary of the Navy, at Joint Services Conference on Professional Ethics, National Defense University, Washington, D.C. 1994*
Corrective: This introduction argues that the subject has been ignored or inaccurately represented. The presentation will correct misunderstandings. Audience members review their own position—and perhaps silently argue or agree with the speaker's views.	As I look around the room, I can see a flicker of recognition. How many of you have heard the term political correctness? That's quite a few. And how many of you have read about political correctness in the news? I'd like to spend the next ten minutes or so talking about what political correctness really means—what it is, and what it isn't—because I believe it's a concept that has been widely misrepresented and misunderstood. *—John Van de Wetering, President, State University of New York at Brockport, 1991*
Narrative: This introduction begins with a relevant story, an anecdote that creates interest in the subject. Audience members wait for the punch line.	There's a story about Edgar Degas, the painter, and a friend of his. Degas' friend was very proud of his new, modern telephone just installed. One day Degas visited for dinner. The friend had purposely arranged to receive a phone call. When the phone rang, he jumped up to answer. He came back to the table beaming with pride. "Well," said Degas, "so that's the telephone. It rings, and you run." *—D. S. Lankford, Marketing Development Vice President, AT&T, 1989*
Hook: This introduction begins with some attention-getting element: a rhetorical question, a startling fact, a challenge. Audience members are encouraged to participate.	Today I'm going to talk about the technology of the future . . . and I'll make a few predictions about what our world will be like over the next 10 to 50 years. That has me a little nervous because anytime you start making predictions, you hope no one nearby has a tape recorder. Here's an example of what I mean. At the Chicago World's Fair way back in 1893, a group of 74 social commentators got together to look 100 years into the future—at the world of 1993. Here are some of their predictions: • Many people will live to be 150. • The government will have grown more simple, as true greatness tends toward simplicity. • Prisons will decline and divorce will be considered unnecessary. • The Nicaraguan canal is as sure to be built as tides are to ebb and flow and the seasons to change. *—Will Kopp, Executive Communication Manager, Battelle, 1993*
Preparatory: This introduction does things such as clarify the purpose, anticipate the method of development, or warn about omissions. Audience members think, "Aha! I need to listen for three particular issues."	Mr. Chairman, and Members of the Committee, I am pleased to participate in this hearing on the appropriate direction for monetary policy in 1993. This morning in my prepared remarks, I want to focus on three issues. The first is what monetary policy can and cannot be expected to do. The second is an evaluation of monetary policy during the past few years, with a comment about the year ahead. And the third is the appropriate role of Congress in overseeing the activities of our nation's central bank. . . . *—W. Lee Hoskins, CEO, The Huntington National Bank, 1992*

final type of introduction listed in Figure 17.8). This preparatory statement should lead smoothly into the main discussion: "This morning I'll discuss three options we have for inventory control. The first one requires adopting bar codes for all stock; it provides the greatest security but also entails the largest initial expenses. . . ."

Development. The **development** of the presentation includes the main points or key arguments and the supporting facts. Your information needs to be organized in a clear, logical manner so that the audience can easily follow the sequence. Because live, in-person presentations don't have a replay button, you need to make the information accessible and memorable to people in the audience the first time they hear it. Thus, for most occasions, you'll use all ten strategies in Figure 17.9 to make your presentations easier for the audience to understand.

Figure 17.9 Ways to Develop an Oral Presentation

STRATEGIES FOR DEVELOPMENT	EXAMPLES
Introduction Incorporate a purpose statement in the introduction.	In this presentation, I introduce the features of the new photocopier and show how these features can make your job much easier.
Incorporate your position into your presentation, either at the beginning (deductive) or at the end (inductive).	The extra initial expense of this photocopier is made up by the savings in personnel time.
Tell the audience how you're organizing the information.	I'll present the features of the photocopier in the order that you're most likely to use them.
Preview what the presentation covers.	By the end of this session, you'll know how to use all the basic operating features, what to do when you see common error messages flashing, and how to complete weekly servicing.
Main Body Identify major points that develop the purpose. Follow up each major point with an example.	Two of the most useful features let you begin with single-sided copies and end up with back-to-back copies that have been automatically collated. For example, imagine that you have 14 laser-printed pages for the departmental newsletter. Put them face down in the tray, push the 2 → 1 button, and then push the sort button. The 14 single-sided pages will turn into 7 collated sheets, printed front and back.
Establish the facts of the situation.	The photocopier you were using took 9.5 seconds per copy; this copier takes only 5.5 seconds per copy.
Refute alternative or opposing views.	Using cartridges for toner is ultimately more efficient and cost-effective even though cartridges are more expensive than buying bulk toner. Replacing the toner cartridge takes about three minutes, and these cartridges can be returned to the local dealer, who will have them refilled.
Use clear transitions to signal a shift from one topic to the next or to indicate a change in perspective.	Now that I've identified the common and special features, I will go through the five most common error messages.
Include summaries of what you've covered at the end of each major point.	So far I've identified the features and explained the most common error messages.
Conclusion Conclude in a way that reviews major points and encourages specific attitudes or actions, draws generalizations, or reestablishes speaker credibility.	*(Review and action)* As you can see, we've covered the basic operating features, learned how to handle the common error messages, and reviewed weekly servicing. With this information you should have no trouble with your first week of operation. As you use the machine this week, keep track of questions you have. I'll try to answer them next week when we meet to learn about using the machine for special projects.

Conclusions and Questions. Rather than just cut a presentation off after making the final key point, a speaker needs to conclude. Again drawing on advice from the ancient Greeks, we identify four possible ways to conclude a presentation: recapitulating, drawing generalizations, encouraging particular attitudes or actions, or reestablishing speaker credibility (Figure 17.10). These approaches work equally well singly or in combination.

Most presentations don't end with the conclusion. Instead, the conclusion is often followed by a question-and-answer session that is every bit as important as the presentation itself. You can reinforce (or, unfortunately, eliminate) the effectiveness of your presentation by your responses to questions.

Figure 17.10 Types of Conclusions for Presentations

TYPE OF CONCLUSION	EXAMPLES FROM BUSINESS SPEECHES
Summarizing or recapitulating: This conclusion restates the facts and central arguments of the main part of the presentation.	[The evidence I've presented supports the position that] organized crime groups are taking advantage of high-tech communication equipment like computers and cellular telephones—trying to stay one step ahead of the law. So what are our options? Are there any solutions? [In summary,] I suggest that there are three places to start. New laws can be passed or existing laws can be modified to empower agencies to combat the changing organized crime problem. Advanced technologies must be continually adapted for use by law enforcement. Finally, we must work on increasing bilateral cooperation between law enforcement agencies around the world. . . . *—William Sessions, Director, FBI, 1992*
Drawing generalizations: This conclusion extends the views in the presentation to their logical consequences by amplifying the speaker's points and minimizing any opposing views.	We in industry must play the role of responsible informant. We have to be more responsive to the public appetite for information. We have to be forthcoming with our expertise. . . . For far too many years, public policy in America has been wrenched this way and that by a prevailing belief—on all sides—that economic growth is incompatible with environmental protection. Increasingly, the evidence from many nations around the world shows us that belief is false . . . that a society must be economically healthy to be ecologically healthy. We are learning that energy, environment, and economic development are three basic human needs. Our policy should aim, not for a trade off between them, but for a synthesis among them. If our society could achieve that, this great nation would find itself once again on the cutting edge . . . and once again, we could say to our competitors, "Beware!" *—Kenneth Derr, CEO, Chevron, 1992*
Encouraging audience attitudes or actions: This conclusion urges the listeners to adopt a particular stance or engage in a particular action.	When you get home, take a close look at your clients and would-be clients, your policyholders and potential policyholders. Choose the one or two who are the most under-insured, who are in the most jeopardy without your services. Make the extra effort to serve these people and eliminate their risk. You can't pursue every potential policyholder to the ends of the earth. But even if you don't make the sale—although I sincerely hope and think you will—you will feel better for making the effort. And it's something extra, a feel-good effort for yourself. You will have assured your peace of mind and done your best to ensure your policyowner's peace of mind. It will emphasize the vital, meaningful nature of our work. Approach each piece of business with the values that you hold within. It is by Moving Beyond, by cherishing the cornerstone values, that we best serve ourselves, our company, our families, and our policyowners. This is important work that we do—and I thank each of you for doing it so well. *—Donald Schuenke, CEO, Northwestern Mutual Life, 1992*
Reestablishing speaker credibility: This conclusion reinforces the ethical appeal of the speaker (and perhaps the unfavorable view of the opposition).	In all things, we do well to remember that we are but temporary custodians of this fragile planet. And I, for one, don't want to pass this remarkable gift on to my children and grandchildren, knowing that we had a chance to do the right thing but, in the end, we just couldn't bring ourselves to face up to our responsibilities. *—Paul Craig Roberts, Distinguished Fellow at the CATO Institute, 1994*

Choosing the Right Words: Style

Style is difficult to define. You hear people say they know it when they hear it, or they recognize it when they see it. But those comments don't help much when you're trying to decide how to make a presentation effective.

Effective style generally includes using vocabulary appropriate for the purpose and audience, using figures of speech that create images and help convey ideas, and using sentences and paragraphs of the appropriate length and structure. Figures of speech, essentially ways of organizing the words you use, are especially valuable in making a presentation clear. Your audience responds not only to what you say but also to how you say it—literally, the sound of the words. While there are many figures of speech, the ones defined and illustrated in Figure 17.11 on page 506 are particularly useful for oral presentations. The terminology is useful as a way to discuss those concepts that can help you plan more effective, appealing presentations.

Figure 17.11 Types of Figures of Speech

FIGURE OF SPEECH	EXAMPLES
Parallelism: placing related ideas in a series of similar words, phrases, or clauses	. . . government of the people, by the people, for the people, shall not perish from the earth. —*Abraham Lincoln, Gettysburg Address, 1863*
Antithesis: juxtaposing contrasting ideas	That's one small step for a man, one giant leap for mankind. —*Neil Armstrong (as he stepped on the moon), 1969*
Repetition: repeating consonants repeating similar vowel sounds	We replace drift and deadlock with renewal and reform. —*Bill Clinton, State of the Union Address, 1994* American businessmen have a love affair with the quick-fix initiatives that we find in the one-minute manager books. This month the mantra is quality. Next month it's restructuring. Then reengineering. Then reinventing. —*Lawrence Bossidy, CEO, Allied Signal, Inc., 1994*
repeating words from one clause to the next	Let there be justice for all. Let there be peace for all. Let there be work, bread, water, and salt for all. Let each know that for each the body, the mind and the soul have been freed to fulfill themselves. —*Nelson Mandela, President of South Africa, 1994*
repeating words in successive clauses, in reverse grammatical order	. . . ask not what your country can do for you; ask what you can do for your country. —*John F. Kennedy, Inaugural Address, 1961*
Metaphor: equating two unlike things that share something in common	Today's Yankee trader knows the lesson of the bamboo seed. The bamboo seed is a nut, enclosed by a very hard skin. You plant it the first year, and add fertilizer and water. Nothing happens. You water and fertilize it for the second year, the third year, and the fourth year, and nothing happens. But when the fifth year arrives, the bamboo grows 90 feet in six weeks. So now we are watering and fertilizing, and so should you. When your business grows 90 feet in six weeks, and someone asks how you did it in such a short time, you'll have the right answer. —*Susan Au Allen, President, U.S. Pan Asian Chamber of Commerce, 1993*
Simile: comparing two unlike things that share something in common	I think of doing business in Japan as being like a game of football. But, first, you need to know which game of football it is that you are playing. . . . Gridiron football is trench warfare; soccer-football is the cavalry. —*M. George Allen, Senior Vice President, 3M, 1994*
Personification: giving human qualities or abilities to abstractions or inanimate objects	I am immensely encouraged that our nation is beginning to **grapple** with these issues [inflation, budget deficit, international trade, and health care], which it had put off during the 80s. —*Robert P. Forrestal, President and CEO, Federal Reserve Bank of America, 1994* [A series of historical events since the eighteenth century] are some of the more notable instances of the on-again, off-again **flirtation** China has had with the West. —*Barbara Hackman Franklin, Former U.N. Secretary of Commerce, 1993*
Rhetorical question: asking a question to make a statement or assertion	Multimedia will not only create a new world—it could very well solve some problems with the old one. We're on the threshold of a very exciting era. You may wonder: How did we get here? —*Bert Roberts, Jr., CEO, MCI, 1993*

Learning the Presentation: Memory

Contemporary audiences respond better to presentations that aren't memorized. Our advice: Don't memorize your presentation unless you're a stage actor presenting the speaker as part of a performance. While you should be very familiar with the content and sequence of your presentation, you can use notecards, outlines, or a sequence of transparencies as occasional prompts.

Notecards. Your notecards, whether consisting of index cards or sheets of paper, can contain the main points of your presentation. They might also include specific facts, details, or statistics as well as any direct quotations that you want to mention. Figure 17.12 shows the seven topic headings on the note card used by Lisa Harry in the formal presentation she gave to her business communication class about updating and redesigning the employee handbook for the Association of Boards of Certification (ABC). Lisa, Document and Technical Coordinator for ABC, was responsible for maintaining this handbook. She gave her 15-minute class presentation in preparation for her formal presentation to her boss, the ABC Director, and to other ABC managers.

Figure 17.12 Notecard for Oral Presentation

1.0	Show how reorganizing will make the sequence of information in the manual more logical.
2.0	Note ABC's vulnerability because of missing policies.
3.0	Note ABC's vulnerability because of outdated policies.
4.0	Emphasize that information needs to be appealing to employees.
5.0	Show how information can be made more accessible to employees.
6.0	Identify problems solved. Acknowledge problems remaining.
7.0	Encourage approval of the proposed revision.

Outlines. If you prefer using a single sheet of paper rather than notecards, you might use a topic outline to organize the main and subordinate ideas of your presentation. A topic outline is usually easier to use than a complete script of your presentation, which you might be tempted to read. The audience didn't come to hear you *read* to them; they want you *talk to* them and *with* them. Even if you prepare the complete text of the presentation (perhaps for publication in a company newsletter or in conference proceedings), your presentation is far more appealing if you do not read.

Figure 17.13 on the next page shows the outline that Lisa Harry decided to use for her formal presentation to her boss, the ABC Director, and to other ABC managers. After her class presentation, Lisa realized that the notes (Figure 17.12) were inadequate. She knew she needed to have a full outline of what she wanted to cover in the presentation. She then used the notes to remind herself what she needed to emphasize in each section of the outline. The outer columns of Figure 17.13 show how her notes coordinated with the outline she used for the formal presentation at ABC.

Outlines also allow you to make changes while you're talking. For example, sometimes you may be on a panel, and the speakers before you take too much time. Because your time is unexpectedly reduced, you need to be able to look at your outline and decide how

TECHNOLOGY

MULTIMEDIA PRESENTATIONS

Multimedia presentation programs, which can be run on most new MS-DOS or Macintosh computers, allow an individual to create presentation materials that incorporate overhead transparency slides, sound, and even videotape. With these programs, the presenter can create custom overheads which can be animated to change as the presentation progresses. These full-color overheads can be presented using a portable computer and a special LCD (liquid crystal display) overhead projector. More elaborate versions incorporate sound—music, spoken testimonials, or sound effects—to enhance the entertainment and persuasive value of the presentation.

The most common software for creating business presentations includes Microsoft's PowerPoint, WordPerfect's Present, and Aldus' Persuasion. Other programs, such as Gold Disk's Astound and Macromedia's Action, are also available. A businessperson can put together a crisp, professional presentation in a few hours on a laptop computer that in the past would have required days of working closely with artists, designers, and photographers.

Since it is difficult to ensure that the presentation site will have the necessary equipment, presenters generally must plan on having their own portable equipment.

Figure 17.13 Outline Excerpt for Oral Presentation

Association of Boards of Certification
Revision of Employee Handbook

Show how reorganizing will make the sequence of information in the manual more logical.

1.0 Reorganize
- 1.1 General employment information
- 1.2 Salary administration
- 1.3 Employee benefits
- 1.4 Work environment

Note ABC's vulnerability because of missing policies.

2.0 Write new policies
- 2.1 Harassment policy
- 2.2 Discipline and termination procedures
- 2.3 Equal employment opportunity policy
- 2.4 Complaint procedures
- 2.5 Resignation policy
- 2.6 Recording hours worked
- 2.7 Leave restrictions

Note ABC's vulnerability because of outdated policies.

3.0 Update old policies
- 3.1 Medical, dental, and optical appointments
- 3.2 Pay period
- 3.3 Payment of benefits
- 3.4 Application for leave
- 3.5 Cancellation
- 3.6 Maternity-paternity leave
- 3.7 Lunch
- 3.8 Flex-time

Emphasize that information needs to be appealing to employees.

4.0 Design attractive format
- 4.1 Cover page
- 4.2 Page template
- 4.3 Formulas
- 4.4 Schedules

Show how information can be made more accessible to employees.

5.0 Create a usable document
- 5.1 Table of contents
- 5.2 Accurate policies
- 5.3 Headings
- 5.4 Page numbers
- 5.5 Typographical cues
  - 5.5.1 Italics
  - 5.5.2 Boldface
  - 5.5.3 Type size

Identify problems solved.

6.0 Problems
- 6.1 Problems solved
  - 6.1.1 Policy examples
  - 6.1.2 Usability testing
  - 6.1.3 Expert testing
  - 6.1.4 Binding

Acknowledge problems remaining.

- 6.2 Problems remaining
  - 6.2.1 Approval and acceptance from staff, supervisor, legal counsel, and board of directors

Encourage approval of the proposed revision.

7.0 Action

to shorten your presentation. Another benefit of an outline is being able to see where you want to make connections to comments made by the speakers before you—easier to do by topic than by stretches of text. You can jot down such connections on your outline as others are speaking.

Cues from Visual Aids. Lisa took the main points from her outline (Figure 17.13) and created a series of transparencies to use during her presentation. Figure 17.14 shows one of the transparencies Lisa created using PowerPoint, an easy-to-use presentation software. Her handwritten notes on her paper copy of the transparency enabled her to place the transparency on the projector and have the related notes in hand.

Using Appearance, Voice, and Body Language: Delivery

People respond to your image before they respond to your message—that is, they start to form opinions based on what you look like and how you sound *before* they listen to what you say. Your professional image is created by a combination of factors: appearance, voice, mannerisms, and body language. Problems in any one of these areas can detract from the overall impression people may receive. This section of the chapter identifies some of the ways you can create a positive professional image.

Figure 17.14 Transparency with Marginal Handwritten Notes

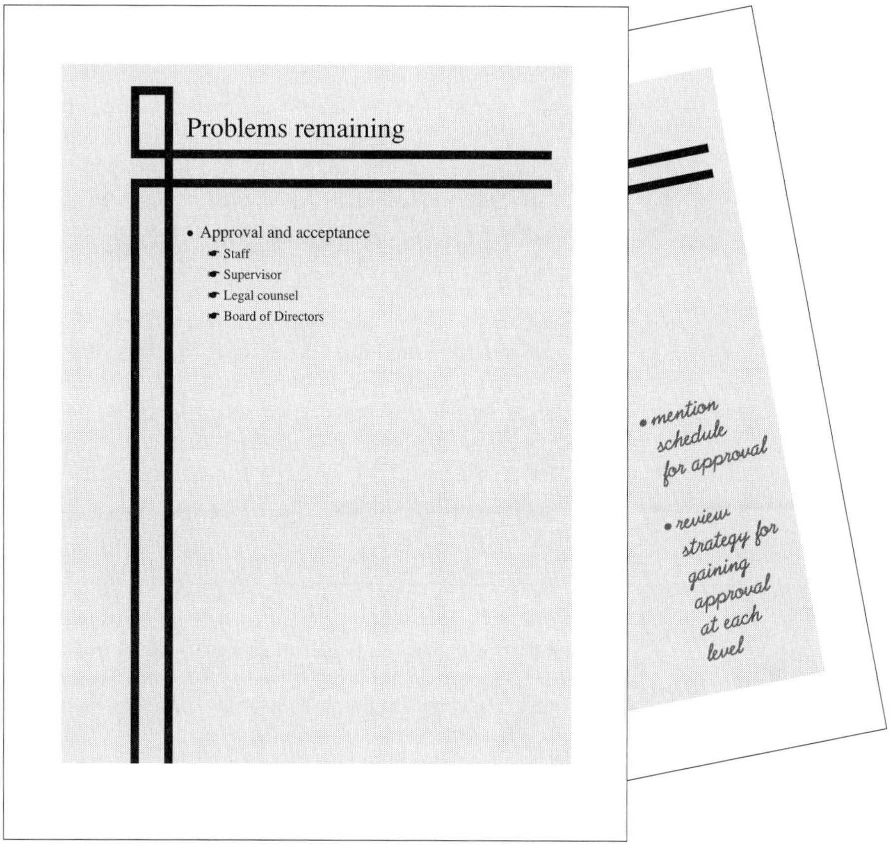

Your decisions about the delivery of your presentation will be influenced by the formality—or informality—of the situation.

Professional Appearance. You need to select clothes and accessories that are appropriate for your speaking occasion. While a navy pin-stripe suit might be appropriate in the boardroom, casual attire and a hardhat are more suitable on the production floor of a manufacturing facility. Beyond basing your decisions on the occasion, though, you need to wear clothes that feel comfortable and familiar. This means that you probably shouldn't wear brand-new clothes because you might be more concerned with how the clothes fit than with the content of the presentation.

You also need to consider the impression that you make with your accessories. Accessories should not detract from your professional image. For example, men and women who wear distracting earrings or bracelets that jingle every time they move might consider other choices when they're making a formal presentation.

What you wear should never attract more attention than what you have to say. Take a few minutes before a presentation—before stepping in front of an audience—to make a final check of clothing, jewelry, and hair. Adjusting zippers or tugging at underwear can spoil an otherwise professional image. Everything should be in place *before* you get up to speak.

Vocal Characteristics. Audiences respond to the sound of a speaker's voice before they respond to the content of the message. Your vocal characteristics—projection, pronunciation, pacing, and pitch—should be used to capture and keep audience attention.

Speakers need to *project* their voices enough to reach everyone in the room, even people sitting in the back. Try to practice in a room that's the same size as the one where you'll make your presentation. If you are speaking in a very large room, use a microphone, but practice speaking with it so you aren't surprised when you hear your voice and so that you don't create electronic feedback.

Speakers who mispronounce words or drop, add, or slur letters or syllables generally lessen their credibility. Your *pronunciation* needs to be accurate. Before a presentation, check the pronunciation of any words you're unsure about, especially foreign or unusual words, technical terms, key points in your presentation, and the names of people.

Your *pacing*—your rate of speech—affects audience reactions. Most people have an average speaking rate of approximately 150 words per minute. A rapid pace demands the audience's full attention, but it also means that people may miss some of the content. A slow pace allows carefully placed emphasis, but some people may become bored or restless. You can increase audience attention by planning variations in pacing that coincide with your need to emphasize certain points.

The *pitch* of your voice—its highness or lowness—influences how appealing you are to listen to. People don't enjoy listening to voices that are whiny, shrill, or nasal. They also don't enjoy listening to the monotone created by an unvarying pitch. Because pitch is controlled by muscle tension, relaxing before a presentation can help your voice sound natural.

A presenter's voice is so important that voice coaching is big business in the workplace. Professionals who do a great deal of speaking often receive specialized coaching to improve their projection, pronunciation, pacing, and pitch. Many companies have a branch of Toast-

SKILLS & STRATEGIES

HANDLING QUESTIONS FROM THE AUDIENCE

You have a number of options for handling questions from an audience. You may choose to accept questions during a presentation if you don't mind being interrupted, if you can keep your place and get back to it after giving an answer, and if the presentation is relatively informal. You can also ask people to hold their questions until the question-and-answer session at the end. In any case, you face a number of potential problems, listed in the accompanying table.

Potential Problem	Discussion
You don't know the answer.	Don't panic. You're not expected to know everything. You should feel comfortable saying something like this: "Although that's a relevant question, I don't have a good answer. However, if you'd like me to find out, contact me after the presentation."
A person in the audience disagrees with you.	Acknowledge the specific areas of disagreement and suggest that multiple interpretations are possible. However, if you feel that the person is incorrect, another response is to focus directly on the area of the conflict. *Example:* I understand your reluctance to approve the retraining of all the support personnel; the expense of such training is high. However, our research shows that in similar-size organizations, the payback period for such retraining is less than 18 months.
One person may monopolize the question time.	Ask if anyone else has a question. If no one does, invite the monopolizer to continue the discussion with you after the presentation.
A person asks about something you have already carefully explained.	Treat the question—and the person—seriously because you can't tell why the person asked the question. Give a straightforward professional response if you can.
A person asks a question that has nothing to do with the topic or that you don't understand.	Ask the person to *rephrase* the question; it may be just poorly worded. Don't ask the person to *repeat* the question, because you might get a repetition of the same question. If rephrasing doesn't clarify the question, you might not be able to offer an answer.
You or the audience can't hear a question.	Ask the person to repeat it. If members of the audience can't hear a question, repeat it for everyone. This repetition has the additional benefit of confirming that you understand the question.
A person in the audience actually makes a statement instead of asking a question.	As a courtesy, you can voice an interest in the person's point of view and follow up by asking if the person has a question.
No one has a question.	Thank the audience and conclude the presentation.

masters, professionals who work with colleagues to help them improve their presentation skills. Toastmasters is an international organization that has effective professional communication as its major goal. Toastmasters will help you rehearse your presentation and make suggestions to assist you in giving a polished presentation.

Mannerisms. The *mannerisms* you use in a presentation also contribute to the professional demeanor you create. Two specific areas involve handling notes and managing mistakes. Handling your notes smoothly creates a positive image. A person who fumbles with notes, shuffles pages, and can't locate a needed transparency gives the impression of being unprepared and disorganized. If you're not using a podium, use a firm backing (e.g., notebook, clipboard) for your notes so that the sheets don't bend and shake.

Mistakes happen. Everyone who has done a great deal of speaking has a collection of "you wouldn't believe" stories to tell. Although presenters try to prevent or minimize mistakes, the way mistakes are handled is often what distinguishes experienced from inexperienced presenters. Accept the likelihood that you will make mistakes. If they're ones that no one else notices, go on as if nothing happened. If it's a mistake that the audience notices, briefly apologize and go on.

Body Language. The final factor in creating your professional image is your *body language*. Your general goal is to appear poised and prepared. If you have something important to say and have prepared carefully, you don't want to waste your efforts through body language that says you're insecure and unprepared. You should avoid the following behaviors that signal nervousness:

- losing control of your hands: playing with keys or loose change in your pocket(s); making lots of dramatic gestures (instead, gesture naturally, as you would in conversation); playing with the pointer, especially the telescoping kind; keeping your hands locked in place at your side; cracking your knuckles
- losing control of your feet: rocking back and forth, standing on one foot, pacing
- losing control of your body: rolling your shoulders, doing knee bends, standing rigidly, clutching or leaning on the podium
- losing control of your visual focus: staring off into space at a point above the audience, staring intently at members of the audience

PREPARING VISUALS AND OTHER SUPPORT MATERIALS

Most people have much stronger visual memories than auditory (hearing) memories. Thus, visual aids can increase your audience's retention of information by approximately 20 percent, which is a big help since most members of an audience remember only about half of what they hear immediately after hearing it. Whenever possible you should show rather than tell, using visuals both as support for complex information and to preview and review key points.

Functions of Visuals in Presentations

Visuals that create appeal can be used on introductory or title slides or transparencies to set the tone. Such visuals might include anything from cartoon figures commenting on the content to elaborate borders that create a distinct image. Visuals that have a decorative function make the presentation more aesthetically appealing (Figure 17.15).

Visuals that depict actual people, processes, and objects reinforce oral information in a presentation by making it more concrete. Such visuals can identify components or parts,

Figure 17.15 Create Visual Appeal

The addition of a decorative element to a presentation reinforced an image the presenter wanted to convey.

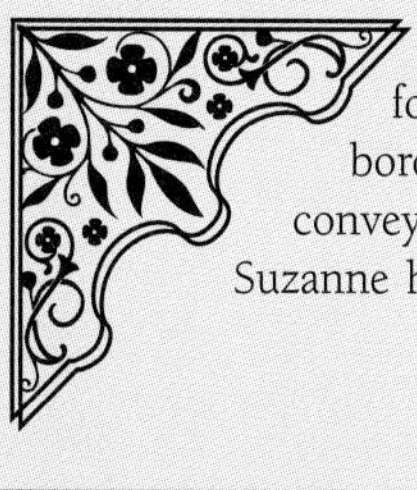

When making a formal presentation to the mall manager about her plan for a new lingerie shop, Suzanne Frantz uses the corner of a Victorian border on all her transparencies, which creates a unifying image and also conveys the sense of elegance. The corner design also sends the message that Suzanne has carefully prepared her materials.

show appearance or structure, or identify locations. Visuals reinforce a speaker's points and increase audience retention of information as shown in the situation in Figure 17.16.

Visuals can provide a framework that helps an audience more easily understand relationships between various aspects of oral information in a presentation. These organizational relationships may be between people or departments in a company or between components in mechanical systems (Figure 17.17).

Visuals help readers understand complex information. A great deal of numeric information is often particularly difficult for an audience to understand without some visual support (Figure 17.18).

Figure 17.16 Show Appearance, Components, and Location

The visuals—in this case, the photograph and the diagrams—gave the audience an accurate picture of what the equipment looked like.

In preparing a sales presentation for a new code reader that would speed grocery store checkouts, Jake Sears was able to put all of the visuals supporting his sales pitch on his portable computer. When he arrived for the presentation, he set up his computer. Among the important visuals were photographs and diagrams of the code reader. Because of his software's capability, Jake was able to rotate the images on his computer so the audience could see the equipment from all sides.

Figure 17.17 Identify Relationships

Visuals can quickly and efficiently illustrate connections that would be more difficult to understand if presented only orally.

In explaining a departmental reorganization plan to two departments that would be combined, Martin Juarez presented three organizational charts. The first, in blue, showed the existing incoming inspection department. The second, in red, detailed the existing in-process inspection department. The third chart highlighted the new combined department, using blue and red for functions and positions that would remain separate and purple for functions and roles that would be combined.

Figure 17.18 Aid Interpretation

Graphs made it easier to understand why there wasn't enough town revenue to support all requests from town departments. Even though many of the requests were important, even essential, some difficult cuts would need to be made.

In preparing to present the proposed budget for the new fiscal year to the town, the Chair of the Finance Committee designed a series of graphs:

- Graph 1 showed all the sources of revenue.
- Graph 2 showed the minimum expenditures for level funding, which equaled the sources of revenue.
- Graph 3 showed the requested additional expenditures. These expenses ranged from big-ticket items such as a rescue vehicle for the fire department and a new roof for the town hall to relatively small expenditures such as funding a lifeguard position for the community beach and paying for certification renewal courses required for the town's tax assessors.

Handouts to Accompany Presentations

Audiences generally like having a handout because it provides visual reinforcement for oral information. However, preparing a handout packet is worth the effort only if you refer to it directly during the presentation or if people in the audience are likely to refer to it afterward. Not only do handouts help the audience follow along with the presentation, they also have additional uses:

- duplicating presentation visuals
- defining complex terminology
- summarizing key points
- listing sources for the presentation and those for further reference
- providing a recap to check after the presentation

There is considerable debate among experts about *when* to distribute a handout. Some say never to distribute a handout until the end of the presentation. If the handout is simply a text of a formal talk, we agree: wait until the end.

Other experts say that the decision to distribute a handout at the beginning or the end depends on the purpose of the handout and the nature of the audience. For example, if the handout duplicates the transparencies and the audience would be likely to take notes on the handout sheets, they need them at the beginning of the presentation, not at the end.

In any case, if you distribute the packet at the beginning of your presentation, you can tell the audience that you will refer to the appropriate pages or sections as you go along. After you refer to a page in the packet, give people a few moments to locate the place. Handout packets don't need to duplicate the presentation; instead, they should highlight or summarize key points and provide information that might be difficult to remember.

Types of Visuals for Presentations

Visual information in a presentation can take many forms. As you decide about the most appropriate visuals to accompany a presentation, you need to consider audience needs and knowledge, your purpose, graphic design resources, finances, time available for presentation, equipment available, and so on. In making your decision, you also need to consider two other important factors: preparation time and audience size.

Computer generated visuals can add interest and authority to your presentations.

Preparation Time. All visuals take time to prepare. Figure 17.19 shows the relative preparation time for various kinds of visuals.

Audience Size. Your visuals need to match the size of the audience and room (Figure 17.20 on page 514). Audiences quickly become annoyed when visuals are too small to see. Presenters who use flip charts and posters displayed on easels should allow 1 inch of letter height for every 10 feet of audience. (So a room that's 20 feet long needs letters in displays to be 2 inches high to be seen in the back of the room.) However, this guideline becomes impractical in a large room, so a presenter should switch from charts to overhead transparencies in medium-size rooms.

Figure 17.19 Match Type of Visual and Preparation Time

VISUAL	LITTLE PREPARATION (DONE ON SITE)	SOME PREPARATION (1 TO 5 HOURS)	LENGTHY PREPARATION (5 HOURS TO MANY DAYS)
Flip chart	•		
Chalkboard	•		
Prepared charts		•	
Prepared transparencies		•	
Demonstrations		•	
35-mm slides		•	•
Physical models			•
Videotapes			•
Films			•
Multimedia presentations			•

Figure 17.20 Match Type of Visual and Room Size

VISUAL	SMALL (UP TO 20) AUDIENCE ROOM	MEDIUM (20 TO 50) AUDIENCE ROOM	LARGE (50+) AUDIENCE ROOM
Flip chart	•		
Chalkboard	•		
Prepared charts	•		
Transparencies	•	• (large screen)	
Demonstrations	•	• (on camera)	
Physical models	•	• (on camera)	
35-mm slides	•	• (large screen)	• (large screen)
Videotapes	•	• (large screen)	• (large screen)
Films	•	• (large screen)	• (large screen)
Multimedia presentations	•	• (large screen)	• (large screen)

Transparencies should use a minimum of 20-point type, though 24-point in some fonts is better. In a very large room, such as an auditorium, 35-mm slides work better.

When audiences can't see your visuals, they get frustrated and restless. Some members may strain to read the visual. Others may turn to the next person and ask what the visual says. In any case, if your visuals are too small to read comfortably, your audience will pay more attention to the inadequacy of the visuals than to the content of your presentation.

Computer Software. Presentation graphics software can make your professional life much easier. These programs enable you to create an outline of the information you want to present, select a template (standard format) for the slides or transparencies, and then adapt or customize these templates to create slides. Such programs also enable you to view each slide individually or to the see the entire sequence. This way, you can easily rearrange them in any order. Presentation software also enables you to print versions of each slide to use on handouts (one, two, three, or more to a page) so that the audience has copies of the transparencies or slides for easy reference as well as for notetaking.[6]

Once the computer graphics are presented, you have your choice of presentation approaches. If you have a portable or laptop computer and an LCD (liquid crystal display) panel, you can project images directly from the computer onto a screen. Most people, however, still make the images into transparencies to display on an overhead projector.

EVALUATING PRESENTATIONS

A presentation's effectiveness depends on how well it addresses the occasion, audience, and purpose. A "good" presentation doesn't always mean the same thing, because different criteria apply for different occasions, purposes, and audiences.

occasion: A presentation given in a monthly project meeting by a marketing intern is going to be evaluated differently from one given at a national convention by a marketing manager with ten years of experience.

purpose: A presentation given to inform new employees about their benefit package is going to be evaluated differently from one given to union members worried about their collective bargaining package.

audience: A presentation given to a group of summer interns will be evaluated differently from one given to a company's department managers.

Figure 17.21 Selected Questions for Evaluating an Oral Presentation

CATEGORY FOR EVALUATION	QUESTIONS FOR EVALUATION
Physical environment	• Is the presentation area organized with the appropriate podium and equipment before the presenter begins? • Is all the equipment working? • Is the presentation area arranged so that all members of the audience have a clear view of the speaker as well as the screen or display area? • Are the visuals large enough that everyone in the audience can see them?
Accuracy and clarity of message	• Is the information accurate and attributed to a verifiable source? • Is the information balanced and unbiased? • Are the concepts, vocabulary, and visuals adapted to the audience? • Do the examples support the main points? Are they relevant and understandable? Are they appropriate for the audience?
Appropriateness of purpose	• Does the speaker acknowledge the audience's purpose in listening? • Are the speaker's purpose and position clearly stated? • Do the content and organization of the information support the purpose?
Adaptation for audience	• Does the presenter focus audience attention with an engaging opening? • Can the audience clearly identify a position and main points? • Is the information organized logically and effectively for the audience? • Do transitions and other revisions for achieving coherence help the members of the audience recognize connections between ideas? • Does the audience have the benefit of periodic previews and reviews? • Are the visuals appropriate for the audience? • Can the audience recognize the conclusion and know what action, if any, is expected of them?
Adaptation for occasion	• Is the informality or formality of the presentation appropriate for the occasion? • Has the presenter appropriately matched the purpose with the occasion?
Preparation and professionalism of speaker	• Is the presenter well prepared? • Is the presenter appropriately poised and professional for the occasion? • Does the presenter speak with sufficient volume and a pleasant tone? • Are the presenter's pronunciation, inflection, and pacing appropriate? • Does the presenter respect time limits? • Does the presenter's body language reinforce the content of the presentation and seem appropriate for the occasion? • Does the speaker have any annoying habits? • Does the presenter use direct eye contact with the entire range of the audience? • Does the presenter handle notes comfortably? • Does the presenter handle audience questions directly and gracefully? • If the presentation is collaborative, are the transitions between speakers smooth?

You probably won't use the same criteria to evaluate every presentation. For a 5-minute presentation given in a monthly project meeting, a speaker who doesn't use notes or any supporting visuals can't be judged on these criteria. In a presentation that is purposely taking a particular side of an issue, a speaker can't be criticized for not being balanced and unbiased. In order to evaluate a presentation, you need to know what criteria apply. The list in Figure 17.21 (page 515), though not inclusive, gives you some suggestions about areas and questions that are often useful for evaluating presentations.

While the questions in Figure 17.21 are useful when you're evaluating others' presentations, they are also useful when you're evaluating yourself. The most efficient way to evaluate yourself is to videotape a practice session and then to view the tape, using the relevant questions to assess your own performance. You will need to recast each question to ask yourself about your own performance, as in Figure 17.22.

You can revise each question along the lines of Figure 17.22 so that you can complete an effective self-assessment. The ability to be constructively self-critical is an important characteristic of successful presenters. Skillful presenters are able to identify what they do effectively as well as identify areas that need improvement, determine the most effective changes, and then implement the corrections.

Figure 17.22 Questions for Evaluating Your Own Oral Presentation

INSTEAD OF ASKING . . .	ASK . . .
• Is the presentation area organized with the appropriate podium and equipment before the presenter begins?	• Will the audience think that the presentation area is well organized?
• Does the presenter focus audience attention with an engaging opening?	• Do I focus audience attention with an engaging opening?
• Is the presenter's pronunciation correct?	• Do I know how to correctly pronounce all the words in my presentation?

MULTICULTURAL

ORAL PRESENTATION TO AN INTERNATIONAL AUDIENCE

Different cultures have varying ideas about what constitutes an effective oral presentation. Americans generally like presentations that seem natural and spontaneous, not "canned" or overly rehearsed. Most other countries, however, expect formality. "Natural" presentations, it is thought, give the impression that the speaker does not respect the audience.

Other expectations also differ. Germans and Swiss, like Americans, prefer a fast-paced, efficient presentation. Your German business partner, however, may become very uncomfortable with the informality you convey if you bring your coffee to your presentation. Latin American and Arab audiences expect a presentation to be in short and separate segments that allow time for questions and reflection about what has been presented. Arabs in particular think a presentation should allow for frequent digressions.

Moreover, audience behavior varies from culture to culture. Japanese audiences, for example, usually sit and nod their heads (which means they understand, not that they agree) and say nothing. However, on some occasions, they may start frenzied talking among themselves. Or, in open discussions, they may suddenly become evasive. What this usually means is that something said is disturbing them. At this point, you should take heed, get off that topic, and go on to something else until you can find out what the problem is.

Another example involves eye contact. To Americans, "looking people in the eye" is a sign of mutual respect. To members of Asian cultures, direct eye contact is considered brash and insolent. Hence, in Asian countries, audiences will avoid eye contact with the presenter by spending most of the time staring down at the floor during a presentation. This usually means the audience is showing respect, not necessarily inattention.

RESPONSE SHEET

ORAL PRESENTATIONS

SPEAKER(S):	AUDIENCE(S):
OCCASION FOR PRESENTING:	TYPE OF PRESENTATION:

WHAT PROBLEM OR ISSUE IS THE SPEAKER (AM I) TRYING TO ADDRESS IN THIS PRESENTATION?

◆ **PURPOSE STATEMENT:** In this presentation, the speaker wants to persuade/inform/demonstrate/train [action] someone [audience] of (or in) something [subject].

In this presentation, ____________ the speaker wants to ____________ ____________ (whom) of (in) ____________.

◆ AUDIENCE KNOWLEDGE AND PRESENTATION ELEMENTS

What does the speaker know about the audience? (List various characteristics.) How can the speaker incorporate that knowledge into the presentation?

- What could the speaker say in the opening that could serve as a relevant, audience-related comment?
- How could the speaker show that the speaker is glad to be there, giving this presentation to this audience?
- What questions will this particular audience ask? How can the speaker incorporate responses to these likely questions into the presentation?
- What rhetorical questions would be appropriate to this presentation?

What can/does the speaker do to encourage audience participation?

◆ PRESENTATION STRATEGIES

What strategies can/does the speaker use to make the presentation accessible and memorable? (Anecdotes? stories? information chunking? etc.)

◆ VISUAL ELEMENTS

What types of visuals can/does the speaker use to augment the presentation?

- chalkboards
- flip charts (hand-drawn during the presentation)
- prepared charts
- transparencies
- demonstrations
- 35-mm slides
- videotapes
- films
- multimedia
- physical models

◆ HANDOUTS

What handouts can/does the speaker use for this presentation? Does the speaker successfully use these handouts to provide a copy of presentation visuals, to define complex terminology, to summarize key points, to list bibliography references, or to provide sources to check? Explain.

ACTIVITIES, EXERCISES, AND ASSIGNMENTS

◆ IN-CLASS ACTIVITIES

1. Refer to Figure 17.1 to answer the following questions.
   a. What kind of visual image does each speaker create?
   b. What do you imagine is the occasion for each presentation?
   c. What strategies might each speaker use to gain audience attention and increase audience engagement?
   d. What kind of introduction might each presenter use?
2. Refer back in the chapter to the Skills and Strategies box, "Handling Questions from the Audience." Imagine that you have just completed a presentation to clerical and secretarial employees about the new health benefits package that will be put into place in your company at the beginning of the year. So far in your question-and-answer session, people in the audience have asked good questions, some that show curiosity about how the health benefit changes will affect them, a few that exhibit some skepticism about whether the changes are actually improvements. Then you acknowledge Sandra Post, who looks angry. She tells a rambling account of unpaid medical expenses that she thought should have been covered under the current plan. What are your options? What do you say? What could defuse the situation? What might escalate the situation?
3. You have been selected to design a training session for warehouse shift supervisors who will need to learn how to enter information into the new computer system for tracking the movement of materials that enter and leave the warehouse. Review the various purposes of presentations. Explain what kind of presentation you would design for these supervisors. What kinds of information would you present? How would you organize it? How would you encourage audience involvement?

◆ INDIVIDUAL AND GROUP EXERCISES

1. Use the presentation evaluation sheet (Figure 17.21) to assess presentations made by your classmates. With the information from this evaluation form, write brief evaluative memos to your classmates that identify their strengths but also make specific suggestions about ways in which they can improve.
2. Use the Response Sheet to review your plan for a presentation prepared for class. Identify areas that need to be revised before you make the presentation.

◆ OUT-OF-CLASS ASSIGNMENTS

1. With your group, select a presentation—by a speaker on campus, in the community, or on television—that you all agree to watch and evaluate. Use the evaluation guidelines in Figure 17.21 to assess this presentation individually. Then get together as a group and compare your evaluations. Make sure to identify the speaker's strengths but also make specific suggestions about ways in which the speaker can improve. Discuss your group's list of strengths and suggestions with others in the class.
2. Plan and present a formal presentation, including transparencies or slides and handouts, about one of your major projects this term, such as your analytical report, proposal, or feasibility report. Use the questions in Figure 17.21 and on the Response Sheet to help you prepare.

CASE

INTEL'S FLAWED PENTIUM CHIP—A PUBLIC RELATIONS QUANDARY[7]

CASE BY ANDREA BREEMER FRANTZ

Background. In November 1994, a math professor doing intricate calculations discovered a glitch in his Pentium microprocessor, Intel's top-of-the-line chip. Initially, Intel denied that the flaw existed. However, further research indicated that the chip could indeed cause errors in complex mathematics calculations. Intel publicly acknowledged that a normal user would encounter an error once every 27,000 years—in other words, next to never.

To address user's concerns, Intel set up a 1-800 phone number through which Intel technicians could determine whether callers' calculations were sufficiently complex to warrant replacement. Because the majority of users would experience no calculation problems, Intel also announced it would continue to distribute the flawed Pentiums until all were sold. However, customers were generally angry with Intel's apparent dismissal of public concerns, and despite Intel CEO Andrew Grove's public Internet apology to users, Intel stock quickly dropped, as did the stock of those manufacturers using the Pentium chip (for example, Dell and Gateway 2000). To counter the public backlash, Intel announced late in December that it would replace its flawed Pentium chip for any customer, no questions asked.

Before Intel's announcement, however, IBM capitalized on Intel's public relations problem by announcing it would no longer distribute computers containing the flawed Pentium chip. Some analysts suggest that IBM's decision to stop distributing Intel's microprocessor was a marketing ploy to slow Pentium sales because of a rival chip IBM would soon be producing (the Power PC).

Task. Clearly, Intel's chief concern at this point is to bolster public relations with customers as well as investors and stockholders. Intel has decided to hire a consulting firm to develop a new media campaign to counter the negativism sparked by the Pentium problems. You are a member of this consulting firm. (Other members may be played by other classmates.) Although the public relations campaign will have many aspects, your team is especially sold on the idea of creating a multimedia presentation to boost Intel's image. Your team will consider these issues:

- Do you openly address the mistake Intel made with the Pentium problems and subsequent public response? Or is it best to put the issue to rest and begin with a fresh appeal?
- How can Intel best address its audience for such a campaign? Whom is it most important to directly address? Individual customers? Large retailers and computer makers? Stockholders and investors? From whom does Intel stand to benefit most in a successful campaign?
- Which media will best complement your plan for a multimedia presentation (for example, print sources such as high-gloss magazines like *U.S. News & World Report* or *Fortune*, television, radio, or an unprecedented World Wide Web campaign)? On the basis of the medium, what sort of persuasive appeal(s) will achieve your goal to bolster customer relations?

You and your team begin by carefully researching Intel and the Pentium problem. In addition, you examine Intel's different promotional campaigns, both successful and unsuccessful, to get a sense for Intel's history for appealing to the public. (To see the types of advertising Intel has done, your best bet is to look at computer magazines such as *MACWORLD*.)

Complication. Rumor has it that Intel CEO Andrew Grove will personally review your campaign plans. Plenty has been written about Grove and his history with Intel. Your team realizes that it needs to address concerns of the person who makes the decisions, and that if that person is indeed Grove, you may have to adjust your presentation plans to suit this audience.

INFLUENCES ON MULTICULTURAL TEAMS

Team interaction can be complex, even difficult, when people on a team come from different cultures. The differences among team members may be the result of geography, ethnicity, education, sociopolitical views, and so on. Figure 1 suggests some of the kinds of cultures you're sure to encounter on workplace teams. While the specific influences will be different, a complexity of cultures almost always comes together when a team is formed.

Clearly, every individual belongs to more than one culture. This Communication Spotlight focuses on multicultural teams, specifically looking at factors that affect team interaction—whether the team has members from different workplace cultures or different national cultures and heritages.

To show how cultures can influence team interaction, we'll describe a team working for a U.S. company called EcoDesign. Their project was to recommend an international advertising campaign for a new line of ergonomic, modular, affordable office furniture made from recycled materials.

Sarah—advertising account executive; grew up in New Jersey; speaks English; in advertising for 7 years, with 2 years at EcoDesign

Figure 1 Cultures Affecting Workplace Professionals

CULTURES AFFECTING TEAM INTERACTION	INQUIRY
Workplace cultures	• Think of IBM vs. Microsoft. • What are some of the cultural differences? (button-down collars vs. blue jeans, approaches to problem solving, reward systems, leadership, corporate hierarchies)
Cultures based on intellectual traditions	• Think of differences between accountants and R&D engineers. • What are some of the cultural differences? (education and training, ways of thinking, organizational commitments and goals)
National cultures	• Think of Mexico and the United States. • What are some of the cultural differences? (perceptions of time, nonverbal cues, collaborative interactions)
Racial and ethnic cultures	• Think of African Americans and Japanese Americans and Caucasian Americans. • What are some of the cultural differences? (experiences in history, socioeconomic conditions, educational and employment opportunities)
Gender cultures	• Think of women and men. • What are some of the cultural differences? (the way they talk, interact, listen, express disagreement)
Political cultures	• Think of Socialists, Republicans, Democrats. • What are some of the cultural differences? (the way they vote, spend money, feel about centralized authority, view the duties of government)
Religious cultures	• Think of Roman Catholics and Baptists. • What are some of the cultural differences? (when and how they celebrate their Sabbath, how they interpret the Bible)

Ed—expert in marketing; grew up in New Mexico; speaks English and some Spanish; in marketing for 12 years, all at EcoDesign

Ahmed—expert in international law; grew up in Saudi Arabia; speaks Arabic, English, and French; in international law for 19 years, 1 year at EcoDesign

Jan—expert in marketing; grew up in Wisconsin; understands some Dutch; in international marketing for 15 years, 4 at EcoDesign

Ling—expert in industrial design; grew up in Singapore; speaks Chinese and English; in design for 5 years, 3 at EcoDesign

Like other workplace teams, this one needed to understand cultural factors that influenced and constrained their work together. They also needed to address the needs of their audience and determine the purpose of their recommendation report and marketing plan.

Given the frequency of multicultural teams, it's a good idea to know how to avoid some of their pitfalls. You increase the likelihood of functioning effectively on multicultural teams if you recognize the factors that influence attitudes and actions:

- cultural attitudes about interpersonal and group interactions
- influences on leadership decisions
- high-context and low-context cultures
- nonverbal factors: kinesics, oculesics, and proxemics

What Influences Attitudes about Group Interaction?

Cultural attitudes influence team structure and interaction. These attitudes result from a person's national culture, as you can see in Figure 2. What Ahmed thought was a normal way to begin work together was seen at best as unnecessary and at worst as inappropriate by other group members.

Figure 2 Differing Perceptions about Interpersonal Relationships

	TEAM EXAMPLE
Ahmed and the other team members had different cultural perceptions about the importance of interpersonal relationships in business.	When the team first formed, Ahmed wanted them to spend some time getting to know each other a little. He was surprised that no one else thought this was very important. He grew distrustful of other members of the team, none of whom displayed any interest in developing interpersonal ties. The other members saw Ahmed's interest in an interpersonal relationship simply as a way to waste time rather than as a way to meld the team into a cohesive unit. The team didn't seem to quickly form the effective working relationships and cooperative attitudes that mark many successful teams.

National cultures may differ in their perception about the importance of strong interpersonal relationships in workplace teams. Tensions may result from differing cultural expectations about appropriate levels of interpersonal relationships. Some cultures typically expect teams to have few interactions beyond those necessary for completing the task. Others typically expect teams to build interpersonal relationships as part of their work together.

Workplace cultures also differ considerably in their perception of the importance of teams. Some organizations believe that the lone individual struggling against the odds is the most motivated or creative or productive. A growing number of companies, however, are seeing the value of teams with a broad representation of professionals. Rather than have a project move from department 1, then to department 2, and finally to department 3, some companies now form a team with representatives from departments 1, 2, and 3 working together.

Teams may find different cultures influencing their productivity. Imagine a hospital team trying to plan a cooperative regional facility that combines equipment and staff, avoids duplication, saves money (and time), and reduces costs. The doctors on the team would be primarily concerned with the quality of patient care, the fiscal officer would be concerned with efficiency and cost, the hospital manager would be concerned with soliciting opinions from the staff and community, and the board of directors would be concerned with credibility and process. Although the team's goal is broadly the same, the concerns of the individual members are different.

The EcoDesign team brought professional biases to the table, as shown in Figure 3. Each team member believed that his or her professional area was central, but did not accord the same importance to the professional areas of the other team members.

Figure 3 Differing Perceptions Based on Professional Area

	TEAM EXAMPLE
Each member of the team believed his or her professional area was central to the success of the project.	Sarah knew the project wouldn't move forward without her expertise to coordinate the efforts of the other members. Ed and Jan, veterans of numerous international marketing campaigns, believed the marketing plan was the single most important part of the project. Ahmed knew that his expertise in international law would eliminate the roadblocks that stymied so many international projects. Ling knew that her successful design history—four international awards in the past five years—was critical.

What Influences Leadership Decisions?

Corporate attitudes about leadership vary considerably. Some companies consistently check that their management reflects the population: their managers and supervisors typically include men and women, professionals in their 30s as well as those in their 60s, people from a range of ethnic and national groups, people who are physically fit and those who are physically challenged, and so on. Other companies (some of whom find themselves in court trying to defend their hiring and promotion practices) consistently have managers who are physically fit white males in their 40s and 50s. In such organizations, women, people of color, people over 60, people who are physically challenged, and so on, are discouraged or ignored if they consider management positions.

Sometimes, as you can see in Figure 4, expectations about team structure and leadership may be based on the workplace culture. For example, the general practice at EcoDesign was to have autocratic teams—that is, teams with a clearly defined leader who made the major decisions and assigned the tasks. This autocratic structure was very efficient and stable, enabling teams to produce consistently high-quality but relatively routine work. The corporate attitudes about leadership at EcoDesign, however, conflicted with the attitudes

Figure 4 Established Leadership Patterns

	TEAM EXAMPLE
Ed was the only member of the team with much knowledge of organizational history. The others came with attitudes and experiences that potentially conflicted with EcoDesign's business-as-usual way of dealing with team leadership and structure. What a workplace or national culture values influences opinions about appropriate team leadership: corporate role, seniority, experience, group choice. The lack of complete support for Sarah as team leader could reduce her effectiveness in coordinating their activities, moving the agenda forward, and resolving affective or procedural conflicts.	From the beginning the team was committed to the project. However, they had difficulty deciding on which member would assume the role of leader. As long as Ed had worked at EcoDesign (since the company started 12 years ago), teams had operated the same way: a dynamic leader with some organizational authority encouraged and controlled the direction and development of the group. Once team members were given task assignments—from brainstorming to presentation planning—they worked well together. Seldom, though, did a team (at least in Ed's memory) work without the clear guidance of a strong leader. Sarah was seen by Jan and Ed as the appropriate choice for the team leader because of her position as an account executive. Ahmed, however, was not sure that Sarah should be the team leader, because she had less seniority and less international experience than he, Ed, or Jan. Ling was willing to go along with whatever the team decided. Sarah was willing to function as the team's facilitator, but because of her successful experiences in a company that encouraged nonhierarchical teams, she wanted the decisions to be made cooperatively. So, although Sarah was the leader, she had less than the full support of the team. None of the team members got exactly what they wanted.

and experiences of some members of the team, especially since the company was branching into more creative ventures. There was some feeling at EcoDesign—rumblings around the water cooler—that creative tasks needed a different kind of team structure.

Where Do Team Members Get Their Information?

Once a team's structure and the leadership roles are established, the members will receive both verbal and nonverbal information from other members of the team. Edward Hall, a researcher who studied cultural differences, believed that responses to nonverbal nuances in communication help people from the same culture understand each other. (And the lack of response is one of the barriers to understanding among people from different cultures.) Hall believed that cultures vary in the reliance people place on nonverbal cues or on verbal cues.

Of course, all people acquire meaning from both verbal and nonverbal messages, but people in some cultures (for example, people from Germany or professionals in corporate communication or engineering) rely more on verbal messages than nonverbal ones. In contrast, people in other cultures (for example, people from Japan or professionals in corporate advertising or negotiations) rely on nonverbal cues as much as on verbal messages. Hall defined these extremes as **low-context cultures** and **high-context cultures:**

- *Low-context cultures* depend primarily on direct verbal messages to communicate. Many people from low-context cultures prefer explicitly stated information. Directness is considered desirable.
- *High-context cultures* such as Japan depend on indirect nonverbal and culturally understood messages to communicate. Many people from high-context cultures prefer that information not be explicitly stated. Directness is often considered rude.

These categories, of course, describe broad cultural characteristics, not necessarily individual behaviors, which are influenced by personality and by the unique mix of cultures that is part of each person.

In low-context cultures, most transmitted information is contained in the message itself. On the other hand, in high-context cultures, the interpretation is primarily determined by the communicators' implicitly shared social and cultural knowledge of the context. This distinction has important implications for communication in organizations. Communication in low-context cultures is more cumbersome, while communication in high-context systems can be rich in meaning, in part because the pattern of messages becomes part of the message itself. However, reaching this level of understanding in a high-context culture takes a lot of time and effort.[1]

Cultures typically can be placed on a high-context culture/low-context culture continuum, as shown in Figure 5 (also see page 441). Team members need to be especially careful not to misinterpret what's going on when team members come from cultures that depend on a different level of context for communication. For example, a German working as a sales representative may presume that any criteria a customer really cares about will be explicitly stated. A Japanese customer may presume that restating what seem to be obvious criteria for a product would be insulting the listening and skills of the sales representative.[2] In contrast, a labor relations arbitrator may be able to settle a labor-management disagreement by attending to more than the paper documents the two sides have been exchanging.

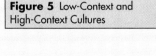

Figure 5 Low-Context and High-Context Cultures

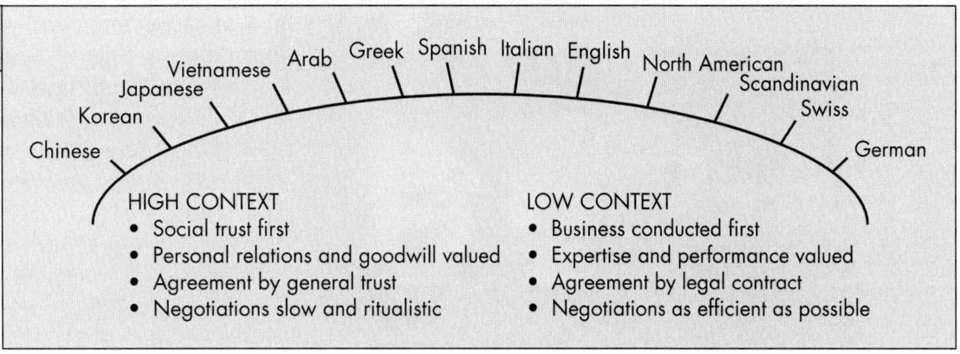

Figure 6 Misreading Contextual Cues

	TEAM EXAMPLE
Ahmed and Ling came from high-context national cultures. Sarah, Ed, and Jan came from low-context national cultures. All of them except Ahmed, however, had chosen professions that depended on context as much as on language to communicate. None of the team members seemed to realize the extent of Ahmed's reservations about Jan's plan.	The team seemed to reach an impasse. Finally Ahmed said, albeit reluctantly, that he'd be willing to try the plan that Jan had proposed. Jan was delighted at the concession—and took it at face value. Ahmed was surprised when the team seemed to get in back of Jan's plan. He expected the team to recognize that his voiced reluctance indicated his very strong opposition, not merely his hesitation. In a high-context culture, team members would have understood Ahmed's body language, his hesitation to support the plan, and his lack of participation in elaborating the plan as indications of his opposition.

The continuum in Figure 5 is intended as a general description of the importance people from various cultures give to verbal and nonverbal messages. You should not use the continuum to stereotype any individuals. However, you can use it as an indicator to help you understand why a team may not be working as effectively as possible. Ahmed, Ed, Jan, Ling, and Sarah may simply be misreading cues, as in Figure 6.

Understanding cultural expectations can make your communications much more effective.

How Can Nonverbal Factors Be Misread?

Nonverbal factors affect all communication. On a team, nonverbal factors such as kinesics (body movement), oculesics (eye movement), and proxemics (use of space) can mean the difference between successful interaction and complete misunderstanding.

Kinesic behaviors, which include all body movement and gestures, mean different things in different cultures. One common example that you might find yourself using is the gesture (with thumb and forefinger touching) that means "OK" in the United States. However, in some countries the gesture is an insult, and in still other countries the gesture is seen as obscene.

Kinesics also includes facial expressions. While *all* people *feel* and *recognize* a range of emotions (happiness, sadness, surprise, fear, anger, sadness, disgust, contempt, interest, bewilderment, and determination), different cultures encourage or discourage the *display* of these emotions. For example, men in many Middle Eastern cultures learn to display their emotions, whereas Asian businessmen and women learn not to.[3]

Sometimes behaviors that are meaningless in one culture have distinct meanings in another culture. For example, most people from the United States and Europe don't know that many people from Arabic cultures consider showing the sole of one's foot or crossing one's legs offensive and disrespectful. Unintentional offense could be given—and the offender wouldn't even know it.[4]

Figure 7 Proxemic Categories

	TYPICAL U.S. PROXEMICS
Public space	> 12 feet
Social space	4–12 feet
Personal space	1.5–4 feet
Intimate space	< 1.5 feet

"**Oculesics**" describes the eye movement and eye contact that goes on during face-to-face communication, what researchers in nonverbal communication call **mutual gaze.** While North Americans favor direct eye contact, many other cultures, including Asian ones, see this directness as insulting. However, mutual gaze is relative. While Americans believe in directness, they shift their gaze periodically. In contrast, people from many Arabic cultures typically use a more intense gaze, with less blinking and shifting of their eyes.

"**Proxemics**" refers to the way people use the space around them. On a team, this would mean not only the space the team chose to work in but also the space between individuals as they worked. Edward Hall described four distances to help us understand how space affects our interactions. Each category in Figure 7 represents increasing intimacy according to mainstream culture in the United States.

We can also draw some generalizations about intercultural proxemics. In general, most people from Latin American, Middle Eastern, and southern European countries are comfortable with *less* distance between the individuals than most people from the United States. Similarly, people from many Asian cultures prefer *more* distance between them than do most people from the United States.[5] This helps explain why you may take a step away from or toward a person you're working with from another culture.

Some of the potential problems that can arise when kinesics, oculesics, and proxemics are misunderstood or misinterpreted are shown in Figure 8.

Figure 8 Reactions to Nonverbal Factors

	TEAM EXAMPLE
Ed saw his posture as relaxing. Ling and Ahmed saw Ed's posture as rude.	At their initial meeting, Ed sprawled back in his chair, right leg crossed over the left. A little while later, he leaned forward, legs apart, elbows on his knees. Ahmed and Ling saw both positions as a sign of Ed's disrespect for the group. Ed just thought he was being relaxed and getting comfortable.
Sarah mistakenly judged emotional reactions on the basis of facial expressions.	Once the discussion got started, people tossed ideas out for the group's consideration. Ahmed thought one of the approaches suggested by Sarah was completely impractical. His face showed his reaction. Ling also thought the idea was impractical, but her facial reaction did not show her opinion; in fact, Ling nodded. By nodding, Ling intended to indicate that she needed to hear more if she were to have any hope of understanding and agreeing with Sarah's point. Interpreting their reactions, Sarah believed that Ahmed disagreed with her but that Ling agreed.
Ahmed intended to convey his commitment to the project and his willingness to settle down to work. Instead, he unintentionally alienated his teammates.	Ahmed's direct, intense eye contact provoked several unintended reactions: Ling felt insulted (because what she thought of as staring is rude in her culture), Sarah felt uncomfortable and embarrassed (because she thought his direct, intense gaze was a sexual come-on), Jan appreciated Ahmed's forthright approach, and Ed felt challenged (because staring is what he thought people did when they challenged each other's positions). These members of the group also felt uncomfortable because they felt as if Ahmed invaded their personal space. Ahmed frequently stood and sat closer than 18 inches from them. Sarah, Jan, and Ed wanted three feet of working space between people. Ling wanted even more space.

To guard against problems inadvertently caused by ignorance about a particular workplace culture, nationality, or ethnic group, members of a team can exchange information about patterns and practices dealing with collaboration and teamwork. Responding to the questions in Figure 9 on the next page requires all the members on a team to reflect about their own practices and preferences. Because these questions focus on attitudes and behaviors that are usually unarticulated, they are useful for improving the multicultural understanding in any group.

Figure 9 Questions to Assess Your Own Attitudes and Behaviors That Influence Interaction on Teams

- When you don't agree with something, are you willing to express objections? criticisms? How do you express your disagreement?
- How do you think disagreements should be resolved? How do you typically resolve disagreements?
- How much attention do you pay to minority positions—that is, points of view expressed by only a few members of your team or group?
- Do you listen just to the words people say, or do you listen to the way they say those words—hesitations, silences, pauses, emphases, omissions, enthusiasm, and so on?
- How do you respond to praise? Do you acknowledge others' contributions? How do you feel when your ideas are appropriated?
- How do you respond to criticism? How do you react to being put on the spot? How likely are you to put other people on the spot?
- Do you think the group should have a leader? What are responsibilities of the leader? What are the responsibilities of the other collaborators?
- When you don't understand something, do you ask for explanations and clarifications?
- Are you willing to suggest an idea or a plan that differs from the one accepted by the majority of the group?

ACTIVITIES AND QUESTIONS FOR DISCUSSION

1. Imagine that you're the supervisor for Ahmed, Ed, Ling, Jan, and Sarah. How would you advise them to help avoid problems that might result from misunderstanding each others' cultures?
2. Do a self-assessment of nonverbal factors in these two situations: (a) working in a team meeting, (b) making a formal presentation. If possible, make a videotape of each situation. Pair with a classmate who will provide detailed feedback about your nonverbal behaviors. Compare your responses with those given by your classmate. Discuss changes that might make your team interactions and formal presentations more effective. Specifically consider these questions:
   - What are some of your kinesic behaviors that might distract other people?
   - What is the range and directness of your eye contact? What do you convey about your confidence?
   - Do you select an appropriate and comfortable distance for speaking? Do you invade other people's space? Do you stay too far away from others?

Communication Spotlight: Revision

USING LOCAL REVISION TO STRENGTHEN BUSINESS DOCUMENTS

When you revise a document, you can begin by reconsidering the global features—that is, you examine whether the document is appropriate for the occasion, audience, and purpose. But making sure the global features are appropriate isn't enough. As you know from reading about levels of edit, one aspect you must check is whether your document follows accepted mechanical and grammatical conventions. Editing that addresses these conventions is generally called **local** (as opposed to *global*) **revision** of a document.

While some mechanical conventions are widely accepted (for example, beginning names with capital letters), others are determined by the occasion and the style guide governing the document (for example, using the optional comma before the "and" in a series of three or more items). Similarly, while some grammatical conventions are widely accepted (for example, making sure subjects and verbs agree), others are determined by the occasion (for example, deciding whether "none" can be singular or plural). To help you with local revision, you need to consider the audience, occasion, and purpose so that you can decide how good is good enough.

Local revision focuses on eliminating problems in specific sentences, phrases, and words—for example, errors in sentence structure, grammar, or mechanics. Figure 1 shows the penultimate (next-to-final) version of an executive summary about the implementation of a new employee safety program in a manufacturing company. Although the information in this draft is accurate, the local-level errors are distracting and unprofessional. How many of these problems can you spot in Figure 1?

Figure 1 Penultimate Version of Executive Summary, Not Yet Copyedited

Executive Summary

The Safety Training for Employees Program, which is proposed to be implimented in an ongoing series of division-wide training seminars and workshops, encourage important changes in employees' workplace safety-related behaviors. Identifying potential risks, situation analysis, and ways to improve working conditions are part of employee training. This concept is crutial since approximately the US Deparment of Labor reports that 96% of all workplace injuries are caused by employees engaged in unsafe actions. Of the 12 incidents reported last year by the division, 10 resulted form employees who ignored established safety procudures. A report criticizing our workplace safety record was compiled by an external safety inspection review team of industrial engineers.

Within the first year of implimenting this training program, other organizations similar to ours have expereinced an average 65% decrease in on the job injuries and accidents. This exceeds the 50% reduction in accidents targeted by our Safety Committee. In addition, organizations similar to ours who have used this training program for five years have reduced its on the job injuries and accidents by 95% over the next several years would save money, and provide employees with a safer workplace.

Our division as spending approximately $3500 each year on unneccessary and avoidable accidents. These funds could be better spent on improving, updating, and upgrading equipment. Considering the reasonable one-time installation fee of $2500, $500 for a safety consultant, and $450 for seminar books, the Safety Training for Employees Program is seen by our Safety Committee as a good, even essential, investment.

The projection is that our division would spend approximatly $1705 less on accidents the first year after the Safety Training for Employees Program is implemented. We would save money each additional year that Safety Training for Employees Program is used because the greatest expense is the initial one-time installation fee. After paying this one-time expense, the program will probable save $1435 at the end of the second year. Savings are expected to increase each year.

This Communication Spotlight uses this executive summary to review five frequent local-level problems in business documents:

- agreement errors
- parallel structure errors
- inappropriate use of active or passive voice
- dangling modifiers
- wordiness

Agreement

The subject and verb of a sentence must **agree** in number—singular subject and singular verb; plural subject and plural verb—even when words or phrases come between the subject and verb. In Figure 2, the subject of the sentence, "Safety Training for Employees Program," is singular, but the verb, "encourage," is plural.

A pronoun, which replaces or substitutes for a noun (often called a referent), needs to agree in gender, person, and number with the noun it replaces. In Figure 3, the noun, "organizations," and the pronoun, "its," disagree in number.

Figure 2 Subject-Verb Agreement

ERROR IN AGREEMENT	ANALYSIS OF AGREEMENT ERROR	CORRECT AGREEMENT
The Safety Training for Employees Program, which is proposed to be implemented in an ongoing series of division-wide seminars and workshops, encourage important changes in employees' workplace safety-related behaviors.	In a simplified form, this is the correct subject-verb agreement in the sentence: The *Safety Training for Employees Program . . . encourages* changes in employees' . . . behaviors. The singular subject of the sentence, *Safety Training for Employees Program,* requires a singular verb, *encourages.*	The Safety Training for Employees Program, which is proposed to be implemented in an ongoing series of division-wide seminars and workshops, encourages important changes in employees' workplace safety-related behaviors.

Figure 3 Noun-Pronoun Agreement

ERROR IN AGREEMENT	ANALYSIS OF AGREEMENT ERROR	CORRECT AGREEMENT
In addition, organizations similar to ours who have used this training program for five years have reduced its on-the-job injuries and accidents by 95%.	In a simplified form, this is the correct noun-pronoun agreement in the sentence: . . . *organizations* have reduced ~~its~~ *their* on-the-job injuries . . . The plural noun, *organizations,* requires a plural pronoun, *their.*	In addition, organizations similar to ours who have used this training program for five years report an average 95% decrease in their on-the-job injuries and accidents.

Parallel Structure

A series of elements—words or phrases in a sentence, items in a list, or related sentences in a paragraph—that convey ideas of equal importance need to be in the same grammatical form. Figure 4 shows a sentence with items in a series that need to be **parallel.**

Active and Passive Voice

Sentences in **active voice** put the doer of the action as the subject of the sentence. Sentences in **passive voice** put the receiver of the action as the subject of the sentence. Sentences in both active voice and passive voice have important uses in business documents. Figure 5 suggests specific reasons to select either active voice or passive voice.

Sometimes you'll have a choice about using either active or passive voice. If it doesn't seem to matter or if you're not sure, you should probably select active voice. In general, your

Figure 4 Parallelism in a Series within a Sentence

ERROR IN PARALLELISM	ANALYSIS OF PARALLELISM ERROR	CORRECT PARALLELISM
Identifying potential risks, situation analysis, and ways to improve working conditions is part of employee training.	Listing the items in a sentence is one way to see if they're in the same grammatical structure: • Identifying potential risks • ~~situation analysis~~ analyzing situations • looking for ways to improve working conditions . . . The three parts of training need to be presented in the same grammatical form—in this case they're gerunds (verbs turned into nouns by adding *-ing*).	Identifying potential risks, analyzing situations, and looking for ways to improve working conditions are part of employee training.

Figure 5 Guidelines for Active and Passive Voice

USE ACTIVE VOICE IF . . .	USE PASSIVE VOICE IF . . .
• the doer of the action is more important than the receiver of the action. • the doer of the action should be emphasized. • the document needs to be easy and interesting to read. • the document should be less wordy.	• the receiver of the action is more important than the doer of the action. • the doer of the action is unknown. • the doer of the action is unimportant. • the doer of the action should be deemphasized.

Figure 6 Active and Passive Voice

PASSIVE VOICE	ANALYSIS OF VOICE	ACTIVE VOICE
A report criticizing our workplace safety record was compiled by an external safety inspection review team of industrial engineers. (19 words)	This is the structure of the passive voice example: A report criticizing our workplace safety record (subject) was compiled (verb) by (preposition) an external safety inspection review team (object of preposition) of (preposition) industrial engineers (object of preposition) This is the structure of the active voice example: An external team of industrial safety engineers (subject) criticized (verb) our safety record (object).	An external team of industrial safety engineers criticized our safety record. (11 words)

audience will have an easier time understanding your document and read it more quickly and easily if you use active voice. Figure 6 on the previous page shows a common problem that results from passive voice—wordiness. Recasting the sentence in active voice reduces the wordiness.

Dangling Modifiers

A **dangling modifier** is a word or phrase that appears to modify the subject of the sentence but doesn't. For example, look at the following sentence:

When choosing a new computer system, a few things must be considered.

The sentence *says* that "things" are doing the choosing. But that can't be. The sentence could be revised in more than one way:

When choosing a new computer system, an office manager must consider several things.

or

A few things must be considered when you are choosing a new computer system.

In Figure 7, the introductory phrase "After paying this one-time expense" should modify the subject, "the program." However, "the program" doesn't pay any expenses. Instead, the expenses are paid by the division of the organization, as the correction shows.

Figure 7 Dangling Modifiers

DANGLING MODIFIER ERRORS	ANALYSIS OF DANGLING MODIFIERS	CORRECT MODIFIERS
After paying this one-time expense, the program is expected to save $1435 at the end of the second year.	This is one way to eliminate the dangling modifier: After paying this one-time expense, ~~the program~~ *our division* is expected to save $1435 at the end of the second year.	After paying this one-time expense, our division is expected to save $1435 by the end of the second year.

Wordiness

Redundant or inflated terms make reading more time-consuming and increase the likelihood that readers will miss the main point. **Wordiness** may simply be the result of excess words, but it may also be the result of passive voice:

Passive voice Considering the reasonable one-time installation fee of $2500, $500 for a safety consultant, and $450 for seminar books, the Safety Training for Employees Program is seen by our Safety Committee as a good, even essential, investment. (37 words)

Active voice Our Safety Committee considers the one-time $2500 installation fee for the Safety Training for Employees Program, $500 for a safety consultant, and $450 for seminar books a good investment. (30 words)

The original sentences in Figure 8 are grammatically correct, but they contain words that add little to the content. The revisions show other ways you can reduce the number of redundant or inflated terms so that your writing is more understandable.

Final Proofreading

Even when the sentences are checked—and doubled-checked—for grammatical and structural errors, you need to proofread for mechanics: punctuation, capitalization, and spelling. When you first read Figure 1, did you notice nine spelling errors (only six of which would

Figure 8 Wordy Sentences

WORDINESS ERRORS	ANALYSIS OF WORDINESS	LESS WORDY SENTENCES
Our division is spending approximately $3,500 each year on unnecessary and avoidable accidents. These funds could be better spent on improving, updating, and upgrading equipment. Considering the reasonable one-time installation fee of $2500, $500 for a safety consultant, and $450 for seminar books, the Safety Training for Employees Program is seen by our Safety Committee as a good, even essential, investment.	These are possible ways to eliminate wordiness: Our division is spending approximately $3,500 each year on ~~unnecessary and avoidable~~ accidents. These funds could be better spent on ~~improving, updating, and~~ upgrading equipment. Considering the ~~reasonable~~ one-time installation fee ~~of~~ $2500, $500 for a safety consultant, and $450 for seminar books, the Safety Training for Employees Program ~~is seen by~~ our Safety Committee ~~as~~ a good, ~~even essential,~~ investment.	Our division is spending approximately $3,500 each year on accidents. These funds could be better spent on upgrading equipment. Our Safety Committee considers the one-time $2,500 installation fee for the Safety Training for Employees Program, $500 for a safety consultant, and $450 for seminar books a good investment.
The Safety Training for Employees Program, which is proposed to be implemented in an ongoing series of division-wide training seminars and workshops, encourages important changes in employees' workplace safety-related behaviors.	The Safety Training for Employees Program, ~~which is proposed~~ to be implemented in a~~n ongoing~~ series of division-wide ~~training seminars and~~ workshops, encourages ~~important~~ changes in employees' ~~workplace safety-related~~ behaviors.	The Safety Training for Employees Program, to be implemented in a series of division-wide workshops, encourages changes in employees' behaviors.

have been caught by the spellchecker), two punctuation errors (one that is repeated twice), and a numerical transposition? Here are the offending items:

Misspelled Words Caught by the Spellchecker	Misspelled Words *Not* Caught by the Spellchecker	Punctuation Errors	Numerical Error
approximately	from (not "form")	Hyphen error: on-the-job	$1750 (not $1705)
crucial	is (not "as")	Comma error: Reducing the number of accidents . . . would save money, and provide employees with a safer workplace.	
department	probably (not "probable")		
experienced			
implemented			
unnecessary			

Don't depend on your spellchecker or grammar checker to catch all the errors you make. For example, the spellchecker can say that "there" and "their" are spelled correctly, but it can't determine if you've used them correctly. A grammar checker can say that 76 percent of your sentences are passive constructions, but it cannot determine if that's an appropriate percentage of passive voice given the occasion, audience, and purpose of your document.

When you think you're done with a document, set it aside for a while (a half hour if that's all the time you have, a day or two if you can). Then read it with a fresh eye—as if you've never seen it before. Give yourself time to read through it several times, each time looking for a different kind of problem. Do a special check for errors that are easy to miss:

- transposed letters ("form" instead of "from")
- substituted letters ("probable" instead of "probably")
- punctuation errors (a comma incorrectly separating a compound verb)
- numerical transposition errors ($1705 instead of $1750, an error that would be caught only by readers familiar with the content)

This final check increases the likelihood that you've produced a document that fulfills the mechanical and grammatical conventions appropriate for the purpose, audience, and occasion.

Adhering to conventions does more than help the reader understand your documents; it also helps create an image of you as a careful, concerned, professional communicator.

Figure 9 shows the final version of the executive summary once the local-level errors have been eliminated.

Figure 9 Final Version of Executive Summary, after Copyediting and Proofreading

Executive Summary

The Safety Training for Employees Program, to be implemented in a series of division-wide workshops, encourages changes in employees' behaviors. Employees are trained to identify potential risks, analyze situations, and look for ways to improve working conditions. This concept is crucial since the US Department of Labor reports that approximately 96% of all workplace injuries are caused by employees engaged in unsafe actions. Employees who ignored established safety procedures caused 10 of the 12 incidents reported last year by the division. An external team of industrial safety engineers criticized our safety record.

Organizations similar to ours who have used this training program for one year report an average 65% decrease in their on-the-job injuries and accidents. This exceeds the 50% reduction in accidents targeted by our Safety Committee. In addition, organizations who have used this training program for five years report an average 95% decrease in their on-the-job injuries and accidents. Reducing the number of accidents in our division by 95% over the next several years would save money and provide employees with a safer workplace.

Our division is spending approximately $3,500 each year on accidents. These funds could be better spent on upgrading equipment. Our Safety Committee considers the one-time $2,500 installation fee for the Safety Training for Employees Program, $500 for a safety consultant, and $450 for seminar books, a good investment.

The projection is that our division would spend approximately $1,750 less on accidents the first year after the Safety Training for Employees Program is implemented. We would save money each additional year that the Safety Training for Employees Program is used because the greatest expense is the initial one-time installation fee. After paying this one-time expense, our division will probably save $1,435 by the end of the second year. Savings are expected to increase each year.

ACTIVITIES AND QUESTIONS FOR DISCUSSION

1. Read the following two sentences—one in active voice, the other in passive voice. Explain possible occasions for which each sentence would be appropriate.

   The team used networked workstations to plan the next phase of the project.

   Networked workstations were used by the team to plan the next phase of the project.

2. Select a document that you have written. Go through it carefully to eliminate agreement errors, parallel structure errors, inappropriate use of active or passive voice, dangling modifiers, and wordiness. Proofread for mechanical errors.

PART VI
PREPARING EMPLOYMENT AND ADMINISTRATIVE MESSAGES

CHAPTER

18

Employment Messages: Resumes and Letters of Application

OUTLINE

A Job Search: The Jeff Foster Story

The Problem-Solving Nature of the Job Search

Planning Documents

Resumes

Letters of Application

Portfolios

CRITERIA FOR EXPLORING CHAPTER 18

What we cover in this chapter	What you will be able to do after reading this chapter
The job search	Create a scenario of a job search situation
Problem solving and the job search	Use various strategies for task definition and problem solution in a job search
Planning documents	Compose personal inventories and create job and company descriptions based on various types of sources
Application letters	Write a letter of application that meets reader expectations and represents your individual credentials
Resumes	Construct effective chronological and functional resumes
Portfolios	Be aware of portfolios as an option for presenting your credentials

Effective communicators know that when you apply for a job, you face two fundamental tasks: presenting information about your qualifications and talking about that information in terms of the reader's or company's needs. In presenting your credentials, you need to *show* that you are qualified, rather than merely state that you are. You also have to dramatize your interest in the company receiving your application, as in Figure 18.1.

CONTEXT

Sarah Watson is applying to be the Communications Director at Countryside Building Sales, which markets building packages to both individuals and firms, as well as to rural cooperatives. After selling a package, Countryside subcontracts a construction crew to erect the building on the buyer's property.

Even though Countryside is only two years old, its owner, Paul French, has a proven track record as a former contractor for various commercial developments in the surrounding eight-county area. French makes good use of his former contacts in subcontracting the construction work. He sees a need to establish further name recognition in the surrounding communities. He wants a publicity campaign with a "down-home" feel to it, and prefers to hire a communications director with some college training in communications, or someone with appropriate work experience. He would like to hire someone with local ties. Sara attempts to address French's concerns in her letter of application (Figure 18.1) and resume (Figure 18.2).

Figure 18.1 Application Letter Presenting Qualifications and Considering Employer Needs

How does the opening establish the context? Is there any concern for links between the applicant's qualifications and the prospective employer's needs this early in the letter?

How does the body of the letter both show the applicant's main selling points and dramatize an interest in the prospective employer?

How does the second-to-last paragraph link personal qualifications to employer's needs?

How does the conclusion facilitate an interview?

Dear Mr. French:

Through a conversation I had with your colleague Mr. David Beesche, I discovered an opening you have for a Communications Director at Countryside Building Sales. I am applying for this position, confident that my coursework and experience qualify me for the job.

Advertising and promotions are a large part of my Speech Communication degree. I have learned written advertising skills through courses such as Planning for Television Production and Publicity Methods. The projects required for these classes involved designing brochures, commercials, and newspaper ads for a particular client. Audience analysis and budget constraints were part of my training in transforming a client's objectives into effective advertising campaign materials.

In addition to the communication skills I developed as part of my degree program, I also had practical experience in this area from my job as a bartender at Town and Country, a local bar and restaurant. I mixed drinks and balanced cash register tapes, but more importantly I created a pleasant atmosphere for cowboys, lawyers, motorcyclists, college students, and church league members alike.

Having been raised only six miles from Pine Bluff, I have a special fondness for the people and surroundings in your community. I feel this familiarity, as well as my wish to settle in the Pine Bluff area, would be an asset to Countryside; I would combine my academic skills with my knowledge of the needs of people living in the surrounding area to present and maintain your company's image as a dependable, locally owned and customer-oriented enterprise.

After you have read my enclosed resume, I would appreciate an opportunity to discuss my qualifications with you in person. I can be reached by calling 816-555-6286. With Countryside Building Sales growing so quickly, I can see your need for a Communications Director. I look forward to hearing from you soon.

Sincerely,

Sarah Watson

Encl.: Resume

Figure 18.2 Resume to Accompany Letter of Application

Sarah Joy Watson

2256 Commerce Street
Kansas City, MO
(816) 555-6286

Education

Bachelor of Arts, May 1993
State University, City, State
Speech Communication/English
GPA: 3.82/4.00

Finished Degree Program in 3 Years
Financed 100% of Educational Expenses

Relevant Coursework

Publicity Methods
Business Communication
Consumer Psychology
Persuasion in Advertising
Planning for Television Production
Multimedia Workshops

Work Experience

Town and Country, Kansas City, MO
Bartender, June 1991–present
- set up conversation areas
- served customers
- balanced inventory with cash receipts

Community Childcare Services, Pine Corners
Caregiver, Summers 1988–1990
- provided infant care for children ages birth-12 months
- prepared care reports for parents and center director

Achievements

Member of PHI BETA KAPPA, liberal arts honorary fraternity
Dean's List and Scholastic Recognition, 1991–present
Federated Women's Club Honors Scholarship, 1991

References

Dr. Allen Makepiece
Professor of Speech
800 Parker Hall
State University
City, State ZIP
816-555-9000, ext. 451

Ms. Kelley Buckner
Director of Multimedia
Corbin Center
State University
City, State ZIP
816-555-6000

Mr. Kit Shephard
Manager
Town and Country
1430 Parkway
Kansas City, MO
816-555-1880

Donna Reynolds
Director
Childcare Services
417 Main Street
Pine Corners
417-555-7656

1. What are Sarah's main qualifications for the position? What are the prospective employer's main needs (consult the Context paragraphs)? How does Sarah link her qualifications to the employer's needs? Why does she mention "cowboys, lawyers, motorcyclists, college students, and church league members"?
2. How do the letter and resume work together to present Sarah's credentials?
3. Except for the job title, the information in the Context paragraphs did not appear in Countryside's job announcement. How does having such information help in a job search? Name several ways Sarah could have found out about this position.

The reason Sarah's application works to get her a job interview is that she knows various skills important to a job search:

- how to use planning documents, such as personal inventories, company descriptions, and job descriptions
- how to handle application forms, design resumes, and write letters of application

A JOB SEARCH: THE JEFF FOSTER STORY

On the first day of a business communication course, Jeff Foster announced, "The main reason I'm taking this course is to learn how to write job letters and resumes. If I know how *that's* done, then I'll be able to get the job I want." Impatient to get started, Jeff studied a checklist of conventions in his text for writing letters of application and drafted the letter shown in Figure 18.3. Satisfied that the letter followed all the conventions precisely (noted in **bold** in the annotations), Jeff immediately sent the letter, along with a resume designed by a resume service, to five target companies conducting on-campus interviews in subsequent weeks. Jeff was both puzzled and upset when his letter did not garner him any interviews.

Figure 18.3 Letter of Application Roughly Applying Conventions

Dear Sirs:

I am applying for the position of Medical Illustrator at MedTech, Inc. I heard of this position from a friend. My major in Biological Pre-Medical Illustration at Michigan State University, my work experience and my portfolio will make me suited for this job.

This position requires artistic skills. At the Eastern State College I began a career in fine arts that makes my work unique. At Michigan State University I began to turn these skills towards medical illustration. After graduation, these skills were honed and put into practice at the internships I held.

During the summer of 19--, while working for the Northeastern Company, I learned and used basic business skills associated with running a business. These include record keeping, communication, goal setting, self motivation and scheduling. While working away from home in Allentown, Pennsylvania, I learned to live independently which made me suited for work outside of my home state.

While attending Michigan State University, I held the positions of Secretary and President of the Biological Pre-Medical Illustration Club. Holding these positions entailed working closely with faculty and members; organizing club functions, trips, and workshops; and planning ways to make our young major grow and expand at the university.

Please contact me by mail or by telephone at (610) 555-0526 and tell me about your plans for working with me.

Sincerely yours,

Jeff Foster

Jeff Foster ***names the position he is applying for and identifies where he heard about the position.*** *He then forecasts how he is qualified with* ***skills representing his strongest qualifications.***

Jeff claims a match between his skills and those needed in the position, which he has researched.

He mentions relevant experience and ***names a desirable personal quality (independence).***

He attempts to arrange an interview, and includes a phone number to facilitate contact.

THE PROBLEM-SOLVING NATURE OF THE JOB SEARCH

When you are searching for a job, you first need to represent the task accurately to yourself. In preparing his letter of application, Jeff had a very simple *representation of the task* of getting a job. To him the key was to follow application letter conventions. This representation, of course, left out a range of other factors important to the occasion:

- how well he implements the conventions in presenting appropriate content
- what he has done to prepare himself for the position and how his achievements rate against those of others
- what personal characteristics he brings to the job and how these might help or hinder him during his search and later employment
- what qualifications the company wants in a candidate applying for the position that year
- how competitive the job market is, depending on the economy, on social legislation (affirmative action rulings, and so forth), and on the desirability of the position and the corporation
- how he knows he is interested in the position in the first place, and how well his interest and his talents match

To improve his representation of the job search, Jeff might have used one of the three problem-solving techniques in Figure 18.4.[1] Using such strategies may help you avoid a representation of the job search that is either too simple, as was Jeff's, or too complex and therefore discouraging. Further, these strategies can help you focus on the most important issues to address in your letter of application.

Figure 18.4 Alternative Strategies for Representing the Job Search

STRATEGY	EXPLANATION AND EXAMPLE
Use an external representation.	Jot down lists, make diagrams, draw a sketch. [*Example:* Jeff might have talked with several people in the profession to get a picture of what the job search in his field is like, and—as a result of these conversations or informational interviews—might have developed a list of steps others have taken to get their positions. Perhaps, for example, Jeff might have discovered that presenting a professional portfolio (one showing previously contracted work) was one key step toward getting a position in his field.]
Work backward.	Make your starting place the original goal, and then work backward, since some problems are easier to solve this way. [*Example:* Jeff works backward from his goal of medical illustrator to his initial considerations of how he decided to go into the field in the first place. He realizes that his internships were crucial to that decision and recognizes he probably should explain his interest in the field with detail from those experiences. *Example:* Mary wants a job teaching elementary school in a small college town. She discovers by talking with officials in the school district that most of the teachers now on staff started by substitute teaching in the district before applying for a full-time position. Mary thus knows to focus her initial efforts on qualifying for the substitute teacher list. As a substitute, Mary can then make herself known in the district and also be on the spot if a full-time opening occurs.]
Propose a hypothesis.	Complete the sentence "Suppose that . . ." in terms of your qualifications or of a company's point of view. [*Examples:* Jeff might have said, "Suppose that there are 150 people wanting the same position I want; what can I do to make my qualifications distinctive?" Mary might have said, "Suppose that the district only hires from within; how can I get my foot in the door?"]

The "traditional" job search method of trial and error can be expensive and discouraging.

Once you have a good representation of the job search, you need *strategies for tackling the task*. Figure 18.5 (next page) shows several problem-solving methods applied to finding a job. Of the strategies in Figure 18.5, the trial-and-error method is least efficient in finding a solution. The other strategies can be used in combination. For example, you might decide to divide the job search into chronological stages. Figure 18.6 (next page) suggests a likely sequence and notes communication tools that support each step. After dividing the task, you might do a means-end analysis for each step that you've identified in the job search.

It is outside the scope of this book to advise you about how to make a career choice. Your adviser and placement office are helpful resources in addressing this issue. Helpful, too, are certain software programs, such as Career Design (Career Design of Atlanta). Career Design is basically a self-help program which aids in identifying individual talents and defining a job that fits well with them. In this chapter, we focus on communication tools that can aid you during the job search.

PLANNING DOCUMENTS

Planning is important to the job application process. "Planning documents" such as personal inventories, job descriptions, and researched descriptions of prospective employers are all factors in a successful job search.

Personal Inventories

Personal Inventories are planning documents used by job applicants at the outset of a job search. Personal inventories have no other audience than the writer. A personal inventory can help you collect preliminary data for the resume, think about the match between your qualifications and the job description, and aid you in preparing for a job interview.

In conducting a personal inventory, you might consider the following:

- What are your goals (short term and long term)? *Setting goals will help you select the job position you want to apply for as well as prepare for job interview questions.*

Figure 18.5 Strategies for Finding Solutions to the Problem of Finding a Job

STRATEGY	EXPLANATION AND EXAMPLE
Trial and error	Searchers don't have or don't use information that indicates that any path is more likely to lead to the goal than any other path. [***Example:*** Jeff decides that not getting an interview so far has just been the "luck of the draw," so he continues by expanding his search, sending the same letter of application and resume to 50 different companies, hoping that one will pan out. ***Example:*** After applying unsuccessfully for five teaching positions, Mary decides that she might be better off applying for jobs in a different field. She applies for business jobs in personnel training, and plans to explore other types of jobs if she isn't immediately successful.]
Means-end analysis	Searchers try to reach a goal by taking a sequence of steps—(1) list differences between current state and the goal, (2) find (an) appropriate way(s) of reducing the difference, (3) compare ways, and (4) pick the one(s) that get(s) you closest to the goal. [***Example:*** Jeff takes a look at his application package. From his adviser's comments, he realizes that he needs to revise his letter to make it more specific. From comments of those in the field, he knows he needs to have a professional portfolio. Jeff decides to revise his letter first and to start compiling a professional portfolio, although he knows that he cannot complete one for his immediate search. ***Example:*** Mary decides that her main goal is to get a teaching position, whether in education or business. She applies for full-time teaching positions even as she works to get herself on the list of substitutes. She also decides to enroll in a community college course entitled "Training in Business and Industry" that is being offered in the evenings in case teaching in the public schools doesn't work out for her.]
Division into parts	Searchers try to make the problem more manageable by dividing it into parts and forming subgoals. [***Example:*** Jeff separates the task of preparing academically from the task of preparing professionally for a position in his field. He decides to extend his university course of study by one semester, giving himself more time to do freelance work, so that he has contract work to include in his portfolio. ***Example:*** Mary investigates what she will have to do to achieve each of these subgoals: to get substitute teaching credentials, to apply for a substitute teaching position, to qualify for full-time certification, to apply and interview for a full-time position, and to enroll in the community college course.]
Pattern matching	Searchers try to learn patterns that have been useful to others and may be useful to them (like application conventions and standard interviewing procedures). [***Example:*** Jeff comes to realize that his initial faith in knowing "how it's done" was well founded, but that his problem came in his simplistic definition of what "it" entailed. Learning from the success of others in his field, Jeff follows their example and—with revised application letter and professional portfolio in hand—has a better chance at being successful himself. [***Example:*** In following the patterns of past teachers, Mary applies to the substitute list in hope of repeating their move from substitute to full-time elementary school teacher.]

Figure 18.6 Likely Chronological Division for Job Search

STEP	COMMUNICATION TOOL
• Decide on the career you want.	Informational interviews (Chapter 11) with those working in areas of likely career interests A personal inventory outlining your skills and preferences
• Determine the position or positions within that field that you are qualified to apply for; determine which companies hire for these positions; answer appropriate job announcements.	Informational interviews with particular companies (Chapter 11) A job description memo based on your research of certain job titles and of those positions within certain companies
• Design one or more resumes appropriate to the position or positions you have decided to apply for.	Conventional or functional resume
• Apply for the position.	Company- and job-specific letters of application
• Interview.	Interviewing skills
• Follow-up.	Thank-you for interview; letters of acceptance, rejection, or resignation (Chapter 19)

TECHNOLOGY

CAREER SOFTWARE IS HELPFUL, BUT...

Various software packages can help you construct a resume. Perfect Resume (Davidson and Associates, Inc.) and Expert Resume Writer (Expert Software), both for PC with Windows, and ResumExpert, for the Macintosh, are three such programs. PFS: Resume & Job Search Pro for Windows (Spinnaker Software) has not only a resume package but also a contact manager and calendar for keeping track of job search appointments and follow-up calls.

Generally inexpensive, nearly all the career software programs offer templates and suggestions on how to write resumes, prospect letters, and application letters. Some also keep a database of important names and addresses and have the ability to merge the information directly into documents and print it on envelopes. Some also include schedule planners which prompt job hunters about important dates (interviews, call-backs, thank-you letters, etc.), and a few even offer practice "interview sessions" in which the computer asks common interview questions and grades the job hunter's responses.

Although such software can ease the task of constructing a resume, you should avoid being a slave to preset categories. Trying to squeeze information about your personal qualifications into a standard format might not prove the best way to represent your individual credentials. You should also understand other limitations of the packages. The programs, for example, give the user a pre-designed resume or letter format and give hints about wording ("use the active voice"), but they do little else. All the sample resumes and letters and varied formats (some programs ask the user questions to fill the blanks in the resume, some just offer a template) can't substitute for knowing how to write these documents.

- What do you expect out of a job (location, salary, hours, workload, authority, achievement, affiliation)? *Knowing what you expect from a job will guide your research into job positions and help you choose the number of positions that you apply for.*
- What skills and training do you possess (academic skills, people skills)? *Focusing on skills and training will help you apply for jobs that you are qualified for. It also helps you formulate the opening of a functional resume, organize your letter of application, and answer interview questions.*
- What academic and work experience have you had? *Reviewing your experience will help you gather data for your application letter and resume.*
- What are your personality characteristics and personal preferences (strengths and weaknesses)? *Knowing your personality characteristics helps you write a portion of the application letter and prepares you for a job interview.*

Perhaps the most challenging aspect of doing a personal inventory is analyzing your personality characteristics. Figure 18.7 shows Janice Ballantyne outlining her characteristics in specific terms. (We will later see how Janice uses these characteristics in specific job application messages.) Preparing a list of positive qualities helps you describe yourself in your letter of application. It also helps you answer questions often asked applicants, such as "Tell me about some of your strengths" or "What makes you feel you would be good at this job?"

Figure 18.7 Sample List of Positive Qualities in Personal Inventory

My personality characteristics are as follows:

Dependable—I am always on time to work, classes and meetings, and when I cannot make it, I always let them know ahead of time.

Hardworking—During my vacations, I paint my parents' barns and other farm buildings and walk their beans, cutting weeds.

Leadership ability—I was elected Vice-President of the Transportation/Logistics Club and was Co-Chairperson for the Club's Open House Display. I have taught Sunday School. I held every office in my 4-H Club.

Organizational ability—When I was a secretary, I organized the departmental files. I organized the Transportation/Logistics Club Open House Display. I organize my daily schedule in order to meet all deadlines.

Quick to learn—I learned my assigned duties when I was a secretary and then asked for additional responsibility.

Good manager of my time—When I was a secretary, I had to manage my time in order to get tests and reports typed with the same deadline. I am able to get my papers and coursework handed in on their due dates.

Responsible—I worked and saved money to pay for my college education. I am continuing to work on being assertive by reading books about it and applying it to my life.

Figure 18.8 Sample Handling of Weaknesses Using a Positive Approach

The writer deals with weaknesses positively. She's "working on" some and has succeeded in addressing others.

> I'm trying to work on some personal attributes right now. I'm a big planner, and sometimes when things don't turn out just right, I let my disappointment get me down. Something I've corrected that I'm pretty proud of is my lack of discipline that ranged from overspending to overworking (committing to too many projects at once). It feels good to be in control finally. I can deliver what I promise.

Being aware of weaknesses is also important. The description of weaknesses in Figure 18.8 is effective because it conveys a positive attitude while at the same time admitting to character faults. Because questions regarding personal strengths and weaknesses are common during job interviews, you are getting a head start on the process by analyzing these in a personal inventory and learning to phrase them positively.

Job and Company Description

Two vital planning documents you need in a job search are descriptions of job openings and of companies offering the positions. Having this information helps you check for matches between your credentials and the companies' criteria for hiring. While companies themselves provide basic information about job openings in their announcements, you will probably benefit from supplementing their public information with your own research. You may consult different types of sources.

- library references
- networking contacts
- job and company advertisements

Doing *library research* is a critical part of a job search. Quite a number of references are available to you. (Chapter 11 pages 318–323 provides a list of such references.) Resources can provide information about a company's vital statistics—corporate officials, size, financial position—and about a range of other issues:

- To discover information about job positions themselves, consult the *Dictionary of Occupational Titles (DOT)* for functional job analyses, the *Occupational Outlook Handbook* for a look at what the future looks like for specific jobs, and *Occupational Briefs* for a sense of the profession.
- To gain an in-depth picture of an organization, acquire a Better Business Bureau's report, data from the Register of Manufacturers for your state or area, or information from the local Chamber of Commerce about the company; call the company to request promotional literature about one of its major products; consult the company's annual report (which can be

MULTICULTURAL

WHAT KIND OF PEOPLE DO CORPORATIONS WANT FOR INTERNATIONAL ASSIGNMENTS?

As more and more companies "go international" and are setting up joint ventures and subsidiaries overseas, there is an increasing need for expatriates to work on international assignments at all corporate levels. However, because an alarmingly high expatriate failure rate exists (between 16 percent and 40 percent of personnel return early, and as high as 70 percent of the assignments in developing countries are aborted), many multinational corporations are setting new employee selection criteria for international assignments. Marvina Schilling reports that companies look for candidates' abilities in three areas:

1. *Self-orientation* focuses on activities and attributes that strengthen self-esteem, self-confidence, and mental health, including the ability to recognize potential conflicts and circumvent negative reactions; to replace pleasurable home activities with substitute activities in the host country; to accomplish tasks with self-confidence, sometimes with little or no help; and to deal with alienation and isolation.
2. *Others-orientation* focuses on activities and attributes that enhance the expatriate's ability to interact effectively with host country nationals (HCNs), including the ability to develop long-lasting friendships with HCNs; to use the local language as often as possible, without fear of being incorrect or sounding silly or stupid, in a desire to understand and relate to HCNs; to pick up on nonverbal body language in the host country, which may have different meanings from what it has in the home country; and to have respect and empathy for others.
3. *Perceptual-orientation* focuses on the ability to understand why foreigners do what they do and includes the ability to wait and accumulate all the facts before jumping to an opinion, stereotype, or incorrect decision, and to be openminded and able to make correct assumptions about the reasons or causes of HCN behavior.

Apart from candidates' abilities in the above areas, other selection criteria include the nature of the candidates' ties to the community or to other family members not going overseas.

obtained from stockbrokers or the company itself); or read articles regarding the company in such periodicals as *Fortune, Forbes, Business Week, Inc.*, and *Electronic Business.*

- To locate articles about a company's people or products, refer to publications such as *The Wall Street Journal Index, New York Times Index,* and *Business Periodicals Index.*

Consider the information gathered by Jennifer Nelson in 1993 about an opening at 3M. Jennifer, majoring in speech pathology, wanted to help children suffering from common language disorders, as well as to do research on ways to address more severe communication problems. Jennifer knew from job placement information at her university career office that 3M was hiring a "research specialist" in its Medical Products Group. Jennifer went to the library to gather information to help her determine whether she fit the job and decide how to target her application. In addition to information about the company's history, product development, and corporate diversity, she found specific information regarding 3M's Medical Products Group, including the fact that the group was currently developing a computer that would allow communication with people afflicted with autism or suffering from strokes or serious head injuries, any of which would prevent them from normal aural communication; and she learned that the group leads the company in sales and earnings, securing multimillion-dollar operating income.

Jennifer supplemented her research about the company with research concerning the job title in general and the specific position at 3M. Jennifer's research (Figure 18.9) helped picture how this particular "research specialist" position fit into the company as a whole, and how it matched her expertise.

Networking is often an excellent source of information about a potential employer. Networking involves consulting not only family and friends, but also people you know from school, your neighborhood, previous job positions, and social and professional organizations. People in any one of these settings might provide a lead to a possible job. Informational interviews (Chapter 11) are one way you can make personal contacts, collect information about a company, and discover matches between your credentials and company needs. You do not necessarily have to intend to apply for a job with a corporation to request an informational interview. Before such an interview, you need to set some time aside to establish your specific goals and to draft a list of 10 to 12 questions to ask. You can then identify the person in the company best suited to help you and can, by telephone or letter, ask for an opportunity to meet. Informational interviews have several benefits:

- You learn about a company's policies, practices, and products.
- You gain a sense of where you stand in the job market.
- You establish additional professional contacts.

Figure 18.9 Job Applicant's Write-Up of Research on Job Position

Research Specialist Position. 3M is in need of a research specialist who is knowledgeable in the area of communication disorders, to convey the special design, comfort, and mechanical needs of the victims of these disorders. Needs must be clearly conveyed from victims, their families, and the specialists to the engineers and designers in order to gain maximum benefit. The technology is part of a breakthrough in this area and enables humans to perform basic communication skills that are necessary for mental and physical health.

The position is under the Life Sciences Sector and Corporate Services Division of the company. The job will be located in the Medical Specialties Department. The research specialist will work closely with several engineers and designers in the medical division. The Department manager is Ronald H. Toensing, who works closely with the Children's Hospital in St. Paul as well as University Hospital in Minneapolis. Both hospitals serve as sources of information. This position requires the following:

1. A degree relating to the study of communication disorders and experience working with those who suffer from the disorders.
2. Excellent skills in communicating ideas and design clearly on a technical level.
3. The ability to relate to others in a way that makes them feel comfortable and open.
4. A twenty-first century way of thinking that allows for change and experimentation.

- You gain interviewing experience.
- You get a chance to evaluate how you would fit with such a company.

Of course, doing preliminary research on the company's vital statistics and on the occupational title itself is essential to preparing good interview questions.

Consider the networking done by Michele Whitehill, a senior majoring in art and design with a minor in advertising. Michele has the long-range goal of becoming art director or creative director of a large advertising agency. From talking with people in the field, Michele knows that to achieve her long-range goal, she must first get experience in creative aspects of advertising, including design and layout. Michele is thus eager to intern with either an ad agency, a newspaper, or a magazine that provides experience in design work.

She discusses with her adviser the internships that are available through her department. Michele also sets up informational interviews with Signature Printing and Publishing, a local firm, and Meredith Publishing, a national publishing house that produces a large number of magazines, including *Better Homes and Gardens.* At these companies, she plans to ask specific questions about how they use Macintosh programs such as Pagemaker and Aldus Freehand or IBM software such as Auto Cad and Draw Paint Deluxe to do layouts. She also plans to discover the qualities these firms most look for in their creative staff. Knowing a company's expectations will help her appropriately emphasize selected information in her credentials.

Many people find their first—and subsequent—jobs through personal and professional contacts.

Job advertisements and announcements in professional journals, newspapers, and university placement offices—as well as attendance at job fairs and corporate open houses, and contact through employment agencies or personal letters of inquiry—are also good resources. For example, Kris Livingston, a graduating senior, wants to apply for a position as a professional writer for a firm specializing in interactive computer disk (CD-i) technology. After he has researched the job title and the company and discussed the position with others in the field, he analyzes information about the job from a position advertisement (represented by Figure 18.10).

Kris' expertise and research are apparent in his analysis. He knows that "documentation" means tracing a project through development and production. He understands that he will be writing to different audiences: to technicians wihin the company and to outside customer-users who are primarily nontechnical. He also picks up on the importance of collaborative and

Figure 18.10 Job Description and Individual Interpretation

KRIS' ANALYSIS	JOB ANNOUNCEMENT EXCERPT
The company wants a writer who can both follow a product through its development and produce a user-friendly description of the product for market.	The position, entitled professional writer, involves gathering product-related information in order to report on it in documentation and manuals. The company is looking for someone with a number of skills:
• *The first bullet indicates collaborative skills are necessary.*	• works with implementors to draw information about the product under development
• *The second implies the company wants someone with discipline and experience as a writer.*	• writes technical descriptions of products/procedures based on specification sheets and a Statement of Requirements (SOR)
• *The third indicates skills needed in translating the technical to nontechnical and vice versa.*	• produces business memos to engineering staff about new developments from market researchers
• *The fourth bullet implies interpersonal as well as collaborative skills.*	• helps senior technical writer
The last paragraph gives "bottom-line" requirements.	The applicant must have a college degree and two years professional writing experience. Also helpful are knowledge of current hardware and software development, basic digital electronics, and company documentation standards.

Figure 18.11 Matches between Job Requirements and Individual Credentials

INFORMATION FROM THE JOB DESCRIPTION	INFORMATION FROM A LIST OF PERSONAL ASSETS (INVENTORY) KRIS HAS COMPILED
Professional Writer: gathers information on CD-i products and reports on it in documentation and manuals	• job fits my goal of professional writer position • software and hardware expertise • computer science major and English minor
Collaborative skills: works with engineers to understand the product under development	• work experience as service technician and customer service representative for MicroProducts
Writing skills: writes technical descriptions of products/procedures based on specification sheets and Statement of Requirements (SOR)	• performance in Technical Writing course • Apple business • article to be published
Technical/nontechnical expertise: produces technical memos to engineering staff about new developments from market researchers and produces manuals that nontechnical folk can use	• automatic data switching device, prototype, user's manual
Collaborative and interpersonal skills: helps senior technical writer	• team projects in various courses • work experience as Customer Service Representative for MicroProducts
Bottom-line requirements: a college degree and two years technical writing experience; knowledge of current hardware and software development, basic digital electronics, and documentation standards	• college degree from California Technological Institute • **two years writing experience: NO** • special achievements involving switching device, article, and Apple

interpersonal skills embedded in the job description. And he recognizes "bottom-line" requirements—qualifications expected of all applicants—when he sees them. Kris then faces the task of framing his qualifications as a fit for these requirements (Figure 18.11).

Kris really wants the position but knows from matching the job description with his list of assets that he is lacking a "bottom-line" requirement: he doesn't have two years of formal professional writing experience. Nevertheless, he does have other experience that might count toward the requirement. Kris' experience is outlined in the resume he eventually constructs for this particular opening (Figure 18.12, page 544). His initial thoughts about how the resume works in terms of the position are represented on the left.

Despite not having worked as a "professional writer," Kris intends to establish that he has had two years of *comparable* writing experience. He has done technical writing at

SKILLS & STRATEGIES

WRITING FOR RESUME BANKS

Resume database services, which enter your qualifications into a central candidate bank, are a booming business. The Resumix system (Santa Clara, California), for example, scans resumes and looks for relevant experience. MicroTrac (Newton Highlands, Massachusetts) matches new resumes with open jobs or sifts through a stack of resumes for a manageable subset for personnel managers to look at individually.

If you choose to write a resume for an electronic resume service, you have to make a few adjustments. For example, you need to know and use "buzzwords" appropriate to the position you are looking for, so that the computer can locate your credentials. If you were looking for a position as an accountant, you would be sure to insert buzzwords like cost accounting, revenue accounting, and CPA to catch the computer's "eye." Since computers and human recruiters read differently, you need to follow separate guidelines for constructing computer-scanned resumes:

- Forget exotic typefaces, underlining, and decorative graphics.
- Send originals and use a laser printer.
- Don't go below 12-point type.
- Use standard 8½" by 11" paper and do not fold.
- Use white or light-beige paper (no blues or grays).
- Avoid double columns.
- Use technical jargon, since computers will target key words (buzzwords) specific to your profession.

These innovations in resume writing and use do not, however, replace the basic function of any resume: to sell your credentials to the prospective employer.

Figure 18.12 Resume for Specific Job Opening

KRIS R. LIVINGSTON
3961 Sierra Madre Road
Arcadia, CA 91006
818-555-8058

I'm going to indicate versatility by implying both software and hardware expertise in my objective.

OBJECTIVE

To secure a position as Professional Writer which takes advantage of my computer engineering background and offers the opportunity to work with innovators in software or hardware development.

Both my major and minor relate to the position directly, so I'm putting education, which is a "bottom-line" requirement, first.

EDUCATION

California Institute of Technology, Pasadena, CA
Bachelor of Science degree, expected December 19--
Major in Computer Science, 3.45 GPA; minor in English, 3.67 GPA
Writing courses in Business Communication and Technical Writing, where I posted the highest scores in the class.

Condie Junior College of Business and Technology, Campbell, CA
A.A. degree, May 19--

My work experience is job related, even though I wasn't a technical writer; I'm showing relevant product knowledge here, as well as appropriate communication and collaborative skills.

EXPERIENCE

8/95–Present — Service Technician, MicroProducts Center, San Jose, CA
Diagnosed and repaired Apple™ computers and peripheral equipment; over phone, helped customers isolate hardware problems; produced service tips and bulletins for sales staff.

8/93–8/95 — Customer Support, MicroProducts Center, San Jose, CA
Resolved customers' software and hardware problems in the store, over the phone, and on-site; worked with salespeople in determining best system configuration for customer needs.

My special achievements should really sell them on my expertise and convince them I can meet my objective.

SPECIAL ACHIEVEMENTS

Started a small software organization for which I used my Apple™ computer to develop, copyright, publish, and market an assembly language utility program for restoring deleted files.

Commissioned to write a hardware construction article for a technically oriented magazine aimed at the Macintosh™ market. The article will describe the construction and use of an audio digitizer which I helped design and for which I developed driving routines. Publication date: November 19--.

Working on an automatic data-switching device for electronic musical instruments which I will offer for sale in kit or assembled form. Have designed and built a working prototype, and am writing assembly instructions and users' manual. Available: September 19--.

I'll provide a list of references to facilitate fast contact.

REFERENCES

Available upon request.

MicroProducts as well as for his entrepreneurial endeavors. Thus, he rightly thinks that he can realistically apply for the position. Kris realizes that he must discuss his credentials in his letter of application (Figure 18.13) in such a way that his prospective employers will also interpret his experience as appropriate and comparable.

You can already see that applying for a position requires both the presentation and interpretation of your credentials to match a specific job situation. You should also be aware that the job search can be a long and sometimes discouraging process. The additional information we present in the rest of this chapter concerning resumes and application letters should help increase your chances of success.

RESUMES

Resumes concisely present an applicant's credentials and include three basic types of information: essential, elective, and elicited.

Essential Information

Certain information is essential to your resume:

- contact information
- education and training
- work experience

Figure 18.13 Letter of Application Interpreting Credentials

Dear Ms. Calavas:

I am applying to be a Professional Writer with PIMA. I am majoring in Computer Science at California Institute of Technology and will be graduating in December of this year.

In addition to the standard programming and data structures classes at California Institute of Technology, I have excelled in several elective courses in computer engineering. The Digital Design and SMOX Design classes were among my favorites. These courses will help me to understand the technology involved in PIMA's CD-i projects and to produce memos to the technical staff.

Throughout my education, I have shown an aptitude for writing. To complement my major in Computer Science, I am currently working on a minor in English. I have done very well in several writing courses, including Technical Writing, which emphasized long reports and team projects. My minor GPA is 3.67 on a 4.0 scale. I received A's in each of my writing courses.

I feel that I would be capable of efficient work for your department because of my depth of understanding of technical subjects and the ability to share my understanding with others. As my enclosed resume indicates, I have four years of experience working with personal computers and dealing with customers on many levels. Through my work at MicroProducts in San Jose, I have learned to communicate my knowledge effectively with others both orally and in writing.

I am a quick learner and have been able to teach myself most of what I know about electronics and computers. Since I purchased my first Apple computer, I have moved on to complete several creative projects involving technical writing, such as the software I published in 19-- and the audio digitizer construction article which will be published in *MacUser* later this year. I am acquainted with both CD-i and CD-ROM. As a technical writer for PIMA, I will readily recognize, understand, and appreciate the technology about which I'll be writing, thus allowing faster completion of documentation projects.

PIMA is a progressive and highly innovative company doing great work with converting popular films to interactive software, and I would be proud to be associated with it. I would appreciate it if you would call me at 818-555-8058 or write me at the above address to arrange a time for an interview to discuss the possibility of employment with your firm.

Sincerely,

(Mr.) Kris Livingston

Encl.

Kris mentions his school in the opening because he thinks it's a plus; the degree is also a bottom-line criterion.

He establishes what's unique about his educational training (his computer engineering experience). He then spells out the connection between his training and the job position.

His training in writing addresses the title of the position. Team projects show collaborative work.

Kris emphasizes his communication skills in terms of end users, an audience mentioned in the job description.

Kris establishes his expertise by detailing successful independent projects and dramatizes an important personal quality: initiative. He matches his qualifications to job requirements.

He compliments the company and requests an interview. Since his name is "generic," Kris indicates his gender in the signature line as a courtesy.

Contact information, which identifies who you are and tells how you can be reached, appears at the opening of your resume. When identifying yourself, you need to use your full legal name. If you wish, you can provide your nickname upon your first personal contact. When listing your address, you should include a temporary address and a permanent address, or a work and a home address, where appropriate. If you list a work telephone number, be sure that your current employer allows employees to use company phones to conduct personal business, however brief.

Information about your *education and training* is essential, especially if you are looking for your first professional position or updating your credentials or changing careers. In any of these cases, your education and training are more likely to provide work-related qualifications than actual work experience. When appropriate, *military* experience can be included either under education or under work experience, depending on whether you want to emphasize the *training* you received or the *duties* you performed. Education and training entries should be listed in reverse chronological order (most recent first). Kris lists his California Institute of Technology (CIT) degree before his Condie Junior College degree (Figure 18.12), because his CIT experience is most recent.

As you tailor your resume to your specific audience, it's sometimes appropriate to list specific courses you've taken or special skills you have acquired. Sarah Watson's resume lists relevant courses from her major (Figure 18.2). Alternatively, you can also list courses that you think will distinguish you as an applicant. For example, if you are majoring in construction engineering, you might choose to list those elective courses outside your major (Business Law, Residential Architecture, Grant and Proposal Writing) that relate directly to the duties of the advertised position.

You may find it important to list special skills, such as computer languages or software familiarity and foreign language capability, in the education section. Or, like Sarah (Figure 18.2), you may want to note that you've financed a certain percentage of your education, especially when that percentage is high and can explain a relative lack of extracurricular activity, which sometimes indicates to employers that you do not like to get involved. Other information appropriate to the education section includes the subject of your thesis, your departmental honors project, and training received in special workshops or company seminars.

Work experience is crucial to include on your resume, whether or not this experience is related to the position for which you are applying. Sometimes applicants present their work experience in two separate sections, grouping past positions as either "job related" or "additional experience." In any case, it is important to avoid gaps in your account. If there are unavoidable gaps in your employment history (due to illness, layoffs, short-lived jobs, etc.), you need to deal with them in your letter of application, your interview, or both.

Like educational experience, work experience should be listed in reverse chronological order. In this list you usually include the dates of employment, the place of employment, your job title, and a listing of your job duties. You can vary how you order these elements. Functional resumes, which we cover later, do not usually list job duties under work experience, but include them implicitly or explicitly in the description of skills that appears at the outset. Figure 18.14 lists job-related and other work experience separately in a chronological resume.

Figure 18.14 Chronological Resume

Angela Courtney Cardello

Current Address
115 Lynn Ave.
Ames, Iowa 50010
515-555-5604

Permanent Address
3030 Mayfair Dr.
Barrington, Illinois 60010
708-555-6434

EDUCATION

IOWA STATE UNIVERSITY, Ames, Iowa BS, May 1994
Apparel Design major with minor in Fashion Merchandising

SELECTED COURSEWORK

Experimental Fashion Design
Fashion Merchandising
Fashion Illustration
Computer Aided Design
Textile and Apparel Industry
Product Development
Sewn Product Analysis
Clothing for Special Needs

JOB RELATED EXPERIENCE

WINNING MOVES, INC. Chicago, Illinois Summer 1993
Design Assistant Intern
- Designed infants and toddlers outerwear for Fall 1994
- Assisted in pattern making, creating sample markers, pricing garments, and designing dyes
- Completed sample requisition forms, purchase orders, and design sheets

Fall 1991
UNIVERSITY THEATRE DEPARTMENT
Costume Shop Assistant
- Responsible for costume construction and alteration

Aug.1988–June 89
MARSHALL FIELDS Vernon Hills, Illinois
Junior Fashion Consultant
- Modeled Clothing
- Worked as a sales associate

OTHER WORK EXPERIENCE

Summers 1990–93
NESTLEREST PARK Lake Zurich, Illinois
Stand Manager
- Assigned employees to daily tasks
- Organized food preparation

June 1989–Sept. 89
CHERNIN'S SHOE STORE Buffalo Grove, Illinois
Sales Associate

HONORS

Dean's List, Fall 1993
1st place Childrenswear Design and 1st place Fashion Illustration: 1993 Textiles and Clothing Department Fashion Show

ACTIVITIES

TEXTILES AND CLOTHING DEPT. FASHION SHOW 1992
Co-Director
- Organized and managed executive board
- Chaired selection committees for music, graphics, choreography

TEXTILES AND CLOTHING DEPT. FASHION SHOW 1991
Presentation Director
- Organized modeling auditions
- Choreographed fashion show

COLLEGE OF FAMILY AND CONSUMER SCIENCES COUNCIL

REFERENCES

Available upon request

Effectively listing job duties is key to writing a good work experience section. Consider Figure 18.15. The listings are effective in that the writer uses *action verbs* in simple past tense to describe her duties. She could have added to the effectiveness of her first set by making the group more parallel.

Figure 18.15 List of Duties Revised for Parallelism

ORIGINAL LIST	REVISED LIST
• Liaison between tenant start-up companies and university	• Served as liaison between tenant start-up companies and university
• Coordinated special promotional projects with director	• Coordinated special promotional projects with director
• Accounting for tenant company rent and services billing	• Provided accounting for tenant company rent and services billing
• Responsible for mass mailings of news releases	• Took responsibility for mass mailings of news releases
• Supplied information for Investors Conference attendees	• Supplied information for Inventors Conference attendees

Elective Information

You may select relevant **elective information**, such as Angela Cardello's Textiles and Clothing Fashion Show experience (Figure 18.14), to highlight your qualifications for the position in question:

- activities
- awards
- civil service ranking
- career goals or objectives
- honors
- interests
- military status
- offices held
- patents
- professional organizations
- publications
- references
- security clearances
- skills
- sports
- test scores
- travels
- volunteer work

You may select several of these options to include on your resume. However, you should limit yourself so that your resume does not become cluttered or lengthy. Although resume length can vary, all of your information should fit on one page, especially for entry-level positions. The one exception to this would be a separate list of references on a second resume sheet (see Appendix A).

Since space is at a premium in resumes, you may want to *combine options* when listing your elective information. For example, Figure 18.16 shows a writer combining "offices held" with extracurricular activities, volunteer work, and special skills under the general heading of "activities." Any number of options can be combined, as long as each can sensibly be placed under the general category heading. Listing a scholarship in Figure 18.16, for example, would not be appropriate, because a scholarship is not an "activity."

Career objectives and references are elective elements that frequently appear on resumes. *Career objectives*, when included, come immediately after the contact information. Objectives serve to identify the type of position you are looking for and to highlight any special qualifications you might have for that position. If you decide to include objectives, you need to make sure that they work for you instead of merely taking up valuable space. Figure 18.17 (page 548) demonstrates the difference between space-wasting and effective objectives.

References are important to any job search. Experts disagree about whether they should be "available upon request" or listed on the resume itself. Figure 18.18 (page 548) summarizes the arguments for each approach. Those in favor of listing references on the resume also point out that most of the arguments for references "available on request" favor the applicant and

Figure 18.16 Grouping That Combines Options for Elective Information

ACTIVITIES	Montana State University Accounting Club Secretary
	Volunteer for Income Tax Assistance Program
	Certified as Small Aircraft Pilot

Figure 18.17 Writing Effective Objectives

SPACE-WASTER OBJECTIVES	OBJECTIVES REVISED FOR EFFECTIVENESS
To obtain a management position in the hospitality industry.	To obtain a junior-level management position in a hotel which takes advantage of my internship training and collaborative work experience.
A challenging career in the field of social work that offers opportunities for growth and advancement.	A position as a case manager for social services that emphasizes child welfare and that incorporates my fluency in Spanish.
A sales position with a progressive organization which uses my experience and education.	Sporting goods sales requiring varsity-level team experience and both a practical and an academic background in marketing.

Figure 18.18 Arguments for Including or Excluding References on a Resume

ARGUMENTS IN FAVOR OF INCLUDING REFERENCES	ARGUMENTS FOR SAYING "REFERENCES AVAILABLE UPON REQUEST"
1. Information about applicants is more credible when it comes from a third party.	1. Applicants prefer to tell prospective employers about themselves personally.
2. Applicants may miss a prospective employer's call and thus miss providing references in a timely manner.	2. Applicants can better keep track of the progress of their job search if these employers must make a request for a list of references.
3. Including references encourages applicants to "customize" their credentials. (Applicants can send out different resumes, each with a separate set of references, based on the job opening.)	3. Applicants can name their references according to potential employer's request for information.
4. Listed references function like a good action close to facilitate a potential employer's contact with references.	4. The people who serve as references should not be called every time a resume is sent.

not the potential employer. You should check with professionals in your field to find out whether or not references are generally included with the resume when applying for jobs.

References can be included in a block at the bottom of a resume, as shown in Figure 18.2, or can be attached as a separate list (see Appendix A). If you list your references on a separate sheet, you need to remember to have your name on the second sheet also, in case it becomes separated from your other materials. You always need to include the reference's name, job title or position, professional address, and phone number.

Before you provide or list a reference, you should talk to the recommenders. You should ask if they can write you a "good" letter of recommendation, offering them an opportunity to state any reservations they might have about your qualifications. Usually, when people are willing to write a letter of recommendation with reservations, you know that they will be as positive as possible about any expressed weaknesses in your credentials. Knowing about perceived weaknesses lets you know what you may need to work on, and what weaknesses to address in an interview.

It is usually better to have a letter from someone who knows you and your capabilities well, warts and all, than from someone who has a prestigious name or title but barely knows your work. At the same time, you should probably restrict yourself to professional references, such as teachers and employers, and exclude personal references, such as ministers and friends. If one of your employers happens to be a friend or a family member, you need to understand that your job performance should be the focus of discussion. In some cases, employers like to see that individuals have both a personal and professional relationship with the recommender.

Many individuals and companies are now refusing to provide references, even for employees in good standing, because of possible legal implications. If, for example, a jury finds that a company is somehow wrong about an employee's performance, the former employee may be in a position to collect a big award.[2] Most courts do allow an employer to provide negative information about a former employee. However, many employers are

ETHICS

WHAT ABOUT WARTS? THE ETHICS OF OMISSION IN EMPLOYMENT COMMUNICATION

Job applicants can misrepresent their credentials by omitting key details. Of course, an applicant can appropriately omit some facts. For example, it might be appropriate not to mention an experience—like a stint working for a political cause—that is not job related and that might not appeal to prospective employers. However, if employers check things out and discover that you misrepresented yourself by omitting a crucial fact, such as being fired from a previous position, you risk losing not only the job but also your professional credibility.

Employers, of course, can also be guilty of deception. John Sculley, the former chairman of Apple Computer, accepted a CEO position with Spectrum Information Technologies and subsequently resigned amid charges of accounting improprieties that he claims he didn't know about when he took the job. Companies sometimes deceive prospective employees when they hire for peak times and don't inform workers that they will be laid off when they are no longer needed.

E. Pendleton James, a New York headhunter, says, "Tell us about any warts you have. What is a wart to you may not be to me." This maxim has a corollary for prospective employees—thoroughly investigate a firm you are considering. You might save yourself from a career blunder if, through such investigation, you discover that the firm you're interested in follows practices that you consider unacceptable.

now including a section on their applications where the applicant consents to allow the prospective employer to obtain references from previous employers. Such a waiver protects a previous employer from liability. Nevertheless, it is becoming increasingly common for companies to verify only employment dates and salary.[3]

Elicited Information

Elicited information is information that you would not normally include on your resume, but which may be appropriate for particular audiences and occasions. For example, you would usually exclude personal data involving birth date or age, gender, marital status, nationality or race, physical characteristics such as height and weight, religious affiliation, and social security number, partly for legal reasons. You would also exclude irrelevant details regarding social organizations and high school experience. However, if a particular job position—such as pilot or flight attendant—has a height requirement, for example, then you would include such information if appropriate and elicited by the employer. Similarly, if a company advertises "applications from women and minorities welcome," then including your gender or race might be advantageous to you if you belong to a class protected by affirmative action. The job position then asks for the inclusion of such detail. You should be aware, however, that constraints arising from Title VII of the Civil Rights Act of 1964 apply to the type of information elicited by employers and affects what you include on your resume (see pages 569–571).

Chronological and Functional Resumes

You can organize the types of resume information discussed in this section in two basic ways. **Chronological resumes** organize a person's activities and accomplishments by time, from the most recent to the least recent (see Figures 18.2, 18.12, and 18.14). **Functional resumes,** which will be discussed shortly, emphasize applicants' skills apart from their employment history. Whether you choose to use a chronological or a functional resume depends, of course, on your audience and your purpose for presenting your skills. Do you wish to emphasize your long, reliable work history in the field, or do you wish an employer to see the skills that you bring to a position which is slightly different from the jobs you've held in the past? Figure 18.19 on the next page should help you in choosing whether to use a chronological or a functional resume.

A major difference in chronological and functional resumes is how the educational and work experience is presented. Figures 18.20 and 18.21 (page 550 and 551) show a chronological resume and a functional resume displaying the same person's credentials. Janice Ballantyne is a graduating senior in transportation and logistics who has had extensive secretarial experience. Her chronological resume (Figure 18.20) emphasizes that work experience. After looking at her resume and showing it to others, Janice discovers that while the resume would be an excellent one if she were applying for an executive secretarial position within a transport company, it does not—except for the objective—help her move to her new career in transportation and logistics. She therefore decides to write a functional resume (Figure 18.21). Because it emphasizes what she can do rather than what she has done, a functional resume supports Janice's move to a new career much better than does her chronological resume.

Figure 18.19 Uses for Chronological and Functional Resumes

CHRONOLOGICAL RESUME	FUNCTIONAL RESUME
You plan to continue a particular career or employment path.	You are changing careers or want to alter your career path.
Your reader specifies "bottom-line" requirements in academic background and employment history. Your reader is a member of a traditional company or organization.	Your reader is looking for certain specific skills and abilities rather than a particular academic background or employment history.
Your current or most recent employer(s) are prestigious.	Your past jobs have been numerous and/or unrelated.
The position builds on past achievements in a particular career.	The position involves freelance work or using old skills to new advantage.

Figure 18.20 Chronological Resume for Janice Ballantyne

Janice includes only one address because where she lives is her permanent address.

Janice offers a dual-headed objective that identifies the job position and names her strengths.

Janice simply lists her degrees.

She provides excellent detail about her five years of secretarial experience.

She lists honors and activities that represent a mixture of leadership and academic achievements.

JANICE M. BALLANTYNE
18551 Ridgewood Dr.
Ames, IA 50010
515-555-2121

CAREER OBJECTIVE

To obtain a position with a firm in the transportation or physical distribution/logistics field that emphasizes operations and that takes advantage of my analytical skills and training in decision theory.

EDUCATION

B.B.A., Transportation/Logistics, December 1994
Iowa State University, Ames, Iowa
GPA: Major - 3.00/4.00

A.A. Degree, Secretarial Science, May 1987
Marshalltown Community College, Marshalltown, Iowa
GPA: Cumulative - 3.33/4.00

EARNED AND PAID 90% OF COLLEGE EDUCATION

WORK EXPERIENCE

Department Head's Secretary, Department of Engineering Science and Mechanics, Iowa State University. Composed and typed letters and memorandums. Supervised two secretaries. Analyzed statistics for class records. Organized and maintained various files and records. (May 1988–May 1992)

Department Head's Secretary, Library Serials Department, Iowa State University. Recorded statistics for over 20,000 serials. Ordered office supplies. Scheduled appointments for the department head. Promoted to the Department of Engineering Science and Mechanics. (June 1987–May 1988)

Secretary, Department of Transportation, Ames, Iowa. Greeted and assisted visitors and callers. Typed correspondence and reports for highway division. (Summers 1986 and 1987)

Secretary, Office Education Department, Marshalltown Community College, Marshalltown, Iowa. Organized and maintained office files. Assisted instructor in preparing coursework, such as typing, duplicating, and recording grades. (January 1986–May 1987, 10 hours/week)

HONORS AND ACTIVITIES

Iowa State University Transportation/Logistics Club Vice President

Delta Nu Alpha Transportation Fraternity

Named Outstanding Office Education Student

Dean's List

Marshalltown Community College Music Scholarship

Marshalltown Savings & Loan Scholarship
National Secretary Scholarship

REFERENCES *[listed below, on separate sheet]*

Figure 18.21 Functional Resume for Janice Ballantyne

Janice describes her objective as a job position, since she wants to clearly signal her new career path from the start.

Janice cites her analytical skills first, since they involve her most recent training appropriate to her new career.

She reduces the emphasis on her secretarial positions while still showing their value in the way she lists her other skills.

Janice uses a modified list format to note her education and work experience.

JANICE M. BALLANTYNE
18551 Ridgewood Dr.
Ames, IA 50010
515-555-2121

POSITION

Assistant Operations Manager with a firm in transportation or physical distribution/logistics

ANALYTICAL SKILLS

- Successfully applied quantitative techniques to production management in Production/Operations Management course at Iowa State University
- Solved problems in physical distribution in Logistics Management and Transportation Carrier Management course
- Analyzed statistics for class records as Department Head's secretary in the Department of Engineering Science and Mechanics

MANAGERIAL SKILLS

- Supervised two secretaries as Department Head's secretary in the Department of Engineering Science and Mechanics
- Coordinated activities of 50-member group as Transportation/Logistics Club vice-president
- Organized the public display for the Transportation/Logistics Club as co-chair for the club's spring festival contribution

INTERPERSONAL SKILLS

- Participated in collaborative projects and wrote successful business messages to various audiences in business communications course
- Dealt with administration, faculty, staff, students and the public when working in various secretarial positions at Iowa State University
- Held leadership positions in the Transportation/Logistics Club and Delta Nu Alpha transportation fraternity.

EDUCATION

B.B.A. Degree, Transportation/Logistics, December 1994
Iowa State University, Ames, Iowa; GPA: Major - 3.00/4.00

A.A. Degree, Secretarial Science, May 1987
Marshalltown Community College, Marshalltown, Iowa; GPA: 3.33/4.00

EXPERIENCE

May 1988–May 1992, Department Head's Secretary, Department of Engineering Science and Mechanics, Iowa State University

June 1987–May 1988, Department Head's Secretary, Library Serials Department, Iowa State University

Summers 1986 & 1987, Secretary, Department of Transportation, Ames, Iowa

REFERENCES *[listed below, on separate sheet]*

LETTERS OF APPLICATION

When you send a resume to a prospective employer, you write an application or cover letter to explain the reason for your correspondence and to highlight your strong points. Letters of application and their accompanying resumes can be solicited or unsolicited. A solicited letter responds to a specific announced job opening in a paper, trade journal, or placement office. An unsolicited letter "prospects" for a position within an organization. Whether solicited or unsolicited, letters of application have several components and tasks in common:

- opening: name the job position and establish the context
- body: develop major selling points and create a match between writer's qualifications and employer's needs
- penultimate (second-to-last) paragraph of body (when appropriate): refer to desirable personal qualities
- close: request an interview and facilitate contact

Letters of application also refer to the resume in some way, sometimes simply with an "enclosure" line.

Remember, too, that letters of application demonstrate "you" attitude by emphasizing reader benefit rather than by using the pronoun "you" (see Chapter 4). Letters of application are one of the few business documents that can appropriately use "I" throughout the message.

Opening

Openings differ in solicited and unsolicited letters of application. A solicited application commonly states the position that you are applying for, mentions where you learned of the position, and includes a "bonus" factor that will make the reader want to read further. The bonus factor might be that you will graduate from a school recognized as excellent in your field or might simply be a forecast statement of the ways in which you qualify for the position. Figure 18.22 shows the factors usually present in the opening of a solicited letter of application.

Unsolicited letters of application must work hard at gaining the reader's attention, since the reader is not in the process of filling a particular position. Writers can make compliments, ask questions, name strong suits or outstanding achievements, refer to important references, or cite excellent matches between what the company does and what the writer can do as ways of sparking interest. Figure 18.23 shows two separate versions of an opening for an unsolicited application letter to the same company.

When writing an unsolicited letter of application, you will need to base the type of attention-getting opening you use on your field. For example, attention getters for an advertising position, which tend to be flashy and imaginative, might be considered inappropriate for applying for a managerial position in a traditional company. In any case, in both solicited and unsolicited letters, it is important that you actually state that you are applying for the position, not simply that you "heard about it" or that you are "interested in it."

Selling Your Credentials

You can sell your qualifications to a prospective employer in two interconnected ways: by detailing specific, appropriate qualifications and by forging a link between those qualifications and the requirements of the position.

In his letter of application (Figure 18.13), Kris Livingston sells his credentials in two ways. First, he *makes generalizations about his abilities* in such statements as "I have excelled in several elective courses in computer engineering," "I have shown an aptitude for writ-

Figure 18.22 Opening of Solicited Application Letter

The writer states he is applying, names the position, states context and adds a bonus forecast.

I am applying for the financial associate position advertised in the Potomac State College *Weekly Bulletin*. As a senior accounting major, I feel my qualifications in business education, work experience, and various other skills would make me a convincing candidate.

Figure 18.23 Two Versions of Unsolicited Application Letter Opening

In 1., the writer selects a formal tone, begins with a match between what she has done and what the company does, pays a compliment, and then notes her graduation from a recognized program.

In 2., the writer names a well-respected reference, applies for the position, forecasts strong qualifications, and shows a match between her qualifications and company needs.

1.

During the course of my college program internship in your Florida park last summer, I was impressed by the dedicated service, unique atmosphere, exceptional staff, and meticulous attention to detail that have given Walt Disney World an internationally prestigious reputation. As a senior in Hotel, Restaurant and Institution Management at Southeastern State University, I am seeking employment in an entry level position in one of your resort's food and beverage departments upon my graduation in May.

2.

Upon the recommendation of Ms. Kelley Ford-Jesperson, supervisor of confections personnel at Walt Disney World, I am applying for an entry-level position in one of your resort's food and beverage departments. I believe my professional training in Southwestern State University's Hotel, Restaurant, and Institution Management program, and my work experience, which is highlighted by a successful internship at Walt Disney World last summer, make me a highly qualified applicant for work in your famous organization.

ing," "I have learned to communicate my knowledge effectively with others both orally and in writing," and "I am a quick learner and have been able to teach myself most of what I know about electronics and computers." Kris selects which abilities to feature according to the criteria for hiring in the job description. Kris, of course, offers support for his general statements in the letter itself and is prepared to offer additional support if there is a subsequent interview.

Second, Kris *suggests direct links between his credentials and the skills necessary for the position* in such statements as "These courses will help me to understand the technology involved in PIMA's CD-i projects and to produce memos to the technical staff," "I feel that I would be capable of efficient work for your department because of my depth of understanding of technical subjects and the ability to share my understanding with others," and "As a technical writer for PIMA, I will readily recognize, understand, and appreciate the technology about which I'll be writing, thus allowing faster completion of documentation projects." These links not only interpret Kris' credentials favorably in terms of the position, but also indicate that Kris has done his research into what the company does and what it wants from a technical writer. That research, even more than the compliment in the last paragraph, dramatizes Kris' interest in the company.

While Kris sells his credentials by creating direct links between his qualifications and the criteria for hiring, Sarah Watson (Figure 18.1) sells hers by emphasizing the parts of her record that correspond to what the prospective employer, Paul French, seems to want. Sarah interprets French's preference for a "down-home approach" and his willingness to hire a person with only "some college" but with appropriate experience as an indication that he has a great deal of respect for practical experience. She, therefore, decides to downplay her academic honors in her letter, which include finishing her four-year program of study in three years, a Phi Beta Kappa membership, and a Federated Women's Club Scholarship. Instead, she details her practical work experience and mentions her personal ties to the area. Although she excludes her impressive honors from the letter, she includes them in a straightforward list on her resume (Figure 18.2). She thus dramatizes her interest in the position by emphasizing those qualifications most important to her prospective employer, while at the same time completely representing her own achievements.

Other strategies help prospective employers see the link between your qualifications and the job requirements. Janice Ballantyne, for example, facilitates the process by ordering the paragraphs of her letter of application (Figure 18.24 on next page) according to the sequence found on her functional resume: *job position, skills, education,* and *work experience.* This direct match between the organization of a letter of application and the sequencing of a resume, while not required, facilitates a reader's interpretation of resume data. Janice is careful to include components expected in a solicited letter of application.

PORTFOLIOS

One of your options in applying for a job is to submit a portfolio along with your resume and letter of application. Some applicants prefer to bring portfolios along with them to their job interviews. Portfolios are displays of assets. Portfolios concerned with your communication assets would showcase your oral and written skills:

- *topics* you can handle
- *audiences* for which you have written
- *designs* you've created
- *visuals* and *graphics* you've designed and used
- *purposes* to which you have responded
- *organizational and developmental* strategies that you've used for various projects
- *presentational* strategies, including use of multimedia
- *genres* or types of writing you're skillful and comfortable with

The assets you choose to include would, of course, depend on what field you are in and which skills you wish to highlight.

The purpose of a portfolio is sales: you are marketing yourself. Because your task is to dramatize your assets, you should be as inclusive as possible. If, for example, you were marketing your communication skills, you would include everything—fiction or nonfiction; written, visual, or oral—that had to do with communication: articles, chapters, stories, books, videotapes of presentations, photos, ad campaigns, work you've edited, work you've

Figure 18.24 Letter of Application Interpreting a Functional Resume

Janice names the position, forecasts areas of match, and states that there is a match between her qualifications and the position.

She organizes her letter according to her skills, a choice that complements her functional resume and her desire to emphasize what she can do and not what she has done.

She uses extracurricular activities to demonstrate her interpersonal skills.

With education, Janice moves from interpreting the skills portion of her functional resume to elaborating on other items.

She includes but deemphasizes her past work experience to signal that she's embarking on a new career.

She requests an interview and facilitates that request. She uses an enclosure line to refer to her resume.

Dear Mr. Haude:

I am applying for the position of Associate Analyst in the Traffic/Distribution Department at Procter and Gamble. I believe my major in Transportation/Logistics from Iowa State University, my work experience, and my activities provide me with the qualifications you are looking for.

While attending Iowa State University, I was able to take courses to develop my analytical skills, which will enable me to identify problems and implement solutions. In the course Production/Operations Management, I learned different applications of quantitative techniques to production management problems such as decision theories. In the courses Logistics Management and Transportation Carrier Management, I studied transportation and physical distribution problems and techniques for solutions.

I have been able to develop my managerial skills through offices I have held, activities I have been involved in and my work experience. I was elected Vice President of the Transportation/Logistics Club. I worked with the professors and the other officers in coordinating club activities. When the president was absent, I would then preside over meetings. I was also Co-Chairperson for the Transportation/Logistics Club Open House Display. I organized and worked with a committee in preparing this display.

Through my activities I enhanced my interpersonal skills. I am a member of the Delta Nu Alpha Transportation Fraternity and attend monthly meetings where I am able to meet with professionals in the transportation/physical distribution field. I belong to volleyball and softball teams, through which I have learned to work as part of a team in accomplishing common goals.

Courses in business communication and speech that I have taken have helped me to develop my communicative skills so I can put my ideas into effect. The business communications course taught me how to write effective business letters. The speech courses taught me effective application of speech communication. I can now apply the techniques I learned about effective communication to interpersonal relations.

While working as a secretary, I had the opportunity to work in a number of different offices. When I worked at Iowa State University, I dealt daily and successfully with administration, faculty, staff, students and the public.

Please write me or call me at (515) 555-2121 to tell me about the possibilities of my working for you. I can plan a trip to Cincinnati to meet and discuss with you ways I could possibly best serve Procter and Gamble.

Sincerely yours,

Janice Ballantyne

Encl.: Resume

substantively contributed to, and so forth. Such work might be presented as excerpts or as entire pieces. It represents a "scrapbook history" of what you've done and a projection of what you will be able to do for an employer.

The physical design of a portfolio has a lot of similarities to a user manual (see Chapter 16). The design should help readers get in and out quickly. At the same time, readers want to learn something useful while they're reading and to keep track of where they are in relation to the whole. You should, therefore, provide guideposts about what readers should particularly notice when reviewing your collection. Possible techniques include brief boxed introductions, marginal annotations, tab dividers to signal major sections, and callouts to identify what you think is important. Your resume, as the first item in the portfolio, can provide the reader with an overview of your credentials and a context for looking at the materials included.

While portfolios have long been common for applicants in visual arts fields, they represent an increasingly attractive alternative for presenting credentials for applicants in a wide range of fields and specialties.

RESPONSE SHEET

LETTER OF APPLICATION

WRITER(S):	AUDIENCE(S):
OCCASION FOR WRITING:	DOCUMENT:

WHAT PROBLEM OR ISSUE IS THE WRITER TRYING TO ADDRESS IN THIS DOCUMENT?

◆ BACKGROUND RESEARCH

What types of personal and professional information will the writer be wise to bring to this application situation?

What does research tell the writer about the prospective employer?

What does research tell the writer about the job position itself?

◆ OPENING

Is the letter of application solicited or unsolicited?

If solicited, does the opening contain specific mention of the job position (title)? Of the context (where the writer heard about the opening)?

If unsolicited, what technique(s) does the writer use to attract reader interest?

In any case, does the opening include a "plus" that will distinguish the applicant from other applicants?

Does the writer actually apply for the position?

◆ BODY

From looking at the body of the letter, can you tell whether or not the letter accompanies a chronological or a functional resume? Explain.

Review the qualifications the writer includes in each paragraph. Comment on the specificity of the qualifications mentioned.

Comment on the writer's attempts to "interpret" the qualifications in terms of the position.

From reading the list of qualifications, *re-create* the job advertisement the writer is answering.

Comment on the writer's attempts to link the qualifications to apparent criteria for hiring.

◆ CLOSE

Does the close ask for an interview? How does the writer facilitate future contact? Suggest improvements where appropriate.

Does the close contain reference to the company where appropriate?

Does the writer refer to the resume at some point in the letter? (An enclosure line counts and is needed in any case.)

RESPONSE SHEET

RESUME

WRITER(S):	**AUDIENCE(S):**
OCCASION FOR WRITING:	**DOCUMENT:**
WHAT PROBLEM OR ISSUE IS THE WRITER TRYING TO ADDRESS IN THIS DOCUMENT?	

◆ BACKGROUND RESEARCH

What types of personal and professional information will the writer be wise to bring to this resume?

What does research tell the writer about the prospective employer?

What does research tell the writer about the job position itself?

Does the writer's research indicate that a *chronological or a functional resume* would be most appropriate. Explain.

◆ ESSENTIAL INFORMATION

Review the contact information listed in the resume. Does the writer list both a current and a permanent address where appropriate? Is there additional information the writer should include (e-mail address, etc.)

Review the information on education and training presented on the resume. If it is a *chronological* resume, are the listings in reverse chronological order?

If it is a *functional* resume, does the writer use educational and training experience to support the skills listed at the outset?

Review the work experience. If it is a *chronological* resume, are the listings in reverse chronological order? Are there gaps in the work history?

If it is a *functional* resume, does the writer support the skills listed with specific, active phrases and experience from the employment history?

◆ ELECTIVE INFORMATION

Comment on the elective information that the writer has chosen to include. Are there suggestions for exclusion or further inclusions?

Where options are somehow grouped together, do the groupings make sense?

Comment on the wording of the objectives if included. Is the objective a space waster?

Comment on the handling of the references.

◆ ELICITED INFORMATION

Locate any information seemingly elicited by the job description. What is the nature of this information, and what does it suggest about the job position itself?

Note any Title VII violations that you spot in the elicited information that is included.

(Note any other suggestions for improvement that you might have regarding any aspect of the resume directly on the draft.)

ACTIVITIES, EXERCISES, AND ASSIGNMENTS

◆ IN-CLASS ACTIVITIES

1. Please refer to Figures 18.1 through 18.3 for the following activity.

   a. Discuss how Figure 18.1 uses the conventional strategies for writing application letters. What differences do you see between how Sarah uses these strategies (Figure 18.1) and how Jeff uses them (Figure 18.3)?

   b. Consider how Sarah's letter (Figure 18.1) and her resume (Figure 18.2) work together. What suggestions for improvement do you have?

   c. How does Sarah prove she has researched the position?

2. Discuss the job search process. Interview several professionals in your field to discover any tips they might have regarding a job search in your professional area. Write a memo about your findings. Then select several of the hints you have discovered and share them with your fellow students. Feel free to add personal experiences to the mix.

3. Assume that you are to give an oral presentation to recent community college graduates about how to write job application letters and resumes so that these documents work together to land the applicant a desirable position. Discuss ways that these graduates can both match their credentials to the job requirements in a letter of application and then link their letters and resumes to make an effective message.

◆ INDIVIDUAL AND GROUP EXERCISES

1. Please refer to Figures 18.25, 18.26, and 18.27 in completing this exercise.

   a. Select the Kitchen Manager's position and match the requirements of the job to the qualifications of the applicant, which include the degree in HRIM.

   b. Select the Front Desk Supervisor's position and match the requirements of the job to the qualifications of the applicant, which include the degree in HRIM.

   c. Using your information from either part a or part b, write the body of an application letter that applies for one of the positions.

   d. Take the qualifications as described in the excerpt from the student's chronological resume (Figure 18.27) as a basis for listing skills in a functional resume. Write the skills portion of a functional resume for this student.

   e. Do you think that the student should use a functional resume for both positions? For only one of the positions? Explain.

CONTEXT

A senior student in Hotel, Restaurant, and Institution Management (HRIM) sees the two positions in Figures 18.25 and 18.26 (page 558) advertised for a resort hotel in the Virginia Beach area. She decides that before she applies for either position, she must match the skills from her work experience, as shown in Figure 18.27 (page 558), to the requirements of each job.

Figure 18.25 Job Description for Kitchen Manager

Kitchen Manager:

Supervises and coordinates activities of food preparation, kitchen, pantry, and storeroom personnel and purchases or requisitions foodstuff and kitchen supplies.

- Plans or participates in planning menus, preparing and apportioning foods, and utilizing food surpluses and leftovers
- Specifies number of servings to be made from any vegetables, meat, beverage and dessert to control portion costs
- Supervises noncooking personnel, such as kitchen helpers, to ensure cleanliness of kitchen and equipment
- Supervises cook and tastes, smells, and observes food to ensure conformance with recipes and appearance standards
- Supervises workers engaged in inventory, storage and distribution of foodstuff and supplies
- Requisitions foodstuffs from purchasing agent
- Hires and discharges employees
- Trains new workers
- Meets with professional staff, customers, or client group to resolve menu inconsistencies or to plan menus for special occasions

Figure 18.26 Job Description for Front Desk Supervisor

Front Desk Supervisor:

Supervises and coordinates activities of front desk and provides communication between employees, guests, and other hotel departments.

- Oversees the happenings at the front desk
- Runs reports and communicates the reports to the staff
- Blocks guests into rooms
- Deals with any problems during the billing process
- Communications with other departments
- Technical skills of the front desk—checking in and out of guests, and operation of the PBX phone system
- Previous supervisory skills to deal with directly subordinate employees

Figure 18.27 List of Qualifications as Taken from Student's Chronological Resume

CAREER RELATED EXPERIENCE

1993–1994 **BEAVER CREEK INN**
Winter Park, CO 80482
NIGHT HOUSEKEEPING SUPERVISOR
- In charge of own staff including evaluations and disciplinary actions
- Held meetings for night staff to discuss assignment of work, potential problems and solutions
- Responsible for turndown service and all public areas

1992–1993 **BORDERLANDS MEXICAN CAFE**
Denver, CO 80011
HEAD WAITRESS
- Scheduling of employees
- Responsible for training new employees

1990–1992 **VACATION HOTEL SOUTH**
Denver, CO 80219
CATERING ASSISTANT
- Helped coordinate events
- Helped coordinate menus for events
- Scheduled employees for events

OTHER WORK

Holidays 1988–1991 **MOVIE THEATRES, INC.**
Denver, CO 80219 - Cashier

Summer 1989 **JESPERS PAINTING SERVICE**
Denver, CO 80012 - Trim-work on homes

ACTIVITIES
Hotel Restaurant Management Club
Club Managers of America Association
Felix House Vice President
National Honor Society
Quality Assurance Committee, Beaver Creek

2. Please use the example in Figure 18.28 to complete this exercise.

   a. Please comment on the opening of this unsolicited letter of application. Remember, in unsolicited letters of application, writers can
      - make compliments
      - name strong suits or outstanding achievements
      - refer to important references
      - cite excellent matches between what the company does and what the writer can do as ways of sparking interest

   Suggest ways that this writer could improve his attempt to engage the reader in the opening of this letter.

Figure 18.28 Draft of Unsolicited Letter of Application

Dear Ms. Peacock:

As an assistant manager in your communication department, I could test and compile on your new word processor line. Having successfully completed my training in communications systems at Ohio State University, I feel I am ready to work for a greatly respected company like RGI.

Along with completing the requirements for my B.S. in electrical engineering, I have also completed the courses necessary for a B.S. in mathematics, both in just 5 years. I chose a double degree program because a good math background is essential to electrical engineers. In order to satisfy the requirements for both degrees I averaged 17–19 credits per semester (12 being considered full-time) and also went to summer class for the past 3 years. I will be graduating on July 24, 19--, with an A-/B+ average for all courses.

For my studies in engineering, I have been fortunate enough to belong to two honor societies. In November 19--, I was asked to join Eta Kappa Nu, which is the honor society for electrical engineering students. And in April 19--, I joined Tau Beta Pi, which honors the top 15% of each engineering class.

In my microelectronics class, I had the opportunity to build a digital voltmeter for a project. Using parts from our lab kit and some I purchased on my own, I finished the voltmeter in two weeks.

For my senior-level technical electives, I chose courses on communications systems, in particular those on the analog subject of antenna theory. I enjoyed this two semester sequence and its lab immensely. I found it particularly gratifying to see how my earlier work in electrical engineering and math prepared me for antenna theory. Because of my enthusiasm and interest in communications systems, I think I could be beneficial to RGI in that area.

To help myself get through school financially, I took a construction job the first two summers of my college career. Here I got valuable experience in working closely with other people. Also I learned what it meant to work hard. Many days we worked 10 to 12 hours. Because of my experience here I believe I could easily learn to work with other engineers at RGI.

RGI is pioneering new research in the field of communications, and I would like to be involved in it. I will be in your area August 1–10 and would like to meet with you personally to discuss how I can contribute to RGI.

Sincerely yours,

b. Please identify and comment on how the writer attempts to connect the skills he has with company needs. Suggest improvements where appropriate.

c. Note the large number of personal pronouns, especially "I's," in this letter. Suggest changes the writer could make to reduce the number of personal pronouns so that he sounds confident but not egotistical.

d. Note that the letter extends to two pages. Suggest ways the writer could reduce the text so that the letter fits on one page.

e. Revise the letter for effectiveness, incorporating both your suggestions and the comments of others.

◆ OUT-OF-CLASS ASSIGNMENTS

1. See if your university provides testing services for students that might provide personality profile information for your inventory. Construct a personal inventory of your assets. Be sure to include strengths and weaknesses. Write down several ways that you could address your weaknesses positively.

2. Locate a job description that would be of interest to you. Using various resources, research both the prospective employer and the job position itself. Write a memo that reports your findings.

3. Construct a chronological resume presenting your qualifications. Construct a functional resume presenting your qualifications. What types of positions would be appropriate to each respective resume? Write a context for each. Using the Response Sheet on resumes as a guide, review another person's resume. Make suggestions where appropriate.

4. Write a letter of application that corresponds to either your chronological or your functional resume. Schedule time to review another person's letter, using the Response Sheet on letters of application as a guide for revision suggestions. Submit both the letter and the resume as a "package" for evaluation.

CASE

PURSUING MAXWELL FINANCIAL GROUP

CASE BY ANDREA BREEMER FRANTZ

Background. Mikayla Ross is a graduating senior with a finance and German double major at Boise State University. Feverishly scanning and testing the job market, Mikayla has sent out approximately 40 resumes and cover letters to a variety of financial services specializing in international investment. If possible, Mikayla would love to find a job that would allow her to use her expertise with the German language as well as her keen abilities with financial planning and investments.

After a serious car accident in the spring of her junior year, which left her paralyzed from the waist down, Mikayla took eight months off from school for physical therapy. She returned the following January to finish her final three semesters. In addition to serving on numerous committees and in

Figure 18.29 Mikayla's Letter of Application

Box 5291
Boise State University
Boise, Idaho 83707
e-mail: mlross@bostate.edu

Mr. Charles Stepanek, Personnel Director
American Financial Services
Box 882, 4th & Washington
Spokane, Washington 98108

February 21, 19--

Dear Mr. Stepanek:

I write in response to your February 15 advertisement in the Boise State University Business Placement Bulletin for a Financial Analyst. Based on my academic emphasis in finance, as well as my strong written, oral and interpersonal communication skills, I feel I would be an asset to the team at American Financial Services and wish to be considered for the position.

As a finance major at Boise State, I gained solid insight into current investment strategies and market analysis. In a recent senior seminar course, I served as team leader of a small group of students hired to consult with AgriPower, a local farm chemical company, about how to invest recent earnings. As a team, we developed a short- and long-range financial plan for AgriPower, based on a great deal of in-depth research into the company and national trends. We then presented our report to the owners of AgriPower, who eventually adopted the plan with only minor adjustments. As team leader, I developed the group's research and presentation strategies, as well as honed my own analytical skills. This course served as the capstone to all of the fundamental and specialized courses I took through the finance program at Boise State because it challenged me to *apply* the knowledge I had previously gained through books and classroom experience.

In addition to my coursework, I have gained practical, hands-on experience at Courier Financial Services, where I recently completed a semester-long internship as a Financial Analyst. Directed by senior Financial Analyst, Brian Lindeman, I observed and participated in numerous planning consultations, and in my last month was allowed to direct three consultations with individuals. Through the experience, I gained invaluable insight into how interpersonal communication, investment knowledge, and solid presentations all combine to make an effective Financial Analyst. I believe this experience, along with my academic background, has prepared me to serve American's needs well as a Financial Analyst. I would bring to American's team an enthusiasm for working with a wide variety of people, a love for analysis and strategic planning, and a commitment to professional ethics.

I would welcome the opportunity to speak with you further about my future with American Financial Services, and am happy to meet with you at your convenience. I may be contacted at the above address and e-mail, or at (912) 555-9293. I look forward to hearing from you.

Sincerely,

Mikayla Ross

various organizations at the university, Mikayla has maintained a 3.85 grade point average. An established leader at the university and in her community, Mikayla was awarded the prestigious Turnbull Award for academic achievement and leadership her senior year.

Mikayla has taken a conventional approach to her job search up to this point, as shown in her letter of application, which she varies slightly for each financial service to which she applies (see Figure 18.29). Through this letter, she has had two telephone interviews and five on-campus interviews. Recently, however, she has heard of a new up-and-coming financial group in Twin Falls, Idaho. The location is very attractive because it is within a day's travel from either Mikayla's friends in Boise or her family in Klamath Falls, Oregon. In addition, the firm is one of the few in the area with a strong emphasis in international consulting. But Mikayla is puzzled by the strange tone of the ad for the position in *The Wall Street Journal* (Figure 18.30).

Unsure of the approach to take in writing this company, Mikayla contacts a friend, who tells her that the staff at Maxwell is an unconventional, lively group. As a group, Maxwell employees are very committed to community betterment: they have helped organize city cleanup projects, headed a playground equipment project in which neighborhood volunteers and businesses contributed both muscle and money to build the playground themselves, and supported two summer league baseball and softball teams. Many of the Maxwell employees are young and actively involved in groups such as the Jaycees. In addition, Maxwell appears to be one of the fastest-growing businesses in the area. Clients seem attracted to the vitality and energy the Maxwell staff embodies.

On the basis of her friend's assessment, Mikayla is even more intrigued about the possibility of working for the unusual financial group. Mikayla also decides that applying to Maxwell will require an unconventional letter of application.

Task. Create an unconventional letter of application for Mikayla which is the result of your brainstorming. Feel free to draw on both verbal and visual strategies to create an effective, unconventional appeal to Maxwell. You may generate additional facts about Mikayla's record and create whatever personality traits you feel Mikayla may possess based on what information is provided here.

Figure 18.30 *Journal* Job Announcement

Financial Analyst

Think you want to be a financial analyst? Someone who crunches numbers and stays glued to CNBC all day? Someone whose mouth waters as you pass the latest *Fortune* and *Smart Money* magazines at the bookstore? Someone who talks investments with Uncle Ralph in the kitchen while the rest of the family watches the Super Bowl?

...Then Don't Apply to Maxwell!

Yes, we're interested in finding the best financial analysts out there. But we also want *real* people with *real* interests and *real* investment *in living.*

If you're interested in joining a fast-paced, client-oriented financial group, you're confident, *and* know how to enjoy yourself outside the office without talking about investments, then perhaps you are who we're looking for.

We have two Financial Analyst positions and one data processing position available beginning in June. Apply with a letter, credentials, and salary requirements to:

Maxwell Financial Group
Carl Brown, Manager
Box #IM30
Twin Falls, Idaho 83301

Complication. Before Mikayla sends the letter to Maxwell, she receives a job offer from a Seattle financial group with whom she interviewed the previous month. Mikayla is still *very* intrigued by Maxwell, but doesn't know whether she should mention the job offer from the other financial group in her application letter to encourage prompt response from Maxwell. The Seattle group has given her two weeks to accept or turn down its offer. Determine what revisions (if any) Mikayla should make to her standard letter of application before sending it to Maxwell. Then write Mikayla's letter to the Seattle financial group expressing ongoing interest in the offered position, but asking for an extra week to make her decision.

CHAPTER

19

Job Interviews and Performance Appraisals

OUTLINE

A Company in Search of a Writer: Associated Insurance Selects a Job Candidate

Interviewing

Follow-Up

Performance Reviews

Letters Addressing Employment Concerns

CRITERIA FOR EXPLORING CHAPTER 19

What we cover in this chapter	What you will be able to do after reading this chapter
Company perspective	Explain how a company's criteria influence the job search
Job interviews	Perform successfully in a job interview
Follow-up procedures	Write thank-yous, letters of acceptance, and other documents that support the job search
Performance review	Understand, develop, and write performance appraisal documents. Explain how Total Quality Management (TQM) and other alternatives shape performance reviews
Letters dealing with employment issues	Write letters of recommendation, termination, and resignation

Professionals in the workplace realize that competence is an issue not only when someone is applying for a job, but also when employees are working on the job. Competencies are underlying skill characteristics people develop to enable them to perform well. Competencies help predict and direct good performance. Figure 19.1 discusses the important link between hiring criteria and subsequent job performance.

CONTEXT

In discussing competence in the workplace, David C. McClelland recounts the problem the U.S. State Department had in selecting junior Foreign Service Information Officers (FSIOs). These young diplomats represent America in foreign countries by staffing libraries, organizing cultural events, and giving talks on America to local groups. "Their real job is to get as many people as possible to like the United States and support U.S. policies." Until 1980, almost all FSIOs were white males.

Figure 19.1 Discussion Connecting Hiring Practices and Competency on the Job

Traditionally, the State Department selected FSIOs through the use of a series of Foreign Service Officer exams. These exams were based on "the skills senior officials thought a modern diplomat needed—essentially knowledge of the liberal arts and culture: American history, western civilization, English usage, and specialties such as economics and government."

The exams, however, had two major drawbacks:

- Minorities and others from less privileged cultures were less likely to pass them.
- There was little relation between high test scores and subsequent success on the job.

The situation caused problems for the diplomatic service and raised legal issues as well: "Given the lack of relation of scores on these tests to on-the-job success, their use potentially represented an act of illegal discrimination and handicapped the U.S. Information Service in its work since its officers did not truly represent the role of minorities in American life."

After studying a group of superstar FSIOs, consultants for the State Department discovered three competency characteristics that differentiated superior from average information officers:

- cross-cultural interpersonal sensitivity
- positive expectations of others
- speed in learning political networks

Subsequently, new kinds of tests which measured these competencies were developed both to predict and to evaluate job performance. Such competency-based testing helped produce superior job performance and retention without race, age, gender, or demographic bias.

1. What differences do you see between the skills senior State Department officials originally thought important in FSIOs and the three main competencies the consultants found to be important?
2. How do potential differences between hiring criteria and subsequent job performance affect a company? Employees within a company? The individuals being hired?
3. What do you think can be done to reduce such differences?

The mismatch between hiring criteria and on-the-job-performance experienced by the State Department in hiring FSIOs points to the importance of two occasions for reviewing a person's performance:

- the job search itself: job interviews and follow-up procedures
- ongoing job performance evaluation: performance reviews and various administrative occasions involving employment concerns

A COMPANY IN SEARCH OF A WRITER: ASSOCIATED INSURANCE SELECTS A JOB CANDIDATE

A three-member selection committee for Associated Insurance has been charged with selecting finalists to be interviewed for a professional writing position in the company. After talking with the "laid-back crew" of writers already on staff and with key management personnel, the committee has established hiring criteria and has set to work reviewing applications. Prior to the discussion (which follows), each member has reviewed the same stack of applications and has made tentative rankings. Their conversation, compiled from several selection-committee meetings, is typical of the type of discussion that takes place in selecting candidates for interviews and shows the job search from a company's perspective. The committee members, Granger, Post, and Meeker, have served together before on several such committees.

Granger: Well, I, for one, was glad for the clear-cut choice this batch offered us.

Post: Oh?

Granger: Now don't start on me again, Post. It's quite obvious that Rutledge is the best choice. He's been employed as a writer by our competitor down the road for the past five years. It would be quite a coup to get him. Besides, he's written a lot of successful proposals.

Post: I'll agree that he has a lot of proposal writing experience, but that's not all writers for us do. In any case, I met him at a convention last year. Very Type A. Very competitive.

Granger: If so, I see that as a plus, not a problem.

Post: Foxx did say something about getting someone who would fit in with that laid-back crew they have down there.

Granger: [*with a pained sigh*] True. Maybe they could *use* a little shaking up.

Meeker: Well, I ranked Booth on top. She has experience in writing policy statements and handling oral presentations. After the P.R. nightmare involving Evanston last year, I thought we could use those types of skills.

Post: I liked Booth too, but I was bothered by the fact that her longer written documents dealt solely with training.

Meeker: Her stuff looked good. Nice format. Super graphics.

Post: Straight out of the most recent software package. I ranked Jennings first. His writing was extremely clear. And his commitment to business ethics as expressed in his letter of application really impressed me. Besides, his strength as a lateral thinker [someone who solves problems using multiple and creative strategies]—mentioned by several of his university references—made him look like a good bet. An up-and-comer. Someone to address future needs.

Granger: I thought we were hiring a professional writer, not an academic. I think you people are trying to make this position into something that it isn't. We are hiring a professional writer. We are hiring someone who can convey information in an effective—okay, "user-friendly"—manner. Now if our business handled radioactive waste or something, maybe I could see weighting our criteria differently. Maybe then we would make ethics or even "lateral thinking" a top priority. But we don't, and we didn't. I can't see why we should make this more complicated than it is. Despite the Evanston flap, Meeker. Despite all that. Evanston was an anomaly, as far as I'm concerned.

Meeker: We *did* initially mention our communication needs as shown by Evanston as a concern in setting our criteria. Perhaps we should review our criteria before we come up with a final ranking?

Granger: Yeah. We do have to get someone in here that will fit. [*clearing his throat*] Rutledge fits in extremely well down the road. . . .

Post: We aren't down the road, Granger. Up a creek, maybe.

INTERVIEWING

A job hunter writes a resume and letter of application to get a job interview. Job interviews are more than just conversations with prospective employers. Interviews are valuable opportunities for both parties to see if the applicant fits comfortably into the company environment. As the Associated Insurance committee discussion suggests, however, the drive to find a fit between the applicant and the situation starts even before the interview begins. In fact, as Chapter 18 has shown, the primary task job candidates face is to find a fit between the job position and their own credentials as they write letters of application. From the employer's point of view, finding that match involves more than an applicant's credentials. It involves the company's past experiences, its present personnel, and its view of its future.

When dressing for a job interview, use a traditional look when you know your future colleagues will also be dressed traditionally or when in doubt.

Unfortunately for both companies and employees, there is not much correlation between interviewing well and actually doing the job well. For this reason, experts now advise that tests become a larger part of the interview situation. Experts now recommend computerized multiple-choice questions based on the job description and corporate style. The computerized test allows human resource personnel to weight answers to favor those factors most predictive of good job performance. Applicants tend to be more honest with a computer than with human interviewers when asked about such things as their goals and preferences.[1]

Experts also recommend that employers identify the most important functions of a job and set up tests to simulate those situations. For example, if receiving visitors is an important part of the job, the company or agency should hire an actor to play the role of a hotel guest while the applicant plays the role of the receptionist. Similarly, if estimating project costs is part of the job, the corporation should set up a case situation that asks the applicant to do an estimate based on a bid or proposal, client expectations, and on-site observation. In short, experts now say that applicants should audition for a job, much in the same way that musicians audition for an orchestra seat or athletes try out for a position on a team.[2]

Until such testing becomes commonplace, full-day interviews are allowing employers to get a picture of how a prospective employee fits into the company. Questions posed by employer and applicant alike dominate such interviews.

Questions Asked by Interviewers

Interviewers ask questions to serve several distinct functions:

- revealing and interpreting achievements
- assessing your motives
- addressing scenarios
- revealing criteria
- projecting the future
- identifying your place in corporate culture
- revealing personal preferences

These separate functions work together to help interviewers assess the match between the applicant and the position. Figure 19.2 on the next page provides a sense of the types of

SKILLS & STRATEGIES

DRESS FOR SUCCESS

Poor personal appearance is a surprisingly common mistake in interviewing. The key is to dress appropriately without being overdressed. Conventional wisdom says clothes should have a traditional look:

- Be understated, not flashy.
- Lean toward neutral colors like dark blue, taupe, and gray (with blue the "power" color).
- Feature jackets, which give the appearance of authority.
- Be complemented by socks or stockings matched to the suit and shoes (shined).
- Accessorize conservatively with simple ties, watches, and jewelry.

For the traditional look, you should also carry a hard-side attaché, rather than a soft-side bag.

However, the question of how to present yourself professionally is not always answered today by a suit and tie. A new category of clothing, dubbed "corporate casual," is in. Designed to bridge the gap between pinstripes and jeans, the corporate casual look is hard to pull off because it can't be purchased off the rack. It requires men to accessorize and to coordinate separate pieces—to mix tweeds with denim or T-shirts with blazers, and to pair such outfits with the new "fun" ties featuring bold graphics or with distinctive jewelry. For women, it includes a choice of three different skirt lengths, or pants or leggings, to go with blazers, softly tailored jackets, or a variety of other tops.

Although dress codes vary across corporations, more and more corporate offices are dressing down Monday through Friday. The more informal attire, however, is mostly an American phenomenon. And the time-honored suit still dominates dress at important corporate meetings and national business conventions.

Interviewees are wise to wear traditional business clothing when interviewing with conservative firms, but to consider a more casual look when interviewing with companies where the dress code is less formal. Informational interviews or networking contacts can clue the interviewee into the appropriate attire for a particular job interview setting.

Figure 19.2 Types of Questions with Samples Asked by Interviewers

Revealing and interpreting achievements	• What was your rank in your college graduating class? • Can you show me some samples of your writing? • Could you describe several problems you've had in your occupational life and how you solved them? • Which of your accomplishments at your present position or former positions are you proudest of? • What would a competitor say about you in terms of your strengths and weaknesses?
Dealing with motives	• Why do you want to leave your present position? • Why did you choose your major? Your university? • What factors are most important to you personally in job satisfaction? • How do you motivate yourself? How do you deal with stress, tension, boredom?
Addressing scenarios	• If you are selected for this position, how would you deal with individuals within the company who may have preferred another candidate? • From what you have been able to learn of the company and the position, what short- and long-term problems do you think you will face, and how would you deal with them? • Assume that we expected significant growth in your area of responsibility and ask you to give us a plan for growth. How would you do that?
Revealing criteria	• Why should we hire you for this position? • What criteria would you use in measuring your own performance over the next year and in following years? • How do you set priorities for your own time? What are these priorities? • What skills or attributes do you think the following should have: an outstanding subordinate, an outstanding peer, an outstanding supervisor of someone at your level?
Projecting the future	• What are your goals or schedule for accomplishment at your present position for the next year? For the next two or three years? • What would your personal goals in this job be for the next year? For the next five or ten years? For the rest of your working career? • From what you know about this company and the position available, what characteristics and accomplishments should we expect in the first six months from the individual we hire? The first five years? • What do you think will be the toughest aspects of the job if you were to accept the position? What will be the most enjoyable aspects? The least enjoyable?
Placing yourself in corporate culture	• Draw me a table of organization where you last worked and tell me where you fit. (Do similarly for our company.) • Describe for me your ideal position. What would the working conditions be like? What kinds of co-workers would you choose? • Under what circumstances would you put your job on the line for something you believed in?
Revealing personal preferences	• Tell me about yourself. • Would you prefer working with people or with numbers? • What are your future educational plans? • What are your salary requirements? • Name me three people in public life you admire most.

questions asked in each of these categories. Not all the questions included in Figure 19.2 are appropriate for entry-level positions. In addition, some of the questions may seem simple, but could require a complex answer. For example, how you describe the problems you've had in your occupational life (third question in right-hand column) could entail a sophisticated analysis of the occasion, the people involved, and the communication within the situation.

Questions Asked by Applicants

As an applicant for a position, you should be prepared to ask as well as answer questions. Like questions asked by prospective employers, the questions you ask as an applicant can represent a range of issues, from evaluation to ethics, from job security to job incentives, from present promotion policies to future plans. Figure 19.3 contains types and examples of the questions that you, as an applicant, might ask during a job interview.

Even though there are a large number of possible questions you as an applicant could ask during an interview, you should probably restrict yourself to asking only a select few. You should definitely avoid asking questions that are readily answered from basic research about the position and company—duties usually associated with the job title, basic company history, and major products and services. When possible, you should ask at least one question that demonstrates that you have indeed researched your potential employer. For example, if you know that the company is part of a new consortium designed to promote community projects, you might ask about the success of a particular program or of the partnership in general.

Traditional job interviews have three basic parts:

- the opening or warm-up
- the question-answer exchange
- the close

Figure 19.3 Questions for Applicants to Ask

About supervisors	• How do you, the supervisor, like to operate in terms of assignments, delegation of responsibility and authority? What do you like in a subordinate? What characteristics don't you like? • How frequently, and in what manner, will I and my supervisor meet on a regular basis, and how will we deal with particular problems? • What contact will I have with my supervisor's boss and others on a higher level? What are the hot issues right now? • What are the company's management style and the philosophy of the top executives?
About incentives and advancement	• How are employees rewarded for excellent performance? • What are the opportunities for advancement and increased responsibility within the company? How easily can employees shift into other areas within the company? • What opportunities are there for growth in my prospective area of responsibility? On what kind of timetable? Is there a commitment to promote from within?
About evaluation	• What are the procedures and criteria for performance evaluations? • What do you and/or my prospective supervisor hope I would accomplish in six months, twelve months, long-term? How are those accomplishments negotiated?
About interaction	• With whom will I interact most frequently, and what are their responsibilities and the nature of our interaction? What in general are their strengths and weaknesses? • What are the limits of my authority and responsibility? What do I have to get permission for? Inform others about after the fact? • Describe the people who thrive in your company. What are their key competencies? Personality traits? • How would you describe the culture of this company? How would you describe company morale? The values and ethics of this corporation?
About expectations	• What experience, training, attributes, operating style, accomplishments, and personality factors should the "ideal" candidate for this job have? • What social requirements does the job entail? • What professional, industrial, community, or public policy involvement do you feel it is necessary for me to have, and in what depth?
About the future	• How secure is this position? • What commitment does the company have to the career development and training of its employees? • What are the major issues your company will face in the next three to five years?

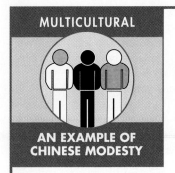

MULTICULTURAL

AN EXAMPLE OF CHINESE MODESTY

Employers in different countries have different evaluation criteria in selecting employees. If you seek jobs overseas, you need to be aware that just "being yourself" according to your own cultural norms may result in your failure to get the job.

For example, Chinese people strive to leave the impression of being polite, humble, modest, and courteous in their first encounter with other people. This behavior originates from the teaching of philosophical Taoism, which sees selflessness and humility as the basis for human conduct. Therefore, if a first-rate Chinese carpenter went to an American furniture company to find a job, the interview dialogue would probably go like this:

Employer: Have you done carpentry work before?

Carpenter: I don't dare say that I have. I have just been in a very modest way involved in the carpenter trade.

Employer: What are you skilled in then?

Carpenter: I won't say "skilled." I have only a little experience in making tables [although he may have been making all kinds of tables for the past 25 years].

Employer: Can you make something now and show us how good you are?

Carpenter: How dare I be so indiscreet as to demonstrate my crude skills in front of a master of the trade like you?

By this time, the American employer might just be fed up and say "I am sorry but we don't take novices" and show him to the door. But, if the employer is more subtle and persistent, the carpenter would probably respond: "If you really insist, I'll try to make a table. Please don't laugh at my crude work." With that he might begin to work on a table, saying a few more times, "Please don't laugh at my crude work . . ." and give the final touches to a perhaps beautiful piece of artwork in the shape of a table.

Interview Basics and Conventions

During the interview, an applicant should note and record the names of the interviewers (properly spelled) and their job titles before leaving the interview site. For details, you can talk with company secretaries or those in charge of setting up the interviews at a placement office or job fair. You should also ask for the interviewers' business cards.

The *opening* is very brief and a very critical portion of the job interview. It usually consists of making introductions, shaking hands, and taking a seat. Surprisingly, the way you handle yourself during these brief moments may determine the outcome of the entire interview. The opening of your interview demands that you look professional, act confident, maintain eye contact, and listen carefully, especially for the interviewer's name and for any cues the interviewer offers.

The *question-answer exchange* is important not only for the information being shared, but also for the personal characteristics you demonstrate during the exchange. You can make a positive impression by:

- listening carefully and picking up on cues given by the interviewers
- offering specific detail to support your answers and being prepared with specific questions to ask your interviewer
- being positive about former teachers, employers, colleagues, your prospective employer, and yourself
- expressing yourself clearly, correctly, and concisely
- being enthusiastic and honestly interested in the position

You should avoid discussions about salary at this stage. If you are asked about salary requirements, you are often wise to state simply that you would expect a salary appropriate to the position. A whole range of factors, including working conditions, collegiality, benefits, corporate policies and environment, and the nature of the surrounding community, will probably influence your happiness with the position more than will salary, so it makes sense to focus on these aspects during your interview.

The *close* is your opportunity to ask any remaining questions (do not extend the interview unnecessarily, however) and to clarify what will happen next. If you are offered the position at this point, you may now want to ask about the salary and benefits involved. It's a good idea to be positive about the offer but to ask for a short period of time to think it over, rather than accept immediately.

Figure 19.4 reviews some guidelines basic to interviewing. You should realize that a lot of this advice is culturally specific. If you were to interview for a position in an international setting, you would be wise to research alternative expectations.

Figure 19.4 Basic Guidelines for Interviewing

Job Interviews: Basic Guidelines

1. Be professional.
   a. Interview only with those companies with which you are sincerely interested in being employed.
   b. Research the company with which you are interviewing and be prepared to "insert" your knowledge of the company into the discussion where appropriate.
   c. Be prepared to discuss specifically your long-term career goals.
   d. Be prepared to ask at least three specific questions of the interviewer at the end of the interview (excluding questions about salary).
   e. Be prompt (call in advance to cancel or reschedule an interview).
2. Assure a good first impression.
   a. Submit a "clean" application form, job letter, and/or resume.
   b. Take care with your personal appearance (see page 565).
   c. Listen for the interviewer's name, and use it, if appropriate, during the interview.
   d. Use a firm handshake and look the interviewer directly in the eye.
3. Maintain that good first impression.
   a. Be positive about your former employers, school, etc.
   b. Be assertive (rather than aggressive or indecisive).
   c. Show tact, courtesy, and tolerance.
   d. Discuss your area of specialization with specific, articulate detail.
   e. Don't relax too much (a little nervousness indicates your interest).
   f. Use body language to work for you (lean forward, face the interviewer squarely, maintain eye contact, use hand motions, avoid crossing arms or legs).
4. Be smart.
   a. Learn how to make negative information positive.
   b. Never make excuses.
   c. Be open to criticism.
   d. Always take the "high road" (avoid cynicism, sarcasm, conceit).
   e. Do not accept a position at the interview; be positive about an offer but ask for a few days (perhaps up to a week) to think it over.
5. Follow-up.
   a. Always write a thank-you note for the interview.
   b. Fulfill any promises made at the interview (providing additional information, etc.) in good speed.
   c. If you decide not to take the job, write a courteous letter informing the company of the "bad news."
   d. If you take the position, write a letter of acceptance if appropriate to your field.

Difficult Interview Situations

Although the common assumption is that interviewers assess, rather than provoke, applicant behavior during interviews, interviewer behavior does influence applicant behavior. For example, if the interviewer smiles and makes eye contact, the applicant will reciprocate by smiling and making eye contact, and the applicant will probably feel more at ease.

Applicants with high self-esteem are not measurably affected by lack of such warm behavior, while applicants with low self-esteem are devastated by cold behavior on the part of the interviewer and, as a result, perform poorly during the interview.[3] Unfortunately, interviewers sometimes have been known to take advantage of this phenomenon and have purposely made the interviewing situation more stressful than it need be to see how applicants respond. In such cases, interviewers might fire questions at a fast pace or react negatively to an applicant's answers. Such practice is not common because, in the end, it tends to reflect negatively on the company.

This does not mean that you will not face difficult interview questions. These questions may arise out of your employment history:

- Why do you want to change jobs?
- Why have you changed jobs so frequently?
- Why did you leave this job?
- Why is there a gap in your work history?
- Why were you let go/fired?

Acceptable reasons for *changing jobs* vary. Changing jobs might be part of your career plan. You might say, "I see this job as an opportunity to move into transportation and logistics, which is a step towards my long-range goal of being an Operations Manager." You might also want additional responsibility. You might say, "I've learned a lot about sales at XYZ Company, and now I want to apply this experience in a larger retail outlet." (Remember, it is important to phrase your answer positively and not to criticize your present employer.) Wishing to relocate is another reason for changing positions. You might have family in the area or have other reasons for wanting to change your location.[4]

Viable reasons for *frequently changing jobs* are often similar to those for changing positions. To make the changes work for you, you need to convince the interviewer that each change brought professional growth and was not due to disloyalty, lack of performance, or inability to get along with colleagues. Similarly, reasons for *leaving a position* are best explained as a matter of professional growth. If you feel that your current employer did not meet your expectations, you need to find some justification for the company's actions. For example, new management might redefine corporate goals in such a way that your position does not involve as much responsibility or innovation as you expected to have at this stage in your career.

As you address *gaps* in your work history, you need to show that your time was well spent. If you were looking for work throughout the period, you might briefly but specifically report on your diligence in trying to secure another position. Perhaps you researched 30 companies in depth before deciding on appropriate firms to send unsolicited resumes. If, on the other hand, you went back to school or participated in a retraining program, you might detail several of the added skills you have gained in the interim. If you have had overriding family responsibilities, you might discuss how these have strengthened some of your personal qualities and will make you a better employee.

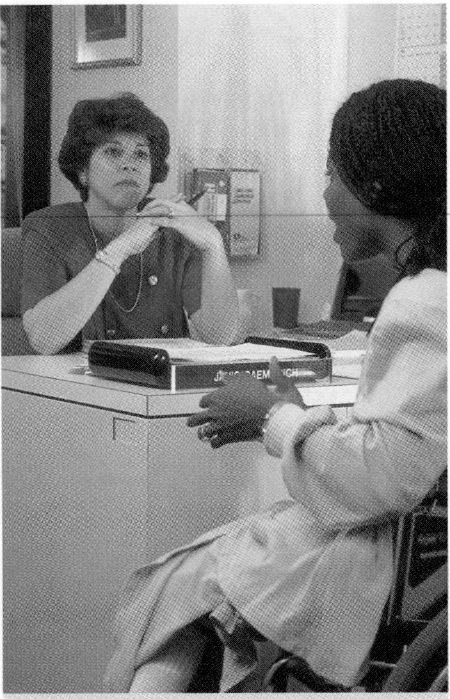
Certain interview questions are prohibited by Title VII of the 1964 Civil Rights Act and by the Americans with Disabilities Act.

In today's economy, more and more applicants are having to deal with being let go or *being fired*. A simple statement that your former employer had to lay off a certain number of workers or that your company was downsizing or consolidating may address the issue of your unemployment. If, in fact, you were fired for your actions, or lack of action, you should admit your mistake and state what you learned from your experience. In any case, it is important not to dwell on the firing but to stress what you can do for the prospective employer.

Other difficulties in interviews may arise out of the situation. For example, your interviewer may speak too much or not enough, or you may be disqualified for the position on the spot. You may run out of time because the interviewer is behind schedule. If you need to draw out the interviewer, you might ask how he or she sees your qualifications in terms of the position. You might also use one of the questions you have prepared in advance (see Figure 19.3) either to elicit a response from the interviewer or to interject yourself into the conversation. If it becomes obvious that the position is not for you, you might define what you can do and ask if there is a position open that better suits your credentials. Finally, if time becomes a problem because of the interviewer's schedule, you need to attempt to reschedule the interview. Whatever the difficulty, you need to be positive throughout the interview process and assertive about getting what you need or want from the opportunity.

ETHICS

WHAT CAN I ASK? THE ETHICS OF DISCLOSURE IN AN EMPLOYMENT INTERVIEW

The Americans with Disabilities Act (ADA) specifically prohibits certain types of questions in the context of a pre-employment inquiry. Once the question is asked, however, a conflict of interest exists for the prospective employee: to assert her legal rights not to answer and potentially create bad feelings or to sacrifice her legal rights and answer, even though the question is illegal.

When you are applying for a position, you are wise to protect yourself, your company, and the rights of prospective employers by knowing pertinent regulations and understanding how they apply to you. A Technical Assistance Manual on the Employment Provisions (Title I) of the Americans with Disabilities Act (EEOC-M-1A, January 1992) summarizes the legal requirements, defines key terms, and provides specific guidelines and examples to help prospective employers and employees avoid violation of the letter and spirit of the ADA. You can call 1-800-669-EEOC (voice) or 1-800-800-3302 (TDD) for more information.

Unfortunately, a difficult interview can arise because the interviewer knowingly or unknowingly asks questions that are prohibited by Title VII of the 1964 Civil Rights Act. Title VII prohibits discrimination in employment on the basis of race, color, religion, sex, or national origin. It is a violation of Title VII to ask information about

- birth (maiden) name or marital status
- sex, height, and weight
- age or date of birth
- religious affiliation
- race or color—even under the guise of requesting "affirmative action" information
- date of citizenship (indicating whether the applicant is naturalized or native-born) or national origin
- specific dates of education (indicating age)
- the branch of military service or type of discharge
- arrest records
- your relationship to a person to be contacted in case of emergency (indicating marital status or lineage)
- memberships in organizations (revealing race, religion, physical handicap, marital status, or ancestry)
- physical handicap
- home ownership

When asked questions prohibited by Title VII, you have every right to decline to answer, but may feel awkward in doing so. Whatever you decide to do, it would be a good idea to take a positive approach and to assume that the violation was unintentional.

FOLLOW-UP

You may follow up your job interview in a number of ways:

- thank-you letter (goodwill message)
- request for a decision or for an extension (persuasive message)
- letter of acceptance (good news message)
- letter declining the position or, if appropriate, a letter of resignation from your current position (bad news message)

It is essential that you immediately thank your interviewer in writing for your job interview. Having asked for a business card, you will be able to address the interviewer by name and title. In your *thank-you* (see Figure 19.5), your first paragraph characteristically reminds the interviewer of the context, your body paragraph assures the reader of your flexibility or commitment to the position and reminds the reader of any special qualifications you may have, and your close expresses confidence and sometimes requests a decision, or asks for further contact.

Sometimes, you may need to ask your prospective employer about a decision on hiring sooner than expected. Or you may need to request an extension on the time you have to reply to an offer. As you would with any other direct request, you would have a context opening that provided necessary background and also provided the main idea, a body that

Figure 19.5 Thank-You for an Interview

The writer opens with the specific context, thanks the reader for her time and consideration, then refers to specific discussion points and shows an eagerness to grow.

The writer closes with confidence. A decision date, if known, would have been included in the close.

I enjoyed speaking with you yesterday about becoming an Account Executive with Thurston and Bates. I left the interview more enthusiastic than ever about the possibility of joining your staff. Thank you for your time and your detailed responses to my questions.

I especially enjoyed our discussion about how Dale Carnegie courses can help in knowing how to gain and maintain a client's interest and commitment to a project. It is an application that I am eager to try.

I feel strongly that I will be able to contribute to the continued success of Thurston and Bates. I look forward to hearing from you regarding your decision.

Figure 19.6 Request for an Extension

The writer shows continued interest in the position while setting the context and making the request. He then offers reasons for the request and again reaffirms interest. He creates goodwill by not assuming the reader will grant the request, by facilitating further contact, by giving a response date, and by thanking the reader.

> I was very pleased to receive your offer of a teaching position on April 1. The offer is attractive because of its balanced combination of teaching and coaching duties. Because I would like more time to consider the offer, I am requesting a two-week extension on the date that I am to return the signed contract.
>
> A two-week extension is necessary because I have just received another offer from a school district in Michigan. Your offer is, frankly, more attractive, but I feel it important to be able to explore the details of both offers in an open discussion with my family.
>
> If you still need my decision by May 1, please let me know right away. I can be reached during business hours at 303-555-2121 or in the evening at 303-555-4536. Otherwise, I will be sure to contact you by May 15. Thank you very much for your consideration.

Figure 19.7 Letter of Acceptance

Opening: *states the good news of the acceptance and compliments the company.*

Body: *deals with miscellaneous details concerning housing and requests additional information concerning transportation.*

Close: *expresses thanks and confidence.*

> I am delighted to accept the position of Assistant Buyer at Goldware's Limited Editions. I was most impressed with your goal of being the innovative leader in fashion for career women.
>
> As we discussed during my on-site interview, I will be arriving in town August 20. I appreciate your kind offer of staying in a motel at the company's expense until I find housing. I have, however, arranged to stay with a friend until I am able to find an apartment. I already have several leads.
>
> I would appreciate your sending me information regarding public transportation. I am especially interested in knowing the location of Interurban stops.
>
> I am excited to begin with Goldware Limited on September 1 and to be sharing in your efforts to bring innovation to the wardrobes of professional women.

explained the reason for the request, and an action close expressing continued interest in the position (Figure 19.6). Such requests need to convey sincere interest in the job position you have been offered through both direct statements and goodwill gestures, such as a willingness to compromise concerning the terms of your request.

Although it may seem redundant after orally accepting an offer and/or signing a written contract, you may want to write a *formal letter of acceptance*. Acceptance letters follow a good news arrangement, with the opening stating your acceptance of the position, the body addressing any miscellaneous details such as forms to be returned or requests for additional information about the community, and the close expressing thanks and confidence about the future (Figure 19.7).

Letters declining a position are essential. These follow a bad news format with a thank-you buffer, reasons for declining the position, and a public relations close. Figure 19.8 is an elegant example of such a letter. The names in the letter have been changed to protect the confidentiality of the persons and organizations involved.

Letters declining a position, just like letters of acceptance, look to the future. You might well have contact with the company whose position you have declined as part of your current job, or you might want to apply to that company again in the future.

PERFORMANCE REVIEWS

Accepting a job position, of course, marks the end of a job search. It also marks the beginning of your employment with a new organization or in a new position and the start of a new round of evaluation based on your job performance. As you will discover, performance evaluations are written annually, semiannually, or quarterly, depending on the company. Almost every employee, regardless of rank or position, is subject to the personnel review process.

A Traditional Performance Review Situation

Jane Baxter's experience should help you picture a typical, traditional performance review process. After six months on the job as a program analyst, Jane arrived at her desk Monday morning to begin debugging the three programs her manager, Lesley, had given her on

Figure 19.8 Letter Declining a Position

The writer begins with a thank-you buffer. Not following common practice in bad news messages, he then immediately reveals his negative decision.

The writer compliments the company and people involved.

He provides reasons for the decision to accept a similar position elsewhere.

The writer provides a cordial close and a commitment to positive relations in the future.

I appreciate very much your attractive offer of a managerial position at Bessey-Price, complete with generous benefits, beginning in August of 19--. I regret to say that I must decline the offer, since I will be accepting a similar position with White, Inc.

I would like to take this opportunity to say that I was extremely impressed by your company. I am confident that I would have enjoyed working with the talented staff at Bessey-Price, and I have recommended your organization highly to others in the insurance industry. I greatly appreciate the time given to me by Mr. Bridges and yourself, your knowledge in answering my questions, and your courtesy in granting me an extension in making what for me was a difficult decision.

My decision involved a complex of factors. My previous experience with the personnel at White, Inc., my spouse's job opportunities for a professional position within the same community, and the presence of family in the area all played a role in my thinking and may well have contributed as much or more to my decision as other considerations such as salary and benefits.

Again, I thank you for your attractive offer and your personal kindness. I will continue to speak highly of Bessey-Price and of those who made my interviews both informative and enjoyable.

Friday. Just as Jane spreads the first program out on her desk and begins tracing the loops, the division secretary stops by and says, "Lesley likes to keep up with performance appraisals, so you'll need to read this evaluation, sign it, and return it to her by 4:00."

Amazed, Jane looks at the evaluation. It consists of a sheet with evaluation criteria noted at the left and numbers filled in at the right. The numbers of this graphic rating scale are complemented by brief essay explanations of Jane's performance on each of her assignments. Under "general comments," Lesley has written, "Jane transferred to Memphis at a very difficult time and has performed remarkably well. I had to depend on Jane, as the Memphis office was for three months void of any programming expertise. Jane showed no reluctance at all to accept the responsibility. Jane is an aggressive individual and at times alienates her coworkers and peers because of her assertiveness. I would rate Jane's overall performance as very good: 2."

Although Jane is at first a bit puzzled by what the numbers mean, she finds the numbers defined on the second page of the evaluation form and sees that her overall performance has been rated in the top 15 percent, so she signs the form and hands it to Lesley at the end of the day. Since Jane is in an organization that uses a very traditional model of performance review, no further meetings need occur, unless Jane has obvious difficulties with her performance. Lesley will continue to observe Jane occasionally, make assessments at the end of each review period, and file a report in Jane's employment file.

Approaches to Performance Review

Although there are various methods for conducting performance appraisals and writing performance reports, you will probably encounter at least one of three basic approaches—described in Figure 19.9 on page 574—after you take a professional position. In order to be specific, every method of review must track and record events in the employee's performance during a review period. Such recording enables an appraisal that is both detailed and illustrative. *Software packages* now provide a convenient means for keeping this ongoing record. Employee Appraiser for Windows, for example, presents the evaluator with a menu of evaluation categories and provides a notebook for logging events in an employee's performance throughout the appraisal period. Other computer performance models are also available.[5]

Accountabilities and Measures

Principles of performance review are not only important to business and industry, but can also be applied to review situations in the classroom as well. Students operating in teams, for example, often find themselves in the position of formally or informally evaluating their fellow team members. Having mutually understood accountabilities (tasks) and measures (evaluation criteria) helps team members know what is expected of them and helps members to make an accurate assessment of each person's contributions.

Figure 19.9 Common Methods of Employee Review

APPROACH	CHARACTERISTICS	VALUE
Easy appraisal	The rater, generally the immediate supervisor, writes a paragraph or more covering an employee's strengths, weaknesses, and potential; similar to written assessments found in letters of recommendation (Figure 19.18).	Advantage: The essay focuses on performance traits that were of particular note during a specific review period. Disadvantage: It is difficult to use for comparison purposes because certain traits may not carry over from one review period to the next.
Graphic rating scale	The rater uses a form to measure an employee on the quality or quantity of his or her performance (outstanding, above average, average, or unsatisfactory; Figure 19.17).	Advantage: The scale evaluates an employee on a set number of skills which then can be compared from period to period. Disadvantage: It is often inappropriately applied to compare workers with different job titles and duties.
Management by Objectives (MBO)	Employee and manager begin and end cycle by meeting to establish and assess job-related goals; together they determine tasks the employee will accomplish during a specific evaluation period (the accountabilities) and the criteria by which these tasks will be measured (the measures).	Advantage: The focus is on two categories of the employee's performance—strengths and weaknesses—and manager and employee agree on terms of review at the outset. Disadvantage: Sometimes there are honest and deep disagreements between the employee's evaluation of his or her performance and the manager's that are tough to negotiate.

Setting up accountabilities and measures is not as easy as it may sound. Tasks need to be defined in concrete terms to avoid misunderstanding and misinterpretation. For example, "updating current accounts" is a specific task that might be defined concretely in terms of frequency and accuracy: "Terry will update all her current sales accounts biweekly with 95 percent accuracy." Some tasks, however, such as promoting good morale among fellow employees, are difficult to describe in concrete terms.

Figure 19.10 shows examples of general task descriptions revised for specificity; the first task is by nature more concrete than the second and third. Words in the initial descriptions like "successfully complete," "participate fully," and "ready cooperation" are open to considerable interpretation. For example, would the employee who wrote three computer programs that ran flawlessly but took two years to design "successfully complete" the task? Would simply talking a lot at meetings count? The revised task descriptions clarify what is expected.

Task descriptions can be used as a basis for accountabilities and measures; the measures tell how the accountability will be assessed. In Figure 19.11, the employee's ability to write four software design programs will be assessed using two criteria: whether the specific deadline of September 1 is met and whether the programs have no more than two errors. With well-defined and measurable or quantifiable accountabilities and measures, evaluation can become a matter of matching established expectations with the actual performance (Figure 19.12).

Figure 19.10 Task Descriptions Revised for Effectiveness

INITIAL TASK DESCRIPTION (BASIS FOR ACCOUNTABILITY)	REVISED TASK DESCRIPTION (BASIS FOR ACCOUNTABILITY)
Successfully complete assigned computer programs	Write four software design programs by September 1 that use multimedia and that contain no more than two programming errors
Participate fully in team meetings	Attend all meetings; arrive on time with tasks stipulated in the day's agenda completed and photocopied for team discussion; contribute ideas and text to draft versions of project
Project purpose clearly and in a manner that elicits ready cooperation	Explain projects so that subordinates are able to work without further guidance 90% of the time

Figure 19.11 Accountabilities and Measures for a Team Project

ACCOUNTABILITIES	MEASURES (CRITERIA FOR ASSESSING ACCOUNTABILITIES)
Write four software design programs using multimedia	Four interactive programs using multimedia **completed by September 1 with no more than two programming errors**

Figure 19.12 The Relationship between Accountabilities, Measures, and Evaluation

ACCOUNTABILITIES	MEASURES	EVALUATION
Write four software design programs using multimedia	Four interactive programs completed by September 1 with no more than two programming errors	Completed three of the four interactive programs by September 1. The fourth program is complete except for acquisition of certain designated video footage. All programs run successfully.

This is not to say that evaluation is ever a cut-and-dried matter. Some accountabilities are extremely difficult to measure or even to describe. For example, a programmer may complete four software programs using multimedia by September 1, but the programs themselves may lack "elegance" (ability to work at maximum speed with minimum complexity). The employee may not be held accountable for "elegance," but her reputation as a good programmer may in the end rest on this abstract quality. Similarly, managerial tasks such as "showing leadership" may be difficult to define at the outset. Specific examples from the manager's behavior may ultimately be used to describe how leadership was shown. In such cases, the evaluator "interprets" the accountability according to the situation and argues for that interpretation; for example, "Sandy showed leadership by designing an introductory pamphlet welcoming our employees transferred from our closed site in Akron." Such matters are often negotiated between reviewer and reviewee.

Wording of evaluations needs careful attention. It should be clear, for example, that strengths are strengths when an overall summary of the performance is made. Instead of saying, "Kay is not our most experienced teller," a summary statement should state, "Kay has regularly met her objectives for the three years she has been employed with us." Similarly, instead of saying, "Jill appears to have no glaring faults or deficiencies as a manager," a summary statement might state, "Jill is an effective manager who has earned the respect of employees and clients alike."

Addressing weaknesses needs similar care. Instead of saying, "Jim is an unproductive programmer," an evaluation might read, "Jim needs to complete 3 engineering design programs with no more than 5 errors. Two programs completed contained 10% of errors over the minimum. One program met the department's quality requirement." With such wording, the evaluator tells what Jim should do, rather than what he did not do. The evaluator also explains specifically how Jim did not meet certain expectations, but softens the assessment by noting in what respect Jim did meet the criteria. This positive approach to negative information is in line with conventions for handling such information in business documents (see Chapter 9). A positive approach also keeps employees motivated and encourages performance review to be a constructive process.

Performance Appraisal Documents

Upon taking a professional position, you may encounter any of a variety of performance appraisal techniques, depending on your employer's preferences. Figure 19.13 (page 576), for example, is a planning document used at some organizations for personnel development and performance review. The "goals" cited in this example are the equivalent of accountabilities, and the "actions" are the equivalent of measures. The job rating and the development rating mentioned in the example are classifications specific to the organization and assess actual performance and improvement respectively.

Figure 19.13 Developmental Plan as Basis for Performance Appraisal

Illustrative Example: "Mary"

Development Goal

Competency Area: Concern for Impact

Job Rating:	Development Rating:	Overall Time Goal: 6/92

SPECIFIC OBJECTIVE

Increase my daily involvement and influence behavior with others outside the unit, especially people who are current or potential users of the unit's services.

Illustrations: I would initiate several meetings a week with department heads and supervisors for the purpose of improving our service and working relationship. I would get involved in committee and task force groups and work to positively influence policy and operating management recommendations.

POTENTIAL OBSTACLES

1. Preference for working on tangible, practical tasks. These are present at all times within the unit and are easy to focus on.
2. Lack of confidence and skill in persuading and influencing others who aren't subordinates.
3. Reluctance to delegate responsibility to subordinates with only periodic review of progress and results.

Development Actions

PRACTICAL ACTION STEPS	**Time Target**
Your Own:	
1. Using a weekly planning calendar, schedule at least five meetings each week with other managers and supervisors. Will write a brief agenda for each meeting noting my goals and areas of mutual business interest.	7/15/91
2. To gain some good ideas about influencing others, will read *The Power Handbook: A Strategic Guide to Organizational and Personal Effectiveness.* Will summarize main points that are especially relevant to my style and development needs.	10/31/91
3. Will attend one internal or external training seminar aimed at skill building in persuasion and personal influence. Will get assistance from my development coach to identify the right resource.	11/1/91
4. Will join one special task force that will provide a regular opportunity to present ideas and recommendations to a group. Will plan specific influence actions and seek feedback from group.	1/1/92
Others:	
Boss: Discuss observations about strengths and weaknesses in the area of influencing others. Review action plan, provide suggestions, and participate in follow-up discussions reviewing progress.	7/10/91 Quarterly
Development Coach: Assist in identifying skill-building seminar and making arrangements. Review development action plan and make suggestions. Participate in behavior practice sessions to increase comfort and skill development.	7/7/91 8/23/91 10/9/91 2/7/92

This type of developmental plan has several advantages:

- It defines objectives in terms of a single, specific competency area; other areas can be defined on separate pages.
- It dramatizes the actions to be taken by the employee in terms of concrete detail and sample illustrations.
- It places specifically defined tasks within a time frame.
- It works to make a perceived weakness a strength.
- It considers potential obstacles.
- It looks to the future.
- It establishes a support network to assist the employee in fulfilling specifically defined tasks.

While Figure 19.13 would aid you at the beginning of a performance review cycle, Figure 19.14 would be important at the end of a review period. Figure 19.14 excerpts portions of an eight-page biennial (every two years) performance review for Robert Carosso, who works for Bull HN Information Systems Inc. Since performance appraisals characteristically contain confidential and propriety information, we are fortunate to have this sample.

CONTEXT

The Bull performance appraisal document, as a whole, features seven sections, with a cover sheet and an end space for signatures. Most detailed is Section A, *Performance against Goals.* This section works like the accountabilities, measures and evaluation set-up discussed in the text. The rest of the document includes Section B, *Teamwork,* which comments on the employee's ability to work as a team player with employer, colleagues, and clients; Section C, *Skills Assessment,* which evaluates skills as well as lists training received during the review period; Section D, *Comment on Competencies,* which invites colleague and customer input; Section E, *Development Agreement,* which covers additional skills the employee would like to develop; Section F, *Overall Assessment,* which contains a summary statement of evaluation; and Section G, *Employee Comment.* Figure 19.14 shows an excerpt from Section A analyzing how Bob met his objectives of team leadership and third-party project management.

Figure 19.14 Excerpts from a Performance Appraisal Document

Criteria/Goal: Team Leadership	**Overall Reviewer's Assessment**
. . . Bob has also been asked, on occasion, to form and lead task teams to solve a particular problem. One such team investigated and solved a problem with the Exchange export function, which was corrupting data in the repository. Another emergency team developed a capability to do repository import/export without user intervention for a potential customer, CNAM. CNAM bought our product.	. . . Bob's work leading the Exchange export team was outstanding. This was a difficult problem to solve given the criticality and the pressure of time.
Third-Party Product Management	
Bob contributed to the initial meetings with Software One, both in the United States and in the U.K. Bob worked with Jim Santos to develop a proposal for a technological partnership with them. Bob went with Jim to the U.K. to meet with Software One, present our proposal, our product architecture, and our questions/issues, and to receive training from them on their products. Bob presented everything that had transpired to the group upon his return. Bob went back to the U.K. again with Cameron McLean and Peter Sawyer to discuss joint product architecture and produce a design study document. After this trip, Bob began facilitating weekly teleconferences between Bull and Software One to discuss process, work products, schedule, equipment, and planning. Our successful joint development of ISD 1.0 was born from these initial efforts.	Bob has provided significant technical expertise to each of the major third-party relationships in which ADI has been involved.

Figure 19.14 demonstrates several qualities important to writing effective performance appraisals:

- Evaluation is based on previously established goals.
- Performance is separated into a number of categories, which can be weighted when appropriate.
- Appraisal has specific detail and cites examples of performance.
- Action and not personality is the focus of the comments.

If there had been criticism of Bob in Figure 19.14, such negative information should have been "sandwiched" between discussions of Bob's good points to maintain good morale. Bob's performance appraisal also serves as an opportunity to address future goals for the next evaluation period.

In today's more team-oriented work environment, team members must sometimes evaluate one another's performance, and management places less emphasis on individual achievements and more on group accomplishments.

Alternatives to Traditional Performance Appraisals

Alternatives to traditional performance appraisals characteristically strive to counteract some problems commonly associated with traditional methods (Figure 19.15 on page 578). Two common alternatives to traditional review that you might encounter are

- Total Quality Management (TQM)
- peer evaluation

Total Quality Management (TQM), adapted from Japanese management models, represents an alternative to individual performance appraisal. TQM stresses improvements in work process rather than employee

Figure 19.15 Improvements for Traditional Performance Review

THE SEVEN DEADLY SINS OF APPRAISALS	STRATEGIES FOR AVOIDING THESE SINS
No discussion. Just sign the form.	Establish a two-way discussion about the appraisal throughout the appraisal period.
One-way discourse. The boss does all the talking.	Encourage employee participation by asking the employee to fill out an appraisal form in advance, citing specific examples of his or her performance.
General, unspecified comments about performance.	Relate performance to fulfillment of clear, well-understood objectives and performance standards (accountabilities and measures).
Surprise ratings.	Fill out the appraisal form and give it to the employee for discussion. Allow employee to respond in writing and include response in performance file.
Wishy-washing ratings.	Determine, at objectives-setting time, what the employee needs to do to earn certain ratings. If the employee will be rated "excellent," "good," "fair," etc., define what makes work "excellent," etc.
Ratings based on comparisons between employees.	Consult others about your evaluation. Be careful to preserve anonymity and confidentiality. Use "360-degree feedback assessment," where feedback is gathered from multiple sources and shared with the employee.
Lack of follow-up.	Convert opportunities for improvement into new objectives for the next performance cycle.

performance. Groups, such as productivity teams, quality circles, and quality-of-work-life groups, concentrate on improving employee performance, and managers integrate their efforts into the entire organization "as part of a larger improvement effort."[6] Figure 19.16 compares performance review under traditional management and under TQM management. In many companies, TQM is used to complement traditional performance appraisal, rather than to replace it.

Peer review means that your performance is evaluated by your fellow workers rather than by your supervisor. Peer review as a *formal* method of evaluation is not always accepted as a good idea by employees. It seems to work best in participatory workplace practices, such as working in collaborative teams. Regular peer evaluation, such as that used and recommended by Hampton Pension Services (Figure 19.17), also helps make peer review a workable alternative. At Hampton, a pension-administration firm, all employees rate each other on how well each worker satisfies ten performance statements. The questions "reflect what the firm as a whole wants the company culture to be."[7] Evaluations are prepared on a computer and anonymously returned for compilation. Answers are quantified and individual scores are used to determine raises and bonuses. A company must be willing to stand by and enforce the results of peer evaluations if this system is to be effective.

Figure 19.16 Comparison of Traditional and TQM Approaches to Performance Review

COMPARING APPROACHES TO PERFORMANCE REVIEW		
ASPECT	TRADITIONAL	TQM
Focus	The individual	The organization or the system of management
Measure of performance	Individual action	Work group collaboration
Employer's goal	Control; documentation	Development; problem solving
Supervisor's role	Referee or judge	Facilitator or coach
Employee's role	Individual achievement and reward	Collaborative achievement and success

TECHNOLOGY

EVALUATING EMPLOYEES BY COMPUTER?

Many companies today are using their computer systems to help them monitor and evaluate the productivity of employees. Companies that install these systems commonly use them to monitor the performance of low-level employees who work primarily at doing repetitive tasks on computer terminals. The system measures the time it takes employees to do various tasks and keeps a record of their productivity. Both managers and employees have access to these productivity reports, thus taking the mystery, fear, and personality conflicts out of employee evaluation sessions. Managers and employees simply go over the reports and discuss what needs to be improved in order to meet standards the computer sets by averaging the productivity of other employees. To managers, then, these systems seem to be an excellent solution to a traditional personnel problem.

The systems, however, are controversial. Although many companies insist that the systems help employers and employees alike by removing interpersonal conflicts and setting realistic productivity goals, others question the ethical correctness, the effect on morale, and the customer service consequences of monitoring employees while they work. Some even see these computers that watch employees while they work as invasions of employee privacy or as the first step to the creation of a totalitarian state dominated by computers.

Even though such perceptions may affect employee morale, the use of these systems is on the rise because they are seen to reduce the stress of performance review.

Figure 19.17 Peer Evaluation Form Using a Graphic Rating Scale

HAMPTON PENSION SERVICES INC. PEER EVALUATION FORM*

Q1: Places organization above self (is a true team player).

Q2: Works additional hours beyond the minimum required by his/her job level or works more diligently than the typical employee.

Q3: If I was starting a business, I would want this person to work for my company.

Q4: Treats new co-workers and existing co-workers in a friendly, respectful, considerate, and professional manner.

Q5: Accepts responsibility for errors without making excuses or being defensive, while striving to minimize the likelihood of repeating them.

Q6: Is very careful to review any work he/she has done before passing it on to another person.

Q7: Is a positive influence in the firm by only criticizing the firm or co-workers when he/she has a well-thought-out suggestion for improvement.

Q8: Is always understanding when I make a mistake that requires him/her to do extra work.

Q9: Avoids bringing personal matters into the office that could have a disruptive impact on his/her co-workers.

Q10: Is always respectful to his/her supervisors and maintains the same working diligence whether his/her supervisor is present or not.

KEY: 1: Strongly Disagree 3: Disagree 5: Sometimes Agree and Sometimes Disagree 7: Agree 10: Very Strongly Agree

As our company expands, there may be co-workers with whom you have little or no contact on a day-to-day basis. For these individuals, there may be a question or two that you are not sure how to answer; therefore, please complete those questions using what you consider to be an "average" choice. *January 1, 1993–June 30, 1993

LETTERS ADDRESSING EMPLOYMENT CONCERNS

A number of letters in business deal directly with employment concerns:

- letters rejecting job applicants
- letters of recommendation
- letters of resignation

Because letters rejecting job applicants are shown in Nick Sanger's story in Chapter 6, they are not discussed here.

Letters of Recommendation

Probably the first letter of recommendation you will be asked to write in your career will be a letter for a colleague. In writing such a letter, your job is to convince the reader that an employee or applicant has the characteristics necessary for success in a particular position. These letters commonly focus on one or more of five categories of character:[8]

- dependability-reliability
- mental quickness
- vigor or initiative
- consideration-cooperation
- urbanity or sophistication

As you write a letter of recommendation, you tailor the letter according to the occasion: you need to know how important each category of character is to the particular job your colleague is seeking. Of course, this means that the person asking for the recommendation needs to provide a written or oral description of the position.

After analyzing the job description, you choose words to describe the candidate that are appropriate to the qualities necessary to the position. For example, words such as "dependable" and "reliable" as well as words such as "tenacious," "confident," and "determined" would be adjectives describing a candidate's dependability-reliability. You will notice that these categories of performance emphasize the personal characteristics that an applicant brings to a position rather than actual knowledge or skills. Your role in writing a recommendation is to predict how the applicant will be able to learn new skills and to get along with other employees. Letters of recommendation are crucial, because employers hire *people*, not sets of credentials.

Letters of recommendation follow conventional formats:

- an opening that establishes the full name of the candidate, the job position (or benefit) the candidate is seeking, the context of the recommendation (solicited, unsolicited), and the duration and nature of the relationship between the writer and the candidate
- a body that contains facts about the candidate that are relevant to the position or benefit sought; specific examples and comparisons are expected
- a close that gives the writer's overall evaluation of the appropriateness of the candidate to the position (or benefit)

Although good letters of recommendation also admit an applicant's weaknesses when appropriate, writers are becoming increasingly hesitant to put anything negative in such letters for fear of legal consequences. Negative factors, however, can and should be included, if the applicant's shortcomings are relevant to the position (or benefit) that is being sought and are serious enough to affect job performance. As you address weaknesses, you need to cite specific detail and to balance criticism with praise, as shown in Figure 19.18.

Figure 19.18 Letter of Recommendation

Opening: establishes that this is a solicited letter and gives the candidate's full name, the writer's relationship with the candidate, and the duration of that relationship.

I am pleased to provide this letter of recommendation for Lyle Allen Deming. I served as Lyle's immediate supervisor from 1990–1993 and have worked together with Lyle as a colleague and friend since his promotion to Director of Training and Development in 1993.

Body: shows examples of Lyle's knowledge and experience appropriate to the position, while developing him as an intelligent, innovative, and sensitive person with fine communication skills.

Lyle has been instrumental in developing competency models for the key job tasks in our company. In developing the models, Lyle combined Behavioral Event Interview (BEI), survey, panel, expert system, and observation data. He was especially innovative in his use of two thematic analysis methods to identify competencies in the BEI data. Due to his efforts, we now have concrete ways of both analyzing the performance of employees in specific positions and training personnel for those positions.

Lyle's work with competency and employee development has also been crucial in creating cross-cultural interpersonal sensitivity among our employees, especially those in managerial positions. Lyle works backward in describing what it takes to be competent in a position by studying those who are recognized as doing an excellent job and developing criteria from their performance. This approach has allowed Lyle to describe excellent performance in terms of what works well at specific sites, including those in Hermosillo, Mexico, and Taipei, Taiwan. His work has increased managers' awareness that cultural differences may change what is effective from site to site.

Lyle complements his intelligence and cross-cultural awareness with his ability to communicate both in large groups and one-on-one. In other words, Lyle not only has the knowledge to be an effective Personnel Director, but he also has the personal qualities to be a success in such a position.

Close: gives a summary assessment of Lyle and his match to the position for which he has applied.

Although we would certainly like to keep Lyle here as our Director of Training and Development, he has my highest recommendation for the position of Personnel Director at your company. He is an excellent choice.

Letters of Resignation

Letters of resignation, Figure 19.19, also follow the pattern of messages that anticipate reader resistance with a buffer showing appreciation, reasons for the decision, the decision to resign, and a goodwill close.

Figure 19.19 Letter of Resignation

The writer's statement of appreciation serves as a buffer.

She offers an explanation for her decision before the "bad news" of the resignation. She offers additional reasons before giving the resignation date.

She uses a goodwill close.

I have very much enjoyed working as a sales associate and, more recently, as an assistant buyer for Dungaree Blues. I feel that I have learned a tremendous amount about the fashion industry while working for your firm.

As you know, one of my long-term goals has been to become a buyer for a fashion house that does a good deal of business overseas. Such a position would allow me to combine my two loves of fashion and travel in a significant way. Recently, I have been offered an assistant buyer's position with Eastwick, Inc. Although this will initially be a lateral move for me, it offers the opportunity of immediate foreign travel and future advancement. I am, therefore, resigning my position with Dungaree Blues, effective November 1.

I will always remember my time with Dungaree Blues with great appreciation. I will especially remember the kindness of all of those who worked with me over the past five years. My best wishes to your future success.

RESPONSE SHEET

JOB INTERVIEW PREPARATION

INTERVIEWEE:	AUDIENCE(S):
OCCASION:	OBJECTIVE(S):

◆ COMPANY PERSPECTIVE

What are the concerns the prospective employer is likely to bring to the interview session?

◆ INTERVIEWER QUESTIONS

What are the questions in each of the categories below that the interviewer is most likely to ask?

Achievements

Motives

Scenarios

Criteria

The future

The interviewee's place in corporate culture

The interviewee's personal preferences

◆ QUESTIONS ASKED BY APPLICANTS

What questions can/should the interviewee be prepared to ask during the interview?

About supervisors

About incentives and advancements

About evaluation

About interaction

About expectations

About the future

Which three questions are most important to ask in this interview situation?

◆ DIFFICULT SITUATIONS

Are there any difficult problems or questions the interviewee will have to address during the interview? (About changing jobs? About leaving a position? About gaps in work history? About being let go or fired?)

How can the interviewee address concerns involving this (these) circumstance(s)?

What does the interviewee regard as the weakest point in interviewing? (Having professional appearance? Appearing nervous rather than confident? Looking the interviewer in the eye? Avoiding negative comments or sarcasm?)

What can the interviewee do to improve performance in this weak area?

◆ FOLLOW-UP

What type(s) of follow-up messages are appropriate to this particular interview situation?

RESPONSE SHEET

PERFORMANCE REVIEW

EVALUATOR:	EMPLOYEE:
OCCASION:	OBJECTIVE(S):

◆ TYPE OF PERFORMANCE REVIEW

What type of performance review is or will be involved (traditional, TQM, alternative, peer)? Explain.

What types of feedback will the employee already have during this performance review period?

◆ ACCOUNTABILITIES AND MEASURES

What are the accountabilities and measures important to this performance review?

Accountabilities	Measures

Are the accountabilities and measures sufficiently specific? (If so, explain why they are effective. If not, suggest improvements.)

◆ EVALUATION

Review the evaluation. How is the evaluation based on previously established goals?

Is the performance separated into a number of categories that can be weighted when appropriate? Is weighting categories appropriate in this case? Explain.

What specific detail or sample illustrations does the evaluator include to demonstrate the reviewed person's performance? Do the examples actually show what the evaluator says they show? Are there ways the evaluator can improve the examples in the evaluation?

Does the evaluation focus on action and not personality? Remarks.

Does the evaluation sandwich any negative information? Explain.

Does the evaluation look to the future? Explain.

◆ FOLLOW-UP

What types of follow-up are planned for this performance review?

ACTIVITIES, EXERCISES, AND ASSIGNMENTS

◆ IN-CLASS ACTIVITIES

1. Please refer to Figure 19.1, the material about FSIOs, for the following activity.

   a. In Figure 19.1, David C. McClelland refers to competencies. In this chapter, we refer to accountabilities. What connection do you see between competencies and accountabilities? How are they similar? Different?

   b. If you were to draw up a list of accountabilities and measures for an FSIO position, what would they be? Draw up such a list.

   c. If you were to apply to be an FSIO with a letter of application and a resume, what credentials would you want to present? How would you show a match between these credentials and the FSIO position?

   d. Assume that you were successful in getting an interview for an FSIO position. Use the Response Sheet on preparing for job interviews to anticipate questions your interviewer might ask and to prepare sample questions of your own.

2. Interviewer questions serve a number of functions, including revealing and interpreting achievements, assessing your motives, addressing scenarios, revealing criteria, projecting the future, identifying your place in corporate culture, and revealing personal preferences. Overall, such questions are designed to "match" the prospective employer and the job applicant. With these functions in mind, work in teams to:

   a. identify a specific job opening with a particular company

   b. design at least five original questions that you might ask a job applicant if you were an interviewer of applicants for this position (refer to the Response Sheet on interviews for assistance)

   c. discuss how the applicant should answer these questions

   d. compose several questions the applicant could ask of the interviewer in the situation you've described

   e. role-play the interview situation that you've designed for other students and ask for their feedback

3. On the basis of what you have learned about working in groups in this class, discuss what you would consider essential *accountabilities* and *measures* for any person participating in team projects. Do you think the collaborative experiences in this class and these accountabilities and measures that you have just established will differ substantially from those in business and industry? Explain.

◆ INDIVIDUAL AND GROUP EXERCISES

1. Job applicants are also responsible for telling the truth in their letters of application and resumes. However, applications involve the interpretation of credentials. And interpretation involves explaining certain "facts" according to your idea of what they mean. Interpretation leaves open the possibility that the prospective employer and the applicant might not see eye to eye about what a certain job experience meant. In other words, the applicant's "truth" might not be the same as the employer's "truth."

   a. Create or relate a scenario that demonstrates differences between the way an applicant and a prospective employer see a particular set of credentials.

   b. Discuss the possible advantages and disadvantages of the fact that credentials are *interpreted* by both employer and applicant.

   c. Discuss possible ways to address the differences in interpretation that you have created or described (in part a).

   d. Write a memo that presents your scenario, summarizes your discussion, and contains a recommendation for action.

2. Please refer to Figure 19.20 in completing this exercise.

CONTEXT

Mr. Drew is interviewing several applicants for a supervisory position at an amusement park. The supervisor would be in charge of scheduling the 60 workers who run the various rides, staffing positions in case of absences, making sure that safety guidelines are followed, and handling any employee or customer complaints. All five applicants being considered, including Louis (Figure 19.20), have had previous amusement park or midway experience. Louis was selected for an interview because of his recommendations. One supervisor wrote, "Louis is among the most charismatic people I've ever known. His leadership is based upon the fact that people of all ages trust and respect him." Louis, now eighteen, has been working in various jobs at amusement parks for four years.

   a. Discuss the interviewer's strengths and weaknesses in the way he is handling the task of interviewing this applicant.

   b. Discuss the applicant's strengths and weaknesses in the way he is responding.

   c. Make concrete suggestions for improvements in both the interviewer's and the applicant's approaches.

Figure 19.20 Excerpt from Job Interview

Mr. Drew:	So, tell me about your experience at America's Theme Park.
Louis:	It was good. Real good. Worked with some interesting people.
Mr. Drew:	Okay. . . . Hmm. Now, were you assigned to do adult rides mainly, or . . . ?
Louis:	Yeah. I especially liked working the roller coaster.
Mr. Drew:	What were the safety features on the roller coasters you worked?
Louis:	The usual. You know, bar in front.
Mr. Drew:	That's all?
Louis:	Well, we had this sign. Kids who couldn't reach a certain mark on it weren't supposed to go on the thing alone.
Mr. Drew:	Did you have any trouble enforcing that?
Louis:	No. I put on my "gang face" and told them to come back with an adult. I did make an exception once when this really short girl showed me her learner's permit. I figured if she was old enough to run me over with a car, she was old enough to ride the coaster solo.
Mr. Drew:	Anything else in terms of safety?
Louis:	There also was a warning that it was a pretty severe ride and people with certain health conditions should be careful.
Mr. Drew:	With all those safety guidelines, was working the ride very stressful?
Louis:	Not stressful. Boring maybe. But sometimes kids at the end of the ride came in with their eyes all bugged out, and it was pretty funny. You know, some kids just like to be scared.
Mr. Drew:	How did you deal with the boredom?
Louis:	Talked with the people before they got on. My Spanish is pretty good, too, so I tried to be on hand to translate if someone couldn't read the warning signs.
Mr. Drew:	How did you know if they could read the signs or not?
Louis:	I asked them. Have you ever said, "Did you read the signs?" two hundred times in six hours?
Mr. Drew:	Was that required?
Louis:	No, it wasn't. But I did it anyway. You know, something to keep things going.
Mr. Drew:	What makes you think you would be a good supervisor?
Louis:	People don't ever give me any trouble. You know, if I ask them to do something, they usually do it.
Mr. Drew:	How do you explain that?
Louis:	My "gang face." . . . No, seriously, I just have a knack for telling people what to do without hurting their feelings or anything.

3. Please refer to Figure 19.21 on the next page in completing this exercise.

CONTEXT

The general competencies listed in Figure 19.21 are important to telemarketers and to those holding sales positions in retail outlets.

a. Review the list of general competencies for sales personnel (Figure 19.21) and discuss any additional categories that you would like to add. Use your experience and that of others involving telemarketers and sales personnel to guide your suggestions.

b. Rate the categories that you have according to importance. Does the company the sales personnel represent or the product being sold make any difference in your rankings? Explain.

c. Working singly or in a small group, convert the categories into specific accountabilities for a particular sales position.

d. Design measures to go with your accountabilities.

4. Please use the example in Figure 19.22 on the next page to complete this exercise.

CONTEXT

Marty Wadsworth worked as a switchboard operator at a financial aid office for 5 months. One month ago, he was moved to the front counter to greet clients, establish their needs, and determine if their problems could be handled on the spot by Mr. Jaffey, a staff member in charge of addressing immediate needs. If their problems required extensive analysis, Marty scheduled an appointment for them with one of the other counselors. Marty's change in job assignment occurred near the end of a 6-month performance review cycle. Even though his new job duties were outlined, no new accountabilities were established. Figure 19.22 shows an essay evaluation of Marty's performance at the end of the 6-month period.

Figure 19.21 General Competencies for Sales Personnel

Relationship building
Maintains work-related friendships
Has and uses networks of contacts

Impact and influence
Establishes credibility of company
Addresses customers' issues and concerns
Predicts effects of own words and actions

Interpersonal understanding
Understands nonverbal behavior
Understands others' attitudes, meanings
Predicts others' reactions

Initiative
Persists, does not give up easily
Seizes opportunities

Achievement orientation
Sets challenging, achievable goals
Uses time efficiently
Improves customer operations

Figure 19.22 Performance Review Essay

As Marty Wadsworth's immediate supervisor, I have seen much to praise in his performance. I also have several suggestions for improvement.

During his tenure as a switchboard operator, Marty showed an uncanny ability to handle conversations on all 8 incoming lines without putting clients on hold for an extensive period of time. He was quick and accurate in his advice concerning financial matters. If callers later came into the office for a scheduled appointment, they almost always made special mention to financial counselors of Marty's efficiency and helpfulness. Marty met or exceeded his goals concerning number of clients handled and courtesy of service during this period.

Because of his ability to diagnose the needs of callers, Marty was moved to the front desk on May 14. Here, he did not prove as successful. In the first place, Marty could not seem to keep track of "who was next" at the counter. A number of clients complained that the "pushier" the customer, the sooner the service. Others complained that once Marty finally noticed them, he seemed abrupt or impatient with his advice. There were no complaints about the accuracy of what he said, and no one suggested that he wasn't trying hard to handle the front-desk situation, which at times can resemble a zoo.

Because of Marty's inability to handle the front desk rush, I am thinking about following Marty's suggestion and instituting a number system, which should help determine which client is next. Marty should also develop strategies for putting counter customers "on hold" when he needs to consult briefly about advice. I feel confident that, with a few adjustments, Marty will be able to handle the pressure of his new position better.

a. Devise one set of accountabilities and measures of Marty's switchboard operator position, and a second set for the front desk position. Are these positions similar enough that they can be evaluated using the same performance guidelines? Explain.

b. Using an appropriate set of accountabilities and measures, evaluate Marty's performance at each respective position. (You may want to invent additional details to support your evaluation.) Discuss any potential problems involved with the fact that Marty's switch in job positions was not reflected in a new or revised performance review document.

c. Convert your accountabilities and measures into a graphic rating scale to measure Marty's performance. What would happen if one graphic rating scale were used to evaluate Marty, Mr. Jaffey, and all others working in the office?

d. Revise Figure 19.22 to improve the way it assesses Marty's performance.

◆ OUT-OF-CLASS ASSIGNMENTS

1. Work in teams to conduct mock interviews for an assortment of job positions. The team will conduct four interviews (each interview will be conducted by team members, with one person being interviewed). Review the suggested questions in the chapter to use as a foundation for developing questions the team would like to ask. Preliminary to the interview, the team needs to

prepare a chart of accountabilities and measures for each position. Team members also must decide what roles each will play. Each person being interviewed can select from any of these potential positions:

- supervisor at a fast-food restaurant
- sales associate for a national chain department store
- assistant ad writer for a radio station
- administrative assistant handling routine correspondence for a manufacturing company

Discuss how the task would change if the interview were an all-day affair.

2. Locate an attractive job opening. Write an application series, including your resume (written in Chapter 18), a copy of the job posting or ad, and a letter of application. Using the Response Sheet on preparing for job interviews, prepare questions for a job interview for this position. Then write a thank-you, and a letter accepting or declining the position.
3. Exchange your application series (written in assignment 2) with a classmate. Using the Response Sheet on performance reviews as a guide, prepare a sample list of accountabilities and measures for the job your classmate has applied for. Then, interview your classmate for this position. Finally, write a letter of recommendation for the person based on the information from the resume, letter of application, and interview.
4. Imagine that you have the opportunity to write your own letter of recommendation. Locate a job opening that you would like to apply for and save the ad or job posting. Using the Response Sheet on performance review, decide the accountabilities and measures that would be appropriate for the job opening you've located. Then identify your strength(s) and shortcoming(s). Determine how your qualifications match the job opening. Now write a letter of recommendation for yourself that is addressed to the prospective employer in the job opening you have selected. In writing this letter, try to make the best of your weaknesses. Consider, however, that you are legally liable for whatever you write.

CASE:
A PERFORMANCE REVIEW FOR PAT REARDON

CASE BY ANDREA BREEMER FRANTZ

Background. After nine years of dedication and hard work, you were recently offered a partnership at Towne, Vogel & Whitehead, a small law firm which has recently handled a number of high-profile environmental law cases. One of your first responsibilities as a new partner is to write performance reviews for all new associates at the firm. Performance reviews usually focus on the following key issues:

- number of cases handled singly
- number of cases handled collaboratively
- relative weight of the cases (For example, how important were they? This usually has less to do with how much revenue a specific case brought in for the firm and more to do with how well the client was served and/or what sort of positive change was effected through the case.)
- win/loss ratio
- billable hours to clients
- attitude and service to the firm
- attitude and service to the community
- other relevant observations related to performance

Though all of the issues are important, frequently it's the last of them ("other") where partners can really show their knowledge of the associates. For example, in your last performance review as an associate, partner Susanne VanZandt Whitehead wrote in detail about your tendency to take losses in the courtroom personally and how such a quality was both a positive and a negative. From that review you learned to maintain a certain level of self-criticism, but also to recognize when circumstances associated with a loss may be beyond your control. Such critiques seek not only to provide specific professional insights to the associate, but also to build strong mentoring relationships between the associate and the partner.

Task. Pat Reardon is an associate who has been with the firm for two years. Reardon has historically been a hard worker and was a top recruit from the University of Chicago in 1991. Since joining TV&W, Reardon has handled a number of sensitive cases, including an environmental pollution case against a major chemical company in the area. During this case, Reardon (as well as the firm) received anonymous threats, but the community largely supported the firm's efforts and they received positive media attention.

Your task is to write a performance review for Pat Reardon based on the information provided. (The review should be addressed directly to Reardon, though the three managing partners of the firm—Towne, Vogel, and Whitehead—will receive copies.)

- *Number of cases handled singly*: 7 (this is an average to moderate load for an associate).
- *Number of cases handled collaboratively*: 18 (this is a heavy load for an associate and indicative of the fact that the other lawyers in the firm want to work with Reardon).
- *Relative weight of the cases*: Reardon carried three notable cases—one as chief counsel and two as an associate to other partners. The case with Reardon as chief counsel dealt with workers' compensation. The two cases with Reardon as an associate involved illegal dumping of waste (both toxic and nontoxic). Through these cases, Reardon began to attract attention as a lawyer willing to take on tough environmental issues in keeping with Towne, Vogel & Whitehead's professional commitment to the environment.
- *Win/loss ratio*: 20 wins, 5 losses (one of the losses was also seen as an "unwinnable" case shortly after the firm agreed to take it).
- *Billable hours*: 240 to 280 per month (well within the average for associates).
- *Attitude and service to firm:* Reardon's attitude and service to the firm are uniformly regarded as very positive. Reardon has demonstrated a willingness to take on tough cases and put in long hours. Other lawyers in the firm appreciate working with such a dedicated young lawyer, and the

secretarial staff has consistently remarked on Reardon's respectful treatment of support staff.

- *Attitude and service to the community*: With little free time, Reardon has still managed to volunteer at the local homeless shelter over Thanksgiving and help raise donations for a bookmobile to visit each of the elementary schools in the area once every two weeks. From talking with Reardon, you also know that a favorite charity is the Leukemia Foundation.

Complication. Though all of these points speak well of Reardon's performance over the review period, there are two issues which complicate an otherwise very favorable assessment.

First, not long ago, while spending a little free time on an Internet law and legal issues news forum, you ran across an essay written by a Washburn University law student. A section of the essay, dated August 1992, was verbatim a part of a summation statement you heard Reardon give only a month ago. Though, as of yet, there are few intellectual property restrictions regarding World Wide Web publications, such appropriation can be seen as unethical by academic standards. When you asked about the idea for the summation, Reardon shrugged and said it had seemed like a creative twist on the argument. Disturbed, you showed Reardon the essay you had read on the net. Reardon admitted the essay prompted the argumentative angle, but denied the entire argument was taken verbatim.

Second, Reardon was recently appointed to the Board of Directors of Globe Petroleum Co., based in Globe, Texas. A tanker for Globe ran into bad weather September 22, 1992, and spilled nearly three-quarters of its cargo of crude oil 20 miles off the coast of Limón, Costa Rica, causing substantial environmental damage. Globe has also been involved in a number of questionable waste management practices, though it has never been formally charged with negligence. You have reservations as to whether Reardon's association with Globe Petroleum is in conflict of interest with Towne, Vogel & Whitehead's public stance on environmental issues. At this point in time, you have not had the opportunity to discuss the appointment with Reardon.

The issue you must address is whether the appropriation of intellectual property and conflict of interest issues can rightfully be addressed in the review under "other relevant observations." Though neither issue is one which will prevent Reardon from being promoted or call into question Reardon's place at the firm, both could be seen as relevant testimonies to Reardon's character.

Communication Spotlight: Collaboration

DESIGNING SUCCESSFUL TEAMS

During your career, you'll work on lots of teams—to solve problems, to investigate new ideas, to complete projects, to oversee quality. Sometimes you'll work on team projects for only a week or two; other times you will be collaborating for months. It's likely that more than three-quarters of the workplace writing you do may involve some type of interaction with other individuals or groups.[1]

Let's look at some of the collaborative interactions at Boyd Environmental Engineering. One project team, for example, designs, develops, markets, and supports innovative safety equipment intended to minimize the risk to technicians who clean up hazardous waste sites. This team creates a variety of documents. It writes marketing brochures, tip sheets, specifications, manuals, monthly progress reports, and press releases. It also writes articles for an internal newsletter, for the annual report, and for the local public media.

Team members often have different areas of expertise.

In order to produce these documents, the various specialists on the team combine their areas of expertise. Marketing specialists conduct surveys. Engineers provide technical information and check technical accuracy. Writers conduct usability tests. The team also elicits the expertise of those outside the teams: Managers at preliminary test sites provide feedback about the equipment and procedures; designers create appealing, market-sensitive logos, graphics, and page designs; lawyers verify the warnings, cautions, and statutory restrictions; consultants produce the training video; and so on.

Reasons for Collaboration

The kind of collaboration going on at Boyd Environmental Engineering is common throughout the 1990s workplace. Well-designed teams work in complex situations because they address recurrent problems:

- the limited time and knowledge of individual professionals
- the diverse needs of multiple audiences using the documents for various purposes
- the complexity of the various situations in which the documents will be used

Whether collaborative interactions are the result of individual choice, circumstance, or management directive, the reasons you'll collaborate generally fall into four categories:

- *Subject*: Some tasks require the expertise of more than one person. The Boyd project team that designed safety equipment to use at hazardous waste sites needed the expertise of design engineers, mechanical engineers, computer engineers, human factors engineers, environmental engineers, civil engineers, marketing specialists, writers, and editors.
- *Process*: Team interaction can generate a variety of viewpoints, which wouldn't occur with one person working individually. The Boyd project team benefited from a process that brought multiple perspectives together.
- *Product*: Some documents (for example, newsletters, user manuals, proposals) are generally better if they're created collaboratively. The Boyd team not only had to create the product, but it had to produce all the documentation. For example, in addition to producing manuals

for operation, maintenance and safety, the team also had to file compliance reports with the appropriate federal agency.

- *Interpersonal benefits*: The collaborative interaction of groups and teams is often more enjoyable than working independently. Such group interaction can produce a less competitive and more cooperative workplace atmosphere. The Boyd team members enjoyed their cooperative spirit as well as the award-winning products they created.

Once you have decided that a task is complex enough to merit a team effort, you need to form a team. The remainder of this Communication Spotlight section focuses on ways you can design teams so that the time the members spend together will be well used and the members will feel good about their work together.

Team Structure: How Is It Organized?

The success of a team depends in part on matching the team's structure to its task. You make decisions about team structure by considering a team's function, the sequence in which tasks are completed, the ways in which responsibilities are divided, and features that characterize the team.

Function. Team structures correspond to three different functions, as shown in Figure 1: problem-resolution teams, creative teams, and tactical teams.

Figure 1 Team Functions

TEAM FUNCTION	APPROACHES	EXAMPLE
Problem-resolution teams • focus on issues that need to be resolved • depend on each member's trusting the other members to be truthful and demonstrate integrity	• Select tasks that require careful investigation. • Do *not* start with predetermined assumptions or conclusions. • Take advantage of team members' expertise. • Collect information from those closest to the problem.	Boyd Environmental Engineering is hired by a city that has tried since the mid-1970s to be environmentally cautious—it uses a city incinerator for electricity; curbside recycling of all glass, plastic, and paper; energy efficiency as a standard requirement for all new construction; and so on. Despite the city's good intentions, the programs are losing lots of money. Boyd draws together a team to help the city figure out how it can maintain its environmental integrity but stop losing money.
Creative teams • focus on exploring possibilities and alternatives • depend on autonomy from the organization's systems and procedures	• Abandon "normative thinking." • Don't reject any ideas prematurely. • Impose few constraints on the team. • Ignore organizational conventions.	Boyd Environmental Engineering decides to venture into new territory. A team is working on developing a new product that is entirely "green"—environmentally safe, able to be recycled—with a large profit potential, geared specifically toward 10- to 15-year-olds in an effort to strengthen their awareness of environmental issues and tap their pocketbooks.
Tactical teams • focus on well-defined operations • depend on an unambiguous definition of the task and of each member's role in completing the task	• Define each role on the team. • Establish clear performance standards for each role. • Assign each team member to a specific role, with well-defined responsibilities. • Direct the implementation of tasks.	Boyd Environmental Engineering is asked by the governor in its state to select a management team to head an emergency cleanup operation. The emergency is at an old industrial dump site that is leaking toxic substances into the local river. Boyd managers will run a military-style operation, with National Guard soldiers doing most of the physical work.

Sequence. The sequence in which tasks are completed influences the structure of a team. In some organizations, projects pass from department team to department team in a *linear* manner. For example, in such an arrangement, a research and development (R&D) team responsible for developing a new water filter for residential customers might have a project first. Then the project might go to mechanical engineering, then to manufacturing, then to marketing, then to documentation, and finally to sales. In this situation, the teams in each department are seen as independent (rather than interdependent). This is the "traditional" approach that has been used successfully in a number of industries.

In contrast, a *concurrent* project team for the same water filter project would have representative members from R&D, engineering, manufacturing, marketing, documentation, and sales all together at the same time. This concurrent structure is based on the assumption that professionals can bring insight to multiple stages and areas in a project. For example, the input from a person in marketing about customer preferences could influence the design by R&D. More and more companies are moving toward concurrent project teams as they realize that projects benefit from the interaction among professionals in multiple areas.

Figure 2 Team Responsibilities

DIVISION-OF-LABOR TEAMS	INTEGRATED TEAMS
Roles on the team and goals and tasks for team members are determined and assigned by managers.	Team members determine roles and goals and then assign tasks.
Tasks are completed in a linear sequence determined by a manager.	Tasks are completed in an order determined by the team.
Team members do only tasks designated by their job description.	Team members contribute their expertise but also contribute in other ways.
Technology manages time and budget.	Technology facilitates team interaction and access to data.
The project is supervised by managers.	The team is managed and assessed cooperatively by the members. Sometimes a facilitator manages administrative details.

Responsibility. A third area of team structure deals with the way members of a team assign their responsibilities. Figure 2 shows two different approaches used to assign work: division-of-labor teams and integrated teams.

Current trends in workplace teams favor integrated, concurrent, self-directed teams. However, a question remains: Should a team manage all aspects of its own work? Some experts say yes,[2] self-directed teams are productive. Thus, the Boyd Environmental Engineering team is probably going to be more productive if it assumes the following responsibilities:

- establishes its own definitions of the task
- determines team membership
- assigns duties for performing the task
- makes decisions regarding all aspects of the team's task
- supervises individual and team training
- evaluates the quality of its product
- assesses its own productivity and effectiveness

Features. Once you know a team's function, the sequence in which tasks are completed, and the ways in which responsibilities are divided, you can use this information to make yourself a more productive member of the team. Figure 3 (page 592) suggests key areas that team members need to consider individually and collectively. Securing common responses to these questions ensures that all team members see the project in the same way—a critical criterion for effective teams.

Figure 3 Team Features

Identify team goals. • What are our team goals? • What must be done to accomplish these goals?
Define individual roles and responsibilities. • What are our individual roles and responsibilities? • How should we communicate with each other—frequency, topics, methods (face-to-face, electronic), and so on?
Select sources and methods of obtaining data and making decisions. • How do we obtain, verify, and/or challenge information? • What methods do we have for tracing decisions?
Agree to make fact-based judgments so information can be verified. • What qualifies as a "fact"? • Have the "facts" been interpreted without bias?

ACTIVITIES AND QUESTIONS FOR DISCUSSION

1. Arrange an interview with a member of a workplace team to learn about the history of the team, the way the team was formed, the way it manages itself, and the way it is rewarded. Consider the following questions as a starting place, and then develop your own questions.

   History of the team

   - What is the function or purpose of your team?
   - Who made the decision to form this team?
   - Have any members of the team worked together before?

   Formation of the team

   - What knowledge, skills, and experiences do members of the team need in order to accomplish the purpose?
   - How were the various members of the team selected?

   Managing the team

   - What is the structure of the team?
   - How are decisions made? How are conflicts resolved?
   - Is there a leader? Why? If there is a leader, how did that person become leader?

   Rewarding the team

   - How is the team rewarded?
   - Do members receive individual acknowledgment? Do they receive group acknowledgment?

   Present the information from your interview in an article that could be published in a company's employee newsletter as a personal account of what makes a team work effectively or ineffectively.

2. Think of a team that you're a member of in this class. Work individually to respond to the questions in Figure 3 in relation to your team. Then meet with your team to answer the questions again—this time collaboratively. Discuss with other members of the team the differences in responses of individuals who have completed the questions before discussing the information with the group.

REVISING, EDITING, AND EVALUATING—CONDUCTING DOCUMENT TESTING

Document testing is one way to find out if the document you write makes sense to readers. The term *document testing* refers broadly to a cluster of techniques used to assess the accuracy, appeal, and appropriateness of a document. Appropriateness includes characteristics such as a document's accessibility, effectiveness, and usability.[1]

Purpose of Document Testing

The overall purpose of document testing is to improve the product or process for the users—whether readers of manuals, reports, or marketing brochures. You can build on questions like the ones in Figure 1 to identify areas that need to be assessed by various forms of document testing. For example, if you have written instructions for operating a remote control camera for video conferencing, you would need to check your instructions for accuracy, appeal, and appropriateness. Figure 1 shows how you can begin with checklist questions—those with a yes or no answer—as a way to get started. Then you can move to probing questions that require explanations.

Figure 1 Generic Document-Testing Questions

CHARACTERISTIC ASSESSED BY TESTING	CHECKLIST QUESTIONS	PROBING QUESTIONS
Accuracy	Is the information verifiable by recognized authorities?	How can the information be verified? What expertise do the experts need?
Appeal	Does the document attract the intended audience?	What makes the document attractive to the audience?
Appropriateness	Does the document meet the needs of the intended audience?	In what ways does the document meet the needs of the intended audience?
	Does the document conform to conventions for the purpose, occasion, and genre?	What conventions does the document use? How will the audience interpret these conventions?
Accessibility	Is the information in the document easy to locate?	What devices are used to make information in the document easy to locate? What reduces accessibility?
Effectiveness	Does the document work the way it was intended?	How will users use the document.
Usability	Can users accomplish what they're supposed to with the document?	What problems do users have accomplishing what they're supposed to?

Types of Document Testing

So that you can decide how to effectively test the documents you write, you'll need to learn some basic information about categories of document testing.[2]

- *Text-based testing* focuses on the document itself—the words, sentences, and paragraphs. Text-based testing emphasizes adherence to conventions and correctness. For example, Does the report have all the expected sections? or, Have spelling errors been eliminated?
- *Expert-based testing* focuses on a number of different areas of specialization: the accuracy of the content, the appropriateness of the organization, or the effectiveness of the design.

- *User-based testing* focuses on the usability of a document. User-based testing can be *concurrent*, assessing a document's usability while a person is using the document; or *retrospective*, assessing a document's usability after a person has finished using it. For example, can users complete the task without frustration or error?

You are probably already familiar with some *retrospective user testing* methods including questionnaires, interviews, focus groups, comprehension tests, and reader-feedback cards. You may be less familiar with methods of *concurrent user testing*: observation, think-aloud protocols, reading protocols, co discovery, and active intervention. Figure 2 summarizes these basic categories, definitions, and methods of document testing.

Regardless of the types of testing you choose, the goal is the same: to make a better document. Every type of document testing provides you with data that you can use to revise your document. Imagine that you have written a new segment about harassment for the company's policy manual. This segment is important, so you decide to reduce the chances of misinterpretation by doing several types of document testing. For example, a computer style checker can give you feedback about the document's sentence structure to help you

Figure 2 Types of Document Testing

CATEGORY OF DOCUMENT TESTING	DEFINITION	METHODS OF TESTING
Text-based testing Is the text conventional and correct?	Concentrates on words, sentences, and paragraphs in a document	• checklists • readability tests • computer programs to assess structural or stylistic features
Expert-based testing Are the content and format approved by qualified experts?	Gathers information from technical reviews, editorial reviews, document design reviews	• technical accuracy • adherence to genre and language conventions • design consistency
Reader-based or usability testing Can the intended audience use the text successfully?	Gets information about a document's usability directly from the users in two ways: 1. *Concurrent testing*—assessment while readers use a document	• *Observations:* Observe the amount of time and apparent ease (or difficulty) a reader or user has in locating information or performing tasks. • *Think-aloud protocols:* Ask a reader or user to think aloud—that is, to say aloud all comments, reactions, and opinions, which you tape-record and often transcribe. • *Reading protocols:* Ask a reader to read aloud as well as to stop at marks (cues) in the text and comment about the context and/or predict what's to come. • *Co-discovery:* Observe two (or occasionally more) users working together to discuss and solve a problem or complete a task. • *Active intervention:* Observe a user and intervene periodically to ask the user to explain what she is doing . . . and why.
	2. *Retrospective testing*—assessment after readers have finished using a document	• questionnaires • interviews • focus groups • comprehension tests • reader-feedback cards

do sentence-level revisions. Similarly, feedback from a subject-matter specialist gives you information to correct parts of the segment that might be interpreted as misrepresenting the state's laws. And observations of the time and apparent ease (or difficulty) a user has in locating information or performing individual tasks or sequences of tasks give you information to make the document more usable.

Create a Testing Plan[3]

You need to decide which documents to test on the basis of these factors:

- *Distribution:* Will a large number of people read the document?
- *Criticality:* Is the document central in decision making or task performance?

Documents that have a wide distribution and that are critical to the organization need to be tested at several points in their development, not just at the end. Most organizations have review processes in place that require some text-based and expert-based tests. User-based testing is far less frequently used, even though it's the only kind of document testing that tells how readers react.

To conduct a user-based test, you need sampling criteria so that you can test a representative portion of a document. The following criteria are commonly used:

- segments that you suspect might have problems for users
- segments of material you see as particularly difficult or complex
- segments that you assess as having special importance

When you user-test a document or the selected segments, you need some way of assessing readers' reactions. Two common measures track reader performance:

- *Time:* how much time people take to find information, perform a task, or recover from errors
- *Frequency:* how many times people return to the instructions, repeat the same error, or show visible frustration, confusion, or satisfaction

Sometimes, though, you might be more interested in measures that assess reader reactions:

- *Ratings:* the ease or difficulty of learning the task, using the product, or understanding the information.
- *Preferences:* readers' opinions about one version versus another or one brand versus another.
- *Predictions of behavior:* readers' responses to specific questions: Would you use this manual? Would you use the revised procedure?
- *Spontaneous comments:* spontaneous, unsolicited comments during an observed or tape-recorded test that indicate attitude: "I'm totally lost here." "That was easy." "At this point I'd call for help."

Reader-based or usability testing can provide valuable information about the scope and severity of problems users might have with a document. Writers with access to testing results can make documents more accurate, appealing, and appropriate for an intended audience.

User-based testing should involve real users doing real tasks. The scenarios you develop to test whether the documents work in particular situations should be short and unambiguous. Figure 3 on the next page summarizes the steps you should take before, during, and after observation of a user.

Once you have completed the document testing, you need to analyze the data you've collected. The analysis identifies places where the document can be improved. In doing this analysis, you can look for trends or patterns as well as for surprises. For example, if you notice that several users go back and reread a particular section of a paragraph in a report, then pause, and then re-read it again, hesitating after certain phrases, you can be fairly certain that this section is causing confusion and needs to be revised.

When you have analyzed the data from the various document tests, you need to organize the problems by their breadth as well as by severity so that you can rank-order the changes that are needed. Because of constraints (usually time and money), you need to decide which changes to make:

- Fix global problems before local problems.

Figure 3 Process of Observations to Collect Data

BEFORE OBSERVING	WHILE OBSERVING	AFTER OBSERVING
• Know the product that the user is using. • Know the goals of the task the user is performing. • Get into the observer role.	• Keep 100% of your attention on the user. • Observe actively. • Record observations, hypotheses, and interpretations. • Write down changes that occur to you. • Censor tendencies to justify or defend your text. • Record all user problems.	• Discuss your interpretation with others. • Ask questions of the user during debriefing. • Make sure you have support from the user for your interpretations.

- Consider whether the effort of the writer to make a particular change is worth the benefit that will result for the reader.

You need to retest the document to be sure that the revision works.

Use the Results of Document Testing

A document that is appropriate for the audience is accessible, effective, and usable. Well-designed documents have numerous benefits:

- saving time and frustration in document design and development
- saving money in service calls, maintenance, training, and revisions
- reducing need for frequent revisions and updates to correct errors
- improving customer service as well as the organization's image

ACTIVITIES AND QUESTIONS FOR DISCUSSION

1. Imagine you have to argue for the development of a testing program in your company. Based on what you have learned about testing, develop a statement advocating the development and implementation of a testing program. Write a brief memo proposal to your manager (who will pass it along up the chain of command).
2. Select a document that you have written or that a team you're on has written. Using the table to help focus your decisions, outline a testing plan for the document.

   a. Identify the document to be tested.

   b. Identify the purpose of testing.

   c. Identify the category of testing as well as the specific type(s):

Text-Based Testing	Expert-Based Testing	User-Based Testing
Type of text-based testing—what text features are being assessed?	Type or focus of expert-based testing—what aspects of the document are being assessed by experts?	Type of user-based testing—how is the usability being assessed?
Date of text-based testing:	Date of expert-based testing:	Date of user-based testing:
Person conducting the text-based testing:	The expert(s) doing the expert-based testing:	The user(s) doing the user-based testing:
Measures used in text-based testing:	Measures used in expert-based testing:	Measures used in user-based testing:

d. Establish the testing situation by completing the following table:

Text-Based Testing	Expert-Based Testing	User-Based Testing
Identify the methods used to assess the text features.	List the questions you want expert(s) to answer.	Create the scenario(s) for the user-based testing.
	1.	Scenario 1
	2.	
	3.	
	4.	Scenario 2
	5.	

3. Implement the test plan that you outlined in item 2. You will need to decide which text-based evaluations to use. You will also need to find experts (unless someone in your group qualifies). Analyze and report the data. Include your recommendations for modifying the document based on the test results.

Appendix A

FORMATS FOR BUSINESS DOCUMENTS

Effective communicators know that format, the way information is arranged on a page, helps readers to move through documents in a predictable and logical fashion. This is not to say that there is only one effective way to format a document. Rather, readers expect to see certain format components in particular types of documents. Thus, format is like those conventions discussed in Chapter 6.

On a basic level, Figure A.1 fulfills the writer's purpose of conveying a new company policy. However, Figure A.1's format discrepancies muddle the overall effectiveness of the message. The revised memo (Figure A.2) addresses these format difficulties. Its concise and readable format not only contributes to clearly presenting information, but also creates a basis for the reader's confidence in the message and in the writer who is presenting it.

CONTEXT Figure A.1 is an internal memo meant to explain and rationalize a company's new petty cash policy. Although the memo is meant to be informal and nonthreatening, it still conveys a company procedure that must be followed. In Figure A.1, awkward or inconsistent formatting lessens the credibility of correspondence, thereby lessening the chances that the correspondence will be taken seriously. In Figure A.2, the format has been redesigned to add to credibility and readability.

SIGNIFICANCE OF FORMATS

Formats are less a question of rigidity than they are of consistency and fulfilling reader expectations. Reader expectations regarding format are often established in company stylesheets and may vary from corporation to corporation (see Chapters 1 and 2). What this appendix contains are basic format guidelines that may be adapted to specific organization constraints.

Most organizations recognize that document appearance acts as an extension of company image. The function of company stylesheets is to make that image consistent. For example, most organizations establish guidelines for how they want headings situated, greetings worded, persons addressed, and so on. Companies also specify how they want these guidelines to appear—whether it be a conventional block style or a customized style. These conventions can be as simple as Marshside's centering of its company logo and address at the top of all memoranda or as complex as AT&T's styleguide, which provides format guidelines for every component of every type of document it produces. Anyone who looks at AT&T documents will find that all correspond to specific guidelines and stylistic features; for example, all logos in document headings are a specific size, all margins in company memoranda are the same, and so on. Regardless of what type of organization you belong to, that organization is going to have some idea about how it wants its image and ideas conveyed through written documents, and you should be aware of these written conventions.

Because formats vary widely—from "traditional" memorandum style to block, modified block, and AMS (Administrative Management Society Simplified Letter format, also called AMS simplified) letter styles—we have provided you with guidelines that will help you format a wide variety of professional documents. The formats provided are not all-inclusive and should not be interpreted as such. These formats do not take away from the fact that you need to be aware of organizational considerations as well as the expectations of your audience. Once you have analyzed the communication context, you can select format components that best serve the needs of a particular communicative situation. In any case, the key is to use guidelines consistently throughout a document. In a business environment, you are judged by the documents you produce. Format inconsistencies within a document translate into inadequate and/or confusing documents, which make you and your organization look less than competent.

With these factors in mind, we have provided you with sections describing formats for business letters, memoranda, envelopes and fax cover sheets, resumes, reports, and brochures.

Figure A.1 Original Version of Petty Cash Memo

- *Tabs for introductory components should be aligned, not staggered.*
- *Because memo format doesn't have a signature line, the name of the sender should be initialed.*
- *"SUBJECT" is a more expected notation than the outdated "RE."*
- *Most readers anticipate the subject line to be written out in ALL CAPS.*
- *Memo format is intended to be direct, so information should be laid out in "chunks"—i.e., the paragraphs should probably not be indented but, rather, be separated by a double space.*
- *Although memos are intended as internal documents, that doesn't mean they should not be proofread as thoroughly as any other document. Note the spelling errors in B. J.'s memo that dilute the credibility of her message.*
- *Memo format uses initials in the "FROM" line as a signature. A signature line such as the one in this memo, while expected in letters, is not expected in memo format.*

Marshside Contracting Company

Ingold Office Park, Suite A-7
North Hwy. 34
West Kingston, RI 02892

DATE: July 23, 199-
TO: Roger Maldski
FROM: B. J. Haughton, Purchasing Supervisor
RE: New Company Petty Cash Policy

The petty cash vouchers on hand to account for the withdrawals from the petty cash fund are $23.09 short of what they should be for the month to date, and I now find it necessary to institute a new system for the disbursement of petty cash funds.

From now on we will need to sign a voucher for any given amount needed to return to the petty cash clerk a reciept for the item purchased as well as the difference in cash between the reciepte3d amount and the amount originally signed for. In this way there will always be cash or signed reciepts for the total amount of petty cash in the fund.

I hope this new policy doesn't create too many problems for you or the business, but it is essential that it be adhered to in order to facilitate the auditing of the business records for income tax purposes.

If you have any suggestions you fell might help improve this system, stop by my office and we can talk it over. This will also give you a chance to see the coffee maker I've installed. Now we won't have to look for change for the vending machine anymore.

Sincerely,

B. J. Haughton, Purchasing Supervisor

Figure A.2 Revised Version of Petty Cash Memo

- *Notice the clean alignment of entries in this revised introductory section.*
- *In memos, the initialing in the "FROM" entry serves as the signature for the document.*
- *"SUBJECT" allows the reader to immediately find what the memo is about, and the use of ALL CAPS in the entry calls the reader's attention to the context of the memo.*
- *Each paragraph is "chunked" into a separate unit, enabling the reader to easily find information in the document.*
- *B. J. does a good job of highlighting important procedural aspects by placing them in a numbered list.*
- *B. J.'s use of a goodwill close provides a feedback mechanism for those receiving and/or having to implement the new policy.*

Marshside Contracting Company
Ingold Office Park, Suite A-7
North Hwy. 34
West Kingston, RI 02892

DATE: July 23, 199-
TO: Roger Maldski
FROM: B. J. Haughton, Purchasing Supervisor
SUBJECT: NEW COMPANY PETTY CASH POLICY

Because the petty cash vouchers on hand are $23.09 short of what they should be for the month to date, I now find it necessary to institute a new system for the disbursement of petty cash funds.

From now on all employees will be required to follow these steps in order to obtain petty cash funds:

1. Sign a voucher for any given amount needed from the petty cash fund.
2. Return a receipt for the item purchased, as well as the difference in cash between the receipted amount and the amount originally signed for.

In this way there will always be cash or signed receipts for the total amount of petty cash in the fund.

Although this new policy may be inconvenient for you as well as the business, it is essential that it be followed to facilitate the auditing of the business records for income tax purposes.

If you have any suggestions you feel might help in revision of the system, stop by my office between 9:00 a.m. and 10:00 a.m. any weekday and we can talk it over.

GENERAL BUSINESS LETTER FORMAT (SEE FIGURES A.3–A.5)

The table accompanying Figure A.3 overviews the basic structural components of all business letters. After reviewing these components, you can then refer to the letter model styles that we've provided in order to see what might work best for the communication situations that you will be encountering. We've included three basic format models that work for most business situations:

- Block (Figure A.3)
- Modified block (Figure A.4)
- AMS simplified (Figure A.5)

Note that although all these styles are different, block and modified block are really variations on the same theme: the variations are basically choices concerning indenting and tabs for addresses, complimentary close, and signature. AMS style, on the other hand, is a much different type of format, one that integrates memo-type components into a letter format.

Additional Business Letter Options

The following additional options for business letters can be seen in Figures A.4 and A.5, with the exception of the second page header shown in this section.

Component	Conventions	Special Cases
Subject line	• should be a double space below salutation • should be in ALL CAPS • acknowledged by placement; "RE" should not be used	• optional; indicates the topic of the correspondence • *AMS*—subject line is required
Attention line	• placed on the second line of the receiver's address	• intended to direct the correspondence to a particular reader or group within an organization, but that *does not mean* that others will not read it • salutation included, even if an attention line is used, if letter is addressed to organization • addresses specific person whenever possible
Enclosure notation	• placed a double space below last line of text (memo) or the signature block (letter)	• optional feature, but often an expected courtesy • more than one enclosure, use the word "Enclosures:" and list the items after colon
Copy notation	• placed a double space below enclosure line	• indicated by "cc," followed by list of recipients • notes others who are receiving copies of the correspondence • can be a necessary persuasive element in a letter of complaint
Postscript	• should be the last item in letter, double-spaced after the item preceding it	• used to update or reinforce information mentioned in the letter • "P.S." optional
Typist line	• placed a double space after signature and title	• needed when someone types the letter other than the letter's author
Second-page heading	• placed one inch from the top of the page • remaining text double-spaced under heading • first line of receiver's address (either personal or company name), page number, and date included	• used if letter is longer than one page

Example of Second-Page Heading

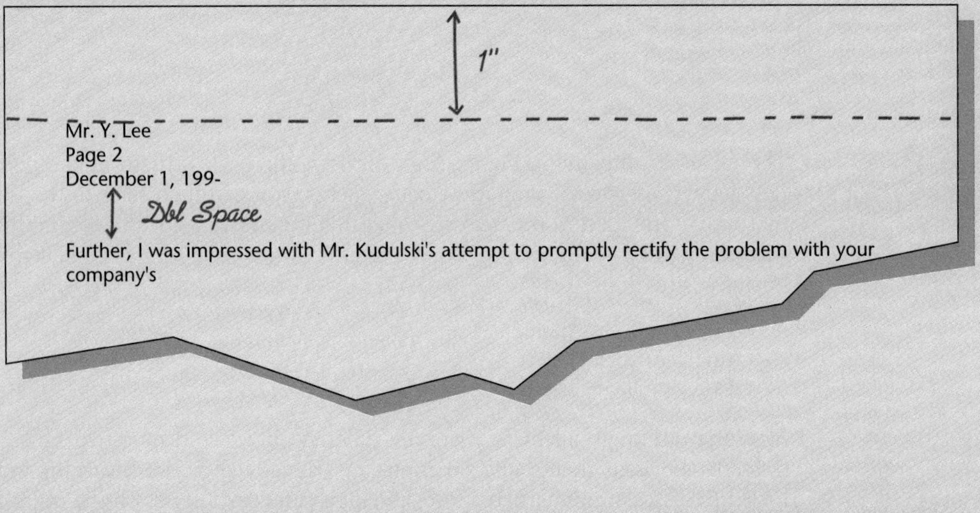
1"
Mr. Y. Lee
Page 2
December 1, 199-
Dbl Space
Further, I was impressed with Mr. Kudulski's attempt to promptly rectify the problem with your company's

The main features of all the letter styles are covered in Figure A.3. These features do not include all the options available to letter writers. For example, optional features such as subject lines, attention lines, second-page headings, enclosure notations, and so on, are discussed below and are integrated into either Figure A.4 or Figure A.5.

The assumption within all of these figures is that, unless otherwise noted, the spacing guidelines given in Figure A.3 are relevant to all the other letter formats presented. Further, in many of the examples, spacing is "flexible." The flexibility of certain spacing guidelines is dependent on the length of your letter and your organization's format specifications. In general, "flexible" in this appendix translates into "between 2 and 8 spaces."

MEMORANDUM FORMAT

There are several standard components of memoranda. These components are integrated into the example shown in Figure A.6. Unlike a letter, which you would attempt to center on the page, a memo will usually start one inch from the top of the page, regardless of length. Of course, the distance from the top of the page may vary according to the style rules of your organization, especially if you are using a centered company heading.

Memo Components

Component	Explanation	Issues and Considerations
Heading	Organizational letterhead should be the first item seen on the memo and should be centered and in all caps.	Optional section, but adds a more professional look to the document and may be expected in some cases.
"TO:" line	Write the name and job title of the people or group to whom you are writing.	If you have established a first-name basis with the addressee, using a first name is preferable to using a formal title, particularly since memos are meant to be informal and are most commonly used as an intraorganizational document.
"DATE:" line	List the entire date.	Important not just as an expected component, but also as a record-keeping device. The date is probably the key referent for follow-up correspondence.
"FROM:" line	This is where the individual or group sending the memo is identified. Should include name and title if appropriate. Must be initialed.	Unlike a letter, the "signature" of a memo is the signaled initials of the person(s) sending the memo
"SUBJECT:" line	This is the section that contextualizes your memo. Readers should know immediately why they should read or not read the memo you sent them. Can be in all caps.	The subject line needs to be relevant and meaningful. Avoid generalities such as "Sales" or "Budget Meeting."

Figure A.3 Standard Business Letter, Block Format

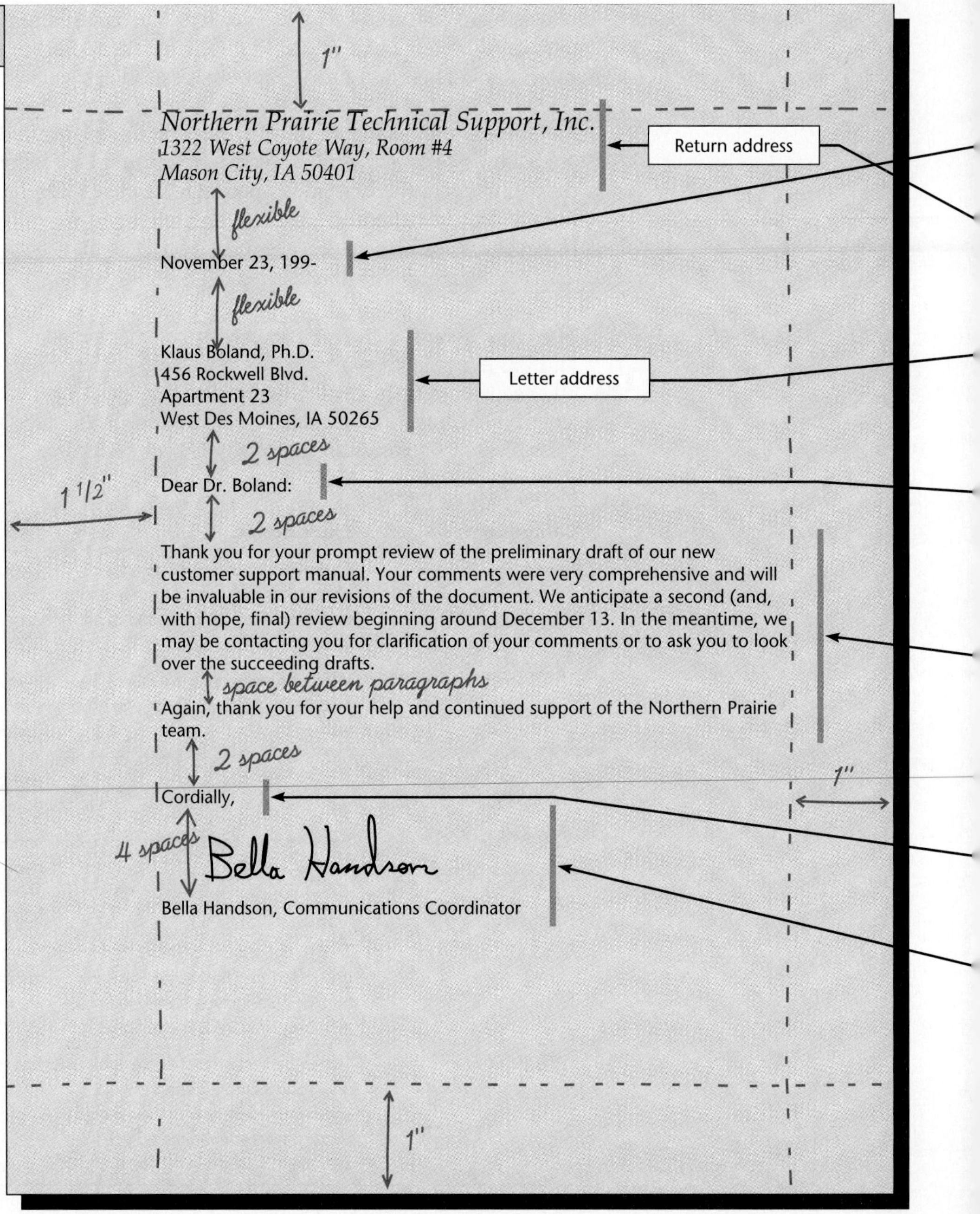

Northern Prairie Technical Support, Inc.
1322 West Coyote Way, Room #4
Mason City, IA 50401

November 23, 199-

Klaus Boland, Ph.D.
456 Rockwell Blvd.
Apartment 23
West Des Moines, IA 50265

Dear Dr. Boland:

Thank you for your prompt review of the preliminary draft of our new customer support manual. Your comments were very comprehensive and will be invaluable in our revisions of the document. We anticipate a second (and, with hope, final) review beginning around December 13. In the meantime, we may be contacting you for clarification of your comments or to ask you to look over the succeeding drafts.

Again, thank you for your help and continued support of the Northern Prairie team.

Cordially,

Bella Handson

Bella Handson, Communications Coordinator

Components of Business Letters

	Explanation	Issues and Considerations
Dateline	• Include month (spelled out), day, and year. • Place approximately 2 inches from top of page: — If *letterhead* is being used, place dateline two spaces below letterhead. — If *standard address* line is used, place dateline immediately below address.	• *Block*—date is aligned with left margin. • *Modified block*—date is placed in the right two-thirds of the page. • *AMS*—same as block.
Addresses: return and letter	• Include name (with Dr., Mr., Ms., etc.) and title of person, company (optional department), street address, city, state abbreviation, and ZIP. • Use nine-digit ZIP, which is now standard and expected.	• Unless the person explicitly refers to him- or herself as "Dr." or "Rev.," defer to "Mr." or "Ms." • Avoid using "Mrs." unless you are absolutely sure that is her preference. • Unless the addressee is in a leadership or noteworthy position, a title is not needed.
Salutation	• Use appropriate courtesy title unless you are on a first-name basis with the addressee. • Use "Ladies and Gentlemen" when addressing a letter to a general and unidentified audience.	• *Mixed style* of punctuation requires a colon after salutation. • *Open style* requires no punctuation after salutation. • *AMS* omits salutation.
Body	• Use single spacing; skip space between paragraphs. • Avoid indenting paragraphs. Indentation is appropriate only when a more "personal" style is wanted—in particular, when correspondence is addressed to customers.	• *Block*—paragraphs are not indented. • *Modified block*—indentation is optional. • *AMS*—paragraphs are not indented.
Complimentary close	• Rely on using *Sincerely* and *Yours truly* in more formal situations, *Cordially* in less formal.	• *Mixed style* of punctuation requires a comma after close. • *Open style* requires no punctuation after close. • *AMS*—close is omitted.
Signature and title	• Place title below signature unless both are short; then a comma can be used to separate.	• *Modified block*—initials after name and title in the"From" section at the top of the page substitute for a signature.

Figure A.4 Business Letter in Modified Block Style

BRANNICK & YONNELL
– ATTORNEYS AT LAW –
124 JEWELL COURT
ST. LOUIS, MO 63104

October 30, 199-

West Metro Insurance Investigators
St. Charles District Office
590 Elroy Road
St. Peters, MO 63076

> Notice that dateline, complimentary close, and signature and title are tabbed at about four inches from the left margin.

Dear Hubert:

I am sending you all the information I have on Mr. Stephanson's motor vehicle transactions.

I would like good documentary evidence from the county treasurer's office on each car bought, owned or sold by Stephanson after January 23, 1994, his last day at work. Also newspaper ads during that period might be interesting, since he said at his depositions that he hadn't offered any cars for sale in the last six months, except his 1989 Chevrolet Suburban.

The person I talked to at the *St. Peters Times Dispatch* front desk on October 19 was Kim Ullet. She was fairly helpful, but their record keeping system is hard to work with.

Let me know what you come up with. The hearing will probably be in December in O'Fallon. If you come up with anything, I will probably need you as a witness to get the evidence into the record.

Thanks for your assistance. Call if you have questions.

Yours truly,

Sally T. Yonnell

Sally T. Yonnell
Senior Partner

gu

> If someone typed the letter other than the author, note it here.

Encl.: copies of vehicles' registrations
copy of loan application
copy of loan acceptance letter

> As a common courtesy, you should inform the reader when there are other documents accompanying the letter. If there are multiple enclosures, they should be noted next to the "Encl." notation.

P.S. I am still searching for the buyer of the Suburban. I think I have the person's name, but he lives in rural Arkansas and has been hard to track down. If I find anything out on this front, I'll let you know.

> Although a bit dated and informal, a postscript notation informs the reader of additional information that is related to the letter but not directly relevant to the letter's main body.

Figure A.5 Business Letter in Simplified AMS Format

SCDS

SOUTHERN CALIFORNIA DESIGN SYSTEMS, #4 ELWAY STREET, LAKEWOOD, CA 90715

If you want to bring the letter to the attention of a particular person within an organization, you can integrate the attention line on the line below the organization's name or two spaces below the receiving organization's entire address.

October 19, 199-

Hillside Office Environments
ATTN: Ms. Matty Wuyn
35A Brohlick Place
Springfield, MO 65806

STATUS OF REFUND REQUEST

AMS simplified requires a subject line written in all capitals and no salutation line.

We appreciate your comments concerning our *Room Service 6.0* interior design software. Feedback from independent interior designers such as yourself is valued and allows us to keep up to date with customer needs and expectations.

We understand the disappointment you must feel when you buy expensive equipment and it doesn't perform as expected. Fortunately, we have just completed updating *Room Service 6.0*, and are pleased to include the updated version, *Room Service Deluxe 1.2*, at no additional charge. We think *Room Service Deluxe* will provide the additional lighting and textural features you wrote to us about, and if you find that *Room Service Deluxe* does give you the features you need, all we ask is that you send back your original copy of *Room Service 6.0* at our cost.

Again, we appreciate your business, and hope that you will find your new software of use and will keep in touch with us.

Best wishes

Notice that the open punctuation in the complimentary close is consistent with the lack of punctuation in the subject line.

M. J. KADULSKI, DISTRICT MANAGER

ou

cc: Y. Lee Vice-President of Customer Service

If a copy of the letter was given to a third party, you should note such at the bottom of the letter. "Carbon copying" can be a useful device in displaying goodwill (such as the example here where the customer is informed that high-level management is informed of her concerns) or a forceful persuasive device, such as sending a carbon copy to your attorney.

Figure A.6 Example of Memo Layout

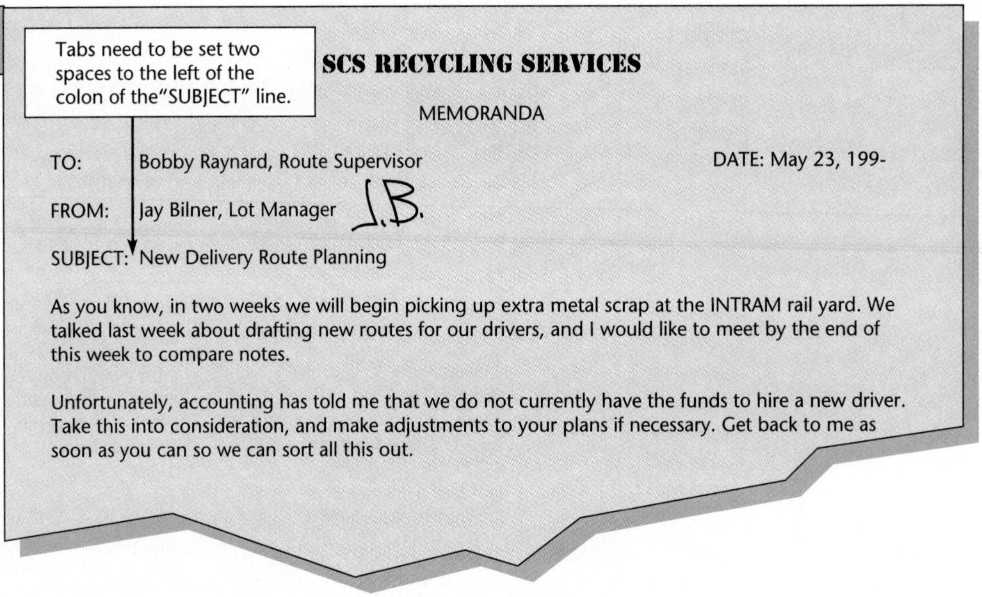
Tabs need to be set two spaces to the left of the colon of the"SUBJECT" line.
SCS RECYCLING SERVICES
MEMORANDA
TO: Bobby Raynard, Route Supervisor
DATE: May 23, 199-
FROM: Jay Bilner, Lot Manager J.B.
SUBJECT: New Delivery Route Planning
As you know, in two weeks we will begin picking up extra metal scrap at the INTRAM rail yard. We talked last week about drafting new routes for our drivers, and I would like to meet by the end of this week to compare notes.
Unfortunately, accounting has told me that we do not currently have the funds to hire a new driver. Take this into consideration, and make adjustments to your plans if necessary. Get back to me as soon as you can so we can sort all this out.

ENVELOPES AND FAX COVER SHEETS

Envelopes and fax cover sheets also have format conventions.

Figure A.7 Envelope Format

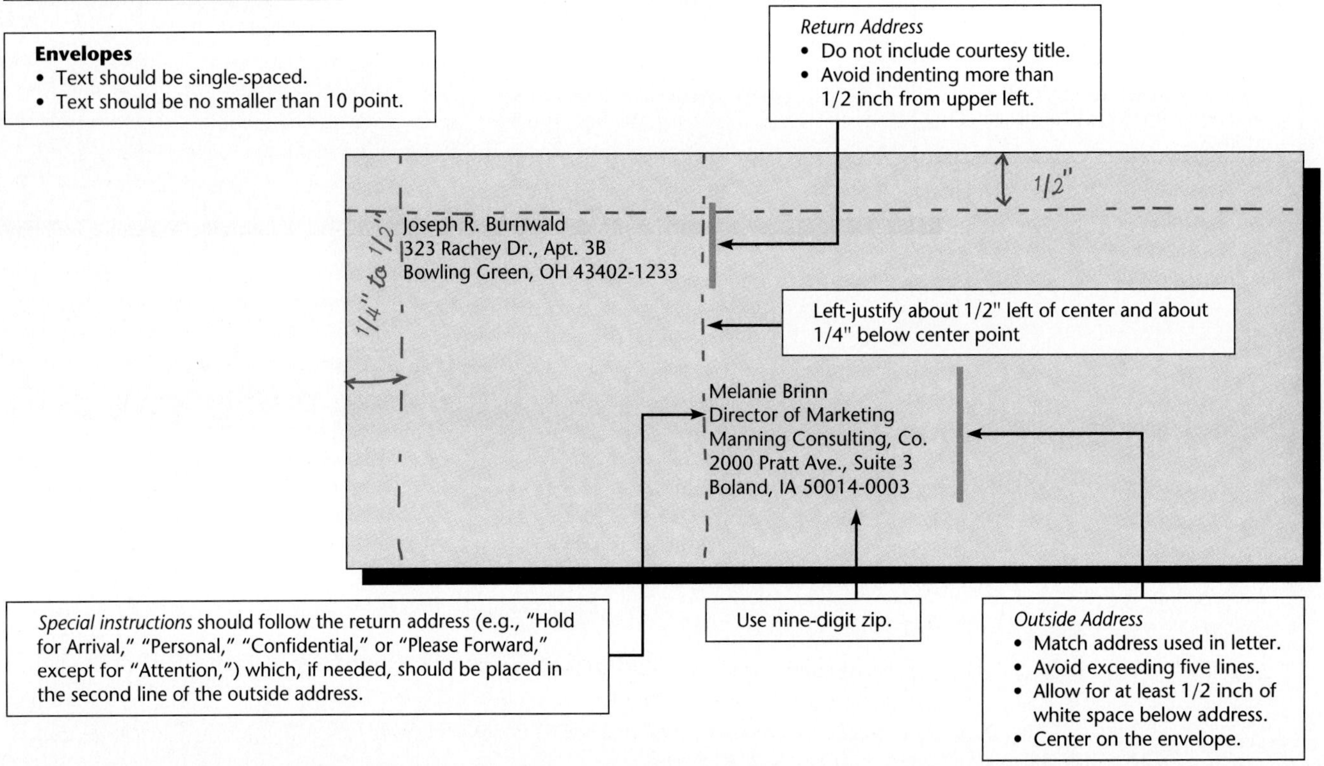

• Text should be no smaller than 10 point.

• Do not include courtesy title.
• Avoid indenting more than 1/2 inch from upper left.

Joseph R. Burnwald
1323 Rachey Dr., Apt. 3B
Bowling Green, OH 43402-1233
Left-justify about 1/2" left of center and about 1/4" below center point
Melanie Brinn

Manning Consulting, Co.
2000 Pratt Ave., Suite 3
Boland, IA 50014-0003
Special instructions should follow the return address (e.g., "Hold for Arrival," "Personal," "Confidential," or "Please Forward," except for "Attention,") which, if needed, should be placed in the second line of the outside address.

Outside Address
• Match address used in letter.
• Avoid exceeding five lines.
• Allow for at least 1/2 inch of white space below address.
• Center on the envelope.

Figure A.8 Fax Cover Sheet

Fax Cover Sheet

- Keep it simple; information should be accessible and expected.
- Make sure all necessary texts are included in order after the cover sheet.

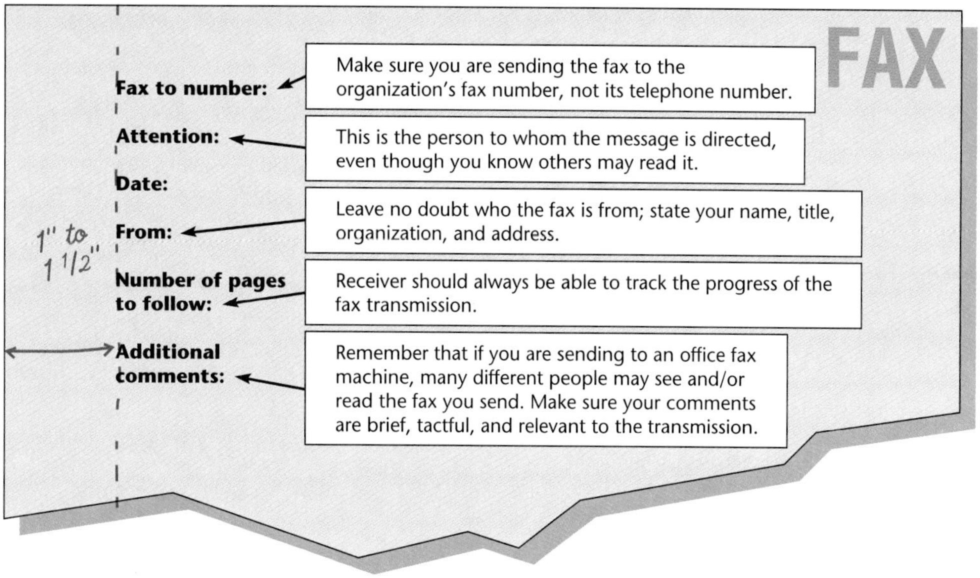

RESUME FORMAT

The resume format component box outlines and explains the general components of resumes. Figures A.9 (Combination Resume), A.10 (Chronological Resume), and A.11 (Skills Resume) show some possible style options to consider when drafting a resume (read Chapter 18 for in-depth discussion of resume rationale and strategy). It is important for you to remember that your resume should draw attention to how your skills, experiences, and abilities are compatible with the needs of the organization to which you are applying. If information is important enough to be put on your resume, it is important enough to stand out. Try to avoid burying your information in paragraph-style sections that force the reader to read the whole section. Make your information easy to see.

Note the explanation at the top of each resume example which suggests how each person has geared his or her skills to the type of position applied for. In particular, notice how Conrad, in Figure A.11, has adapted his skills to a position that, while perhaps not in the same field as his previous jobs, values the same skills he derived from his previous employment.

Look at the pre-drafting checklist for resumes for an overview of resume drafting considerations. In particular, you need to be aware of the following when drafting the best resume for a given situation:

- the audience's expectations
- your strengths, skills, and experiences and how they fit the audience's needs and expectations
- the visual power of your resume
- the resume's overall features and how they come together to create the text that will define you to a potential employer

Figure A.9 Combination Resume

Notice how all the sections stand out due to effective use of white space and bulleting.

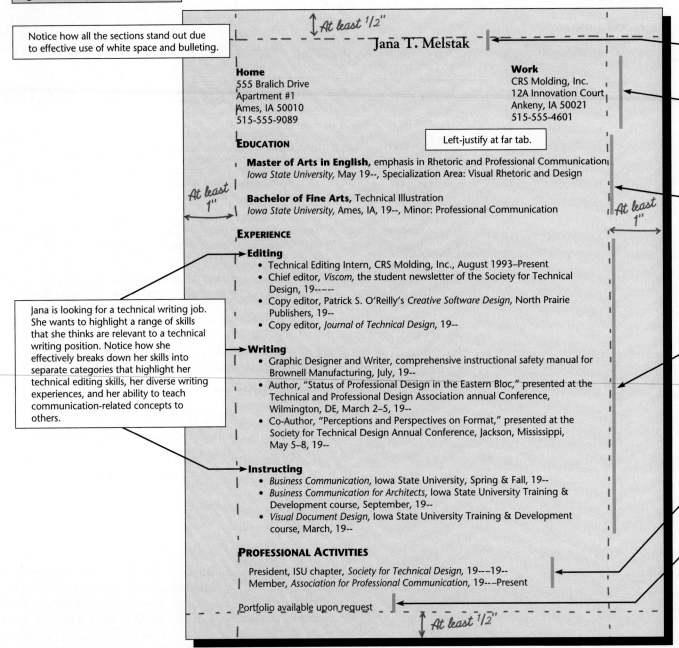

At least 1/2"

Jana T. Melstak

Home
555 Bralich Drive
Apartment #1
Ames, IA 50010
515-555-9089

Work
CRS Molding, Inc.
12A Innovation Court
Ankeny, IA 50021
515-555-4601

Left-justify at far tab.

EDUCATION

Master of Arts in English, emphasis in Rhetoric and Professional Communication
Iowa State University, May 19--, Specialization Area: Visual Rhetoric and Design

Bachelor of Fine Arts, Technical Illustration
Iowa State University, Ames, IA, 19--, Minor: Professional Communication

At least 1"

At least 1"

EXPERIENCE

Editing

- Technical Editing Intern, CRS Molding, Inc., August 1993–Present
- Chief editor, *Viscom,* the student newsletter of the Society for Technical Design, 19-----
- Copy editor, Patrick S. O'Reilly's *Creative Software Design*, North Prairie Publishers, 19--
- Copy editor, *Journal of Technical Design*, 19--

Jana is looking for a technical writing job. She wants to highlight a range of skills that she thinks are relevant to a technical writing position. Notice how she effectively breaks down her skills into separate categories that highlight her technical editing skills, her diverse writing experiences, and her ability to teach communication-related concepts to others.

Writing

- Graphic Designer and Writer, comprehensive instructional safety manual for Brownell Manufacturing, July, 19--
- Author, "Status of Professional Design in the Eastern Bloc," presented at the Technical and Professional Design Association annual Conference, Wilmington, DE, March 2–5, 19--
- Co-Author, "Perceptions and Perspectives on Format," presented at the Society for Technical Design Annual Conference, Jackson, Mississippi, May 5–8, 19--

Instructing

- *Business Communication*, Iowa State University, Spring & Fall, 19--
- *Business Communication for Architects*, Iowa State University Training & Development course, September, 19--
- *Visual Document Design*, Iowa State University Training & Development course, March, 19--

PROFESSIONAL ACTIVITIES

President, ISU chapter, *Society for Technical Design*, 19---19--
Member, *Association for Professional Communication*, 19---Present

Portfolio available upon request

At least 1/2"

Resume Format Components

Component	Rationale
Name	Essentially, this is what sets the context for the entire document—i.e., all resume entries will be attributed to *your name*. Center your name about an inch below the top of the page and use ALL CAPS and/or **Bold** to make it stand out.
Address	Remember, you want to make it as easy as possible for the person reading your resume to contact you. Include your present address as well as another address where you can be reached. • *Work address* is an option, but make sure that your current employer won't have a problem with people calling you at work. • *Permanent address* may be a better secondary option. This address should be of a place where you will be sure to be given the message (e.g., parent's house).
Education	The highest-level heading in this section should parallel what you feel is more suitable to the specific position applied for. If your degree matches the position, foreground your degree; if you are applying for a job not directly related to your degree, or if you think your college carries a level of prestige, foreground the college.
Experience	Focus only on college-age experience. Depending on the extent of your experience, you may want to divide your experiences into specific sub-categories. However, avoid too many subcategories; you want to sell skills, experience, and/or specific training. Whichever of these categories is most suitable to the position applied for, foreground that area. The other categories should be used to supplement and support your resume's main selling points.
Professional activities, honors, and awards	Much like the Experiences section, this section should reflect only college-age experience. Avoid entries that may be misinterpreted as reflecting bias in some way. Make sure to note if you "won" or were "elected" or "chosen" for awards or organizational positions.
References	Often, too much emphasis is placed on the References section of the resume. Most people applying for a job have references, and employers know it. As a rule of thumb, only include references if you need to fill up the bottom 2 or 3 inches of your resume. Using "References available upon request" is obvious and should be avoided. A preferable option is to have a separate list of references (see Figure A.12) available for readers. That way, you have another tangible item to give them. The more they see your name, the more likely you are to stand out.

Figure A.10 Chronological Resume

As noted in his "Objective" section, Manuel is looking for a job that will allow him to utilize his bilingual abilities. In order to show that he can supplement those communicative abilities with solid business experience, Manuel decided to use a chronological format that illustrates his professional development.

Manual R. Radis

Present Address
5463$^{1}/_{2}$ 6th Street Place
Garland, TX 75044
(214) 555-0908

Permanent Address
2309 Tellera Drive
Edinburg, TX 78539
(210) 555-1322

Statements of objectives should be used when position applied for may not directly relate to background and/or education.

OBJECTIVE To secure a customer service position with an innovative company that would benefit from my business and bilingual communication skills

EDUCATION **Bachelor of Arts in English, minor in Economics**, May 19--
University of Texas at Dallas, Richardson, TX
Overall GPA: 3.24/4.00
- Vice-President, *UTD Mexican-American Student Association*, 19--
- Secretary, *Society for Business Writers*, 19--
- Member, *Dean's List*, Fall 19-- –Fall 19--
- Recipient, South Texas Merit Scholarship, 19--

EMPLOYMENT

February 19-- to Present

Document Designer and Writer, ABN Telemarketing, Mesquite, TX
Major Responsibilities:
- Design training documents to be used by new employees
- Write and edit company documents
- Participate actively in business meetings
- Communicate ideas and concepts in both Spanish and English to a broad variety of people

Although dates are foregrounded, there is still the need to show specific skills learned on a job.

November 19-- to January 19--

Copy Editor, *Texas Economist*, Dallas, TX
Major Responsibilities:
- Copy edited all aspects of trade journal text
- Translated several pieces for the *International News* section of journal
- Wrote business correspondence and newsbriefs

Instead of putting a high school job at the bottom of the page, Manuel fills out the bottom of his resume with References. Although a reference list is not necessary, it is a better addition to a resume than another job listing that may not add anything to your professional profile.

August 19-- to November 19--

Shift Manager, Waiter, and Greeter, Lula's Restaurant and Lounge Dallas, TX. Major responsibilities:
- Served over 400 customers a night
- Coordinated staffing and special events
- Supervised over 15 waiters, greeters, bussers, and food prep workers
- Trained all levels of staff in customer service and company policies

REFERENCES

Chooses the professor he is closest to and who is knowledgeable about his communication skills

Dr. Thurman P. Longley
Professor of English
University of Texas at Dallas
Richardson, TX 75080
(214) 555-4321

Dr. Mohammed Muruk
Professor of Economics
University of Texas at Dallas
Richardson, TX 75080
(214) 555-8973

Millie P. Stephans
CEO, ABN Telemarketing
Suite 6, The Mackey Building
67 North 10th Street
Mesquite TX, 75149
(214) 555-4302

Chooses a professor who is familiar with his professional, business-related skills.

Chooses a boss who can speak to his business experience.

Figure A.11a Skills Resume

Conrad has been successful at sales and retail management positions, but would like to enter the insurance and financial planning industry. Although he has no direct experience in this industry, Conrad thinks that he has learned many skills that would be attractive to insurance and finance recruiters. He chose a skills-oriented strategy that foregrounds both professional and personal skills and then details the extensive work history that provided him his varied skills and experiences.

Conrad V. Yeung
1253 Delmara Avenue, #3
Los Angeles, CA 90035
(213) 555-2569

PROFESSIONAL SKILLS

- Sell high volume of electronic, audio, and video equipment in a high traffic location
- Supervise and evaluate all levels of store workers
- Train professionals in selling and motivational skills
- Analyze customer needs and satisfy those needs promptly and efficiently
- Develop and maintain a budget and profitably manage cash flow

Notice how Conrad chose action verbs that stand out as someone skims down the line of entries.

PERSONAL SKILLS

- Motivate others, especially new employees
- Set and accomplish personal and organizational goals
- Communicate information clearly and concisely
- Generate creative ideas
- Plan and manage projects through to completion
- Interact in a professional, friendly manner

EXPERIENCE

Foregrounds his management/supervisory experience over his selling experience even though the events aren't necessarily chronological.

Management/Supervision:

Store Manager
Super V Electronics, Mountain View Shopping Center, Los Angeles, CA
August 1994–Present

Consistent use of adverbs again makes for ease of scanning and creates a "high-energy" look.

- Effectively coordinate and supervise all activities at top store in region
- Consistently exceed personal sales goals
- Thoroughly train and motivate employees
- Profitably develop budget and maintain financial responsibility for over $5 million dollars in store merchandise

Shipping/Receiving Supervisor
Mori Electronics Distribution Center, Long Beach, CA
August 1991–December 1992

- Accurately maintained extensive shipping/receiving records
- Pro-actively analyzed and solved potential problem areas
- Effectively supervised 12 dock and office workers
- Thoroughly learned customs regulations and extensive inventory database tracking system

Figure A.11b Skills Resume

Two-page resumes need a heading and page number at the top of the second page.

Yeung Resume 2

Should be even with name on first page

Store Manager
Eddie's Records and Tapes, Santa Monica, CA
June 1986–August 1987
- Effectively administered all daily store operations
- Efficiently interacted with various-sized international and regional distributors
- Developed promotions and community-service activities

Sales/Customer Service:

Sales Representative
Super V Electronics, Bakersfield, CA, and Los Angeles, CA
January 1993–August 1994
- Successfully met or surpassed sales quotas every month of employment
- Consistently provided excellent customer service
- Continually depicted a positive and professional image

Sales Representative and Selling Team Leader
MarliCo Wholesale Club, Reno, NV
October 1989–August 1991
- Progressively worked way up to top salesperson of the region
- Repeatedly achieved Customer Service Award (5 time winner)

EDUCATION

Bachelor of Arts, Philosophy
California State University–Los Angeles, Los Angeles, CA, 1986

AWARDS/RECOGNITION

Salesperson of the Year, Western District, January 28, 1994
Outstanding Achievement Award, September 23, 1992
Salesperson of the Month, September, 1993; January, March, June, 1993
Team Leadership Award, July 1991

REFERENCES

Mr. Sol Nelvy, District Manager
Super V Electronics, Inc.
1200 Seaview Avenue, Suite 4A
Placentia, CA 92670
(714) 555-8738

Chooses immediate boss; obviously, this reference does not have a problem with Conrad's looking for other work.

Mr. Mike Randoli, Store Manager
Super V Electronics, Inc.
145 Southern Hills Mall
Palo Alto, CA 94303
(415) 555-5678

Former business associate who is also successful

Ms. Randi I. Littler, Regional Manager
Tanaka Electronics Co.
545A Tanaka Boulevard
Sunnyvale, CA 94087
(408) 555-9090

A representative of a company that sells products in Conrad's store

Mr. Eddie McKeehan, Owner (Retired)
Eddie's Records and Tapes
7 Surfway Lane
Honolulu, HI 96846
(808) 555-0631

Personal reference who is also a former boss

Note that sometimes references are included on a separate sheet (Figure A.12).

Notice that Jana has divided up her references into two categories: those that can attest to her professional abilities and those that can attest to her personal attributes. This is not to say that there is not overlap between the two: those in the professional category should be able to attest to Jana's personal traits, and her personal references should be knowledgeable of her professional abilities.

Figure A.12 Separate Reference Page for a Resume

References for Jana T. Melstak

Professional

Darren G. Hayes, Chief Designer CRS Molding, Inc. 12A Innovation Court Ankeny, IA 50021-0000	Sara E. Dovel, Publications Editor Society for Technical Design #5 The Harrison Bulding Lexington, KY 40509-0000	Janet O. Ibers, Technical Writer Bownell Manufacturing 4 North 78th Court Des Moines, IA 50325-0000

Personal

Gary M. Radour Professor of Design Iowa State University Ames, IA 50011-0000 (515) 555-0769	Myron O. Baley, Architect Mallon, Morry, and Associates 659 Union Drive Dubuque, IA 52001-0000 (319) 555-8886	Martha P. Pewford Professor of English Iowa State University Ames, IA 50011-0000 (515) 555-7117

Before you begin drafting your resume, you should consider the following:

- Remember that your resume is how you are initially identified by the reader; sell the skills and experiences that will create a positive mental image of you and distinguish you as the best candidate for the position.
- Structure your resume's contents in a skimmable and scannable fashion by properly using white space, bullets, action verbs, and logical and consistent headings.
- Include only information that is true and relevant; avoiding "fluffing up" your positions or skills.
- Make sure that job titles, place of employment, location, and dates are included for job entries, and that degree (spelled out), college, location, and (anticipated) graduation date are included for education entries.
- PROOFREAD for spelling, punctuation, parallelism, and consistency.

REPORT FORMAT

The following table provides overviews and descriptions of components found in formal reports. Figures A.13 through A.17 are examples of these components. Organizations vary widely in terms of the "look" they try to create.

Organizational preferences are important. For example, when considering how to paginate the bibliographic section (Figure A.16) and the report's appendix (Figure A.17), remember that some organizations prefer to put page numbers in these sections and some do not.

You may also want to familiarize yourself with several software options that can efficiently design and format particular sections of reports, such as bibliographies and tables of contents.

These are factors you will need to consider before you begin writing your report (consult chapters 14 and 15 for more information):

- Awareness of the level of knowledge your intended audience has about your subject matter; the less knowledge they have, the more formal and comprehensive the report.
- Awareness of your organizational report style—there may be certain standard expectations about the look, organization, and content of reports.
- Regardless of what style you choose, consistency is of the utmost importance—know the style and draft your correspondence in accordance with the conventions of that style.

The following discussion notes standard report components, which are shown in Figures A.13, A.14, and A.15.

Standard Report Components

Component	Explanation	Issues and Considerations
Letter of transmittal (Figure A.13)	Will probably contain three main paragraphs: 1. introduces report's subject and purpose 2. focuses on one or two key points—e.g., central problem, recommendations 3. courtesy close, call to action	The letter of transmittal provides a context for the report that follows. Readers should be provided with enough information so they will know what to expect in the report.
Title page (Figure A.14)	Should contain three main sections (all centered): 1. report title	• Title type style should match highest-level heading found in text (e.g., ALL CAPS). • If report title is more than one line in length, double-space between lines and divide the lines according to logical units.
	2. person or group for whom the report is prepared	• Receiver line should be preceded by "prepared for" and then a space. • Receiver line should note title, company, and company address.
	3. identification of report writer(s)	• Preparer line should be preceded by "prepared by" and then a space. • Preparer line should note title, company, and company address. • Receiver line should include date after address and a space.
Table of contents (Figure A.15)	Three functions: 1. locating device for topics 2. forecasts extent and nature of topics 3. shows logical arrangement and relationship of parts	• A table of contents can serve as an outline while drafting report. • You should match entries to page numbers using a dotted line (easy for eyes to follow). • You also should space out entries; overcrowding can hinder referencing. • You need to match headings to highest-level heading style found in text.
Text body	Generally, all reports will have certain basic components—Overview, Background, Recommendations, Evidence, and Discussion—in basically the same order.	• All sections of the report must be easy to find (by good use of white space and by logical arrangement of headings). • Remember that reports are persuasive documents that are not to be weighted down with extraneous materials; this dilutes the power of the report.
Appendixes (Figure A.16)	If appendixes are used, they need to be listed in a separate section after the Table of Contents.	• Make sure that a section of appendixes is necessary. • Appendixes should be used only if visuals are referred to in multiple sections of the report.
Bibliography/works cited (Figure A.17)	In order to make a report credible, outside research data must be used to support the report's ideas and argumentative points. In so doing, all outside sources must be attributed within the text (footnotes, parenthetical citation, etc.) and in the bibliography.	• All outside sources must be cited. • You should become knowledgeable of your organization's style preference and use it properly and consistently.

Figure A.13 Letter of Transmittal

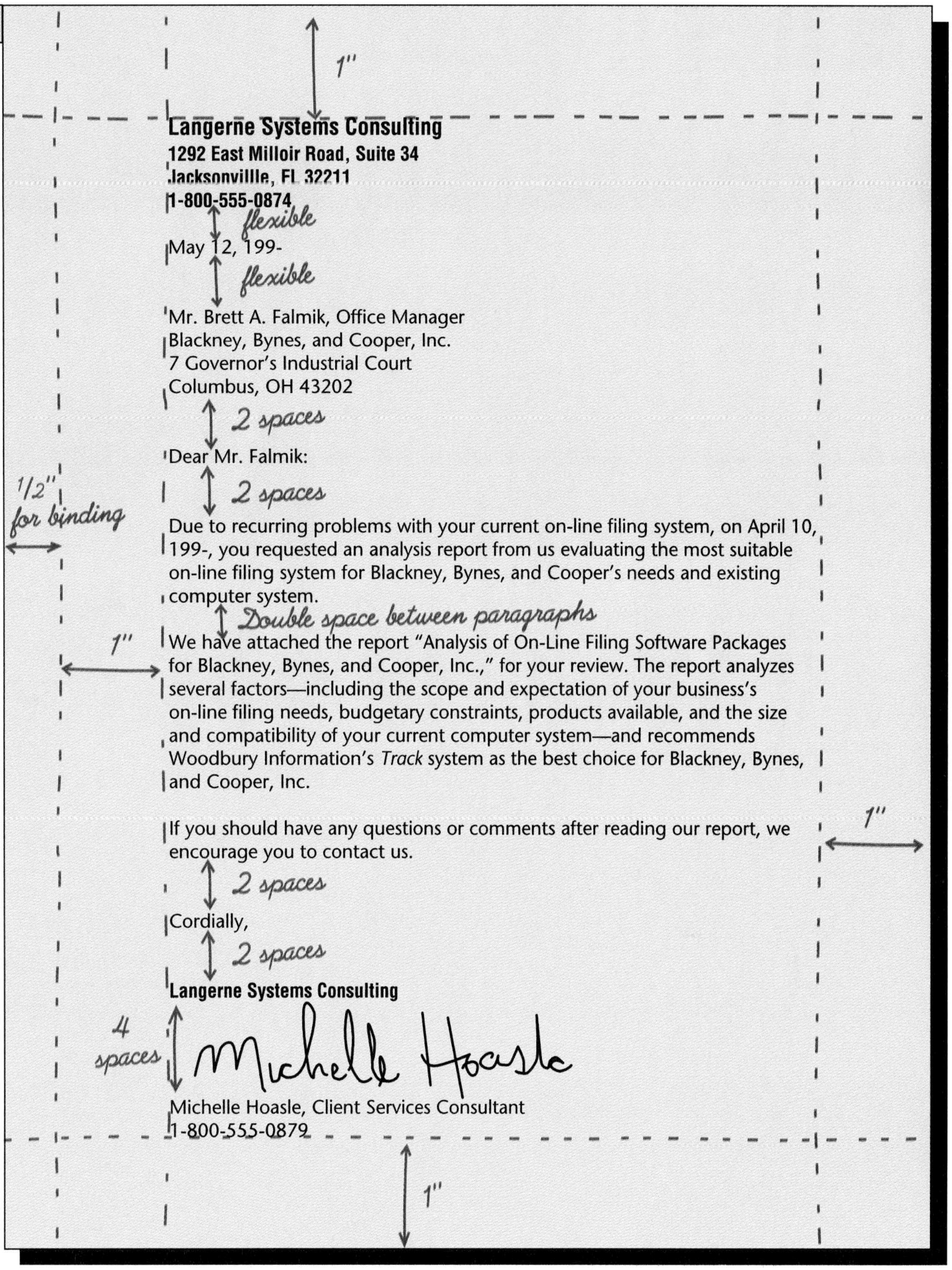

Langerne Systems Consulting
1292 East Milloir Road, Suite 34
Jacksonville, FL 32211
1-800-555-0874

May 12, 199-

Mr. Brett A. Falmik, Office Manager
Blackney, Bynes, and Cooper, Inc.
7 Governor's Industrial Court
Columbus, OH 43202

Dear Mr. Falmik:

Due to recurring problems with your current on-line filing system, on April 10, 199-, you requested an analysis report from us evaluating the most suitable on-line filing system for Blackney, Bynes, and Cooper's needs and existing computer system.

We have attached the report "Analysis of On-Line Filing Software Packages for Blackney, Bynes, and Cooper, Inc.," for your review. The report analyzes several factors—including the scope and expectation of your business's on-line filing needs, budgetary constraints, products available, and the size and compatibility of your current computer system—and recommends Woodbury Information's *Track* system as the best choice for Blackney, Bynes, and Cooper, Inc.

If you should have any questions or comments after reading our report, we encourage you to contact us.

Cordially,

Langerne Systems Consulting

Michelle Hoasle

Michelle Hoasle, Client Services Consultant
1-800-555-0879

Figure A.14 Title Page of a Report

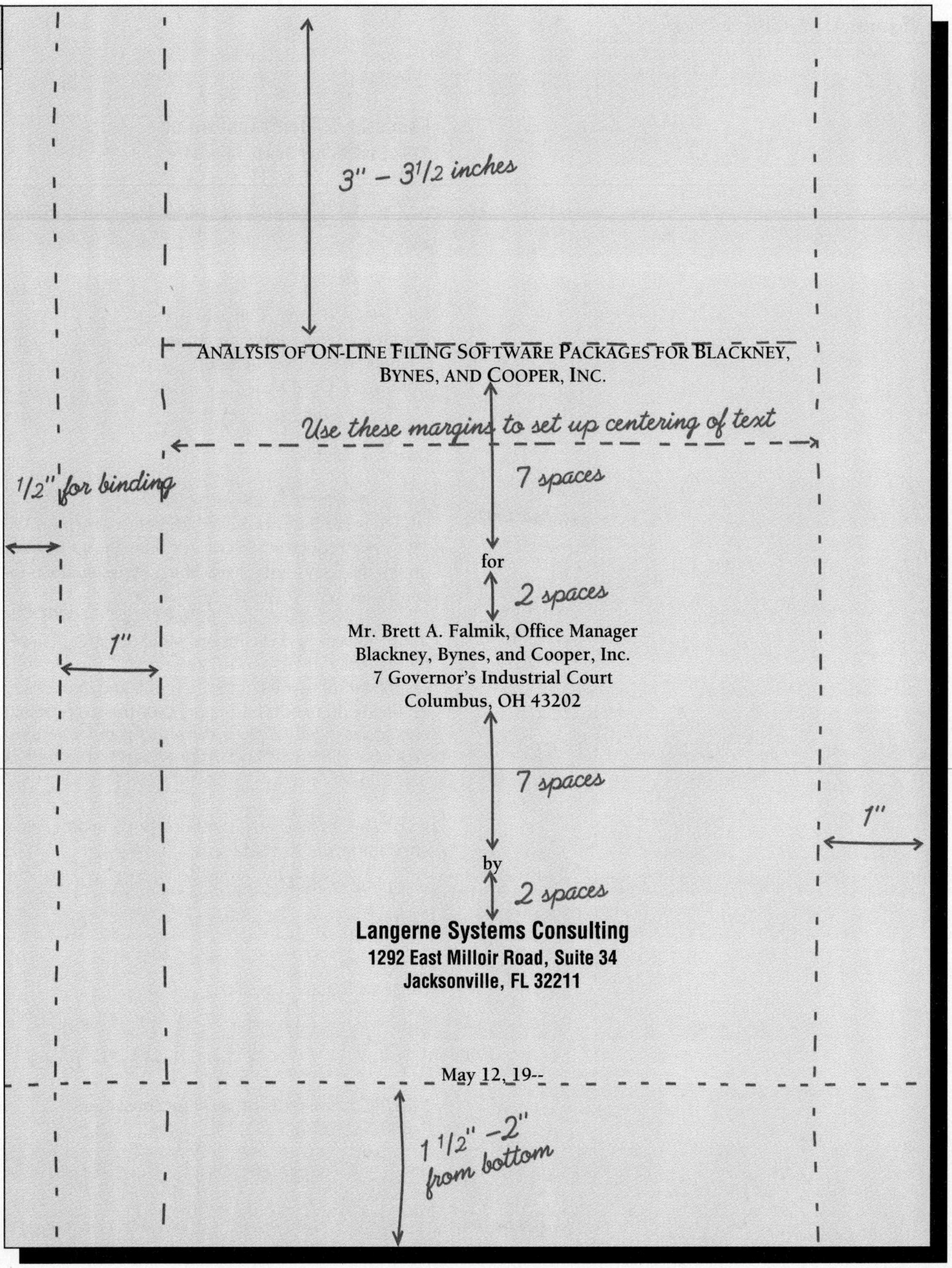

ANALYSIS OF ON-LINE FILING SOFTWARE PACKAGES FOR BLACKNEY, BYNES, AND COOPER, INC.

for

Mr. Brett A. Falmik, Office Manager
Blackney, Bynes, and Cooper, Inc.
7 Governor's Industrial Court
Columbus, OH 43202

by

Langerne Systems Consulting
1292 East Milloir Road, Suite 34
Jacksonville, FL 32211

May 12, 19--

Figure A.15 Report Table of Contents

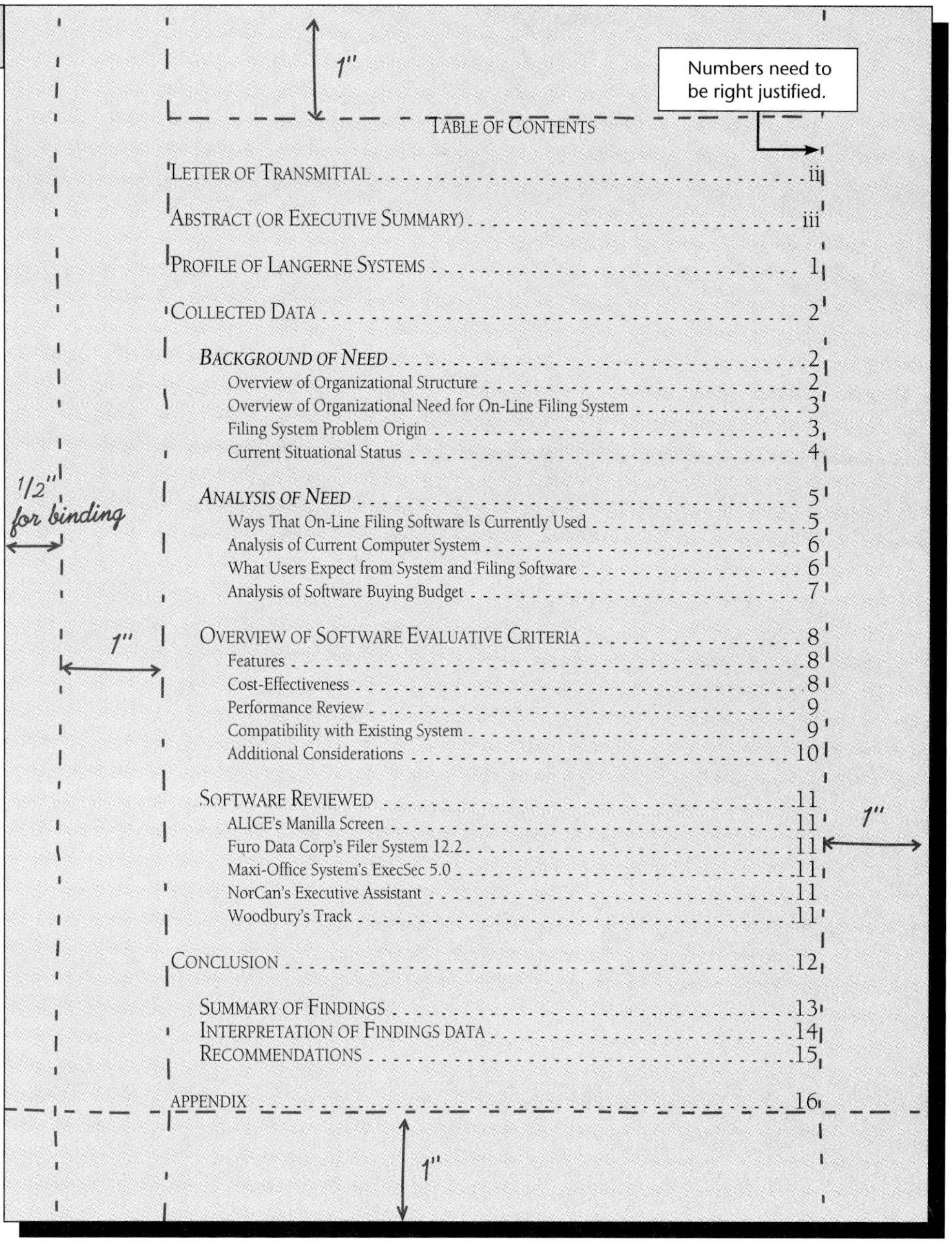

TABLE OF CONTENTS

LETTER OF TRANSMITTAL ii

ABSTRACT (OR EXECUTIVE SUMMARY) iii

PROFILE OF LANGERNE SYSTEMS 1

COLLECTED DATA 2

BACKGROUND OF NEED 2
Overview of Organizational Structure 2
Overview of Organizational Need for On-Line Filing System 3
Filing System Problem Origin 3
Current Situational Status 4

ANALYSIS OF NEED 5
Ways That On-Line Filing Software Is Currently Used 5
Analysis of Current Computer System 6
What Users Expect from System and Filing Software 6
Analysis of Software Buying Budget 7

OVERVIEW OF SOFTWARE EVALUATIVE CRITERIA 8
Features 8
Cost-Effectiveness 8
Performance Review 9
Compatibility with Existing System 9
Additional Considerations 10

SOFTWARE REVIEWED 11
ALICE's Manilla Screen 11
Furo Data Corp's Filer System 12.2 11
Maxi-Office System's ExecSec 5.0 11
NorCan's Executive Assistant 11
Woodbury's Track 11

CONCLUSION 12

SUMMARY OF FINDINGS 13
INTERPRETATION OF FINDINGS DATA 14
RECOMMENDATIONS 15

APPENDIX 16

Bibliography

- Familiarize yourself with the chosen bibliographic style used by your organization and be consistent in your usage of that style.
- Bibliographic entries are single spaced within the entry, but double spaced between entries.

Figure A.16 Bibliography Page Excerpt

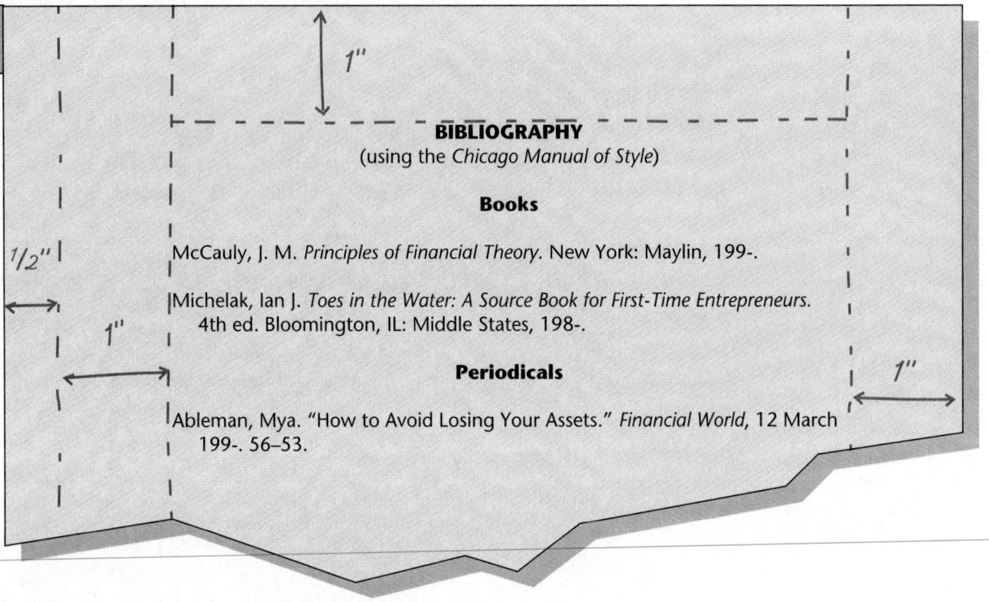

BIBLIOGRAPHY
(using the *Chicago Manual of Style*)

Books

McCauly, J. M. *Principles of Financial Theory.* New York: Maylin, 199-.

Michelak, Ian J. *Toes in the Water: A Source Book for First-Time Entrepreneurs.* 4th ed. Bloomington, IL: Middle States, 198-.

Periodicals

Ableman, Mya. "How to Avoid Losing Your Assets." *Financial World,* 12 March 199-. 56–53.

Appendix

- An appendix provides a central location for supporting texts or graphs that are frequently referred to in the text or are more illustrative than essential.

Figure A.17 Appendix Page Excerpt

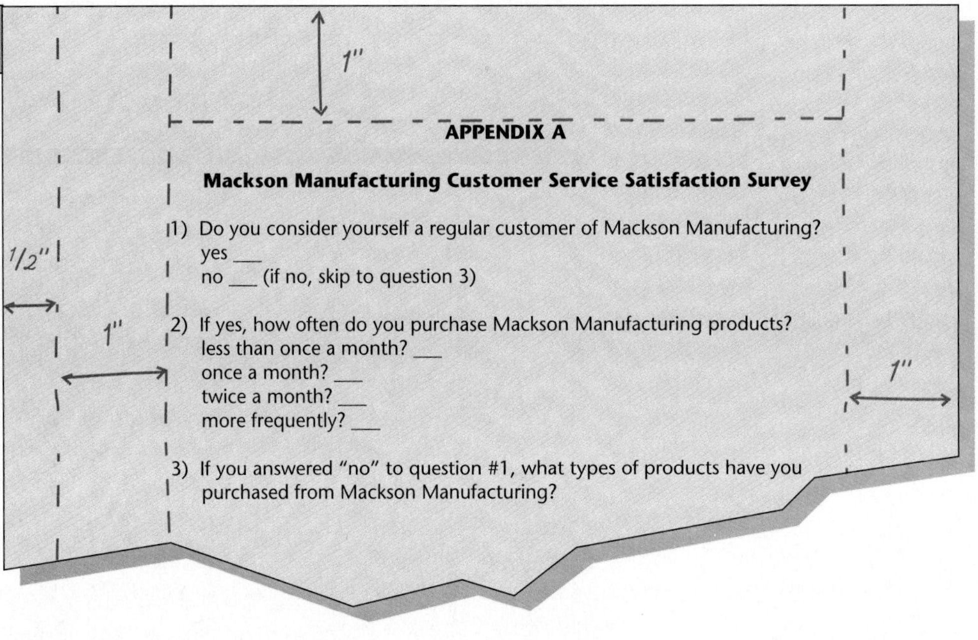

APPENDIX A

Mackson Manufacturing Customer Service Satisfaction Survey

1) Do you consider yourself a regular customer of Mackson Manufacturing?
yes ___
no ___ (if no, skip to question 3)

2) If yes, how often do you purchase Mackson Manufacturing products?
less than once a month? ___
once a month? ___
twice a month? ___
more frequently? ___

3) If you answered "no" to question #1, what types of products have you purchased from Mackson Manufacturing?

BROCHURE FORMAT

Brochures can be created in a variety of formats. You have probably seen two-fold brochures or brochures with horizontal folds and so on. Figure A.18 shows the general folding guidelines for brochures. We chose the three-fold example as a way to emphasize the types of things that you will need to consider in any brochure you produce (Figure A.19).

The key underlying consideration for you to remember when you are drafting brochures is that brochures should provide enough information to engage the reader and move them to action, without burdening them with too much detail. Most people come to a brochure voluntarily. Despite this aspect of reader cooperation, those writing brochures benefit from using persuasive strategies in designing their brochure (review, for example, the AIDA convention for presenting sales information, Chapter 10). Your document must grab the reader's attention. It must be eye-catching and appealing enough to make a reader want to pick it up and read it. Further, once the reader has picked up the brochure, you want to move them through it, establishing links between what you are talking about and their needs (establish *interest*). You then highlight key points you want them to remember, creating *desire* and then motivating them to take some *action*-after they have read the document. Brochures are limited in scope, but that does not mean they are limited in effectiveness. You need to remember, though, that the document's effectiveness is directly related to how easy the information is to find and process.

Figure A.18 Brochure Folds and Panels

The style of brochure you choose depends in part on the availability of mechanical facilities for folding. Before you design your brochure, check that the necessary folding machine is available. Otherwise the brochure could become an expensive, time-consuming hand-folding operation.

Most professionals printers have folding machines that will do two kinds of folds:

- *parallel folds:* Each fold is parallel to the other, whether in a two-panel brochure or in a computer printout that uses an accordion fold.
- *right angle folds:* Each fold is at right angles to the preceding fold, as in formal invitations that have two right angle folds.

There are various fold options:

- *four-panel brochure:* This is the simplest type of brochure, with only one fold along either the long (A) or short (B) dimension. These brochures are typically used as bill stuffers, price lists, instruction sheets, and so on.

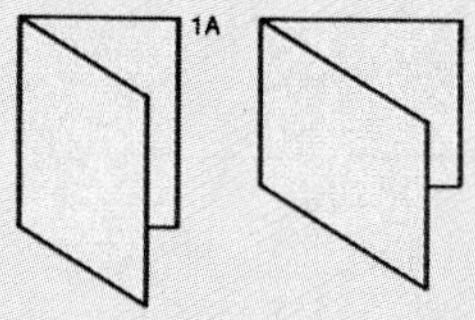

- *six-panel brochure:* This brochure is made with two parallel folds, either regular (A) or accordion (B). These brochures are typically used as envelope stuffers, promotional flyers, and so on.

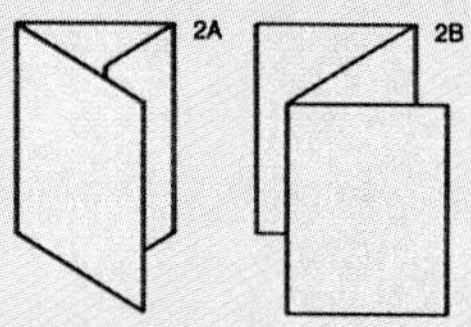

- *eight-panel brochure:* This brochure has three typical variations—(1) one parallel and one right angle fold, (2) two parallel folds and one accordion fold, and (3) three parallel accordion folds. Versions A and B can be bound and trimmed as booklets. Version A can also be opened up to present a poster for display.

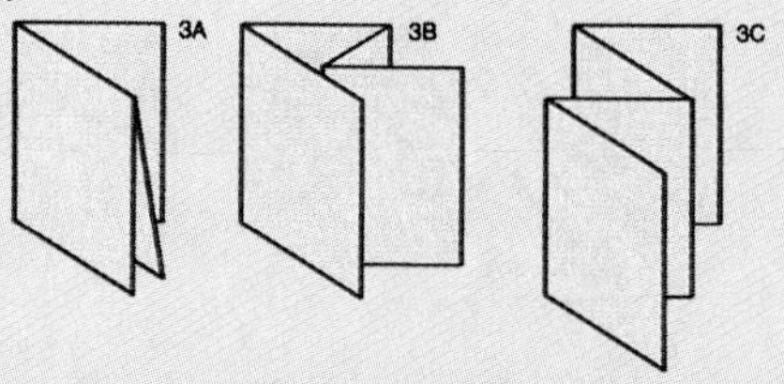

You also need to consider folding when you are calculating the cost. Most printers have a per fold charge, so an 8 1/2″ × 11″ piece of paper made into a four panel brochure will probably cost less than the same size paper made into a six-panel or eight-panel brochure.

Source: *Pocket Pal: A Graphics Arts Production Handbook.* International Paper Company. 1983.

Figure A.19 Sample Brochure Panels

The key to an effective brochure is to focus on one main selling point and make all the information brief and easy to find. The purpose of a brochure is to catch the reader's interest enough so they will take the next step: calling or writing for more information.

Cover Panel*—This should contain the "hook," an eye-catching feature that is short, visible, and helps target the audience you would like to pick up and read the brochure.*

Interior Panel*—Once you have caught the reader's attention enough to persuade them to open your brochure, you need to provide brief and "chunked" details that will make the reader want to find more information. The inner section of a persuasive brochure is the interest and desire section (see Chapter 10). Also, notice this brochure's use of a graphic as a central feature of the middle section.*

Back Panel*—Just as in a business letter, there needs to be an implied invitation to the reader to seek more information. You should make sure you provide the reader with the details necessary to contact the organization or persons noted in the brochure.*

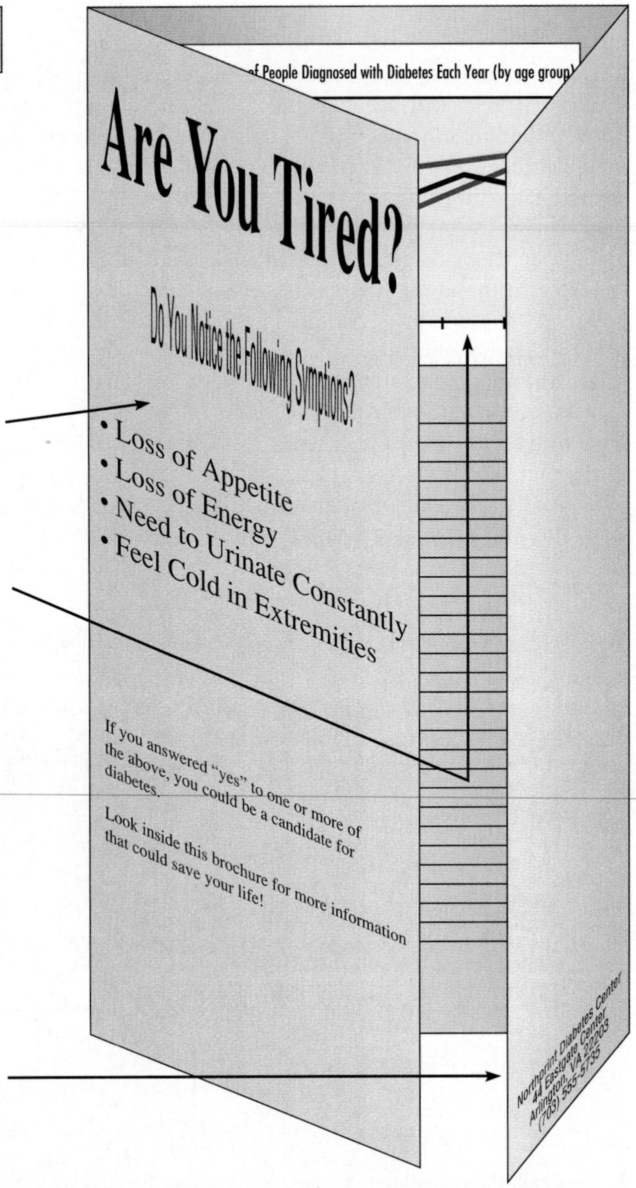

People Diagnosed with Diabetes Each Year (by age group
Are You Tired?
Do You Notice the Following Symptoms?
• Loss of Appetite
• Loss of Energy
• Need to Urinate Constantly
• Feel Cold in Extremities
If you answered "yes" to one or more of the above, you could be a candidate for diabetes.
Look inside this brochure for more information that could save your life!
Northprint Diabetes Center
44 Eastgate Center
Arlington, VA 22203
(703) 555-5735

Appendix B

DOCUMENTATION AND CITATION

Using Documentation and Citation

Documentation and Citation Formats

Journal Articles
- —Single Author
- —Two or Three Authors
- —More Than Three Authors

Interviews
- —Personal
- —With . . .

Reference Books
- —Signed Article in a Reference Book
- —Unsigned Article in a Reference Book

Newspapers
- —Signed Article from a Daily Newspaper
- —Unsigned Article from a Daily Newspaper

Books
- —One Author
- —Two or Three Authors
- —More Than Three Authors
- —Anonymous Authors
- —With an Editor
- —With an Author and an Editor
- —Edition Other Than the First
- —Corporate Author

Multivolume Works

Electronic Resources
- —CD ROM (and Abstract On)
- —On-Line Journal Article—General Access
- —Software—With Author
- —Software—No Author
- —Electronic Data File or Database
- —On-Line Journal—Subscriber Based

Proceedings
- —Proceedings of a Conference
- —Paper Given at a Conference

Media
- —TV Program
- —Audio Recording
- —Film

USING DOCUMENTATION AND CITATION

Documenting and citing the information you use not only shows that you are a careful researcher, but it enables your readers to make decisions about the credibility of your argument based on these resources. Careless, inadequate, or incomplete documentation and citation not only reflect badly on your professionalism, in some cases omitting documentation and citation is illegal.

- **Documentation** typically refers to the source lists that appear at the end of a document. When these lists are called *Sources*, *References*, or *Bibliography*, they typically list all sources used in the preparation of a document. When the list is called *Sources Cited*, it typically lists only sources actually referred to in the document.
- **Citation** typically refers to the in-text or end-of-document references for specific materials. These in-text notes (usually in parentheses or brackets), bottom-of-page footnotes, or end-of-document notes identify the source for quoted or paraphrased information. While text citations appear in the text or at the end of the document, citations for data in visuals (say, from the U.S. Census Bureau) or for entire visuals are typically placed immediately after the visual.

Whenever you use information from another source, you must cite the original source. Specifically, you need to provide citations in these circumstances:

- when you quote material directly, using the exact words from the original source
- when you paraphrase or summarize material, using your own words but generally reflecting the content and organization of the original source
- when you refer to any information (theories, practices, examples, and so on) that is unique to or typically associated with a specific person, publication, or organization
- when you use data or information from a source as the content for a visual
- when you use an entire visual of any sort

In some documents you may have to also provide a list documenting all of your sources. Whether this documentation is necessary depends on the guidelines of the organization you are working for or the publication you are writing for.

While many companies have their own guidelines for documentation and citation, many others depend on widely used standard formats. These are three of the most commonly used manuals:

- *Chicago Manual of Style*
- *Publication Manual of the American Psychological Association*, usually referred to as the *APA Manual*
- *MLA Handbook*, published by the Modern Language Association

Many businesses use the formats in the *Chicago Manual* or some variation of these formats. However, while many academic departments also use the formats in the *Chicago Manual*, others prefer formats in the *APA Manual* or the *MLA Handbook*. Appendix B provides *Chicago*, *APA*, and *MLA* documentation and citation formats for the most common kinds of sources you will use in preparing business documents.

DOCUMENTATION AND CITATION FORMATS

JOURNAL ARTICLES

Journal Article—Single Author

MLA Style

Nudell, Mayer. "Expose Yourself for Career Success." *Security Management* 36 (September 1992): 80.

In text: (Nudell 80)

Footnote: [1]Mayer Nudell, "Expose Yourself for Career Success," *Security Management* 36 (September 1992): 80.

APA Style

Nudell, Mayer. (1992, September). Expose yourself for career success. *Security Management, 36,* 80.

In text: (Nudell, 1992, p. 80)

Chicago Manual of Style

Nudell, Mayer. 1992. Expose yourself for career success. *Security Management* 36:80.

In text: (Nudell 1992, 80)

Footnote: [1]Nudell, "Expose yourself for career success," *Security Management* 36 (September 1992): 80.

Journal Article—Two or Three Authors

MLA Style

Longenecker, Clinton O., and Patrick R. Liverpool. "Making Yourself All Ears." *Management World* 17 (September–October 1988): 22–3.

In text: (Longenecker and Liverpool 22)

Footnote: [1]Clinton O. Longenecker and Patrick R. Liverpool, "Making Yourself All Ears," *Management World* 17 (September–October 1988): 22–3.

APA Style

Longenecker, Clinton O., Liverpool, Patrick R. (1988, September/October). Making yourself all ears. *Management World, 17,* 22–3.

In text: (Longenecker and Liverpool 1988, 22)

Chicago Manual of Style

Longenecker, Clinton O., and Patrick R. Liverpool. 1988. Making yourself all ears. *Management World* 17 (September/October): 22–3.

In text: (Longenecker and Liverpool 1988, 22)

Footnote: [1]Longenecker and Liverpool, "Making yourself all ears," *Management World* 17 (September/October 1988): 22–3.

Journal Article—More Than Three Authors

MLA Format

Aguilar, A., D. Martinez-Carrera, F. Parra, M. Sanchez-Hernandez, P. Morales, and M. Sobal. "Economic and Financial Analysis of a Rural Mushroom Farm in Cuetzalan, Puebla, Mexico." *Micologia Neotropical Aplicada* 6 (1993): 81–94.

Or: Aguilar, A., et al. "Economic and Financial Analysis of a Rural Mushroom Farm in Cuetzalan, Puebla, Mexico." *Micologia Neotropical Aplicada* 6 (1993): 81–94.

In text (follows the form of the bibliography): (Aguilar, Martinez-Carrera, Parra, Sanchez-Hernandez, Morales, and Sobal 81)

Or: (Aguilar, et al. 81)

Footnote: [1]A. Aguilar, D. Martinez-Carrera, F. Parra, M. Sanchez-Hernandez, P. Morales, and M. Sobal, "Economic and Financial Analysis of a Rural Mushroom Farm in Cuetzalan, Puebla, Mexico," *Micologia Neotropical Aplicada* 6 (1993): 81–94.

APA Style

Aguilar, A., Martinez-Carrera, D., Parra, F., Sanchez-Hernandez, M., Morales, P., and Sobal, M. (1993). Economic and financial analysis of a rural mushroom farm in Cuetzalan, Puebla, Mexico. *Micologia Neotropical Aplicada* 6, 81–94.

In text (first mention): (Aguilar, Martinez-Carrera, Parra, Sanchez-Hernandez, Morales, and Sobal 81)

(subsequent mentions): (Aguilar et al., 1993, 81)

Chicago Manual of Style

Aguilar, A., D. Martinez-Carrera, F. Parra, M. Sanchez-Hernandez, P. Morales, and M. Sobal. 1993. Economic and financial analysis of a rural mushroom farm in Cuetzalan, Puebla, Mexico. *Micologia Neotropical Aplicada* 6: 81–94.

In text: (Aguilar et al. 1993, 81)

Footnote: [1]A. Aguilar et al., "Economic and financial analysis of a rural mushroom farm in Cuetzalan, Puebla, Mexico," *Micologia Neotropical Aplicada* 6 (1993): 81–94.

INTERVIEWS

Interview—Personal

MLA Style

Gates, William. Personal interview. 10 October 1994.

In text: No in-text citation format suggested for personal interviews.

Chicago Manual of Style

Gates, William. Interview with author. Richmond, Washington. 10 October 1994.

References to interviews are best mentioned in the text.

Footnote: William Gates, personal interview with author, Richmond, Washington, 10 October 1994.

Interview—With . . .

MLA Style

Drucker, Peter. "Managing in a Post-Capitalist Marketplace." Interview. With Tom Brown. *Industry Week* 243 (January 3, 1994): 12–14+.

In text: (Drucker 12)

REFERENCE BOOKS

Signed Article in a Reference Book

MLA Style

Krooss, Herman. "Business and Industry, History of." *Collier's Encyclopedia.* 1989 ed., 20–27.

In text: (Krooss 20–27)

[1]Herman Krooss, "Business and Industry, History of," *Collier's Encyclopedia,* 1989 ed. 20–27.

APA Style

Krooss, Herman. (1989). Business and industry, history of. In *Collier's Encyclopedia* (1989 ed., Vol. 5, pp. 20–27). New York: Macmillan.

In text: (Krooss, 1989, 20–27)

Unsigned Article in a Reference Book

MLA Style

"Keynes, John Maynard." *Collier's Encyclopedia.* 1989 ed.

APA Style

Keynes, John Maynard. In *Collier's Encyclopedia* (1989 ed., Vol. 14, p. 59). New York: Macmillan.

In text: (Keynes, 1989, 59)

Chicago Manual of Style

Footnote: [1]*Collier's Encyclopedia,* 1989 ed., s.v. "Keynes, John Maynard."

NEWSPAPERS

Signed Article from a Daily Newspaper

MLA Style

Sims, Calvin. "Eisner Says Euro Disney May Close." *New York Times* 1 Jan. 1994, late ed.: 43+.

In text: (Sims 43)

Footnote: [1]Calvin Sims, "Eisner Says Euro Disney May Close," *New York Times* 1 Jan. 1994, late ed.: 43+.

APA Style

Sims, Calvin. (1994, January 1). Eisner says Euro Disney may close. *New York Times,* late ed., p. 43+.

In text: (Sims, 1994, 43)

Chicago Manual of Style

Footnote: [1]Calvin Sims, "Eisner Says Euro Disney May Close," *New York Times,* 1 January 1994, late New York edition.

Unsigned Article from a Daily Newspaper

MLA Style

"Stocks Drop Sharply with Mexico Strife." *New York Times* 4 Jan. 1994, late ed.: D3.

In text: ("Stocks Drop" D3)

Footnote: [1]"Stocks Drop Sharply with Mexico Strife," *New York Times* 4 Jan. 1994, late ed.: D3.

APA Style

Stocks drop sharply with Mexico strife. (1994, January 4). *New York Times,* late ed., p. D3.

In text: (Stocks drop, 1994, p. D3)

Chicago Manual of Style

Footnote: [1]"Stocks Drop Sharply with Mexico Strife," *New York Times* 4 January 1994, late New York edition.

BOOKS

Book—One Author

MLA Style

Cronin, Mary J. *Doing Business on the Internet: How the Electronic Highway Is Transforming American Companies.* New York: Van Nostrand Reinhold, 1994.

In text: (Cronin 153)

Footnote: [1]Mary J. Cronin, *Doing Business on the Internet: How the Electronic Highway Is Transforming American Companies* (New York: Van Nostrand Reinhold, 1994) 153.

APA Style

Cronin, Mary J. (1994). *Doing business on the Internet: How the electronic highway is transforming American companies.* New York: Van Nostrand Reinhold.

In text: (Cronin, 1994, 153)

Chicago Manual of Style

Cronin, Mary J. 1994. *Doing business on the Internet: How the electronic highway is transforming American companies.* New York: Van Nostrand Reinhold.

In text: (Cronin 1994, 153)

Footnote: [1]Mary J. Cronin. *Doing Business on the Internet* (New York: Van Nostrand Reinhold, 1994), 153.

Book—Two or Three Authors

MLA Style

Edwards, Jeremy, and Klaus Fischer. *Banks, Finance and Investment in Germany.* Cambridge: Cambridge University Press, 1994.

In text: (Edwards and Fischer 153)

Footnote: [1]Jeremy Edwards and Klaus Fischer, *Banks, Finance and Investment in Germany* (Cambridge: Cambridge University Press, 1994) 153.

APA Style

Edwards, Jeremy, Fischer, Klaus. (1994). *Banks, finance and investment in Germany.* Cambridge: Cambridge University Press.

In text: (Edwards and Fischer, 1994, 153)

Chicago Manual of Style

Edwards, Jeremy, and Klaus Fischer. 1994. *Banks, finance and investment in Germany.* Cambridge: Cambridge University Press.

In text: (Edwards and Fischer 1994, 153)

Footnote: [1]Jeremy Edwards and Klaus Fischer, *Banks, Finance and Investment in Germany* (Cambridge: Cambridge University Press, 1994), 153.

Book—More Than Three Authors

MLA Style (Switches to "et al." for More Than Three Authors)

Edwards, P. K., et al. *Beyond the Workplace: Managing Industrial Relations in the Multi-Establishment Enterprise.* New York: B. Blackwell, 1988.

In text: (Edwards et al. 153)

Footnote: [1]P. K. Edwards et al. *Beyond the Workplace: Managing Industrial Relations in the Multi-Establishment Enterprise* (New York: B. Blackwell, 1988) 153.

APA Style (Switches to "et al." in the In-Text Citation for More Than Three Authors)

Edwards, P. K., Martin, Roderick, Purcell, John, Sisson, Keith. (1988). *Beyond the workplace: Managing industrial relations in the multi-establishment enterprise.* New York: B. Blackwell.

In text: (Edwards et al., 1988, 153)

Chicago Manual of Style (Switches to "et al." in the In-Text Citation for More Than Three Authors)

Edwards, P. K., Roderick Martin, John Purcell, and Keith Sisson. 1988. *Beyond the workplace: Managing industrial relations in the multi-establishment enterprise.* New York: B. Blackwell.

In text: (Edwards et al. 1988, 153)

Footnote: [1]P.K. Edwards et al., *Beyond the Workplace: Managing Industrial Relations in Multi-Establishment Enterprise* (New York: B. Blackwell, 1988), 153.

Book—Anonymous Authors

MLA Style

Literary Market Place: The Directory of American Book Publishing. 1993 ed. New York: Bowker, 1993.

In text: (*Literary Market Place* 153)

Footnote: [1]*Literary Market Place: The Directory of American Book Publishing,* 1993 ed. (New York: Bowker, 1993) 153.

APA Style

Literary market place: The directory of American book publishing (1993 ed.). (1993). New York: Bowker.

In text: (*Literary market place,* 1993, 153)

Chicago Manual of Style

Literary market place: The directory of American book publishing. 1993. New York: Bowker.

In text: (*Literary market place* 1993, 153)

Footnote: [1]*Literary Market Place: The Directory of American Book Publishing* (New York: Bowker, 1993), 153.

Book—With an Editor

MLA Style

Boisot, Max, ed. *East-West Business Collaboration: The Challenge of Governance in Post-Structuralist Enterprises.* London; New York: Routledge, 1994.

In text: (Boisot 153)

Footnote: [1]Max Boisot, ed., *East-West Business Collaboration: The Challenge of Government in Post-Structuralist Enterprises* (London; New York: Routledge, 1994) 153.

APA Style

Boisot, Max (Ed.). (1994) *East-west business collaboration: The challenge of governance in post-structuralist enterprises.* London; New York: Routledge.

In text: (Boisot, 1994, 153)

Chicago Manual of Style

Boisot, Max, ed. 1994. *East-west business collaboration: The challenge of governance in post-structuralist enterprises.* London; New York: Routledge.

In text: (Boisot 1994, 153)

Footnote: [1]Max Boisot, ed., *East-West Business Collaboration: The Challenge of Governance in Post-Structuralist Enterprises* (London; New York: Routledge, 1994), 153.

Book—With an Author and an Editor

MLA Style

Lee, Andrew W. *Backyard Market Gardening: The Entrepreneur's Guide to Selling What You Grow.* George DeVault, ed. Burlington, VT: Good Earth Publishing, 1993.

In text: (Lee 153)

Footnote: [1]Andrew W. Lee, *Backyard Market Gardening: The Entrepreneur's Guide to Selling What You Grow,* ed. George DeVault (Burlington, VT: Good Earth Publishing, 1993) 153.

Chicago Manual of Style

Lee, Andrew W. 1993. *Backyard market gardening: The entrepreneur's guide to selling what you grow.* Edited by George DeVault. Burlington, VT: Good Earth Publishing.

In text: (Lee 1993, 153)

Footnote: [1]Andrew W. Lee, *Backyard Market Gardening: The Entrepreneur's Guide to Selling What You Grow,* ed. George DeVault (Burlington, VT: Good Earth Publishing, 1993), 153.

Book—Edition Other Than the First

MLA Style

Jensen, Daniel L., et al. *Advanced Accounting.* 3rd ed. New York: McGraw-Hill, 1994.

In text: (Jensen et al. 153)

Footnote: [1]Daniel L. Jensen et al., *Advanced Accounting,* 3rd ed. (New York: McGraw-Hill, 1994) 153.

APA Style

Jensen, Daniel L. (1994). *Advanced Accounting* (3rd ed.). New York: McGraw-Hill.

In text: (Jensen et al., 1994, 153)

Chicago Manual of Style

Jensen, Daniel L. 1994. *Advanced Accounting.* 3rd ed. New York: McGraw-Hill.

In text: (Jensen et al. 1994, 153)

Footnote: [1]Daniel L. Jensen et al., *Advanced Accounting,* 3rd ed. (New York: McGraw-Hill, 1994), 153.

Book—Corporate Author

MLA Style

Arthur Andersen and Company. *The Arthur Andersen North American Business Sourcebook.* Chicago: Triumph Books, 1993.

In text: (Arthur Andersen and Company 153)

Footnote: [1]Arthur Andersen and Company, *The Arthur Andersen North American Business Sourcebook* (Chicago: Triumph Books, 1993) 153.

APA Style

Arthur Andersen and Company. (1993). *The Arthur Andersen North American business sourcebook.* Chicago: Triumph Books.

In text: (Arthur Andersen and Company, 1993, 153)

Chicago Manual of Style

Arthur Andersen and Company. 1993. *The Arthur Andersen North American business sourcebook.* Chicago: Triumph Books.

In text: (Arthur Andersen and Company 1993, 153)

Footnote: [1]Arthur Andersen and Company, *The Arthur Andersen North American Business Sourcebook* (Chicago: Triumph Books, 1993), 153.

MULTIVOLUME WORKS

MLA Style

Dun and Bradstreet's Key Business Directory of Latin America. 2 vols. Bethlehem, PA: Dun and Bradstreet Information Services, 1993.

In text: (Dun and Bradstreet 2: 153)

Footnote: [1]*Dun and Bradstreet's Key Business Directory of Latin America,* vol. 2 (Bethlehem, PA: Dun and Bradstreet Information Services, 1993) 153.

APA Style

Dun and Bradstreet's key business directory of Latin America. (Vols. 1–2). (1993). Bethlehem: PA: Dun and Bradstreet Information Services.

In text: (Dun and Bradstreet, 1993, 2:153)

Chicago Manual of Style

Dun and Bradstreet's key business directory of Latin America. 1993. 2 vols. Bethlehem, PA: Dun and Bradstreet Information Services.

In text: (Dun and Bradstreet 1993, 2:153)

Footnote: [1]*Dun and Bradstreet's Key Business Directory of Latin America,* vol. 2 (Bethlehem, PA: Dun and Bradstreet Information Services, 1993), 153.

ELECTRONIC RESOURCES

CD ROM (and Abstract On)

MLA Format

Weidman, Christine Ingleborg. "Prices for Earnings Expectations: The Role of Loss Functions." *ProQuest.* CD-ROM. 1994.

APA Style

Weidman, Christine Ingeborg. (1994). *Prices for Earnings Expectations: The Role of Loss Functions* [CD-ROM]. Abstract from: ProQuest File: Dissertation Abstracts Item: 9409570

On-Line Journal Article—General Access

APA Style

Haynes, Jenny. (1994, Summer). Checklist on market makers [17 paragraphs]. *NASDAQ Financial Executive Journal* [on-line serial], 4(2). Available: http://www.law.cornell.edu/nasdaq/nasdtoc.html

Chicago Manual of Style

Haynes, Jenny. 1994. Checklist on market makers. In *NASDAQ Financial Executive Journal* (Vol. 4, no. 2) [on-line serial] Ithaca, New York: Cornell University Law School. [Available from http://www/law.cornell.edu/nasdaq/nasdtoc.html]

Software—With Author

MLA Format

Wright, Will. *Sim City 2000.* Computer software. Orinda, CA: Maxis, 1993.

APA Style

Wright, Will. (1993). Sim City 2000 [computer software]. Orinda, CA: Maxis.

Chicago Manual of Style

Wright, Will. Sim City 2000, Maxis, Orinda, CA.

Software—No Author

MLA Format

Lotus 1-2-3. Release 2. Computer software. Lotus Development Corporation, 1993.

APA Style

Lotus 1-2-3 (Rel. 2) [Computer software]. (1993). Cambridge, MA: Lotus Development Corporation.

Chicago Manual of Style

Lotus 1-2-3 Rel. 2, Lotus Development Corporation, Cambridge, MA.

Electronic Data File or Database

APA Style

Census Basic Tables for U.S. Metro Areas. [Internet web text]. (1990). Columbia, Missouri: Missouri State Census Data Center [Producer and Distributor]. Available: gopher://bigcat.missouri.edu/00/reference/census/us/basictables/us.text/metro.areas

On-Line Journal—Subscriber Based

APA Style

Stuck, B. W. "Centrex keeps on going and going" (June 1994). *Business Communications Review* Available: by request to BCR@enews.com

Chicago Manual of Style

Stuck, B. W. 1994. Centrex keeps on going and going. In *Business Communications Review* (June) [on-line serial]. Available: by request to BCR@enews.com

PROCEEDINGS

Proceedings of a Conference

MLA Format

Kawabe, Nobuo, and Eisuke Daito, eds. *International Conference on Business History.* Tokyo: University of Tokyo Press, 1993.

In text: (Kawabe and Daito 153)

Footnote: [1]Nobuo Kawabe and Eisuke Daito, eds., *International Conference on Business History* (Tokyo: University of Tokyo Press, 1993), 153.

APA Style

Kawabe, Nobuo, and Daito, Eisuke (Eds.), (1993). *International Conference on Business History.* Tokyo: University of Tokyo Press.

In text: (Kawabe and Daito, 1993, 153)

Paper Given at a Conference

MLA Format

Hillmer, Barbara, and Michelle Violanti. " 'Kiss Dagwood Bumstead Goodbye': A Communication Perspective on Downsizing." Annual Meeting of the Speech Communication Association, Miami, FL, November 18–21, 1993.

In text: (Hillmer and Violanti 153)

Footnote: [1]Barbara Hillmer and Michelle Violanti, " 'Kiss Dagwood Bumstead Goodbye': A Communication Perspective on Downsizing," Annual Meeting of the Speech Communication Association, Miami, FL, November 18–21, 1993, 153.

APA Style

Hillmer, Barbara, and Violanti, Michelle. (1993, November). *"Kiss Dagwood Bumstead goodbye": A communication perspective on downsizing.* Paper presented at the Annual Meeting of the Speech Communication Association, Miami, FL.

In text: (Hillmer and Violanti, 1993, 153)

Chicago Manual of Style

Hillmer, Barbara, and Michelle Violanti. 1993. Kiss Dagwood Bumstead goodbye: A communication perspective on downsizing. Paper presented at symposium. Annual Meeting of the Speech Communication Association, Miami, FL.

In text: (Hillmer and Violanti 1993, 153)

Footnote: [1]Barbara Hillmer and Michelle Violanti, " 'Kiss Dagwood Bumstead Goodbye': A Communication Perspective on Downsizing," Annual Meeting of the Speech Communication Association, Miami, FL, November 18–21, 1993, 153.

MEDIA

TV Program

MLA Format

"Another Trojan Horse." *CBS Sunday Morning.* Prod. Cathy Lewis. CBS. 26 November 1995.

Footnote: [1]"Another Trojan Horse," *CBS Sunday Morning,* Prod. Cathy Lewis, CBS, 26 November 1995.

APA Style

Another Trojan Horse. In Cathy Lewis (Producer), *CBS Sunday Morning.* New York: CBS.

Audio Recording

MLA Format

Joerger, Eugene, Business Combinations and Intangible Assets. New York: CP Audio, 1970.

APA Style

Joerger, Eugene (Speaker). (1970). *Business combinations and intangible assets* (Cassette recording). New York: CP Audio.

Chicago Manual of Style

Joerger, Eugene. "Business Combinations and Intangible Assets." New York: CP Audio, 1970.

Film

MLA Format

Roger and Me. dir. Michael Moore. Burbank, CA: Warner Brothers, 1990.

Footnote: [1]*Roger and Me,* dir. Michael Moore, Burbank, CA: Warner Bros., 1990.

APA Style

Moore, Michael (Director). 1990. *Roger and Me* [Film]. Burbank, CA: Warner Brothers.

Chicago Manual of Style

Moore, Michael (director). *Roger and Me.* Burbank, CA: Warner Brothers, 1990.

Appendix C

USAGE HANDBOOK

What's the Difference between Correctness and Conventions?

Ways to Use This Handbook

Murray's Draft: The Importance of Grammar and Mechanics in Business Documents

1. Sentences
- 1.1 Sentence Fragments
- 1.2 Comma Splices and Run-On Sentences
- 1.3 Subject-Verb Agreement
- 1.4 Pronoun-Antecedent Agreement
- 1.5 Pronoun Reference
- 1.6 Dangling Modifiers
- 1.7 Misplaced Modifiers
- 1.8 Parallel Structure

2. Punctuation—Beyond the Period, Exclamation Point, and Question Mark
- 2.1 Apostrophe
- 2.2 Brackets
- 2.3 Colon
- 2.4 Comma
- 2.5 Dash
- 2.6 Ellipsis
- 2.7 Hyphen
- 2.8 Parentheses
- 2.9 Quotation Marks
- 2.10 Semicolon
- 2.11 Slash

3. Numbers—Figures or Words?

Revisiting Murray's Draft

WHAT'S THE DIFFERENCE BETWEEN CORRECTNESS AND CONVENTIONS?

Correctness in business documents is based on what a particular workplace culture agrees is acceptable for its documents. Many companies follow standards available in published manuals (such as the *Chicago Manual of Style*) or in company styleguides (such as the *UPS Stylebook*).

What's absolute? Virtually nothing. People in particular cultures and situations within those cultures determine what's acceptable. This level of acceptance works as a convention that is usually seen as a standard of correctness, regardless of what other cultures do. Violating the standard in a particular culture—whether a different country or a different company—is usually regarded as a mistake.

- Are fragments absolutely forbidden? No. Both of the following forms might be acceptable in different situations:

  Employee reaction to the proposed restructuring of the department. Negative!

  Employee reaction to the proposed restructuring of the department. The reaction has been uniformly negative.
- Is spelling fixed? No. Spelling varies from culture to culture.

  Depending on the culture, both "behavior" and "behaviour" are acceptable.

  Depending on the culture, both "catalog" and "catalogue" are acceptable.
- Commas? No. The use of commas varies from culture to culture.

  The paper clips, extra pens, and pads of paper are in the supply closet.

  The paper clips, extra pens and pads of paper are in the supply closet.
- Capitalization? No. Both the "up" style (using uppercase letters in all conventional situations) and the "down" style (using minimal capitalization) are commonly used.

  The entrance to the Marketing Department is on Spear Avenue.

  The entrance to the marketing department is on Spear avenue.

Part of your responsibility as a professional is to learn the conventions and standards of correctness that are used in your workplace culture. Two keys to professional documents include using conventions appropriate for the situation and using consistent conventions within the same document, visual, or presentation.

WAYS TO USE THIS HANDBOOK

You can use this Handbook in a number of different ways:

- as a reference when you need to review a particular point of grammar, mechanics, or style
- as a source to learn new information about grammar, mechanics, or style
- as a way to help you understand the options you have in revising your documents

MURRAY'S DRAFT: THE IMPORTANCE OF GRAMMAR AND MECHANICS IN BUSINESS DOCUMENTS

Murray Caton was asked by Cynthia Jorgenson, his manager in the Human Relations Department, to draft the complaint procedure for the sexual harassment section in the company's policy handbook, which was being substantially revised. Although the review cycle for the procedure Murray drafted would be extensive, Cynthia made it clear that she wanted reviewers to focus on the substance of the procedure—the steps in the process, the legal ramifications, and so on; she did not want readers distracted by mechanical and grammatical problems with Murray's writing.

The accompanying excerpt is a copy of the draft that Murray submitted to Cynthia. Use this draft to give yourself a quick, informal diagnostic test. Before you look at the sample text, have a blank sheet of paper handy so that you can place it over the left-hand column identifying Murray's miscues. As you read the text, write the miscues you find on the paper. When you're finished reading, see if you've identified the same miscues as those listed in the left-hand column.

To use this Handbook most effectively, concentrate only on the sections discussing the miscues that you had the most difficulty identifying. Then see if you can correct the miscues in Murray's draft. A corrected version of Murray's draft appears at the end of the Handbook. Because most of the miscues can be corrected in more than one way, this corrected version represents one option the writer had in revising the draft. (See Chapter 5 for a discussion about how miscues affect the *ethos* of a document.)

punctuation error
agreement error
parallel structure error in list
punctuation error
unnecessary repetition
parallel structure error in list
punctuation error
parallel structure error
punctuation error
spelling error, punctuation error

Sexual Harassment

Sexual harassment, by definition, is any verbal, physical, or environmental sexual misconduct; any unwelcome sexual advance; or any unwelcome sexual behavior. Sexual harassment is against state and federal law when:

- Sexual requests or conduct are made either explicitly or implicitly a condition of employment.
- Agree to or reject such conduct by an individual is used as the basis for an employment decision.
- The conduct in question interferes with an individuals work performance by creating an intimidating, hostile, offensive, or uncomfortable working environment.

If you feel you are the victim of sexual harassment, these following steps need to be followed by the complainant and the company to remedy the situation:

1) The complainant should review the company's complaint policy.
2) Complaint investigation (by the company)
3) Decision making and action (by the company).

1. Review the Complaint Policy

Report your sexual harassment complaint, either written or orally, to the Vice President or Employment Specialist of the Human Resources department or to your supervisor. The Vice President and Employment Specialist of Human Resources will be in charge of conducting the investigation. The Vice President, and Employment Specialist have been specifically trained to handle sexual harassment complaints. If you do not feel comfortable discussing your complaint with human resource personnel you may speak to higher levels of management without the risk of adverse consequences. Any report of sexual harassment will be taken seriously by this company.

agreement error
agreement error
dangling modifier
spelling error
fragment
numeral error
dangling modifier
parallel structure error
punctuation error, pronoun reference
spelling error
spelling error
spelling error, run-on sentence

A supervisor must report any instance of sexual harassment that they witness or are aware of, to the Vice President or Employment Specialist of Human Resources. Failure to comply with this policy result in disciplinary actions up to termination.

All incidents of sexual harassment must be reported. Once reported, an investigation of the compalint will take place immediately and confidentially.

Retaliation against the complainant not tolerated. Retaliation may include, but is not limited to, threats, harassment by fellow employees, or continued harassment by the accused. Disciplinary action, up to termination, will be taken if such behavior occurs.

Every new employee will be required to attend a sexual harassment policy program within 3 months of employment. These programs will be administered by the Human Resources Department. Upon employment, the program has required attendance.

2. Complaint Investigations

If you feel you have been the victim of sexual harassment you will need to document the date and time it occurred, the people involved (the alleged harasser and any witnesses), and a detailed description of what took place.

Your complaint needs to be presented to the Vice President or Employment Specialist of the Human Resources department or a manager as quickly as possible. If to much time is wasted, relevant information may be forgotten.

Once the complaint is filled, the Vice President or Employment Specialist of Human Resources or you manager will contact all parties involved, this includes the complainant, the accused, and any witnesses.

parallel structure error	**3. Making Decisions and Initiating Actions** The decision about whether sexual harassment has taken place will be contingent on our company's definition of sexual harassment.
spelling error	If the accused is found guilty, disciplinary action will be imposed immediately. Disiplinary action may include, but is not limited to, formal written reprimand, probational period, suspension from work without pay, or termination of employment.
pronoun error *pronoun error* *parallel structure error*	If the accused is found not guilty, they will be informed why and how it was made. Retaliation against the complainant for filing the complaint will not be tolerated. Retaliation may include, but is not limited to, making threats, harassment by fellow employees, or harassing the person who was accused.
spelling error, spelling error	All steps of the complaint process will be documented and placed in the complainant's and accused's personal files. All information is completely confidentail. The Human Resource department will also keep a separate file about the complaint itself.

1 SENTENCES

Complete, easy-to-read sentences are expected in virtually all business and professional communication.

1.1 Sentence Fragments

A sentence fragment is an incomplete sentence that is missing either a subject or a verb, or is a subordinate idea that needs to be connected to a main idea. The fragment can be corrected either by completing the thought or connecting the fragment to another sentence.

sentence fragment #1 Telecommuting or telework began to develop as an economic opportunity in the late 1960s and early 1970s. When futurists first grappled with the tremendous waste inherent in having millions of workers physically commute to an office five days a week.

The text beginning "When futurists first grappled with the tremendous waste . . ." is a fragment in the form of a subordinate clause. To eliminate the fragment, you need to make it into a complete sentence or connect it to another sentence. Some of the options for eliminating the fragment follow:

revisions Telecommuting or telework began to develop as an economic opportunity in the late 1960s and early 1970s, when futurists first grappled with the tremendous waste inherent in having millions of workers physically commute to an office five days a week.

or

In the late 1960s and early 1970s, when futurists first grappled with the tremendous waste inherent in having millions of workers physically commute to an office five days a week, telecommuting or telework began to develop as an economic opportunity.

or

Telecommuting or telework began to develop as an economic opportunity in the late 1960s and early 1970s. During those years, futurists first grappled with the tremendous waste inherent in having millions of workers physically commute to an office five days a week.

1.2 Comma Splices and Run-On Sentences

Comma splices and run-on sentences are caused by mistakenly linking or fusing two or more sentences. *Comma splices* are caused by connecting two sentences with only a comma. *Run-on sentences* (sometimes called fused sentences) occur when two sentences are written as if they are a single sentence, without internal punctuation separating the clauses.

If the two ideas are not closely connected, the inappropriately linked clauses can be made into two separate sentences. If the two ideas are closely related and of equal importance, the independent clauses (complete sentences) can be connected using one of three conventions:

1. Use a coordinate conjunction (*and, but, or, nor, for, so, yet*) that is preceded by a comma to link two independent clauses (complete sentences).
2. Use a semicolon to link two independent clauses (complete sentences) that are closely related and of equal importance.
3. Use a conjunctive adverb, usually preceded by a semicolon and followed by a comma, to link two independent clauses (complete sentences). These are common conjunctive adverbs: *accordingly, also, besides, hence, however, moreover, nevertheless, otherwise, therefore, thus, still.*

comma splices

Generally, regional companies are doing well. Cooper Electronics is in excellent shape, sales were up 12 percent, sales for FY97 [fiscal year 1997] ended at $758 million, with a net income of $73 million. Computer Components Corporation did well until the final quarter, total sales for FY96 were up 7 percent with gross income of $8.3 million, net income was $74 million. FY97 was somewhat less successful for Hart Hardware, annual sales were down 20 percent, FY97 should swing up.

identification of comma splices

Generally, regional companies are doing well. Cooper Electronics is in excellent shape, sales were up 12 percent, sales for FY97 [fiscal year 1997] ended at $758 million, with a net income of $73 million. Computer Components Corporation did well until the final quarter, total sales for FY96 were up 7 percent, with gross income of $8.3 million, net income was $74 million. FY97 was somewhat less successful for Hart Hardware, annual sales were down 20 percent, FY97 should swing up.

revision

Generally, regional companies are doing well. Cooper Electronics is in excellent shape. Sales were up 12 percent, and sales for FY97 [fiscal year 1997] ended at $758 million, with a net income of $73 million. Computer Components Corporation did well until the final quarter. Total sales for FY96 were up 7 percent. Gross income was $8.3 million; net income was $74 million. FY97 was somewhat less successful for Hart Hardware. Annual sales were down 20 percent; FY97 should swing up.

run-on sentence #1

Alternative software configurations are available in training sessions employees learn to modify the software to fit their own requirements.

revisions

Various software configurations are available. In training sessions, employees learn to modify the software to fit their own requirements.

or

Various software configurations are available in training sessions. Employees learn to modify the software to fit their own requirements.

run-on sentence #2

Given the heavy use of the printer in our office, the printer's cartridge needs to be replaced about once a month and the cost runs about $60 per cartridge.

revisions

Given the heavy use of the printer in our office, the printer's cartridge needs to be replaced about once a month, and the cost runs about $60 per cartridge.

or

Given the heavy use of the printer in our office, the printer's cartridge needs to be replaced about once a month; the cost runs about $60 per cartridge.

or

Given the heavy use of the printer in our office, the printer's cartridge needs to be replaced about once a month. The cost runs about $60 per cartridge.

1.3 Subject-Verb Agreement

The subject and verb of a sentence must agree in number—that is, use a singular subject with a singular verb; use a plural subject with a plural verb.

agreement error Because of inadequate training for new employees, increases in the number of claims being filed, and complex insurance regulations, the time to process claim forms are increasing.

The subject and verb—"time" and "are"—must agree. The singular subject "time" requires a singular verb. Or the plural verb "are" requires a plural subject.

agreement Because of inadequate training for new employees, increases in the number of claims being filed, and complex insurance regulations, the *time* to process claim forms *is* increasing.
or
Because of inadequate training for new employees, increases in the number of claims being filed, and complex insurance regulations, the *times* to process claim forms *are* increasing.

Agreement errors can also result from using the wrong verb with a compound subject. Two or more subjects joined by *and* take a plural verb, even if one or more of the subjects is singular.

agreement error An ergonomically designed workstation and the adjustable chair was ordered for each of the department's employees.

agreement An ergonomically designed *workstation* and the adjustable *chair were* ordered for each of the department's employees.

Decisions are sometimes more complicated, though. Specifically, if two subjects joined by *and* are commonly perceived as a single unit, then they use a singular verb. For example, "track and field" is usually perceived as a single athletic event.

agreement The *advertising and marketing* of the product *is* an important concern.

In this example, *advertising and marketing* are perceived as a single concern, so the term uses a singular verb *is*. However, two or more subjects joined by *or* take a verb that agrees with the closest subject.

agreement error An adjustable chair, new bookcases, or a tilt pad for their monitor are among the choices employees can select when their offices are renovated.

agreement An adjustable chair, new bookcases, or a tilt pad for their monitor is among the choices employees can select when their offices are renovated.
or
An adjustable chair, a tilt pad for their monitor, or new bookcases are among the choices employees can select when their offices are renovated.
or
An adjustable chair, new bookcases, and a tilt pad for their monitor are among the choices employees can select when their offices are renovated.

When the subject of a sentence is an indefinite pronoun (a word such as *each* or *everyone*), the subject usually takes a singular verb. Indefinite pronouns do not refer to any specific person or thing.

agreement error Everyone in this company are affected by the plans to expand the options for health insurance.

agreement *Everyone* in this company *is* affected by the plans to expand the options for health insurance.

When an indefinite pronoun functions as an adjective preceding a compound subject, the sentence uses a singular verb.

agreement error Each proposal, test plan, and test report written by the marketing staff are submitted to the editorial group for copy editing.

agreement *Each* proposal, test plan, and test report written by the marketing staff *is* submitted to the editorial group for copy editing.

When "each" is used adverbially, it is associated *only* with plural subjects and verbs.

agreement The trainees were *each* given a parking permit, a computer access code, and an office key.

Some collective nouns can take either a singular or a plural verb, depending on the meaning. When the collective noun refers to the group as a single entity, use a singular verb. When the group's members are being considered as individuals, use a plural verb. Notice also that the pronouns (in this case, *their* and *its*) change, depending on whether the team is seen as a single entity or as a group of individuals.

agreement with collective nouns	The marketing team has reported its survey results. (*The team is presented as a single entity, one team.*) *or* The marketing team have reported their survey results. (*The team is presented as a group of individuals.*)

A common subject-verb agreement error results from making a linking verb agree with the complement rather than the subject of the sentence.

agreement error	An important part of marketing research are opinions from a representative random sample of potential customers.
agreement	An important *part* of marketing research *is* opinions from a representative random sample of potential customers. *or* *Opinions* from a representative random sample of potential customers *are* an important part of marketing research.

1.4 Pronoun-Antecedent Agreement

A pronoun substitutes for a noun. An antecedent is a noun or pronoun earlier in the sentence (or an immediately preceding sentence) to which a pronoun refers. A pronoun must agree with its antecedent in three ways:

- *gender:* feminine, masculine, neuter
- *person:* first, second, third
- *number:* singular, plural

Errors in pronoun-antecedent agreement often confuse readers. Many errors result from the misuse of indefinite pronouns, which are pronouns that do not refer to a specific person, idea, or thing. These are the most common indefinite pronouns:

all	everybody	nobody
another	everyone	none
any	everything	nothing
anybody	few	one
anyone	many	several
anything	more	some
both	most	somebody
each	neither	someone
either	no one	something

With the exception of such obvious plurals as *all, few, many, more, most, several,* and *some,* indefinite pronouns are third-person singular. When indefinite pronouns are antecedents to other pronouns, they generally require singular pronouns.

pronoun-antecedent agreement error	*Everyone* brought *their* favorite games to the company picnic.

The error results because "everyone" is singular and "their" is plural. The correction can substitute "his" only if all the company employees are male, "her" only if all employees are female. To write "Everyone brought his games to the picnic" would be inaccurate if both men and women employees brought games. However, to write "Everyone brought his or her games to the company picnic" would be awkward. The most appropriate correction bypasses the stylistic problem of using *his/her* or *his or her* by making both the antecedent and the pronoun plural.

pronoun-antecedent agreement	*All* employees brought *their* games to the company picnic.

Collective nouns used as antecedents can take either a singular or a plural pronoun, depending on the meaning. When the collective noun refers to the group acting together, the pronoun should be singular.

pronoun-antecedent agreement	The *team* discussed changes in department structure at *its* weekly meeting. (The team is seen as a single entity, working as a unit.) *or* The *team* wrote *their* recommendations for changes in department structure. (The members of the team are acting independently, each writing recommendations.)

1.5 Pronoun Reference

Pronouns can cause ambiguity and confusion for readers if the antecedents are not clear. Most problems result from inappropriate use of these pronouns:

it	they
that	this
there	which
these	you

Reserve *you* for situations in which you directly address readers. Use *it, this, that, which*, or *there* when you can identify a specific antecedent. These pronouns usually do not present a problem in conversation, but they can make your writing wordy, vague, and sometimes confusing. You can easily rewrite common expressions that use pronouns ineffectively.

It is believed . . . → Our team believes that . . .
There are several competitors . . . → Several competitors include . . .

Pronouns that have implied antecedents need to be replaced by clear nouns that eliminate the vague references.

pronoun-antecedent agreement error	Most computers have the capacity for you to set parameters so that your work is automatically saved at regular specified intervals. *It* reduces unnecessary work delays and frustrations.

What is the antecedent of "it"? Computers? Capability? Parameters? Automatically saved? Specified intervals? For the sentence to be more effective, "it"—which has no clear antecedent—needs to be replaced by words that make clear what "it" means.

pronoun-antecedent agreement	Most computers have the capability of setting parameters so that work is automatically saved at regular specified intervals. *Activating the automatic save feature* reduces unnecessary work delays and frustrations.

1.6 Dangling Modifiers

A dangling modifier is a word or phrase that, by its position, looks as if it should modify the subject of a sentence, but actually doesn't. A modifier dangles because there is no word in the sentence that it logically modifies. A dangling modifier gives the reader misleading and sometimes inaccurate information and may cause unintended humor. Sometimes you can eliminate the dangling modifier, you can add or change the subject of the independent clause, or you can change the dangling modifier into a subordinate clause. Occasionally, rewriting the entire sentence produces the best result.

dangling modifier	To compete successfully in the interactive video market, product quality must be improved.

Although readers can probably figure out what the writer means, the phrase "To compete successfully in the interactive video market" can't logically modify the sentence's subject, "product quality"; product quality doesn't compete.

no dangling modifier	To compete successfully in the interactive video market, our company must improve product quality. (*A subject responsible for the actions—in this case, competing successfully and improving product quality—is added to the sentence.*) *or* Our company must improve product quality in order to compete successfully in the interactive video market. (*The order of the sentence is reversed so that the main clause comes first and the phrase follows.*) *or* If our company is to compete successfully in the interactive video market, we must improve product quality. (*The phrase is revised so that it is a clause that has a subject that is a synonym for the new subject of the sentence.*)

dangling modifier Once established as a corporation, comprehensive health coverage for employees will be necessary.

"Comprehensive health coverage" can't be "established as a corporation," regardless of what the sentence says.

no dangling modifier Comprehensive health coverage for employees will be necessary once the corporation is established.

or

The employees need comprehensive health coverage once the corporation is established.

or

Once we establish a corporation, comprehensive health coverage for employees will be necessary.

1.7 Misplaced Modifiers

Misplaced words and phrases confuse readers and increase the likelihood that readers will interpret information in a way different from what the writer intended. Adverbs can be correctly placed in several locations in a sentence, so they are easy to inadvertently misplace. These words can be particularly troublesome:

almost	merely
even	nearly
exactly	only
hardly	scarcely
just	simply

Placing phrases and subordinate clauses close to the words they are intended to modify helps reduce potential problems.

modifier placement

Only the administrative assistant had access to the computer security code.

The *only* administrative assistant had access to the computer security code.

The administrative assistant *only* had access to the computer security code.

The administrative assistant had access to the *only* computer security code.

modifier placement

Just the finance officer approved the budget this afternoon.

The finance officer *just* approved the budget this afternoon.

The finance officer approved *just* the budget this afternoon.

The finance officer approved the budget *just* this afternoon.

1.8 Parallel Structure

Parallel structure presents ideas or facts of equivalent importance in equivalent grammatical structures.

error in parallelism Telecommuting has had a favorable impact on many aspects of business, including reducing the need for office space, an improvement in quality of service, maintenance of jobs in impoverished areas, decentralized operations, and allowing parents with small children or persons with reduced mobility to come into the labor market.

analysis of error in parallelism Telecommuting has had a favorable impact on many aspects of business, including *reducing* the need for office space,
~~an improvement~~ *improving* ~~in~~ quality of service,
~~maintenance~~ *maintaining* jobs in impoverished areas,
~~decentralized~~ *decentralizing* operations, and
allowing parents with small children or persons with reduced mobility to come into the labor market.

parallel elements Telecommuting has had a favorable impact on many aspects of business, including reducing the need for office space, improving quality of service, maintaining jobs in impoverished areas, decentralizing operations, and allowing parents with small children or persons with reduced mobility to come into the labor market.

Source: Robert Moskowitz (1994), "Telecommuting: Bringing the Work Home," *Hemispheres* (April): 33–36.

2 PUNCTUATION—BEYOND THE PERIOD, EXCLAMATION POINT, AND QUESTION MARK

(*Note:* Conventions discussed in this section are based on the 14th edition of *The Chicago Manual of Style.*)

2.1 Apostrophe

2.1.1 Use an apostrophe to indicate possession. Add an apostrophe plus s ('s) to singular nouns and indefinite pronouns to form the possessive. Use an apostrophe plus s ('s) to form possessives of plural nouns that don't end in s.

possession A broken water pipe damaged files in the company's data processing center.

The personnel manager examined everyone's employment history.

The on-site women's locker room made it easier for employees to participate in a midday aerobics class.

2.1.2 Use an apostrophe to indicate omission of one or more letters or figures.

omission hadn't = had not

must've = must have (*never* must of)

'96 = 1996

2.1.3 Avoid common errors that confuse *it's* (it is) and *its* (possessive form of *it*), *you're* (you are) and *your* (possessive form of *you*). Never use apostrophes with such possessive pronouns as *hers, theirs*, or *ours*.

incorrect The department confirmed it's decision by taking a formal vote.

revision The department confirmed its decision by taking a formal vote.

incorrect Its too late to change your insurance deductible for this year.

revision Its too late to change your insurance deductible for this year.

incorrect Her's is the only workstation that has not been networked yet.

revision Hers is the only workstation that has not been networked yet.

incorrect The decision to shift to a flex-time schedule is their's alone.

revision The decision to shift to a flex-time schedule is theirs alone.

2.2 Brackets

2.2.1 Use brackets to enclose comments or explanations inserted in a quotation.

signaling insertions Sales increased last month [March 1997].

The project director [Brian Jackson] requested an extension because of equipment malfunctions.

2.2.2 Use *sic* (meaning "so" or "thus") in brackets to indicate an error in the original document.

signaling errors The delivery date is listed on the invoice as 2-31-96 [*sic*].

2.3 Colon

2.3.1 Use a colon as a convention in salutations, publication data, time, titles.

salutation Dear Ms. Greenough:

publication data (June 1996): 742

time 2:45 p.m.

title *Communication Processes and Merger Success: An Exploratory Study of Four Financial Institution Mergers*

2.3.2 Use a colon to introduce a list or series when the words preceding are a complete sentence. Do *not* use a colon if the words preceding the list or series are not a complete sentence.

colon Training satisfaction is determined by assessing these factors: amount and availability of training, time for learning, support for training, documentation, progress evaluations.

colon preceding bulleted list Training satisfaction is determined by assessing these factors:

- amount and availability of training
- time for learning
- support for training
- documentation
- progress evaluations

***Note:* A complete sentence precedes colon. There is no period at the end of the list.**

no colon Training satisfaction is determined by amount and availability of training, time for learning, support for training, documentation, progress evaluations.

2.4 Comma

2.4.1 Use a comma as a convention in dates, numbers, addresses, and informal salutations and with titles or degrees.

date April 15, 1996 (comma needed)

15 April 1996 (no comma needed)

numbers $576,253

address Management Communication Quarterly
Sage Publications, Inc.
2455 Teller Road
Thousand Oaks, CA 91320

salutation Dear Sandy,

degree Jennifer M. Samuels, M.B.A.

2.4.2 Use a comma to separate two sentences (that is, two independent clauses) connected with a coordinating conjunction—*and, but, or, for, so, yet*. Place a comma preceding the conjunction. Writers do have to be careful not to indulge in "hypercorrection," which occurs if they simply insert a comma every time they see an "and." Commas are only necessary when the "and" connects two independent clauses or when it connects the final item in a series of three or more items.

comma and coordinating conjunction The company picnic was announced for September 20 at Wayland Park, and the rain date was set for September 27.

no comma needed The company picnic was scheduled for September 20 at Wayland Park and the rain date for September 27.

2.4.3 Use commas to separate items in a series. Place a comma following each item in the series, except the final one. The comma preceding the "and" is optional; however, using this comma in business communication can reduce ambiguity.

commas and items in a series The interest rates for new business loans depend on a variety of factors including prime rate, geographic location, duration of loan, and amount borrowed.

Prior work history, academic preparation, attitude, and recommendations are all factors in assessing a candidate's suitability.

We expect the new on-site child-care facility to decrease absenteeism, improve positive attitudes, and increase productivity for all workers.

***Note:* The items in each series are parallel.**

Do *not* use commas to separate compound elements—for example, two nouns, two verbs, or two modifiers.

incorrect The hardware, and software come bundled together for one price.

revision The hardware and software come bundled together for one price.

incorrect The presentation for potential investors was too long, and boring.

revision The presentation for potential investors was too long and boring.

incorrect The personnel director reviewed and determined raises for each employee.

revision The personnel director reviewed and determined raises for each employee.

2.4.4 Use a comma to separate introductory phrases and subordinate clauses from the main sentence.

comma with introductory phrases and clause Because networking the department's computers would take a full day, all employees were asked to work at home.

All employees were asked to work at home because networking the department's computers would take a full day.

***Note:* If the order of main and subordinate clauses is reversed, with main clause first, no comma is used.**

2.5 Dash

Use a dash (made with an -em- dash [—] on your computer keyboard) to signal a break in thought. Do *not* set off a dash with spaces.

dash The survey—which had an astounding 73 percent return rate—provided data for analyzing international communication practices in agribusiness.

2.6 Ellipsis

Use ellipsis points (three spaced dots) to indicate that something in a quotation has been omitted. If the omission comes at the end of a sentence, the first dot is the period, followed by the three dots of the ellipsis. Brackets are used to indicate letters, words, or phrases added to make the edited text make sense.

original quotation

Besides these factors within the merged organizations, two elements in the external environment of the acquired firms also seemed to influence employees' communication needs. The first was *geographic distance.* Where the merger sites were widely separated, more desire for supportive communication behaviors was reported. When the merger sites were in close proximity, less use and need for this kind of communication was expressed.

Satisfaction with the communication they received also appears to be influenced by the merged firms' *location.* Employees of acquired firms located in rural areas seemed less critical of their acquirers' communication behavior overall than were employees of the acquired firms in more suburban and urban areas. Employees of acquired firms in rural areas had fewer alternate employment opportunities and were grateful just to keep their jobs after the merger.

Source: Myrna M. Cornett-DeVito and Paul G. Friedman (1995), "Communication Processes and Merger Success: An Exploratory Study of Four Financial Institution Mergers," *Management Communication Quarterly* 9 (1, August): 63.

quotation with omission indicated "[T]wo elements in the external environment of the acquired firm also seemed to influence employees' communication needs. The first was *geographic distance. . . .* [The second was] *location. . . .* "

***Note:* Brackets indicate added material that was not part of the original quotation.**

2.7 Hyphen

2.7.1 Use a hyphen to signal the break of a word, showing that the word is carried over to the next line. Break words *only* at the end of a syllable.

hyphen with word break at end of line The remarkable growth of the new company is exceeded only by the extraordinarily strong enthusiasm and loyalty of its employees.

2.7.2 Use a hyphen to create compound modifiers that precede a noun.

hyphen with compound modifiers preceding nouns

We ordered only high-density disks.

The three-day training session had to be rescheduled.

The redesigned workspaces were separated by 6-foot module dividers.

The 22-member production team required effective, experienced leadership.

The carefully packaged parts arrived undamaged.

The laboratory was located in an environmentally controlled facility.

***Note:* When the first word of a compound modifier ends in -ly, no hyphen is used.**

2.7.3 Use a hyphen in all words that begin with *self.*

hyphen with words beginning with *self*

self-assessment

self-employment

self-regulation

2.7.4 Use a hyphen to avoid ambiguity.

avoid ambiguity

co-op: The health food co-op has more than 300 members.
coop: The old chicken coop was replaced by an environmentally controlled building.

re-cover: Because of the intense heat, the plants were re-covered.
recover: Despite being severely damaged in an ice storm, the plants in front of our headquarters would recover.

2.7.5 Use hyphens in fractions and ratios that function as adjectives preceding a noun.

fractions and ratios

The board of directors requires a two-thirds majority to pass resolutions.

The vote was carried by a two-to-one margin.

2.7.6 Use hyphens in compound numbers from twenty-one through ninety-nine.

compound numbers

We received fifty-seven applications for internal transfers to staff the new market research facility.

2.8 Parentheses

2.8.1 Use parentheses to separate supplementary information within a single sentence or to enclose one or more sentences.

parentheses for supplementary information

A flex-time schedule (defined as an 8-hour day occurring any time between 6 a.m. and 8 p.m.) is an option for some employees.

2.8.2 Use parentheses to separate acronyms from the rest of the text the first time they are introduced.

parentheses for acronyms

Activate a teller machine with this card and your Personal Identification Number (PIN).

2.9 Quotation Marks

2.9.1 Use quotation marks to indicate the titles of articles from periodicals and newspapers.

titles of articles

"Leader Behaviors Affecting Team Performance" in the *Journal of Business Communication*

"Its Product Is for Men but Osborn Markets It to Women" in *The Wall Street Journal*

***Note:* Underline or italicize titles of books, journals, and newspapers.**

2.9.2 Use quotation marks to enclose short direct quotations. Longer quotations (more than three lines) should be single spaced and indented from the regular margins; these longer quotations do not use quotation marks.

short direct quotations

Mr. Dederick argued that the productivity gain is "probably a statistical phenomenon" and that "we're not going to get numbers like this again" soon.

Source: Christiana Duff (1995), "Productivity Was Up Sharply in Second Quarter," *The Wall Street Journal* (September 8): A-2.

long direct quotation The Amerus Bank information booklet for customers opening new accounts explains liability disclosures:

> Tell us AT ONCE if you believe your card has been lost or stolen. Telephoning is the best way of keeping your possible losses down. You could lose all the money in your account (plus your maximum overdraft line of credit). If you tell us within 2 business days, you can lose no more than $50 if someone used your card without your permission. . . .

2.9.3 Place commas and periods inside quotation marks. Place colons and semicolons outside quotation marks. Place question marks, exclamation points, and dashes inside the quotation marks only if the punctuation is part of the quotation; otherwise, place them outside the quotation marks.

quotation marks and punctuation "A journeyman welder is like a free agent in baseball," said Walt Elish, Executive Director of the Economic Development Corporation of Waukesha County, Wisconsin.

Source: Raju Narisetti (1995), "Manufacturers Decry a Shortage of Workers While Rejecting Many," *The Wall Street Journal* (September 8): A-1.

2.10 Semicolon

2.10.1 Use a semicolon to separate two closely related sentences.

semicolon connecting two sentences Beginning May 1, the independent audit team will spend five days at our facility; the report will be available at the end of the month.

2.10.2 Use a semicolon to separate two sentences connected by a conjunctive adverb. Precede the conjunctive adverb with a semicolon; follow it with a comma.

semicolon with conjunctive adverb As early as last quarter, we started to identify internal processes that need to be modified; however, the audit report will identify additional areas for improvement.

2.10.3 Use a semicolon to separate items in a series if individual items themselves contain commas.

semicolon with series Follow these guidelines for protecting your ATM card: keep card away from sunlight, heat or anything magnetic; don't write your PIN number on your card; do not loan your card to anyone.

2.11 Slash

Use a slash to separate elements in dates, to indicate a fraction, and in place of *per*. Be careful to avoid a slash when it might unintentionally be read as a symbol for division.

dates 9/23/95 (September 23, 1995)

fractions 3/4 (three-quarters)

per /test run (per test run)

3 NUMBERS—FIGURES OR WORDS?

(*Note:* These conventions for use of figures and words are based on those suggested in the 14th edition of *The Chicago Manual of Style.*)

3.1

For most business documents, use words for numbers one through nine and figures for all other numbers.

figures or words Our division was first in sales increases.

The marketing department of the company has two floors.

Paul ranked 17th in a field of 427 taking the qualifying exam for a promotion.

The company's film and slide library is housed in 15,000 square feet of the building with special humidity and temperature controls.

3.2

Use words rather than figures at the beginning of a sentence. If this is awkward, rewrite the sentence.

awkward Five thousand two hundred thirty-two registered dealers visited the trade show during the first day.

conventional During the first day, 5,232 registered dealers visited the trade show.

3.3

Express very large, round numbers (over six digits) by a figure followed by million, billion, trillion, and so on.

large numbers Revenues exceeded $1.5 million for the final quarter.

3.4

Use figures for physical quantities—distances, lengths, areas, volumes, pressures, and so on.

physical quantities The new office provides 2,700 square feet more than the present facilities.

When the river rose 19 inches, the warehouse was at risk of flooding.

The report's headings were in 12-point Helvetica.

3.5

Use figures with symbols or abbreviations.

symbols and abbreviations We had to order special 35-mm film to shoot photos at night.

The marketing brochure showed that the computer monitor tilted a 20°.

The report's headings were in 12-pt. Helvetica.

3.6

Use figures for all percentages and decimal fractions.

percentages and decimals Our personnel manager estimated that the new training program would reduce the turnover by at least 23 percent.

3.7

Use figures to indicate age.

age Retirement benefits can begin as early as age 55.

Professionals in their 30s often have to juggle complex personal and professional responsibilities.

The 62-year-old sales manager filed a grievance for age discrimination.

REVISITING MURRAY'S DRAFT

At the beginning of this appendix, you read a draft of the complaint procedure that Murray Caton submitted to Cynthia Jorgenson in his company's Human Relations Department. Despite Cynthia's request that the draft have few grammatical and mechanical miscues, Murray simply didn't do a careful job of editing. In fact, Cynthia commented that she sometimes wasn't sure what he meant and returned his draft with the miscues marked. Murray was forced to scurry around to learn exactly what she meant by "lack of parallel structure," "dangling modifier," and "pronoun error." He was surprised that eliminating the problems turned out to be more than a last-minute clean-up task.

You're about to read a revision, a more polished version that Murray produced after he reviewed the kind of information that's in this appendix. This information showed Murray how to eliminate grammatical and mechanical problems in his early draft. After you read Murray's revised draft, compare the changes he made with the ones you suggested when you first read the earlier draft. As you compare your revision with Murray's, consider how each possible revision might affect the audience, how it responds to the occasion, and how it fulfills the purpose of the document.

Sexual Harassment

Sexual harassment, by definition, is any verbal, physical, or environmental sexual misconduct; any unwelcome sexual advance; or any unwelcome sexual behavior. Sexual harassment is against state and federal law when any of these conditions occur:

- Sexual requests or conduct is made either explicitly or implicitly a condition of employment.
- Agreement to or rejection of such conduct by an individual is used as the basis for an employment decision.
- The conduct in question interferes with an individual's work performance by creating an intimidating, hostile, offensive, or uncomfortable working environment.

If you feel you are the victim of sexual harassment, these steps need to be followed by the complainant and the company to remedy the situation:

1) Review of the company's complaint policy (by the complainant)
2) Complaint investigation (by the company)
3) Decision making and action (by the company)

1. Learning the Complaint Policy

Report your sexual harassment complaint, either written or oral, to the Vice President or Employment Specialist of the Human Resources department or to your supervisor. The Vice President and Employment Specialist of Human Resources will be in charge of conducting the investigation. The Vice President and Employment Specialist have been specifically trained to handle sexual harassment complaints. If you do not feel comfortable discussing your complaint with human resource personnel, you may speak to higher levels of management without the risk of adverse consequences. Any report of sexual harassment will be taken seriously by this company.

Supervisors must report any instance of sexual harassment that they witness or are aware of to the Vice President or Employment Specialist of Human Resources. Failure to comply with this policy will result in disciplinary actions up to termination.

Once an incident of sexual harassment is reported, investigation of the complaint will take place immediately and confidentially.

Retaliation against the complainant will not be tolerated. Retaliation may include, but is not limited to, threats, harassment by fellow employees, or continued harassment by the accused. Disciplinary action, up to termination, will be taken if such behavior occurs.

Every new employee will be required to attend a sexual harassment policy program within three months of employment. These programs will be administered by the Human Resource Department. Upon employment, you will be informed of the program that you are required to attend.

2. Investigating Complaints

If you feel you have been the victim of sexual harassment, you will need to document the date and time the behavior occurred as well as the people involved (the alleged harasser and any witnesses) and then provide a detailed description of what took place.

Your complaint needs to be presented to the Vice President or Employment Specialist of the Human Resources department or a manager as quickly as possible. If too much time is wasted, relevant information may be forgotten.

Once the complaint is filed, the Vice President or Employment Specialist of Human Resources or your manager will contact all parties involved: this includes the complainant, the accused, and any witnesses.

3. Making Decisions and Initiating Actions

The decision about whether sexual harassment has taken place will be contingent on our company's definition of sexual harassment.

If the accused is found guilty, disciplinary action will be imposed immediately. Disciplinary action may include, but is not limited to, formal written reprimand, probational period, suspension from work without pay, or termination of employment.

If the accused is found not guilty, the complainant will be informed why and how the decision was made. Retaliation against the complainant for filing the complaint will not be tolerated. Retaliation may include, but is not limited to, threats, harassment by fellow employees or any harassment by the person accused.

All steps of the complaint process will be documented and placed in the complainant's and accused's personnel files. All information is completely confidential. The Human Resource department will also keep a separate file about the complaint itself.

NOTES

Chapter 1

[1]Mary Leslie Mohan (1993), *Organizational Communication and Cultural Vision: Approaches for Analysis*, State University of New York Press, New York, 2–11.

[2]Thomas A. Falsey (1989), *Corporate Philosophies and Mission Statements: A Survey and Guide for Corporate Communicators and Management*, Quorum Books, New York.

[3]Richard Pascale (1984), "Fitting Employees into the Company Culture," *Fortune* 109 (May 28): 28–30+.

[4]Alecia Swasy (1993), *Soap Opera: The Inside Story of Procter & Gamble*, Random House, New York.

[5]Margo L. Smith (1990), "'Back Home We Use Fish That Size for Bait': Developing Joint Ventures in Latin America," *Cross-Cultural Management and Organizational Culture* 42 (February): 133–44.

[6]Tomoko Hamada and Ann Jordan, eds. (1990), *Cross-Cultural Management and Organizational Culture*, Williamsburg, VA: Dept. of Anthropology, College of William and Mary.

[7]Michele Wender Zak (1994), "'It's Like a Prison in There'—Organizational Fragmentation in a Demographically Diversified Workplace," *Journal of Business and Technical Communication* 8 (July): 281–98.

[8]Marion G. Sobol, Gail E. Farrelly, and Jessica S. Taper (1992), *Shaping the Corporate Image: An Analytical Guide for Executive Decision Makers*, Quorum Books, New York, 12.

[9]James G. Gray, Jr. (1986), *Managing the Corporate Image: The Key to Public Trust*, Quorum Books, Westport, Conn.

[10]Michael Nash (1983), "The Organization's Image," *Managing Organizational Performance,* San Francisco, CA: Jossey-Bass Publishers.

[11]John Couretas (1984), "The Corporate Image Facelift: How to Avoid 'Techno-Dread' with a Bambi Sound-Alike, and Other Tales," *Business Marketing* 69 (February): 46–48+.

Chapter 2

[1]Information taken from Helen Rothschild Ewald and Donna Stine (1983), "Speech Act Theory and Business Communication Convention," *Journal of Business Communication* 20(3): 13–25.

[2]"Where 1990s-Style Management Is Already Hard at Work" (1989), *Business Week* (October 23): 92–93.

[3]J. David Johnson (1993) offers this observation as well as an insightful analysis of corporate communication in *Organizational Communication Structure*, Ablex Publishing, Norwood, N.J.

[4]Marilyn H. Lewis and N.L. Reinsch, Jr. (1988), "Listening in Organizational Environments," *Journal of Business Communication* 25(3): 49–67.

[5]See Stephen Toulmin, Richard Rieke, and Allan Janik (1979) *An Introduction to Reasoning*, Macmillan Publishing Company, Inc., New York.

[6]"When Your Workplace Is Divided by a Common Language," (1991), *Personnel* 68 (July): 14.

Chapter 3

[1]Philip H. Mirvis, Amy L. Sales, and Edward J. Hackett (1991), "The Implementation and Adoption of New Technology in Organizations: The Impact on Work, People, and Culture," *Human Resource Management* 30: 113–39.

[2]Howard Gleckman with John Carey, Russell Mitchell, Tim Smart, and Chris Roush (1993), "The Technology Payoff," *Business Week* (June 14): 57–68.

[3]G. Christian Hill (1994), "All Together Now: Internal Computer Networks Are Changing the Way Companies—and Their Employees—Do Business," *The Wall Street Journal* (November 14): R1, R8.

[4]David Woodruff (1993), "High Tech Keeps a Retailer from Wilting," *Business Week* (June 14): 64.

[5]Jared Sandberg, "Net Working: Corporate America Is Falling in Love with the Internet," *The Wall Street Journal* (November 14): R14, R33.

[6]Bill Richards (1994), "The Future Is Now," *The Wall Street Journal* (November 14): R10, R25.

[7]Richards.

[8]Lotus Notes promotional brochure.

[9]David Kirkpatrick (1994), "Why Microsoft Can't Stop Lotus Notes," *Fortune* (December 12): 141–57.

[10]Bill Richards, op. cit.

[11]Russ Lockwood (1990), "Multimedia in Business: The New Presentations," *Personal Computing* (June 29): 116–26.

[12]Joseph Schorr (1993), "A Road Map to Multimedia Presentation," *Macworld* (November): 114–19.

[13]Schorr.

Communication Spotlight I

[1]Leavitt; Shaw

[2]J. David Johnson (1993), *Organizational Communication Structure,* Ablex Publishing, Norwood, N.J. (modified from Chapter 3, Network analysis, pp. 33–58).

Chapter 5

[1]Marc Hequet (1993) "The Intricacies of Interviewing," *Training* 30 (April): 31–34.

[2]Kristin R. Woolever and Helen M. Loeb (1994), *Writing for the Computer Industry*, Prentice Hall, Englewood Cliffs, NJ.

[3]Entire genres of writing are sometimes classified according to their dominant purpose. A good example of such classification can be found in James L. Kinneavy's *A Theory of Discourse*, where genres such as scientific writing and textbooks are classified as "referential discourse," having an informative aim, and other genres including political speeches, legal oratory, and editorials are classified as "persuasive discourse" (p. 61). James L. Kinneavy (1980), *A Theory of Discourse: The Aims of Discourse,* Norton, New York.

[4]Ramage and Beane

[5]Our thanks to Smokey McKinney (Potowatomi), co-chair of the symposium committee, for his help in interpreting the artwork.

Chapter 6

[1]See Dorothy Augustine and W. Ross Winterowd (1986), "Speech Acts and the Reader-Writer Connection," in Bruce T. Peterson, ed., *Convergences: Transactions in Reading and Writing,* National Council of Teachers of English, Urbana, Ill., 127–148.

[2]Aristotle, *Art of Rhetoric* I.i.10–11.

[3]Persuasive documents in other types of writing do not always put the most important argument last. Forensic discourse, for example, puts the most important argument first and repeats it at the end as well, under the assumption that juries will most likely be listening at the beginning and at the end of an attorney's presentation.

[4]Some of the examples presented in this portion of the text come from an article written by Helen Rothschild Ewald and Donna Stine (1993) entitled "Speech Act Theory and Business Communication Convention," *Journal of Business Communication* 20 (3): 13–25.

[5]We are consciously using terms from speech act theory to label these ineffective ways of departing from conventions. Speech act theory is introduced in Chapter 2.

Chapter 7

[1]Annette T. Rottenberg (1994), *Elements of Argument,* St. Martin's Press, New York. This introductory text provides clear, effective definitions and examples of formal argument.

[2]Stephen Toulmin, Richard Beke, and Allan Janik (1979), *An Introduction to Reasoning,* Macmillan, New York; and Sonya K. Foss (1996), *Rhetorical Criticism: Exploration and Practice,* 2nd ed., Waveland Press, Prospect Heights, IL.

[3]Paul Bator (1980), "Aristotlean and Rogerian Rhetoric," *College Composition and Communication* XXXI (Dec.): 427–32.

[4]Lisa Ede and Andrea Lunsford (1989), *Singular Texts/Plural Authors,* Southern Illinois University Press, Carbondale.

[5]Rebecca E. Burnett (1990), "Benefits of Collaborative Planning in the Business Communication Classroom," *Bulletin of the Association for Business Communication* 53 (2):9–17. This work is part of the Making Thinking Visible Project at Carnegie-Mellon University, funded by the Howard Heinz Endowment of Pittsburgh Foundation and sponsored by the Center for the Study of Writing at Berkeley and Carnegie-Mellon.

[6]G. William Page (1989), "Using Project Management Software in Planning," *Journal of the American Planning Association* 55 (Autumn): 494–499.

Communication Spotlight II

[1]Flower et al., Detection, Diagnosis . . .

[2]Barbara Sitko (1993), "Exploring Feedback: Writers Meet Readers," in Ann M. Penrose and Barbara M. Sitko, eds., *Hearing Ourselves Think: Cognitive Research in the College Writing Classroom,* Oxford University Press, New York, 170–187.

Chapter 8

[1]The information and quotes about humor in this section are derived from: "Add Humor to Workplace Memos," (1992), *Personnel Journal* 71 (June): 67; Gerald Cohen (1992), "Humanizing Technical Communication," *Technical Communication* (third quarter): 468–69; "How Kodak Made Room for Humor," (1992), *Personnel Journal* 71 (June): 66; Lisa E. Phillips (1992), "Using Humor in Business Ads Can Get Ticklish," *Business Marketing* (May): 56; and Ron Zemke (1991), "Humor in Training: Laugh and the World Learns with You—Maybe," *Training* 28 (August): 26–29.

Communication Spotlight III

[1]Modified from Donelson R. Forsythe (1983), *An Introduction to Group Dynamics,* Brooks/Cole, Pacific Grove, Calif.

[2]Roger Fisher, William Ury, and Bruce Patton (1991), *Getting to Yes,* 2nd ed., Houghton Mifflin, Boston.

Chapter 11

[1]Barbara Peterson, Director of 3M Information Services, telephone interview, February 14, 1995.

Chapter 12

[1]Charles Kostelnick (1989), "Visual Rhetoric: A Reader-Oriented Approach to Graphics and Designs," *The Technical Writing Teacher* XVI (Winter): 77–88.

Chapter 13

[1]Edward R. Tufte (1983), *The Visual Display of Quantitative Information,* Graphics Press, Cheshire, CT.

Communication Spotlight IV

[1]Walden Miller, Manager of Technical Documentation, OptImage, telephone interview, October 1994.

[2]Janis Foreman (1993), "Task Groups and Their Writing: Relationships between Group Characteristics and Group Reports," *Technical Communication Quarterly* 2(1): 75–88.

Chapter 15

[1]Richard C. Freed, Shervin Freed, and Joe Romano (1995), *Writing Winning Business Proposals: Your Guide to Landing the Client, Making the Sale, Persuading the Boss,* McGraw-Hill, Inc., New York.

Chapter 16

[1]Modified from David E. Clement (1987), "Human Factors, Instructions and Warnings, and Products Liability," *IEEE Transactions on Professional Communicaiton* 30(3): 149–56.

Chapter 17

[1](1991) "Critical Link Between Presentation Skills, Upward Mobility," *Supervision* 52 (October): 24.

[2]Floyd Wickman (1992), "Getting Them to 'Buy In' to Your Message," *Supervisory Management.*

[3]Modified from Kittie W. Watson and Larry L. Barker (1992), Training 101: Both Sides of the Platform," *Training & Development* 46(November): 15–17.

[4]Frank O'Meara (1993), "Presentation Tips from Old, Dead Greeks," *Training* 30(May): 69–71.

[5]Edward P. J. Corbett (1990), *Classical Rhetoric for the Modern Student,* 3rd Edition. New York: Oxford University Press.

[6]Preston Gralla (1992), "A Step-By-Step Guide," *PC Computing* (May): 1–17; Phillip Robinson (1994), "Electronic Presentations Can Be Tough to Get Up and Running," *The Boston Globe* (March 22): 45.

[7]Background information regarding Intel and Pentium chip is based on *Newsweek: 1994 in Perspectives*, special issue, December 26, 1994: 13; *U.S. News & World Report*, December 12, 1994; and *Fortune*, January 16, 1995.

Communication Spotlight V

[1]David Johnson (1993), *Organizational Communication Structure*, Ablex, Norwood, NJ.

[2]David A. Victor (1992), *International Business Communication*, HarperCollins, New York.

[3]Ibid.

[4]Ibid.

[5]O. Michael Watson (1970), *Proxemic Behavior: A Cross-Cultural Study*, Mouton, The Hague.

Chapter 18

[1]The information in this figure and the next is based in part on information taken from John R. Hayes (1987), *The Complete Problem Solver*, Laurence Erlbaum Associates, Hillsdale, N.J.

[2]Junda Woo (1993), "Quick Slander Actions Threaten Employers," *The Wall Street Journal* (November 26): B1+.

[3]Max Messmer (1993), "Nothing but the Truth," *Small Business Reports* 18 (March): 11–14.

Chapter 19

[1]Suzanne Oliver (1993), "Slouches Make Better Operators," *Forbes* (August 16): 104–5.

[2]L. M. Sixel (1994), "Experts Advise More Tests on Interviews," *Houston Chronicle*, 2 Star Edition (October 1).

[3]Robert C. Liden, Christopher L. Martin, and Charles K. Parsons (1993), "Interviewer and Applicant Behaviors in Employment Interviews," *Academy of Management Journal* 36: 372–86.

[4]Paul R. Saunders (1993), "Job Interviewing: How to Make It Work for You!" *Journal of Systems Management* 44 (July): 17–20+. Many of the examples in this section were suggested by Saunders' discussion.

[5]James R. Grisemer (1993), "The Power of Performance Measurement: A Computer Performance Model and Examples from Colorado Cities," *Government Finance Review* 9 (October): 17–21.

[6]James S. Bowman (1994), "At Last, an Alternative to Performance Appraisal: Total Quality Management," *Public Administration Review* 54 (March–April): 129–36.

[7]Theodore B. Kinni (1993), "Judge and Be Judged: Hampton Pension Services Has an Antidote for the Dreaded Performance Appraisal," *Industry Week* (August 2): 45+.

[8]Michael G. Aamondt, Devon A. Bryan, and Alan J. Whitcomb (1993), "Predicting Performance with Letters of Recommendation," *Public Personnel Management* 22 (Spring): 81–89.

Communication Spotlight VI

Collaboration:

[1]Andrea Lunsford and Lisa Ede (1990), *Singular Texts/Plural Authors: Perspective on Collaborative Writing*, Southern Illinois University Press, Carbondale; Paul Anderson (1985), "What Survey Research Tells Us about Writing at Work," in L. Odell and D. Goswami, eds., *Writing in Nonacademic Settings*, Guilford Press, New York, 3–83; and Lester Faigley and Thomas P. Miller (1982), "What We Learn from Writing on the Job," *College English* 44: 557–69.

[2]Deborah S. Bosley (1991), "Designing Effective Technical Communication Teams," *Technical Communication* 38 (4): 504–12.

Revision:

[1]Rebecca E. Burnett (1994), "Reviewing the Practice of Document Testing," *ABC Bulletin*: 47–48, 58.

[2]Karen A. Schriver (1989), "Evaluating Text Quality: The Continuum from Text-Focused to Reader-Focused Methods," *IEEE Transaction on Professional Communication* 32: 238–55.

[3]Modified from discussions in J. S. Dumas and J. C. Redish (1993), *A Practical Guide to Usability Testing*, Ablex Publishing, Norwood, N.J.; R. A. Grice and L. S. Ridgway (1991), "Information Product Testing," in Thomas T. Barker, ed., *Perspectives on Software Documentation: Inquiries and Innovations*, Baywood Publishing, Amityville, N.Y.; J. Ramey (1989), "A Selected Bibliography: A Beginner's Guide to Usability Testing," *IEEE Transaction on Professional Communication* 32: 310–16; J. Rubin (1994), *Handbook of Usability Testing*, John Wiley & Sons, New York; Schriver, op. cit.; and Patricia Sullivan (1989), "Beyond a Narrow Conception of Usability Testing," *IEEE Transaction on Professional Communication* 32: 256–64.

SOURCES

Chapter 1

Skills and Strategies, Page 7 Linda Flower and John R. Hayes (1981), "A Cognitive Process Theory of Writing," *College Composition and Communication* 32: 365–87; and Linda Flower, Karen A. Schriver, Linda Carey, Christina Haas, and John R. Hayes (1992), "Planning in Writing: The Cognition of a Constructive Process," in Stephen P. Witte, Neil Nakadate, and Roger D. Cherry, eds., *A Rhetoric of Doing,* Southern Illinois University Press, Carbondale, 181–243.

Ethics, Page 12 Table: Do's and don'ts taken from Amy Dunkin (1991), "Blowing the Whistle without Paying the Piper," *Business Week* (June 3): 138–39. Text: Barbara Ettorre (1994), "Whistle-blowers: Who's the Real Bad Guy?" *Management Review* 83 (May): 18–23; James E. Porter (1993), "The Role of Law, Policy, and Ethics in Corporate Composing: Toward a Practical Ethics for Professional Writing," in Nancy Roundy Blyler and Charlotte Thralls, eds., *Professional Communication: The Social Perspective,* Sage Publications, Newbury Park, Calif., 128–41; and Kevin M. Smith and John M. Oseth (1993), "The Whistleblowing Era: A Management Perspective," *Employee Relations* 19 (Autumn): 179–92.

Multicultural, Page 13 Craig Coulter (1994), "Cultural Sensitivity–It Isn't Easy, but It Is Right," *Passages* (May): 2; Rene Olie (1990), "Cultural Issues in Transnational Business Ventures." Tomoko Hamada and Ann Jordan, eds. *Cross-Cultural Management and Organizational Culture.* Williamsburg, VA: Dept. of Anthropology, College of William and Mary, 145–172; and Alecia Swasy (1993), "Don't Sell Thick Diapers in Tokyo," *New York Times* (October 3): 9.

Technology, Page 18 Samuel E. Bleecker (1994), "The Virtual Organization," *Futurist* (March–April): 9–12+; and John A. Byrne (1993), "The Virtual Corporation," *Business Week* (February 8): 98–102.

Figure 1.23, Page 28 Joseph Bruchac (1991), *Native American Stories,* Fulcrum Publishing, Golden, Colo.; John G. Niehardt (1979), *Black Elk Speaks: Being the Life Story of a Holy Man of the Oglala Sioux,* University of Nebraska Press, Lincoln; and Joanne Martin (1988), "Stories and Scripts in Organizational Settings," *Comprehension: Perspectives from Cognitive Psychology, Linguistics, Artificial Intelligence and Education,* Lawrence Erlbaum Associates, Hillsdale, N.J., 255–305.

Chapter 2

Figure 2.1, Page 34 Adapted from Barbara Minto (1987), *The Pyramid Principle: Logic in Writing and Thinking,* Minto International, Inc., London; and Helen Rothschild Ewald (1983), *Writing as Process: Invention and Convention,* Charles E. Merrill, Columbus, Ohio.

Figure 2.11, Page 44 Based in part on David Krackhardt and Jeffrey R. Hanson (1993),"Informal Networks: The Company behind the Chart," *Harvard Business Review* 71 (July–August): 104–11.

Ethics, Page 45 David Bjerklie (1993), "E-Mail: The Boss Is Watching," *Technology Review* (April): 14–15; and Michele Simms (1994), "Defining Privacy in Employee Health Screening Cases: Ethical Ramifications Concerning the Employee/Employer Relationship," *Journal of Business Ethics* 13: 315–25.

Figure 2.13, Page 47 Adapted from information in Robert Benfari and Jean Knox (1991), *Understanding Your Management Style,* D.C. Heath and Company, Lexington, MA.

Multicultural, Page 48 Table: Adapted from Mary Munter (1993), "Cross-Cultural Communication for Managers," *Business Horizons* (May–June): 69–78. Text: Richard M. Hodgetts and Jane W. Gibson (1989), "Communicating Effectively in Multicultural Markets," IEEE/*International Professional Communication Conference,* Garden City, N.Y.: 269–272; and Geert Hofstede (1984), *Culture's Consequences: International Differences in Work-Related Values,* Sage Publications, Beverly Hills, Calif.

Technology, Page 49 Jeffrey Hsu and Tony Lockwood (1993), "Collaborative Computing," *Byte* 18 (March): 112–34; and Alice LaPlante (1993), "'90s Style Brainstorming," *Forbes* 152 (October 25): 44–46.

Figure 2.15, Page 49 Adapted from Steven Golen (1990), "A Factor Analysis of Barriers to Effective Listening," *Journal of Business Communication* 27(1): 25–35.

Figure 2.21, Page 54 Adapted from Stephen Toulmin, Richard Rieke, and Allan Janik (1979), *An Introduction to Reasoning,* Macmillan Publishing Co., Inc., New York.

Figure 2.25, Page 56 "When Your Workplace Is Divided by a Common Language" (1991) *Personnel* 68 (July): 14.

Figure 2.27, Page 59 Material based on information in Rosabeth Moss Kanter (1983), "Change Masters and the Intricate Architecture of Corporate Culture Change," *Management Review* 72 (October): 18–78.

Chapter 3

Figure 3.14, Page 71 U.S. West Communications (1994), *Solutions for the Information Highway.*

Figure 3.15, Page 73 Chris Reidy (1994), "No Lines On-Line," *Boston Globe* (December 6): 43.

Figure 3.16, Page 74 Jared Sandberg (1994), "Net Working: Corporate America Is Falling in Love with the Internet," *The Wall Street Journal* (November 14): R14, R33.

Ethics, Page 74 Bob Filipczak (1994), "The Electronic Water-cooler," *Training* (March): 43.; and "Work Week: New Year's Promises," (1995), *The Wall Street Journal* (January 3): 1.

Technology, Page 76 Liora Alschuler (1993), special section, "Standard General Markup Language," Introduction, *Technical Communication* 40 (May): 208–9.; and Elizabeth Gilmore (1993), "Introducing Today's SGML," *Technical Communication* 40 (May): 210–18.

Multicultural, Page 79 Dave Kansas (1993), "The Icon Crisis: Tiny Pictures Cause Confusion," *The Wall Street Journal* (November 17): B1.; and Patricia A. Williams and Pamela S. Beason (1990), *Writing Effective Software Documentation,* Scott, Foresman and Company, Glenview, Ill.

Figure 3.23, Page 82 Michael Schrage (1994), "Pros and Cons of Anonymous Corporate E-Mail," *Boston Globe* (April 3): 69.

Figure 3.24, Page 83 Michael Schrage (1994), "Robert's Electronic Rules of Order," *The Wall Street Journal* (November 29).

Figure 3.25, Page 83 Michael Schrage (1992), "When Technology Heightens Office Tensions," *The Wall Street Journal* (October 5): A12.

Figure 3.26, Page 84 John R. Wilke (1993), "Computer Links Erode Hierarchical Nature of Workplace Culture," *The Wall Street Journal* (December 9): 1.

Figure 3.27, Page 88 Evan I. Schwartz (1993) "The Power of Software: New Approaches Are Starting to Get Big Results," *Business Week* (June 14): 76.

Communication Spotlight I

Figure 1, Page 92 Adapted from Benne & Sheats (1948), quoted in Donelson R. Forsyth (1990), *Group Dynamics* 2nd ed., Brooks/Cole, Pacific Grove, CA, p. 113.

Figure 2, Page 93 Adapted from Benne & Sheats (1948), quoted in Donelson R. Forsyth (1990), *Group Dynamics* 2nd ed., Brooks/Cole, Pacific Grove, CA, p. 113.

Chapter 4

Ethics, Page 104 Erik Larson (1992), *The Naked Consumer: How Our Private Lives Become Public Commodities,* Henry Holt and Company, New York.

Technology, Page 105 "Putting Census Data in Entrepreneurs' Hands" (1994), *The Wall Street Journal* 76 (February 24): B4; and Ben Smith and Howard Eglowstein (1993), "Putting Your Data on the Map," *Byte* 18 (January): 188–90+.

Skills & Strategies, Page 122 Leon E. Wynter (1993), "Braided Hair Collides with Office Norms," *The Wall Street Journal* (May 3): B1; Pearl G. Aldrich (1985), "Skirting Sexism," *Nation's Business* (December): 34–36; Bill Daily and Miriam Finch (1993), "Benefiting from Nonsexist Language in the Workplace," *Business Horizons* 36 (March–April): 30–34; and "Navigating the Differences" (1993), *Training and Development* 47 (April): 29–37.

Chapter 5

Figure 5.2, Page 131 Americans with Disabilities Act of 1990, Pub. L. No. 101–336, USCA 12101 et seq. West (1990); and Charles Alan Drugel (1993), "AIDS and the ADA: Maneuvering through a Legal Minefield," *Labor Law Journal* (July): 408–21.

Technology, Page 137 Michelle Neely Martinez (1994) "How to Avoid Accidents on the Electronic Highway," *HR Magazine* 39 (July): 74–77; Trevor Nelson (1994), "Stick to 'Snail Mail,'" *The Wall Street Journal* 76 (June 8): A16; and Shannon Peters (1994), "Standard Policy Clears Confusion over E-Mail," *Personnel Journal* 73 (June): 123–24.

Ethics, Page 138 Norbert Elliot, Eric Katz, and Robert Lynch (1993), "The *Challenger* Tragedy: A Case Study in Organizational Communication and Professional Ethics," *Business and Professional Ethics Journal* 12 (Summer): 91–108; and Patrick Moore (1992), "When Politeness Is Fatal: Technical Communication and the *Challenger* Accident," *Journal of Business and Technical Communication* 6 (July): 269–92.

Multicultural, Page 146 D. Lawrence Kincaid (1987), *Communication Theory: Eastern and Western Philosophy,* Academic Press, Boston.

Skills & Strategies, Page 152 Brad Edmonson (1993), "Return of the Jungle," *American Demographics* (March):2.

Chapter 6

Multicultural, Page 164 Brenda R. Sims and Stephen Guice (1992), "Differences between Business Letters from Native and Nonnative Speakers of English," *Journal of Business Communication* 29 (1): 23–39.

Technology, Page 165 Victor J. Cosentino (1994), "Virtual Legality," *Byte* 19 (March): 278; Jared Sandberg (1993), "Up in Flames," *The Wall Street Journal* 76 (November 15): R12; and John Seabrook (1994), "My First Flame," *New Yorker* 70 (June 6): 70–79.

Ethics, Page 177 Anne G. Perkins (1994) "The Costs of Deception," *Harvard Business Review* (May–June): 10–11; and Robert Tomsho (1994), "How Greyhound Lines Re-engineered Itself Right into a Deep Hole," *The Wall Street Journal* 76 (October 20): A1.

Chapter 7

Multicultural, Page 193 Kathy Spencer and Peggy Yates (1990), "Tell It to the World: Technical Communication in the Global Marketplace," In *Proceedings of the 37th International Technical Communication Conference,* RT-149–152.

Ethics, Page 197 Thomas A. Falsey (1989), *Corporate Philosophies and Mission Statements: A Survey and Guide for Corporate Communicators and Management,* Quorum Books, New York; and James R. Gregory with Jack G. Wiechmann (1991), *Marketing Corporate Images: The Company as Your Number One Product,* NTC Business Books, Lincolnwood, Ill.

Figure 7.13, Page 200 Canadian Handbook of Flexible Benefits.

Technology, Page 207 Wendy Pickering (1994), "Project 4.0 Works in the Office," *Datamation* 40 (March 15): 64+; Jan Watts (1991), "Keep Your Projects on Time, on Budget," *PC Computing* 4 (June): 161–166+; and Lamont Wood (1988), "The Promise of Project Management," *Byte* 13 (November): 180–188+.

Chapter 8

Multicultural, Page 223 S. Jenkins and J. Hinds (1987), "Business Letter Writing: English, French, and Japanese," *TESOL Quarterly,* 21(2): 327–49.

Skills & Strategies, Page 227 Information from "Cross-Cultural Dos and Don'ts" (1991), *Personnel Journal* 70: 28+.

Technology, Page 233 Brian Cox (1994), "Savings in Costs and Time Boost Video Conferencing," *National Underwriter* (Life & Health/Financial Services Edition) 98 (January 24): 2+; and Elliot M. Gold (1994), "PCs Rewrite the Rules for Videoconferencing," *Data Communications* 23 (March): 95–98+.

Ethics, Page 239 John Bryan (1992), "Down the Slipperly Slope: Ethics and the Technical Writer as Marketer," *Technical Communication Quarterly* 1: 73–88.

Chapter 9

Technology, Page 254 Scott Cunningham and Alan L. Porter (1992), "Communication Networks: A Dozen Ways They'll Change Our Lives," *Futurist* 26: 19–22.

Ethics, Page 261 Kim Sydow Campbell (1990), "Negative Messages and Speech Act Theory," *Journal of Business Communication* 27 (Fall): 357–75; and Phillip V. Lewis and Henry E. Speck III (1990), "Ethical Orientations for Understanding Business Ethics," *Journal of Business Communication* 27 (Summer): 213–32.

Multicultural, Page 272 Penelope Brown and Stephen Levinson (1978), "Universals in Language Use: Politeness Phenomena," in Esther N. Goody, ed., *Questions and Politeness: Strategies in Social Interaction,* Cambridge University Press, Cambridge; Yueguo Gu (1990), "Politeness Phenomena in Modern Chinese," *Journal of Pragmatics* 14(2): 237–57; Hiroki Kato and Joan S. Kato (1992), *Understanding and Working with the Japanese Business World,* Prentice Hall, Englewood

Cliffs, N.J.; and LuMing R. Mao (1994), "Beyond Politeness Theory: 'Face' Revisited and Renewed," *Journal of Pragmatics* 21: 487–511.

Chapter 10

Skills & Strategies, Page 281 David Roberts and Helen Rothschild Ewald (1993), Course Materials on Designing Brochures; *Pocket Pal: A Graphics Arts Production Handbook,* International Paper Company.

Ethics, Page 288 Kenneth E. Anderson (1991), "A History of Communication Ethics," in Karen Joy Greenberg, ed., *Conversations on Communication Ethics,* Ablex Publishing, Norwood, N.J., 3–19; Eric Benderoff (1992), "Long Run or Short Term, Direct Mail Works," *Professional Builder and Remodeler* 57 (May): 67; Cynthia Massino (1993), "5,243% Return on Investment!" *Bank Marketing* (March): 21; and Pamela Sebastian (1994), "Charity Tries Two Letters to Melt Cold Hearts," *The Wall Street Journal* (November 22): B1.

Technology, Page 295 Peter Lewis (1994), "An Ad (Gasp!) in Cyberspace," *New York Times* (April 19): D1–D2; and Michael Rothschild (1994), "Stagecoach Days on the Infohighway," *Forbes* 153 (February 28 supp. ASAP): 25–26.

Multicultural, Page 296 Carl A. Nelson (1990), *Global Success: International Business Tactics for the 1990s,"* Liberty Hall Press, Blue Ridge Summit, Pa.

Communication Spotlight III

Figure 1, Page 305 Roger Fisher, William Ury, and Bruce Patton (1991), *Getting to Yes,* 2nd ed., Houghton Mifflin, Boston.

Chapter 11

Skills and Strategies, Page 323 Natalie A. Updegrove (1990), "Database Searching: Information Retrieval for Nutrition Professionals," *Journal of Nutrition Education* 22 (October): 241–247.

Multicultural, Page 328 Sondra Thiederman (1991), *Bridging Cultural Barriers for Corporate Success: How to Manage the Multicultural Workforce.* Lexington Books, Lexington, Mass.

Technology, Page 331 Allison Class (1991), "Advanced-Level Spreadsheets," *Accountancy* 107 (March): 122+; Nicholas Daniels (1992), "Spreadsheets under Scrutiny," *Byte* 17 (11) (1992 Essential Guide to Windows issue): 70–+; and Stephen Rather (1991), "Simplified Spreadsheet Models Are Key Research Tool," *Marketing News* 25 (January 7): 15+.

Figure 11.14, Page 333 Modified from Darrell Huff (1954), *How to Lie with Statistics,* W. W. Norton, New York.

Ethics, Page 336 Herbert Michaelson (1990), "How an Author Can Avoid the Pitfalls of Practical Ethics," *IEEE Transactions on Professional Communication* 33(2): 58–61; M. Jimmie Killingsworth and Scott P. Sanders (1990), "Complementarity and Compensation: Bridging the Gap between Writing and Design," *Technical Writing Teacher* 17(3): 204–221.

Case Background, Pages 339–340 Bureau of the Census, U.S. Department of Commerce.

Chapter 12

Technology, Page 347 Charlotte LeGates (1993), "Professional-Looking Publishing from Desktop Computers," *HRMagazine* 38: 29+; Patrick Marshall (1993), "Meet the Press," *Inc.* 15 (Technology Guide, Winter): 66–68+; and Russ Risko (1994), "It's Not All Roses," *Managing Office Technology* 39 (January): 11.

Ethics, Page 357 Stuart Bass (1994), "Strict Construction of Health Insurance Contracts," *Labor Law Journal* 45 (2): 90–101; Mitchell E. Macdonald (1990), "High Court to Shippers: 'Read the Fine Print,'" *Traffic Management* 29 (7): 15–16; and Miles A. Tinker (1963), *Legibility of Print,* Iowa State University Press, Ames.

Multicultural, Page 361 William Horton (1993), "The Almost Universal Language: Graphics for International Documentation," *Technical Communication* 40 (Fourth Quarter): 682–93.

Chapter 13

Figure 13.1, Page 367 Institute on World Affairs. (1993). Promotional brochure.

Multicultural, Page 370 William Horton (1993) "The Almost Universal Language: Graphics for International Documents," *Technical Communication* 40 (Fourth Quarter): 682–93.

Figure 13.7, Page 373 Delta Air Lines.

Figure 13.8, Page 374 *The Boston Globe.*

Figure 13.10, Page 375 *Tieline.* January 1994, vol 7, no 1, p. 3.

Figure 13.11, Page 376 J. E. Miller and M. Porter (1985), *Supervision in the Hospitality Industry,* John Wiley & Sons.

Figure 13.15, Page 378 Prudential Securities (February 1994), *Ideas for Investors,* p. 2., North Palm Beach, Fla.

Technology, Page 378 Dave Andrews (1994), "Graphics Gets Down to Basics," *Byte* 19 (January): 28; and Walter S. Mossberg (1994), "Graphics Software That's Friendly Even to Non-Artists," *The Wall Street Journal* (January 27): B1.

Figure 13.25, Page 384 Ben & Jerry's, *Call for Kids,* Waterbury, VT.

Figure 13.28, Page 386 U.S. Census.

Figure 13.29, Page 386 "Heinz Affiliates Aid Earthquake Victims," *Heinz Quarterly,* Third Quarter 1994, H.J. Heinz Company, Pittsburgh, PA, p. 11.

Figure 13.31, Page 388 Bob Shaw (1994), "When Charts Are Sloppy, Numbers Can Deceive," *Des Moines Register* (13 May): 13A.

Ethics, Page 389 Douglas Jehl (1994), "Warning to China on Trade: U.S. Adds It to List on Product Piracy," *New York Times* (April 30): 39, 47; Mitchell Kapor (1993), "Innocent Felons," *Forbes* (February 15): 208; and Penny M. Simpson, Debasish Banjeree, and Claude L. Simpson (1994), "Softlifting: A Model of Motivating Factors," *Journal of Business Ethics* 13 (6): 431–38.

Figure 13.37, Page 391 *The Des Moines Register,* January 1994, p. 3.

Figure 13.39, Page 395 "Don't Make Your Child's College Education More Expensive Than It Has to Be," *FYI: A Financial Newsletter for Clients and Friends of Waddell & Reed,* Volume Six, Number 1, p. 2.

Communication Spotlight IV

Collaboration:

Figure 2, Page 399 Modified from Rebecca E. Burnett (1990), "Benefits of Collaborative Planning in the Business Communication Classroom," *Bulletin of the Association for Business Communication* 53 (2): 9–17.

Revision:

Figure 1, Page 403 Used with permission of Theresa Humpal and Deborah Fauser, Business Communication 302, Iowa State University.

Figure 2, Page 404 Used with permission of Jason McAlexander, Carrie Matlock, and Rachel Woods.

Chapter 14

Ethics, Page 407 Randall Poe (1994), "Can We Talk? CEOs Speak Frankly in the New Breed of Annual Reports," *Across the Board* 31: 16–23.

Technology, Page 419 Jim Heid (1993), "Word Processing with Style Sheets," *Macworld* 10 (March): 203+; and *User's Guide to Microsoft Word* (1993), Microsoft Corporation, Redmond, Wash.

Multicultural, Page 421 John Hinds (1987), "Reader versus Writer Responsibility: A New Typology," in Ulla Connor and Robert B. Kaplan, eds., *Writing across Languages: Analysis of L2 Text,* Addison-Wesley Publishing Co., Reading, Mass., 141–52; John Mackin (1989), "Surmounting the Barrier between Japanese and English Technical Documents," *Technical Communication* 36 (Fourth Quarter): 346–51; Gail Nash (1987), "Cross-Cultural Communication and Technical Communication," in *Proceedings of the 34th International Technical Communications Conference* ET188–ET190; and Iris I. Varner (1987), "Internationalizing Business Communication Courses," *Bulletin of the Association for Business Communication* (December): 7–11.

Chapter 15

Skills and Strategies, Page 439 Materials developed and copyrighted by Richard C. Freed as class lecture notes (1991); and Richard C. Freed, Shervin Freed, and Joe Romano (1995), *Writing Winning Business Proposals: Your Guide to Landing the Client, Making the Sale, Persuading the Boss,* McGraw-Hill, Inc., New York.

Multicultural, Page 441 Edward T. Hall and Mildred R. Hall (1987), *Hidden Differences: Doing Business with the Japanese,* Anchor Press, New York; and Hiroki Kato and Joan S. Kato (1992), *Understanding and Working with the Japanese Business World,* Prentice Hall, Englewood Cliffs, N.J.

Technology, Page 445 "Perspectives on Multimedia" (1992), *Computerland Magazine* (May–June): 17–19.

Ethics, Page 455 Table: Based on data in Senator William Proxmire (1980), *The Fleecing of America,* Houghton Mifflin Company, Boston; Text: Pierre L. Van den Berghe (1970), *Academic Gamesmanship,* Abelard-Schuman, London, 108; and Bill Lawren (1984), "Air Conditioned Underwear," *Omni* 7 (November): 43.

Chapter 16

Multicultural, Page 472 Gerald Albaum, J. Strandskov, E. Duerr, and L. Dowd (1989), *International Marketing and Exporting Management,* Addison-Wesley Publishing Co., Reading, Mass.

Figure 16.7, Page 473 Used with permission. Public Affairs Department, AAA Iowa.

Technology, Page 481 William Horton (1993), "Horton's Laws of On-Line Documentation," *Technical Communication* 40 (May): 318–19; and Sandra Oster (1994), "Indexes in Computer Documentation," *Technical Communication* 41 (February): 41–50.

Skills and Strategies, Page 484 Pamela S. Helyar (1992), "Products Liability: Meeting Legal Standards for Adequate Instructions," *Journal of Technical Writing and Communication* 22(2): 125–47.

Ethics, Page 486 John Bryan (1994), "The Devil Is in the Details—but So Are the Saints," in Rebecca E. Burnett, *Teaching Technical Communication: Instructor's Resource Manual for Technical Communication,* 3rd ed., 51–69; David E. Clement (1987), "Human Factors, Instructions and Warnings, and Products Liability," *IEEE Transactions on Professional Communication* 30(3): 149–56; and Kristin Woolever (1990), "Corporate Language and the Law: Avoiding Liability in Corporate Communications," *IEEE Transactions on Professional Communication* 33(2): 94–98.

Chapter 17

Ethics, Page 501 Gary Kurzbard and George J. Siomkos (1992), "Crafting a Damage Control Plan: Lessons from Perrier," *Journal of Business Strategy* (March–April): 39–43; and Lyle Sussman, Penny Ricchio, and James Belohlav (1983), "Corporate Speeches as a Source of Corporate Values: An Analysis across Years, Themes, and Industries," *Strategic Management Journal* 4(2): 187–196.

Figure 17.8, Page 503 John B. Dalton (1994), "The Character of Readiness: The Ethics of Moral Behavior," *Vital Speeches of the Day* 60(10): 296–298. Delivered to the Joint Services Conference on Professional Ethics, National Defense University, Washington, DC, January 27, 1994; John E. Van De Wetering (1991), "Political Correctness: The Insult and the Injury," *Vital Speeches of the Day* 58(4): 100–103. Delivered to the Rotary Club, Rochester, New York, September 3, 1991; D. S. Lankford (1990), "High Definition Video Technology: Telecommunications Infrastructure," *Vital Speeches of the Day* 56(8): 241–244; Will Kopp (1994), "Inventing the Future: Battelle's Vision of Tomorrow's Technology," *Vital Speeches of the Day* 60(8): 244–248; and W. Lee Hoskins (1993), "What Monetary Policy Can and Cannot Do: Price Stability," *Vital Speeches of the Day* 59(10): 290. Delivered before the Joint Economic Committee of the Congress of the United States, Washington, DC, December 30, 1992.

Figure 17.10, Page 505 William S. Sessions, "Combatting Organized Crime: The American Experience," *Vital Speeches of the Day* 59(9): 262–265. Delivered at A Symposium on Organized Crime, hosted by the Bavarian Interior Ministry, Federal Republic of Germany, Munich, Germany, December 4, 1992; Kenneth T. Derr, "Beware the Cutting Edge: Environmental Conservation and the Oil Industry," *Vital Speeches of the Day* 59(3): 93–96. Delivered to the American Legislative Exchange Council Annual Conference, Colorado Springs, Colorado, August 7, 1992; Donald J. Schuenke, "The Key to Moving Beyond: The Values That You Hold Within," *Vital Speeches of the Day* 59(3): 86–89. Delivered to the 1992 Annual Meeting of Agents, Milwaukee, Wisconsin, July 20, 1992; and Paul Craig Roberts, "Nature Is a More Gentle Adversary than the Government: The Stealing of Property Rights by Our Government," *Vital Speeches of the Day* 60(12): 371–373. Delivered before the American Farm Bureau Federation's 75th Annual Meeting, Fort Lauderdale, FL, January 10, 1994.

Figure 17.11, Page 506 Bill Clinton, "State of the Union," *Vital Speeches of the Day* 60(9): 258–264. Delivered before the Joint Session of Congress, Washington, DC, January 26, 1994; Lawrence A. Bossidy (1994), "America's Corporations Are Back in the Lead," *Vital Speeches of the Day* 60(13): 386–389. Delivered before the Economic Club of Detroit, Detroit, Michigan, February 14, 1994; Nelson Mandela, "Glory and Hope: Let There Be Work, Bread, Water, and Salt for All," *Vital Speeches of the Day* 60(16): 486. Delivered to the People of South Africa, Pretoria, South Africa, May 10, 1994; Susan Au Allen, "Bountiful Voyages: Doing Business in Asia," *Vital Speeches of the Day* 60(8): 253–256. Delivered to the International Asian Expo, Anaheim, California, December 4, 1993; M. George Allen (1994), "Succeeding in Japan," *Vital Speeches of the Day* 60(14): 424–432. Delivered before the Louisiana/Japan Association, New Orleans, Louisiana, February 17, 1994; Robert P. Forrestal (1994), "The Outlook for the United States in 1994," *Vital Speeches of the Day* 60(10): 303–305. Delivered to the Atlanta Rotary Club, Atlanta, GA, January 24, 1994; Barbara Hackman Franklin, "China: The Emerging Economic Colossus, *Vital Speeches of the Day* 60(6): 171–174. Delivered at the University of Hartford, Hartford, Connecticut, November 2, 1993; and Bert C. Roberts, Jr. "Information Highways Delivering and Shaping: The Multimedia World of Tomorrow," *Vital Speeches of the Day* 60(8): 235–236. Delivered to the Town Hall of California, Los Angeles, California, December 2, 1993.

Technology, Page 507 Priscilla C. Brown (1993), "Color Helps the Sell," *Business Marketing* (January): 58; Selinda Chiquoine (1993), "Perfectly Presentable Presentations," *Byte* 17 (Spring): 16; and Mark A. Clarkson (1993), "Presentations to Go," *Byte* 17 (Spring): 99–104.

Multicultural, Page 516 Ronald E. Duke, J. S. Fielden, and J. S. Hill (1991), "International Communication: An Executive Primer," *Business Horizons* 34 (January–February): 20–25.

Communication Spotlight V

Figure 1, Page 520 Roger Fisher, William Ury, and Bruce Patton (1991), *Getting to Yes,* 2nd ed., Houghton Mifflin, Boston.

Figure 5, Page 523 Mary Munter (1993), "Cross-Cultural Communication for Managers," *Business Horizons* 36 (May–June): 69–78. (Adapted from Hall, 1976).

Chapter 18

Technology, Page 539 Laurianne McLaughlin (1993), "Software to the Rescue for Creating Your Résumé," *PC World* 11 (October): 113; and Walter Mossberg (1994), "Four Programs to Ease PC Users into a Job Search," *The Wall Street Journal* (May 5): B1.

Multicultural, Page 540 Marvina Schilling (1993), "Avoid Expatriate Culture Shock," *HRMagazine* (July): 58–63.

Skills and Strategies, Page 543 Bill Leonard (1993), "Resume Databases to Dominate Field," *HRMagazine* (April): 59–60; Janine S. Pouliot (1994), "A Computerized Hiring Search," *Nation's Business* 82 (February): 32; Esther Dyson (1990), "What to Do with that Stack of Resumes," *Forbes* (October 15): 200; Larry Stevens (1993), "Resume Scanning Simplifies Tracking," *Personnel Journal* 72 (April): 77–79, for discussion of the scanning programs SmartSearch2 and Restrac; and Stanley W. Angrist (1994), "Looking for Work in the Information Age," *The Wall Street Journal* (January 19): A16. See also Joyce Kennedy and Thomas Morrow (1994), *Electronic Resume Revolution,* John Wiley, New York; and Margaret Mannix (1992), "Writing a Computer-Friendly Resume," *U.S. News & World Report* (October 26): 90+.

Ethics, Page 549 Timothy D. Schellhardt (1994), "While the Recruiter Checks Your Resume, Investigate the Firm's," *The Wall Street Journal* (February 23): B1.

Chapter 19

Figure 19.1, Page 563 Lyle M. Spencer, Jr., and Signe M. Spencer (1993), *Competence at Work: Models for Superior Performance,* John Wiley & Sons, Inc., New York.

Skills and Strategies, Page 565 Teri Agins (1994), "Between Suits and Jeans: The Corporate Casual Look," *The Wall Street Journal* (January 21): B1+; Daniel J. McConville (1994), "The Casual Corporation," *Industry Week* 234 (June 20): 12–17; Paul R. Saunders (1993), "Job Interviewing: How to Make It Work for You!" *Journal of Systems Management* 44 (July): 17–20+; and Ginger Colon (1994), "Dress to Sell," *Sales and Marketing Management* 146 (March): 108.

Multicultural, Page 568 Robert A. Kapp (1993), *Communicating with China,* Intercultural Press, Chicago.

Figure 19.13, Page 576 Lyle M. Spencer, Jr., and Signe M. Spencer (1993), *Competence at Work: Models for Superior Performance,* John Wiley & Sons, New York, p. 319.

Figure 19.15, Page 578 Adapted from Supervisory Management (1994).

Figure 19.16, Page 578 Adapted from David A. Waldman and Ron S. Kennett (1990), "Improve Performance by Appraisal," *HRMagazine* 35 (July): 66–69.

Technology, Page 579 N. Faye Angel (1989), "Evaluating Employees by Computer," *Personnel Administrator* 34 (November): 67–68+; and Rebecca A. Grant, Christopher A. Higgins, and Richard H. Irving (1988), "Computerized Performance Monitors: Are They Costing You Customers?" *Sloan Management Review* 29 (Spring): 39–45.

Figure 19.17, Page 579 Theodore B. Kinni (1993), "Judge and Be Judged: Hampton Pension Services Has an Antidote for the Dreaded Performance Appraisal," *Industry Week* (August 2): 45+.

Figure 19.21, Page 586 Adapted from Lyle M. Spencer, Jr. and Signe M. Spencer (1993), *Competence at Work: Models for Superior Performance,* John Wiley & Sons, Inc., New York.

Communication Spotlight VI

Collaboration:

Figure 1, Page 590 Adapted from Carl E. Larson and Frank M. J. LaFasto (1989), *TeamWork: What Must Go Right/What Can Go Wrong,* Sage Publishing, Newbury Park, CA.

Figure 2, Page 591 M. Jimmie Kinningsworth and Betsy Goebel Jones (1989), "Division of Labor or Integrated Teams: A Crux in the Management of Technical Communication," *Technical Communication* (36)3: 210–21.

Figure 3, Page 592 Carl E. Larson and Frank M. J. LaFasto (1989), *TeamWork: What Must Go Right/What Can Go Wrong,* Sage Publishing, Newbury Park, CA.

Revision:

Figure 2, Page 594 Modified from J. S. Dumas and J. C. Redish (1993), *A Practical Guide to Usability Testing,* Ablex Publishing, Norwood, N.J.; and Karen A. Schriver (1989), "Evaluating Text Quality: The Continuum from Text-Focused to Reader-Focused Methods," *IEEE Transaction on Professional Communication* 32: 238–55.

Indexes

NAME/ORGANIZATION INDEX

A

ABC/DEF, Inc., 15, 17–19, 29
Across the Smiles, 26
Action, 507
Action Technologies Inc., 85
Addison, Jon, 78–79
Adobe Illustrator, 77
Agstar Seed Company, 410, 413
Alcoa, 97
Aldus Freehand, 542
Aldus PageMaker, 77, 196, 542
Aldus Persuasion, 77, 80–81, 507
Allen, M. George, 506
Allen Susan Au, 506
Alliance Insurance, Inc., 155
Allied Signal, Inc., 506
American Association for Advertising Agencies, 283
American Automobile Association (AAA), 472
American Institute of Certified Public Accountants, 2, 28
American Medical Association, 249
American Surgical Products, Inc. (ASPI), 59–60
America Online, 295
Amnesty International, 298
Anderson, Charles, 217–218
Andrews, Jim, 413
Apple Computer, 549
Applegate, Lynda M., 85
Apple Macintosh, 75, 79, 105, 196, 478, 507
Apple Valley Transportation Authority (AVTA), 15, 18–19, 29
Arabian Health Care Supply Corporation, 407–408
ARCO, 20
Aristotle, 138
Armstrong, Gary, 144–146
Armstrong, Neil, 506
Associated Insurance, 564
Association of Boards of Certification (ABC), 507
Astound, 507
AT&T, 72, 470, 503
Auto Cad, 542
Ayer Directory: Newspapers, Magazines, and Trade Publications, 321

B

Bagwell, Kris, 85
Ballantyne, Janice, 539, 549–551, 553
Barker, Larry, 496
Batelle, 503
Bathish, Louis, 407–408
Bauer, Frank, 59
Bauer, John, 59
Baxter, Jane, 572–573
Beaman, R. W., 45
L.L. Bean, 73, 234, 236
Becton-Dickinson, 408
The Bell Curve: Intelligence and Class Structure in American Life, 30–31
Bellencamp, John, 100, 107
Ben & Jerry's, 378
Better Business Bureau, 540
Better Homes and Gardens, 542
BIOBeef, 10
Birmingham Savings Bank, 234
Black and Decker, 103
Black Elk, 28
Blanke, Wilma, 364
Bloomingdales, 103
Blue Cross and Blue Shield of Iowa (BCBSI), 350, 486
Boeing Aerospace, 76
Boisjoly, Roger, 138
Booker, James, Jr., 158–159
Booker, Rob, 63
Booker Paper Company, 158–159
Book-of-the-Month Club, 296
Bossidy, Lawrence, 506
Boyd Environmental Engineering, 589, 590
Brady, Sarah, 286
Bridge, Alva, 89
Bronham, Malcolm, 3
Brown, Penelope, 272
Bruchac, Joseph, 28
Burger, Lucille, 28
Business Communications Review, 325
Business Week, 72, 108, 299, 498, 541

C

Cabletron Systems Inc., 84
Campbell, Kim Sydow, 261
Cannes Dew, 131–133
Cardello, Angela Courtney, 546, 547
Career Design, 537
Carson, Alex, 413
Cartoon Channel, 85
Carver-Smith, Sam, 158
Catalog of Federal Domestic Assistance, 440
Celestial Seasonings, Inc., 7, 22, 448, 451
CE Software, 77
Challenger, 138
Chapin, Sandy, 45–46
Chapman, Carl, 429–430
Charnish, Allan, 74
Chase Manhattan Bank, 84
Chemical Banking Corp., 84
Chevron Corp., 85
The Chicago Manual of Style, 94
Ching, Hsing-luen, 188–189
Cholla Ilbo, 296
Cigna Corporation, 76, 82
Cisco Systems, Inc., 84
Claris Draw, 77
Clark, David, 317–318, 320–321, 323, 325
Clinton, Bill, 288
Coastland Travel and Ferry Services, 251
Comedy Central, 85
Commerce Business Daily, 440
Comp-U-Safe, 111
Computerworld, 63
Coopers & Lybrand, 63, 85
The Coordinator, 85
Corbett, William J., 2, 28
Corometrics Medical Systems, 407–408, 414–415
Cory, Sean, 368
Countryside Building Sales, 534
Cross, Glen, 434
Cunningham, Scott, 254

D

Dae-Waon, Kim, 296
Dalton, John B., 503
DataGraph, 62
Davidson and Associates, Inc., 539
Davis, Union, 158
Deitchman, John, 85
Dell, 518

Delta Manufacturing, 440, 442
Deming, Lyle Allen, 580
DeSimone, L. D., 9, 242
Dictionary of Occupational Titles, 540
Dirkes, Mary Jo, 85
Domino's Pizze, 104
Draw Paint Deluxe, 542
Dyson, Esther, 85

E

Eastman Kodak, 23, 76
EasyFlow, 467
Easy Home Care, 296
EcoDesign, 520–523
EDS, 63
El Camino Associates, 456–460
Electronic Business, 541
Elliott, Kerrie, 195
Employee Appraiser for Windows, 573
EnviroFirm, 492–493
Epson, 45
Expert Resume Writer, 539
Exxon, 252

F

Farney, Grovery, 158
Farnsworth, Estelle, 249
Fauser, Deborah, 402
Federal Deposit Insurance Corporation (FDIC), 330
Federal Grants and Contracts Weekly, 440
Federal National Mortgage Association, 72
Federal Register, 440
Federal Reserve Bank of America, 506
Financial Management Systems, 317
Financial Trust, 303
First Boston Corp., 84
First National Bank, 316–317
Fischer, Jerry, 131–133
Fisher, Roger, 304
Fitzgerald, A. Ernest, 12
Flesch Readability Index, 118
Foley, Susan, 344, 346
Forbes, 541
Ford-Jesperson, Kelley, 552
Foreman, Janis, 401
Forrestal, 506
Forrester, Leah, 365
Forrester Research, 84
Fortune, 7, 12, 20, 82, 299, 498, 519, 541
Foster, Jeff, 536
Foster, Lance, 147
Frank's Nursery and Crafts, Inc., 72–73
Frantz, Andrea Breemer, 88, 127, 158, 210, 249, 277, 339, 363, 396, 434, 464, 490, 559, 587
Freeman-Ruiz, 157
French, Paul, 534
Frox, Inc., 456

G

Gaines, Kelley, 131–133
Gateway 2000, 518
Geist Software, 62–68, 81, 83
Gibson, Brian, 369–370
Global Enterprises, 39–41, 44, 58
Globe Petroleum, 588
GMBL Hotel, 442
Goedken, Loras, 437–438, 445
Gold Disk, 507
Goldman, Craig, 84
Green, Robert, 121–122
Grice, H. P., 38, 239
Groundwater Service and Supply, 413
Grove, Andrew, 518–519
Growfast, Inc., 145
Gunning Fog Index, 118

H

Hach, Kitty, 28
Hach Company, 28
Hahn, Harley, 75
Hahne Accounting, 111
Hamilton, Judy, 30, 303
Hamilton Construction, 127–128
Hampshire Inn, 468
Hampton Pension Services, 578
Handgun Control, Inc., 286
Hansen Enterprises, 413
Harry, Lisa, 507
Harvey, Brenda, 368
Hatari Hotel, 88–89
Hathaway, Jason, 195
Heartland Development, 268
Helyar, Pamela S., 484
Henry Street Settlement House, 22
Hewlett-Packard, 76, 470
Hey, Elizabeth, 309–312
High Horse, 28
Hill, Lena, 218
Hoffman, Steve, 62
Hoover, Janelle, 368
Horn, Robert, 485
Hoskins, W. Lee, 503
Houghton, Ed, 423
Hughes, Robert, 122
Humpal, Theresa, 402
Huntington National Bank, 503

I

IBM, 28, 63, 72, 75, 105, 193, 518, 542
Inc., 541
INCON, 45
Integrated Services Digital Network (ISDN), 254
Intel Corp., 18, 72, 518–519
International Data Corporation, 76
The Internet: Complete Reference, 75
The Internet Business Journal, 325

J

Jackson Bicycle Works, 447
Jacobs, Sally, 79–80
James, E. Pendleton, 549
Jamison Cable, 252–253
JCPenney, 73
Jefferson, Wyndell, 196
Jennings, William, 85
Johnson, J. David, 43
Johnson, Paul, 84
Johnson, Rachel, 272
Johnson & Higgins, 85
Johnson & Johnson, 20, 197
Journal of Business Strategy, 299
Juarez, Martin, 512
Juarez, Rob, 127

K

Kansas, David, 79
Kay-Bee Toys, 103
Kehoe, Brendan P., 75
Kelsey, Jim, 3, 5
Kennedy, Gene, 272
Kennedy, John F., 506
Kenny Rogers' Roasters, 103
Kimberly-Clark, 408
Kirkman, Kay, 113
Kline, Sandra, 423
Kopp, Will, 503
KPMG Peat Warwick, 62, 63
Kraft Velveeta Shells, 104
Kramer, Kate, 34–38

L

Lacombe, Greg, 127
Lankford, D. S., 503
League of Women Voters, 142
Levinson, Stephen, 272
Library of Congress, 318, 320
Library of Congress Guide to Subject Headings, 321
Lincoln, Abraham, 506
Lippincott & Margulies, 21
Livingston, Kris, 542–545, 553
Loeb, Helen M., 134
Lotus 1-2-3, 77
Lotus Development Corp., 84
Lotus Freelance, 77
Lotus Notes, 63, 76–78, 85

M

Macmillan Publishing, 73
MacProject II, 79
Macromedia, 507
MACWORLD, 519
Major League Baseball, 277–278
Mandela, Nelson, 506
Manzi, Jim, 84
Mao, LuMing Robert, 272
Marcel, Rene, 468–469
Margolin, Clifford, 89
Maslow, Abraham, 293
Mason, Jim, 437
Matlock, Carrie, 402–403
Matsushita Electric, 73
Maxwell, Gates, 45
Maxwell Financial Group, 559–561
Mayo, Alice, 158

McAlexander, 402–403
McClelland, David C., 563, 584
McDonnell, Kate, 131–133
McDonnell Douglas Corporation, 472
McDonough, Brian J., 277
MCI, 72, 506
McKinney, Smokey, 28
Michaelson, Herbert, 336
Microsoft Access, 77
Microsoft Corporation, 79
Microsoft Excel, 77
Microsoft PowerPoint, 77, 80–81, 507
Microsoft Project, 77
Microsoft Word, 76, 77, 80, 95, 419, 484
MicroTrac, 543
Miller, Mike, 10
Miller, Walden, 398, 400, 480
Mills, Daniel, 277
Minnesota Department of Natural Resources, 240, 242
Minto, Barbara, 33, 55
MLA Style Manual, 94
Molitor, Kate, 62
Morton Thiokol, 138
MTV Networks, 85
Muncie, Ellen, 216–218

N

NameLab, 21
Nasdaq Financial Executive Journal, 325
National Museum of Women, 294
National Paper Board Co., 276
National Rifle Association (NRA), 286
Nature Conservancy, 240, 242–24, 289, 294
Nelson, Bill, 311–312
Nelson, Jennifer, 541
Nelson, Kent C., 22
Nestle's, 103
Newswire, 323–324
The New York Times, 498
The New York Times Index, 323, 541
The New York Times Manual of Style and Usage, 94
Nicklodeon, 85
North, Oliver, 291
Northwest Airlines, 2–3, 25–26, 28, 33, 44, 52, 94, 105, 95, 323–324, 329, 332
Novell Inc., 84

O

Oberon Consolidated, Inc., 45–46
Occupational Briefs, 540
Occupational Outlook Handbook, 540
Occupational Safety and Health Administration (OSHA), 192
Octel Communications, 81
O'Leary, Rene, 434
O'Malley, Frank, 249
Orlikowsky, Wanda, 85
Overseas Private Investment Corporation (OPIC), 299

P

Palermo, Ann, 76
Pamphlet, Inc., 316–317, 332
Parkview West, 136, 137
Pascale, Richard, 13
Patton, Bruce, 304
Pentium chip, 518–519
Perfect Resume, 539
Perkins Restaurant, 402
Peters, Tom, 62, 63
Peterson, Barbara, 318
PFS: Resume & Job Search Pro for Windows, 539
Philips Media OptImage, 13–14, 29–30, 41–44, 46–48, 58, 356, 360, 480
Pizza Place, 464–465
Porter, Alan, 254
Potter, Donald, 85
Powell, Colin, 138
Price Waterhouse, 77, 85
Principal Financial Group, 309–312, 354, 357, 473
Procter & Gamble, 13
Prodigy, 295
Progressive Insurance, 72
The Pyramid Principle: Logic in Writing and Thinking, 33

Q

QuickTime, 77, 80–81

R

Ramirez Rope, 15–16, 19, 29, 30
Read Rite, 73
Real Estate Tax Services of Arizona, Inc. (RETS), 352
Reardon, Pat, 587–588
Reed, Tara, 63
Renze, Janet, 456
Research Monitor News, 440
Research Monitor Profile, 440
ResumExpert, 539
Resumix, 543
Riley, Charles, 85
Robert B. Wolter Inc. (RBWI), 276
Roberts, Bert, Jr., 506
Roberts, Pat, 465
Rock Springs Art Gallery/Historical Museum, 396–397
Rollins, Beth, 493
Ross, Mikayla, 559–561

S

Sage, Barbara, 493
Sanchez, Randy, 456
Sandburg, Bill, 276
Sands Environmental Services, 413
Sanger, Nick, 260, 272
Santiago, J. T., 278
Schmidt, Harry, 62
Schorr, Joseph, 80–81
Schrage, Michael, 85
Scott Construction, 448, 451
Sculley, John, 549
Seamless, 408
Securities and Exchange Commission, 76
The Serials Directory: An International Reference Book, 318
Service Merchandise, 73
Seybold, Patricia, 85
Seybold Office Computing Group, 85
Shannon, Claude, 81
Shea, Donald, 85
Shell Oil, 76
Sheraton, Taylor, 426–427
Shoars, Alana, 45
Signature Printing and Publishing, 542
Silicon Graphics, 78
Simmons Pump, 21
Smith, Art, 222, 223
Smith Kline, 408
Smithson, Sam, 89
SNAP Hardware, 15–16, 19, 29–30
Solar Industries, 437–439
Sommers, Lee, 492
Spectrum Information Technologies, 549
Spencer, Kathy, 193
Spiegel, 73
Spinnaker Software, 539
Sprint, 72
Stanley Works, 11–12
Steding, Tom, 81
Stevens, Katherine, 195–196
Stolichnaya, 104
Stout, Rick, 75
Stricker, Denise Steel, 323–324
Styles, William, 122
Sumino, Ayisha, 88
Supervisory Management, 496

T

Target, 73
Tasters Choice, 103
TeamVision, 77
Tedlock, Dave, 139–140, 282–283, 287
Tedlock Advertising, 20–21, 140, 282–283, 287, 352
TelePad Corporation, 18
Thompson, Burke, 363–365
Thompson, Frasier, 363–365
Thompson, Jeremiah, 407–408, 414–415
Thompson, Keith, 363
Thompson, Suzi, 363, 365
Thompson Appliances, 363–365
Thornberg, Julie, 39–41, 58
3Com Corp., 81, 83
3M, 7–9, 15, 20, 24–26, 97, 227–228, 240, 242, 299, 318, 379, 406–407, 506, 541
Time, 384
Timex, 104
Toastmasters, 510–511
Toulmin, Stephen, 53, 199, 452
Towne, Vogel & Whitehead, 587–588
Training and Development, 496
Tucson Psychiatric Institute, 287
Tufte, Edward, 387
Turner Broadcasting System Inc., 85

Turow, J. P., 341
Tylenol, 20, 63, 197

U

U.S. News & World Report, 519
Ulrich's International Periodicals Directory, 321–322
United Funds, 343
United Parcel Service (UPS), 3–7, 10, 26, 43, 44, 90, 97, 197–199, 298, 360
  Community Internship Program, 21–22
United States Air Force, 12
United States Army Intelligence School, 149
United States Census Bureau, 103–104, 340
United States Congress, 3
United States Defense Department, 11
United States Education Department, 298, 339
United States Energy Department, 339
United States Navy, 503
United States Postal Service, 254
United States Small Business Administration, 364
United States Supreme Court, 45
United States Transportation Department, 104
Ury, William, 304
USA Today, 325

V

Van de Wetering, Joohn, 503
Ventura Publishing, 77
Viacom Inc., 85
Visa, 73

W

Waddell & Reed, Inc., 343
Wadsworth, Marty, 585, 586
The Wall Street Journal, 73, 79, 84–85, 498, 560
The Wall Street Journal Index, 323, 541
Walt Disney World, 552
Wass, Kim, 25, 142, 221, 236, 239, 297, 472, 487
Watson, Kittie, 496
Watson, Sarah Joy, 534–536, 545, 553
Watson, Thomas, Sr., 28
Watson Mountaineering, 78
Web Form, Inc., 421
Wells, Herbert, 397
Westwood Associates, 426
White, Jack, 59
White, Jeff, 413
White, Thomas, 85
Whitehead, Susanne VanZandt, 587
Whitehill, Michele, 542
Wickman, Floyd, 496
Wilke, John R., 84
Willig, Al, 127
Wilson, Bill, 84
Wood, Don, 81
Woods, Rachel, 402–403
Woolever, Kristin R., 134, 486
Worchester Family Clinic (WFC), 249
WordPerfect, 76, 77, 80, 419, 484, 507
Worldwide Entertainment Corporation (WEC), 188–189
Writing Effective Software Documentation, 79
Writing for the Computer Industry, 134
Wymark, 210–211

Y

Yates, Peggy, 193
Young & Rubicam Inc., 85
Youth Programs and Shelter Services (YPSS), 434

Z

Zak, Michele Wender, 18
Zen and the Art of Internet: A Beginner's Guide, 75

SUBJECT INDEX

A

Abstract indexes, 323
Abstracts, 420–421
Accessibility, business messages and, 146
Accuracy, business messages and, 140
Acronyms, 193
Active listening, oral presentations and, 496–499
Active voice, 528–530
Advance organizers, 482
Advertising, Internet and, 295
Affective conflict, 212
Agendas, 48–50
Agreement, subject and verb, 528
AIDA plan, 286–288, 292
AIDS, 155
American with Disabilities Act (ADA), 131–133, 570
Annual reports, 23
  ethics and, 407
Anonymity, electronic networks and, 82
Antithesis, 506
Appeals
  to audience's emotions and values, 144–147
  to communicator's character, 139–144
  to integrity of communication, 148–150
  purpose and, 138–152
Appendixes, 428–429
Application letters, 551–553
  you-attitude and, 110–111
Argument
  claims in, 191–194
  components of, 197–202
  message-centered, 199–200
  reader-centered, 200–201
  writer-centered, 197–199
    line of, 194–197
    comparative-advantage, 195
    criteria-goals, 195–196
    need-plan, 194–195
    net-benefit, 196–197
Assessment section, 449–451
Assumptions-based model, 38–39
Audience, purpose and, 134, 137–138
Audience analysis, 100–102
  instructional documents and, 479
  message and, 107
  occasion and, 107–108
  reader characteristics and, 102–105
  using personal interviews and surveys, 104
  using secondary sources and databases, 103
  writer-reader relationship and, 107
  writing strategies and, 108–110
Audience cooperation, 222–227
  messages assuming, 227
  strategies to encourage, 223–226
  web of business materials anticipating, 240
Audience resistance
  overcoming, 258–259
  reasons for, 253–258
Audioconferencing, 233
Average, 332

B

Background, 422, 424–425, 440–442
Backing, 200
Backward planning, 403
Bar graphs, 377–378, 382, 390
Benefits section, 444–445
Bibliographic databases, 323
Bibliography, 428
Body language, oral presentations and, 508–511
Brochures, instructional, 471–473
Budget narrative, 446
Buffer, 121
  for negative messages, 261
Bulleted lists, 14
Business communication
  Speech Act maxims and, 38
  technology and, 84–85
Business documents
  applying design principles to, 348–360
  chunking information in, 348–352
  claims in argument, 191–194
  components of argument, 197–202
  creating visual coherence in, 353–357
  establishing emphasis in, 357–360
  global revision strengthening, 309–312
  international, graphics for, 370
  labeling chunks in, 352–353
  line of argument, 194–197
  local revision strengthening, 527–532
  planning of
  collaborative, 202–204
    constructive, 191
    knowledge-driven, 190–191
    schema-driven, 189–190
  redesigning, 360–361
  revision, 216–219
  team-written, eliminating problems in, 402–404
  visual tools for organizing, 204–207
Business graphics, 376
Business letters
  collection, 289–291
  cultural differences in, 223
  fund-raising, 288–289
  sales, 292–293
Business messages
  goodwill, 234–239
  negative
    composing, 259–271
    constructing buffers for, 261
    direct approach in, 263
  occasions for, 260
  positive close in, 263
  persuasive, 283–291
    implied reader and, 284–286
  planning, 188–189
  positive, 232–234
  routine or neutral, 227–232
  sales, 292–296
    humor in, 293–294
Business reports
  argument sequence in, 427
  components of, functions of, 416–429
  documentary, 409–413
  evaluative, 413–415
    conventions of, 417
  formal, characteristics of, 409
  including details for readers, 427–429
  informal, characteristics of, 409
  introduction of, 421–425
  investigative, 413
  orienting readers of, 417–421
  persuading readers, 426–427
  purposes of, 408–416
  reinforcing business relationships, 407–408

C

Call report, 45
Card catalog, 320–323
Career objectives, in resumes, 547
Career software, 539
Cartoon drawing, 386
Causal fallacies, 336
CD-ROM databases, 323
Central tendency, measures of, 332
Certified mail, 34–35
  set of instructions concerning, 36
Change, audience resistance and, 254–256
Chartjunk, 387–388, 390–391
Chronological resume, 546, 549–550
Chunking information, 348–352
Civil Rights Act of 1964, 571
Claim, 133–134
Claim adjustments
  negative, 269–271
Claim letters, 265–269
Claims of fact, 192
Claims of policy, 193–194
Claims of value, 192–193
Clarity, business messages and, 149
Codes of ethics, 9–12
Collaborative planning, 202–204
Collection letters, 289–291
Common criteria, 10
Communication
  business, technology and, 84–85
  corporate, corporate image and, 22–26
  difficulties in, 16
  electronic. *See* Electronic communication
  formal channels of, 41–43

informal channels of, 43–44
integrity of, appeals to, 148–150
intercultural, 14–15
nonverbal, 15–16
organizational culture expressed in, 3–5
problem areas in, 39
technologies, 68–81
verbal, 15–16
Communication networks, 41–46
Communication process, 35–41
assumptions-based model of, 38–39
reciprocal models of, 37
transmission models of, 35–36
Communication task, problem-solving approach to defining, 34
Communicator
appeals to character, 139–144
purposes tied to, 135–136
Company description, job search and, 540–544
Company image, promoting, 299
Comparative-advantage line of argument, 195
Complaints, 265–269
Compliance reports, 417
Composing process, 51–56
Comprehensiveness, business messages and, 149–150
Computer anxiety, 72
Computer decision making, meetings and, 49
Computerized databases, 323
Computer networks, 72–81
Computers, 72–81
employee evaluation and, 579
mainframe, 75
on-line documentation, 481
personal, 75
types of hardware, 74–75
workplace culture and, 84–85
Conference program, designing, 344–346
Conflict, 212–214
affective, 212
procedural, 212–213
substantive, 214
Congratulations, 239
Constraints, instructional documents and, 480
Constructive planning, 191
Contact information, 545
Convention-driven purpose, 136
Corporate communications, corporate image and, 22–26
Corporate framework, communication style within, 34–35
Corporate goals, 7–9
Corporate image, 19–21
community and, 21–22
corporate communications and, 22–26
Corporate librarian, responsibilities of, 319
Corporate newspapers, 26
Corporate principles, 12
Corporation, virtual, 18
Correctness, business messages and, 141
Courtesy, business messages and, 146–147
Credit approvals, 233–234
Criteria, 9–12
common, 10
situated, 10–11
Criteria-goals line of argument, 195–196
Cross-references, 482

D

Dangling modifiers, 530
Database management software, 77–79
Databases
computerized, 323
search strategies for, 324
Deductive plan, 263
Design, applying functions and principles of, 346–348
Design elements, 482
Desktop publishing, 347
Desktop publishing software, 77
Detail selection, 116–117
Directives, 46–47
Direct-mail packages, 294–296, 301
Direct plan, 263
Direct requests, 229–232
Distortion, visuals and, 382–386
Diversity, 6–7
Documentary reports, 409–413
Documentation
international, 193
symbols in, 472
on-line, 481
Document cycling plan, 58
Documents. *See* Business documents
instructional. *See* Instructional documents
Document testing, 593–597
purpose of, 593
types of, 593–595
Document webs, 240
Drawing and graphing software, 77
Dress codes, 565
Dumb terminals, 75

E

Electronic communication, 62
technologies, 68–81
issues relating to, 81–84
Electronic Communications Privacy Act of 1986 (ECPA), 45
Electronic lists and groups, 75
Electronic networks
anonymity and, 82
information overload and, 81–82
lack of interpersonal contact and, 82–83
organizational values and, 83–84
Elicited information, 549
E-mail, 62–68, 137
ethics and, 45
junk, 81
requesting and receiving information using, 323–324
Employment. letters addressing, 579–581
Ergo propter hoc, 335
Ethernet, 81
Ethics, 9–12
annual reports and, 407
corporate mission statements and, 197
e-mail and, 45
employment interview and, 570
graphic displays and, 336
Internet access and, 74
junk mail appeals and, 288
mailing lists and, 104
omission in employment communication and, 549
oral presentations and, 501
phrasing negative messages and, 261
positive messages and, 239
proposal writing and, 455
purpose for communicating and, 138
sleight-of-hand text and, 357
software piracy and, 387
of warning, 486
Evaluative reports, 413–415
conventions of, 417
Executive summaries, 420–421
Expert-based document testing, 593–594
Expertise, audience resistance and, 258
Explicit purpose, 134

F

Facsimile (fax) equipment, 71–72
Fallacies, 333–336
Feasibility reports
assessment section of, 449–451
business proposals and, 437–438
characteristics of, 438–440
components of, 441
criteria in, 448
evaluation of, 453–455
implementation sections of, 451
overview of alternatives in, 448–449
single-option, 452
Feedback, revising after, decision tree of, 217
Figures of speech, 506
File transfer protocol (FTP), 74
Flow charts, 204, 206, 374, 377, 478–479
symbols in, 478
Focus groups, 328
Formal channels, 41–43
Formal reports, you-attitude and, 111
Formal tables, 374, 375
Format selection, 117–118
Four P's, 296
FTP (file transfer protocol), 74
Function, team structures and, 590
Functional resume, 549–551
Fund-raising letters, 288–289

G

Gantt chart, 204–207
Genres, 110

Global revision, 216
business documents and, 309–312
factors to consider in, 95
Glossaries, 484
Goods and services, promoting, 297–298
Goodwill messages, 234–239
Gopher, 325
Graphic displays, ethics and, 336
Graphic elements, 346
Graphics
business, 376
for international documents, 370
Graphs, 375–378
distorting numeric information, 389
Grids, 348–349
Grounds, 199
Group membership, audience resistance and, 256–258
Groupware, 62, 76–78
Guidelines, establishing, 94–97

H

Handouts, oral presentations and, 512–513
Hard bargaining, 304–305
Hardware, types of, 74–75
Help menu, 481
Heuristics, 52–56
Hierarchy of needs, 293
High-context culture, 441, 523
Humor
audience cooperation and, 226
sales messages and, 293–294

I

Iconography, international, 79
Idea section, 444
Identification, 147
Imaging software, 77
Implementation section, 445–446, 451
Implicit purpose, 134
Implied reader, 284–286
Indexes, 484
Indirect approach, 259
Inductive approach, 259
Inferential fallacies, 335
Informal channels, 43–44
Informal tables, 373
Information
audience resistance and, 253–254
collecting and interpreting, 316–317
interpreting, 329–336
locating and selecting sources of, 317–329
Informational interviews, 325–328
Informational sheets, 469–470
Information mapping, 485
Information overload, 81–82
Inquiries, 229–232
Instructional brochures, 471–473
Instructional documents
alternative, 484–485
conventional elements in, 481–487
liability and, 485–487
orienting readers, 481–484
planning, 477–480
testing, 480
types of, 469–477
Instructional sheets, 469–470
Integrated pattern, 449, 450
Integrity, 148–150
Intercultural communication, 14–15
International documentation, 193
graphics for, 370
symbols in, 472
International iconography, 79
International marketing, 296
Internet, 73–74
advertising and, 295
increases in companies registered on, 74
requesting and receiving information using, 325
Interpersonal relationships, differing perceptions about, 521
Invention, oral presentations and, 501–502
Investigative reports, 413
Invitations, 236–238
Invoked reader, 284–286
ISO 9000, 315, 413
Isotype, 376

J

Job advertisements, 542
Job description, job search and, 540–544
Job interviews, 564–571
conventions in, 568
difficult situations in, 569–571
follow-up and, 571–572
questions asked by applicants, 567
questions asked by interviewers, 565–566
Job search
planning documents and, 537–544
portfolios and, 553–554
problem-solving nature of, 536–537
resumes and, 544–553
Junk mail appeals, ethics and, 288
Justification, 350

K

Kinesic behaviors, 524
Knowledge-driven planning, 190–191

L

Lake View T-shirt controversy, 490
Leadership decisions, influences on, 522–523
Leading, 344, 350–351
Letters of application, 551–553
you-attitude and, 110–111
Letters of inquiry, 229–232
Letters of recommendation, 579–580
Letters of resignation, 581
Letters of transmittal, 418
Liability, instructional documents and, 485–487
Library resources, 318–323
License agreements, 467
Line graphs, 374, 376, 392
Line of argument, 194–197
comparative-advantage, 195
criteria-goals, 195–196
need-plan, 194–195
net-benefit, 196–197
Listening, 48
active, oral presentations and, 496–499
developing team skills and, 399
guidelines for, 49
Listservs, 74
Local revision, 216
business documents and, 527–532
Logic errors, assessing, 332–336
Low-context culture, 441, 523

M

Mailing lists, ethics and, 104
Mailings, response rates for, 115
Mainframe computers, 75
Main idea, 133–134
Management background sheet, 4–5
Management styles, 46–47
Manipulation, visuals and, 382–386
Mannerisms, oral presentations and, 511
Manuals, 473–475
Marketing, international, 296
Market reports, 417
Mean, 332
Measures of central tendency, 332
Median, 332
Meetings, 46–51
Memo of transmittal, 418
Memory, oral presentations and, 506–508
Message-centered components, 199–200
Messages. *See* Business messages
Metaphor, 506
Methods statement, 423
Milestone charts, 374
Minutes, 50–51
Mission statements, 7–9
ethics and, 197
Mixed pattern, 449, 451
Mode, 332
Multiculturalism
associations of color, 361
Chinese modesty, 568
communication goals and purposes, 146
cultural differences in business letters, 223
effects of culture on report writing, 421
graphics for international documents, 370
high- and low-context cultures, 441
international assignments, 540
international documentation, 193
international iconography, 79
international marketing, 296
negative face, 272
oral presentation to international audience, 516

symbols in international documentation, 472
target audiences, demographics, and language choice, 103
understanding foreign-born employees, 328–329
unlucky number 4, 13
Multicultural teams, influences on, 520–526
Multimedia presentations, 507
Multimedia software, 80–81
Multiple bar graph, 378, 382, 384
Mutual gaze, 525

N

Need-plan line of argument, 194–195
Needs section, 442–444, 463
Negative adjustments, 269–271
Negative face, 272
Negative messages
composing, 259–271
constructing buffers for, 261
direct approach in, 263
occasions for, 260
positive close in, 263
you-attitude and, 111
Negative responses, 264
Negotiation, on workplace teams, 304–308
Net benefit line of argument, 196–197
Networking, 541–544
Networks, 92–93
Newsletters, 25–26
Newspaper indexes, 321–323
News releases, 295
Nonverbal communication, 15–16
difficulties in, 16
North American Free Trade Agreement (NAFTA), 3–4
Notecards, oral presentations and, 507

O

Occasion, 10, 37
instructional documents and, 479–480
purposes tied to, 136–137
Oculesics, 525
On-line databases, 323
On-line documentation, 481
Operational purpose, 135–136
Oral presentations
active listening and, 496–499
conclusions for, 505
delivery and, 508–511
development of, 503–504
ethics and, 501
evaluating, 513–516
introductions for, 502–503
invention and, 501–502
memory and, 506–508
organization and, 502–504
preparation for, 492–496, 501–511
purposes of, 499–501
style and, 505
visuals and, 511–514
Order acknowledgments, 234
Orders, negative information about, 264–265
Order substitution, negative message indicating, 266
Organization, oral presentations and, 502–504
Organizational chart, 41–42
Organizational climate, 46
Organizational culture, 5–7
expressed in communication, 3–5
Organizational sequencing, 114–116
Organizational values, electronic networks and, 83–84
Organizations, composing process within, 51–56
Orphan, 344
Outlines, oral presentations and, 507–508
Overview, 422–423

P

Pacing, oral presentations and, 510
Paralanguage, 328
Parallelism, 506
Parallel structure, 528
Partitioned pattern, 449–450
Passive voice, 152, 528–530
Peer review, 578
Performance appraisals, 572–579
accountabilities and measures in, 573–575
alternatives to, 577–579
approaches to, 573
documents in, 575–577
Periodical indexes, 321–323
Persona, 142
Personal computers (PCs), 75
Personal inventories, 537–540
Personification, 506
Persuasive messages, 283–291
implied reader and, 284–286
Persuasive requests, 286–288
Photographs, 378–379, 386
Pie graphs, 376, 381
Pitch, oral presentations and, 510
Planning
collaborative, 202–204
constructive, 191
knowledge-driven, 190–191
schema-driven, 189–190
Planning documents, job search and, 537–544
Policy manual, 474–475
Population map, 380, 387–388
Portfolios, 553–554
Positional bargaining, 304–305
Positive messages, 232–234
Positive responses, 232–233
Positive wording, 112
Presentation software, 77
Press packages, 299
Press releases, 24–25
occasions for, 24
Prework communications meetings (PCMs), 4–6, 197–199
Problem-solution analysis, 55
Problem-solution line of argument, 194–195
Procedural conflict, 212–213
Procedures manual, 473–474
Professional appearance, oral presentations and, 509
Professional journals, 322
Program evaluation and review technique (PERT), 207
Project management tools, 204–207
Project planning software, 77, 79–80
Promotional packages, 297–299
Pronoun use, 110–112
Proofreading, 530–532
Proposals
argumentative elements in, 452, 453
background section of, 440–442
benefits section of, 444–445
characteristics of, 438–440
components of, 440–447
ethics and, 455
evaluation of, 453–455
feasibility studies and, 437–438
idea section of, 444
implementation section of, 445–456
needs section of, 442–444, 463
recommendation sections of, 446–447
Propositions, 502
Purpose
appeals and, 138–152
characteristics of, 133–135
convention-driven, 136
explicit, 134
implicit, 134
operational, 135–136
primary, 136–137
secondary, 136
tied to audience, 137–138
tied to communicator, 135–136
tied to message, 136
tied to occasion, 136–137
types of, 135–138

Q

Qualifiers, 200
Questions, developing team skills and, 399–400

R

Readability, 118–122
contextual aspect of, 122
reader expectations and attitudes and, 121–122
stylistic features and, 118–121
Readability formulas, 118–119
Reader-based document testing, 594
Reader benefit, 112–113
Reader-centered components, 200–201
Reader expectations, purpose and, 138
Reader resistance, 252–253
Reader use, 113
Rebuttals, 200
Reciprocal models, 37
Recommendation reports, 417, 452

Recommendation sections, 446–447
Reference databases, 323
Reference resources, 319
References, in resumes, 547–549
Referral databases, 323
Reflecting, developing team skills and, 400–401
Relative status, 107
Repetition, 506
Reports. *See* Business reports
Request for price quotation (RFQ), 439
Request for proposals (RFP), 439
Responsibility, team structures and, 591
Resumes, 544–551
  chronological, 546, 549–550
  elective information in, 547–549
  elicited information in, 549
  essential information in, 544–547
  functional, 549–551
Review instructions, 476–477
Revision
  global, 216
    business documents and, 309–312
    factors to consider in, 95
  local, 216
    business documents and, 527–532
Rhetorical question, 506
Rogerian strategies, 200–202

S

Sales letters, 292–293
Sales messages, 292–296
  humor in, 293–294
Sans serif font, 355
Scatter graphs, 376–377, 381
Schema-driven planning, 189–190
Selling point, selecting, 282–283
Sequence, team structures and, 590–591
Serif font, 355
Sexual harassment, 475
Shared agreement, 453
Shared factors, 6–7
Shared goals, audience resistance and, 256–258
Sharing, developing team skills and, 400
Shoptalk, 18–19
Simile, 506
Simple bar graph, 377, 382–383
Situated criteria, 10–11
Skills & strategies
  avoiding offensive language, 122
  conventions for creating visuals, 371
  designing brochures, 281
  document's outline working, 425
  dressing for success, 565
  guidelines for writing instructional material, 484
  how to say no, 262
  maintaining cross-cultural goodwill, 227
  naming your subject, 52
  oral presentations, 510
  overcoming computer anxiety, 72
  passive voice, 152
  proposals, 439
  selecting databases, 323
  using serif and sans serif typefaces, 355
  writing for resume banks, 543
Sliding bar graph, 378, 382, 385
Sneaks, 12
Soft bargaining, 304–305
Soft-lifting, 387
Software
  career, 539
  communication problems solved with, 77
  employment appraisal, 573
  oral presentations and, 512–513
  types of, 76–81
Software piracy, 387
Source databases, 323
Spatial elements, 346
Speech Act theorists, 38–39
Spreadsheet software, 77, 331
Stakeholding, 197
Stance, 108, 330–332
Stance placement, 197
Standard General Markup Language (SGML), 76
Standards, establishing, 94–97
Structured writing, 485, 486
Style, oral presentations and, 505
Style manuals, sources of, 94–96
Style selection, 117–118
Stylesheets, 12–14
  concerns, 13
  principles and style, 14
Subdivided bar graph, 377, 382–383
Subdivided 100 percent bar graph, 378, 382, 384
Subject matter expert (SME), 310–311
Substantive conflict, 214
Surface feature map, 380, 387–388
Surveys, 328–329
  types of questions for, 329

T

Table of contents, 421–422
Tables
  formal, 374–375
  informal, 373
Tattletales, 12
Teams, 90–93
  members
    interpersonal functions of, 91
    task functions of, 90
  multicultural, influences on, 520–526
  nonhierarchical, 91–92
  successful, designing, 589–592
  traditional, 90–91
  workplace, negotiation on, 304–308
Team skills, developing, 398–401
Technology
  automatic style, 419
  business graphics, 376
  career software, 539
  communicating to large audiences, 105
  computer-generated presentations, 445
  computerized employee evaluation, 579
  computers, 76
  conducting business long-distance, 233
  desktop publishing, 347
  e-mail, 137
  Integrated Services Digital Network, 254
  Internet ads, 295
  meetings and computer decision making, 49
  multimedia presentations, 507
  number crunching, 331
  on-line documentation, 481
  projects by computer, 207
  virtual corporation, 18
Teleconferencing, 233
Telephone information instruction card, 468
Telephone systems, 69–71
Telnet, 325
Text-based document testing, 593–594
Textual elements, 346
Thank-yous, 239
Title, 420
Title page, 420
Tone, 142–144
Total Quality Management (TQM), performance appraisals and, 577–578
Trade magazines, 322
Transmission models, 35–36
Transmittals, 228–229
Troublemakers, 12
Tuning in, 398
Typeface, 354–356
Type size, 356–357
Typographic devices, 358–360

U

United States Congress, 3
Universal Product Code, 72–73
Usability document testing, 594
User-based document testing, 594
Usernet groups, 74

V

Verbal communication, 15–16
  difficulties in, 16
Videoconferencing, 233
Virtual corporation, 18
Visual coherence, creating, 353–357
Visuals
  adapting to audience needs, 369–370
  conveying image and content, 368
  creating appeal, 380, 389
  functions of, 370–381
  identifying chronology, 374
  identifying location, 379–380
  identifying relationships, 375–378
  oral presentations and, 511–514
  organizing data, 372–374
  questions for assessing, 396

showing appearance, 378–379
use and misuse of, 381–388
Voice, oral presentations and, 508–511

W

Warnier-Orr diagrams, 204–205
Warrants, 199–200
Webs, 92–93
Welcome messages, 236–238
Whistleblowers, 12
White space, 348, 350–352
Wordiness, 530
Word processing software, 77
Work experience, in resumes, 546
Workplace culture, computers and, 84–85
Workplace professionals, cultures affecting, 520
Workplace teams, negotiation on, 304–308
Works cited, 428
World Wide Web (WWW), 74, 325, 588
Writer-centered components, 197–199
Writing strategies, audience analysis and, 108–110

Y

You-attitude, 110–113

CREDITS

FIGURE CREDITS:

1.1, 1.2: Courtesy of Northwest Airlines; 1.3, 1.4, 1.5: Courtesy of United Parcel Service; 1.6a , 1.6b, 1.7: Courtesy of 3M; 1.8: Courtesy of United Parcel Service; 1.13, 1.14: Philips Media OptImage; 1.15, 1.16: Courtesy of Tedlock Marketing, Advertising, and Public Relations; 1.17: Courtesy of United Parcel Service; 1.18: Courtesy of Celestial Seasonings; 1.19: Courtesy of Eastman Kodak; 1.21: Courtesy of 3M; 1.22: Courtesy of Dr. Kim Wass; 1.23: Courtesy of Smokey McKinney; 1.24, 2.9, 2.10: Courtesy of OptImage; 2.12: Courtesy of Oberon; 2.19: Courtesy of Northwest Airlines; 3.1: Courtesy of Tribune Media Services; 3.16: *Wall Street Journal*; 3.21: Courtesy of Microsoft; 3.22: *Forbes*; 3.23: *The Boston Globe*; 3.24–3.26: *Wall Street Journal*; 3.27: *Business Week*; Communication Spotlight I: Revision, Figure 2: Courtesy of OptImage; 4.7, 4.8: Courtesy of Northwest Airlines; 4.18–4.20: Courtesy of Iowa State University Foundation; 5.12: Courtesy of Tedlock Marketing, Advertising, and Public Relations; 5.16: Courtesy of the League of Women Voters; 5.17–5.19: Courtesy of Dr. Kim Wass; 5.27: Courtesy of Ames Public Schools; 5.28: Courtesy of Iowa State University and Lance Foster; 6.1: Courtesy of The Greenwood Trust Company; 6.15: Courtesy of Neal Bowers; 6.21a, 6.21b, 6.21c: Courtesy of The Greenwood Trust Company; 7.12: Courtesy of United Parcel Service; 7.19: Courtesy of Blue Cross/Blue Shield; 7.20, 7.21: Courtesy of Microsoft; 7.22: Courtesy of Ames Public Schools, Communication Spotlight II: Revision, Figure 2: Courtesy of Oxford University Press; 8.1: Courtesy of Dr. Kim Wass; 8.8: Courtesy of Copyworks; 8.9: Courtesy of 3M; 8.11: Courtesy of United Parcel Service; 8.25: Courtesy of L. L. Bean; 8.27: Courtesy of Neil Nakadate; 8.29: Courtesy of Dr. Kim Wass; 8.32: Courtesy of 3M; 8.33, 8.34: Courtesy of The Nature Conservancy, Minnesota Chapter; 8.37: Courtesy of Ames Concrete Contracters; 9.1: Courtesy of Northwest Airlines; 9.2: Courtesy of Tedlock Marketing, Advertising, and Public Relations; 9.5: Courtesy of the U.S. Postal Service; 9.9: Courtesy of the *Journal of Basic Writing*; 9.15: Courtesy of Iowa State University Childhood Development Center; 10.1: Courtesy of Robert A. Cook; 10.2, 10.3a, 10.3b, 10.6: Courtesy of Tedlock Marketing, Advertising, and Public Relations; 10.8a, 10.8b: Courtesy of The Nature Conservancy;10.14: Courtesy of Tedlock Marketing, Advertising, and Public Relations; 10.15: Courtesy of Northwest Airlines; Communication Spotlight for Part III: Revision, Figures 1–5: Courtesy of The Principal Financial Group; 11.10: Courtesy of Northwest Airlines; 12.1: Courtesy of Waddell and Reed; 12.3: Courtesy of Working Assets; 12.6: Courtesy of QMS Supplies and Accessories; 12.10: Courtesy of Waddell and Reed; 12.11: Courtesy of Blue Cross/Blue Shield; 12.13: Courtesy of Tedlock Marketing, Advertising, and Public Relations; 12.16: Courtesy of The Principal Financial Group; 12.18, 12.23: Courtesy of OptImage; 12.24: Courtesy of United Parcel Service; 13.2 (top): NASA Headquarters; 13.8: *The Boston Globe*; 13.12: Courtesy of Microsoft; 13.15: Courtesy of Prudential Securities; 13.17: Courtesy of GT Global Communication Fund; 13.22: Courtesy of Claris Corporation; 13.24 (top): Courtesy of Arthur Anderson & Co.; 13.24 (bottom): Courtesy of Hewlett Packard Company; 13.25: Courtesy of Ben and Jerry's; 13.26: Courtesy of 3M; 13.27 (bottom) Magellan Geographix; 13.28: Courtesy of *The Lowell Sun;* 13.29: Courtesy of H.J. Heinz; 13.30 (top): Courtesy of Procter & Gamble; (middle): Robert Mankoff/The Cartoon Bank; (bottom): Steve Weber/Stock Boston; 13.31: Courtesy of Lehman Brothers; 13.38: Courtesy of the *Des Moines Register*; 13.39: Courtesy of Waddell and Reed; 14.2: Courtesy of Corometrics; 14.9: Courtesy of Seneca Oil; 14.11: Courtesy of Corometrics; 15.27: Courtesy of Janet Renze, Grant and Proposal Writing Course, Iowa State University; 15.29: Courtesy of United Parcel Service; 16.5: Courtesy of Hewlett Packard; 16.6: Courtesy of Dr. Kim Wass; 16.7: Courtesy of AAA Iowa; 16.8: Courtesy of The Principal Financial Group; 16.10a, 16.10b, 16.10c: Courtesy of Ricoh Copiers; 16.14a, 16.14b, 16.15, 16.16: Courtesy of Blue Cross/Blue Shield; 16.17: Courtesy of Dr. Kim Wass; 17.1 (left): Brad Markel/Gamma Liaison, Inc.; 17.1 (right): Pat McDonogh;19.17: Courtesy of *Industry Week*.

PHOTO CREDITS:

Page 37: M. Antman/The Image Works; Page 49: Phil Schofield Photography; Page 63: Tribune Media Services; Page 73: IBM; Page 80: Antonio Ribeiro/Gamma-Liaison, Inc.; Page 102: Don Smetzer/Tony Stone Images; Page 108: Telegraph Colour Library/FPG International; Page 131: Stephen Frisch/Stock Boston; Page 138: Martin Simon/SABA Press Photos, Inc.; Page 145: Save The Children; Page 163 (left): Bob Daemmrich/Stock Boston; Page 163 (right): John Zolner/Uniphoto Picture Agency; Page 165: Steve Benbow/Stock Boston; Page 175: Twentieth Century Fox/Neal Peters Collection; Page 189: C/B Productions/The Stock Market; Page 197: UPI/Bettmann; Page 200: Bill Horsman/Stock Boston; Page 212: Kerbs/Monkmeyer Press; Page 224: Bruce Stoddard/FPG International; Page 228: Jon Feingersh/The Stock Market; Page 241: Paul Sundberg; Page 252: Greg Gibson/AP/Wide World Photos; Page 258: Bob Daemmrich/The Image Works; Page 260: David H. Wells/The Image Works; Page 281: Neal Peters/Neal Peters Collection; Pages 290, 298: Teri Stratford; Page 310: Hewlett Packard; Page 316: Michael Krasowitz/FPG International; Page 327: Bill Truelow/Gamma-Liaison, Inc.; Page 328: Lawrence Migdale/Stock Boston; Page 350: Bob Galbraith/AP/World Wide Photos; Page 357: David Young Wolff/Tony Stone Images; Page 403: Siteman/Monkmeyer Press; Page 407: L.D. Bohm Studios, Inc/Gamma-Liaison, Inc.; Page 417: Wagner: SABA Press Photos, Inc.; Page 426: Louis Psihoyos/Matrix International; Page 475: Wayne Sorce; Page 477: Photofest; Page 509: Steve Wolf; Page 513: IBM; Page 524 (top): Gabe Palmer/The Stock Market; Page 524 (bottom): Ken Ross/FPG International; Page 537: Chuck Savage/The Stock Market; Page 542: Collins/Monkmeyer Press; Page 565: David Stoecklein/The Stock Market; Page 570: Robert E. Daemmrich/Tony Stone Images; Page 577: Kevin Horan; Page 589: Peter Beck/The Stock Market